COLLEGE
ATLAS OF THE WORLD

SECOND EDITION

NATIONAL GEOGRAPHIC, WASHINGTON, D.C.

A LEGACY OF SERVICE TO GEOGRAPHY

John Wiley & Sons, Inc. is the worldwide leader in geography publishing. We began our partnership with geography education in 1911 and continue to publish college texts, professional books, journals and technology products that help teachers teach and students learn. We are committed to making it easier for students to visualize spatial relationships, think critically about their interactions with the environment and appreciate the earth's dynamic landscapes and diverse cultures.

To serve our customers we have partnered with the AAG, the AGS and the NCGE while building extraordinary relationships with *National Geographic* that allow us to pair authoritative maps, photos and content with our market-leading books.

Our authors are a group of accomplished researchers whose contributions have shaped the discipline over the last century, combined with a new generation of insightful scholars who are dedicated to their students and the discipline. Together, their contributions have served multiple generations, and will continue to impact the discipline for many years to come.

Visit us online at http://www.wiley.com/college/geography

Library of Congress Cataloging in Publication data
is available upon request.

ISBN-13: 978-0-470-88887-2

NATIONAL GEOGRAPHIC

Explore the World! Research and make your own maps. Learn how you can be involved and care for our planet Earth. *National Geographic* and *John Wiley & Sons, Inc.* will help you start your adventure. For your passport to the World of Maps and Geography go to:

www.wiley.com/college/atlas

MapMachine

Locate nearly any place on Earth, print free maps of continents, countries, and learn about the places you explore.
http://java.nationalgeographic.com/studentatlas/

XPEDITIONS

Xpeditions is home to the U.S. National Geography Standards—and to thousands of ideas, tools, and interactive adventures that bring them to life.
http://www.nationalgeographic.com/xpeditions/atlas/

WileyPLUS

WileyPLUS integrates the entire digital textbook with resources—including map quizzes and exclusive NGS video—to help you master the material no matter what your learning style. Go to:
www.wiley.com/college/atlas

GeoDiscoveries

GeoDiscoveries is an easy to use website to help reinforce and illustrate key concepts from the text through the use of animations, videos, and interactive exercises. Students can use the resources for tutorials as well as self-quizzing to complement the textbook and enhance understanding of geography. Easy integration of this content into course management systems and homework assignments gives instructors the opportunity to integrate multimedia with their syllabi and with more traditional reading and writing assignments. Resources include: Animations, Videos, Simulations, and Interactive Exercises. Go to:
www.wiley.com/college/geodiscoveries

ConceptCaching

ConceptCaching.com allows instructors to share photographs that they have taken during their fieldwork as well as leisure travel with students and other instructors. All caches are placed in spatial context and linked according to their thematic content. Photographs and GPS coordinates are "cached" and categorized along core concepts of geography. Professors can access the online image database or submit their own by visiting
www.ConceptCaching.com

WILEY
Publishers Since 1807

NATIONAL GEOGRAPHIC

COLLEGE
ATLAS OF THE WORLD

SECOND EDITION

Founded in 1888, the National Geographic Society is one of the largest nonprofit scientific and educational organizations in the world. It reaches more than 375 million people worldwide each month through its official journal, NATIONAL GEOGRAPHIC, and its other magazines; the National Geographic Channel; television documentaries; radio and music programs; films; books; videos and DVDs; maps; live events; exhibits; and interactive media. National Geographic has funded more than 9,200 scientific research projects and supports an education program promoting geographic literacy.

For more information, please call
1-800-NGS LINE (647-5463)
or write to the following address:
National Geographic Society
1145 17th Street N.W.
Washington, D.C. 20036-4688 U.S.A.

Log on to nationalgeographic.com

More on National Geographic Maps and its products
at **natgeomaps.com** or call 1-800-962-1643

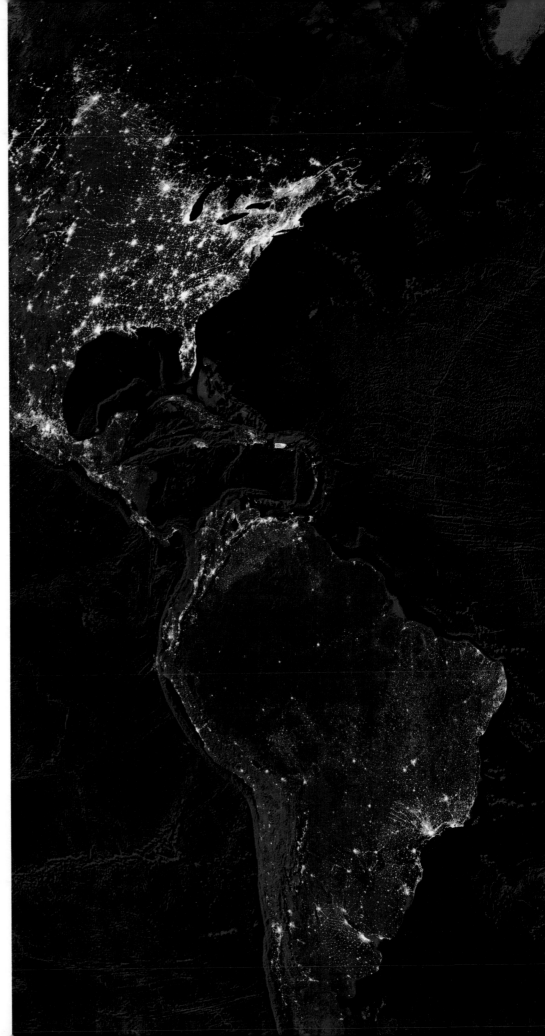

PREFACE

This atlas was created digitally by cartographers working on two continents. The mapmakers performed their work on networked computers using Geographic Information Systems (GIS) software. They communicated instantaneously via email and trans-Atlantic conference calls and swapped digital files via the Internet. They used desktop graphics programs to refine map designs and tapped other software to help position thousands of place-names on political maps. For thematic maps, they utilized imagery captured by satellites, manipulated elevation data gathered by radar instruments carried into orbit by astronauts, and tapped Earth data gathered by thousands of sensors scattered across the face of the planet.

The tools used to make this book—that we cartographers take for granted as standard methods of the trade—would have been considered almost miraculous by the gentlemen who founded the National Geographic Society in 1888 on a late winter evening in Washington, D.C. Among their ranks were Alexander Graham Bell, inventor of the telephone, and John Wesley Powell, leader of the first expedition through the rapids of the Grand Canyon.

The mission the founders articulated for the fledgling Society was "the increase and diffusion of geographic knowledge." They sensed, perhaps, that the Age of Exploration was drawing to a close and that scientific inquiry would replace discovery and conquest. They likely surmised that a globe whose limits were finite would require conservation and stewardship. They no doubt recognized that new mass communication technologies, including telephony and photography, could be used to spread knowledge.

They would have been visionaries indeed if they could have foreseen how the next century's new information technologies would transform geography itself. The cumulative revolution wrought by computers, satellite and aerial photography, global positioning systems satellites, GIS, and the Internet turned geographers from the relatively passive pursuits of observing and documenting the planet to the active endeavors of analysis, synthesis, prediction, and decision making. Geography can now assimilate and present—in its unique expression, cartography—a vast array of high-quality information, giving us an incomparable basis for understanding our world and taking action in it. Bell and Powell would be thrilled.

Today, scientists, businesspeople, soldiers, policy makers, and informed citizens of every country on Earth tap geographic knowledge via their computers, laptops, handheld devices—and modern atlases. The book in your hands is a conduit to a complex and nuanced view of the world you are entering. In time, you will take the world itself into your hands—to preserve, improve, and make safer and more prosperous.

Chief Cartographer
National Geographic Society

5

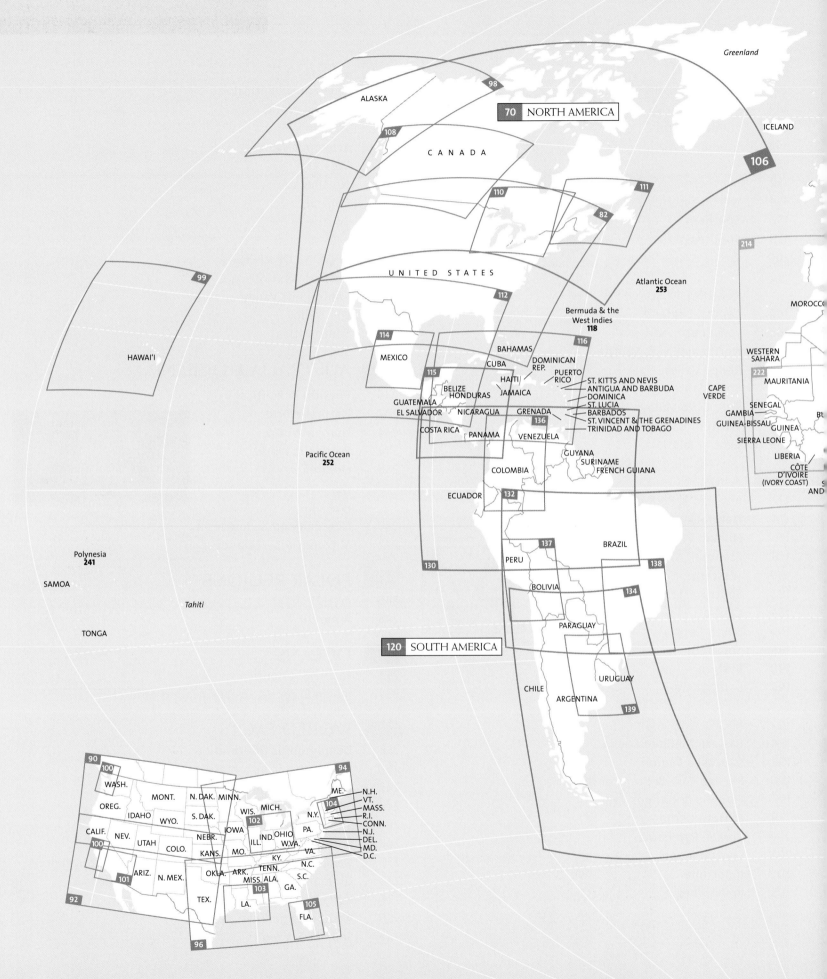

Greenland

ALASKA

70 NORTH AMERICA

ICELAND

C A N A D A

106

98

108

110

111

82

214

99

Atlantic Ocean
253

MOROCCO

U N I T E D   S T A T E S

112

HAWAI'I

Bermuda & the
West Indies
118

114

116

WESTERN
SAHARA

MEXICO

BAHAMAS

CUBA

DOMINICAN
REP.

PUERTO
RICO

222 MAURITANIA

CAPE
VERDE

115

HAITI

ST. KITTS AND NEVIS

BELIZE

JAMAICA

ANTIGUA AND BARBUDA

SENEGAL

HONDURAS

DOMINICA

GUATEMALA

ST. LUCIA

GAMBIA

EL SALVADOR

NICARAGUA

GRENADA

BARBADOS

GUINEA-BISSAU

GUINEA

136

ST. VINCENT & THE GRENADINES

COSTA RICA

TRINIDAD AND TOBAGO

SIERRA LEONE

PANAMA

VENEZUELA

Pacific Ocean
252

LIBERIA

GUYANA

CÔTE
D'IVOIRE
(IVORY COAST)

SURINAME

COLOMBIA

FRENCH GUIANA

AND

ECUADOR

132

BRAZIL

137

Polynesia
241

PERU

138

SAMOA

130

BOLIVIA

134

Tahiti

PARAGUAY

TONGA

120 SOUTH AMERICA

URUGUAY

CHILE

ARGENTINA

139

90

100

94

WASH.

MONT.

N. DAK.

MINN.

ME.

N.H.
VT.

OREG.

IDAHO

WYO.

S. DAK.

WIS.

MICH.

104

MASS.

R.I.

102

N.Y.

CONN.

CALIF.

NEV.

UTAH

NEBR.

IOWA

IND.

OHIO

PA.

N.J.

100

COLO.

ILL.

W.VA.

DEL.

MD.

KANS.

MO.

KY.

VA.

D.C.

ARIZ.

N. MEX.

OKLA.

ARK.

TENN.

N.C.

101

MISS.

ALA.

S.C.

92

TEX.

LA.

103

GA.

105

FLA.

96

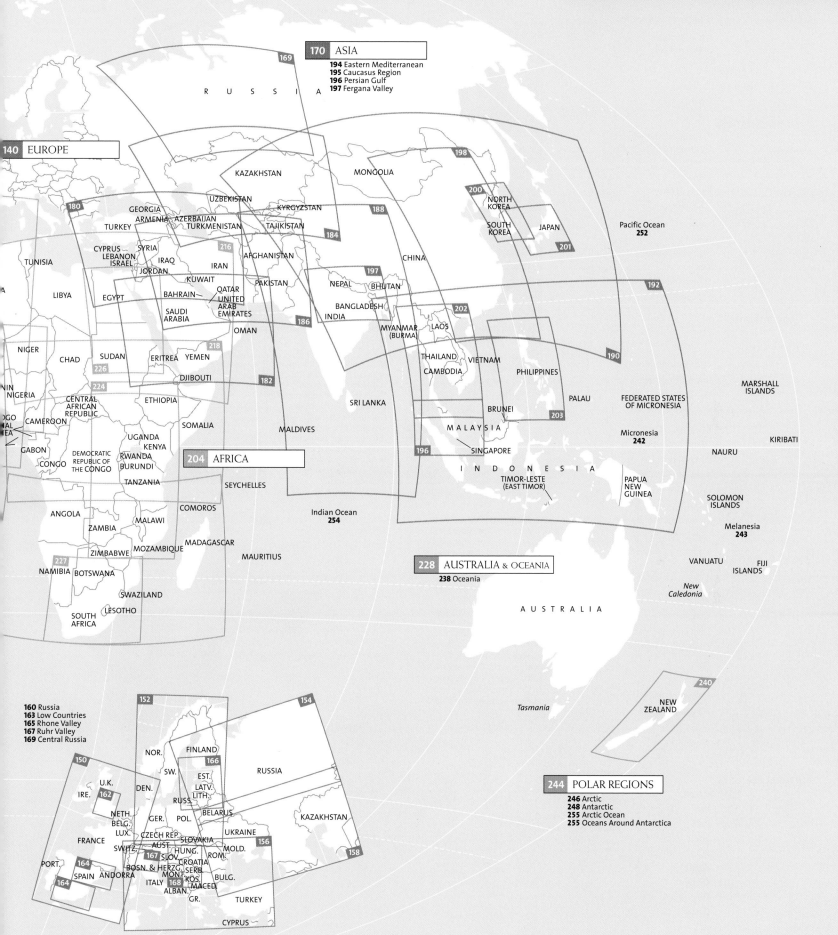

170 ASIA
- **194** Eastern Mediterranean
- **195** Caucasus Region
- **196** Persian Gulf
- **197** Fergana Valley

140 EUROPE

204 AFRICA

228 AUSTRALIA & OCEANIA
- **238** Oceania

160 Russia
163 Low Countries
165 Rhone Valley
167 Ruhr Valley
169 Central Russia

244 POLAR REGIONS
- **246** Arctic
- **248** Antarctic
- **255** Arctic Ocean
- **255** Oceans Around Antarctica

RUSSIA
KAZAKHSTAN
MONGOLIA
UZBEKISTAN
KYRGYZSTAN
GEORGIA
ARMENIA AZERBAIJAN
TURKEY TURKMENISTAN TAJIKISTAN
NORTH KOREA
SOUTH KOREA
JAPAN
Pacific Ocean **252**
CYPRUS SYRIA
LEBANON IRAQ
ISRAEL JORDAN
KUWAIT
IRAN
AFGHANISTAN
CHINA
TUNISIA
LIBYA
EGYPT
BAHRAIN QATAR
UNITED ARAB EMIRATES
SAUDI ARABIA
PAKISTAN
NEPAL
BHUTAN
BANGLADESH
INDIA
MYANMAR (BURMA)
LAOS
OMAN
NIGER
CHAD
SUDAN
ERITREA YEMEN
DJIBOUTI
THAILAND
VIETNAM
CAMBODIA
PHILIPPINES
PALAU
MARSHALL ISLANDS
NIGERIA
CENTRAL AFRICAN REPUBLIC
ETHIOPIA
SOMALIA
SRI LANKA
MALDIVES
BRUNEI
FEDERATED STATES OF MICRONESIA
CAMEROON
GABON CONGO
DEMOCRATIC REPUBLIC OF THE CONGO
UGANDA KENYA
RWANDA BURUNDI
MALAYSIA
SINGAPORE
Micronesia **242**
NAURU
KIRIBATI
TANZANIA
SEYCHELLES
INDONESIA
ANGOLA
ZAMBIA
MALAWI
COMOROS
MADAGASCAR
MAURITIUS
TIMOR-LESTE (EAST TIMOR)
PAPUA NEW GUINEA
SOLOMON ISLANDS
Melanesia **243**
ZIMBABWE MOZAMBIQUE
Indian Ocean **254**
VANUATU
FIJI ISLANDS
NAMIBIA BOTSWANA
SWAZILAND
SOUTH AFRICA LESOTHO
New Caledonia
AUSTRALIA
Tasmania
NEW ZEALAND

NOR.
FINLAND
SW.
RUSSIA
U.K.
IRE.
DEN.
EST.
LATV.
LITH.
RUSS.
BELARUS
NETH.
BELG.
LUX.
GER.
POL.
UKRAINE
KAZAKHSTAN
FRANCE
CZECH REP.
SLOVAKIA
SWITZ. AUST. HUNG. MOLD.
PORT.
ANDORRA
SPAIN
SLOV. CROATIA ROM.
BOSN. & HERZG. SERB.
MONT. KOS.
ITALY ALBAN. MACED.
BULG.
GR.
TURKEY
CYPRUS

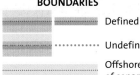

BOUNDARIES

	Defined
··········	Undefined or disputed
	Offshore line of separation

CITIES

✹ ✷ ⊛ ⊙   Capitals

● ● ·   Towns

TRANSPORTATION

UNDER CONSTRUCTION	Passenger railroad High-speed
UNDER CONSTRUCTION	Main line
→)═══(← ─)── ─(←	Tunnel
	Railroad ferry
UNDER CONSTRUCTION	Superhighway
UNDER CONSTRUCTION	Road
	Auto ferry
	Highway tunnel
- - - -	Trail
✈	Scheduled air service
⚲	Spaceport

WATER FEATURES

	Drainage
	Intermittent drainage
	Intermittent lake
	Dry salt lake
	Swamp
─ ─ ─	Channel
°	Water hole or well
	Limit of drift ice
	Bank or shoal
	Coral reef
302 200 84	Depth curves and soundings in meters
	Falls or rapids

PHYSICAL FEATURES

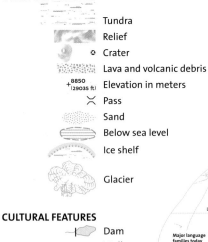

	Tundra
	Relief
✪	Crater
	Lava and volcanic debris
+8850 (29035 ft)	Elevation in meters
⤬	Pass
	Sand
	Below sea level
	Ice shelf
	Glacier

CULTURAL FEATURES

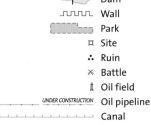

	Dam
⌐⌐⌐⌐⌐	Wall
	Park
⊡	Site
∴	Ruin
⤬	Battle
⛏	Oil field
UNDER CONSTRUCTION	Oil pipeline
	Canal

BOUNDARIES AND POLITICAL DIVISIONS

Red dots:
Claimed boundary; India claims the entire region of Kashmir—including areas now controlled by Pakistan and China

Broken boundary dots:
Disputed boundary; the line of control, a cease-fire line dating back to 1972, separates Indian and Pakistani forces

Single color band:
Internal country boundary

Double color band:
International boundary

Internal region type:
In this case, Punjab, a state of India

Most political boundaries depicted in this Atlas are stable and uncontested. Those that are disputed receive special treatment. Disputed areas are shown in a gray color, including the Palestinian territories (West Bank and Gaza Strip) and separatist states still claimed by other countries.

International boundaries and disputed territories, where scale permits, reflect de facto status at time of publication.

CITIES AND TOWNS

Star with ring:
Administrative capital for internal regions, such as provinces, states, and territories in Australia, Canada, Mexico, United Kingdom, and the United States

Small type and town spot:
City or town with fewer than 100,000 people

Bull's-eye:
Administrative capital for internal regions in most countries and for dependent territories

Star with double ring:
National capital; larger type size shows Dublin as a city between 100,000 and one million people

The regional political maps that form the bulk of this Atlas depict four categories of cities or towns. The largest cities, over five million, are shown in capital letters (for example, **LONDON**).

▼ WORLD THEMATIC MAPS

Thematic maps show the spatial distribution of physical or cultural phenomena in a way that is graphically illuminating and useful. This thematic map on language was created by National Geographic Maps, using a combination of data on subjects such as cultures, linguistics, and migrations, as well as consultation with experts. Thematic maps also use quantitative sources in the presentation of topics such as economics or health.

Major language families today

- Afro-Asiatic
- Altaic
- Austro-Asiatic
- Austronesian
- Dravidian
- Indo-European
- Japanese/Korean
- Kam-Tai
- Niger-Congo
- Nilo-Saharan
- Sino-Tibetan
- Uralic
- Other

▲ CONTINENTAL THEMATIC MAPS

This Atlas contains three spreads of thematic maps for each continent covering human, natural, and economic topics. The map shown here of Africa's vegetation, derived from satellite imagery, on-the-ground analysis, and population data for urban areas, was compiled using data from the University of Maryland Global Land Cover Facility.

TRANSPORTATION

Dashed red line:
Trail or track

Red line:
Road or highway

Double red line:
Superhighway; this includes interstates, motorways, and other limited-access highways

Plane symbol:
Airport with scheduled service

Dark gray line:
Passenger railroad

Double gray line:
High-speed passenger railroad

Red dots:
Intracoastal waterway

Dashed red line in water:
Car or passenger ferry

Superhighways and roads produce a dense network as they crisscross the Philadelphia area, but good roads and highways are rare in many parts of the world.

OTHER FEATURES

Brown dot pattern:
Sand

Blue circle:
Well or water hole

Dashed blue line:
Outlines intermittent lakes or dry salt lakes; here it marks the former shoreline of Lake Chad

Blue dot pattern:
Dry salt lake bed; often arid salt flats or pans that become ephemeral lakes after rainstorms

Blue line:
River

Blue swamp pattern:
Swamp, marsh, or other wetland

Blue line and dots:
Intermittent drainage; usually flows due to seasonal rains

Blue area with blue outline:
Perennial lake

Cross:
Mountain summit; elevation in meters—also in feet for highest elevations

Ironically, water features web this largely semiarid region of central Africa. Water is key to life on Earth. Lack of water can lead to desertification and human migration.

"*When people at a party ask me where I'm from and I say Morocco, the conversation often comes to a complete halt. Even if they know nothing about my country, people could ask where it is. Then they might ask me about its languages or religions or its physical appearance.*"

Amine Elouazzani, an American college graduate, could have at best been describing how to use the *National Geographic Collegiate Atlas of the World.* A well-educated person should know how to ask good questions and be able to read, understand, and appreciate maps. Use the political and thematic maps in this Atlas to orient yourself to the world at present and to inform your direction for the future.

The maps in the political, or reference, section of this Atlas show international boundaries, cities, national parks, road networks, and other features. They are organized by continent, and each section begins with an overview of the continent's physical and human geography. In the index, most entries are keyed to place-names on the political maps, citing the page number, followed by their geographic coordinates. The thematic maps at the front of the Atlas explore topics in depth, revealing the rich patchwork and infinite interrelatedness of our changing planet. In selecting from the vast storehouse of knowledge about the Earth, the Atlas editors relied upon proven data sources, such as the World Health Organization, United Nations, World Wildlife Fund, U.S. Census Bureau, and U.S. Department of Commerce.

Maps inform us, feed our curiosity, and help us shape our inquiry in spatial and temporal terms. They enable us to move beyond our boundaries and engage in conversation with each other.

▼ GRAPHS, CHARTS, AND TABLES

Conveying relationships, facts, and trends quickly and efficiently is the work of these types of displays. They are diagrams that compare information in visual form. Three common types are the bar graph, the line graph, and the circle (or pie) chart. This Atlas uses all three conventions. The bar graph below, from the Health & Literacy thematic spread, compares male and female literacy rates for a range of countries and in relation to world averages. The viewer gains immediate insight not only into the level of literacy in a society but also into the relative value and status accorded to women. These graphic presentations summarize complex data and are most valuable when they generate deep and penetrating inquiry.

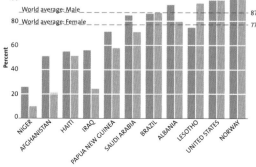

Male and female literacy rates, 2005 estimate
(as a percentage of total population age 15 and over)

GeoBytes

UNIQUE SPECIES
Madagascar and the Indian Ocean islands are home to many species found nowhere else. Of the region's 13,000 plant species, more than 89% are endemic, meaning that is the only place on Earth they live.

FRAGILE POPULATIONS
Nearly half of the world's tortoises and freshwater turtles are threatened.

HUMAN HEALTH
Medicines derived from plants and animals are the primary source of health care for 80% of the world's population.

ECONOMIC VALUE
Scientists estimate that ecosystems worldwide provide goods and services, such as nutrient recycling and waste treatment, valued at more than $20 trillion a year.

EXTINCTION RISK
One in every eight birds and one in every four mammals face a high risk of extinction in the near future.

BEETLEMANIA
Beetles are the most diverse life-form on Earth. More than a thousand different kinds can live on a single tree in the forests of South America.

▲ TEXT AND GEOBYTES
A blue box on each spread is headed GeoBytes—short, striking facts chosen on a need-to-know or fun-to-know basis. Each thematic spread is introduced with a text block that discusses the theme and alludes to the graphic presentations. Each map or graphic is anchored by explanatory text for a complete and coherent unit.

▼ OTHER UNIQUE FEATURES
The Atlas employs a variety of images and mapping techniques to express data. A cartogram, for instance, depicts the size of an object, such as a country, in relation to an attribute, not geographic space. Grounded in research by the Population Reference Bureau, this cartogram represents countries by unit of population, with only a suggestive nod to geographical location. An economic cartogram shows the relative prosperity of the countries of the world. In both cases, editors chose cartograms as the most visually striking way to convey the information. On a map showing the distribution of human population, LandScan global population databases were used, as the most reliable and visually striking tool. While this Atlas is distinguished by its thematic maps, individual thematic maps are, in turn, distinguished by the number of variables analyzed. For example, a thematic map on economy shows Gross Domestic Product by agriculture, manufacturing, and services. Another on land cover parses out pasture, cropland, and forest.

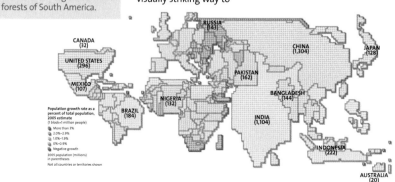

Population growth rate as a percent of total population, 2005 estimate
(1 block=1 million people)

MAP SCALE RELATIONSHIPS IN THIS ATLAS

MAP PROJECTIONS

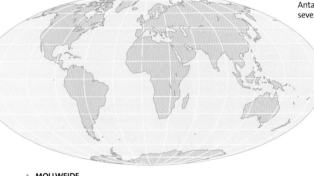

▲ **LAMBERT AZIMUTHAL EQUAL-AREA**
Distortion away from the center makes this projection a poor choice for world maps but useful for fairly circular regions. It is used on the Trade & Globalization spread, pages 56-57, in the Income Group, 2005, map.

▼ **ORTHOGRAPHIC**
Designed to show Earth as seen from a distant point in space, the orthographic is usually used to portray hemispheres. Distortion at the edges, however, compresses landmasses.

▲ **ALBERS CONIC EQUAL-AREA**
The Albers is a good format for mapping mid-latitude regions that are larger east to west than

north to south. Most maps of the United States in the Atlas appear on this projection.

▲ **AZIMUTHAL EQUIDISTANT**
Mapmakers can choose any center point, from which directions and distances are true, but in outer areas shapes and sizes are distorted. On this projection, Antarctica, the Arctic Ocean, and several continents appear.

▲ **MOLLWEIDE**
In 1805, Carl B. Mollweide, a German mathematician, devised this elliptical equal-area projection that represents

relative sizes accurately but distorts shapes at the edges. Many thematic maps in the Atlas use the Mollweide.

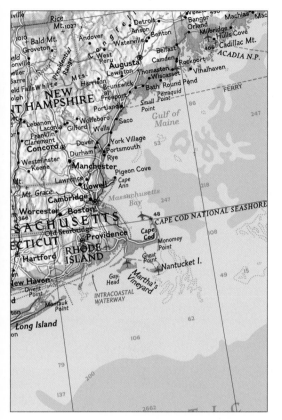

Map scale describes the relationship between distance on a map and distance on the ground. It is usually presented as a ratio or fraction in any of three ways. Verbal scale is a written description of scale, such as "one centimeter equals 100 kilometers," meaning one centimeter on the map is equal to 100 kilometers on the ground. A graphic scale is a bar or line with tick marks showing units such as kilometers or miles that graphically represent scale. A representative fraction (RF) or ratio scale indicates how much the size of a physical area was reduced to fit on the map by showing the relationship between one unit on the map and one unit of the same length on the ground. For example, if the scale is in centimeters and reads 1:10,000,000 (or 1/10,000,000), then each centimeter on the map represents 100 kilometers on the ground.

Political maps in this Atlas were created in a range of scales from global cartographic databases that merged data from maps NGS created in the past. These "seamless" databases give NGS the ability to map anywhere in the world at an appropriate scale.

From left to right, these four maps illustrate the relationship between the scale of a map and the area shown. The area shown decreases as scale increases, while the level of detail shown increases. Smaller scale maps such as the U.S. map on the far left (1:36,000,000) show more area but only the largest features are visible. Large scale maps, such as the map of Cape Cod (1:1,750,000), show a small area but in greater detail.

WINKEL TRIPEL
First developed by Oswald Winkel in 1921, this "tripel" projection avoids the congestion and compression of polar areas that are common to many projections. The shapes of countries and islands closely resemble their true shapes as one would see on a globe.

INTERRUPTED GOODE HOMOLOSINE
To minimize distortion of shape and preserve horizontal scale, this projection interrupts the globe. Its equal-area quality makes it suitable for mapping distributions of various kinds of information.

BUCKMINSTER FULLER
Also known as the "Dymaxion map," this projection created by Richard Buckminster Fuller in the mid-20th century mostly retains the relative size of each part of the globe. Because the continents are not split, one can better see the interconnectedness of the Earth's landmasses.

MERCATOR
Named for Gerardus Mercator, the Flemish geographer who invented it in 1569, this most famous of all map projections was intended for navigation. Useful for showing constant bearings as straight lines, the Mercator greatly exaggerates areas at higher latitudes.

ECKERT EQUAL-AREA
Produced by German educator Max Eckert, this projection represents the Poles by a line one-half the length of the Equator. Polar regions are less compressed than on elliptical projections; low-latitude landmasses are elongated.

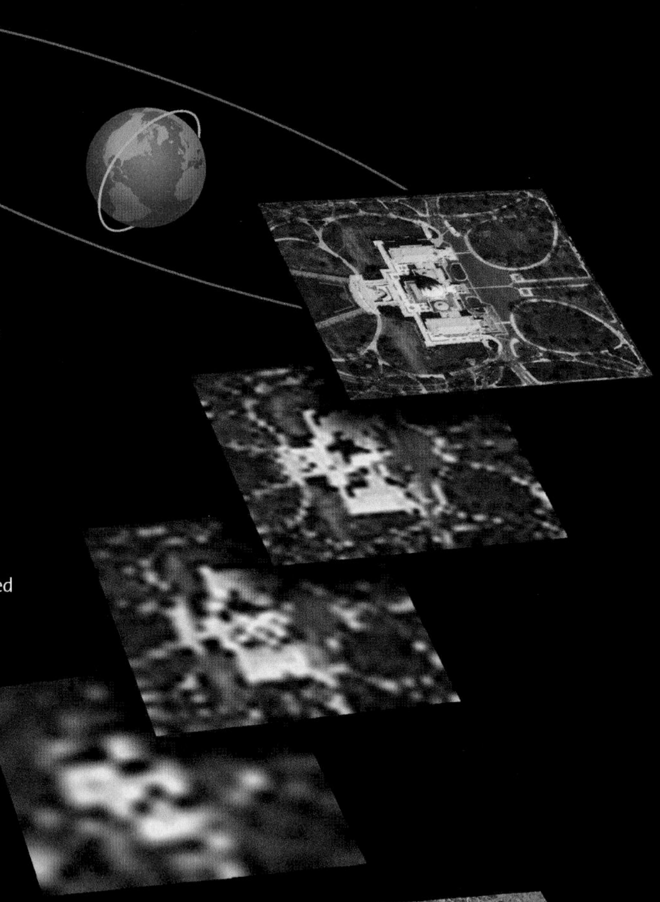

EYES IN THE SKY

Geostationary satellites follow the Earth's path 35,888 kilometers (22,300 miles) above, giving us a wide window to life below. Low-altitude satellites cross the Equator and the Poles many times per day and eventually view most of the planet.

COMING IN FOCUS

With increased spatial resolution, details emerge in these computer-generated images based on an aerial photograph of the U.S. Capitol in Washington, D.C. From bottom to top, they mimic the 30 (98)-, 15 (49)-, 10 (33)-, and 1-meter (3-feet) resolution of commercial satellites.

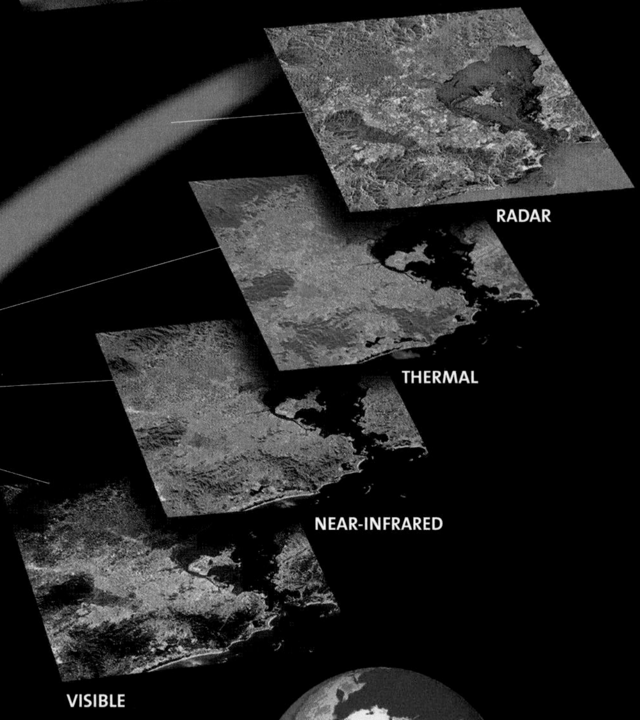

RADAR

THERMAL

NEAR-INFRARED

VISIBLE

RANGE OF SIGHT

From short wavelengths to long, these images give us a detailed view of Rio de Janeiro. They show, from bottom to top, the area as seen in visible light; vegetation (red) as seen in near-infrared; heat (bright colors) in thermal; and the city's features (black and white) as seen in radar.

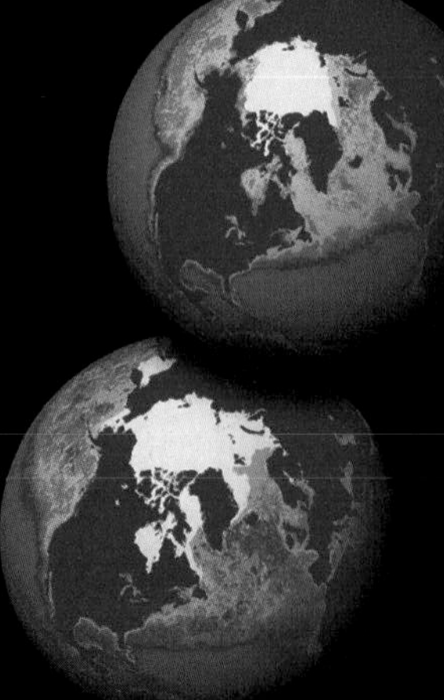

SPOTTING CHANGE

Composite images compiled from low-altitude satellite data illustrate seasonal changes across the globe. Polar ice (white) creeps southward in February (bottom) and by September (top) it has retreated and phytoplankton flourishes (red, orange, and yellow).

The human eye sees only a tiny fraction of the spectrum of electromagnetic radiation that illuminates the world, a narrow band known as "visible" radiation. With the aid of remote sensing, we are able to view a wider range of that spectrum, including infrared, thermal, and microwave bands. From space, we are also able to view large expanses of the Earth, as well as small areas, in great detail. From an altitude of 730 kilometers (454 miles), Landsat 7 can view features as small as 15 meters (49 feet) across. Scientists use remote-sensing satellite data to understand global processes on the Earth's surface, in the oceans, and in the lower atmosphere.

This mosaic image of North America illustrates some of the types of remotely sensed data that scientists have access to today. The eastern third of the continent shows clusters of light on the Earth's surface visible from space at night, helping us better understand urbanization and population density. False-color is used in the middle of the continent to show surface-feature classes. Reds and purples represent different classes or types of vegetation; blues show arid land. Images like this are useful for environmental monitoring. The westernmost part of the continent is in true color. The greener areas are more densely vegetated and less populated. Vibrant colors of the oceans represent sea-surface temperature. Areas in red are the warmest; the blues are the coolest.

To create this image, data were extracted from a number of datasets—the Advanced Very High Resolution Radiometer (AVHRR), the Moderate Resolution Imaging Spectroradiometer (MODIS), and versions 4, 5, and 7 of the Landsat Enhanced Thematic Mapper (ETM). The base of the image was enhanced with shaded relief produced from Shuttle Radar Topography Mission (SRTM) digital elevation model (DEM) data.

IMAGE BY ROBERT STACEY, WORLDSAT INTERNATIONAL INC.

A century ago balloonists recorded bird's-eye views of the landscape below on film. Today satellites take increasingly detailed pictures of Earth, penetrating darkness and clouds to create composite images of the land and seafloor and to map once-elusive features such as the ozone hole. Remote sensing—the examination of the Earth from a distance—has widespread applications, from military surveillance to archeological exposure. And, by layering different sets of remotely sensed data, scientists can study relationships between phenomena such as shrinking polar ice and rising global temperatures.

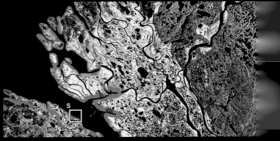

Satellite images from 1973 to 1999 were used to measure change along Canada's Beaufort Sea coastline, an area highly sensitive to erosion. This image illustrates areas of rapid erosion (red), moderate erosion (orange), no detectable erosion (green), and accretion (blue).

This image shows the widespread flooding that occurred throughout North Carolina in late September 1999 after the region was hit by Hurricanes Dennis and Floyd. Flooded areas are shown in light blue, rivers in dark blue, roads in red, and the coastline in green.

Nearly 4,450 hectares (11,000 acres) burned in the February 2006 Sierra fire in Orange County, California. Deep red tones in the center of this Landsat image show the burned areas on February 12th, the day the fire was contained.

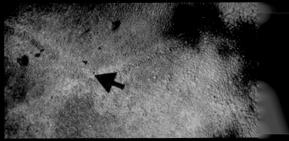

With the help of remote-sensing imagery, archeologists have identified ancient footpaths in the Arenal Region of Costa Rica. These 2,500-year-old footpaths are being used to study the prehistoric religious, economic, political, and social organization of the region.

UNDERSTANDING OUR WORLD THROUGH GIS

Geographic Information Systems (GIS) is a digitally organized collection of computer hardware, software, methodology, and data assemblage and storage. GIS supports the capture, manipulation, and analysis of place-based information. A highly adaptable tool, GIS provides the means to store and display geographic data and to analyze and describe patterns, distributions, and phenomena. Because so many human and environmental issues can be usefully considered in geographic terms, GIS is becoming increasingly common across a range of enterprises. Foresters use GIS data to inventory trees. Epidemiologists model and predict the spread of disease. Policy makers, environmentalists, and city planners employ GIS technologies to analyze issues and provide dramatic visualizations for matters ranging from wildfire management in the western United States to the rates of suburban sprawl in India's burgeoning cities. The attraction of GIS comes from the magnitude of its analytical capabilities that, in turn, derive from once-unimaginable powers of manipulation of spatial data to suit specific needs. For example, a table with latitude/longitude coordinates of car crashes can be overlaid with a road network to route emergency service vehicles and estimate their arrival time. Combine the crash incident database with other geospatial data, such as terrain, weather, transportation infrastructure, or socioeconomic characteristics, and traffic planners can determine contributing factors to accidents and recommend preventative action. More and more, GIS is the analytical tool for understanding patterns and processes that affect our lives.

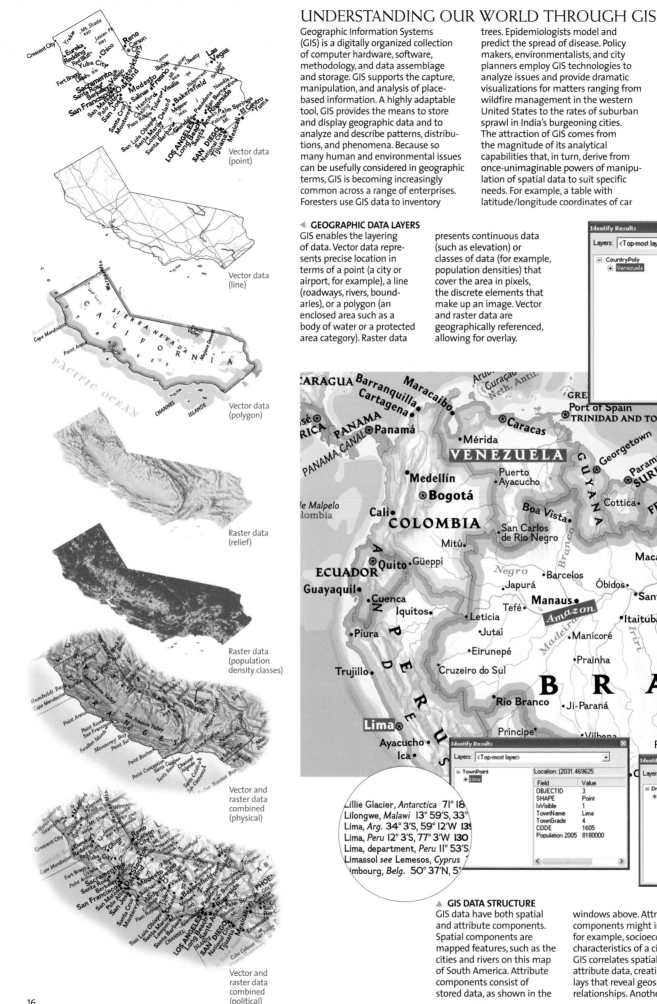

Vector data (point)

Vector data (line)

Vector data (polygon)

Raster data (relief)

Raster data (population density classes)

Vector and raster data combined (physical)

Vector and raster data combined (political)

◄ **GEOGRAPHIC DATA LAYERS**
GIS enables the layering of data. Vector data represents precise location in terms of a point (a city or airport, for example), a line (roadways, rivers, boundaries), or a polygon (an enclosed area such as a body of water or a protected area category). Raster data presents continuous data (such as elevation) or classes of data (for example, population densities) that cover the area in pixels, the discrete elements that make up an image. Vector and raster data are geographically referenced, allowing for overlay.

▲ **GIS DATA STRUCTURE**
GIS data have both spatial and attribute components. Spatial components are mapped features, such as the cities and rivers on this map of South America. Attribute components consist of stored data, as shown in the windows above. Attribute components might include, for example, socioeconomic characteristics of a city. GIS correlates spatial and attribute data, creating overlays that reveal geospatial relationships. Another use of GIS is digital indexing, which constituted a major advance over laborious and error-prone manual compilation. This Atlas used customized GIS software to coordinate place-names with latitude and longitude (bubble).

URBAN PLANNING

GIS can be used to inventory and visualize urban land use patterns. The strict code of zoning laws and classifications common to cities and towns requires an accurate database management system. GIS can not only manage the zoning database but can also portray the data in a map. Such visualization can help clarify development issues, plan resource allocations, or identify park and open space needs. Maps with specific GIS overlays can provide common ground for discussion in public forums that may address questions of, for example, school zones, land ownership, or sprawl.

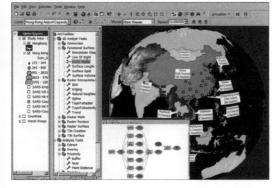

TRANSPORTATION

Many applications of GIS exist within the transportation sector and work particularly well when coupled with the pinpoint accuracy of Global Positioning System (GPS) technology. Freight shipping companies frequently turn to GIS to estimate arrival times of their trucks, using real-time traffic information, digital representations of nationwide transportation infrastructure, and GPS information. Individual drivers have become accustomed to using GIS and GPS for finding directions and avoiding traffic jams.

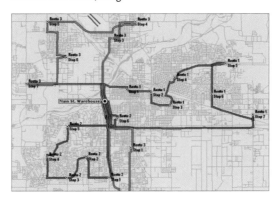

At the dawn of the Age of Exploration, the problem facing mapmakers was a dearth of information. With geospatial data flowing from satellite imagery, aerial photography, on-the-ground surveying, quantitative data, and archival records, the challenge for cartographers became how to manage a wealth of information. Geographic Information Systems (GIS), a sophisticated and versatile digital tool set with a wide range of applications, provides a solution. The data management capabilities of this digital technology make geospatial information readily available for analysis, modeling, and mapping. Scientists use GIS to inventory plant and animal species in their native habitats. Disaster relief managers identify at-risk areas and evacuation routes. The 2004 U.S. presidential election marked the first time that GIS software was used to collate and present near-real-time voting tallies. While GIS allows the layering of information, on-board and handheld Global Positioning System (GPS) devices pinpoint location. Today, geospatial concepts permeate ordinary life to an extraordinary degree.

EMERGENCY MANAGEMENT

In emergency management, GIS can be used to model potential disasters, track real-time weather, plan and adjust evacuation routes, define disaster areas, and inventory damage. Predicting and tracking wildfire helps fire management crews plan and allocate resources. GIS can show the before-and-after appearance of the land affected by a disaster, which can help recovery and show how to plan ahead for next time.

DEMOGRAPHICS & CENSUS

The U.S. Census Bureau stores demographic and socioeconomic data at numerous levels, even at the county, tract, or city-block level. Applying spatial analysis techniques to such archival data can reveal patterns, trends, and distributions. The findings can be put to various uses, including encouraging economic development or indicating the results of elections.

HEALTH

During the 2002-03 SARS outbreak in China, an Internet GIS server allowed for the rapid collection and dissemination of data to health officials and the public. This application tracked the spread of the disease, detected patterns, and distributed accurate information. GIS is currently being used to monitor the H5N1 strain of avian flu around the world, combining outbreaks with pertinent data such as wildfowl migration routes and locations of poultry farms.

CONSERVATION

Mapping the effects of human population growth and deforestation on Asian elephant habitat highlights the versatility of GIS. Satellite images, demographic data, and elephant locations derived from radio tracking and GPS yielded a comprehensive database and visualization of elephant viability in Myanmar (formerly Burma). The study demonstrated that the rate of deforestation caused by human population growth was lower here than in most countries of Southeast Asia and that as a result elephant populations were less affected .

Earth was born of an agglomeration of dust and rock, gravity sucking ever more fragments into its mass as the young planet wobbled in its orbital path. Early on, an infant planet about the size of Mars struck Earth. With the aggregation of solid particles from the impact, the Moon took shape. Earth stabilized in its orbit around the Sun. A bombardment of comets and asteroids pocked the Moon; Earth absorbed meteor hits with little visible impact. Continents drifted and collided, oceans filled the basins. Another great agent of change, life in the form of massive colonies of photosynthesizing cyanobacteria pumped oxygen into the atmosphere. Oxygen-breathing organisms evolved on land. Now humans—all six billion and more—have become a major force. Our burning of fossil fuels pumps carbon dioxide, a major greenhouse gas, into the atmosphere and heats the planet. Industrial and agricultural chemicals, human effluent, and rubbish pollute land, air, and water. Travel, more common and speedier than ever before, spreads ideas, commerce, culture, alien plant and animal species, and diseases at an unprecedented rate. Resources of food and fuel are unevenly distributed. Ideologies clash; turmoil and wars devastate societies. Yet good will, learning, and ingenuity may be marshaled to mitigate adverse consequences. Earth goes forward on its own course and in its own time. The adventure continues, and geography helps to write the record.

The human footprint on planet Earth

Most impacted

Least impacted

PHYSICAL REGIONS
This artist-rendered relief map depicts Earth's land-forms above and below the surface of the ocean. Major mountain systems are shaded to emphasize their elevation. The Himalaya tower over India's Ganges plain; the Andes and Rocky Mountains reign over the Americas. All are dwarfed by the Mid-Atlantic Ridge, a submarine mountain range that stretches from Iceland to near Antarctica.

WESTERN HEMISPHERE

WINKEL TRIPEL PROJECTION, CENTRAL MERIDIAN 0°
SCALE 1:96,338,000
1 centimeter = 963 kilometers; 1 inch = 1520 miles at the equator

0 500 1000 1500 2000 2500
KILOMETERS

0 500 1000 1500 2000 2500
STATUTE MILES

EASTERN
HEMISPHERE

POLITICAL BOUNDARIES

The world is divided into 194 independent countries, with colors on the map showing the extents of national sovereignty. International boundaries only occasionally mark true cultural boundaries; they are more often a complex artifact of colonialism, conquest, religious conversion, and conflict. The political map is a useful but all-too-neat construct for a bewilderingly complicated world.

ARCTIC REGION

0   600 km

0   600 mi

Azimuthal Equidistant Projection

ANTARCTIC REGION

0 600 km
0 600 mi
Azimuthal Equidistant Projection
• Research station

HISTORICAL EARTH AND TECTONICS

Cataclysms such as volcanoes and earthquakes, which occur most often along plate boundaries, capture attention, but the tectonic movement that underlies them is imperceptibly slow. How slow? The Mid-Atlantic Ridge, for example, which is being built up by magma oozing between the North American and African plates, grows at about the speed of a human fingernail.

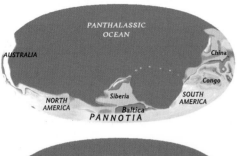

◀ 600 MILLION YEARS AGO
A supercontinent, known as Rodina, split apart, and oceans filled the basins. Fragments collided, thrusting up mountain ranges. Glaciers spread, twice covering the Equator. A new polar supercontinent, Pannotia, formed.

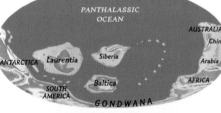

◀ 500 MILLION YEARS AGO
A breakaway chunk of Pannotia drifted north, splitting into three masses—Laurentia (North America), Baltica (northern Europe), and Siberia. In shallow waters, the first multicellular animals with exoskeletons appeared, and the Cambrian explosion of life took off.

◀ 300 MILLION YEARS AGO
Laurentia collided with Baltica and later with Avalonia (Britain and New England). The Appalachian mountains arose along the edge of the supercontinent, Pangaea, as a new ice age ensued.

◀ 200 MILLION YEARS AGO
Dinosaurs roamed the Pangaean land mass, which stretched nearly from Pole to Pole and almost encircled Tethys, the oceanic ancestor of the Mediterranean Sea. The Pacific's predecessor, the immense Panthalassic Ocean, surrounded the supercontinent.

◀ 100 MILLION YEARS AGO
Pangaea broke apart. The Atlantic poured in between Africa and the Americas. India split away from Africa, and Antarctica and Australia were stranded near the South Pole.

◀ 50 MILLION YEARS AGO
A meteorite wiped out the dinosaurs. Drifting continental fragments collided—Africa into Eurasia, pushing up the Alps; India into Asia, raising the Himalaya. Birds and once-tiny mammals began to fill the ecological niche vacated by dinosaurs.

◀ PRESENT DAY
Formation of the Isthmus of Panama and the split of Australia from Antarctica changed ocean currents, cooling the air. Ice sheets gouged out the Great Lakes just 20,000 years ago. Since then, warmer temperatures have melted ice, and sea levels have risen.

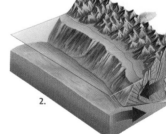

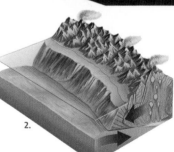

Tectonic feature

Plate boundary
- ᴧᴧ Divergent
- ▲▲ Convergent
- ┼┼ Transform zone

Plate motion
- → Divergent (arrow length proportional to plate motion speed)
- → Convergent
- ◯ Hot spot

Major tectonic event in the last 100 years

Earthquake
- ● Ten deadliest
- △ Ten costliest
- · Other

Volcanic eruption
- △ Notable
- ᴧ Known during the past 10,000 years

1. SEAFLOOR SPREADING
Adjacent oceanic plates slowly diverge, at the rate of a few centimeters a year. Along such boundaries—the Mid-Atlantic Ridge and the East Pacific Rise—molten rock (magma) pours forth to form new crust (lithosphere).

2. SUBDUCTION
When two massive plates collide, the older, colder, denser one—usually the oceanic plate meeting a continental plate—takes a dive. Pushed into the interior of the Earth, it is transformed into molten material that may rise again in volcanic eruption. Subduction also causes earthquakes, raises coastal mountains, and creates island arcs such as the Aleutians and the Lesser Antilles.

E arth's crust may appear stable and fixed, but, as earthquakes and volcanic activity remind us, Earth's crust is in constant motion, propelled by the heat and pressure of a 2,900-kilometer (1,800-mile)-thick zone of molten rock surrounding a metallic core. Earth's brittle surface—the lithosphere—is cracked into great rafts of rock, called plates, averaging 97 kilometers (60 miles) thick and thousands of kilometers wide. As the plates shift, they change the face of the planet, raising up mountains, generating earthquakes and tsunamis, and firing volcanoes.

GeoBytes

FIRST SEISMOGRAPH
The Chinese invented the first device to register earthquakes in the first century A.D.

"THE BIG ONE"
The North American West Coast is one of the most earthquake-threatened regions in the world.

TECTONICS THEORY
Plate tectonics has proven as central to Earth sciences as the discovery of the structure of the atom has been to physics and chemistry and the theory of evolution to biology.

NEW NEIGHBORS
Moving slowly to the northwest, the Pacific plate carries a sliver of California, including Los Angeles, which will become a suburb of San Francisco—in a few million years.

RISKY BEHAVIOR
Today, 500 million people live within striking distance of 550 or so active volcanoes.

Map labels:

TIC OCEAN
EURASIAN PLATE
ASIA
URAL MOUNTAINS
GREENLAND
Iceland
Grimsvötn, Iceland
Surtsey, Iceland
Shiveluch, Russia
Bezymyannaya, Russia
Ksudach, Russia
Azores
New England
EUROPE
ALPS
1999 (August) Turkey
1999 (November) Turkey
1998 Armenia
1980 Italy
1908 Messina, Italy
1948 Ashgabat Turkmenistan
1932 Gansu Province, China
1927 Qinghai, China
1920 Gansu Province, China
2005 Kashmir
Plateau of Tibet
HIMALAYA
Mt. Everest 8,850
1994 Kuril Islands, Russia; Hokkaido, Japan
1976 Tangshan, China
2004 Niigata, Japan
1923 Kanto, Japan
1995 Kobe, Japan
NORTH PACIFIC OCEAN
RING OF FIRE
ARABIAN PLATE
Nubia Plate
Tibesti Uplift
Afar
AFRICA
AFRICAN PLATE
Cape Verde
INDIAN PLATE
1999 Taiwan
Pinatubo, Philippines
Taal, Philippines
PHILIPPINE PLATE
PACIFIC PLATE
Caroline
EQUATOR
2004 Sumatra, Indonesia
East Africa
Kilimanjaro 5,895
Somali Plate
Comoros
St. Helena
SOUTH ATLANTIC OCEAN
Madagascar
Réunion
INDIAN OCEAN
CAPRICORN PLATE
Edge of diffuse plate boundary
Location uncertain
Rabaul Caldera, Papua New Guinea
Ulawun, Papua New Guinea
Merapi, Indonesia
Kelut, Indonesia
Agung, Indonesia
Lamington, Papua New Guinea
AUSTRALIAN PLATE
AUSTRALIA
Walvis Ridge
Crozet
Kerguelen
Bouvet
East Australia
Mt. Kosciuszko 2,228
Ruapehu, New Zealand
Tasmantid
ANTARCTIC PLATE
ANTARCTICA

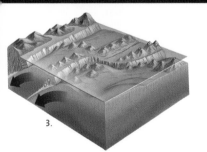

3. ACCRETION
As ocean plates advance on continental edges or island arcs and slide under them, seamounts on the ocean floor are skimmed off and pile up in submarine trenches. The buildup can fuse with continental plates, as most geologists agree was the case with Alaska and much of western North America.

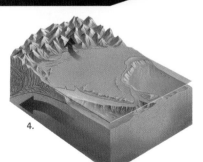

4. COLLISION
When continental plates meet, the resulting forces can build impressive mountain ranges. Earth's highest landforms—the Himalaya and adjacent Tibetan Plateau—were born when the Indian plate rammed into the Eurasian plate 50 million years ago.

5. FAULTING
Boundaries at which plates slip alongside each other are called transform faults. An example is California's San Andreas fault, which accommodates the stresses between the North American and Pacific plates. Large and sudden displacements—strike-slip movements—can create high-magnitude earthquakes.

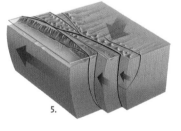

6. HOT SPOTS
A column of magma rising from deep in the mantle, a hot spot is a thermal plume that literally burns a hole in Earth's rocky crust. The result? Volcanoes, geysers, and new islands. Eruptions occur at plate boundaries, such as in Iceland and the Galápagos, as well as within plates, such as the volcanoes of Hawai'i and the geysers of Yellowstone.

EOLIAN LANDFORMS
Sand dunes

BARCHAN
The most common type of sand dune, the points of these crescent-shaped dunes lie downwind.

LONGITUDINAL
These are narrow, lengthy sand ridges that lie parallel to the prevailing wind direction.

PARABOLIC
Similar in shape to barchans, the points of these crescent-shaped dunes lie upwind.

TRANSVERSE
Looking like sandy sea waves, these dunes form perpendicular to the prevailing wind.

STAR
Formed by winds blowing from many directions, these pyramidal sand mounds grow upward.

GeoBytes

LOESS PLATEAU, CHINA
The thickest known loess (windblown silt) deposits are 335 meters (1,100 feet) deep. The plateau possesses fertile soil and high cliffs.

GANGES RIVER DELTA
The world's largest delta is formed by the Ganges and Brahmaputra Rivers. Its area is about the size of Ireland.

PERU–BOLIVIA ALTIPLANO
Second only to Tibet's plateau in elevation and extent, the Altiplano is a basin 4,000 meters (13,000 feet) high.

LAKE BAIKAL, RUSSIA
This lake lies in the planet's deepest fault-generated trough, a rift about 9 kilometers (5.6 miles) deep.

ICE SHEETS
These dome-shaped masses of glacier ice cover Greenland and Antarctica today. Glaciers blanketed most of Canada 12,000 years ago.

HIGH PLATEAUS
Possessing gentle slopes over much of their area, high plateaus are distinctly elevated above surrounding land. An example: the Colorado Plateau. Rivers on plateaus often cut deep valleys or canyons.

PLAINS
The legacy of exogenic forces after millions of years, these gently sloping regions result from eroded sediments that are transported and deposited by glaciers, rivers, and oceans.

WIDELY SPACED MOUNTAINS
Found, for instance, in the Great Basin in the U.S., this feature consists of heavily eroded mountains, where the eroded material fills the adjacent valleys.

MOUNTAINS
Mountains are formed by tectonic folds and faults and by magma moving to the surface. Mountains exhibit steep slopes, form elongated ranges, and cover one-fifth of the world's land surface.

LANDFORMS OF THE WORLD
The map shows the seven landforms that make up the Earth.

Major landform types
- Mountains
- Widely spaced mountains
- High plateaus
- Hills and low plateaus
- Depressions
- Plains
- Ice sheets

LANDFORMS

VOLCANIC
1. Crater Lake, Oregon
The caldera, now filled by Crater Lake, was produced by an eruption some 7,000 years ago.

VOLCANIC
2. Misti Volcano, Peru
A stratovolcano, or composite volcano, it is composed of hardened lava and volcanic ash.

VOLCANIC
3. Mount Fuji, Japan
Japan's highest peak at 3,776 meters (12,388 feet), Mt. Fuji is made up of three superimposed volcanoes.

EXOGENIC
4. Isle of Skye, Scotland
A pinnacle of basalt lava, known as the Old Man of Storr, resulted from millions of years of erosion.

KARST
5. Southern China
Steep-sided hills, or tower karst, dominate a karst landscape, where rainfall erodes limestone rock.

FLUVIAL LANDFORMS

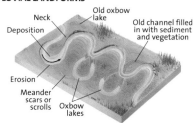

Neck · Old oxbow lake · Deposition · Old channel filled in with sediment and vegetation · Erosion · Meander scars or scrolls · Oxbow lakes

▲ MEANDERS
Meanders are the smooth, rounded bends of rivers that increase in size as a floodplain widens. Meanders form as faster currents erode the river's outer banks while adding sediment to the inner banks. Erosion eventually cuts off the meander, creating an oxbow lake. Floods can suddenly change a river's course.

GLACIAL LANDFORMS

▼ GLACIAL
Glaciers fill river valleys and bury them in ice. Ice sheets, including the ones that covered parts of North America and Europe, can be hundreds of meters thick. Migrating glacial ice transforms preglacial topography as it grinds away rock in its path. Debris, carried by the ice, is deposited when the glacier stops advancing—further changing the terrain.

Meltwater · Ice dammed lake · Ice sheet · Ice block · Tunnel

Esker formed by stream under ice sheet · Drumlin shaped by overriding glacier · Kettle lakes formed when ice blocks melt · Terminal moraines formed at margins of ice

▲ POSTGLACIAL
Mountain glaciers leave behind sharp-edged ridges and steep-sided valleys—causing waterfalls to plunge down sheer slopes. Areas that were covered with ice sheets, such as the Canadian Shield, exhibit stony soils, lowlands dotted with lakes, and grooved bedrock surfaces.

Map labels: Greenland · Brooks Ra. · Alaska Ra. · Rocky Mountains · Great Plains · Canadian Shield · NORTH AMERICA · Great Basin · Ozark Plateau · Appalachian Mts. · Colorado Plateau · Sa. Madre Oriental · Coastal Plain · Sa. Madre Occidental · Hawaiian Islands · PACIFIC OCEAN · EQUATOR · ATLANTIC OCEAN · Guiana Highlands · Amazon Basin · SOUTH AMERICA · Brazilian Highlands · Andes · Altiplano · Pampas · Patagonia · ATLANTIC OCEAN

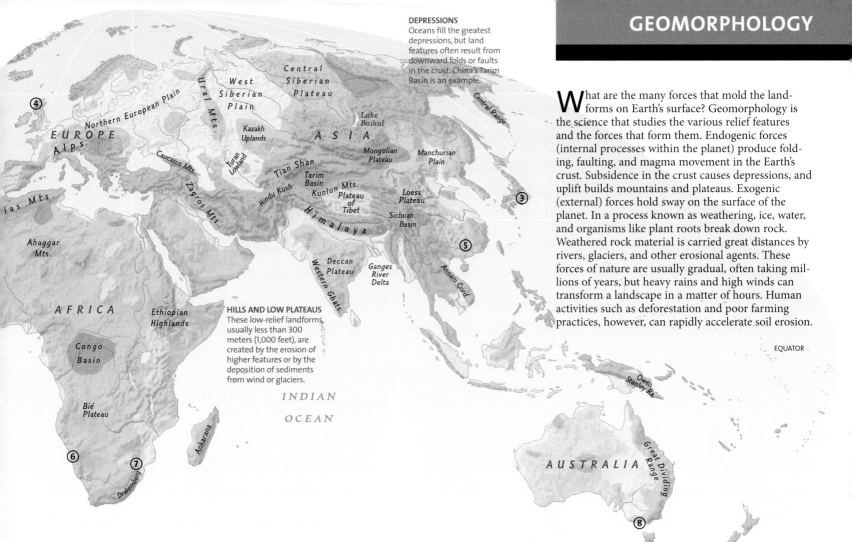

DEPRESSIONS
Oceans fill the greatest depressions, but land features often result from downward folds or faults in the crust. China's Tarim Basin is an example.

HILLS AND LOW PLATEAUS
These low-relief landforms, usually less than 300 meters (1,000 feet), are created by the erosion of higher features or by the deposition of sediments from wind or glaciers.

What are the many forces that mold the landforms on Earth's surface? Geomorphology is the science that studies the various relief features and the forces that form them. Endogenic forces (internal processes within the planet) produce folding, faulting, and magma movement in the Earth's crust. Subsidence in the crust causes depressions, and uplift builds mountains and plateaus. Exogenic (external) forces hold sway on the surface of the planet. In a process known as weathering, ice, water, and organisms like plant roots break down rock. Weathered rock material is carried great distances by rivers, glaciers, and other erosional agents. These forces of nature are usually gradual, often taking millions of years, but heavy rains and high winds can transform a landscape in a matter of hours. Human activities such as deforestation and poor farming practices, however, can rapidly accelerate soil erosion.

EOLIAN
6. Namibia, Africa
Arid conditions and windstorms combine to build some of the tallest sand dunes in Africa.

FLUVIAL
7. Blyde River Canyon, Africa
South Africa's Blyde River carved a steep, colorful canyon some 800 meters (2,600 ft) deep.

COASTAL
8. Victoria, Australia
Ocean waves erode coastal cliffs, leaving behind sea stacks made of more resistant rock.

POSTGLACIAL
9. Kejimkujik, Nova Scotia
Drumlins, shaped by overriding glaciers, are elliptical mounds paralleling past glacial movement.

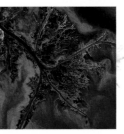

FLUVIAL
10. Mississippi River Delta
Deltas result from the deposition of river sediments and vary in shape and size depending on discharge, currents, and waves.

OTHER LANDFORMS
11. Meteor Crater, Arizona
Some 150 visible impact craters exist on Earth; others may have eroded away or been covered.

▲ **EOLIAN LANDFORMS**
Eolian (from Aeolus, the Greek god of the winds) describes landforms shaped by the wind, and it works best as a geomorphic agent when wind velocity is high—and moisture and vegetation are low.

Desert dunes are the most common eolian landform. During the last glaciation, however, strong winds carried vast clouds of silt that were deposited as loess (a fine-grained, fertile soil).

▲ **WATERSHEDS**
The map above shows the watersheds, or drainage basins, of Earth's largest river systems. Rivers rise in mountains or plateaus, eroding and depositing sediments along their entire length. Erosional landforms created by rivers include mesas and canyons; depositional (aggradational) landforms include levees and deltas.

Major watersheds
- Ten largest
- Other

▲ **ICE AGES**
A glacier is a mass of ice moving slowly down a slope or valley. Glacial ice that spreads over vast non-mountainous areas is known as an ice sheet. For millions of years ice sheets have gone through cycles of advancing over continents—and then melting back. The most recent glacial period ended some 10,000 years ago.

Greatest extent of ice during last ice age

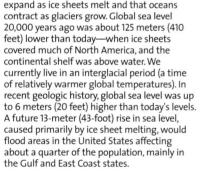

□ Maximum glaciation 20,000 years ago

Present-day

□ Projected sea level rise: 13m (43ft)

▲ SEA LEVEL CHANGES

Earth's hydrologic cycle shows that oceans expand as ice sheets melt and that oceans contract as glaciers grow. Global sea level 20,000 years ago was about 125 meters (410 feet) lower than today—when ice sheets covered much of North America, and the continental shelf was above water. We currently live in an interglacial period (a time of relatively warmer global temperatures). In recent geologic history, global sea level was up to 6 meters (20 feet) higher than today's levels. A future 13-meter (43-foot) rise in sea level, caused primarily by ice sheet melting, would flood areas in the United States affecting about a quarter of the population, mainly in the Gulf and East Coast states.

▶ A SLICE OF EARTH

A cross-section shows that the oceanic crust includes plains, volcanoes, and ridges. The abyssal plains, deepest parts of the the the oceanic floor, can reach greater than 3,000 meters (9,840 feet) beneath the surface of the ocean. Underwater volcanoes are called seamounts if they rise more than 1,000 meters (3,300 feet) above the seafloor. The Mid-Atlantic Ridge is a vast submarine mountain range beneath the Atlantic Ocean. Surrounding most continents is an underwater extension of the landmass known as a continental shelf—a shallow, submerged plain. Continental slopes connect the continental shelf with the oceanic crust in the form of giant escarpments that can descend some 2,000 meters (6,600 feet).

▼ EARTH'S HIGHS AND LOWS

This computer-generated image of the Earth is a digital elevation model—color-coded to show elevation differences. The image was derived from satellite altimetry and shipboard echo-sounding measurements. The deepest point, Challenger Deep at 10,971 meters (35,994 feet) below sea level, is dark blue , while the highest point, Mount Everest at 8,850 meters (29,035 feet) above sea level, is brown. Antarctica, the world's highest continent thanks to its thick ice sheet, shows up in shades of red, with a 2,300 meters (7,546 feet) average elevation. Also red is Greenland's ice sheet, about one-eighth the size of Antarctica's. Green expanses highlight lowland areas, and the adjacent aqua-hued regions reveal underwater continental shelves.

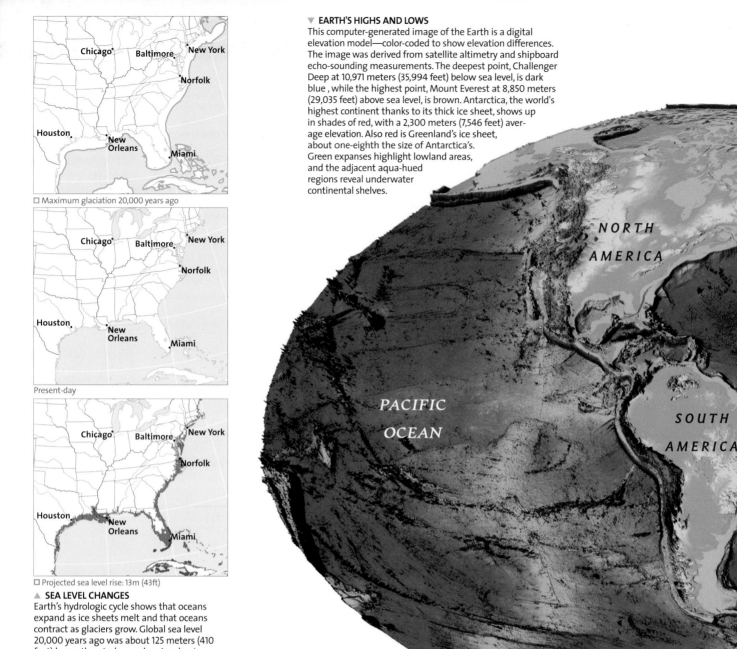

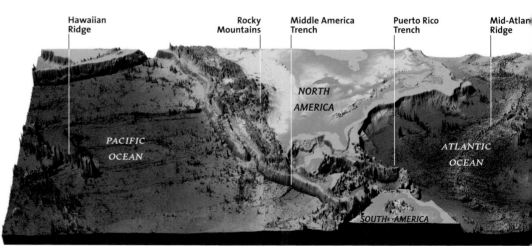

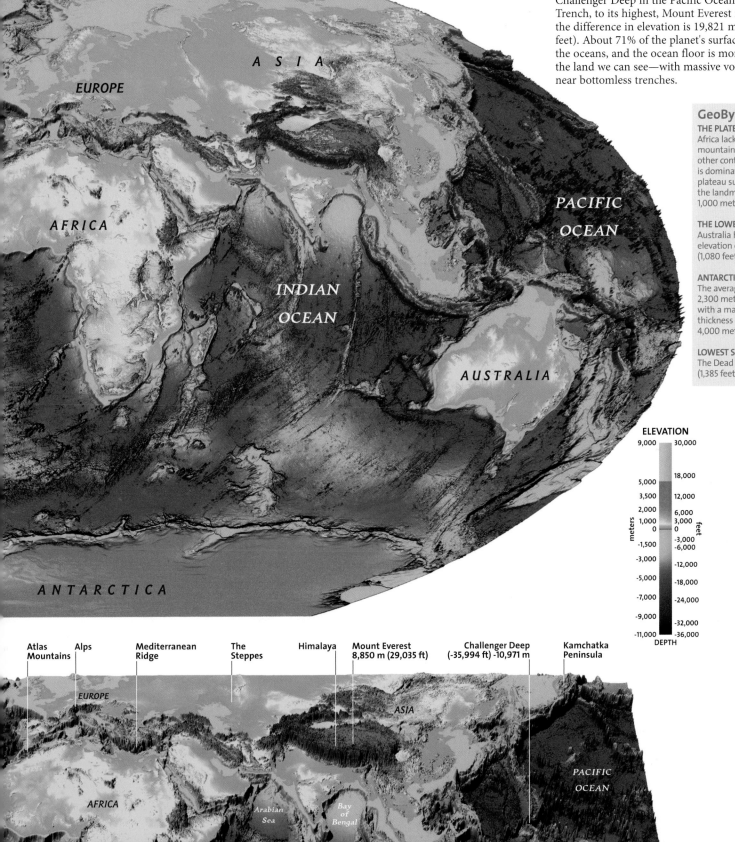

The continental surface and ocean floor have evolved over billions of years, producing enormous variations in relief. From Earth's deepest point, Challenger Deep in the Pacific Ocean's Mariana Trench, to its highest, Mount Everest in the Himalaya, the difference in elevation is 19,821 meters (65,029 feet). About 71% of the planet's surface lies beneath the oceans, and the ocean floor is more varied than the land we can see—with massive volcanoes and near bottomless trenches.

GeoBytes

THE PLATEAU CONTINENT
Africa lacks the long mountain ranges of the other continents. Instead, it is dominated by extensive plateau surfaces. Much of the landmass lies above 1,000 meters (3,300 feet).

THE LOWEST CONTINENT
Australia has an average elevation of only 330 meters (1,080 feet).

ANTARCTIC ICE SHEET
The average elevation is 2,300 meters (7,546 feet), with a maximum ice thickness of more than 4,000 meters (13,120 feet).

LOWEST SURFACE POINT
The Dead Sea lies 422 meters (1,385 feet) below sea level.

Polar circulation

Midlatitude westerlies

Northeast trade winds at surface

Equator

Southeast trade winds at surface

Hadley cells

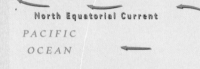

▲ HADLEY CELLS
Air that rises at the Equator and converges in the sub-tropics forms Hadley cells, while other equatorial trade winds blow east-west. Westerlies dominate higher latitudes.

GeoBytes

WATTS FROM THE SUN
Each year the sun deposits 324 watts—enough energy for five 60-watt electric bulbs—into every square meter of Earth. Most are absorbed by the tropical zones.

ENERGY BOUNCE
About 30% of the sun's energy is reflected back to space. Only 70% is absorbed by the atmosphere and surface of the planet.

CLOUD BUFFERS
Clouds can cool the planet surface by their shade or warm it by absorbing infrared radiation from the Earth.

INDUSTRY'S ROLE
The world's industrialized areas have produced more than 60% of the carbon dioxide emissions that contribute to global warming.

▼ SEASONS AND ROTATION OF THE EARTH
The tilt of the Earth on its axis causes seasonal change. Summer arrives when the rays become more direct and their heat is more concentrated. Winter's cold comes as the sun's rays slant at a steeper angle and cover a larger area.

Spring Equinox
Northern Hemisphere

Winter Solstice
Northern Hemisphere

Summer Solstice
Northern Hemisphere

Fall Equinox
Northern Hemisphere

North Pole

Tropic of Cancer

Equator

Tropic of Capricorn

South Pole

Climatic zones
(based on modified Köppen system)

Humid equatorial climate (A)
■ No dry season (Af)
■ Short dry season (Am)
□ Dry winter (Aw)

Dry climate (B)
□ Semiarid (BS) } h = hot
□ Arid (BW)   } k = cold

Humid temperate climate (C)
■ No dry season (Cf)
■ Dry winter (Cw)
□ Dry summer (Cs)

Humid cold climate (D)
□ No dry season (Df)
□ Dry winter (Dw)

Cold polar climate (E)
■ Tundra and ice

Highland climate (H)
□ Unclassified highlands

Ocean current
→ Cold
⇒ Warm

a = hot summer
b = cool summer
c = short, cool summer
d = very cold winter

Map labels

ARCTIC O

Beaufort Gyre

ARCTIC CIRCLE

Greenland Current

North

Labrador Current

Subarctic Current

Alaska Current

North Pacific Drift

California Current

Gulf Stream

North Atlantic Drift

Canary Current

PACIFIC OCEAN

North Equatorial Current

North Equatorial Current

ATLANTIC OCEAN

Equatorial Countercurrent

Equatorial Countercurrent

South Equatorial Current

South Equatorial Current

South Subtropical Current

Peru Current

Brazil Current

Falkland Current

Weddell Gyre

Cfc, Dfc, Dfb, Dfa, Cfb, Csb, BWk, Csa, BSk, BSh, BWh, Cfa, Af, Am, Aw, Cwa, Cfb, H, E

From Arctic desert to equatorial rain forest, climate is the average of the elements of weather over time and dictates conditions for the viability of life. Climatic patterns are established primarily by the energy of the sun and the distribution of solar radiation, which is greatest at the Equator and least at the Poles, and is modified by altitude and distance from the sea. The Köppen system used here classifies Earth's climatic zones based on precipitation, temperature, and vegetation. These zones can shift over time. In recent decades, human activities, such as the burning of fossil fuels that increase greenhouse gases in the atmosphere, are contributing to worldwide temperature variations.

Mean annual precipitation
(in thousand millimeters)

More than 3.0 | 2.0 - 3.0 | 1.5 - 2.0 | 1.0 - 1.5 | .60 - 1.0 | .40 - .60 | .20 - .40 | .10 - .20 | Less than .10 | Non-land area | No data available

▲ **PRECIPITATION**
Rainfall hugs the Equator but migrates alternately north-south to the summer hemispheres, when land is warmer than surrounding seas and rising hot air draws in moisture.

▼ **TEMPERATURE**
Temperatures vary seasonally and with latitude as the Earth offers first one, than the other, hemisphere to more direct sunlight. Temperatures are modified by ocean currents and vegetation and are depressed by altitude.

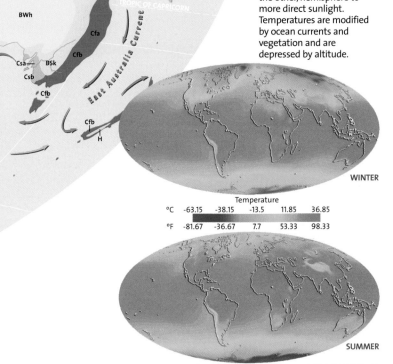

WINTER

Temperature

| °C | -63.15 | -38.15 | -13.5 | 11.85 | 36.85 |
| °F | -81.67 | -36.67 | 7.7 | 53.33 | 98.33 |

SUMMER

Surface currents along the eastern boundaries of the ocean basins transport colder water equatorward, while western boundary currents carry warmer waters poleward. Warm Gulf Stream water keeps northern Europe warmer than Canada.

PACIFIC OCEAN

INDIAN OCEAN

North Equatorial Current
Equatorial Countercurrent
South Equatorial Current

Kuroshio Current

North Equatorial Current
Equatorial Countercurrent

South Subtropical Current

Aguhas Current

West Australia Current

East Australia Current

West Wind Drift
West Wind Drift

TROPIC OF CANCER
EQUATOR
TROPIC OF CAPRICORN
ANTARCTIC CIRCLE

Black Sea
Caspian Sea
Mediterranean Sea

TRACKING WEATHER PATTERNS

▼ PRESSURE AND PREDOMINANT WINDS

The sun's direct rays shift from south of the Equator in January to north in July, creating large temperature differences over the globe.

These, in turn, lead to air density differences and the creation of high and low pressure areas. Winds result from air attempting to

equalize these pressure differences, but the influence of the rotating planet deflects them from a straight line path.

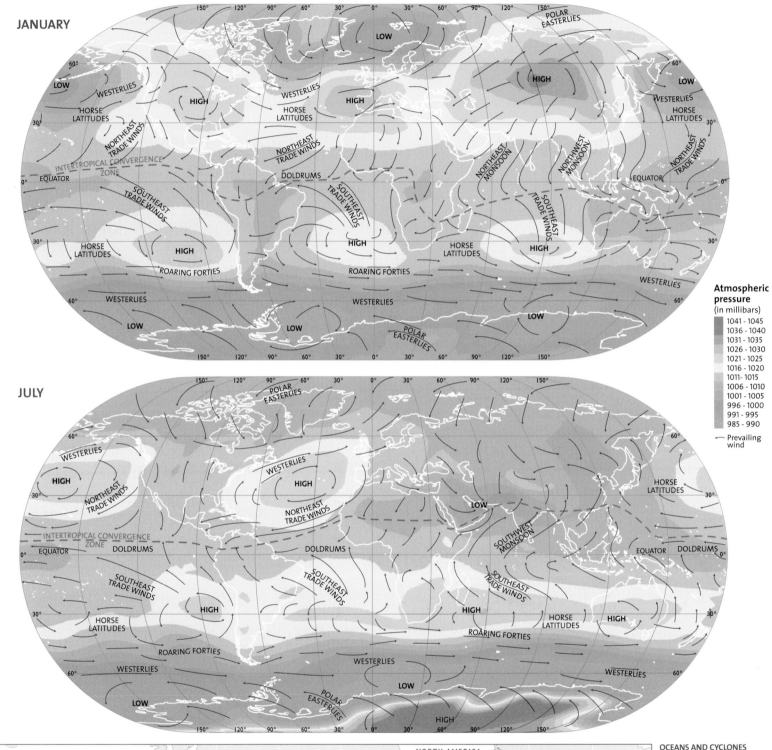

JANUARY

JULY

Atmospheric pressure
(in millibars)

1041 - 1045
1036 - 1040
1031 - 1035
1026 - 1030
1021 - 1025
1016 - 1020
1011 - 1015
1006 - 1010
1001 - 1005
996 - 1000
991 - 995
985 - 990

← Prevailing wind

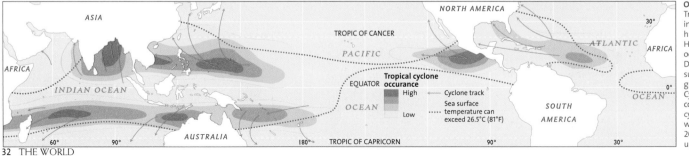

Tropical cyclone occurance

High
Low

← Cyclone track
···· Sea surface temperature can exceed 26.5°C (81°F)

OCEANS AND CYCLONES

Tropical cyclones (called typhoons in the Eastern Hemisphere and hurricanes in the Western Hemisphere) are most likely to occur in areas of greatest heating. Dotted lines show where the sea surface temperature can be greater than 26.5°C (81°F). Cyclones last until they move over cooler water or hit land. When a cyclone encounters warmer waters, as Hurricane Katrina did in 2005 in the Gulf of Mexico, it picks up energy and strength.

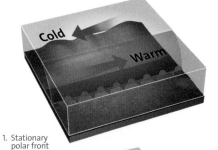

1. Stationary polar front

2. Cyclogenesis

3. Low pressure cell—undeveloped

4. Low pressure cell—developed

5. Occlusion

GeoBytes

CHRISTMAS GIFTS
El Niño, The Child, is named for the Christ Child, because the oceanic temperature rise traditionally comes around Christmas.

MONSIEUR CORIOLIS
The Coriolis Effect, the apparent force exerted on winds and ocean currents by the rotation of the earth, was first described by Gastave-Gaspard Coriolis, a French mathematician, in 1835.

SUPER STORMS
One hurricane during its life cycle can expend as much energy as 10,000 nuclear bombs.

BIG STORMS
Frontal systems are the most common weather feature in the mid-latitudes and give precipitation to large, populated areas of the globe. Most occluded fronts have a life of 3 to 6 days.

Weather is the state of the atmosphere--as indicated by temperature, moisture, wind speed and direction, and barometric pressure--at a specific time and place. Although still frustratingly difficult to predict, weather acts in some known patterns. Variations in ocean temperatures off the South American coast influence storm formation and rainfall around the globe. Jet streams that speed around the planet can usher in winter storms. And the right combination of warm water, wind, and energy from heated water vapor can cook up lethal hurricanes and typhoons that can overwhelm shorelines and cities.

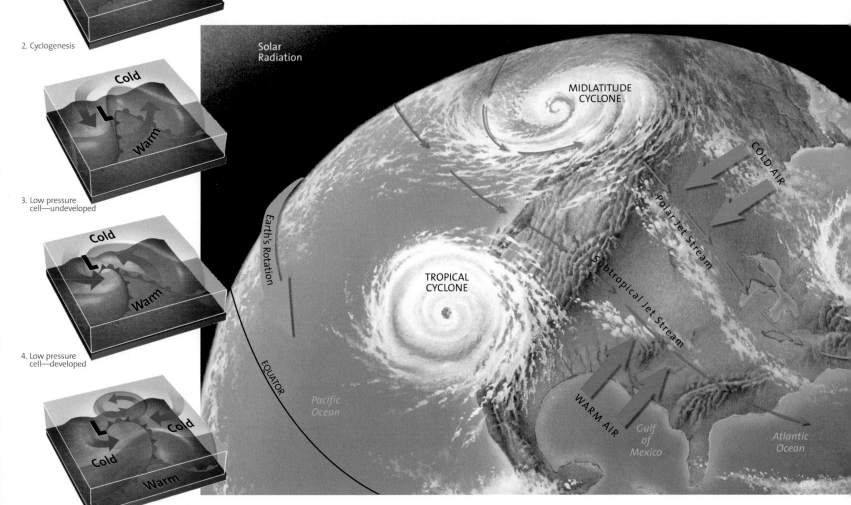

Solar Radiation

MIDLATITUDE CYCLONE

COLD AIR

Polar Jet Stream

Subtropical Jet Stream

TROPICAL CYCLONE

Earth's Rotation

EQUATOR

Pacific Ocean

WARM AIR

Gulf of Mexico

Atlantic Ocean

▲ FORMATION OF A MID-LATITUDE CYCLONE

Mid-latitude cyclones are found between 35° and 70° of latitude in the zone of the westerly winds. Most are occluded fronts. (1) Characterized by intense, heavy precipitation, cold polar air—with a boundary known as a front—meets warm tropical air. (2) A wave develops along the frontal boundary as the opposing air masses interact. Cyclogenesis (the birth of a cyclone) begins. (3) The faster-moving cold air forces the warm air to lift above the cold. (4) Full rotation develops, counterclockwise in the Northern Hemisphere and clockwise in the Southern Hemisphere. (5) Complete occlusion occurs as the warm air, fully caught-up by the cold air, has been lifted away from the surface. Because the warm air is completely separated from the surface, the characteristics of the cold air are felt on the ground in the form of unsteady, windy, and wet weather.

◄ EL NIÑO AND LA NIÑA

El Niño, an anomaly of sea-surface height or "relief" of the sea, brings warm water to South America's west coast, leading to severe short-term changes in world weather. La Niña, a cooling of those waters, has opposite effects.

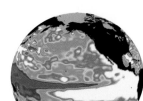

Sea surface height anomaly

| cm | -12 | -8 | -4 | 0 | 4 | 8 | 12 |
| in | -5 | -3 | -2 | 0 | 2 | 3 | 5 |

▲ HOW WEATHER HAPPENS

Weather is ultimately the atmospheric response to unequal inputs of solar energy over the globe, as a surplus of heat in low latitudes is transferred to higher latitudes by air motion and by mid-latitude storms. Part of that dynamic are jet streams—rivers of westerly winds speeding as fast as 400 kph (250 mph) in the upper atmosphere, which are also instrumental in the genesis of storms: The Polar Front Jet, which snakes along the front between Arctic and warmer continental air, is instrumental in the formation and direction of cyclonic North Pacific winter storms; the Subtropical Jet blows along the boundary of tropical circulation cells and can also abet storm formation, bringing warm, moist air and precipitation into the continent. Weather patterns are also influenced by the different properties of oceans and continents to absorb or reflect heat, which creates pressure differences that give rise to moving air masses.

◄ **OUR LAYERED OCEAN**
With depth, the ocean's five layers get colder, darker, saltier, denser, and more devoid of life.

200 meters (660 feet)
The epipelagic is the sunlit zone where photosynthesis by plants can take place and where the vast majority of all marine animals live.

1,000 meters (3,300 feet)
Only some light penetrates the mesopelagic, or twilight zone. Thus no plants grow, but large fish and whales hunt and bioluminescent fish first appear.

3,960 meters (13,000 feet)
No light reaches the midnight zone, or bathypelagic, but sperm whales and rays are known to hunt here for food.

6,100 meters (20,000 feet)
Pressure is crushing in the abyssopelagic, or abyss zone, home to bizarre angler fish and invertebrates such as sponges and sea cucumbers.

10,060 meters (33,000 feet)
The hadalpelagic zone penetrates into the deepest ocean trenches yet is home to small crustaceans called isopods.

Marine Sediments
The vast majority of the Earth's biologically fixed carbon lies in marine sediments trapped at the bottom of the seas. Carbon deposits from past eras are seen in current landforms upthrust from the oceans, such as the white cliffs of Dover.

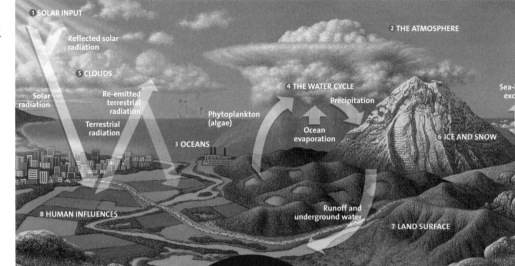

① **SOLAR INPUT**
Reflected solar radiation
⑤ **CLOUDS**
Solar radiation
Re-emitted terrestrial radiation
Terrestrial radiation
② **THE ATMOSPHERE**
④ **THE WATER CYCLE**
Precipitation
Phytoplankton (algae)
Ocean evaporation
③ **OCEANS**
Sea-ice heat exchange
⑥ **ICE AND SNOW**
Runoff and underground water
⑧ **HUMAN INFLUENCES**
⑦ **LAND SURFACE**

▲ **WHAT SHAPES EARTH'S CLIMATE**
Much of the sun's heat (1) is held in the atmosphere (2) by greenhouses gases as well as in the top layer of oceans. Oceans (3) distribute heat; evaporation lifts moisture (4). Clouds (5) reflect heat and cool Earth; they also warm it by trapping heat. Ice and snow (6) reflect sunlight, cooling Earth. Land (7) can influence the formation of clouds, and human use (8) can alter natural processes.

▲ **GREENHOUSE HEAT TRAP**
The atmosphere acts like a greenhouse, allowing sunlight to filter through. Gases such as carbon dioxide, methane, ozone, and nitrous oxide help the atmosphere hold heat. This heating is key in Earth's ability to stay warm and sustain life.

THE GREENHOUSE EFFECT
Greenhouse gases
Solar radiation
Trapped heat

GeoBytes

BIOGENESIS
The evolution of the biosphere is thought to have begun some 3.5 billion years ago.

A NEW SCIENCE
In 1926 a Soviet scientist, Vladimir I. Vernadsky, argued that human reason is capable of ensuring the sustainability of the biosphere.

BOTTOM BIOMASS
The microbes that live deep beneath the Earth's surface could exceed all animal and plant life on the surface by biomass.

WORLD OF BIOMES
Scientists divide the biosphere into a number of biomes that consist of broadly similar flora and fauna. Terrestrial biomes include deserts, forests, and grasslands; oceanic ones are coral reefs, estuaries, oceans, and the deep abyssal zone.

BIRDS SOAR ABOVE
High-flying birds, such as the Ruppell's vulture and the bar-headed geese, are found at altitudes greater than Mt. Everest's nearly 9,140 meters (30,000 feet).

▶ **EARTH'S GREEN BIOMASS**
Earth's vegetative biomass, the foundation of most life on the planet, is measured by chlorophyll-producing plants. Both land and sea process an equal amount of carbon—50 to 60 billion metric tonnes per year. Photoplankton provides the basis of measurement in the oceans; green-leaf mass on land.

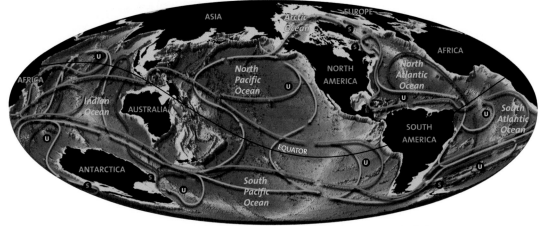

OCEAN CIRCULATION
Ocean circulation, driven by wind, density, and Earth's rotation, conveys heat energy around the globe. Tropical surface waters move toward the Poles, cool, sink, and loop around to upwell near the Equator. The Gulf Stream, for example, warms northern Europe. Other, density-driven currents flow vertically to replenish deeper waters.

Ocean circulation

- ▬ Warmer than 3.5°C (38.3°F)
- ▬ 1°C – 3.5°C
- ▬ Cooler than 1°C (33.8°F)
- **S** Sinking
- **U** Upwelling

The biosphere is Earth's thin layer of life. Containing all known life in the solar system, the biosphere, if viewed from miles above the planet, would be at a scale no thicker than this page. Although the biosphere is 19 kilometers (12 miles) from top to bottom, the bulk of it ocean depths, most living things occupy a three-kilometer-wide (two-mile-wide) band extending from the sunlit ocean layer to the snowline of high mountains. The biosphere––and its communities of plants and animals––interacts with the other key spheres of physical geography: the lithosphere, Earth's solid outer crust; the atmosphere, the layer of air above; and the hydrosphere, the oceans and all water on and within Earth. The ecosystems of the biosphere are in constant flux as the planet turns, as weather and climate shift, and as the human impacts of forestry, agriculture, and urbanization affect the fundamental components of the biosphere––carbon dioxide and other gases, water, and the photosynthesis of plants.

Key to images
Ocean: Chlorophyll concentration

| >.01 | .05 | .2 | 1 | 2 | 5 | 20 | 50 |

(a (mg/m³))
Land cover: Normalized Difference Vegetation Index (NDVI)

Max.   Min.

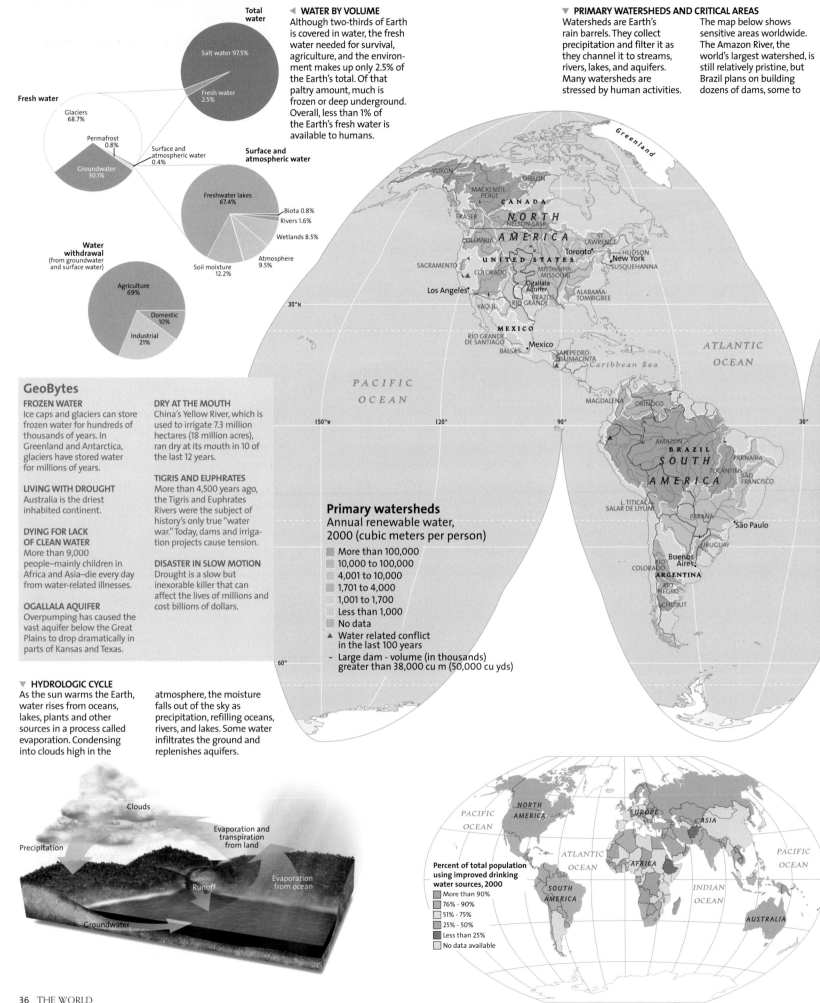

WATER BY VOLUME

Although two-thirds of Earth is covered in water, the fresh water needed for survival, agriculture, and the environment makes up only 2.5% of the Earth's total. Of that paltry amount, much is frozen or deep underground. Overall, less than 1% of the Earth's fresh water is available to humans.

Total water
- Salt water 97.5%
- Fresh water 2.5%

Fresh water
- Glaciers 68.7%
- Permafrost 0.8%
- Groundwater 30.1%
- Surface and atmospheric water 0.4%

Surface and atmospheric water
- Freshwater lakes 67.4%
- Biota 0.8%
- Rivers 1.6%
- Wetlands 8.5%
- Atmosphere 9.5%
- Soil moisture 12.2%

Water withdrawal
(from groundwater and surface water)
- Agriculture 69%
- Domestic 10%
- Industrial 21%

GeoBytes

FROZEN WATER
Ice caps and glaciers can store frozen water for hundreds of thousands of years. In Greenland and Antarctica, glaciers have stored water for millions of years.

LIVING WITH DROUGHT
Australia is the driest inhabited continent.

DYING FOR LACK OF CLEAN WATER
More than 9,000 people–mainly children in Africa and Asia–die every day from water-related illnesses.

OGALLALA AQUIFER
Overpumping has caused the vast aquifer below the Great Plains to drop dramatically in parts of Kansas and Texas.

DRY AT THE MOUTH
China's Yellow River, which is used to irrigate 7.3 million hectares (18 million acres), ran dry at its mouth in 10 of the last 12 years.

TIGRIS AND EUPHRATES
More than 4,500 years ago, the Tigris and Euphrates Rivers were the subject of history's only true "water war." Today, dams and irrigation projects cause tension.

DISASTER IN SLOW MOTION
Drought is a slow but inexorable killer that can affect the lives of millions and cost billions of dollars.

HYDROLOGIC CYCLE

As the sun warms the Earth, water rises from oceans, lakes, plants and other sources in a process called evaporation. Condensing into clouds high in the atmosphere, the moisture falls out of the sky as precipitation, refilling oceans, rivers, and lakes. Some water infiltrates the ground and replenishes aquifers.

Clouds
Precipitation
Evaporation and transpiration from land
Runoff
Evaporation from ocean
Groundwater

PRIMARY WATERSHEDS AND CRITICAL AREAS

Watersheds are Earth's rain barrels. They collect precipitation and filter it as they channel it to streams, rivers, lakes, and aquifers. Many watersheds are stressed by human activities. The map below shows sensitive areas worldwide. The Amazon River, the world's largest watershed, is still relatively pristine, but Brazil plans on building dozens of dams, some to

Primary watersheds
Annual renewable water, 2000 (cubic meters per person)
- More than 100,000
- 10,000 to 100,000
- 4,001 to 10,000
- 1,701 to 4,000
- 1,001 to 1,700
- Less than 1,000
- No data
- ▲ Water related conflict in the last 100 years
- – Large dam - volume (in thousands) greater than 38,000 cu m (50,000 cu yds)

Percent of total population using improved drinking water sources, 2000
- More than 90%
- 76% - 90%
- 51% - 75%
- 25% - 50%
- Less than 25%
- No data available

power aluminum smelters. In Africa and Asia, lack of access to water and water-related diseases are the main problems. In Europe and the Middle East, overuse, pollution, and disagreement over diverting water are the major challenges. Hope rests in better planning and community-scale projects.

It's as vital to life as air. Yet fresh water is one of the rarest resources on Earth. Only 2.5% of Earth's water is fresh, and of that the usable portion for humans is less than 1% of all fresh water, or 0.01% of all water on Earth. Water is constantly recycling through Earth's hydrologic cycle. But population growth and pollution are combining to make less and less available per person per year, while global climate change adds new uncertainty.

Efficiency, conservation, and technology can help ensure that the water you absorb today will still be usable and clean hundreds of years from now.

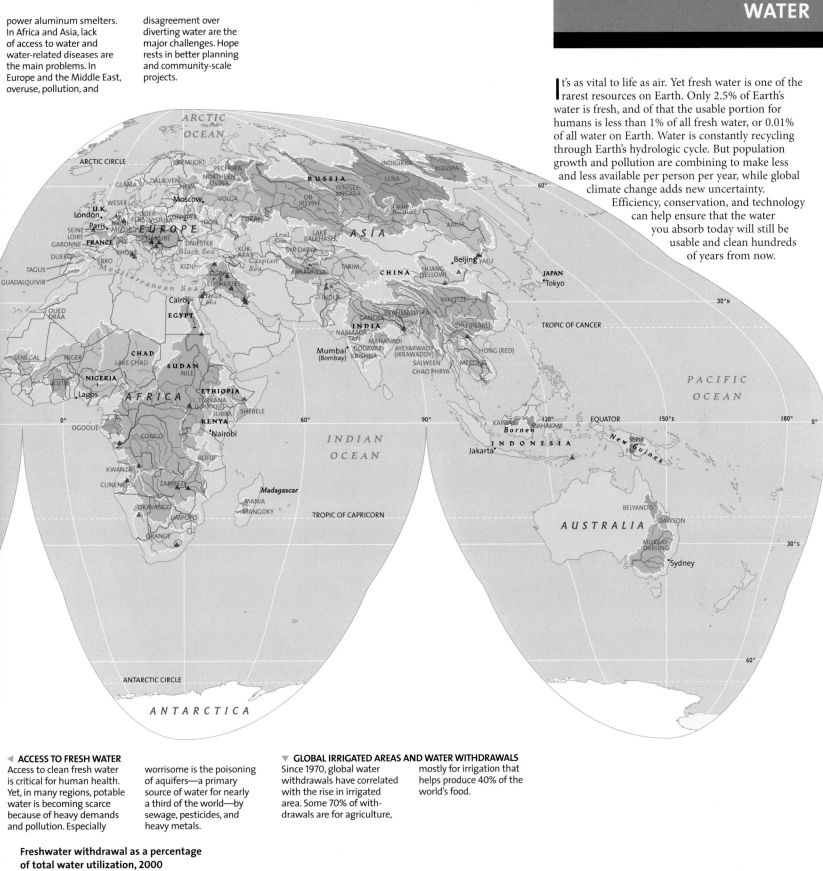

◀ ACCESS TO FRESH WATER

Access to clean fresh water is critical for human health. Yet, in many regions, potable water is becoming scarce because of heavy demands and pollution. Especially worrisome is the poisoning of aquifers—a primary source of water for nearly a third of the world—by sewage, pesticides, and heavy metals.

▼ GLOBAL IRRIGATED AREAS AND WATER WITHDRAWALS

Since 1970, global water withdrawals have correlated with the rise in irrigated area. Some 70% of withdrawals are for agriculture, mostly for irrigation that helps produce 40% of the world's food.

Freshwater withdrawal as a percentage of total water utilization, 2000

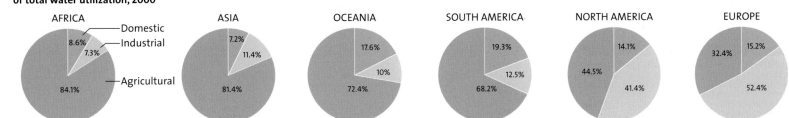

AFRICA — Domestic, Industrial, Agricultural
8.6%, 7.3%, 84.1%

ASIA
7.2%, 11.4%, 81.4%

OCEANIA
17.6%, 10%, 72.4%

SOUTH AMERICA
19.3%, 12.5%, 68.2%

NORTH AMERICA
14.1%, 44.5%, 41.4%

EUROPE
15.2%, 32.4%, 52.4%

GLOBAL LAND COVER COMPOSITION

OTHER 31.42%
0.1% Built-up
7.99% Cropland
Barren (Desert and Polar Ice) 23.33%
Closed shrubland 4.49%
Grassland 8.05%
Open shrubland 13.08%

GRASSLAND OR SHRUBLAND 41.63%

Wooded grassland 16.01%

FOREST 26.96%
Woodland 11.3%
Evergreen broadleaf 8.26%
Evergreen needleleaf 3.82%
Mixed 2.27%
Deciduous broadleaf 0.96%
Deciduous needleleaf 0.35%

Three characteristics underlie these categories: life-form (woody, herbaceous, or bare); leaf type (needle or broad); and leaf duration (evergreen or deciduous).

EVERGREEN NEEDLELEAF FOREST
Tree height exceeds 5 m (16 ft); more than 60% of this land is canopied by forest. Typical example: boreal (northern) region. On tree plantations, trees are logged for paper and building products.

EVERGREEN BROADLEAF FOREST
More than 60% of the land is covered by a forest canopy, with trees over 5 m (16 ft). Such forests dominate in the tropics and are home to great biodiversity, when not cleared for mechanized farms, ranches, and tree plantations.

Land Cover

Forest
- Evergreen needleleaf
- Evergreen broadleaf
- Deciduous needleleaf
- Deciduous broadleaf
- Mixed forest
- Woodland

Grassland or shrubland
- Wooded grassland
- Closed shrubland
- Open shrubland
- Grassland

Other
- Cropland
- Barren (Desert and Polar Ice)
- Built-up

DECIDUOUS NEEDLELEAF FOREST
A forest canopy covers more than 60% of the land; tree height exceeds 5 m (16 ft). This class is dominant only in Siberia, taking the form of larch forests.

DECIDUOUS BROADLEAF FOREST
More than 60% of the land is covered by a forest canopy; tree height exceeds 5 m (16 ft). In temperate regions, much of this forest has been converted to cropland.

MIXED FOREST
Both needle and deciduous types of trees appear. This type is largely found between temperate deciduous and boreal evergreen forests.

WOODLAND
Land has herbaceous or woody understory; trees exceed 5 m (16 ft) and may be deciduous or evergreen. Highly degraded in long-settled human environments, such as in West Africa.

WOODED GRASSLAND
Woody or herbaceous under-stories are punctuated by trees. Examples are African savannah as well as open boreal borderland between trees and tundra.

CLOSED SHRUBLAND
Found where prolonged cold or dry seasons limit plant growth, this cover is dominated by bushes or shrubs not exceeding 5 m (16 ft). Tree canopy is less than 10%.

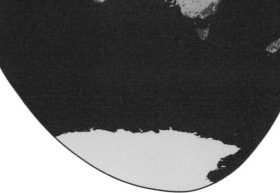

Satellite data provide the most reliable picture of global vegetative cover over time. Few natural communities of plants and animals have remained the same; most have been altered by humans.

The "natural" vegetation reflects what would grow there, given ideal conditions. The map at left is based on a year of global satellite imagery from the Advanced Very High Resolution Radiometer (AVHRR) at a spatial resolution of one kilometer.

By recording the data at different wavelengths of the electro-magnetic spectrum, scientists can derive land cover type through spectral variation. Changes in vegetation are captured in the satellite record, contributing to a rich data bank for Earth studies in areas such as conservation, biodiversity assessments, and land resource management.

GeoBytes

PLANT SPECIES
Approximately, 250,000 plant species occupy the biomes of the Earth, with an estimated 10 to 15% still to be discovered.

RICH IN BIODIVERSITY
Evergreen broadleaf forests are typical of rain forests, which represent approximately one-half of Earth's remaining forests, occupying 7% of land area worldwide.

THREATS TO FORESTS
Forests everywhere are under pressure from logging, mining, global warming, slash-and-burn agriculture, and desertification.

OPEN SHRUBLAND
Shrubs are dominant, not exceeding 2 m (6.5 ft) in height. They can be evergreen or deciduous. This type occurs in semiarid or severely cold areas.

GRASSLAND
Occurring in a wide range of habitats, this landscape has continuous herbaceous cover. The American Plains and central Russia are the premier examples.

CROPLAND
Crop-producing fields constitute over 80% of the land. Temperate regions are home to large areas of mechanized farming; in the developing world, plots are small.

BARREN (DESERT)
The land never has more than 10% vegetated cover. True deserts, such as the Sahara, as well as areas succumbing to desertification, are examples.

BUILT-UP
This class was mapped using the populated places layer that is part of the "Digital Chart of the World" (Danko, 1992). It represents the most densely inhabited areas.

BARREN (POLAR ICE)
Permanent snow cover characterizes this class, the greatest expanses of which are in the polar regions, as well as on high elevations in Alaska and the Himalaya.

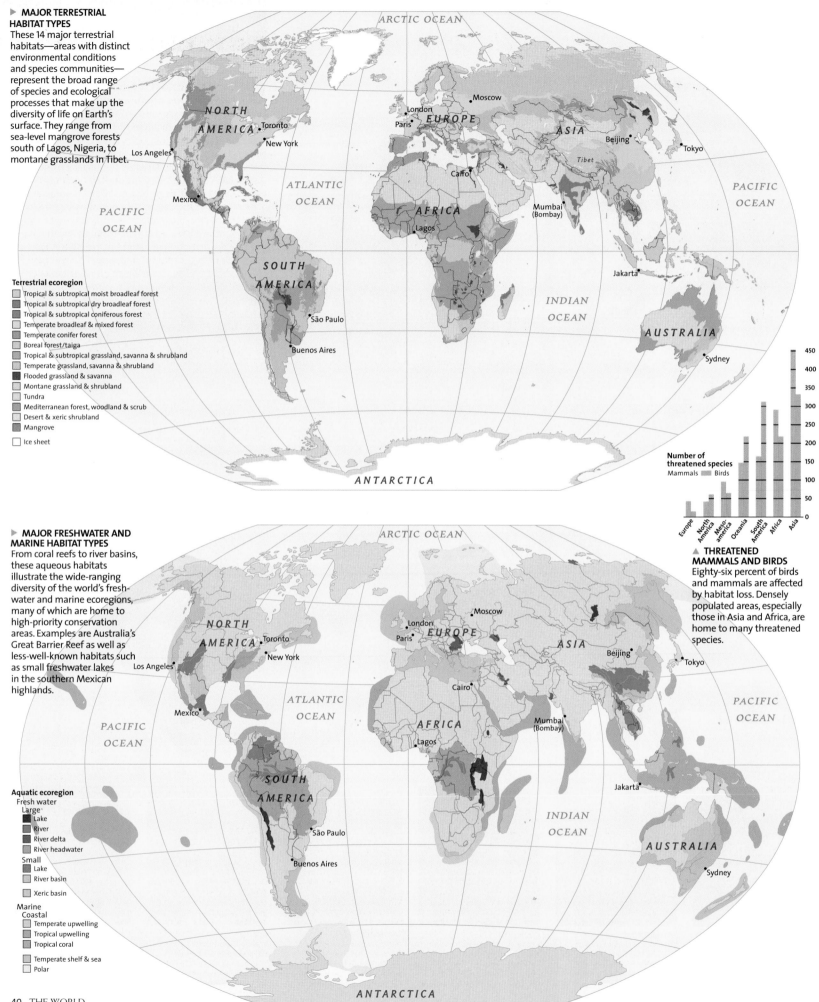

► MAJOR TERRESTRIAL HABITAT TYPES

These 14 major terrestrial habitats—areas with distinct environmental conditions and species communities—represent the broad range of species and ecological processes that make up the diversity of life on Earth's surface. They range from sea-level mangrove forests south of Lagos, Nigeria, to montane grasslands in Tibet.

Terrestrial ecoregion
- Tropical & subtropical moist broadleaf forest
- Tropical & subtropical dry broadleaf forest
- Tropical & subtropical coniferous forest
- Temperate broadleaf & mixed forest
- Temperate conifer forest
- Boreal forest/taiga
- Tropical & subtropical grassland, savanna & shrubland
- Temperate grassland, savanna & shrubland
- Flooded grassland & savanna
- Montane grassland & shrubland
- Tundra
- Mediterranean forest, woodland & scrub
- Desert & xeric shrubland
- Mangrove

- Ice sheet

Number of threatened species
Mammals ▮ Birds

▲ THREATENED MAMMALS AND BIRDS

Eighty-six percent of birds and mammals are affected by habitat loss. Densely populated areas, especially those in Asia and Africa, are home to many threatened species.

► MAJOR FRESHWATER AND MARINE HABITAT TYPES

From coral reefs to river basins, these aqueous habitats illustrate the wide-ranging diversity of the world's fresh-water and marine ecoregions, many of which are home to high-priority conservation areas. Examples are Australia's Great Barrier Reef as well as less-well-known habitats such as small freshwater lakes in the southern Mexican highlands.

Aquatic ecoregion
Fresh water
Large
- Lake
- River
- River delta
- River headwater

Small
- Lake
- River basin

- Xeric basin

Marine
Coastal
- Temperate upwelling
- Tropical upwelling
- Tropical coral

- Temperate shelf & sea
- Polar

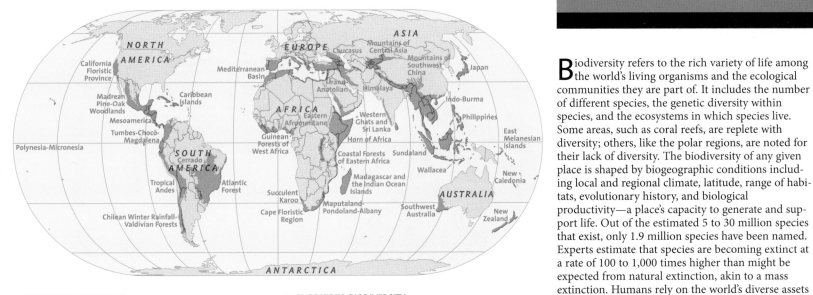

Biodiversity refers to the rich variety of life among the world's living organisms and the ecological communities they are part of. It includes the number of different species, the genetic diversity within species, and the ecosystems in which species live. Some areas, such as coral reefs, are replete with diversity; others, like the polar regions, are noted for their lack of diversity. The biodiversity of any given place is shaped by biogeographic conditions including local and regional climate, latitude, range of habitats, evolutionary history, and biological productivity—a place's capacity to generate and support life. Out of the estimated 5 to 30 million species that exist, only 1.9 million species have been named. Experts estimate that species are becoming extinct at a rate of 100 to 1,000 times higher than might be expected from natural extinction, akin to a mass extinction. Humans rely on the world's diverse assets for survival—food, medicine, clean air, drinkable water, habitable climates—yet it is our activities that pose the greatest threat to the world's biodiversity.

▲ BIODIVERSITY HOTSPOTS

What areas are vital for conserving biodiversity? Conservation International identified 34 "hotspots," defined as habitat holding at least 1,500 endemic plant species and having lost 70% of its original extent.

▼ THREATS TO BIODIVERSITY

The greatest threats to biodiversity—habitat loss and fragmentation, invasion of non-native species, pollution, and unsustainable exploitation—are all caused by human economic activity and population growth.

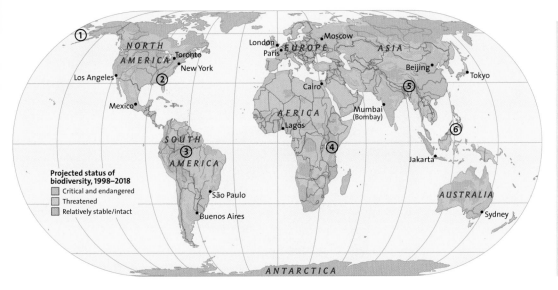

Projected status of biodiversity, 1998–2018
- Critical and endangered
- Threatened
- Relatively stable/intact

GeoBytes

UNIQUE SPECIES
Madagascar and the Indian Ocean islands are home to many species found nowhere else. Of the region's 13,000 plant species, more than 89% are endemic, meaning that is the only place on Earth they live.

FRAGILE POPULATIONS
Nearly half of the world's tortoises and freshwater turtles are threatened.

HUMAN HEALTH
Medicines derived from plants and animals are the primary source of health care for 80% of the world's population.

ECONOMIC VALUE
Scientists estimate that ecosystems worldwide provide goods and services, such as nutrient recycling and waste treatment, valued at more than $20 trillion a year.

EXTINCTION RISK
One in every eight birds and one in every four mammals face a high risk of extinction in the near future.

BEETLEMANIA
Beetles are the most diverse life-form on Earth. More than a thousand different kinds can live on a single tree in the forests of South America.

1. THE BERING SEA
The Bering Sea, separating Alaska and Russia, is one of the world's most diverse marine environments. Polar bears, seals, sea lions, walruses, whales, enormous populations of seabirds, and more than 400 species of fish, crustaceans, and mollusks live in this ecoregion. It is also home to one of the world's largest salmon runs. Global warming, pollution, overfishing, and mining are major threats to this region's biodiversity.

2. SOUTHEASTERN U.S. RIVERS AND STREAMS
From Appalachian streams to saltwater marshes along the Atlantic and Gulf coasts, this ecoregion harbors hundreds of species of fish, snails, crayfish, and mussels. A single river in the region, the Cahaba River in Alabama, has more fish species per mile than any other river in North America. Population growth and increasing streamside development, dams, and water diversion for irrigation are long-term threats.

3. THE AMAZON RIVER AND FLOODED FORESTS
More than 3,000 species of freshwater fish and many mammals, including the pink river dolphin, inhabit this ecoregion. The Amazon Basin is Earth's largest watershed and is noted for having the world's largest expanse of seasonally flooded forests, habitat for a wide array of migratory species. Selective logging and the conversion of floodplains for ranching and agricultural use are threats to the region.

4. RIFT VALLEY LAKES
This cluster of freshwater and alkaline lakes spread across East Africa's Great Lakes region. It is home to nearly 800 species of cichlid fishes, all derived from a common ancestor, a process called species radiation. These radiations are an extraordinary example of evolutionary adaptation. The lakes also provide important bird habitat—half of the world's flamingo population lives here. Threats to the region include deforestation, pollution, and the spread of non-native species.

5. EASTERN HIMALAYAN BROADLEAF AND CONIFER FORESTS
Snaking across the lowlands and foothills of the Himalaya, this ecoregion supports a remarkable diversity of plants and animals, including endangered mammals such as the clouded leopard, Himalayan black bear, and the golden langur. These sub-alpine forests are also a significant endemic bird area. Because forests are slow to regenerate, conversion to cropland and timber extraction are serious threats to this region's biodiversity.

6. SULU-SULAWESI SEAS
Extensive coral reefs, mangroves, and seagrass beds make this one of the richest habitats for reef animals and plants in the world. More than 450 species of coral, six of the world's eight species of marine turtles, and numerous species of fish, sharks, and whales live in this marine ecoregion between Indonesia, Malaysia, and the Philippines. These reefs continue to be threatened by coastal erosion, pollution, and overfishing.

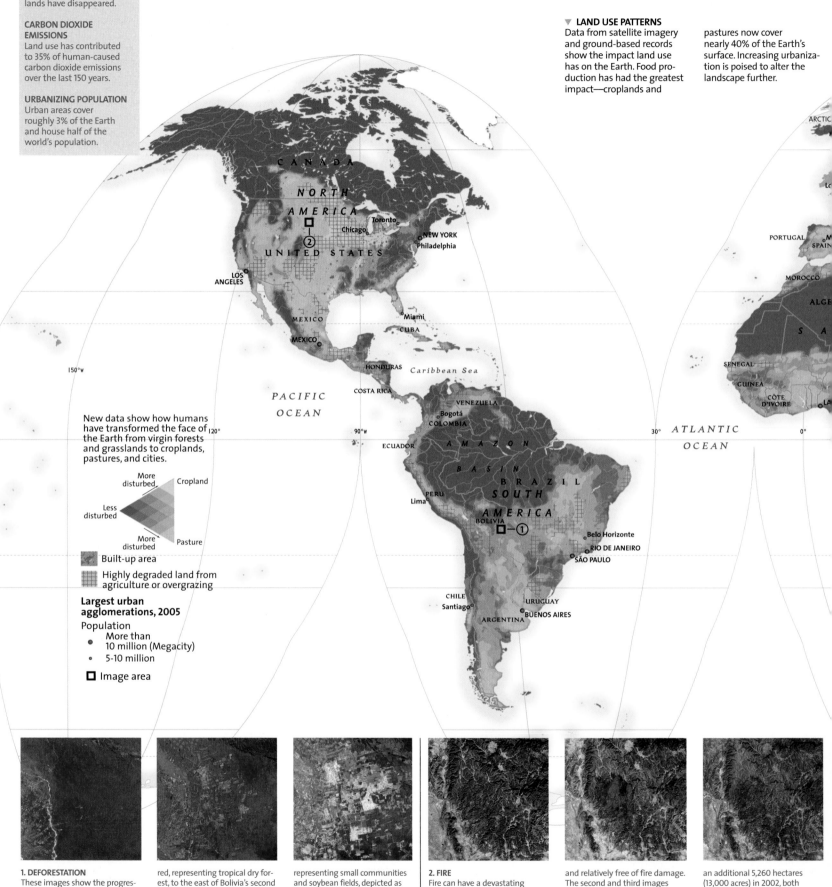

▼ **LAND USE PATTERNS**
Data from satellite imagery and ground-based records show the impact land use has on the Earth. Food production has had the greatest impact—croplands and pastures now cover nearly 40% of the Earth's surface. Increasing urbanization is poised to alter the landscape further.

New data show how humans have transformed the face of the Earth from virgin forests and grasslands to croplands, pastures, and cities.

More disturbed — Cropland
Less disturbed
More disturbed — Pasture

Built-up area

Highly degraded land from agriculture or overgrazing

Largest urban agglomerations, 2005

Population
- More than 10 million (Megacity)
- 5-10 million

□ Image area

1. DEFORESTATION
These images show the progression of deforestation and increasing agricultural development in Bolivia. The first image (1975) shows a large expanse of solid red, representing tropical dry forest, to the east of Bolivia's second largest city, Santa Cruz. The other two images (1992 and 2000, respectively) show an increasing number of open patches representing small communities and soybean fields, depicted as light-colored rectangles, in areas that were once forested.

2. FIRE
Fire can have a devastating and immediate impact on the landscape. In 1999, the Black Hills of South Dakota were covered with vegetation, shown in green, and relatively free of fire damage. The second and third images show the same area after the Jasper fire of 2000 destroyed nearly 34,000 hectares (84,000 acres) and a smaller fire burned an additional 5,260 hectares (13,000 acres) in 2002, both shown in red. It will take decades for the area to recover.

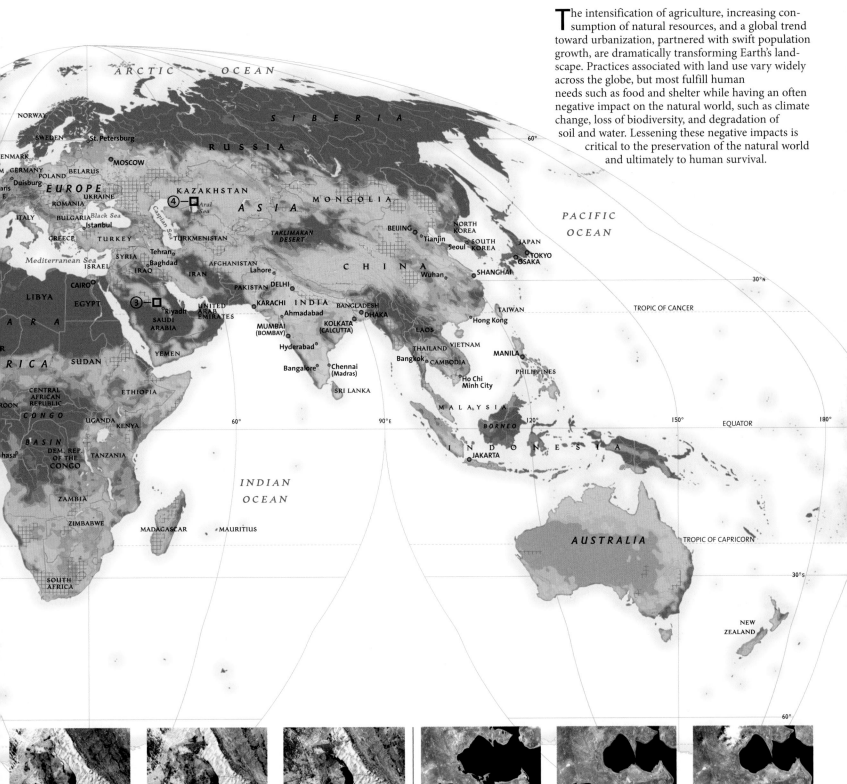

The intensification of agriculture, increasing consumption of natural resources, and a global trend toward urbanization, partnered with swift population growth, are dramatically transforming Earth's landscape. Practices associated with land use vary widely across the globe, but most fulfill human needs such as food and shelter while having an often negative impact on the natural world, such as climate change, loss of biodiversity, and degradation of soil and water. Lessening these negative impacts is critical to the preservation of the natural world and ultimately to human survival.

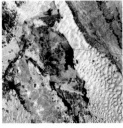

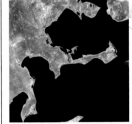
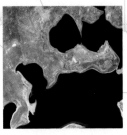
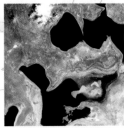

3. AGRICULTURAL DEVELOPMENT
Agriculture in Saudi Arabia has undergone dramatic changes in the last 30 years. The first image (1972) shows little agricultural development. The oasis cities of Buraydah and 'Unayzah are barely noticeable. By 1986, there is a striking increase in center-pivot irrigation, seen as red circles, for crops such as wheat, and the cities are larger. The 2003 image reveals a vast expansion of irrigated lands surrounding the rapidly growing cities.

4. FRESHWATER LOSS
Over the last three decades, the volume of the Aral Sea has shrunk by 75%. This can be attributed to water being diverted to irrigate cotton and rice fields in Central Asia. These images from 1973, 1987, and 2000, show the drastic changes to the Aral Sea's shoreline, which has receded up to 121 kilometers (75 miles). Sea level has also dropped more than 16 meters (52 feet).

▶ POPULATION DENSITY

Population density can be measured as the average number of people per square unit in a given area (arithmetic density). Populations, however, are not evenly distributed. Often, they're gathered around arable land. By comparing populations to farmland (physiologic density), statistics can be more meaningful.

Egypt, for example, where nearly 90% of the citizens are clustered in the Nile Valley, has a modest overall density of 74 people per sq km (191 people per sq mi), but a physiologic density of 3,089 people per agricultural sq km (8,000 people per agricultural sq mi), among the world's highest.

RUSSIA (143)
CANADA (32)
UNITED STATES (296)
MEXICO (107)
BRAZIL (184)
NIGERIA (132)
PAKISTAN (162)
CHINA (1,304)
JAPAN (128)
BANGLADESH (144)
INDIA (1,104)
INDONESIA (222)
AUSTRALIA (20)

Population growth rate as a percent of total population, 2005 estimate
(1 block=1 million people)

- More than 3%
- 2.0%–2.9%
- 1.0%–1.9%
- 0%–0.9%
- Negative growth

2005 population (millions) in parentheses
Not all countries or territories shown

▲ POPULATION CARTOGRAM

The world appears quite different when countries are sized proportional to their populations and mapped. Underpopulated Canada, the world's second largest country, is reduced to a small strip above the United States, while small, crowded Japan looms large. India and China become the global giants.

▶ POPULATION PYRAMIDS

When population is expressed in bars representing age and gender and stacked up (males left, females right), country profiles emerge that have ramifications for the future. Countries with high birthrates and high percentages of young, such as Nigeria, look like pyramids. Countries such as Italy, whose birth rate is below the replacement fertility level of 2.1 children per couple, show bulges in the higher age brackets. The United States clearly shows the "baby boom" of children born in the years after World War II.

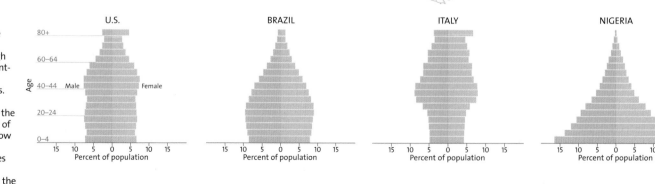

U.S. / BRAZIL / ITALY / NIGERIA

Age: 80+, 60–64, 40–44 (Male / Female), 20–24, 0–4
Percent of population: 15 10 5 0 5 10 15

Year: A.D. 1 50 100 150 200 250 300 350 400 450 500 550 600 650 700 750 800 850 900 950 100

Geographers approach the study of human populations, or demography, from a spatial perspective, asking why density, distribution, resources, births, deaths, and migrations vary from place to place. Earth's population, now at 6.5 billion, grows by 80 million a year, or 1.2% annually. The bulk of the increase occurs in developing countries in Asia, Africa, and Latin America. Physiologic density—the number of people per unit of agricultural land—shows concentrations in Asia, in particular in China and India; in Europe, from Britain into Russia; along the eastern seaboard of the United States; and in West Africa in Nigeria and along the Nile Valley.

GeoBytes

COUNTING HEADS
Most governments conduct a population census every ten years, although the process is expensive and accuracy is difficult to attain for most.

PACKED NEIGHBORHOODS
The most densely populated place in the world is Macau, a Chinese Special Administrative Region, with 18,960 people per sq km (47,400 people per sq mi). The least dense is Greenland.

IOWA VS. BANGLADESH
Bangladesh's rural population density is up to 12,950 per sq km (5,000 per sq mi) in an area the size of Iowa. In Iowa, the figure is fewer than 145 per sq km (55 per sq mi).

SHEER NUMBERS
The most populated country is the People's Republic of China, with 1.3 billion. The least populated jurisdiction is Pitcairn Island in the Pacific, with 46 people.

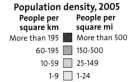

Population density, 2005

People per square km	People per square mi
More than 195	More than 500
60-195	150-500
10-59	25-149
1-9	1-24
Less than 1	Less than 1

INDIA

LAOS

AUSTRALIA

15 10 5 0 5 10 15
Percent of population

15 10 5 0 5 10 15
Percent of population

15 10 5 0 5 10 15
Percent of population

REGIONAL POPULATION GROWTH
Earth's population has burgeoned since 1800, from approximately one billion to today's 6.5 billion. Africa is sustaining high fertility rates (average number of children per woman) and is projected to contain 21% of the world's population by 2050.

- Asia
- Africa
- Latin America
- Europe
- North America
- Australia & Oceania

Projected growth

Number of people (in billions)

1050 1100 1150 1200 1250 1300 1350 1400 1450 1500 1550 1600 1650 1700 1750 1800 1850 1900 1950 2000 2050
Year

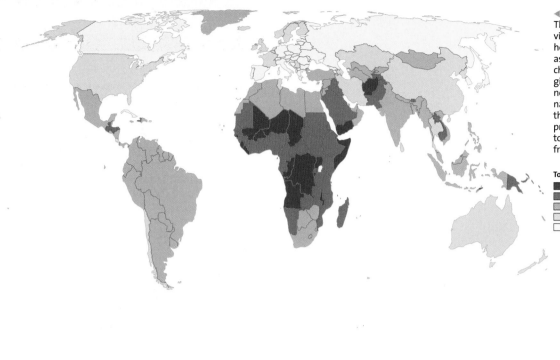

FERTILITY

The nations of central Africa virtually leap off the map as hotbeds of fertility, measured as the average number of children born to women in a given population. In contrast, northern industrialized nations, such as Canada and the Czech Republic, are not producing enough babies to keep their populations from decreasing.

Total fertility rate, 2005
- More than 5.9
- 4.0-5.9
- 2.2-3.9
- 1.6-2.1
- Less than 1.6

MIGRANT POPULATION

Modern migrations flow toward jobs and money. Immigrants from poor economies now provide workers for oil-rich Middle East nations and for Western Europe, the United States, Canada, and Australia. South America's French Guiana attracts migrants from neighboring countries because of its guaranteed minimum wage and good health and educational systems. Some 175 million people have moved to another country, or about 3% of the world's population.

Percent migrant population, 2000
- More than 40%
- 18%-40%
- 8%-17%
- 2%-7%
- Less than 2%
- No data available

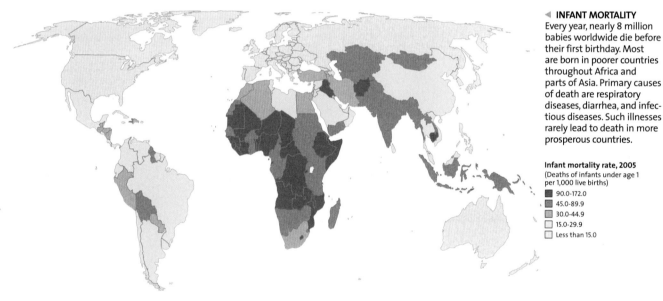

INFANT MORTALITY

Every year, nearly 8 million babies worldwide die before their first birthday. Most are born in poorer countries throughout Africa and parts of Asia. Primary causes of death are respiratory diseases, diarrhea, and infectious diseases. Such illnesses rarely lead to death in more prosperous countries.

Infant mortality rate, 2005
(Deaths of infants under age 1 per 1,000 live births)
- 90.0-172.0
- 45.0-89.9
- 30.0-44.9
- 15.0-29.9
- Less than 15.0

URBAN POPULATION

Cities, notably in developing countries, are growing at nearly twice the rate of the overall world population increase, and almost half the world's people now live in urban areas. Many newcomers hope to escape rural poverty and find work, although lack of skills condemns millions to slums.

Percent urban population, 2005
- More than 75%
- 60%-74%
- 40%-59%
- 20%-39%
- Less than 20%

LIFE EXPECTANCY

The gap in life expectancy between developed and developing nations has narrowed as better medical care and education have lowered the infant mortality rate. Many Africans, however, die early. A male Zambian can expect to live only 38 years, while the average Japanese male ages to 78.

Life expectancy at birth, 2005
(in years)
- 70 or older
- 60-69
- 50-59
- 40-49
- 39 or younger

URBAN GROWTH

Coal-belt cities in industrialized Europe have stabilized, but Asian and African cities have exploded with growth as millions abandon rural life for the urban promises of prosperity and better health. The population of Lagos, Nigeria, for example, could increase by nearly 6 million by 2015.

Urban growth, 1955-2005
(Population in millions)
- More than 275
- 150-274
- 75-149
- 25-74
- Less than 25
- No data available

Growth of largest urban agglomerations, 1955-2015

- 2015 (projected)
- 2005
- 1955

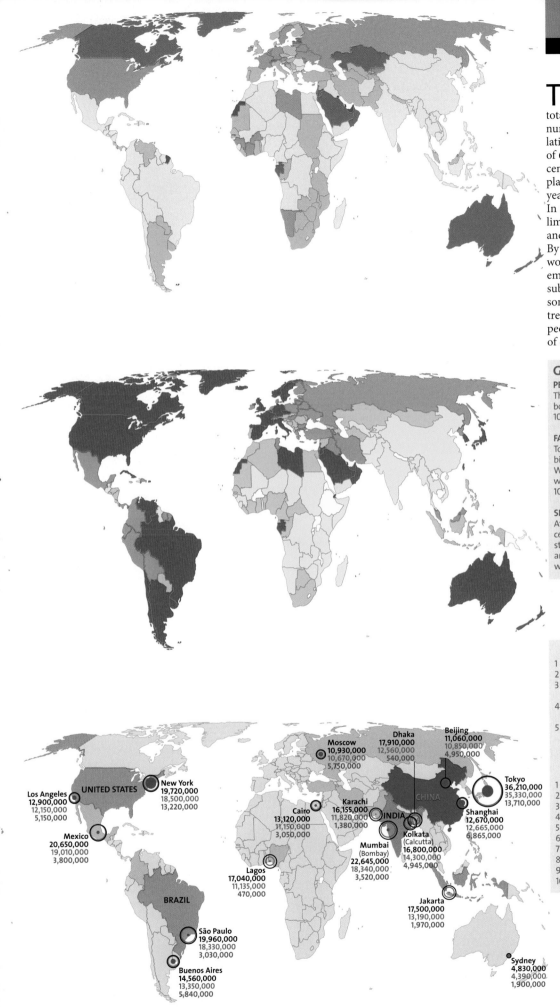

The 21st century will witness substantial world population growth, even as the rate of growth slows, total fertility rates decline, and populations age. Sheer numbers will increase simply because the base population is so great; the benchmark figure of 6 billion was reached in October 1999. By mid-century, up to 10 billion humans may be sharing the planet. Of the 80 million people being added each year, some 90% are born into developing countries. In some African and Muslim countries, one key to limiting growth is improving the status of women and their access to education and contraception. By 2050, the elderly could constitute 22% of the world's population, affecting economies, savings, employment, and health care. The toll of AIDS in sub-Saharan Africa and adult male mortality in some Eastern European countries are disturbing trends. In the future, cities will grow, and more people will cross international boundaries in search of employment and security.

GeoBytes

PEOPLE THROUGH TIME
The total number of humans born since 50,000 B.C. is 106 billion.

FAST FORWARD
Today the world gains one billion people every 11 years. With current growth rates, world population could reach 10 billion by 2050.

SIX BILLION STRONG
At the beginning of the 21st century, world population stood at 6.4 billion people, or an estimated 6% of the total who have ever lived.

SMALL CITIES
Pre-Industrial Age cities were comparatively small. Rome, the largest city of antiquity, had only 350,000 people.

NATIVITY DISCREPANCY
The death rate of mothers during childbirth in developing countries is 22 times higher than that of women in the developed world.

MOST CHILDREN
In 2005, the the highest fertility rate in the world was in Niger, where women averaged eight children.

MOST POPULOUS COUNTRIES, Mid-2005

1	China	1,303,701,000	6	Pakistan	162,420,000
2	India	1,103,596,000	7	Bangladesh	144,233,000
3	United States	296,483,000	8	Russia	143,025,000
4	Indonesia	221,932,000	9	Nigeria	131,530,000
5	Brazil	184,184,000	10	Japan	127,728,000

MOST DENSELY POPULATED PLACES, Mid-2005

		Population density per sq km	(sq mi)
1	Macau	18,960	(47,400)
2	Monaco	16,500	(33,000)
3	Singapore	6,509	(16,847)
4	Hong Kong	6,338	(16,400)
5	Gibraltar	4,143	(9,667)
6	Vatican City	1,995	(3,990)
7	Malta	1,282	(3,320)
8	Bermuda	1,170	(2,952)
9	Bahrain	1,020	(2,639)
10	Maldives	987	(2,557)

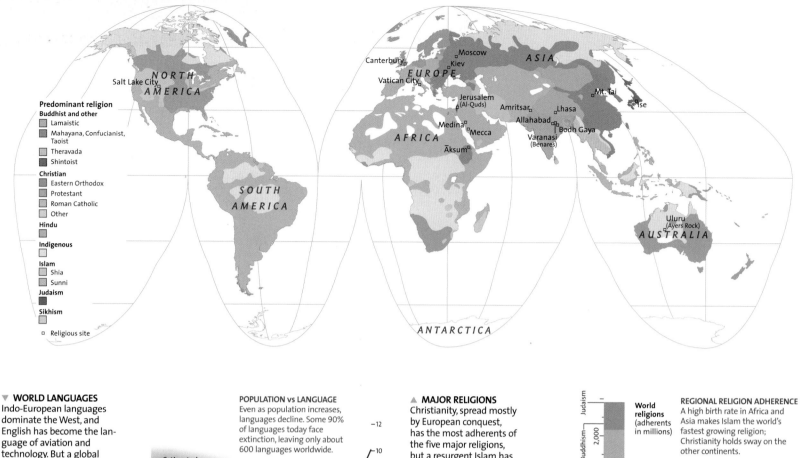

Predominant religion

Buddhist and other
- Lamaistic
- Mahayana, Confucianist, Taoist
- Theravada
- Shintoist

Christian
- Eastern Orthodox
- Protestant
- Roman Catholic
- Other

Hindu

Indigenous

Islam
- Shia
- Sunni

Judaism

Sikhism

▫ Religious site

▼ **WORLD LANGUAGES**
Indo-European languages dominate the West, and English has become the language of aviation and technology. But a global language is not yet at hand. More people speak Mandarin Chinese than speak English, Spanish, German, and French combined. Half of the 6,000 languages in the world today are spoken by fewer than 10,000 people; a quarter by fewer than a thousand. Only a score are on the tongues of millions. After Mandarin Chinese and English, Hindi ranks third.

POPULATION vs LANGUAGE
Even as population increases, languages decline. Some 90% of languages today face extinction, leaving only about 600 languages worldwide.

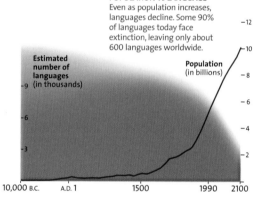

Estimated number of languages (in thousands)

Population (in billions)

▲ **MAJOR RELIGIONS**
Christianity, spread mostly by European conquest, has the most adherents of the five major religions, but a resurgent Islam has blossomed on the African-Asian axis. Hinduism and Buddhism today maintain wide blocs of the faithful in Asia, while the homeland of Judaism in Israel is a beleaguered bastion.

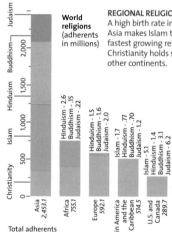

World religions (adherents in millions)

Total adherents in italics

Asia 2,453.1
- Hinduism - 2.6
- Buddhism - .15
- Judaism - .22

Africa 755.1
- Hinduism - 1.5
- Buddhism - 1.6
- Judaism - 2.0

Europe 592.1
- Islam - 1.7
- Hinduism - .77
- Buddhism - .70
- Judaism - 1.2

Latin America and the Caribbean 514.5
- Islam - 5.1
- Hinduism - 1.4
- Buddhism - 3.1
- Judaism - 6.2

U.S. and Canada 289.7
- Islam - .41
- Hinduism - .42
- Buddhism - .50
- Judaism - .10

Australia and Oceania 27.6

REGIONAL RELIGION ADHERENCE
A high birth rate in Africa and Asia makes Islam the world's fastest growing religion; Christianity holds sway on the other continents.

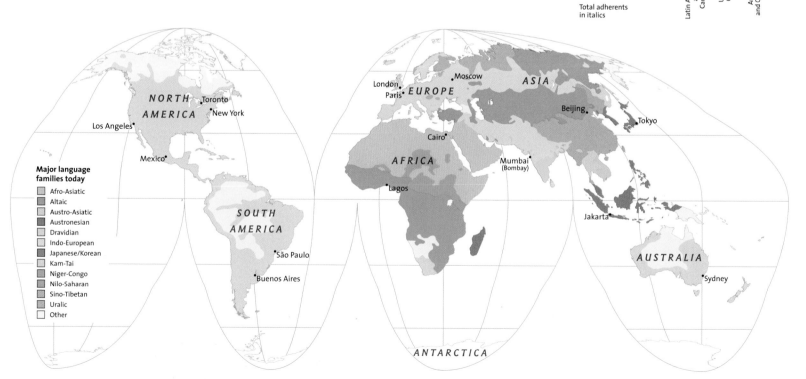

Major language families today
- Afro-Asiatic
- Altaic
- Austro-Asiatic
- Austronesian
- Dravidian
- Indo-European
- Japanese/Korean
- Kam-Tai
- Niger-Congo
- Nilo-Saharan
- Sino-Tibetan
- Uralic
- Other

Religious adherence

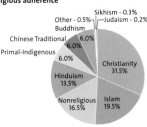

- Other - 0.5%
- Judaism - 0.2%
- Sikhism - 0.3%
- Buddhism 6.0%
- Chinese Traditional 6.0%
- Primal-Indigenous 6.0%
- Hinduism 13.5%
- Nonreligious 16.5%
- Islam 19.5%
- Christianity 31.5%

RELIGIOUS ADHERENCE
The classification of religion and adherents has changed over time. In Western thought and early "world-religion" writing, three religions were recognized: Judaism, Christianity, and Paganism. As Eastern history was more understood, other faiths were added to the list of world religions. Around 1800, the "big five" religions were classified as Judaism, Christianity, Islam, Hinduism, and Buddhism. Most recently, nonreligious has been added as an important segment.

SATELLITE IMAGES OF HOLY SITES
The Old City of Jerusalem surrounds Al' Aqsa Mosque and the Dome of the Rock (left). Al' Aqsa is the second oldest mosque in Islam after the Kaaba in Mecca and is third in holiness after the mosques in Mecca and Medina. It holds up to 400,000 worshippers at one time. The shrine of the Dome of the Rock, built in A.D. 692, commemorates the Prophet Muhammad's ascension to heaven. Also visible is the Western (Wailing) Wall of the Jews, the holiest site in the Jewish world. Part of the retaining wall supporting the Temple of Jerusalem built by Herod in 20 B.C., it is visited by Jews from all over the world. Here, too, is the Via Dolorosa, the traditional route of Christ's crucifixion. Christians pray along the route. The streets of Mecca huddle around the Kaaba (center), Islam's holiest shrine. At Allahabad, the Ganges and Yamuna Rivers (right) draw over 30 million Hindus to bathe in their waters during the Maha Kumbh Mela, the largest gathering of human beings ever recorded.

GeoBytes

FIRST URBANITES
The Sumerians developed the first city on the broad alluvial plain of the Tigris and Euphrates Rivers.

ACROSS THE STRAIT
Walking dry-shod across a land bridge, ancestors of Native Americans crossed into present-day Alaska from Siberia more than 14,000 years ago.

A TROVE OF LANGUAGES
Papua New Guinea is home to more than 800 languages.

CHINA KEPT OUTSIDERS OUT
The rulers of ancient China were so fearful of external influences that they shut off their kingdom for centuries. The quarantine led to technological stagnation.

STONE TOOLS IN AN AGE OF EXPLORATION
In Australia, Africa, South America, and India's Andaman and Nicobar Islands, European explorers found indigenous people living with Stone Age technology.

From the food we eat to the values we cherish, culture is at the heart of how we live and understand our human world. Not just a collection of customs, rituals, or artifacts, culture is a complex building up of ideas, innovation, and ideologies. Distinct cultures emerged in river valleys, along coastlines, on islands, and across land masses, as humans spread to every continent but Antarctica. Conquest and trade helped dominant cultures to expand. Today, electronic communication, transportation networks, and economic globalization bring major cultures closer. Cultural perceptions can play a part in misunderstanding and conflict. Yet cultures arose in the first place in response to a human need for stability and progress.

OLD CITY OF JERUSALEM, ISRAEL

MECCA, SAUDI ARABIA

ALLAHABAD, INDIA

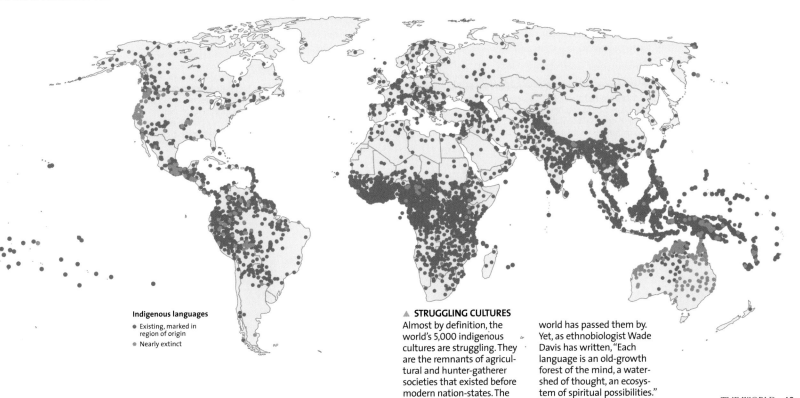

Indigenous languages

- Existing, marked in region of origin
- Nearly extinct

▲ **STRUGGLING CULTURES**
Almost by definition, the world's 5,000 indigenous cultures are struggling. They are the remnants of agricultural and hunter-gatherer societies that existed before modern nation-states. The world has passed them by. Yet, as ethnobiologist Wade Davis has written, "Each language is an old-growth forest of the mind, a watershed of thought, an ecosystem of spiritual possibilities."

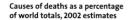

Causes of deaths as a percentage of world totals, 2002 estimates

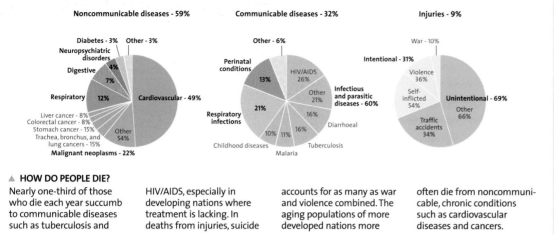

Noncommunicable diseases - 59%
- Diabetes - 3%
- Other - 3%
- Neuropsychiatric disorders 4%
- Digestive 7%
- Respiratory 12%
- Cardiovascular - 49%
- Other 54%
- Liver cancer - 8%
- Colorectal cancer - 8%
- Stomach cancer - 15%
- Trachea, bronchus, and lung cancers - 15%
- Malignant neoplasms - 22%

Communicable diseases - 32%
- Other - 6%
- Perinatal conditions 13%
- HIV/AIDS 26%
- Other 21%
- Infectious and parasitic diseases - 60%
- Respiratory infections 21%
- 16%
- Diarrhoeal 16%
- Childhood diseases 10%
- Malaria 11%
- Tuberculosis

Injuries - 9%
- War - 10%
- Intentional - 31%
- Violence 36%
- Self-inflicted 54%
- Unintentional - 69%
- Other 66%
- Traffic accidents 34%

▲ HOW DO PEOPLE DIE?

Nearly one-third of those who die each year succumb to communicable diseases such as tuberculosis and HIV/AIDS, especially in developing nations where treatment is lacking. In deaths from injuries, suicide accounts for as many as war and violence combined. The aging populations of more developed nations more often die from noncommunicable, chronic conditions such as cardiovascular diseases and cancers.

▼ CARDIOVASCULAR DISEASE

Cardiovascular diseases—heart diseases and stroke—seem to be by-products of the more affluent lifestyle that afflicts the developed world, especially in Russia and Eastern Europe. Stress, alcohol abuse, smoking, inactivity, and diets lacking in fruits and vegetables and rich in cholesterol and saturated fats are risk factors that exacerbate the diseases that kill some 17 million people a year, nearly one-third of all deaths.

▼ HIV/AIDS

Acquired Immunodeficiency Syndrome (AIDS) came to the world's attention in the 1980s. Since then, more than 25 million people have died of the disease, which is carried by the Human Immunodeficiency Virus (HIV). Although HIV/AIDS symptoms can be stabilized by modern drugs, 40 million people remain infected at the end of 2005. Many of these live in countries where poverty, denial, lack of health-delivery systems, and drug production and patent problems limit access to prevention and treatment strategies.

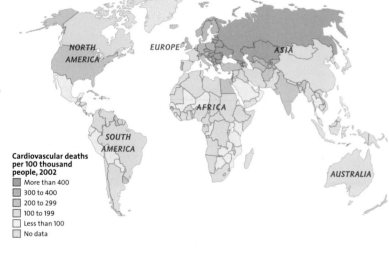

Cardiovascular deaths per 100 thousand people, 2002
- More than 400
- 300 to 400
- 200 to 299
- 100 to 199
- Less than 100
- No data

Percentage of adults (ages 15-49) living with HIV/AIDS, 2003
- 20.0% - 38.0%
- 10.0% - 19.9%
- 5.0% - 9.9%
- 2.0% - 4.9%
- 0.1% - 1.9%
- No data available

▼ DOCTORS WITHIN BORDERS

A shortage of physicians is critical in sub-Saharan African countries. Liberia and Eritrea, for example, had only three doctors for every 100,000 people in 2004. In contrast, Italy had 606, and Cuba, where health care is centralized, had 590. Now the gap between haves and have-nots is widening as many formerly socialist countries decentralize health care and physicians emigrate from poor societies to wealthier.

▼ MALARIA RAVAGES TROPICS

Malaria is a mostly tropical, parasitic disease transmitted from human to human by mosquito bites. Worldwide, over 500 million people suffer from illness caused by the malaria parasite. In sub-Saharan Africa exposure to malaria-infected mosquitoes is so intense that over a million people die each year. Use of insecticide-treated mosquito nets and new drugs to alleviate the disease will continue to make a difference while scientists work to develop an effective vaccine.

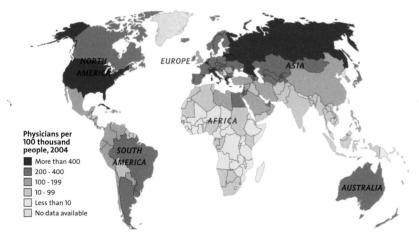

Physicians per 100 thousand people, 2004
- More than 400
- 200 - 400
- 100 - 199
- 10 - 99
- Less than 10
- No data available

Malaria endemicity
- More than 50% (Holo-Hyperendemic)
- 10% - 50% (Mesoendemic)
- Less than 10% (Hypoendemic)
- No malaria

Endemicity is measured by the percentage of children infected with the parasite.

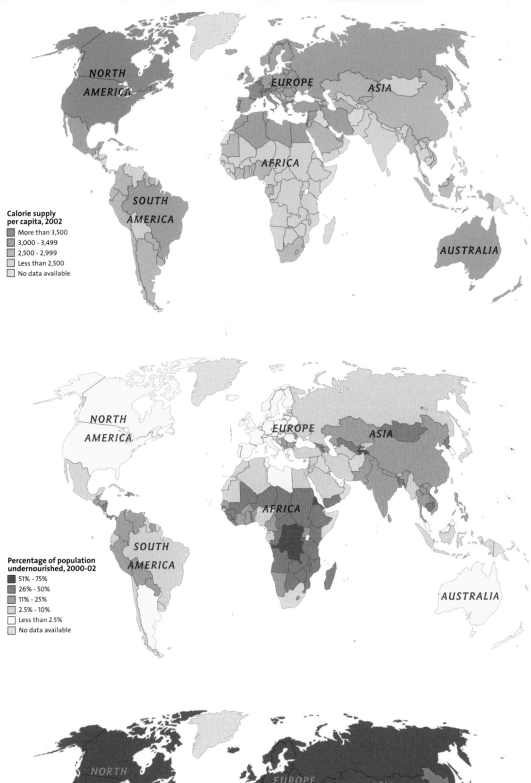

**Calorie supply
per capita, 2002**

- More than 3,500
- 3,000 - 3,499
- 2,500 - 2,999
- Less than 2,500
- No data available

**Percentage of population
undernourished, 2000-02**

- 51% - 75%
- 26% - 50%
- 11% - 25%
- 2.5% - 10%
- Less than 2.5%
- No data available

Literacy rate, 2005 estimate
(as a percentage of total
population age 15 and over)

- 96% - 100%
- 86% - 95%
- 76% - 85%
- 51% - 75%
- Less than 51%
- No data available

Developed and developing nations show major differences in the rates and causes of death, with AIDS the most significant difference. Cardiovascular disease, the major cause of death in the developed world, is an increasing contributor to mortality in developing nations. Closely tied to health measurements are literacy rates—the percentage of a population who can read—mainly because literacy is an indicator of the reach and effectiveness of a nation's educational system. Educating girls and women improves health indices not only for females but for families. Girls' education makes a difference—in lowered infant mortality and overall mortality rates and in increased rates at which health care is sought.

◀ CALORIE CONSUMPTION

How many calories do people need to stay healthy? At least 2,500 a day. But Afghans consume a paltry 1,523 a day, and one-third of sub-Saharan African children are undernourished. In wealthy countries, such as the United States, high calorie intake means a high rate of obesity—a risk factor for heart disease, diabetes, and cancer. Middle-income countries, such as Mexico and Brazil, are beginning to confront their own epidemics of obesity.

◀ HUNGER

Although the world produces 20% more food than its population can consume, nearly a billion people suffer from chronic hunger, a condition provoked by drought, war, social conflicts, and inept public policy. Some five million children under age five die each year from lack of food. In sub-Saharan Africa, where desertification has overtaken agricultural lands and there is little irrigation, drought precedes famine.

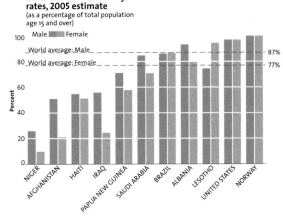

**Male and female literacy
rates, 2005 estimate**
(as a percentage of total population
age 15 and over)

Male ▓▓ Female

World average: Male — 87%
World average: Female — 77%

NIGER, AFGHANISTAN, HAITI, IRAQ, PAPUA NEW GUINEA, SAUDI ARABIA, BRAZIL, ALBANIA, LESOTHO, UNITED STATES, NORWAY

◀ LITERACY

A nation's success depends on an educated population; thus illiteracy remains strongly tied to poverty. In some regions of Asia, Africa, and the Middle East, women suffer much higher rates of illiteracy than men, a reflection of a systematic social bias against them and a denial or discouragement of women's access to education.

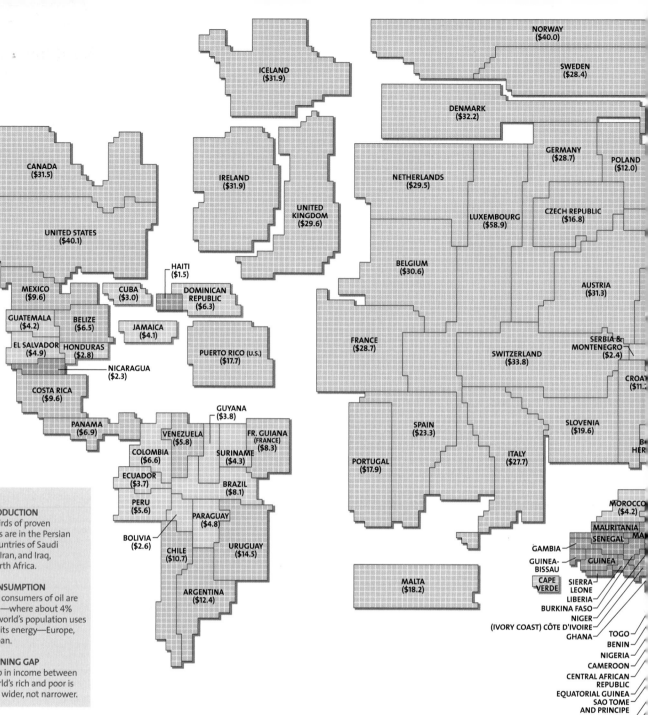

▶ CURRENT GDP POPULATION DATA

Cartograms are value-by-area maps. As a graphic representation that depicts the size of an object (such as a country) in relation to an attribute (such as Gross Domestic Product or GDP per capita), cartograms do not delineate geographic space but rather express a thematic relationship. In the cartogram at right, each block represents one hundred U.S. dollars. With some geographical facsimile, countries are associated with neighboring countries and land masses, but the size of an individual country is related to its Gross Domestic Product per capita, that is, the value of final goods and services produced within a country in a year, divided by population. Luxembourg, a tiny inland area, is the giant among the nations of the world in terms of GDP per capita, at $58,900. The United States is next, at $40,100. Russia ranks a middling 82, at $9,800, in GDP per capita. Ranked 231 and 232 are Malawi and Timor-Leste (East Timor), at $600 and $400, respectively.

GeoBytes

HUNTING AND GATHERING
This mode of production supported people for more than 95% of the time humans have lived on Earth.

NEOLITHIC REVOLUTION
Around 10,000 B.C., agriculture ushered in settled societies and increasing populations.

FIVE COUNTRIES
The largest deposits of strategic minerals, essential to industry, are concentrated in Canada, the U.S., Russia, South Africa, and Australia.

OIL PRODUCTION
Two-thirds of proven reserves are in the Persian Gulf countries of Saudi Arabia, Iran, and Iraq, and North Africa.

OIL CONSUMPTION
Largest consumers of oil are the U.S.—where about 4% of the world's population uses 30% of its energy—Europe, and Japan.

A WIDENING GAP
The gap in income between the world's rich and poor is getting wider, not narrower.

Map labels (GDP per capita, in thousands of U.S. dollars):

NORWAY ($40.0)
ICELAND ($31.9)
SWEDEN ($28.4)
DENMARK ($32.2)
CANADA ($31.5)
IRELAND ($31.9)
GERMANY ($28.7)
POLAND ($12.0)
NETHERLANDS ($29.5)
UNITED KINGDOM ($29.6)
LUXEMBOURG ($58.9)
CZECH REPUBLIC ($16.8)
UNITED STATES ($40.1)
BELGIUM ($30.6)
AUSTRIA ($31.3)
HAITI ($1.5)
MEXICO ($9.6)
CUBA ($3.0)
DOMINICAN REPUBLIC ($6.3)
SERBIA & MONTENEGRO ($2.4)
GUATEMALA ($4.2)
BELIZE ($6.5)
JAMAICA ($4.1)
FRANCE ($28.7)
CROA[TIA] ($11.2)
EL SALVADOR ($4.9)
HONDURAS ($2.8)
PUERTO RICO (U.S.) ($17.7)
SWITZERLAND ($33.8)
NICARAGUA ($2.3)
COSTA RICA ($9.6)
GUYANA ($3.8)
SLOVENIA ($19.6)
PANAMA ($6.9)
VENEZUELA ($5.8)
FR. GUIANA (FRANCE) ($8.3)
COLOMBIA ($6.6)
SURINAME ($4.3)
SPAIN ($23.3)
ITALY ($27.7)
ECUADOR ($3.7)
BRAZIL ($8.1)
PORTUGAL ($17.9)
PERU ($5.6)
PARAGUAY ($4.8)
BOLIVIA ($2.6)
CHILE ($10.7)
URUGUAY ($14.5)
MOROCCO ($4.2)
MAURITANIA
GAMBIA
SENEGAL
MA[LI]
GUINEA-BISSAU
GUINEA
CAPE VERDE
SIERRA LEONE
MALTA ($18.2)
LIBERIA
ARGENTINA ($12.4)
BURKINA FASO
NIGER
(IVORY COAST) CÔTE D'IVOIRE
GHANA
TOGO
BENIN
NIGERIA
CAMEROON
CENTRAL AFRICAN REPUBLIC
EQUATORIAL GUINEA
SAO TOME AND PRINCIPE
CONGO
DEM. REP. OF THE CONGO

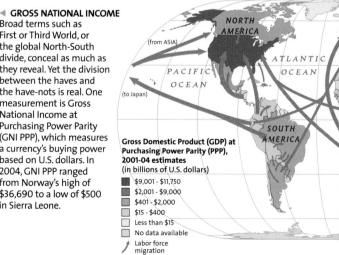

◀ GROSS NATIONAL INCOME

Broad terms such as First or Third World, or the global North-South divide, conceal as much as they reveal. Yet the division between the haves and the have-nots is real. One measurement is Gross National Income at Purchasing Power Parity (GNI PPP), which measures a currency's buying power based on U.S. dollars. In 2004, GNI PPP ranged from Norway's high of $36,690 to a low of $500 in Sierra Leone.

Gross National Income (GNI) per capita, 2002-04
(in U.S. dollars)
- More than $20,000
- $5,000 - $19,999
- $2,000 - $4,999
- $1,000 - $1,999
- $500 - $999
- $90 - $499
- No data available

Gross Domestic Product (GDP) at Purchasing Power Parity (PPP), 2001-04 estimates
(in billions of U.S. dollars)
- $9,001 - $11,750
- $2,001 - $9,000
- $401 - $2,000
- $15 - $400
- Less than $15
- No data available
- Labor force migration

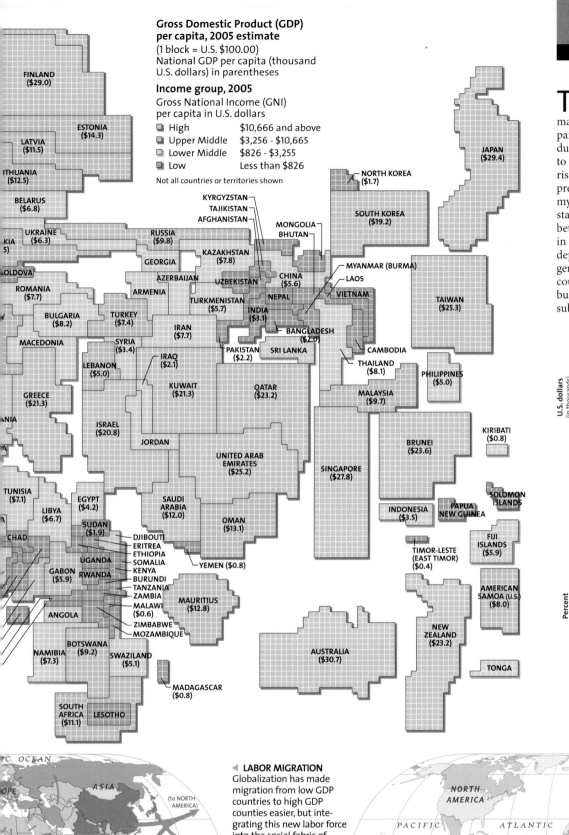

Gross Domestic Product (GDP) per capita, 2005 estimate
(1 block = U.S. $100.00)
National GDP per capita (thousand U.S. dollars) in parentheses

Income group, 2005
Gross National Income (GNI) per capita in U.S. dollars

High	$10,666 and above
Upper Middle	$3,256 - $10,665
Lower Middle	$826 - $3,255
Low	Less than $826

Not all countries or territories shown

FINLAND ($29.0)
ESTONIA ($14.3)
LATVIA ($11.5)
LITHUANIA ($12.5)
BELARUS ($6.8)
UKRAINE ($6.3)
...KIA (5)
...OLDOVA
ROMANIA ($7.7)
BULGARIA ($8.2)
MACEDONIA
GREECE ($21.3)
...ANIA
TUNISIA ($7.1)
LIBYA ($6.7)
CHAD
NAMIBIA ($7.3)
SOUTH AFRICA ($11.1)
LESOTHO
BOTSWANA ($9.2)
SWAZILAND ($5.1)
ANGOLA
GABON ($5.9)
UGANDA
RWANDA
MAURITIUS ($12.8)
MADAGASCAR ($0.8)
DJIBOUTI
ERITREA
ETHIOPIA
SOMALIA
KENYA
BURUNDI
TANZANIA
ZAMBIA
MALAWI ($0.6)
ZIMBABWE
MOZAMBIQUE
YEMEN ($0.8)
EGYPT ($4.2)
SUDAN ($1.9)
SAUDI ARABIA ($12.0)
OMAN ($13.1)
UNITED ARAB EMIRATES ($25.2)
JORDAN
ISRAEL ($20.8)
LEBANON ($5.0)
SYRIA ($3.4)
IRAQ ($2.1)
KUWAIT ($21.3)
QATAR ($23.2)
IRAN ($7.7)
TURKEY ($7.4)
ARMENIA
AZERBAIJAN
GEORGIA
RUSSIA ($9.8)
KAZAKHSTAN ($7.8)
TURKMENISTAN ($5.7)
UZBEKISTAN
KYRGYZSTAN
TAJIKISTAN
AFGHANISTAN
PAKISTAN ($2.2)
INDIA ($3.1)
NEPAL
BHUTAN
MONGOLIA
BANGLADESH ($2.0)
SRI LANKA
MYANMAR (BURMA)
LAOS
CHINA ($5.6)
VIETNAM
THAILAND ($8.1)
CAMBODIA
MALAYSIA ($9.7)
SINGAPORE ($27.8)
BRUNEI ($23.6)
INDONESIA ($3.5)
PHILIPPINES ($5.0)
TAIWAN ($25.3)
NORTH KOREA ($1.7)
SOUTH KOREA ($19.2)
JAPAN ($29.4)
PAPUA NEW GUINEA
SOLOMON ISLANDS
KIRIBATI ($0.8)
TIMOR-LESTE (EAST TIMOR) ($0.4)
FIJI ISLANDS ($5.9)
AMERICAN SAMOA (U.S.) ($8.0)
NEW ZEALAND ($23.2)
AUSTRALIA ($30.7)
TONGA

The world's economies are increasingly interrelated. The exchange of farm products, natural resources, manufactured goods, and services benefits trading partners by allowing them to sell what they best produce at home and buy what is economical for them to purchase from overseas. Regional trade is on the rise, as agreements among countries offer each other preferential access to markets, improving the economy of neighboring blocs of countries and the general standard of living. Nevertheless, the stark difference between high- and low-income countries is apparent in a cartogram, which depicts quantitative data not dependent on scale or area. Dominant economies generally occupy the Northern Hemisphere. Oil-rich countries in the Middle East hold their own. The burden of poverty falls mainly on countries in sub-Saharan Africa and in Asia.

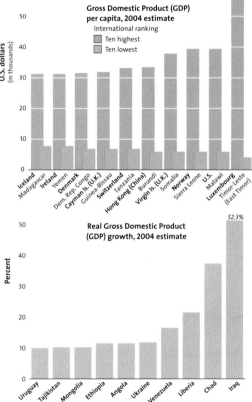

Gross Domestic Product (GDP) per capita, 2004 estimate
International ranking
- Ten highest
- Ten lowest

$58.9

U.S. dollars (in thousands)

Iceland, Madagascar, Ireland, Yemen, Denmark, Dem. Rep. Congo, Cayman Is. (U.K.), Guinea-Bissau, Switzerland, Tanzania, Hong Kong (China), Burundi, Virgin Is. (U.K.), Somalia, Norway, Sierra Leone, U.S., Malawi, Luxembourg, Timor-Leste (East Timor)

Real Gross Domestic Product (GDP) growth, 2004 estimate

52.3%

Percent

Uruguay, Tajikistan, Mongolia, Ethiopia, Angola, Ukraine, Venezuela, Liberia, Chad, Iraq

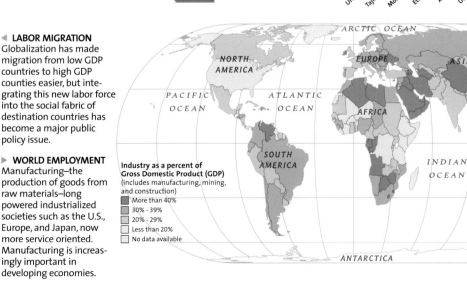

◄ **LABOR MIGRATION**
Globalization has made migration from low GDP countries to high GDP counties easier, but integrating this new labor force into the social fabric of destination countries has become a major public policy issue.

(to NORTH AMERICA)
(from SOUTH AMERICA)

► **WORLD EMPLOYMENT**
Manufacturing—the production of goods from raw materials—long powered industrialized societies such as the U.S., Europe, and Japan, now more service oriented. Manufacturing is increasingly important in developing economies.

Industry as a percent of Gross Domestic Product (GDP)
(includes manufacturing, mining, and construction)

	More than 40%
	30% - 39%
	20% - 29%
	Less than 20%
	No data available

ARCTIC OCEAN
NORTH AMERICA
EUROPE
ASIA
PACIFIC OCEAN
ATLANTIC OCEAN
AFRICA
SOUTH AMERICA
INDIAN OCEAN
PACIFIC OCEAN
AUSTRALIA
ANTARCTICA

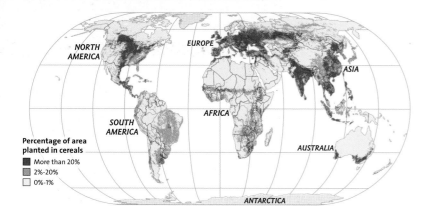

Percentage of area planted in cereals
- More than 20%
- 2%-20%
- 0%-1%

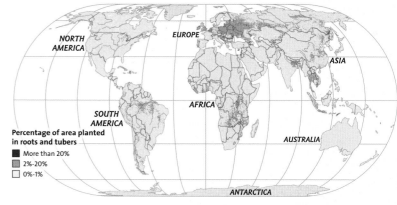

Percentage of area planted in roots and tubers
- More than 20%
- 2%-20%
- 0%-1%

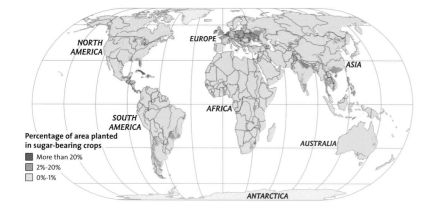

Percentage of area planted in sugar-bearing crops
- More than 20%
- 2%-20%
- 0%-1%

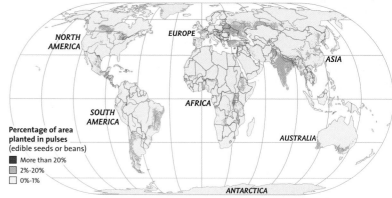

Percentage of area planted in pulses (edible seeds or beans)
- More than 20%
- 2%-20%
- 0%-1%

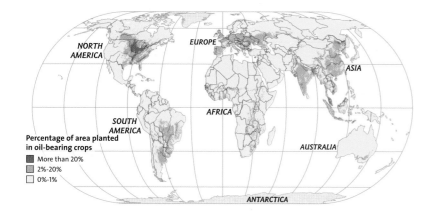

Percentage of area planted in oil-bearing crops
- More than 20%
- 2%-20%
- 0%-1%

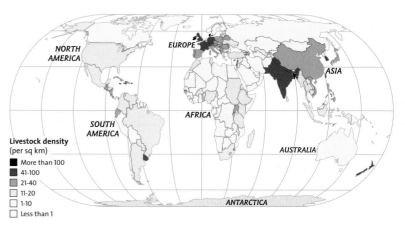

Livestock density (per sq km)
- More than 100
- 41-100
- 21-40
- 11-20
- 1-10
- Less than 1

▲ **CEREALS**
Cereal grains, including barley, maize, millet, rice, rye, sorghum, and wheat, are agricultural staples across the globe. They cover 61% of the world's cultivated land and contribute more calories and protein to the human diet than any other food group.

▲ **SUGAR-BEARING CROPS**
Our taste for sweetness is met by two sugar-bearing crops: sugarcane and sugar beets. Sugarcane is grown in the subtropics, mostly in the Caribbean and Florida. Sugar beets thrive in the temperate latitudes of the Northern Hemisphere, primarily in Europe.

▲ **OIL-BEARING CROPS**
Major oil-bearing crops—soybeans, groundnuts, rapeseed, sunflower, and oil palm fruit—account for 10% of the total calories available for human consumption. Asia and the Americas are the largest producers of these crops, with soybeans contributing the greatest share.

▲ **ROOTS AND TUBERS**
Although cultivation of tubers such as cassava, potatoes, sweet potatoes, taro, and manioc makes up less than 5% of the world's harvested area, these foods are staples across the globe and are critical to subsistence farming in Africa, Asia, and Latin America.

▲ **PULSES**
Pulses—the edible seeds of legumes such as dry beans, chick-peas, and lentils—have two to three times as much protein as most cereals. They are cultivated broadly, but nearly 90% of the world's crop is consumed in developing countries.

▲ **ANIMAL PRODUCTS**
Consumption of meat, milk, and eggs, all high-protein foods, is unequal across the globe. Wealthier industrialized nations consume 30% more meat than developing nations. With population growth, rising incomes, and urbanization, worldwide demand for animal products is increasing.

◀ **MAIZE**
Corn, or maize, was domesticated 6,000 years ago in Mexico. It is now intensively grown in the United States, China, along Africa's Rift Valley, and throughout Eastern Europe. Although it remains a staple food, more than 70% of the world's harvest is for animal feed.

◀ **WHEAT**
Wheat—the most widely grown cereal—is cultivated across the globe. Most of it is grown, however, in the temperate latitudes of the Northern Hemisphere. Wheat, mainly in baked goods, is a major source of calories for more than half of the world's population.

◀ **RICE**
Rice plays a dominant role in the agriculture and diet of Asia. Nearly 90% of the world's rice is consumed and produced in Asia, mostly on small family farms. Larger scale commercial cultivation of rice takes place in the southern United States, southern Australia, and the Amazon Basin.

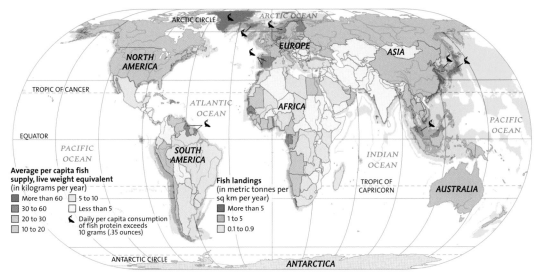

Average per capita fish supply, live weight equivalent (in kilograms per year)
- More than 60
- 30 to 60
- 20 to 30
- 10 to 20
- 5 to 10
- Less than 5
- Daily per capita consumption of fish protein exceeds 10 grams (.35 ounces)

Fish landings (in metric tonnes per sq km per year)
- More than 5
- 1 to 5
- 0.1 to 0.9

More than 850 million people worldwide do not have access to adequate food. Hunger, found across the globe and even in the richest countries, is chronic in rural areas of the developing world, places not always well suited for agriculture or managed for sustainable yield. Other countries with climates and soils better suited to agriculture, such as the United States, grow and consume far more food than is required to meet the needs of their populations. We are faced with closing this gap between the hungry and the overfed at a time when the world's population, mostly in developing countries, is expected to grow by three billion over the next 50 years. Lack of space for cropland expansion, climate change, and environmental stresses such as deforestation, desertification, and erosion add to the challenge of agricultural management and productivity.

▲ FISHERIES AND AQUACULTURE

Fish is a vital source of protein for much of the world. Yet the world's primary fisheries are under stress from overfishing and environmental degradation. The tonnage of fish caught in the wild has remained relatively stable over the past five years, while tonnage of fish produced by aquaculture has increased markedly. Aquaculture, primarily in freshwater environments, now accounts for more than 30% of total fish production. China leads in aquaculture production, growing more than two-thirds of all farm-raised fish.

World diets, 2003 (as a percentage of daily calorie consumption)

Cerals* - excluding beer
Fruits* - excluding wine
Milk* - excluding butter

NORTH AMERICA
- Cereals* 29%
- Starchy roots - 2%
- Sweeteners 17%
- Vegetable oils 14%
- Fruits* - 3%
- Alcoholic beverages - 3%
- Meat 11%
- Animal fats - 3%
- Milk* 9%
- Other 9%

EUROPE
- 31%, 7%, 9%, 5%, 12%, 5%, 3%, 11%, 12%, 5%

AUSTRALIA & OCEANIA
- 25%, 8%, 8%, 4%, 16%, 7%, 3%, 4%, 5%, 11%, 12%

SOUTH AMERICA
- 34%, 8%, 6%, 2%, 11%, 3%, 4%, 10%, 17%, 5%, 1% 2%

ASIA
- 54%, 10%, 3% 2%, 8%, 9%, 7%, 4%

AFRICA
- 50%, 9%, 3% 1% 3% 2% 4%, 8%, 6%, 14%, 8%

▲ WHAT THE WORLD EATS

The foods people eat vary widely and are chosen on the basis of availability, income, and cultural preference. Cereals, arguably the most significant food source worldwide, make up a large percentage of diets in Africa and Asia. High caloric foods—sugars, meats, and oils—make up a significant portion of diets in Oceania, the Americas, and Europe.

▼ GENETICALLY MODIFIED AGRICULTURE

Planting of genetically modified (GM) or "biotech" crops, mainly soybeans, corn, cotton, and canola, is still conservative but on the rise despite continued debate over ecological impacts and human health hazards. GM crops first became an industry in 1996. Some 75% of GM planting today is in countries such as the United States, Argentina, Canada, and Brazil. Some developing nations are beginning to grow GM crops in hopes of increasing output in areas where traditional crops do not meet the needs of the population.

▶ DISTRIBUTION OF CROPS

The distribution of the world's staple crops varies across the globe. Wheat, maize, and barley thrive in the temperate climates of the United States, Europe, and Australia, whereas sugarcane is better suited to the tropical climate of the Caribbean. Rice thrives in high rainfall areas of Asia, and drought-resistant crops such as millet and sorghum are staples of drier places, such as the Sahel on the southern fringe of the Sahara Desert in Africa.

PERCENTAGE OF WORLD CROP PRODUCTION BY REGION

Highest producers		Lowest producers	
Conterminous U.S.	**87%**	**Caribbean**	**60%**
Maize	28%	Sugarcane	36%
Wheat	26%	Maize	8%
Soybean	24%	Pulses*	6%
Cotton	5%	Rice	6%
Sorghum	4%	Cassava	4%
Central Asia	**87%**	**Eastern Africa**	**59%**
Wheat	51%	Maize	27%
Barley	23%	Pulses*	10%
Cotton	9%	Sorghum	9%
Millet	2%	Cassava	8%
Rye	2%	Rice	5%
Australia & New Zealand	**85%**	**East Asia**	**57%**
Wheat	51%	Rice	20%
Barley	18%	Wheat	17%
Pulses*	11%	Maize	12%
Sorghum	3%	Soybean	5%
Sugarcane	2%	Rapeseed	3%
Southern Africa	**84%**	**Southern Europe**	**51%**
Maize	54%	Wheat	21%
Wheat	15%	Barley	16%
Sunflower	6%	Maize	6%
Sorghum	5%	Sunflower	6%
Sugarcane	4%	Pulses*	2%
*Pulses-edible seeds or beans			

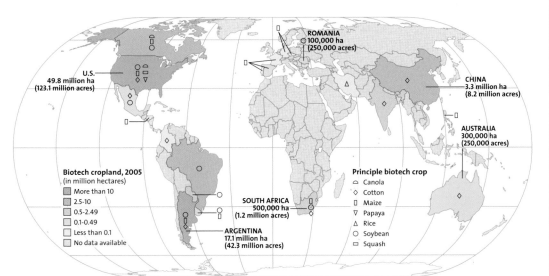

U.S. 49.8 million ha (123.1 million acres)

ROMANIA 100,000 ha (250,000 acres)

CHINA 3.3 million ha (8.2 million acres)

AUSTRALIA 300,000 ha (250,000 acres)

SOUTH AFRICA 500,000 ha (1.2 million acres)

ARGENTINA 17.1 million ha (42.3 million acres)

Biotech cropland, 2005 (in million hectares)
- More than 10
- 2.5-10
- 0.5-2.49
- 0.1-0.49
- Less than 0.1
- No data available

Principle biotech crop
- Canola
- Cotton
- Maize
- Papaya
- Rice
- Soybean
- Squash

GeoBytes

AGRICULTURAL HEARTLANDS
The world's largest agricultural areas are in China, Australia, the United States, Kazakhstan, the Russian Federation, Brazil, Argentina, India, and Saudi Arabia.

GM CROPS
Nearly 30% of the world's total area of soybeans, maize, cotton, and canola is planted with genetically modified (GM) varieties.

UNEQUAL CONSUMPTION
On average, people in North America and Europe consume more than 3,000 calories per day, whereas people in some African countries consume barely half that. In countries such as Eritrea, the Democratic Republic of the Congo, and Burundi, up to 70% of the population is undernourished.

▶ TRADE BLOCS

Common interests encourage neighboring countries to form trade blocs to benefit from increased trade and growth. Trade blocs steer a course between protectionism and unbridled capitalism. Such agreements fall into two classes: free trade zones, such as NAFTA (North American Free Trade Agreement), which removes internal tariffs but allows participants to set external tariffs; and customs unions, such as the EU (European Union), in which all agree to common outside tariffs.

Most active regional trade blocs, 2005

- Agadir Agreement
- Andean Community
- APEC - Asia-Pacific Economic Cooperation
- ASEAN - Association of Southeast Asian Nations
- CACM - Central American Common Market
- CARICOM - Caribbean Community and Common Market
- CEMAC - Economic and Monetary Community of Central Africa
- COMESA - Common Market for Eastern and Southern Africa
- EAC - East African Community
- ECOWAS - Economic Community of West African States
- EU - European Union
- EurAsEC - Eurasian Economic Community
- GCC - Gulf Cooperation Council
- MERCOSUR - Southern Common Market
- NAFTA - North American Free Trade Agreement
- PARTA - Pacific Regional Trade Agreement
- SAARC - South Asian Association for Regional Cooperation
- SACU - Southern African Customs Union

- Not an active bloc member

GeoBytes

LARGEST TRADE BLOC
The European Union (EU) member states account for nearly one-third of the global economy, making the EU the largest economic body in the world.

LARGEST ECONOMY
The country with the largest economy is the United States, with an income of more than $12 trillion.

LARGEST ASIAN ECONOMY
Japan has the world's second largest economy at $4.7 trillion—the biggest in Asia.

LARGEST EUROPEAN ECONOMY
Germany maintains the largest economy in Europe, with a national income of more than $2.4 trillion.

LARGEST SOUTH AMERICAN ECONOMY
The Brazilian economy, which exceeds $550 billion, dominates South America.

▶ WORLD DEBT

Debt hinders many developing countries. The World Bank classifies countries by debt level. A country with debt at or above 80% of its gross national income (GNI) is classified as severely indebted and in danger of defaulting on loans.

Estimated external debt as a percentage of Gross Domestic Product (GDP) at Purchasing Power Parity, 2002-04 estimates
(GDP PPP based upon U.S. dollars)

- More than 100%
- 30% - 100%
- 15% - 29%
- 5% - 14%
- Less than 5%
- No data available

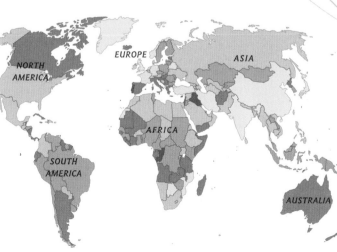

▲ TRADE FLOW

International trade of goods is a major avenue of globalization. The arrows above show the value of trade between major regions of the world. More than half of world trade occurs between high-income areas such as Japan, the United States, and Western Europe. Trade is increasing, however, between these high-income countries and developing countries in Asia, South America, and Africa. Lowered trade barriers offer opportunities for low-income countries, although still limited. Labor-intensive merchandise, such as textiles, can be produced and exported at a low cost from developing

To multinational corporations, globalization means that products can be produced in multiple locations and distributed worldwide. To consumers, globalization means lower prices. To governments, globalization can mean job losses, multinational mergers, and price-fixing cartels. While the benefits of globalization have not been universally shared, it has been a force in bringing economic growth. The World Trade Organization (WTO) works with governments and international organizations to regulate trade and reduce economic inequality among countries. Global integration increases the flow of trade, capital, information, and people across borders by reducing or eliminating trade restrictions and customs barriers. Globalization presents both challenges and opportunities—for new markets, jobs, and export-led growth.

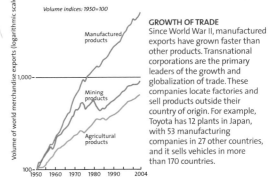

GROWTH OF TRADE
Since World War II, manufactured exports have grown faster than other products. Transnational corporations are the primary leaders of the growth and globalization of trade. These companies locate factories and sell products outside their country of origin. For example, Toyota has 12 plants in Japan, with 53 manufacturing companies in 27 other countries, and it sells vehicles in more than 170 countries.

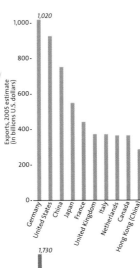

MERCHANDISE EXPORTS
China has risen quickly to become the third-largest exporter of merchandise after Germany. China's growth rate exceeds that of any large industrial country. From 2000 to 2004, the value of merchandise exports grew by 24% annually, largely due to the undervalued Chinese currency that makes exports cheap.

MERCHANDISE IMPORTS
The United States is by far the world's largest importer—the U.S. trade deficit (more imports than exports) approached $725 billion in 2005. China's growing trade surplus is fueling an economic boom in that country.

---

nations. Trade in agricultural commodities is a key issue between developing and high-income countries. Two billion families in the world make a living from farming. About 60 countries are dependent on commodities for more than 40% of their export income—in some African countries the figure

is 80%. Stormy meetings of the World Trade Organization (WTO) focus on making the European Union (EU) and the United States end subsidies to their farmers to increase trade opportunities for developing nations.

Income Group, 2005
Gross National Income (GNI) per capita in U.S. dollars

High	$10,066 and above
Upper middle	$3,256 - $10,065
Lower middle	$826 - $3,255
Low	Less than $826
No data available	

Interregional merchandise trade
(in billions of U.S. dollars)

- $240 and above
- $120 - $240
- $60 - $119
- $30 - $59
- $5 - $29
- Less than $5

● Stock exchange (World Federation of Exchanges member)

Single-commodity-dependent economy
(commodity comprising more than 40 percent of total exports)

- □ Agriculture
- ◇ Cotton
- ⊜ Crude oil and petroleum products
- ⚓ Fishing
- ✕ Gems, metals, and minerals
- △ Machinery and equipment
- ▣ Textiles and apparel

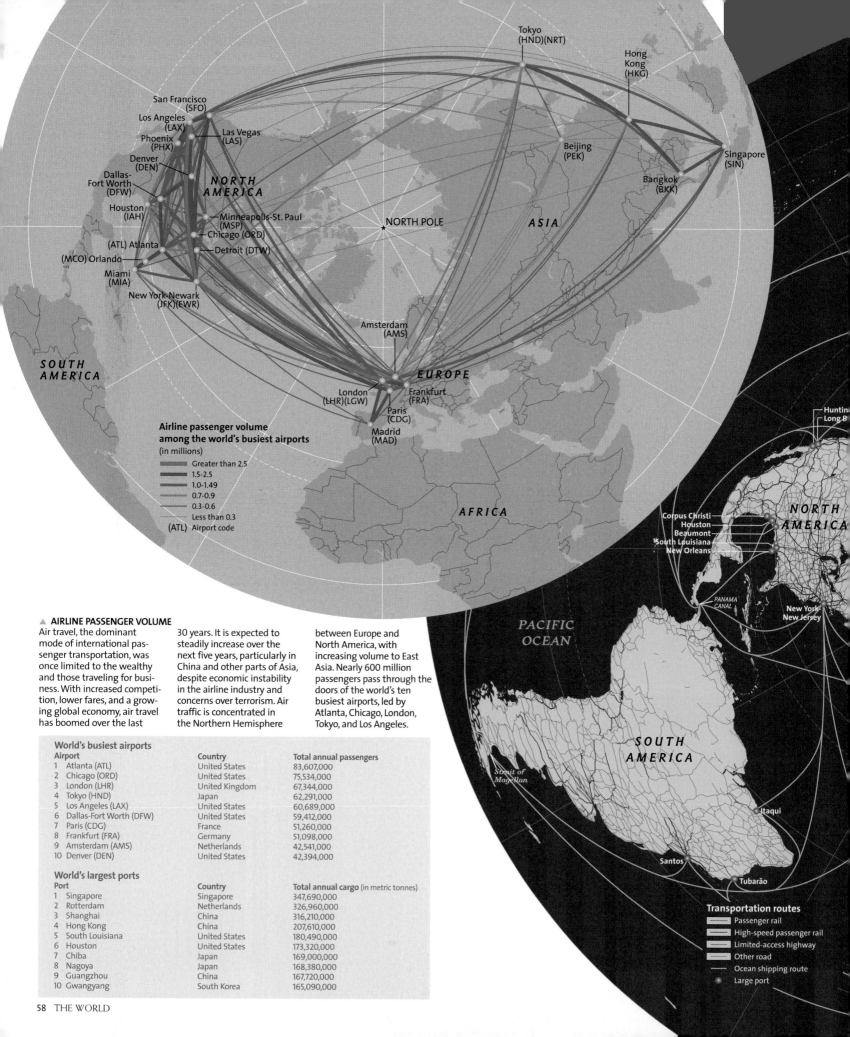

Airline passenger volume among the world's busiest airports
(in millions)

- Greater than 2.5
- 1.5-2.5
- 1.0-1.49
- 0.7-0.9
- 0.3-0.6
- Less than 0.3
- (ATL) Airport code

▲ AIRLINE PASSENGER VOLUME

Air travel, the dominant mode of international passenger transportation, was once limited to the wealthy and those traveling for business. With increased competition, lower fares, and a growing global economy, air travel has boomed over the last 30 years. It is expected to steadily increase over the next five years, particularly in China and other parts of Asia, despite economic instability in the airline industry and concerns over terrorism. Air traffic is concentrated in the Northern Hemisphere between Europe and North America, with increasing volume to East Asia. Nearly 600 million passengers pass through the doors of the world's ten busiest airports, led by Atlanta, Chicago, London, Tokyo, and Los Angeles.

World's busiest airports

	Airport	Country	Total annual passengers
1	Atlanta (ATL)	United States	83,607,000
2	Chicago (ORD)	United States	75,534,000
3	London (LHR)	United Kingdom	67,344,000
4	Tokyo (HND)	Japan	62,291,000
5	Los Angeles (LAX)	United States	60,689,000
6	Dallas-Fort Worth (DFW)	United States	59,412,000
7	Paris (CDG)	France	51,260,000
8	Frankfurt (FRA)	Germany	51,098,000
9	Amsterdam (AMS)	Netherlands	42,541,000
10	Denver (DEN)	United States	42,394,000

World's largest ports

	Port	Country	Total annual cargo (in metric tonnes)
1	Singapore	Singapore	347,690,000
2	Rotterdam	Netherlands	326,960,000
3	Shanghai	China	316,210,000
4	Hong Kong	China	207,610,000
5	South Louisiana	United States	180,490,000
6	Houston	United States	173,320,000
7	Chiba	Japan	169,000,000
8	Nagoya	Japan	168,380,000
9	Guangzhou	China	167,720,000
10	Gwangyang	South Korea	165,090,000

Transportation routes

- Passenger rail
- High-speed passenger rail
- Limited-access highway
- Other road
- Ocean shipping route
- Large port

Throughout history, the movement of goods and people linked places and their economies. Early transport was undertaken on foot or by animals such as horses and camels. Long distances were traveled over water by pole and current-propelled boats, then by oar and later by sail. With the introduction of mechanical means of transport--steamboats, railroad locomotives, and eventually automobiles and airplanes--movement from place to place accelerated rapidly. Speed, efficiency, and safety are some of the metrics of modern transportation systems. Today, people and goods move quickly about the world via a web of land, sea, and air networks that together keep the global economy humming.

GeoBytes

SAVING TIME BY CANAL
With the opening of the Suez Canal in 1869, the journey from London to Mumbai (Bombay) shrunk from nearly six months to about two months.

SAVING TIME BY TRAIN
First launched in Japan in 1964, high-speed trains can carry passengers at speeds exceeding 300 kph (186 mph). Europe, East Asia, and the U.S. have adopted fast trains to provide national, inter-urban transport.

◄ **TRANSPORTATION ROUTES**
Nearly all of the world's freight headed for international destinations is transported via ships in standardized containers. These sealed metal containers have dramatically altered the face of international freight transport. They are designed to be easily transferred from one mode of transport to another, for instance, from a ship to a train, thereby increasing efficiency and reducing cost. As with passenger airline traffic, maritime freight traffic is concentrated. The largest 10 ports, led by Singapore, Rotterdam, Shanghai, Hong Kong, and South Louisiana, handle more than 50% of global freight traffic.

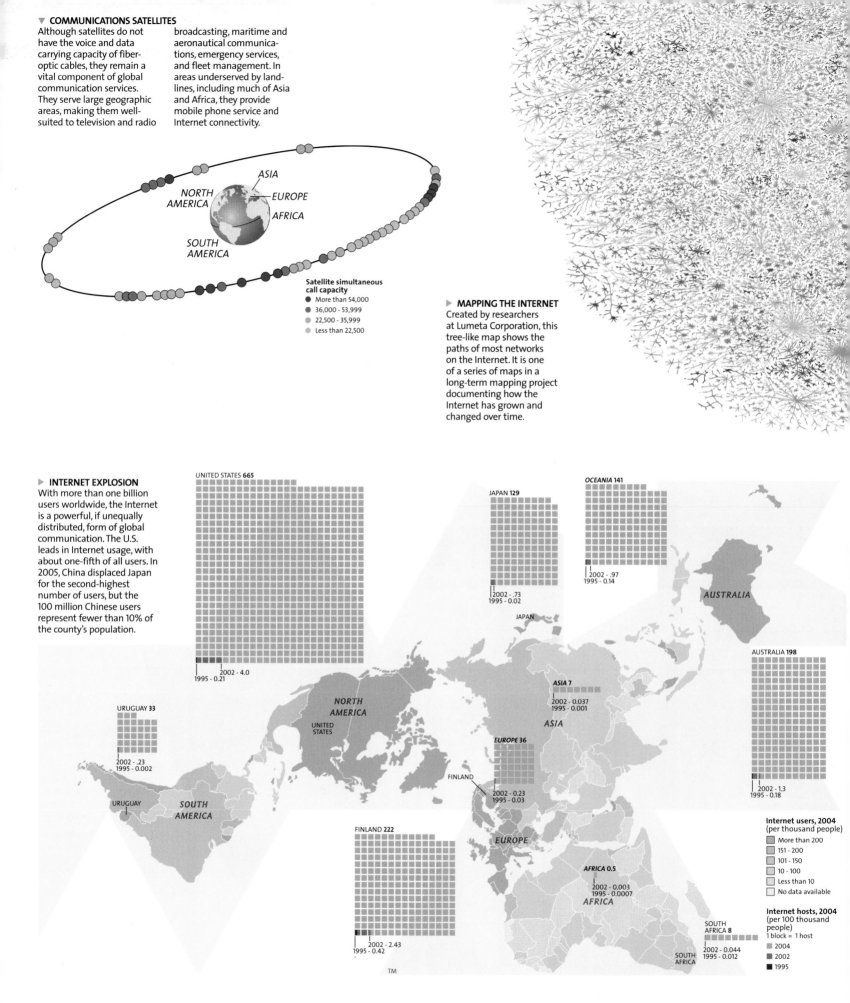

▼ COMMUNICATIONS SATELLITES

Although satellites do not have the voice and data carrying capacity of fiber-optic cables, they remain a vital component of global communication services. They serve large geographic areas, making them well-suited to television and radio broadcasting, maritime and aeronautical communications, emergency services, and fleet management. In areas underserved by land-lines, including much of Asia and Africa, they provide mobile phone service and Internet connectivity.

ASIA
NORTH AMERICA
EUROPE
AFRICA
SOUTH AMERICA

Satellite simultaneous call capacity
- More than 54,000
- 36,000 - 53,999
- 22,500 - 35,999
- Less than 22,500

▶ MAPPING THE INTERNET

Created by researchers at Lumeta Corporation, this tree-like map shows the paths of most networks on the Internet. It is one of a series of maps in a long-term mapping project documenting how the Internet has grown and changed over time.

▶ INTERNET EXPLOSION

With more than one billion users worldwide, the Internet is a powerful, if unequally distributed, form of global communication. The U.S. leads in Internet usage, with about one-fifth of all users. In 2005, China displaced Japan for the second-highest number of users, but the 100 million Chinese users represent fewer than 10% of the county's population.

UNITED STATES **665**
2002 - 4.0
1995 - 0.21

JAPAN **129**
2002 - .73
1995 - 0.02

OCEANIA **141**
2002 - .97
1995 - 0.14

AUSTRALIA

AUSTRALIA **198**
2002 - 1.3
1995 - 0.18

NORTH AMERICA
UNITED STATES

ASIA **7**
2002 - 0.037
1995 - 0.001

ASIA

EUROPE **36**
2002 - 0.23
1995 - 0.03

FINLAND

URUGUAY **33**
2002 - .23
1995 - 0.002

URUGUAY
SOUTH AMERICA

FINLAND **222**
2002 - 2.43
1995 - 0.42

EUROPE

AFRICA **0.5**
2002 - 0.003
1995 - 0.0007

AFRICA

SOUTH AFRICA **8**
2002 - 0.044
1995 - 0.012

SOUTH AFRICA

Internet users, 2004
(per thousand people)
- More than 200
- 151 - 200
- 101 - 150
- 10 - 100
- Less than 10
- No data available

Internet hosts, 2004
(per 100 thousand people)
1 block = 1 host
- 2004
- 2002
- 1995

TM

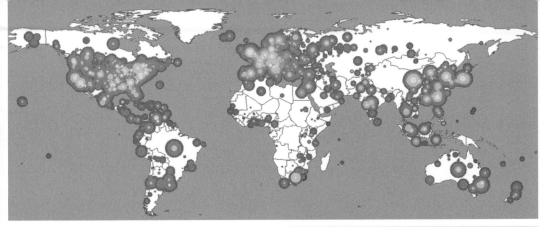

▲ SPREAD OF A COMPUTER VIRUS
This map shows the spread of the CodeRed worm on July 19, 2001, which disproportionately affected small businesses and home users. Some 360,000 computers were infected, spreading in early (yellow), middle (orange), and late (red) zones. Clearly, not all software programs are benign. Programs designed to intentionally disrupt, damage, or interfere with computer functions, files, and data are commonly referred to as computer viruses. Much like human-spread viruses, they range in complexity, severity and speed of transmission. One particularly fast-spreading type of virus is called worms. They spread themselves automatically by controlling other software programs such as email.

GeoBytes

EXPLOSIVE GROWTH
In 1981, the Internet had barely more than 200 host computers. Today there are more than 400 million, with millions more being added every month.

MOBILE WORLD
More than 75% of the world's population lives within range of a mobile phone network, whereas only 50% have access to a fixed-line telephone.

TV AND RADIO
In the last thirty years, television viewers in the developing world have multiplied 55 fold. The number of radios per 1,000 habitants has more than doubled.

U.S. OWNS THE SKIES
The United States owns more than half of the world's satellites, with Russia a distant second. Other satellite holders include Japan and China. Satellites serve a mix of civilian, commercial, and military uses.

Advances in and widespread use of communication technologies have quickly changed the face of international communication. Enormous amounts of data can be shared nearly instantaneously, and voice communication is now possible across much of the globe. Neither would have been possible a few decades ago when nearly all telecommunication services were carried over copper wire. The Internet has fostered entrepreneurship, helped open new markets, created new industries and jobs, and provided accessibility to and sharing of vast amounts of information. Cellular phones have made voice communication a reality for many who previously had no access to land-line phone service. And without the widespread network of fiber-optic cables, the rapid transmission of volumes of data and crystal-clear voice communication—hallmarks of international communication today—would not be possible. Although these technologies have helped foster communication and economic activity across the globe, they are not truly global. Many areas, both in the developed and developing world, do not have access to these technologies, creating a divide between the digital haves and have-nots.

▶ CONNECTING THE PLANET
The world is increasingly connected by underground and undersea fiber-optic cables and cellular networks. Fiber-optic cables allow for lightening-fast transmission of email, data, and voice calls, whereas cellular technology has extended phone service to parts of the world previously without any land-line service, including rural regions in Asia and Africa.

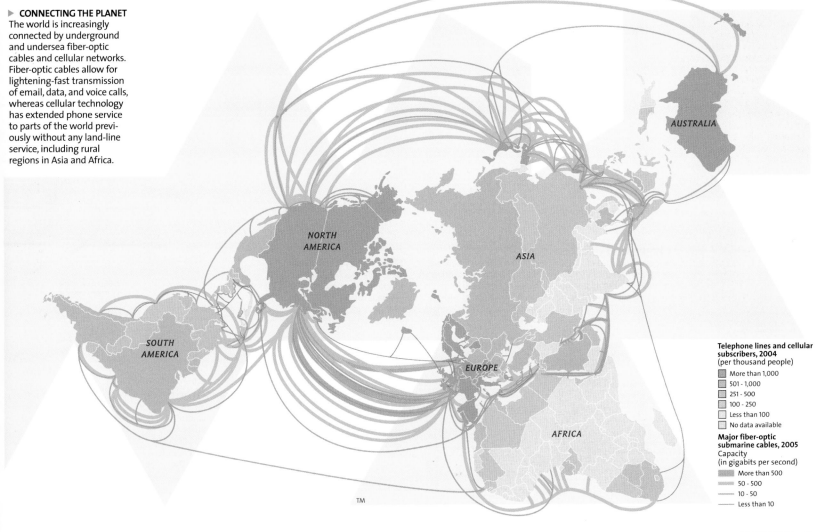

Telephone lines and cellular subscribers, 2004
(per thousand people)
- More than 1,000
- 501 - 1,000
- 251 - 500
- 100 - 250
- Less than 100
- No data available

Major fiber-optic submarine cables, 2005
Capacity
(in gigabits per second)
- More than 500
- 50 - 500
- 10 - 50
- Less than 10

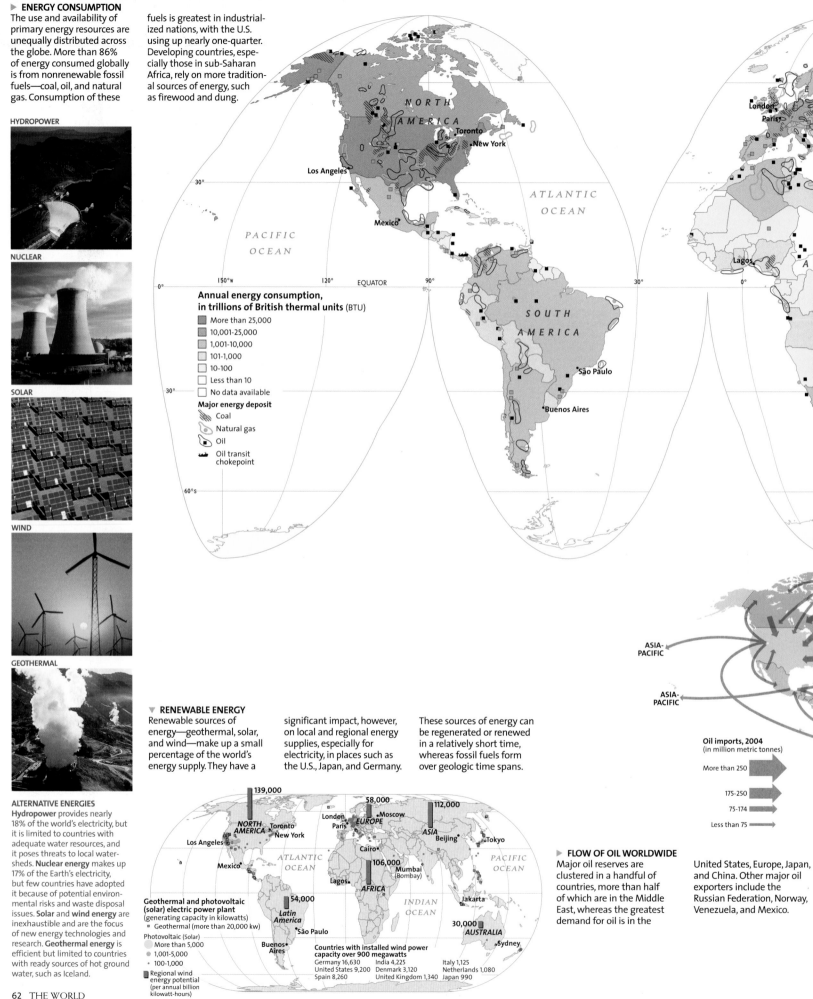

▶ ENERGY CONSUMPTION

The use and availability of primary energy resources are unequally distributed across the globe. More than 86% of energy consumed globally is from nonrenewable fossil fuels—coal, oil, and natural gas. Consumption of these fuels is greatest in industrialized nations, with the U.S. using up nearly one-quarter. Developing countries, especially those in sub-Saharan Africa, rely on more traditional sources of energy, such as firewood and dung.

HYDROPOWER

NUCLEAR

SOLAR

WIND

GEOTHERMAL

ALTERNATIVE ENERGIES

Hydropower provides nearly 18% of the world's electricity, but it is limited to countries with adequate water resources, and it poses threats to local watersheds. **Nuclear energy** makes up 17% of the Earth's electricity, but few countries have adopted it because of potential environmental risks and waste disposal issues. **Solar** and **wind energy** are inexhaustible and are the focus of new energy technologies and research. **Geothermal energy** is efficient but limited to countries with ready sources of hot ground water, such as Iceland.

Annual energy consumption, in trillions of British thermal units (BTU)

- More than 25,000
- 10,001-25,000
- 1,001-10,000
- 101-1,000
- 10-100
- Less than 10
- No data available

Major energy deposit
- Coal
- Natural gas
- Oil
- Oil transit chokepoint

▼ RENEWABLE ENERGY

Renewable sources of energy—geothermal, solar, and wind—make up a small percentage of the world's energy supply. They have a significant impact, however, on local and regional energy supplies, especially for electricity, in places such as the U.S., Japan, and Germany. These sources of energy can be regenerated or renewed in a relatively short time, whereas fossil fuels form over geologic time spans.

Geothermal and photovoltaic (solar) electric power plant
(generating capacity in kilowatts)
- ▪ Geothermal (more than 20,000 kw)

Photovoltaic (Solar)
- ● More than 5,000
- ● 1,001-5,000
- · 100-1,000

▪ Regional wind energy potential (per annual billion kilowatt-hours)

Countries with installed wind power capacity over 900 megawatts

Germany 16,630	India 4,225	Italy 1,125
United States 9,200	Denmark 3,120	Netherlands 1,080
Spain 8,260	United Kingdom 1,340	Japan 990

▶ FLOW OF OIL WORLDWIDE

Major oil reserves are clustered in a handful of countries, more than half of which are in the Middle East, whereas the greatest demand for oil is in the United States, Europe, Japan, and China. Other major oil exporters include the Russian Federation, Norway, Venezuela, and Mexico.

Oil imports, 2004
(in million metric tonnes)
- More than 250
- 175-250
- 75-174
- Less than 75

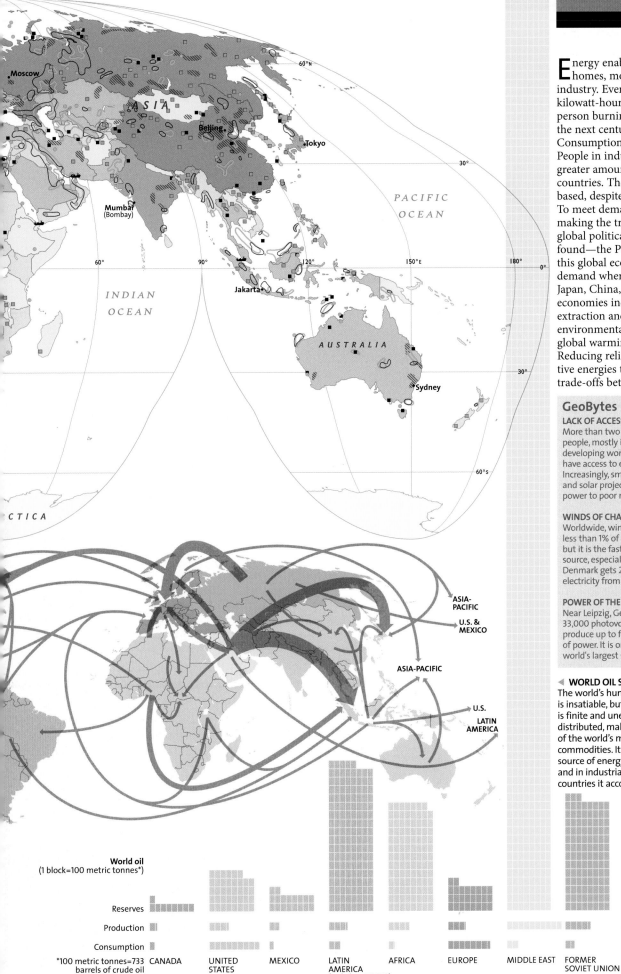

Moscow

A S I A

Beijing

Tokyo

PACIFIC
OCEAN

Mumbai
(Bombay)

Jakarta

INDIAN
OCEAN

AUSTRALIA

Sydney

C T I C A

60°N

30°

PACIFIC
OCEAN

60°

90°

120°

150°E

180°

0°

30°

60°S

Energy enables us to cook our food, heat our homes, move about our planet, and run industry. Everyday the world uses some 320 billion kilowatt-hours of energy—equivalent to each person burning 22 lightbulbs nonstop, and over the next century demand may increase threefold. Consumption is not uniform across the globe. People in industrialized countries consume far greater amounts of energy than those in developing countries. The world's energy supply is still fossil-fuel based, despite advances in alternative energy sources. To meet demand, many countries must import fuels, making the trade of energy a critical, often volatile global political issue. Instability where most oil is found—the Persian Gulf, Nigeria, Venezuela—make this global economic powerline fragile. Insatiable demand where most energy is consumed—the U.S., Japan, China, India, Germany—makes national economies increasingly dependent. Furthermore, extraction and use of fossil fuel have serious environmental effects, such as air pollution and global warming. The challenge for the future? Reducing reliance on fossil fuels, developing alternative energies to meet demand, and mediating the trade-offs between the environment and energy.

GeoBytes

LACK OF ACCESS
More than two billion people, mostly in the developing world, do not have access to electricity. Increasingly, small-scale wind and solar projects bring power to poor rural areas.

WINDS OF CHANGE
Worldwide, wind supplies less than 1% of electric power, but it is the fastest growing source, especially in Europe. Denmark gets 20% of its electricity from wind.

POWER OF THE SUN
Near Leipzig, Germany, some 33,000 photovoltaic panels produce up to five megawatts of power. It is one of the world's largest solar arrays.

GOING NUCLEAR
France gets 78% of its electricity from nuclear power. Developing nations, such as China and India, are building new reactors to reduce pollution and meet soaring energy demands.

GROWING PAINS
China is fueling its economic growth with huge quantities of coal, and it suffers from energy-related environmental problems. China is second only to the United States in greenhouse gas emissions that contribute to global warming.

◄ **WORLD OIL SUPPLY**
The world's hunger for oil is insatiable, but the supply is finite and unequally distributed, making it one of the world's most valuable commodities. It is the leading source of energy worldwide, and in industrialized countries it accounts for more than one-third of all energy consumed. Pressure on the world's oil supply continues to mount as both industrialized and developing countries grow more dependent on it to meet increasing energy needs.

ASIA-
PACIFIC

U.S. &
MEXICO

ASIA-PACIFIC

U.S.

LATIN
AMERICA

World oil
(1 block=100 metric tonnes*)

Reserves

Production

Consumption

*100 metric tonnes=733
barrels of crude oil

CANADA

UNITED
STATES

MEXICO

LATIN
AMERICA
(excluding MEXICO)

AFRICA

EUROPE

MIDDLE EAST

FORMER
SOVIET UNION

ASIA-PACIFIC

▼ FLIGHT FROM CONFLICT

By the end of 2004, the number of refugees worldwide reached an estimated 9.2 million, and the flows of people uprooted from their homes because of war, violence, and oppression showed no sign of abating in 2005. The bar graph below indicates the scale of refugee displacement and sanctuary. In Colombia, decades of conflict have led to a vast number of internal displaced persons (IDPs), shown by the brown bar. The blue bar shows the number of Colombians who have fled their homes. Large numbers of Afghans are displaced internally (brown bar) and have left the country. Pakistan has given residence to many (brown bar). Germany and the United States shelter refugees from around the world (brown bars).

United Nations High Commission for Refugees trucks evacuate people from Srebrenica during the Bosnian conflict in 1993.

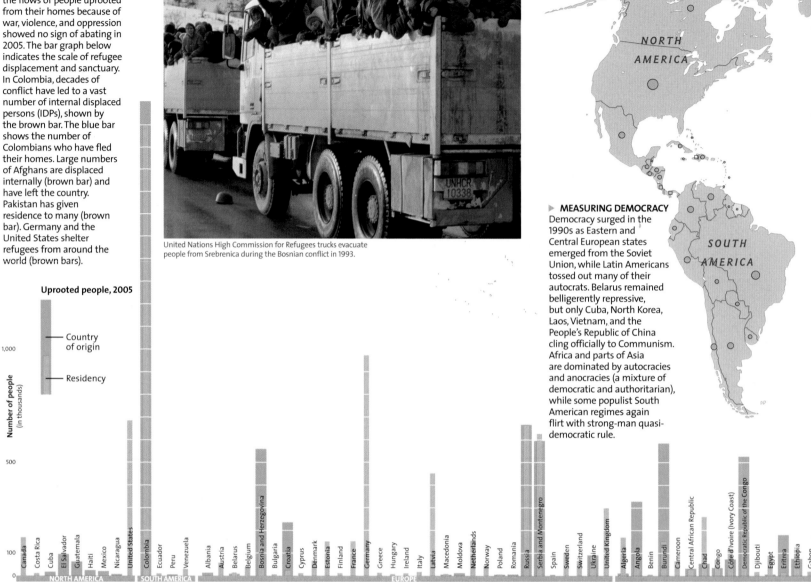

Uprooted people, 2005

— Country of origin

— Residency

Number of people (in thousands)

1,000

500

100

NORTH AMERICA: Canada, Costa Rica, Cuba, El Salvador, Guatemala, Haiti, Mexico, Nicaragua, United States

SOUTH AMERICA: Colombia, Ecuador, Peru, Venezuela

EUROPE: Albania, Austria, Belarus, Belgium, Bosnia and Herzegovina, Bulgaria, Croatia, Cyprus, Denmark, Estonia, Finland, France, Germany, Greece, Hungary, Ireland, Italy, Latvia, Macedonia, Moldova, Netherlands, Norway, Poland, Romania, Russia, Serbia and Montenegro, Spain, Sweden, Switzerland, Ukraine, United Kingdom

Algeria, Angola, Benin, Burundi, Cameroon, Central African Republic, Chad, Congo, Côte d'Ivoire (Ivory Coast), Democratic Republic of the Congo, Djibouti, Egypt, Eritrea, Ethiopia, Gabon

▶ MEASURING DEMOCRACY

Democracy surged in the 1990s as Eastern and Central European states emerged from the Soviet Union, while Latin Americans tossed out many of their autocrats. Belarus remained belligerently repressive, but only Cuba, North Korea, Laos, Vietnam, and the People's Republic of China cling officially to Communism. Africa and parts of Asia are dominated by autocracies and anocracies (a mixture of democratic and authoritarian), while some populist South American regimes again flirt with strong-man quasi-democratic rule.

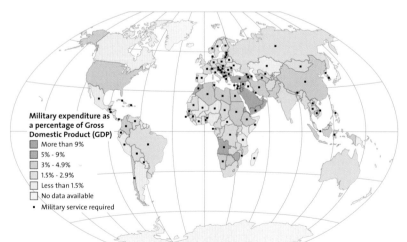

▲ DEFENSE SPENDING

Military spending soaks up a large percentage of GDP (Gross Domestic Product) in many countries that can ill afford it. Angola, whose 26-year-old civil war ended in 2002, is awash in arms. The states of the Middle East, some with weak economies and beset by popular insurrections, continue to maintain large defense forces. A resurgent China flexes new military muscle. The United States spends as much on defense as the rest of the world combined. More than 80 nations, headed by both democracies and totalitarian governments, require military service of their youth.

Military expenditure as a percentage of Gross Domestic Product (GDP)

- More than 9%
- 5% - 9%
- 3% - 4.9%
- 1.5% - 2.9%
- Less than 1.5%
- No data available
- ▪ Military service required

▲ BIOLOGICAL WEAPONS

Only a small volume of a toxic biological agent, if properly dispersed, could cause massive casualties in a densely populated area. Moreover, its manufacture could be virtually undetectable, as only a small facility is needed, and much of the material and equipment has legitimate medical and agricultural use. Although only about 8 countries have offensive biological weapons programs, that number is expected to grow with the increased international flow of technology, goods, and information.

Biological weapons possession

- Known
- Possible
- Possible offensive research program

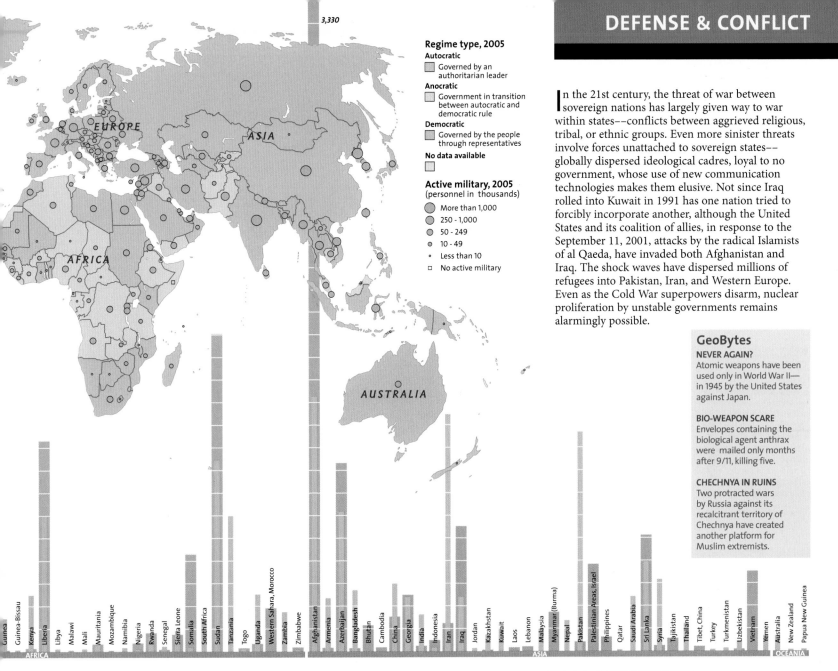

Regime type, 2005

Autocratic
Governed by an authoritarian leader

Anocratic
Government in transition between autocratic and democratic rule

Democratic
Governed by the people through representatives

No data available

Active military, 2005
(personnel in thousands)
More than 1,000
250 - 1,000
50 - 249
10 - 49
Less than 10
No active military

EUROPE
ASIA
AFRICA
AUSTRALIA

3,330

In the 21st century, the threat of war between sovereign nations has largely given way to war within states--conflicts between aggrieved religious, tribal, or ethnic groups. Even more sinister threats involve forces unattached to sovereign states-- globally dispersed ideological cadres, loyal to no government, whose use of new communication technologies makes them elusive. Not since Iraq rolled into Kuwait in 1991 has one nation tried to forcibly incorporate another, although the United States and its coalition of allies, in response to the September 11, 2001, attacks by the radical Islamists of al Qaeda, have invaded both Afghanistan and Iraq. The shock waves have dispersed millions of refugees into Pakistan, Iran, and Western Europe. Even as the Cold War superpowers disarm, nuclear proliferation by unstable governments remains alarmingly possible.

GeoBytes

NEVER AGAIN?
Atomic weapons have been used only in World War II— in 1945 by the United States against Japan.

BIO-WEAPON SCARE
Envelopes containing the biological agent anthrax were mailed only months after 9/11, killing five.

CHECHNYA IN RUINS
Two protracted wars by Russia against its recalcitrant territory of Chechnya have created another platform for Muslim extremists.

Guinea | Guinea-Bissau | Kenya | Liberia | Libya | Malawi | Mali | Mauritania | Mozambique | Namibia | Nigeria | Rwanda | Senegal | Sierra Leone | Somalia | South Africa | Sudan | Tanzania | Togo | Uganda | Western Sahara, Morocco | Zambia | Zimbabwe

AFRICA

Afghanistan | Armenia | Azerbaijan | Bangladesh | Bhutan | Cambodia | China | Georgia | India | Indonesia | Iran | Iraq | Jordan | Kazakhstan | Kuwait | Laos | Lebanon | Malaysia | Myanmar (Burma) | Nepal | Pakistan | Palestinian Areas, Israel | Philippines | Qatar | Saudi Arabia | Sri Lanka | Syria | Tajikistan | Thailand | Tibet, China | Turkey | Turkmenistan | Uzbekistan | Vietnam | Yemen

ASIA

Australia | New Zealand | Papua New Guinea

OCEANIA

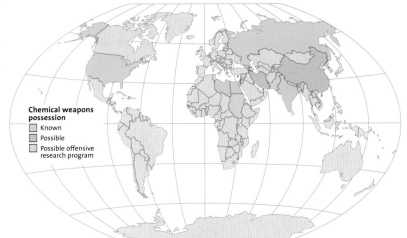

▲ CHEMICAL WEAPONS

Only 9 sovereign nations, including the United States, Russia, South Korea, and India, acknowledge chemical weapon stockpiles, but little doubt remains that additional countries and subnational groups also have them. Under the Chemical Weapons Convention (CWC), member countries are scheduled to destroy stockpiles by 2007, although Russia and the United States have received extensions. Terror groups seldom acknowledge international treaties, and materials for chemical weapons are readily available to those who would have them.

Chemical weapons possession
Known
Possible
Possible offensive research program

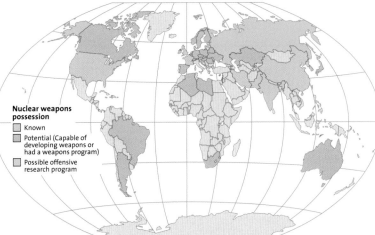

▲ NUCLEAR WEAPONS

The United States, United Kingdom, China, France, and Russia remain the world's only declared nuclear weapon states under the Nuclear Non-Proliferation Treaty, but Pakistan and India have conducted nuclear tests, and Israel is believed also to possess arsenals. Libya recently gave up its nuclear program, and Belarus, Kazakhstan, and Ukraine all relinquished Soviet nuclear weapons on their territories. But on October 9, 2006, North Korea tested a nuclear weapon. Iran, another country with nuclear ambitions, is enriching uranium and building its first nuclear power plant.

Nuclear weapons possession
Known
Potential (Capable of developing weapons or had a weapons program)
Possible offensive research program

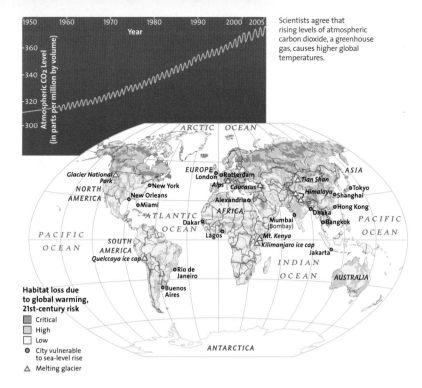

Scientists agree that rising levels of atmospheric carbon dioxide, a greenhouse gas, causes higher global temperatures.

Habitat loss due to global warming, 21st-century risk
- ☐ Critical
- ☐ High
- ☐ Low
- ⊙ City vulnerable to sea-level rise
- △ Melting glacier

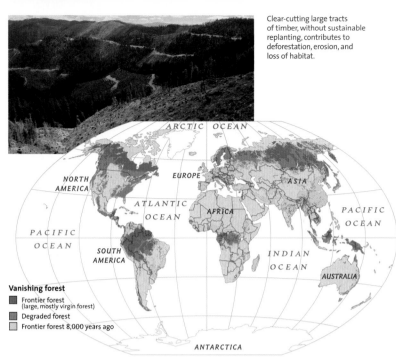

Clear-cutting large tracts of timber, without sustainable replanting, contributes to deforestation, erosion, and loss of habitat.

Vanishing forest
- ■ Frontier forest (large, mostly virgin forest)
- ■ Degraded forest
- ☐ Frontier forest 8,000 years ago

▲ GLOBAL WARMING

Temperatures across the world are increasing at a rate not seen at any other time in the last 10,000 years. Although climate variation is a natural phenomenon, human activities that release carbon dioxide and other greenhouse gases into the atmosphere—industrial processes, fossil fuel consumption, deforestation, and land use change—are contributing to this warming trend. Scientists predict that if this trend continues, one-third of plant and animal habitats will be dramatically altered and more than one million species will be threatened with extinction in the next 50 years. And even small increases in global temperatures can melt glaciers and polar ice sheets, raising sea levels and flooding coastal cities and towns.

▲ DEFORESTATION

Of the 13 million hectares (32 million acres) of forest lost each year, mostly to make room for agriculture, more than half are in South America and Africa, where many of the world's tropical rain forests and terrestrial plant and animal species can be found. Loss of habitat in such species-rich areas takes a toll on the world's biodiversity. Deforested areas also release, instead of absorb, carbon dioxide into the atmosphere, contributing to global climate change. Deforestation can also affect local climates by reducing evaporative cooling, leading to decreased rainfall and higher temperatures.

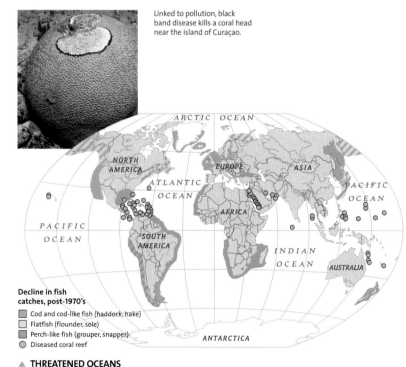

Linked to pollution, black band disease kills a coral head near the island of Curaçao.

Decline in fish catches, post-1970's
- ☐ Cod and cod-like fish (haddock, hake)
- ☐ Flatfish (flounder, sole)
- ☐ Perch-like fish (grouper, snapper)
- ⊙ Diseased coral reef

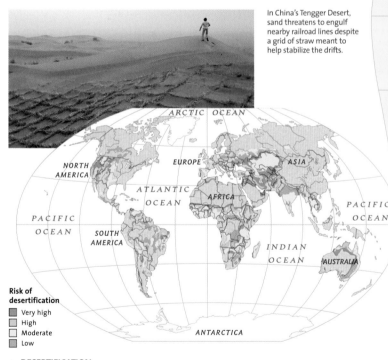

In China's Tengger Desert, sand threatens to engulf nearby railroad lines despite a grid of straw meant to help stabilize the drifts.

Risk of desertification
- ■ Very high
- ☐ High
- ☐ Moderate
- ☐ Low

▲ THREATENED OCEANS

Oceans cover more than two-thirds of the Earth's surface and are home to at least half of the world's biodiversity, yet they are the least understood ecosystems. The combined stresses of overfishing, pollution, increased carbon dioxide emissions, global climate change, and coastal development are having a serious impact on the health of oceans and ocean species. Over 70% of the world's fish species are depleted or nearing depletion, and 50% of coral reefs worldwide are threatened by human activities.

▲ DESERTIFICATION

Climate variability and human activities, such as grazing and conversion of natural areas to agricultural use, are leading causes of desertification, the degradation of land in arid, semiarid, and dry subhumid areas. The environmental consequences of desertification are great—loss of topsoil, increased soil salinity, damaged vegetation, regional climate change, and a decline in biodiversity. Equally critical are the social consequences—more than 2 billion people live in and make a living off these dryland areas, covering about 41% of Earth's surface.

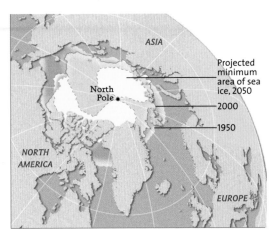

▲ POLAR ICE CAP
Over the last 50 years, the extent of polar sea ice has noticeably decreased. Since 1970 alone, an area larger than Norway, Sweden, and Denmark combined has melted. This trend is predicted to accelerate as temperatures rise in the Arctic and across the globe.

GeoBytes

ACIDIFYING OCEANS
Oceans are absorbing an unprecedented 20 to 25 million tonnes (22 to 28 millions tons) of carbon dioxide each day, increasing the water's acidity.

ENDANGERED REEFS
Some 95% of coral reefs in Southeast Asia have been destroyed or are threatened.

RECORD TEMPERATURES
The 1990s were the warmest decade on record in the last century.

WARMING ARCTIC
While the world as a whole has warmed nearly 0.6°C (1°F) over the last hundred years, parts of the Arctic have warmed 4 to 5 times as much in only the last 50 years.

DISAPPEARING RAIN FORESTS
Scientists predict that the world's rain forests will disappear within the next one hundred years if the current rate of deforestation continues.

OIL POLLUTION
Nearly 1.3 million tonnes (1.4 million tons) of oil seep into the world's oceans each year from the combined sources of natural seepage, extraction, transportation, and consumption.

ACCIDENTAL DROWNINGS
Entanglement in fishing gear is one of the greatest threats to marine mammals.

A FAREWELL TO FROGS?
Worldwide, almost half of the 5,700 named amphibian species are in decline.

With the growth of scientific record keeping, observation, modeling, and analysis, our understanding of Earth's environment is improving. Yet even as we deepen our insight into environmental processes, we are changing what we are studying. At no other time in history have humans altered their environment with such speed and force. Nothing occurs in isolation, and stress in one area has impacts elsewhere. Our agricultural and fishing practices, industrial processes, extraction of resources, and transportation methods are leading to extinctions, destroying habitats, devastating fish stocks, disturbing the soil, and polluting the oceans and the air. As a result, biodiversity is declining, global temperatures are rising, polar ice is shrinking, and the ozone layer continues to thin.

▼ POLLUTION
No corner of the earth is immune to pollution, be it in the air, soil, or water. Concentrations of pollution can be found in the industrial centers of North America, Europe, and, increasingly, Asia—and areas downwind or downstream from them. Shipping routes are sources of pollution, from oil spills to garbage dumpings.

Environmental stress factor
Accident
* ★ Industrial
* ● Oil rig explosion
* ➝ Oil spill
* ⟳ Acid rain

Deforestation
* ☐ Temperate forest
* ▨ Tropical forest
* ☐ Desertification
* ∿ Pollution from shipping

▶ OZONE DEPLETION
First noted in the mid-1980s, the springtime "ozone hole" over the Antarctic continues to grow. With sustained efforts to restrict chlorofluorocarbons (CFCs) and other ozone-depleting chemicals, scientists have begun to see what they hope is a leveling off in the rate of depletion. Stratospheric ozone shields the Earth from the sun's ultraviolet radiation. Thinning of this protective layer puts people at risk for skin cancer and cataracts. It can also have devastating effects on the Earth's biological functions.

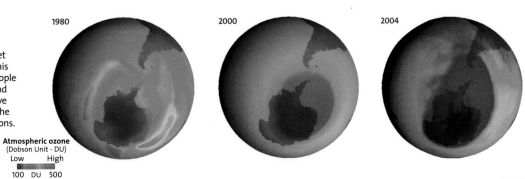

Atmospheric ozone
(Dobson Unit - DU)
Low   High
100   DU   500

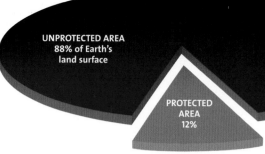

UNPROTECTED AREA
88% of Earth's land surface

PROTECTED AREA 12%

 **PERCENTAGE PROTECTED**
Protected areas worldwide represent 12% of the Earth's land surface, according to the U.N. Environmental Programme World Conservation Monitoring Centre. Only 0.5% of the marine environment is within protected areas—an amount considered inadequate by conservationists because of the increasing threats of overfishing and coral reef loss worldwide.

HAWAI'I VOLCANOES NATIONAL PARK, HAWAI'I
The park includes two of the world's most active volcanoes, Kilauea and Mauna Loa. The landscape shows the results of 70 million years of volcanism, including calderas, lava flows, and black sand beaches. Lava spreads out to build the island, and seawater vaporizes as lava hits the ocean at 1,149°C (2,100° F). The national park, created in 1916, covers 10% of the island of Hawai'i and is a refuge for endangered species, like the hawksbill turtle and Hawaiian goose. It was made a World Heritage site in 1987.

GALÁPAGOS NATIONAL PARK, ECUADOR
Galápago means tortoise in Spanish, and at one time 250,000 giant tortoises roamed the islands. Today about 15,000 remain, and three of the original 14 subspecies are extinct—and the Pinta Island tortoise may be extinct soon. In 1959, Ecuador made the volcanic Galápagos Islands a national park, protecting the giant tortoises and other endemic species. The archipelago became a World Heritage site in 1978, and a marine reserve surrounding the islands was added in 2001.

WESTERN UNITED STATES
An intricate public lands pattern—including national forests, wilderness areas, wildlife refuges, and national parks such as Arches (above)—embraces nearly half the surface area of 11 western states. Ten out of 19 World Heritage sites in the United States are found here. It was in the West that the modern national park movement was born in the 19th century with the establishment of Yellowstone and Yosemite National Parks.

MADIDI NATIONAL PARK, BOLIVIA
Macaws may outnumber humans in Madidi, Bolivia's second largest national park, established in 1995. A complex community of plants, animals, and native Indian groups share this 18,900-sq-km (7,300-sq-mi) reserve, part of the Tropical Andes biodiversity hotspot. Indigenous communities benefit from ecotourism.

AMAZON BASIN, BRAZIL
Indigenous peoples help manage reserves in Brazil that are linked with Jaú National Park. The park and reserves are part of the Central Amazon Conservation Complex, a World Heritage site covering more than 60,000 sq km (23,000 sq mi). It is the largest protected area in the Amazon Basin and one of the most biologically rich regions on the planet.

ARCTIC REGIONS
Polar bears find safe havens in Canadian parks, such as on Ellesmere Island, and in Greenland's huge protected area—Earth's largest—that preserves the island's frigid northeast. In 1996 countries with Arctic lands adopted the Circumpolar Protected Areas Network Strategy and Action Plan to help conserve ecosystems. Today 15% of Arctic land area is protected.

PROTECTED AREAS WORLDWIDE
What are protected areas? Most people agree that such territories are dedicated to protecting and maintaining biodiversity and are often managed through legal means. Yellowstone National Park, established in 1872, is often cited as the start of the modern era of protected areas. From a mere handful in 1900, the number of protected areas worldwide now exceeds 104,790, covering more than 20 million sq km (7.7 million sq mi). North America claims the most protected land of any region, amounting to almost 18% of its territory. South Asia, at about 7%, has the least amount of land under some form of protection. Not all protected areas are created or managed equally, and management categories developed by IUCN range from strict nature reserve to areas for sustainable use. Management effectiveness varies widely and can be affected by such factors as conservation budgets, and political stability. Throughout the world—but especially in tropical areas—protected areas are threatened by illegal hunting, overfishing, pollution, and the removal of native vegetation. Countries and international organizations no longer choose between conservation and development; rather the goal for societies is to balance the two for equitable and sustainable resource use.

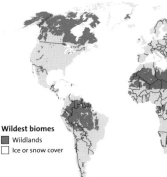

Wildest biomes
- ■ Wildlands
- □ Ice or snow cover

◄ WILDEST AREAS

Although generally far from cities, the world's remaining wild places play a vital role in a healthy global ecosystem. The boreal (northern) forests of Canada and Russia, for instance, help cleanse the air we breathe by absorbing carbon dioxide and providing oxygen. With the human population increasing by an estimated one billion over the next 15 years, many wild places could fall within reach of the plow or under a cloud of smog.

For millennia, lands have been set aside as sacred ground or as hunting reserves for the powerful. Today, great swaths are protected for recreation, habitat conservation, biodiversity preservation, and resource management. Some groups may oppose protected spaces because they want access to resources now. Yet local inhabitants and governments are beginning to see the benefits of conservation efforts and sustainable use for human health and future generations.

SAREKS NATIONAL PARK, SWEDEN

This remote 1,970-sq-km (760-sq-mi) park, established in 1909 to protect the alpine landscape, is a favorite of backcountry hikers. It boasts some 200 mountains more than 1,800 m (5,900 ft) high, narrow valleys, and about 100 glaciers. Sareks forms part of the Laponian Area World Heritage site and has been a home to the Saami (or Lapp) people since prehistoric times.

AFRICAN RESERVES

Some 120,000 elephants roam Chobe National Park in northern Botswana. Africa has more than 7,500 national parks, wildlife reserves, and other protected areas, covering about 9% of the continent. Protected areas are under enormous pressure from expanding populations, civil unrest and war, and environmental disasters.

WOLONG NATURE RESERVE, CHINA

Giant pandas freely chomp bamboo in this 2,000-sq-km (772-sq-mi) reserve in Sichuan Province, near the city of Chengdu. Misty bamboo forests host a number of endangered species, but the critically endangered giant panda—among the rarest mammals in the world—is the most famous resident. Only about 1,600 giant pandas exist in the wild.

KAMCHATKA, RUSSIA

Crater lakes, ash-capped cones, and diverse plant and animal species mark the Kamchatka Peninsula—a World Heritage site—located between the icy Bering Sea and Sea of Okhotsk. The active volcanoes and glaciers form a dynamic landscape of great beauty, known as "The Land of Fire and Ice." Kamchatka's remoteness and rugged landscape help fauna flourish, producing record numbers of salmon species and half of the Steller's sea-eagles on Earth.

GUNUNG PALUNG NATIONAL PARK, INDONESIA

A tree frog's perch could be precarious in this 900-sq-km (347-sq-mi) park on the island of Borneo, in the heart of the Sundaland biodiversity hotspot. The biggest threat to trees and animals in the park and region is illegal logging. Gunung Palung contains a wider range of habitats than any other protected area on Borneo, from mangroves to lowland and cloud forests. A number of endangered species, such as orangutans and sun bears, depend on the dense forests.

AUSTRALIA & NEW ZEALAND

Uluru, a red sandstone monolith (formerly known as Ayers Rock), and the vast Great Barrier Reef, one of the largest marine parks in the world, are outstanding examples of Australia's protected areas—which make up more than 10% of the country's area and conserve a diverse range of unique ecosystems. About a third of New Zealand is protected, and it is a biodiversity hotspot because of threats to flightless native birds, such as the kakapo and kiwi. Cats, stoats, and other predators, introduced to New Zealand by settlers, kill thousands of birds each year.

ANTARCTICA

The Antarctic Treaty, signed in 1959, regulates the continent and the marine environment (south of 60° south latitude) as a "natural reserve devoted to peace and science." The Treaty is recognized as one of the most successful international agreements. The annual Antarctic Treaty Consultative Meeting brings national representatives together to discuss topics such as scientific cooperation and environmental protection.

Spanning some 8,040 kilometers (5,000 miles) from the bleak shores of the Arctic Ocean to the tropical forest of Panama, North America's more than 24 million square kilometers (9 million square miles) constitute the third largest continent. Besides the Arctic Ocean, the Atlantic and Pacific Oceans bound it. Ancient eastern mountains and young western peaks bracket it. Volcanoes and earthquakes punctuate it, and storms roll across its expanse. Major rivers carve it: The St. Lawrence empties the Great Lakes; the Mississippi and its tributaries drain the heartland of the United States. Rocks of the Canadian Shield mark its age: They formed nearly four billion years before the arrival of the first human occupants, sometime between 13,000 and 40,000 years ago. Woodland peoples ranged widely in pursuit of game, the Mississippian people erected great mounds, and the Maya and the Aztec civilizations farmed irrigated croplands and built colossal structures. From the 15th century, arriving Europeans reduced many native cultures by force of arms. Their invisible weapons—the rapid, widespread, and lethal agents of imported infectious diseases—devastated vastly more. Settlers surged into depopulated and fertile lands. The result: crops and livestock to feed the many; steamboats and railroads to carry many more into the interior. Not all newcomers came of their own will; more than four million Africans were brought to North America as slaves to work on the sugar plantations of the Caribbean and on the cotton plantations of the U.S. South. Seeking freedom and fortune, more than 20 million immigrants came to the United States between 1880 and 1920. Mines disgorged raw materials for growing industries, maiming the countryside. Roads were laid out to bear automobiles and trucks, link regions, and carry people over mountains, plains, and deserts. No continent has been so transformed in so brief a time.

IMAGE BY ROBERT STACEY, WORLDSAT INTERNATIONAL INC.

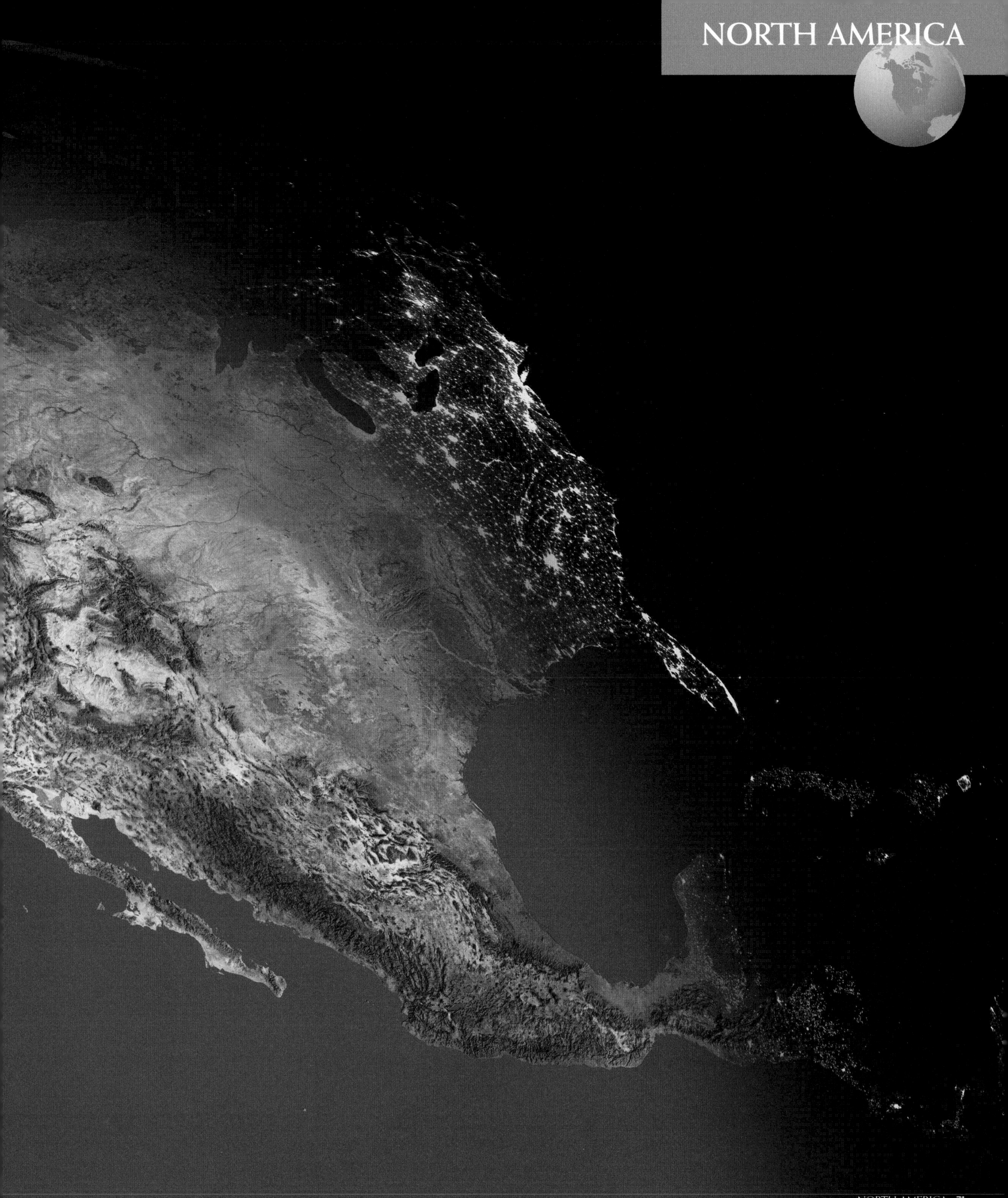

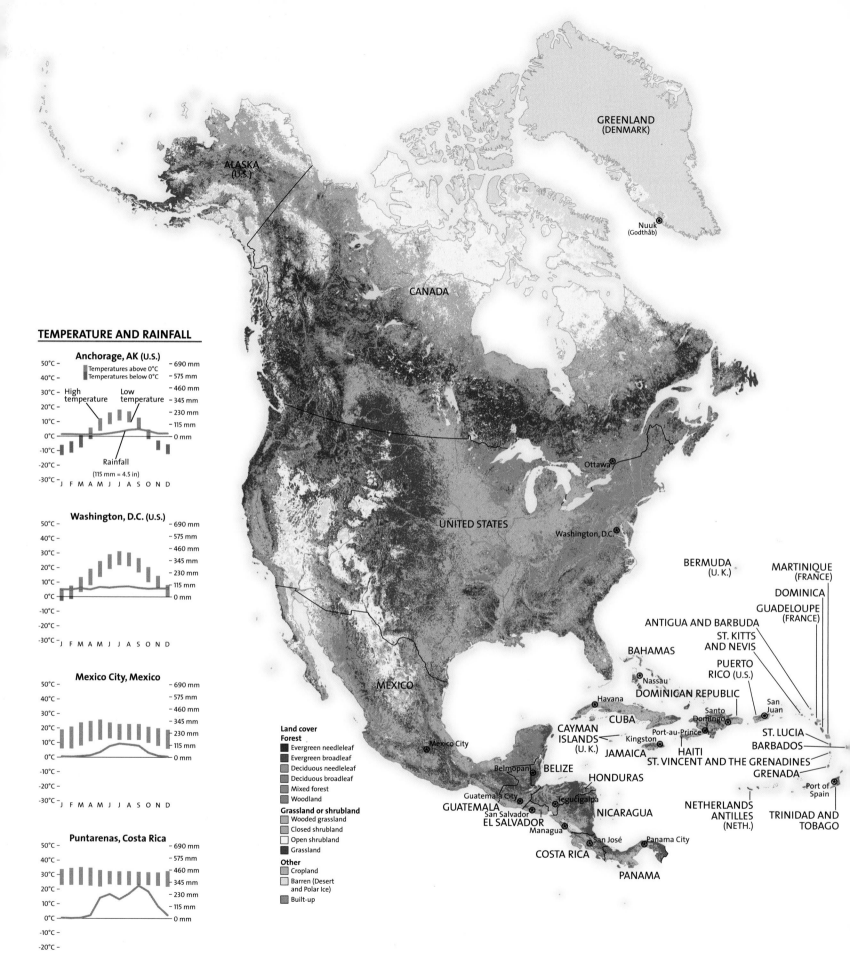

TEMPERATURE AND RAINFALL

Anchorage, AK (U.S.)

■ Temperatures above 0°C
■ Temperatures below 0°C

High temperature
Low temperature
Rainfall
(115 mm = 4.5 in)

J F M A M J J A S O N D

Washington, D.C. (U.S.)

J F M A M J J A S O N D

Mexico City, Mexico

J F M A M J J A S O N D

Puntarenas, Costa Rica

J F M A M J J A S O N D

Land cover
Forest
■ Evergreen needleleaf
■ Evergreen broadleaf
□ Deciduous needleleaf
□ Deciduous broadleaf
□ Mixed forest
□ Woodland

Grassland or shrubland
□ Wooded grassland
□ Closed shrubland
□ Open shrubland
■ Grassland

Other
□ Cropland
□ Barren (Desert and Polar Ice)
■ Built-up

ALASKA (U.S.)

GREENLAND (DENMARK)

Nuuk (Godthåb)

CANADA

UNITED STATES

Ottawa

Washington, D.C.

BERMUDA (U.K.)

MARTINIQUE (FRANCE)

DOMINICA

GUADELOUPE (FRANCE)

ANTIGUA AND BARBUDA

ST. KITTS AND NEVIS

BAHAMAS

PUERTO RICO (U.S.)

Nassau

DOMINICAN REPUBLIC

Havana

San Juan

CUBA

Santo Domingo

MEXICO

CAYMAN ISLANDS (U.K.)

Port-au-Prince

ST. LUCIA

BARBADOS

Kingston

JAMAICA

HAITI

ST. VINCENT AND THE GRENADINES

Mexico City

GRENADA

Belmopan

BELIZE

HONDURAS

Port of Spain

Guatemala City

Tegucigalpa

NETHERLANDS ANTILLES (NETH.)

TRINIDAD AND TOBAGO

GUATEMALA

San Salvador

NICARAGUA

EL SALVADOR

Managua

San José

Panama City

COSTA RICA

PANAMA

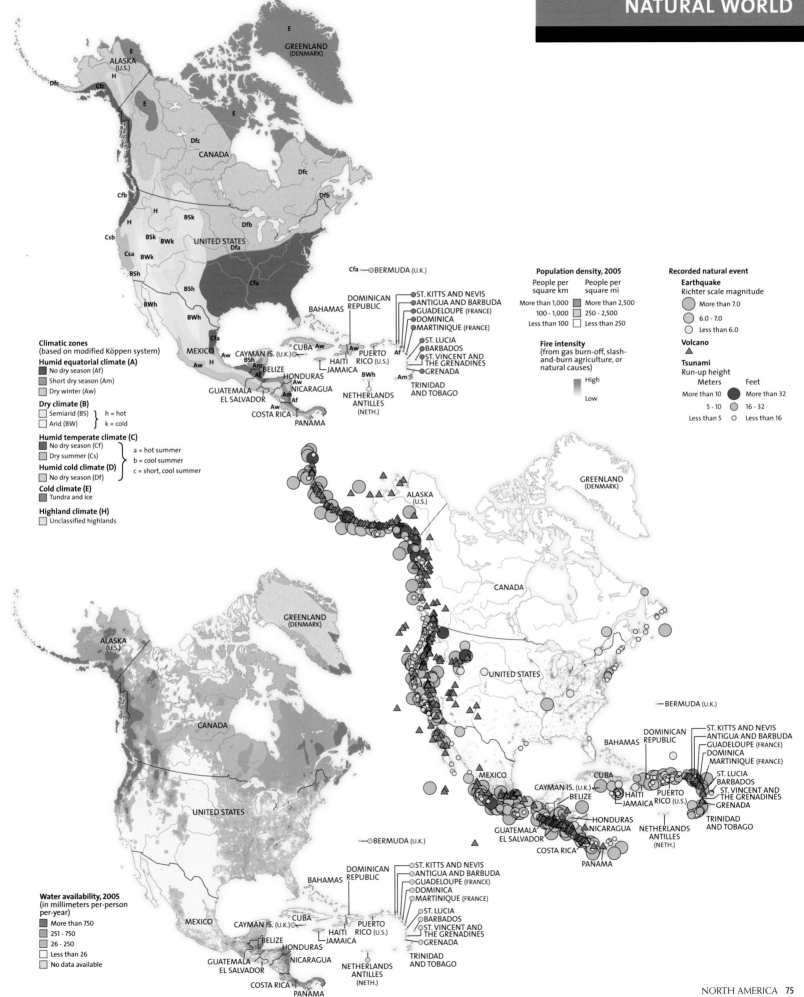

Climatic zones
(based on modified Köppen system)

Humid equatorial climate (A)
- No dry season (Af)
- Short dry season (Am)
- Dry winter (Aw)

Dry climate (B)
- Semiarid (BS) } h = hot
- Arid (BW)   } k = cold

Humid temperate climate (C)
- No dry season (Cf)
- Dry summer (Cs)

Humid cold climate (D)
- No dry season (Df)

a = hot summer
b = cool summer
c = short, cool summer

Cold climate (E)
- Tundra and ice

Highland climate (H)
- Unclassified highlands

Population density, 2005

People per square km	People per square mi
More than 1,000	More than 2,500
100 - 1,000	250 - 2,500
Less than 100	Less than 250

Fire intensity
(from gas burn-off, slash-and-burn agriculture, or natural causes)

High

Low

Recorded natural event

Earthquake
Richter scale magnitude
- More than 7.0
- 6.0 - 7.0
- Less than 6.0

Volcano

Tsunami
Run-up height

Meters	Feet
More than 10	More than 32
5 - 10	16 - 32
Less than 5	Less than 16

Water availability, 2005
(in millimeters per-person per-year)
- More than 750
- 251 - 750
- 26 - 250
- Less than 26
- No data available

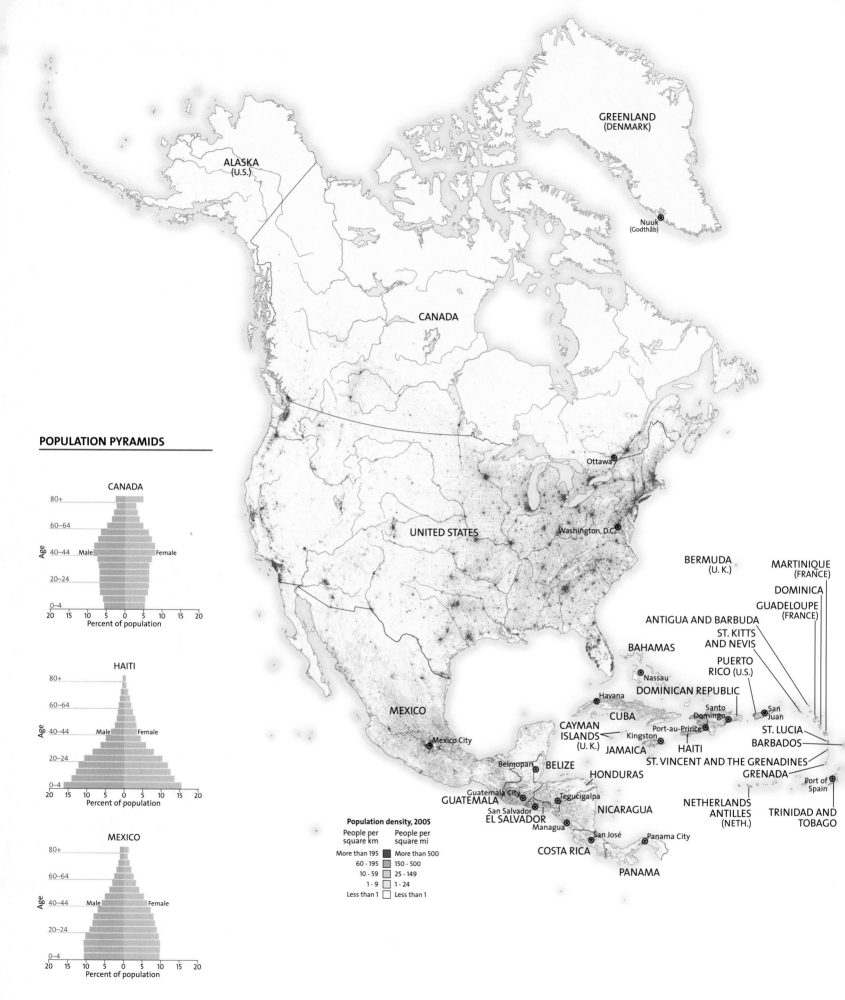

POPULATION PYRAMIDS

CANADA

Age

80+

60–64

40–44   Male   Female

20–24

0–4

20 15 10 5 0 5 10 15 20
Percent of population

HAITI

Age

80+

60–64

40–44   Male   Female

20–24

0–4

20 15 10 5 0 5 10 15 20
Percent of population

MEXICO

Age

80+

60–64

40–44   Male   Female

20–24

0–4

20 15 10 5 0 5 10 15 20
Percent of population

GREENLAND
(DENMARK)

ALASKA
(U.S.)

Nuuk
(Godthåb)

CANADA

Ottawa

UNITED STATES

Washington, D.C.

BERMUDA
(U.K.)

MARTINIQUE
(FRANCE)

DOMINICA

GUADELOUPE
(FRANCE)

ANTIGUA AND BARBUDA

ST. KITTS
AND NEVIS

BAHAMAS

PUERTO
RICO (U.S.)

Nassau

DOMINICAN REPUBLIC

Havana

MEXICO

CUBA

Santo
Domingo

San
Juan

ST. LUCIA

CAYMAN
ISLANDS
(U.K.)

Port-au-Prince

BARBADOS

Mexico City

Kingston

JAMAICA

HAITI

ST. VINCENT AND THE GRENADINES

Belmopan

BELIZE

GRENADA

Port of
Spain

Guatemala City

Tegucigalpa

HONDURAS

NETHERLANDS
ANTILLES
(NETH.)

TRINIDAD AND
TOBAGO

GUATEMALA

San Salvador

EL SALVADOR

Managua

NICARAGUA

San José

Panama City

COSTA RICA

PANAMA

Population density, 2005

People per square km	People per square mi
More than 195	More than 500
60 - 195	150 - 500
10 - 59	25 - 149
1 - 9	1 - 24
Less than 1	Less than 1

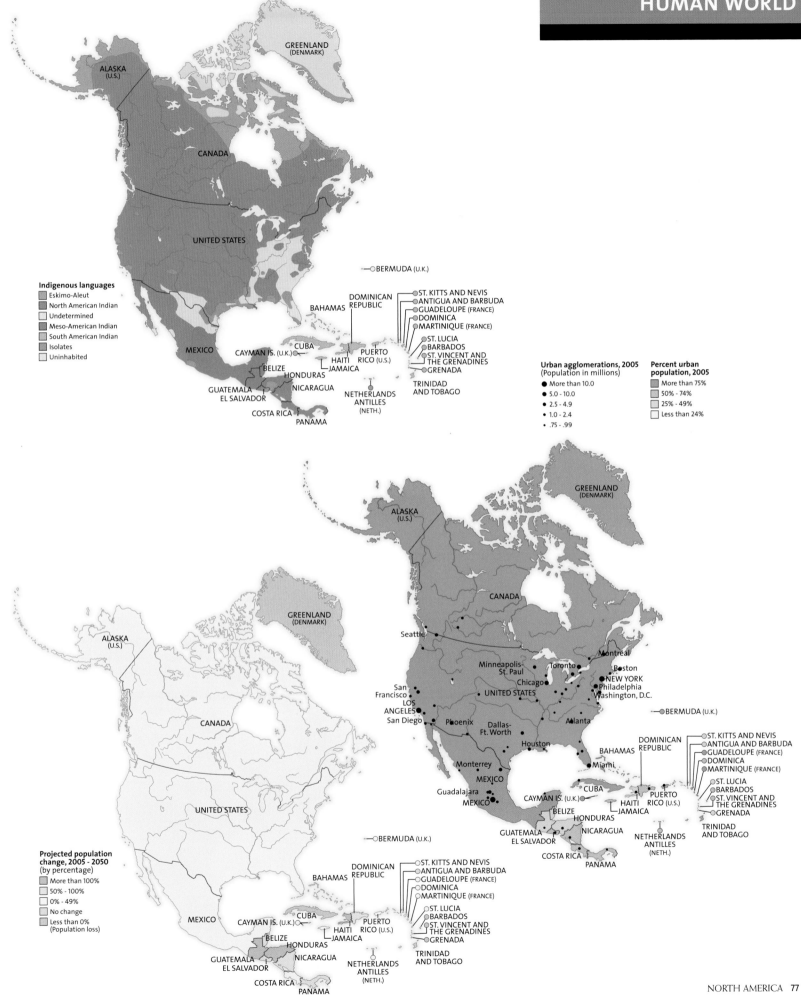

Indigenous languages
- Eskimo-Aleut
- North American Indian
- Undetermined
- Meso-American Indian
- South American Indian
- Isolates
- Uninhabited

Urban agglomerations, 2005
(Population in millions)
- ● More than 10.0
- ● 5.0 - 10.0
- ● 2.5 - 4.9
- ● 1.0 - 2.4
- • .75 - .99

Percent urban population, 2005
- More than 75%
- 50% - 74%
- 25% - 49%
- Less than 24%

Projected population change, 2005 - 2050
(by percentage)
- More than 100%
- 50% - 100%
- 0% - 49%
- No change
- Less than 0% (Population loss)

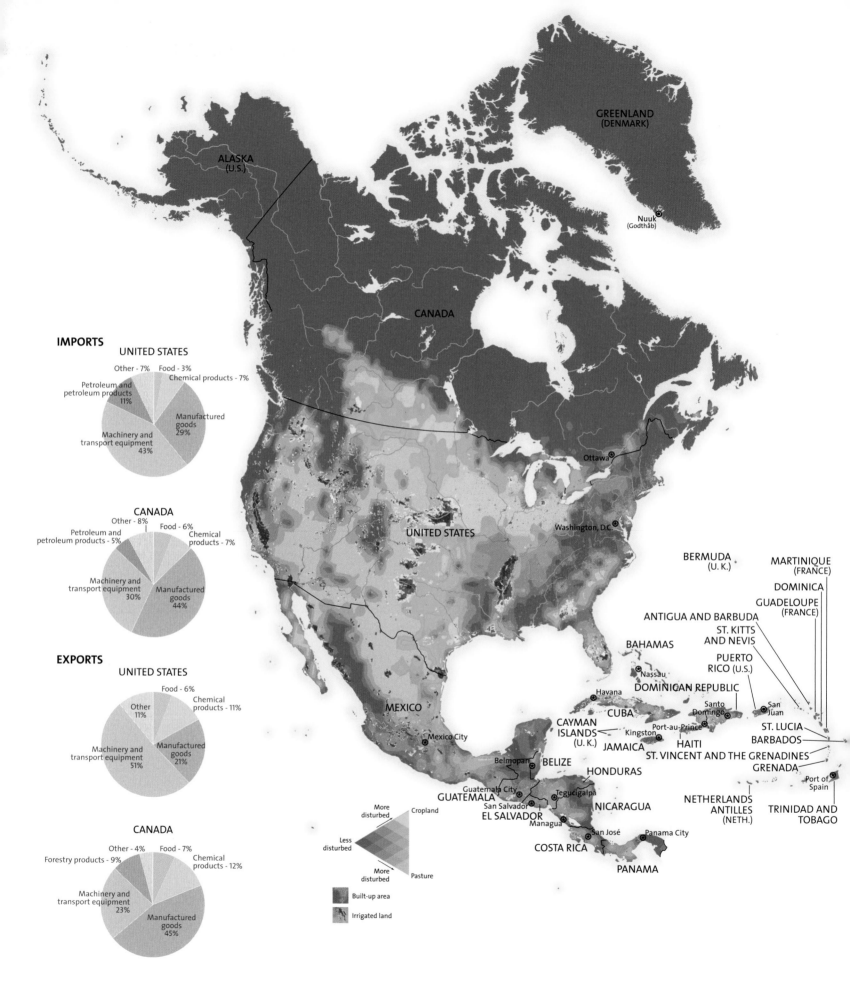

ALASKA
(U.S.)

GREENLAND
(DENMARK)

Nuuk
(Godthåb)

CANADA

IMPORTS

UNITED STATES

Other - 7%　Food - 3%
Chemical products - 7%
Petroleum and
petroleum products
11%
Manufactured
goods
29%
Machinery and
transport equipment
43%

CANADA

Other - 8%　Food - 6%
Petroleum and
petroleum products - 5%
Chemical
products - 7%
Machinery and
transport equipment
30%
Manufactured
goods
44%

Ottawa

Washington, D.C.

UNITED STATES

EXPORTS

UNITED STATES

Food - 6%
Other
11%
Chemical
products - 11%
Machinery and
transport equipment
51%
Manufactured
goods
21%

MEXICO

Mexico City

BERMUDA
(U.K.)

MARTINIQUE
(FRANCE)

DOMINICA

GUADELOUPE
(FRANCE)

ANTIGUA AND BARBUDA
ST. KITTS
AND NEVIS

BAHAMAS

PUERTO
RICO (U.S.)

Nassau

DOMINICAN REPUBLIC

Havana

Santo
Domingo

San
Juan

CUBA

CAYMAN
ISLANDS
(U.K.)

Kingston

Port-au-Prince

ST. LUCIA

BARBADOS

JAMAICA

HAITI

ST. VINCENT AND THE GRENADINES

CANADA

Other - 4%　Food - 7%
Forestry products - 9%
Chemical
products - 12%
Machinery and
transport equipment
23%
Manufactured
goods
45%

Belmopan

BELIZE

HONDURAS

Guatemala City

GUATEMALA

Tegucigalpa

San Salvador

EL SALVADOR

Managua

NICARAGUA

GRENADA

Port of
Spain

NETHERLANDS
ANTILLES
(NETH.)

TRINIDAD AND
TOBAGO

San José

Panama City

COSTA RICA

PANAMA

More
disturbed　Cropland

Less
disturbed

More
disturbed　Pasture

Built-up area

Irrigated land

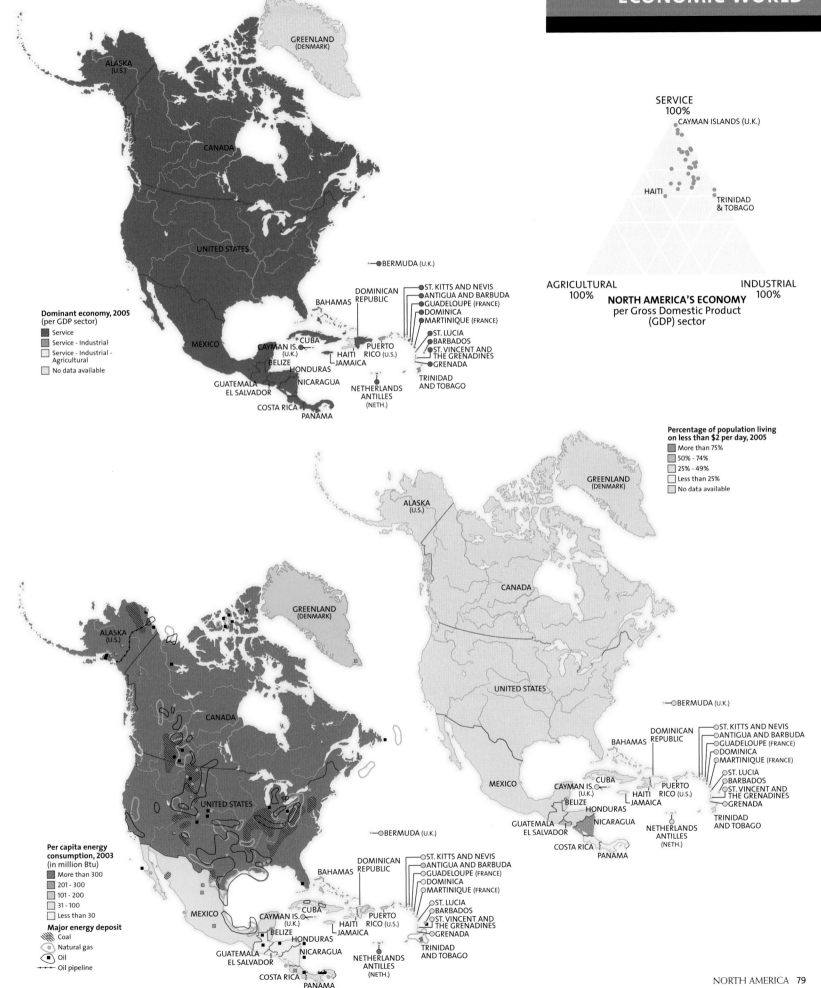

SERVICE 100%

CAYMAN ISLANDS (U.K.)

HAITI

TRINIDAD & TOBAGO

AGRICULTURAL 100%

INDUSTRIAL 100%

NORTH AMERICA'S ECONOMY
per Gross Domestic Product (GDP) sector

Dominant economy, 2005
(per GDP sector)
- Service
- Service - Industrial
- Service - Industrial - Agricultural
- No data available

GREENLAND (DENMARK)

ALASKA (U.S.)

CANADA

UNITED STATES

MEXICO

BERMUDA (U.K.)

BAHAMAS

DOMINICAN REPUBLIC

CUBA

CAYMAN IS. (U.K.)

HAITI

JAMAICA

PUERTO RICO (U.S.)

BELIZE

HONDURAS

GUATEMALA

EL SALVADOR

NICARAGUA

COSTA RICA

PANAMA

NETHERLANDS ANTILLES (NETH.)

ST. KITTS AND NEVIS
ANTIGUA AND BARBUDA
GUADELOUPE (FRANCE)
DOMINICA
MARTINIQUE (FRANCE)
ST. LUCIA
BARBADOS
ST. VINCENT AND THE GRENADINES
GRENADA

TRINIDAD AND TOBAGO

Percentage of population living on less than $2 per day, 2005
- More than 75%
- 50% - 74%
- 25% - 49%
- Less than 25%
- No data available

GREENLAND (DENMARK)

ALASKA (U.S.)

CANADA

UNITED STATES

MEXICO

BERMUDA (U.K.)

DOMINICAN REPUBLIC

BAHAMAS

CUBA

CAYMAN IS. (U.K.)

BELIZE

HAITI

JAMAICA

PUERTO RICO (U.S.)

HONDURAS

GUATEMALA

EL SALVADOR

NICARAGUA

COSTA RICA

PANAMA

NETHERLANDS ANTILLES (NETH.)

ST. KITTS AND NEVIS
ANTIGUA AND BARBUDA
GUADELOUPE (FRANCE)
DOMINICA
MARTINIQUE (FRANCE)
ST. LUCIA
BARBADOS
ST. VINCENT AND THE GRENADINES
GRENADA

TRINIDAD AND TOBAGO

Per capita energy consumption, 2003
(in million Btu)
- More than 300
- 201 - 300
- 101 - 200
- 31 - 100
- Less than 30

Major energy deposit
- Coal
- Natural gas
- Oil
- Oil pipeline

ALASKA (U.S.)

GREENLAND (DENMARK)

CANADA

UNITED STATES

MEXICO

BERMUDA (U.K.)

BAHAMAS

DOMINICAN REPUBLIC

CUBA

CAYMAN IS. (U.K.)

HAITI

JAMAICA

PUERTO RICO (U.S.)

BELIZE

HONDURAS

GUATEMALA

EL SALVADOR

NICARAGUA

COSTA RICA

PANAMA

NETHERLANDS ANTILLES (NETH.)

ST. KITTS AND NEVIS
ANTIGUA AND BARBUDA
GUADELOUPE (FRANCE)
DOMINICA
MARTINIQUE (FRANCE)
ST. LUCIA
BARBADOS
ST. VINCENT AND THE GRENADINES
GRENADA

TRINIDAD AND TOBAGO

D A

Lower Red L.
Leech Lake
Mille Lacs L.
MINNESOTA
St Paul
Des Moines
Des Moines
IOWA
C O
L

Eagle Mt. 701
Isle Royale
Mesabi Ra.
Keweenaw Peninsula
Upper Peninsula
WISCONSIN
Timms Hill 595
Wolf
Wisconsin
Madison
Lake Winnebago
Lake Superior

Lake Michigan
Strs. of Mackinac
MICHIGAN
Muskegon
Lower Peninsula
Grand
Lansing
St. Clair
Lake Huron
Saginaw Bay

Georgian Bay

Lake Ontario
Niagara Falls
Finger Lakes
NEW YORK
Catskill Mountains
Albany

St. Lawrence
Lake Champlain
Adirondack Mountains
Mt. Marcy 1629
Mt. Mansfield 1339
Montpelier
VT.
Green Mountains
N.H.
White Mts.
Mt. Washington 1917
Merrimack
Concord
Boston
MASS.
Hartford
CONN.
Providence
R.I.

MAINE
Mt. Katahdin 1606
Moosehead Lake
Augusta
Mt. Desert I.
Gulf of Maine

Cape Cod
Nantucket I.
Martha's Vineyard
Long Island Sd.
Long Island

Cedar
Iowa
Rock
ILLINOIS
Springfield
Charles Mound 376
Mississippi
INDIANA
Indianapolis
Wabash
Campbell Hill 472
OHIO
Columbus
Gt. Miami
Scioto
Maumee

PENNSYLVANIA
Harrisburg
Allegheny
Susquehanna
Delaware
New York
Trenton
NEW JERSEY
Pine Barrens

Jefferson City
Missouri
Osage
Harry S. Truman Res.
Lake of the Ozarks
MISSOURI
Taum Sauk Mt. 540
Ozark Plateau

Kaskaskia
Ohio
KENTUCKY
Frankfort
Kentucky
Lake Barkley
Lake Cumberland
Kentucky Lake
Nashville
Cumberland
TENNESSEE

WEST VIRGINIA
Charleston
Mt. Davis 1024
Washington D.C.
Annapolis
Dover
DEL.
MARYLAND
Potomac
Chesapeake Bay
Delaware Bay
Chincoteague Bay

Richmond
James
VIRGINIA
Roanoke
Tar
Cape Charles
Great Dismal Swamp
Albemarle Sound

Boston Mountains
Magazine Mt. 839
Little Rock
Ouachita Mountains
Lake Ouachita
ARKANSAS
White
Black
St. Francis
Saline
Ouachita

Black Mt.
Clinch
Clingmans Dome 2025
Great Smoky Mts.
Mt. Mitchell 2037
Woodall Mountain
Tennessee

Raleigh
Neuse
NORTH CAROLINA
Pee Dee
Cape Lookout
Cape Hatteras
Pamlico Sound

ATLANTIC OCEAN

Driskill Mt. 163
MISSISSIPPI
Jackson
Yazoo
Mississippi
Pearl
ALABAMA
Tombigbee
Black Belt
Alabama
Coosa
Cheaha Mt. 734
Montgomery
GEORGIA
Atlanta
Chattahoochee
Flint
Oconee
Ocmulgee
Altamaha
Savannah

SOUTH CAROLINA
Columbia
Santee
Cape Fear
Pee Dee
Sea Islands

Shreveport
Red
Sabine
LOUISIANA
Baton Rouge
Lake Pontchartrain
Marsh I.
Timbalier Bay
Mississippi River Delta
Breton Sound
Mississippi Sd.
Mobile Bay
Pensacola
Cape San Blas
Apalachee Bay
L. Seminole
Tallahassee
Okefenokee Swamp
Suwannee

Galveston Bay
io Bay

Gulf of Mexico

FLORIDA
Tampa Bay
Charlotte Harbor
Cape Romano
Cape Sable
Dry Tortugas
Marquesas Keys
Florida Keys
Cape Canaveral
Kissimmee
Peace
Lake Okeechobee
The Everglades
Biscayne Bay
Straits of Florida
BAHAMAS
TROPIC OF CANCER

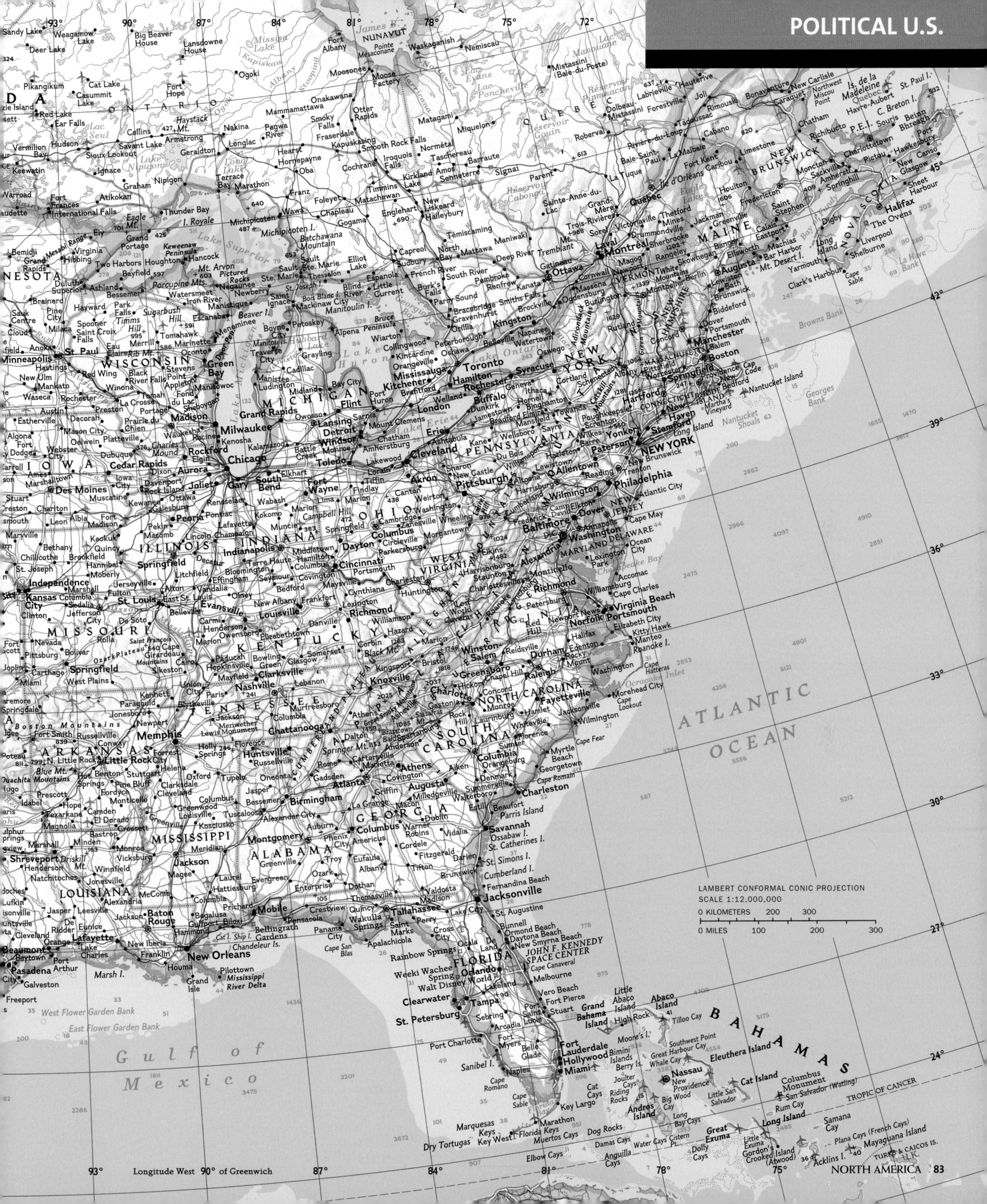
ATLANTIC OCEAN
Gulf of Mexico
BAHAMAS
ONTARIO
QUEBEC
NUNAVUT
NEW BRUNSWICK
NOVA SCOTIA
P.E.I.
MAINE
VERMONT
NEW HAMPSHIRE
MASSACHUSETTS
RHODE ISLAND
CONNECTICUT
NEW YORK
NEW JERSEY
PENNSYLVANIA
DELAWARE
MARYLAND
WEST VIRGINIA
VIRGINIA
NORTH CAROLINA
SOUTH CAROLINA
GEORGIA
FLORIDA
ALABAMA
MISSISSIPPI
LOUISIANA
ARKANSAS
TENNESSEE
KENTUCKY
OHIO
INDIANA
ILLINOIS
MICHIGAN
WISCONSIN
IOWA
MISSOURI
Lake Superior
Lake Michigan
Lake Huron
Lake Erie
Lake Ontario
TROPIC OF CANCER
LAMBERT CONFORMAL CONIC PROJECTION
SCALE 1:12,000,000
0 KILOMETERS 200 300
0 MILES 100 200 300
93° 90° 87° 84° 81° 78° 75° 72°
45° 42° 39° 36° 33° 30° 27° 24°
Longitude West 90° of Greenwich

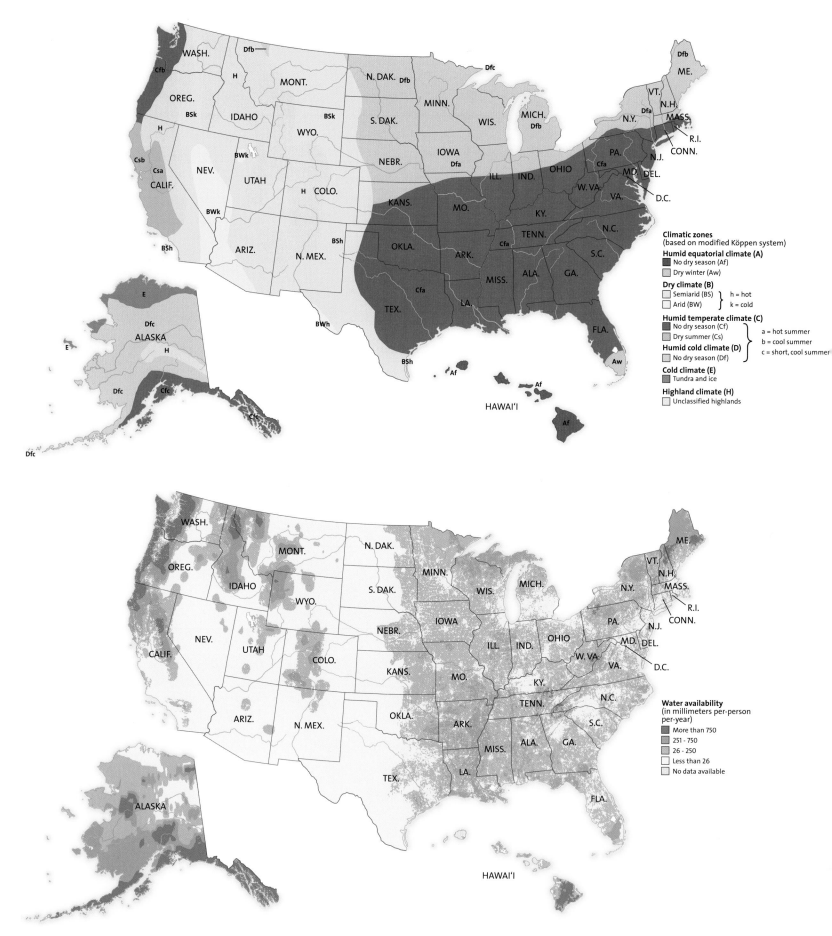

Climatic zones
(based on modified Köppen system)

Humid equatorial climate (A)
- No dry season (Af)
- Dry winter (Aw)

Dry climate (B)
- Semiarid (BS)   h = hot
- Arid (BW)   k = cold

Humid temperate climate (C)
- No dry season (Cf)
- Dry summer (Cs)

a = hot summer
b = cool summer
c = short, cool summer

Humid cold climate (D)
- No dry season (Df)

Cold climate (E)
- Tundra and ice

Highland climate (H)
- Unclassified highlands

Water availability
(in millimeters per-person per-year)
- More than 750
- 251 - 750
- 26 - 250
- Less than 26
- No data available

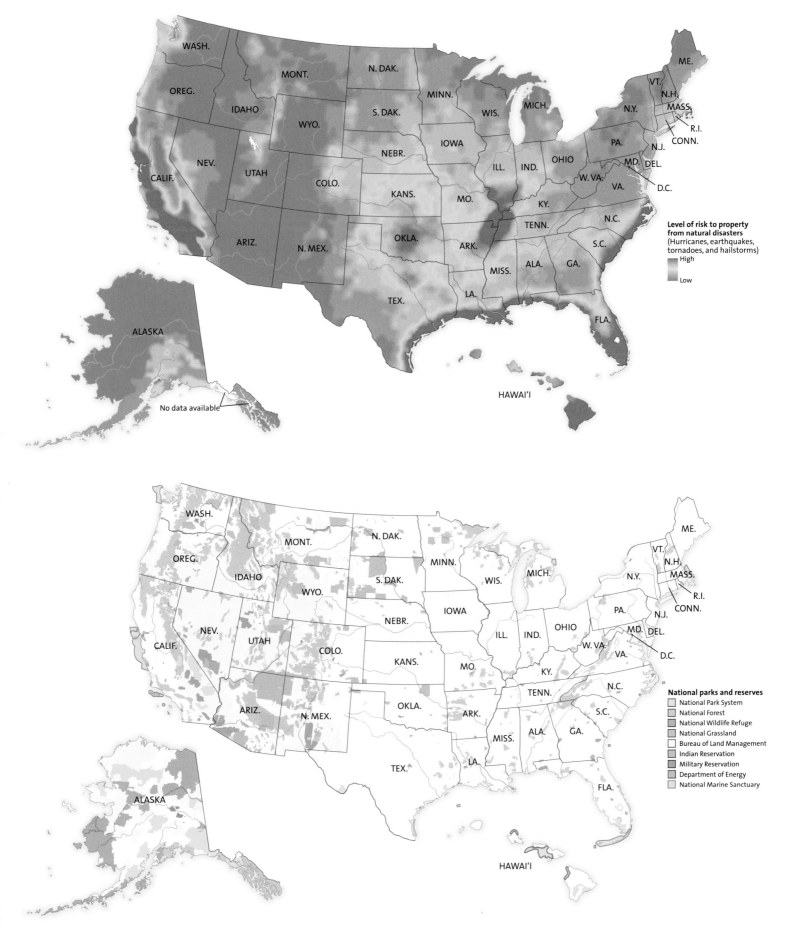

Level of risk to property from natural disasters
(Hurricanes, earthquakes, tornadoes, and hailstorms)

High

Low

No data available

National parks and reserves
- National Park System
- National Forest
- National Wildlife Refuge
- National Grassland
- Bureau of Land Management
- Indian Reservation
- Military Reservation
- Department of Energy
- National Marine Sanctuary

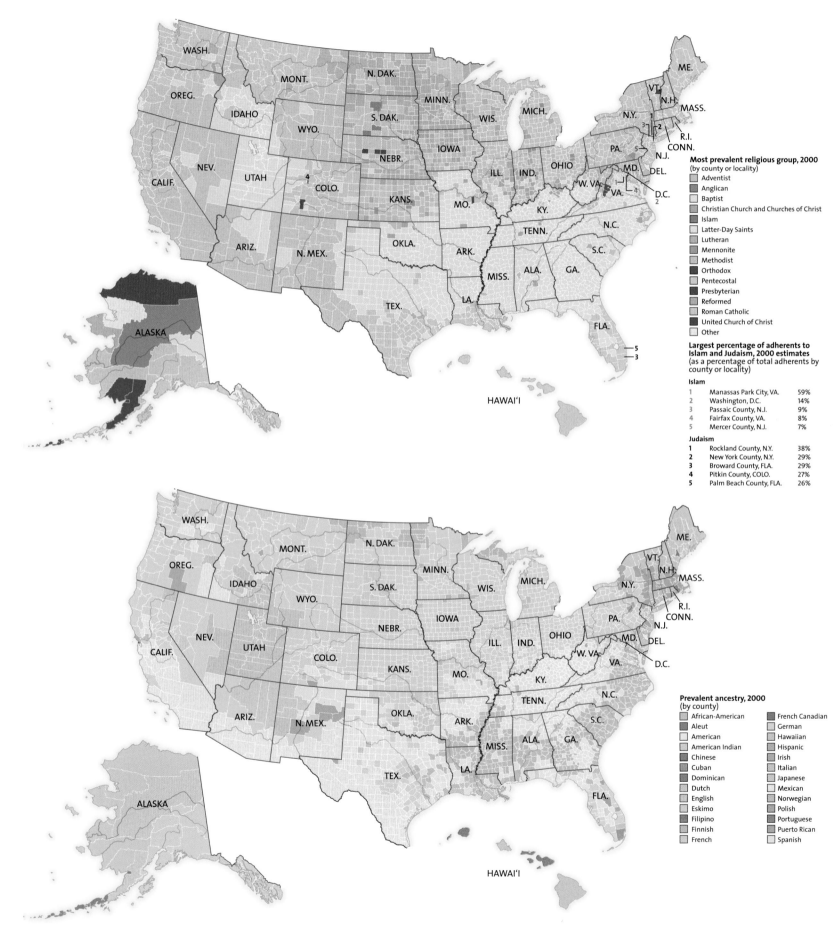

Most prevalent religious group, 2000
(by county or locality)

- Adventist
- Anglican
- Baptist
- Christian Church and Churches of Christ
- Islam
- Latter-Day Saints
- Lutheran
- Mennonite
- Methodist
- Orthodox
- Pentecostal
- Presbyterian
- Reformed
- Roman Catholic
- United Church of Christ
- Other

Largest percentage of adherents to Islam and Judaism, 2000 estimates
(as a percentage of total adherents by county or locality)

Islam

1	Manassas Park City, VA.	59%
2	Washington, D.C.	14%
3	Passaic County, N.J.	9%
4	Fairfax County, VA.	8%
5	Mercer County, N.J.	7%

Judaism

1	Rockland County, N.Y.	38%
2	New York County, N.Y.	29%
3	Broward County, FLA.	29%
4	Pitkin County, COLO.	27%
5	Palm Beach County, FLA.	26%

Prevalent ancestry, 2000
(by county)

- African-American
- Aleut
- American
- American Indian
- Chinese
- Cuban
- Dominican
- Dutch
- English
- Eskimo
- Filipino
- Finnish
- French
- French Canadian
- German
- Hawaiian
- Hispanic
- Irish
- Italian
- Japanese
- Mexican
- Norwegian
- Polish
- Portuguese
- Puerto Rican
- Spanish

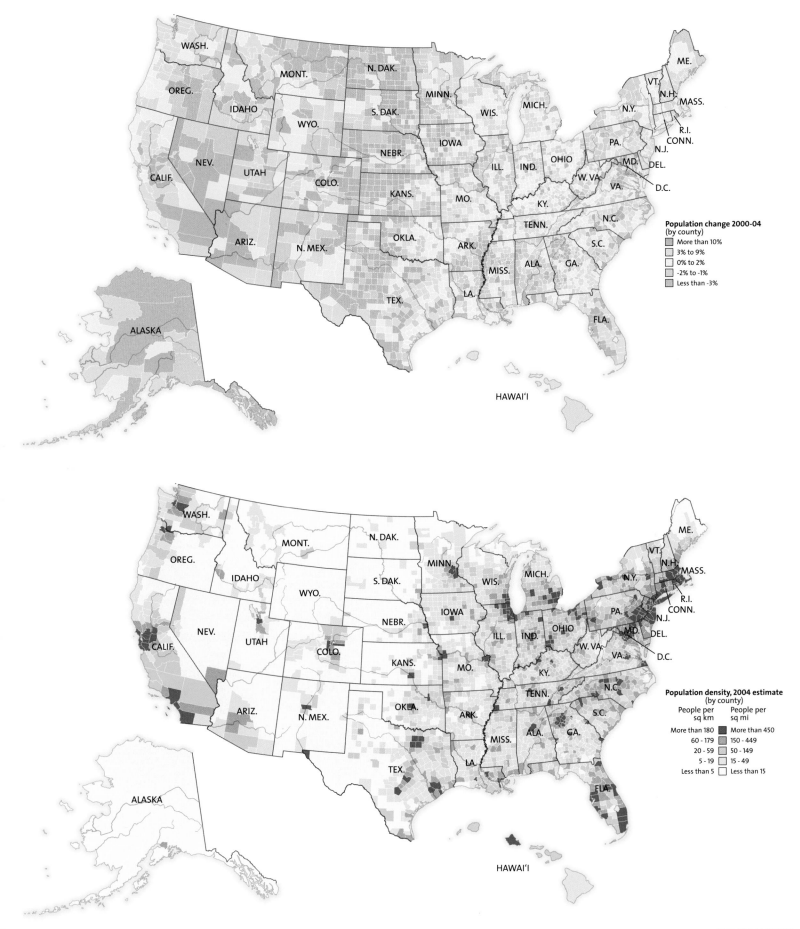

Population change 2000-04
(by county)
- More than 10%
- 3% to 9%
- 0% to 2%
- -2% to -1%
- Less than -3%

Population density, 2004 estimate
(by county)

People per sq km	People per sq mi
More than 180	More than 450
60 - 179	150 - 449
20 - 59	50 - 149
5 - 19	15 - 49
Less than 5	Less than 15

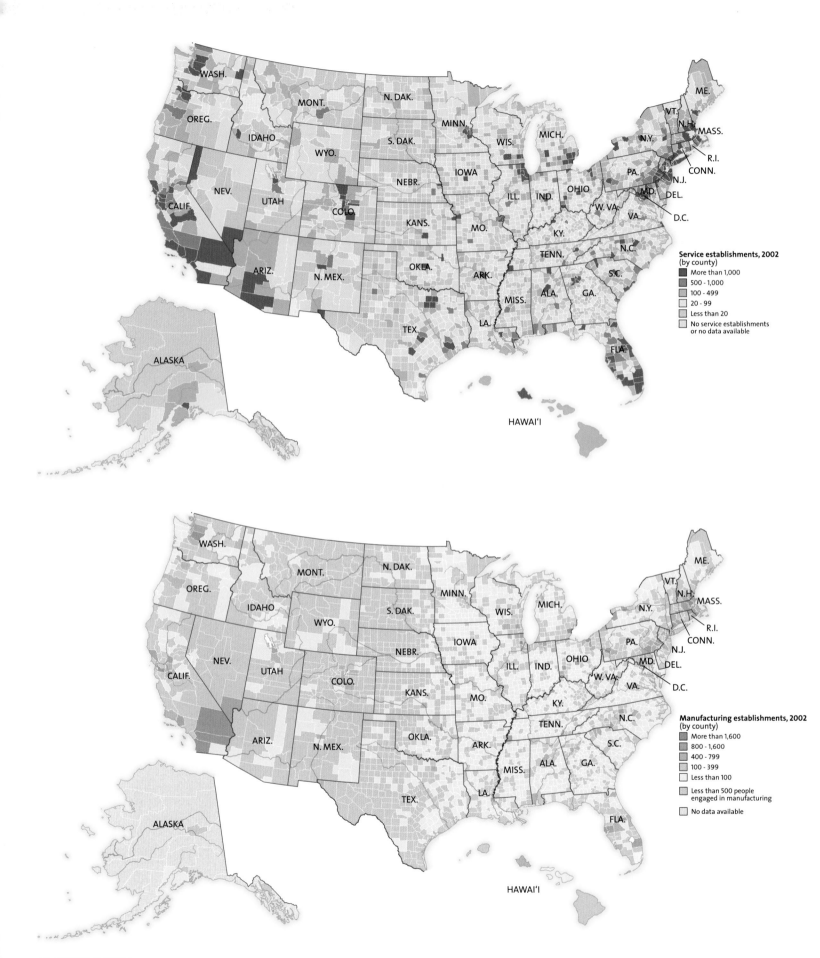

Service establishments, 2002
(by county)

- More than 1,000
- 500 - 1,000
- 100 - 499
- 20 - 99
- Less than 20
- No service establishments or no data available

Manufacturing establishments, 2002
(by county)

- More than 1,600
- 800 - 1,600
- 400 - 799
- 100 - 399
- Less than 100
- Less than 500 people engaged in manufacturing
- No data available

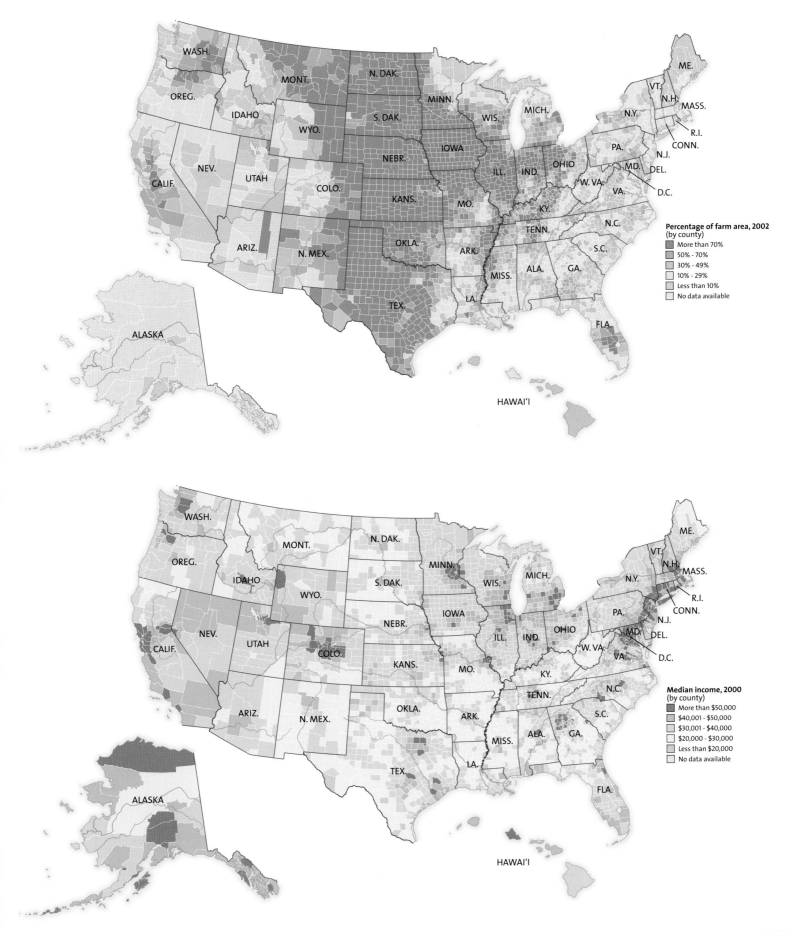

Percentage of farm area, 2002
(by county)

- More than 70%
- 50% - 70%
- 30% - 49%
- 10% - 29%
- Less than 10%
- No data available

Median income, 2000
(by county)

- More than $50,000
- $40,001 - $50,000
- $30,001 - $40,000
- $20,000 - $30,000
- Less than $20,000
- No data available

NORTHWESTERN U.S.

Provinces / States: CANADA · SASKATCHEWAN · MANITOBA · ONTARIO · MONTANA · NORTH DAKOTA · SOUTH DAKOTA · MINNESOTA · WYOMING · NEBRASKA · IOWA · COLORADO · KANSAS · MISSOURI

Selected cities and features:

- Saskatoon, Regina, Winnipeg, Moose Jaw, Swift Current, Medicine Hat
- Bismarck, Minot, Williston, Grand Forks, Fargo
- Pierre, Rapid City, Sioux Falls, Aberdeen, Watertown
- Bismarck, Mandan, Jamestown
- Billings, Miles City, Glendive, Great Falls
- Cheyenne, Casper, Laramie, Sheridan
- Denver, Lakewood, Westminster, Arvada, Boulder, Fort Collins, Colorado Springs, Pueblo, Grand Junction
- Omaha, Lincoln, North Platte, Scottsbluff
- Sioux City, Council Bluffs
- Wichita

Parks and features: Theodore Roosevelt Nat. Park · Badlands N.P. · Wind Cave N.P. · Bighorn Canyon N.R.A. · Upper Missouri River Breaks N.M. · Grasslands N.P. · Riding Mountain N.P. · Rocky Mt. N.P. · Dinosaur N.M. · Black Canyon of the Gunnison N.M. · Colorado N. Mem. · Arches N.P. · Canyonlands N.P. · Flaming Gorge N.R.A. · Fossil Butte N.M. · Fort Peck Lake · Lake Sakakawea · Lake Oahe

(Map of the Southwestern United States showing parts of Wyoming, Colorado, Nebraska, Kansas, Oklahoma, New Mexico, Texas, and northern Mexico including Chihuahua, Coahuila, and Sonora.)

State and region names:
WYOMING · COLORADO · NEBRASKA · KANSAS · OKLAHOMA · NEW MEXICO · TEXAS · MEXICO · CHIHUAHUA · COAHUILA · SONORA · NUEVO LEÓN · TAMAULIPAS · ROCKY MOUNTAINS · SANGRE DE CRISTO MOUNTAINS · GUADALUPE MOUNTAINS · LLANO ESTACADO · EDWARDS PLATEAU · SIERRA MADRE OCCIDENTAL

Selected cities: Denver, Aurora, Lakewood, Arvada, Westminster, Boulder, Fort Collins, Colorado Springs, Pueblo, Grand Junction, Durango, Lincoln, North Platte, Wichita, Dodge City, Oklahoma City, Amarillo, Lubbock, Wichita Falls, Fort Worth, Arlington, Abilene, Albuquerque, Santa Fe, Las Cruces, El Paso, Ciudad Juárez, San Antonio, Austin, Waco, Chihuahua

National parks and monuments: ROCKY MOUNTAIN N.P., DINOSAUR NAT. MON., ARCHES N.P., CANYONLANDS N.P., MESA VERDE N.P., BLACK CANYON OF THE GUNNISON N.P., CANYON DE CHELLY NAT. MON., PETRIFIED FOREST N.P., EL MALPAIS NAT. MON., BANDELIER N.M., CHACO CULTURE N.H.P., SALINAS PUEBLO MISSIONS N.M., WHITE SANDS NAT. MON., CARLSBAD CAVERNS N.P., GUADALUPE MOUNTAINS N.P., BIG BEND N.P., AMISTAD N.R.A., LAKE MEREDITH N.R.A., SAGUARO N.P., FLAMING GORGE N.R.A.

Mountain peaks: Mt. Elbert 4399, Mt. Harvard 4395, Pikes Pk. 4301, Longs Pk. 4345, Mt. Wilson 4342, Wheeler Pk. 4011, Sandia Crest 3255, Mt. Taylor 3445

MANITOBA

ONTARIO

NORTH DAKOTA

SOUTH DAKOTA

MINNESOTA

NEBRASKA

IOWA

WISCONSIN

MICHIGAN

KANSAS

MISSOURI

ILLINOIS

INDIANA

OHIO

OKLAHOMA

ARKANSAS

KENTUCKY

TENN.

Lake Superior

Lake Nipigon

VOYAGEURS N.P.

ISLE ROYALE N.P.

APOSTLE ISLANDS N.L.

PICTURED ROCKS N.L.

PUKASKWA N.P.

OZARK PLATEAU

OZARK N.S.R.

BUFFALO NAT. RIVER

CUMBERLAND PLATEAU

MAMMOTH CAVE N.P.

LAND BETWEEN THE LAKES

Thunder Bay

Duluth

Minneapolis

St. Paul

Sioux Falls

Omaha

Lincoln

Des Moines

Cedar Rapids

Madison

Milwaukee

Grand Rapids

Rockford

Chicago

Naperville

Aurora

Joliet

Gary

South Bend

Fort Wayne

Peoria

Springfield

Indianapolis

Columbus

Dayton

Cincinnati

Louisville

Lexington

Topeka

Kansas City

Independence

Overland Park

Wichita

Jefferson City

St. Louis

Springfield

Tulsa

Marquette

Sault Sainte Marie

Ann Arbor

Toledo

Warren

Livonia

Lansing

Flint

COLORADO
KANSAS
MISSOURI
OKLAHOMA
ARKANSAS
TEXAS
LOUISIANA
MISSISSIPPI
NEW MEXICO
COAHUILA
NUEVO LÉON
TAMAULIPAS
SAN LUIS POTOSÍ
ZACATECAS
MEXICO
ILL.

GULF OF MEXICO

Wichita Amarillo Lubbock Wichita Falls Oklahoma City Tulsa Fort Worth Dallas Garland Plano Mesquite Arlington Abilene Waco Austin San Antonio Houston Pasadena Beaumont Baton Rouge Lafayette New Orleans Metairie Shreveport Little Rock Hot Springs Springfield Memphis Jackson Vicksburg Corpus Christi Laredo Nuevo Laredo Brownsville Matamoros McAllen Reynosa Monterrey Saltillo Ciudad Victoria Monclova

Red Hills Wolf Creek Canadian Washita North Pease Red River Ozark Plateau Boston Mountains Ouachita Mountains Kiamichi Mts. Magazine Mt. Blue Mountain Sabine EDWARDS PLATEAU LLANO ESTACADO CAPROCK ESCARPMENT Rio Grande Pecos Eufaula Lake Lake Conroe BIG THICKET NAT. PRES. AMISTAD N.R.A. RIO GRANDE WILD & SCENIC RIVER PADRE ISLAND NATIONAL SEASHORE Baffin Bay Alazan Bay Corpus Christi Bay Matagorda Peninsula Galveston Atchafalaya Bay Caillou Bay Terrebonne Bay Isles Dernieres Point au Fer West Bay

FLOWER GARDEN BANKS NATIONAL MARINE SANCTUARY
West Flower Garden Bank East Flower Garden Bank
Claypile Bank Stetson Bank

CUMBRES DE MONTERREY N.P.
OZARK NAT. SCENIC RIVERWAYS
BUFFALO NAT. RIVER
HOT SPRINGS N.P.

Black Mesa Rabbit Ear Mountain Palo Duro Canyon Castle Mt. King Mt. Taum Sauk Mt. St. Francois Mountains

LAMBERT CONFORMAL CONIC PROJECTION
SCALE 1:6,000,000
0 KILOMETERS 100 150
0 MILES 50 100 150

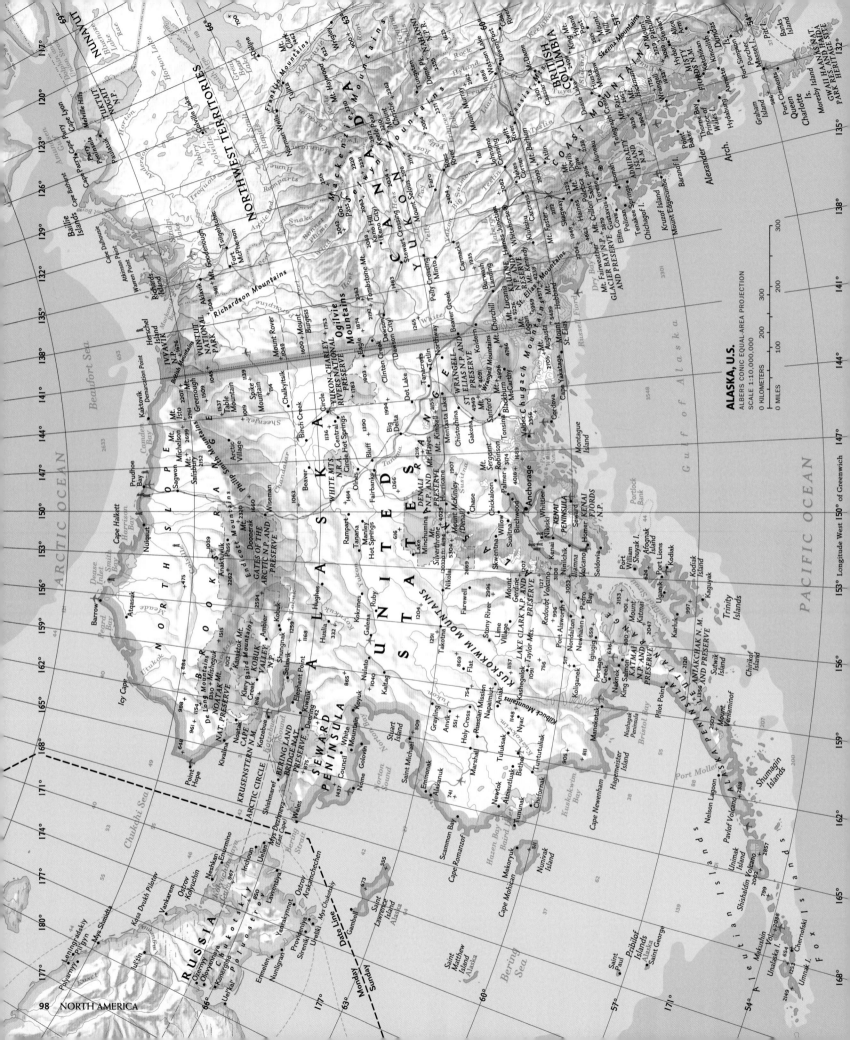

ALASKA, U.S.

ALBERS CONIC EQUAL-AREA PROJECTION

SCALE 1:10,000,000

HAWAI'I, U.S.

OBLIQUE MERCATOR PROJECTION

SCALE 1:10,000,000

0 KILOMETERS 100 200 300

0 MILES 100 200 300

PAPAHĀNAUMOKUĀKEA MARINE NATIONAL MONUMENT

Created on June 15, 2006, this protected area includes atolls, reefs, and small islands extending over 2,000 kilometers (1,400 mi.) northwest of the main Hawaiian Islands. This area contains nearly 70 percent of all coral reefs within U.S. waters with over 7,000 marine species including corals, sea turtles, and Hawaiian monk seals. It is the largest protected area ever created in the U.S. at nearly 360,000 square kilometers (140,000 sq. mi.).

TROPIC OF CANCER

PACIFIC OCEAN

North Western Hawaiian Islands

Kure Atoll (Ocean Island)

Midway Islands
Sand I. Eastern I.

Pearl and Hermes Atoll

Lisianski Island

Neva Shoal

Laysan Island

Maro Reef

Gardner Pinnacles

La Perouse Pinnacle
French Frigate Shoals

Necker Island

Nihoa

KAUA'I
Wai'oli Mission
Kīlauea Lighthouse
Kaulu Paoa Heiau
Mākaleha Mts.
Anahola
Mānā
First Sugar Mill
Hauola Place of Refuge

NI'IHAU
Kamalino
Pāni'au
Kawaihoa Point

Nihoa

Ka'ula

Kaua'i
Ni'ihau

O'ahu
Honolulu

Lāna'i
Kaho'olawe

Moloka'i
KALAUPAPA N.H.P.
Maui

Hawai'i
HALEAKALĀ N.P.
Mauna Kea
HAWAI'I VOLCANOES N.P.
Kalae (South Point)

Kaua'i Channel

Kaiwi Channel

Kalohi Channel

'Alenuihaha Channel

Pu'uomahuka Heiau
Kahuku Point
Lā'ie
Polynesian Cultural Center
Ka'ena Point
Old Sugar Mill
HICKAM A.F.B.
Honolulu
U.S.S. ARIZONA MEM. WW II VALOR IN THE PACIFIC NAT. MON.
Pearl Harbor
He'eia
Kāne'ohe Bay
Diamond Head

O'AHU

MOLOKA'I
Kapuāiwa Coconut Grove
Garden of the Gods
Maunaloa
Kalaupapa
KALAUPAPA N.H.P.

LĀNA'I

KAHO'OLAWE

MAUI
Ha'ikū
HALEAKALĀ N.P.
Kahe'a Heiau & Petroglyphs
Wailohonu Petroglyphs

Kealaikahiki Channel

Pailolo Channel

HAWAI'I
Kamehameha I Birthplace
Kukuihaele
KOHALA
HAMAKUA
Mauna Kea
Pepe'ekeo
Hilo Bay
HILO
Hilo
PUNA
Kapoho Crater
Kea'au Ranch
HAWAI'I VOLCANOES N.P.
Petroglyphs
Pu'ukoholā Heiau National Historic Site
Petroglyphs
Mākole'a Point
Kailua-Kona
KALOKO-HONOKŌHAU N.H.P.
Captain Cook Monument
PU'UHONUA O HŌNAUNAU N.H.P.
KONA
Mauna Loa
KA'Ū
Kauná Point
Nā'ālehu
Heiau o Kalalea

PRINCIPAL HAWAIIAN ISLANDS

MERCATOR PROJECTION

SCALE 1:4,000,000

0 KILOMETERS 20 40 60 80 100

0 MILES 20 40 60 80 100

The state of Hawai'i includes all islands and reefs in the chain that extends from the island of Hawai'i to Kure, except Midway Islands, which are administered as a wildlife refuge by the U.S. Fish and Wildlife Service.

PACIFIC OCEAN

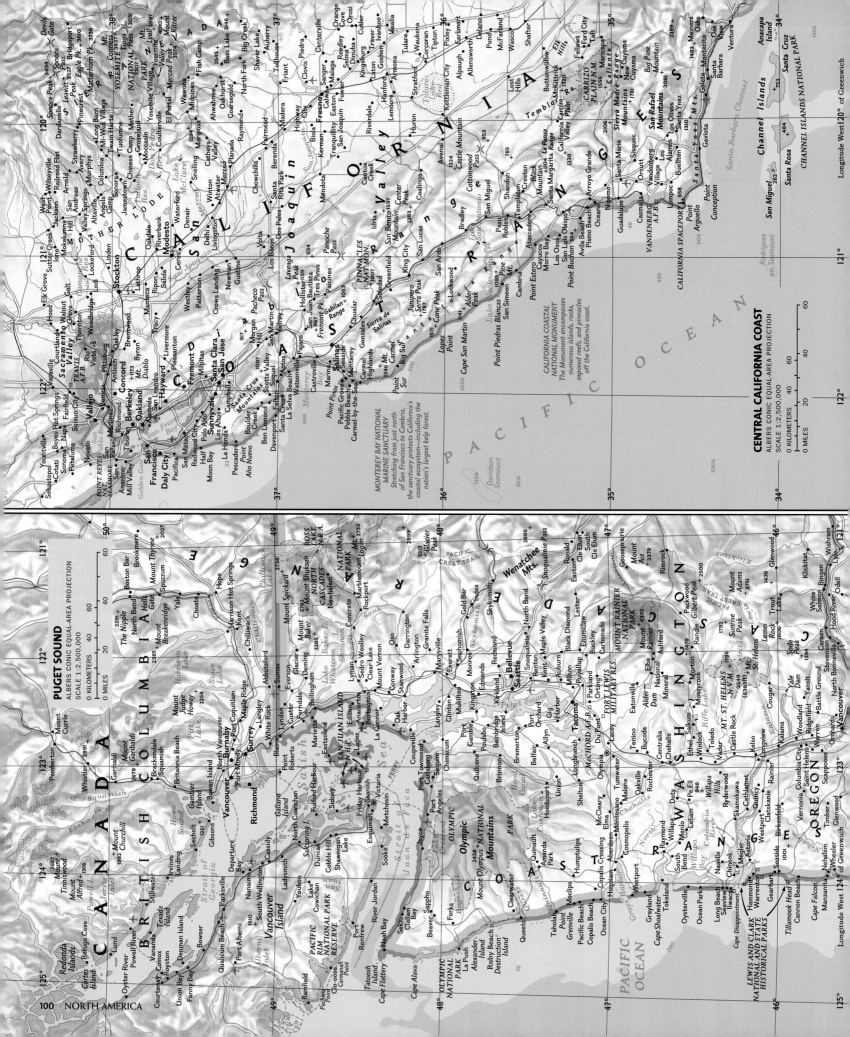

SOUTHERN CALIFORNIA

ALBERS CONIC EQUAL-AREA PROJECTION
SCALE 1:2,500,000

Longitude West 119° of Greenwich

SOUTHERN GREAT LAKES

ALBERS CONIC EQUAL-AREA PROJECTION
SCALE 1:3,000,000

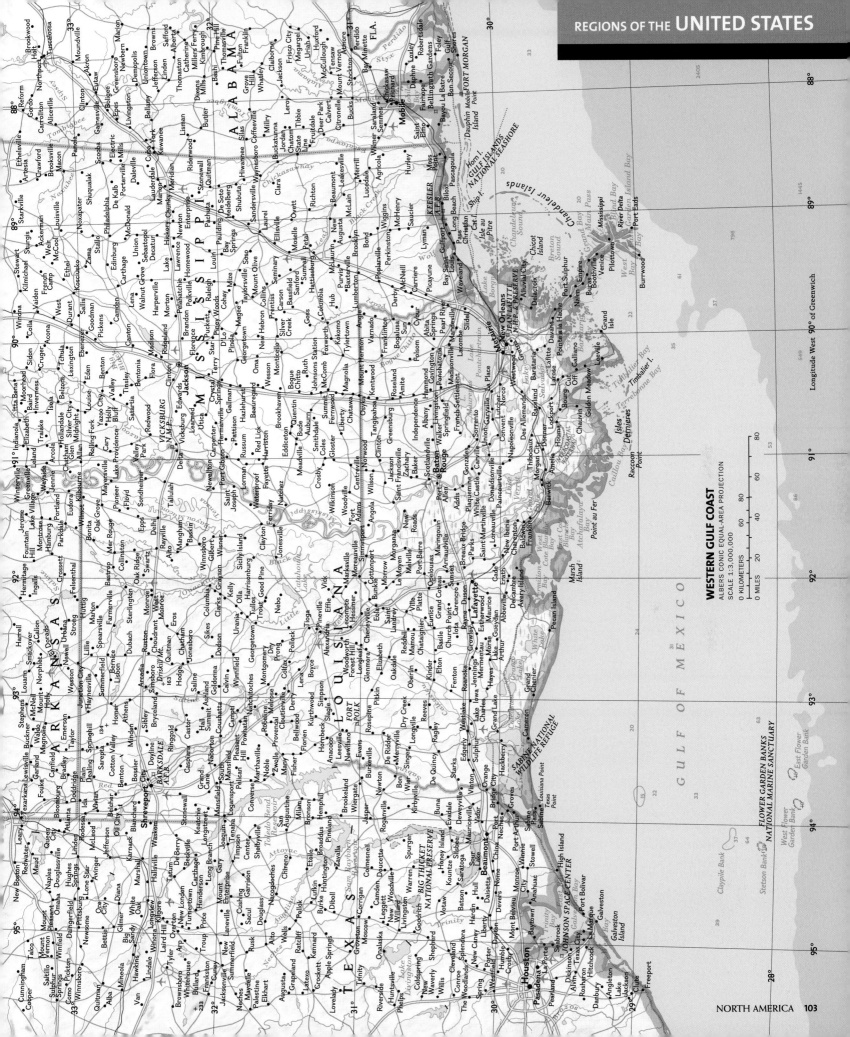

WESTERN GULF COAST

ALBERS CONIC EQUAL-AREA PROJECTION
SCALE 1:13,000,000

GULF OF MEXICO

SOUTHERN NEW ENGLAND

ALBERS CONIC EQUAL-AREA PROJECTION

SCALE 1:1,750,000

0 KILOMETERS   30   40   50

0 MILES   10   20   30   40   50

Longitude West 72° of Greenwich

PENINSULAR FLORIDA
ALBERS CONIC EQUAL-AREA PROJECTION
SCALE 1:2,500,000

AZIMUTHAL EQUIDISTANT PROJECTION
SCALE 1:16,000,000

0 KILOMETERS   300   400

0 MILES   100   200   300   400

WESTERN CANADA

ALBERS CONIC EQUAL-AREA PROJECTION

SCALE 1:6,000,000

0 KILOMETERS 100   150
0 MILES   50   100   150

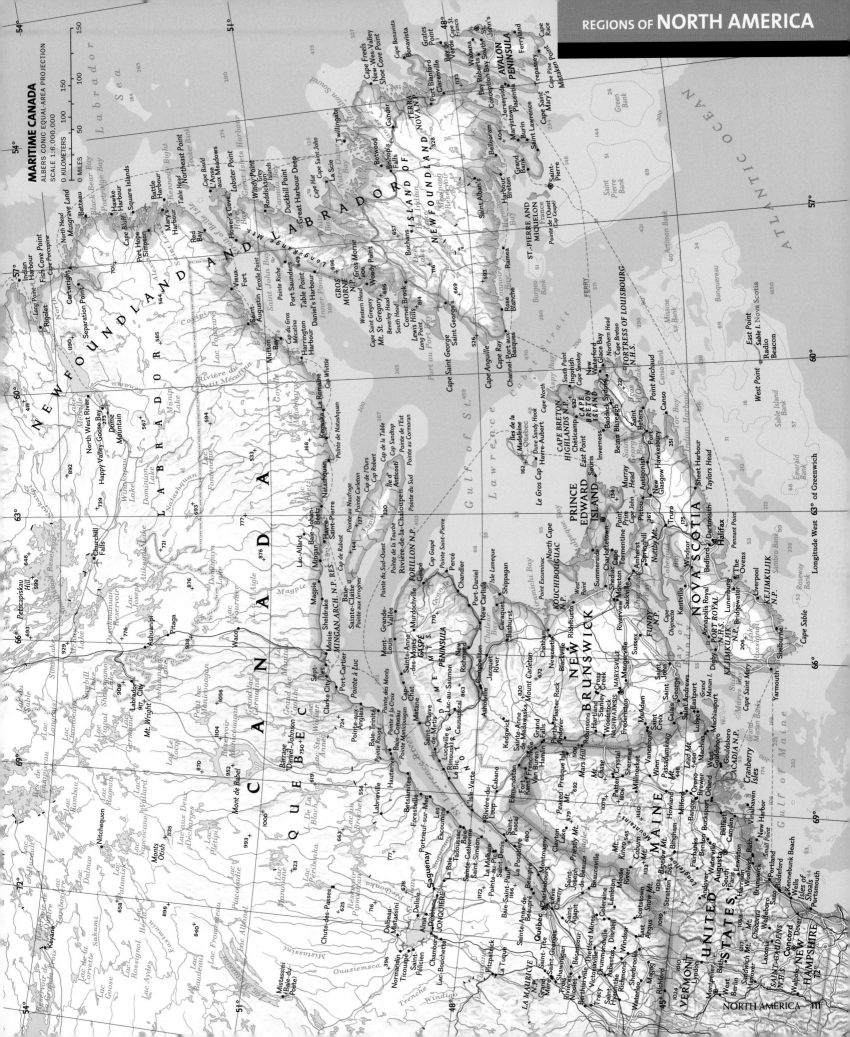

National Parks of Mexico
(Selected national parks are numbered in blue on the map.)

1	Cañón de Río Blanco	9	Los Mármoles
2	Cañón del Sumidero	10	Nevado de Toluca
3	Cumbres de Monterrey	11	Palenque
4	El Gogorrón	12	Pico de Orizaba
5	Iztaccíhuatl–Popocatépetl	13	Pico de Tancítaro
6	Lago de Camécuaro	14	Sierra de San Pedro Mártir
7	Lagunas de Chacahua	15	Volcán Nevado de Colima
8	La Malinche		

ALBERS CONIC EQUAL-AREA PROJECTION
SCALE 1:10,000,000

0 KILOMETERS   200   300

0 MILES   100   200   300

TROPIC OF CANCER

PACIFIC OCEAN

National Parks and Biotopes of Guatemala
(Selected protected areas are numbered in blue on the map.)

16 Sierra del Lacandón
17 Laguna del Tigre–Río Escondido
18 Laguna del Tigre
19 Mirador–Río Azul
20 Naachtún Dos Lagunas
21 Mirador–Río Azul
22 Tikal

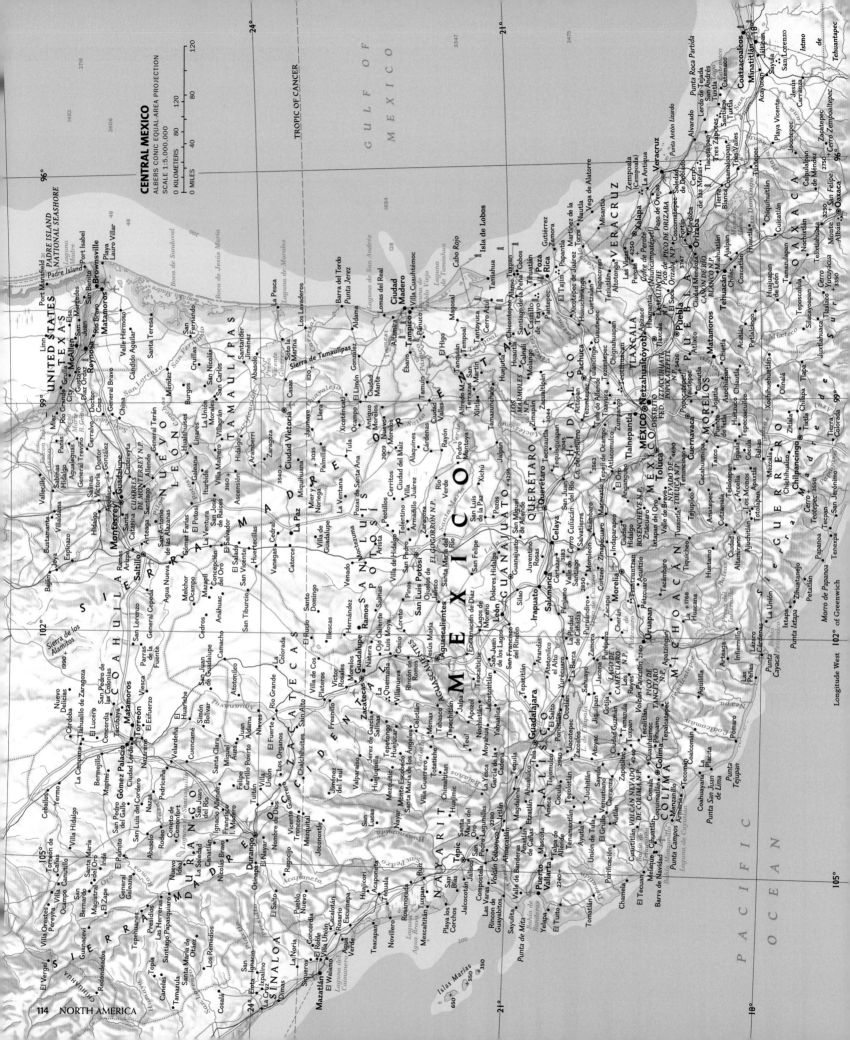

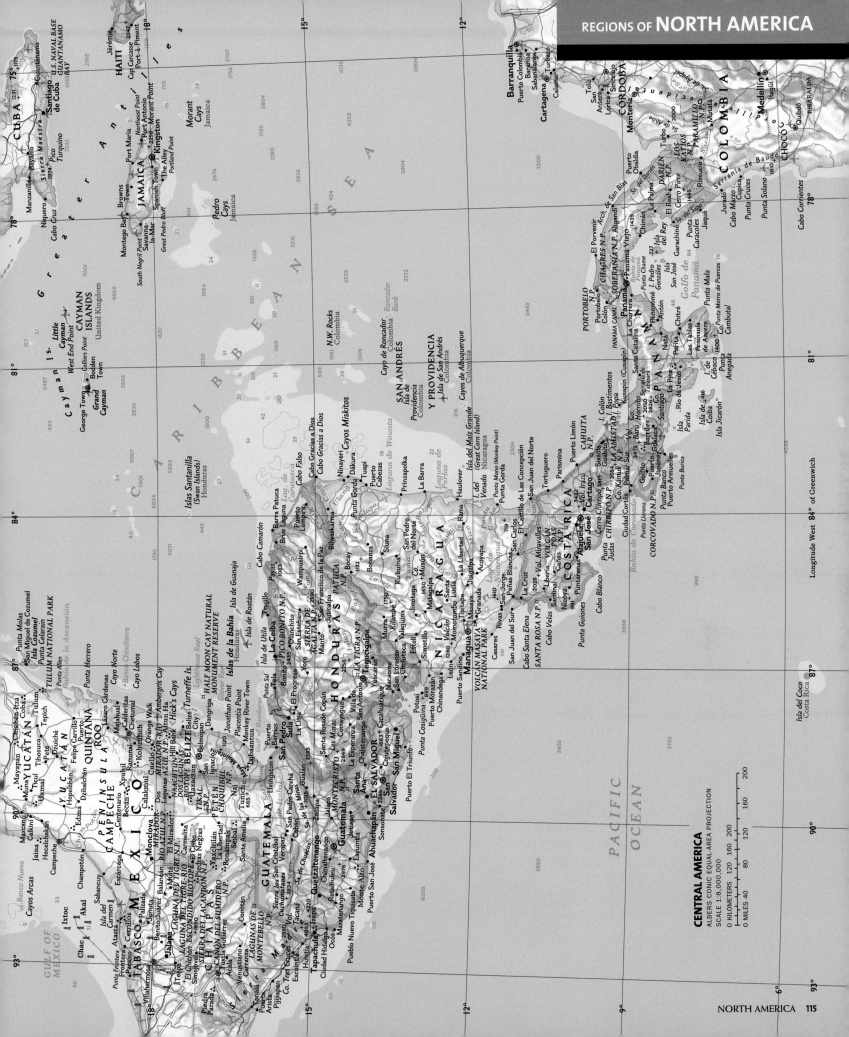

CENTRAL AMERICA
ALBERS CONIC EQUAL-AREA PROJECTION
SCALE 1:8,000,000
0 KILOMETERS 40 80 120 160 200
0 MILES 40 80 120 160 200

Longitude West 84° of Greenwich

Gulf of Mexico

FLORIDA
UNITED STATES

Port Charlotta • Arcadia • Stuart
West Palm Beach
Fort Myers • Belle Glade • Grand Bahama I.
Sanibel Island • Naples • Delray Beach • Freeport
Cape Romano • Pompano Beach • High Rock
BIG CYPRESS NAT. PRESERVE • Fort Lauderdale • Bimini Islands
Everglades City • Hollywood • Moore's I.
Homestead • Miami • Southwest Point
EVERGLADES N.P. • Cape Sable • Berry Islands
Key Largo • Nassau • New Providence
Marquesas Keys • Keys • Flamingo Point
Key West • Florida • Marathon • Deadman's Cays • Dog Rocks • Kemps Bay
Elbow Cays • Damas Cays • Anguilla Cays • Cistern Point

Cooper's Town
Tilloo Cay
Little Abaco Island • Abaco Island
Grand Bahama I.
Abaco Island
Andros Island • Big Wood Cay
Little San Salvador
Eleuthera Island • Rock Sound
Exuma Sound
Great Exuma
Long Cay • Little Exuma • Deadman
Gt. Guana Cay • Concep

Gulf of Mexico

Isla Pérez
Arrecife Alacránes
CAMPECHE BANK
Bancos Ingleses
Banco Nuevo
Cayos Arcas

MÉXICO
YUCATÁN
Progreso • Dzilam de Bravo • El Cuyo
Sisal • Chelem • Chiquilá
Hunucmá • Dzibilchaltún • Isla Holbox
Mérida • Izamal • Tizimín • Isla Mujeres / I. Cancún
Maxcanú • Acanceh • Piste • Valladolid • Cancún
Muna • Mayapán • Chichén Itzá • Cobá
Uman • Ticul • Peto • Puerto Morelos
Jaina • Campeche • Tepich • Punta Molas / Isla Cozumel
Champotón • Hopelchén • Felipe Carrillo Puerto • Punta Celarain

CAMPECHE
QUINTANA ROO
YUCATAN PENINSULA
Edzná • Dzibalchén • Punta Allen
Sabancuy • Dzuiché • Vigia Chico
Escárcega • Calderitas • Punta Herrero
Centenario • Chetumal
Balancán • Monclova • Cayo Norte
El Mirador • Calakmul • Banco Chinchorro
TABASCO • Xpuhil • Cayo Lobos
Tenosique • Kohunlich • Orange Walk
El Ceibo • Uaxactún • Cuello • Ambergris Cay

GUATEMALA
Cobán • Livingston • Puerto Barrios
Sierra de los Cuchumatanes
PETÉN • Flores • Tikal • San Ignacio • Belmopan
Piedras Negras • Tikal N.P. • BELIZE
Yaxchilán • Bonampak • La Libertad • Dangriga
CHIAPAS • Seibal • Naj Tunich • Maya Mts.
Santa Amelia • San Luis
Jonathan Point • Placentia Point • Monkey River Town

HONDURAS
Sierra de las Minas • Copán • Las Minas
Zacapa • Gualán • Yoro
Chiquimula • Santa Rosa de Copán
Guatemala • MONTECRISTO N.P. • Comayagua • Villa de San Antonio
Chimaltenango • Escuintla • La Esperanza • LA TIGRA N.P. • Tegucigalpa
Santa Ana • Ahuachapán • Nacaome • San Lorenzo • Murra
EL SALVADOR
San José • Sonsonate • Cojutepeque
San Salvador • Puerto El Triunfo • San Miguel
Punta San Juan • Golfo de Fonseca • Punta Cosigüina • Choluteca

NICARAGUA
Somotillo • Estelí • Jinotega • Matagalpa
Chinandega • La Trinidad • Somoto • Potosí
León • Lago de Managua • Jinotega
Managua • Tipitapa • La Libertad
Masaya • Granada • Rama
VOLCÁN MASAYA N.P. • Acoyapa • Bluefields
Casares • Rivas • Punta Gorda
San Jorge • San Juan del Sur • San Carlos • Punta Mono (Monkey Point)
Cabo Santa Elena • Peñas Blancas • El Castillo de La Concepción
SANTA ROSA N.P. • Liberia • Altamira
Cabo Velas • Cañas • Tortuguero • TORTUGUERO N.P.

COSTA RICA
Nicoya • Esparza • Parismina
Puntarenas • San José • Puerto Limón
Punta Guiones • Cartago • CAHUITA N.P.
Cabo Blanco • CHIRRIPÓ N.P. • LA AMISTAD N.P.
Punta Judas • Ciudad Cortés • Palmar

PANAMA
OMAR TORRIJOS N.P. • SOBERANÍA N.P. • CHAGRES N.P. • Panamá
CORCOVADO N.P. • Puerto Armuelles • Golfo de Panamá
Archipiélago de San Blas

CUBA
La Habana (Havana) • GUANABACOA • Matanzas
La Esperanza • Artemisa • Corralillo • Quemado de Güines
PINAR DEL RÍO • LA HABANA • Colón • VILLA CLARA
Pinar del Río • Mantua • MATANZAS • Caibarién
Ciudad Sandino • Los Palacios • Cienfuegos • Santa Clara • CIEGO DE ÁVILA
Nueva Gerona • Península de Zapata • Cruces • SANCTI SPÍRITUS
Cabo Francés • Cabo San Antonio • Cayo Largo • Sancti Spíritus • Ciego de Ávila
I. DE LA JUVENTUD • Cayo del Rosario • Cayos de Dios • CAMAGÜEY
Camagüey • CUBA • Minas
Contramaestre • LAS TUNAS • Gibara
Santa Cruz del Sur • Guáimaro • Guayabal • Las Tunas • Holguín
Niquero • GRANMA • Bayamo • SANTIAGO DE CUBA
Cabo Cruz • Sierra Maestra • Santiago de Cuba

JAMAICA
Montego Bay • St. Ann's Bay • Port Maria
North Negril Point • Browns Town • Northeast Point • Port Antonio
South Negril Point • Savanna-la-Mar • Spanish Town • Kingston • Morant Point
Great Pedro Bluff • The Alley • Portland Point

CAYMAN ISLANDS U.K.
George Town • Grand Cayman
Little Cayman • West End Point

GREATER ANTILLES

CARIBBEAN

Islas Santanilla (Swan Islands) Honduras
North West Rocks Colombia
Cayos Miskitos
SAN ANDRÉS Y PROVIDENCIA
Isla de Providencia Colombia • Roncador Bank
Islas del Maíz Nicaragua
Isla de San Andrés Colombia
I. del Maíz Grande (Great Corn Island) Nicaragua

Isla de Guanaja
Islas de la Bahía
Isla de Roatán
Isla de Utila
Gulf of Honduras
La Ceiba • PICO BONITO N.P. • Trujillo • Cabo Camarón
Puerto Cortés • Punta Sal • Tela
San Pedro Sula • El Progreso • Olanchito • Payas • Brus Laguna
Quimistán • La Lima • San Esteban • Barra Patuca
Comayagua • Manto • San Francisco de la Paz • Wampusirpi
Juticalpa • Puerto Lempira
PATUCA N.P. • Bocay • Bilwaskarma • Cabo Gracias a Dios
Kilambé • Siuna • Kuikuina • Ninayeri • Punta Gorda • Dákura
Yalagüina • San Pedro del Norte • Tuapí • Puerto Cabezas
La Barra • Prinzapolka • Laguna de Perlas
Haulover • Laguna de Perlas

PACIFIC OCEAN

Bahía de Barbacoas
SUCRE
Carmen de Bolívar
Sincelejo
Barranquilla
Puerto Colombia
ATLÁNTICO
Cartagena
Turbaco
CÓRDOBA
Montería
ANTIOQUIA
Planeta Rica

TROPIC OF CAPRICORN

Longitude West 72° of Greenwich

ATLANTIC OCEAN

24°

21°

18°

15°

12°

San Salvador (Watling)
Samana Cay
Plana Cays (French Cays)
Mayaguana I. 40
TURKS AND CAICOS ISLANDS U.K.
Little Inagua Island
West Caicos
East Caicos
Caicos Is.
Turks Islands
Ambergris Cays
Cockburn Town
Great Inagua Island
Matthew Town 48
Mouchoir Passage

Baracoa
Punta de Maisí
Île de la Tortue
Monte Cristi
Cabo Isabela
HISPANIOLA
Cabo Francés Viejo
Abreú
Cabo Cabrón
Cabo Samaná
GUANTÁNAMO BAY
Jean-Rabel
Cap-à-Foux +902
Anse-Rouge
Cap-Haïtien
Dessalines
HAITI
Saint-Marc
Cordillera Central
Imbert
Puerto Plata
Mao
Santiago
San Francisco de Macorís
Samaná
Bahía Escocesa
Cabo San Rafael

Baracoa
Saint-Marc
Anse-à-Galets
Hinche
Comendador
DOMINICAN REPUBLIC
Sabana de La Mar
El Macao
I. de la Gonâve
Pointe Ouest
Grande Cayemite 778
Miragoâne Jacmel
Port-au-Prince
Duvergé
San Juan
Santo Domingo
Higüey
Cabo Engaño
Massif de la Hotte
Les Cayes
Côtes-de-Fer
Cabral
Azua
Baní
Nizao
San Pedro de Macorís
La Romana
Punta Higüero
Barahona
Isla Saona
I. Mona
P.R.

ANTILLES

Isla Beata
Cabo Beata
Cabo Rojo
San Germán
Mayagüez
Ponce
Utuado
San Juan
Cayey
PUERTO RICO United States

Vieques
P.R.
St. Croix
Christiansted
U.S. VIRGIN ISLANDS U.S.

U.K. Virgin Islands
Anegada
BRITISH VIRGIN ISLANDS
Tortola
St. John
St. Thomas
Charlotte Amalie
Road Town
Sombrero
ANGUILLA U.K.
The Valley
St. Martin France & Neth. Antilles
St.-Barthélemy France
Gustavia
Saba Neth. Antilles
St. Eustatius Neth. Antilles
Barbuda
ST. KITTS AND NEVIS
Basseterre
Nevis
St. John's
Antigua
ANTIGUA AND BARBUDA
Montserrat U.K.
Plymouth
MONTSERRAT

C A R I B B E A N   S E A

LESSER ANTILLES
LEEWARD ISLANDS
GUADELOUPE France
Basse-Terre
Grande-Terre
Basse-Terre
Pointe-à-Pitre
La Désirade
Les Saintes
Marie-Galante
Guadeloupe Passage

MONTSERRAT
Eruptions from Soufriere Hills volcano since 1995 have forced the evacuation of southern Montserrat—including its capital, Plymouth.

Dominica Passage
Roseau
DOMINICA
Martinique Passage
Mgne. Pelée
Fort-de-France
Sainte-Marie
Martinique
MARTINIQUE France
Pointe d'Enfer
St. Lucia Channel
Castries
ST. LUCIA
St. Vincent Passage
WINDWARD ISLANDS
Kingstown
ST. VINCENT AND THE GRENADINES
Bequia
Canouan
Union
Carriacou
Hillsborough
GRENADA
St. George's
Pt. Salines
Speightstown
Bridgetown
BARBADOS

NETHERLANDS ANTILLES
The Netherlands Antilles consist of the islands of Curaçao and Bonaire off Venezuela and Saba, St. Eustatius, and southern St. Martin (St. Maarten) in the Leeward Islands. Aruba separated from the Netherlands Antilles in 1986.

Punta Gallinas
Bahía Honda
Bahía de Portete
Punta de la Guajira
Cabo de la Vela
ARUBA Neth.
Oranjestad
NETHERLANDS ANTILLES
Curaçao
Willemstad
Bonaire
Islas de Aves Venez.
Islas Los Roques Venez.
La Blanquilla
Venezuela
Los Hermanos
ARCHIPIÉLAGO LOS ROQUES N.P.
Cayo Grande
Tobago
TRINIDAD AND TOBAGO
Charlotteville
Canaan

Santa Marta
Ríohacha
GUAJIRA
Uribia
Paraguaipoa
Puerto López
Punto Fijo
Peninsula de Paraguaná
Punta Cardón
MÉDANOS DE CORO N.P.
Coro
La Vela de Coro
Mirimire
Chichiriviche
Puerto Cumarebo
MORROCOY N.P.
Tucacas
Puerto Cabello
VARGAS
La Guaira
CAPITAL DIST.
Caracas
NUEVA ESPARTA
La Asunción
I. de Margarita
I. Cubagua
I. Coche
Peninsula de Paria
Macuro
Galera Point +940
Río Caribe
Gulf of Paria
Port of Spain
San Fernando
Trinidad
Delaware Bank

Valledupar
CÉSAR
Rosario
Caracolí
MAGDALENA
OMBIA
Mara
Maracaibo
Machiques
PERIJÁ N.P.
SIERRA de Perijá
Cabimas
Lagunillas
Mene Grande
Lago de Maracaibo
ZULIA
Santa Ana
TRUJILLO
Bobures
Betijoque
Valera
Encontrados
BOLÍVAR
NORTE DE SANTANDER
MÉRIDA
Mérida
Barinas
BARINAS
Cordillera de Mérida

FALCÓN
San Rafael
Dabajuro
Churuguara
San Felipe
LARA
Carora
Barquisimeto
YARACUY
Valencia
CARABOBO
Maracay
San Juan de los Morros
ARAGUA
MIRANDA
Los Teques
Río Chico
Guanta
Barcelona
Puerto Píritu
MONAGAS
Maturín
SUCRE
Cumaná
Aragua de Barcelona
Narical +2660
San Mateo
Anaco
Pedernales
MARIUSA N.P.
Punta Araguapiche

Acarigua
San Carlos
COJEDES
PORTUGUESA
Guanare
El Baúl
Calabozo
GUÁRICO
AGUARO-GUARIQUITO N.P.
Ortiz
El Sombrero
Zaraza
VENEZUELA
San José de Amacuro
Waini Point
Grico
Nipa
Leona
Caripito
Coporito
Tucupita
DELTA AMACURO
Barrancas
Curiapo
El Pao
Oficina
Ciudad Soledad
Ciudad Bolívar
Morawhanna
ANZOÁTEGUI
Serranía de Imataca
GUYANA

NORTH AMERICA 117

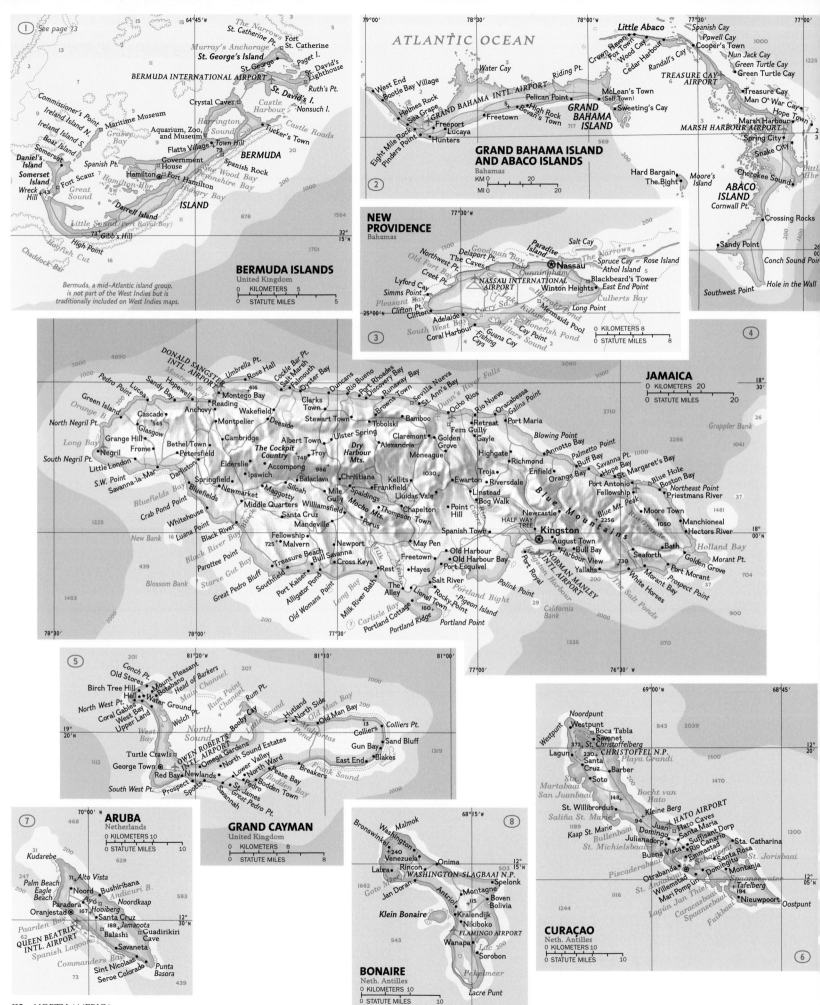

BERMUDA ISLANDS
United Kingdom

Bermuda, a mid-Atlantic island group,
is not part of the West Indies but is
traditionally included on West Indies maps.

1 See page 73

KILOMETERS 5
STATUTE MILES 5

2 GRAND BAHAMA ISLAND
AND ABACO ISLANDS
Bahamas

KM 0   20
MI 0   20

ATLANTIC OCEAN

3 **4** NEW PROVIDENCE
Bahamas

KILOMETERS 8
STATUTE MILES 8

JAMAICA

KILOMETERS 20
STATUTE MILES 20

5 GRAND CAYMAN
United Kingdom

KILOMETERS 8
STATUTE MILES 8

7 ARUBA
Netherlands

KILOMETERS 10
STATUTE MILES 10

8 BONAIRE
Neth. Antilles

KILOMETERS 10
STATUTE MILES 10

6 CURAÇAO
Neth. Antilles

KILOMETERS 10
STATUTE MILES 10

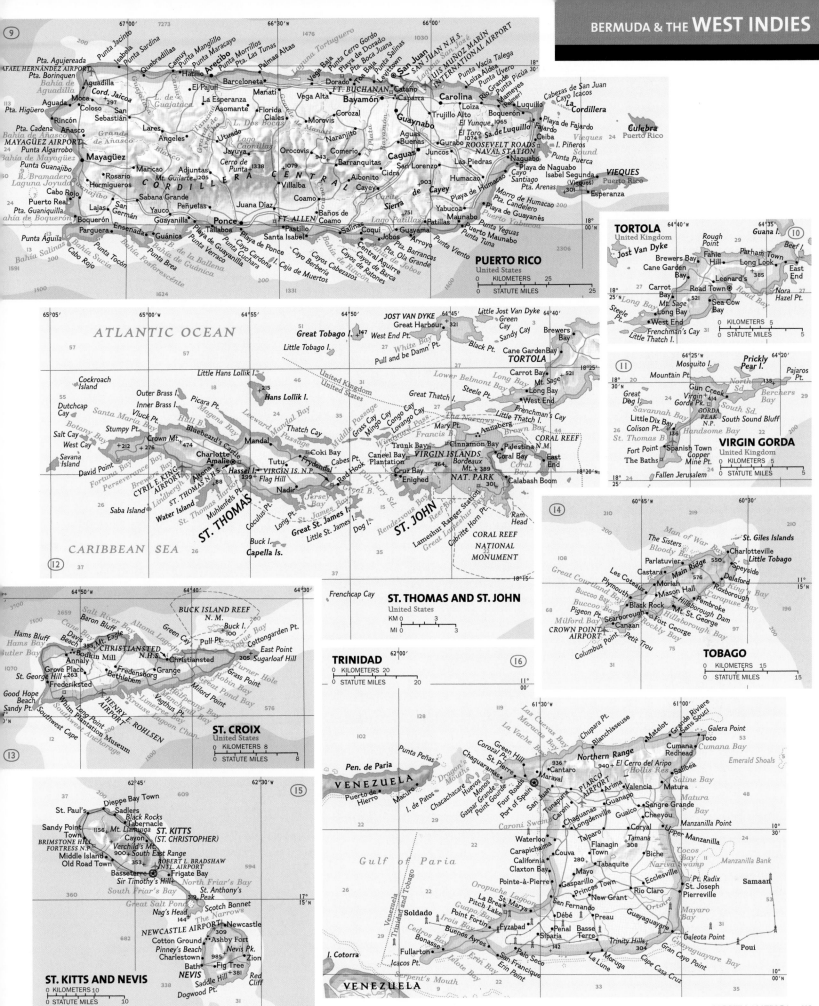

Two features dominate South America: the Andes, extending 7,242 kilometers (4,500 miles), is the world's longest and second highest mountain range; the Amazon—the world's largest river by volume and, at 6,679 kilometers (4,150 miles), the second longest—flows through the largest, most biologically rich rain forest on Earth. Some of the people in the Amazon Basin are among the least touched by the modern world, although the press of logging, agriculture, and settlement has devastated much of the forest and its scattered inhabitants. Other South American features also stand out. The Pantanal, spanning parts of Brazil, Paraguay, and Bolivia with flooded grasslands and savannas, is 17 times the size of the Florida Everglades and home to a kaleidoscopic diversity of plant and animal life. The vast grassy plains of the Argentine Pampas nourish livestock, but the Atacama Desert of Chile supports little life. Its dry, clear, thin air, however, makes it ideal for astronomical observatories. In the Andes, the Inca empire expanded between 1438 and 1527, stretching from modern Colombia to western Argentina. Weakened by internal dissension, the Inca succumbed to Francisco Pizarro's forces in 1533. Spaniards looted its golden treasures and forced native slave labor to work gold and silver mines; Portuguese overlords imported millions of slaves from Africa to work Brazilian plantations. Not until the early 19th century under Simón Bolívar, the Liberator of the Americas, did the desire for independence coalesce and rebellion spread rapidly. Yet even after the colonial period, strife continued during the 20th century with coups, civil wars, and cross-border disputes. Today mining of industrial mineral ores, fishing, forestry, petroleum extraction, and commercial agriculture support the continent's economies, but prosperity does not reach all its people. Populist leaders in countries such as Venezuela and Bolivia are raising their voices, while indigenous peoples' activists are gaining new influence.

IMAGE BY ROBERT STACEY, WORLDSAT INTERNATIONAL INC.

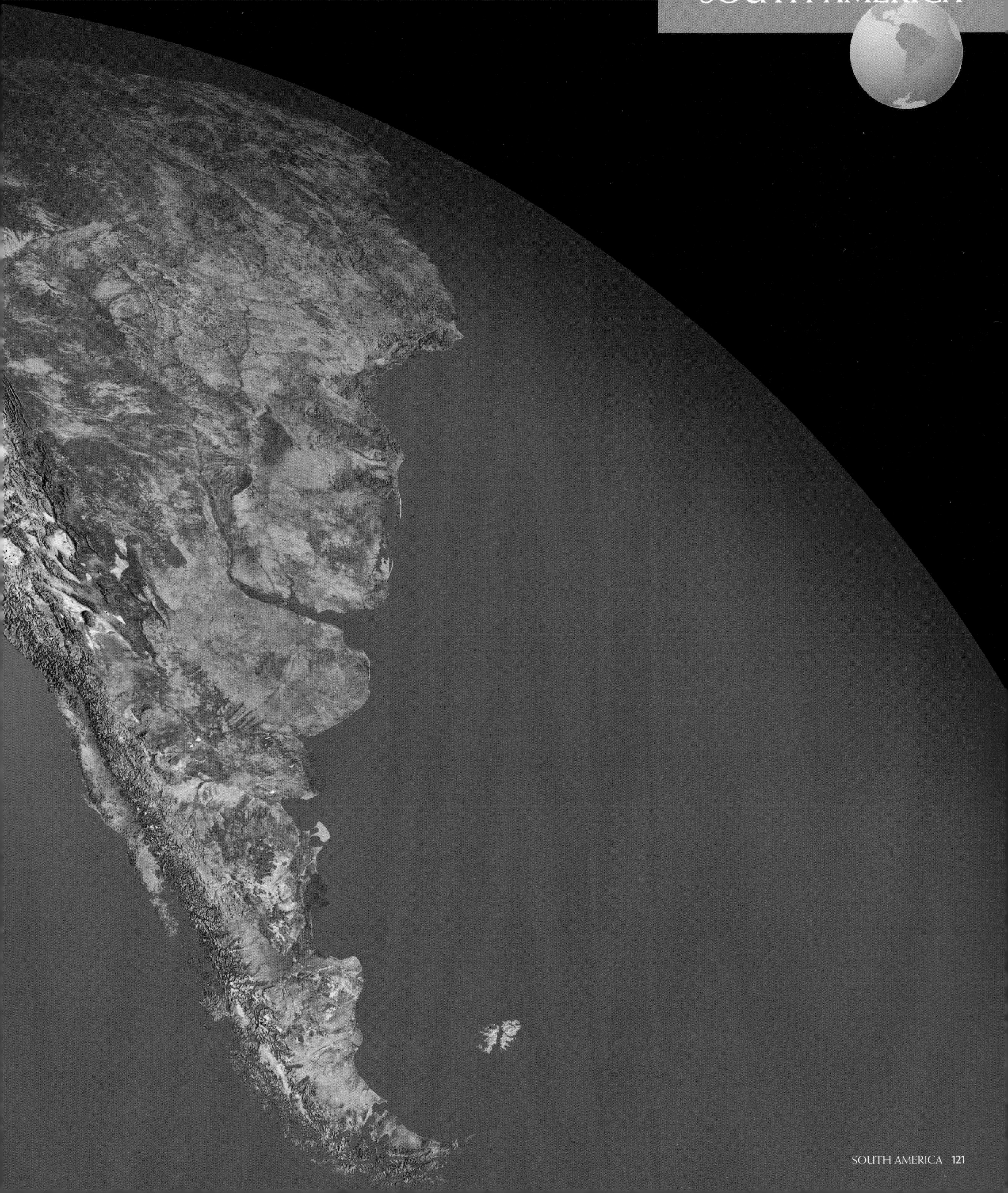

CARIBBEAN Sea

90° 80° 70° Longitude West 50° of Greenwich 40°

GUATEMALA HONDURAS
Coco
EL SALVADOR NICARAGUA
Tegucigalpa
Managua
Volcán Irazú 3412
San José 3819
COSTA RICA
Panama City
PANAMA
Golfo de Panamá

Caribbean Sea

Golfo de Venezuela
Barranquilla
Maracaibo 5775
Lago de Maracaibo
Isla de Margarita
Port of Spain
Caracas
TRINIDAD AND TOBAGO
Orinoco River Delta

Lesser Antilles

ATLANTIC OCEAN

10°

VENEZUELA
Georgetown
Paramaribo
Angel Falls
GUYANA
2735 Mt. Roraima
2579 GUIANA HIGHLANDS
SURINAME
FRENCH GUIANA
Cayenne
5007
Source of the Orinoco 5007
Serra de Tumucumaque

4080
Medellín
Bogotá
COLOMBIA
Cali 3750
2994 Pico de Neblina
Cabo Norte
Mouths of the Amazon
ILHA DE MARAJÓ

EQUATOR 0°
Quito
ECUADOR
Caquetá
A M A Z O N
Belém
Baía de São Marcos
0°

Galápagos Islands
Guayaquil
Golfo de Guayaquil
Putumayo
Napo
Amazon (Solimões)
Manaus
Amazon
Fortaleza

Punta Pariñas
Punta Negra
Marañón
Javari
Juruá
Madeira
Tapajós
Xingu
Ponta do Calcanhar

PACIFIC
Nev. Huascarán 6768
S e l v a s   B A S I N
Purus
Aripuaña
Iriri
Araguaia
Parnaíba
10°
P E R U
Lima
Mamoré
1995
Juruena
Teles Pires
Tocantins
B R A Z I L
BRAZILIAN
Recife

6425
Nev. Coropuna
Source of the Amazon
Lago Titicaca
La Paz
1995
PLANALTO DO MATO GROSSO
1995
HIGHLANDS
Salvador

BOLIVIA
Sucre
Pantanal
Goiânia
Brasília

OCEAN
20°
Isla San Félix
Isla San Ambrosio
CHILE
Volcán Llullaillaco 6723
PARAGUAY
Asunción
Gran Chaco
Belo Horizonte
2890
Bandeira
20°

TROPIC OF CAPRICORN
Cerro Ojos del Salado 6880
Cerro del Toro 6880
Salinas Ambargasta
Salinas Grandes
Paraná
Iguazú Falls
Curitiba
São Paulo
Rio de Janeiro
Cabo Frío
Cabo de Santa Marta Grande

Islas Juan Fernández
Highest point in South America
Cerro Aconcagua 6959 (22831 ft)
Córdoba
Entre Ríos
Uruguay
URUGUAY
Porto Alegre
Lagoa dos Patos

30°
Santiago
A R G E N T I N A
Buenos Aires
Montevideo
Río de la Plata
Bahía Samborombón
30°

4709 Volcán Domuyo
Pampa
ATLANTIC

Negro
Bahía Blanca
OCEAN

Golfo San Matías
PENÍNSULA VALDÉS
40°
Archipiélago de los Chonos
Golfo San Jorge
Cabo Tres Puntas
40°

Península de Taitao 1372
Patagonia
Lowest point in South America
Laguna del Carbón
-105 (-344 ft)
Bahía Grande

West Falkland
Stanley
East Falkland

Strait of Magellan
Falkland Islands

AZIMUTHAL EQUIDISTANT PROJECTION
SCALE 1:31,000,000
0 KILOMETERS 600 800
0 MILES 200 400 600 800

Tierra del Fuego

Scotia Sea
Cape Disappointment
South Georgia

50°
Cabo de Hornos (Cape Horn)
100° 90° 80° 70° 60° 50° 40° 30° 20°
50°

ATLANTIC OCEAN

PACIFIC OCEAN

ATLANTIC OCEAN

Caribbean Sea

Countries and regions:

GUATEMALA, HONDURAS, EL SALVADOR, NICARAGUA, COSTA RICA, PANAMA, VENEZUELA, COLOMBIA, ECUADOR, PERU, BOLIVIA, CHILE, ARGENTINA, URUGUAY, PARAGUAY, BRAZIL, GUYANA, SURINAME, FRENCH GUIANA, TRINIDAD AND TOBAGO

ST. LUCIA, ST. VINCENT & THE GRENADINES, GRENADA, BARBADOS, Aruba (Neth.), Bonaire, Curaçao, Neth. Antilles

Selected cities and features:

Tegucigalpa, Puerto Cabezas, León, Granada, Bluefields, Managua, San José, COSTA RICA, Vol. Irazú 3412, Pto. Limón, Colón, Panamá, PANAMA, David, Puerto Armuelles, Golfo de Panamá

Santa Marta, Barranquilla, Cartagena, Maracaibo, +5775, Amuay, Puerto Cabello, La Guaira, Cumaná, Port of Spain, Caracas, Maturín, Mérida, Montería, Cúcuta, Bucaramanga, Ciudad Bolívar, Ciudad Guayana, Morawhanna

Bello, Medellín, Manizales, BOGOTÁ, Ibagué, Villavicencio, Puerto Ayacucho, Georgetown, Nieuw Amsterdam, Paramaribo, St.-Laurent du Maroni, Cayenne, Angel Falls, Luepa, Mt. Roraima 2739, Oiapoque

Buenaventura, Cali, COLOMBIA, Popayán, Calamar, San Carlos, Boa Vista, Caracaraí, Lethem, 5007, Cottica, Calçoene, Amapá, Cabo Norte, Bailique

San Lorenzo, Tumaco, Pasto, Esmeraldas, Mitú, Pico de Neblina 2994, Novo Paraíso, 5007, Macapá

Quito, Ibarra, Chimborazo, Güeppí, La Pedrera, Japurá, Fonte Boa, Carvoeiro, Monte Alegre, Gurupá, ILHA DE MARAJÓ, Bragança, São Luís, Chaves, Belém, Abaetetuba, Curralinho

Manta, Portoviejo, ECUADOR, São Paulo de Olivença, Iquitos, Leticia, Tefé, Óbidos, Parintins, Santarém, Camocim, Sobral, Fortaleza

Guayaquil, Cuenca, Machala, Loja, Tumbes, Coari, Itacoatiara, Manaus, Itaituba, Tucuruí, Brejo, Parnaíba, Bacabal, Caxias, Ipu, Aracati, Ponta do Calcanhar

Punta Pariñas, Talara, Paita, Piura, Punta Negra, Tarapoto, Jutaí, Borba, Manicoré, Marabá, Imperatriz, Teresina, Crateús, Iguatu, Mossoró, Natal

Chiclayo, Cajamarca, Contamana, Eirunepé, Lábrea, Prainha, Humaitá, Calama, Barra do São Manuel, Jacareacanga, Carolina, Juazeiro do Norte, Campina Grande, João Pessoa

Pacasmayo, Trujillo, PERU, Cruzeiro do Sul, Pucallpa, Boca do Acre, Madeira, Cachimbo, Araguaína, Conceição do Araguaia, Pedro Afonso, Patos, Recife, Caruaru

Chimbote, Huaraz, Huánuco, Rio Branco, Guajará-Mirim, Porto Velho, Ji-Paraná, Itaúba, BRAZIL, Porto Nacional, Barra, Xique Xique, Juazeiro, Garanhuns, Arapiraca, Propriá, Penedo, Maceió

Cerro de Pasco, LIMA, Callao, Huancayo, Cobija, Riberalta, Príncipe da Beira, Vilhena, Itaúba, Sinop, Parecis, Peixe, Barreiras, Sítio do Mato, Jequié, Itabuna, Estância, Alagoinhas

Huancavelica, Ayacucho, Puerto Maldonado, Trinidad, PLANALTO DO MATO GROSSO, Vila Bela da Santíssima Trindade, Porangatu, Carinhanha, Januária, Feira de Santana, Ilhéus

Pisco, Ica, Nasca, Cusco, Abancay, Juliaca, Nev. Coropuna 6425, L. Titicaca, 1078, Cáceres, Cuiabá, Anápolis, Brasília, Vitória da Conquista, Canavieiras

Arequipa, Matarani, Moquegua, La Paz, BOLIVIA, Cochabamba, Santa Cruz, San José de Chiquitos, Rio Verde, Goiânia, Uberlândia, Pirapora, Diamantina, Governador Valadares, Caravelas

Tacna, Arica, +1995, Oruro, Potosí, Sucre, Camiri, Corumbá, Coxim, Araguari, Curvelo, Uberaba, Montes Claros, 2890, Vitória

Pisagua, Salar de Uyuni, Tarija, Mariscal Estigarribia, Aguaray, Campo Grande, São José do Rio Preto, Ribeirão Preto, Bandeira 2890, Belo Horizonte, Juiz de Fora

Tocopilla, Calama, Gran Chaco, Concepción, Londrina, Campinas, Sorocaba, Volta Redonda, Nova Friburgo, Campos

Mejillones, Antofagasta, 6723, San Salvador de Jujuy, PARAGUAY, Asunción, Villarrica, Araçatuba, Bauru, SÃO PAULO, Santos, RIO DE JANEIRO

Taltal, Volcán Llullaillaco, Cerro Ojos del Salado, San Miguel de Tucumán, Formosa, Curitiba, Iguape, Paranaguá, Iguaçu Falls

Diego de Almagro, Chañaral, Caldera, 6880, Belén, Resistencia, Corrientes, Posadas, Joinville

Huasco, Sarco, Cerro del Toro 6880, Catamarca, Santiago del Estero, Mercedes, Goya, Uruguaiana, Passo Fundo, Imbituba, Florianópolis, Tubarão

La Serena, La Rioja, Bagé, Caxias do Sul, Porto Alegre

CHILE, Ovalle, San Juan, Córdoba, Salto, Paysandú, Pelotas, Rio Grande

Los Vilos, Cerro Aconcagua 6959, Mendoza, Río Cuarto, Paraná, URUGUAY, Treinta-y-Tres

Islas Juan Fernández, Valparaíso, Santiago, San Luis, Rosario, Rocha, Montevideo

Rancagua, Curicó, Talca, ARGENTINA, San Rafael, Pehuajó, Olavarría, Tandil

Chillán, 4709, Concepción, Santa Rosa, Tres Arroyos, Necochea, Mar del Plata

Los Ángeles, Temuco, Zapala, Neuquén, Río Colorado, Bahía Blanca

Valdivia, Negro, Viedma, Golfo San Matías, PENÍNSULA VALDÉS

Osorno, San Carlos de Bariloche, Camarones, Golfo San Jorge

Puerto Montt, Ancud, Puerto Madryn, Rawson

Isla Grande de Chiloé, Esquel, Puerto Aisén, Balmaceda, 4035, Comodoro Rivadavia, Cabo Tres Puntas

Archipiélago de los Chonos, Monte San Valentín, Las Heras, Puerto Deseado

Puerto San Julián, -105, Puerto Santa Cruz, Puerto Coig

El Calafate, Río Turbio, Yacimiento Río Turbio, Puerto Natales, Stanley, Falkland Islands (Islas Malvinas) U.K.

Manantiales, ISLA GRANDE DE TIERRA DEL FUEGO, Río Grande, Punta Arenas, Ushuaia, Cabo de Hornos (Cape Horn)

Galápagos Islands (Archipiélago de Colón) Ecuador, Puerto Baquerizo Moreno

Isla San Félix, Isla San Ambrosio, Chile

EQUATOR, TROPIC OF CAPRICORN

Administered by United Kingdom (claimed by Argentina), South Georgia I. U.K., Scotia Sea

AZIMUTHAL EQUIDISTANT PROJECTION
SCALE 1:31,000,000
0 KILOMETERS   600   800
0 MILES   200   400   600   800

Longitude West of Greenwich

SOUTH AMERICA 123

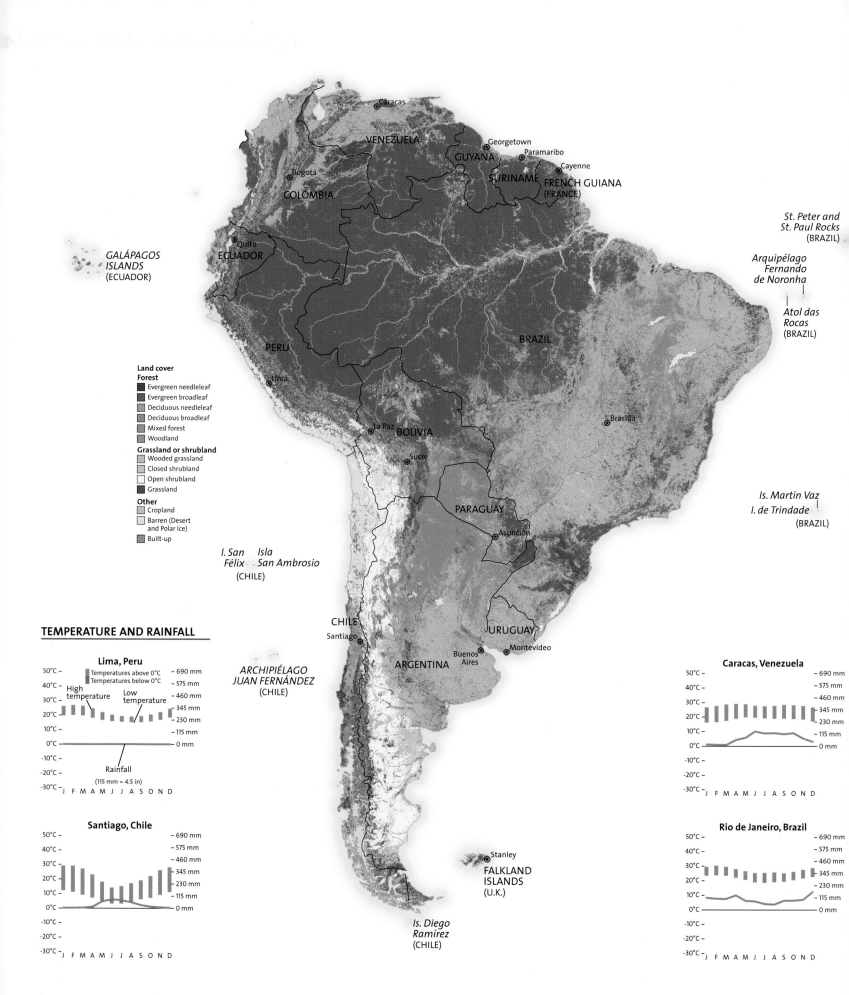

GALÁPAGOS
ISLANDS
(ECUADOR)

VENEZUELA
Caracas

Georgetown
GUYANA
Paramaribo
Bogotá
SURINAME   Cayenne
COLOMBIA   FRENCH GUIANA
                     (FRANCE)

Quito
ECUADOR

St. Peter and
St. Paul Rocks
(BRAZIL)

Arquipélago
Fernando
de Noronha

PERU   BRAZIL   Atol das
                                    Rocas
Lima   (BRAZIL)

Land cover
Forest
Evergreen needleleaf
Evergreen broadleaf
Deciduous needleleaf
Deciduous broadleaf
Mixed forest
Woodland

Grassland or shrubland
Wooded grassland
Closed shrubland
Open shrubland
Grassland

Other
Cropland
Barren (Desert
and Polar Ice)
Built-up

La Paz
BOLIVIA
Sucre

Brasília

Is. Martin Vaz
I. de Trindade
(BRAZIL)

PARAGUAY

I. San   Isla
Félix   San Ambrosio
(CHILE)

Asunción

TEMPERATURE AND RAINFALL

Lima, Peru

50°C –   – 690 mm
40°C –   – 575 mm
High   Low   – 460 mm
30°C – temperature temperature – 345 mm
20°C –   – 230 mm
10°C –   – 115 mm
0°C –   – 0 mm
-10°C –   Rainfall
-20°C –
          (115 mm = 4.5 in)
-30°C – J F M A M J J A S O N D

Temperatures above 0°C
Temperatures below 0°C

CHILE
Santiago

ARCHIPIÉLAGO
JUAN FERNÁNDEZ
(CHILE)

URUGUAY
Montevideo
Buenos
Aires
ARGENTINA

Caracas, Venezuela

50°C –   – 690 mm
40°C –   – 575 mm
30°C –   – 460 mm
20°C –   – 345 mm
10°C –   – 230 mm
0°C –   – 115 mm
-10°C –   – 0 mm
-20°C –
-30°C – J F M A M J J A S O N D

Santiago, Chile

50°C –   – 690 mm
40°C –   – 575 mm
30°C –   – 460 mm
20°C –   – 345 mm
10°C –   – 230 mm
0°C –   – 115 mm
-10°C –   – 0 mm
-20°C –
-30°C – J F M A M J J A S O N D

Rio de Janeiro, Brazil

50°C –   – 690 mm
40°C –   – 575 mm
30°C –   – 460 mm
20°C –   – 345 mm
10°C –   – 230 mm
0°C –   – 115 mm
0°C –   – 0 mm
-10°C –
-20°C –
-30°C – J F M A M J J A S O N D

Stanley
FALKLAND
ISLANDS
(U.K.)

Is. Diego
Ramírez
(CHILE)

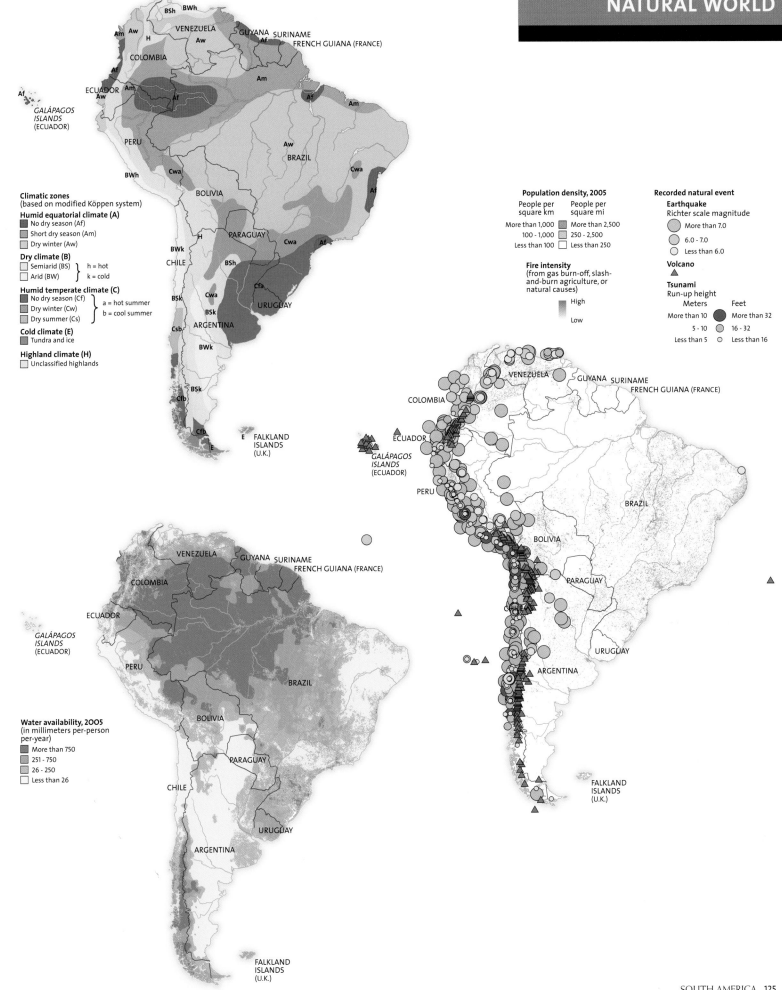

Climatic zones
(based on modified Köppen system)

Humid equatorial climate (A)
- No dry season (Af)
- Short dry season (Am)
- Dry winter (Aw)

Dry climate (B)
- Semiarid (BS)   } h = hot
- Arid (BW)   } k = cold

Humid temperate climate (C)
- No dry season (Cf)
- Dry winter (Cw)   } a = hot summer
- Dry summer (Cs)   } b = cool summer

Cold climate (E)
- Tundra and ice

Highland climate (H)
- Unclassified highlands

Population density, 2005

People per square km	People per square mi
More than 1,000	More than 2,500
100 - 1,000	250 - 2,500
Less than 100	Less than 250

Fire intensity
(from gas burn-off, slash-and-burn agriculture, or natural causes)

High
Low

Recorded natural event

Earthquake
Richter scale magnitude
- More than 7.0
- 6.0 - 7.0
- Less than 6.0

Volcano

Tsunami
Run-up height

Meters	Feet
More than 10	More than 32
5 - 10	16 - 32
Less than 5	Less than 16

Water availability, 2005
(in millimeters per-person per-year)
- More than 750
- 251 - 750
- 26 - 250
- Less than 26

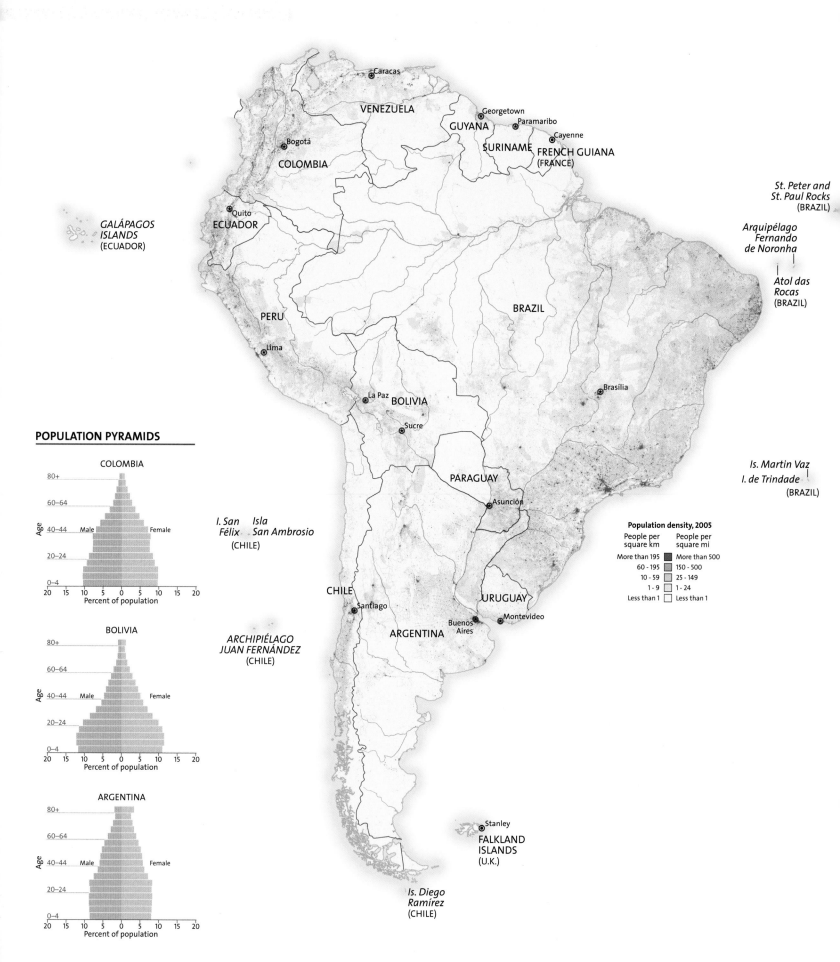

Caracas

VENEZUELA

Georgetown
GUYANA
Paramaribo
SURINAME
Cayenne
FRENCH GUIANA
(FRANCE)

Bogotá

COLOMBIA

St. Peter and
St. Paul Rocks
(BRAZIL)

Quito
ECUADOR

GALÁPAGOS
ISLANDS
(ECUADOR)

Arquipélago
Fernando
de Noronha

Atol das
Rocas
(BRAZIL)

PERU

BRAZIL

Lima

Brasília

POPULATION PYRAMIDS

La Paz
BOLIVIA

Sucre

Is. Martin Vaz
I. de Trindade
(BRAZIL)

COLOMBIA

PARAGUAY

Asunción

I. San
Félix
Isla
San Ambrosio
(CHILE)

Population density, 2005

People per
square km

People per
square mi

More than 195

More than 500

60 - 195

150 - 500

10 - 59

25 - 149

1 - 9

1 - 24

Less than 1

Less than 1

BOLIVIA

ARCHIPIÉLAGO
JUAN FERNÁNDEZ
(CHILE)

CHILE

URUGUAY

Santiago

Montevideo

Buenos
Aires

ARGENTINA

ARGENTINA

Stanley

FALKLAND
ISLANDS
(U.K.)

Is. Diego
Ramírez
(CHILE)

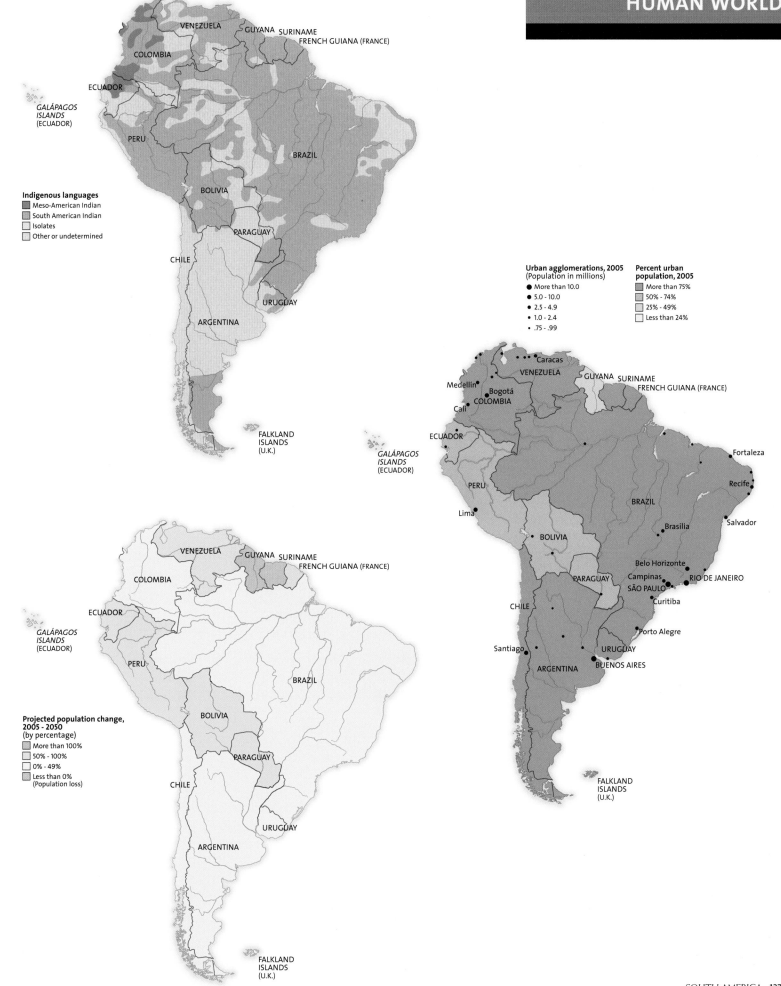

Indigenous languages
- Meso-American Indian
- South American Indian
- Isolates
- Other or undetermined

Urban agglomerations, 2005
(Population in millions)
- ● More than 10.0
- ● 5.0 - 10.0
- ● 2.5 - 4.9
- • 1.0 - 2.4
- · .75 - .99

Percent urban population, 2005
- More than 75%
- 50% - 74%
- 25% - 49%
- Less than 24%

Projected population change, 2005 - 2050
(by percentage)
- More than 100%
- 50% - 100%
- 0% - 49%
- Less than 0% (Population loss)

GALÁPAGOS ISLANDS (ECUADOR)

VENEZUELA
GUYANA
SURINAME
FRENCH GUIANA (FRANCE)
COLOMBIA
ECUADOR
PERU
BRAZIL
BOLIVIA
PARAGUAY
CHILE
URUGUAY
ARGENTINA
FALKLAND ISLANDS (U.K.)

Caracas
Medellín
Bogotá
Cali
Lima
Fortaleza
Recife
Brasília
Salvador
Belo Horizonte
Campinas
RIO DE JANEIRO
SÃO PAULO
Curitiba
Porto Alegre
Santiago
BUENOS AIRES

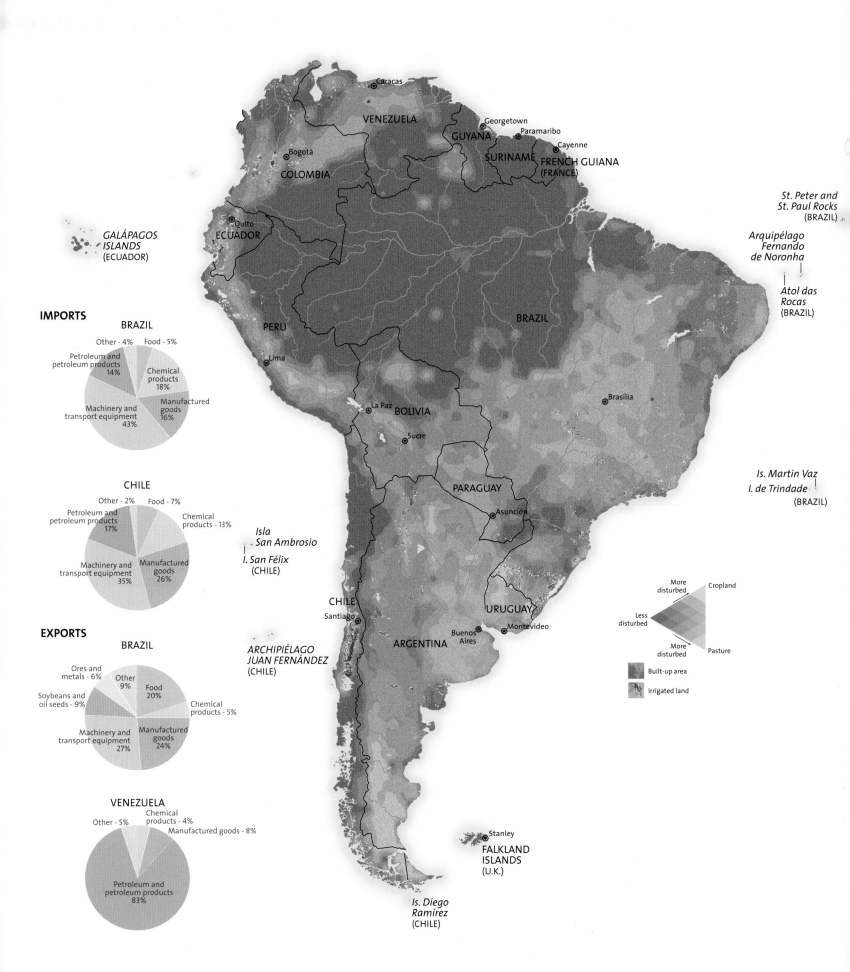

Caracas

VENEZUELA

Bogotá

COLOMBIA

Georgetown
Paramaribo
GUYANA
Cayenne
SURINAME
FRENCH GUIANA
(FRANCE)

St. Peter and
St. Paul Rocks
(BRAZIL)

Quito
ECUADOR

GALÁPAGOS
ISLANDS
(ECUADOR)

Arquipélago
Fernando
de Noronha

Atol das
Rocas
(BRAZIL)

PERU

BRAZIL

IMPORTS

BRAZIL

Lima

Brasília

Other - 4%   Food - 5%
Petroleum and
petroleum products
14%

Chemical
products
18%

Machinery and
transport equipment
43%

Manufactured
goods
16%

La Paz   BOLIVIA

Sucre

Is. Martin Vaz
I. de Trindade
(BRAZIL)

CHILE

Other - 2%   Food - 7%
Petroleum and
petroleum products
17%

Chemical
products - 13%

Machinery and
transport equipment
35%

Manufactured
goods
26%

PARAGUAY

Asunción

Isla
San Ambrosio
I. San Félix
(CHILE)

More
disturbed   Cropland

Less
disturbed

More
disturbed   Pasture

Built-up area

Irrigated land

EXPORTS

BRAZIL

CHILE

URUGUAY

Santiago

Montevideo

Ores and
metals - 6%
Soybeans and
oil seeds - 9%

Other
9%   Food
20%

Chemical
products - 5%

Machinery and
transport equipment
27%

Manufactured
goods
24%

ARCHIPIÉLAGO
JUAN FERNÁNDEZ
(CHILE)

Buenos
Aires

ARGENTINA

VENEZUELA

Chemical
products - 4%
Other - 5%   Manufactured goods - 8%

Petroleum and
petroleum products
83%

Stanley
FALKLAND
ISLANDS
(U.K.)

Is. Diego
Ramírez
(CHILE)

Dominant economy, 2005
(per GDP sector)

- Service
- Service - Industrial
- Service - Industrial - Agricultural
- No data available

GALÁPAGOS ISLANDS (ECUADOR)

VENEZUELA
GUYANA
SURINAME
FRENCH GUIANA (FRANCE)
COLOMBIA
ECUADOR
PERU
BRAZIL
BOLIVIA
PARAGUAY
CHILE
URUGUAY
ARGENTINA
FALKLAND ISLANDS (U.K.)

SERVICE 100%

PERU
SURINAME
VENEZUELA
GUYANA

AGRICULTURAL 100%   **INDUSTRIAL 100%**

SOUTH AMERICA'S ECONOMY
per Gross Domestic Product
(GDP) sector

Per capita energy consumption, 2003
(in million Btu)

- More than 300
- 201 - 300
- 101 - 200
- 31 - 100
- Less than 30

Major energy deposit

- Coal
- Natural gas
- Oil
- Oil pipeline

VENEZUELA
GUYANA
SURINAME
FRENCH GUIANA (FRANCE)
COLOMBIA
ECUADOR
GALÁPAGOS ISLANDS (ECUADOR)
PERU
BRAZIL
BOLIVIA
PARAGUAY
CHILE
ARGENTINA
URUGUAY
FALKLAND ISLANDS (U.K.)

VENEZUELA
GUYANA SURINAME
FRENCH GUIANA (FRANCE)
COLOMBIA
ECUADOR
GALÁPAGOS ISLANDS (ECUADOR)
PERU
BRAZIL
BOLIVIA
PARAGUAY
CHILE
URUGUAY
ARGENTINA
FALKLAND ISLANDS (U.K.)

**Percentage of population living
on less than $2 per day, 2005**

- More than 75%
- 50% - 74%
- 25% - 49%
- Less than 25%
- No data available

CARIBBEAN

San Salvador
EL SALVADOR
HONDURAS
Murra Siuna
Kilambé Kuikuina
San Pedro del Norte
Prinzapolka
SAN ANDRÉS Roncador Bank
Y PROVIDENCIA
I. de Providencia Colombia
Neth. ARUBA
Oranjestad
Punta Gallinas
Cabo de la Vela
Península de La Guajira
Pen. de Paraguaná
Punta Fijo

San Miguel
Puerto El Triunfo
Punta San Juan
Somotillo
Jinotega
Estelí
Co. Musún
La Barra
Isla de San Andrés Colombia
SIERRA NEVADA DE SANTA MARTA
Santa Marta
Riohacha
San Rafael
Paraguaipoa
Golfo de Venezuela

NICARAGUA
León
Managua
Masaya
VOLCÁN MASAYA N.P.
Tipitapa
La Libertad
Rama
Bluefields
Haulover
Green Point
Punta Gorda
Lago de Nicaragua
Barranquilla
ATLÁNTICO
Cartagena
Valledupar
CÉSAR
Machiques
Maracaibo
ZULIA
Barquisimet

COSTA RICA
Vol. Miravalles
Liberia
Nicoya
Tortuguero
Parismina
Puerto Limón
CAHUITA N.P.
San José
PORTOBELO
Portobelo N.P.
El Porvenir
Piña
CHAGRES N.P.
Aligandí
Carmen de Bolívar
Tolú
San Antero
Lorica
Sincelejo
Magangué
SUCRE
San Marcos
CÓRDOBA
Montería
El Banco
Ocaña
TRUJILLO
Valera
Bobures
Mérida
Barinas
PICO SIERRA NEVADA N.P.

SANTA ROSA N.P.
Cabo Santa Elena
Punta Guiones
Cabo Blanco
Golfo de Nicoya
LA AMISTAD N.P.
Ciudad Cortés
CORCOVADO N.P.
Puerto Jiménez
Puerto Armuelles
Golfo de Chiriquí
Co. Chirripó
Co. Kámuk
Vol. Barú
Co. Hornito
PANAMÁ
Chimán
Puerto Obaldía
LOS KATÍOS N.P.
Mutatá
Valdivia
ANTIOQUIA
PARAMILLO N.P.
PAMPLONA
San Cristóbal
EL TAMA N.P.
Arauca

Chitré
Península de Azuero
Punta Mala
Co. Cambutal
Golfo de Panamá
Co. Pirré
Jaqué
Riosucio
Cupica
Punta Solano
Medellín
Bello
Envigado
Vélez
Socorro
SANTANDER
Bucaramanga
EL COCUY N.P.
Rondón
ARAUCA

Isla del Coco
Costa Rica
Cabo Corrientes
Bajo Baudó
Quibdó
Sonsón
Manizales
RISARALDA
Honda
Monterrey
Yopal
CASANARE
San Luis de Palenque
Orocué

ADMINISTRATIVE AREAS OF VENEZUELA AND THEIR CAPITALS
(Numbered in blue where not labeled on map)

1 **Aragua** (Maracay)
2 **Capital District** (Caracas)
3 **Miranda** (Los Teques)
4 **Vargas** (La Guaira)

Punta Charambirá
I. de Malpelo Colombia
Pereira
Armenia
QUINDÍO
Ibagué
BOGOTÁ CAPITAL DISTRICT
Villavicencio
META
Puerto López
Restrepo
El Porvenir
San José de Ocuné
VICH

Tuluá
VALLE DEL CAUCA
Palmira
TOLIMA
SUMAPAZ N.P.
San Martín
Granada
COLOMBIA
Mapiripana
Trinida
GUAVIARE
Calamar
Mitú
VAUPÉS

FARALLONES DE CALI N.P.
Cali
Neiva
HUILA
SERRANÍA DE LA MACARENA
San José del Guaviare
Miraflores

Punta Reyes
Punta Guascama
SANQUIANGA N.P.
Popayán
CAUCA
Timbío
Mercaderes
Garzón
Florencia
CORDILLERA DE LOS PICACHOS N.P.
Co. Otare
CAQUETÁ
CHIRIBIQUETE N.P.

Cabo Manglares
Valdez
NARIÑO
Pasto
Mocoa
Tres Esquinas
LA PAYA N.P.

Esmeraldas
Punta Galera
Cabo de San Francisco
Muisne
San Lorenzo
Túquerres
Tulcán
PUTUMAYO
Putumayo
Güeppi
Puerto Leguízamo
Araracuara
Guamareyes
AMAZONAS
CAHUINARÍ N.P.
Puerto Miraña

EQUATOR
Ibarra
Otavalo
Cayambe
SUMACO-NAPO GALERAS N.P.
Nuevo Rocafuerte
Santa María

Isla Pinta
Isla Marchena
Isla Genovesa
I. Darwin
I. Wolf
Santo Domingo de los Colorados
Quito
COTOPAXI N.P.
Cotopaxi
Tena
LLANGANATES N.P.
YASUNÍ N.P.
Puerto Curaray
Santa Clotilde
Bellavista

I. Isabela
I. San Salvador
Fernandina
Puerto Villamil
I. Santa Cruz
Puerto Ayora
Isla San Cristóbal
Puerto Baquerizo Moreno
Bahía de Caráquez
Chone
Manta
Quevedo
Ambato
Riobamba
SANGAY N.P.
Macas
Cononaco
Posto Cunambo
Puerto Curaray

Montecristi
Portoviejo
MACHALILLA N.P.
ECUADOR
Sangay
Yaupí
Andoas

GALÁPAGOS ISLANDS
(Archipiélago de Colón)
Ecuador
I. Santa María
Isla Española

Guayaquil
Eloy Alfaro
Salinas
Santa Elena
La Libertad
Playas
Isla Puná
Balao
Machala
Cuenca
Pasaje
Zamora
Soledad
Santa Rosa
Sinchiyacu
Iquitos
Francisco de Orellana
Pebas
AMACAYACU N.P.
Santa Rit

Golfo de Guayaquil
Tumbes
Zorritos
TUMBES
CERROS DE AMOTAPE N.P.
Zaruma
Macará
Loja
Borja
Puerto América
LORETO
Tamshiyacu
Caballococha
Remate de Males
Caxias
Atalaia
Letíc

PACIFIC OCEAN
Lobitos
Punta Pariñas
Lagunitos
Paita
Catacaos
Piura
AMAZONAS
CAJAMARCA
San Ignacio
Puerto América
San Isidro
Lagunas
Tamánco
Nauta
Requena
Santa Cruz
Negro
Eirunepé

Punta Aguja
Punta Negra
Bayóvar
Isla Lobos de Tierra
Motupe
Chachapoyas
Jumbilla
Moyobamba
SAN MARTÍN
Lamas
Navarro
Yurimaguas
Rodrigues
Ipixuna
Envira

LAMBAYEQUE
Lambayeque
Bambamarca
Cajamarca
Orellana
Contamana
São Salvador
SERRA DO DIVISOR
Cruzeiro do Sul
Feijó

Chiclayo
Mocupe
Pacasmayo
San Pedro de Lloc
Bolívar
Huamachuco
San Jerónimo
Tarauacá

Puerto Chicama
Paiján
LA LIBERTAD
ABISEO N.P.
RÍO
Tirután
Pucallpa
Masisea
Puerto Alegre
Marechal Thaumaturgo

Trujillo
Virú
Cabana
Pomabamba
Uchiza
Puerto Portillo
Foz do Jordão
Santa Rosa do Purus
Esperanza
Assis Bras

Chimbote
Casma
Huaraz
ANCASH
Nevado Huascarán
HUASCARÁN N.P.
TINGO MARÍA N.P.
HUÁNUCO
Huánuco
YANACHAGA CHEMILLÉN N.P.
Sheboya
Bolognesi
Ulbio

Huarmey
Punta Cabeza de Lagarto
Punta Las Zorras
Patívilca
Huaura
PASCO
Cerro de Pasco
Gran Pajonal
Atalaya
Sepahua

AZIMUTHAL EQUIDISTANT PROJECTION
SCALE 1:12,000,000
0 KILOMETERS 200 300
0 MILES 100 200 300

Huaral
Palpa
Huacho
Merced
Satipo
JUNÍN
Chancay
La Oroya
Camisea
MANU NATIONAL PARK

LIMA
Callao
Lima
Chosica
Huancayo
Pampas
Pariacaca
Co. Payne

San Vicente de Cañete
Cerro Azul
Imperial
Huancavelica
CUS
San Bartolo
Santa Bárbara
Vilcabamba
Machu Picchu
Cusco

Tambo de Mora
Pisco
ICA
AYACUCHO
Ayacucho
APURÍMAC
Abancay
Mil
Sintuya
Inambari
Quillabamba
MADRE DE DIO

Ica
Quince
BAHÍA SONENE
Macusani
PUNO

SEA

ATLANTIC
OCEAN

St. LUCIA
Castries
Kingstown
ST. VINCENT
AND THE
GRENADINES
Bridgetown
BARBADOS
Tobago Basin
GRENADA
St. George's
Charlotteville Tobago
TRINIDAD AND TOBAGO
Port of Spain

ARCHIPIÉLAGO
LOS ROQUES N.P.
Is. de
Aves
Venez.
Is. Los
Roques
Venez.
Isla
Blanquilla
Venez.
Isla La Tortuga
Venez.
Isla de Margarita
La Asunción
Nueva
Esparta
Mochima
N.P.
Isla Coche
Galeota
Point
San Fernando
Gulf of
Paria
Punta Araguapiche

CORO
Bonaire
MORROCOY N.P.
Chichiriviche
Tucacas
La Guaira
Caracas
Petare
Los Teques
Maracay
Puerto La Cruz
Cumaná
Carúpano
SUCRE
Maturín
MONAGAS
Pedernales
DELTA
AMACURO
Curiapo
San José
de Amacuro
MARIUSA
N.P.
Tucupita
Barrancas

NEZUELA
GUÁRICO
ANZOÁTEGUI
Ciudad Guayana
Morawhanna
Shell Beach
Mabaruma
Hosororo

BOLÍVAR
Ciudad Bolívar
Guri Dam
El Pao
Matthew's Ridge
Port Kaituma
Charity

EQUATOR

AMAZONAS
BRAZIL
PARÁ
MARANHÃO

BOLIVIA
MATO GROSSO
GOIÁS
BAHIA

SOUTH AMERICA 131

ANTARES
Anajás
Belém
Bragança
Muaná
Castanhal
Viseu
Abaetetuba
Capitão Poço
Curralinho
Cametá
Camiranga
I. Mangunça
Cururupu
Mocajuba
Porfirio
Canindé
Guimarães
ALCÁNTARA SPACEPORT
LENÇÓIS MARANHENSES N.P.
São João de Cortes
Tucuruí
São Luís
I. de São Luís
I. do Caju
Primeira Cruz
I. das Canárias
Ponta dos Patos
Marabá
Itupiranga
Represa de Tucuruí
Serra do Gurupi
Peri Mirim
São Bento
Mortos
Ilha Grande de Santa Isabel
Parnaíba
Camocim
Granja
Paracuru
Remansão
Jatobal
São Raimundo
Viana
Penalva
Arari
Rosário
Morrinhos
Açaraú
Acaraú
Caucaia
Fortaleza
do Araguaia
Santa Inês
Itapecuru Mirim
Urbano Santos
Sobral
Tianguá
Ipu
Maranguape
Cascavel
Tocantinópolis
MARANHÃO
Bacabal
Chapadinha
Brejo
Piripiri
Piracuruca
Pacujá
Fortim
Aracati
São Geraldo do Araguaia
Coelho Neto
Porto
Barras
Campo Maior
Ipueiras
Baturité
Russas
Mossoró
Macau
Araguatins
Presidente Dutra
Pedreiras
Peritoró
União
Oiticica
Tamboril
Quixadá
RIO GRANDE DO NORTE
Porto Franco
Caxias
Timon
Teresina
CEARÁ
Independência
Caraúbas
Currais Novos
Ceará Mirim
Natal
Araguaína
Barra do Corda
Grajaú
Colinas
Parnarama
Regeneração
Tauá
Iguatu
Orós
Patu
Caicó
Goianinha
Filadélfia
Carolina
Riachão
Balsas
Mirador
Amarante
Jucás
Icó
Sousa
Pombal
Jardim do Seridó
Guarabira
Rio Tinto
TOCANTINS
Palmeirante
Serra das Alpercatas
Pastos Bons
Barão de Grajaú
Floriano
Picos
Fronteiras
Cajazeiras
Conceição
PARAÍBA
João Pessoa
Conceição do Araguaia
Loreto
Benedito Leite
Uruçuí
PIAUÍ
Jaicós
Simplício Mendes
Crato
Juazeiro do Norte
Sumé
Paulista
Olinda
Recife

SÃO PAULO
MINAS GERAIS
BAHIA
RIO DE JANEIRO
ESPÍRITO SANTO

ATLANTIC OCEAN

Arquipélago de Fernando de Noronha Brazil
Atol das Rocas Brazil

Salvador (Bahia)
Vitória da Conquista
Brasília
DISTRITO FED.
Goiânia
Anápolis
Uberlândia
Belo Horizonte
Juiz de Fora
RIO DE JANEIRO
Niterói
Cabo Frio
SÃO PAULO
Santos
São Vicente
Curitiba
Florianópolis

AZIMUTHAL EQUIDISTANT PROJECTION
SCALE 1:12,000,000
0 KILOMETERS 200 300
0 MILES 100 200 300
Longitude West 45° of Greenwich
TROPIC OF CAPRICORN
SOUTH AMERICA 133

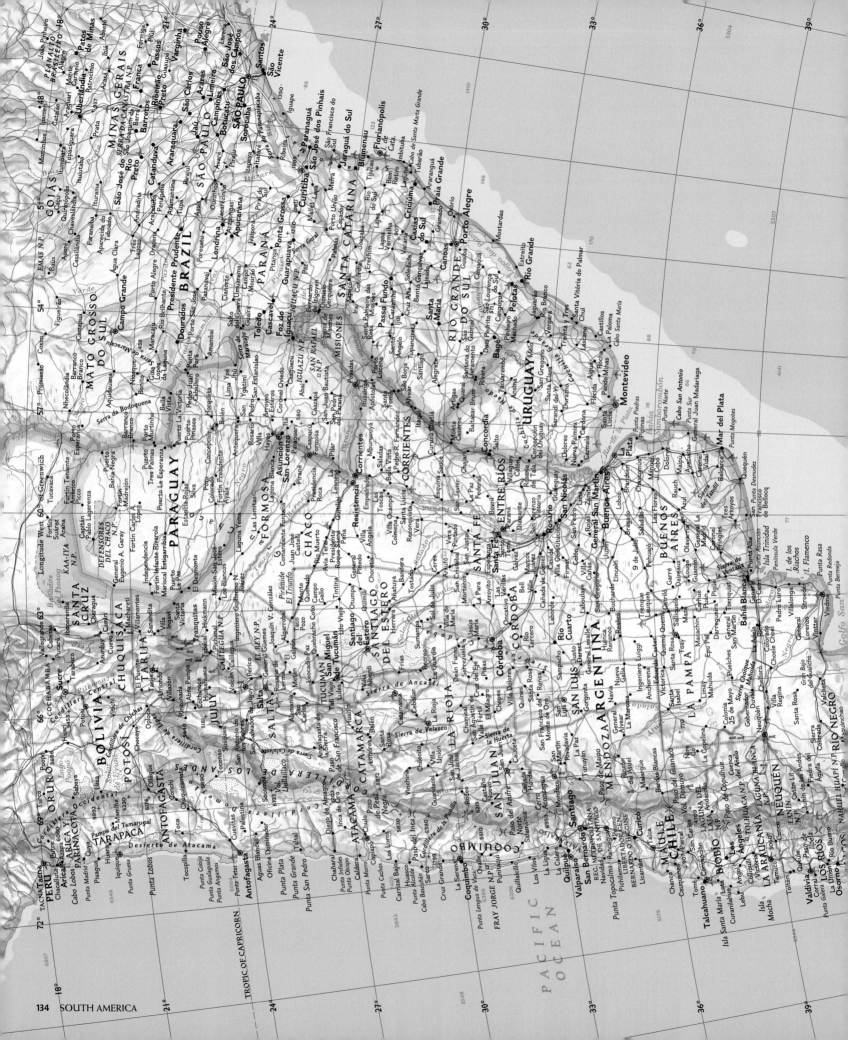

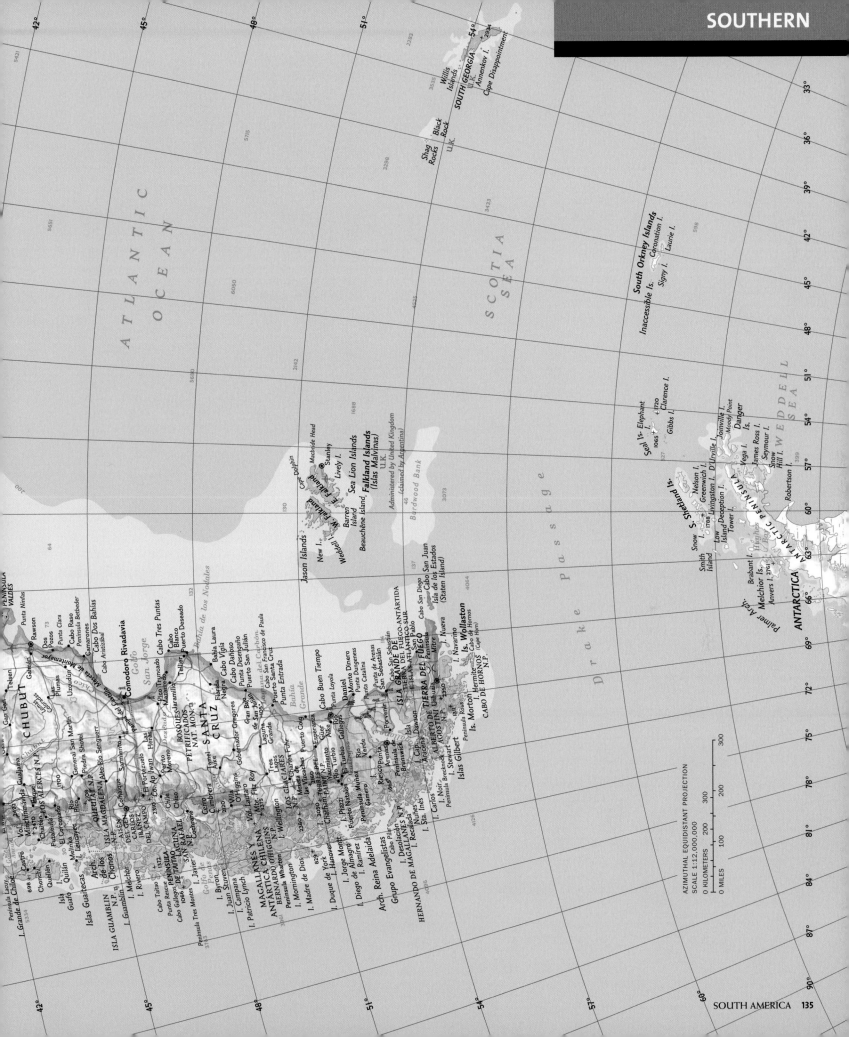

ALTIPLANO

AZIMUTHAL EQUIDISTANT PROJECTION

SCALE 1:6,000,000

0 KILOMETERS 100 150

0 MILES 50 100 150

PACIFIC OCEAN

SOUTHEASTERN BRAZIL

AZIMUTHAL EQUIDISTANT PROJECTION

SCALE 1:7,000,000

0 KILOMETERS 100 150 200

0 MILES 50 100 150 200

States / Regions

TOCANTINS
MATO GROSSO
GOIÁS
DISTRITO FEDERAL
BAHIA
MINAS GERAIS
MATO GROSSO DO SUL
SÃO PAULO
PARANÁ
SANTA CATARINA
RIO GRANDE DO SUL
ESPÍRITO SANTO
RIO DE JANEIRO
B R A Z I L

Selected cities and towns

Araguaçu, Porangatu, Mutunópolis, Estrela do Norte, Mara Rosa, São Miguel do Araguaia, Bandeirante, Cocalinho, Ministro João Alberto, Mozarlândia, Itapaci, Barro Alto, Nova América, Rubiataba, Ceres, Uruana, Rialma, Rianápolis, Goianésia, Gabriel de Goiás, Goiás, Itaberaí, Jaraguá, Pirenópolis, Anápolis, Luziânia, Brasília, Corumbá de Goiás, Inhumas, Anicuns, Trindade, Goiânia, Leopoldo de Bulhões, Silvânia, Bela Vista de Goiás, Hidrolândia, Orizona, Piracanjuba, Pires do Rio, Urutaí, Ipameri, Catalão, Goiatuba, Itumbiara

Cavalcante, Nova Roma, Posse, Iaciara, Alto Paraíso de Goiás, Lajes N.P., Chapada dos Veadeiros, São Domingos de Goiás, Campos Belos, São João da Aliança, Formoso, Buritis, Unaí, Brasília de Minas, Bonfinópolis de Minas, São Romão, São Francisco, Januária, Itacarambi

Correntina, Santa Maria da Vitória, Cocos, Carinhanha, Coribe, Manga, Matias Cardoso, Monte Azul, Espinosa, Mato Verde, Rio Pardo de Minas, Porteirinha, Salinas, Comercinho, Grão Mogol, Medina, Araçuaí, Virgem da Lapa, Minas Novas, Turmalina, Carai, Novo Cruzeiro, Ladainha, Poté, Teófilo Otoni

Bom Jesus da Lapa, Riacho de Santana, Livramento do Brumado, Rio de Contas, Barra da Estiva, Caetité, Guanambi, Palmas de Monte Alto, Urandi, Caculé, Condeúba, Piatã, Manuel Vitorino, Jequié, Poções, Anagé, Vitória da Conquista, Itambé, Encruzilhada, Cândido Sales, Pedra Azul, Jordânia, Itapetinga

Uberlândia, Patos de Minas, Patrocínio, Araxá, Uberaba, Divinópolis, Belo Horizonte, Sete Lagoas, Sabará, Itabira, Montes Claros, Pirapora, Diamantina, Governador Valadares, Colatina, Vitória, Vila Velha, Cariacica, Vitória da Conquista

São José do Rio Preto, Catanduva, Ribeirão Preto, Franca, Barretos, Araraquara, São Carlos, Bauru, Jaú, Araras, Rio Claro, Limeira, Piracicaba, Campinas, Jundiaí, Sorocaba, São Paulo, Santo André, Santos, São Vicente, Taubaté, São José dos Campos, Guaratinguetá, Pindamonhangaba, Resende, Volta Redonda, Barra Mansa, Nova Iguaçu, Duque de Caxias, Niterói, Rio de Janeiro, Cabo Frio, Macaé, Campos, Juiz de Fora, Barbacena, Varginha, Poços de Caldas

Londrina, Apucarana, Maringá, Ponta Grossa, Curitiba, Paranaguá, São José dos Pinhais, Cascavel, Guarapuava, Joinville, Blumenau, Itajaí, Florianópolis, Criciúma, Tubarão, Lajes, Passo Fundo

Physical features

Serra do Roncador, Rio das Mortes, Rio Araguaia, Serra do Espigão Mestre, CHAPADA DIAMANTINA N.P., CHAPADA DOS VEADEIROS, GRANDE SERTÃO VEREDAS N.P., Rio São Francisco, Serra do Espinhaço, PLANALTO, MONTE PASCOAL N.P., Serra do Mar, SERRA DA CANASTRA N.P., SERRA DA BOCAINA NAT. PARK, EMAS N.P., IGUAÇU N.P., SÃO JOAQUIM N.P., Rio Paraná, Rio Paranapanema, Três Marias Dam, Jurumirim Dam, ATLANTIC OCEAN, TROPIC OF CAPRICORN

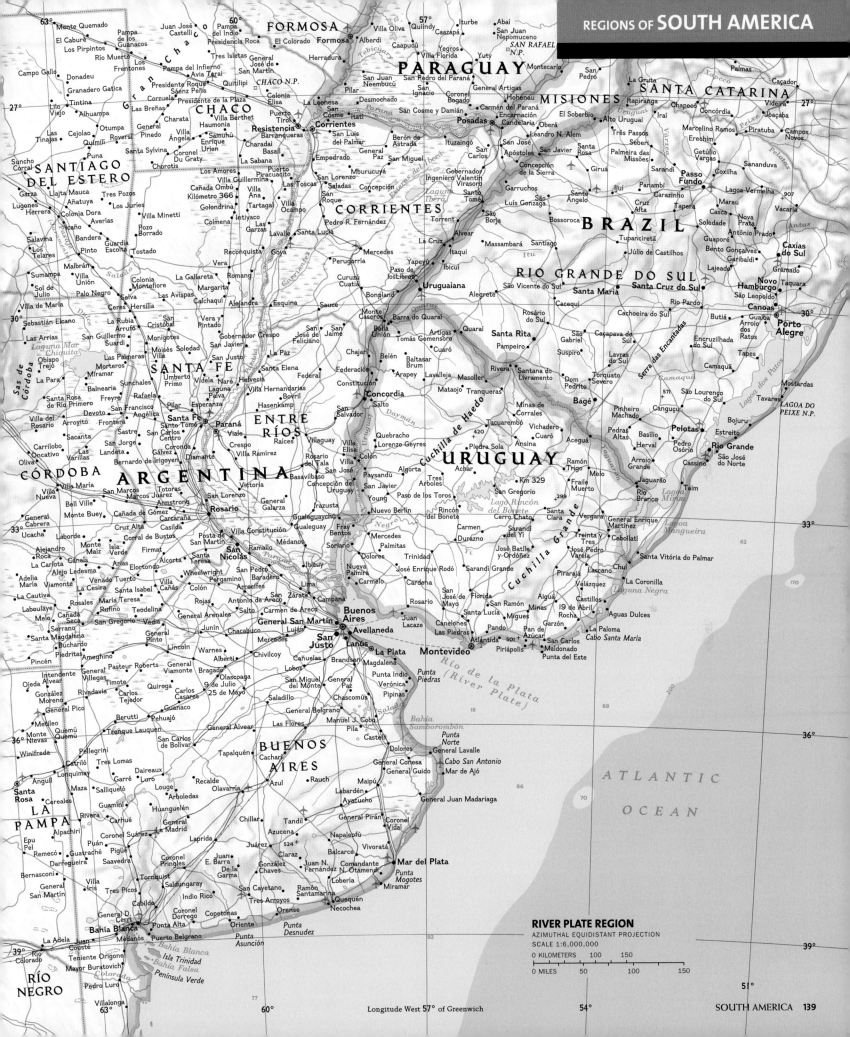

PARAGUAY

FORMOSA

CHACO

SANTIAGO DEL ESTERO

CORRIENTES

MISIONES

SANTA CATARINA

BRAZIL

RIO GRANDE DO SUL

SANTA FE

ENTRE RÍOS

URUGUAY

CÓRDOBA

ARGENTINA

BUENOS AIRES

LA PAMPA

RÍO NEGRO

ATLANTIC OCEAN

Río de la Plata (River Plate)

RIVER PLATE REGION

AZIMUTHAL EQUIDISTANT PROJECTION

SCALE 1:6,000,000

0 KILOMETERS   100   150

0 MILES   50   100   150

The second smallest continent, Europe has a population density second only to Asia. Its name comes from Europa, a Phoenician woman who, according to Greek myth, was seduced by the god Zeus and carried off to Crete. From the Ural Mountains in the east to peninsulas and islands in the west, Europe has had an influence in the world that far outweighs its size: From the continent's seaports in Portugal, Spain, Italy, England, France, and Holland, Europeans set out in the last 600 years and left their imprint throughout the world. The Minoan, Greek, and Roman societies that gave rise to Western civilization were Mediterranean kin and sometimes antagonists to, among others, Phoenicia, Tyre, Judea, Egypt, and Carthage. The welter of peoples, nations, philosophies, religions, arts, and customs that make up Europe and, in the 19th and 20th centuries, the various "isms"—national-, imperial-, Marx-, Nazi-, and others—kept Europe in flux throughout its history, from the fall of Rome to the jittery cold peace that followed World War II. While numerous rivers and plains gave passage for commerce and conquest, the mountain fastnesses of the Pyrenees and Alps and hard passages of the North Sea and English Channel stood as barriers against invaders. The tendency of Europe to fracture has been mended by cooperative enterprises such as the economic Common Market, followed by the European Union. The EU now has 27 members, including eight former Soviet Bloc countries, and three applicants. While members maintain open borders to each other, and 16 countries use a common currency, the Euro, the adoption of a common constitution has been rejected by voters in France and the Netherlands. Difficulties in assimilating, employing, and acculturating immigrants from former colonial states and Muslim countries challenge European societies, long steeped in democratic ideas of equality and free expression.

IMAGE BY ROBERT STACEY, WORLDSAT INTERNATIONAL INC.

Land cover
Forest
- Evergreen needleleaf
- Evergreen broadleaf
- Deciduous needleleaf
- Deciduous broadleaf
- Mixed forest
- Woodland

Grassland or shrubland
- Wooded grassland
- Closed shrubland
- Open shrubland
- Grassland

Other
- Cropland
- Barren (Desert and Polar Ice)
- Built-up

Franz Josef Land (RUSSIA)

SVALBARD (NORWAY)
Longyearbyen

Novaya Zemlya (RUSSIA)

Reykjavik ICELAND

FAROE ISLANDS (DENMARK)

NORWAY
SWEDEN
FINLAND
RUSSIA

Oslo
Helsinki
Stockholm
Tallinn
ESTONIA
Riga
LATVIA
Moscow

IRELAND
Dublin

UNITED KINGDOM

DENMARK
Copenhagen
NETHERLANDS
BELGIUM
London
Amsterdam
Brussels
Berlin
GERMANY
POLAND
Warsaw

LITHUANIA
Vilnius
RUSSIA
Minsk
BELARUS

CHANNEL IS. (U.K.)
Paris
LUXEMBOURG
Prague
CZECH REP.
SLOVAKIA
Vienna
Bratislava
Budapest
Kiev
UKRAINE

FRANCE
SWITZERLAND
Bern
AUSTRIA
SLOVENIA
HUNGARY
Ljubljana
Zagreb
ROMANIA
Chisinau
MOLDOVA

KAZAKHSTAN

LIECHTENSTEIN
SAN MARINO
CROATIA
BOSNIA AND HERZEGOVINA
Belgrade
SERBIA
Bucharest

PORTUGAL
Madrid
Lisbon
SPAIN
MONACO
ANDORRA
VATICAN CITY
ITALY
Rome
MONTENEGRO
Podgorica
KOSOVO
Prishtina
Sarajevo
Skopje
BULGARIA
Sofia
TURKEY
Istanbul
AZERBAIJAN
GEORGIA

GIBRALTAR (U.K.)
ALBANIA
Tirana
MACEDONIA
GREECE
Athens

Valletta MALTA
Nicosia
CYPRUS

TEMPERATURE AND RAINFALL

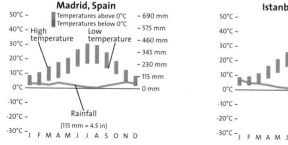

Madrid, Spain
- Temperatures above 0°C
- Temperatures below 0°C
- High temperature
- Low temperature
- Rainfall
- (115 mm = 4.5 in)

J F M A M J J A S O N D

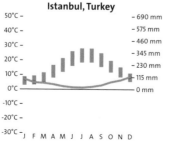

Istanbul, Turkey

J F M A M J J A S O N D

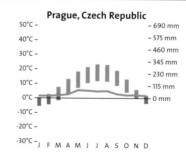

Prague, Czech Republic

J F M A M J J A S O N D

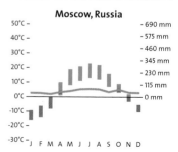

Moscow, Russia

J F M A M J J A S O N D

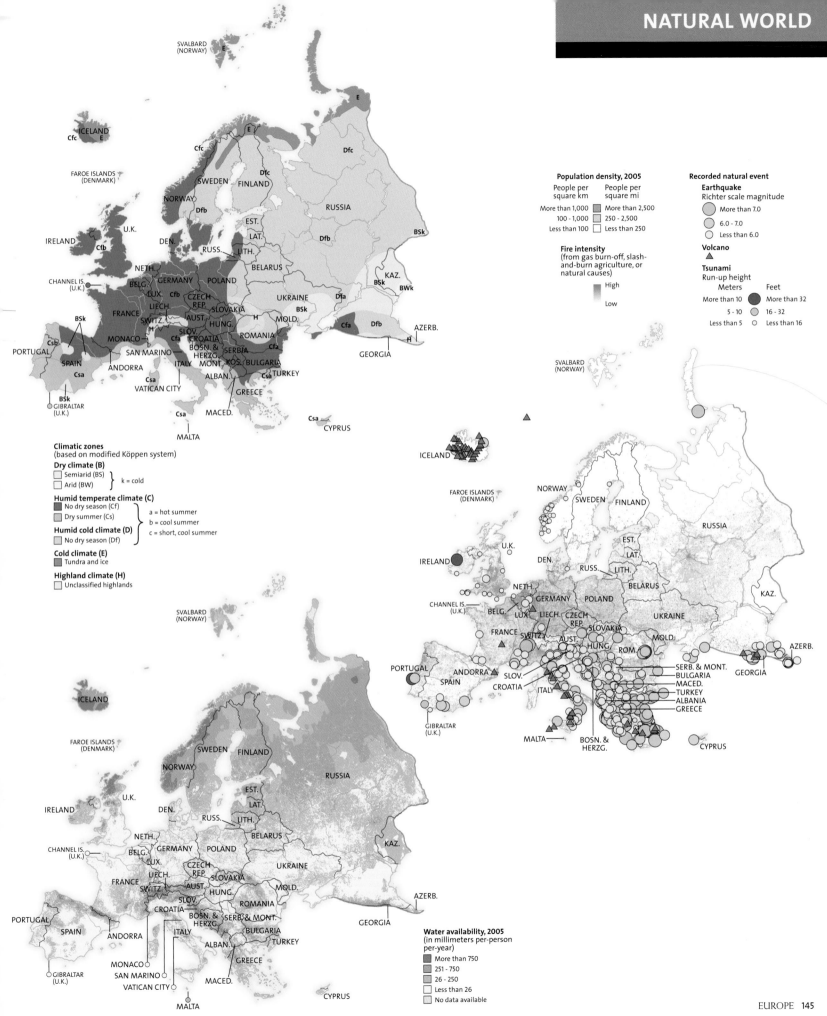

Franz Josef Land
(RUSSIA)

SVALBARD
(NORWAY)
⊕ Longyearbyen

Novaya
Zemlya
(RUSSIA)

Reykjavík ⊕ ICELAND

FAROE ISLANDS
(DENMARK)

SWEDEN

NORWAY

FINLAND

RUSSIA

Oslo ⊕   Helsinki ⊕

UNITED
KINGDOM   Stockholm ⊕   Tallinn ⊕
                                          ESTONIA
IRELAND ⊕ Dublin   DENMARK   Riga ⊕   Moscow ⊕
                          Copenhagen ⊕   LATVIA
                          NETHERLANDS   LITHUANIA
                          BELGIUM   RUSSIA Vilnius ⊕
London ⊕   ⊕ Amsterdam   Minsk ⊕   KAZAKHSTAN
CHANNEL IS.   Berlin ⊕   POLAND   BELARUS
(U.K.)   Brussels ⊕   GERMANY   Warsaw ⊕
                          Paris ⊕   Prague ⊕   Kiev ⊕
                          LUXEMBOURG   CZECH REP.   UKRAINE
                          FRANCE   SLOVAKIA
                                          Vienna ⊕ Bratislava ⊕   Chişinău ⊕   AZERBAIJAN
                          Bern ⊕   AUSTRIA Budapest ⊕   GEORGIA
                          SWITZERLAND   Ljubljana ⊕ HUNGARY   MOLDOVA
                                          SLOVENIA Zagreb ⊕ ROMANIA
PORTUGAL   LIECHTENSTEIN   CROATIA   Bucharest ⊕
                          SAN   BOSNIA AND
                          MARINO   HERZEGOVINA ⊕ Sarajevo Belgrade ⊕
                          MONACO   SERBIA AND   BULGARIA
Lisbon ⊕   Madrid ⊕   VATICAN ITALY   MONTENEGRO Sofia ⊕
                          CITY ⊕ Rome   Podgorica ⊕   TURKEY
SPAIN   ANDORRA   Tirana ⊕ Skopje ⊕   Istanbul ⊕
                                          ALBANIA
GIBRALTAR (U.K.)   MACEDONIA GREECE
                                          Athens ⊕
                          Valletta ⊕ MALTA   Nicosia ⊕
                                                      CYPRUS

Population density, 2005

People per   People per
square km   square mi

More than 195   More than 500
60 - 195   150 - 500
10 - 59   25 - 149
1 - 9   1 - 24
Less than 1   Less than 1

POPULATION PYRAMIDS

BOSNIA AND HERZEGOVINA

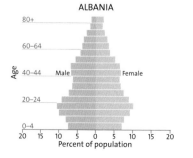

ALBANIA

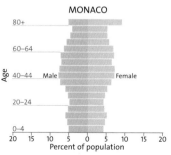

MONACO

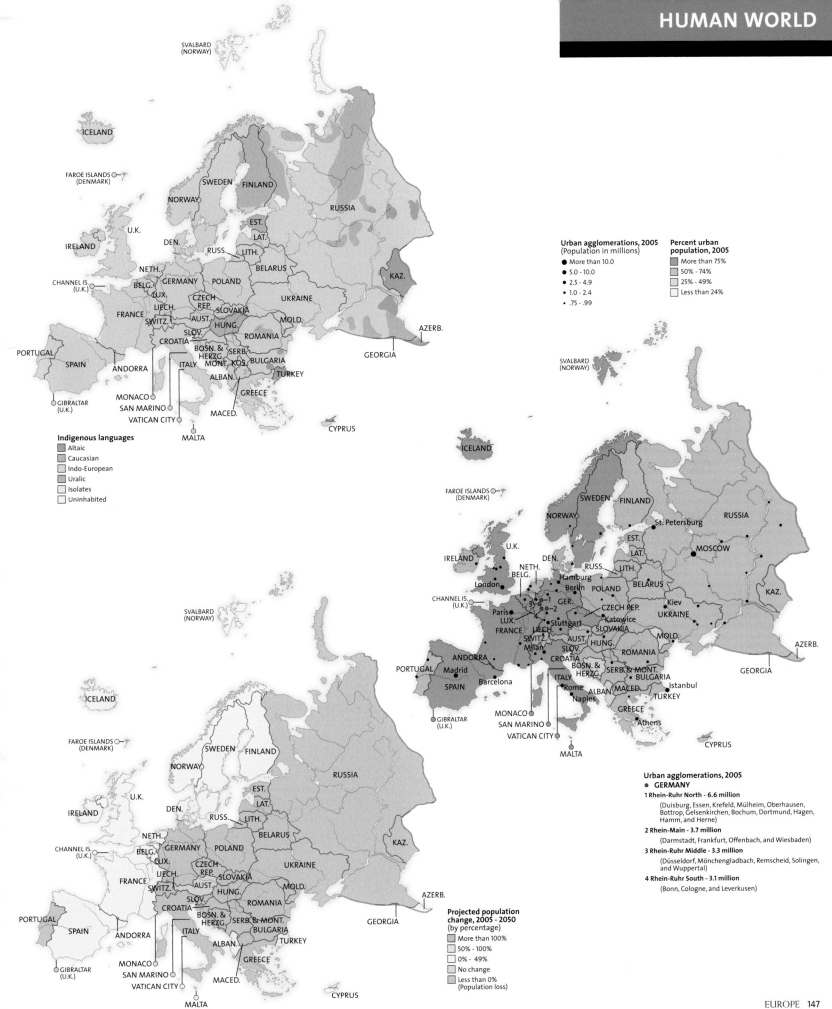

Urban agglomerations, 2005
(Population in millions)

● More than 10.0
● 5.0 - 10.0
● 2.5 - 4.9
• 1.0 - 2.4
· .75 - .99

Percent urban population, 2005

More than 75%
50% - 74%
25% - 49%
Less than 24%

Indigenous languages

Altaic
Caucasian
Indo-European
Uralic
Isolates
Uninhabited

Urban agglomerations, 2005
● GERMANY

1 Rhein-Ruhr North - 6.6 million
(Duisburg, Essen, Krefeld, Mülheim, Oberhausen, Bottrop, Gelsenkirchen, Bochum, Dortmund, Hagen, Hamm, and Herne)

2 Rhein-Main - 3.7 million
(Darmstadt, Frankfurt, Offenbach, and Wiesbaden)

3 Rhein-Ruhr Middle - 3.3 million
(Düsseldorf, Mönchengladbach, Remscheid, Solingen, and Wuppertal)

4 Rhein-Ruhr South - 3.1 million
(Bonn, Cologne, and Leverkusen)

Projected population change, 2005 - 2050
(by percentage)

More than 100%
50% - 100%
0% - 49%
No change
Less than 0% (Population loss)

Franz Josef Land
(RUSSIA)

SVALBARD
(NORWAY)
Longyearbyen

Novaya
Zemlya
(RUSSIA)

Reykjavík ⊗ ICELAND

FAROE ISLANDS
(DENMARK)

RUSSIA

SWEDEN

NORWAY   FINLAND

Oslo ⊗   Helsinki ⊗

UNITED   Stockholm ⊗   Tallinn
KINGDOM   ESTONIA

IRELAND Dublin ⊗   Riga
                                LATVIA   Moscow ⊗
                                LITHUANIA
DENMARK   Vilnius ⊗
London ⊗ Copenhagen ⊗   RUSSIA
NETHERLANDS   Minsk ⊗   KAZAKHSTAN
BELGIUM   BELARUS

CHANNEL IS. Amsterdam ⊗ Berlin ⊗
(U.K.)   Brussels ⊗   POLAND
             GERMANY   Warsaw ⊗
                                                Kiev ⊗
Paris ⊗   Prague ⊗
LUXEMBOURG   CZECH REP.   UKRAINE
                          SLOVAKIA
FRANCE   Bern ⊗ Vienna ⊗ Bratislava   AZERBAIJAN
SWITZERLAND   AUSTRIA   Chişinău ⊗ GEORGIA
             Ljubljana ⊗ HUNGARY Budapest
LIECHTENSTEIN SLOVENIA Zagreb ⊗   MOLDOVA
             SAN   CROATIA   ROMANIA
PORTUGAL   MARINO BOSNIA AND Belgrade ⊗ Bucharest
             MONACO   HERZEGOVINA SERBIA
Lisbon ⊗   VATICAN ITALY Sarajevo ⊗ Prishtina BULGARIA
             CITY MONTENEGRO   Sofia ⊗
     Madrid ⊗   Rome ⊗ Podgorica   TURKEY
SPAIN   ANDORRA KOSOVO Skopje ⊗
                          Tirana   Istanbul ⊗
                          ALBANIA
GIBRALTAR (U.K.)   MACEDONIA

                          GREECE
                          Athens ⊗

Valletta ⊗ MALTA   Nicosia ⊗
                                    CYPRUS

More
disturbed ◣ Cropland
Less
disturbed
More
disturbed ◣ Pasture

▨ Built-up area
▨ Irrigated land

IMPORTS

GERMANY

Petroleum and
petroleum products - 8%
Other 8%
Food 6%
Chemical products - 10%
Machinery and transport equipment 38%
Manufactured goods 30%

UNITED KINGDOM

Petroleum and
petroleum products - 4%
Other 6%
Food - 6%
Chemical products - 10%
Machinery and transport equipment 46%
Manufactured goods 28%

EXPORTS

FRANCE

Other - 6%
Beverages - 3%
Food 8%
Chemical products 14%
Machinery and transport equipment 45%
Manufactured goods 24%

GERMANY

Medical and
pharmaceutical products - 2%
Food - 3%
Other 8%
Chemical products - 12%
Machinery and transport equipment 52%
Manufactured goods 23%

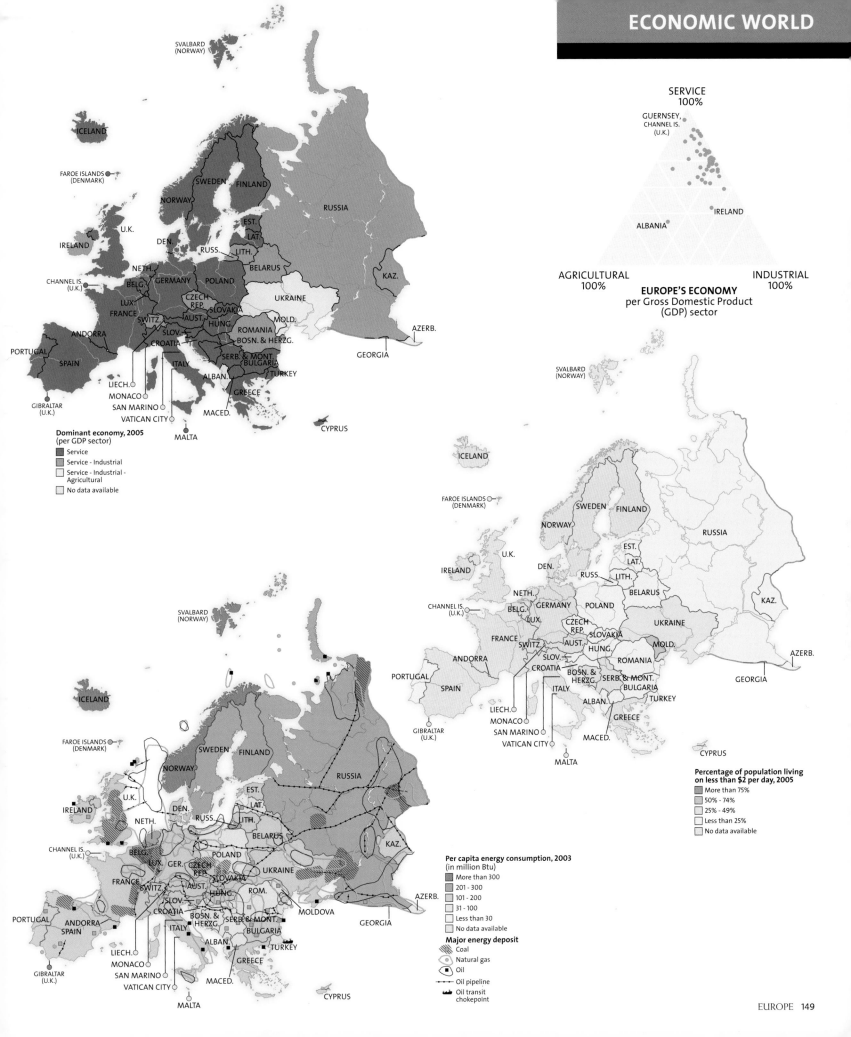

Dominant economy, 2005
(per GDP sector)
- Service
- Service - Industrial
- Service - Industrial - Agricultural
- No data available

SERVICE
100%

GUERNSEY,
CHANNEL IS.
(U.K.)

IRELAND

ALBANIA

AGRICULTURAL
100%

INDUSTRIAL
100%

EUROPE'S ECONOMY
per Gross Domestic Product
(GDP) sector

**Percentage of population living
on less than $2 per day, 2005**
- More than 75%
- 50% - 74%
- 25% - 49%
- Less than 25%
- No data available

Per capita energy consumption, 2003
(in million Btu)
- More than 300
- 201 - 300
- 101 - 200
- 31 - 100
- Less than 30
- No data available

Major energy deposit
- Coal
- Natural gas
- Oil
- Oil pipeline
- Oil transit chokepoint

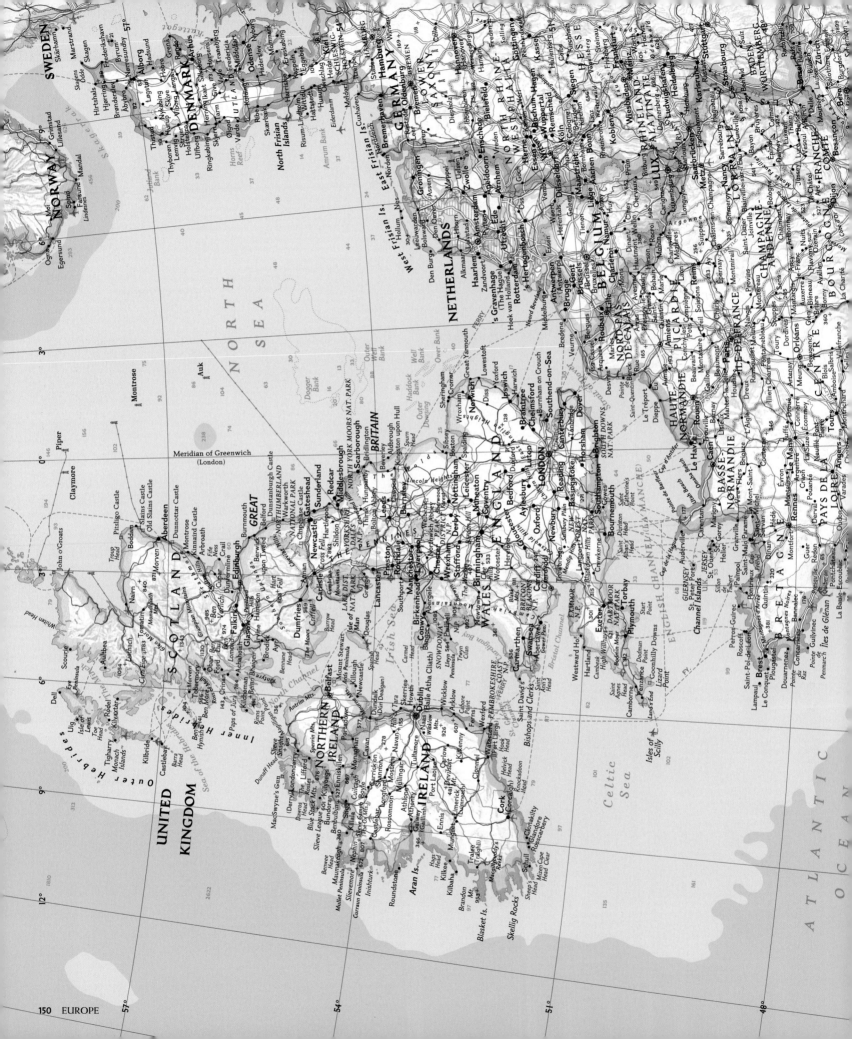

AZIMUTHAL EQUIDISTANT PROJECTION
SCALE 1:6,000,000

0 KILOMETERS   100   150
0 MILES   50   100   150

POLAND

BELARUS

UKRAINE

ROMANIA

MOLDOVA

TRANSYLVANIA

BULGARIA

TURKEY

RUSSIA

CRIMEA

SMOLENSK

BRYANSK

KALUGA

TULA

OREL

KURSK

LIPETSK

TAMBOV

BELGOROD

VORONEZH

ROSTOV

KRASNODAR

KARACH CHERK

ABKHAZIA

BLACK SEA

SEA OF AZOV

MARMARA DENIZI

MOSKVA

Kyiv (Kiev)

Minsk

Bucureşti (Bucharest)

ISTANBUL (CONSTANTINOPLE)

AZIMUTHAL EQUIDISTANT PROJECTION
SCALE 1:6,000,000

0 KILOMETERS 100 150

0 MILES 50 100 150

LOW COUNTRIES
ALBERS CONIC EQUAL-AREA PROJECTION
SCALE 1:2,500,000

0 KILOMETERS 40 60 80
0 MILES 20 40 60 80

NORTH SEA

West Frisian Islands

ENGLAND

NETHERLANDS

FRIESLAND
GRONINGEN
DRENTHE
OVERIJSSEL
NORTH HOLLAND
FLEVOLAND
SOUTH HOLLAND
UTRECHT
GELDERLAND
ZEELAND
NORTH BRABANT
LIMBURG

LOWER SAXONY
NORTH RHINE-WESTPHALIA
GERMANY
RHINELAND-PALATINATE

BELGIUM
FLANDERS
WALLONIA
BRUSSELS-CAPITAL

LUXEMBOURG
SAARLAND
LORRAINE
ALSACE

FRANCE
NORD-PAS-DE-CALAIS
PICARDIE
HAUTE-NORMANDIE
ILE-DE-FRANCE
CHAMPAGNE-ARDENNE
CENTRE
BOURGOGNE

Amsterdam
's Gravenhage (The Hague)
Rotterdam
Utrecht
Groningen
Eindhoven
Antwerpen (Antwerp)
Brussels (Bruxelles, Brussel)
Gent
Brugge
Namur
Liège
Charleroi
Köln (Cologne)
Düsseldorf
Münster
Bonn
Koblenz
Saarbrücken
Luxembourg
Paris
Reims
Amiens
Lille
Calais
Dunkerque (Dunkirk)
Metz
Nancy
Strasbourg

English Channel (La Manche)
Strait of Dover

EUROPE 163

FRANCE

ÎLE-DE-FRANCE
CHAMPAGNE-ARDENNE
LORRAINE
ALSACE
GERMANY
BADEN-WÜRTTEMBERG
ORLÉANAIS
CENTRE
BOURGOGNE
FRANCHE-COMTÉ
SWITZERLAND
LIMOUSIN
AUVERGNE
LYONNAIS
RHÔNE-ALPES
VALLE D'AOSTA
AQUITAINE
MASSIF CENTRAL
DAUPHINÉ
ITALY
PIEDMONT
GUIENNE
LANGUEDOC-ROUSSILLON
CÉVENNES N.P.
MIDI-PYRÉNÉES
PROVENCE-ALPES-CÔTE D'AZUR
MONACO
MEDITERRANEAN SEA
Golfe du Lion

RHONE VALLEY
ALBERS CONIC EQUAL-AREA PROJECTION
SCALE 1:2,500,000

0 KILOMETERS 60
0 MILES 20 40 60

Longitude East 5° of Greenwich

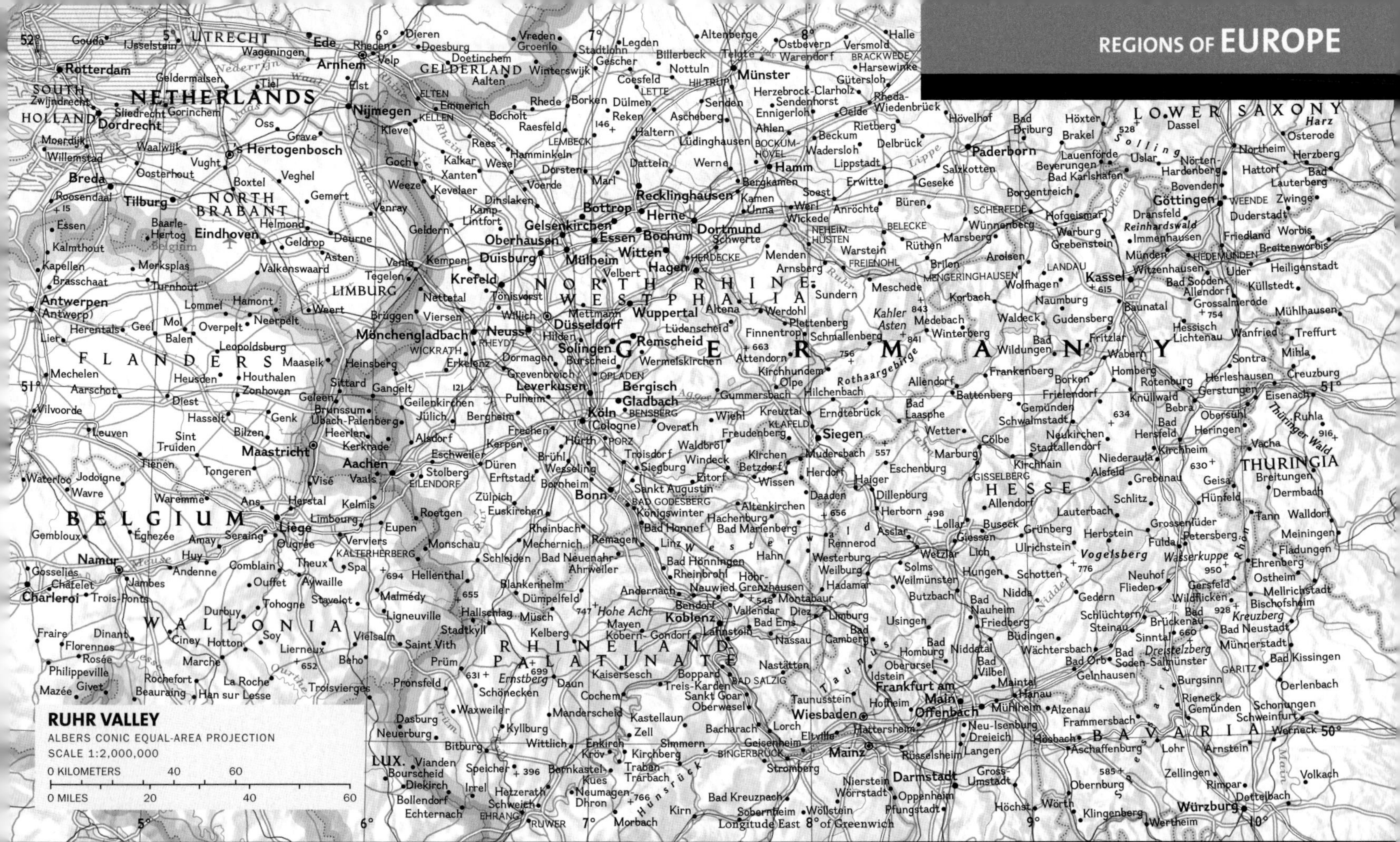
NETHERLANDS
BELGIUM
FLANDERS
WALLONIA
NORTH BRABANT
LIMBURG
GELDERLAND
NORTH RHINE-WESTPHALIA
GERMANY
RHINELAND-PALATINATE
HESSE
LOWER SAXONY
THURINGIA
BAVARIA
LUX.
Rotterdam
Utrecht
Nijmegen
Antwerpen (Antwerp)
Maastricht
Liège
Aachen
Köln (Cologne)
Düsseldorf
Duisburg
Essen
Dortmund
Bonn
Koblenz
Frankfurt am Main
Wiesbaden
Mainz
Darmstadt
Kassel
Würzburg
Longitude East 8° of Greenwich

RUHR VALLEY

ALBERS CONIC EQUAL-AREA PROJECTION
SCALE 1:2,000,000
0 KILOMETERS 40 60
0 MILES 20 40 60

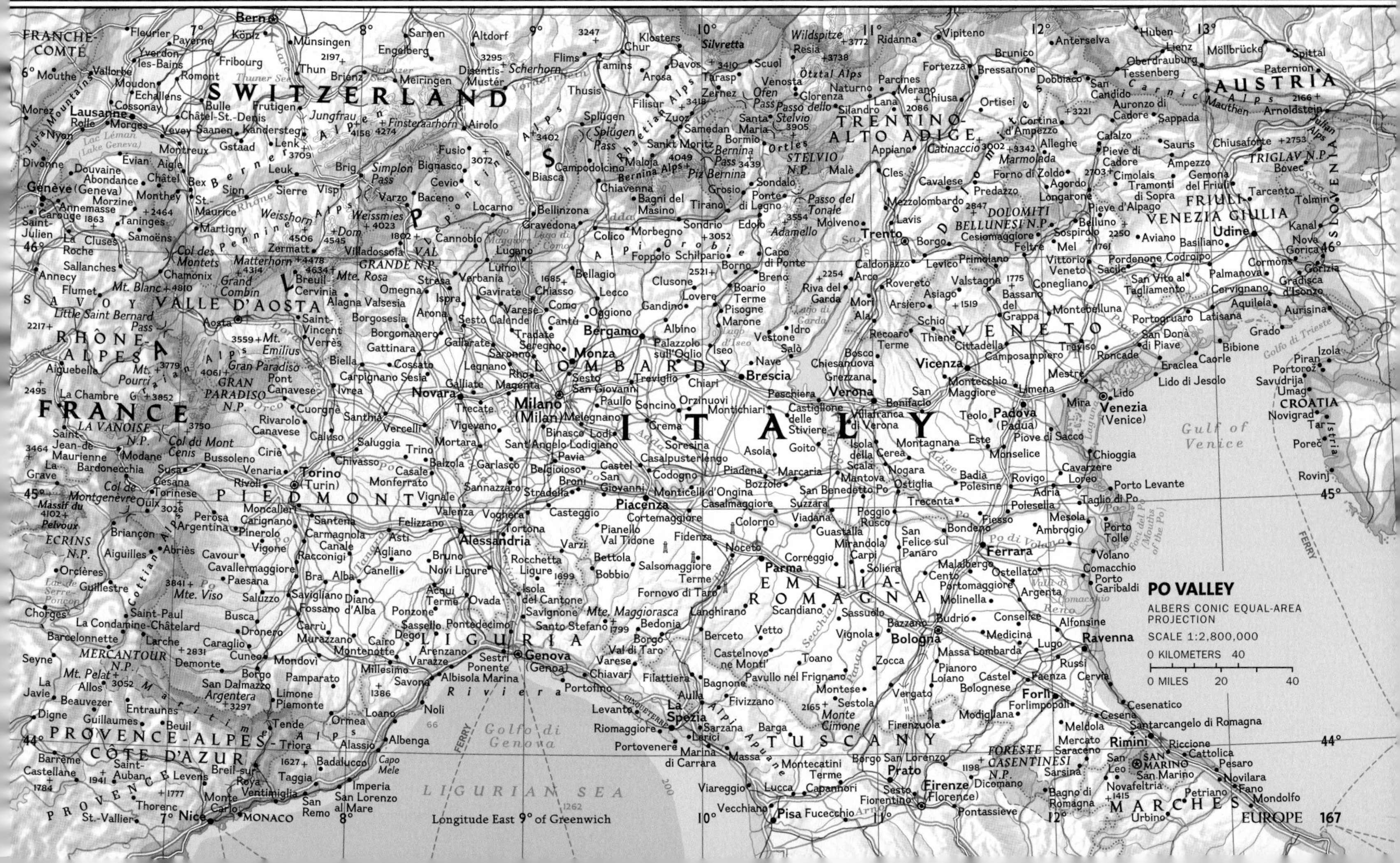
SWITZERLAND
AUSTRIA
FRANCE
ITALY
SLOVENIA
CROATIA
MONACO
SAN MARINO
FRANCHE-COMTÉ
RHÔNE-ALPES
PROVENCE-ALPES-CÔTE D'AZUR
VALLE D'AOSTA
PIEDMONT
LOMBARDY
TRENTINO-ALTO ADIGE
VENETO
FRIULI VENEZIA GIULIA
LIGURIA
EMILIA-ROMAGNA
TUSCANY
MARCHES
Bern
Genève (Geneva)
Torino (Turin)
Milano (Milan)
Genova (Genoa)
Venezia (Venice)
Bologna
Firenze (Florence)
Gulf of Venice
LIGURIAN SEA
Golfo di Genova
Longitude East 9° of Greenwich

PO VALLEY

ALBERS CONIC EQUAL-AREA PROJECTION
SCALE 1:2,800,000
0 KILOMETERS 40
0 MILES 20 40

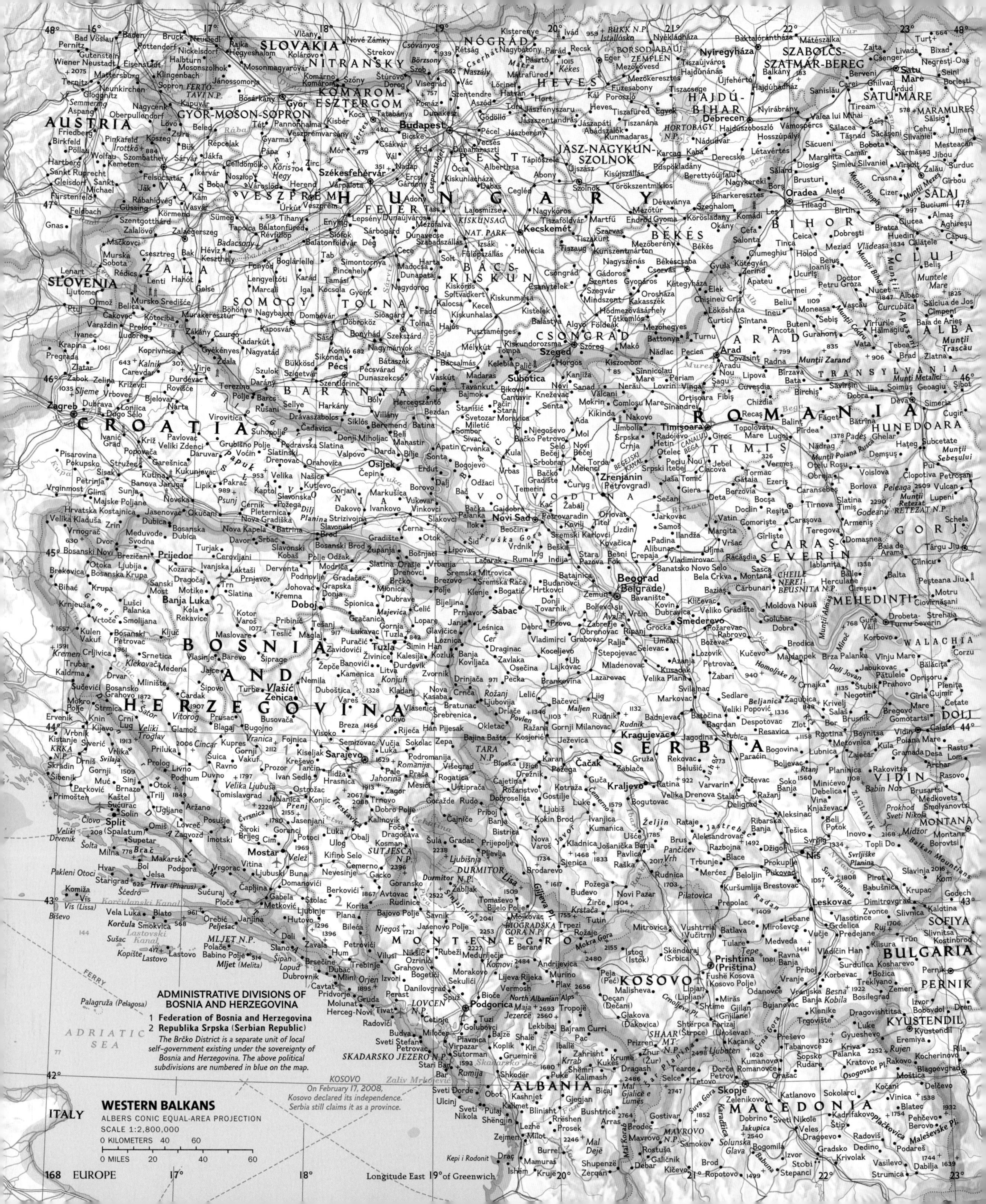

WESTERN BALKANS
ALBERS CONIC EQUAL-AREA PROJECTION
SCALE 1:2,800,000
0 KILOMETERS 40 60
0 MILES 20 40 60
ADMINISTRATIVE DIVISIONS OF BOSNIA AND HERZEGOVINA
1 Federation of Bosnia and Herzegovina
2 Republika Srpska (Serbian Republic)
The Brčko District is a separate unit of local self-government existing under the sovereignty of Bosnia and Herzegovina. The above political subdivisions are numbered in blue on the map.
KOSOVO
On February 17, 2008, Kosovo declared its independence. Serbia still claims it as a province.
Longitude East 19° of Greenwich
AUSTRIA
SLOVAKIA
HUNGARY
SLOVENIA
CROATIA
ROMANIA
BOSNIA AND HERZEGOVINA
SERBIA
MONTENEGRO
KOSOVO
ALBANIA
MACEDONIA
BULGARIA
ITALY
ADRIATIC SEA
Budapest
Zagreb
Beograd (Belgrade)
Sarajevo
Podgorica
Prishtina (Priština)
Skopje
Split (Spalatum)
Mostar
Novi Sad
Timişoara
Oradea
Arad
Debrecen
Szeged
Pécs
Osijek
Banja Luka
Tuzla
Niš
Kragujevac
Dubrovnik
Tiranë
SOFIYA

CENTRAL RUSSIA

ALBERS CONIC EQUAL-AREA PROJECTION

SCALE 1:10,000,000

So large and so diverse—covering almost two-thirds of Earth's land surface and inhabited by 60% of humanity—Asia is as much a world as a continent. Earth's most violent tectonic collision continues here, as the Indian subcontinent rams into Asia and thrusts up the Himalaya and the Tibetan Plateau. The resulting land demarcation has effectively isolated large sections of Asia from each other and, in particular, has kept the two most populous countries—China and India, which between them contain half the continent's population—as counterweights to one another, demographically, culturally, economically, and politically. Asia's vast landmass embraces a wide range of terrain and peoples, from the lightly populated steppes of central Russia to the deserts of the contentious Middle East, from the perilous floodplain of Bangladesh to the teeming western islands of the Indonesian archipelago. Home to the faiths of Judaism, Christianity, Islam, Hinduism, Buddhism, Taoism, Shintoism—and more tongues than religions—the continent supports both megacities and Shangri-La pockets of solitude. Once primarily a source of raw materials and crops such as rubber, tin, petroleum, timber, and rice, Asia now manufactures goods, from children's toys to high-end electronics, that flood the rest of the world. Japan led the economic boom. China, India, Korea, Singapore, and others are extending it. Prosperity remains elusive for less-developed countries, such as Afghanistan and Timor-Leste (East Timor), which have per-capita incomes only one-fourth of that in the region overall. Other regional issues include cross-border migration, trafficking of people and drugs, trans-boundary spread of diseases, spillover of conflicts, and looming environmental hazards.

IMAGE BY ROBERT STACEY, WORLDSAT INTERNATIONAL INC.

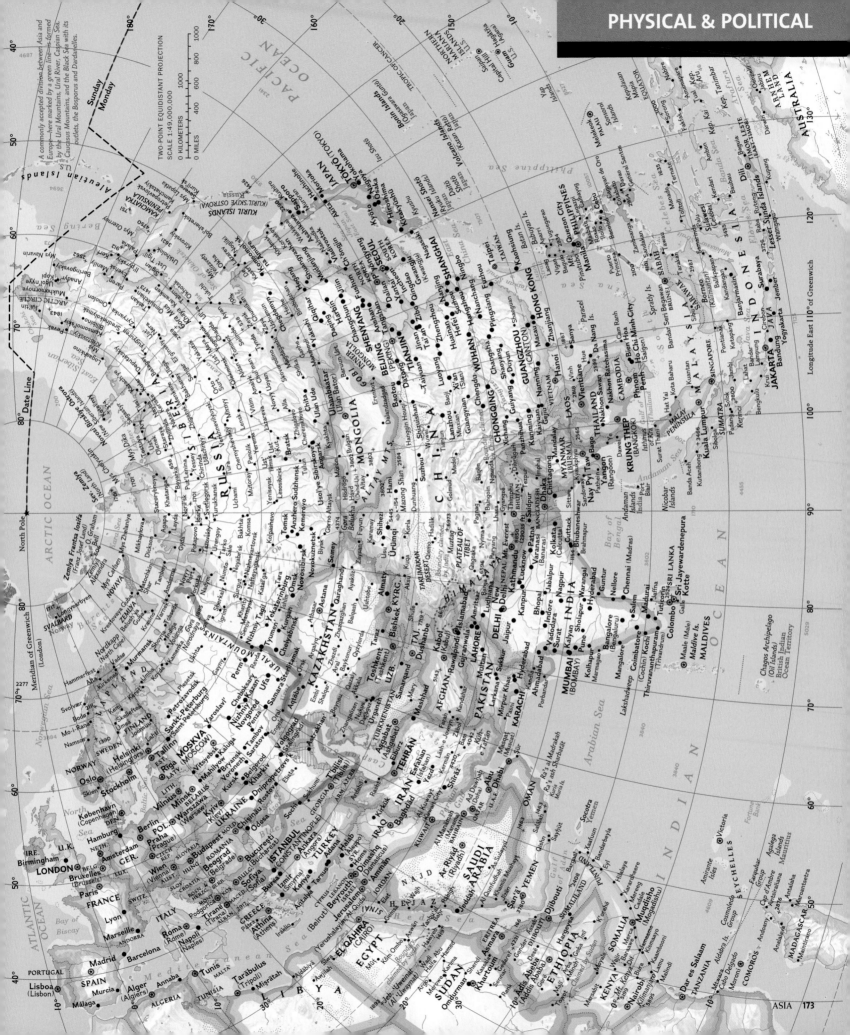

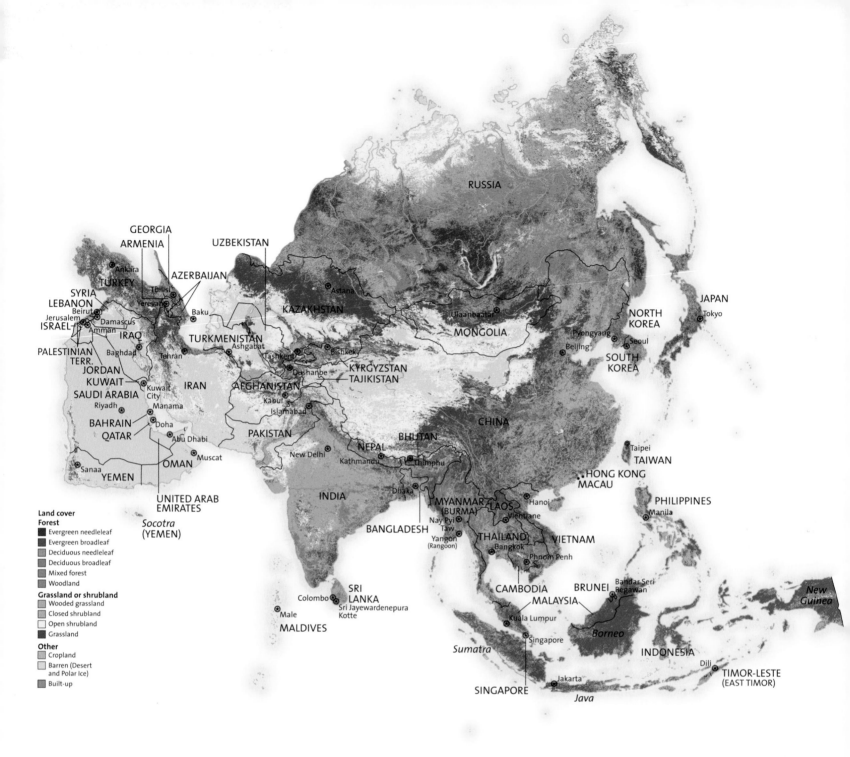

RUSSIA

GEORGIA
ARMENIA
AZERBAIJAN
UZBEKISTAN
Ankara
TURKEY
SYRIA
LEBANON
Tbilisi
Yerevan
Baku
KAZAKHSTAN
Astana
Ulaanbaatar
MONGOLIA
JAPAN
Tokyo
Jerusalem
Beirut
Damascus
Amman
ISRAEL
IRAQ
PALESTINIAN
TERR.
JORDAN
KUWAIT
SAUDI ARABIA
Baghdad
TURKMENISTAN
Ashgabat
Tashkent
Bishkek
KYRGYZSTAN
TAJIKISTAN
NORTH
KOREA
Pyongyang
Beijing
Seoul
SOUTH
KOREA
Tehran
Dushanbe
Kuwait
City
Manama
IRAN
AFGHANISTAN
Kabul
Riyadh
BAHRAIN
QATAR
Doha
Abu Dhabi
Islamabad
CHINA
Taipei
TAIWAN
Muscat
OMAN
PAKISTAN
NEPAL
BHUTAN
New Delhi
Kathmandu
Thimphu
HONG KONG
MACAU
Sanaa
YEMEN
UNITED ARAB
EMIRATES
INDIA
Dhaka
MYANMAR
(BURMA)
LAOS
Hanoi
Vientiane
PHILIPPINES
Manila
Socotra
(YEMEN)
BANGLADESH
Nay Pyi
Taw
Yangon
(Rangoon)
THAILAND
Bangkok
VIETNAM

Land cover
Forest
Evergreen needleleaf
Evergreen broadleaf
Deciduous needleleaf
Deciduous broadleaf
Mixed forest
Woodland
Grassland or shrubland
Wooded grassland
Closed shrubland
Open shrubland
Grassland
Other
Cropland
Barren (Desert
and Polar Ice)
Built-up

Phnom Penh
SRI
LANKA
Colombo
Sri Jayewardenepura
Kotte
Male
MALDIVES
CAMBODIA
BRUNEI
Bandar Seri
Begawan
MALAYSIA
Kuala Lumpur
Borneo
New
Guinea
Sumatra
Singapore
INDONESIA
Dili
TIMOR-LESTE
(EAST TIMOR)
SINGAPORE
Jakarta
Java

TEMPERATURE AND RAINFALL

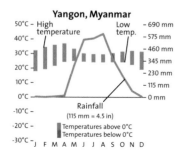

Yangon, Myanmar

High temperature
Low temp.
Rainfall
(115 mm = 4.5 in)
Temperatures above 0°C
Temperatures below 0°C

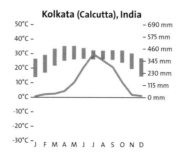

Kolkata (Calcutta), India

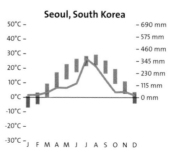

Seoul, South Korea

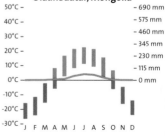

Ulaanbaatar, Mongolia

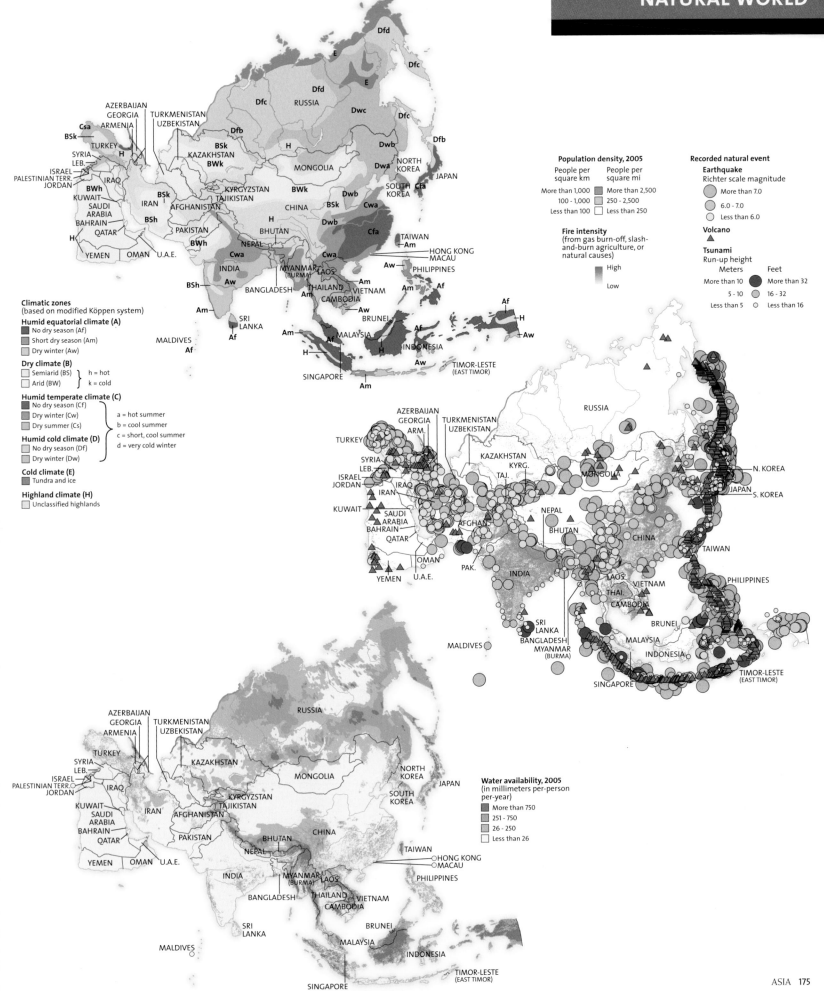

Climatic zones
(based on modified Köppen system)

Humid equatorial climate (A)
- No dry season (Af)
- Short dry season (Am)
- Dry winter (Aw)

Dry climate (B)
- Semiarid (BS) } h = hot
- Arid (BW) } k = cold

Humid temperate climate (C)
- No dry season (Cf)
- Dry winter (Cw)   a = hot summer
- Dry summer (Cs)   b = cool summer
                       c = short, cool summer
Humid cold climate (D)   d = very cold winter
- No dry season (Df)
- Dry winter (Dw)

Cold climate (E)
- Tundra and ice

Highland climate (H)
- Unclassified highlands

Population density, 2005

People per square km	People per square mi
More than 1,000	More than 2,500
100 - 1,000	250 - 2,500
Less than 100	Less than 250

Fire intensity
(from gas burn-off, slash-and-burn agriculture, or natural causes)
- High
- Low

Recorded natural event

Earthquake
Richter scale magnitude
- More than 7.0
- 6.0 - 7.0
- Less than 6.0

Volcano ▲

Tsunami
Run-up height

Meters	Feet
More than 10	More than 32
5 - 10	16 - 32
Less than 5	Less than 16

Water availability, 2005
(in millimeters per-person per-year)
- More than 750
- 251 - 750
- 26 - 250
- Less than 26

Population density, 2005

People per square km	People per square mi
More than 195	More than 500
60 - 195	150 - 500
10 - 59	25 - 149
1 - 9	1 - 24
Less than 1	Less than 1

POPULATION PYRAMIDS

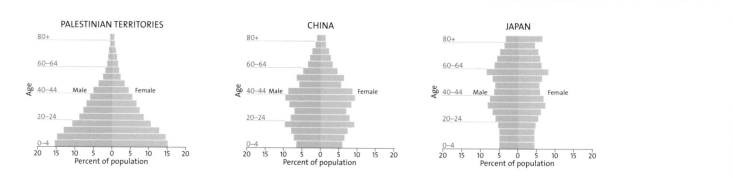

PALESTINIAN TERRITORIES

CHINA

JAPAN

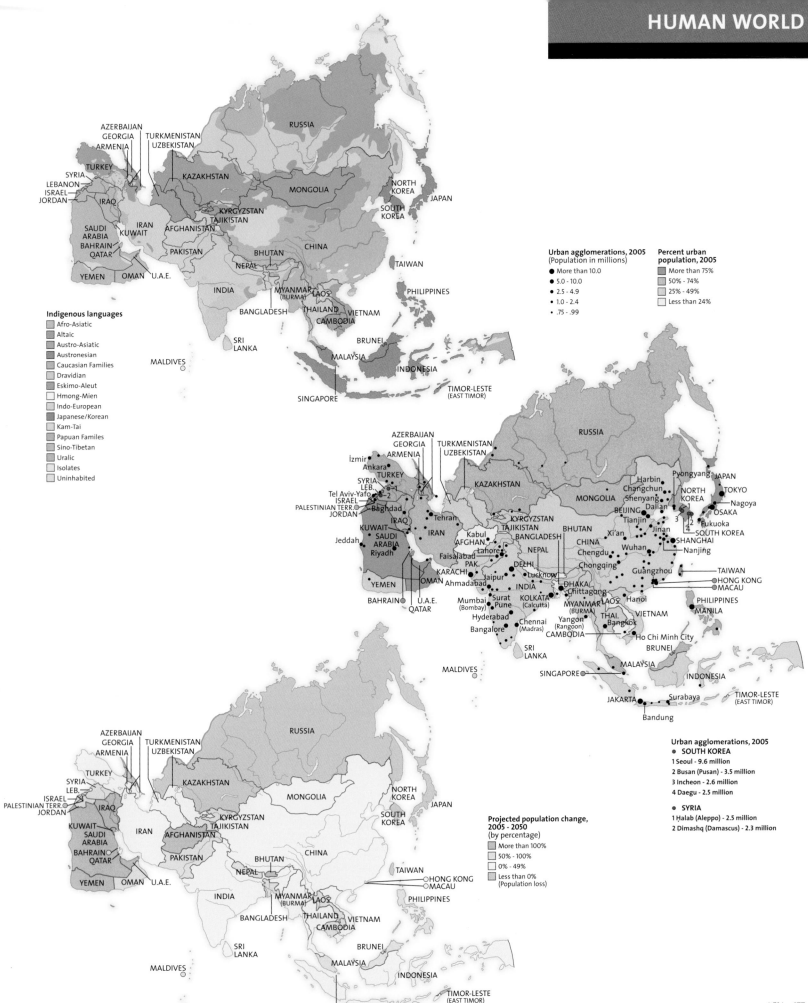

Indigenous languages
- Afro-Asiatic
- Altaic
- Austro-Asiatic
- Austronesian
- Caucasian Families
- Dravidian
- Eskimo-Aleut
- Hmong-Mien
- Indo-European
- Japanese/Korean
- Kam-Tai
- Papuan Familes
- Sino-Tibetan
- Uralic
- Isolates
- Uninhabited

Urban agglomerations, 2005
(Population in millions)
- More than 10.0
- 5.0 - 10.0
- 2.5 - 4.9
- 1.0 - 2.4
- .75 - .99

Percent urban population, 2005
- More than 75%
- 50% - 74%
- 25% - 49%
- Less than 24%

Urban agglomerations, 2005
- **SOUTH KOREA**
1 Seoul - 9.6 million
2 Busan (Pusan) - 3.5 million
3 Incheon - 2.6 million
4 Daegu - 2.5 million

- **SYRIA**
1 Ḥalab (Aleppo) - 2.5 million
2 Dimashq (Damascus) - 2.3 million

Projected population change, 2005 - 2050
(by percentage)
- More than 100%
- 50% - 100%
- 0% - 49%
- Less than 0% (Population loss)

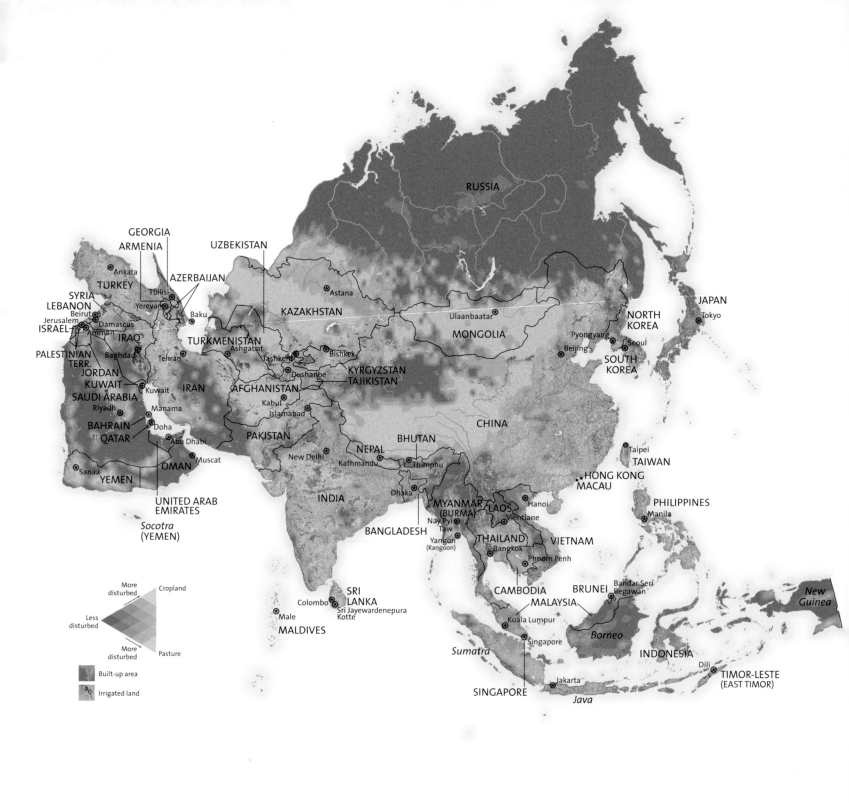

GEORGIA
ARMENIA
UZBEKISTAN
Ankara
TURKEY
AZERBAIJAN
Tbilisi
SYRIA
LEBANON
Yerevan
Baku
Jerusalem
Beirut
Damascus
ISRAEL
Amman
IRAQ
PALESTINIAN
TERR.
Baghdad
JORDAN
KUWAIT
SAUDI ARABIA
Kuwait
Riyadh
Manama
BAHRAIN
Doha
QATAR
Abu Dhabi
OMAN
Muscat
Sanaa
YEMEN
UNITED ARAB
EMIRATES
Socotra
(YEMEN)

RUSSIA
Astana
KAZAKHSTAN
Ulaanbaatar
MONGOLIA
TURKMENISTAN
Ashgabat
Tashkent
Bishkek
KYRGYZSTAN
Dushanbe
TAJIKISTAN
Tehran
IRAN
AFGHANISTAN
Kabul
Islamabad
PAKISTAN
New Delhi
Kathmandu
NEPAL
BHUTAN
Thimphu
CHINA
Dhaka
INDIA
BANGLADESH
MYANMAR
(BURMA)
Nay Pyi
Taw
Yangon
(Rangoon)
LAOS
Vientiane
THAILAND
Bangkok
Phnom Penh
CAMBODIA
VIETNAM
Hanoi

JAPAN
Tokyo
NORTH
KOREA
Pyongyang
Beijing
Seoul
SOUTH
KOREA
Taipei
TAIWAN
HONG KONG
MACAU
PHILIPPINES
Manila

SRI
LANKA
Colombo
Sri Jayewardenepura
Kotte
Male
MALDIVES

BRUNEI
Bandar Seri
Begawan
MALAYSIA
Kuala Lumpur
Borneo
Singapore
Sumatra
SINGAPORE
Jakarta
Java
INDONESIA
Dili
TIMOR-LESTE
(EAST TIMOR)
New
Guinea

More
disturbed
Cropland
Less
disturbed
More
disturbed
Pasture
Built-up area
Irrigated land

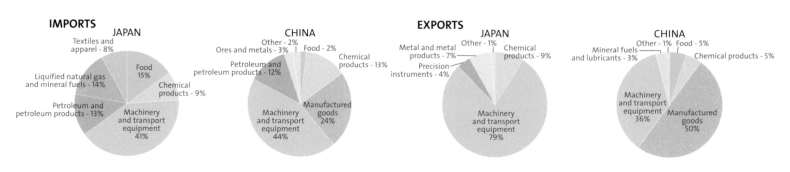

IMPORTS

JAPAN

Textiles and apparel - 8%
Food 15%
Liquified natural gas and mineral fuels - 14%
Chemical products - 9%
Petroleum and petroleum products - 13%
Machinery and transport equipment 41%

CHINA

Other - 2%
Ores and metals - 3%
Food - 2%
Petroleum and petroleum products - 12%
Chemical products - 13%
Manufactured goods 24%
Machinery and transport equipment 44%

EXPORTS

JAPAN

Metal and metal products - 7%
Other - 1%
Chemical products - 9%
Precision instruments - 4%
Machinery and transport equipment 79%

CHINA

Mineral fuels and lubricants - 3%
Other - 1%
Food - 5%
Chemical products - 5%
Machinery and transport equipment 36%
Manufactured goods 50%

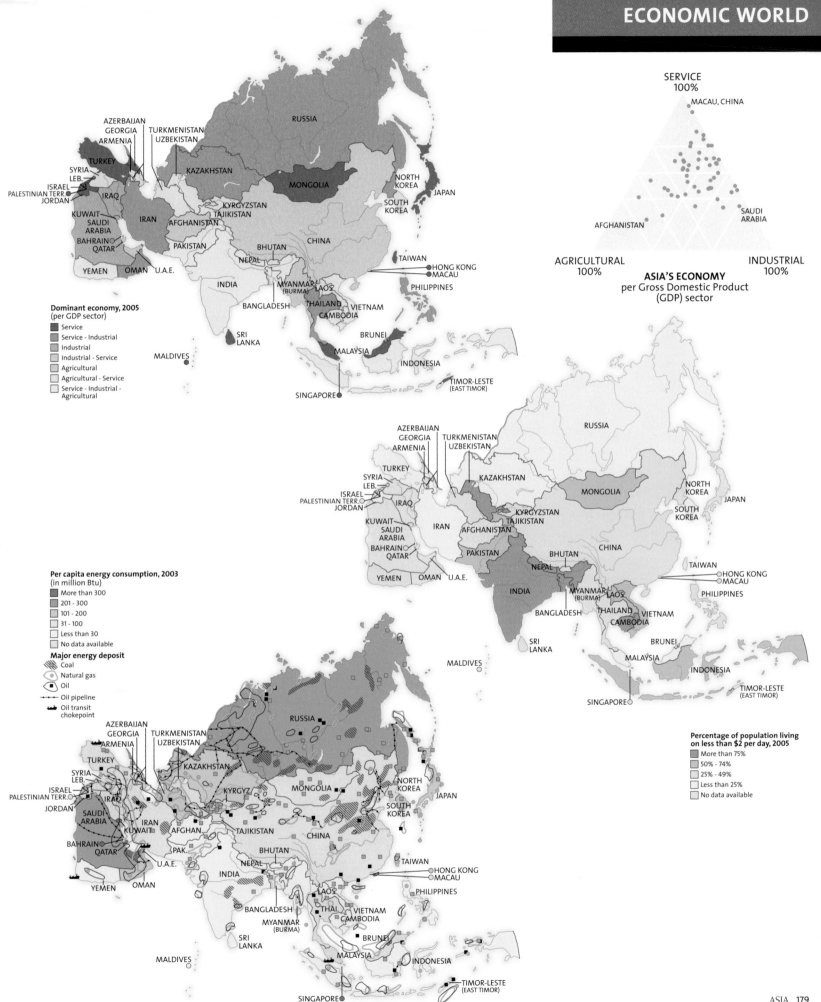

SERVICE 100%

MACAU, CHINA

AFGHANISTAN

SAUDI ARABIA

AGRICULTURAL 100%

INDUSTRIAL 100%

ASIA'S ECONOMY
per Gross Domestic Product (GDP) sector

Dominant economy, 2005
(per GDP sector)
- Service
- Service - Industrial
- Industrial
- Industrial - Service
- Agricultural
- Agricultural - Service
- Service - Industrial - Agricultural

Per capita energy consumption, 2003
(in million Btu)
- More than 300
- 201 - 300
- 101 - 200
- 31 - 100
- Less than 30
- No data available

Major energy deposit
- Coal
- Natural gas
- Oil
- Oil pipeline
- Oil transit chokepoint

Percentage of population living on less than $2 per day, 2005
- More than 75%
- 50% - 74%
- 25% - 49%
- Less than 25%
- No data available

Ābādān
Bandar-e Emān Behbehān 51° Dow Gonbadān 54° Shahr-e Rafsanjān 57° Kermān 60°
Khomeynī Ardakān Marv Bābak Baghīn Māhān
Al Fāw Bandar-e Deylam Gachsāran Dasht Persepolis Mashīz Noṣratābād
Būbīyān +3219 Zarqan Qal'eh-ye 'Askar Keshīt
ah Bandar-e Rīg Kāzerūn Borazjān Sirjān 4374+ 4420 Bām Fahraj Shūr Qila Nok Kundi Dalbandin
waŷt Khārk Shīrāz 4+ Kūh-e Hazārān Bāft Darzīn Gaz Kūh-e Safed Mīrjāveh Yakmach Kharan
ait) Bushgan Estahbān Kūh-e Laleh Zār Jīroft 3962+ Kūh-e Jebāl Bārez Rīgān Taftān Qila Ladgasht Zayakī Jangal
Rīshahr Būshehr Ahram Fasā Dārāb 4042 2817+ Kūh-e PAKISTAN
Az Zawr Forozan 44 Firūzābād Aliabad IRAN Khāsh Gazū Qila Ladgasht
ımadı Khvormūj Jahrom Ṭārom Dowlatābād Kahnūj Bāzmān+ Gazak Īrānshahr 2146+ Kūhak
Ra's al Mish'āb Deyyer Ṭāheri Jūyom Sa'ādatābād 3280 Hasan Hāmūn-e 3489 Panjgūr +1623 27°
Safaniya Langī Rūdān Jaz Mūrīān Zāboli Esfandak
Ra's Nāy Band Gāvbandī Lār Bandar 'Abbās Mīnāb Sanderek Maskūtān Espakeh Qaṣr-e Sarbāz BALUCHISTAN Diz
Zawr Abū Bastak Hormoz Kūhestak Remeshk Nīkshahr Pīshīn
Manīfah 'Alī Jana Bandar-e Māqām Qeshm Angohrān Kūrān Dap Bāhū Mand Hoshab
Berri Al Jubayl Ra's Tannūrah Lāvān Bandar-e Qeshm Sīrīk Sūrāk Kalāt Turbat Kandrach
Niṭa Fadhili Ṭufayḥ Al Qaṭīf Charak Bandar-e Bāsa'īdū Hengām Jāsk Hūmedān Chāhbār Polān Suntsar
Fazran Az Zahrān Ad Dammām Kish Lengeh Abū Ra's al Kumzār Gavāter Pasni
ay'īrah 172 BAHRAIN Reshadat Mūsā Khaymah Ra's al 2081 Bay'ah Gwāter Bay Gwadar Ras Astola Ras Ormara
Al Manāmah Sīrrī Musandam Dadnah Jīwani Nuh Island
Al 'Uqayr (Manama) Umm al Qaywayn Adh Ummara
Al Hufūf Awali Al Khawr Īran Sharjah Dhayd Ormara
(Hofūf) Az Mubarraz Al Jumaylīyah Umm Ajmān Mīnā' Jabal 'Alī Al Fujayrah
Ghawar Oil Field Dukhān Ad Dawḥah Shaif Dubai Shinaș
rais Umm Zirkūh Abu Dhabi
Mazalij Harmalīyah Sa'īd Al Bunduq Zakum Shināṣ 1132 GULF OF OMAN 3275
As Salwā QATAR Ra's Abū Qumayyiṣ Ṣuḥār
Harad Ra's Abū Dalmā Mubarras Abū al Al 'Ayn As Sīb 24°
Khawr Duwayhin Sīr Banī Abyaḍ Masqaṭ (Muscat) TROPIC OF CANCER
A As Ṣufuq Yās Al Mughayrā Ṭarīf Jabal Ḥafīt 1166 Al Qābil 3348 4256
+240 Bab Danķ Al Khābūrah Maṭrah
UNITED ARAB EMIRATES Ar Rustāq 'Alāyat
Al Khunn Yabrīn Bu Hasa Jabal ash Shām Samā'il Qurayyāt
Bi'r Humar An Nashshāsh Asab 'Ibrī 2980 Nizwā Qalhāt
Fardān Zarrarah Bahlah 2152+ Ra's al Ḥadd
Al 'Ubaylah Shaybah Umm az Lekhwair Natih Adam Bilād Banī Ṣūr
Zumūl Jibāl Fahud Al Mintirib Bū 'Alī As Suwayḥ
Al Quraynī Umm as Samīm Huwaisah O Ra's Jibsh 21°
Al Ḥadidah Ghaba North M Al Ashkharah
(meteorite craters) Saih A
Nihayda Qarn Alam
Rub' al Khālī N Dawwah +276
(Empty Quarter) Khalūf Jazīrat Maṣīrah 3447
mpty Quarter) Kalbān (Masira)
Haymā' Khalīj
Al Ḥadidah Jiddat Maṣīrah
145 al Ḥarāsīs 132+ Duqm
Ra's
Dawkah Mazrag al Madrakah
Saddat ash +350 Ash Marmūl Ghubbat
Shuqqah Shiṣar Qaharīr Ṣawqirah 3921
Sanāw +270 Sharbatāt Ṣawqirah
Shihan Thamarīt Ra's ash Sharbatāt
Ḥāsik Al Ḥallānīyah
Thamūd ZUFĀR Ṭaqah 1463 Kuria Muria Is. 18°
Habarūt Salālah Ḥāsik
E N +865 Damqawt Rakhyūt Mirbāṭ Ra's
Tarīm Ra's Darbat 'Alī Ṣadḥ Mirbāṭ
ām Wādī al Maṣilah Al Ghaydah ARABIAN
AMAWT Nishtūn Ghubbat al
Qamar SEA
akh Qishn Ra's Fartak 4188
+1730 2410 Ra's Sharwayn
Al Ghaydah Ḥarrah Sayḥūt 15°
Ash Shiḥr
awlā Ar Riyān
aṭar Al Mukallā
Mijdahah 4470
Ra's al Kalb
E N 4137
ADEN
3630 4133
2341

183 ASIA

Qalansīyah Ḥadiboh 12°
Ra's Shū'ab Qāḍub +1503
'Abd al Kūrī Socotra (Suquṭrā)
Yemen Yemen
Caluula Al Ikhwān
Bandar Murcaayo Bereeda Cape (The Brothers)
SOMALIA 51° Gwardafuy 54° 57° 60° 63°

LAMBERT CONFORMAL CONIC PROJECTION
SCALE 1:8,000,000
0 KILOMETERS 120 160 200
0 MILES 40 80 120 160 200

TURKMENISTAN

UZBEKISTAN

TAJIKISTAN

CHINA

Garagum

Türkmenabat
(Chärjew)

Aşgabat
(Ashgabat)

Mashhad

Neyshābūr

Qūchān

Herat

AFGHANISTAN

HAZARAJAT

Kabol
(Kabul)

ISLAMABAD
CAP. TERR.

Islamabad

Rawalpindi

Peshawar

KHYBER-
PAKHTUNKHWA

JAMMU AND
KASHMIR

AZAD
KASHMIR

Srinagar

LINE OF CONTROL

KASHMIR

GILGIT-
BALTISTAN

HINDU KUSH

WAKHAN

BADAKHSHAN

PAMIRS

Karakoram Range

Kandahar

SISTAN

PUSHT-I-RUD

Dasht-e
Khash

BALOCHISTAN

Quetta

PAKISTAN

PUNJAB

LAHORE

Faisalabad

Multan

Bahawalpur

Amritsar

Jullundur

INDIA

RAJASTHAN

Great Indian Desert

Bikaner

Fatehpur

Ajmer

Beawar

Udaipur

Zāhedān

BALUCHISTAN

Sukkur

Larkana

SINDH

Hyderabad

Nawabshah

KIRTHAR
N.P.

KARACHI

GUJARAT

Ahmadabad

Gandhinagar

Rajkot

Jamnagar

Porbandar

Junagadh

Surat

Vadodara

Bharuch

Bhavnagar

GULF OF OMAN

ARABIAN
SEA

TROPIC OF CANCER

Mouths of
the Indus

Muscat
(Masqaţ)

LAMBERT CONFORMAL CONIC PROJECTION
SCALE 1:8,000,000
0 KILOMETERS 120 160 200
0 MILES 40   80   120   160   200

ASIA 187

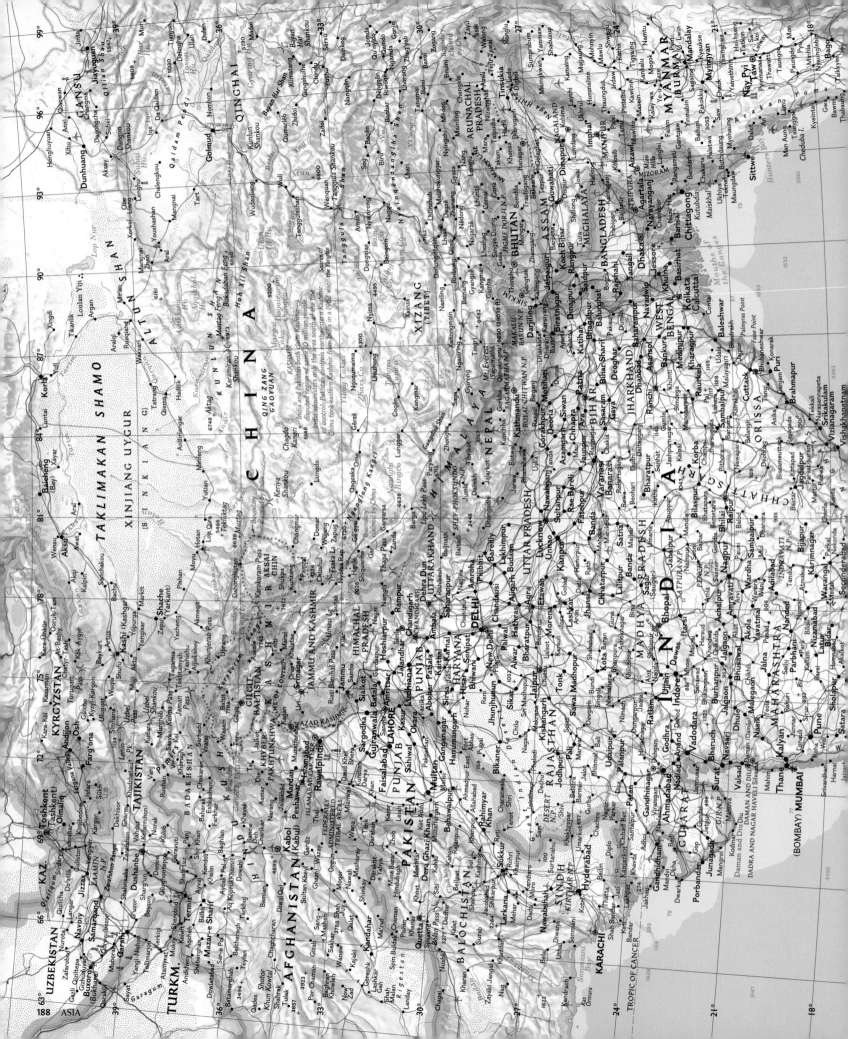

ARABIAN SEA

BAY OF BENGAL

INDIAN OCEAN

ANDAMAN SEA

ANDAMAN AND NICOBAR ISLANDS
India

INDONESIA

ANDHRA PRADESH

KARNATAKA

KERALA

TAMIL NADU

SRI LANKA

MALDIVES

LAKSHADWEEP
India

Pagoda Point
Preparis North Channel
Preparis South Channel
Narcondam Island
Landfall I.   Cape Price
N. Andaman
Mayabandar
Interview I.
Middle Andaman
Outram I.
Henry Lawrence I.
Havelock I.
S. Andaman
Herbertabad   Port Blair
Rutland I.
N. Sentinel I.
Nachuge   Chetamale
Little   Toibalawe
Andaman
Ten Degree Channel
Car Nicobar
Kakana
Katchall I. Camorta I.
Misha
Little Nicobar   Laful
Dakoank   Teniaa
Kanalla Bananga
Henhoaha Great Nicobar
Great Channel
We
Breueh
Peunasoe   Sigli
Banda Aceh   Tangse
Calang
Keudepanga
Ujung Dewa
Kepulauan
Banyak
Duncan Passage

Machilipatnam (Bandar)
Chirala
Ongole
Nellore
SHAR SPACE LAUNCH CENTER
Chennai (Madras)
Kanchipuram
Puducherry (Pondicherry)
PUDUCHERRY
Cuddalore
Kumbakonam
Point Pedro
Chundikkulam
Mullaittivu
Kuchchaveli
Trincomalee
Kinniyai
Valaichchenai
Batticaloa
MADURU OYA N.P.
Kattankudi
Akkaraipattu
Panama
RUHUNA (YALA) N.P.
Tissamaharama
Ambalantota
Jaffna
Kilinochchi
Talaimannar   Kallakkara
WILPATTU N.P.
Anuradhapura
Isaiyanvilai Puttalam
Gulf of Mannar
Mannar
Negombo
Colombo
Sri Jayewardenepura Kotte
Panadura
Matugama
Ambalangoda
Matara
Kandy
Nuwara Eliya
Badulla

Kurnool
Machilipatnam
Adoni
Markapur
Kondukur
Kavali
Atmakur
Proddatur
Kadapa
Cuddapah
Rajampet
Rayachoti
Kalahasti
Chittoor
Vellore
Polur
Villupuram
Attur
Kallakurichi
Tiruchchirappalli
Pudukkottai
Madurai
Karaikal
Tiruchirappalli
Tanjore
Thanjavur
Mettur
Salem
Dindigul
Tirunelveli
Thoothukudi
Tuticorin
Nagercoil
Kanniyakumari

Raichur
Kalaburagi
Gulbarga
Tikal
Bellary
Bellari
Hospet
Chitradurga
Davangere
Shimoga
Shivamogga
Bengaluru
Bangalore
Hosur
Kolar
Hindupur
Vaniyambadi
Coimbatore
Pollachi
Palani
Ernakulam
Trichur (Thrissur)
Cochin (Kochi)
Alleppey (Alappuzha)
Kollam
Thiruvananthapuram (Trivandrum)
Attingal

Belgaum
Hubli
Dharwad
Gadag
Bagalkot
Panaji
GOA
Karwar
Kumta
Bhatkal
Mangalore
Kasaragod
Kannur
Kozhikode (Calicut)
Thalassery (Tellicherry)
Puttur
Hosdurg
Malvan
Kolhapur

Kavaratti
LAKSHADWEEP India
Minicoy Island
Nine Degree Channel
Eight Degree Channel
Suheli Par
Byramgore Reef
Cherbaniani Reef
Sesostris Bank
Bassas de Pedro
Cora Divh
Angria Bank

Ihavandiffulu Atoll
Muladu
Tiladummati Atoll
North Malosmadulu Atoll
South Malosmadulu Atoll
Miladummadulu Atoll
Fadiffolu Atoll
Helengili
Male Atoll
Maale (Male)
South Male Atoll
Felidu Atoll
Wadu
Kendikolu
Ari Atoll
Nilandu Atoll
Mulaku Atoll
Gadifuri
Kolumadulu Atoll
Kandudu
Haddummati Atoll
Gang
Isdu
Fahala
Nilandu
Maldive Is. One and Half Degree Channel
Equatorial Channel
Hitadu   Midu
Fua Mulaku
Addu Atoll
Gan
Nadale
Suvadiva Atoll
Feridu
Ukulahu
Mandu
Huvadu
Feridu
North Malosmadulu Atoll

Moresby Islands
Salomon Is.
Nelsons Island
Peros Banhos Is.
Three Brothers
Eagle Islands
I. Lubine   Coin
Chagos Archipelago (Oil Islands)
British Indian Ocean Territory
Egmont Islands
Diego Garcia

LAMBERT CONFORMAL CONIC PROJECTION
SCALE 1:12,000,000

0 KILOMETERS   100   200   300
0 MILES   100   200   300

Longitude East 81° of Greenwich

EQUATOR

SEA OF OKHOTSK

OSTROV SAKHALIN

KURIL ISLANDS (KURIL'SKIYE OSTROVA)
Russia

Simushir

Urup

Iturup (Etorofu)

Kunashir (Kunashiri)

Habomai Islands

HOKKAIDŌ
Asahikawa
Sapporo
Hakodate

Aomori
Hachinohe
Morioka
Kamaishi
Akita
Ishinomaki
Sakata
Yamagata
Sendai
Niigata
Nagaoka
Utsunomiya
Maebashi
Mito
Toyama
Nagano
TŌKYŌ
Kanazawa
Fuji
Yokohama
Kōfu
Yokosuka
HONSHŪ
Nagoya
Hamamatsu
Kyōto
Toyohashi
Kōbe
Ōsaka
Wakayama
Hiroshima
Kure
Kōchi
Kitakyūshū
Matsuyama
SHIKOKU
Fukuoka
Sasebo
Kumamoto
Nagasaki
Miyazaki
Shibushi
KYŪSHŪ
Kagoshima
KAGOSHIMA SPACE CENTER
Kanoya
TANEGASHIMA SPACE CENTER
Sata Misaki
Tanega Shima
Yaku Shima
Tokara Rettō

SEA OF JAPAN
(EAST SEA)

La Perouse Str.
Wakkanai
Rebun Tō
Rishiri Tō
Mombetsu
Abashiri
Kushiro
Obihiro
Muroran
Okushiri Tō
Tsugaru Kaikyō
Hirosaki

Oki Shotō

Hachijō Jima

Muko Jima Rettō

Bonin Islands
(Ogasawara Guntō)

Chichi Jima Rettō

Haha Jima Rettō

Kita Iwo Jima

Volcano Is.
(Kazan Rettō)
Japan

Iwo Jima (Sulphur Island)

Minami Iwo Jima

PACIFIC OCEAN

J A P A N

I Z U S H O T Ō

PHILIPPINE SEA

EAST CHINA SEA

Amami Ō Shima
Tokuno Shima
Okino Erabu Shima
Okinawa
Naha

NANSEI SHOTŌ (RYUKYU ISLANDS)

Daitō Islands

TROPIC OF CANCER

Miyako
Ishigaki
Iriomote

TAIWAN
The People's Republic of China claims Taiwan as its 23rd province. Taiwan's government (Republic of China) maintains that there are two political entities. The islands of Dongsha, Kinmen, Matsu and Penghu are administered by Taiwan.

Taipei (Taibei)
Chilung (Keelung)
Hsinchu
Changhua
Hualien
TAIWAN
Tainan
Taitung
Kaohsiung
Hengchun

Matsu
Haitan Dao
Kinmen (Quemoy)
Penghu (Pescadores)

Taiwan Strait

Bashi Channel

Dongsha (Pratas I.)

Itbayat
Basco
Batan Is.
Calayan
Babuyan Is.
Fuga
Camiguin
Aparri
Laoag
Cape Bojeador
PHILIPPINES
LUZON
Luzon Strait

HONG KONG, S.A.R.
Macau, S.A.R.
Shenzhen
DONGGUAN
Shantou
Chaozhou
Kaohsiung
Jiangmen
Zhaoqing
GUANGDONG
Dingnan
Changting
Shaoguan
Ganzhou
Quanzhou
Xiamen
Nanping
FUJIAN
Fuzhou
Shangyou
Ji'an
Nanchang
JIANGXI
Jingdezhen
Shangrao
Quzhou
Linhai
Wenzhou
Fu'an
Ningde
Wuyi Shan
Hengyang
Changsha
HUNAN

WUHAN
HEBEI
Huangshi
Jiujiang
Anqing
Hefei
ANHUI
Fuyang
Nanyang
HENAN
Xinyang
Nanjing
Wuxi
Suzhou
SHANGHAI
SHANGHAI SHI
Hangzhou
Shaoxing
ZHEJIANG
Ningbo
Anlu
Jingmen

Three Gorges Dam

Nantong
Changzhou
Zhenjiang
Yangzhou
JIANGSU
Huaiyin
Shuyang
Xuzhou
Shangqiu
Kaifeng
Zhengzhou
Jining

NEI MONGOL

CHITA
Bambuyka
Tsipikan
Kalakan
Mogocha
Amazar
Skovorodino
Dzhalinda
Tygda
Shimanovsk
Svobodnyy Cosmodrome
Belogorsk
Blagoveshchensk
Heihe
Raychikhinsk
Obluch'ye
Birobidzhan
Khabarovsk
Vyazemskiy
Bikin
Svetlaya
Amgu
Terney

AMUR
Khrebet Dzhagdy
Tugur
Nikolayevsk na Amure
Bogorodskoye
De Kastri
Aleksandrovsk-Sakhalinskiy
Poronaysk
Makarov
Mys Terpeniya
Zaliv Terpeniya
Dolinsk
Kholmsk
Nevel'sk
Yuzhno-Sakhalinsk
Korsakov
Gornozavodsk
Mys Aniva

KHABAROVSK
Komsomol'sk na Amure
Vanino

JEWISH AUTON. REG.
Khor

Stanovoy Khrebet
Tynda
Chumikan
Uda
Torom

Never
Zeya
Huma
Fevral'sk
Ushumun
Magdagachi

Mohe
Heilong Jiang

Chita
Nerchinsk
Sretensk
Vershino Darasunskiy
Kurlya
Shilka
Olovyannaya
Aginskoye
Borzya
Krasnokamensk
Zabaykalsk
Manzhouli
Hailar
Choybalsan
Baruun Urt
Tamsagbulag
Manzhouli
Hulun Nur
Ovoot
Dong Ujimqin Qi
Sonid Youqi
Xilinhot
Linxi
Kailu
Duolun
Chifeng
Chengde
Zhangjiakou
Xuanhua

BEIJING (PEKING)
BEIJING SHI
Tangshan
Tianjin (Tientsin)
TIANJIN SHI
Tanggu
Baoding
Shijiazhuang
HEBEI
Yangquan
Yuci
Xingtai
Handan
Anyang
Changzhi
SHANXI
Dezhou
Jinan
Zibo
Weifang
Weihai
Yantai
SHANDONG
Qingdao
Lianyungang
Jining
Linyi
Xuzhou

Hulun Nur

Arxan
Lindian
Qiqihar
HEILONGJIANG
Suihua
Anda
Hulan
Harbin
Fuyu
Baicheng
Taonan
Ulanhot
JILIN
Jilin
Changchun
Dunhua
Siping
Shuangliao
Tieling
Tongliao
Kailu
Kaili

Dongbei (Manchuria)
Yichun
Hegang
Jiamusi
Yilan
Jixi
Lishuzhen
Dal'nerechensk
Hulin
Mudanjiang
Ning'an
Ussuriysk
Artem
Vladivostok
Nakhodka
MARITIME TERRITORY
Khrebet Sikhote Alin'

Dahinggan Ling

Nenjiang
Nehe
Bugt

Yilehuli Shan

Xiao Hinggan Ling

SHENYANG
Anshan
Benxi
Fushun
LIAONING
Jinzhou
Dandong
Sinŭiju
NORTH KOREA
P'yŏngyang
Namp'o
Wŏnsan
Hŭngnam
Hyesan
Ch'ŏngjin
Najin
Unggi
Tonghua
Tumen

Demarcation Line, July 27, 1953

Dalian (Dairen)
Lüshun
Kaesŏng
Incheon (Inch'ŏn)
SEOUL
Chuncheon
Cheongju
SOUTH KOREA
Daejeon (Taejon)
Jeonju
Daegu (Taegu)
Gwangju (Kwangju)
Masan
Busan (Pusan)
Mokpo
Jeju
Jeju-Do
S. Korea
Cheongju

YELLOW SEA

Korea Strait (Tsushima Strait)

Tangshan

JIANGSU

Huaiyin

YELLOW SEA

Fuzhou

GUANGDONG

LAMBERT CONFORMAL CONIC PROJECTION
SCALE 1:16,000,000

0 KILOMETERS 300 400

0 MILES 100 200 300 400

Longitude East 132° of Greenwich

ASIA 191

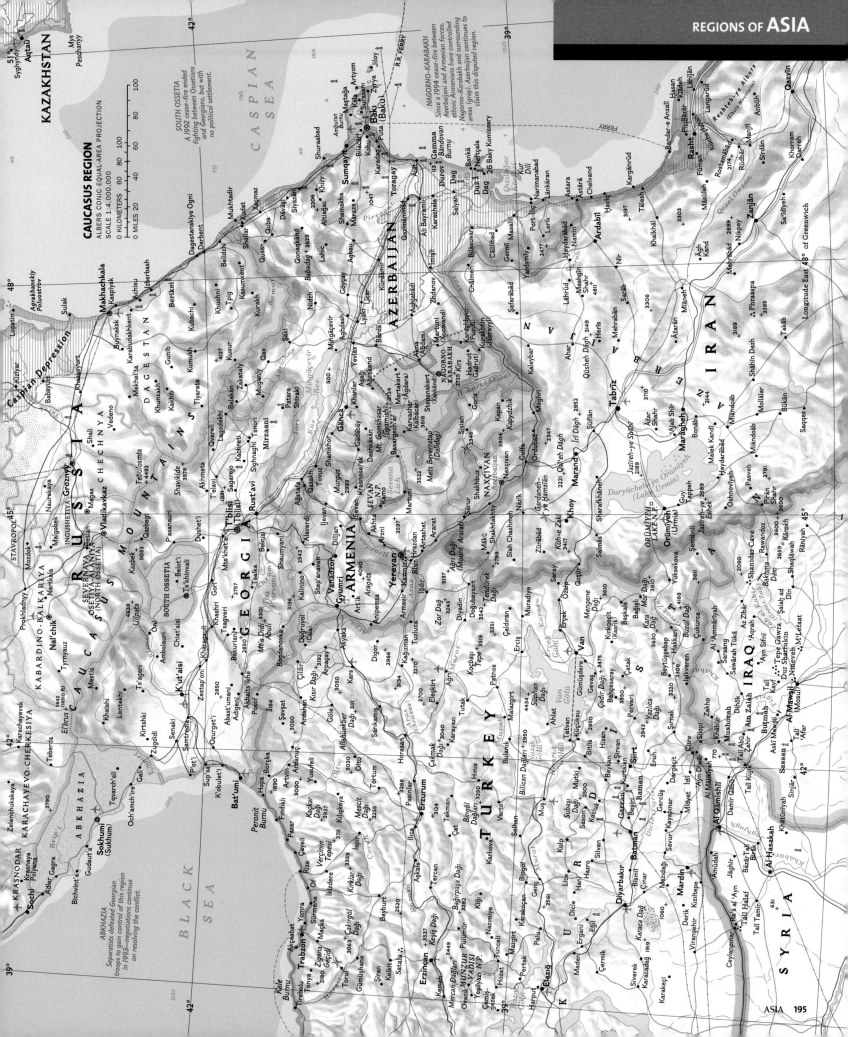

CAUCASUS REGION
ALBERS CONIC EQUAL-AREA PROJECTION
SCALE 1:4,000,000

SOUTH OSSETIA
A 1992 cease-fire ended
fighting between Ossetians
and Georgians, but with
no political settlement.

NAGORNO-KARABAKH
Since a 1994 cease-fire between
Azerbaijani and Armenian forces,
ethnic Armenians have controlled
Nagorno-Karabakh and surrounding
areas (gray). Azerbaijan continues to
claim this disputed region.

ABKHAZIA
Separatists defeated Georgian
troops to gain control of this region
in 1993—negotiations continue
on resolving the conflict.

KAZAKHSTAN

CASPIAN SEA

BLACK SEA

RUSSIA

GEORGIA

ARMENIA

AZERBAIJAN

TURKEY

IRAN

IRAQ

SYRIA

FERGANA VALLEY
ALBERS CONIC EQUAL-AREA PROJECTION
SCALE 1:4,500,000

0 KILOMETERS 60 80 100 120
0 MILES 40 60 80 100 120

GANGES VALLEY
ALBERS CONIC EQUAL-AREA PROJECTION
SCALE 1:8,000,000

0 KILOMETERS 120 160 200
0 MILES 40 80 120 160 200

EASTERN CHINA

ALBERS CONIC EQUAL-AREA PROJECTION

SCALE 1:8,000,000

0 KILOMETERS 40 80 120 160 200

0 MILES 40 80 120 160 200

TAIWAN

The People's Republic of China claims Taiwan as
its 23rd province. Taiwan's government maintains
that there are two political entities.
Of China) maintains that there are two political entities.
The islands of Dongshu, Kinmen, Matsu, and Penghu
are administered by Taiwan.

PROVINCES AND PROVINCE-LEVEL CITIES WITH CAPITALS

NORTH KOREA

1 **Chagang** (Kanggye)
2 **Hamgyong, North** (Ch'ŏngjin)
3 **Hamgyong, South** (Hamhŭng)
4 **Hwanghae, North** (Sariwŏn)
5 **Hwanghae, South** (Haeju)
6 **Kangwon** (Wŏnsan)
7 **Phyongan, North** (Sinŭiju)
8 **Phyongan, South** (P'yŏng-sŏng)
9 **Pyongyang City**
10 **Raseon City**
11 **Ryanggang** (Hyesan)

SOUTH KOREA

12 **Busan City**
13 **Chungcheong, North** (Cheongju)
14 **Chungcheong, South** (Daejeon)
15 **Daegu City**
16 **Daejeon City**
17 **Gangwon** (Chuncheon)
18 **Gwangju City**
19 **Gyeonggi** (Suwon)
20 **Gyeongsang, North** (Daegu)
21 **Gyeongsang, South** (Changwon)
22 **Incheon City**
23 **Jeju** (Jeju) off map
24 **Jeolla, North** (Jeonju)
25 **Jeolla, South** (Namak)
26 **Seoul City**
27 **Ulsan City**

The above political subdivisions are numbered in blue on the map.

KOREAN PENINSULA
ALBERS CONIC EQUAL-AREA PROJECTION
SCALE 1:4,000,000

The Democratic People's Republic of Korea is referred to as North Korea. The Republic of Korea is known as South Korea.

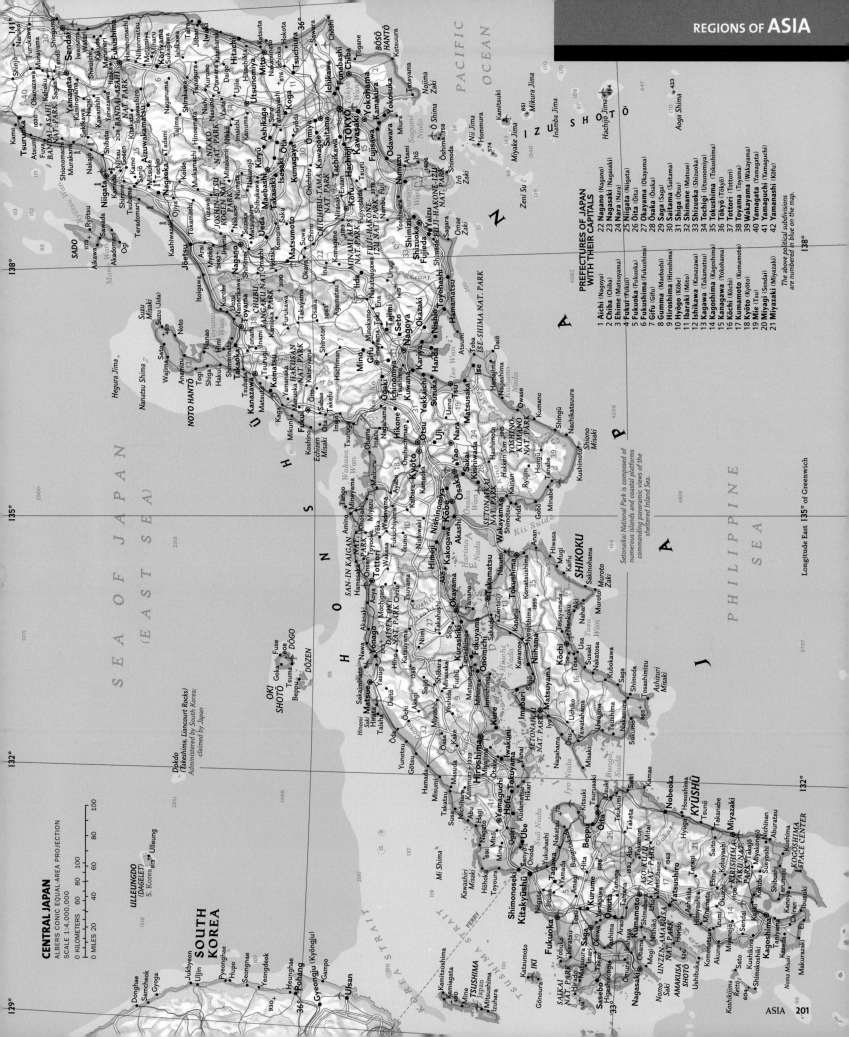

Indochina refers historically to French Indochina,
which comprised Vietnam, Laos, and Cambodia.
Physical geographers extend the region
to include Thailand, Myanmar (Burma),
and peninsular Malaysia.

INDOCHINA

ALBERS CONIC EQUAL-AREA PROJECTION

SCALE 1:8,000,000

0 KILOMETERS 120 160 200

0 MILES 40 80 120 200

PHILIPPINES
ALBERS CONIC EQUAL-AREA PROJECTION
SCALE 1:7,000,000

0 KILOMETERS 100   150   200

0 MILES   50   100   150   200

SPRATLY ISLANDS
The scattered islands and reefs called the Spratly
Islands are claimed by Brunei, China, Malaysia,
the Philippines, Taiwan, and Vietnam. The Spratlys
possess rich fishing grounds and potential oil.

S O U T H   C H I N A   S E A

Vereker
Banks
Tungsha Tao
(Pratas I.)

Stewart
Seamount

Macclesfield
Banks

Scarborough Shoal

Reed Tablemount

Brown Bank

Seahorse Shoal

Lys Shoal
Loaita Bank
Tizard Bank
Union Reefs
Sabina Shoal
Carnatic Reef
Investigator Shoal
Commodore Reef

S P R A T L Y   I S L A N D S

P H I L I P P I N E   S E A

Benham Seamount

Batan Islands
+1008
Basco

Luzon Strait

Balintang Channel
1088

Babuyan Islands
543
794

Babuyan Channel

Mayraira Point
Cape Bojeador
Bangui
Claveria
Bacarra   Abulug   Santa Ana
Laoag   Aparri
San Nicolas   Buguey
Batac   Kabugao
Espiritu   2361
Cabugao   *Mount Sicapoo*
Bangued   Tuguegarao
Vigan
Narvacan   Lubuagan   Bontoc
Candon
Santa Cruz   Ilagan
Bangar   Roxas
Bacnotan
San Fernando   *Mount Pulog* 2934
Baguio   Bayombong
Cape Bolinao   **LUZON**
Lingayen   1850   Casiguran
Dagupan   San Jose
Santa Cruz   **San Carlos**   Cuyapo   Baler
Masinloc   2037   Victoria   Cape Encanto
Palauig   **Tarlac**   Gapan
Angeles   **Cabanatuan**
San Narciso   San Fernando
Olongapo   Malolos
Bataan Peninsula   **Manila** **Quezon City**
Corregidor   **Cavite**

Iligan Point
Valley Head
Baguio Point
Aubarede Point
Divilacan Bay
NORTHERN SIERRA MADRE NATIONAL PARK
Palanan
Cape San Ildefonso
Polillo Islands

Lingayen Gulf

Lamon Bay

Lag. de Bay

Manila Bay

Lubang Island
Paluan
Mount Halcon
Mamburao   2505
Santa Cruz
Sablayan
MINDORO
2488   *Mount Baco*
Roxas
San Jose

Calapan
Boac
Pola
Marinduque

Jose Panganiban   Paracale
Santa Cruz   Daet
Pandan Point
Lucena   Panganiban (Payo)
Batangas   **Lipa**   *Tayabas Bay*   *Catanduanes*
San Pablo   *Ragay Gulf*   Mt. Isarog   Virac
Mulanay   Naga   1850
Iriga   2462   Mayon Volcano
Ligao   **Legazpi**
Burias   Magallanes   Sorsogon
Bulan   Gubat
Sibuyan   Ticao   Catarman   Allen

Mindoro Strait   *Tablas Strait*   *Sibuyan Sea*
Yog Point
San Miguel Bay

Busuanga   Romblon
Bintuan   Sibuyan 2050
Culion   Santa Fe
Culion   Masbate
Calamian Group   Nabas   *Masbate*   Catbalogan
Pandan   Kalibo   **Roxas**
El Nido   659   Culasi   2117   Ajuy   Cataingan
703   *Cuyo Islands*   *Mount Nangtud*   **PANAY**
Taytay   Cuyo   Alimodian
Roxas   1603   San Jose   Dao   **Iloilo**   Cadiz   Bogo
Cleopatra Needle   **Bacolod**   Borbon
PALAWAN   La Carlota   908   **Cebu**
Puerto Princesa   Isabela   **San Carlos**   **CEBU**
Aborlan   Inagauan   *Cagayan Islands*   Cauayan   870
Birong   1709   Sipalay   Tanjay   Tagbilaran
Malabuñgan   Hinoba-an   *Panay Gulf*   **BOHOL**
Quezon   Aboabo   Bayawan   Oslob   Siquijor
2100   Siaton   Dumaguete   Zamboanguita
Bonobono   Brooke's Point   Zamboanguita
Canipaan   Cape   Rio Tuba   *Tubbataha Reefs*
Buliluyan

Samar
SAMAR
Oras
Wright   Sulat
Catbalogan   Calbiga
Carigara   Basey
Tacloban   General MacArthur
1350   Guiuan
Ormoc   *Leyte Gulf*
Baybay   **LEYTE**
Sogod
Saint Bernard   Loreto
Dinagat
Siargao
Guindulman   Dapa
Placer   Lanuza
Surigao
2012
Salay   Mt. Hilonghilong
1713   Hilonghilong
Buenavista   **Butuan**

Imuruan Bay   *Ulugan Bay*
Malampaya Sound

Sulu Sea
Cagayan Islands

Dipolog   Baliangao
Manukan   Oroquieta   Gingoog
Sindangan   **Cagayan de Oro**
Liloy   1224   **Ozamis**   Tubod
Siocon   **Pagadian**   **Iligan**   Malaybalay   2896
Kabasalan   2316   **Marawi**   Lingig
Alicia   *Lake Lanao*   **MINDANAO**   Cateel
Sibuco   Malabang   Kibawe   Compostela
Zamboanga   Kabawe   Tagum   2810   Baganga
Isabela   Margosatubig   Carmen   Maco
Lamitan   **Cotabato**   Babak   Manay
1011   Datu Piang   *Mount Apo* 2954   **Davao**
Basilan   Lebak   Isulan   Buluan   Digos   1633
Palimbang   Koronadal   Padada   Mati
2083   Tupi   *Davao Gulf*
Kiamba   **General Santos**   *Cape San Agustin*
Glan   Jose Abad Santos
Tinaca Point   886   *Sarangani Islands*

Iligan Bay
Illana Bay
Moro Gulf
Sibuguey Bay
Basilan Strait

Pangutaran
Pangutaran Group
Jolo   Jolo
Parang
Luuk
Tapul
Siasi

Sulu Archipelago
Bongao   533
Tawi Tawi

Celebes Sea   *Sarangani Bay*

INDONESIA   *Miangas (Palmas)*
Kepulauan Karakaralong   *Kepulauan Nanusa*

Sikuati   Kudat
Bandau   Tandik
Senaja
Kota Belud   1219
Tuaran   *KINABALU PARK*
4101
Kota   *Kinabalu*
Kinabalu   Ranau
CROCKER RANGE N.P.
MALAYSIA
Tambunan   Lamag
Bingkor   Sukau
Beaufort   Pintasan
Melalap   Lintang
Weston   Pinangah
Bandar   Lahad Datu
Seri Begawan   *Darvel Bay*
BRUNEI   **S A B A H**
Brunei Bay

Sandakan

Banggi
Cagayan Sulu I.
Balabac
Balabac
Balabac Strait
Labuk Bay
Sugut
Tanjong Sugut
Sibutu Passage

Longitude East 123° of Greenwich

ASIA 203

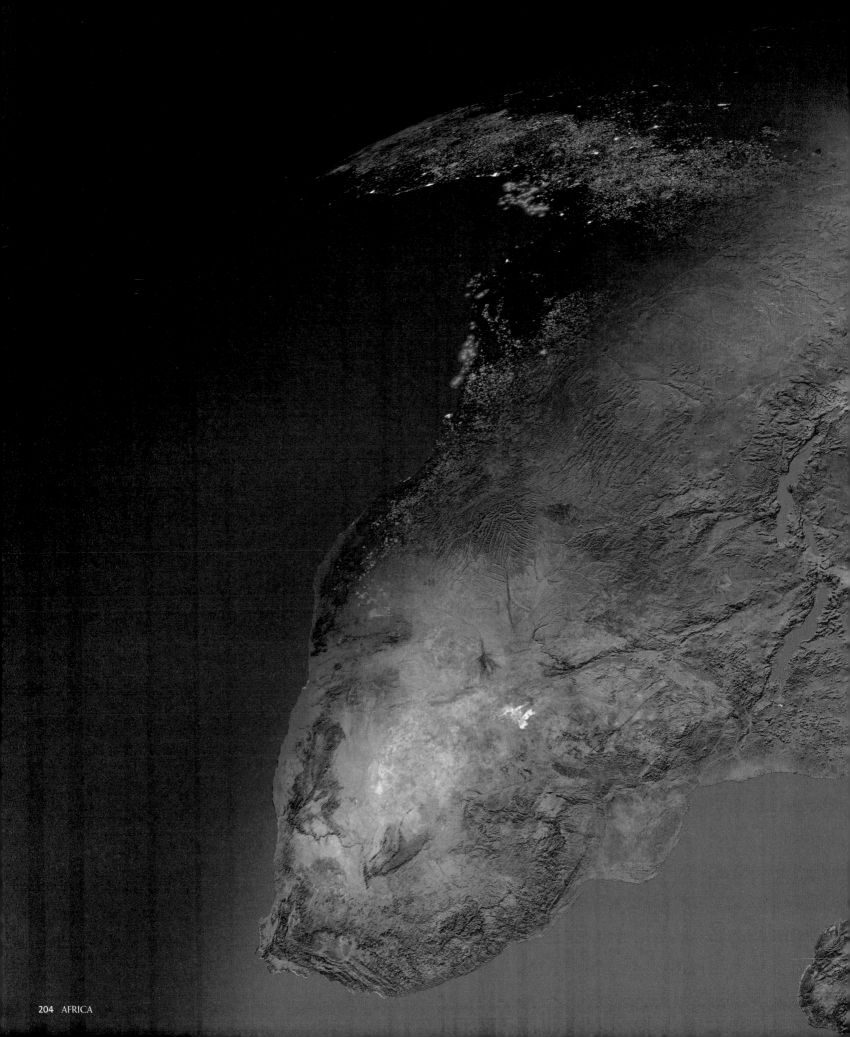

Mother continent of us all, Africa gave rise to modern humans; through mitochondrial DNA analysis, scientists now calculate that all living humans are related to a single woman who lived in Africa 150,000 years ago. Africa is the only continent to reach into both north and south temperate zones, with a broad tropical belt that acted as a barrier to the spread of agriculture. The continent also lacked animals that could be domesticated, such as cows and sheep. Its magnificent wild animals evolved in conjunction with hunters and developed a healthy wariness of humans. That same co-evolution made it easier for microbes to jump from animals to humans. One contemporary metamorphosis, HIV/AIDS, now infects approximately 20% of the population of some sub-Saharan countries. European colonization engulfed the continent in the 19th and early 20th centuries, driven partly by the discovery of gold and diamonds. Beginning in the 1960s, independence has divided Africa into 53 nations, 15 of them landlocked, where loyalties to tribe and religion often run deeper than nationhood. Civil wars have erupted between rival ethnic groups, notably between the Hutu and Tutsi in central Africa and in Darfur, Sudan, between black Africans and pro-government Arab militias. African nations today also grapple with corruption, disease, poverty, environmental degradation, and population pressure. Although Africa remains largely rural, urban centers such as Lagos, Nairobi, and Johannesburg are mushrooming. On the plus side, oil production in West Africa could double in the next decade, raising the possibility of a new Africa-centric approach to resource use. The rivers of Africa can generate hydroelectric power. The wild animals are a draw for ecotourists. The forests of the Congo Basin could be logged sustainably. Technology, such as cell phones, is improving communications. And in the land of the first mother, women are becoming empowered, as shown by the environmental activist, Wangari Maathai, Nobel Peace Prize laureate from Kenya.

IMAGE BY ROBERT STACEY, WORLDSAT INTERNATIONAL INC.

AZIMUTHAL EQUIDISTANT PROJECTION
SCALE 1:37,000,000

0 KILOMETERS   600 800 1000

0 MILES 200   400   600   800 1000

MADEIRA IS.
(PORTUGAL)

CANARY IS.
(SPAIN)

Algiers
Tunis
Rabat
TUNISIA
MOROCCO
Tripoli
Cairo

WESTERN
SAHARA
(MOROCCO)

ALGERIA
LIBYA
EGYPT

Nouakchott
CAPE
VERDE
MAURITANIA
MALI
Praia
Dakar
NIGER
CHAD
SUDAN
Khartoum
ERITREA
Asmara
SENEGAL
GAMBIA Banjul
Bamako
Niamey
N'Djamena
DJIBOUTI
Djibouti
GUINEA-BISSAU
Bissau
BURKINA
FASO
NIGERIA
ETHIOPIA
SOMALIA
GUINEA
Conakry
CÔTE
D'IVOIRE
(IVORY COAST)
Ouagadougou
BENIN
Abuja
Addis Ababa
Freetown
TOGO
GHANA
CENTRAL
AFRICAN
REPUBLIC
SIERRA LEONE
Yamoussoukro
Lomé
Porto-Novo
Monrovia
Accra
Cotonou
Bangui
LIBERIA
Abidjan
CAMEROON
Mogadishu
Malabo
Yaoundé
EQUATORIAL GUINEA
RIO MUNI
UGANDA
KENYA
SAO TOME
AND PRINCIPE
São
Tomé
Libreville
CONGO
Kampala
Nairobi
GABON
Brazzaville
Kinshasa
Kigali
RWANDA
Victoria
CABINDA
(ANGOLA)
DEMOCRATIC
REPUBLIC OF
THE CONGO
Bujumbura
BURUNDI
SEYCHELLES
Luanda
Dodoma
Dar es Salaam
TANZANIA
Moroni
ANGOLA
ZAMBIA
Lilongwe
MALAWI
COMOROS
Lusaka
MOZAMBIQUE
Harare
Antananarivo
NAMIBIA
ZIMBABWE
MADAGASCAR
MAURITIUS
Windhoek
Port
Louis
BOTSWANA
RÉUNION
(FRANCE)
Gaborone
Pretoria
(Tshwane)
Maputo
Mbabane
Lobamba
SWAZILAND
Bloemfontein
Maseru
LESOTHO
SOUTH
AFRICA
Cape Town

Land cover
Forest
- Evergreen needleleaf
- Evergreen broadleaf
- Deciduous needleleaf
- Deciduous broadleaf
- Mixed forest
- Woodland

Grassland or shrubland
- Wooded grassland
- Closed shrubland
- Open shrubland
- Grassland

Other
- Cropland
- Barren (Desert and Polar Ice)
- Built-up

TEMPERATURE AND RAINFALL

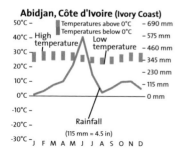

Abidjan, Côte d'Ivoire (Ivory Coast)

High temperature
Low temperature
Temperatures above 0°C
Temperatures below 0°C

Rainfall
(115 mm = 4.5 in)

J F M A M J J A S O N D

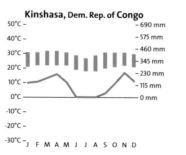

Kinshasa, Dem. Rep. of Congo

J F M A M J J A S O N D

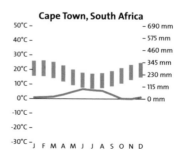

Cape Town, South Africa

J F M A M J J A S O N D

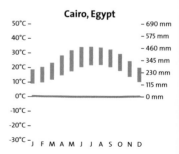

Cairo, Egypt

J F M A M J J A S O N D

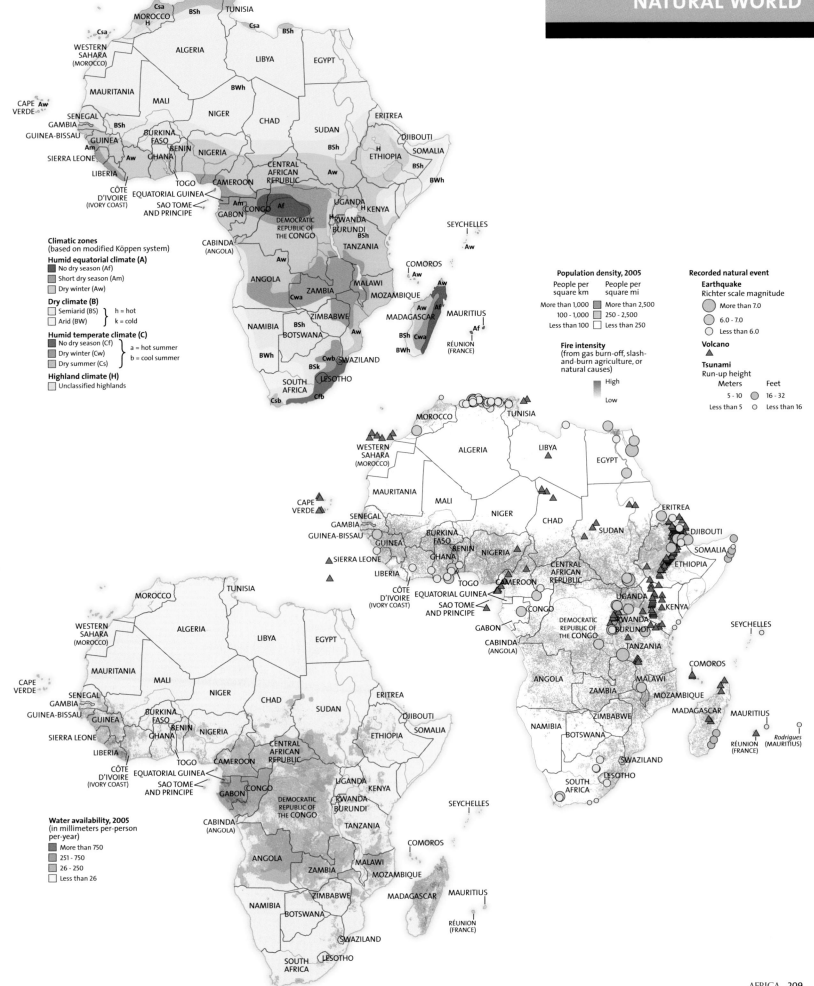

Climatic zones
(based on modified Köppen system)

Humid equatorial climate (A)
- No dry season (Af)
- Short dry season (Am)
- Dry winter (Aw)

Dry climate (B)
- Semiarid (BS) h = hot
- Arid (BW) k = cold

Humid temperate climate (C)
- No dry season (Cf) a = hot summer
- Dry winter (Cw) b = cool summer
- Dry summer (Cs)

Highland climate (H)
- Unclassified highlands

Population density, 2005
People per square km | People per square mi
More than 1,000 | More than 2,500
100 - 1,000 | 250 - 2,500
Less than 100 | Less than 250

Fire intensity
(from gas burn-off, slash-and-burn agriculture, or natural causes)
High
Low

Recorded natural event

Earthquake
Richter scale magnitude
- More than 7.0
- 6.0 - 7.0
- Less than 6.0

Volcano

Tsunami
Run-up height
Meters | Feet
5 - 10 | 16 - 32
Less than 5 | Less than 16

Water availability, 2005
(in millimeters per-person per-year)
- More than 750
- 251 - 750
- 26 - 250
- Less than 26

Population density, 2005

People per square km	People per square mi
More than 195	More than 500
60 - 195	150 - 500
10 - 59	25 - 149
1 - 9	1 - 24
Less than 1	Less than 1

POPULATION PYRAMIDS

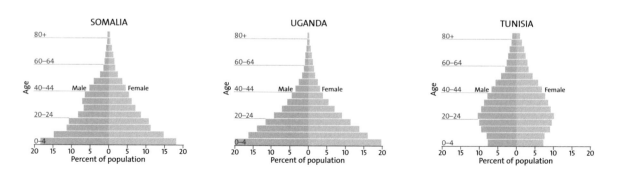

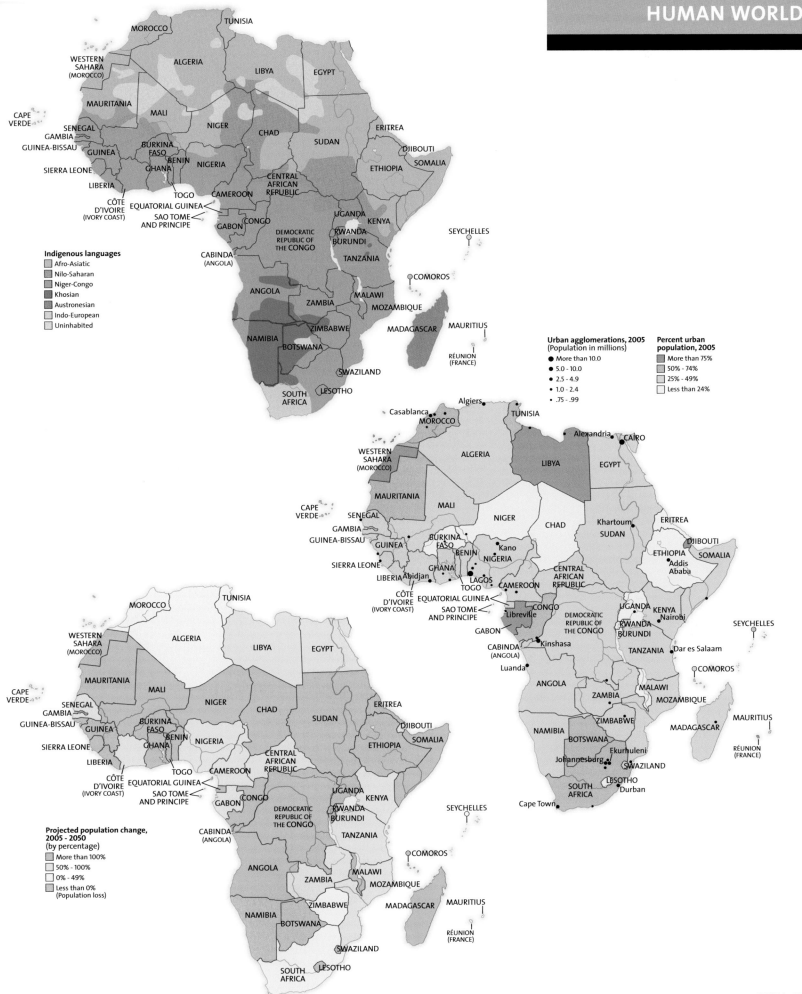

Indigenous languages
- Afro-Asiatic
- Nilo-Saharan
- Niger-Congo
- Khosian
- Austronesian
- Indo-European
- Uninhabited

Urban agglomerations, 2005
(Population in millions)
- ● More than 10.0
- ● 5.0 - 10.0
- ● 2.5 - 4.9
- ● 1.0 - 2.4
- · .75 - .99

Percent urban population, 2005
- More than 75%
- 50% - 74%
- 25% - 49%
- Less than 24%

Projected population change, 2005 - 2050
(by percentage)
- More than 100%
- 50% - 100%
- 0% - 49%
- Less than 0% (Population loss)

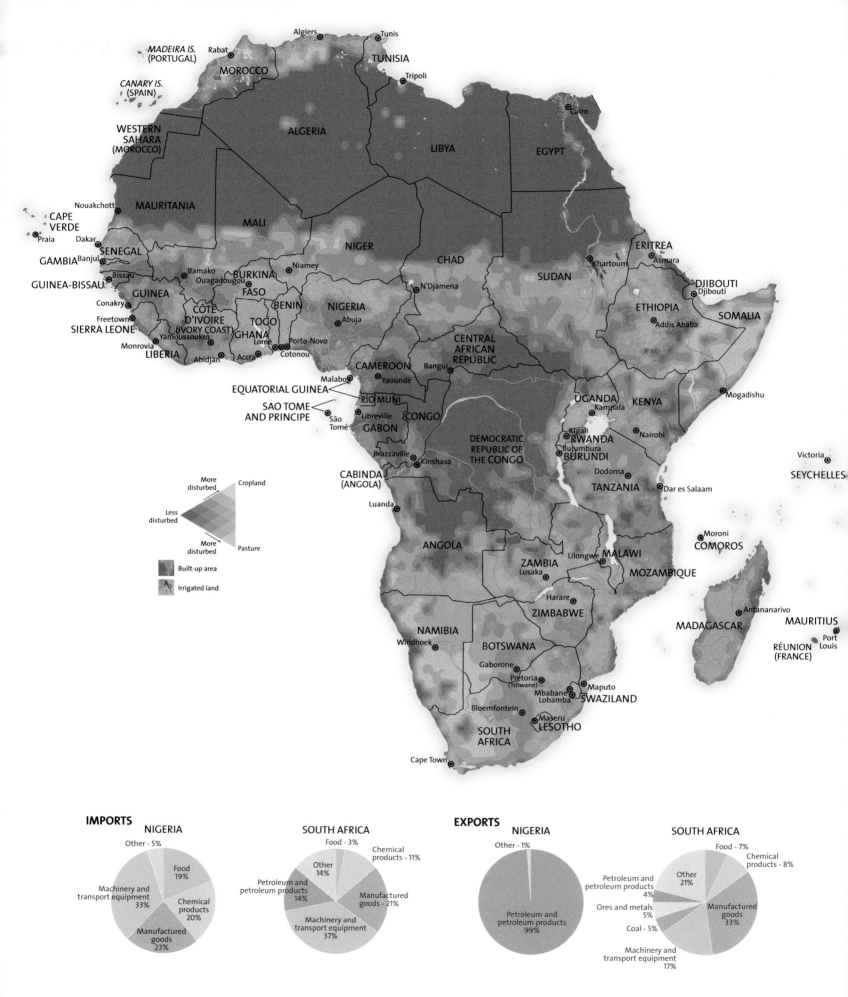

Algiers · Tunis
MOROCCO · Rabat · Tripoli
TUNISIA
MADEIRA IS. (PORTUGAL)
CANARY IS. (SPAIN)
WESTERN SAHARA (MOROCCO)
ALGERIA
LIBYA
EGYPT
Cairo
MAURITANIA
Nouakchott
MALI
NIGER
CHAD
SUDAN
Khartoum
ERITREA
Asmara
CAPE VERDE
Praia · Dakar
SENEGAL
Niamey
N'Djamena
DJIBOUTI
Djibouti
GAMBIA Banjul
GUINEA-BISSAU
Bissau
BURKINA FASO
Ouagadougou
Bamako
NIGERIA
Abuja
CENTRAL AFRICAN REPUBLIC
Bangui
ETHIOPIA
Addis Ababa
SOMALIA
GUINEA
Conakry
CÔTE D'IVOIRE (IVORY COAST)
BENIN
TOGO
GHANA
Lomé
Porto-Novo
Cotonou
CAMEROON
Yaoundé
UGANDA
Kampala
KENYA
Nairobi
Mogadishu
SIERRA LEONE
Freetown
Yamoussoukro
Accra
Monrovia
LIBERIA
Abidjan
Malabo
EQUATORIAL GUINEA
RIO MUNI
CONGO
Libreville
São Tomé
GABON
DEMOCRATIC REPUBLIC OF THE CONGO
RWANDA
Kigali
Bujumbura
BURUNDI
Dodoma
TANZANIA
Dar es Salaam
Victoria
SEYCHELLES
SAO TOME AND PRINCIPE
Brazzaville
Kinshasa
CABINDA (ANGOLA)
Luanda
ANGOLA
ZAMBIA
Lusaka
Lilongwe MALAWI
MOZAMBIQUE
Moroni
COMOROS
Harare
ZIMBABWE
MADAGASCAR
Antananarivo
MAURITIUS
Port Louis
RÉUNION (FRANCE)
NAMIBIA
Windhoek
BOTSWANA
Gaborone
Pretoria (Tshwane)
Maputo
Mbabane
Lobamba
SWAZILAND
Bloemfontein
Maseru
LESOTHO
SOUTH AFRICA
Cape Town

More disturbed — Cropland
Less disturbed
More disturbed — Pasture
Built-up area
Irrigated land

IMPORTS

NIGERIA
Other - 5%
Food 19%
Machinery and transport equipment 33%
Chemical products 20%
Manufactured goods 23%

SOUTH AFRICA
Food - 3%
Chemical products - 11%
Other 14%
Petroleum and petroleum products 14%
Manufactured goods - 21%
Machinery and transport equipment 37%

EXPORTS

NIGERIA
Other - 1%
Petroleum and petroleum products 99%

SOUTH AFRICA
Food - 7%
Chemical products - 8%
Other 21%
Petroleum and petroleum products 4%
Ores and metals 5%
Coal - 5%
Machinery and transport equipment 17%
Manufactured goods 33%

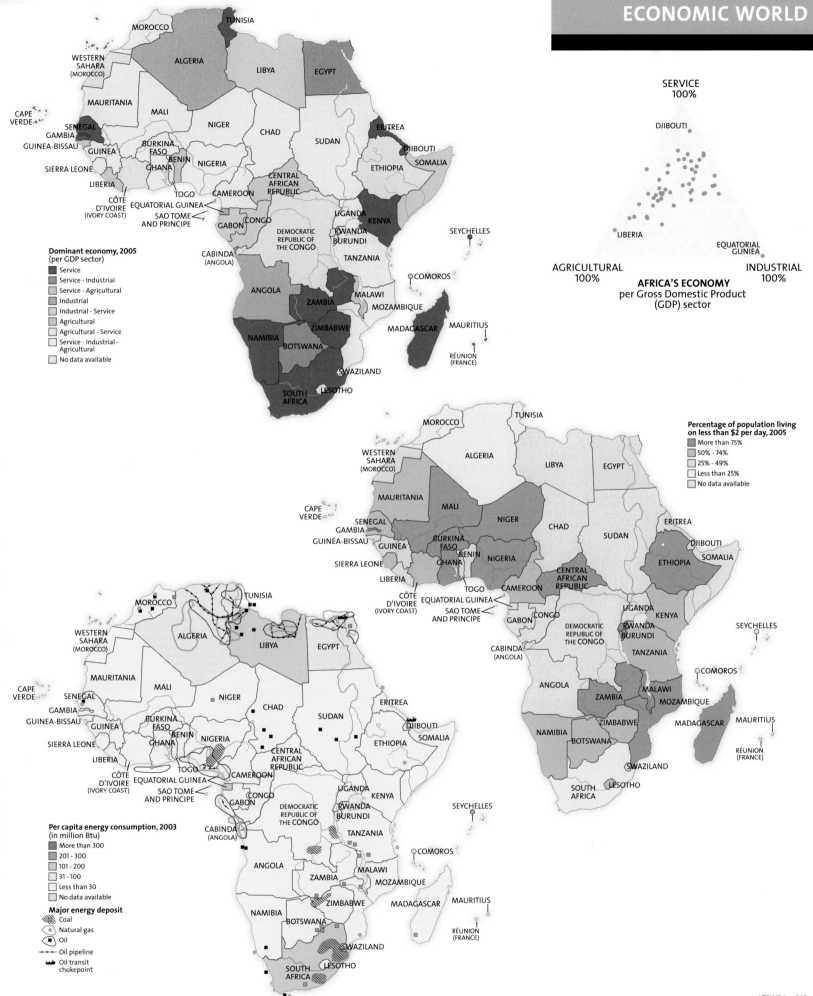

Dominant economy, 2005
(per GDP sector)
- Service
- Service - Industrial
- Service - Agricultural
- Industrial
- Industrial - Service
- Agricultural
- Agricultural - Service
- Service - Industrial - Agricultural
- No data available

SERVICE
100%

DJIBOUTI

LIBERIA

EQUATORIAL
GUNIEA

AGRICULTURAL
100%

INDUSTRIAL
100%

AFRICA'S ECONOMY
per Gross Domestic Product
(GDP) sector

**Percentage of population living
on less than $2 per day, 2005**
- More than 75%
- 50% - 74%
- 25% - 49%
- Less than 25%
- No data available

Per capita energy consumption, 2003
(in million Btu)
- More than 300
- 201 - 300
- 101 - 200
- 31 - 100
- Less than 30
- No data available

Major energy deposit
- Coal
- Natural gas
- Oil
- Oil pipeline
- Oil transit chokepoint

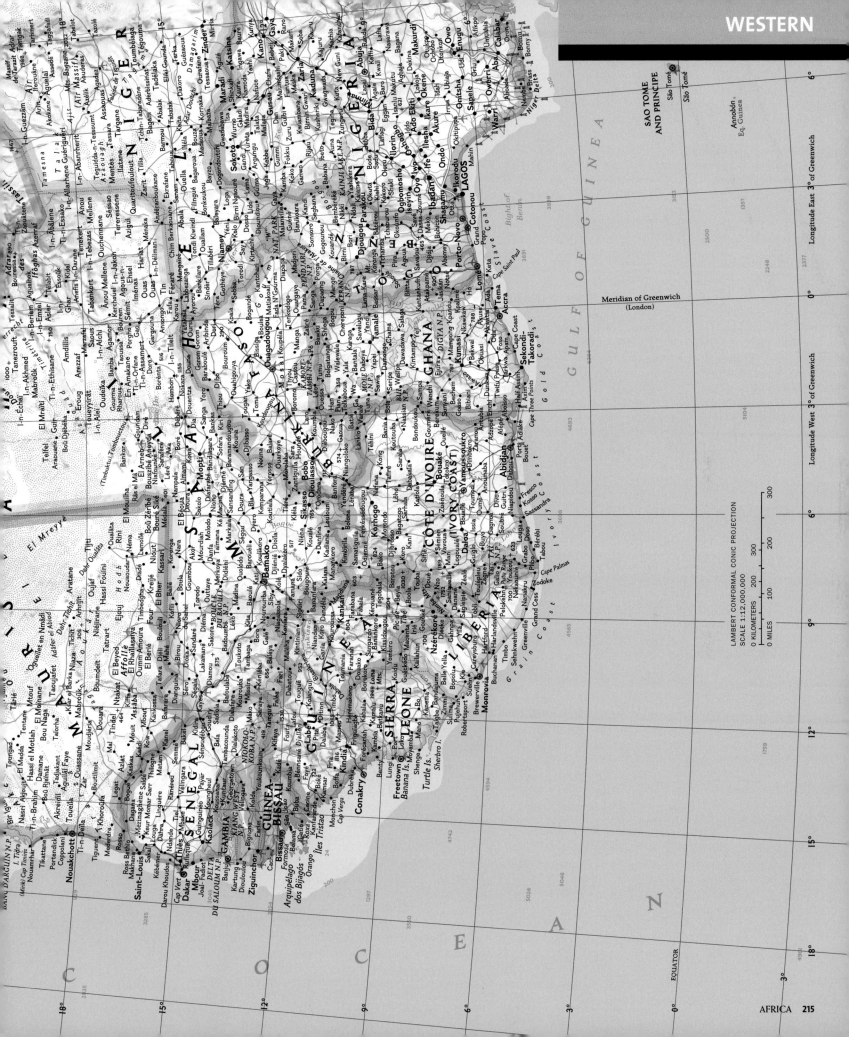

LAMBERT CONFORMAL CONIC PROJECTION
SCALE 1:12,000,000

0 KILOMETERS 200 300

0 MILES 100 200 300

TURKEY
Konya
Adana
Adıyaman
Diyarbakır
Batman
Mardin
Şanlıurfa
Gaziantep
Iskenderun
Hatay (Antioch)
Halab (Aleppo)
Ar Raqqah
CYPRUS
Lefkosia (Lefkoşa, Nicosia)
SYRIA
Ḩimş (Homs)
Tadmur
Al Lādhiqīyah (Latakia)
LEBANON
Beyrouth (Beirut)
Dimashq (Damascus)
Haifa
Tel Aviv-Yafo
Jerusalem
ISRAEL
'Ammān
JORDAN
Be'ér Sheva
GAZA STRIP
WEST BANK
Dead Sea
IRAQ
Al Mawşil (Mosul)
Kirkūk
As Sulaymānīyah
Baghdād
Karbalā'
An Najaf
Al Başrah
SYRIAN DESERT
MESOPOTAMIA
Euphrates
Tigris
IRAN
TEHRĀN
Hamadān
Kermānshāh
Qom
Kāshān
Eşfahān (Isfahan)
Shīrāz
Yazd
Kermān
Ahvāz
Ābādān
Būshehr
Bandar-e 'Abbās
Dasht-e Kavīr (Salt Desert)
KHORASAN
ZAGROS MOUNTAINS
KUWAIT
SAUDI ARABIA
Ar Riyāḑ (Riyadh)
Ad Dammām
Al Madīnah (Medina)
Makkah (Mecca)
Jeddah
Aţ Ţā'if
An Nafūd
Ar Rub' al Khālī (Empty Quarter)
Al Hufūf (Hofuf)
BAHRAIN
Al Manāmah (Manama)
QATAR
Ad Dawḩah (Doha)
UNITED ARAB EMIRATES
Abu Dabi
Dubai
Sharjah
OMAN
Strait of Hormuz
PERSIAN GULF
Gulf of Oman
YEMEN
Şan'ā' (Sanaa)
'Adan (Aden)
Al Ḩudaydah
Ta'izz
ḨAḐRAMAWT
Socotra
GULF OF ADEN
RED SEA
ERITREA
Asmara
ETHIOPIA
DJIBOUTI
Djibouti
SOMALIA
SOMALILAND
PUNTLAND
Hargeysa
INDIAN OCEAN
EGYPT
SINAI
El Suweis (Suez)
Aswân
Luxor
Lake Nasser
SUDAN
Khartoum
Omdurman
Port Sudan
Kassala
Nubian Desert
WHITE NILE
BLUE NILE
Tana Hāyk'
Bahir Dar
Gonder
Mek'ele
Dire Dawa
Harer
Cape Gwardafuy
33°
36°
39°
42°
45°
48°
51°
33°
30°
27°
24°
21°
18°
15°
12°
9°

LAMBERT CONFORMAL CONIC PROJECTION
SCALE 1:12,000,000
0 KILOMETERS 200   300
0 MILES   100   200   300

COASTAL WEST AFRICA
ALBERS CONIC EQUAL-AREA PROJECTION
SCALE 1:8,000,000

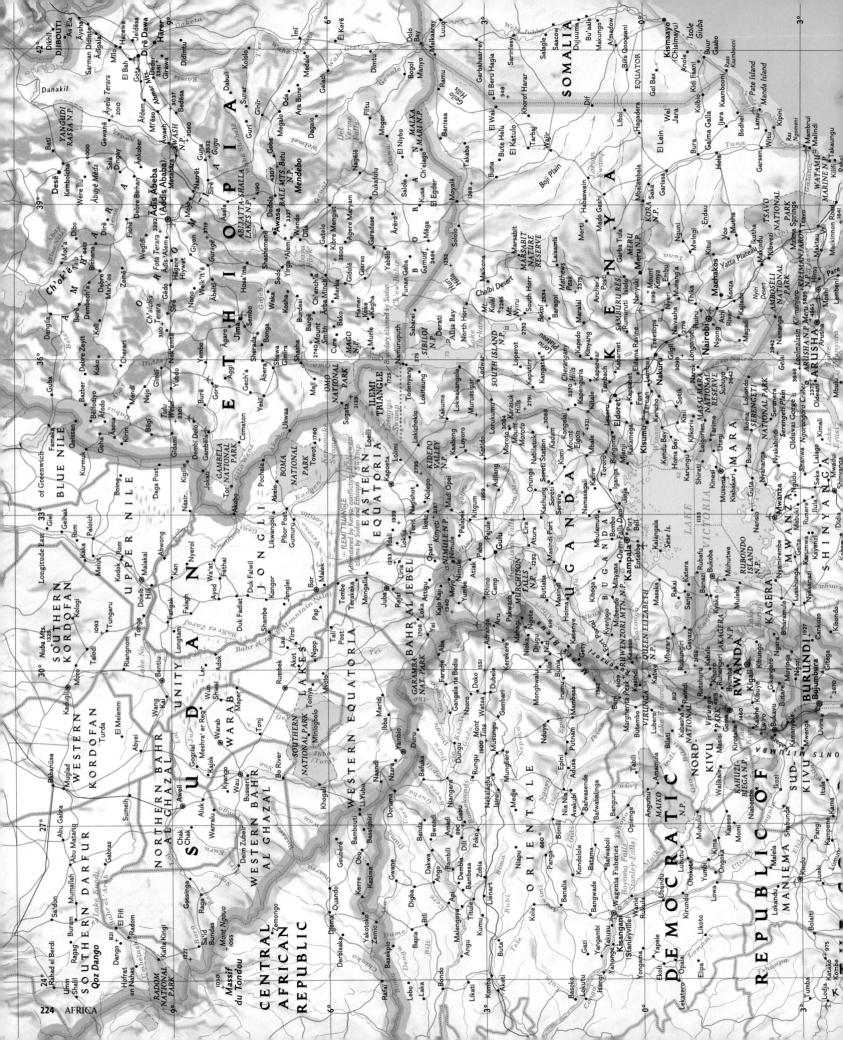

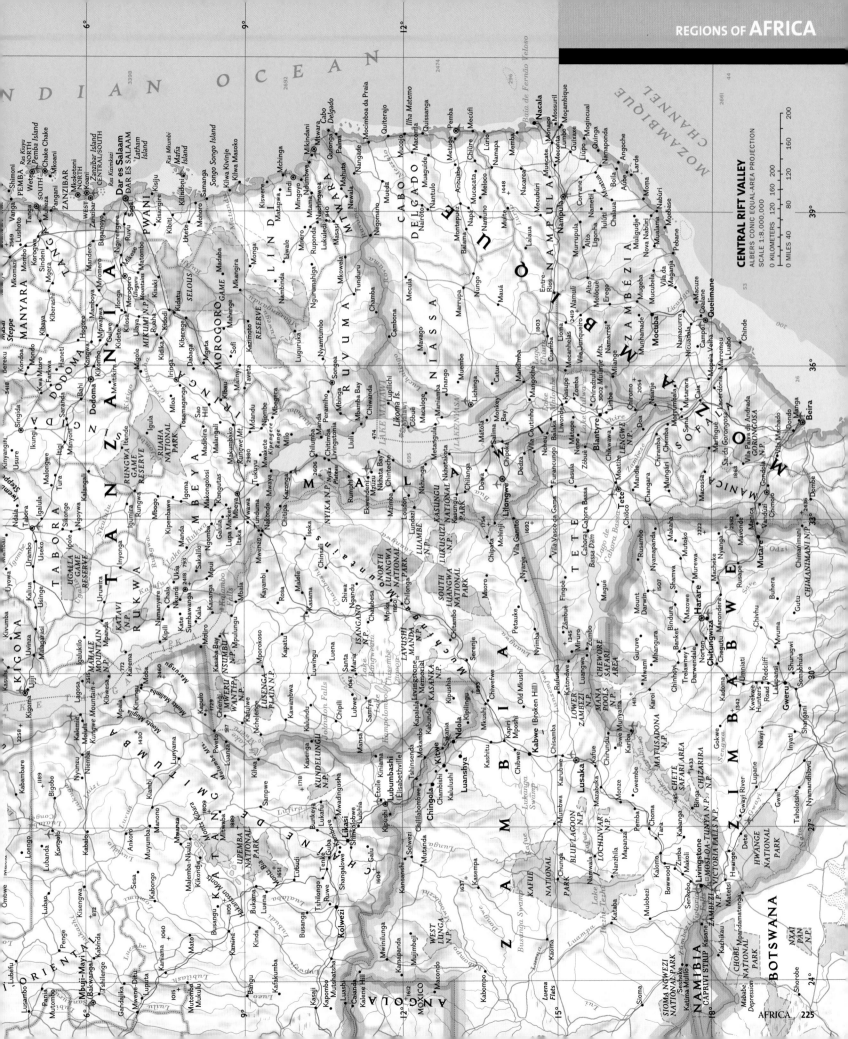

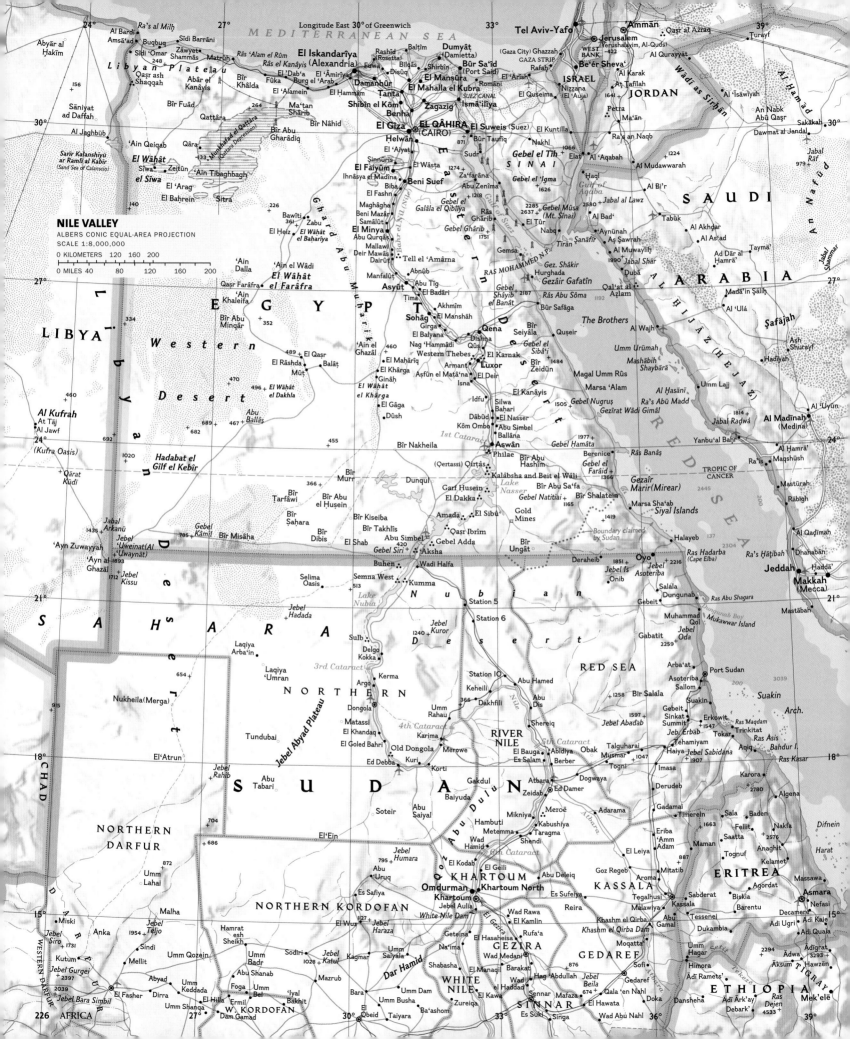

island nation and smallest, flattest continent, with a territory about the size of the United States, Australia has gone on a planetary walkabout since it broke away from the supercontinent of Gondwana about 55 million years ago. Isolated, dry, and scoured by erosion, Australia developed unique animals, notably marsupials such as kangaroos, and plants, such as more than 600 eucalyptus species. The land surface has been stable enough to preserve some of the world's oldest rocks and mineral deposits, dating to the original formation of Earth's crust. Precambrian fossils include stromatolites—photosynthetic bacteria that generated oxygen in the early atmosphere and whose descendants still grow mounded in shallow lagoons, such as in Shark Bay in western Australia. In contrast, New Zealand's two principal islands, about the size of Colorado, are younger and tell of a more violent geology that raised high volcanic mountains above deep fjords, leaving landscapes reminiscent of Europe's Alps, Norway's coast, and Scotland's moors. Both nations were first inhabited by seafarers, Australia as long as 50,000 years ago, New Zealand little more than a thousand. From the late 18th century to the early 20th, both were British colonies. Both have transformed themselves from commerce based on exports of beef and hides, lamb and wool, to fully integrated industrialized and service-oriented economies. Both have striven with varying success to accommodate aboriginal peoples, as well as recent immigrants—many from Vietnam and China and many of the Muslim faith—as part of a diverse, modern society. Oceania, roughly those islands of the southwest Pacific that include Polynesia, Micronesia, and Melanesia, was settled by indigenous expeditions sailing in multihulled vessels. These adventurers settled nearly every inhabitable Pacific island and perhaps made landfall as far distant as South America before Europeans appeared over the horizon in the 17th century. Today these islands are in various states of nationhood or dependency, prosperity or poverty, and often ignored if not outright exploited.

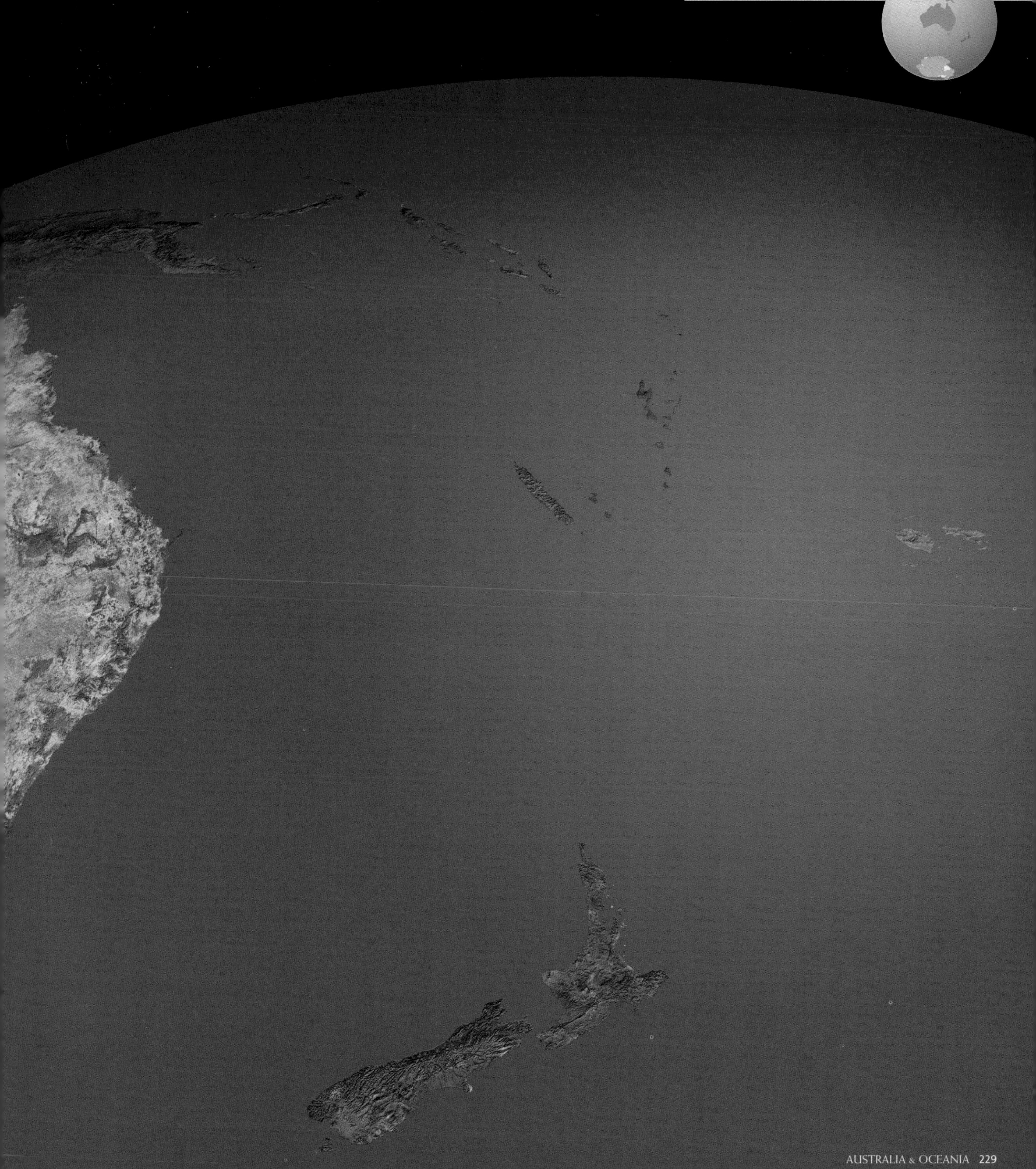

SOLOMON SEA

TROBRIAND IS.
Goodenough I. 2566
D'ENTRECASTEAUX IS.
Woodlark Is.
LOUISIADE ARCHIPELAGO
Normanby I. 3876 Misima
Fergusson I.
Tagula
Rossel I.

CORAL SEA

TROPIC OF CAPRICORN

Lord Howe I.
Ball's Pyramid

TASMAN SEA

Owen Stanley Mt. Victoria 4035m
Hood Point
PAPUA NEW GUINEA
Port Moresby

NEW GUINEA

Flinders Entrance
Olinda Entrance
Pandora Entrance
Cape York
Port Musgrave
Cape York
Albatross Bay
Mt. Carter 671
Archer
Mitchell

Magdelaine Cays

Herald Cays

Tregrosse Islets

Great Barrier Reef

Hinchinbrook Island
Palm Is.

Cumberland Islands
Shaw Island

Percy Isles

Townshend I.

Keppel Bay

Capricorn Group
Bunker Group
Hervey Bay
Fraser Island

Moreton I.
N. Stradbroke I.

Cape Byron

Brisbane 1381

Sydney

Canberra, A.C.T.
Mt. Kosciuszko 2228 highest point in Australia

JERVIS BAY TERRITORY

BASS STRAIT

FURNEAUX GROUP
Flinders I.

TASMAN SEA

Mt. Ossa 1617
Hobart

TASMANIA

Cape Pillar
Storm Bay
Bruny I.

GREAT DIVIDING RANGE

QUEENSLAND

GREAT ARTESIAN BASIN

NEW SOUTH WALES

VICTORIA

Melbourne

ARAFURA SEA

GULF OF CARPENTARIA

Croker Island
Coburg Peninsula
Melville I.
Bathurst I.
Darwin

ARNHEM LAND

Groote Eylandt

NORTHERN TERRITORY

Barkly Tableland

CENTRAL LOWLANDS

SOUTH AUSTRALIA

Lake Eyre
LAKE EYRE BASIN

Flinders Ranges

Adelaide

Kangaroo I.

GREAT AUSTRALIAN BIGHT

Nullarbor Plain

WESTERN AUSTRALIA

GREAT SANDY DESERT

GIBSON DESERT

GREAT VICTORIA DESERT

Uluru (Ayers Rock)
MacDonnell Ranges
Musgrave Ranges

Kimberley Plateau

INDIAN OCEAN

TIMOR SEA

TIMOR-LESTE (EAST TIMOR)

TIMOR

INDONESIA

FLORES
Savu Sea
SUMBA
SUMBAWA

Bali Sea
BALI
JAVA
Surabaya

LOMBOK

Perth

Rottnest I.

Cape Leeuwin

Geographe Bay
Cape Naturaliste

Shark Bay

North West Cape

Exmouth Gulf

AUSTRALIA & OCEANIA

AZIMUTHAL EQUIDISTANT PROJECTION
SCALE 1:19,000,000

0 KILOMETERS 100 200 300 400 500
0 MILES 100 200 300 400 500

Longitude East 130° of Greenwich

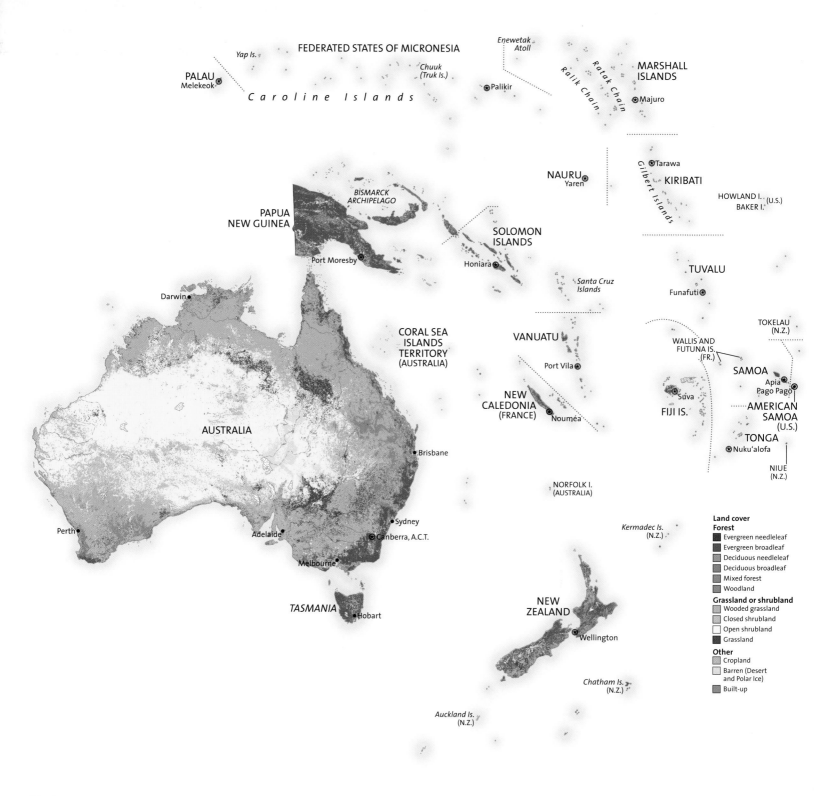

FEDERATED STATES OF MICRONESIA

Enewetak Atoll

Yap Is.

Chuuk (Truk Is.)

MARSHALL ISLANDS

PALAU
⊛ Melekeok

C a r o l i n e   I s l a n d s

⊛ Palikir

Ralik Chain

Ratak Chain

⊛ Majuro

NAURU
⊛ Yaren

⊛ Tarawa

KIRIBATI

Gilbert Islands

HOWLAND I. (U.S.)
BAKER I. (U.S.)

BISMARCK ARCHIPELAGO

PAPUA NEW GUINEA

SOLOMON ISLANDS

TUVALU

Funafuti ⊛

• Port Moresby

Honiara •

Santa Cruz Islands

TOKELAU (N.Z.)

Darwin •

CORAL SEA ISLANDS TERRITORY (AUSTRALIA)

VANUATU

WALLIS AND FUTUNA IS. (FR.)

SAMOA
Apia ⊛
Pago Pago ⊛

• Port Vila

AUSTRALIA

NEW CALEDONIA (FRANCE)

Nouméa •

Suva •

FIJI IS.

AMERICAN SAMOA (U.S.)

TONGA
⊛ Nuku'alofa

NIUE (N.Z.)

• Brisbane

Perth •

Adelaide •
Sydney •
⊛ Canberra, A.C.T.

Melbourne •

NORFOLK I. (AUSTRALIA)

Kermadec Is. (N.Z.)

Land cover
Forest
■ Evergreen needleleaf
■ Evergreen broadleaf
■ Deciduous needleleaf
■ Deciduous broadleaf
■ Mixed forest
■ Woodland

Grassland or shrubland
■ Wooded grassland
■ Closed shrubland
□ Open shrubland
■ Grassland

Other
□ Cropland
□ Barren (Desert and Polar Ice)
■ Built-up

TASMANIA

• Hobart

NEW ZEALAND

• Wellington

Chatham Is. (N.Z.)

Auckland Is. (N.Z.)

TEMPERATURE AND RAINFALL

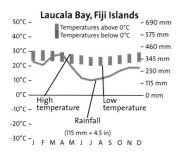

Laucala Bay, Fiji Islands

■ Temperatures above 0°C
■ Temperatures below 0°C

High temperature
Low temperature
Rainfall
(115 mm = 4.5 in)

J F M A M J J A S O N D

Auckland, New Zealand

Rainfall
(115 mm = 4.5 in)

J F M A M J J A S O N D

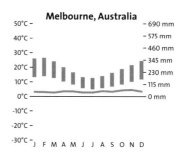

Melbourne, Australia

J F M A M J J A S O N D

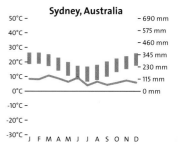

Sydney, Australia

J F M A M J J A S O N D

The entire extent of Oceania encompasses the islands of the Central and South Pacific, including Hawai'i, New Zealand, and Australia.

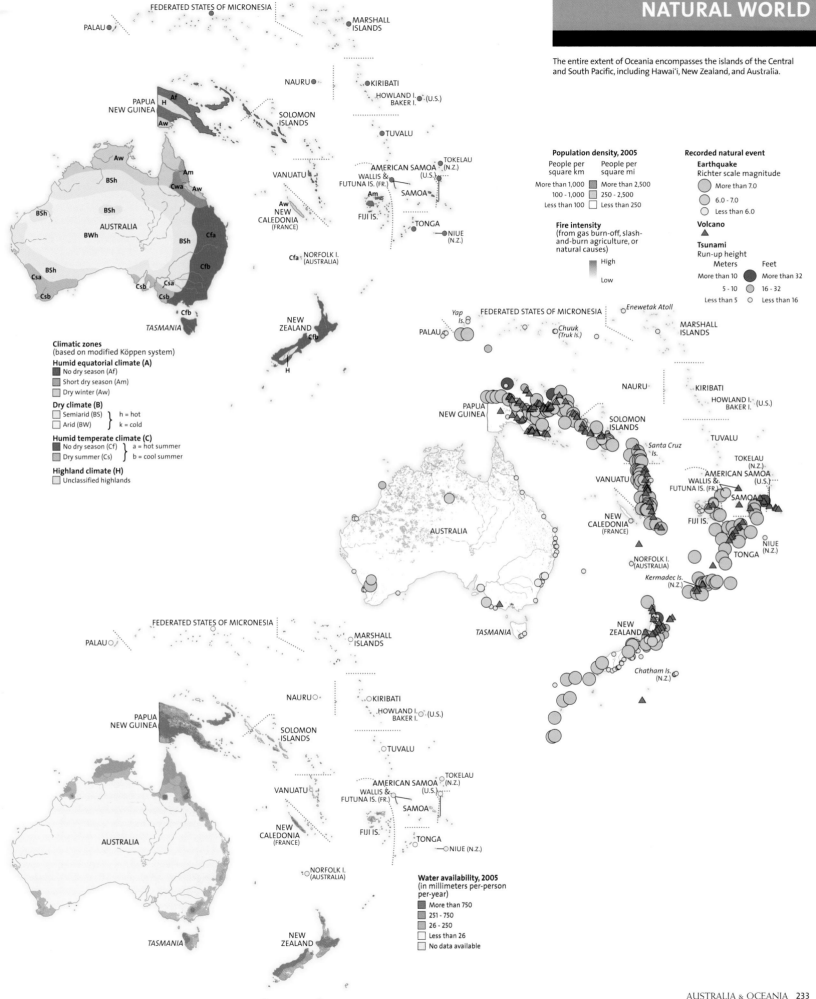

FEDERATED STATES OF MICRONESIA
PALAU
MARSHALL ISLANDS
NAURU
KIRIBATI
HOWLAND I.
BAKER I. (U.S.)
PAPUA NEW GUINEA
Af
H
Aw
SOLOMON ISLANDS
TUVALU
Aw
BSh
Am
Cwa
Aw
TOKELAU (N.Z.)
AMERICAN SAMOA (U.S.)
BSh
BSh
VANUATU
WALLIS & FUTUNA IS. (FR.)
Am
SAMOA
BWh
AUSTRALIA
Aw
NEW CALEDONIA (FRANCE)
FIJI IS.
TONGA
BSh
Cfa
NIUE (N.Z.)
BSh
Csa
Cfb
Cfa
NORFOLK I. (AUSTRALIA)
Csb
Csb
Csb
Cfb
TASMANIA

Climatic zones
(based on modified Köppen system)

Humid equatorial climate (A)
- No dry season (Af)
- Short dry season (Am)
- Dry winter (Aw)

Dry climate (B)
- Semiarid (BS) } h = hot
- Arid (BW) } k = cold

Humid temperate climate (C)
- No dry season (Cf) } a = hot summer
- Dry summer (Cs) } b = cool summer

Highland climate (H)
- Unclassified highlands

NEW ZEALAND
Cfb
H

Population density, 2005

People per square km		People per square mi
More than 1,000	▓	More than 2,500
100 - 1,000	▒	250 - 2,500
Less than 100	☐	Less than 250

Fire intensity
(from gas burn-off, slash-and-burn agriculture, or natural causes)
High
Low

Recorded natural event

Earthquake
Richter scale magnitude
○ More than 7.0
○ 6.0 - 7.0
○ Less than 6.0

Volcano ▲

Tsunami
Run-up height

Meters		Feet
More than 10	●	More than 32
5 - 10	●	16 - 32
Less than 5	○	Less than 16

Yap Is.
FEDERATED STATES OF MICRONESIA
Enewetak Atoll
PALAU
Chuuk (Truk Is.)
MARSHALL ISLANDS
NAURU
KIRIBATI
HOWLAND I.
BAKER I. (U.S.)
PAPUA NEW GUINEA
SOLOMON ISLANDS
TUVALU
Santa Cruz Is.
TOKELAU (N.Z.)
VANUATU
WALLIS & FUTUNA IS. (FR.)
AMERICAN SAMOA (U.S.)
SAMOA
NEW CALEDONIA (FRANCE)
FIJI IS.
AUSTRALIA
NIUE (N.Z.)
TONGA
NORFOLK I. (AUSTRALIA)
Kermadec Is. (N.Z.)
TASMANIA
NEW ZEALAND
Chatham Is. (N.Z.)

FEDERATED STATES OF MICRONESIA
PALAU
MARSHALL ISLANDS
NAURU
KIRIBATI
HOWLAND I.
BAKER I. (U.S.)
PAPUA NEW GUINEA
SOLOMON ISLANDS
TUVALU
VANUATU
TOKELAU (N.Z.)
AMERICAN SAMOA (U.S.)
WALLIS & FUTUNA IS. (FR.)
SAMOA
NEW CALEDONIA (FRANCE)
FIJI IS.
AUSTRALIA
TONGA
NIUE (N.Z.)
NORFOLK I. (AUSTRALIA)
TASMANIA
NEW ZEALAND

Water availability, 2005
(in millimeters per-person per-year)
- More than 750
- 251 - 750
- 26 - 250
- Less than 26
- No data available

FEDERATED STATES OF MICRONESIA

Enewetak Atoll

Yap Is.

PALAU
Koror ⊗

Chuuk (Truk Is.)

⊗ Palikir

C a r o l i n e   I s l a n d s

MARSHALL
ISLANDS

Ralik Chain

Ratak Chain

⊗ Majuro

⊗ Tarawa

NAURU ⊗
Yaren

KIRIBATI

Gilbert Islands

HOWLAND I. (U.S.)
BAKER I.

BISMARCK
ARCHIPELAGO

PAPUA
NEW GUINEA

Port Moresby ⊗

SOLOMON
ISLANDS

Honiara ⊗

Santa Cruz Islands

TUVALU

Funafuti ⊗

TOKELAU
(N.Z.)

Darwin ●

CORAL SEA
ISLANDS
TERRITORY
(AUSTRALIA)

VANUATU

Port-Vila ⊗

NEW
CALEDONIA
(FRANCE)

Nouméa ⊗

FIJI IS.

Suva ⊗

WALLIS AND
FUTUNA IS.
(FR.)

SAMOA
Apia ⊗
Pago Pago ⊗

AMERICAN
SAMOA
(U.S.)

AUSTRALIA

Brisbane ●

TONGA
⊗ Nuku'alofa

NIUE
(N.Z.)

NORFOLK I.
(AUSTRALIA)

Perth ●

Adelaide ●
Canberra, A.C.T. ⊗

Sydney ●

Melbourne ●

Kermadec Is.
(N.Z.)

TASMANIA

Hobart ●

NEW
ZEALAND

Wellington ⊗

Population density, 2005

People per square km	People per square mi
More than 195	More than 500
60 - 195	150 - 500
10 - 59	25 - 149
1 - 9	1 - 24
Less than 1	Less than 1

Chatham Is.
(N.Z.)

Auckland Is.
(N.Z.)

POPULATION PYRAMIDS

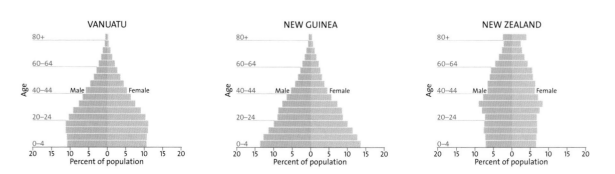

VANUATU

NEW GUINEA

NEW ZEALAND

Indigenous languages
Australian
- Aboriginal
- Undetermined

- Austronesian
- Papuan
- Uninhabited

Population of capitals and urban agglomerations, 2005 (in thousands)
- ● More than 4,000
- ● 1,260 - 3,999
- ● 420 - 1,259
- • 140 - 419
- • 7 - 139

Percent urban population, 2005
- More than 75%
- 50% - 74%
- 25% - 49%
- Less than 24%
- Uninhabited

Projected population change, 2005 - 2050 (by percentage)
- More than 100%
- 50% - 100%
- 0% - 49%
- Less than 0% (Population loss)

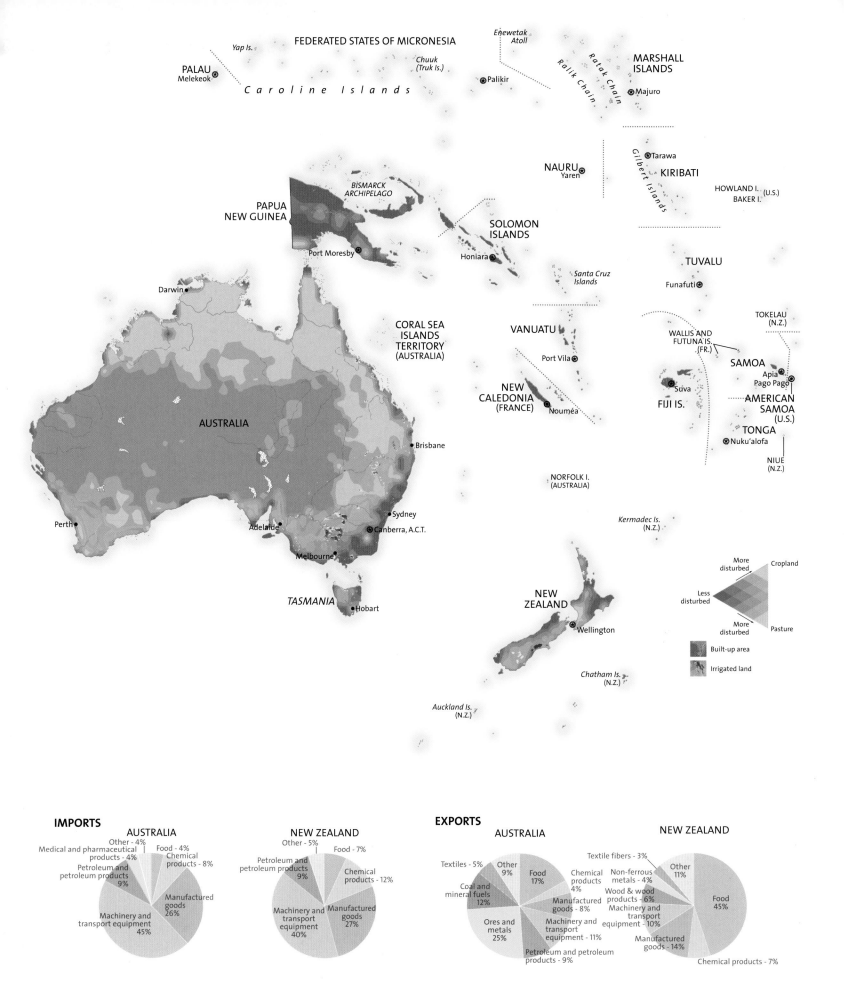

FEDERATED STATES OF MICRONESIA

Yap Is.

PALAU
Melekeok ⊗

Enewetak Atoll

Chuuk (Truk Is.)

⊗Palikir

MARSHALL ISLANDS

C a r o l i n e   I s l a n d s

Ralik Chain

Ratak Chain

●Majuro

⊗Tarawa

NAURU
Yaren ⊗

Gilbert Islands

KIRIBATI

HOWLAND I. (U.S.)
BAKER I.

BISMARCK ARCHIPELAGO

PAPUA NEW GUINEA

Port Moresby ⊗

SOLOMON ISLANDS

Honiara ⊗

Santa Cruz Islands

TUVALU

Funafuti ⊗

TOKELAU (N.Z.)

Darwin ●

CORAL SEA ISLANDS TERRITORY (AUSTRALIA)

VANUATU

Port Vila ⊗

WALLIS AND FUTUNA IS. (FR.)

SAMOA
Apia ⊗
Pago Pago ⊗

AMERICAN SAMOA (U.S.)

AUSTRALIA

NEW CALEDONIA (FRANCE)

Nouméa ●

FIJI IS.

Suva ●

TONGA
⊗Nuku'alofa

NIUE (N.Z.)

Brisbane ●

Perth ●

Adelaide ●

Sydney ●
⊗Canberra, A.C.T.

Melbourne ●

NORFOLK I. (AUSTRALIA)

Kermadec Is. (N.Z.)

More disturbed — Cropland

Less disturbed

TASMANIA

Hobart ●

NEW ZEALAND

⊗Wellington

Chatham Is. (N.Z.)

More disturbed — Pasture

Built-up area

Irrigated land

Auckland Is. (N.Z.)

IMPORTS

AUSTRALIA

Other - 4%
Medical and pharmaceutical products - 4%
Food - 4%
Chemical products - 8%
Petroleum and petroleum products 9%
Manufactured goods 26%
Machinery and transport equipment 45%

NEW ZEALAND

Other - 5%
Food - 7%
Petroleum and petroleum products 9%
Chemical products - 12%
Machinery and transport equipment 40%
Manufactured goods 27%

EXPORTS

AUSTRALIA

Textiles - 5%
Other 9%
Food 17%
Coal and mineral fuels 12%
Chemical products 4%
Manufactured goods - 8%
Ores and metals 25%
Machinery and transport equipment - 11%
Petroleum and petroleum products - 9%

NEW ZEALAND

Textile fibers - 3%
Non-ferrous metals - 4%
Other 11%
Wood & wood products - 6%
Machinery and transport equipment - 10%
Food 45%
Manufactured goods - 14%
Chemical products - 7%

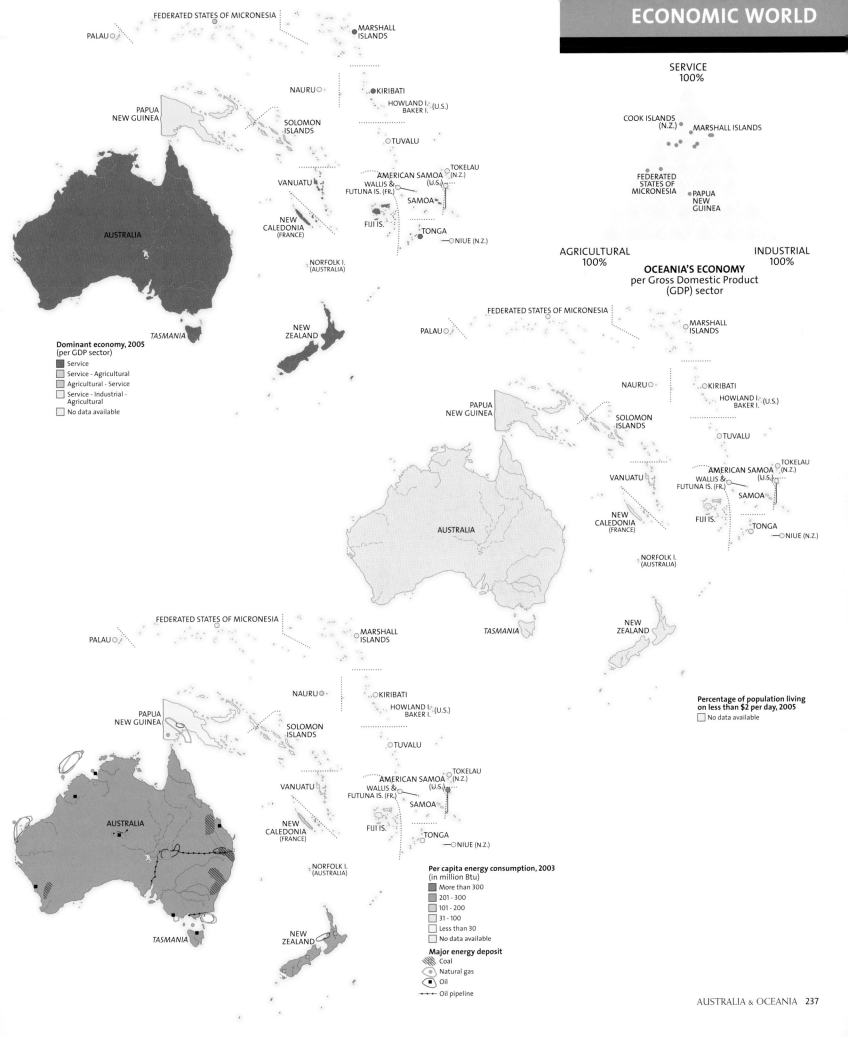

FEDERATED STATES OF MICRONESIA

PALAU

MARSHALL ISLANDS

NAURU

KIRIBATI

HOWLAND I.
BAKER I. (U.S.)

PAPUA NEW GUINEA

SOLOMON ISLANDS

TUVALU

TOKELAU (N.Z.)

AMERICAN SAMOA (U.S.)

WALLIS & FUTUNA IS. (FR.)

VANUATU

SAMOA

NEW CALEDONIA (FRANCE)

FIJI IS.

TONGA

NIUE (N.Z.)

AUSTRALIA

NORFOLK I. (AUSTRALIA)

TASMANIA

NEW ZEALAND

Dominant economy, 2005
(per GDP sector)
- Service
- Service - Agricultural
- Agricultural - Service
- Service - Industrial - Agricultural
- No data available

SERVICE
100%

COOK ISLANDS (N.Z.)

MARSHALL ISLANDS

FEDERATED STATES OF MICRONESIA

PAPUA NEW GUINEA

AGRICULTURAL
100%

INDUSTRIAL
100%

OCEANIA'S ECONOMY
per Gross Domestic Product
(GDP) sector

FEDERATED STATES OF MICRONESIA

PALAU

MARSHALL ISLANDS

NAURU

KIRIBATI

HOWLAND I.
BAKER I. (U.S.)

PAPUA NEW GUINEA

SOLOMON ISLANDS

TUVALU

TOKELAU (N.Z.)

AMERICAN SAMOA (U.S.)

WALLIS & FUTUNA IS. (FR.)

VANUATU

SAMOA

NEW CALEDONIA (FRANCE)

FIJI IS.

TONGA

NIUE (N.Z.)

AUSTRALIA

NORFOLK I. (AUSTRALIA)

TASMANIA

NEW ZEALAND

Percentage of population living on less than $2 per day, 2005
- No data available

FEDERATED STATES OF MICRONESIA

PALAU

MARSHALL ISLANDS

NAURU

KIRIBATI

HOWLAND I.
BAKER I. (U.S.)

PAPUA NEW GUINEA

SOLOMON ISLANDS

TUVALU

TOKELAU (N.Z.)

AMERICAN SAMOA (U.S.)

WALLIS & FUTUNA IS. (FR.)

VANUATU

SAMOA

NEW CALEDONIA (FRANCE)

FIJI IS.

TONGA

NIUE (N.Z.)

AUSTRALIA

NORFOLK I. (AUSTRALIA)

TASMANIA

NEW ZEALAND

Per capita energy consumption, 2003
(in million Btu)
- More than 300
- 201 - 300
- 101 - 200
- 31 - 100
- Less than 30
- No data available

Major energy deposit
- Coal
- Natural gas
- Oil
- Oil pipeline

This is a map of Australia & Oceania showing East Asia, Southeast Asia, and the Western Pacific region.

RUSSIA

MONGOLIA · Ulaanbaatar · Öndörhaan · Choybalsan · Baruun Urt · Saynshand (Buyant-Uhaa)

Ulan Ude · Chita · Shilka · Baley · Sretensk · Olovyannaya · Borzya · Aginskoye · Khilok

GOBI

110° 120° 130° 140° 150° 160° 170°

50°

Mogocha · Skovorodino · Ushumun · Shimanovsk · Svobodnyy · Chegdomyn · Komsomol'sk na Amure · Amur · Heilong · De Kastri · Lazarev

Nikolayevsk na Amure · Okha · Nogliki

OSTROV SAKHALIN · Aleksandrovsk Sakhalinskiy

SEA OF OKHOTSK · POLUOSTROV KAMCHATKA · Petropavlovsk Kamchatskiy · Bol'sheretsk · Severo Kuril'sk · Mys Lopatka

Near Islands · Attu · Ra...
ALE...

Romanovka · Manzhouli · Hailar · Yakeshi · Ganhe · Nenjiang · Nehe · Yichun · Hegang · Jiamusi · Shuangyashan · Birobidzhan · Khabarovsk · Vyazemskiy · Poronaysk · Kholmsk · Yuzhno Sakhalinsk · Korsakov

Zalantun · Ulanhot · Arxan · Yitulihe · Blagoveshchensk · Heihe

CHINA · Qiqihar · Daqing · Baicheng · Harbin · Mudanjiang · Jixi · Qitaihe · Dal'negorsk · Ozero Khanka · Wakkanai · HOKKAIDŌ · +1426 · KURIL ISLANDS (KURIL'SKIYE OSTROVA) · La Perouse Strait

SHENYANG · Changchun · Tongliao · Jilin · Ch'ŏngjin · Vladivostok · Nakhodka · Asahikawa · +2290 · Sapporo · Chitose · Kushiro

3802 · Taibus Qi · Duolun · Xilinhot · Erenhot · Hanggin Houqi · Baotou · Datong · Zhangjiakou · Anshan · Fushun · Hamhŭng · NORTH KOREA · Dandong · Anju · Wŏnsan · P'yŏngyang · Hakodate · Muroran · Aomori · Hachinohe · Akita · Morioka · Hirosaki

40°

Wuda · Shizuishan · BEIJING (PEKING) · Tianjin · Dalian · Incheon · SEOUL · Niigata · Kanazawa · HONSHŪ

Taiyuan · Shijiazhuang · Handan · Jinan · Zibo · Qingdao · Daejeon · Daegu · Busan · Kyōto · Nagoya · TŌKYŌ · Yokohama · 2341 · NORTH

Baoji · Xi'an (Sian) · Luoyang · Zhengzhou · Kaifeng · Heze · Tai'an · Zaozhuang · Xuzhou · SOUTH KOREA · Gwangju · Hiroshima · Kōbe · Osaka · 3776 · Japan

Xiangfan · Hefei · Anqing · Nanjing · Suzhou · Wuxi · SHANGHAI · Fukuoka · Kitakyūshū · Kumamoto · KYŪSHŪ · Izu Shotō

WUHAN · Hangzhou · Shaoxing · Ningbo · Nagasaki · Tokara Rettō · Nansei Shotō (Ryukyu Islands)

30°

CHONGQING · Changsha · Nanchang · Jinhua · Quzhou · Wenzhou · EAST CHINA SEA · Bonin Islands (Ogasawara Guntō) · 2259

Zunyi · Shaoyang · Pingxiang · Hengyang · Nanping · Fuzhou · Ganzhou · Naha · Okinawa · Daitō Shotō

Guiyang · Duyun · Guilin · GUANGZHOU (CANTON) · Taipei (Taibei) · 7507 · Iwo To (Iwo Jima) · Volcano Islands (Kazan Rettō) · Japan · Minami Tori Shima (Marcus) · Japan

Nanning · Foshan · HONG KONG · Shantou · Kaohsiung · TAINAN · TAIWAN · Sakishima Shotō

Zhanjiang · Haikou · Batan Islands · Babuyan Islands

20°

Dongfang · 1867+ · Hainan · Sanya · Laoag · Vigan · Aparri · Tuguegarao · LUZON · Luzon Strait · Wake Island U.S.

Quang Tri · Da Nang · Paracel Islands · Baguio · +2934 · PHILIPPINE SEA · NORTHERN MARIANA ISLANDS U.S. · Capital Hill Saipan (11) · Tinian · Rota

VIETNAM · 2598 · Qui Nhon · Mount Pinatubo · 2934+ · Quezon City · Manila · Naga · Legazpi · PHILIPPINES · U.S. Guam ⊛ Hagåtña (Agana) (12)

Buon Me Thuot · Nha Trang · Cam Ranh · SOUTH CHINA SEA · Spratly Islands · Masbate · Roxas · Iloilo · Bacolod · Cebu · Calbayog · Yap Islands · M I C R O N E S I A

10°

Bien Hoa · Ho Chi Minh City (Saigon) · Con Son · Palawan · Puerto Princesa · 2100+ · 10057 · Bikini Atoll · Enewetak Atoll · Ratak Chain · MARSHALL ISLANDS

Kinabalu · 4101 · Cagayan de Oro · Cotabato · Davao · MINDANAO · General Santos · 2954 · Ngulu Atoll · 8527 · Melekeok · Senyavin Is. · Palikir Pohnpei (Ponape) (17) · Majuro (14)

Bandar Seri Begawan · BRUNEI · Sandakan · Zamboanga · Tawau · Sonsorol Islands · PALAU (13) · CAROLINE ISLANDS · Chuuk (Truk Islands) (18) · FEDERATED STATES OF MICRONESIA · Kosrae (Kusaie) (19) · Jaluit Atoll (15)

MALAYSIA · Sibu · 2987+ · Tarakan · Kepulauan Sangihe · Kepulauan Talaud · Kepulauan Mapia · Mortlock Islands · 4261

Sangkulirang · Tolitoli · Celebes Sea · Kepulauan Mapia · M E L A · Kapingamarangi Atoll · Tarawa (Bairiki) (16) · GILBERT ISLANDS

0° · BORNEO · Samarinda · Palu · Gorontalo · 1635+ · Ternate · EQUATOR · Ninigo Group · N E S I A

Pontianak · 3000+ · Sorong · Sarmi · Admiralty Islands · Mussau Islands · NAURU (20)

Ketapang · Balikpapan · SULAWESI · 3455 · Kendari · Fakfak · Jayapura · Aitape · Wewak · Kavieng · New Ireland · Green Islands · Nukumanu Islands · M

Tanjungpandan · Kandangan · Parepare · Ambon · Nabire · Amamapare · Namatanai · BISMARCK ARCHIPELAGO · +4509 · Rabaul · 2743+ · Bougainville · 2438 · Ontong Java Atoll · E

Banjarmasin · Makassar (Ujung Pandang) · Baubau · Kep. Kai · Tual · Kepulauan Aru · 46 · Kepi · Muting · NEW GUINEA · Madang · Lae · Huon Gulf · New Britain · 2447+ · SOLOMON ISLANDS (21) · L

10°

JAKARTA · Bandung · Surabaya · Tasikmalaya · Yogyakarta · JAVA · Jember · Bali · 3726 · Raba · Flores · Ruteng · Waingapu · Dili · Baguia · PAPUA NEW GUINEA · Daru · Port Moresby · Trobriand Is. · Honiara ⊛ Guadalcanal · Stewart Islands · Duff Islands · TUVALU (1) · A

Sumbawa · Sumba · Timor · TIMOR-LESTE (EAST TIMOR) · Kupang · Arafura Sea · Merauke · Gulf of Papua · Samarai · D'Entrecasteaux Is. · Louisiade Archipelago · 1280 · Santa Cruz Islands · Vanikolo Is. · N

Lesser Sunda Islands · 7125 · INDIAN OCEAN · Heywood Shoal · Seringapatam Reef · Scott Reef · Lynher Bank · Wessel Islands · Nhulunbuy · Weipa · Coen · Cooktown · Flora Reef · Willis Islets · CORAL · Lihou Reefs · Torres Is. · Banks Islands · Rotuma Fiji · Vanua Lev...

Timor Sea · Holothuria Banks · Joseph Bonaparte Gulf · Oenpelli · Jabiru · Aurukun · Espiritu Santo · 1879 · VANUATU (22) · FIJI ISLANDS (23) · Vitu Levu

Darwin · Wyndham · Kununurra · Ngukurr · Borroloola · Gulf of Carpentaria · Normanton · Georgetown · 1622+ · Cairns · Innisfail · Townsville · Ayr · Îles Chesterfield · Éfaté ⊛ Port Vila · Ceva-i-Ra...

20°

AUSTRALIA · Broome · Derby · Fitzroy Crossing · Halls Creek · Newcastle Waters · Burketown · Croydon · GREAT DIVIDING RANGE · Bowen · Mackay · Swain Reefs · NEW CALEDONIA · France · Nouméa · Loyalty Islands

Roebourne · Dampier · Marble Bar · Mt. Ord · 937 · Lake Argyle · 1628+ Mount Panié

Onslow · Exmouth · North West Cape · Great Sandy Desert · Mount Isa · Cloncurry · Charters Towers · Camooweal · Winton · Dajarra · Barrow Creek · Tennant Creek

110° 120° 130° 140° 150° Longitude East 160° of Greenwich 170°

SEA

Islands of
Four Mountains
Andreanof Is.
IAN ISLANDS
United States

Unalaska
2149
Fox Islands

ALEUTIAN ISLANDS

Queen
Charlotte
Islands

CANADA

4016
Mt.
Waddington

Kamloops   Kelowna
Medicine Hat
Lethbridge

Calgary

Swift
Current

50°

Vancouver
Island

Vancouver

Victoria

Havre

Tacoma   Seattle
Olympia   +Mt. Rainier
4392
2550+Mt.
St. Helens
Portland
Salem
Redmond
Coos Bay
Eugene
+2665
Medford
Klamath Falls
Eureka
Lassen Pk.+
4317   Alturas
Mt. Shasta
3187+

Spokane
Missoula
Walla Walla   Butte

Great Falls
Helena

Billings

Borah Peak
+
Boise   3859   Idaho Falls

Worland

UNITED STATES

Great Salt
Lake

Cape Mendocino

Salt Lake City   Provo

40°

P A C I F I C   O C E A N

Reno
Sacramento
Oakland
San Francisco
San Jose
4418.Mt.
Whitney
Bakersfield
Santa Barbara
Los Angeles
Long Beach
San Diego
Tijuana

Carson City
Ely

86.

Fresno

Las Vegas

Flagstaff

Albuquerque

Riverside   Phoenix

Mexicali   Tucson
Douglas
3444   Nogales

30°

I. de Guadeloupe
Mexico

Hermosillo

Guaymas
MEXICO

Los
Mochis

La Purísima

Midway
Islands

Pearl and Hermes
Atoll

Gardner
Pinnacles

H   A
W
A   United States
I
I

Punta Eugenia

TROPIC OF CANCER

Islas
Marías

Cabo San Lucas

La Paz

5121

Kaua'i
O'ahu
Honolulu   Moloka'i
Maui
Mauna Kea
4205+
Hawai'i

Islas
Revillagigedo
Mexico

20°

Johnston Atoll
U.S.

P
O
L
Y

Clipperton
Fr.

10°

5037

5121

3091

Kingman Reef
Palmyra Atoll U.S.
Teraina (Washington I.)
Tabuaeran (Fanning I.)

EQUATOR

5121

0°

5529

L
I
N
E

Howland Island
U.S.
Baker Island

Kiritimati
③ (Christmas I.)
Kiribati

Jarvis Island
U.S.

I
S
L
A
N
D
S

S O U T H   P A C I F I C   O C E A N

5121

PHOENIX ISLANDS

TOKELAU N.Z.

MARQUESAS
ISLANDS

4526

Ua Huka
Hiva Oa

10°

ti

I
R
I
B
A
T
I

Pukapuka Atoll
(Danger Islands)

C
O
O
K

I
S
L
A
N
D
S

Îles
Wallis
Fr.

SAMOA
② AMERICAN
Savai'i   SAMOA
Apia   U.S.
Pago Pago
Tutuila ④   Manu'a Is. ⑤

SAMOA ISLANDS

Rangiroa

Manihi

T U A M O T U   A R C H I P E L A G O

Lau
Group

New
Zealand

Niue

Hervey
Islands

Bora Bora   Huahine
Raiatea   ⑦ Papeete
Tahiti
SOCIETY ISLANDS
FRENCH
POLYNESIA
France

Groupe
Actéon

MERCATOR PROJECTION
SCALE 1:35,000,000
0 KILOMETERS   600 800 1000
0 MILES 200   400   600   800 1000
⑬ Red circled numbers are reference keys
to larger scale maps on pages 241–243.

TONGA ISLANDS

Ha'apai Group

Nuku'alofa   TONGA
Tongatapu ⑨
Group

⑥ Rarotonga

AUSTRAL ISLANDS (TUBUAI IS.)

Îs. du Duc de Glouster

Îles Gambier

20°

170°   160°   Longitude West 160° of Greenwich   150°   140°   130°   120°   110°

NEW ZEALAND
ALBERS CONIC EQUAL-AREA PROJECTION
SCALE 1:5,750,000

0 KILOMETERS 100 150
0 MILES 50 100 150

TASMAN SEA

NORTH ISLAND

Cape Reinga
North Cape
Te Hapua
Te Kao
Cape Karikari
Ninety Mile Beach
Mangonui
Kaeo
Cape Brett
Ahipara
Mangamuka
Paihia
Opua
Kawakawa
Pawarenga
Moerewa
Panguru
Rawene
Whakapara
Waimamaku
Pakotai
Hikurangi
Donnellys Crossing
Kaihu
Kamo
Whangarei
Waiotira
Marsden Point
Te Kopuru
Waipu
Ruawai
Maungaturoto
Port Fitzroy
Paparoa
Great Barrier I.
Wellsford
Tryphena
Leigh
Matakana
Cape Colville
North Head
East Coast Bays
Colville
Coromandel
Helensville
Whitianga
Waitemata
COROMANDEL PEN.
Auckland
Howick
Tairua
Manukau
Papakura
Whangamata
Pukekohe
Pokeno
Thames
Tuakau
Waitakaruru
Te Kauwhata
Paeroa
Waihi
Huntly
Te Aroha
Ngaruawahia
Waitoa
Mount Maunganui
Pukemiro
Raglan
Hamilton
Te Puke
Maketu
Cape Runaway
Hicks Bay
Kawhia
Cambridge
Matata
Te Araroa
Te Kaha
Otorohanga
Putaruru
Whakatane
Hikurangi
Tikitiki
Waitomo Caves
Rotorua
Te Teko
Opotiki
Torere
Ruatoria
Te Kuiti
Hangatiki
Atiamuri
Mt.
Te Puia Springs
Benneydale
TE UREWERA N.P.
Motu
Arowhana
Tokomaru Bay
Awakino
Ongarue
Ruatahuna
Matawai
Tolaga Bay
Mokau
Taringamotu
Okahukura
Taupo
Minginui
Te Karaka
Ormond
Taumarunui
Waitahanui
Kakahi
Turangi
Ruakituri
Whangara
Uruti
Tuai
Mt. Ngauruhoe
Patutahi
Gisborne
Waitara
Kakahi
Raupunga
Whakapunake
New Plymouth
Urenui
National Park
Mt. Ruapehu
Fraserton
Oakura
Lepperton
Te Pohue
Putorino
Wairoa
EGMONT N.P.
Rahotu
Toko
Raetihi
TONGARIRO N.P.
Waiouru
Kaweka
Tutira
Mahia Pen.
(Mt. Egmont) Mt. Taranaki
Eltham
Waioru
Esdale
Napier
Opunake
Manaia
Hawera
Taihape
Taradale
Cape Kidnappers
Altona
Kakatahi
Utiku
Pakipaki
Kakaramea
Waverley
Mangaweka
Waipawa
Waimarama
Waitotara
Kai Iwi
Wanganui
Waipukurau
Rata
Takapau
Pukehou
Castlecliff
Marton
Feilding
Omakere
Bulls
Palmerston North
Porangahau
Foxton
Taumatawhakatangihangakoauauotamateapokaiwhenuakitanatahu
Levin
Shannon
Pongaroa
Cape Turnagain
Otaki
Ohau
Alfredton
Akitio
Waikanae
Mitre
Mauriceville
Porirua
Carterton
Tinui
Castlepoint
Wellington
Lower Hutt
Greytown
Martinborough
NEW

SOUTH ISLAND

Cape Farewell
Pakawau
Collingwood
Rockville
D'Urville I.
Takaka
ABEL TASMAN N.P.
French Pass
Riwaka
Mt. Stokes
KAHURANGI NATIONAL PARK
Tasman
Karamea
Tapawera
Stoke
Picton
Seddonville
Tadmor
Havelock
Blenheim
Granity
Mt. Owen
Hector
Owen River
Wairau Valley
Waimangaroa
Westport
Murchison
Seddon
Charleston
Mt. Uriah
Tapuaenuku
Ward
Cape Campbell
PAPAROA N.P.
Reefton
Molesworth
Cape Palliser
Mount Ross
Barrytown
Maruia
NELSON LAKES N.P.
Manakau
Rapahoe
Ikamatua
Hanmer Springs
Kekerengu
Greymouth
Ngahere
Clarence
Arahura
Dobson
Kaikoura
Hokitika
Moana
Waiau
Oaro
Kumara Junction
Rotherham
Parnassus
Kowhitirangi
Otira
Culverden
Cheviot
Ross
ARTHUR'S PASS N.P.
Hawarden
Domett
Arthur's Pass
Omihi
Scargill
Waipara
Amberley
Harihari
Springfield
Oxford
Franz Josef
Whataroa
Lake Coleridge
Belfast
Rangiora
Fox Glacier
Methven
Rolleston
Christchurch
(Mt. Cook) Aoraki
AORAKI (MT. COOK) N.P.
Mayfield
Lincoln
Lyttelton
Haast
Hinds
Ashburton
BANKS PEN.
Jackson Head
Lake Tekapo
Geraldine
Akaroa
Jackson Bay
Fairlie
Orari
MT. ASPIRING N.P.
Lake Pukaki
Pleasant Point
Temuka
Mt. Aspiring
Twizel
Cave
Timaru
Omarama
Waimate
Saint Andrews
Milford Sound
Otematata
Makikihi
Mount Tutoko
Hakataramea
Studholme Junction
Coronet Pk.
Tarras
Kurow
Morven
Glenavy
Glenorchy
Arrowtown
Cromwell
Duntroon
Enfield
Oamaru
FIORDLAND
Queenstown
Clyde
Omakau
Maheno
Kakanui
The Remarkables
Kingston
Ranfurly
Totara
Hampden
NATIONAL
Te Anau
Coal Creek
Palmerston
Athol
Flat
Karitane
Waikouaiti
PARK
Manapouri
Mossburn
Roxburgh
Hyde
Seacliff
Waitati
Dipton
Edievale
Ettrick
Port Chalmers
Dusky Sound
Riversdale
Kelso
Waikouaiti
Mosgiel
Dunedin
Orawia
Winton
Tapanui
Lawrence
Green Island
Waipahi
Waihola
Thornbury
Gore
Milton
Otautau
Browns
Balclutha
Waikiwi
Clinton
Kaitangata
Otatara
Invercargill
Tahakopa
Owaka
FOVEAUX
Mt. Anglem
Bluff
Tiwai Point
Waikawa
STEWART I.
(RAKIURA)
Mason Bay
Half Moon Bay
RAKIURA NATIONAL PARK
Mt. Allen

ZEALAND

PACIFIC OCEAN

Mernoo Bank

Pegasus Bay

Canterbury Bight

Longitude East 174° of Greenwich

Polynesia

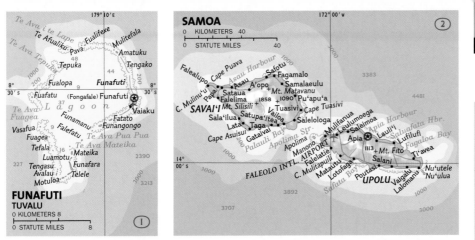

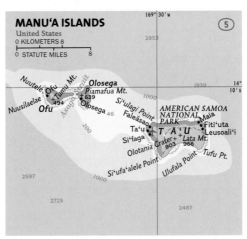

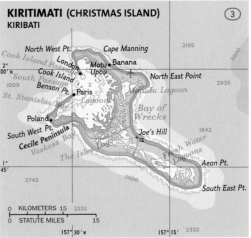

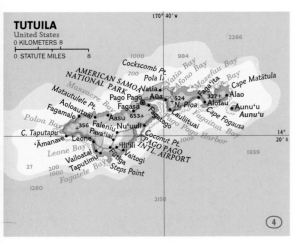

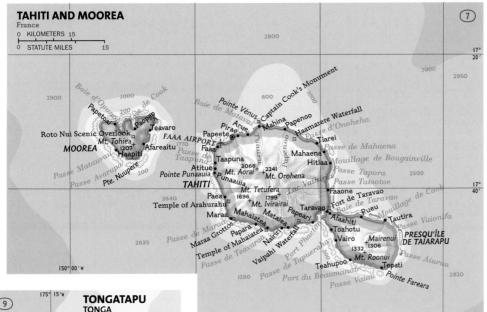

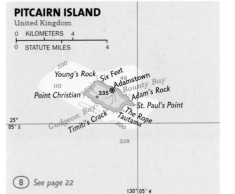

Micronesia

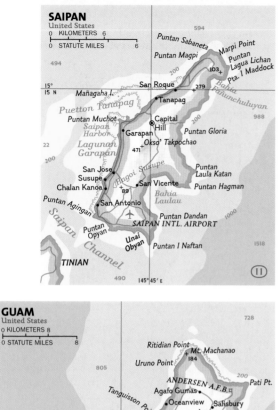

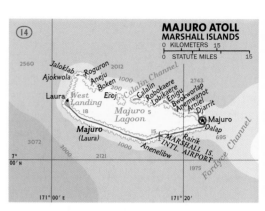

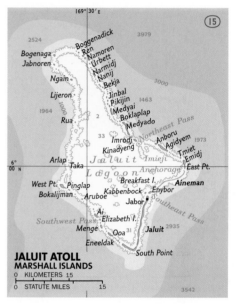

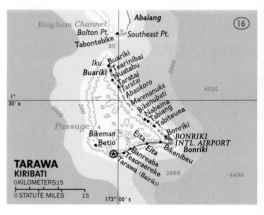

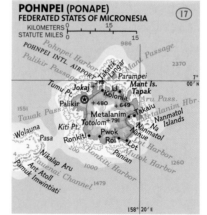

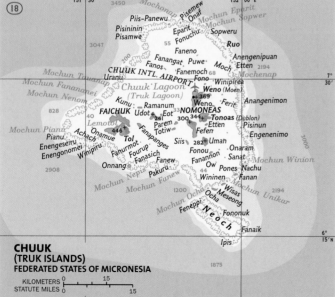

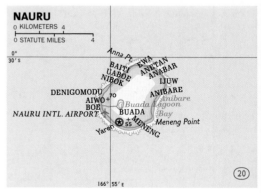

Melanesia

Pinipel
Green Islands
Nissan
Jangain
Yovo
Kilinailau Is.
Veharnu
Tauu Is.
Nukumanu Atoll
Nogu Dabu

PACIFIC

Ontong Java Atoll
(Lord Howe Atoll)
Pelau
Avaha
Ke Loma
Ke Ila
Kukolu
Luaniua

OCEAN

Papua New Guinea
Solomon Islands

Lemanmanu
Cape Hanpan
Hanahan
Gagan
Buka
Ieta
Sohano
Taiof
Dios
Puto
Cape L'Avedy
Cape Nehus

Roncador Reef

Bougainville
Amun
Mt.
Balbi
Wakunai
Cape Mabiri
Tarara
Kieta
Cape Moltke
Bagana
Torokina
Mt. Takuan
Taki
Motupena Pt.
Jaba
Boku
Tabago
Mamagota
Kaukauai
Buin
Balla'lae
Fauro
Shortland
Halola
Falamae
Mono
Treasury Islands
Stirling I.

Malevanga
Cape Alexander
Laluai Pt.
Kumbakale
Voza
Choiseul
Panggoe
Sasamungga
Varungga Pt.
Tasure
Luti
Rob Roy
Vaghena
Amayon Islands
Ghaghe
Barora Fa
Kia
Barora Ite
Santa Isabel
Ghatere
Dadale
Mt. Kubonitu
Buala
Susubona
Tatamba
Sepi
San Jorge I.
Vikenara Pt.

Edwards Bank

Dai (Ndai)
Ramos I.
Cape Astrolabe
Manaoba
Maluu
Kwailibesi
Dala
Daringali
Cape Aracides
Leli
Auki
Olomburi
Malaita
Anoano
Tarapaina
Maramasike
Sa'a
Cape Zelee
Hadja
Ulawa

Sorezaru Pt.
Vella Lavella
Baga
Maravae
Kolombangara
Kundu
Ranongga
Simbo
Gizo
Vonavona
Munda
Hapai
New Georgia
New Georgia Group
Rendova
Lokuru
Tombe
Seghe
Vangunu
Mt. Vangunu
Mbulo
Nggatokae
Mborokua
Russell Is.
Nandina
Pavuvu
Alokan
C. Esperance
Maravovo
Honiara
Guadalcanal
Wanderer Bay
Cape Hunter
Ndundu
Mt. Popomanaseu
Florida Islands
Savo
Nggela Sule
Nggela
Tulaghi
Tutumu
Aola
Kaoka Bay
Avu Avu
Mbalo
Rokera
Paruru

Three Sisters Is.
Heuru
Uki
Anuta
Pamua
Kirakira
Wanione
San Cristobal
Wainoari
Mwaniwowo
Santa Ana
Santa Catalina

Bellona Island

SOLOMON ISLANDS
0 KILOMETERS 75
0 STATUTE MILES 75

Manggautu
Rennell
Tinggoa

CORAL SEA

Hiu
Métoma
Tégua
Torres
Loh
Islands
Toga
Vétaounde
Uréparapara
Reef Islands
(Rowa Islands)
Mt. Sürétiméat
Mota Lava
Mota
Vanua Lava
Wasaka
BANKS ISLANDS
Santa Maria
Avire
Mérig
Makéone
Méré Lava
Cape Cumberland
Olpoi
Nokuku
Sakao (Lathi)
Cape Queiros
Malao
Espiritu
Santo
Aoba
Marino
Maéwo
Wusi
Kolé
Nangiré
Narovorovo
Luganville
PEKOA
AIRPORT
Nduindui
Nazareth
Malo
Namaram
Pentecost
(Île Pentecôte)
Ranwas
Norsup
Port Stanley
Selwyn Strait
Lakatoro
Méghem
Marum Volcano
Malakula
Mt. Pénot
Ambrym
Lamap
Paama
Lopévi (Ulvéah)
Tomman
Moriu
Epi
Maskelynes Is.
Votlo
Shepherd
Islands
Laïka
Tongoa (Kuwaé)
Tongariki
Émaé
Makura
Monument (Étarik)
Matan
Mataso
Nguna
Moso
Émao
Lélépa
Efaté (Île Vaté)
Devil's Pt.
BAUERFIELD AIRPORT
Port-Vila

Mt. Santop
Potnarvin
Dillon's Bay
Erromango
Pilbarra Point

Lowital
Aniwa
Tanna
Waïsisi
Isangel
Yasur Volcano
Mt. Tukosméra
Futuna

VANUATU
0 KILOMETERS 80
0 STATUTE MILES 80

Anatom
(Kéamu)
Anelghowhat

FIJI ISLANDS
0 KILOMETERS 80
0 STATUTE MILES 80

Cikobia
Vetauua
Nukudamu
Udu Pt.
Tawake
Ringgold Isles
Nukubasaga
Kia
Mali
Labasa
Yalewa Kalou
Nukuira
Naduri
VANUA LEVU
Rabi (Rambi)
Cobia
Yanuca
Koroko
Kioa
Qamea
Laucala
Wailagi Lala
Yasawa
Nacula
Savusavu
Somosomo
Naitaba
Yaqeta
Nabouwalu
Taveuni
Lomaloma
Mago
Munia
Viwa
Vatia
Rakiraki
Makale
Namenalala
Koro
Nakodu
Vatu Vara
Vekai
Katafaga
Waya
Vatukoula
Tavua
Tomanivi
Makogai
Wakaya
Cicia
Tuvuca
Yaroua
Nailaga
Ba
Navai
Levuka
Ovalau
Batiki
Nairai
Nayau
Lautoka
NADI
INTL AIRPORT
VITI LEVU
Vunindawa
Bau
Moturiki
Gau
Malolo
Nadi
Momi
Nausori
Suva
Vanua Masi
Lomawai
Sigatoka
Korolevu
Navua
Naitonitoni
Beqa
Vanuca
Vatulele
Moala
Tavu Na Sici
Totoya
Vuaqava
Komo
Moce
Kadavu
Vunisea
Ono
Buliya
Cape Washington
Matuku
Marabo
Ogea Levu
Ogea Driki
(Turtle) Vatoa

The North Pole marks one end of the Earth's axis of rotation where it pierces the icy Arctic Ocean. The corresponding but much colder South Pole sits at 2,835 meters (9,300 feet) of elevation with a continent around it. Greenland is like a smaller Antarctica, about three times the size of Texas, with ice averaging more than one and a half kilometers (one mile) deep. Both poles were first reached on foot by adventuring explorers in the early 20th century. Both polar regions have been used for extensive scientific investigations as, for example, in drilling deep ice cores to analyze the climate and atmosphere of prehistoric times. Polar regions have profound effects on the world's environment and climate. Earth's magnetic field emerges from them and deflects harmful incoming solar radiation. The polar waters contribute to oceanic currents that transport cold and warm water around the globe. The poles have provided data that give early warning of worldwide problems caused by human actions—in Antarctica's case depletion of the ozone layer that blocks harmful ultraviolet radiation. In the north, mounting evidence suggests that the Arctic Ocean is warming, and its surface ice is rapidly melting. This trend might finally open the long-sought Northwest Passage to shipping and permit open-water drilling for petroleum. It might also severely restrict polar bear and other animal habitats while devastating hunting and other life ways of native Arctic peoples. Thawing of surface ice will likely also accelerate global warming by provoking significant changes in ocean circulation and lead to rising sea levels.

IMAGE BY ROBERT STACEY, WORLDSAT INTERNATIONAL INC.

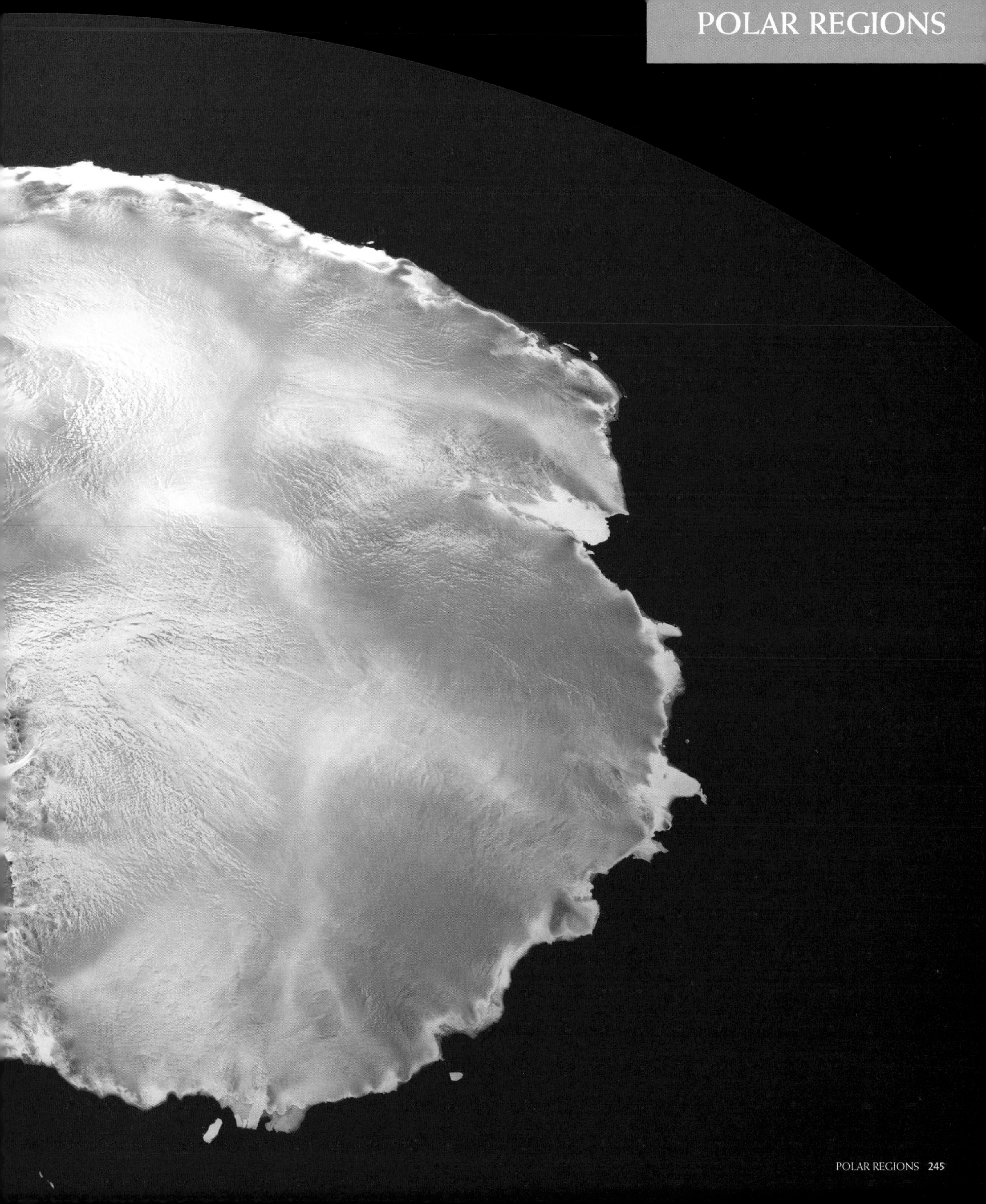

ICE

Pack ice responds to prevailing winds and ocean currents. Tabular icebergs up to 700 sq km (270 sq mi) in area sometimes break away from the northern edge of small ice shelves. These ice islands float slowly in erratic clockwise patterns around the North American side of the Arctic Ocean, completing full circuits in five to ten years, until they disintegrate or move into the Atlantic. Each year hundreds of much smaller bergs break off – calve – from the Greenland ice sheet and Canada's glaciers and move southward into the North Atlantic shipping lanes. After the sinking of the Titanic in 1912, leading maritime nations formed the International Ice Patrol to monitor icebergs and to study polar currents and iceberg dynamics.

AZIMUTHAL EQUIDISTANT PROJECTION
SCALE 1:20,000,000

0 KILOMETERS 300 400 500
0 MILES 200 300 400 500

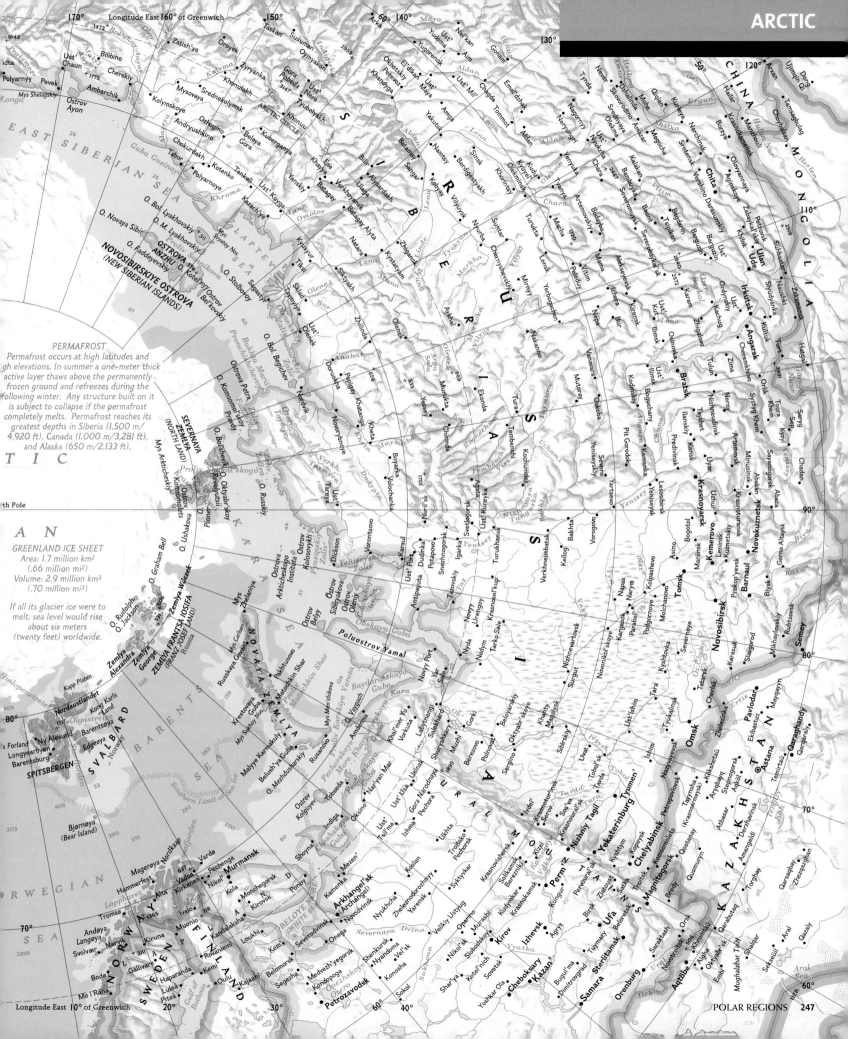

PERMAFROST

Permafrost occurs at high latitudes and gh elevations. In summer a one-meter thick active layer thaws above the permanently frozen ground and refreezes during the following winter. Any structure built on it is subject to collapse if the permafrost completely melts. Permafrost reaches its greatest depths in Siberia (1,500 m/ 4,920 ft), Canada (1,000 m/3,281 ft), and Alaska (650 m/2,133 ft).

GREENLAND ICE SHEET

Area: 1.7 million km² (.66 million mi²)
Volume: 2.9 million km³ (.70 million mi³)

If all its glacier ice were to melt, sea level would rise about six meters (twenty feet) worldwide.

ANTARCTIC PENINSULA AREA STATIONS

Argentina
1 Jubany
Brazil
2 Comandante Ferraz
Chile
3 Bernardo O'Higgins
4 Eduardo Frei
5 Estación Marítima Antártica
6 Julio Escudero

China
7 Great Wall
Korea, South
8 King Sejong
Poland
9 Arctowski
Russia
10 Bellingshausen
Uruguay
11 Artigas

Research Stations: ⊛ Year-round   ○ Other

ICE SHELVES
Large areas of floating glacier ice fringe the coast of Antarctica. The two largest ice shelves are the Ross Ice Shelf and the Ronne Ice Shelf, both separated by glacier ice that is grounded below sea level. Large tabular icebergs periodically calve from ice shelves.

A SEA OF ICE
When winter comes, the ocean surface around Antarctica begins to freeze. Spreading over an average of 77,700 square kilometers (30,000 sq. miles) a day, the ring of sea ice eventually covers more than 18 million square kilometers (7 million sq. miles), an area larger than the continent itself. Reducing the ocean's absorption of atmospheric carbon dioxide and blocking ocean-atmosphere heat exchange, sea ice plays a role in shaping regional climate that in turn has impacts over much of the globe.

CLIMATE
The southern polar region is substantially colder than its northern counterpart. The lofty ice sheet reflects as much as 90 percent of solar radiation back to space, whereas in the Arctic Ocean ice partly melts in summer and the dark waters absorb heat. The temperature difference between the equatorial and polar regions drives atmospheric circulation. Because the South Pole is colder than the North, winds are stronger in the Southern Hemisphere. The ice sheet contains a climate record that extends back at least 200,000 years at some locations. Ice cores preserve a record of past atmospheric composition, volcanic eruptions, and other environmental information.

Bentley Subglacial Trench is the lowest known point in Antarctica at -2,555 m (-8,383 ft)

Longitude West of Greenwich

WEIGHT OF THE ICE SHEET The ice mass covering Antarctica is so heavy that it depresses the Earth's crust more than 914 meters (3,000 feet). Ice-free continental shelves actually tilt in toward the land, rather than sloping away toward the deep seafloor.

ICE DESERT Although Antarctica stores some 72 percent of the world's fresh water as ice, precipitation on six million sq km (2.3 million sq mi) of the continents's interior averages less than five cm (two inches) a year, similar to the amount of rainfall in the driest part of the Sahara.

A FIFTH OCEAN? The Atlantic, Indian, and Pacific Oceans merge into icy waters around Antarctica. Some define this as an ocean—calling it the Antarctic Ocean, Austral Ocean, or Southern Ocean. While most accept four oceans, including the Arctic, there is no international agreement on the name and extent of a fifth ocean.

World's coldest place: Annual average temperature –56.7°C (–70.1°F)

A record low temperature of minus 89.2°C (–128.6°F) was recorded here on July 21, 1983.

THICKEST ICE Echo-sounding from aircraft has identified an ice thickness of 4,776 m (15,670 ft). Bedrock was found at 2,341 m (7,680 ft) below sea level.

AZIMUTHAL EQUIDISTANT PROJECTION
SCALE 1:18,000,000

PACIFIC OCEAN

ATLANTI

The first color images beamed home from satellites in lunar orbit illustrated with startling visual impact a fact long known: Earth is truly a water planet. The great interconnected oceans cover 70 percent of it. Hidden from plain sight beneath that blue surface lie trenches, ridges, rises, abyssal plains, and immense, snaking mountain ranges. Earth's highest mountain, from base to top, is not Everest, but the almost mile-higher Mauna Kea, a volcano that broke the Pacific Ocean's surface during the creation of Hawai'i. Primitive oceans and atmospheres were born from release and condensation of gases including water vapor spewing from the hot young planet. More water was added by bombardment of water-rich comets. The combination of Earth's size and distance from the Sun allowed water to persist as a liquid and set the stage for the origins of life. Without oceans Earth's climate would be much more extreme, perhaps unlivable, with much hotter hot zones and much colder frigid zones. Ocean currents set in motion by the planet's rotation, shaped by landmasses, and maintained by flow and counterflow between Polar and Equatorial regions keep Earth mostly temperate. Even small variations in these patterns can have large effects. The systematic variation of oceanic patterns in the Pacific called "El Niño" brings stormy weather to the United States and Peru, for instance, while a rise in Atlantic sea surface temperature feeds the formation, frequency, and severity of hurricanes. A matter of present concern is the melting of Arctic sea ice because of global warming accelerated by human activities. Introduction of cold fresh meltwater into the North Atlantic circulation system may suppress or deflect the Gulf Stream. That current warms northwest Europe, and its substantial weakening could lead to widespread economic and political hardships.

IMAGE BY ROBERT STACEY, WORLDSAT INTERNATIONAL INC.

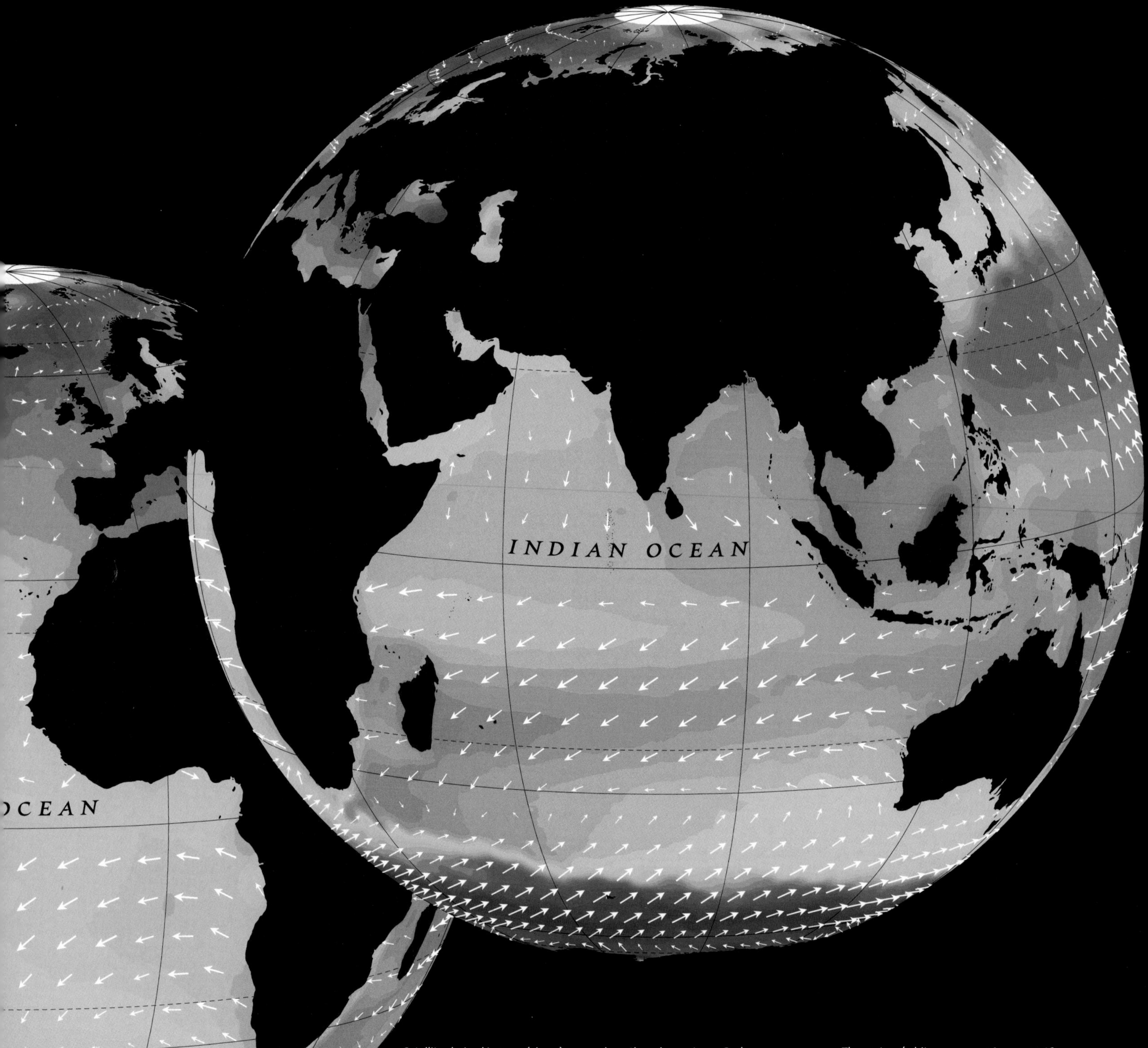

INDIAN OCEAN

OCEAN

Satellite-derived images (above) depict a ten-year average of the hills and valleys, or shape, of the changing ocean surface. These undulations range over a few meters in height, and flow occurs along the color contours. Such topographic maps are like the weather maps for ocean currents, aiding oceanographers, fisher-men, and navigators in studying the ocean and utilizing its resources. The vectors (white arrows) show ocean velocity caused exclusively by the effect of wind on the top layer of the ocean (called the Ekman Drift).

Ekman Drift
(in cm/second)

→ 17

→ 8

→ 1

Departure from mean sea level

| Meters | -2.6 | -2.4 | -2.2 | -2.0 | -1.8 | -1.6 | -1.4 | -1.2 | -1.0 | -0.8 | -0.6 | -0.4 | -0.2 | 0.0 | 0.2 | 0.4 | 0.6 | 0.8 | 1.0 | 1.2 |

No data available

| Feet | -8.5 | -7.9 | -7.2 | -6.6 | -5.9 | -5.2 | -4.6 | -3.9 | -3.3 | -2.6 | -2.0 | -1.3 | -0.7 | 0.0 | 0.7 | 1.3 | 2.0 | 2.6 | 3.3 | 3.9 |

ATLANTIC OCEAN
MERCATOR PROJECTION
SCALE 1:62,600,000

0 KILOMETERS 1200 1600
0 MILES 400 800 1200 1600

GREENLAND

FOXE BASIN

HUDSON BAY

ICELAND
• Reykjavík
Surtsey

FAROE ISLANDS

SCANDINAVIA
Bergen
Oslo • Stockholm
• Helsinki
GULF OF BOTHNIA
BALTIC SEA
• Hamburg

NORTH SEA
Dublin BRITISH ISLES
CELTIC SEA
ENGLISH CHANNEL
BAY OF BISCAY

NORTH AMERICA

DAVIS STRAIT
Nuuk (Godthåb)
Tasiilaq (Ammassalik)
DENMARK STRAIT

NORTHWEST ATLANTIC
LABRADOR SEA
CONTINENTAL SHELF
CONTINENTAL SLOPE

St. Lawrence
Montréal • Québec
Chicago • Halifax
Boston • New York
GULF OF ST. LAWRENCE
St. John's
Cape Breton Island
Grand Banks of Newfoundland
Flemish Cap

IMARSSUAK SEACHANNEL
Eirik Ridge
Gloria Ridge
CHARLIE-GIBBS FRACTURE ZONE
MID-OCEAN CANYON

REYKJANES RIDGE
MAURY SEACHANNEL
Rockall
WYVILLE THOMSON RIDGE
PORCUPINE PLAIN
PORCUPINE BANK
BISCAY PLAIN

EUROPE
Marseille
Lisbon
CORSICA
SARDINIA
TYRRHENIAN SEA
SICILY
BALEARIC IS.
Rome
ADRIATIC SEA
Danube
Athens
CRETE
MEDITERRANEAN SEA
Tripoli

AZORES
Pico
OCEANOGRAPHER FRACTURE ZONE

MID ATLANTIC RIDGE

SOHM PLAIN

Gulf of Maine
Sable Island
CONTINENTAL SLOPE
Laurentian Fan
New England Seamounts
Hudson Canyon
Cape Hatteras
CONTINENTAL SHELF
Bermuda Islands
BERMUDA RISE
HATTERAS PLAIN
Blake-Bahama Ridge
BLAKE PLATEAU
BAHAMA ISLANDS

Corner Seamounts
ATLANTIS FRACTURE ZONE
KANE FRACTURE ZONE

MADEIRA ISLANDS
Strait of Gibraltar
Rabat
Algiers

CANARY ISLANDS
CAPE VERDE PLAIN

New Orleans
GULF OF MEXICO
Mexico Basin
Campeche Bank
Havana
CUBA
Miami
Atlantic Ocean's deepest point
HISPANIOLA
NARES PLAIN
Puerto Rico Trench
(-28232 ft)
Cayman Trench

AFRICA
Nouakchott
Dakar
CAPE VERDE ISLANDS

CENTRAL AMERICA
MIDDLE AMERICA TRENCH
GREATER ANTILLES
LESSER ANTILLES
AVES RIDGE
Trinidad
Panama City
DEMERARA PLAIN
VEMA FRACTURE ZONE
DOLDRUMS FRACTURE ZONE

GAMBIA PLAIN
Freetown
SIERRA LEONE RISE
Abidjan • Accra
Lagos
Bioko
Libreville
EQUATOR

PACIFIC OCEAN
GALÁPAGOS ISLANDS
COCOS RIDGE
CARNEGIE RIDGE

SOUTH AMERICA
Georgetown
Amazon Fan
CONTINENTAL SHELF
Belém
CEARA PLAIN
St. Peter and St. Paul Rocks
Fernando de Noronha
ROMANCHE FRACTURE ZONE
CHAIN FRACTURE ZONE

PERNAMBUCO PLAIN
ASCENSION FRACTURE ZONE
Congo Canyon
São Tomé
Luanda
Congo
Zambezi
ANGOLA PLAIN
St. Helena
MID ATLANTIC RIDGE

Amazon
Paraguay
Paraná
Lima
PERU-CHILE TRENCH
NASCA RIDGE
San Félix Island
San Ambrosio Island
Juan Fernández Islands

SOUTH PACIFIC OCEAN

CHILE RISE

Rio de Janeiro
São Paulo
Santos Plateau
Victoria Seamount
Trindade
Martin Vaz Islands
RIO GRANDE RISE

Montevideo
Buenos Aires
Gulf of San Jorge
CONTINENTAL SLOPE
CONTINENTAL RISE
ARGENTINE PLAIN
Zapiola Ridge

Tristan da Cunha Group
Discovery Tablemount

WALVIS RIDGE
Orange
CAPE PLAIN
Cape of Good Hope
Cape Town
CONTINENTAL SHELF
CONTINENTAL SLOPE

MID ATLANTIC RIDGE

INDIAN OCEAN

MERCATOR PROJECTION

SCALE 1:51,400,000

0 KILOMETERS 400 800 1200

0 MILES 400 800 1200

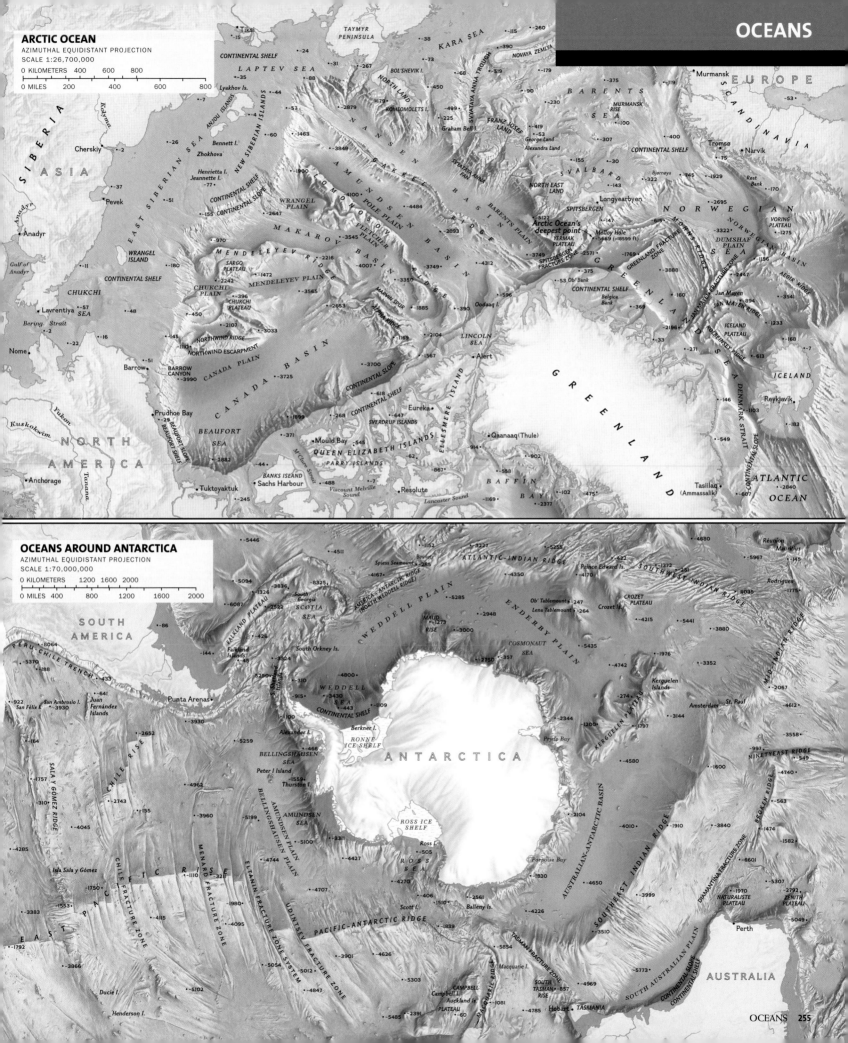

NATIONAL GEOGRAPHIC SOCIETY'S PLACE-NAMES POLICY

In keeping with the National Geographic Society's 122-year chartered purpose as a not-for-profit scientific and educational organization, the Society's cartographic policy is one of portraying de facto situations; that is, to portray to the best of our judgment a current reality. National Geographic strives to be apolitical, to consult multiple authoritative sources, and to make independent decisions based on extensive research. When there are conflicting or variant names, National Geographic does not purport to be the arbiter or determiner of a single name, but simply tries to provide the reader of the map sufficient information in which the reality of conflicting naming claims can be presented. International boundaries and disputed territories, where scale permits, reflect de facto status at the time of publication of our maps and atlases.

The Society's policy for naming geographic features is governed by a representative council of Society cartographers. This council meets frequently to assess available information about naming issues and, based on the best information and research available, seeks to make an independent judgment about future changes or clarifications on its maps, as well as to correct any errors. It is the policy of the Society to correct any errors as quickly as possible on the next published version of a particular map or Atlas.

Depending on the type of map (whether physical or political), the Society uses either conventional (English) or native spellings, or, where space permits, a combination of both. For example, when a commonly recognized form of a well-known place-name, such as Bombay, differs from the official national form – Mumbai—the conventional form is listed in parenthesis: Mumbai (Bombay). The Society does not follow any single source in making its naming determinations. Decisions regarding the naming assigned to geographic places, locations, bodies of water, and the like are checked against a number of external entities, including: the Board on Geographic Names; recognized reference books such as encyclopedias, dictionaries, geographical dictionaries, other atlases, independent academic texts and other similar sources; international bodies such as the United Nations, the European Community, and the like; as well as the policies of individual governmental entities. Names commonly recognized as alternatives or variants by such sources are often used on our maps. In such instances, the primary name is determined by using the form recognized by the de facto controlling country of the area, or by using the generally held conventional form of the name. On occasion where warranted and where space permits, explanatory notes stating the basis or context of a recognized variant naming are provided. Current examples of the application of this variant naming policy are: Falkland Islands (Islas Malvinas); Sea of Japan (East Sea).

National Geographic Maps frequently applies a secondary place-name in parenthesis ( ) after a recognized primary form of a place-name. This treatment is used even when the primary name is more widely recognized, provided that the variant name is used widely enough that National Geographic considers the inclusion of both to have real reference and educational value for the users of its products. Some instances of this use and examples are listed below.

Conventional Names

Used when the commonly recognized form (conventional) of a well-known place name differs from the official national form. The conventional form is listed in parenthesis. Conventional names are recognized as an official variant form for a place-name by multiple reference sources. On physical maps only the conventional form is generally used.

= Roma (Rome)
= Mumbai (Bombay)
= Ghazzah (Gaza City)

If a feature crosses over multiple countries (usually a river), the official national form is labeled within that specific country with the conventional in parentheses. As the feature moves into another country, then that country's official form is used as the primary name.

= Donau (Danube)
= Duna (Danube)
= Dunaj (Danube)
= Dunărea (Danube)
= Dunav (Danube)
= Dunay (Danube)

Historic Names

Given same treatment as conventional names.

= İstanbul (Constantinople)
= Guangzhou (Canton)
= Ho Chi Minh City (Saigon)

Variant Names: Similar to conventional names, but are not necessarily officially recognized as an official variant. Often used by the media.

= Al Fallūjah (Fallujah)

Names with shared possession

When a name (usually a border mountain) is jointly controlled by more then one country and has multiple official names, the general rule is to list the conventional name first and then list the official names together in parentheses. Order of the secondary names can vary. The country that is the main subject of the map would be first. If both countries are the subject of the map, the names are listed in order of the country.

• Mount Everest (Sagarmāthā, Qomolangma): for a map of South Asia when Nepal is the map subject.
• Mount Everest (Qomolangma, Sagarmāthā): for a map of China or when both countries are the map subject.

Disputed Names

When a name has differing forms recognized by different countries. The primary name is determined by using the form recognized by the de facto controlling country of the area, or using the generally held conventional form of the name.

Cyprus
= Lefkosia (Nicosia, Lefkoşa)
= Ammochostos (Famagusta, Gazimagusa)
= Keryneia (Kyrenia, Girne)
Dokdo
= Dokdo (Takeshima, Liancourt Rocks)
Southern Kuril Islands
= Iturup (Etorofu)
= Kunashir (Kunashiri)
Other Features
= English Channel (La Manche)
= Falkland Islands (Islas Malvinas)
= Sea of Japan (East Sea)

Possession Labels

National Geographic Maps applies possession labels in red type to non-contiguous territorial areas (generally islands), identifying the country that has political control of it. Where an area is controlled by one country but is also claimed by another, a longer red note identifying the controlling country and the party claiming ownership is given in red type.

= Falkland Islands (Islas Malvinas)-United Kingdom
  Administered by United Kingdom (claimed by Argentina)
= Senkaku Shotō (Diaoyu Islands)-Japan
  Administered by Japan (claimed by China and Taiwan)

Map Notes

Where scale permits, explanatory notes, as those listed below, are added to our maps to explain the current political situation of disputed possessions or territories.

Abkhazia:
ABKHAZIA
Separatists defeated Georgian troops to gain control of this region in 1993-negotiations continue on resolving the conflict.

Cyprus:
DIVIDED CYPRUS
Cyprus was partitioned in 1974 following a coup backed by Greece and an invasion by Turkey. The island is composed of a Greek Cypriot south with an internationally recognized government and a Turkish Cypriot north (gray) with a government recognized only by Turkey. The UN patrols the dividing line and works toward reunification of the island.

Kashmir:
KASHMIR
India and Pakistan both claim Kashmir-a disputed region of some 10 million people. India administers only the area south of the line of control; Pakistan controls northwestern Kashmir. China took eastern Kashmir from India in a 1962 war.

Kosovo:
KOSOVO
On February 17, 2008, Kosovo declared its independence. Serbia still claims it as a province.

Kuril Islands:
KURIL ISLANDS
The southern Kuril Islands of Iturup (Etorofu), Kunashir (Kunashiri), Shikotan, and the Habomai group were lost by Japan to the Soviet Union in 1945. Japan continues to claim these Russian-administered islands.

Nagorno-Karabakh:
NAGORNO-KARABAKH
Since a 1994 cease-fire between Azerbaijani and Armenian forces, ethnic Armenians have controlled Nagorno-Karabakh and surrounding areas (gray). Azerbaijan continues to claim this disputed region.

Paracel Islands:
PARACEL ISLANDS
Occupied by China in 1974, which calls them Xisha Qundao; claimed by Vietnam, which calls them Hoàng Sa.

Somaliland:
SOMALILAND
In 1991 the Somali National Movement declared Somaliland an independent republic (in gray) with Hargeysa as the capital. It is not internationally recognized.

South Ossetia:
SOUTH OSSETIA
A 1992 cease-fire ended fighting between Ossetians and Georgians, but with no political settlement.

Taiwan:
TAIWAN (short form)
The People's Republic of China claims Taiwan as its 23rd province. Taiwan's government (Republic of China) maintains that there are two political entities.

TAIWAN (long form)
The People's Republic of China claims Taiwan as its 23rd province. Taiwan's government (Republic of China) maintains that there are two political entities. The islands of Matsu, Pescadores, Pratas, and Quemoy are administered by Taiwan.

Transdniestria:
TRANSDNIESTRIA
Since the break-up of the Soviet Union, Ukrainian and Russian minorities have been struggling for independence from Moldova.

West Bank and Gaza:
WEST BANK & GAZA STRIP
Captured by Israel in the 1967 Six Day War, a 1993 peace agreement gives areas of the West Bank and Gaza limited Palestinian autonomy. The future for these autonomous areas and 3 million Palestinians is subject to Israeli-Palestinian negotiations.

Western Sahara:
WESTERN SAHARA
Western Sahara, formerly Spanish Sahara, was divided by Morocco and Mauritania in 1976. Morocco has administered the territory since Mauritania's withdrawal in August 1979. The United Nations does not recognize this annexation, and Western Sahara remains in dispute.

Data used to create the thematic maps and tables in this atlas are reflective of its original publication date. The datasets used represent the most current available in 2005-06.

CONTINENT/Country	Capital	Language	Religion	Area sq km
NORTH AMERICA				
Antigua and Barbuda	Saint John's	English, local dialects	Anglican, other Protestant, Roman Catholic	442
Bahamas	Nassau	English, Creole	Baptist, Anglican, Roman Catholic	13,939
Barbados	Bridgetown	English	Protestant, Roman Catholic	430
Belize	Belmopan	English, Spanish, Mayan, Garifuna, Creole	Roman Catholic, Protestant	22,965
Canada	Ottawa	English, French	Roman Catholic, Protestant	9,984,670
Costa Rica	San José	Spanish, English	Roman Catholic, Evangelical	51,100
Cuba	La Habana (Havana)	Spanish	Roman Catholic, Protestant, Jehovah's Witness, Jewish, Santeria	110,860
Dominica	Roseau	English, French patios	Roman Catholic, Protestant	751
Dominican Republic	Santo Domingo	Spanish	Roman Catholic	48,442
El Salvador	San Salvador	Spanish, Nahua	Roman Catholic, Evangelical	21,041
Grenada	Saint George's	English, French patios	Roman Catholic, Anglican, other Protestant	344
Guatemala	Guatemala (Guatemala City)	Spanish, Amerindian languages	Roman Catholic, Protestant, indigenous Mayan beliefs	108,889
Haiti	Port-au-Prince	French, Creole	Roman Catholic, Protestant, Voodoo	27,750
Honduras	Tegucigalpa	Spanish, Amerindian dialects	Roman Catholic	112,492
Jamaica	Kingston	English, patois English	Protestant, Roman Catholic, other spiritual beliefs	10,991
Mexico	México (Mexico City)	Spanish, various Mayan, Nahuatl, and other indigenous languages	Roman Catholic	1,964,375
Nicaragua	Managua	Spanish, English, indigenous languages	Roman Catholic, Protestant	130,000
Panama	Panamá (Panama City)	Spanish, English	Roman Catholic, Protestant	75,517
Saint Kitts and Nevis	Basseterre	English	Anglican, other Protestant	269
Saint Lucia	Castries	English, French patios	Roman Catholic, Protestant	616
Saint Vincent and the Grenadines	Kingstown	English, French patios	Anglican, Methodist, Roman Catholic, other Protestant	389
Trinidad and Tobago	Port-of-Spain	English, Hindi, French, Spanish	Roman Catholic, Hindu, Anglican, Muslim, Presbyterian	5,128
United States	Washington, D.C.	English, Spanish	Protestant, Roman Catholic, Jewish	9,826,630
NORTH AMERICA: TERRITORIES AND AREAS OF SPECIAL STATUS				
Denmark				
Greenland	Nuuk (Godthåb)	Greenlandic (East Inuit), Danish, English	Evangelical Lutheran	2,166,086
France				
Guadeloupe	Basse-Terre	French, Creole patios	Roman Catholic, Hindu, pagan African	1,706
Martinique	Fort-de-France	French, Creole patios	Roman Catholic, Protestant	1,101
Saint-Pierre and Miquelon	St.-Pierre	French	Roman Catholic	241
Netherlands				
Aruba	Oranjestad	Dutch, Papiamento, English, Spanish	Roman Catholic, Protestant	193
Netherlands Antilles	Willemstad, Curaçao	Dutch, Papiamento, English, Spanish	Roman Catholic, Protestant	809
United Kingdom				
Anguilla	The Valley	English	Anglican, Methodist	96
Bermuda	Hamilton	English, Portuguese	Protestant, Anglican, Roman Catholic	53
British Virgin Islands	Road Town	English	Methodist, Anglican	153
Cayman Islands	George Town	English	Protestant, Roman Catholic	262
Montserrat	Plymouth (abandoned)	English	Anglican, Methodist, Roman Catholic	102
Turks and Caicos Islands	Cockburn Town	English	Baptist, Anglican, Methodist	430
United States				
Navassa Island	Administered from Washington, D.C.	. . .	. . .	5
Puerto Rico	San Juan	Spanish, English	Roman Catholic, Protestant	9,084
Virgin Islands	Charlotte Amalie	English, Spanish, Creole	Protestant, Roman Catholic	386
SOUTH AMERICA				
Argentina	Buenos Aires	Spanish, English, Italian, German, French	Roman Catholic	2,780,400
Bolivia	La Paz (Administrative) Sucre (Constitutional)	Spanish, Quechua, Aymara	Roman Catholic	1,098,581
Brazil	Brasília	Portuguese, Spanish, English, French	Roman Catholic	8,547,403
Chile	Santiago	Spanish	Roman Catholic, Protestant	756,096
Colombia	Bogotá	Spanish	Roman Catholic	1,141,748
Ecuador	Quito	Spanish, Quechua	Roman Catholic	283,560
Guyana	Georgetown	English, Amerindian dialects, Creole, Hindi, Urdu	Christian, Hindu, Muslim	214,969
Paraguay	Asunción	Spanish, Guarani	Roman Catholic	406,752
Peru	Lima	Spanish, Quechua, Aymara	Roman Catholic	1,285,216
Suriname	Paramaribo	Dutch, English, Sranang Tongo (Taki-Taki), Hindustani, Javanese	Hindu, Protestant (Moravian), Roman Catholic, Muslim	163,265
Uruguay	Montevideo	Spanish, Portunol, Brazilero	Roman Catholic	176,215
Venezuela	Caracas	Spanish, indigenous dialects	Roman Catholic	912,050
SOUTH AMERICA: TERRITORIES AND AREAS OF SPECIAL STATUS				
France				
French Guiana	Cayenne	French	Roman Catholic	86,504
United Kingdom				
Falkland Islands	Stanley	English	Anglican, Roman Catholic	12,173
EUROPE				
Albania	Tiranë (Tirana)	Albanian, Greek	Muslim, Albanian Orthodox, Roman Catholic	28,748
Andorra	Andorra la Vella	Catalan, French, Castilian (Spanish)	Roman Catholic	468
Austria	Wien (Vienna)	German	Roman Catholic, Protestant	83,858
Belarus	Minsk	Belarusian, Russian	Eastern Othodox, Roman Catholic, Protestant, Jewish, Muslim	207,595
Belgium	Bruxelles (Brussels)	Dutch, French, German	Roman Catholic, Protestant	30,528
Bosnia and Herzegovina	Sarajevo	Croatian, Serbian, Bosnian	Muslim, Orthodox, Roman Catholic	51,129
Bulgaria	Sofiya (Sofia)	Bulgarian	Bulgarian Orthodox, Muslim	110,994
Croatia	Zagreb	Croatian	Roman Catholic, Orthodox	56,542
Cyprus	Lefkosia (Lefkosa, Nicosia)	Greek, Turkish, English	Greek Orthodox, Muslim	9,251
Czech Republic	Praha (Prague)	Czech	Roman Catholic, Protestant, atheist	78,866
Denmark	København (Copenhagen)	Danish, Faroese, Greenlandic	Evangelical Lutheran	43,098
Estonia	Tallinn	Estonian, Russian, Ukrainian	Evangelical Lutheran, Russian Orthodox, Eastern Orthodox	45,227
Finland	Helsinki (Helsingfors)	Finnish, Swedish	Evangelical Lutheran	338,145
France	Paris	French	Roman Catholic	543,965
Germany	Berlin	German	Protestant, Roman Catholic	357,022
Greece	Athina (Athens)	Greek	Greek Orthodox	131,957
Hungary	Budapest	Hungarian	Roman Catholic, Calvinist, Lutheran	93,030
Iceland	Reykjavik	Icelandic, English, Nordic languages, German	Evangelical Lutheran	103,000
Ireland	Baile Átha Cliath (Dublin)	English, Irish	Roman Catholic	70,273
Italy	Roma (Rome)	Italian, German, French, Slovene	Roman Catholic	301,333
Latvia	Riga	Latvian, Lithuanian, Russian	Lutheran, Roman Catholic, Russian Orthodox	64,589
Liechtenstein	Vaduz	German, Alemannic dialect	Roman Catholic, Protestant	160
Lithuania	Vilnius	Lithuanian, Polish, Russian	Roman Catholic, Lutheran, Russian Orthodox, Protestant	65,300
Luxembourg	Luxembourg	Luxembourgish, German, French	Roman Catholic	2,586
Macedonia	Skopje	Macedonian, Albanian, Turkish	Macedonian Orthodox, Muslim	25,713
Malta	Valletta	Maltese, English	Roman Catholic	316
Moldova	Chisinau	Moldovan, Russian, Gagauz	Eastern Orthodox	33,800
Monaco	Monaco	French, English, Italian, Monegasque	Roman Catholic	2
Montenegro (Mid-2006 Data)	Podgorica	Montenegrin, Serbian, Albanian	Orthodox, Muslim, Roman Catholic	13,812

Area (sq mi)	Population Mid-2005 (in 1,000s)	Projected pop. change 2005-2050	Pop density sq km (sq mi)	Urban pop.	Natural increase	Total fertility / infant mortality rate	Pop. <15 / >65	Life expectancy: Male/Female	HIV/AIDS Pop. 15-49 2003-04	CONTINENT / Country Formal Name
										NORTH AMERICA
(171)	80	0%	181 (468)	37%	1.39%	2.30 / 20.90	26.40% / 7.80%	69.00 / 73.80	- - -	Antigua and Barbuda
(5,382)	319	46%	23 (59)	89%	1.17%	2.20 / 12.70	29.60% / 5.20%	66.60 / 72.73	3.00%	Commonwealth of The Bahamas
(166)	258	-2%	600 (1,554)	50%	0.63%	1.80 / 13.20	21.80% / 11.80%	70.00 / 74.10	1.50%	Barbados
(8,867)	292	64%	13 (33)	49%	2.25%	3.30 / 31.00	36.30% / 4.10%	66.70 / 73.50	2.40%	Belize
(3,855,101)	32,225	14%	3 (8)	79%	0.30%	1.50 / 5.40	17.90% / 13.10%	77.20 / 82.10	0.30%	Canada
(19,730)	4,331	46%	85 (220)	59%	1.33%	2.00 / 9.25	30.00% / 5.60%	76.30 / 81.10	0.60%	Republic of Costa Rica
(42,803)	11,275	-2%	102 (263)	76%	0.44%	1.50 / 5.80	20.90% / 10.30%	75.29 / 79.09	0.10%	Republic of Cuba
(290)	70	17%	93 (241)	71%	0.80%	1.90 / 22.20	27.80% / 7.90%	71.20 / 77.20	- - -	Commonwealth of Dominica
(18,704)	8,862	50%	183 (474)	64%	1.70%	2.90 / 31.00	33.60% / 5.20%	66.40 / 69.30	1.70%	Dominican Republic
(8,124)	6,881	57%	327 (847)	59%	2.03%	3.00 / 24.60	32.90% / 5.00%	67.10 / 73.00	0.70%	Republic of El Salvador
(133)	101	-14%	294 (759)	39%	1.16%	2.10 / 17.40	35.00% / 7.80%	- - - / - - -	- - -	Grenada
(42,042)	12,701	120%	117 (302)	39%	2.79%	4.40 / 39.00	41.90% / 4.00%	63.01 / 68.87	1.10%	Republic of Guatemala
(10,714)	8,288	127%	299 (774)	36%	1.87%	4.70 / 80.30	41.80% / 3.40%	51.00 / 53.70	5.60%	Republic of Haiti
(43,433)	7,212	104%	64 (166)	47%	2.79%	4.10 / 32.00	41.40% / 3.80%	67.40 / 74.30	1.80%	Republic of Honduras
(4,244)	2,666	28%	243 (628)	52%	1.29%	2.40 / 24.40	30.70% / 7.20%	71.80 / 75.20	1.20%	Jamaica
(758,449)	107,029	30%	54 (141)	75%	1.85%	2.60 / 24.90	30.60% / 4.80%	73.10 / 77.60	0.30%	United Mexican States
(50,193)	5,774	88%	44 (115)	59%	2.70%	3.80 / 35.50	41.90% / 3.10%	65.65 / 70.36	0.20%	Republic of Nicaragua
(29,157)	3,232	55%	43 (111)	62%	1.76%	2.70 / 20.64	29.30% / 5.60%	72.25 / 77.36	0.90%	Republic of Panama
(104)	48	33%	178 (462)	33%	0.98%	2.30 / 16.70	28.00% / 8.30%	67.58 / 71.65	- - -	Federation of Saint Kitts and Nevis
(238)	163	44%	265 (685)	30%	0.99%	2.20 / 14.20	30.40% / 7.40%	72.00 / 76.70	- - -	Saint Lucia
(150)	111	-12%	285 (740)	55%	1.13%	2.10 / 18.10	30.40% / 6.30%	70.30 / 73.70	- - -	Saint Vincent and the Grenadines
(1,980)	1,305	-6%	254 (659)	74%	0.65%	1.60 / 18.60	21.20% / 6.60%	67.31 / 73.73	3.20%	Republic of Trinidad and Tobago
(3,794,083)	296,483	42%	30 (78)	79%	0.58%	2.00 / 6.60	20.90% / 12.40%	74.80 / 80.10	0.60%	United States of America
										NORTH AMERICA: TERRITORIES AND AREAS OF SPECIAL STATUS
(836,086)	57	0%	0.03 (0.07)	83%	0.85%	2.40 / 8.90	25.90% / 5.40%	64.10 / 69.50	- - -	Overseas Region of Denmark
(658)	450*	5%	264 (684)	100%	1.04%	2.20 / 6.40	23.10% / 8.90%	74.50 / 81.10	- - -	French Overseas Department
(425)	397	10%	361 (934)	95%	0.66%	2.00 / 7.50	23.10% / 10.10%	75.20 / 81.70	- - -	French Overseas Department
(93)	7	-14%	29 (75)	89%	0.25%	- - - 0	19.90% / 11.48%	- - - / - - -	- - -	French Overseas Territorial Collectivity
(75)	97	13%	503 (1,293)	47%	0.70%	2.00 / 2.60	21.00% / 10.60%	75.30 / 82.20	- - -	Overseas Region of the Netherlands
(312)	187	35%	231 (605)	69%	0.78%	2.20 / 8.80	23.40% / 9.60%	72.10 / 78.70	- - -	Overseas Region of the Netherlands
(37)	13	23%	135 (351)	100%	0.61%	1.70 / 14.40	28.00% / 8.00%	77.90 / 78.02	- - -	British Overseas Territory
(21)	62	2%	1,170 (2,952)	100%	0.67%	2.10 / 0	19.40% / 11.30%	75.20 / 79.30	- - -	British Overseas Territory
(59)	22	55%	144 (373)	61%	1.05%	2.00 / 17.86	25.61% / 4.91%	70.20 / 78.60	- - -	British Overseas Territory
(101)	44	105%	168 (436)	100%	1.18%	2.20 / 8.00	22.00% / 7.10%	76.70 / 81.80	- - -	British Overseas Territory
(39)	5	0%	49 (128)	13%	-0.30%	- - - / - - -	22.70% / 16.43%	- - - / - - -	- - -	British Overseas Territory
(166)	21	100%	49 (127)	45%	1.98%	3.20 / 16.90	32.50% / 3.70%	72.30 / 76.80	- - -	British Overseas Territory
(2)	0	- - -	- - - - - -	- - -	- - -	- - - / - - -	- - - / - - -	- - - / - - -	- - -	Territory of the United States
(3,507)	3,912	-4%	431 (1,115)	94%	0.65%	1.80 / 9.80	22.20% / 12.20%	72.90 / 80.70	- - -	Self-Governing Commonwealth in Association with the United States
(149)	109	-6%	282 (732)	93%	0.93%	2.30 / 3.10	24.40% / 9.70%	74.90 / 82.70	- - -	Territory of the United States
										SOUTH AMERICA
(1,073,518)	38,592	39%	14 (36)	89%	1.06%	2.40 / 16.80	27.20% / 9.90%	70.60 / 78.10	0.70%	Argentine Republic
(424,164)	8,922	62%	8 (21)	63%	2.11%	3.85 / 54.00	37.10% / 4.30%	61.80 / 65.99	0.10%	Republic of Bolivia
(3,300,169)	184,184	41%	22 (56)	81%	1.41%	2.40 / 27.00	28.90% / 5.80%	67.60 / 75.20	0.70%	Federative Republic of Brazil
(291,930)	16,136	27%	21 (55)	87%	1.03%	2.05 / 7.80	24.20% / 7.20%	72.99 / 79.04	0.30%	Republic of Chile
(440,831)	46,039	44%	40 (104)	75%	1.68%	2.60 / 25.60	31.70% / 4.90%	69.17 / 75.32	0.70%	Republic of Colombia
(109,483)	13,032	56%	46 (119)	61%	2.12%	3.30 / 29.00	33.23% / 6.69%	71.30 / 77.00	0.30%	Republic of Ecuador
(83,000)	751	-35%	3 (9)	36%	1.28%	2.30 / 49.00	28.40% / 4.80%	59.81 / 65.86	2.50%	Co-operative Republic of Guyana
(157,048)	6,158	67%	15 (39)	54%	1.73%	2.90 / 37.00	32.30% / 4.40%	68.60 / 73.12	0.50%	Republic of Paraguay
(496,224)	27,947	53%	22 (56)	73%	1.61%	2.70 / 33.00	32.20% / 5.20%	67.34 / 72.42	0.50%	Republic of Peru
(63,037)	447	-4%	3 (7)	74%	1.42%	2.60 / 26.00	29.10% / 5.80%	65.75 / 72.51	1.70%	Republic of Suriname
(68,037)	3,419	23%	19 (50)	93%	0.59%	2.20 / 15.00	23.80% / 13.30%	71.29 / 79.20	0.30%	Oriental Republic of Uruguay
(352,144)	26,749	57%	29 (76)	87%	1.80%	2.70 / 19.58	30.70% / 4.60%	69.90 / 75.81	0.70%	Bolivarian Republic of Venezuela
										SOUTH AMERICA: TERRITORIES AND AREAS OF SPECIAL STATUS
(33,400)	195	91%	2 (6)	75%	2.63%	3.90 / 12.40	35.00% / 3.80%	71.70 / 79.20	- - -	French Overseas Department
(4,700)	3	3%	0.25 (0.64)	79%	0.55%	- - - / - - -	- - - / - - -	- - - / - - -	- - -	British Overseas Territory
										EUROPE
(11,100)	3,170	13%	110 (286)	42%	0.93%	2.00 / 8.40	27.29% / 8.10%	71.70 / 76.40	- - -	Republic of Albania
(181)	74	-3%	158 (409)	92%	0.71%	1.30 / 3.86	14.90% / 12.60%	- - - / - - -	- - -	Principality of Andorra
(32,378)	8,151	0%	97 (252)	54%	0.05%	1.40 / 4.50	16.30% / 15.49%	75.90 / 81.60	0.30%	Republic of Austria
(80,153)	9,776	-13%	47 (122)	72%	-0.55%	1.20 / 7.70	16.20% / 14.30%	62.70 / 74.70	- - -	Republic of Belarus
(11,787)	10,458	5%	343 (887)	97%	0.05%	1.60 / 4.40	17.40% / 17.02%	75.58 / 81.69	0.20%	Kingdom of Belgium
(19,741)	3,840	-19%	75 (195)	43%	0.09%	1.20 / 7.60	18.30% / 12.20%	71.30 / 76.70	< 0.05%	Bosnia and Herzegovina
(42,855)	7,741	-34%	70 (181)	70%	-0.52%	1.30 / 11.60	14.20% / 17.10%	68.70 / 75.60	< 0.05%	Republic of Bulgaria
(21,831)	4,438	-14%	78 (203)	56%	-0.29%	1.30 / 6.30	16.60% / 16.30%	71.20 / 78.30	< 0.05%	Republic of Croatia
(3,572)	965	12%	104 (270)	65%	0.40%	1.60 / 6.20	20.49% / 10.90%	74.80 / 79.10	- - -	Republic of Cyprus
(30,450)	10,212	-8%	129 (335)	77%	-0.09%	1.20 / 3.70	15.20% / 13.90%	72.03 / 78.51	0.10%	Czech Republic
(16,640)	5,418	1%	126 (326)	72%	0.16%	1.80 / 4.39	18.90% / 14.90%	74.89 / 79.48	0.20%	Kingdom of Denmark
(17,462)	1,345	-23%	30 (77)	69%	-0.28%	1.50 / 7.00	15.97% / 16.18%	66.04 / 76.90	1.10%	Republic of Estonia
(130,558)	5,246	1%	16 (40)	62%	0.19%	1.80 / 3.10	17.50% / 15.90%	75.30 / 82.30	0.10%	Republic of Finland
(210,026)	60,742	5%	112 (289)	76%	0.43%	1.90 / 3.90	18.57% / 16.40%	76.70 / 83.80	0.40%	French Republic
(137,847)	82,490	-9%	231 (598)	88%	-0.14%	1.30 / 4.32	14.70% / 18.00%	75.59 / 81.34	0.10%	Federal Republic of Germany
(50,949)	11,100	-4%	84 (218)	60%	0.01%	1.30 / 5.10	14.60% / 17.50%	76.40 / 81.10	0.20%	Hellenic Republic
(35,919)	10,086	-12%	108 (281)	65%	-0.37%	1.30 / 6.60	15.60% / 15.50%	68.29 / 76.53	0.10%	Republic of Hungary
(39,769)	295	21%	3 (7)	94%	0.83%	2.00 / 2.40	22.60% / 11.80%	78.70 / 82.50	0.20%	Republic of Iceland
(27,133)	4,125	14%	59 (152)	60%	0.83%	2.00 / 4.78	20.85% / 11.15%	75.10 / 80.30	0.10%	Republic of Ireland
(116,345)	58,742	-11%	195 (505)	90%	0.04%	1.30 / 4.80	14.20% / 19.20%	76.80 / 82.50	0.50%	Italian Republic
(24,938)	2,300	-23%	36 (92)	68%	-0.50%	1.30 / 9.40	15.40% / 16.20%	65.90 / 76.90	0.60%	Republic of Latvia
(62)	35	26%	219 (565)	21%	0.39%	1.30 / 2.90	18.00% / 10.80%	78.70 / 82.10	- - -	Principality of Liechtenstein
(25,212)	3,415	-16%	52 (135)	67%	-0.31%	1.30 / 7.90	17.70% / 15.00%	66.48 / 77.85	0.10%	Republic of Lithuania
(998)	457*	41%	177 (458)	91%	0.41%	1.60 / 3.85	18.80% / 14.10%	74.90 / 81.50	0.20%	Grand Duchy of Luxembourg
(9,928)	2,039	-2%	79 (205)	59%	0.44%	1.50 / 11.30	20.40% / 10.80%	70.80 / 75.70	< 0.05%	Republic of Macedonia
(122)	405	-10%	1,282 (3,320)	91%	0.21%	1.50 / 7.20	18.20% / 13.00%	75.78 / 80.48	0.20%	Republic of Malta
(13,050)	4,206	-21%	124 (322)	45%	-0.18%	1.20 / 14.40	19.80% / 9.90%	64.50 / 71.60	0.20%	Republic of Moldova
(1)	33	67%	16,500 (33,000)	100%	0.64%	- - - / - - -	13.23% / 22.43%	- - - / - - -	- - -	Principality of Monaco
(5,333)	600	-4%	43 (113)	- - -	0.30%	1.70 / 8.00	21.00% / 12.00%	- - - / - - -	- - -	Republic of Montenegro

CONTINENT/Country	Capital	Language	Religion	Area sq km
Netherlands	Amsterdam	Dutch, Frisian	Roman Catholic, Protestant, Muslim	41,528
Norway	Oslo	Norwegian	Evangelical Lutheran	323,758
Poland	Warszawa (Warsaw)	Polish	Roman Catholic	312,685
Portugal	Lisboa (Lisbon)	Portuguese, Mirandese	Roman Catholic	92,345
Romania	Bucuresti (Bucharest)	Romanian, Hungarian, German	Eastern Orthodox, Protestant, Catholic	238,391
Russia	Moskva (Moscow)	Russian	Russian Orthodox, Muslim, other	17,075,400
San Marino	San Marino	Italian	Roman Catholic	61
Serbia (Mid -2006 Data)	Belgrade	Serbian, Hungarian, Bosnian, Albanian	Orthodox, Muslim, Roman Catholic, Protestant	88,361
Slovakia	Bratislava (Pressburg)	Slovak, Hungarian	Roman Catholic, atheist, Protestant	49,035
Slovenia	Ljubljana	Slovenian, Serbo-Croatian	Roman Catholic, other	20,273
Spain	Madrid	Castilian Spanish, Catalan, Galician, Basque	Roman Catholic	505,988
Sweden	Stockholm	Swedish	Lutheran, Roman Catholic	449,964
Switzerland	Bern	German, French, Romanisch	Roman Catholic, Protestant	41,284
Ukraine	Kyiv (Kiev)	Ukrainian, Russian, Romanian, Polish, Hungarian	Ukrainian Orthodox, Ukrainian Catholic (Uniate), Protestant, Jewish	603,700
United Kingdom	London	English, Welsh, Scottish form of Gaelic	Anglican, Roman Catholic, other Protestant, Muslim	242,910
Vatican City	Vatican City	Italian, Latin, French	Roman Catholic	0.4
EUROPE: TERRITORIES AND AREAS OF SPECIAL STATUS				
Denmark				
Faroe Islands	Tórshavn	Faroese, Danish	Evangelical Lutheran	1,399
Norway				
Svalbard	Longyearbyen	Norwegian, Russian	Evangelical Lutheran, Russian Orthodox	62,049
United Kingdom				
Channel Islands (Guernsey and Jersey)	Saint Peter Port, Guernsey Saint Helier, Jersey	English, French, Norman French dialect	Anglican, Roman Catholic, Baptist	194
Gibraltar	Gibraltar	English, Spanish, Italian, Portuguese	Roman Catholic, Church of England	7
Isle of Man	Douglas	English, Manx Gaelic	Anglican, Roman Catholic, Methodist, Baptist	572
ASIA				
Afghanistan	Kabol (Kabul)	Pashtu, Afghan Persian (Dari), Uzbek, Turkmen, 30 minor languages	Sunni and Shiite Muslim	652,090
Armenia	Yerevan	Armenian, Russian	Armenian Apostolic	29,743
Azerbaijan	Baku	Azerbaijani, Russian, Armenian	Muslim, Russian Orthodox, Armenian Orthodox	86,600
Bahrain	Al Manamah (Manama)	Arabic, English, Farsi, Urdu	Shiite and Sunni Muslim	717
Bangladesh	Dhaka	Bangla (Bengali), English	Muslim, Hindu	147,570
Bhutan	Thimphu	Dzonkha, Tibetan and Nepali dialects	Lamaistic Buddhist, Hindu	46,500
Brunei	Bandar Seri Begawan	Malay, English, Chinese	Muslim, Buddhist, Christian, indigenous beliefs	5,765
Cambodia	Phnom Penh	Khmer, French, English	Theravada Buddhist	181,035
China	Beijing (Peking)	Chinese (Mandarin), Cantonese, other dialects and minority languages	Toist, Buddhist, Muslim	9,596,960
Georgia	Tbilisi (Tiflis)	Georgian, Russian, Armenian, Azeri	Georgian Orthodox, Muslim, Russian Orthodox	69,700
India	New Delhi	Hindi, English, 14 other official languages	Hindu, Muslim, Christian, Sikh, Buddhist, Jain, Parsi	3,287,270
Indonesia	Jakarta	Bahasa Indonesia, English, Dutch, Javanese, and other local dialects	Muslim, Protestant, Roman Catholic, Hindu, Buddhist	1,922,570
Iran	Tehran	Persian, Turkic, Kurdish, various local dialects	Shiite and Sunni Muslim	1,648,000
Iraq	Baghdad	Arabic, Kurdish, Assyrian, Armenian	Shiite and Sunni Muslim	437,072
Israel	Jerusalem (Yerushalayim, Al-Quds)	Hebrew, Arabic, English	Jewish, Muslim, Christian	22,145
Japan	Tokyo	Japanese	Shinto, Buddhist	377,887
Jordan	Amman	Arabic, English	Sunni Muslim, Christian	89,342
Kazakhstan	Astana	Kazakh (Qazaq), Russian	Muslim, Russian Orthodox	2,717,300
Korea, North	Pyongyang	Korean	Buddhist, Confucianist	120,538
Korea, South	Seoul	Korean, English widely taught	Christian, Buddhist	99,250
Kuwait	Kuwait City	Arabic, English	Sunni and Shiite Muslim, Christian, Hindu, Parsi	17,818
Kyrgyzstan	Bishkek	Kyrgyz, Russian	Muslim, Russian Orthodox	199,900
Laos	Viangchan (Vientiane)	Lao, French, English, varous ethnic languages	Buddhist, Animist, other	236,800
Lebanon	Beyrouth (Beirut)	Arabic, French, English, Armenian	Muslim, Christian	10,452
Malaysia	Kuala Lumpur	Bahasa Melayu, English, Chinese /regional dialects, indigenous languages	Muslim, Buddhist, Daoist, Hindu, Christian, Sikh, Shamanist	329,847
Maldives	Maale (Male)	Maldivian Dhivehi, (dialect of Sinhala), English	Sunni Muslim	298
Mongolia	Ulaanbaatar (Ulan Bator)	Khalkha Mongol, Turkic, Russian	Tibetan Buddhist, Lamaism	1,564,116
Myanmar (Burma)	Yangon (Rangoon)	Burmese, minor languages	Buddhist, Christian, Muslim	676,552
Nepal	Kathmandu	Nepali, English, many other languages and dialects	Hindu, Buddhist, Muslim	147,181
Oman	Masqat (Muscat)	Arabic, English, Baluchi, Urdu, Indian dialects	Ibadhi Muslim, Sunni Muslim, Shiite Muslim, Hindu	309,500
Pakistan	Islamabad	Punjabi, Sindhi, Siraiki, Pashtu, Urdu, English	Sunni and Shiite Muslim, Christian, Hindu	796,095
Philippines	Manila	Filipino (based on Tagalog), English, and 8 major dialects	Roman Catholic, Protestant, Muslim, Buddhist	300,000
Qatar	Ad Dawhah (Doha)	Arabic, English	Muslim	11,521
Saudi Arabia	Ar Riyad (Riyadh)	Arabic	Muslim	1,960,582
Singapore	Singapore	Chinese, Malay, Tamil, English	Buddhist, Muslim, Christian, Hindu, Sikh, Taoist, Confucianist	660
Sri Lanka	Colombo	Sinhala, Tamil, English	Buddhist, Hindu, Christian, Muslim	65,525
Syria	Dimashq (Damascus)	Arabic, Kurdish, Armenian, Aramaic, Circassian, French, English	Sunni, Alawite, Druze and other Muslim sects, Christian	185,180
Tajikistan	Dushanbe	Tajik, Russian	Sunni and Shiite Muslim	143,100
Thailand	Krung Thep (Bangkok)	Thai, English, ethnic and regional dialects	Buddhist, Muslim	513,115
Timor-Leste (East Timor)	Dili	Tetum, Portuguese, Bahasa, Indonesian, English	Christian (mostly Roman Catholic)	14,609
Turkey	Ankara (Angora)	Turkish, Kurdish, Arabic, Armenian, Greek	Muslim (mostly Sunni)	779,452
Turkmenistan	Asgabat (Ashgabat)	Turkmen, Russian, Uzbek	Muslim, Eastern Orthodox	488,100
United Arab Emirates	Abu Zaby (Abu Dhabi)	Arabic, Persian, English, Hindi, Urdu	Sunni and Shiite Muslim, Christian, Hindu, other	77,700
Uzbekistan	Toshkent (Tashkent)	Uzbek, Russian, Tajik	Muslim, Eastern Orthodox	447,400
Vietnam	Hanoi	Vietnamese, English, French, Chinese, Khmer, local languages	Buddhist, Hoa Hao, Cao Dai, Christian, indigenous beliefs, Muslim	331,114
Yemen	Sana (Sanaa)	Arabic	Sunni and Shiite Muslim	536,869
ASIA: TERRITORIES AND AREAS OF SPECIAL STATUS				
China				
Hong Kong	- - -	Chinese (Cantonese), English	Local religions, Christian	1092
Macau	- - -	Portuguese, Chinese (Cantonese)	Buddhist, Roman Catholic	25
Taiwan	Taipei (Taipei)	Mandarin Chinese, Taiwanese	Mixture of Buddhist, Confucian, and Taoist; Christian	35,980
Israel - Palestinian Areas	- - -	Arabic, Hebrew, English	Muslim (mostly Sunni), Jewish, Christian	- - -
Gaza Strip	- - -	Arabic, Hebrew, English	Muslim (mostly Sunni), Jewish	365
West Bank	- - -	Arabic, Hebrew, English	Muslim (mostly Sunni), Jewish, Christian	5,655
United Kingdom				
British Indian Ocean Territory	Administered from London	English	- - -	44
AFRICA				
Algeria	Alger (Algiers)	Arabic, French, Berber dialects	Sunni Muslim	2,381,741
Angola	Luanda	Portuguese, Bantu	Indigenous beliefs, Roman Catholic, Protestant	1,246,700
Benin	Cotonou (Administrative) Porto-Novo (Constitutional)	French, Fon, Yoruba, tribal languages	Indigenous beliefs, Christian, Muslim	112,622
Botswana	Gaborone	English, Setswana	Indigenous beliefs, Christian	581,730
Burkina Faso	Ouagadougou	French, native African languages	Muslim, indigenous beliefs, Christian	274,200
Burundi	Bujumbura	Kirundi, French, Swahili	Roman Catholic, indigenous beliefs, Muslim, Protestant	27,834
Cameroon	Yaoundé	French, English, 24 major African language groups	Indigenous beliefs, Christian, Muslim	475,442
Cape Verde	Praia	Portuguese, Crioulo (Kriolu)	Roman Catholic, Protestant	4,036
Central African Republic	Bangui	French, Sangho, Arabic, tribal languages	Indigenous beliefs, Protestant, Roman Catholic, Muslim	622,984
Chad	N'Djamena	French, Arabic, Sara, Sango, more than 120 different languages and dialects	Muslim, Christian, animist	1,284,000

Area (sq mi)	Population Mid-2005 (in 1,000s)	Projected pop. change 2005-2050	Pop density sq km (sq mi)	Urban pop.	Natural increase	Total fertility / infant mortality rate	Pop. <15 / >65	Life expectancy: Male / Female	HIV/AIDS Pop. 15-49 2003-04	CONTINENT / Country Formal Name
(16,034)	16,296	4%	392 (1,016)	62%	0.35%	1.70 / 4.14	18.55% / 13.80%	76.20 / 80.80	0.20%	Kingdom of the Netherlands
(125,004)	4,620	21%	14 (37)	78%	0.34%	1.80 / 3.20	19.70% / 14.70%	77.50 / 82.33	0.10%	Kingdom of Norway
(120,728)	38,163	-15%	122 (316)	62%	0.02%	1.20 / 6.75	17.20% / 12.96%	70.52 / 78.90	0.10%	Republic of Poland
(35,655)	10,576	-12%	115 (297)	53%	0.04%	1.40 / 4.10	15.70% / 16.80%	74.00 / 80.57	0.40%	Portuguese Republic
(92,043)	21,612	-29%	91 (235)	53%	-0.19%	1.30 / 16.70	16.40% / 14.40%	67.50 / 74.80	< 0.05%	Romania
(6,592,850)	143,025	-23%	8 (22)	73%	-0.55%	1.40 / 12.40	15.70% / 13.40%	58.80 / 72.00	1.10%	Russian Federation
(24)	30	0%	492 (1,250)	84%	0.33%	1.20 / 6.70	15.00% / 16.00%	77.80 / 84.20	- - -	Republic of San Marino
(34,116)	9,500	-10%	107 (278)	- - -	0.10%	1.80 / 10.0	19.00% / 15.00%	- - - / - - -	- - -	Republic of Serbia
(18,932)	5,382	-12%	110 (284)	56%	0.01%	1.20 / 7.80	17.60% / 11.60%	69.80 / 77.80	< 0.05%	Slovak Republic
(7,827)	1,998	-5%	99 (255)	51%	-0.10%	1.20 / 4.00	14.47% / 15.20%	73.20 / 80.70	< 0.05%	Republic of Slovenia
(195,363)	43,484	1%	86 (223)	76%	0.13%	1.30 / 3.57	14.50% / 16.80%	76.90 / 83.60	0.70%	Kingdom of Spain
(173,732)	9,029	18%	20 (52)	84%	0.11%	1.70 / 3.10	17.57% / 17.25%	78.35 / 82.68	0.10%	Kingdom of Sweden
(15,940)	7,446	-4%	180 (467)	68%	0.17%	1.40 / 4.30	16.20% / 15.80%	77.90 / 83.00	0.40%	Swiss Confederation
(233,090)	47,110	-29%	78 (202)	68%	-0.70%	1.20 / 9.50	15.27% / 15.53%	62.64 / 74.06	1.40%	Ukraine
(93,788)	60,068	12%	247 (640)	89%	0.17%	1.70 / 5.20	18.34% / 15.97%	75.90 / 80.50	0.20%	United Kingdom of Great Britain and Northern Ireland
(0.2)	0.798	25%	1,995 (3,990)	100%	-0.90%	- - - / - - -	- - - / - - -	- - - / - - -	- - -	State of the Vatican City (The Holy See)
										EUROPE: TERRITORIES AND AREAS OF SPECIAL STATUS
(540)	50	16%	36 (93)	38%	0.70%	2.50 / 2.80	23.60% / 13.20%	77.00 / 81.00	- - -	Overseas Region of Denmark
(23,957)	3	-0.02%	.05 (.13)	- - -	-1.99%	- - - / - - -	- - - / - - -	- - - / - - -	0.00%	Norwegian Dependency
(75)	149	15%	768 (1,987)	31%	0.23%	1.40 / 3.40	14.70% / 12.60%	75.54 / 80.33	- - -	British Crown Dependencies
(3)	29	-7%	4,143 (9,667)	100%	0.48%	- - - / 5.50	- - - / - - -	- - - / - - -	- - -	British Overseas Territory
(221)	78	6%	136 (353)	52%	0.01%	1.60 / 3.30	17.80% / 16.70%	- - - / - - -	- - -	British Crown Dependency
										ASIA
(251,773)	29,929	174%	46 (119)	22%	2.56%	6.80 / 171.90	44.90% / 2.40%	41.40 / 41.80	- - -	Transitional Islamic State of Afghanistan
(11,484)	3,033	8%	102 (264)	65%	0.25%	1.40 / 36.10	22.31% / 10.78%	67.49 / 74.97	0.10%	Republic of Armenia
(33,436)	8,388	38%	97 (251)	51%	0.99%	2.00 / 9.80	26.40% / 6.80%	69.60 / 75.20	< 0.05%	Republic of Azerbaijan
(277)	731	58%	1,020 (2,639)	87%	1.81%	2.80 / 8.00	27.90% / 2.52%	73.10 / 74.80	0.20%	Kingdom of Bahrain
(56,977)	144,233	60%	977 (2,531)	23%	1.88%	3.00 / 65.00	34.66% / 3.38%	61.00 / 61.80	- - -	People's Republic of Bangladesh
(17,954)	970	108%	21 (54)	21%	2.55%	4.70 / 60.50	40.00% / 4.30%	61.65 / 64.74	- - -	Kingdom of Bhutan
(2,226)	363	62%	63 (163)	74%	1.88%	2.60 / 8.30	31.80% / 2.60%	71.70 / 76.60	< 0.05%	Negara Brunei Darussalam
(69,898)	13,329	85%	74 (191)	15%	2.18%	4.50 / 95.10	37.10% / 3.20%	52.13 / 59.62	2.60%	Kingdom of Cambodia
(3,705,405)	1,303,701	10%	136 (352)	37%	0.59%	1.60 / 27.20	21.50% / 7.60%	70.40 / 73.70	0.10%	People's Republic of China
(26,911)	4,501	-19%	65 (167)	52%	0.01%	1.40 / 24.80	18.60% / 13.30%	68.00 / 74.80	0.10%	Republic of Georgia
(1,269,221)	1,103,596	48%	336 (870)	28%	1.68%	3.00 / 60.00	35.90% / 4.43%	60.80 / 62.50	0.90%	Republic of India
(742,308)	221,932	39%	115 (299)	42%	1.56%	2.60 / 45.70	29.71% / 4.72%	66.44 / 70.44	0.10%	Republic of Indonesia
(636,296)	69,515	47%	42 (109)	67%	1.20%	2.10 / 32.10	29.70% / 4.30%	68.83 / 71.74	0.10%	Islamic Republic of Iran
(168,754)	28,807	121%	66 (171)	68%	2.72%	5.10 / 94.00	42.00% / 2.80%	57.30 / 60.40	< 0.05%	Republic of Iraq
(8,550)	7,105	55%	321 (831)	92%	1.55%	2.90 / 5.10	28.35% / 9.90%	77.50 / 81.50	0.10%	State of Israel
(145,902)	127,728	-21%	338 (875)	79%	0.08%	1.30 / 2.80	13.80% / 19.80%	78.36 / 85.33	< 0.05%	Japan
(34,495)	5,795	79%	65 (168)	79%	2.40%	3.70 / 22.10	36.90% / 3.00%	70.60 / 72.40	< 0.05%	Hashemite Kingdom of Jordan
(1,049,155)	15,079	-1%	6 (14)	57%	0.58%	2.00 / 61.00	27.20% / 7.50%	60.50 / 71.50	0.20%	Republic of Kazakhstan
(46,540)	22,912	15%	190 (492)	60%	0.92%	2.00 / 21.00	27.00% / 7.90%	68.70 / 74.20	- - -	Democratic People's Republic of Korea
(38,321)	48,294	-12%	487 (1,260)	80%	0.51%	1.20 / 5.10	19.10% / 9.10%	73.38 / 80.44	< 0.05%	Republic of Korea
(6,880)	2,589	172%	145 (376)	96%	1.73%	4.00 / 9.60	25.60% / 1.60%	76.70 / 78.50	- - -	State of Kuwait
(77,182)	5,172	60%	26 (67)	35%	1.34%	2.60 / 55.00	33.00% / 6.00%	64.50 / 72.20	0.10%	Kyrgyz Republic
(91,429)	5,924	96%	25 (65)	19%	2.33%	4.80 / 88.00	40.20% / 3.50%	53.25 / 55.75	0.10%	Lao People's Democratic Republic
(4,036)	3,779	31%	362 (936)	87%	1.58%	2.20 / 17.20	28.10% / 6.20%	71.90 / 75.10	0.10%	Lebanese Republic
(127,355)	26,121	80%	79 (205)	62%	2.09%	3.30 / 10.00	33.00% / 4.60%	70.40 / 76.20	0.40%	Malaysia
(115)	294	83%	987 (2,557)	27%	1.40%	2.80 / 18.00	36.10% / 4.20%	71.30 / 72.30	- - -	Republic of Maldives
(603,909)	2,646	46%	2 (4)	57%	1.55%	2.50 / 58.00	31.00% / 3.60%	61.90 / 65.90	< 0.05%	Mongolia
(261,218)	50,519	26%	75 (193)	29%	1.22%	2.70 / 75.00	29.30% / 4.60%	57.35 / 62.93	1.20%	Union of Myanmar
(56,827)	25,371	89%	172 (446)	14%	2.21%	3.70 / 64.40	38.50% / 3.50%	61.76 / 62.50	0.50%	Kingdom of Nepal
(119,500)	2,436	50%	8 (20)	76%	1.83%	3.40 / 16.20	32.82% / 2.78%	72.22 / 75.43	0.10%	Sultanate of Oman
(307,374)	162,420	82%	204 (528)	34%	2.41%	4.80 / 85.10	41.80% / 4.00%	60.90 / 62.60	0.10%	Islamic Republic of Pakistan
(115,831)	84,765	68%	283 (732)	48%	2.26%	3.50 / 29.00	35.49% / 3.94%	66.93 / 72.18	< 0.05%	Republic of the Philippines
(4,448)	768	44%	67 (173)	92%	1.79%	3.30 / 11.20	25.40% / 2.20%	69.40 / 72.10	- - -	State of Qatar
(756,985)	24,573	101%	13 (32)	86%	2.73%	4.50 / 23.00	37.20% / 2.70%	69.93 / 73.76	- - -	Kingdom of Saudi Arabia
(255)	4,296	21%	6,509 (16,847)	100%	0.53%	1.30 / 1.90	20.10% / 7.99%	77.40 / 81.30	0.20%	Republic of Singapore
(25,299)	19,722	14%	301 (780)	30%	1.30%	2.00 / 11.20	26.70% / 6.40%	70.70 / 75.40	< 0.05%	Democratic Socialist Republic of Sri Lanka
(71,498)	18,389	91%	99 (257)	50%	2.67%	3.70 / 22.30	37.10% / 3.20%	70.60 / 73.10	< 0.05%	Syrian Arab Republic
(55,251)	6,813	60%	48 (123)	27%	2.32%	4.10 / 89.00	40.00% / 4.00%	60.85 / 66.13	< 0.05%	Republic of Tajikistan
(198,115)	65,002	13%	127 (328)	31%	0.72%	1.70 / 20.00	22.80% / 7.30%	67.90 / 75.00	1.50%	Kingdom of Thailand
(5,640)	947	245%	65 (168)	8%	2.70%	6.40 / 94.00	41.30% / 2.80%	54.14 / 56.25	- - -	Democratic Republic of Timor-Leste
(300,948)	72,907	38%	94 (242)	65%	1.39%	2.40 / 38.30	29.30% / 5.60%	66.40 / 71.00	- - -	Republic of Turkey
(188,456)	5,240	40%	11 (28)	47%	1.56%	2.90 / 73.90	32.10% / 4.40%	58.24 / 66.74	< 0.05%	Turkmenistan
(30,000)	4,618	101%	59 (154)	78%	1.36%	2.50 / 7.90	25.30% / 0.97%	75.50 / 79.76	- - -	United Arab Emirates
(172,742)	26,444	45%	59 (153)	37%	1.59%	2.70 / 61.70	34.70% / 4.70%	63.32 / 69.72	0.10%	Republic of Uzbekistan
(127,844)	83,305	38%	252 (652)	26%	1.29%	2.20 / 18.00	29.20% / 6.50%	70.00 / 73.00	0.40%	Socialist Republic of Vietnam
(207,286)	20,727	243%	39 (100)	26%	3.30%	6.20 / 74.80	45.70% / 3.90%	58.80 / 62.50	0.10%	Republic of Yemen
										ASIA: TERRITORIES AND AREAS OF SPECIAL STATUS
(422)	6,921	27%	6,338 (16,400)	100%	0.17%	1.00 / 2.50	14.90% / 12.00%	78.60 / 84.60	0.10%	Special Administrative Region of China
(10)	474	13%	18,960 (47,400)	99%	0.39%	0.80 / 3.47	17.10% / 8.10%	- - - / - - -	- - -	Special Administrative Region of China
(13,891)	22,731	-13%	632 (1,636)	78%	0.36%	1.20 / 5.35	19.34% / 9.48%	73.35 / 79.05	- - -	
- - -	3,762	197%	625 (1,619)	57%	3.40%	5.60 / 20.70	45.50% / 3.10%	70.70 / 73.80	- - -	Areas of Special Status
(141)	- - -	- - -	- - - - - -	- - -	- - -	- - - / - - -	- - - / - - -	- - - / - - -	- - -	Area of Special Status
(2,183)	- - -	- - -	- - - - - -	- - -	- - -	- - - / - - -	- - - / - - -	- - - / - - -	- - -	Area of Special Status
(17)	- - -	- - -	- - - - - -	- - -	- - -	- - - / - - -	- - - / - - -	- - - / - - -	- - -	British Overseas Territory
										AFRICA
(919,595)	32,814	35%	14 (36)	49%	1.53%	2.40 / 31.60	30.70% / 5.20%	72.50 / 74.40	0.10%	People's Democratic Republic of Algeria
(481,354)	15,375	173%	12 (32)	33%	2.56%	6.80 / 139.00	45.60% / 2.40%	38.85 / 41.99	3.90%	Republic of Angola
(43,484)	8,439	162%	75 (194)	40%	2.92%	5.90 / 105.00	43.60% / 2.60%	52.97 / 54.52	1.90%	Republic of Benin
(224,607)	1,640	-14%	3 (7)	54%	-0.34%	3.10 / 56.80	39.40% / 3.80%	34.20 / 35.30	37.30%	Republic of Botswana
(105,869)	13,925	184%	51 (132)	17%	2.53%	6.20 / 81.00	46.00% / 2.90%	42.19 / 45.70	1.80%	Burkina Faso
(10,747)	7,795	193%	280 (725)	9%	2.84%	6.80 / 66.90	46.60% / 2.60%	48.70 / 49.80	6.00%	Republic of Burundi
(183,569)	16,380	88%	34 (89)	48%	2.26%	5.00 / 74.00	43.60% / 3.00%	47.10 / 49.00	5.50%	Republic of Cameroon
(1,558)	476	94%	118 (306)	53%	2.26%	4.00 / 31.00	41.90% / 6.20%	66.16 / 72.16	- - -	Republic of Cape Verde
(240,535)	4,238	53%	7 (18)	41%	1.74%	4.90 / 94.10	43.20% / 4.20%	43.20 / 44.40	13.50%	Central African Republic
(495,755)	9,657	206%	8 (19)	24%	2.72%	6.30 / 101.00	48.00% / 2.80%	45.00 / 48.40	4.80%	Republic of Chad

CONTINENT/Country	Capital	Language	Religion	Area sq km
Comoros	Moroni	Arabic, French, Shikomoro	Sunni Muslim, Roman Catholic	1,862
Congo	Brazzaville	French, Lingala, Monokutuba	Christian, animist, Muslim	342,000
Congo, Dem. Rep. of the	Kinshasa (Léopoldville)	French, Lingala, Kingwana, Kikongo, Tshiluba	Roman Catholic, Protestant, Kimbanguist, Muslim, traditional	2,344,885
Côte d'Ivoire (Ivory Coast)	Abidjan (Administrative) Yamoussoukro (Legislative)	French, Dioula, 60 native dialects	Christian, Muslim, indigenous beliefs	322,462
Djibouti	Djibouti	French, Arabic, Somali, Afar	Muslim, Christian	23,200
Egypt	El Qâhira (Cairo)	Arabic, English, French	Sunni Muslim, Coptic Christian	1,002,000
Equatorial Guinea	Malabo	Spanish, French, pidgin English, Fang Bubi, Ibo	Roman Catholic, pagan practices	28,051
Eritrea	Asmara	Afar, Arabic, Tigre, Kunama, Tigrinya	Muslim, Coptic Christian, Roman Catholic, Protestant	121,144
Ethiopia	Adis Abeba (Addis Ababa)	Amharic, Tigrinya, Orominga, Guaraginga, Somali, Arabic	Muslim, Ethiopian Orthodox, animist	1,133,380
Gabon	Libreville	French, Fang, Myene, Nzebi, Bapounou/Eschira, Bandjabi	Christian, indigenous beliefs	267,667
Gambia	Banjul	English, Mandinka, Wolof, Fula	Muslim, Christian	11,295
Ghana	Accra	English, Akan, Moshi-Dagomba, Ewe, Ga	Christian, indigenous beliefs, Muslim	238,537
Guinea	Conakry	French, local languages	Muslim, Christian, indigenous beliefs	245,857
Guinea-Bissau	Bissau	Portuguese, Crioulo, African languages	Indigenous beliefs, Muslim, Christian	36,125
Kenya	Nairobi	English, Kiswahili, numerous indigenous languages	Protestant, Roman Catholic, indigenous beliefs, Muslim	580,367
Lesotho	Maseru	English, Sesotho, Zulu, Xhosa	Christian, indigenous beliefs	30,355
Liberia	Monrovia	English, 20 ethnic languages	Indigenous beliefs, Christian, Muslim	111,370
Libya	Tarabulus (Tripoli)	Arabic, Italian, English	Sunni Muslim	1,759,540
Madagascar	Antananarivo	French, Malagasy	Indigenous beliefs, Christian, Muslim	587,041
Malawi	Lilongwe	English, Chichewa	Protestant, Roman Catholic, Muslim	118,484
Mali	Bamako	French, Bambara, numerous African languages	Muslim, indigenous beliefs	1,240,192
Mauritania	Nouakchott	Hassaniya Arabic, Wolof, Pulaar, Soninke, French	Muslim	1,030,700
Mauritius	Port Louis	English, French, Creole, Hindi, Urdu, Hakka, Bhojpuri	Hindu, Christian, Muslim, Protestant	2,040
Morocco	Rabat	Arabic, Berber dialects, French	Muslim	710,850
Mozambique	Maputo	Portuguese, indigenous dialects	Indigenous beliefs, Christian, Muslim	799,380
Namibia	Windhoek	English, Afrikaans, German, indigenous languages	Christian, indigenous beliefs	824,292
Niger	Niamey	French, Hausa, Djerma	Muslim, indigenous beliefs, Christian	1,267,000
Nigeria	Abuja	English, Hausa, Yoruba, Igbo, Fulani	Muslim, Christian, indigenous beliefs	923,768
Rwanda	Kigali	Kinyarwanda, French, English, Kiswahili	Roman Catholic, Protestant, Adventist, Muslim	26,338
Sao Tome and Principe	SãoTomé	Portuguese	Roman Catholic, Evangelical, Protestant, Seventh-Day Adventist	1,001
Senegal	Dakar	French, Wolof, Pulaar Diola, Jola, Mandinka	Muslim, Christian	196,722
Seychelles	Victoria	English, French, Creole	Roman Catholic, Anglican	455
Sierra Leone	Freetown	English, Mende, Temne, Krio	Muslim, indigenous beliefs, Christian	71,740
Somalia	Muqdisho (Mogadishu)	Somali, Arabic, Italian, English	Sunni Muslim	637,657
South Africa	Pretoria(Tshwane)(Admin.) Bloemfontein (Judicial) Cape Town (Legislative)	Afrikaans, English, Ndebele, Pedi, Sotho, Swazi, Tsonga, Tswana, Venda, Xhosa,	Christian, indigenous beliefs, Muslim, Hindu	1,219,090
Sudan	Khartoum	Arabic, Nubian, Ta Bedawie, many local dialects	Sunni Muslim, indigenous beliefs, Christian	2,505,813
Swaziland	Mbabane (Administrative) Lobamba (Legislative and Royal)	English, siSwati	Indigenous beliefs, Roman Catholic, Muslim	17,363
Tanzania	Dar es Salaam (Administrative) Dodoma (Legislative)	Kiswahili, Kiungujo, English, Arabic, many local languages	Christian, Muslim, indigenous beliefs	945,087
Togo	Lomé	French, Ewe, Mina, Kabye, Dagomba	Indigenous beliefs, Christian, Muslim	56,785
Tunisia	Tunis	Arabic, French	Muslim	163,610
Uganda	Kampala	English, Ganda, Luganda, many local languages	Roman Catholic, Protestant, indigenous beliefs, Muslim	241,139
Zambia	Lusaka	English, indigenous languages	Christian, Muslim, Hindu	752,614
Zimbabwe	Harare	English, Shona, Sindebele	Syncretic (part Christian, part indigenous beliefs), Christian,	390,757
AFRICA: TERRITORIES AND AREAS OF SPECIAL STATUS				
France				
Mayotte	Mamoudzou	Mahorian, French	Muslim, Christian	374
Réunion	St.-Denis	French, Creole	Roman Catholic, Hindu, Muslim, Buddhist	2,507
Morocco				
Western Sahara	- - -	Hassaniya Arabic, Moroccan Arabic	Muslim	252,120
Norway				
Bouvet Island	Administered from Oslo	- - -	- - -	59
South Africa				
Prince Edward Islands	Administered from Bisho, Eastern Cape Province	- - -	- - -	335
United Kingdom				
Saint Helena	Jamestown	English	Anglican (majority)	411
AUSTRALIA & OCEANIA				
Australia	Canberra, A.T.C.	English, native languages	Protestant, Roman Catholic	7,692,024
Fiji Islands	Suva	English, Fijian, Hindustani	Christian, Hindu, Muslim	18,376
Kiribati	Tarawa	English, I-Kiribati	Roman Catholic, Protestant	811
Marshall Islands	Majuro	English, Marshallese, Japanese	Christian (mostly Protestant)	181
Micronesia	Palikir	English, Turkese, Pohnpeian, Yapese, Kosraean, Ulithian	Roman Catholic, Protestant	702
Nauru	Yaren	Nauruan, English	Protestant, Roman Catholic	21
New Zealand	Wellington	English, Maori	Protestant, Roman Catholic	270,534
Palau	Koror	English, Palauan, Japanese, 3 additional local languages	Roman Catholic, Protestant, Modekngei (indigenous)	489
Papua New Guinea	Port Moresby	715 indigenous languages	Protestant, indigenous beliefs, Roman Catholic	462,840
Samoa	Apia	Samoan, English	Christian	2,831
Solomon Islands	Honiara	Melanesian pidgin, 120 indigenous languages, English	Protestant, Roman Catholic, indigenous beliefs	28,370
Tonga	Nuku'alofa	Tongan, English	Christian	748
Tuvalu	Funafuti	Tuvaluan, English, Samoan	Church of Tuvalu (Congregationalist), Seventh-Day Adventist, Baha'i	26
Vanuatu	Port-Vila	English, French, more than 100 local languages	Protestant, Catholic, indigenous beliefs	12,190
AUSTRALIA & OCEANIA: TERRITORIES AND AREAS OF SPECIAL STATUS				
Australia				
Ashmore and Cartier Islands	Administered from Canberra, A.T.C.	- - -	- - -	5
Christmas Island	The Settlement	English, Chinese, Malay	Buddhist, Muslim, Christian	135
Cocos (Keeling) Islands	West Island	Malay (Cocos dialect), English	Sunni Muslim	14
Coral Sea Islands Territory	Administered from Canberra, A.T.C.	- - -	- - -	3
Norfolk Island	Kingston	English, Norfolk	Protestant, Roman Catholic	35
France				
Clipperton Island	- - -	- - -	- - -	7
French Polynesia	Papeete, Tahiti	French, Tahitian	Protestant, Roman Catholic	4,167
New Caledonia	Nouméa	French, 33 Melanesia-Polynesian dialects	Roman Catholic, Protestant	19,060
Wallis and Futuna	Matâ'utu	French, Wallisian (indigenous Polynesian language)	Roman Catholic	161
New Zealand				
Cook Islands	Avarua	English, Maori	Christian	240
Niue	Alofi	Niuean, English	Ekalesia Niue (a Protestant Church)	263
Tokelau	Administered from Wellington	Tokelauan, English	Congregational Christian Church	12
United Kingdom				
Pitcairn Islands	Adamstown	English, Pitcairnese	Seventh-Day Adventist	47
United States				
American Samoa	Pago Pago	Samoan, English	Christian Congregationalist	233
Baker Island	Administered from Washington, D.C.	- - -	- - -	2
Guam	Hagåtña (Agana)	English, Chamorro, Japanese	Roman Catholic	561
Northern Mariana Islands	Saipan	English, Chamorro, Carolinian	Christian, traditional beliefs	464

Area (sq mi)	Population Mid-2005 (in 1,000s)	Projected pop. change 2005-2050	Pop density sq km (sq mi)	Urban pop.	Natural increase	Total fertility / infant mortality rate	Pop. <15 / >65	Life expectancy: Male / Female	HIV/AIDS Pop. 15-49 2003-04	CONTINENT / Country Formal Name
(719)	671	173%	360 (933)	33%	3.04%	5.40 / 96.30	42.70% / 2.90%	57.90 / 62.30	---	Union of the Comoros
(132,047)	3,999	243%	12 (30)	52%	3.09%	6.30 / 72.00	45.60% / 2.90%	50.62 / 53.09	4.90%	Republic of the Congo
(905,365)	60,764	201%	26 (67)	30%	3.06%	6.70 / 94.70	47.70% / 2.50%	49.00 / 51.80	4.20%	Democratic Republic of the Congo
(124,503)	18,154	87%	56 (146)	46%	2.23%	5.20 / 118.00	41.10% / 3.10%	45.80 / 47.80	7.00%	Republic of Côte d'Ivoire
(8,958)	793	95%	34 (89)	82%	1.85%	4.20 / 99.80	41.00% / 2.70%	51.08 / 53.84	2.90%	Republic of Djibouti
(386,874)	74,033	70%	74 (191)	43%	2.01%	3.20 / 37.00	36.30% / 4.50%	67.49 / 71.83	< 0.05%	Arab Republic of Egypt
(10,831)	504	127%	18 (47)	45%	2.29%	5.90 / 102.00	42.50% / 3.80%	43.45 / 45.55	---	Republic of Equatorial Guinea
(46,774)	4,670	118%	39 (100)	19%	2.62%	5.40 / 49.70	44.80% / 3.40%	56.10 / 59.00	2.70%	State of Eritrea
(437,600)	77,431	120%	68 (177)	15%	2.50%	5.90 / 100.00	43.78% / 2.98%	46.51 / 48.61	4.40%	Federal Democratic Republic of Ethiopia
(103,347)	1,384	65%	5 (13)	81%	2.11%	4.30 / 57.30	40.00% / 4.30%	55.29 / 57.57	8.10%	Gabonese Republic
(4,361)	1,595	155%	141 (366)	26%	2.79%	5.50 / 76.00	44.80% / 2.70%	51.30 / 55.00	1.20%	Republic of The Gambia
(92,100)	22,019	115%	92 (239)	44%	2.25%	4.50 / 64.00	40.20% / 3.30%	56.50 / 59.30	2.20%	Republic of Ghana
(94,926)	9,453	204%	38 (100)	33%	2.66%	5.90 / 94.20	44.40% / 3.10%	47.90 / 50.40	3.20%	Republic of Guinea
(13,948)	1,586	235%	44 (114)	32%	2.96%	7.10 / 120.00	45.80% / 3.00%	42.83 / 46.08	---	Republic of Guinea-Bissau
(224,081)	33,830	92%	58 (151)	36%	2.23%	4.90 / 77.00	42.60% / 2.30%	48.09 / 46.30	6.70%	Republic of Kenya
(11,720)	1,804	-29%	59 (154)	13%	-0.13%	3.50 / 92.10	37.80% / 4.90%	35.80 / 34.80	28.90%	Kingdom of Lesotho
(43,000)	3,283	224%	29 (76)	45%	2.90%	6.80 / 142.00	45.90% / 2.20%	40.97 / 43.46	5.90%	Republic of Liberia
(679,362)	5,766	88%	3 (8)	86%	2.39%	3.50 / 26.80	34.50% / 4.10%	73.90 / 78.30	0.30%	Great Socialist People's Libyan Arab Jamahiriya
(226,658)	17,308	141%	29 (76)	26%	2.74%	5.20 / 87.70	44.79% / 2.83%	52.50 / 56.80	1.70%	Republic of Madagascar
(45,747)	12,341	260%	104 (270)	14%	3.16%	6.50 / 99.60	46.40% / 2.90%	43.41 / 46.03	14.20%	Republic of Malawi
(478,841)	13,518	211%	11 (28)	30%	3.24%	7.10 / 133.00	47.00% / 2.70%	46.83 / 48.28	1.90%	Republic of Mali
(397,955)	3,069	144%	3 (8)	40%	2.73%	5.90 / 97.00	43.30% / 3.40%	49.90 / 53.10	0.60%	Islamic Republic of Mauritania
(788)	1,243	21%	609 (1,577)	42%	0.87%	1.90 / 14.40	24.90% / 6.50%	68.57 / 75.29	---	Republic of Mauritius
(274,461)	30,704	47%	43 (112)	57%	1.55%	2.50 / 40.40	30.40% / 4.85%	68.00 / 72.10	0.10%	Kingdom of Morocco
(308,642)	19,420	94%	24 (63)	32%	2.15%	5.50 / 119.00	44.20% / 2.70%	41.01 / 42.78	12.20%	Republic of Mozambique
(318,261)	2,031	-12%	2 (6)	33%	1.07%	4.20 / 50.70	39.50% / 3.50%	46.00 / 46.10	21.3%	Republic of Namibia
(489,191)	13,957	259%	11 (29)	21%	3.41%	8.00 / 153.00	48.10% / 1.90%	44.37 / 43.53	1.20%	Republic of Niger
(356,669)	131,530	96%	142 (369)	44%	2.38%	5.90 / 100.00	43.40% / 2.90%	43.39 / 44.44	5.40%	Federal Republic of Nigeria
(10,169)	8,722	101%	331 (858)	17%	2.27%	5.70 / 107.00	43.80% / 2.30%	41.87 / 45.26	5.10%	Republic of Rwanda
(386)	153	93%	153 (396)	38%	2.54%	4.10 / 82.00	38.40% / 4.20%	61.87 / 63.83	---	Democratic Republic of Sao Tome and Principe
(75,955)	11,658	98%	59 (153)	43%	2.57%	5.10 / 83.00	42.10% / 3.00%	54.35 / 56.76	0.80%	Republic of Senegal
(176)	81	11%	178 (460)	50%	1.00%	2.10 / 16.00	25.50% / 7.80%	66.17 / 76.10	---	Republic of Seychelles
(27,699)	5,525	150%	77 (199)	37%	2.27%	6.50 / 165.00	41.40% / 3.20%	38.72 / 41.58	---	Republic of Sierra Leone
(246,201)	8,592	197%	13 (35)	33%	2.88%	7.00 / 120.00	44.80% / 2.70%	45.70 / 49.00	---	Somalia
(470,693)	46,923	3%	38 (100)	53%	0.72%	2.80 / 43.00	32.90% / 4.00%	50.00 / 53.00	21.50%	Republic of South Africa
(967,500)	40,187	110%	16 (42)	36%	2.74%	5.20 / 67.14	44.20% / 2.20%	56.20 / 58.50	2.30%	Republic of the Sudan
(6,704)	1,138	-34%	66 (170)	25%	0.34%	3.90 / 74.80	42.70% / 3.20%	33.90 / 36.80	38.80%	Kingdom of Swaziland
(364,900)	36,481	96%	39 (100)	32%	2.44%	5.70 / 68.00	44.90% / 2.60%	43.20 / 45.00	7.00%	United Republic of Tanzania
(21,925)	6,145	120%	108 (280)	33%	2.72%	5.40 / 93.00	42.60% / 3.00%	52.26 / 56.20	4.10%	Togolese Republic
(63,170)	10,043	21%	61 (159)	65%	1.10%	2.10 / 21.10	26.70% / 6.80%	71.10 / 75.10	< 0.05%	Tunisian Republic
(93,104)	26,907	387%	112 (289)	12%	3.24%	6.90 / 88.40	50.50% / 2.30%	47.60 / 48.30	7.10%	Republic of Uganda
(290,586)	11,227	95%	15 (39)	35%	1.85%	5.70 / 95.00	44.80% / 2.90%	37.88 / 36.92	16.50%	Republic of Zambia
(150,872)	13,010	21%	33 (86)	34%	1.11%	3.80 / 62.00	39.60% / 3.40%	39.90 / 41.10	24.60%	Republic of Zimbabwe
										AFRICA: TERRITORIES AND AREAS OF SPECIAL STATUS
(144)	181	207%	484 (1,257)	28%	3.07%	5.60 / ---	42.10% / 1.70%	57.80 / 62.00	---	French Overseas Territorial Collectivity
(968)	782	36%	312 (808)	89%	1.44%	2.50 / 6.10	27.30% / 7.20%	71.20 / 79.60	---	French Overseas Department
(97,344)	341	163%	1 (4)	93%	1.98%	3.90 / 53.00	34.30% / 3.30%	62.23 / 65.71	---	Area of Special Status
(23)	0	---	--- ---	---	---	--- / ---	--- / ---	--- / ---	---	Territory of Norway
(129)	0	---	--- ---	---	---	--- / ---	--- / ---	--- / ---	---	Territory of South Africa
(159)	6	---	15 (38)	35%	-0.10%	1.50 / 0	19.10% / 9.20%	74.10 / 80.00	---	British Overseas Territory
										AUSTRALIA & OCEANIA
(2,969,906)	20,351	29%	3 (7)	91%	0.61%	1.80 / 4.50	19.80% / 13.00%	77.80 / 82.80	0.10%	Commonwealth of Australia
(7,095)	842	11%	46 (119)	46%	1.47%	2.70 / 15.60	29.80% / 4.20%	65.65 / 70.04	0.10%	Republic of the Fiji Islands
(313)	92	128%	113 (294)	43%	1.80%	4.30 / 43.00	40.10% / 3.30%	58.20 / 67.30	---	Republic of Kiribati
(70)	59	75%	326 (843)	68%	3.01%	4.40 / 35.00	41.60% / 2.70%	66.60 / 70.40	---	Republic of the Marshall Islands
(271)	108	-10%	154 (399)	22%	2.14%	4.40 / 40	40.30% / 3.70%	66.50 / 67.00	---	Federated States of Micronesia
(8)	13	77%	619 (1,625)	100%	1.78%	3.70 / 12.10	41.00% / 1.60%	57.30 / 64.50	---	Republic of Nauru
(104,454)	4,107	23%	15 (39)	86%	0.73%	2.00 / 5.58	21.60% / 12.04%	76.30 / 81.10	0.10%	New Zealand
(189)	21	24%	43 (111)	70%	0.87%	2.10 / 15.40	23.90% / 5.40%	66.64 / 74.54	---	Republic of Palau
(178,703)	5,887	80%	13 (33)	13%	2.10%	4.10 / 71.00	40.10% / 2.30%	54.67 / 55.79	0.60%	Independent State of Papua New Guinea
(1,093)	188	-15%	66 (172)	22%	2.40%	4.30 / 17.80	40.70% / 4.47%	71.80 / 73.80	---	Independent State of Samoa
(10,954)	472	93%	17 (43)	16%	2.60%	4.50 / 66.00	40.10% / 3.20%	61.90 / 63.10	---	Solomon Islands
(289)	102	68%	136 (353)	33%	1.81%	3.10 / 19.00	39.49% / 5.20%	69.80 / 71.70	---	Kingdom of Tonga
(10)	10	80%	385 (1,000)	47%	1.72%	3.70 / 35.00	36.20% / 5.70%	61.70 / 65.10	---	Tuvalu
(4,707)	218	78%	18 (46)	21%	2.57%	4.20 / 34.00	41.70% / 3.30%	65.60 / 69.00	---	Republic of Vanuatu
										AUSTRALIA & OCEANIA: TERRITORIES AND AREAS OF SPECIAL STATUS
(2)	0	---	--- ---	---	---	--- / ---	--- / ---	--- / ---	---	Australian External Territory
(52)	0.474	111%	4 (9)	---	---	--- / ---	--- / ---	--- / ---	---	Australian External Territory
(5)	0.632	58%	45 (126)	---	---	--- / ---	--- / ---	--- / ---	---	Australian External Territory
(1)	0	---								Australian External Territory
(14)	2	0%	57 (143)	80%	0.15%	--- / 0	--- / ---	--- / ---	---	Australian External Territory
(3)	0	---	--- ---	---	---	--- / ---	--- / ---	--- / ---	---	French Possession
(1,608)	255	40%	61 (159)	53%	1.32%	2.50 / 5.20	30.80% / 4.30%	66.90 / 68.16	---	French Overseas Territory
(7,359)	227	61%	12 (31)	71%	1.35%	2.40 / 8.60	29.40% / 6.30%	69.80 / 75.80	---	French Overseas Territory
(62)	15	33%	93 (242)	0%	1.35%	2.70 / 5.50	--- / ---	--- / ---	---	French Overseas Territory
(93)	13	23%	54 (140)	63%	1.52%	3.70 / 16.90	30.00% / 5.90%	68.40 / 71.50	---	Self-Governing in Free Association with New Zealand
(102)	1.617	24%	6 (16)	34%	1.07%	3.00 / 29.40	29.60% / 9.30%	69.80 / 71.20	---	Self-Governing in Free Association with New Zealand
(5)	1.538	30%	128 (308)	0%	2.40%	4.90 / 33.00	--- / ---	67.80 / 70.40	---	Territory of New Zealand
(18)	0.045	0%	1 (3)	---	---	--- / ---	26.40% / 15.00%	--- / ---	---	British Overseas Territory
(90)	63	-33%	270 (700)	89%	2.31%	3.90 / 15.40	38.70% / 3.30%	70.70 / 79.80	---	Territory of the United States
(1)	0	---	--- ---	---	---	--- / ---	--- / ---	--- / ---	---	Territory of the United States
(217)	169	45%	301 (779)	93%	1.59%	2.60 / 6.20	30.46% / 5.30%	75.50 / 80.40	---	Territory of the United States
(179)	80	79%	172 (447)	90%	1.52%	1.70 / 7.00	22.50% / 1.50%	70.70 / 79.80	---	Commonwealth in Political Union with the United States

CONTINENT/Country	GDP per capita in U.S. dollars Mid-2005 estimate	Services as % of GDP Sector 2003	Industry as % of GDP Sector 2003	Agriculture as % of GDP Sector 2003	Total estimated value of imports in million U.S. dollars 2005	Total estimated value of exports in million U.S. dollars 2005	% of population with access to electricity 2003
NORTH AMERICA							
Antigua and Barbuda	$11,000	76.8%	18.0%	4.0%	$735	$214	- - -
Bahamas	$20,200	90.0%	7.0%	3.0%	$5,806	$1,507	- - -
Barbados	$17,000	78.0%	16.0%	6.0%	$1,476	$209	- - -
Belize	$6,800	67.3%	15.0%	17.7%	$622	$350	- - -
Canada	$34,000	71.3%	26.4%	2.3%	$317,700	$364,800	- - -
Costa Rica	$11,100	62.5%	28.7%	8.8%	$9,690	$7,005	95.7%
Cuba	$3,500	67.9%	25.5%	6.6%	$6,916	$2,388	97.0%
Dominica	$5,500	58.0%	24.0%	18.0%	$234	$74	- - -
Dominican Republic	$7,000	58.1%	30.6%	11.2%	$9,747	$5,818	66.8%
El Salvador	$4,700	59.4%	32.1%	8.5%	$6,678	$3,586	70.8%
Grenada	$5,000	68.4%	23.9%	7.7%	$276	$40	- - -
Guatemala	$4,700	58.5%	19.3%	22.3%	$7,744	$3,940	66.7%
Haiti	$1,700	50.0&	20.0%	30.0%	$1,471	$391	34.0%
Honduras	$2,900	55.8%	30.7%	13.5%	$4,161	$1,726	54.5%
Jamaica	$4,400	65.0%	29.8%	5.2%	$4,144	$1,593	90.0%
Mexico	$10,000	69.6%	26.4%	4.0%	$223,700	$213,700	- - -
Nicaragua	$2,900	56.3%	25.7%	17.9%	$2,952	$1,550	48.0%
Panama	$7,200	76.2%	16.3%	7.5%	$8,734	$7,481	76.1%
Saint Kitts and Nevis	$8,800	68.7%	28.3%	3.0%	$405	$70	- - -
Saint Lucia	$5,400	76.6%	18.0%	5.4%	$410	$82	- - -
Saint Vincent and the Grenadines	$2,900	66.9%	24.4%	8.7%	$225	$37	- - -
Trinidad and Tobago	$16,700	50.0%	48.8%	1.2%	$6,011	$9,161	99.0%
United States	$41,800	79.4%	19.7%	0.9%	$1,727,000	$927,500	- - -
NORTH AMERICA: TERRITORIES AND AREAS OF SPECIAL STATUS							
Denmark							
Greenland	$20,000	- - -	- - -	- - -	$601	$480	- - -
France							
Guadeloupe	$7,900	68.0%	17.0%	15.0%	$1,700	$140	- - -
Martinique	$14,400	83.0%	11.0%	6.0%	$2,000	$250	- - -
Saint-Pierre and Miquelon	$7,000	- - -	- - -	- - -	$70	$7	- - -
Netherlands							
Aruba	$21,800	- - -	- - -	- - -	$875	$80	- - -
Netherlands Antilles	$16,000	84.0%	15.0%	1.0%	$4,383	$2,076	- - -
United Kingdom							
Anguilla	$7,500	78.0%	18.0%	4.0%	$81	$2.6	- - -
Bermuda	$69,900	89.0%	10.0%	1.0%	$8,078	$1,469	- - -
British Virgin Islands	$38,500	92.0%	6.2%	1.8%	$187	$25.3	- - -
Cayman Islands	$32,300	95.4%	3.2%	1.4%	$457	$1.2	- - -
Montserrat	$3,400	- - -	- - -	- - -	$17	$0.7	- - -
Turks and Caicos Islands	$11,500	- - -	- - -	- - -	$176	$169	- - -
United States							
Navassa Island	- - -	- - -	- - -	- - -	- - -	- - -	- - -
Puerto Rico	$18,600	56.0%	43.0%	1.0%	$29,100	$46,900	- - -
Virgin Islands	$14,500	80.0%	19.0%	1.0%	- - -	- - -	- - -
SOUTH AMERICA							
Argentina	$13,100	54.1%	34.8%	11.1%	$28,800	$40,000	94.6%
Bolivia	$2,900	55.1%	30.1%	14.9%	$1,845	$2,371	60.4%
Brazil	$8,400	75.1%	19.1%	5.8%	$78,020	$115,100	94.9%
Chile	$11,300	56.9%	34.3%	8.8%	$30,090	$38,030	99.0%
Colombia	$7,900	58.3%	29.4%	12.3%	$20,420	$23,060	81.0%
Ecuador	$4,300	63.6%	28.7%	7.7%	$8,436	$9,224	80.0%
Guyana	$4,600	41.8%	19.9%	38.3%	$682	$587.2	- - -
Paraguay	$4,900	48.5%	24.2%	27.2%	$3,832	$3,130	74.7%
Peru	$5,900	60.4%	29.3%	10.3%	$12,150	$15,950	73.0%
Suriname	$4,100	65.0%	22.0%	13.0%	$750	$881	- - -
Uruguay	$9,600	59.9%	27.3%	12.8%	$3,540	$3,550	98.0%
Venezuela	$6,100	54.4%	41.1%	4.5%	$24,630	$52,730	94.0%
SOUTH AMERICA: TERRITORIES AND AREAS OF SPECIAL STATUS							
France							
French Guiana	$8,300	- - -	- - -	- - -	$625	$155	- - -
United Kingdom							
Falkland Islands	$25,000	- - -	- - -	- - -	$90	$125	- - -
EUROPE							
Albania	$4,900	56.1%	19.2%	24.7%	$2,473	$708.8	- - -
Andorra	$24,000	- - -	- - -	- - -	$1,077	$58	- - -
Austria	$32,700	65.9%	31.7%	2.3%	$118,800	$122,500	- - -
Belarus	$6,900	60.1%	30.1%	9.8%	$16,940	$16,140	- - -
Belgium	$31,400	72.2%	26.5%	1.3%	$264,500	$269,600	- - -
Bosnia and Herzegovina	$6,800	53.0%	32.1%	14.9%	$6,800	$2,700	- - -
Bulgaria	$9,600	57.5%	30.7%	11.7%	$15,900	$11,670	- - -
Croatia	$11,600	61.5%	30.1%	8.4%	$18,930	$10,300	- - -
Cyprus	$21,600	76.0%	19.9%	4.1%	$5,552	$1,237	- - -
Czech Republic	$19,500	57.1%	39.4%	3.5%	$76,590	$78,370	- - -
Denmark	$34,600	71.5%	26.4%	2.1%	$74,690	$84,950	- - -
Estonia	$16,700	67.0%	28.5%	4.5%	$9,189	$7,439	- - -
Finland	$30,900	66.0%	30.5%	3.5%	$56,450	$67,880	- - -
France	$29,900	72.8%	24.5%	2.7%	$473,300	$443,400	- - -
Germany	$30,400	69.4%	29.4%	1.1%	$801,000	$1,016,000	- - -
Greece	$22,200	69.3%	23.8%	6.9%	$48,200	$18,540	- - -
Hungary	$16,300	65.3%	31.4%	3.3%	$64,830	$61,750	- - -
Iceland	$35,600	79.2%	9.6%	11.2%	$4,582	$3,215	- - -
Ireland	$41,000	49.0%	46.0%	5.0%	$65,470	$102,000	- - -
Italy	$29,200	69.5%	27.8%	2.6%	$369,200	$371,900	- - -
Latvia	$13,200	71.0%	24.4%	4.5%	$8,559	$5,749	- - -
Liechtenstein	$25,000	- - -	- - -	- - -	$917	$2,470	- - -
Lithuania	$13,700	59.0%	33.8%	7.3%	$13,330	$10,950	- - -
Luxembourg	$55,600	78.9%	20.5%	0.6%	$18,740	$13,390	- - -
Macedonia	$7,800	57.3%	30.4%	12.2%	$3,196	$2,047	- - -
Malta	$19,900	74.0%	23.0%	3.0%	$3,859	$2,744	- - -
Moldova	$1,800	52.8%	24.7%	22.5%	$2,230	$1,040	- - -
Monaco	$27,000	- - -	- - -	- - -	- - -	- - -	- - -
Montenegro	$3,800	- - -	- - -	- - -	- - -	- - -	- - -

Telephone mainlines per 1,000 people 2003	Arable & permanent cropland area 2003 sq km (sq mi)	Forested area as % of total land area 2000	Protected areas as % of total land area 2003	Average annual deforestation: % change 1990 - 2000 (Negative number indicates an increase in forest area.)	Carbon dioxide emissions : metric tonnes per capita 2000	CONTINENT / Country Formal Name
						NORTH AMERICA
- - -	100 (39)	21.4%	- - -	- - -	4.9	Antigua and Barbuda
415	120 (46)	51.5%	- - -	- - -	5.9	Commonwealth of The Bahamas
497	170 (66)	4.0%	- - -	- - -	4.4	Barbados
113	1,020 (394)	72.5%	- - -	- - -	3.1	Belize
629	521,150 (201,217)	33.6%	11.1%	0.0%	14.2	Canada
251	5,250 (2,027)	46.8%	23.0%	0.8%	1.4	Republic of Costa Rica
51	37,880 (14,626)	24.7%	69.1%	-1.3%	2.8	Republic of Cuba
304	210 (81)	61.3%	- - -	- - -	1.4	Commonwealth of Dominica
115	15,960 (6,162)	28.4%	51.9%	0.0%	3.0	Dominican Republic
116	9,100 (3,514)	14.4%	0.4%	4.6%	1.1	Republic of El Salvador
290	120 (46)	12.2%	- - -	- - -	2.1	Grenada
71	20,500 (7,915)	36.3%	20.0%	1.7%	0.9	Republic of Guatemala
17	11,000 (4,247)	3.8%	0.4%	5.7%	0.2	Republic of Haiti
48	14,280 (5,514)	41.5%	6.4%	1.0%	0.7	Republic of Honduras
170	2,840 (1,097)	31.3%	- - -	1.5%	4.2	Jamaica
158	273,000 (105,406)	33.7%	10.2%	1.1%	4.3	United Mexican States
37	21,610 (8,344)	42.7%	17.8%	3.0%	0.7	Republic of Nicaragua
122	6,950 (2,683)	57.7%	21.7%	1.6%	2.2	Republic of Panama
500	80 (31)	14.7%	- - -	- - -	- - -	Federation of Saint Kitts and Nevis
320	180 (69)	27.9%	- - -	- - -	- - -	Saint Lucia
234	140 (54)	27.4%	- - -	- - -	- - -	Saint Vincent and the Grenadines
250	1,220 (471)	44.1%	6.0%	0.8%	20.5	Republic of Trinidad and Tobago
621	1,755,000 (677,609)	33.1%	25.9%	-0.2%	19.8	United States of America
						NORTH AMERICA: TERRITORIES AND AREAS OF SPECIAL STATUS
- - -	- - - - - -	- - -	- - -	- - -	- - -	Overseas Region of Denmark
- - -	250 (97)	47.2%	- - -	- - -	- - -	French Overseas Department
- - -	210 (81)	43.9%	- - -	- - -	- - -	French Overseas Department
- - -	30 (12)	13.0%	- - -	- - -	- - -	French Overseas Territorial Collectivity
- - -	20 (8)	2.2%	- - -	- - -	- - -	Overseas Region of the Netherlands
- - -	80 (31)	1.5%	- - -	- - -	- - -	Overseas Region of the Netherlands
- - -	- - - - - -	71.4%	- - -	- - -	- - -	British Overseas Territory
- - -	10 (4)	20.0%	- - -	- - -	- - -	British Overseas Territory
- - -	40 (15)	24.4%	- - -	- - -	- - -	British Overseas Territory
- - -	10 (4)	48.4%	- - -	- - -	- - -	British Overseas Territory
- - -	20 (8)	35.0%	- - -	- - -	- - -	British Overseas Territory
- - -	10 (4)	80.0%	- - -	- - -	- - -	British Overseas Territory
- - -	- - - - - -	- - -	- - -	- - -	- - -	Territory of the United States
346	830 (320)	46.0%	3.5%	0.2%	2.3	Self-Governing Commonwealth in Association with the United States
- - -	30 (12)	27.9%	- - -	- - -	- - -	Territory of the United States
						SOUTH AMERICA
219	289,000 (111,584)	12.1%	6.6%	0.8%	3.9	Argentine Republic
72	32,560 (12,571)	54.2%	13.4%	0.3%	1.3	Republic of Bolivia
223	666,000 (257,144)	57.2%	6.7%	0.4%	1.8	Federative Republic of Brazil
221	23,070 (8,907)	21.5%	18.9%	0.1%	3.9	Republic of Chile
179	38,500 (14,865)	58.5%	10.2%	0.4%	1.4	Republic of Colombia
122	29,850 (11,525)	39.2%	18.3%	1.2%	2.0	Republic of Ecuador
- - -	5,100 (1,969)	76.7%	- - -	- - -	2.1	Co-operative Republic of Guyana
46	31,360 (12,108)	46.5%	3.5%	0.5%	0.7	Republic of Paraguay
67	43,100 (16,641)	53.7%	6.1%	0.4%	1.1	Republic of Peru
152	680 (263)	94.7%	- - -	- - -	5.0	Republic of Suriname
- - -	14,120 (5,452)	8.6%	0.3%	-5.0%	1.6	Oriental Republic of Uruguay
111	34,000 (13,127)	54.1%	63.8%	0.4%	6.5	Bolivarian Republic of Venezuela
						SOUTH AMERICA: TERRITORIES AND AREAS OF SPECIAL STATUS
- - -	160 (62)	91.8%	- - -	- - -	- - -	French Overseas Department
- - -	- - - - - -	0.0%	- - -	- - -	- - -	British Overseas Territory
						EUROPE
83	6,990 (2,699)	29.0%	3.8%	0.8%	0.9	Republic of Albania
438	10 (4)	35.6%	- - -	- - -	- - -	Principality of Andorra
481	14,620 (5,645)	46.7%	33.0%	-0.2%	7.6	Republic of Austria
311	56,810 (21,934)	38.0%	6.3%	-3.2%	5.9	Republic of Belarus
489	8,580 (3,313)	22.0%	2.6%	-0.2%	10.0	Kingdom of Belgium
245	11,010 (4,251)	43.1%	0.5%	0.0%	4.8	Bosnia and Herzegovina
380	35,340 (13,645)	32.8%	4.5%	-0.6%	5.3	Republic of Bulgaria
417	15,840 (6,116)	38.2%	7.5%	-0.1%	4.5	Republic of Croatia
572	1,400 (541)	18.9%	- - -	- - -	8.5	Republic of Cyprus
360	32,990 (12,738)	34.3%	16.1%	-0.0%	11.6	Czech Republic
669	22,740 (8,780)	11.8%	34.0%	-0.2%	8.4	Kingdom of Denmark
341	5,610 (2,166)	53.9%	11.8%	-0.6%	11.7	Republic of Estonia
492	22,180 (8,564)	73.9%	9.3%	-0.0%	10.3	Republic of Finland
566	195,730 (75,572)	28.3%	13.3%	-0.4%	6.2	French Republic
657	120,400 (46,487)	31.7%	31.9%	0.0%	9.6	Federal Republic of Germany
454	38,310 (14,792)	29.1%	3.6%	-0.9%	8.2	Hellenic Republic
349	48,040 (18,548)	21.5%	7.0%	-0.4%	5.4	Republic of Hungary
660	70 (27)	0.5%	- - -	- - -	7.7	Republic of Iceland
491	11,840 (4,571)	9.7%	1.7%	-3.0%	11.1	Republic of Ireland
484	106,970 (41,301)	33.9%	7.9%	-0.3%	7.4	Italian Republic
285	18,500 (7,143)	47.4%	13.4%	-0.4%	2.5	Republic of Latvia
583	40 (15)	43.1%	- - -	- - -	- - -	Principality of Liechtenstein
239	29,850 (11,525)	33.5%	10.3%	-0.2%	3.4	Republic of Lithuania
798	630 (243)	33.5%	- - -	- - -	19.4	Grand Duchy of Luxembourg
271	6,120 (2,363)	35.8%	7.1%	0.0%	5.5	Republic of Macedonia
521	110 (42)	1.1%	- - -	- - -	7.2	Republic of Malta
219	21,430 (8,274)	10.0%	1.4%	-0.2%	1.5	Republic of Moldova
1040	- - - - - -	0.0%	- - -	- - -	- - -	Principality of Monaco
- - -	- - - - - -	- - -	- - -	- - -	- - -	Republic of Montenegro

CONTINENT/Country	GDP per capita in U.S. dollars Mid-2005 estimate	Services as % of GDP Sector 2003	Industry as % of GDP Sector 2003	Agriculture as % of GDP Sector 2003	Total estimated value of imports in million U.S. dollars 2005	Total estimated value of exports in million U.S. dollars 2005	% of population with access to electricity 2003
Netherlands	$30,500	73.1%	24.5%	2.4%	$326,600	$365,100	- - -
Norway	$42,300	61.0%	37.5%	1.5%	$58,120	$111,200	- - -
Poland	$13,300	66.1%	30.7%	3.1%	$95,670	$92,720	- - -
Portugal	$19,300	63.9%	30.2%	5.9%	$60,350	$38,800	- - -
Romania	$8,200	52.0%	36.1%	11.9%	$38,150	$27,720	- - -
Russia	$11,100	60.7%	34.2%	5.2%	$125,000	$245,000	- - -
San Marino	$34,600	- - -	- - -	- - -	- - -	- - -	- - -
Serbia	$4,400	- - -	- - -	- - -	- - -	- - -	- - -
Slovakia	$16,100	66.6%	29.7%	3.7%	$34,480	$32,390	- - -
Slovenia	$21,600	60.3%	36.9%	2.8%	$19,620	$18,530	- - -
Spain	$25,500	67.1%	29.6%	3.3%	$271,800	$194,300	- - -
Sweden	$29,800	70.3%	27.9%	1.8%	$104,400	$126,600	- - -
Switzerland	$32,300	64.5%	34.0%	1.5%	$135,000	$148,600	- - -
Ukraine	$7,200	45.6%	40.3%	14.1%	$37,180	$38,220	- - -
United Kingdom	$30,300	72.4%	26.6%	1.0%	$483,700	$372,700	- - -
Vatican City	- - -	- - -	- - -	- - -	- - -	- - -	- - -
EUROPE: TERRITORIES AND AREAS OF SPECIAL STATUS							
Denmark							
Faroe Islands	$22,000	62.0%	11.0%	27.0%	$639	$533	- - -
Norway							
Svalbard	- - -	- - -	- - -	- - -	- - -	- - -	- - -
United Kingdom							
Channel Islands	- - -	- - -	- - -	- - -	- - -	- - -	- - -
Gibraltar	$27,900	86.0%	13.0%	1.0%	$2,967	$271	- - -
Isle of Man	$28,500	- - -	- - -	- - -	- - -	- - -	- - -
ASIA							
Afghanistan	$800	20.0%	20.0%	60.0%	$3,870	$471	2.0%
Armenia	$4,500	37.3%	39.2%	23.5%	$1,500	$800	- - -
Azerbaijan	$4,800	31.1%	54.5%	14.3%	$4,656	$6,117	- - -
Bahrain	$23,000	58.3%	41.0%	0.7%	$7,830	$11,170	- - -
Bangladesh	$2,100	52.0%	26.3%	21.8%	$12,970	$9,372	20.4%
Bhutan	$1,400	27.3%	39.5%	33.2%	$196	$154	- - -
Brunei	$23,600	50.0%	45.0%	5.0%	$1,641	$4,514	- - -
Cambodia	$2,200	35.9%	29.7%	34.5%	$3,538	$2,663	15.8%
China	$6,800	33.1%	52.3%	14.6%	$631,800	$752,200	98.6%
Georgia	$3,300	54.1%	25.5%	20.5%	$2,500	$1,400	- - -
India	$3,300	51.2%	26.6%	22.2%	$113,100	$76,230	43.0%
Indonesia	$3,600	39.9%	43.6%	16.6%	$62,020	$83,640	53.4%
Iran	$8,300	47.6%	41.2%	11.3%	$42,500	$55,420	97.9%
Iraq	$3,400	27.8%	58.6%	13.6%	$19,570	$17,780	95.0%
Israel	$24,600	59.5%	37.7%	2.8%	$43,190	$40,140	100.0%
Japan	$31,500	74.0%	24.7%	1.3%	$451,100	$550,500	- - -
Jordan	$4,700	71.8%	26.0%	2.2%	$8,681	$4,226	95.0%
Kazakhstan	$8,200	53.9%	38.3%	7.8%	$17,510	$30,090	- - -
Korea, North	$1,700	56.3%	40.4%	3.3%	$2,819	$1,275	20.0%
Korea, South	$20,400	62.2%	34.6%	3.2%	$248,400	$277,600	- - -
Kuwait	$19,200	39.1%	60.5%	0.4%	$12,230	$44,430	100.0%
Kyrgyzstan	$2,100	38.4%	22.9%	38.7%	$937	$759	- - -
Laos	$1,900	25.5%	25.9%	48.6%	$541	$379	- - -
Lebanon	$6,200	67.7%	20.0%	12.2%	$8,855	$1,782	95.0%
Malaysia	$12,100	41.8%	48.5%	9.7%	$118,700	$147,100	96.9%
Maldives	$3,900	62.0%	18.0%	20.0%	$645	$123	- - -
Mongolia	$1,900	57.0%	14.9%	28.1%	$1,011	$852	90.0%
Myanmar (Burma)	$1,700	34.5%	8.9%	56.6%	$2,183	$2,514	5.0%
Nepal	$1,400	37.8%	21.6%	40.6%	$1,696	$626	15.4%
Oman	$13,200	3.1%	55.8%	41.1%	$8,709	$19,010	94.0%
Pakistan	$2,400	53.2%	23.5%	23.3%	$21,260	$14,850	52.9%
Philippines	$5,100	53.2%	32.3%	14.5%	$42,660	$41,250	87.4%
Qatar	$27,400	41.5%	58.2%	0.3%	$6,706	$24,900	- - -
Saudi Arabia	$12,800	40.3%	55.2%	4.5%	$44,930	$165,000	97.7%
Singapore	$28,100	65.0%	34.9%	0.1%	$187,500	$212,400	100.0%
Sri Lanka	$4,300	54.7%	26.3%	19.0%	$8,370	$6,442	62.0%
Syria	$3,900	48.0%	28.6%	23.5%	$5,973	$6,344	85.9%
Tajikistan	$1,200	56.4%	20.2%	23.4%	$1,250	$950	- - -
Thailand	$8,300	46.3%	44.0%	9.8%	$107,000	$105,800	82.1%
Timor-Leste (East Timor)	$400	57.4%	17.2%	25.4%	$202	$10	- - -
Turkey	$8,200	64.7%	21.9%	13.4%	$101,200	$72,490	- - -
Turkmenistan	$8,000	28.8%	42.7%	28.5%	$4,175	$4,700	- - -
United Arab Emirates	$43,400	37.5%	58.5%	4.0%	$60,150	4103,100	96.0%
Uzbekistan	$1,800	43.1%	21.7%	35.2%	$4,140	$5,360	- - -
Vietnam	$2,800	38.2%	40.0%	21.8%	$34,440	$31,340	75.8%
Yemen	$900	45.0%	40.0%	15.0%	$4,190	$6,387	50.0%
ASIA: TERRITORIES AND AREAS OF SPECIAL STATUS							
China							
Hong Kong	$32,900	88.0%	12.0%	0.0%	$291,600	$286,300	- - -
Macau	$22,000	92.7%	7.2%	0.1%	$3,478	$3,465	- - -
Taiwan	$27,600	67.4%	30.9%	1.7%	$172,900	$185,100	- - -
Israel - Palestinian Areas					$1,952	$270	- - -
Gaza Strip	$600	63.0%	28.0%	9.0%	- - -	- - -	- - -
West Bank	$1,100	63.0%	28.0%	9.0%	- - -	- - -	- - -
United Kingdom							
British Indian Ocean Territory	- - -	93.0%	2.0%	5.0%	- - -	- - -	- - -
AFRICA							
Algeria	$7,200	34.7%	55.1%	10.2%	$22,530	$49,590	98.0%
Angola	$3,200	26.6%	64.6%	8.8%	$8,165	$26,800	12.0%
Benin	$1,100	50%	14.4%	35.7%	$1,043	$827	22.0%
Botswana	$10,500	52.5%	45.2%	2.4%	$3,370	$3,680	22.0%
Burkina Faso	$1,300	50.1%	18.9%	31.0%	$992	$395	13.0%
Burundi	$700	32.0%	19.0%	49.0%	$200	$52	- - -
Cameroon	$2,400	39.1%	16.7%	44.2%	$2,514	$3,236	20.0%
Cape Verde	$6,200	73.4%	19.7%	6.8%	$500	$73	- - -
Central African Republic	$1,100	14.3%	24.9%	60.8%	$203	$131	- - -
Chad	$1,500	40.9%	13.5%	45.6%	$749,100	$3,016	- - -

Telephone mainlines per 1,000 people 2003	Arable & permanent cropland area 2003 sq km (sq mi)	Forested area as % of total land area 2000	Protected areas as % of total land area 2003	Average annual deforestation: % change 1990 - 2000 (Negative number indicates an increase in forest area.)	Carbon dioxide emissions : metric tonnes per capita 2000	CONTINENT / Country Formal Name
614	9,440 (3,645)	10.8%	14.2%	-0.3%	8.7	Kingdom of the Netherlands
713	8,730 (3,371)	30.7%	6.8%	-0.4%	11.1	Kingdom of Norway
319	129,010 (49,811)	30.0%	12.4%	-0.1%	7.8	Republic of Poland
411	23,110 (8,923)	41.3%	6.6%	-1.7%	5.8	Portuguese Republic
199	98,720 (38,116)	27.7%	4.7%	-0.2%	3.8	Romania
242	1,243,730 (480,207)	47.9%	7.8%	-0.0%	9.9	Russian Federation
763	10 (4)	1.6%	- - -	- - -	- - -	Republic of San Marino
- - -	- - - - - -	- - -	- - -	- - -	- - -	Republic of Serbia
241	15,640 (6,039)	40.1%	22.8%	-0.3%	6.6	Slovak Republic
407	2,020 (780)	62.8%	6.0%	-0.2%	7.3	Republic of Slovenia
434	187,150 (72,259)	35.9%	8.5%	-0.6%	7.0	Kingdom of Spain
736	26,720 (10,317)	66.9%	9.1%	-0.0%	5.3	Kingdom of Sweden
744	4,330 (1,672)	30.9%	30.0%	-0.4%	5.4	Swiss Confederation
216	333,870 (128,908)	16.5%	3.9%	-0.3%	6.9	Ukraine
591	57,080 (22,039)	11.8%	20.9%	-0.8%	9.6	United Kingdom of Great Britain and Northern Ireland
- - -	- - - - - -	0.0%	- - -	- - -	- - -	State of the Vatican City (The Holy See)
						EUROPE: TERRITORIES AND AREAS OF SPECIAL STATUS
- - -	30 (12)	0.1%	- - -	- - -	- - -	Overseas Region of Denmark
- - -	- - - - - -	- - -	- - -	- - -	- - -	Norwegian Dependency
- - -	- - - - - -	4.1%	- - -	- - -	- - -	British Crown Dependencies
- - -	- - - - - -	0.0%	- - -	- - -	- - -	British Overseas Territory
- - -	- - - - - -	6.1%	- - -	- - -	- - -	British Crown Dependency
						ASIA
2	80,480 (31,074)	1.3%	0.3%	- - -	0.0	Transitional Islamic State of Afghanistan
148	5,600 (2,162)	10.0%	7.6%	-1.3%	1.1	Republic of Armenia
114	20,120 (7,768)	11.3%	6.1%	-1.3%	3.6	Republic of Azerbaijan
268	60 (23)	0.6%	- - -	- - -	29.1	Kingdom of Bahrain
5	84,190 (32,506)	6.7%	0.8%	-1.3%	0.2	People's Republic of Bangladesh
34	1,280 (494)	68.0%	- - -	- - -	0.5	Kingdom of Bhutan
256	170 (66)	52.8%	- - -	- - -	- - -	Negara Brunei Darussalam
3	38,070 (14,699)	59.2%	18.5%	0.6%	0.0	Kingdom of Cambodia
209	1,548,500 (597,879)	21.2%	7.8%	-0.9%	2.2	People's Republic of China
133	10,660 (4,116)	39.7%	2.3%	0.0%	1.2	Republic of Georgia
46	1,697,390 (655,366)	22.8%	5.2%	-0.1%	1.1	Republic of India
39	344,000 (132,819)	48.8%	20.6%	1.2%	1.3	Republic of Indonesia
220	182,480 (70,456)	6.8%	4.8%	0.0%	4.9	Islamic Republic of Iran
28	60,190 (23,239)	1.9%	0.0%	0.0%	3.3	Republic of Iraq
458	4,280 (1,653)	8.3%	15.8%	-4.9%	10.0	State of Israel
472	47,360 (18,286)	68.2%	6.8%	0.0%	9.3	Japan
114	4,000 (1,544)	0.9%	3.4%	0.0%	3.2	Hashemite Kingdom of Jordan
130	226,860 (87,591)	1.2%	2.7%	-2.2%	8.1	Republic of Kazakhstan
41	29,000 (11,197)	51.4%	2.6%	0.0%	8.5	Democratic People's Republic of Korea
538	18,460 (7,127)	63.5%	6.9%	0.1%	9.1	Republic of Korea
198	180 (69)	0.3%	1.5%	-5.2%	21.9	State of Kuwait
76	13,650 (5,270)	4.5%	12.5%	-2.6%	0.9	Kyrgyz Republic
12	10,310 (3,981)	69.9%	3.6%	0.4%	0.1	Lao People's Democratic Republic
199	3,130 (1,208)	13.3%	0.5%	0.3%	3.5	Lebanese Republic
182	75,850 (29,286)	63.6%	5.7%	1.2%	6.2	Malaysia
102	130 (50)	3.0%	- - -	- - -	1.8	Republic of Maldives
56	12,000 (4,633)	6.5%	11.5%	0.5%	3.1	Mongolia
7	109,810 (42,398)	49.0%	0.3%	1.4%	0.2	Union of Myanmar
16	24,900 (9,614)	25.4%	8.9%	1.8%	0.1	Kingdom of Nepal
84	800 (309)	3.1%	14.0%	0.0%	8.2	Sultanate of Oman
27	201,300 (77,722)	2.5%	4.9%	1.1%	0.8	Islamic Republic of Pakistan
41	107,000 (41,313)	24.0%	5.7%	1.4%	1.0	Republic of the Philippines
261	210 (81)	- - -	- - -	- - -	69.6	State of Qatar
155	37,980 (14,664)	1.3%	38.3%	0.0%	18.1	Kingdom of Saudi Arabia
450	20 (8)	3.4%	4.9%	0.0%	14.7	Republic of Singapore
49	19,160 (7,398)	29.9%	13.5%	1.6%	0.6	Democratic Socialist Republic of Sri Lanka
123	54,210 (20,931)	2.5%	- - -	0.0%	3.3	Syrian Arab Republic
37	10,570 (4,081)	2.9%	4.2%	-0.5%	0.6	Republic of Tajikistan
105	176,870 (68,290)	28.4%	13.9%	0.7%	3.3	Kingdom of Thailand
- - -	1,900 (734)	53.7%	- - -	- - -	- - -	Democratic Republic of Timor-Leste
268	260,130 (100,437)	13.2%	1.6%	-0.2%	3.3	Republic of Turkey
77	22,660 (8,749)	8.8%	4.2%	0.0%	7.5	Turkmenistan
281	2,540 (981)	3.7%	0.0%	-2.8%	18.1	United Arab Emirates
67	50,400 (19,460)	8.0%	2.0%	-0.2%	4.8	Republic of Uzbekistan
54	89,800 (34,672)	39.7%	3.7%	-0.5%	0.7	Socialist Republic of Vietnam
28	16,690 (6,444)	1.0%	- - -	1.8%	0.5	Republic of Yemen
						ASIA: TERRITORIES AND AREAS OF SPECIAL STATUS
559	- - - - - -	- - -	- - -	- - -	5.0	Special Administrative Region of China
- - -	- - - - - -	- - -	- - -	- - -	- - -	Special Administrative Region of China
- - -	- - - - - -	- - -	- - -	- - -	- - -	
- - -	1,950 (753)	1.5%	- - -	- - -	- - -	Areas of Special Status
- - -	- - - - - -	- - -	- - -	- - -	- - -	Area of Special Status
- - -	- - - - - -	- - -	- - -	- - -	- - -	Area of Special Status
- - -	- - - - - -	- - -	- - -	- - -	- - -	British Overseas Territory
						AFRICA
69	82,150 (31,718)	1.0%	5.0%	-1.3%	2.9	People's Democratic Republic of Algeria
7	35,900 (13,861)	47.4%	6.6%	0.2%	0.5	Republic of Angola
9	29,170 (11,263)	21.3%	11.4%	2.3%	0.3	Republic of Benin
75	3,800 (1,467)	21.1%	18.5%	0.9%	2.3	Republic of Botswana
5	49,000 (18,919)	29.0%	11.5%	0.2%	0.1	Burkina Faso
3	13,550 (5,232)	5.9%	5.7%	9.0%	0.0	Republic of Burundi
7	71,600 (27,645)	45.6%	4.5%	0.9%	0.4	Republic of Cameroon
156	490 (189)	20.7%	- - -	- - -	0.3	Republic of Cape Verde
2	20,240 (7,815)	36.5%	8.7%	0.1%	0.1	Central African Republic
2	36,300 (14,016)	9.5%	9.1%	0.6%	0.00	Republic of Chad

CONTINENT/Country	GDP per capita in U.S. dollars Mid-2005 estimate	Services as % of GDP Sector 2003	Industry as % of GDP Sector 2003	Agriculture as % of GDP Sector 2003	Total estimated value of imports in million U.S. dollars 2005	Total estimated value of exports in million U.S. dollars 2005	% of population with access to electricity 2003
Comoros	$600	47.2%	11.9%	40.9%	$115	$34	- - -
Congo	$1,300	33.8%	60.1%	6.2%	$807	$2,209	20.9%
Congo, Dem. Rep. of the	$700	34.0%	11.0%	55.0%	$1,319	$1,108	6.7%
Côte d'Ivoire (Ivory Coast)	$1,600	55.2%	18.6%	26.2%	$4,759	$6,490	50.0%
Djibouti	$1,300	80.7%	15.8%	3.5%	$987	$250	- - -
Egypt	$3,900	49.8%	34%	16.1%	$24,100	$14,330	93.8%
Equatorial Guinea	$50,200	4.3%	88.9%	6.8%	$1,864	$6,727	- - -
Eritrea	$1,000	61.4%	24.7%	13.9%	$677	$33.6	17.0%
Ethiopia	$900	47.4%	10.7%	41.8%	$2,722	$612	4.7%
Gabon	$6,800	29.8%	62.1%	8.1%	$1,533	$5,813	31.0%
Gambia	$1,900	55.2%	14.6%	30.1%	$197	$140.3	- - -
Ghana	$2,500	39.3%	24.9%	35.8%	$4,273	$2,911	45.0%
Guinea	$2,000	39.0%	36.4%	24.6%	$680	$612	- - -
Guinea-Bissau	$800	17.9%	13.3%	68.7%	$176	$116	- - -
Kenya	$1,100	64.7%	19.6%	15.8%	$5,126	$3,173	7.9%
Lesotho	$2,500	39.8%	43.5%	16.6%	$1,166	$603	5.0%
Liberia	$1,000	17.7%	5.4%	76.9%	$4,839	$910	- - -
Libya	$11,400	45.6%	45.7%	8.7%	$10,820	$30,790	99.8%
Madagascar	$900	55.4%	15.4%	29.2%	$1,400	$951	8.0%
Malawi	$600	46.7%	14.9%	38.4%	$645	$364	5.0%
Mali	$1,200	35.5%	26.1%	38.4%	$1,858	$323	- - -
Mauritania	$2,200	50.8%	30.0%	19.3%	$1,124	$784	- - -
Mauritius	$13,100	63.3%	30.6%	6.1%	$2,507	$1,949	100.0%
Morocco	$4,200	53.6%	29.6%	16.8%	$18,150	$9,472	71.1%
Mozambique	$1,300	42.8%	31.2%	26.1%	$2,041	$1,690	7.2%
Namibia	$7,000	63.6%	25.6%	10.8%	$2,350	$2,040	34.0%
Niger	$900	43.4%	16.8%	39.9%	$588	$222	- - -
Nigeria	$1,400	24.2%	49.5%	26.4%	$25,950	$52,160	40.0%
Rwanda	$1,500	36.5%	21.9%	41.6%	$243	$98	- - -
Sao Tome and Principe	$1,200	68.4%	14.6%	17.0%	$38	$8	
Senegal	$1,800	62%	21.2%	16.8%	$2,405	$1,526	30.1%
Seychelles	$7,800	61.7%	35.1%	3.3%	$460	$312	- - -
Sierra Leone	$800	16.5%	30.8%	52.7%	$531	$185	- - -
Somalia	$600	25.0%	10.0%	65.0%	$576	$241	- - -
South Africa	$12,000	65.2%	31.0%	3.8%	$52,970	$50,910	66.1%
Sudan	$2,100	41.0%	20.3%	38.7%	$5,028	$6,989	30.0%
Swaziland	$5,000	36.2%	51.5%	12.2%	$2,149	$1,991	- - -
Tanzania	$700	38.6%	16.4%	45.0%	$2,391	$1,581	10.5%
Togo	$1,700	37.1%	22.2%	40.8%	$1,047	$768	9.0%
Tunisia	$8,300	59.8%	28.1%	12.1%	$12,860	$10,300	94.6%
Uganda	$1,800	46.4%	21.2%	32.4%	$1,608	$768	3.7%
Zambia	$900	50.2%	27%	22.8%	$1,934	$1,947	12.0%
Zimbabwe	$2,300	57.6%	24.3%	18.1%	$2,059	$1,644	39.7%
AFRICA: TERRITORIES AND AREAS OF SPECIAL STATUS							
France							
Mayotte	$2,600	- - -	- - -	- - -	$141	$3.44	- - -
Réunion	$6,200	73.0%	19.0%	8.0%	$2,500	$214	- - -
Morocco							
Western Sahara	- - -	- - -	- - -	- - -	- - -	- - -	- - -
Norway							
Bouvet Island	- - -	- - -	- - -	- - -	- - -	- - -	- - -
South Africa							
Prince Edward Islands	- - -	- - -	- - -	- - -	- - -	- - -	- - -
United Kingdom							
Saint Helena	$2,500	87.0%	10.0%	3.0%	$45	$19	- - -
AUSTRALIA & OCEANIA							
Australia	$31,900	71.2%	25.9%	2.9%	$119,600	$103,000	- - -
Fiji Islands	$6,000	56.8%	27.0%	16.2%	$1,235	$862	- - -
Kiribati	$800	74.9%	10.9%	14.2%	$62	$17	- - -
Marshall Islands	$2,300	70.0%	16.0%	14.0%	$54	$9	- - -
Micronesia	$3,900	46.0%	4.00%	50.0%	$149	$22	- - -
Nauru	$5,000	- - -	- - -	- - -	$20	$17	- - -
New Zealand	$25,200	68.0%	27.4%	4.6%	$24,570	$22,210	- - -
Palau	$5,800	- - -	- - -	- - -	$99	$18	- - -
Papua New Guinea	$2,600	35.2%	39.4%	25.7%	$1,651	$2,833	- - -
Samoa	$5,600	63.0%	23.0%	14.0%	$285	$94	- - -
Solomon Islands	$1,700	47.0%	11.0%	42.0%	$159	$171	- - -
Tonga	$2,300	56.4%	15.1%	28.5%	$122	$34	- - -
Tuvalu	$1,100	- - -	- - -	- - -	$31	$1	- - -
Vanuatu	$2,900	62.0%	12.0%	26.0%	$233	$205	- - -
AUSTRALIA & OCEANIA: TERRITORIES AND AREAS OF SPECIAL STATUS							
Australia							
Ashmore and Cartier Islands	- - -	- - -	- - -	- - -	- - -	- - -	- - -
Christmas Island	- - -	- - -	- - -	- - -	- - -	- - -	- - -
Cocos (Keeling) Islands	- - -	- - -	- - -	- - -	- - -	- - -	- - -
Coral Sea Islands Territory	- - -	- - -	- - -	- - -	- - -	- - -	- - -
Norfolk Island	- - -	- - -	- - -	- - -	$18	$1.5	- - -
France							
Clipperton Island	- - -	- - -	- - -	- - -			- - -
French Polynesia	$17,500	78.0%	18.0%	4.0%	$1,437	$385	- - -
New Caledonia	$15,000	65.0%	30.0%	5.0%	$1,636	$999	- - -
Wallis and Futuna	$3,800	- - -	- - -	- - -	$0.3	$0.25	- - -
New Zealand							
Cook Islands	$5,000	75.2%	7.8%	17.0%	$51	$9.1	- - -
Niue	$3,600	- - -	- - -	- - -	$2	$0.137	- - -
Tokelau	$1,000	- - -	- - -	- - -	$0.3	$0.098	- - -
United Kingdom							
Pitcairn Islands	- - -	81.0%	13.6%	5.4%	- - -	- - -	- - -
United States							
American Samoa	$5,800	- - -	- - -	- - -	$105	$10	- - -
Baker Island	- - -	- - -	- - -	- - -	- - -	- - -	- - -
Guam	$15,000	78.0%	15.0%	7.0%	$701	$45	- - -
Northern Mariana Islands	$12,500	- - -	- - -	- - -	- - -	- - -	- - -

Telephone mainlines per 1,000 people 2003	Arable & permanent cropland area 2003 sq km (sq mi)	Forested area as % of total land area 2000	Protected areas as % of total land area 2003	Average annual deforestation: % change 1990 - 2000 (Negative number indicates an increase in forest area.)	Carbon dioxide emissions : metric tonnes per capita 2000	CONTINENT / Country Formal Name
17	1,320 (510)	2.9%	- - -	- - -	0.1	Union of the Comoros
2	5,470 (2,112)	65.8%	6.5%	0.1%	0.5	Republic of the Congo
0	78,000 (30,116)	58.9%	5.0%	0.4%	0.1	Democratic Republic of the Congo
14	69,000 (26,641)	32.7%	6.0%	3.1%	0.7	Republic of Côte d'Ivoire
15	10 (4)	0.2%	- - -	- - -	0.6	Republic of Djibouti
127	34,240 (13,220)	0.1%	9.7%	-3.4%	2.2	Arab Republic of Egypt
18	2,300 (888)	58.2%	- - -	- - -	0.4	Republic of Equatorial Guinea
9	5,650 (2,181)	15.4%	4.3%	0.3%	0.1	State of Eritrea
6	117,690 (45,440)	11.9%	16.9%	0.8%	0.1	Federal Democratic Republic of Ethiopia
29	4,950 (1,911)	84.5%	0.7%	0.0%	2.8	Gabonese Republic
28	3,200 (1,236)	41.7%	2.3%	-1.0%	0.2	Republic of The Gambia
13	63,850 (24,653)	24.2%	5.6%	1.7%	0.3	Republic of Ghana
3	17,500 (6,757)	27.4%	0.7%	0.5%	0.2	Republic of Guinea
8	5,500 (2,124)	73.7%	- - -	0.9%	0.2	Republic of Guinea-Bissau
10	52,120 (20,124)	6.2%	8.0%	0.5%	0.3	Republic of Kenya
13	3,340 (1,290)	0.3%	0.2%	0.0%	- - -	Kingdom of Lesotho
- - -	6,020 (2,324)	32.7%	1.7%	2.0%	0.1	Republic of Liberia
136	21,500 (8,301)	0.1%	0.1%	-1.4%	10.9	Great Socialist People's Libyan Arab Jamahiriya
4	35,500 (13,707)	22.1%	4.3%	0.9%	0.1	Republic of Madagascar
8	25,900 (10,000)	36.2%	11.2%	2.4%	0.1	Republic of Malawi
5	47,000 (18,147)	10.3%	3.7%	0.7%	0.1	Republic of Mali
14	5,000 (1,931)	0.3%	1.7%	2.7%	1.2	Islamic Republic of Mauritania
285	1,060 (409)	18.2%	7.8%	0.6%	2.4	Republic of Mauritius
40	93,760 (36,201)	9.8%	0.7%	0.0%	1.3	Kingdom of Morocco
5	45,800 (17,683)	24.6%	8.4%	0.2%	0.1	Republic of Mozambique
66	8,200 (3,166)	9.3%	13.6%	0.9%	1.0	Republic of Namibia
2	145,000 (55,985)	1.0%	7.7%	3.7%	0.1	Republic of Niger
7	334,000 (128,958)	12.2%	3.3%	2.6%	0.3	Federal Republic of Nigeria
3	14,700 (5,676)	19.5%	6.2%	3.9%	0.1	Republic of Rwanda
46	550 (212)	28.4%	- - -	- - -	0.6	Democratic Republic of Sao Tome and Principe
22	25,070 (9,680)	45.0%	11.6%	0.7%	0.4	Republic of Senegal
256	70 (27)	88.9%	- - -	- - -	2.8	Republic of Seychelles
5	6,450 (2,490)	38.5%	2.1%	2.9%	0.1	Republic of Sierra Leone
10	10,710 (4,135)	11.4%	0.8%	1.0%	- - -	Somalia
107	157,120 (60,664)	7.6%	5.5%	0.1%	7.4	Republic of South Africa
27	174,200 (67,259)	28.4%	5.2%	1.4%	0.2	Republic of the Sudan
44	1,920 (741)	31.5%	3.5%	-1.2%	0.4	Kingdom of Swaziland
4	51,000 (19,691)	39.9%	29.8%	0.2%	0.1	United Republic of Tanzania
12	26,300 (10,154)	7.1%	7.9%	3.4%	0.4	Togolese Republic
118	49,300 (19,035)	6.8%	0.3%	-0.2%	1.9	Tunisian Republic
2	73,500 (28,379)	18.4%	24.6%	2.0%	0.1	Republic of Uganda
8	52,890 (20,421)	57.1%	31.9%	2.4%	0.2	Republic of Zambia
26	33,500 (12,934)	45.3%	12.1%	1.5%	1.2	Republic of Zimbabwe
						AFRICA: TERRITORIES AND AREAS OF SPECIAL STATUS
	- - - - - -	14.7%	- - -	- - -	- - -	French Overseas Territorial Collectivity
- - -	390 (151)	33.6%	- - -	- - -	- - -	French Overseas Department
- - -	50 (19)	3.8%	- - -	- - -	- - -	Area of Special Status
- - -	- - - - - -	- - -	- - -	- - -	- - -	Territory of Norway
- - -	- - - - - -	- - -	- - -	- - -	- - -	Territory of South Africa
- - -	40 (15)	6.5%	- - -	- - -	- - -	British Overseas Territory
						AUSTRALIA & OCEANIA
542	479,350 (185,078)	21.3%	13.4%	0.0%	18.0	Commonwealth of Australia
124	2,850 (1,100)	54.7%	- - -	- - -	0.9	Republic of the Fiji Islands
51	370 (143)	3.0%	- - -	- - -	0.3	Republic of Kiribati
83	100 (39)	- - -	- - -	- - -	- - -	Republic
103	360 (139)	90.6%	- - -	- - -	- - -	Federated
- - -	- - - - - -	0.0%	- - -	- - -	- - -	Republic of Nauru
448	33,720 (13,019)	31.0%	29.6%	-0.5%	8.3	New Zealand
- - -	60 (23)	87.6%	- - -	- - -	- - -	Republic of Palau
12	8,750 (3,378)	65.0%	2.3%	0.4%	0.5	Independent State
73	1,290 (498)	60.4%	- - -	- - -	0.8	Independent State of Samoa
13	770 (297)	77.6%	- - -	- - -	0.4	Solomon Islands
113	260 (100)	5.0%	- - -	- - -	1.2	Kingdom of Tonga
	20 (8)	33.3%	- - -	- - -	- - -	Tuvalu
31	1,050 (405)	36.1%	- - -	- - -	0.4	Republic of Vanuatu
						AUSTRALIA & OCEANIA: TERRITORIES AND AREAS OF SPECIAL STATUS
- - -	- - - - - -	- - -	- - -	- - -	- - -	Australian External Territory
- - -	- - - - - -	- - -	- - -	- - -	- - -	Australian External Territory
- - -	- - - - - -	- - -	- - -	- - -	- - -	Australian External Territory
- - -		- - -	- - -	- - -	- - -	Australian External Territory
- - -	- - - - - -	- - -	- - -	- - -	- - -	Australian External Territory
- - -	- - - - - -	- - -	- - -	- - -	- - -	French Possession
- - -	250 (97)	28.7%	- - -	- - -	- - -	French Overseas Territory
- - -	10 (4)	39.2%	- - -	- - -	- - -	French Overseas Territory
- - -	60 (23)	35.3%	- - -	- - -	- - -	French Overseas Territory
- - -	60 (23)	66.5%	- - -	- - -	- - -	Self-Governing in Free Association with New Zealand
- - -	70 (27)	54.2%	- - -	- - -	- - -	Self-Governing in Free Association with New Zealand
- - -	- - - - - -	0.0%	- - -	- - -	- - -	Territory of New Zealand
- - -	- - - - - -	83.3%	- - -	- - -	- - -	British Overseas Territory
- - -	50 (19)	89.4%	- - -	- - -	- - -	Territory of the United States
- - -	- - - - - -	- - -	- - -	- - -	- - -	Territory of the United States
- - -	120 (46)	47.1%	- - -	- - -	- - -	Territory of the United States
- - -	80 (31)	72.4%	- - -	- - -	- - -	Commonwealth in Political Union with the United States

GEOGRAPHIC COMPARISONS

THE EARTH

MASS: 5,973,600,000,000,000,000,000,000 metric tons
TOTAL AREA: 510,066,000 sq km
LAND AREA: 148,647,000 sq km (29.1%)
WATER AREA: 361,419,000 sq km (70.9%)
POPULATION Mid-2005: 6,477,000,000

THE CONTINENTS

	AREA (SQ KM)	PERCENT OF LAND
Asia	44,570,000	30.0
Africa	30,065,000	20.2
North America	24,474,000	16.5
South America	17,819,000	12.0
Antarctica	13,209,000	8.9
Europe	9,947,000	6.7
Australia	7,692,000	5.2

HIGHEST POINT ON EACH CONTINENT

	METERS
Mount Everest, Asia	8,850
Cerro Aconcagua, South America	6,959
Mount McKinley (Denali), North America	6,194
Kilimanjaro, Africa	5,895
El'brus, Europe	5,642
Vinson Massif, Antarctica	4,897
Mount Kosciuszko, Australia	2,228

LOWEST SURFACE POINT ON EACH CONTINENT

	METERS
Dead Sea, Asia	-422
Lake Assal, Africa	-156
Laguna del Carbón, South America	-105
Death Valley, North America	-86
Caspian Sea, Europe	-28
Lake Eyre, Australia	-16
Bentley Subglacial Trench, Antarctica	-2,555

POPULATION OF EACH CONTINENT, Mid-2005

	POPULATION	PERCENT OF WORLD TOTAL
Asia	3,921,000,000	60.5
Africa	906,000,000	14.0
Europe	730,000,000	11.3
North America	515,000,000	7.9
South America	373,000,000	5.8
Australia	20,400,000	0.3
Islands of the Pacific	13,000,000	0.2

THE OCEANS

	AREA (SQ KM)	PERCENT OF EARTH'S WATER AREA
Pacific	169,479,000	46.8
Atlantic	91,526,400	25.3
Indian	74,694,800	20.6
Arctic	13,960,100	3.9

DEEPEST POINT IN EACH OCEAN

	METERS
Challenger Deep, Pacific Ocean	-10,971
Puerto Rico Trench, Atlantic Ocean	-8,605
Java Trench, Indian Ocean	-7,125
Molloy Deep, Arctic Ocean	-5,669

LARGEST SEAS BY AREA

		AREA (SQ KM)	AVERAGE DEPTH (METERS)
1	Coral Sea	4,184,000	2,471
2	South China Sea	3,596,000	1,180
3	Caribbean Sea	2,834,000	2,596
4	Bering Sea	2,520,000	1,832
5	Mediterranean Sea	2,469,000	1,572
6	Sea of Okhotsk	1,625,000	814
7	Gulf of Mexico	1,532,000	1,544
8	Norwegian Sea	1,425,000	1,768
9	Greenland Sea	1,158,000	1,443
10	Sea of Japan (East Sea)	1,008,000	1,647

LONGEST RIVERS

		KM
1	Nile, Africa	7,081
2	Amazon, South America	6,679
3	Chang Jiang (Yangtze), Asia	6,244
4	Mississippi-Missouri, North America	6,083
5	Yenisey-Angara, Asia	5,810
6	Huang (Yellow), Asia	5,778
7	Ob-Irtysh, Asia	5,520
8	Amur, Asia	5,504
9	Lena, Asia	5,150
10	Congo, Africa	5,118

METRIC CONVERSION TABLES

CONVERSION FROM METRIC MEASURES

SYMBOL	WHEN YOU KNOW	MULTIPLY BY	TO FIND	SYMBOL
LENGTH				
cm	centimeters	0.393701	inches	in
m	meters	3.280840	feet	ft
m	meters	1.093613	yards	yd
km	kilometers	0.621371	miles	mi
AREA				
cm²	square centimeters	0.155000	square inches	in²
m²	square meters	10.76391	square feet	ft²
m²	square meters	1.195990	square yards	yd²
km²	square kilometers	0.386102	square miles	mi²
ha	hectares	2.471054	acres	--
MASS				
g	grams	0.035274	ounces	oz
kg	kilograms	2.204623	pounds	lb
t	metric tonnes	1.102311	short tons	--
VOLUME				
mL	milliliters	0.061024	cubic inches	in³
mL	milliliters	0.033814	liquid ounces	liq oz
L	liters	2.113376	pints	pt
L	liters	1.056688	quarts	qt
L	liters	0.264172	gallons	gal
m³	cubic meters	35.31467	cubic feet	ft³
m³	cubic meters	1.307951	cubic yards	yd³
TEMPERATURE				
°C	degrees Celsius (centigrade)	9/5 & add 32	degrees Fahrenheit	°F

CONVERSION TO METRIC MEASURES

SYMBOL	WHEN YOU KNOW	MULTIPLY BY	TO FIND	SYMBOL
LENGTH				
in	inches	2.54	centimeters	cm
ft	feet	0.3048	meters	m
yd	yards	0.9144	meters	m
mi	miles	1.609344	kilometers	km
AREA				
in²	square inches	6.4516	square centimeters	cm²
ft²	square feet	0.092903	square meters	m²
yd²	square yards	0.836127	square meters	m²
mi²	square miles	2.589988	square kilometers	km²
--	acres	0.404686	hectares	ha
MASS				
oz	ounces	28.349523	grams	g
lb	pounds	0.453592	kilograms	kg
--	short tons	0.907185	metric tonnes	t
VOLUME				
in³	cubic inches	16.387064	milliliters	mL
liq oz	liquid ounces	29.57353	milliliters	mL
pt	pints	0.473176	liters	L
qt	quarts	0.946353	liters	L
gal	gallons	3.785412	liters	L
ft³	cubic feet	0.028317	cubic meters	m³
yd³	cubic yards	0.764555	cubic meters	m³
TEMPERATURE				
°F	degrees Fahrenheit	5/9 after subtracting 32	degrees Celsius (centigrade)	°C

URBAN AGGLOMERATIONS, 2005
(Population in thousands)

City	Country	Population
Tokyo	Japan	35,327
Mexico City	Mexico	19,013
New York-Newark	United States	18,498
Mumbai (Bombay)	India	18,336
São Paulo	Brazil	18,333
Delhi	India	15,334
Kolkata (Calcutta)	India	14,299
Buenos Aires	Argentina	13,349
Jakarta	Indonesia	13,194
Shanghai	China	12,665
Dhaka	Bangladesh	12,560
Los Angeles-Long Beach-Santa Ana,	United States	12,146
Karachi	Pakistan	11,819
Rio de Janeiro	Brazil	11,469
Osaka-Kōbe	Japan	11,286
Cairo	Egypt	11,146
Lagos	Nigeria	11,135
Beijing	China	10,849
Metro Manila	Philippines	10,677
Moscow	Russia	10,672
Paris	France	9,854
Istanbul	Turkey	9,760
Seoul	South Korea	9,592
Tianjin	China	9,346
Chicago	United States	8,711
Lima	Peru	8,180
London	United Kingdom	7,615
Bogotá	Colombia	7,594
Tehran	Iran	7,352
Hong Kong	China,	7,182
Chennai (Madras)	India	6,915
Bangkok	Thailand	6,604
Rhein-Ruhr North	Germany	6,566
(Duisburg, Essen, Krefeld, Mülheim, Oberhausen, Bottrop, Gelsenkirchen, Bochum, Dortmund, Hagen, Hamm and Herne)		
Bangalore	India	6,532
Lahore	Pakistan	6,373
Hyderabad	India	6,145
Wuhan	China	6,003
Baghdad	Iraq	5,910
Kinshasa	Dem. Rep. Congo	5,717
Santiago	Chile	5,623
Riyadh	Saudi Arabia	5,514
Miami	United States	5,380
Brasília	Brazil	5,341
Philadelphia	United States	5,325
Saint Petersburg	Russia	5,315
Belo Horizonte	Brazil	5,304
Ahmadabad	India	5,171
Madrid	Spain	5,145
Toronto	Canada	5,060
Ho Chi Minh City	Vietnam	5,030
Chongqing	China	4,975
Shenyang	China	4,916
Dallas-Fort Worth	United States	4,612
Khartoum	Sudan	4,495
Pune (Poona)	India	4,485
Barcelona	Spain	4,424
Sydney	Australia	4,388
Singapore	Singapore	4,372
Boston	United States	4,313
Atlanta	United States	4,284
Houston	United States	4,283
Washington, D.C.	United States	4,190
Chittagong	Bangladesh	4,171
Hanoi	Vietnam	4,147
Yangon (Rangoon)	Myanmar (Burma)	4,082
Bandung	Indonesia	4,020
Milan	Italy	4,007
Detroit	United States	3,980
Guadalajara	Mexico	3,881
Jeddah	Saudi Arabia	3,807
Porto Alegre	Brazil	3,795
Alexandria	Egypt	3,760
Casablanca	Morocco	3,743
Rhein-Main	Germany	3,721
(Darmstadt, Frankfurt, Offenbach and Wiesbaden)		
Surat	India	3,671
Melbourne	Australia	3,663
Ankara	Turkey	3,593
Recife	Brazil	3,527
Busan (Pusan)	South Korea	3,527
Monterrey	Mexico	3,517
Abidjan	Côte d'Ivoire (Ivory Coast)	3,516
Montréal	Canada	3,511
Chengdu	China	3,478
Phoenix-Mesa	United States	3,393
San Francisco-Oakland	United States	3,342
Salvador	Brazil	3,331
Berlin	Germany	3,328
Rhein-Ruhr Middle	Germany	3,325
(Düsseldorf, Mönchengladbach, Remscheid, Solingen and Wuppertal)		
Kabul	Afghanistan	3,288
Johannesburg	South Africa	3,288
Pyongyang	North Korea	3,284

Abbreviations

A.	*Arroio, Arroyo*
A.C.T.	*Australian Capital Territory*
A.F.B.	*Air Force Base*
A.F.S.	*Air Force Station*
A.R.B.	*Air Reserve Base*
Adm.	*Administrative*
Af.	*Africa*
Afghan.	*Afghanistan*
Ala.	*Alabama*
Alas.	*Alaska*
Alban.	*Albania*
Alg.	*Algeria*
Alta.	*Alberta*
Amer.	*America-n*
Amzns.	*Amazonas*
Anch.	*Anchorage*
And. & Nic.	*Andaman and Nicobar Islands*
And. Prad.	*Andhra Pradesh*
Antil.	*Antilles*
Arch.	*Archipelago, Archipiélago*
Arg.	*Argentina*
Ariz.	*Arizona*
Ark.	*Arkansas*
Arkh.	*Arkhangel'sk*
Arm.	*Armenia*
Arun. Prad.	*Arunachal Pradesh*
Astrak.	*Astrakhan'*
Atl. Oc.	*Atlantic Ocean*
Aust.	*Austria*
Austral.	*Australia*
Auton.	*Autonomous*
Azerb.	*Azerbaijan*
B.	*Baai, Baía, Baie, Bahía, Bay, Bugt, Buḩayrat*
B. Aires	*Buenos Aires*
B.C.	*British Columbia*
B. Qazaq.	*Batys Qazaqstan*
Bashk.	*Bashkortostan*
Bayq.	*Bayqongyr*
Belg.	*Belgium*
Bol.	*Bolivia*
Bol.	*Bol'sh-oy, -aya, -oye*
Bosn. & Herzg.	*Bosnia and Herzegovina*
Br.	*Branch*
Braz.	*Brazil*
Bulg.	*Bulgaria*
Burya.	*Buryatiya*
C.	*Cabo, Cap, Cape, Capo*
C.H.	*Court House*
C.P.	*Conservation Park*
C.R.	*Costa Rica*
C.S.I. Terr.	*Coral Sea Islands Territory*
Cach.	*Cachoeira*
Calif.	*California*
Can.	*Canada*
Cap.	*Capitán*
Catam.	*Catamarca*
Cd.	*Ciudad*
Cen. Af. Rep.	*Central African Republic*
Cga.	*Ciénaga*
Chan.	*Channel*
Chand.	*Chandigarh*
Chap.	*Chapada*
Chech.	*Chechnya*
Chely.	*Chelyabinsk*
Chhat.	*Chhattīsgarh*
Chongq.	*Chongqing Shi*
Chuk.	*Chukotskiy*
Chuv.	*Chuvashiya*
Chyrv.	*Chyrvony, -aya, -aye*
Cmte.	*Comandante*
Cnel.	*Coronel*
Co.-s.	*Cerro-s*
Col.	*Colombia*
Colo.	*Colorado*
Conn.	*Connecticut*
Cord.	*Cordillera*
Corr.	*Corrientes*
Cr.	*Creek, Crique*
D.	*Danau*
D. & Diu	*Daman and Diu*
D. & Nagar	*Dadra and Nagar Haveli*
D.C.	*District of Columbia*
D.F.	*Distrito Federal*
Del.	*Delaware*
Dem.	*Democratic*
Den.	*Denmark*
Dist.	*District, Distrito*
Dom. Rep.	*Dominican Republic*
Dr.	*Doctor*
Dz.	*Dzong*
E.	*East-ern*
E. Ríos	*Entre Ríos*
E. Santo	*Espírito Santo*
Ea.	*Estancia*
Ecua.	*Ecuador*
El Salv.	*El Salvador*
Emb.	*Embalse*
Eng.	*England*
Ens.	*Ensenada*
Entr.	*Entrance*
Eq.	*Equatorial*
Est.	*Estación*
Est.	*Estonia*
Ét.	*Étang*
Eth.	*Ethiopia*
Eur.	*Europe*
Ez.	*Ezers*
F.	*Fiume*
F.S.M.	*Federated States of Micronesia*
Falk. Is.	*Falkland Islands*
Fd.	*Fiord, Fiordo, Fjord*
Fed.	*Federal, Federation*
Fin.	*Finland*
Fk.	*Fork*
Fla.	*Florida*
Fn.	*Fortín*
Fr.	*France, French*
Ft.	*Fort*
Fy.	*Ferry*
G.	*Golfe, Golfo, Gulf*
G. Altay	*Gorno-Altay*
G.R.	*Game Reserve*
Ga.	*Georgia*
Geb.	*Gebergte, Gebirge*
Gen.	*General*
Ger.	*Germany*
Gez.	*Gezîra-t, Gezîret*
Gezr.	*Gezâir*
Gl.	*Glacier*
Gob.	*Gobernador*
Gr.	*Greece,*
Gr.	*Gross-er*
Gral.	*General*
Gt.	*Great-er*
Guang.	*Guangdong*
H.K.	*Hong Kong*
Hbr.	*Harbor, Harbour*
Hdqrs.	*Headquarters*
Heilong.	*Heilongjiang*
Hi. Prad.	*Himachal Pradesh*
Hist.	*Historic, -al*
Hond.	*Honduras*
Hts.	*Heights*
Hung.	*Hungary*
Hwy.	*Highway*
I.H.S.	*International Historic Site*
I.-s.	*Île-s, Ilha-s, Isla-s, Island-s, Isle, Isol-a, -e*
Ice.	*Iceland*
Ig.	*Igarapé*
Igr.	*Ingeniero*
Ill.	*Illinois*
Ind.	*Indiana*
Ind. Oc.	*Indian Ocean*
Ingush.	*Ingushetiya*
Intl.	*International*
Ire.	*Ireland*
It.	*Italy*
J.	*Järvi, Joki*
J. & Kash.	*Jammu and Kashmir*
J.A.R.	*Jewish Autonomous Region*
Jab., Jeb.	*Jabal, Jebel*
Jam.	*Jamaica*
Jct.	*Jonction, Junction*
Jez.	*Jezero, Jezioro*
Jhark.	*Jharkhand*
K.	*Kanal*
K. Balka.	*Kabardino-Balkariya*
K. Cherk.	*Karachayevo-Cherkesiya*
K. Mansi	*Khanty-Mansi*
Kalin.	*Kaliningrad*
Kalmy.	*Kalmykiya*
Kamchat.	*Kamchatka*
Kans.	*Kansas*
Karna.	*Karnataka*
Kaz.	*Kazakhstan*
Kemer.	*Kemerovo*
Kep.	*Kepulauan*
Kh.	*Khor*
Khabar.	*Khabarovsk*
Khak.	*Khakasiya*
Khr.	*Khrebet*
Km.	*Kilómetro*
Kól.	*Kólpos*
Kör.	*Körfez,-i*
Koryak.	*Koryakskiy*
Kos.	*Kosovo*
Kr.	*Krasn-yy, -aya, -oye*
Krasnod.	*Krasnodar*
Krasnoy.	*Krasnoyarsk*
Ky.	*Kentucky*
Kyrg.	*Kyrgyzstan*
L.	*Lac, Lago, Lake, Límni, Loch, Lough*
La.	*Louisiana*
Lag.	*Laguna*
Lakshad.	*Lakshadweep*
Latv.	*Latvia*
Ldg.	*Landing*
Leb.	*Lebanon*
Lib.	*Libya*
Liech.	*Liechtenstein*
Lith.	*Lithuania*
Lux.	*Luxembourg*
M.	*Mal-yy, -aya, -oye*
M.C.A.S.	*Marine Corps Air Station*
M. Gerais	*Minas Gerais*
M. Grosso	*Mato Grosso*
M. Grosso S.	*Mato Grosso do Sul*
M. Prad.	*Madhya Pradesh*
Maced.	*Macedonia*
Mahar.	*Maharashtra*
Mal.	*Mal-y-y, -aya, -aye*
Man.	*Manitoba*
Mangg.	*Mangghystaū*
Maran.	*Maranhão*
Mass.	*Massachusetts*
Md.	*Maryland*
Me.	*Maine*
Medit. Sea	*Mediterranean Sea*
Meghal.	*Meghalaya*
Mex.	*Mexico*
Mgne.	*Montagne*
Mich.	*Michigan*
Minn.	*Minnesota*
Miss.	*Mississippi*
Mo.	*Missouri*
Mold.	*Moldova*
Mon.	*Monument*
Mont.	*Montana, Montenegro*
Mor.	*Morocco*
Mord.	*Mordoviya*
Mt.-s.	*Mont-s, Mount-ain-s*
Mte.-s.	*Monte-s*
Mti., Mtii.	*Munţi-i*
Mun.	*Municipal*
Murm.	*Murmansk*
N.	*North-ern*
N.A.S.	*Naval Air Station*
N.B.	*National Battlefield*
N.B.	*New Brunswick*
N.B.P.	*National Battlefield Park*
N.B.S.	*National Battlefield Site*
N.C.	*National Cemetery*
N.C.	*North Carolina*
N.C.A.	*National Conservation Area*
N. Dak.	*North Dakota*
N.E.	*North East*
N.H.	*New Hampshire*
N.H.P.	*National Historic, -al Park*
N.H.S.	*National Historic Site*
N. Ire.	*Northern Ireland*
N.J.	*New Jersey*
N.L.	*National Lakeshore*
N.M.	*National Monument*
N.M.P.	*National Military Park*
N. Mem.	*National Memorial*
N. Mem. P.	*National Memorial Park*
N. Mex.	*New Mexico*
N. Mongol	*Nei Mongol*
N.P.	*National Park*
N.R.	*Nature Reserve*
N.R.A.	*National Recreation Area*
N.S.	*Nova Scotia, National Seashore*
N.S.R.	*National Scenic Riverway*
N.S.R.A.	*National Seashore Recreational Area*
N.S.T.	*National Scenic Trail*
N.S.W.	*New South Wales*
N.T.	*Northern Territory*
N.T.C.	*Naval Training Center*
N.T.S.	*Naval Training Station*
N.V.M.	*National Volcanic Monument*
N.W.T.	*Northwest Territories*
N.Y.	*New York*
N.Z.	*New Zealand*
Nat. Mem.	*National Memorial*
Nat. Mon.	*National Monument*
Nat. Park	*National Park*
Nebr.	*Nebraska*
Neth.	*Netherlands*
Nev.	*Nevada, Nevado*
Nfld. & Lab.	*Newfoundland and Labrador*
Nicar.	*Nicaragua*
Niz. Nov.	*Nizhniy Novogorod*
Nizh.	*Nizhn-iy, -yaya, -eye*
Nor.	*Norway*
Nov.	*Nov-yy, -aya, -aye, -oye*
Novg.	*Novgorod*
Novo.	*Novosibirsk*
Nr.	*Nørre*
O.	*Ostrov, Oued*
Oc.	*Ocean*
Of.	*Oficina*
Okla.	*Oklahoma*
Ong. Qazaq.	*Ongtüstik Qazaqstan*
Ont.	*Ontario*
Ør.	*Øster*
Oreg.	*Oregon*
Orenb.	*Orenburg*
Oz.	*Ozero*
P.	*Paso, Pass, Passo*
P.E.I.	*Prince Edward Island*
P.N.G.	*Papua New Guinea*
P.R.	*Puerto Rico*
Pa.	*Pennsylvania*
Pac. Oc.	*Pacific Ocean*
Pak.	*Pakistan*
Pan.	*Panama*
Pant.	*Pantano*
Parag.	*Paraguay*
Parq. Nac.	*Parque Nacional*
Pass.	*Passage*
Peg.	*Pegunungan*
Pen.	*Peninsula, Péninsule*
Per.	*Pereval*
Pern.	*Pernambuco*
Pivd.	*Pivdennyy*
Pk.	*Peak*
Pl.	*Planina*
Plat.	*Plateau*
Pol.	*Poland*
Pol.	*Poluostrov*
Por.	*Porog*
Port.	*Portugal*
Pres.	*Presidente*
Prov.	*Province, Provincial*
Pt.-e.	*Point-e*
Pta.	*Ponta, Punta*
Pto.	*Puerto*
Q.	*Quebrada*
Qarag.	*Qaraghandy*
Qnsld.	*Queensland*
Que.	*Quebec*
Qyzyl.	*Qyzylorda*
R.	*Río, River, Rivière*
R. Gr. Norte	*Rio Grande do Norte*
R. Gr. Sul	*Rio Grande do Sul*
R.I.	*Rhode Island*
R. Jan.	*Rio de Janeiro*
R. Negro	*Río Negro*
Ra.-s.	*Range-s*
Raja.	*Rajasthan*
Reg.	*Region*
Rep.	*Republic*
Res.	*Reservoir, Reserve, Reservatório*
Rk.	*Rock*
Rom.	*Romania*
Russ.	*Russia*
S.	*South-ern*
S.A.R.	*Special Administrative Region*
S. Aust.	*South Australia*
S.C.	*South Carolina*
S. Dak.	*South Dakota*
S. Estero	*Santiago del Estero*
S. Paulo	*São Paulo*
S.W.	*Southwest*
Sa.-s.	*Serra, Sierra-s*
Sal.	*Salar, Salina*
Sask.	*Saskatchewan*
Scot.	*Scotland*
Sd.	*Sound*
Sel.	*Selat*
Ser.	*Serranía*
Serb.	*Serbia*
Sev.	*Severn-yy, -aya, -oye*
Sev. Oset.	*Severnaya Osetiya-Alaniya*
Sgt.	*Sargento*
Shand.	*Shandong*
Shy. Qazaq.	*Shyghys Qazaqstan*
Sk.	*Shankou*
Slov.	*Slovenia*
Solt. Qazaq.	*Soltüstik Qazaqstan*
Sp.	*Spain, Spanish*
Spr.-s.	*Spring-s*
Sq.	*Square*
Sr.	*Sønder*
St.-e.	*Saint-e, Sankt, Sint*
St. Peter.	*Saint Petersburg*
Sta., Sto.	*Santa, Station, Santo*
Sta. Cata.	*Santa Catarina*
Sta. Cruz.	*Santa Cruz*
Stavr.	*Stavropol'*
Str.-s.	*Straat, Strait-s*
Sv.	*Svyat-oy, -aya, -oye*
Sverd.	*Sverdlovsk*
Sw.	*Sweden*
Switz.	*Switzerland*
Syr.	*Syria*
T. Fuego	*Tierra del Fuego*
T. Nadu	*Tamil Nadu*
Taj.	*Tajikistan*
Tartar.	*Tartarstan*
Tas.	*Tasmania*
Tel.	*Teluk*
Tenn.	*Tennessee*
Terr.	*Territory*
Tex.	*Texas*
Tg.	*Tanjung*
Thai.	*Thailand*
Tocant.	*Tocantins*
Trin.	*Trinidad*
Tun.	*Tunisia*
Turk.	*Turkey*
Turkm.	*Turkmenistan*
U.A.E.	*United Arab Emirates*
U.K.	*United Kingdom*
U. Prad.	*Uttar Pradesh*
U.S.	*United States*
Udmur.	*Udmurtiya*
Uj.	*Ujung*
Ukr.	*Ukraine*
Ulyan.	*Ul'yanovsk*
Uru.	*Uruguay*
Uttar.	*Uttarakhand*
Uzb.	*Uzbekistan*
Va.	*Virginia*
Val.	*Valle*
Vdkhr.	*Vodokhranilishche*
Vdskh.	*Vodoskhovyshche*
Venez.	*Venezuela*
Verkh.	*Verkhn-iy, -yaya, -eye*
Vic.	*Victoria*
Vol.	*Volcán, Volcano*
Volg.	*Volgograd*
Voz.	*Vozyera, -yero, -yera*
Vozv.	*Vozvyshennost'*
Vr.	*Vester*
Vt.	*Vermont*
Vyal.	*Vyaliki, -ikaya, -ikaye*
W.	*Wadi, Wâdi, Wādī, Webi*
W.	*West-ern*
W. Aust.	*Western Australia*
W. Bengal	*West Bengal*
W.H.	*Water Hole*
W. Va.	*West Virginia*
Wash.	*Washington*
Wis.	*Wisconsin*
Wyo.	*Wyoming*
Y. Nenets	*Yemal-Nenets*
Yar.	*Yarymadasy*
Yaro.	*Yaroslavl'*
Yu.	*Yuzhn-yy, -aya, -oye*
Zakh.	*Zakhod-ni, -nyaya, -nye*
Zal.	*Zaliv*
Zap.	*Zapadn-yy, -aya, -oye*
Zimb.	*Zimbabwe*

Foreign Terms

Aaglet	*well*
Aain	*spring*
Aauinat	*spring*
Āb	*river, water*
Ache	*stream*
Açude	*reservoir*
Ada,-si	*island*
Adrar	*mountain-s, plateau*
Aguada	*dry lake bed*
Aguelt	*water hole, well*
'Ain, Aïn	*spring, well*
Aïoun-et	*spring-s, well*
Aivi	*mountain*
Akra, Akrotírio	*cape, promontory*
Alb	*mountain, ridge*
Alföld	*plain*
Alin'	*mountain range*
Alpe-n, -s	*mountain-s*
Altiplanicie	*high-plain, plateau*
Alto	*hill-s, mountain-s, ridge*
Älv-en	*river*
Āmba	*hill, mountain*
Anou	*well*
Anse	*bay, inlet*
Ao	*bay, cove, estuary*
Ap	*cape, point*
Archipel, Archipiélago	*archipelago*
Arcipelago, Arkhipelag	*archipelago*
Arquipélago	*archipelago*
Arrecife-s	*reef-s*
Arroio, Arroyo	*brook, gully, rivulet, stream*
Ås	*ridge*
Ava	*channel*
Aylagy	*gulf*
'Ayn	*spring, well*
Ba	*intermittent stream,river*
Baai	*bay, cove, lagoon*
Bāb	*gate, strait*
Badia	*bay*
Bælt	*strait*
Bagh	*bay*
Bahar	*drainage basin*
Bahía	*bay*
Bahr, Baḩr	*bay, lake, river, sea, wadi*
Baía, Baie	*bay*
Bajo-s	*shoal-s*
Ban	*village*
Bañado-s	*flooded area, swamp-s*
Banc, Banco-s	*bank-s, sandbank-s, shoal-s*
Bandao	*peninsula*
Baño-s	*hot spring-s, spa*
Baraj-ı	*dam, reservoir*
Barra	*bar, sandbank*
Barrage, Barragem	*dam, lake, reservoir*
Barranca	*gorge, ravine*
Bazar	*marketplace*
Belentligi	*plateau*
Ben, Beinn	*mountain*
Belt	*strait*
Bereg	*bank, coast, shore*
Berg-e	*mountain-s*
Bil	*lake*
Biq'at	*plain, valley*
Bir, Bîr, Bi'r	*spring, well*
Birket	*lake, pool, swamp*
Bjerg-e	*mountain-s, range*
Boca, Bocca	*channel, river, mouth*
Bocht	*bay*
Bodden	*bay*
Boğaz, -ı	*strait*
Bögeni	*reservoir*
Boka	*gulf, mouth*
Bol'sh-oy, -aya, -oye	*big*
Bolsón	*inland basin*
Boubairet	*lagoon, lake*
Bras	*arm, branch of a stream*
Braţ, -ul	*arm, branch of a stream*
Bræ-er	*glacier*
Bre, -en	*glacier, ice cap*
Bredning	*bay, broad water*
Bruch	*marsh*
Bucht	*bay*
Bugt-en	*bay*
Buḩayrat, Buheirat	*lagoon, lake,marsh*
Bukhta, Bukta, Bukt-en	*bay*
Bulak, Bulaq	*spring*
Bum	*hill, mountain*
Burnu, Burun	*cape, point*
Busen	*gulf*
Buuraha	*hill-s, mountain-s*
Büyük	*big, large*
Cabeza-s	*head-s, summit-s*
Cabo	*cape*
Cachoeira	*rapids, waterfall*
Cal	*hill, peak*
Caleta	*cove, inlet*
Campo-s	*field-s, flat country*
Canal	*canal, channel, strait*
Caño	*channel, stream*
Cao Nguyen	*mountain, plateau*
Cap, Capo	*cape*
Capitán	*captain*
Càrn	*mountain*
Castillo	*castle, fort*
Catarata-s	*cataract-s, waterfall-s*
Causse	*upland*
Çay	*brook, stream*
Cay-s, Cayo-s	*island-s, key-s, shoal-s*
Cerro-s	*hill-s, peak-s*
Chaîne, Chaînons	*mountain chain, range*
Chapada-s	*plateau, upland-s*
Chedo	*archipelago*
Chenal	*river channel*
Chersónisos	*peninsula*
Chhung	*bay*
Chi	*lake*
Chiang	*bay*
Chiao	*cape, point, rock*
Ch'ih	*lake*
Chink	*escarpment*
Chott	*intermittent salt lake, salt marsh*
Chou	*island*
Ch'ü	*canal*
Ch'üntao	*archipelago, islands*
Chute-s	*cataract-s, waterfall-s*
Chyrvony, -aya, -aye	*red*
Ciénaga	*marsh*
Cima	*mountain, peak, summit*
Ciudad	*city*
Co	*lake*
Col	*pass*
Collina, Colline	*hill, mountains*
Con	*island*
Cordillera	*mountain chain*
Corno	*mountain, peak*
Coronel	*colonel*
Corredeira	*cascade, rapids*
Costa	*coast*
Côte	*coast, slope*
Coxilha, Cuchilla	*range of low hills*
Crique	*creek, stream*
Csatorna	*canal, channel*
Cul de Sac	*bay, inlet*
Da	*great, greater*
Daban	*pass*
Dağ, -ı, Dāgh	*mountain*
Dağlar, -ı	*mountains*
Dahr	*cliff, mesa*
Dake	*mountain, peak*
Dal-en	*valley*
Dala	*steppe*
Dan	*cape, point*
Danau	*lake*
Dao	*island*
Dar'ya	*lake, river*
Daryācheh	*lake, marshy lake*
Dasht	*desert, plain*
Dawan	*pass*
Dawḩat	*bay, cove, inlet*
Deniz, -i	*sea*
Dent-s	*peak-s*
Deo	*pass*
Desēt	*hummock, island, land-tied island*
Desierto	*desert*
Détroit	*channel, strait*
Dhar	*hills, ridge, tableland*
Ding	*mountain*
Distrito	*district*
Djebel	*mountain, range*
Do	*island-s, rock-s*
Doi	*hill, mountain*
Dome	*ice dome*
Dong	*village*
Dooxo	*floodplain*
Dzong	*castle, fortress*
Eiland-en	*island-s*
Eilean	*island*
Ejland	*island-s*
Elv	*river*
Embalse	*lake, reservoir*
Emi	*mountain, rock*
Enseada, Ensenada	*bay, cove*
Ér	*rivulet, stream*
Erg	*sand dune region*
Est	*east*
Estación	*railroad station*
Estany	*lagoon, lake*
Estero	*estuary, inlet, lagoon, marsh*
Estrecho	*strait*
Étang	*lake, pond*
Eylandt	*island*
Ežeras	*lake*
Ezers	*lake*

Falaise *cliff, escarpment*
Farvand-et *channel, sound*
Fell *mountain*
Feng *mount, peak*
Fiord-o *inlet, sound*
Fiume *river*
Fjäll-et *mountain*
Fjällen *mountains*
Fjärd-en *fjord*
Fjarðar, Fjörður *fjord*
Fjeld *mountain*
Fjell-ene *mountain-s*
Fjöll *mountain-s*
Fjord-en *inlet, fjord*
Fleuve *river*
Fljót *large river*
Flói *bay, marshland*
Foci *river mouths*
Főcsatorna *principal canal*
Förde *fjord, gulf, inlet*
Forsen *rapids, waterfall*
Fortaleza *fort, fortress*
Fortín *fortified post*
Foss-en *waterfall*
Foum *pass, passage*
Foz *mouth of a river*
Fuerte *fort, fortress*
Fwafwate *waterfalls*

Gacan-ka *hill, peak*
Gal *pond, spring, waterhole, well*
Gang *harbor*
Gangri *peak, range*
Gaoyuan *plateau*
Garaet, Gara'et *lake, lake bed, salt lake*
Gardaneh *pass*
Garet *hill, mountain*
Gat *channel*
Gata *bay, inlet, lake*
Gattet *channel, strait*
Gaud *depression, saline tract*
Gave *mountain stream*
Gebel *mountain-s, range*
Gebergte *mountain range*
Gebirge *mountains, range*
Geçidi *mountain pass, passage*
Geçit *mountain pass, passage*
Gezâir *islands*
Gezîra-t, Gezîret *island, peninsula*
Ghats *mountain range*
Ghubb-at, -et *bay, gulf*
Giri *mountain*
Gjiri *bay*
Gletscher *glacier*
Gobernador *governor*
Gobi *desert*
Gol *river, stream*
Göl, -ü *lake*
Golets *mountain, peak*
Golf, -e, -o *gulf*
Gor-a, -y, Gór-a, -y *mountain,-s*
Got *point*
Gowd *depression*
Goz *sand ridge*
Gran, -de *great, large*
Gryada *mountains, ridge*
Guan *pass*
Guba *bay, gulf*
Guelta *well*
Guntō *archipelago*
Gunung *mountain*
Gura *mouth, passage*
Guyot *table mount*

Ḩadabat *plateau*
Haehyŏp *strait*
Haff *lagoon*
Hai *lake, sea*
Haihsia *strait*
Haixia *channel, strait*
Hakau *reef, rock*
Hakuchi *anchorage*
Halvø, Halvøy-a *peninsula*
Hama *beach*
Hamada, Ḩammādah *rocky desert*
Hamn *harbor, port*
Hāmūn, Hamun *depression, lake*
Hana *cape, point*
Hantō *peninsula*
Har *hill, mound, mountain*
Ḩarrat *lava field*
Hasi, Hassi *spring, well*
Hauteur *elevation, height*
Hav-et *sea*
Havn, Havre *harbor, port*
Hawr *lake, marsh*
Hāyk' *lake, reservoir*
Hegy, -ség *mountain, -s, range*
Heiau *temple*
Ho *canal, lake, river*
Hoek *hook, point*
Hög-en *high, hill*
Höhe, -n *height, high*
Høj *height, hill*
Holm, -e, Holmene *island-s, islet -s*
Ḩolot *dunes*
Hon *island-s*
Hor-a, -y *mountain, -s*
Horn *horn, peak*
Houma *point*
Hoved *headland, peninsula, point*
Hraun *lava field*
Hsü *island*
Hu *lake, reservoir*
Huk *cape, point*
Hüyük *hill, mound*

Idehan *sand dunes*
Igarapé *creek, stream*
Île-s, Ilha-s, Illa-s, Îlot-s *island-s, islet-s*
Îlet, Ilhéu-ș *islet, -s*
Irhil *mountain-s*
'Irq *sand dune-s*
Isblink *glacier, ice field*
Is-en *glacier*
Isebræ *glacier*
Isfjord *ice fjord*
Iskappe *ice cap*
Isla-s, Islote *island-s, islet*
Isol-a, -e *island, -s*
Istmo *isthmus*
Iwa *island, islet, rock*

Jabal, Jebel *mountain-s, range*
Järv, -i, Jaure, Javrre *lake*
Jazā'ir, Jazīrat, Jazīreh *island-s*
Jehīl *lake*
Jezero, Jezioro *lake*
Jiang *river, stream*
Jiao *cape*
Jībal *hill, mountain, ridge*
Jima *island-s, rock-s*
Jøkel, Jökull *glacier, ice cap*
Joki, Jokka *river*
Jökulsá *river from a glacier*
Jūn *bay*

Kaap *cape*
Kafr *village*
Kaikyō *channel, strait*
Kaise *mountain*
Kaiwan *bay, gulf, sea*
Kanal *canal, channel*
Kangerlua *fjord*
Kangri *mountain, peak*
Kap, Kapp *cape*
Kavīr *salt desert*
Kefar *village*
Kënet' *lagoon, lake*
Kep *cape, point*
Kepulauan *archipelago, islands*
Khalīg, Khalīj *bay, gulf*
Khirb-at, -et *ancient site, ruins*
Khrebet *mountain range*
Kinh *canal*
Klint *bluff, cliff*
Kō *bay, cove, harbor*
Ko *island, lake*
Koh *island, mountain, range*
Köl-i *lake*
Kólpos *gulf*
Kong *mountain, king*
Körfez, -i *bay, gulf*
Kosa *spit of land*
Kou *estuary, river mouth*
Kowtal-e *pass*
Krasn-yy, -aya, -oye *red*
Kronprince *crown prince*
Kryazh *mountain range, ridge*
Kuala *estuary, river mouth*
Kuan *mountain pass*
Kūh, Kūhhā *mountain-s, range*
Kul', Kuli *lake*
Kum *sandy desert*
Kundo *archipelago*
Kuppe *hill-s, mountain-s*
Kust *coast, shore*
Kyst *coast*
Kyun *island*

La *pass*
Lac, Lac-ul, -us *lake*
Lae *cape, point*
Lago, -a *lagoon, lake*
Lagoen, Lagune *lagoon*
Laguna-s *lagoon-s, lake-s*
Laht *bay, gulf, harbor*
Laje *reef, rock ledge*
Laut *sea*
Lednik *glacier*
Leida *channel*
Lhari *mountain*
Li *village*
Liedao *archipelago, islands*
Liehtao *archipelago, islands*
Liman-ı *bay, estuary*
Límni *lake*
Ling *mountain-s, range*
Linn *pool, waterfall*
Lintasan *passage*
Liqen *lake*
Llano-s *plain-s*
Loch, Lough *lake, arm of the sea*
Loma-s *hill-s, knoll-s*
Mal *mountain, range*
Mal-yy, -aya, -oye *little, small*
Mamarr *pass, path*
Man *bay*
Mar, Mare *large lake, sea*
Marsa, Marsá *bay, inlet*
Masabb *mouth of river*
Massif *massif, mountain-s*
Mauna *mountain*
Mēda *plain*
Meer *lake, sea*
Melkosopochnik *undulating plain*
Mesa, Meseta *plateau, tableland*
Mierzeja *sandspit*
Minami *south*
Mios *island*
Misaki *cape, peninsula, point*
Mochun *passage*
Molsron *harbor*
Mong *town, village*
Mont-e, -i, -s *mount, -ain, -s*
Montagne, -s *mount, -ain, -s*
Montaña, -s *mountain, -s*
More *sea*
Morne *hill, peak*
Morro *bluff, headland, hill*
Motu, -s *islands*
Mouïet *well*
Mouillage *anchorage*
Muang *town, village*
Mui *cape, point*
Mull *headland, promontory*
Munkhafad *depression*
Munte *mountain*
Munți-i *mountains*
Muong *town, village*
Mynydd *mountain*
Mys *cape*

Nacional *national*
Nada *gulf, sea*
Næs, Näs *cape, point*
Nafūd *area of dunes, desert*
Nagor'ye *mountain range, plateau*
Nahar, Nahr *river, stream*
Nakhon *town*
Namakzār *salt waste*
Ne *island, reef, rock-s*
Neem *cape, point, promontory*
Nes, Ness *peninsula, point*
Nevado-s *snow-capped mountain-s*
Nez *cape, promontory*
Ni *village*
Nísi, Nísia, Nisís, Nísoi *island-s, islet-s*
Nisídhes *islets*
Nizhn-iy, -yaya, -eye *lower*
Nizmennost' *low country*
Noord *north*
Nord-re *north-ern*
Nørre *north-ern*
Nos *cape, nose, point*
Nosy *island, reef, rock*
Nov-yy, -aya, -aye, -oye *new*
Nudo *mountain*
Numa *lake*
Nunatak, -s, -ker *peak-s surrounded by ice cap*
Nur *lake, salt lake*
Nuruu *mountain range, ridge*
Nut-en *peak*
Nuur *lake*

O-n, Ø-er *island-s*
Oblast' *administrative division, province, region*
Oceanus *ocean*
Odde-n *cape, point*
Øer-ne *islands*
Oficina *nitrate plant*
Oglat *group of wells*
Oguilet *well*
Ór-os, -i *mountain, -s*
Órmos *bay, port*
Ort *place, point*
Øst-er *east*
Ostrov, -a, Ostrv-o, -a *island, -s*
Otoci, Otok *islands, island*
Ouadi, Oued *river, watercourse*
Øy-a *island*
Øyane *islands*
Ozer-o, -a *lake, -s*

Pää *mountain, point*
Palus *marsh*
Pampa-s *grassy plain-s*
Pantà *lake, reservoir*
Pantanal *marsh, swamp*
Pao, P'ao *lake*
Parbat *mountain*
Parque *park*
Pas, -ul *pass*
Paso, Passo *pass*
Passe *channel, pass*
Pasul *pass*
Pedra *rock*
Pegunungan *mountain range*
Pellg *bay, bight*
Peña *cliff, rock*
Pendi *basin*
Penedo-s *rock-s*
Péninsule *peninsula*
Peñón *point, rock*
Pereval *mountain pass*
Pertuis *strait*
Peski *sands, sandy region*
Phnom *hill, mountain, range*
Phou *mountain range*
Phu *mountain*
Piana-o *plain*
Pic, Pik, Piz *peak*
Picacho *mountain, peak*
Pico-s *peak-s*
Pistyll *waterfall*
Piton-s *peak-s*
Pivdennyy *southern*
Plaja, Playa *beach, inlet, shore*
Planalto, Plato *plateau*
Planina *mountain, plateau*
Plassen *lake*
Ploskogor'ye *plateau, upland*
Pointe *point*
Polder *reclaimed land*
Poluostrov *peninsula*
Pongo *water gap*
Ponta, -l *cape, point*
Ponte *bridge*
Poolsaar *peninsula*
Portezuelo *pass*
Porto *port*
Poulo *island*
Praia *beach, seashore*
Presa *reservoir*
Presidente *president*
Presqu'île *peninsula*
Prins *prince*
Prinsesse *princess*
Prokhod *pass*
Proliv *strait*
Promontorio *promontory*
Průsmyk *mountain pass*
Przylądek *cape*
Puerto *bay, pass, port*
Pulao *island-s*
Pulau, Pulo *island*
Puncak *peak, summit, top*
Punt, Punta, -n *point, -s*
Pun *peak*
Pu'u *hill, mountain*
Puy *peak*

Qā' *depression, marsh, mud flat*
Qal'at *fort*
Qal'eh *castle, fort*
Qanâ *canal*
Qārat *hill-s, mountain-s*
Qaṣr *castle, fort, hill*
Qila *fort*
Qiryat *settlement, suburb*
Qolleh *peak*
Qooriga *anchorage, bay*
Qoz *dunes, sand ridge*
Qu *canal*
Quebrada *ravine, stream*
Qullai *peak, summit*
Qum *desert, sand*
Qundao *archipelago, islands*
Qurayyāt *hills*

Raas *cape, point*
Rabt *hill*
Rada *roadstead*
Rade *anchorage, roadstead*
Rags *point*
Ramat *hill, mountain*
Rand *ridge of hills*
Rann *swamp*
Raqaba *wadi, watercourse*
Ras, Râs, Ra's *cape*
Ravnina *plain*
Récif-s *reef-s*
Regreg *marsh*
Represa *reservoir*
Reservatório *reservoir*
Restinga *barrier, sand area*
Rettō *chain of islands*
Ri *mountain range, village*
Ría *estuary*
Ribeirão *stream*
Río, Rio *river*
Roca-s *cliff, rock-s*
Roche-r, -s *rock-s*
Rosh *mountain, point*
Rt *cape, point*
Rubha *headland*
Rupes *scarp*

Saar *island*
Saari, Sari *island*
Sabkha-t, Sabkhet *lagoon, marsh, salt lake*
Sagar *lake, sea*
Sahara, Ṣaḩrā' *desert*
Sahl *plain*
Saki *cape, point*
Salar *salt flat*
Salina *salt pan*
Salin-as, -es *salt flat-s, salt marsh-es*
Salto *waterfall*
Sammyaku *mountain range*
San *hill, mountain*
San, -ta, -to *saint*
Sandur *sandy area*
Sankt *saint*
Sanmaek *mountain range*
São *saint*
Sarīr *gravel desert*
Sasso *mountain, stone*
Savane *savanna*
Scoglio *reef, rock*
Se *reef, rock-s, shoal-s*
Sebjet *salt lake, salt marsh*
Sebkha *salt lake, salt marsh*
Sebkhet *lagoon, salt lake*
See *lake, sea*
Selat *strait*
Selkä *lake, ridge*
Semenanjung *peninsula*
Sen *mountain*
Seno *bay, gulf*
sermeq, sermia *glacier*
Serra, Serranía *range of hills or mountains*
Severn-yy, -aya, -oye *northern*
Sgùrr *peak*
Sha *island, shoal*
Sha'īb *ravine, watercourse*
Shamo *desert*
Shan *island-s, mountain-s, range*
Shankou *mountain pass*
Shanmo *mountain range*
Sharm *cove, creek, harbor*
Shatt, Shaṭṭ *large river*
Shi *administrative division, municipality*
Shima *island-s, rock-s*
Shō *island, reef, rock*
Shotō *archipelago*
Shott *intermittent salt lake*
Shuiku *reservoir*
Shuitao *channel*
Shyghanaghy *bay, gulf*
Sierra *mountain range*
Silsilesi *mountain chain, ridge*
Sint *saint*
Sinus *bay, sea*
Sjö-n *lake*
Skarv-et *barren mountain*
Skerry *rock*
Slieve *mountain*
Sø, Sø-er *lake, lake-s*
Sønder, Søndre *south-ern*
Sopka *conical mountain, volcano*
Sor *lake, salt lake*
Sør, Sör *south-ern*
Sory *salt lake, salt marsh*
Spitz-e *peak, point, top*
Sredn-iy, -yaya, -eye *central, middle*
Stagno *lake, pond*
Stantsiya *station*
Stausee *reservoir*
Stenón *channel, strait*
Step'-i *steppe-s*
Štít *summit, top*
Stor-e *big, great*
Straat *strait*
Straum-en *current-s*
Strelka *spit of land*
Stretet, Stretto *strait*
Su *reef, river, rock, stream*
Sud *south*
Sudo *channel, strait*
Suidō *channel, strait*
Şummān *rocky desert*
Sund *sound, strait*
Sunden *channel, inlet, sound*
Svyat-oy, -aya, -oye *holy, saint*
Sziget *island*

Tagh *mountain-s*
Tall *hill, mound*
T'an *lake*
Tanezrouft *desert*
Tang *plain, steppe*
Tangi *peninsula, point*
Tanjong, Tanjung *cape, point*
Tao *island-s*
Tarso *hill-s, mountain-s*
Tassili *plateau, upland*
Tau *mountain-s, range*
Taūy *hills, mountains*
Tchabal *mountain-s*
Te Ava *tidal flat*
Tel-l *hill, mound*
Telok, Teluk *bay*
Tepe, -si *hill, peak*
Tepuí *mesa, mountain*
Terara *hill, mountain, peak*
Testa *bluff, head*
Thale *lake*
Thang *plain, steppe*
Tien *lake*
Tierra *land, region*
Ting *hill, mountain*
Tir'at *canal*
Tō *lake, pool*
To, Tō *island-s, rock-s*
Tonle *lake*
Tope *hill, mountain, peak*
Top-pen *peak-s*
Träsk *bog, lake*
Tso *lake*
Tsui *cape, point*
Tübegi *peninsula*
Tulu *hill, mountain*
Tunturi-t *hill-s, mountain-s*

Uad *wadi, watercourse*
Udde-m *point*
Ujong, Ujung *cape, point*
Umi *bay, lagoon, lake*
Ura *bay, inlet, lake*
'Urūq *dune area*
Uul, Uula *mountain, range*
'Uyûn *springs*

Vaara *mountain*
Vaart *canal*
Vær *fishing station*
Vaïn *channel, strait*
Valle, Vallée *valley, wadi*
Vallen *waterfall*
Valli *lagoon, lake*
Vallis *valley*
Vanua *land*
Varre *mountain*
Vatn, Vatten, Vatnet *lake, water*
Veld *grassland, plain*
Verkhn-iy, -yaya, -eye *higher, upper*
Vesi *lake, water*
Vest-er *west*
Via *road*
Vidda *plateau*
Vig, Vík, Vik, -en *bay, cove*
Vinh *bay, gulf*
Vodokhranilishche *reservoir*
Vodoskhovyshche *reservoir*
Volcan, Volcán *volcano*
Vostochn-yy, -aya, -oye *eastern*
Vötn *stream*
Vozvyshennost' *plateau, upland*
Vozyera, -yero, -yera *lake-s*
Vrchovina *mountains*
Vrch-y *mountain-s*
Vrh *hill, mountain*
Vrŭkh *mountain*
Vyaliki, -ikaya, -ikaye *big, large*
Vysočina *highland*

Wabē *stream*
Wadi, Wâdi, Wādī *valley, watercourse*
Wâhât, Wāḩat *oasis*
Wald *forest, wood*
Wan *bay, gulf*
Water *harbor*
Webi *stream*
Wiek *cove, inlet*

Xia *gorge, strait*
Xiao *lesser, little*

Yanchi *salt lake*
Yang *ocean*
Yarymadasy *peninsula*
Yazovir *reservoir*
Yölto *island group*
Yoma *mountain range*
Yü *island*
Yumco *lake*
Yunhe *canal*
Yuzhn-yy, -aya, -oye *southern*

Zaki *cape, point*
Zaliv *bay, gulf*
Zan *mountain, ridge*
Zangbo *river, stream*
Zapadn-yy, -aya, -oye *western*
Zatoka *bay, gulf*
Zee *bay, sea*
Zemlya *land*
Zhotasy *mountains*

A

150 Mile House, *Can.* 52°7' N, 121°57" W **108**
19 de Abril, *Uru.* 34°23' S, 54°5' W **139**
23 August, *Rom.* 43°55' N, 28°35' E **156**
25 de Mayo, *Arg.* 35°26' S, 60°12' W **139**
26 Baky Komissary, *Azerb.* 39°18' N, 49°10' E **195**
2nd Cataract, fall(s), *Sudan* 21°54' N, 30°50' E **226**
31 de Janeiro, *Angola* 6°53' S, 15°18' E **218**
31 de Março, Pico, peak, *Braz.* 0°48' N, 66°0' W **136**
3rd Cataract, fall(s), *Sudan* 19°55' N, 29°47' E **226**
6th Cataract, fall(s), *Sudan* 16°29' N, 32°36' E **182**
9 de Julio, *Arg.* 35°26' S, 60°54' W **139**
A Coruña, *Sp.* 43°21' N, 8°27' W **150**
Aa, river, *Ger.* 52°26' N, 7°28' E **163**
Aachen, *Ger.* 50°46' N, 6°5' E **167**
Aagaard Islands, *Indian Ocean* 65°36' S, 52°31' E **248**
Aalsmeer, *Neth.* 52°15' N, 4°45' E **163**
Aalst, *Belg.* 50°56' N, 4°2' E **163**
Aalten, *Neth.* 51°55' N, 6°34' E **167**
Äänekoski, *Fin.* 62°36' N, 25°41' E **152**
Aansluit, *S. Af.* 26°46' S, 22°30' E **227**
Aapajärvi, *Fin.* 67°13' N, 27°16' E **152**
Aarau, *Switz.* 47°22' N, 8°1' E **156**
Aare, river, *Switz.* 47°6' N, 7°20' E **165**
Aarschot, *Belg.* 50°58' N, 4°49' E **167**
Aasiaat (Egedesminde), *Den.* 68°45' N, 52°53' W **106**
Aavasaksa, *Fin.* 66°23' N, 23°42' E **152**
Aba, *Dem. Rep. of the Congo* 3°51' N, 30°17' E **224**
Aba, *Nig.* 5°9' N, 7°23' E **222**
Abā as Sa'ūd, *Saudi Arabia* 17°27' N, 44°8' E **182**
Abacaxis, river, *Braz.* 5°29' S, 58°39' W **130**
Abaclia, *Mold.* 46°22' N, 28°55' E **156**
Abaco Island, *Bahamas* 26°0' N, 77°0' W **118**
Abaco Islands, *North Atlantic Ocean* 27°0' N, 77°0' W **118**
Abadab, Jebel, peak, *Sudan* 18°52' N, 35°52' E **182**
Ābādān, *Iran* 30°20' N, 48°21' E **180**
Ābādeh, *Iran* 31°6' N, 52°39' E **180**
Abádszalók, *Hung.* 47°29' N, 20°35' E **168**
Abaeté, *Braz.* 19°9' S, 45°25' W **138**
Abaetetuba, *Braz.* 1°45' S, 48°54' W **130**
Abag Qi (Xin Hot), *China* 44°1' N, 114°56' E **198**
Abaí, *Parag.* 26°1' S, 55°53' W **139**
Abaji, *Nig.* 8°28' N, 6°55' E **222**
Abajo Mountains, *Utah, U.S.* 37°57' N, 109°50' W **90**
Abajo Peak, *Utah, U.S.* 37°49' N, 109°31' W **92**
Abak, *Nig.* 4°57' N, 7°47' E **222**
Abakaliki, *Nig.* 6°17' N, 8°5' E **222**
Abakan, *Russ.* 53°42' N, 91°25' E **184**
Abakan, river, *Russ.* 52°22' N, 89°24' E **184**
Abala, *Congo* 1°19' S, 15°34' E **218**
Abala, spring, *Niger* 14°56' N, 3°27' E **222**
Abalak, *Niger* 15°19' N, 6°11' E **222**
Abalemma, spring, *Alg.* 20°57' N, 5°55' E **222**
Abalemma, spring, *Niger* 16°18' N, 7°49' E **222**
Abalessa, *Alg.* 22°55' N, 4°49' E **214**
Abancay, *Peru* 13°40' S, 72°52' W **137**
Abapó, *Bol.* 18°52' S, 63°30' W **137**
Ābār al Hazīm, spring, *Jordan* 31°35' N, 37°13' E **194**
Abâr el Kanâyis, spring, *Egypt* 31°0' N, 26°47' E **180**
Abarán, *Sp.* 38°12' N, 1°24' W **164**
Abarqū, *Iran* 31°6' N, 53°19' E **180**
Abasān, *Gaza Strip, Israel* 31°18' N, 34°21' E **194**
Abashiri, *Japan* 43°53' N, 144°8' E **190**
Abasolo, *Mex.* 27°10' N, 101°26' W **96**
Abasolo, *Mex.* 25°18' N, 104°41' W **114**
Abasolo, *Mex.* 24°2' N, 98°23' W **114**
Abast'umani, *Ga.* 41°45' N, 42°48' E **195**
Abatskiy, *Russ.* 56°15' N, 70°27' E **184**
Abau, *P.N.G.* 10°10' S, 148°43' E **192**
Abava, river, *Latv.* 57°6' N, 22°18' E **166**
Abay, *Kaz.* 41°18' N, 68°51' E **197**
Ābay (Blue Nile), river, *Eth.* 11°15' N, 38°15' E **224**
Ābaya Hāyk', lake, *Eth.* 6°24' N, 37°45' E **224**
Abaza, *Russ.* 52°42' N, 90°7' E **184**
Abba, *Cen. Af. Rep.* 5°18' N, 15°9' E **218**
Abbaye, Point, *Mich., U.S.* 46°59' N, 88°13' W **94**
Abbeville, *Ala., U.S.* 31°33' N, 85°15' W **96**
Abbeville, *Fr.* 50°5' N, 1°49' E **163**
Abbeville, *La., U.S.* 29°57' N, 92°8' W **103**
Abbey, *Can.* 50°43' N, 108°46' W **90**
Abbotsford, *Can.* 49°2' N, 122°17' W **100**
Abbotsford, *Wis., U.S.* 44°57' N, 90°19' W **110**
Abbotsford, site, *U.K.* 55°34' N, 2°51' W **150**
Abbottabad, *Pak.* 34°7' N, 73°14' E **186**
'Abda (Eboda), ruin(s), *Israel* 30°47' N, 34°43' E **194**
Abdelmalek Ramdan, *Alg.* 36°6' N, 0°15' E **150**
Abdera, ruin(s), *Gr.* 40°55' N, 24°52' E **156**
Abdi, *Chad* 12°40' N, 21°18' E **216**
Abdulino, *Russ.* 53°38' N, 53°43' E **154**
Ab-e Istadeh-ye Moqor, lake, *Afghan.* 32°25' N, 66°51' E **186**
Ab-e Vakhan (Oxus), river, *Afghan.* 37°8' N, 72°26' E **186**
Abéché, *Chad* 13°48' N, 20°49' E **216**
Ābeltī, *Eth.* 8°9' N, 37°32' E **224**
Abelvær, *Nor.* 64°44' N, 11°14' E **152**
Abenab, *Namibia* 19°19' S, 18°7' E **220**
Abengourou, *Côte d'Ivoire* 6°41' N, 3°30' W **222**
Abenójar, *Sp.* 38°52' N, 4°22' W **164**
Abeokuta, *Nig.* 7°12' N, 3°22' E **222**
Ābera, *Eth.* 7°12' N, 35°57' E **224**
Aberaeron, *U.K.* 52°13' N, 4°15' W **162**
Abercorn see Mbala, *Zambia* 8°53' S, 31°23' E **224**
Aberdare, *U.K.* 51°42' N, 3°26' W **162**
Aberdeen, *Idaho, U.S.* 42°57' N, 112°50' W **90**
Aberdeen, *Md., U.S.* 39°30' N, 76°11' W **94**
Aberdeen, *Miss., U.S.* 33°49' N, 88°33' W **96**
Aberdeen, *N.C., U.S.* 35°7' N, 79°26' W **96**
Aberdeen, *Ohio, U.S.* 38°39' N, 83°45' W **102**
Aberdeen, *S. Af.* 32°29' S, 24°4' E **227**
Aberdeen, *S. Dak., U.S.* 45°26' N, 98°30' W **90**
Aberdeen, *U.K.* 57°8' N, 2°8' W **150**
Aberdeen, *Wash., U.S.* 46°58' N, 123°50' W **100**
Aberdeen Lake, lake, *Can.* 64°17' N, 101°1' W **106**
Aberdyfi, *U.K.* 52°32' N, 4°2' W **162**
Aberedw, *U.K.* 52°6' N, 3°20' W **162**
Abergavenny, *U.K.* 51°49' N, 3°1' W **162**
Abergele, *U.K.* 53°17' N, 3°35' W **162**
Abersychan, *U.K.* 51°44' N, 3°3' W **162**
Abert, Lake, *Oreg., U.S.* 42°42' N, 120°35' W **82**
Abertawe see Swansea, *U.K.* 51°37' N, 3°57' W **162**
Abertillery, *U.K.* 51°43' N, 3°8' W **162**
Aberystwyth, *U.K.* 52°25' N, 4°4' W **162**
Abez', *Russ.* 66°28' N, 61°49' E **169**
Abhā, *Saudi Arabia* 18°11' N, 42°30' E **182**
Ābhē Bid Hāyk', lake, *Eth.* 11°2' N, 40°54' E **216**
Abibe, Serranía de, *Col.* 7°44' N, 76°42' W **136**
'Abidiya, *Sudan* 18°12' N, 33°59' E **182**
Abidjan, *Côte d'Ivoire* 5°20' N, 4°12' W **222**
Abijatta-Shalla Lakes National Park, *Eth.* 7°16' N, 37°53' E **224**
Abilene, *Kans., U.S.* 38°53' N, 97°12' W **90**
Abilene, *Tex., U.S.* 32°26' N, 99°44' W **92**
Abingdon, *Mo., U.S.* 40°47' N, 90°24' W **94**
Abingdon, *U.K.* 51°40' N, 1°18' W **162**
Abingdon, *Va., U.S.* 36°42' N, 81°59' W **96**
Abington, *Conn., U.S.* 41°51' N, 72°1' W **104**
Abiquiu, *N. Mex., U.S.* 36°11' N, 106°19' W **92**
Abisko, *Nor.* 68°20' N, 18°47' E **152**
Abita Springs, *La., U.S.* 30°28' N, 90°2' W **103**
Abitau, river, *Can.* 60°23' N, 108°5' W **108**
Abitibi, Lake, *Can.* 48°36' N, 80°21' W **110**
Ābīy Ādī, *Eth.* 13°34' N, 38°59' E **182**
Abja Paluoja, *Est.* 58°6' N, 25°20' E **166**
Abkhazia, special sovereignty, *Ga.* 42°59' N, 41°14' E **195**
Abnūb, *Egypt* 27°18' N, 31°8' E **180**
Åbo see Turku, *Fin.* 60°27' N, 22°15' E **166**
Aboa, station, *Antarctica* 73°4' S, 13°21' W **248**
Aboabo, *Philippines* 9°9' N, 118°7' E **203**
Abohar, *India* 30°9' N, 74°11' E **186**
Aboisso, *Côte d'Ivoire* 5°25' N, 3°15' W **222**
Abomey, *Benin* 7°13' N, 1°57' E **222**
Abondance, *Fr.* 46°16' N, 6°44' E **167**
Abong Mbang, *Cameroon* 3°59' N, 13°12' E **218**
Abongabong, peak, *Indonesia* 4°14' N, 96°41' E **196**
Abony, *Hung.* 47°11' N, 20°1' E **168**
Aborlan, *Philippines* 9°27' N, 118°33' E **203**
Abou Deïa, *Chad* 11°27' N, 19°18' E **216**
Abou Goulem, *Chad* 13°35' N, 21°39' E **216**
Abra Pampa, *Arg.* 22°42' S, 65°44' W **137**
Abrantes, *Port.* 39°29' N, 8°16' W **214**
Abreojos, Punta, *Mex.* 26°44' N, 114°58' W **112**
Abreschviller, *Fr.* 48°38' N, 7°5' E **163**
Abreú, *Dom. Rep.* 19°41' N, 69°59' W **116**
Abreuvoir Timg'aouine, spring, *Alg.* 21°40' N, 4°29' E **222**
Abriès, *Fr.* 44°48' N, 6°54' E **167**
Abrolhos, Arquipželago dos, *South Atlantic Ocean* 18°35' S, 39°25' W **132**
Abruka Saar, island, *Est.* 58°0' N, 22°32' E **166**
Abruzzi, adm. division, *It.* 41°59' N, 13°13' E **156**
Abruzzi, Mount, *Can.* 50°26' N, 115°13' W **90**
Absalom, Mount, *Antarctica* 80°26' S, 26°24' W **248**
Absaroka Range, *Wyo., U.S.* 44°17' N, 110°13' W **90**
Absarokee, *Mont., U.S.* 45°29' N, 109°26' W **90**
Abu, *Japan* 34°28' N, 131°28' E **200**
Abū al Abyaḑ, island, *U.A.E.* 24°17' N, 53°46' E **182**
Abū 'Alī, island, *Saudi Arabia* 27°21' N, 49°32' E **180**
Abu 'Aweigîla, *Egypt* 30°50' N, 34°6' E **194**
Abu Ballâs, peak, *Egypt* 24°27' N, 27°33' E **226**
Abū Dālī, *Syr.* 34°40' N, 36°53' E **194**
Abu Deleiq, *Sudan* 15°50' N, 33°45' E **182**
Abu Dhabi, *U.A.E.* 24°25' N, 54°14' E **196**
Abu Dis, *Sudan* 19°5' N, 33°38' E **182**
Abu Dulu, Qoz, *Sudan* 15°50' N, 31°47' E **182**
Abu Gabra, *Sudan* 11°4' N, 26°43' E **224**
Abu Gamal, *Sudan* 15°6' N, 36°24' E **182**
Abu Gubeiha, *Sudan* 11°26' N, 31°17' E **218**
Abu Hamed, *Sudan* 19°31' N, 33°19' E **182**
Abu Hashim, *Sudan* 12°59' N, 34°21' E **182**
Abū Kamāl, *Syr.* 34°27' N, 40°54' E **180**
Abu Matariq, *Sudan* 10°56' N, 26°14' E **224**
Abū Mūsá, island, *Iran* 25°55' N, 54°49' E **180**
Abū Nā'im, spring, *Lib.* 28°57' N, 18°46' E **216**
Abu Qurqâș, *Egypt* 27°58' N, 30°47' E **180**
Abu Road, *India* 24°28' N, 72°47' E **186**
Abu Safah, oil field, *Saudi Arabia* 27°5' N, 50°39' E **196**
Abu Saiyal, spring, *Sudan* 17°16' N, 31°12' E **182**
Abu Shagara, Ras, *Sudan* 21°6' N, 37°15' E **182**
Abu Shanab, *Sudan* 13°55' N, 27°43' E **226**
Abu Simbel, *Egypt* 24°25' N, 33°0' E **182**
Abu Simbel, site, *Egypt* 22°19' N, 31°29' E **182**
Abu Sôma, Râs, *Egypt* 26°31' N, 34°1' E **180**
Abu Sufyan, *Sudan* 11°55' N, 26°21' E **216**
Abu Șuweir, *Egypt* 30°32' N, 32°4' E **194**
Abu Tabari, spring, *Sudan* 17°30' N, 28°29' E **226**
Abu Tîg, *Egypt* 27°3' N, 31°14' E **180**
Abu 'Uruq, *Sudan* 15°53' N, 30°25' E **226**
Abu Zabad, *Sudan* 12°20' N, 29°13' E **216**
Abu Zenîma, *Egypt* 29°2' N, 33°6' E **180**
Abuja, *Nig.* 9°4' N, 7°2' E **222**
Abulug, *Philippines* 18°25' N, 121°26' E **203**
Abumombazi, *Dem. Rep. of the Congo* 3°32' N, 22°2' E **218**
Abunã, *Braz.* 9°42' S, 65°22' W **137**
Abunã, river, *South America* 10°24' S, 67°6' W **137**
Ābūr, *Jordan* 30°48' N, 35°42' E **194**
Aburatsu, *Japan* 31°34' N, 131°23' E **201**
Ābuyē Mēda, peak, *Eth.* 10°30' N, 39°43' E **224**
Abwong, *Sudan* 9°5' N, 32°9' E **224**
Abyad, *Sudan* 13°44' N, 26°29' E **226**
Abyad Plateau, Jebel, *Sudan* 19°0' N, 26°57' E **226**
Abyār al Ḩakīm, spring, *Lib.* 31°35' N, 23°27' E **180**
Åbybro, *Den.* 57°8' N, 9°43' E **150**
Abyei, *Sudan* 9°34' N, 28°26' E **224**
Abyek, *Iran* 36°1' N, 50°36' E **180**
Açailândia, *Braz.* 4°57' S, 47°42' W **130**
Acala, *Mex.* 16°34' N, 92°49' W **115**
Acámbaro, *Mex.* 20°0' N, 100°43' W **114**
Acancéh, *Mex.* 20°47' N, 89°27' W **116**
Acandí, *Col.* 8°31' N, 77°19' W **136**
Acaponeta, *Mex.* 22°29' N, 105°22' W **114**
Acaponeta, river, *Mex.* 23°39' N, 105°17' W **114**
Acapulco, *Mex.* 16°51' N, 99°55' W **112**
Acaraí, Serra, *Guyana* 1°50' N, 57°38' W **130**
Acaraú, *Braz.* 2°55' S, 40°7' W **132**
Acari, *Peru* 15°28' S, 74°35' W **137**
Acari, river, *Braz.* 5°32' S, 60°5' W **130**
Acari, river, *Peru* 15°19' S, 74°37' W **137**
Acaricuara, *Col.* 0°36' N, 70°22' W **136**
Acarigua, *Venez.* 9°34' N, 69°13' W **136**
Acatenango, Volcán de, *Guatemala* 14°28' N, 90°58' W **115**
Acatlán, *Mex.* 18°11' N, 98°5' W **114**
Acayucan, *Mex.* 17°56' N, 94°55' W **114**
Accomac, *Va., U.S.* 37°42' N, 75°41' W **94**
Accous, *Fr.* 42°58' N, 0°35' E **164**
Accra, *Ghana* 5°34' N, 0°22' E **222**
Accrington, *U.K.* 53°45' N, 2°23' W **162**
Aceguá, *Braz.* 31°52' S, 54°12' W **139**
Achacachi, *Bol.* 16°8' S, 68°43' W **137**
Achaguas, *Venez.* 7°47' N, 68°16' W **136**
Achahoish, *U.K.* 55°56' N, 5°34' W **150**
Achalpur, *India* 21°17' N, 77°30' E **188**
Achar, *Uru.* 32°25' S, 56°10' W **139**
Achegour, spring, *Niger* 19°4' N, 11°45' E **222**
Acheng, *China* 45°32' N, 126°55' E **198**
Achénouma, *Niger* 19°14' N, 12°57' E **216**
Acheux, *Fr.* 50°4' N, 2°33' E **163**
Achikulak, *Russ.* 44°31' N, 44°47' E **158**
Achinsk, *Russ.* 56°16' N, 90°41' E **169**
Achisu, *Russ.* 42°37' N, 47°45' E **195**
Achit, *Russ.* 56°48' N, 57°56' E **154**
Achna, *Northern Cyprus, Cyprus* 35°2' N, 33°46' E **194**
Acht, Hohe, peak, *Ger.* 50°22' N, 6°58' E **167**
Achuyevo, *Russ.* 45°44' N, 37°43' E **156**
Achwa (Moroto), river, *Uganda* 2°14' N, 32°58' E **224**
Achwa, river, *Uganda* 3°31' N, 32°12' E **224**
Acıgöl, lake, *Turk.* 37°49' N, 29°43' E **156**
Acıpayam, *Turk.* 37°25' N, 29°20' E **156**
Acîș, *Rom.* 47°30' N, 22°48' E **168**
Ackerman, *Miss., U.S.* 33°17' N, 89°11' W **103**
Ackley, *Iowa, U.S.* 42°32' N, 93°3' W **94**
Acklins and Crooked Islands, adm. division, *Bahamas* 22°52' N, 74°50' W **116**
Acklins Island, *Bahamas* 22°22' N, 75°3' W **116**
Acle, *U.K.* 52°38' N, 1°32' E **163**
Acobamba, *Peru* 12°53' S, 74°33' W **137**
Acoma Pueblo, site, *N. Mex., U.S.* 34°54' N, 107°40' W **92**
Acomayo, *Peru* 13°56' S, 71°41' W **137**
Acona, *Miss., U.S.* 33°15' N, 90°2' W **103**
Aconcagua, Cerro, *Arg.* 32°33' S, 69°57' W **134**
Aconchi, *Mex.* 29°49' N, 110°14' W **92**
Aconi, Point, *Can.* 46°21' N, 60°50' W **111**
Acora, *Peru* 16°1' S, 69°46' W **137**
Açores see Azores, islands, *Port.* 39°29' N, 27°35' W **207**
Acoyapa, *Nicar.* 11°55' N, 85°9' W **115**
Acqui Terme, *It.* 44°41' N, 8°28' E **167**
Acrae, ruin(s), *It.* 37°1' N, 14°47' E **156**
Acre, adm. division, *Braz.* 9°34' S, 70°21' W **137**
Acre, river, *Braz.* 10°24' S, 68°2' W **137**
Acre see 'Akko, *Israel* 32°55' N, 35°4' E **194**
Ács, *Hung.* 47°41' N, 18°2' E **156**
Actéon, Groupe, islands, *South Pacific Ocean* 21°2' S, 137°14' W **238**
Actium, ruin(s), *Gr.* 38°55' N, 20°39' E **156**
Acton, *Calif., U.S.* 34°28' N, 118°13' W **101**
Acton, *Me., U.S.* 43°31' N, 70°55' W **104**
Actopan, *Mex.* 20°15' N, 98°56' W **114**
Açuã, river, *Braz.* 7°39' S, 64°12' W **130**
Acuitzio, *Mex.* 19°29' N, 101°21' W **114**
Acuruaú, river, *Braz.* 8°44' S, 71°25' W **130**
Açurizal, *Braz.* 15°11' S, 56°24' W **132**
Acworth, *N.H., U.S.* 43°12' N, 72°18' W **104**
Ad Dahnā', *Saudi Arabia* 26°39' N, 46°15' E **196**
Ad Dakhla, *Western Sahara, Mor.* 23°42' N, 15°58' W **214**
Ad Ḑāli', *Yemen* 13°41' N, 44°44' E **182**
Ad Dammām, *Saudi Arabia* 26°23' N, 50°5' E **196**
Ad Dār al Ḩamrā', *Saudi Arabia* 27°21' N, 37°41' E **180**
Ad Dawādimī, *Saudi Arabia* 24°29' N, 44°23' E **182**
Ad Dawḩah (Doha), *Qatar* 25°13' N, 51°25' E **196**
Ad Dibdibah, region, *Asia* 28°10' N, 46°32' E **180**
Ad Dilam, *Saudi Arabia* 23°57' N, 47°13' E **196**
Ad Dīwānīyah, *Iraq* 31°59' N, 44°51' E **180**
Ad Durūz, Jabal, peak, *Syr.* 32°39' N, 36°41' E **194**
Ada, *Ghana* 5°46' N, 0°34' E **222**
Ada, *Minn., U.S.* 47°16' N, 96°32' W **90**
Ada, *Ohio, U.S.* 40°45' N, 83°50' W **102**
Ada, *Okla., U.S.* 34°45' N, 96°40' W **92**
Ada, *Serb.* 45°48' N, 20°7' E **168**
Adâfer el Abiod, region, *Africa* 18°47' N, 10°37' W **222**
Adailo, *Eritrea* 14°26' N, 40°50' E **182**
Adair, Bahía de, *Mex.* 31°22' N, 114°33' W **80**
Adair, Cape, *Can.* 71°24' N, 71°5' W **106**
Adak, *Nor.* 65°20' N, 18°34' E **152**
Adak, island, *Alas., U.S.* 51°18' N, 176°44' W **160**
Adaleh, spring, *Eth.* 7°27' N, 46°22' E **218**
Adam, *Oman* 22°23' N, 57°30' E **182**
Adam, Mount, *U.K.* 51°37' S, 60°5' W **134**
Adam Peak, *Nev., U.S.* 41°9' N, 117°24' W **90**
Adamantina, *Braz.* 21°41' S, 51°5' W **138**
Adamello, peak, *It.* 46°9' N, 10°27' E **167**
Adamovka, *Russ.* 51°32' N, 59°53' E **154**
Adams, *Mass., U.S.* 42°36' N, 73°8' W **104**
Adams, *Minn., U.S.* 43°33' N, 92°43' W **94**
Adams, *Wis., U.S.* 43°56' N, 89°49' W **94**
Adams, Cape, *Antarctica* 75°10' S, 61°57' W **248**
Adams Lake, *Can.* 51°15' N, 120°1' W **90**
Adams, Mount, *Wash., U.S.* 46°11' N, 121°33' W **100**
Adams Mountain, *Mass., U.S.* 42°40' N, 72°55' W **104**
Adam's Peak, *Sri Lanka* 6°46' N, 80°24' E **188**
Adams Point, *Mich., U.S.* 45°24' N, 83°41' W **94**
Adamstown, *Pitcairn Is., U.K.* 25°0' S, 130°0' W **241**
Adamsville, *Tenn., U.S.* 35°13' N, 88°23' W **96**
Adamuz, *Sp.* 38°1' N, 4°32' W **164**
'Adan (Aden), *Yemen* 12°46' N, 44°59' E **182**
'Adan aș Șughrá, *Yemen* 12°35' N, 44°1' E **182**
Adana, *Turk.* 36°59' N, 35°18' E **156**
Adapazarı, *Turk.* 40°46' N, 30°25' E **156**
Adar Doutchi, region, *Africa* 14°33' N, 5°50' E **222**
Adarama, *Sudan* 17°3' N, 34°54' E **182**
Adare Peninsula, *Antarctica* 71°10' S, 175°59' E **248**
Addington, *Okla., U.S.* 34°13' N, 97°58' W **92**
Addis, *La., U.S.* 30°19' N, 91°17' W **103**
Addis Ababa see Ādīs Ābeba, *Eth.* 8°58' N, 38°34' E **224**
Addison, *Vt., U.S.* 44°5' N, 73°19' W **104**
Addo, *S. Af.* 33°34' S, 25°42' E **227**
Addo Elephant National Park, *S. Af.* 33°31' S, 25°41' E **227**
Addu Atoll, *Maldives* 0°54' N, 72°39' E **188**
Addy, *Wash., U.S.* 48°20' N, 117°50' W **90**
Adel, *Ga., U.S.* 31°7' N, 83°26' W **96**
Adel, *Oreg., U.S.* 42°11' N, 119°54' W **90**
Adelaide, *Austral.* 34°59' S, 138°14' E **230**
Adelaide Island, *Antarctica* 66°56' S, 72°20' W **248**
Adelaide Peninsula, *Can.* 67°53' N, 97°8' W **106**
Adelanto, *Calif., U.S.* 34°35' N, 117°26' W **101**
Adélfi, islands, *Aegean Sea* 36°26' N, 26°40' E **156**
Adelia María, *Arg.* 33°39' S, 64°2' W **139**
Adélie Coast, *Antarctica* 66°59' S, 145°40' E **248**
Adelunga Toghi, peak, *Uzb.* 42°7' N, 70°59' E **197**
Ademuz, *Sp.* 40°3' N, 1°18' W **164**
Aden, Gulf of 12°29' N, 45°45' E **173**
Aden see 'Adan, *Yemen* 12°46' N, 44°59' E **182**
Adenau, *Ger.* 50°23' N, 6°57' E **163**
Aderbissinat, *Niger* 15°39' N, 7°53' E **222**
Aderg, peak, *Mauritania* 21°24' N, 11°58' W **222**
Adh Dhayd, *U.A.E.* 25°16' N, 55°48' E **196**
Adhoi, *India* 23°23' N, 70°29' E **186**
Ādī Ārk'ay, *Eth.* 13°29' N, 37°55' E **182**
Adi Kaie, *Eritrea* 14°47' N, 39°22' E **182**
Adi Quala, *Eritrea* 14°38' N, 38°49' E **182**
Ādī Ramets', *Eth.* 13°49' N, 37°22' E **182**
Adi Ugri, *Eritrea* 14°52' N, 38°50' E **182**
Adiaké, *Côte d'Ivoire* 5°12' N, 3°20' W **214**
Adie Inlet, *Antarctica* 66°40' S, 63°15' W **248**
Ādīgala, *Eth.* 10°23' N, 42°17' E **224**
Adige, river, *It.* 45°11' N, 11°20' E **167**
Adigeni, *Ga.* 41°41' N, 42°42' E **195**
Ādīgrat, *Eth.* 14°16' N, 39°26' E **182**
Adilabad, *India* 19°40' N, 78°33' E **188**
Adilang, *Uganda* 2°42' N, 33°28' E **224**
Adin, *Calif., U.S.* 41°11' N, 120°58' W **90**
Adīrī, *Lib.* 27°32' N, 13°13' E **216**
Adirondack Mountains, *N.Y., U.S.* 43°57' N, 76°16' W **106**
Ādīs Ābeba (Addis Ababa), *Eth.* 8°58' N, 38°34' E **224**
Ādīs 'Alem, *Eth.* 9°2' N, 38°21' E **224**
Adıyaman, *Turk.* 37°45' N, 38°16' E **180**
Adjud, *Rom.* 46°5' N, 27°10' E **156**
Adlavik Islands, *North Atlantic Ocean* 54°39' N, 62°27' W **106**
Adler, *Russ.* 43°28' N, 40°0' E **195**
Admiralty Island, *Alas., U.S.* 57°30' N, 133°39' W **106**
Admiralty Islands, *Bismarck Sea* 3°32' S, 145°14' E **192**
Ado, *Nig.* 6°37' N, 2°55' E **222**
Ado Ekiti, *Nig.* 7°38' N, 5°13' E **222**
Adobe Flat, *Nev., U.S.* 40°2' N, 119°8' W **90**
Adok, *Sudan* 8°7' N, 30°17' E **224**
Adolfo López Mateos, *Mex.* 28°26' N, 107°23' W **92**
Adolfo López Mateos, Presa, lake, *Mex.* 25°10' N, 108°53' W **81**
Adoni, *India* 15°38' N, 77°16' E **188**
Adony, *Hung.* 47°6' N, 18°51' E **168**
Adorf, *Ger.* 50°19' N, 12°15' E **152**
Adour, river, *Fr.* 43°24' N, 1°10' W **214**
Adra, *Sp.* 36°44' N, 3°1' W **164**
Adranga, *Dem. Rep. of the Congo* 2°53' N, 30°25' E **224**
Adrar, *Alg.* 27°55' N, 0°18' E **214**
Adrar, region, *Mauritania* 20°22' N, 14°7' W **222**
Adraskan, *Afghan.* 33°38' N, 62°18' E **186**
Adré, *Chad* 13°26' N, 22°12' E **216**
Adria, *It.* 45°4' N, 12°1' E **167**
Adrian, *Mich., U.S.* 41°52' N, 84°2' W **102**
Adrian, *Minn., U.S.* 43°36' N, 95°56' W **90**
Adrian, *Tex., U.S.* 35°15' N, 102°40' W **92**
Adrianople see Edirne, *Turk.* 41°39' N, 26°34' E **156**
Adriatic Sea 41°51' N, 17°3' E **156**
Adun Gol, *China* 42°4' N, 107°56' E **198**
Adusa, *Dem. Rep. of the Congo* 1°24' N, 28°4' E **224**
Ādwa, *Eth.* 14°9' N, 38°52' E **182**
Adwick le Street, *U.K.* 53°33' N, 1°12' W **162**
Adycha, river, *Russ.* 66°53' N, 135°23' E **160**
Adygeya, adm. division, *Russ.* 44°59' N, 40°1' E **158**
Adzopé, *Côte d'Ivoire* 6°3' N, 3°52' W **222**
Adz'vavom, *Russ.* 66°36' N, 59°17' E **169**
Aegae, ruin(s), *Gr.* 38°8' N, 22°13' E **156**
Aegean Sea 36°34' N, 23°7' E **156**
Aegir Ridge, *Norwegian Sea* 65°42' N, 4°7' W **255**
Aegna, island, *Est.* 59°37' N, 24°35' E **166**
Aegviidu, *Est.* 59°15' N, 25°35' E **166**
Afadé, *Cameroon* 12°15' N, 14°39' E **216**
Afam, *Nig.* 4°45' N, 7°23' E **222**
Afándou, *Gr.* 36°17' N, 28°10' E **156**
Afar, region, *Africa* 12°59' N, 40°4' E **182**
Āfdem, *Eth.* 9°27' N, 41°0' E **224**
Affollé, *Mauritania* 16°21' N, 11°11' W **222**
Afghanistan 34°0' N, 66°0' E **186**
Afgooye, *Somalia* 2°5' N, 45°8' E **218**
Afgooye Caddo, *Somalia* 3°12' N, 45°33' E **218**
'Afīf, *Saudi Arabia* 23°53' N, 42°56' E **182**
Afikpo, *Nig.* 5°55' N, 7°55' E **222**
Afiq, *Israel* 32°46' N, 35°42' E **194**
Åfjord, *Nor.* 63°57' N, 10°14' E **152**
Aflou, *Alg.* 34°6' N, 2°5' E **214**
Afmadow, *Somalia* 0°28' N, 42°4' E **224**
Āfodo, *Eth.* 10°13' N, 34°47' E **224**
Afognak Island, *Alas., U.S.* 57°51' N, 151°54' W **98**
Afonso Cláudio, *Braz.* 20°6' S, 41°10' W **138**
Afqā, *Leb.* 34°4' N, 35°53' E **194**
Africa 1°0' N, 17°0' E **207**
Afşin, *Turk.* 38°14' N, 36°53' E **156**
Afton, *Okla., U.S.* 36°41' N, 94°58' W **94**
Afton, *Wyo., U.S.* 42°42' N, 110°55' W **82**
Afuá, *Braz.* 0°10' N, 50°23' W **130**
'Afula, *Israel* 32°36' N, 35°17' E **194**
Afyon, *Turk.* 38°44' N, 30°31' E **156**
Agadem, *Niger* 16°49' N, 13°17' E **216**
Agadez, *Niger* 16°59' N, 7°58' E **222**
Agadir, *Mor.* 30°25' N, 9°37' W **214**
Agaie, *Nig.* 8°59' N, 6°18' E **222**
Agalega Islands, *Indian Ocean* 12°45' S, 55°37' E **173**
Agamenticus, Mount, *Me., U.S.* 43°13' N, 70°44' W **104**
Agamor, spring, *Mali* 17°16' N, 3°178' E **222**
Agana see Hagåtña, *Guam, U.S.* 13°0' N, 145°0' E **242**
Agapa, *Russ.* 71°43' N, 89°24' E **173**
Agapovka, *Russ.* 53°20' N, 59°12' E **154**
Agar, *India* 23°43' N, 76°3' E **197**
Āgaro, *Eth.* 7°49' N, 36°37' E **224**
Agartala, *India* 23°47' N, 91°18' E **197**
Agaruut, *Mongolia* 43°18' N, 109°26' E **198**
Agassiz Fracture Zone, *South Pacific Ocean* 39°32' S, 131°55' W **252**
Agata, *Russ.* 66°51' N, 93°40' E **169**
Agata, Ozero, lake, *Russ.* 67°14' N, 92°22' E **169**
Agate, *Colo., U.S.* 39°27' N, 103°57' W **90**
Agats, *Indonesia* 5°34' S, 138°4' E **192**
Agattu, island, *Alas., U.S.* 52°17' N, 171°43' E **160**
Agawam, *Mass., U.S.* 42°3' N, 72°37' W **104**
Agbaja, *Nig.* 7°58' N, 6°38' E **222**
Agboville, *Côte d'Ivoire* 5°51' N, 4°12' W **222**
Ağdam see Akna, *Azerb.* 39°59' N, 46°54' E **195**
Ägdara see Martakert, *Asia* 40°12' N, 46°47' E **195**
Agde, *Fr.* 43°19' N, 3°27' E **164**
Agde, Cap d', *Fr.* 43°11' N, 3°30' E **165**
Agdz, *Mor.* 30°41' N, 6°29' W **214**
Agematsu, *Japan* 35°47' N, 137°43' E **201**
Agen, *Fr.* 44°14' N, 0°36' E **214**
Åger, *Sp.* 41°59' N, 0°46' E **164**
Agere Maryam, *Eth.* 5°37' N, 38°16' E **224**
Agger, river, *Ger.* 50°55' N, 7°20' E **167**
Aggi, *Eth.* 7°55' N, 35°38' E **224**
Āghā Jārī, *Iran* 30°43' N, 49°53' E **180**
Aghaylas, *Western Sahara, Mor.* 22°28' N, 14°23' W **214**
Aghdash, *Azerb.* 40°39' N, 47°28' E **195**
Aghireșu, *Rom.* 46°51' N, 23°14' E **168**
Aghjabädi, *Azerb.* 40°2' N, 47°28' E **195**
Aghsu, *Azerb.* 40°34' N, 48°25' E **195**
Aghwinit, *Western Sahara, Mor.* 22°11' N, 13°10' W **214**
Agia Napa, *Cyprus* 34°59' N, 33°59' E **194**
Agiabampo, Estero de 26°15' N, 110°30' W **80**
Agimont, *Belg.* 50°9' N, 4°45' E **163**
Agin Buryat, adm. division, *Russ.* 51°4' N, 114°22' E **190**
Aginskoye, *Russ.* 51°6' N, 114°30' E **190**
Ágio Óros (Mount Athos), *Gr.* 40°14' N, 23°2' E **156**
Ágios Nikólaos, *Gr.* 35°12' N, 25°40' E **180**
Agios Sergios, *Northern Cyprus, Cyprus* 35°11' N, 33°52' E **194**
Aglat Jrayfiya, spring, *Western Sahara, Mor.* 25°1' N, 14°18' W **214**
Agliano, *It.* 44°47' N, 8°13' E **167**
Agmar, *Mauritania* 25°18' N, 10°48' W **214**
Agnes, Mount, *Austral.* 26°55' S, 128°44' E **230**
Agnibilékrou, *Côte d'Ivoire* 7°5' N, 3°12' W **222**
Agnières, *Fr.* 44°41' N, 5°53' E **150**
Agno, river, *Philippines* 16°6' N, 120°49' E **203**
Agön, island, *Sw.* 61°29' N, 17°17' E **166**
Agoncillo, *Sp.* 42°25' N, 2°18' W **164**
Agordat, *Eritrea* 15°32' N, 37°53' E **182**
Agordo, *It.* 46°17' N, 12°2' E **167**
Agostinho, *Braz.* 9°58' S, 68°33' W **137**
Agoua, *Benin* 8°17' N, 1°57' E **222**
Agouénit, *Mauritania* 16°41' N, 7°34' W **222**
Agouma, *Gabon* 1°35' S, 10°11' E **218**
Agous-n-Ehsel, spring, *Mali* 16°20' N, 1°44' E **222**
Agout, river, *Fr.* 43°44' N, 1°47' E **165**
Agra, *India* 27°9' N, 77°59' E **197**
Agrakhanskiy Poluostrov, *Russ.* 43°41' N, 47°7' E **195**
Agramunt, *Sp.* 41°46' N, 1°6' E **164**

Agraouri, spring, *Niger* 18°16′ N, 14°14′ E 222
Agreda, *Sp.* 41°50′ N, 1°55′ W 164
Ağrı Dağı (Ararat, Mount), *Turk.* 39°42′ N, 44°15′ E 195
Ağrı (Karaköse), *Turk.* 39°43′ N, 43°3′ E 195
Agrichay, river, *Azerb.* 41°18′ N, 46°42′ E 195
Agricola, *Miss., U.S.* 30°47′ N, 88°30′ W 103
Agrigento, *It.* 37°18′ N, 13°34′ E 216
Agrihan, island, *U.S.* 18°37′ N, 144°36′ E 192
Agrínio, *Gr.* 38°35′ N, 21°22′ E 143
Agryz, *Russ.* 56°30′ N, 53°2′ E 154
Ağstafa, *Azerb.* 41°6′ N, 45°26′ E 195
Agua Brava, Laguna, lake, *Mex.* 22°8′ N, 105°49′ W 114
Água Clara, *Braz.* 20°25′ S, 52°56′ W 138
Agua Nueva, *Mex.* 25°5′ N, 101°7′ W 114
Agua Preta, river, *Braz.* 1°58′ S, 64°53′ W 130
Agua Prieta, *Mex.* 31°18′ N, 109°34′ W 92
Agua Tibia Mountain, *Calif., U.S.* 33°24′ N, 117°1′ W 101
Agua Verde, *Mex.* 22°55′ N, 105°58′ W 114
Aguachica, *Col.* 8°19′ N, 73°38′ W 136
Aguaclara, *Col.* 4°43′ N, 73°2′ W 136
Aguadas, *Col.* 5°35′ N, 75°26′ W 136
Agualeguas, *Mex.* 26°18′ N, 99°33′ W 114
Aguanga, *Calif., U.S.* 33°26′ N, 116°52′ W 101
Aguapeí, *Braz.* 16°12′ S, 59°41′ W 132
Aguapeí, Serra do, peak, *Braz.* 16°5′ S, 59°29′ W 132
Aguarey, *Arg.* 22°13′ S, 63°51′ W 137
Aguarico, river, *Ecua.* 0°18′ N, 76°27′ W 136
Aguaro-Guariquito National Park, *Venez.* 8°21′ N, 66°34′ W 136
Aguas Blancas, *Chile* 24°11′ S, 69°54′ W 132
Aguas Dulces, *Uru.* 34°20′ S, 53°50′ W 139
Águas Formosas, *Braz.* 17°5′ S, 40°59′ W 138
Aguas Negras, *Peru* 0°27′ N, 75°23′ W 136
Aguascalientes, *Mex.* 21°50′ N, 102°23′ W 114
Aguascalientes, adm. division, *Mex.* 21°45′ N, 102°53′ W 114
Aguelal, spring, *Niger* 18°44′ N, 8°6′ E 222
Aguelhok, *Mali* 19°27′ N, 0°50′ E 222
Agueraktem, spring, *Mauritania* 23°11′ N, 6°24′ W 214
Aguié, *Niger* 13°28′ N, 7°33′ E 222
Aguilâl Faye, spring, *Mauritania* 18°27′ N, 14°47′ W 222
Aguilar, *Colo., U.S.* 37°24′ N, 104°40′ W 92
Aguilar de Campoo, *Sp.* 42°46′ N, 4°16′ W 150
Águilas, *Sp.* 37°24′ N, 1°36′ W 164
Aguililla, *Mex.* 18°44′ N, 102°45′ W 114
Aguja, Cabo de la, *Col.* 11°20′ N, 75°3′ W 116
Aguja, Punta, *Peru* 5°43′ S, 82°17′ W 130
Agujita, *Mex.* 27°52′ N, 101°10′ W 92
Āgula'i, *Eth.* 13°40′ N, 39°36′ E 182
Agulhas Basin, *Indian Ocean* 46°55′ S, 24°17′ E 254
Agulhas, Cape, *S. Af.* 35°7′ S, 20°3′ E 227
Agulhas Plateau, *Indian Ocean* 39°48′ S, 26°43′ E 254
Agustín Codazzi, *Col.* 10°2′ N, 73°16′ W 136
Aha Hills, *Botswana* 19°49′ S, 20°57′ E 220
Ahaggar (Hoggar), *Alg.* 21°56′ N, 4°32′ E 222
Ahaggar National Park, *Alg.* 23°5′ N, 4°38′ E 214
Ahar, *Iran* 38°30′ N, 47°3′ E 195
Ahaus, *Ger.* 52°4′ N, 7°0′ E 163
Ahelleguen, spring, *Alg.* 25°36′ N, 7°2′ E 214
Ahipara, *N.Z.* 35°11′ S, 173°10′ E 240
Ahlainen, *Fin.* 61°40′ N, 21°36′ E 166
Ahlat, *Turk.* 38°43′ N, 42°26′ E 195
Ahlatlıbel, ruin(s), *Turk.* 39°48′ N, 32°38′ E 156
Ahlen, *Ger.* 51°46′ N, 7°54′ E 167
Ahmadabad, *India* 22°59′ N, 72°36′ E 186
Ahmadi, oil field, *Kuwait* 29°2′ N, 48°1′ E 196
Ahmadpur East, *Pak.* 29°9′ N, 71°16′ E 186
Ahmar Mountains, *Eth.* 9°9′ N, 40°49′ E 224
Ahmeyine, spring, *Mauritania* 20°53′ N, 14°28′ W 222
Ahnet, region, *Africa* 25°8′ N, 2°58′ E 214
Ahoada, *Nig.* 5°6′ N, 6°37′ E 222
Ahome, *Mex.* 25°53′ N, 109°10′ W 112
Ahoskie, *N.C., U.S.* 36°17′ N, 77°1′ W 96
Ahram, *Iran* 28°51′ N, 51°20′ E 196
Ahrensburg, *Ger.* 53°40′ N, 10°13′ E 152
Ähtäri, *Fin.* 62°32′ N, 24°4′ E 152
Ahtme, *Est.* 59°17′ N, 27°27′ E 166
Ahua 'Umi Heiau, site, *Hawai'i, U.S.* 19°37′ N, 155°50′ W 99
Ahuacatlán, *Mex.* 21°2′ N, 104°30′ W 114
Ahuachapán, *El Salv.* 13°56′ N, 89°52′ W 115
Ahualulco, *Mex.* 20°41′ N, 103°59′ W 114
Ahvāz (Ahwāz), *Iran* 31°19′ N, 48°41′ E 180
Ahvenanmaa see Åland, island, *Fin.* 60°26′ N, 19°33′ E 166
Ahwahnee, *Calif., U.S.* 37°22′ N, 119°44′ W 100
A'war, *Yemen* 13°32′ N, 46°42′ E 182
Ahwāz see Ahvāz, *Iran* 31°19′ N, 48°41′ E 180
Ai Qurayyāt, *Saudi Arabia* 31°19′ N, 37°20′ E 180
Aiari, river, *Braz.* 1°15′ N, 69°5′ W 136
Aichi, adm. division, *Japan* 35°3′ N, 136°54′ E 201
Aigialousa, *Northern Cyprus, Cyprus* 35°32′ N, 34°11′ E 194
Aigle, *Switz.* 46°20′ N, 6°58′ E 167
Aigle, Lac à l', lake, *Can.* 51°12′ N, 65°54′ W 111
Aigoual, Mont, peak, *Fr.* 44°7′ N, 3°32′ E 165
Aiguá, *Uru.* 34°14′ S, 54°44′ W 139
Aiguebelle, *Fr.* 45°32′ N, 6°18′ E 167
Aigües, *Sp.* 38°29′ N, 0°22′ E 164
Aiguilles, *Fr.* 44°47′ N, 6°51′ E 167
Aijiekebey, *China* 37°11′ N, 75°22′ E 184
Aikawa, *Japan* 38°2′ N, 138°15′ E 201
Aiken, *S.C., U.S.* 33°33′ N, 81°44′ W 96
Aileach, Grianan of, peak, *Ire.* 55°0′ N, 7°33′ W 150
Ailet Jridani, *Tun.* 35°6′ N, 10°1′ E 156
Ailigas, peak, *Fin.* 69°25′ N, 25°49′ E 152
Ailly-sur-Noye, *Fr.* 49°45′ N, 2°20′ E 163
Aim, *Russ.* 58°49′ N, 134°4′ E 160
Aimorés, *Braz.* 19°29′ S, 41°5′ W 138
Aimorés, Serra dos, *Braz.* 18°14′ S, 41°22′ W 132
'Aïn Azaz, spring, *Alg.* 27°5′ N, 3°30′ E 214
Aïn Ben Tili, *Mauritania* 25°57′ N, 9°34′ W 214
Aïn Cheikr, spring, *Alg.* 22°9′ N, 9°535′ E 222
'Ain Dalla, spring, *Egypt* 27°18′ N, 27°19′ E 180
'Aïn Deheb, *Alg.* 34°51′ N, 1°31′ E 214
Aïn Djasser, *Alg.* 35°53′ N, 6°17′ E 150
'Aïn el Berd, *Alg.* 35°20′ N, 0°31′ E 150
'Ain el Ghazâl, spring, *Egypt* 25°47′ N, 30°31′ E 180
'Aïn el Hadjel, *Alg.* 35°36′ N, 3°55′ E 214
'Ain el Qideirât (Kadesh-Barnea), spring, *Egypt* 30°39′ N, 34°25′ E 194
'Ain el Wâdi, spring, *Egypt* 27°22′ N, 28°12′ E 180
'Ain Khaleifa, spring, *Egypt* 26°44′ N, 27°46′ E 180
'Aïn M'lila, *Alg.* 36°0′ N, 6°34′ E 150
'Aïn Oussera, *Alg.* 35°26′ N, 2°55′ E 150
'Ain Qeiqab, spring, *Egypt* 29°35′ N, 24°56′ E 180
Ain, river, *Fr.* 45°52′ N, 5°17′ E 165
'Aïn Sefra, *Alg.* 32°50′ N, 0°39′ E 143
'Aïn Sefra, *Alg.* 32°47′ N, 0°37′ E 214
'Aïn Souf, spring, *Alg.* 28°6′ N, 2°14′ E 214
'Aïn Taïba, spring, *Alg.* 30°18′ N, 5°49′ E 214
'Aïn Temouchent, *Alg.* 35°17′ N, 1°9′ W 150
'Ain Tibaghbagh, spring, *Egypt* 29°6′ N, 26°24′ E 180
'Aïn Tidjoubar, spring, *Alg.* 27°46′ N, 1°22′ E 214
'Aïn Tiguift, spring, *Alg.* 26°12′ N, 3°38′ E 214
Ain Zalah, oil field, *Iraq* 36°44′ N, 42°24′ E 195
Aïna, river, *Congo* 1°30′ N, 13°14′ E 218
Ainaži, *Latv.* 57°51′ N, 24°20′ E 166
Aínos National Park, *Gr.* 38°8′ N, 20°34′ E 156
Aínsa, *Sp.* 42°25′ N, 0°7′ E 164
Ainsworth, *Nebr., U.S.* 42°31′ N, 99°53′ W 90
Aipe, *Col.* 3°13′ N, 75°18′ W 136
Aiquile, *Bol.* 18°12′ S, 65°13′ W 137
Aïr (Aïr Massif), region, *Africa* 17°26′ N, 6°28′ E 222
Air Force Island, *Can.* 67°34′ N, 76°15′ W 106
Aïr Massif see Aïr, region, *Africa* 17°26′ N, 6°28′ E 222
Airaines, *Fr.* 49°57′ N, 1°55′ E 163
Airbangis, *Indonesia* 0°14′ N, 99°22′ E 196
Airdrie, *Can.* 51°18′ N, 114°2′ W 90
Aire, *Fr.* 50°38′ N, 2°24′ E 163
Aire, river, *Fr.* 49°3′ N, 5°9′ E 163
Airiselkä, *Fin.* 66°16′ N, 23°56′ E 152
Airolo, *Switz.* 46°32′ N, 8°36′ E 167
Aisén del General Carlos IbŽañez del Campo, adm. division, *Chile* 48°43′ S, 77°8′ W 134
Aishalton, *Guyana* 2°28′ N, 59°9′ W 130
Aisne, river, *Fr.* 49°22′ N, 2°54′ E 163
Aïssa, Djebel, peak, *Alg.* 32°52′ N, 0°38′ E 214
Aït Baha, *Mor.* 30°3′ N, 9°10′ W 214
Aït Ourir, *Mor.* 31°36′ N, 7°43′ W 214
Aitape, *P.N.G.* 3°14′ S, 142°19′ E 238
Aitkin, *Minn., U.S.* 46°30′ N, 93°43′ W 94
Aitona, *Sp.* 41°29′ N, 0°27′ E 164
Aiviekste, river, *Latv.* 56°47′ N, 26°29′ E 166
Aix, Mount, *Wash., U.S.* 46°46′ N, 121°17′ W 100
Aix-en-Othe, *Fr.* 48°13′ N, 3°45′ E 163
Aix-en-Provence, *Fr.* 43°31′ N, 5°26′ E 150
Aizawl, *India* 23°39′ N, 92°42′ E 197
Aizpute, *Latv.* 56°42′ N, 21°36′ E 166
Aizuwakamatsu, *Japan* 37°29′ N, 139°54′ E 201
'Ajab Shīr, *Iran* 37°28′ N, 45°54′ E 195
Ajaccio, *Fr.* 41°55′ N, 8°41′ E 156
Ajajú, river, *Col.* 0°59′ N, 73°20′ W 136
Ajalpan, *Mex.* 18°21′ N, 97°16′ W 114
Ajax Peak, *Mont., U.S.* 45°18′ N, 113°49′ W 90
Ajdābiyā, *Lib.* 30°44′ N, 20°15′ E 216
Ajir, region, *Africa* 18°0′ N, 6°22′ E 222
Ajka, *Hung.* 47°5′ N, 17°34′ E 168
'Ajlūn, *Jordan* 32°20′ N, 35°44′ E 194
'Ajmān, *U.A.E.* 25°26′ N, 55°28′ E 196
Ajmer, *India* 26°27′ N, 74°38′ E 186
Ajo, *Ariz., U.S.* 32°22′ N, 112°51′ W 92
Ajo, Mount, *Ariz., U.S.* 32°0′ N, 112°45′ W 92
Ajuana, river, *Braz.* 1°1′ S, 65°40′ W 136
Ajuchitlán, *Mex.* 18°7′ N, 100°31′ W 114
Ajuy, *Philippines* 11°11′ N, 122°59′ E 203
Ak Dağlar, peak, *Turk.* 36°30′ N, 29°29′ E 156
Ak Dovurak, *Russ.* 51°7′ N, 90°31′ E 184
Aka, *Mali* 15°25′ N, 4°12′ W 222
Aka, river, *Dem. Rep. of the Congo* 4°3′ N, 29°25′ E 224
Akadomari, *Japan* 37°53′ N, 138°25′ E 201
Akagera National Park, *Rwanda* 1°48′ S, 30°38′ E 224
Akagi, *Japan* 34°59′ N, 132°43′ E 201
Akaki, *Cyprus* 35°7′ N, 33°7′ E 194
Akal, oil field, *Mex.* 19°26′ N, 92°7′ W 115
Akalkot, *India* 17°31′ N, 76°11′ E 188
Akanthou, *Northern Cyprus, Cyprus* 35°21′ N, 33°44′ E 194
Akaroa, *N.Z.* 43°50′ S, 172°58′ E 240
Akasaki, *Japan* 35°28′ N, 133°40′ E 201
Akashi, *Japan* 34°40′ N, 134°59′ E 201
Akaska, *S. Dak., U.S.* 45°19′ N, 100°8′ W 90
Akbulak, *Russ.* 51°1′ N, 55°38′ E 158
Akçaabat, *Turk.* 41°1′ N, 39°31′ E 195
Akçadağ, *Turk.* 38°17′ N, 37°57′ E 180
Akçakışla, *Turk.* 39°31′ N, 36°19′ E 156
Akçakoca, *Turk.* 41°4′ N, 31°8′ E 156
Akçay, *Turk.* 39°35′ N, 26°50′ E 156
Akçay, *Turk.* 36°35′ N, 29°43′ E 156
Akchâr, region, *Africa* 20°12′ N, 15°6′ W 222
Akdağ, peak, *Turk.* 38°29′ N, 26°25′ E 156
Akdağ, peak, *Turk.* 36°47′ N, 32°8′ E 156
Akdağmadeni, *Turk.* 39°39′ N, 35°54′ E 156
Akdepe, *Turkm.* 42°3′ N, 59°23′ E 180
Akelo, *Sudan* 6°55′ N, 33°38′ E 224
Akera see Hakari, river, *Azerb.* 39°28′ N, 46°37′ E 195
Åkernes, *Nor.* 58°44′ N, 7°29′ E 152
Akespe, *Kaz.* 46°48′ N, 60°32′ E 184
Aketi, *Dem. Rep. of the Congo* 2°45′ N, 23°46′ E 224
Akhalts'ikhe, *Ga.* 41°39′ N, 42°57′ E 195
Akhisar, *Turk.* 38°54′ N, 27°50′ E 156
Akhmeta, *Ga.* 42°1′ N, 45°17′ E 195
Akhmīm, *Egypt* 26°38′ N, 31°42′ E 180
Akhta, *Arm.* 40°28′ N, 44°45′ E 195
Akhtopol, *Bulg.* 42°7′ N, 27°54′ E 156
Akhtuba, river, *Russ.* 47°55′ N, 46°29′ E 158
Akhtubinsk, *Russ.* 48°17′ N, 46°10′ E 158
Aki, *Japan* 33°30′ N, 133°54′ E 201
Akie, river, *Can.* 57°15′ N, 124°59′ W 108
Akimiski Island, *Can.* 53°8′ N, 84°10′ W 106
Akita, *Japan* 39°48′ N, 140°10′ E 190
Akitio, *N.Z.* 40°37′ S, 176°23′ E 240
Akjoujt, *Mauritania* 19°43′ N, 14°24′ W 222
Akka, *Mor.* 29°24′ N, 8°15′ W 214
Akkala, *Uzb.* 43°40′ N, 59°32′ E 207
Akkaraipattu, *Sri Lanka* 7°14′ N, 81°52′ E 188
Akkarvik, *Nor.* 70°3′ N, 20°30′ E 152
'Akko (Acre), *Israel* 32°55′ N, 35°4′ E 194
Akkuş, *Turk.* 40°48′ N, 36°59′ E 156
Aklavik, *Can.* 68°13′ N, 135°6′ W 98
Aklera, *India* 24°24′ N, 76°34′ E 197
Akmenė, *Lith.* 56°15′ N, 22°41′ E 166
Akmeqit, *China* 37°7′ N, 77°0′ E 184
Akna (Ağdam), *Azerb.* 39°59′ N, 46°54′ E 195
Aknīste, *Latv.* 56°8′ N, 25°46′ E 166
Akō, *Japan* 34°45′ N, 134°22′ E 201
Akobo, *Sudan* 7°45′ N, 33°0′ E 224
Ākobo, river, *Africa* 7°0′ N, 34°13′ E 224
Akokane, *Niger* 18°43′ N, 7°9′ E 222
Akola, *India* 20°41′ N, 77°1′ E 188
Akom, *Cameroon* 2°50′ N, 10°34′ E 218
Akonolinga, *Cameroon* 3°50′ N, 12°15′ E 218
Akor, *Mali* 14°52′ N, 6°59′ W 222
Akosombo, *Ghana* 6°20′ N, 2°119′ E 222
Akosombo Dam, *Ghana* 6°1′ N, 0°14′ E 222
Akot, *India* 21°6′ N, 77°5′ E 188
Akot, *Sudan* 6°31′ N, 30°4′ E 224
Akpatok Island, *Can.* 60°24′ N, 72°3′ W 106
Akqi, *China* 40°56′ N, 78°33′ E 184
Akrabat, *Turkm.* 35°29′ N, 61°45′ E 186
'Akramah, ruin(s), *Lib.* 31°59′ N, 23°31′ E 180
Akranes, *Ice.* 64°21′ N, 22°0′ W 143
Akreidil, spring, *Mauritania* 18°29′ N, 15°39′ W 222
Akron, *Ala., U.S.* 32°52′ N, 87°44′ W 103
Akron, *Colo., U.S.* 40°9′ N, 103°13′ W 90
Akron, *Ind., U.S.* 41°1′ N, 86°1′ W 102
Akron, *Iowa, U.S.* 42°48′ N, 96°34′ W 90
Akron, *Mich., U.S.* 43°33′ N, 83°31′ W 102
Akron, *Ohio, U.S.* 41°5′ N, 81°31′ W 102
Akrotiri, *Cyprus* 34°35′ N, 32°56′ E 194
Akrotírio Apolitáres, *Gr.* 35°50′ N, 23°21′ E 156
Akrotírio Dafnoúdi, *Gr.* 38°18′ N, 19°38′ E 156
Akrotírio Doukáto, *Gr.* 38°35′ N, 19°40′ E 156
Akrotírio Gérakas, *Gr.* 36°46′ N, 23°7′ E 156
Akrotírio Ginas, *Gr.* 36°4′ N, 28°5′ E 156
Akrotírio Griá, *Gr.* 37°49′ N, 24°58′ E 156
Akrotírio Hélatros, *Gr.* 35°12′ N, 27°2′ E 156
Akrotírio Kafiéas, *Gr.* 38°9′ N, 24°37′ E 156
Akrotírio Kapélo, *Gr.* 36°4′ N, 23°4′ E 156
Akrotírio Katomfri, *Gr.* 36°50′ N, 24°36′ E 156
Akrotírio Keáli, *Gr.* 35°49′ N, 22°34′ E 156
Akrotírio Kílopas, *Gr.* 37°3′ N, 23°37′ E 156
Akrotírio Korakas, *Gr.* 39°23′ N, 25°29′ E 156
Akrotírio Maléas, *Gr.* 36°22′ N, 23°13′ E 156
Akrotírio Mestá, *Gr.* 38°15′ N, 25°6′ E 156
Akrotírio Moúnda, *Gr.* 37°59′ N, 19°56′ E 156
Akrotírio Pláka, *Gr.* 35°4′ N, 26°19′ E 156
Akrotírio Spánda, *Gr.* 35°41′ N, 23°46′ E 156
Akrotírio Spathí, *Gr.* 36°16′ N, 22°58′ E 156
Akrotírio Stavrí, *Gr.* 37°13′ N, 24°54′ E 156
Akrotírio Stenó, *Gr.* 37°14′ N, 24°58′ E 156
Akrotírio Ténaro (MatapŽas, Taenarum), *Gr.* 36°13′ N, 21°38′ E 156
Aksaray, *Turk.* 38°21′ N, 34°1′ E 156
Aksarka, *Russ.* 66°29′ N, 67°47′ E 169
Aksay, *China* 39°25′ N, 94°14′ E 188
Aksay, *Russ.* 47°56′ N, 43°59′ E 158
Aksayqin Hu, lake, *China* 35°8′ N, 78°55′ E 188
Akşehir, *Turk.* 38°20′ N, 31°25′ E 156
Akşehir Gölü, lake, *Turk.* 38°32′ N, 31°9′ E 156
Akseki, *Turk.* 37°2′ N, 31°47′ E 156
'Aksha, ruin(s), *Egypt* 22°4′ N, 31°12′ E 182
Ak-Shyyrak, *Kyrg.* 41°54′ N, 78°43′ E 184
Aksu, *China* 41°9′ N, 80°15′ E 184
Aksu, *Kaz.* 42°34′ N, 52°43′ E 158
Aksu, river, *China* 40°58′ N, 80°24′ E 184
Aksū, river, *Kaz.* 45°44′ N, 79°0′ E 184
Āksum, *Eth.* 14°7′ N, 38°41′ E 182
Aktag, peak, *China* 36°43′ N, 84°36′ E 184
Aktash, *Russ.* 50°21′ N, 87°48′ E 184
Ak-Tektir, *Kyrg.* 42°6′ N, 72°26′ E 197
Akto, *China* 39°8′ N, 75°54′ E 184
Aktogay, *Kaz.* 48°51′ N, 60°6′ E 158
Aktsyabrski, *Belarus* 52°36′ N, 28°58′ E 152
Akujärvi, *Fin.* 68°40′ N, 27°42′ E 152
Akula, *Dem. Rep. of the Congo* 2°20′ N, 20°15′ E 218
Akune, *Japan* 32°1′ N, 130°13′ E 201
Akure, *Nig.* 7°18′ N, 5°11′ E 222
Akureyri, *Ice.* 65°41′ N, 18°16′ W 246
Akuse, *Ghana* 6°4′ N, 9°535′ E 222
Akwatia, *Ghana* 6°0′ N, 0°48′ E 214
Akyaka, *Turk.* 40°45′ N, 43°32′ E 195
Āl 'Ābis, *Saudi Arabia* 18°1′ N, 43°9′ E 182
Al 'Adam, *Lib.* 31°53′ N, 23°57′ E 180
Al A'madī, *Kuwait* 29°3′ N, 48°4′ E 180
Al Akhḍar, *Saudi Arabia* 28°3′ N, 37°7′ E 180
Al' Amādīyah, *Iraq* 37°7′ N, 43°29′ E 180
Al' Amārah, *Iraq* 31°53′ N, 47°9′ E 180
Al 'Ammārīyah, *Iraq* 37°6′ N, 43°22′ E 195
Al 'Ānāt, *Syr.* 32°20′ N, 36°48′ E 194
Al 'Aqabah, *Jordan* 29°34′ N, 35°4′ E 180
Al 'Aqīq, *Saudi Arabia* 20°40′ N, 41°22′ E 182
Al 'Arīḍah, *Leb.* 34°38′ N, 35°59′ E 194
Al Arṭāwīyah, *Saudi Arabia* 26°29′ N, 45°23′ E 180
Al As'ad, *Saudi Arabia* 27°50′ N, 37°22′ E 180
Al Ashkharah, *Oman* 21°52′ N, 59°32′ E 182
Al 'Athāmīn, peak, *Iraq* 30°20′ N, 43°33′ E 180
Al 'Ayn, *U.A.E.* 24°10′ N, 55°38′ E 196
Al 'Ayzarīyah, *Israel* 31°45′ N, 35°15′ E 194
Al Bad', *Saudi Arabia* 28°26′ N, 35°4′ E 180
Al Badī', *Saudi Arabia* 22°5′ N, 46°30′ E 207
Al Bā'ah, *Saudi Arabia* 20°3′ N, 41°33′ E 182
Al Ba'rah, spring, *Kuwait* 29°35′ N, 47°59′ E 196
Al Bardī, *Lib.* 31°46′ N, 25°3′ E 180
Al Basīt, Ra's, *Syr.* 35°50′ N, 35°50′ E 156
Al Başrah, *Iraq* 30°29′ N, 47°49′ E 180
Al Bayād, *Saudi Arabia* 23°42′ N, 47°48′ E 196
Al Biqā' (Bekaa Valley), region, *Leb.* 33°43′ N, 35°51′ E 194
Al Bi'r, *Saudi Arabia* 28°51′ N, 36°15′ E 180
Al Bir Lahlou, *Western Sahara, Mor.* 26°23′ N, 9°32′ W 214
Al Bīrah, *West Bank, Israel* 31°53′ N, 35°12′ E 194
Al Birk, *Saudi Arabia* 18°8′ N, 41°36′ E 182
Al Birkah, *Lib.* 24°50′ N, 10°8′ E 216
Al Bunduq, oil field, *U.A.E.* 25°2′ N, 52°25′ E 196
Al Burayj, *Gaza Strip, Israel* 31°25′ N, 34°24′ E 194
Al Buraymī, *Oman* 24°11′ N, 55°49′ E 196
Al Burjayn, *Tun.* 35°40′ N, 10°35′ E 156
Al Dafyānah, *Jordan* 32°18′ N, 36°38′ E 194
Al Fallūjah (Fallujah), *Iraq* 33°19′ N, 43°46′ E 180
Al Farciya, *Western Sahara, Mor.* 27°8′ N, 9°52′ W 214
Al Fāw, *Iraq* 29°59′ N, 48°28′ E 196
Al Fayḍah, *Saudi Arabia* 25°15′ N, 44°25′ E 182
Al Fujayrah, *U.A.E.* 25°10′ N, 56°18′ E 196
Al Fuqahā', *Lib.* 27°50′ N, 16°20′ E 216
Al Furāt (Euphrates), river, *Syr.* 35°43′ N, 39°21′ E 180
Al Furāt, river, *Iraq* 32°7′ N, 44°56′ E 180
Al Ghārīyah, *Syr.* 32°23′ N, 36°39′ E 194
Al Ghayḍah, *Yemen* 16°12′ N, 52°14′ E 182
Al Ghayḍah, *Yemen* 14°55′ N, 49°58′ E 182
Al Ghayl, *Saudi Arabia* 22°33′ N, 46°18′ E 182
Al Ghayl, *Yemen* 16°3′ N, 44°48′ E 182
Al Ghazālah, *Saudi Arabia* 26°42′ N, 41°22′ E 180
Al Ghuwayr, *Jordan* 31°8′ N, 35°45′ E 194
Al Ḥaddār, *Saudi Arabia* 21°56′ N, 45°58′ E 182
Al Ḥadīdah, *Saudi Arabia* 21°32′ N, 50°30′ E 182
Al Ḥadīthah, *Iraq* 34°8′ N, 42°27′ E 180
Al Haggounia, *Western Sahara, Mor.* 27°25′ N, 12°26′ W 214
Al Ḥallānīyah, island, *Oman* 17°35′ N, 55°22′ E 182
Al Ḥamād, *Saudi Arabia* 31°17′ N, 37°38′ E 180
Al Ḥamīdīyah, *Syr.* 34°42′ N, 35°56′ E 194
Al Ḥammār, Hawr, lake, *Iraq* 30°49′ N, 46°38′ E 180
Al Ḥamrā', *Lib.* 29°39′ N, 12°0′ E 216
Al Ḥamrā', *Saudi Arabia* 23°55′ N, 38°51′ E 182
Al Ḥamūd, *Jordan* 31°17′ N, 35°47′ E 194
Al Ḥanākīyah, *Saudi Arabia* 24°50′ N, 40°29′ E 182
Al Ḥaqw, *Saudi Arabia* 17°33′ N, 42°40′ E 182
Al Ḥarīq, *Saudi Arabia* 23°35′ N, 46°33′ E 196
Al Harūj al Aswad, *Lib.* 28°27′ N, 17°15′ E 216
Al Ḥasakah, *Syr.* 36°31′ N, 40°46′ E 195
Al Ḥasānī, island, *Saudi Arabia* 25°1′ N, 36°30′ E 182
Al Ḥawīyah, *Saudi Arabia* 21°26′ N, 40°31′ E 182
Al Ḥawrah, *Yemen* 13°51′ N, 47°33′ E 182
Al Ḥayy, *Iraq* 32°9′ N, 46°5′ E 180
Al Ḥījānah, *Syr.* 33°21′ N, 36°32′ E 194
Al Ḥijāz (Hejaz), region, *Saudi Arabia* 26°54′ N, 36°41′ E 180
Al Ḥillah, *Iraq* 32°27′ N, 44°26′ E 180
Al Ḥillah (Hauta), *Saudi Arabia* 23°28′ N, 46°52′ E 196
Al Ḥimá, spring, *Saudi Arabia* 18°13′ N, 44°30′ E 182
Al Ḥişn, *Jordan* 32°28′ N, 35°53′ E 194
Al Hoceima, *Mor.* 35°14′ N, 3°57′ W 150
Al Ḥudaydah, *Yemen* 14°48′ N, 42°56′ E 182
Al Hufūf (Hofuf), *Saudi Arabia* 25°21′ N, 49°34′ E 196
Al Ḥulwah, *Saudi Arabia* 23°23′ N, 46°49′ E 182
Al Ḥunayy, *Saudi Arabia* 24°58′ N, 48°46′ E 196
Al Hūwah, *Saudi Arabia* 23°0′ N, 45°48′ E 182
Al Ikhwān (The Brothers), islands, *Yemen* 11°24′ N, 52°52′ E 182
Al 'Irqah, *Yemen* 13°40′ N, 47°19′ E 182
Al 'Īsāwīyah, *Saudi Arabia* 30°41′ N, 38°1′ E 180
Al Jabalash Sharqī (Anti-Lebanon), *Leb.* 34°5′ N, 36°21′ E 194
Al Jaghbūb, *Lib.* 29°45′ N, 24°30′ E 180
Al Jawf, *Lib.* 24°10′ N, 23°16′ E 216
Al Jawf, *Saudi Arabia* 29°54′ N, 39°51′ E 143
Al Jazīrah, spring, *Lib.* 25°43′ N, 21°7′ E 216
Al Jehrā, *Kuwait* 29°21′ N, 47°40′ E 196
Al Jīb, *West Bank, Israel* 31°50′ N, 35°10′ E 194
Al Jifāra, *Tun.* 32°1′ N, 11°10′ E 214
Al Jīzah, *Jordan* 31°41′ N, 35°57′ E 194
Al Jubayl, *Saudi Arabia* 26°59′ N, 49°39′ E 196
Al Jubaylah, *Saudi Arabia* 24°52′ N, 46°28′ E 196
Al Jumaylīyah, *Qatar* 25°36′ N, 51°7′ E 196
Al Jumaymah, spring, *Saudi Arabia* 29°41′ N, 43°37′ E 180
Al Junaynah, *Saudi Arabia* 20°15′ N, 42°50′ E 182
Al Kahfah, *Saudi Arabia* 27°2′ N, 43°3′ E 180
Al Karak, *Jordan* 31°10′ N, 35°42′ E 194
Al Kawm, *Syr.* 35°12′ N, 38°51′ E 180
Al Khābūrah, *Oman* 23°54′ N, 57°7′ E 196
Al Khalīl (Hebron), *West Bank, Israel* 31°31′ N, 35°6′ E 194
Al Kharfah, *Saudi Arabia* 22°11′ N, 46°41′ E 182
Al Kharj, *Saudi Arabia* 24°10′ N, 47°20′ E 196
Al Khāşirah, *Saudi Arabia* 23°29′ N, 43°44′ E 182
Al Khawr, *Qatar* 25°41′ N, 51°30′ E 196
Al Khīrān, *Kuwait* 28°36′ N, 48°21′ E 196
Al Khiyam, *Leb.* 33°19′ N, 35°36′ E 194
Al Khubar, *Saudi Arabia* 26°13′ N, 50°8′ E 196
Al Khufayfīyah, *Saudi Arabia* 24°54′ N, 44°44′ E 182
Al Khums, *Lib.* 32°42′ N, 14°16′ E 216
Al Khunn, *Saudi Arabia* 23°16′ N, 49°15′ E 182
Al Khuraybah, *Yemen* 15°7′ N, 48°20′ E 182
Al Khurmah, *Saudi Arabia* 21°51′ N, 42°3′ E 182
Al Kifl, *Iraq* 32°16′ N, 44°24′ E 180
Al Kūfah (Kufah), *Iraq* 32°5′ N, 44°27′ E 186
Al Kufrah (Kufra Oasis), *Lib.* 24°20′ N, 23°44′ E 226
Al Kūt, *Iraq* 32°34′ N, 45°49′ E 180
Al Kuwayt (Kuwait City), *Kuwait* 29°20′ N, 47°52′ E 196
Al La'bān, *Jordan* 30°54′ N, 35°42′ E 194
Al Labwah, *Leb.* 34°11′ N, 36°21′ E 194
Al Lādhiqīyah (Latakia), *Syr.* 35°31′ N, 35°47′ E 194
Al Lajā, *Syr.* 32°53′ N, 36°19′ E 194
Al Lawz, Jabal, peak, *Saudi Arabia* 28°38′ N, 35°13′ E 180
Al Lidām, *Saudi Arabia* 20°27′ N, 44°48′ E 182
Al Līth, *Saudi Arabia* 20°8′ N, 40°18′ E 182
Al Luḥayyah, *Yemen* 15°41′ N, 42°42′ E 182
Al Luwaymī, *Saudi Arabia* 27°54′ N, 42°12′ E 180
Al Ma'ānīyah, spring, *Iraq* 30°42′ N, 42°57′ E 180
Al Madīnah (Medina), *Saudi Arabia* 24°26′ N, 39°34′ E 182
Al Madwar, *Jordan* 32°17′ N, 35°59′ E 194
Al Mafraq, *Jordan* 32°20′ N, 36°12′ E 194
Al Mahbas, *Western Sahara, Mor.* 27°27′ N, 9°2′ W 214
Al Maḥrūqah, *Lib.* 27°29′ N, 14°0′ E 216
Al Majma'ah, *Saudi Arabia* 25°52′ N, 45°23′ E 182
Al Malāqī, spring, *Lib.* 26°53′ N, 16°49′ E 216
Al Mālikīyah, *Syr.* 37°11′ N, 42°4′ E 195
Al Manāmah (Manama), *Bahrain* 26°10′ N, 50°27′ E 196
Al Manzil, *Jordan* 31°3′ N, 36°0′ E 194
Al Marj (Barce), *Lib.* 32°30′ N, 20°53′ E 216
Al Mashrafah, *Syr.* 34°50′ N, 36°52′ E 194
Al Mawşil (Mosul), *Iraq* 36°20′ N, 43°0′ E 195
Al Mayādīn, *Syr.* 35°0′ N, 40°24′ E 180
Al Mayyāh, *Saudi Arabia* 27°50′ N, 42°49′ E 180
Al Mazra'ah, *Jordan* 31°17′ N, 35°32′ E 194
Al Mazzah, *Syr.* 33°30′ N, 36°14′ E 194
Al Mintirib, *Oman* 22°24′ N, 58°49′ E 182
Al Minyah, *Leb.* 34°28′ N, 35°56′ E 194
Al Mismīyah, *Syr.* 33°7′ N, 36°23′ E 194
Al Mubarraz, *Saudi Arabia* 25°27′ N, 49°35′ E 196
Al Mudawwarah, *Jordan* 29°23′ N, 36°2′ E 180
Al Mughayrā', *U.A.E.* 24°3′ N, 53°31′ E 196
Al Mukallā, *Yemen* 14°33′ N, 49°6′ E 182
Al Mukhā, *Yemen* 13°20′ N, 43°14′ E 182
Al Musayyib, *Iraq* 32°47′ N, 44°21′ E 180
Al Mushannaf, *Syr.* 32°44′ N, 36°46′ E 194
Al Muwaqqar, ruin(s), *Jordan* 31°48′ N, 36°2′ E 194
Al Muwayh, *Saudi Arabia* 22°43′ N, 41°37′ E 182
Al Muwayliḥ, *Saudi Arabia* 27°41′ N, 35°28′ E 180
Al Qābil, *Oman* 23°52′ N, 55°51′ E 196
Al Qaḍīmah, *Saudi Arabia* 22°19′ N, 39°8′ E 182
Al Qadmūs, *Syr.* 35°5′ N, 36°9′ E 194
Al Qā'im, *Iraq* 34°17′ N, 41°11′ E 180
Al Qa'īyah, *Saudi Arabia* 24°19′ N, 43°32′ E 182
Al Qā'īyah, spring, *Saudi Arabia* 26°28′ N, 45°33′ E 196
Al Qāmishlī, *Syr.* 37°2′ N, 41°16′ E 195
Al Qārah, *Yemen* 13°41′ N, 45°15′ E 182
Al Qaryah ash Sharqīyah, *Lib.* 30°23′ N, 13°33′ E 216
Al Qaryatayn, *Syr.* 34°10′ N, 37°17′ E 180
Al Qaşr, *Jordan* 31°18′ N, 35°44′ E 194
Al Qaţīf, *Saudi Arabia* 26°32′ N, 49°59′ E 196
Al Qaţrānah, *Jordan* 31°14′ N, 36°1′ E 194
Al Qaţrūn, *Lib.* 24°53′ N, 14°29′ E 216
Al Qawārishah, *Lib.* 32°1′ N, 20°5′ E 216
Al Qaws, site, *Lib.* 30°26′ N, 18°21′ E 216
Al Qayşūmah, *Saudi Arabia* 28°18′ N, 46°9′ E 196
Al Qunayţirah (Quneitra), *Syr.* 33°7′ N, 35°49′ E 194
Al Qunfudhah, *Saudi Arabia* 19°6′ N, 41°7′ E 182
Al Qurayn, spring, *Saudi Arabia* 21°51′ N, 53°48′ E 182
Al Qurayyah, *Syr.* 32°32′ N, 36°35′ E 194
Al Qurnah, *Iraq* 30°55′ N, 47°22′ E 180
Al Quşayr, *Syr.* 34°30′ N, 36°34′ E 194
Al Quşūrīyah, *Saudi Arabia* 23°43′ N, 44°37′ E 182
Al Quţayfah, *Syr.* 33°43′ N, 36°35′ E 194
Al Quway'īyah, *Saudi Arabia* 24°2′ N, 45°15′ E 182
Al 'Ubaylah, *Saudi Arabia* 21°58′ N, 50°56′ E 182
Al 'Udaysah, *Leb.* 33°15′ N, 35°32′ E 194
Al 'Ulá, *Saudi Arabia* 26°36′ N, 37°51′ E 180
Al 'Uqaylah, *Lib.* 30°13′ N, 19°11′ E 216
Al 'Uqayr, *Saudi Arabia* 25°38′ N, 50°8′ E 196
Al 'Uwaynāt see 'Uweinat, Jebel, peak, *Sudan* 21°51′ N, 24°58′ E 226
Al 'Uwaynāt (Serdeles), *Lib.* 25°47′ N, 10°33′ E 216
Al 'Uwaynid, *Saudi Arabia* 24°54′ N, 45°48′ E 182
Al 'Uwayqīlah, *Saudi Arabia* 30°18′ N, 42°12′ E 180
Al 'Uyūn, *Saudi Arabia* 26°30′ N, 43°40′ E 180
Al 'Uyūn, *Saudi Arabia* 24°33′ N, 39°33′ E 182
Al 'Uzayr, *Iraq* 31°19′ N, 47°23′ E 180
Al Wābirīyah, spring, *Lib.* 27°24′ N, 18°5′ E 216
Al Wafra, *Kuwait* 28°35′ N, 47°57′ E 196
Al Wajh, *Saudi Arabia* 26°15′ N, 36°27′ E 180
Al Wakrah, *Qatar* 25°6′ N, 51°35′ E 196
Al Wannān, *Saudi Arabia* 26°53′ N, 48°26′ E 196
Al Waqbah, spring, *Saudi Arabia* 28°52′ N, 45°26′ E 196
Al Warī'ah, *Saudi Arabia* 27°47′ N, 47°32′ E 196
Al Yādūdah, *Jordan* 31°50′ N, 35°54′ E 194
Ala, *It.* 45°45′ N, 11°0′ E 167
Alà, Monti di, *It.* 40°33′ N, 8°47′ E 156
Ala-Archa National Park, site, *Kyrg.* 42°35′ N, 74°19′ E 197
Alabama, adm. division, *Ala., U.S.* 31°51′ N, 88°21′ W 96
Alabama, river, *Ala., U.S.* 31°12′ N, 87°54′ W 103
Alabaster, *Ala., U.S.* 33°14′ N, 86°49′ W 96
Alaca, *Turk.* 40°8′ N, 34°50′ E 156
Alaca Dağ, peak, *Turk.* 37°28′ N, 32°4′ E 156
Alacahöyük, ruin(s), *Turk.* 40°13′ N, 34°37′ E 156
Alaçam, *Turk.* 41°35′ N, 35°36′ E 156
Alacant see Alicante, *Sp.* 38°20′ N, 0°30′ E 164
Alachua, *Fla., U.S.* 29°47′ N, 82°30′ W 105
Alacón, *Sp.* 41°1′ N, 0°43′ E 164
Aladağ, peak, *Turk.* 37°42′ N, 35°5′ E 156
Aladağ, peak, *Turk.* 37°56′ N, 32°0′ E 156
Ālagē, Āmba, peak, *Eth.* 12°57′ N, 39°23′ E 182

Alagir, Russ. 43°3′ N, 44°14′ E 180
Alagna Valsesia, It. 45°51′ N, 7°56′ E 167
Alagoas, adm. division, Braz. 9°35′ S, 37°52′ W 132
Alagoinhas, Braz. 12°10′ S, 38°24′ W 132
Alagón, Sp. 41°45′ N, 1°8′ W 164
Alai Mountains, Kyrg. 39°53′ N, 72°4′ E 184
Alaior, Sp. 39°55′ N, 4°8′ E 164
Alajärvi, Fin. 62°59′ N, 23°46′ E 152
Alajärvi, Fin. 64°58′ N, 28°45′ E 152
Alajuela, C.R. 10°0′ N, 84°12′ W 115
Alakanuk, Alas., U.S. 62°34′ N, 164°50′ W 98
Alakoko Fishpond, site, Hawai'i, U.S. 21°56′ N, 159°25′ W 99
Alaköl, lake, Kaz. 46°20′ N, 81°30′ E 184
Alakurtti, Russ. 66°58′ N, 30°24′ E 152
Alalakh, ruin(s), Turk. 36°11′ N, 36°16′ E 156
Alalaú, river, Braz. 0°23′ N, 60°19′ W 130
'Alam el Rûm, Râs, Egypt 31°25′ N, 27°18′ E 226
Alama, Cen. Af. Rep. 5°29′ N, 21°51′ E 218
Alamagan, island, U.S. 17°32′ N, 144°34′ E 192
Alameda, Calif., U.S. 37°46′ N, 122°17′ W 100
Alameda, Can. 49°15′ N, 102°19′ W 90
Alameda, N. Mex., U.S. 35°10′ N, 106°38′ W 92
Alameda, Sp. 37°13′ N, 4°40′ W 164
Alamedilla, Sp. 37°36′ N, 3°15′ W 164
Alamillo, Sp. 38°39′ N, 4°47′ W 164
Alamitos, Sierra de los, peak, Mex. 26°19′ N, 102°22′ W 114
Alamo, Ind., U.S. 39°58′ N, 87°4′ W 102
Álamo, Mex. 20°54′ N, 97°41′ W 114
Alamo, Tenn., U.S. 35°48′ N, 89°6′ W 96
Alamo Lake, Ariz., U.S. 34°18′ N, 113°36′ W 101
Alamo, river, Calif., U.S. 32°55′ N, 115°31′ W 101
Alamo, river, Mex. 26°31′ N, 99°57′ W 114
Alamogordo, N. Mex., U.S. 32°54′ N, 105°57′ W 92
Álamos, Mex. 29°12′ N, 110°8′ W 92
Álamos, river, Mex. 26°56′ N, 109°8′ W 80
Alanäs, Nor. 64°8′ N, 15°39′ E 152
Åland (Ahvenanmaa), island, Fin. 60°26′ N, 19°33′ E 166
Alanís, Sp. 38°2′ N, 5°44′ W 164
Alanta, Lith. 55°21′ N, 25°17′ E 166
Alantika Mountains, Cameroon 8°35′ N, 12°15′ E 216
Alanya (Coracesium), Turk. 36°31′ N, 32°1′ E 180
Alapayevsk, Russ. 57°50′ N, 61°38′ E 154
Alappuzha see Alleppey, India 9°29′ N, 76°20′ E 188
Alaquines, Mex. 22°6′ N, 99°36′ W 114
Alarcón, Sp. 39°32′ N, 2°5′ W 164
Alas Purwo National Park, Indonesia 8°40′ S, 114°4′ E 238
Alas, river, Indonesia 3°22′ N, 97°44′ E 196
Alaşehir, Turk. 38°21′ N, 28°31′ E 156
Alaska, adm. division, Alas., U.S. 64°46′ N, 156°29′ W 98
Alaska, Gulf of 57°56′ N, 149°1′ W 98
Alaska Highway, Can. 57°34′ N, 122°49′ W 108
Alaska Peninsula, North America 58°0′ N, 157°11′ W 98
Alaska Plain, North Pacific Ocean 55°0′ N, 143°0′ W 252
Alaska Range, North America 62°13′ N, 153°16′ W 98
Alassio, It. 44°0′ N, 8°10′ E 167
Alasuolijärvi, lake, Fin. 66°17′ N, 27°9′ E 152
Älät, Azerb. 39°56′ N, 49°23′ E 195
Alatoz, Sp. 39°5′ N, 1°22′ W 164
Alatyr', Russ. 54°47′ N, 46°37′ E 154
Alava, Cape, Wash., U.S. 48°4′ N, 124°53′ W 100
Alaverdi, Arm. 41°6′ N, 44°38′ E 195
Alāyat Samā'il, Oman 23°14′ N, 58°3′ E 182
Alazeya, river, Russ. 70°55′ N, 153°45′ E 160
Alba, It. 44°41′ N, 8°2′ E 167
Alba, Tex., U.S. 32°46′ N, 95°38′ W 103
Alba, adm. division, Rom. 46°13′ N, 22°59′ E 156
Alba, Foum el, pass, Mali 20°40′ N, 3°37′ W 222
Alba Iulia, Rom. 46°3′ N, 23°35′ E 168
Albac, Rom. 46°27′ N, 22°58′ E 168
Albacete, Sp. 38°58′ N, 1°51′ W 164
Albalá del Caudillo, Sp. 39°14′ N, 6°11′ W 164
Albalate del Arzobispo, Sp. 41°7′ N, 0°31′ E 164
Albanel, Lac, lake, Can. 50°52′ N, 74°31′ W 106
Albania 40°43′ N, 19°44′ E 156
Albano, Braz. 2°29′ S, 57°32′ W 130
Albany, Ga., U.S. 31°34′ N, 84°10′ W 96
Albany, Ind., U.S. 40°18′ N, 85°14′ W 102
Albany, Ky., U.S. 36°40′ N, 85°8′ W 96
Albany, La., U.S. 30°29′ N, 90°35′ W 103
Albany, Mo., U.S. 40°13′ N, 94°19′ W 94
Albany, N.Y., U.S. 42°38′ N, 73°50′ W 104
Albany, Ohio, U.S. 39°13′ N, 82°13′ W 102
Albany, Oreg., U.S. 44°36′ N, 123°6′ W 90
Albany, Tex., U.S. 32°43′ N, 99°18′ W 92
Albany, Wis., U.S. 42°42′ N, 89°26′ W 102
Albany Island, Can. 52°20′ N, 82°53′ W 81
Albany, river, Can. 51°8′ N, 89°34′ W 110
Albares, Sp. 40°17′ N, 3°0′ W 164
Albarracín, Sp. 40°24′ N, 1°28′ W 164
Albemarle Sound 35°57′ N, 77°15′ W 80
Albenga, It. 44°3′ N, 8°13′ E 167
Albens, Fr. 45°46′ N, 5°56′ E 150
Alberdi, Parag. 26°12′ S, 58°4′ W 139
Alberese, It. 42°40′ N, 11°5′ E 156
Alberic, Sp. 39°6′ N, 0°31′ E 164
Alberni Inlet 48°57′ N, 124°47′ W 100
Albert, Fr. 50°0′ N, 2°39′ E 163
Albert Icefield, Can. 50°49′ N, 118°18′ W 90
Albert Kanaal, canal, Belg. 51°8′ N, 4°47′ E 163
Albert Lea, Minn., U.S. 43°37′ N, 93°23′ W 94
Albert Markham, Mount, Antarctica 81°20′ S, 159°13′ E 248
Albert, Mount, Can. 53°31′ N, 66°47′ W 111
Alberta, Ala., U.S. 32°13′ N, 87°25′ W 103
Alberta, adm. division, Can. 54°43′ N, 116°17′ W 108
Alberti, Arg. 35°1′ S, 60°18′ W 139
Albertirsa, Hung. 47°14′ N, 19°37′ E 168
Alberton, Mont., U.S. 46°59′ N, 114°29′ W 90
Albertville, Ala., U.S. 34°15′ N, 86°12′ W 96
Albi, Fr. 43°54′ N, 2°9′ E 150
Albia, Iowa, U.S. 41°1′ N, 92°47′ W 94
Albin, Wyo., U.S. 41°25′ N, 104°6′ W 90
Albina, Suriname 5°31′ N, 54°6′ W 130
Albina, Ponta, Angola 15°56′ S, 11°11′ E 220
Albinia, It. 42°31′ N, 11°13′ E 156
Albino, It. 45°46′ N, 9°47′ E 167
Al'bino, Russ. 59°22′ N, 83°4′ E 169
Albion, Mich., U.S. 42°14′ N, 84°45′ W 102
Albion, Nebr., U.S. 41°39′ N, 98°1′ W 90
Albion, N.Y., U.S. 43°14′ N, 78°13′ W 110
Albisola Marina, It. 44°19′ N, 8°30′ E 167
Albocàsser, Sp. 40°21′ N, 0°2′ E 164
Alborán, Isla de, island, Sp. 35°54′ N, 3°2′ W 164
Alboran Sea 35°34′ N, 4°26′ W 150
Alborea, Sp. 39°15′ N, 1°23′ W 164
Ålborg, Den. 57°1′ N, 9°55′ E 150
Ålborg Bugt 56°51′ N, 9°52′ E 152
Alborz, oil field, Iran 34°39′ N, 51°0′ E 180
Alborz, Reshteh-ye (Elburz Mountains), Iran 36°43′ N, 49°25′ E 195
Albota de Jos, Mold. 45°56′ N, 28°29′ E 158
Albox, Sp. 37°23′ N, 2°10′ W 164
Albreda, Can. 52°37′ N, 119°10′ W 108
Albuquerque, N. Mex., U.S. 35°5′ N, 106°39′ W 92
Albury, Austral. 36°4′ S, 146°57′ E 231
Alby, Nor. 62°29′ N, 15°27′ E 152
Alca, Peru 15°10′ S, 72°46′ W 137
Alcácer do Sal, Port. 38°21′ N, 8°31′ W 150
Alcadozo, Sp. 38°38′ N, 1°59′ W 164
Alcalà de Xibert, Sp. 40°17′ N, 0°12′ E 164
Alcalá de Henares, Sp. 40°28′ N, 3°22′ W 164
Alcalá de los Gazules, Sp. 36°27′ N, 5°44′ W 150
Alcalá la Real, Sp. 37°28′ N, 3°56′ W 164
Alcalde, Punta, Chile 28°34′ S, 72°35′ W 134
Alcamo, It. 37°59′ N, 12°58′ E 156
Alcanar, Sp. 40°32′ N, 0°28′ E 164
Alcañiz, Sp. 41°1′ N, 0°7′ E 164
Alcántara, Sp. 39°42′ N, 6°53′ W 150
Alcantara Lake, Can. 60°55′ N, 109°3′ W 108
Alcântara Spaceport, Braz. 2°18′ S, 44°32′ W 132
Alcantarilla, Sp. 37°58′ N, 1°14′ W 164
Alcaraz, Sp. 38°39′ N, 2°29′ W 164
Alcarràs, Sp. 41°33′ N, 0°30′ E 164
Alcaudete, Sp. 37°35′ N, 4°5′ W 164
Alcázar de San Juan, Sp. 39°23′ N, 3°13′ W 164
Alchevs'k, Ukr. 48°27′ N, 38°44′ E 158
Alcoa, Tenn., U.S. 35°47′ N, 83°58′ W 96
Alcoak, Cerro, peak, Bol. 22°26′ S, 66°54′ W 137
Alcocer, Sp. 40°28′ N, 2°36′ W 150
Alcoi see Alcoy, Sp. 38°41′ N, 0°29′ E 164
Alcolea, Sp. 37°55′ N, 4°41′ W 164
Alcolea del Pinar, Sp. 41°1′ N, 2°29′ W 164
Alconbury, U.K. 52°21′ N, 0°16′ E 162
Alcorcón, Sp. 40°19′ N, 3°51′ W 150
Alcorisa, Sp. 40°52′ N, 0°24′ E 164
Alcorta, Arg. 33°33′ S, 61°8′ W 139
Alcoutim, Port. 37°27′ N, 7°31′ W 150
Alcoy (Alcoi), Sp. 38°41′ N, 0°29′ E 164
Alcubierre, Sierra de, Sp. 41°44′ N, 0°29′ W 164
Alcúdia, Sp. 39°50′ N, 3°7′ E 164
Alcudia, Sierra de, Sp. 38°37′ N, 4°35′ W 164
Aldabra Islands, Indian Ocean 9°54′ S, 45°17′ E 218
Aldama, Mex. 28°49′ N, 105°56′ W 92
Aldama, Mex. 22°53′ N, 98°5′ W 114
Aldan, Russ. 58°39′ N, 125°29′ E 160
Aldan, river, Russ. 58°50′ N, 130°46′ E 160
Aldaz, Mount, Antarctica 75°57′ S, 123°51′ W 248
Aldbrough, U.K. 53°49′ N, 0°7′ E 162
Aldea Moret, Sp. 39°26′ N, 6°24′ W 164
Aldeburgh, U.K. 52°9′ N, 1°35′ E 163
Alden, Point, Antarctica 66°56′ S, 142°24′ E 248
Alder Dam, Wash., U.S. 46°48′ N, 122°26′ W 100
Alder Peak, Calif., U.S. 35°52′ N, 121°25′ W 100
Aldershot, U.K. 51°14′ N, 0°46′ E 162
Aldora, Ga., U.S. 33°2′ N, 84°12′ W 96
Aledo, Mo., U.S. 41°12′ N, 90°45′ W 94
Aleg, Mauritania 17°3′ N, 13°57′ W 222
Alegranza, island, Sp. 29°23′ N, 13°30′ W 214
Alegre, Braz. 20°48′ S, 41°35′ W 138
Alegre, Braz. 18°18′ S, 47°7′ W 138
Alegre, river, Braz. 15°11′ S, 59°48′ W 132
Alegres Mountain, N. Mex., U.S. 34°9′ N, 108°16′ W 92
Alegrete, Braz. 29°49′ S, 55°50′ W 139
Alejandra, Arg. 29°53′ S, 59°50′ W 139
Alejandro Roca, Arg. 33°26′ S, 63°43′ W 139
Alejo Ledesma, Arg. 33°37′ S, 62°37′ W 139
Alekhovshchina, Russ. 60°25′ N, 33°54′ E 154
Aleksandro Nevskiy, Russ. 53°26′ N, 40°12′ E 154
Aleksandrov, Russ. 56°23′ N, 38°42′ E 154
Aleksandrov Gay, Russ. 50°9′ N, 48°35′ E 158
Aleksandrovac, Serb. 43°27′ N, 21°2′ E 168
Aleksandrovka, Russ. 52°40′ N, 54°25′ E 154
Aleksandrovsk, Russ. 59°10′ N, 57°36′ E 154
Aleksandrovsk Sakhalinskiy, Russ. 50°47′ N, 142°22′ E 190
Aleksandrovskoye, Russ. 56°47′ N, 85°37′ E 169
Alekseyevka, Russ. 52°18′ N, 48°3′ E 158
Alekseyevka, Russ. 50°40′ N, 38°41′ E 158
Alekseyevka, Russ. 52°35′ N, 51°15′ E 154
Alekseyevsk, Russ. 57°49′ N, 108°40′ E 160
Aleksin, Russ. 54°30′ N, 37°10′ E 154
Aleksinac, Serb. 43°32′ N, 21°42′ E 168
Além Paraíba, Braz. 21°54′ S, 42°44′ W 138
Alemania, Arg. 25°37′ S, 65°38′ W 134
Alenquer, Braz. 1°59′ S, 54°49′ W 130
'Alenuihāhā Channel, Hawai'i, U.S. 20°17′ N, 156°24′ W 99
Alépé, Côte d'Ivoire 5°30′ N, 3°42′ W 222
Aleppo see Ḩalab, Syr. 36°11′ N, 37°9′ E 156
Aléria, Fr. 42°5′ N, 9°32′ E 156
Alert, Can. 82°29′ N, 61°46′ W 246
Alert Bay, Can. 50°31′ N, 126°50′ W 90
Alerta, Peru 10°46′ S, 71°50′ W 137
Alès, Fr. 44°7′ N, 4°4′ E 214
Aleşd, Rom. 47°4′ N, 22°23′ E 168
Alessandria, It. 44°54′ N, 8°37′ E 167
Ålesund, Nor. 62°27′ N, 6°2′ E 160
Alet, Fr. 42°59′ N, 2°14′ E 164
Aleutian Basin, Bering Sea 56°6′ N, 179°52′ E 252
Aleutian Islands, Bering Sea 54°5′ N, 164°2′ W 98
Aleutian Range, North America 56°36′ N, 158°49′ W 98
Aleutian Trench, North Pacific Ocean 49°58′ N, 174°26′ W 252
Alevina, Mys, Russ. 58°36′ N, 148°19′ E 160
Alexander, N. Dak., U.S. 47°49′ N, 103°40′ W 90
Alexander Archipelago, North Pacific Ocean 56°25′ N, 135°30′ W 98
Alexander Bay, S. Af. 28°43′ S, 16°27′ E 207
Alexander, Cape, Antarctica 67°21′ S, 61°14′ W 248
Alexander City, Ala., U.S. 32°56′ N, 85°57′ W 112
Alexander Island, Wash., U.S. 47°44′ N, 124°42′ W 100
Alexander, Mount, Austral. 22°39′ S, 115°23′ E 230
Alexandra Falls, Can. 60°42′ N, 116°54′ W 108
Alexandra Land, Russ. 81°0′ N, 47°0′ E 255
Alexandra, Zemlya, islands, Zemlya Alexandra 80°31′ N, 33°19′ E 160
Alexandria, Can. 52°38′ N, 122°27′ W 108
Alexandria, Can. 45°19′ N, 74°39′ W 94
Alexandria, Ind., U.S. 40°16′ N, 85°41′ W 102
Alexandria, Ky., U.S. 38°57′ N, 84°24′ W 102
Alexandria, La., U.S. 31°17′ N, 92°28′ W 103
Alexandria, Minn., U.S. 45°52′ N, 95°23′ W 90
Alexandria, N.H., U.S. 43°36′ N, 71°48′ W 104
Alexandria, Rom. 43°59′ N, 25°20′ E 156
Alexandria, S. Af. 33°39′ S, 26°24′ E 227
Alexandria, S. Dak., U.S. 43°37′ N, 97°46′ W 90
Alexandria, Va., U.S. 38°48′ N, 77°4′ W 94
Alexandria Bay, N.Y., U.S. 44°19′ N, 75°55′ W 94
Alexandria see El Iskandarîya, Egypt 31°10′ N, 29°55′ E 180
Alexandrium, ruin(s), West Bank, Israel 32°4′ N, 35°26′ E 194
Alexandroúpoli, Gr. 40°52′ N, 25°52′ E 180
Alexis Creek, Can. 52°5′ N, 123°19′ W 108
Alexis, river, Can. 52°28′ N, 57°29′ W 111
Aley, Leb. 33°48′ N, 35°36′ E 194
Aleysk, Russ. 52°32′ N, 82°53′ E 184
Aleza Lake, Can. 54°6′ N, 122°4′ W 108
Alfambra, Sp. 40°32′ N, 1°2′ W 164
Alfândega da FŽe, Port. 41°20′ N, 6°59′ W 150
Alfaro, Sp. 42°10′ N, 1°45′ W 164
Alfenas, Braz. 21°28′ S, 45°56′ W 138
Alföld, Hung. 46°44′ N, 20°4′ E 168
Alfonsine, It. 44°29′ N, 12°2′ E 167
Alford, U.K. 53°15′ N, 0°11′ E 162
Alfred, Me., U.S. 43°28′ N, 70°44′ W 104
Alfred, Mount, Can. 50°10′ N, 124°4′ W 100
Alfredo M. Terrazas, Mex. 21°26′ N, 98°52′ W 114
Alfredton, N.Z. 40°41′ S, 175°53′ E 240
Alfreton, U.K. 53°6′ N, 1°24′ W 162
Alfta, Nor. 61°19′ N, 16°0′ E 152
Algarrobal, Arg. 25°29′ S, 64°1′ W 134
Algeciras, Sp. 36°7′ N, 5°28′ W 164
Algemesí, Sp. 39°11′ N, 0°26′ E 150
Algena, Eritrea 17°15′ N, 38°30′ E 182
Alger, Mich., U.S. 44°7′ N, 84°7′ W 102
Alger (Algiers), Alg. 36°44′ N, 2°56′ E 150
Alger, Mount, Can. 56°55′ N, 130°4′ W 108
Algeria 28°10′ N, 1°37′ W 214
Algha, Kaz. 49°57′ N, 57°20′ E 158
Alghabas, Kaz. 50°39′ N, 52°4′ E 158
Alghero, It. 40°33′ N, 8°19′ E 156
Algiers see Alger, Alg. 36°44′ N, 2°56′ E 150
Alginet, Sp. 39°16′ N, 0°29′ E 164
Algoa Bay 33°54′ S, 25°43′ E 227
Algodones, Mex. 32°42′ N, 114°45′ W 101
Algoma, Wis., U.S. 44°35′ N, 87°28′ W 94
Algona, Iowa, U.S. 43°3′ N, 94°14′ W 94
Algonac, Mich., U.S. 42°36′ N, 82°33′ W 102
Algonquin Park, Can. 45°32′ N, 78°35′ W 94
Algorta, Uru. 32°26′ S, 57°24′ W 139
Algy o, Hung. 46°19′ N, 20°13′ E 168
Alhama de Granada, Sp. 37°0′ N, 3°59′ W 164
Alhama de Murcia, Sp. 37°50′ N, 1°27′ W 164
Alhambra, Sp. 38°53′ N, 3°4′ W 164
Alhaurín el Grande, Sp. 36°38′ N, 4°42′ W 164
Alhuampa, Arg. 27°7′ S, 62°35′ W 139
Äli Bayramlı, Azerb. 39°56′ N, 48°54′ E 195
'Ali Sabīh, Djibouti 11°7′ N, 42°43′ E 218
Alia, Sp. 39°26′ N, 5°13′ W 164
Aliabad, Iran 28°33′ N, 55°47′ E 196
Aliaga, Sp. 40°40′ N, 0°42′ E 164
Alibunar, Serb. 45°5′ N, 20°58′ E 168
Alicante (Alacant), Sp. 38°20′ N, 0°30′ E 164
Alice, S. Af. 32°47′ S, 26°51′ E 227
Alice, Tex., U.S. 27°43′ N, 98°4′ W 92
Alice Arm, Can. 55°28′ N, 129°33′ W 108
Alice Creek, river, Can. 58°22′ N, 113°21′ W 108
Alice, Punta, It. 39°18′ N, 17°11′ E 156
Alice Town, Bahamas 25°43′ N, 79°17′ W 105
Alicedale, S. Af. 33°18′ S, 26°2′ E 227
Aliceville, Ala., U.S. 33°7′ N, 88°9′ W 103
Alicia, Philippines 7°33′ N, 122°57′ E 203
Alida, Can. 49°22′ N, 101°51′ W 90
Alida, peak, Gr. 39°6′ N, 21°11′ E 156
Alif, oil field, Yemen 15°45′ N, 46°7′ E 182
Aligandí, Pan. 9°13′ N, 78°2′ W 115
Aligarh, India 27°52′ N, 78°4′ E 197
Alijos, Rocas, islands, North Pacific Ocean 25°9′ N, 116°16′ W 112
'Ālika Cone, peak, Hawai'i, U.S. 19°15′ N, 155°47′ W 99
Alima, river, Congo 1°21′ S, 15°44′ E 218
Alimodian, Philippines 10°50′ N, 122°24′ E 203
Alindao, Cen. Af. Rep. 5°3′ N, 21°14′ E 218
Alingsås, Nor. 57°55′ N, 12°33′ E 152
Alins, Sp. 42°32′ N, 1°18′ E 164
Alinskoye, Russ. 63°19′ N, 87°36′ E 169
Alipur, Pak. 29°24′ N, 70°54′ E 186
Aliquippa, Pa., U.S. 40°37′ N, 80°15′ W 94
Alişar Hüyük (Alishar), ruin(s), Turk. 39°34′ N, 35°7′ E 156
Aliseda, Sp. 39°25′ N, 6°43′ W 164
Alishar see Alişar Hüyük, ruin(s), Turk. 39°34′ N, 35°7′ E 156
Alittjåkko, peak, Nor. 67°53′ N, 17°20′ E 152
Alivéri, Gr. 38°24′ N, 24°2′ E 156
Aliwal North, S. Af. 30°43′ S, 26°42′ E 227
Alix, Can. 52°22′ N, 113°11′ W 108
Alkmaar, Neth. 52°37′ N, 4°43′ E 163
Alla, Russ. 54°43′ N, 110°49′ E 173
Allada, Benin 6°45′ N, 2°9′ E 222
Allagash Falls, Me., U.S. 46°45′ N, 70°14′ W 94
Allagash Lake, lake, Me., U.S. 46°16′ N, 69°59′ W 94
Allahabad, India 25°26′ N, 81°49′ E 197
Allahabad, Pak. 28°55′ N, 70°53′ E 186
Allahüekber Dağı, peak, Turk. 40°33′ N, 42°28′ E 195
Allakaket, Alas., U.S. 66°30′ N, 152°26′ W 106
Allan Creek, river, Can. 60°20′ N, 130°53′ W 108
Allan Hills, Antarctica 76°41′ S, 158°26′ E 248
Allan Mountain, Idaho, U.S. 45°34′ N, 114°7′ W 90
Allan Water, Can. 50°14′ N, 90°12′ W 94
Allanmyo, Myanmar 19°23′ N, 95°12′ E 202
Allanridge, S. Af. 27°48′ S, 26°38′ E 227
Allanton, N.Z. 45°57′ S, 170°16′ E 240
Allegan, Mich., U.S. 42°31′ N, 85°51′ W 102
Alleghe, It. 46°25′ N, 12°1′ E 167
Allegheny Mountains, North America 37°1′ N, 82°33′ W 96
Allegheny Mountains, W. Va., U.S. 39°57′ N, 78°49′ W 106
Allen, Philippines 12°31′ N, 124°18′ E 203
Allen, Mount, N.Z. 47°8′ S, 167°43′ E 240
Allen, Punta, Mex. 19°51′ N, 88°7′ W 115
Allendale, S.C., U.S. 33°0′ N, 81°19′ W 96
Allendale Town, U.K. 54°53′ N, 2°16′ W 162
Allende, Mex. 28°19′ N, 100°51′ W 92
Allende, Mex. 25°18′ N, 100°0′ W 114
Allendorf, Ger. 50°40′ N, 8°47′ E 167
Allensworth, Calif., U.S. 35°51′ N, 119°24′ W 100
Allentown, Pa., U.S. 40°35′ N, 75°30′ W 94
Allentsteig, Aust. 48°41′ N, 15°20′ E 156
Alleppey (Alappuzha), India 9°29′ N, 76°20′ E 188
Allerton, Ill., U.S. 39°54′ N, 87°56′ W 102
Allgäuer Alpen, Ger. 47°27′ N, 9°48′ E 156
Allia Bay, site, Kenya 3°38′ N, 36°16′ E 224
Alliance, Can. 52°25′ N, 111°47′ W 108
Alliance, Nebr., U.S. 42°5′ N, 102°53′ W 90
Alliance, Ohio, U.S. 40°54′ N, 81°7′ W 102
Allier, river, Fr. 44°53′ N, 3°36′ E 165
Allison Peninsula, Antarctica 73°1′ S, 85°31′ W 248
Alliston, Can. 44°8′ N, 79°51′ W 94
Allo, Sp. 42°34′ N, 2°2′ W 164
Allos, Fr. 44°14′ N, 6°37′ E 167
Alluvial City, La., U.S. 29°49′ N, 89°43′ W 103
Allyn, Wash., U.S. 47°22′ N, 122°50′ W 100
Alma, Can. 48°30′ N, 71°40′ W 94
Alma, Ga., U.S. 31°31′ N, 82°28′ W 96
Alma, Kans., U.S. 38°59′ N, 96°18′ W 90
Alma, Mich., U.S. 43°22′ N, 84°40′ W 102
Alma, Nebr., U.S. 40°5′ N, 99°23′ W 90
Alma Peak, Can. 56°43′ N, 127°38′ W 108
Almacelles, Sp. 41°43′ N, 0°26′ E 164
Almadén, Sp. 38°46′ N, 4°51′ W 164
Almagro, Sp. 38°52′ N, 3°42′ W 164
Almami, Mali 14°55′ N, 5°2′ W 222
Almansa, Sp. 38°51′ N, 1°6′ W 164
Almanza, Sp. 42°38′ N, 5°4′ W 150
Almanzor, peak, Sp. 40°13′ N, 5°23′ W 150
Almas, Braz. 11°35′ S, 47°9′ W 130
Almaş, Rom. 46°56′ N, 23°8′ E 168
Almaş, Munţii, Rom. 44°42′ N, 22°4′ E 168
Almas, river, Braz. 15°8′ S, 49°18′ W 138
Almassora see Almazora, Sp. 39°57′ N, 0°3′ W 150
Almaty, Kaz. 43°15′ N, 76°57′ E 184
Almaty, adm. division, Kaz. 44°42′ N, 75°55′ E 184
Almazán, Sp. 41°28′ N, 2°32′ W 164
Almaznoe, Kaz. 50°13′ N, 54°14′ E 158
Almazora (Almassora), Sp. 39°57′ N, 0°3′ W 150
Almeirim, Braz. 1°31′ S, 52°36′ W 130
Almelo, Neth. 52°20′ N, 6°39′ E 163
Almena, Kans., U.S. 39°53′ N, 99°43′ W 90
Almenar, Sp. 41°46′ N, 0°34′ E 164
Almenara, Braz. 16°11′ S, 40°45′ W 138
Almenara, peak, Sp. 38°32′ N, 2°29′ W 164
Almendra, Sp. 41°34′ N, 5°54′ W 150
Almendralejo, Sp. 38°41′ N, 6°25′ W 164
Almere, Neth. 52°20′ N, 5°9′ E 163
Almería, Sp. 36°49′ N, 2°28′ W 164
Al'met'yevsk, Russ. 54°51′ N, 52°17′ E 154
Almina, Punta, Sp. 35°53′ N, 5°17′ W 164
Almo, Idaho, U.S. 42°6′ N, 113°38′ W 92
Almonaster la Real, Sp. 37°51′ N, 6°48′ W 164
Almond Mountain, Can. 49°17′ N, 118°42′ W 90
Almont, Mich., U.S. 42°55′ N, 83°4′ W 102
Almonte, Can. 45°13′ N, 76°11′ W 94
Almonte, Sp. 37°15′ N, 6°31′ W 164
Almonte, river, Sp. 39°32′ N, 6°18′ W 164
Almoradí, Sp. 38°6′ N, 0°48′ E 164
Almudévar, Sp. 42°2′ N, 0°36′ E 164
Almuñécar, Sp. 36°43′ N, 3°41′ W 164
Almunge, Sw. 59°52′ N, 18°0′ E 166
Almuradiel, Sp. 38°30′ N, 3°30′ W 164
Almus, Turk. 40°22′ N, 36°53′ E 156
Almvik, Nor. 57°49′ N, 16°27′ E 152
Alnif, Mor. 31°8′ N, 5°12′ W 214
Aloja, Latv. 57°45′ N, 24°52′ E 166
Alonsa, Can. 50°48′ N, 98°59′ W 90
Alor, island, Indonesia 8°9′ S, 124°15′ E 192
Alor Setar, Malaysia 6°4′ N, 100°24′ E 196
Álora, Sp. 36°49′ N, 4°43′ W 164
Alot, India 23°45′ N, 75°31′ E 197
Aloysius, Mount, Austral. 26°3′ S, 128°22′ E 230
Alpachiri, Arg. 37°25′ S, 63°44′ W 139
Alpaugh, Calif., U.S. 35°53′ N, 119°30′ W 100
Alpedrinha, Port. 40°5′ N, 7°29′ W 150
Alpena, Mich., U.S. 45°3′ N, 83°28′ W 94
Alpera, Sp. 38°56′ N, 1°14′ W 164
Alpercatas, Serra das, Braz. 6°24′ S, 46°9′ W 130
Alpha Ridge, Arctic Ocean 85°33′ N, 120°28′ W 255
Alpine, Ariz., U.S. 33°50′ N, 109°7′ W 92
Alpine, Calif., U.S. 32°50′ N, 116°47′ W 101
Alpine, Tex., U.S. 30°20′ N, 103°40′ W 92
Alps, mountains, Europe 44°14′ N, 6°2′ E 165
Al-Quds see Jerusalem, Israel 31°46′ N, 35°9′ E 194
Alsace, adm. division, Fr. 47°41′ N, 7°21′ E 150
Alsace, region, Europe 48°41′ N, 7°17′ E 163
Alsask, Can. 51°23′ N, 109°59′ W 90
Alsdorf, Ger. 50°52′ N, 6°10′ E 167
Alsea, river, Oreg., U.S. 44°18′ N, 124°1′ W 90
Alsfeld, Ger. 50°45′ N, 9°16′ E 167
Alstahaug, Nor. 65°53′ N, 12°23′ E 152
Alstead, N.H., U.S. 43°8′ N, 72°22′ W 104
Alston, U.K. 54°48′ N, 2°26′ W 162
Alsunga, Latv. 56°58′ N, 21°32′ E 166
Alta, Iowa, U.S. 42°39′ N, 95°19′ W 90
Alta, Nor. 69°56′ N, 23°12′ E 152
Alta Coloma, peak, Sp. 37°34′ N, 3°36′ W 164
Alta Sierra, Calif., U.S. 35°43′ N, 118°34′ W 101
Altagracia, Venez. 10°43′ N, 71°32′ W 136
Altagracia de Orituco, Venez. 9°51′ N, 66°25′ W 136
Altamachi, Bol. 16°54′ S, 66°23′ W 137
Altamachi, river, Bol. 16°4′ S, 66°58′ W 137
Altamaha, river, Ga., U.S. 31°52′ N, 82°32′ W 80
Altamira, Braz. 1°38′ N, 67°12′ W 136
Altamira, Braz. 3°13′ S, 52°16′ W 130
Altamira, Chile 25°48′ S, 69°53′ W 132
Altamira, Col. 2°4′ N, 75°50′ W 136
Altamira, C.R. 10°29′ N, 84°22′ W 116
Altamira, Mex. 22°23′ N, 97°56′ W 114
Altamont, Ill., U.S. 39°3′ N, 88°45′ W 102
Altamont, N.Y., U.S. 42°42′ N, 74°3′ W 104
Altamura, Isla de, island, Mex. 24°52′ N, 109°26′ W 112
Altan Xiret see Ejin Horo Qi, China 39°33′ N, 109°44′ E 198
Altano, Capo, It. 39°15′ N, 7°47′ E 156
Altar, Mex. 30°43′ N, 111°51′ W 92
Altar, Desierto de, Mex. 32°29′ N, 114°39′ W 101
Altares, Mex. 28°50′ N, 103°22′ W 92
Altata, Mex. 24°37′ N, 107°56′ W 112
Altaville, Calif., U.S. 38°5′ N, 120°34′ W 100
Altavista, Va., U.S. 37°6′ N, 79°18′ W 96
Altay, China 47°53′ N, 88°12′ E 184
Altay, Mongolia 46°18′ N, 96°16′ E 190
Altay, Russ. 60°18′ N, 68°55′ E 169
Altay, adm. division, Russ. 52°16′ N, 81°43′ E 184
Altay Mountains, Asia 53°12′ N, 81°13′ E 184
Altayskiy, Russ. 51°57′ N, 85°25′ E 184
Altdorf, Ger. 48°33′ N, 12°6′ E 152
Altdorf, Switz. 46°52′ N, 8°38′ E 167
Altea, Sp. 38°36′ N, 0°3′ W 164
Altena, Ger. 51°16′ N, 7°39′ E 167
Altenberge, Ger. 52°2′ N, 7°28′ E 167
Altenbruch, Ger. 53°48′ N, 8°46′ E 163
Altenkirchen, Ger. 50°41′ N, 7°39′ E 167
Alter do Chão, Braz. 2°30′ S, 55°2′ W 130
Altiağac, Azerb. 40°51′ N, 48°57′ E 195
Altınekin, Turk. 38°17′ N, 32°52′ E 156
Altıntaş, Turk. 39°4′ N, 30°7′ E 156
Altınyayla, Turk. 36°59′ N, 29°32′ E 156
Altiplano, Bol.-Peru 18°49′ S, 68°8′ W 137
Altkirch, Fr. 47°37′ N, 7°13′ E 150
Alto, La., U.S. 32°20′ N, 91°52′ W 103
Alto, Tex., U.S. 31°38′ N, 95°5′ W 103
Alto Araguaia, Braz. 17°22′ S, 53°17′ W 138
Alto, Cerro, peak, Tex., U.S. 31°54′ N, 106°1′ W 92
Alto Chicapa, Angola 10°54′ S, 19°12′ E 220
Alto Garças, Braz. 16°58′ S, 53°32′ W 132
Alto Ligonha, Mozambique 15°32′ S, 38°17′ E 224
Alto Molócuè, Mozambique 15°37′ S, 37°42′ E 224
Alto Paraguai, Braz. 14°36′ S, 56°36′ W 132
Alto Paraíso de Goias, Braz. 14°8′ S, 47°31′ W 138
Alto Paraná, Braz. 23°6′ S, 52°30′ W 138
Alto Parnaíba, Braz. 9°7′ S, 45°59′ W 132
Alto Purús, river, Peru 10°46′ S, 71°45′ W 137
Alto Río Senguerr, Arg. 45°3′ S, 70°50′ W 134
Alto Sucuriú, Braz. 19°17′ S, 52°50′ W 138
Alto Taquari, Braz. 17°52′ S, 53°18′ W 138
Alto Uruguai, Braz. 27°22′ S, 54°9′ W 139
Alto Yuruá, river, Braz. 9°10′ S, 72°49′ W 137
Alton, Calif., U.S. 40°33′ N, 124°9′ W 90
Alton, Iowa, U.S. 42°57′ N, 96°2′ W 90
Alton, Mo., U.S. 38°53′ N, 90°11′ W 94
Alton, N.H., U.S. 43°27′ N, 71°14′ W 104
Alton, N.Z. 39°40′ S, 174°25′ E 240
Alton, U.K. 51°8′ N, 0°59′ E 162
Alton Bay, N.H., U.S. 43°28′ N, 71°16′ W 104
Alton, oil field, Austral. 27°55′ S, 149°8′ E 230
Altona, Can. 49°5′ N, 97°34′ W 90
Altona, Ger. 53°33′ N, 9°58′ E 150
Altoona, Wis., U.S. 44°47′ N, 91°26′ W 94
Altotonga, Mex. 19°45′ N, 97°15′ W 114
Altrincham, U.K. 53°23′ N, 2°21′ W 162
Altun Ha, ruin(s), Belize 17°45′ N, 88°29′ W 115
Altunhisar, Turk. 37°59′ N, 34°21′ E 156
Alturas, Calif., U.S. 41°29′ N, 120°34′ W 90
Altus, Okla., U.S. 34°37′ N, 99°20′ W 92
Aluk, Sudan 8°23′ N, 27°29′ E 224
Alūksne, Latv. 57°25′ N, 27°0′ E 166
Aluniş, Rom. 46°53′ N, 24°50′ E 156
Alunite, Nev., U.S. 35°58′ N, 114°55′ W 101
Alupka, Ukr. 44°25′ N, 34°0′ E 156
Alushta, Ukr. 44°40′ N, 34°20′ E 156
Alustante, Sp. 40°36′ N, 1°40′ W 164
Alva, Okla., U.S. 36°47′ N, 98°40′ W 92
Alvajärvi, Fin. 63°26′ N, 25°21′ E 152
Alvarado, Mex. 18°45′ N, 95°45′ W 114
Alvarado, Tex., U.S. 32°24′ N, 97°11′ W 96
Alvarães, Braz. 3°15′ S, 64°56′ W 130
Álvaro Obregón, Presa, lake, Mex. 28°1′ N, 111°16′ W 81
Alvdal, Nor. 62°5′ N, 10°39′ E 152
Alvear, Arg. 29°4′ S, 56°33′ W 139
Alvin, Ill., U.S. 40°18′ N, 87°36′ W 102

Alvin, *Tex., U.S.* 29°24' N, 95°14' W **103**
Alvinston, *Can.* 42°49' N, 81°51' W **102**
Alvito, *Port.* 38°14' N, 8°0' W **150**
Alvkarleby, *Sw.* 60°32' N, 17°22' E **166**
Alvorada, *Braz.* 12°33' S, 49°9' W **130**
Alvord, *Tex., U.S.* 33°21' N, 97°42' W **92**
Alvord Desert, *Oreg., U.S.* 42°35' N, 118°19' W **90**
Älvros, *Nor.* 62°3' N, 14°37' E **152**
Älvsbyn, *Nor.* 65°40' N, 20°58' E **152**
Alwar, *India* 27°33' N, 76°36' E **197**
Alxa Zuoqi, *China* 38°51' N, 105°44' E **198**
Alyangula, *Austral.* 13°52' S, 136°30' E **173**
Alysardakh, *Russ.* 65°53' N, 131°29' E **160**
Alytus, *Lith.* 54°23' N, 24°1' E **166**
Alyzia, ruin(s), *Gr.* 38°40' N, 20°49' E **156**
Alzada, *Mont., U.S.* 45°0' N, 104°24' W **90**
Alzenau, *Ger.* 50°5' N, 9°3' E **167**
Alzira, *Sp.* 39°7' N, 0°29' E **214**
Am Dam, *Chad* 12°45' N, 20°28' E **216**
Am Djéména, *Chad* 13°6' N, 17°19' E **216**
Am Djeress, spring, *Chad* 16°7' N, 22°54' E **226**
Am Khoumi, *Chad* 12°48' N, 19°43' E **216**
Am Léiouna, *Chad* 12°47' N, 21°49' E **216**
Am Timan, *Chad* 11°0' N, 20°18' E **216**
Am Zoer, *Chad* 14°11' N, 21°22' E **216**
Amacayacu National Park, *Col.* 3°48' S, 70°34' W **136**
Amada Gaza, *Cen. Af. Rep.* 4°45' N, 15°10' E **218**
Amada, ruin(s), *Egypt* 22°41' N, 32°11' E **182**
Amadi, *Dem. Rep. of the Congo* 3°37' N, 26°45' E **224**
Amadi, *Sudan* 5°30' N, 30°21' E **218**
Amadjuak Lake, *Can.* 64°49' N, 73°51' W **106**
Amadora, *Port.* 38°45' N, 9°15' W **150**
Amagansett, *N.Y., U.S.* 40°58' N, 72°10' W **104**
Amagi, *Japan* 33°24' N, 130°39' E **201**
Amaiur-Maia, *Sp.* 43°11' N, 1°28' W **164**
Åmål, *Nor.* 59°2' N, 12°38' E **152**
Amal, oil field, *Lib.* 29°23' N, 21°3' E **216**
Amalfi, *Col.* 6°57' N, 75°5' W **136**
Amalyk, *Russ.* 57°31' N, 116°39' E **173**
Amamapare, *Indonesia* 4°47' S, 136°38' E **238**
Amambaí, *Braz.* 23°6' S, 55°16' W **134**
Amambaí, river, *Braz.* 22°48' S, 54°50' W **132**
Amambaí, Serra de, *Braz.* 23°18' S, 55°51' W **132**
Amami Ō Shima, island, *Japan* 28°23' N, 129°46' E **190**
Amamula, *Dem. Rep. of the Congo* 0°19' N, 27°46' E **224**
Amanda, *Ohio, U.S.* 39°38' N, 82°45' W **102**
Amanda Park, *Wash., U.S.* 47°25' N, 123°53' W **100**
Amangeldi, *Kaz.* 50°11' N, 65°13' E **184**
Amaniú, river, *Braz.* 1°19' S, 67°42' W **136**
Amanos Dağları, *Turk.* 36°14' N, 36°0' E **156**
Amantea, *It.* 39°9' N, 16°4' E **156**
Amapá, *Braz.* 10°19' S, 69°28' W **137**
Amapá, *Braz.* 2°2' N, 50°50' W **130**
Amapá, adm. division, *Braz.* 1°12' N, 53°2' W **130**
Amarante, *Braz.* 6°17' S, 42°51' W **132**
Amardalay, *Mongolia* 46°7' N, 106°22' E **198**
Amargosa, *Braz.* 13°1' S, 39°38' W **138**
Amargosa Desert, *Nev., U.S.* 36°47' N, 116°46' W **101**
Amargosa Range, *Calif., U.S.* 36°17' N, 116°48' W **101**
Amargosa Valley, *Nev., U.S.* 36°38' N, 116°25' W **101**
Amarillo, *Tex., U.S.* 35°10' N, 101°51' W **92**
Amarkantak, *India* 22°40' N, 81°46' E **197**
Amaro, Monte, peak, *It.* 42°4' N, 14°1' E **156**
Amarpur, *India* 23°30' N, 91°37' E **197**
Amarwara, *India* 22°19' N, 79°10' E **197**
Amasa, *Mich., U.S.* 46°14' N, 88°27' W **94**
Amasia see Amasya, *Turk.* 40°40' N, 35°50' E **156**
Amasine, *Western Sahara, Mor.* 25°48' N, 13°20' W **214**
Amasra, *Turk.* 41°44' N, 32°24' E **156**
Amasya (Amasia), *Turk.* 40°40' N, 35°50' E **156**
Amatari, *Braz.* 3°16' S, 58°55' W **130**
Amataurá, *Braz.* 3°32' S, 68°4' W **136**
Amatepec, *Mex.* 18°38' N, 100°9' W **114**
Amathous, ruin(s), *Cyprus* 34°42' N, 33°5' E **194**
Amatlán de Cañas, *Mex.* 20°49' N, 104°27' W **114**
Amavon Islands, *Solomon Sea* 7°0' S, 158°0' E **242**
Amay, *Belg.* 50°33' N, 5°18' E **167**
Amazar, *Russ.* 53°50' N, 120°55' E **190**
Amazon Fan, *North Atlantic Ocean* 5°17' N, 46°22' W **253**
Amazon see Amazonas, river, *Braz.* 3°8' S, 55°59' W **123**
Amazonas, adm. division, *Braz.* 5°31' S, 65°36' W **130**
Amazonas (Amazon), river, *Braz.* 3°8' S, 55°59' W **123**
Amazonas see Solimões, river, *Braz.* 2°50' S, 66°35' W **123**
Amazônia National Park, *Braz.* 4°19' S, 57°15' W **130**
Amb, *Pak.* 34°14' N, 72°48' E **186**
Āmba Gīyorgīs, *Eth.* 12°41' N, 37°37' E **218**
Āmba Maryam, *Eth.* 11°23' N, 39°16' E **182**
Ambala, *India* 30°21' N, 76°50' E **197**
Ambalangoda, *Sri Lanka* 6°16' N, 80°4' E **188**
Ambalantota, *Sri Lanka* 6°7' N, 81°4' E **188**
Ambarchik, *Russ.* 69°33' N, 162°14' E **160**
Ambato, *Ecua.* 1°21' S, 78°48' W **130**
Ambato Boeny, *Madagascar* 16°27' S, 46°44' E **220**
Ambatolampy, *Madagascar* 19°24' S, 47°27' E **220**
Ambatondrazaka, *Madagascar* 18°0' S, 48°24' E **207**
Ambazac, *Fr.* 45°57' N, 1°23' E **150**
Ambelau, island, *Indonesia* 4°17' S, 127°15' E **192**
Ambergris Cay, island, *Belize* 17°58' N, 87°52' W **115**
Ambergris Cays, islands, *North Atlantic Ocean* 21°19' N, 72°57' W **116**
Amberley, *Can.* 44°1' N, 81°42' W **102**
Amberley, *N.Z.* 43°10' S, 172°44' E **240**
Amberley, *U.K.* 50°54' N, 0°32' E **162**
Ambidédi, *Mali* 14°34' N, 11°50' W **222**
Ambikapur, *India* 23°7' N, 83°12' E **197**
Ambilobe, *Madagascar* 13°13' S, 49°2' E **220**
Ambla, *Est.* 59°10' N, 25°48' E **166**
Ambler, *Alas., U.S.* 67°5' N, 157°52' W **98**
Ambleside, *U.K.* 54°25' N, 2°58' W **162**
Ambleteuse, *Fr.* 50°48' N, 1°36' E **163**
Ambo, *Peru* 10°11' S, 76°10' W **130**
Amboasary, *Madagascar* 25°4' S, 46°26' E **220**
Ambodifotatra, *Madagascar* 16°58' S, 49°51' E **220**
Ambohimahasoa, *Madagascar* 21°6' S, 47°13' E **220**
Ambohimanga Atsimo, *Madagascar* 20°53' S, 47°36' E **220**
Amboise, *Fr.* 47°24' N, 0°58' E **150**
Amboiva, *Angola* 11°34' S, 14°44' E **220**
Ambolauri, *Ga.* 42°28' N, 43°9' E **195**
Ambon, *Indonesia* 3°41' S, 128°3' E **192**
Amboró National Park, *Bol.* 17°42' S, 64°48' W **137**
Amborompotsy, *Madagascar* 20°35' S, 46°14' E **220**
Amboseli National Park, *Kenya* 2°50' S, 37°15' E **224**
Amboy, *Ill., U.S.* 41°42' N, 89°20' W **102**
Amboy Crater, *Calif., U.S.* 34°31' N, 115°48' W **101**
Ambre, Cap d', *Madagascar* 12°1' S, 49°15' E **220**
Ambre, Montagne d', peak, *Madagascar* 12°41' S, 48°58' E **220**
Ambriz, *Angola* 7°51' S, 13°6' E **218**
Ambrogio, *It.* 44°55' N, 11°55' E **167**
Ambrósio, *Braz.* 2°53' S, 68°19' W **136**
Amburan Burnu, *Azerb.* 40°36' N, 49°49' E **195**
Amchitka, island, *Alas., U.S.* 51°7' N, 177°20' E **160**
Amderma, *Russ.* 69°42' N, 61°41' E **169**
Amdillis, spring, *Mali* 18°24' N, 0°17' E **222**
Amdo, *China* 32°19' N, 91°44' E **188**
Ameca, *Mex.* 20°33' N, 104°3' W **114**
Ameca, river, *Mex.* 20°55' N, 105°12' W **114**
Ameghino, *Arg.* 34°51' S, 62°28' W **139**
Ameland, island, *Neth.* 53°28' N, 5°37' E **163**
Amelia, *La., U.S.* 29°40' N, 91°7' W **103**
Amenia, *N.Y., U.S.* 41°50' N, 73°34' W **104**
America-Antarctic Ridge (North Weddell Ridge), *South Atlantic Ocean* 59°0' S, 16°0' W **255**
American Highland, *Antarctica* 74°55' S, 76°3' E **248**
American, river, *Wash., U.S.* 46°53' N, 121°26' W **100**
American Samoa, *United States* 14°0' S, 171°0' W **238**
Americus, *Ga., U.S.* 32°3' N, 84°15' W **112**
Amersfoort, *S. Af.* 27°2' S, 29°51' E **227**
Amery, *Wis., U.S.* 45°18' N, 92°23' W **94**
Amery Ice Shelf, *Antarctica* 71°16' S, 69°44' E **248**
Ames, *Iowa, U.S.* 42°0' N, 93°37' W **94**
Amesbury, *Mass., U.S.* 42°50' N, 70°57' W **104**
Amesbury, *U.K.* 51°10' N, 1°47' W **162**
Amga, *Russ.* 61°1' N, 131°52' E **160**
Amga, river, *Russ.* 59°34' N, 126°34' E **160**
Amgu, *Russ.* 45°56' N, 137°30' E **190**
Amguema, river, *Russ.* 67°26' N, 178°38' W **98**
Amguid, *Alg.* 26°26' N, 5°23' E **214**
Amhara, region, *Africa* 12°12' N, 36°11' E **182**
Amherst, *Can.* 45°49' N, 64°13' W **111**
Amherst, *N.H., U.S.* 42°51' N, 71°38' W **104**
Amherst, *N.Y., U.S.* 42°58' N, 78°50' W **94**
Amherst, *Ohio, U.S.* 41°23' N, 82°14' W **102**
Amherst, *Tex., U.S.* 33°59' N, 102°23' W **92**
Amherst, *Va., U.S.* 37°34' N, 79°4' W **96**
Amherstburg, *Can.* 42°5' N, 83°6' W **102**
Amhovichy, *Belarus* 53°6' N, 27°50' E **158**
Amiata, Monte, peak, *It.* 42°53' N, 11°32' E **156**
Amidon, *N. Dak., U.S.* 46°27' N, 103°19' W **90**
Amiens, *Fr.* 49°52' N, 2°18' E **163**
Amili, *India* 28°23' N, 95°50' E **188**
Amino, *Japan* 35°39' N, 135°1' E **201**
Aminuis, *Namibia* 23°43' S, 19°18' E **227**
Amiot Islands, *South Pacific Ocean* 67°26' S, 74°9' W **248**
Amioun, *Leb.* 34°17' N, 35°48' E **194**
Amirante Isles, *Indian Ocean* 4°41' S, 51°23' E **173**
Amirante Trench, *Indian Ocean* 9°12' S, 53°16' E **254**
Amisk Lake, lake, *Can.* 54°33' N, 102°35' W **108**
Amisk, river, *Can.* 54°40' N, 112°29' W **108**
Amistad National Recreation Area, *Tex., U.S.* 29°32' N, 101°42' W **96**
Amistad Reservoir, lake, *Tex., U.S.* 29°33' N, 101°44' W **92**
Amisus see Samsun, *Turk.* 41°17' N, 36°20' E **158**
Amite, *La., U.S.* 30°42' N, 90°31' W **103**
Amity, *Ark., U.S.* 34°14' N, 93°28' W **96**
Amla, *India* 21°56' N, 78°9' E **197**
Åmli, *Nor.* 58°45' N, 8°29' E **152**
Amlia, island, *Alas., U.S.* 52°10' N, 173°59' W **160**
'Amm Adam, *Sudan* 16°21' N, 36°4' E **182**
'Ammān (Philadelphia), *Jordan* 31°56' N, 35°53' E **194**
Ammanford, *U.K.* 51°47' N, 4°0' W **162**
Ammänsaari, *Fin.* 64°50' N, 28°52' E **152**
Ammarfjället, peak, *Nor.* 66°4' N, 15°30' E **152**
Ammarnäs, *Nor.* 65°57' N, 16°10' E **152**
Ammeloe, *Ger.* 52°4' N, 6°47' E **167**
Ammochostos (Famagusta, Gazimagusa), *Northern Cyprus, Cyprus* 35°7' N, 33°56' E **194**
Amo, *Ind., U.S.* 39°41' N, 86°37' W **102**
Āmol, *Iran* 36°36' N, 52°17' E **180**
Amolar, *Braz.* 18°1' S, 57°31' W **132**
Amos, *Can.* 48°34' N, 78°8' W **94**
Amot, *Mor.* 27°57' N, 10°6' W **214**
Åmot, *Nor.* 59°36' N, 7°57' E **152**
Åmotfors, *Nor.* 59°47' N, 12°24' E **152**
Amoúdia, peak, *Gr.* 37°31' N, 25°56' E **156**
Amoy see Xiamen, *China* 24°25' N, 118°6' E **198**
Ampani, *India* 19°34' N, 82°36' E **188**
Ampanihy, *Madagascar* 24°39' S, 44°42' E **220**
Amparafaravola, *Madagascar* 17°36' S, 48°13' E **220**
Amparihy Est, *Madagascar* 23°58' S, 47°22' E **220**
Amparo, *Braz.* 22°42' S, 46°47' W **138**
Ampato, Nevado, peak, *Peru* 15°52' S, 71°55' W **137**
Ampere, *Braz.* 25°57' S, 53°30' W **139**
Ampezzo, *It.* 46°23' N, 12°47' E **167**
Amphiareion, ruin(s), *Gr.* 38°17' N, 23°43' E **156**
Amphitrite Point, *Can.* 48°43' N, 125°48' W **90**
Amposta, *Sp.* 40°42' N, 0°34' E **164**
Ampthill, *U.K.* 52°1' N, 0°30' E **162**
Amqui, *Can.* 48°27' N, 67°27' W **94**
'Amrān, *Yemen* 15°40' N, 43°57' E **182**
Amravati, *India* 20°56' N, 77°46' E **188**
Amreli, *India* 21°36' N, 71°12' E **186**
'Amrīt (Marathus), ruin(s), *Syr.* 34°50' N, 35°52' E **194**
'Amrīt, ruin(s), *Syr.* 34°48' N, 35°49' E **156**
Amritsar, *India* 31°39' N, 74°52' E **186**
Amroha, *India* 28°54' N, 78°28' E **188**
Amsā'ad, *Lib.* 31°37' N, 25°2' E **180**
'Amshīt, *Leb.* 34°9' N, 35°38' E **194**
Amsterdam, *Neth.* 52°22' N, 4°50' E **163**
Amsterdam, *N.Y., U.S.* 42°56' N, 74°12' W **104**
Amsterdam, island, *Fr.* 37°45' S, 78°0' E **254**
Amstetten, *Aust.* 48°7' N, 14°51' E **152**
Amston, *Conn., U.S.* 41°37' N, 72°21' W **104**
Amu Darya, river, *Uzb.* 41°1' N, 61°42' E **184**
Amuay, *Venez.* 11°51' N, 70°4' W **123**
'Āmūdah, *Syr.* 37°6' N, 40°57' E **195**
Amukta, island, *Alas., U.S.* 52°4' N, 171°7' W **160**
Amuku Mountains, *Guyana* 2°4' N, 58°12' W **130**
Amundsen Basin *Arctic Ocean* 88°0' N, 90°0' E **255**
Amundsen Gulf 70°20' N, 123°56' W **98**
Amundsen, Mount, *Antarctica* 67°13' S, 101°28' E **248**
Amundsen Plain *South Pacific Ocean* 65°0' S, 125°0' W **255**
Amundsen Sea 73°41' S, 105°21' W **248**
Amundsen-Scott South Pole, station, *Antarctica* 89°59' S, 164°21' W **248**
Amur, adm. division, *Russ.* 53°36' N, 124°46' E **190**
Amur, river, *Russ.* 51°18' N, 138°37' E **190**
Amurang, *Indonesia* 1°13' N, 124°28' E **192**
Amurrio, *Sp.* 43°2' N, 3°1' W **164**
Amusco, *Sp.* 42°10' N, 4°28' W **150**
Amvrosiyivka, *Ukr.* 47°44' N, 38°26' E **158**
Amydery'a, *Turkm.* 37°56' N, 65°18' E **197**
An, *Myanmar* 19°46' N, 94°7' E **202**
An Khe, *Vietnam* 13°58' N, 108°40' E **202**
An Nabī Shīt, *Leb.* 33°52' N, 36°6' E **194**
An Nabk, *Syr.* 34°1' N, 36°44' E **194**
An Nabk Abū Qaṣr, spring, *Saudi Arabia* 30°18' N, 38°41' E **180**
An Nafūd, *Saudi Arabia* 28°35' N, 39°18' E **180**
An Najaf (Najaf), *Iraq* 31°58' N, 44°19' E **180**
An Namatah, *Jordan* 30°48' N, 35°32' E **194**
An Nashshāsh, *U.A.E.* 23°1' N, 54°3' E **182**
An Nāṣirīyah, *Syr.* 33°52' N, 36°48' E **194**
An Nāṣirīyah (Nasiriyah), *Iraq* 31°5' N, 46°11' E **180**
An Nawfalīyah, *Lib.* 30°41' N, 17°49' E **143**
An Nimāṣ, *Saudi Arabia* 19°2' N, 42°9' E **182**
An Nu'ayrīyah, *Saudi Arabia* 27°28' N, 48°27' E **196**
An Pass, *Myanmar* 19°59' N, 94°17' E **202**
An Phuoc, *Vietnam* 11°36' N, 108°54' E **202**
An Uaimh see Navan, *Ire.* 53°38' N, 6°42' W **150**
Ana María, Cayos, islands, *Caribbean Sea* 21°11' N, 79°29' W **116**
Anabar, river, *Russ.* 70°31' N, 114°9' E **160**
Anabarskiy Zaliv 73°25' N, 108°6' E **160**
Anacapa Island, *North Pacific Ocean* 34°4' N, 119°29' W **100**
Anaco, *Venez.* 9°26' N, 64°30' W **116**
Anacoco, *La., U.S.* 31°14' N, 93°21' W **103**
Anaconda, *Mont., U.S.* 46°7' N, 112°58' W **90**
Anaconda Range, *Mont., U.S.* 45°49' N, 113°46' W **90**
Anacortes, *Wash., U.S.* 48°28' N, 122°38' W **100**
Anactorium, ruin(s), *Gr.* 38°55' N, 20°45' E **156**
Anadyr', *Russ.* 64°38' N, 177°6' E **160**
Anadyr, Gulf of see Anadyrskiy Zaliv 66°48' N, 179°18' W **160**
Anadyr', river, *Russ.* 66°42' N, 169°30' E **160**
Anadyrskiy Zaliv (Anadyr, Gulf of) 66°48' N, 179°18' W **160**
Anáfi, *Gr.* 36°20' N, 25°46' E **156**
Anáfi, island, *Gr.* 36°24' N, 25°52' E **180**
Anagé, *Braz.* 14°45' S, 41°10' W **138**
Anaghit, *Eritrea* 16°20' N, 38°35' E **182**
'Ānah, *Iraq* 34°25' N, 41°58' E **180**
Anaheim, *Calif., U.S.* 33°50' N, 117°56' W **101**
Anahim Lake, *Can.* 52°28' N, 125°20' W **108**
Anahola, *Hawai'i, U.S.* 22°8' N, 159°19' W **99**
Anáhuac, *Mex.* 27°13' N, 100°9' W **96**
Anáhuac, *Mex.* 24°27' N, 101°31' W **114**
Anahuac, *Tex., U.S.* 29°45' N, 94°41' W **103**
Anai Mudi, peak, *India* 10°8' N, 76°55' E **188**
Anaï, spring, *Alg.* 24°9' N, 11°27' E **214**
Anajás, *Braz.* 1°0' N, 49°58' W **130**
Anak, *N. Korea* 38°29' N, 125°29' E **200**
Anaktuvuk Pass, *Alas., U.S.* 68°11' N, 151°54' W **98**
Analalava, *Madagascar* 14°38' S, 47°47' E **220**
Analavelona, peak, *Madagascar* 22°36' S, 44°2' E **220**
Anamã, *Braz.* 3°33' S, 61°30' W **130**
Anambas, Kepulauan, islands, *South China Sea* 2°41' N, 105°43' E **196**
Anamizu, *Japan* 37°13' N, 136°54' E **201**
Anamoose, *N. Dak., U.S.* 47°51' N, 100°15' W **90**
Anamosa, *Iowa, U.S.* 42°6' N, 91°17' W **94**
Anamu, river, *Braz.* 0°42' N, 56°51' W **130**
Anamur, *Turk.* 36°5' N, 32°51' E **156**
Anamur Burnu, *Azerb.* 36°2' N, 32°4' E **156**
Anan, *Japan* 33°52' N, 134°37' E **201**
Ananchichi, *Belarus* 52°31' N, 27°39' E **152**
Anand, *India* 22°33' N, 73°0' E **186**
Anan'yiv, *Ukr.* 47°43' N, 29°58' E **156**
Anapa, *Russ.* 44°54' N, 37°23' E **156**
Anápolis, *Braz.* 16°21' S, 48°59' W **138**
Anār, *Iran* 30°51' N, 55°18' E **180**
Anārak, *Iran* 33°20' N, 53°42' E **180**
Ånäset, *Nor.* 64°14' N, 21°2' E **152**
Anastasia Island, *Fla., U.S.* 29°52' N, 81°16' W **105**
Anatahan, island, *U.S.* 16°12' N, 144°27' E **192**
Anatolia (Asia Minor), region, *Asia* 38°39' N, 30°18' E **180**
Anatolikí Makedonía Kai Thráki, adm. division, *Gr.* 41°5' N, 15°57' E **156**
Anatone, *Wash., U.S.* 46°7' N, 117°9' W **90**
Añatuya, *Arg.* 28°28' S, 62°49' W **139**
Anauá, river, *Braz.* 0°57' N, 60°9' W **130**
Anaurilândia, *Braz.* 22°2' S, 52°48' W **138**
Añavieja, *Sp.* 41°51' N, 1°56' W **164**
Anavilhanas, Arquipélago das, *South America* 3°13' S, 62°22' W **130**
Anbyŏn, *N. Korea* 39°2' N, 127°31' E **200**
Ancares, Sierra de, *Sp.* 42°54' N, 7°7' W **150**
Ancash, adm. division, *Peru* 9°4' S, 78°36' W **130**
Ancasti, Sierra de, *Arg.* 28°4' S, 65°55' W **132**
Anchieta, *Braz.* 20°51' S, 40°44' W **138**
Anchorage, *Alas., U.S.* 61°5' N, 149°53' W **98**
Anchorena, *Arg.* 35°40' S, 65°23' W **134**
Anclitas, Cayo, island, *Cuba* 20°30' N, 79°14' W **116**
Ancona, *It.* 43°36' N, 13°30' E **167**
Ancram, *N.Y., U.S.* 42°2' N, 73°40' W **104**
Ancuabe, *Mozambique* 13°2' S, 39°54' E **224**
Ancud, *Chile* 41°59' S, 73°55' W **123**
Ancud, Golfo de 42°13' S, 73°45' W **134**
Ancy-le-Franc, *Fr.* 47°46' N, 4°9' E **150**
Anda, *China* 46°22' N, 125°24' E **198**
Andacollo, *Arg.* 37°13' S, 70°40' W **134**
Andahuaylas, *Peru* 13°41' S, 73°24' W **137**
Andalgalẑa, *Arg.* 27°36' S, 66°19' W **132**
Åndalsnes, *Nor.* 62°33' N, 7°42' E **152**
Andalusia, *Ala., U.S.* 31°18' N, 86°28' W **96**
Andalusia, adm. division, *Sp.* 37°27' N, 4°53' W **164**
Andaman and Nicobar Islands, *India* 11°25' N, 92°50' E **192**
Andaman Basin, *Andaman Sea* 9°56' N, 95°4' E **254**
Andaman Islands, *Andaman Sea* 12°47' N, 94°43' E **202**
Andaman Sea 15°15' N, 94°7' E **188**
Andapa, *Madagascar* 14°39' S, 49°40' E **220**
Andara, *Namibia* 18°3' S, 21°32' E **220**
Andaraí, *Braz.* 12°49' S, 41°21' W **138**
Andavaka, Cap, *Madagascar* 25°40' S, 46°43' E **220**
Andeg, *Russ.* 67°55' N, 53°10' E **169**
Andelot-Blancheville, *Fr.* 48°14' N, 5°17' E **163**
Andenne, *Belg.* 50°29' N, 5°5' E **167**
Andéranboukane, *Mali* 15°27' N, 3°2' E **222**
Andermatt, *Switz.* 46°38' N, 8°36' E **167**
Andernach, *Ger.* 50°26' N, 7°23' E **167**
Anderson, *Calif., U.S.* 40°26' N, 122°19' W **90**
Anderson, *Ind., U.S.* 40°5' N, 85°41' W **102**
Anderson, *Mo., U.S.* 36°38' N, 94°27' W **96**
Anderson, *S.C., U.S.* 34°29' N, 82°40' W **96**
Anderson Dome, *Antarctica* 72°28' S, 87°2' W **248**
Anderson Massif, *Antarctica* 78°56' S, 82°12' W **248**
Anderson Ranch Dam, *Idaho, U.S.* 43°28' N, 115°37' W **90**
Anderson, river, *Can.* 68°35' N, 127°50' W **98**
Andersson Island, *Antarctica* 63°39' S, 59°14' W **134**
Andes, Cordillera de los, mountains, *South America* 9°47' S, 74°52' W **123**
Andhra Pradesh, adm. division, *India* 16°19' N, 79°37' E **188**
Andijon, *Uzb.* 40°46' N, 72°21' E **197**
Andikira, *Gr.* 38°22' N, 22°36' E **156**
Andikíthira, island, *Gr.* 35°48' N, 22°23' E **180**
Andilálou, ruin(s), *Gr.* 41°29' N, 24°9' E **156**
Andilamena, *Madagascar* 17°2' S, 48°33' E **220**
Andir, river, *China* 36°34' N, 84°8' E **184**
Andirá, *Braz.* 3°45' S, 66°17' W **136**
Andırın, *Turk.* 37°34' N, 36°21' E **156**
Andirlangar, *China* 37°37' N, 83°47' E **184**
Andkhvoy, *Afghan.* 36°55' N, 65°8' E **186**
Andoany (Hell-Ville), *Madagascar* 13°24' S, 48°17' E **207**
Andoas, *Peru* 2°57' S, 76°25' W **136**
Andomskiy Pogost, *Russ.* 61°14' N, 36°39' E **154**
Andong, *S. Korea* 36°33' N, 128°43' E **200**
Andorra la Vella, *Andorra* 42°29' N, 1°26' E **164**
Andorra 42°29' N, 1°26' E **164**
Andover, *Me., U.S.* 44°37' N, 70°46' W **94**
Andover, *N.H., U.S.* 43°26' N, 71°50' W **104**
Andover, *U.K.* 51°12' N, 1°30' W **162**
Andovoranto, *Madagascar* 18°57' S, 49°5' E **220**
Andøya, island, *Nor.* 69°24' N, 14°6' E **160**
Andradina, *Braz.* 20°56' S, 51°24' W **138**
Andreapol', *Russ.* 56°39' N, 32°18' E **154**
Andreba, *Madagascar* 17°40' S, 48°33' E **220**
Andrew, *Can.* 53°52' N, 112°20' W **108**
Andrews, *Ind., U.S.* 40°50' N, 85°37' W **102**
Andrews, *S.C., U.S.* 33°26' N, 79°34' W **96**
Andrews, *Tex., U.S.* 32°18' N, 102°33' W **92**
Andreyevka, *Russ.* 52°20' N, 51°50' E **158**
Andrijevica, *Mont.* 42°43' N, 19°47' E **168**
Androka, *Madagascar* 25°1' S, 44°7' E **220**
Ándros, island, *Gr.* 37°54' N, 24°57' E **180**
Androscoggin, river, *Me., U.S.* 44°23' N, 71°6' W **104**
Andryushino, *Russ.* 59°17' N, 62°59' E **154**
Andryushkino, *Russ.* 69°9' N, 154°31' E **160**
Andújar, *Sp.* 38°2' N, 4°3' W **164**
Andulo, *Angola* 11°31' S, 16°41' E **220**
Aneby, *Nor.* 57°49' N, 14°46' E **152**
Anefis I-n-Darane, *Mali* 18°2' N, 0°37' E **222**
Anegada, island, *U.K.* 18°43' N, 65°1' W **116**
Anegada, Punta, *Pan.* 7°14' N, 81°48' W **115**
Añelo, Cuenca del, *Arg.* 37°56' S, 69°57' W **134**
Anenii Noi, *Mold.* 46°52' N, 29°13' E **156**
Aneroid, *Can.* 49°42' N, 107°18' W **90**
Anet, *Fr.* 48°51' N, 1°26' E **163**
Aneta, *N. Dak., U.S.* 47°39' N, 98°0' W **90**
Aneto, peak, *Sp.* 42°37' N, 0°39' E **164**
Aney, *Niger* 19°27' N, 12°54' E **216**
Anfah, *Leb.* 34°21' N, 35°44' E **194**
Angamos, Punta, *Chile* 23°1' S, 71°22' W **132**
Angang, *S. Korea* 35°58' N, 129°15' E **200**
Angangueo, *Mex.* 19°36' N, 100°17' W **114**
Ang'angxi, *China* 47°7' N, 123°48' E **198**
Angara, river, *Russ.* 58°38' N, 98°21' E **246**
Angarsk, *Russ.* 52°43' N, 103°32' E **190**
Angaur (Ngeaur), island, *Palau* 7°0' N, 134°0' E **242**
Ånge, *Nor.* 62°31' N, 15°37' E **152**
Ángel de la Guarda, Isla, island, *Mex.* 29°35' N, 113°31' W **112**
Angel Falls, *Venez.* 4°34' N, 63°39' W **123**
Angeles, *Philippines* 15°8' N, 120°35' E **203**
Angélica, *Arg.* 31°33' S, 61°32' W **139**
Angelina, river, *Tex., U.S.* 31°30' N, 94°50' W **103**
Angels Camp, *Calif., U.S.* 38°4' N, 120°33' W **100**
Angermünde, *Ger.* 53°1' N, 14°0' E **152**
Angers, *Fr.* 47°28' N, 0°33' E **150**
Angerville, *Fr.* 48°18' N, 1°59' E **163**
Angical, *Braz.* 12°0' S, 44°40' W **132**
Angie, *La., U.S.* 30°57' N, 89°49' W **103**
Angkor, ruin(s), *Cambodia* 13°28' N, 103°45' E **202**
Angle Inlet, *Minn., U.S.* 49°18' N, 95°7' W **90**
Anglem, Mount, *N.Z.* 46°46' S, 167°48' E **240**
Anglès, *Sp.* 41°56' N, 2°38' E **164**
Angleton, *Tex., U.S.* 29°9' N, 95°26' W **103**
Anglure, *Fr.* 48°35' N, 3°48' E **163**
Ango, *Dem. Rep. of the Congo* 3°58' N, 25°52' E **224**
Angoche, *Mozambique* 16°12' S, 39°57' E **224**
Angohrān, *Iran* 26°33' N, 57°50' E **196**
Angol, *Chile* 37°49' S, 72°43' W **134**
Angola 12°18' S, 17°4' E **220**
Angola, *Ind., U.S.* 41°38' N, 85°0' W **102**
Angola, *La., U.S.* 30°56' N, 91°34' W **103**
Angola, *N.Y., U.S.* 42°38' N, 79°3' W **94**
Angola Plain, *South Atlantic Ocean* 15°4' S, 3°22' E **253**
Angora see Ankara, *Turk.* 39°55' N, 32°43' E **156**
Angostura, *Col.* 0°28' N, 72°30' W **136**
Angostura, *Mex.* 25°21' N, 108°10' W **112**
Angostura, Presa de la, *Mex.* 30°32' N, 109°47' W **92**
Angoulême, *Fr.* 45°39' N, 0°10' E **150**
Angouma, *Gabon* 1°11' N, 12°19' E **218**
Angoumois, region, *Europe* 45°50' N, 0°49' E **165**
Angra dos Reis, *Braz.* 23°2' S, 44°20' W **138**
Angren, *Uzb.* 41°1' N, 70°14' E **197**
Angtassom, *Cambodia* 11°1' N, 104°39' E **202**
Angu, *Dem. Rep. of the Congo* 3°27' N, 24°26' E **224**
Angüés, *Sp.* 42°6' N, 0°9' E **164**
Anguil, *Arg.* 36°31' S, 64°2' W **139**
Anguilla, *U.K.* 18°48' N, 69°45' W **116**
Anguilla Cays, *North Atlantic Ocean* 23°19' N, 79°28' W **116**
Anguille, Cape, *Can.* 47°49' N, 60°20' W **111**
Angumu, *Dem. Rep. of the Congo* 0°7' N, 27°39' E **224**
Anguo, *China* 38°26' N, 115°21' E **198**
Angutikha, *Russ.* 65°58' N, 87°24' E **169**
Angvik, *Nor.* 62°53' N, 8°3' E **152**
Anhua, *China* 28°23' N, 111°3' E **198**
Anhui, adm. division, *China* 31°34' N, 117°12' E **198**
Aniak, *Alas., U.S.* 61°24' N, 159°45' W **98**
Anicuns, *Braz.* 16°32' S, 49°58' W **138**
Anie, Pic d', peak, *Fr.* 42°55' N, 0°45' E **164**
Anikhovka, *Russ.* 51°29' N, 60°15' E **154**
Animas, *N. Mex., U.S.* 31°57' N, 108°47' W **92**
Animas Peak, *N. Mex., U.S.* 31°33' N, 108°50' W **92**
Ánimas, Punta de las, *Mex.* 28°44' N, 114°7' W **112**
Anin, *Myanmar* 15°41' N, 97°46' E **202**
Aniñón, *Sp.* 41°26' N, 1°43' W **164**
Anipemza, *Arm.* 40°26' N, 43°36' E **195**
Anishinabi Lake, lake, *Can.* 50°26' N, 94°1' W **90**
Anita, *Chile* 20°29' S, 69°51' W **137**
Anita, *Pa., U.S.* 40°59' N, 78°59' W **94**
Aniva, *Mys, Russ.* 45°46' N, 142°25' E **190**
Anivorano, *Madagascar* 18°47' S, 48°58' E **220**
Anixab, *Namibia* 20°58' S, 14°46' E **220**
Anjalankoski, *Fin.* 60°41' N, 26°51' E **166**
Anjiang, *China* 27°16' N, 110°11' E **198**
Anjosvarden, peak, *Nor.* 62°24' N, 14°7' E **152**
Anjou Islands, *East Siberian Sea* 74°45' N, 144°8' E **255**
Anjou, region, *Europe* 47°39' N, 1°10' W **150**
Anju, *N. Korea* 39°35' N, 125°44' E **198**
Anka, spring, *Sudan* 14°37' N, 24°51' E **226**
Ankang, *China* 32°36' N, 109°3' E **198**
Ankara (Angora), *Turk.* 39°55' N, 32°43' E **156**
Ankaramena, *Madagascar* 21°58' S, 46°39' E **220**
Ankarede, *Nor.* 64°49' N, 14°12' E **152**
Ankasakasa, *Madagascar* 16°22' S, 44°50' E **220**
Ankazoabo, *Madagascar* 22°15' S, 44°28' E **220**
Ankazobe, *Madagascar* 18°20' S, 47°8' E **220**
Anklam, *Ger.* 53°51' N, 13°41' E **152**
Ānkober, *Eth.* 9°31' N, 39°42' E **224**
Ankofa, peak, *Madagascar* 16°23' S, 48°27' E **220**
Ankoro, *Dem. Rep. of the Congo* 6°48' S, 26°52' E **224**
Ankpa, *Nig.* 7°21' N, 7°36' E **222**
Anlong, *China* 25°0' N, 105°26' E **198**
Anlu, *China* 31°14' N, 113°42' E **198**
Ann Arbor, *Mich., U.S.* 42°15' N, 83°46' W **102**
Ann, Cape, *Mass., U.S.* 42°36' N, 70°36' W **104**
Anna, *Mo., U.S.* 37°27' N, 89°14' W **96**
Anna Paulowna, *Neth.* 52°52' N, 4°50' E **163**
Annaba (Bône), *Alg.* 36°53' N, 7°45' E **156**
Annai, *Guyana* 3°55' N, 59°7' W **130**

Annan, U.K. 54°59′ N, 3°16′ W 150
Annapolis, Md., U.S. 38°58′ N, 76°37′ W 94
Annapolis Royal, Can. 44°43′ N, 65°31′ W 111
Annecy, Fr. 45°54′ N, 6°7′ E 167
Annecy, Lac d', lake, Fr. 45°52′ N, 6°0′ E 165
Annemasse, Fr. 46°11′ N, 6°14′ E 167
Annenkov Island, U.K. 54°35′ S, 38°57′ W 134
Annenskiy Most, Russ. 60°44′ N, 37°6′ E 154
Annette, Alas., U.S. 55°2′ N, 131°38′ W 108
Anniston, Ala., U.S. 33°38′ N, 85°50′ W 96
Annobón, island, Equatorial Guinea 1°32′ S, 4°43′ E 214
Annweiler, Ger. 49°11′ N, 7°56′ E 163
Año Nuevo, Point, Calif., U.S. 37°10′ N, 122°33′ W 100
Anoka, Minn., U.S. 45°10′ N, 93°22′ W 94
Anole, Somalia 0°54′ N, 41°57′ E 224
Anori, Braz. 3°49′ S, 61°42′ W 130
Anotaie, river, Braz. 3°23′ N, 52°15′ W 130
Ânou Mellene, spring, Mali 17°27′ N, 0°32′ E 222
Ânou Mellene, spring, Mali 18°0′ N, 3°58′ E 222
Anou Meniet, spring, Alg. 24°59′ N, 4°19′ E 214
Anou-I-n-Ouzzal, spring, Alg. 20°40′ N, 2°27′ E 222
Anoumaba, Côte d'Ivoire 6°14′ N, 4°32′ W 222
Anping, China 41°9′ N, 123°28′ E 200
Anpu, China 21°25′ N, 110°2′ E 198
Anqing, China 30°36′ N, 116°59′ E 198
Anren, China 26°42′ N, 113°17′ E 198
Anröchte, Ger. 51°33′ N, 8°19′ E 167
Ans, Belg. 50°40′ N, 5°29′ E 167
Ansai, China 36°53′ N, 109°21′ E 198
Ansan, S. Korea 37°18′ N, 126°52′ E 198
Ansbach, Ger. 49°18′ N, 10°33′ E 152
Anse-à-Foleur, Haiti 19°53′ N, 72°37′ W 116
Anse-à-Galets, Haiti 18°50′ N, 72°53′ W 116
Anselmo, Nebr., U.S. 41°36′ N, 99°53′ W 90
Anseong, S. Korea 37°0′ N, 127°16′ E 200
Anse-Rouge, Haiti 19°39′ N, 73°3′ W 116
Anshan, China 41°7′ N, 122°59′ E 200
Anshun, China 26°16′ N, 105°54′ E 198
Ansina, Uru. 31°54′ S, 55°29′ W 139
Ansley, Nebr., U.S. 41°16′ N, 99°23′ W 92
Anson, Me., U.S. 44°47′ N, 69°55′ W 94
Anson, Tex., U.S. 32°44′ N, 99°54′ W 92
Ansongo, Mali 15°39′ N, 0°28′ E 222
Ansonia, Conn., U.S. 41°20′ N, 73°5′ W 104
Ansonia, Ohio, U.S. 40°12′ N, 84°39′ W 102
Ansonville, Can. 48°45′ N, 80°42′ W 94
Anta, Peru 13°29′ S, 72°9′ W 137
Antabamba, Peru 14°24′ S, 72°53′ W 137
Antakya, Turk. 36°10′ N, 36°6′ E 143
Antalaha, Madagascar 15°1′ S, 50°13′ E 207
Antalya, Turk. 36°52′ N, 30°43′ E 156
Antalya Körfezi 36°30′ N, 30°36′ E 180
Antanambe, Madagascar 16°27′ S, 49°48′ E 220
Antananarivo, Madagascar 18°59′ S, 47°21′ E 220
Antanifotsy, Madagascar 19°40′ S, 47°20′ E 220
Antarctic Ridge South Atlantic Ocean 62°0′ S, 10°0′ W 255
Antarctic Sound 62°24′ S, 58°49′ W 248
Antarctica 81°0′ S, 0°0′ E 248
Antarctica 71°33′ S, 29°36′ E 248
Antas, river, Braz. 28°48′ S, 51°2′ W 139
Antelope, Oreg., U.S. 44°53′ N, 120°44′ W 90
Antelope Lake, lake, Can. 50°13′ N, 108°54′ W 90
Antelope Peak, Nev., U.S. 39°23′ N, 116°33′ W 90
Antelope Point, peak, Mont., U.S. 45°45′ N, 109°11′ W 90
Antelope Range, Nev., U.S. 39°3′ N, 116°34′ W 90
Antelope Valley, Calif., U.S. 34°47′ N, 118°27′ W 101
Antequera, Parag. 24°5′ S, 57°12′ W 132
Antequera, Sp. 37°1′ N, 4°34′ W 164
Anterselva, It. 46°52′ N, 12°5′ E 167
Anthony, Fla., U.S. 29°17′ N, 82°7′ W 105
Anthony, Kans., U.S. 37°8′ N, 98°2′ W 92
Anthony, N. Mex., U.S. 32°1′ N, 106°38′ W 112
Anti Atlas, mountains, Mor. 30°17′ N, 8°12′ W 214
Antibes, Cap d', Fr. 43°28′ N, 7°8′ E 165
Anticosti, Île d', island, Can. 48°50′ N, 63°33′ W 81
Antifer, Cap d', Fr. 49°39′ N, 0°14′ E 150
Antigo, Wis., U.S. 45°8′ N, 89°9′ W 94
Antigonish, Can. 45°36′ N, 62°0′ W 111
Antigua and Barbuda 17°0′ N, 62°0′ W 116
Antigua, island, Antigua and Barbuda 17°5′ N, 61°41′ W 116
Antiguo Morelos, Mex. 22°32′ N, 99°6′ W 114
Anti-Lebanon see Al Jabalash Sharqī, Leb. 34°5′ N, 36°21′ E 194
Antilla, Cuba 20°51′ N, 75°44′ W 116
Anti-m-Misaou, spring, Alg. 21°57′ N, 3°4′ E 222
Antimony, Utah, U.S. 38°6′ N, 111°59′ W 92
Antioch, Calif., U.S. 38°0′ N, 121°50′ W 100
Antioch, Ill., U.S. 42°28′ N, 88°6′ W 102
Antioch see Hatay, Turk. 36°12′ N, 36°8′ E 156
Antioquia, Col. 6°34′ N, 75°51′ W 136
Antioquia, adm. division, Col. 6°56′ N, 76°39′ W 136
Antipatris, ruin(s), Israel 32°5′ N, 34°54′ E 194
Antipayuta, Russ. 69°4′ N, 76°54′ E 169
Antisana, peak, Ecua. 0°31′ N, 78°23′ W 136
Antler Peak, Nev., U.S. 40°35′ N, 117°13′ W 90
Antlers, Okla., U.S. 34°12′ N, 95°37′ W 96
Antofagasta, Chile 23°40′ S, 70°25′ W 132
Antofagasta, adm. division, Chile 22°1′ S, 70°14′ W 137
Antofagasta de la Sierra, Arg. 26°5′ S, 67°22′ W 132
Antón, Pan. 8°24′ N, 80°16′ W 115
Anton, Tex., U.S. 33°48′ N, 102°11′ W 92
Anton Chico, N. Mex., U.S. 35°11′ N, 105°10′ W 92
Antón Lizardo, Punta, Mex. 18°49′ N, 95°58′ W 114
Antonibe, Madagascar 15°8′ S, 47°25′ E 220
Antonina, Braz. 25°27′ S, 48°43′ W 138
Antoniny, Ukr. 49°48′ N, 26°53′ E 152
Antônio Prado, Braz. 28°53′ S, 51°16′ W 139
Antonito, Colo., U.S. 37°3′ N, 106°1′ W 92
Antonovo, Kaz. 49°21′ N, 51°45′ E 158
Antons, Lac des, lake, Can. 52°49′ N, 74°20′ W 111
Antopal', Belarus 52°12′ N, 24°45′ E 152
Antrim Mountains, U.K. 54°52′ N, 6°38′ W 150
Antropovo, Russ. 58°24′ N, 43°6′ E 154
Antsirabe, Madagascar 19°53′ S, 47°7′ E 207
Antsirabe, Madagascar 14°0′ S, 49°58′ E 220
Antsirañana, Madagascar 12°26′ S, 49°16′ E 220
Antsla, Est. 57°48′ N, 26°31′ E 166
Antsohihy, Madagascar 14°53′ S, 47°59′ E 220
Anttila, Fin. 65°7′ N, 29°48′ E 154
Anttila, Fin. 61°2′ N, 26°49′ E 166
Anttis, Nor. 67°16′ N, 22°48′ E 152
Anttola, Fin. 61°34′ N, 27°35′ E 166
Antu, China 42°32′ N, 128°18′ E 200
Antubia, Ghana 6°18′ N, 2°51′ W 222
Antufash, Jazīrat, island, Yemen 15°45′ N, 42°7′ E 182
Antwerp, Ohio, U.S. 41°9′ N, 84°44′ W 102
Antwerpen (Antwerp), Belg. 51°13′ N, 4°24′ E 167
Anuppur, India 23°7′ N, 81°42′ E 197
Anupshahr, India 28°20′ N, 78°15′ E 197
Anuradhapura, Sri Lanka 8°22′ N, 80°22′ E 188
Anvers Island, Antarctica 64°36′ S, 66°3′ W 134
Anvik, Alas., U.S. 62°30′ N, 160°23′ W 98
Anxi, China 25°5′ N, 118°13′ E 198
Anxi, China 40°31′ N, 95°47′ E 188
Anxiang, China 29°24′ N, 112°12′ E 198
Anxin, China 38°57′ N, 115°54′ E 198
Anyang, China 36°5′ N, 114°19′ E 198
Anyang, S. Korea 37°22′ N, 126°54′ E 200
Anyi, China 28°49′ N, 115°28′ E 198
Anyi, China 35°5′ N, 111°4′ E 198
Anykščiai, Lith. 55°32′ N, 25°8′ E 166
Anyou, China 18°11′ N, 109°34′ E 198
Anyuan, China 25°6′ N, 115°24′ E 198
Anyue, China 30°5′ N, 105°22′ E 198
Anza, Calif., U.S. 33°33′ N, 116°42′ W 101
Anzá, Col. 6°18′ N, 75°54′ W 136
Anze, China 36°8′ N, 112°10′ E 198
Anzhero Sudzhensk, Russ. 56°3′ N, 86°8′ E 169
Anzhu, Ostrova, islands, Ostrov Kotel'nyy;Ostrov Faddeyevskiy 75°26′ N, 135°19′ E 160
Anzio, It. 41°26′ N, 12°37′ E 156
Anzoátegui, adm. division, Venez. 8°48′ N, 64°48′ W 116
Aohan Qi, China 42°17′ N, 119°55′ E 198
Aoiz, Sp. 42°47′ N, 1°21′ W 164
Aokas, Alg. 36°38′ N, 5°14′ E 150
Aomori, Japan 40°51′ N, 140°48′ E 190
Aoraki (Cook, Mount), N.Z. 43°45′ S, 170°4′ E 240
Aosta, It. 45°44′ N, 7°19′ E 167
Aouchich, spring, Mauritania 22°4′ N, 12°4′ W 222
Aouderas, Niger 17°38′ N, 8°25′ E 222
Aougoundou, Lac, lake, Mali 15°47′ N, 5°12′ W 222
'Aouinet Bel Egrâ, spring, Alg. 26°52′ N, 6°53′ W 214
Aoukâr, plain, Mali 23°48′ N, 5°5′ W 214
Aoukâr, region, Africa 17°48′ N, 10°56′ W 222
Aoulef, Alg. 26°59′ N, 1°5′ E 214
Aoya, Japan 35°29′ N, 133°58′ E 201
Aozi, Chad 21°3′ N, 18°40′ E 216
Aozou, Chad 21°49′ N, 17°26′ E 216
Ap Iwan, Cerro, peak, Chile 46°13′ S, 71°59′ W 134
Apa, river, South America 22°10′ S, 57°17′ W 132
Apache, Okla., U.S. 34°52′ N, 98°22′ W 96
Apache Mountain, N. Mex., U.S. 33°55′ N, 108°41′ W 92
Apache Mountains, Tex., U.S. 31°9′ N, 104°30′ W 92
Apahida, Rom. 46°48′ N, 23°46′ E 156
Apalachicola, Fla., U.S. 29°43′ N, 85°0′ W 96
Apam, Ghana 5°19′ N, 0°47′ E 222
Apamea, ruin(s), Syr. 35°24′ N, 36°21′ E 194
Apaporis, river, Col. 0°17′ N, 71°46′ W 136
Aparecida do Taboado, Braz. 20°5′ S, 51°8′ W 138
Aparri, Philippines 18°18′ N, 121°40′ E 203
Apateu, Rom. 46°37′ N, 21°46′ E 168
Apatin, Serb. 45°39′ N, 18°58′ E 168
Apatity, Russ. 67°34′ N, 33°19′ E 152
Apatzingán, Mex. 19°5′ N, 102°22′ W 114
Apaxtla, Mex. 18°8′ N, 99°53′ W 114
Ape, Latv. 57°31′ N, 26°43′ E 166
Apeldoorn, Neth. 52°13′ N, 5°57′ E 163
Apen, Ger. 53°13′ N, 7°50′ E 163
Apere, Bol. 12°7′ S, 66°17′ W 137
Apere, river, Bol. 15°6′ S, 66°7′ W 137
Aphaea, ruin(s), Gr. 37°44′ N, 23°26′ E 156
Api, Dem. Rep. of the Congo 3°41′ N, 25°28′ E 224
Apia, Samoa 14°0′ S, 172°0′ W 241
Apiacá, river, Braz. 9°19′ S, 57°6′ W 130
Apiacás, Serra dos, Braz. 9°38′ S, 57°21′ W 130
Apiaí, Braz. 24°38′ S, 48°58′ W 138
Apiaú, Serra do, Braz. 2°53′ N, 61°48′ W 130
Apidiá, river, Braz. 12°33′ S, 61°11′ W 130
Apizaco, Mex. 19°23′ N, 98°11′ W 114
Aplao, Peru 16°6′ S, 72°31′ W 137
Apo, Mount, Philippines 6°59′ N, 125°11′ E 203
Apodaca, Mex. 25°46′ N, 100°12′ W 114
Apodi, Chapada do, Braz. 5°8′ S, 38°11′ W 132
Apollonia, ruin(s), Alban. 40°41′ N, 19°21′ E 156
Apollonia see Sozopol, Bulg. 42°25′ N, 27°42′ E 156
Apollonia see Sūsah, Lib. 32°52′ N, 21°59′ E 143
Apolo, Bol. 14°41′ S, 68°31′ W 137
Apopka, Fla., U.S. 28°40′ N, 81°31′ W 105
Apopka, Lake, Fla., U.S. 28°38′ N, 81°44′ W 105
Aporé, Braz. 18°57′ S, 52°3′ W 138
Aporé, river, Braz. 19°9′ S, 51°35′ W 138
Apostle Islands, Lake Superior 47°6′ N, 90°53′ W 94
Apóstoles, Arg. 27°55′ S, 55°44′ W 139
Apostolos Andreas, Cape, Northern Cyprus, Cyprus 35°34′ N, 34°34′ E 194
Apostolos Andreas Monastery, site, Northern Cyprus, Cyprus 35°40′ N, 34°32′ E 194
Apoteri, Guyana 4°0′ N, 58°34′ W 130
Apozol, Mex. 21°28′ N, 103°7′ W 114
Appalachian Mountains, North America 47°54′ N, 68°40′ W 82
Appennini, mountains, Europe 44°37′ N, 8°30′ E 167
Appiano, It. 46°27′ N, 11°15′ E 167
Apple Springs, Tex., U.S. 31°12′ N, 94°59′ W 103
Apple Valley, Calif., U.S. 34°30′ N, 117°12′ W 101
Appleby, U.K. 54°34′ N, 2°29′ W 162
Appleton, Wis., U.S. 44°16′ N, 88°25′ W 94
Appleton City, Mo., U.S. 38°10′ N, 94°2′ W 94
Apriķi, Latv. 56°49′ N, 21°31′ E 166
Apsheron Yarymadasy, Azerb. 40°21′ N, 49°19′ E 180
Apsheronsk, Russ. 44°26′ N, 39°48′ E 180
Aptera, ruin(s), Gr. 35°26′ N, 24°1′ E 156
Aptos, Calif., U.S. 36°59′ N, 121°53′ W 100
Apuane, Alpi, It. 43°57′ N, 10°17′ E 167
Apucarana, Braz. 23°36′ S, 51°31′ W 138
Apuí, Braz. 1°11′ N, 69°14′ W 136
Apuka, Russ. 60°30′ N, 169°28′ E 160
Apulia, adm. division, It. 41°1′ N, 15°35′ E 156
Apure, adm. division, Venez. 7°4′ N, 70°6′ W 136
Apurímac, adm. division, Peru 13°58′ S, 73°41′ W 137
Apurímac, river, Peru 13°27′ S, 73°16′ W 137
Apurito, Venez. 7°55′ N, 68°28′ W 136
Apuseni, Munţii, Rom. 46°38′ N, 22°39′ E 168
Aq Kopruk, Afghan. 36°4′ N, 66°54′ E 186
Aqaba, Gulf of 28°52′ N, 34°11′ E 180
Aqadyr, Kaz. 48°13′ N, 72°52′ E 184
Aqchan, Afghan. 36°57′ N, 66°14′ E 186
Aqiq, Sudan 18°9′ N, 38°7′ E 182
Aqköl, Kaz. 46°40′ N, 49°6′ E 158
Aqköl, Kaz. 43°24′ N, 70°46′ E 184
Aqköl, Kaz. 45°0′ N, 75°39′ E 184
Aqköl, Kaz. 52°0′ N, 70°59′ E 184
Aqmola, adm. division, Kaz. 51°31′ N, 68°23′ E 184
Aqqikkol Hu, lake, China 37°10′ N, 87°39′ E 188
Aqqystaū, Kaz. 47°14′ N, 51°4′ E 158
'Aqrah, Iraq 36°45′ N, 43°47′ E 195
Aqsay, Kaz. 51°10′ N, 52°58′ E 158
Aqshataū, Kaz. 49°25′ N, 54°45′ E 158
Aqshataū, Kaz. 47°58′ N, 73°59′ E 184
Aqsū, Kaz. 52°27′ N, 71°58′ E 184
Aqsū, Kaz. 42°25′ N, 69°50′ E 197
Aqsūat, Kaz. 47°47′ N, 82°49′ E 184
Aqsū-Ayuly, Kaz. 48°45′ N, 73°42′ E 184
Aqsūgek, Kaz. 44°37′ N, 74°28′ E 184
Aqtaū, Kaz. 43°38′ N, 51°14′ E 195
Aqtaysay, Kaz. 49°40′ N, 54°1′ E 158
Aqtöbe, Kaz. 50°15′ N, 57°12′ E 158
Aqtöbe, adm. division, Kaz. 48°43′ N, 56°0′ E 158
Aqtoghay, Kaz. 48°12′ N, 75°2′ E 184
Aqtoghay, Kaz. 46°55′ N, 79°39′ E 184
Aquarius Mountains, Ariz., U.S. 35°1′ N, 113°36′ W 101
Aquidauana, Braz. 20°29′ S, 55°48′ W 134
Aquileia, It. 45°46′ N, 13°21′ E 167
Aquiles SerdŽan, Mex. 28°35′ N, 105°55′ W 92
Aquitaine, adm. division, Fr. 44°10′ N, 1°18′ W 150
Aqyrab, Kaz. 50°35′ N, 55°8′ E 158
Aqzhal, Kaz. 49°13′ N, 81°23′ E 184
Aqzhar, Kaz. 47°35′ N, 83°45′ E 184
Aqzhayyq, Kaz. 50°50′ N, 51°17′ E 158
Ar Horqin Qi (Tianshan), China 43°55′ N, 120°7′ E 198
Ar Rabbah, Jordan 31°16′ N, 35°44′ E 194
Ar Rafīd, Syr. 32°57′ N, 35°53′ E 194
Ar Ramādī, Iraq 33°23′ N, 43°14′ E 180
Ar Ramthā, Jordan 32°33′ N, 36°0′ E 194
Ar Raqqah, Syr. 35°54′ N, 39°2′ E 180
Ar Rashādīyah, Jordan 30°42′ N, 35°37′ E 194
Ar Rass, Saudi Arabia 25°50′ N, 43°28′ E 182
Ar Rastan (Arethusa), Syr. 34°55′ N, 36°44′ E 194
Ar Rawḑah, Saudi Arabia 21°12′ N, 42°47′ E 182
Ar Riyāḑ (Riyadh), Saudi Arabia 24°35′ N, 46°35′ E 186
Ar Riyān, Yemen 14°40′ N, 49°21′ E 182
Ar Rub' al Khālī (Empty Quarter), Saudi Arabia 24°33′ N, 54°53′ E 196
Ar Rummān, Jordan 32°9′ N, 35°49′ E 194
Ar Ruşayfah, Jordan 32°1′ N, 36°2′ E 194
Ar Rustāq, Oman 23°23′ N, 57°24′ E 182
Ar Ruţbah, Iraq 33°3′ N, 40°14′ E 180
Ara, India 25°32′ N, 84°37′ E 197
Āra Ārba, Eth. 6°31′ N, 41°17′ E 224
'Arab al Mulk, Syr. 35°16′ N, 35°55′ E 194
'Arabah, Wādī al, Israel-Jordan 30°23′ N, 35°1′ E 194
Arabian Basin, Arabian Sea 10°36′ N, 65°57′ E 254
Arabian Gulf see Persian Gulf 26°40′ N, 51°30′ E 196
Arabian Sea 13°38′ N, 58°38′ E 173
Araç, Turk. 41°15′ N, 33°19′ E 156
Araç, river, Turk. 41°9′ N, 32°58′ E 158
Aracaju, Braz. 10°54′ S, 37°5′ W 132
Aracati, Braz. 4°35′ S, 37°43′ W 132
Aracatu, Braz. 14°27′ S, 41°29′ W 138
Araçatuba, Braz. 21°11′ S, 50°27′ W 138
Aracena, Sp. 37°53′ N, 6°35′ W 164
Aracena, Sierra de, Sp. 37°58′ N, 6°51′ W 164
Aracruz, Braz. 19°51′ S, 40°19′ W 132
Araçuaí, Braz. 16°52′ S, 42°4′ W 138
Araçuaí, river, Braz. 17°50′ S, 43°0′ W 138
'Arad, Israel 31°14′ N, 35°12′ E 194
Arad, Rom. 46°11′ N, 21°19′ E 168
Arad, adm. division, Rom. 46°9′ N, 21°5′ E 156
Arada, Chad 15°1′ N, 20°39′ E 216
Araden, ruin(s), Gr. 35°12′ N, 23°57′ E 156
Aradu Nou, Rom. 46°9′ N, 21°20′ E 168
Arafali, Eritrea 15°1′ N, 39°42′ E 182
Arafura Sea 9°12′ S, 134°22′ E 192
Araga, spring, Niger 17°25′ N, 11°36′ E 222
Aragarças, Braz. 15°58′ S, 52°14′ W 138
Aragats, peak, Arm. 40°30′ N, 44°8′ E 195
Arago, Cape, Oreg., U.S. 43°20′ N, 124°41′ W 90
Aragon, adm. division, Sp. 41°26′ N, 1°15′ W 164
Aragua, adm. division, Venez. 10°3′ N, 67°40′ W 136
Aragua de Barcelona, Venez. 9°29′ N, 64°52′ W 116
Araguacema, Braz. 8°50′ S, 49°37′ W 130
Araguaçu, Braz. 12°52′ S, 49°56′ W 138
Araguaia National Park, Braz. 11°14′ S, 50°56′ W 130
Araguaia, river, Braz. 15°22′ S, 51°48′ W 132
Araguaína, Braz. 7°12′ S, 48°16′ W 130
Araguao, Boca 9°11′ N, 61°20′ W 116
Araguapiche, Punta, Venez. 9°21′ N, 60°53′ W 116
Araguari, Braz. 18°40′ S, 48°15′ W 138
Araguari, river, Braz. 18°56′ S, 48°13′ W 138
Araguatins, Braz. 5°39′ S, 48°8′ W 130
Arahal, Sp. 37°15′ N, 5°34′ W 164
Arahura, N.Z. 42°42′ S, 171°4′ E 240
Arai, Japan 37°0′ N, 138°14′ E 201
Araia, Sp. 42°52′ N, 2°19′ W 164
Arak, Alg. 25°18′ N, 3°44′ E 214
Arāk, Iran 34°6′ N, 49°42′ E 180
Araka, spring, Niger 18°54′ N, 15°24′ E 216
Arakamchechen, Ostrov, island, Russ. 64°44′ N, 172°1′ W 98
Arakan Yoma, Myanmar 19°6′ N, 94°18′ E 202
Aral, China 38°8′ N, 90°43′ E 188
Aral, China 40°40′ N, 81°28′ E 184
Aral, Kaz. 46°54′ N, 61°36′ E 184
Aral Mangy Qaraqumy, Kaz. 47°11′ N, 61°51′ E 184
Aral Sea, lake 45°32′ N, 58°10′ E 160
Aralqi, China 39°27′ N, 87°44′ E 188
Aralqum, Kaz. 44°8′ N, 58°11′ E 180
Aralsor Köli, lake, Kaz. 49°0′ N, 48°1′ E 158
Araltobe, Kaz. 50°31′ N, 60°6′ E 158
Aramac, Austral. 23°0′ S, 145°16′ E 231
Aramberri, Mex. 24°4′ N, 99°50′ W 114
Aramits, Fr. 43°6′ N, 0°44′ E 164
Arampampa, Bol. 18°0′ S, 65°58′ W 137
Ārān, Iran 34°9′ N, 51°30′ E 180
Aran Islands, Celtic Sea 53°12′ N, 10°30′ W 150
Aranda de Duero, Sp. 41°40′ N, 3°44′ W 164
Arandas, Mex. 20°41′ N, 102°22′ W 114
Arani, Bol. 17°38′ S, 65°41′ W 137
Aranjuez, Sp. 40°1′ N, 3°36′ W 164
Aranos, Namibia 24°5′ S, 19°7′ E 227
Aransas Pass, Tex., U.S. 27°53′ N, 97°9′ W 96
Arantes, river, Braz. 19°25′ S, 50°20′ W 138
Arantur, Russ. 60°59′ N, 63°37′ E 169
Aranyaprathet, Thai. 13°44′ N, 102°31′ E 202
Arao, Japan 32°57′ N, 130°26′ E 201
Araouane, Mali 18°53′ N, 3°34′ W 222
Arapa, Laguna, lake, Peru 15°11′ S, 70°11′ W 137
Arapaho, Okla., U.S. 35°33′ N, 98°58′ W 96
Arapey, Uru. 30°57′ S, 57°33′ W 139
Arapiraca, Braz. 9°45′ S, 36°42′ W 132
Arapkir, Turk. 39°1′ N, 38°31′ E 180
Arapongas, Braz. 23°26′ S, 51°28′ W 138
Araracuara, Col. 0°29′ N, 72°17′ W 136
Araranguá, Braz. 28°58′ S, 49°29′ W 138
Araraquara, Braz. 21°48′ S, 48°12′ W 138
Araras, Braz. 9°5′ S, 68°6′ W 137
Araras, Braz. 6°13′ S, 54°34′ W 130
Araras, Braz. 22°22′ S, 47°23′ W 138
Ararat, Arm. 39°50′ N, 44°40′ E 195
Ararat, Mount see Ağrı Dağı, Turk. 39°39′ N, 44°12′ E 180
Ararat, Mount see Ağrı Dağı, peak, Turk. 39°42′ N, 44°15′ E 195
Arari, Braz. 3°28′ S, 44°46′ W 132
Araria, India 26°5′ N, 87°27′ E 197
Araripe, Chapada do, Braz. 7°34′ S, 40°28′ W 132
Araruama, Braz. 22°52′ S, 42°22′ W 138
Aras (Araxes), river, Asia 40°0′ N, 42°18′ E 195
Arataca, Braz. 15°18′ S, 39°24′ W 138
Aratane, spring, Mauritania 18°24′ N, 8°33′ W 222
Arataú, river, Braz. 3°14′ S, 50°37′ W 130
Arauá, river, Braz. 4°14′ S, 64°51′ W 130
Arauca, Col. 7°0′ N, 70°47′ W 136
Arauca, adm. division, Col. 6°39′ N, 71°44′ W 136
Arauca, river, Venez. 7°27′ N, 67°58′ W 136
Araucária, Braz. 25°36′ S, 49°24′ W 138
Arauquita, Col. 6°58′ N, 71°22′ W 136
Araxá, Braz. 19°36′ S, 46°56′ W 138
Araxes see Aras, river, Turk. 40°0′ N, 42°18′ E 195
Arayit Dağı, peak, Turk. 39°17′ N, 31°39′ E 156
Ārba Minch', Eth. 5°59′ N, 37°37′ E 224
Arba'at, Sudan 19°46′ N, 36°57′ E 182
Arbazh, Russ. 57°41′ N, 48°24′ E 154
Arbela see Irbid, Jordan 32°32′ N, 35°51′ E 194
Arbīl, Iraq 36°10′ N, 43°59′ E 180
Arboledas, Arg. 36°51′ S, 61°28′ W 139
Arborea, It. 39°46′ N, 8°34′ E 156
Arborfield, Can. 53°6′ N, 103°40′ W 108
Arborg, Can. 50°53′ N, 97°13′ W 90
Arbrå, Nor. 61°29′ N, 16°19′ E 152
Arbre du Ténéré, site, Niger 17°44′ N, 10°5′ E 222
Arbroath, U.K. 56°33′ N, 2°38′ W 150
Arc, Fr. 47°27′ N, 5°33′ E 150
Arc Dome, peak, Nev., U.S. 38°49′ N, 117°26′ W 90
Arc, river, Fr. 45°23′ N, 6°17′ E 165
Arcachon, Fr. 44°36′ N, 1°15′ W 214
Arcadia, Fla., U.S. 27°13′ N, 81°52′ W 105
Arcadia, Ind., U.S. 40°10′ N, 86°1′ W 102
Arcadia, La., U.S. 32°31′ N, 92°56′ W 103
Arcadia, Mich., U.S. 44°29′ N, 86°14′ W 94
Arcadia, Peru 1°3′ S, 75°18′ W 136
Arcadia, Wis., U.S. 44°15′ N, 91°29′ W 94
Arcanum, Ohio, U.S. 39°59′ N, 84°32′ W 102
Arcas, Cayos, islands, Gulf of Mexico 20°19′ N, 92°6′ W 115
Arcata, Calif., U.S. 40°52′ N, 124°6′ W 90
Arcelia, Mex. 18°16′ N, 100°16′ W 114
Archangel see Arkhangel'sk, Russ. 64°35′ N, 40°37′ E 154
Archar, Bulg. 43°48′ N, 22°54′ E 168
Archbold, Ohio, U.S. 41°30′ N, 84°18′ W 102
Archeï, spring, Chad 16°53′ N, 21°44′ E 216
Archena, Sp. 38°6′ N, 1°19′ W 164
Archer, Fla., U.S. 29°32′ N, 82°32′ W 105
Archer Bay 13°40′ S, 141°24′ E 230
Archer Bend National Park, Austral. 13°35′ S, 141°56′ E 238
Archer City, Tex., U.S. 33°34′ N, 98°38′ W 92
Archer Point, Antarctica 68°54′ S, 161°17′ E 248
Archer, river, Austral. 13°39′ S, 141°16′ E 231
Archer's Post, Kenya 0°36′ N, 37°40′ E 224
Archerwill, Can. 52°25′ N, 103°52′ W 108
Archidona, Sp. 37°5′ N, 4°24′ W 164
Archipiélago de Colón see Galápagos Islands, Ecuador 0°13′ N, 92°2′ W 130
Archipiélago Los Roques National Park, Caribbean Sea 11°50′ N, 67°27′ W 136
Archman, Turkm. 38°33′ N, 57°9′ E 180
Arci, Monte, peak, It. 39°46′ N, 8°41′ E 156
Arcis, Fr. 48°32′ N, 4°8′ E 163
Arco, Idaho, U.S. 43°38′ N, 113°18′ W 90
Arco, It. 45°55′ N, 10°52′ E 167
Arco, Paso del, pass, Arg. 38°47′ S, 71°6′ W 134
Arcola, Ill., U.S. 39°41′ N, 88°19′ W 102
Arcola, Miss., U.S. 33°14′ N, 90°53′ W 103
Arcos, Braz. 20°17′ S, 45°34′ W 138
Arcos de Jalón, Sp. 41°12′ N, 2°17′ W 150
Arcoverde, Braz. 8°24′ S, 37°1′ W 132
Arctic Bay, Can. 73°3′ N, 85°8′ W 73
Arctic Ocean 79°19′ N, 170°44′ W 246
Arctic Red, river, Can. 66°40′ N, 132°38′ W 98
Arctic Village, Alas., U.S. 68°6′ N, 145°32′ W 98
Arctowski, station, Antarctica 62°12′ S, 58°12′ W 134
Arda, river, Bulg. 41°30′ N, 25°42′ E 156
Ardabīl, Iran 38°15′ N, 48°18′ E 195
Ardahan, Turk. 41°5′ N, 42°40′ E 195
Ardakān, Iran 32°14′ N, 54°3′ E 180
Ardakān, Iran 30°14′ N, 51°59′ E 196
Årdal, Nor. 61°14′ N, 7°43′ E 152
Årdal, Nor. 59°8′ N, 6°11′ E 152
Ardales, Sp. 36°51′ N, 4°51′ W 164
Ardanuç, Turk. 41°9′ N, 42°2′ E 195
Ardaşşawwān, Jordan 30°58′ N, 36°46′ E 194
Ardatov, Russ. 54°47′ N, 46°19′ E 154
Ardencaple Fjord 74°46′ N, 25°23′ W 246
Ardestān, Iran 33°20′ N, 52°25′ E 180
Ardmore, Okla., U.S. 34°9′ N, 97°7′ W 92
Ardmore, S. Dak., U.S. 43°1′ N, 103°40′ W 90
Ardres, Fr. 50°51′ N, 1°58′ E 163
Ards Peninsula, U.K. 54°21′ N, 6°3′ W 150
Ardud, Rom. 47°38′ N, 22°53′ E 168
Ardvrach Castle, site, U.K. 58°9′ N, 5°6′ W 150
Ardvule, Rubha, U.K. 57°15′ N, 8°1′ W 150
Åre, Nor. 63°24′ N, 13°3′ E 152
Arena, Point, U.S. 38°47′ N, 124°3′ W 90
Arenápolis, Braz. 14°28′ S, 56°53′ W 132
Arenas, Punta de, Arg. 53°3′ S, 68°13′ W 134
Arendal, Nor. 58°27′ N, 8°43′ E 152
Arendsee, Ger. 52°53′ N, 11°30′ E 152
Arenys de Mar, Sp. 41°34′ N, 2°33′ E 164
Arenzano, It. 44°23′ N, 8°41′ E 167
Arequipa, Peru 16°24′ S, 71°35′ W 137
Arequipa, adm. division, Peru 16°8′ S, 73°31′ W 137
Ārēro, Eth. 4°43′ N, 38°48′ E 224
Arês, Braz. 6°14′ S, 35°8′ W 132
Areskutan, peak, Nor. 63°26′ N, 12°55′ E 152
Arethusa see Ar Rastan, Syr. 34°55′ N, 36°44′ E 194
Arévalo, Sp. 41°3′ N, 4°44′ W 150
Arezzaf, spring, Mali 18°5′ N, 1°47′ W 222
Arezzo, It. 43°27′ N, 11°52′ E 156
Arga Sala, river, Russ. 68°51′ N, 107°46′ E 160
Argaman, West Bank, Israel 32°8′ N, 35°30′ E 194
Argamasilla de Alba, Sp. 39°7′ N, 3°7′ W 164
Argamasilla de Calatrava, Sp. 38°44′ N, 4°5′ W 164
Argan, China 40°6′ N, 88°17′ E 188
Argatay, Mongolia 45°33′ N, 108°4′ E 198
Argelès, Fr. 42°32′ N, 3°0′ E 164
Argens, river, Fr. 43°25′ N, 6°3′ E 165
Argenta, It. 44°36′ N, 11°49′ E 167
Argentario, Monte, peak, It. 42°23′ N, 11°5′ E 156
Argentera, peak, It. 44°10′ N, 7°17′ E 165
Argenteuil, Fr. 48°55′ N, 2°13′ E 163
Argentina 35°22′ S, 67°13′ W 134
Argentine Plain, South Atlantic Ocean 46°42′ S, 48°15′ W 253
Argentré, Fr. 48°3′ N, 0°34′ E 150
Argeş, adm. division, Rom. 44°57′ N, 24°28′ E 156
Arghandab Dam, Afghan. 32°2′ N, 65°50′ E 186
Argo, Sudan 19°30′ N, 30°27′ E 226
Argolas, Braz. 20°26′ S, 40°25′ W 138
Argonaut Mountain, Can. 51°49′ N, 118°25′ W 90
Argonne, Fr. 49°43′ N, 4°51′ E 167
Árgos, Gr. 37°35′ N, 22°41′ E 180
Argos, Ind., U.S. 41°13′ N, 86°14′ W 102
Argoub, Western Sahara, Mor. 23°35′ N, 15°51′ W 214
Arguello, Point, Calif., U.S. 34°30′ N, 120°49′ W 100
Arguin, Cap d', Mauritania 20°25′ N, 16°42′ W 214
Argungu, Nig. 12°43′ N, 4°31′ E 222
Argus, Calif., U.S. 35°44′ N, 117°25′ W 101
Argus, Dome, Antarctica 79°52′ S, 74°47′ E 248
Argus Range, Calif., U.S. 36°0′ N, 117°34′ W 101
Arguut, Mongolia 45°28′ N, 102°18′ E 190
Argyle, Mich., U.S. 43°33′ N, 82°56′ W 102
Argyle, Minn., U.S. 48°18′ N, 96°51′ W 90
Argyle, N.Y., U.S. 43°14′ N, 73°31′ W 104
Argyle, Lake, Austral. 16°12′ S, 128°11′ E 230
Arhebeb, spring, Mali 21°5′ N, 0°8′ E 222
Arhrîjît, Mauritania 18°21′ N, 9°15′ W 222
Århus, Den. 56°9′ N, 10°11′ E 150
Ari Atoll, Maldives 3°33′ N, 72°22′ E 188
Ariamsvlei, Namibia 28°7′ S, 19°50′ E 227
Ariana, Tun. 36°51′ N, 10°11′ E 156
Arias, Arg. 33°39′ S, 62°23′ W 139
Aribinda, Burkina Faso 14°14′ N, 0°52′ E 222
Arica, Chile 18°34′ S, 70°20′ W 137

Arica, Col. 2°9′ S, 71°46′ W 136
Arica, Peru 1°39′ S, 75°12′ W 136
Arica y Parinacota, adm. division, Chile 18°28′ S, 70°18′ W 137
Arid, Mount, Austral. 34°1′ S, 122°58′ E 230
Arida, Japan 34°4′ N, 135°7′ E 201
Aridal, Western Sahara, Mor. 25°59′ N, 13°48′ W 214
Arīḩā, Syr. 35°48′ N, 36°35′ E 156
Arīḩā (Jericho), West Bank, Israel 31°51′ N, 35°27′ E 194
Arija, Sp. 42°57′ N, 3°59′ W 164
Arikaree, river, Colo., U.S. 39°48′ N, 102°40′ W 90
Arimã, Braz. 5°47′ S, 63°42′ W 130
Arinos, Braz. 15°54′ S, 46°4′ W 138
Arinos, river, Braz. 10°28′ S, 58°34′ W 132
Ariogala, Lith. 55°15′ N, 23°29′ E 166
Aripao, Venez. 7°19′ N, 65°4′ W 130
Ariporo, river, Col. 5°57′ N, 71°13′ W 136
Aripuanã, Braz. 9°59′ S, 59°28′ W 130
Aripuanã, river, Braz. 7°52′ S, 60°35′ W 130
Aripuanã, river, Braz. 11°15′ S, 59°41′ W 130
Ariquemes, Braz. 9°57′ S, 63°6′ W 130
Arismendi, Venez. 8°29′ N, 68°22′ W 136
Arista, Mex. 22°37′ N, 100°51′ W 114
Aristizábal, Cabo, Arg. 45°23′ S, 66°29′ W 134
Arivechi, Mex. 28°54′ N, 109°10′ W 92
Ariza, Sp. 41°18′ N, 2°4′ W 164
Arizona, adm. division, Ariz., U.S. 34°22′ N, 112°38′ W 92
Arizpe, Mex. 30°19′ N, 110°12′ W 92
Arjona, Col. 10°16′ N, 75°22′ W 136
Ark, The, peak, Antarctica 80°43′ S, 26°3′ W 248
Arka, Russ. 60°10′ N, 142°13′ E 160
Arkadak, Russ. 51°53′ N, 43°35′ E 158
Arkadelphia, Ark., U.S. 34°6′ N, 93°5′ W 96
Arkansas, adm. division, Ark., U.S. 35°4′ N, 93°21′ W 96
Arkansas City, Kans., U.S. 37°2′ N, 97°3′ W 92
Arkansas, river, Okla., U.S. 35°13′ N, 95°34′ W 80
Arkanū, Jabal, peak, Lib. 22°16′ N, 24°40′ E 226
Arkhangel'sk, Russ. 64°32′ N, 40°54′ E 160
Arkhangel'sk, adm. division, Russ. 63°2′ N, 38°58′ E 154
Arkhangel'sk (Archangel), Russ. 64°35′ N, 40°37′ E 154
Arkhangel'skoye, Russ. 44°34′ N, 44°3′ E 158
Arkhangel'skoye, Russ. 51°28′ N, 40°52′ E 158
Arklow, Ire. 52°47′ N, 6°10′ W 150
Arkona, Kap, Ger. 54°42′ N, 13°34′ E 152
Arkösund, Nor. 58°28′ N, 16°53′ E 152
Arkticheskiy, Mys, Russ. 81°1′ N, 79°59′ E 160
Arkticheskogo Instituta, Ostrova, island, Russ. 75°29′ N, 77°0′ E 160
Arkul', Russ. 57°19′ N, 50°9′ E 154
Arlanzón, Sp. 42°18′ N, 3°27′ W 164
Arles, Fr. 43°41′ N, 4°40′ E 214
Arlington, Ga., U.S. 31°25′ N, 84°43′ W 96
Arlington, Ill., U.S. 41°28′ N, 89°15′ W 102
Arlington, Mass., U.S. 42°24′ N, 71°10′ W 104
Arlington, N.Y., U.S. 41°41′ N, 73°54′ W 104
Arlington, Oreg., U.S. 45°42′ N, 120°12′ W 90
Arlington, S. Dak., U.S. 44°20′ N, 97°9′ W 94
Arlington, Tex., U.S. 32°43′ N, 97°7′ W 92
Arlington, Vt., U.S. 43°4′ N, 73°10′ W 104
Arlington, Wash., U.S. 48°10′ N, 122°7′ W 100
Arlit, Niger 18°50′ N, 7°14′ E 222
Arlon, Belg. 49°40′ N, 5°48′ E 163
Arly, river, Fr. 45°44′ N, 6°31′ E 165
Arma, Kans., U.S. 37°31′ N, 94°42′ W 94
Armada, Mich., U.S. 42°50′ N, 82°53′ W 102
Armadale Castle, site, U.K. 57°2′ N, 6°1′ W 150
Armadillo, Mex. 22°13′ N, 100°40′ W 114
Armant, Egypt 25°36′ N, 32°27′ E 182
Armavir, Arm. 40°9′ N, 44°2′ E 195
Armavir, Russ. 44°59′ N, 41°6′ E 158
Armenia 40°14′ N, 44°43′ E 195
Armenia, Col. 4°28′ N, 75°45′ W 136
Armenia Mountain, Pa., U.S. 41°44′ N, 77°0′ W 94
Armeniş, Rom. 45°13′ N, 22°18′ E 168
Armentières, Fr. 50°40′ N, 2°53′ E 163
Armeria, Mex. 18°55′ N, 104°0′ W 114
Armero, Col. 4°57′ N, 74°55′ W 136
Armijo, N. Mex., U.S. 35°2′ N, 106°41′ W 92
Armilla, Sp. 37°8′ N, 3°38′ W 164
Armit, Can. 52°49′ N, 101°47′ W 108
Armizonskoye, Russ. 55°56′ N, 67°39′ E 184
Armona, Calif., U.S. 36°19′ N, 119°43′ W 100
Armour, S. Dak., U.S. 43°18′ N, 98°21′ W 90
Armstrong, Arg. 32°49′ S, 61°35′ W 139
Armstrong, Can. 50°18′ N, 89°2′ W 110
Armstrong, Can. 50°26′ N, 119°12′ W 90
Armutcuk, Turk. 41°20′ N, 31°31′ E 156
Armyans'k, Ukr. 46°5′ N, 33°41′ E 156
Arnaoutis, Cape, Cyprus 35°5′ N, 32°4′ E 194
Arnaud, Can. 49°16′ N, 97°6′ W 90
Arnaudville, La., U.S. 30°23′ N, 91°57′ W 103
Arnbach, Aust. 46°44′ N, 12°23′ E 167
Årnes, Nor. 60°7′ N, 11°28′ E 152
Arnett, Okla., U.S. 36°7′ N, 99°46′ W 92
Arnhem, Neth. 51°59′ N, 5°54′ E 167
Arnhem Land, region, Australia 11°54′ S, 131°40′ E 192
Arnold, Calif., U.S. 38°15′ N, 120°22′ W 100
Arnold, Nebr., U.S. 41°25′ N, 100°12′ W 90
Arnold, river, Austral. 14°50′ S, 133°57′ E 230
Arnolds Park, Iowa, U.S. 43°21′ N, 95°8′ W 90
Arnoldstein, Aust. 46°33′ N, 13°42′ E 167
Arnot, Can. 55°45′ N, 96°45′ W 108
Arnsberg, Ger. 51°23′ N, 8°4′ E 167
Arnstein, Ger. 49°58′ N, 9°58′ E 167
Aroa, Venez. 10°25′ N, 68°54′ W 136
Aroab, Namibia 26°50′ S, 19°43′ E 227
Aroánia, Óri, peak, Gr. 37°57′ N, 22°8′ E 156
Arock, Oreg., U.S. 42°55′ N, 117°31′ W 90
Arolsen, Ger. 51°23′ N, 9°1′ E 167
Aroma, Sudan 15°46′ N, 36°8′ E 182
Aroma Park, Ill., U.S. 41°4′ N, 87°48′ W 102
Aron, India 25°57′ N, 77°54′ E 197
Arona, It. 45°45′ N, 8°32′ E 167
Arosa, Switz. 46°46′ N, 9°38′ E 167
Ærøskøbing, Den. 54°53′ N, 10°24′ E 150
Arowhana, peak, N.Z. 38°8′ S, 177°45′ E 240
Arp, Tex., U.S. 32°13′ N, 95°4′ W 103
Arpa, river, Asia 40°28′ N, 43°31′ E 195
Arpaçay, Turk. 40°52′ N, 43°19′ E 195
Arpajon, Fr. 48°35′ N, 2°14′ E 163
Arqalyq, Kaz. 50°13′ N, 66°54′ E 184
Arque, Bol. 17°51′ S, 66°22′ W 137
Arques, Fr. 50°44′ N, 2°18′ E 150
Arquía, Col. 7°58′ N, 77°7′ W 136
'Arrābah, West Bank, Israel 32°24′ N, 35°11′ E 194
Arraias, Braz. 12°56′ S, 46°58′ W 130
Arras, Alban. 41°45′ N, 20°18′ E 168
Arras, Fr. 50°17′ N, 2°47′ E 163
Arreau, Fr. 42°54′ N, 0°20′ E 164
Arrecifes, Arg. 34°4′ S, 60°7′ W 139
Arrée, Montagnes d', Fr. 48°29′ N, 4°12′ W 150
Arriate, Sp. 36°47′ N, 5°9′ W 164
Arris, Alg. 35°12′ N, 6°17′ E 150
Arroio dos Ratos, Braz. 30°6′ S, 51°44′ W 139
Arroio Grande, Braz. 32°12′ S, 53°7′ W 139
Arrojado, river, Braz. 13°40′ S, 45°16′ W 138
Arrou, Fr. 48°6′ N, 1°7′ E 163
Arroux, river, Fr. 46°45′ N, 4°8′ E 165
Arrowhead, river, Can. 60°18′ N, 123°11′ W 108
Arrowsmith, Ill., U.S. 40°26′ N, 88°38′ W 102
Arrowtown, N.Z. 44°57′ S, 168°51′ E 240
Arrowwood, Can. 50°44′ N, 113°10′ W 90
Arroyito, Arg. 31°27′ S, 63°4′ W 139
Arroyo de la Luz, Sp. 39°28′ N, 6°36′ W 164
Arroyo Grande, Calif., U.S. 35°8′ N, 120°35′ W 100
Arroyo Hondo, N. Mex., U.S. 36°31′ N, 105°40′ W 92
Arroyo Verde see Puerto Lobos, Arg. 42°2′ S, 65°5′ W 134
Arroyos y Esteros, Parag. 25°5′ S, 57°7′ W 132
Arrufó, Arg. 30°13′ S, 61°44′ W 139
Ars-en-Ré, Fr. 46°12′ N, 1°33′ W 150
Arshaly, Kaz. 50°49′ N, 72°11′ E 184
Arshaty, Kaz. 49°17′ N, 86°36′ E 184
Arsiero, It. 45°48′ N, 11°20′ E 167
Arsikere, India 13°20′ N, 76°14′ E 188
Arsk, Russ. 56°7′ N, 49°54′ E 154
Arsuk, Den. 61°13′ N, 48°8′ W 106
Artashat, Arm. 39°58′ N, 44°32′ E 195
Arteaga, Mex. 25°25′ N, 100°52′ W 114
Arteaga, Mex. 18°24′ N, 102°16′ W 114
Artem, Russ. 43°26′ N, 132°21′ E 190
Artemisa, Cuba 22°49′ N, 82°46′ W 116
Artemivs'k, Ukr. 48°35′ N, 37°57′ E 158
Artemovsk, Russ. 54°24′ N, 93°22′ E 190
Artemovskiy, Russ. 58°19′ N, 114°40′ E 160
Artemovskiy, Russ. 57°22′ N, 61°47′ E 154
Artenay, Fr. 48°4′ N, 1°51′ E 150
Artesa de Segre, Sp. 41°53′ N, 1°3′ E 164
Artesia, Miss., U.S. 33°23′ N, 88°38′ W 103
Artesia, N. Mex., U.S. 32°50′ N, 104°25′ W 92
Artesian, S. Dak., U.S. 43°59′ N, 97°57′ W 90
Arthez, Fr. 43°28′ N, 0°37′ E 150
Arthog, U.K. 52°42′ N, 4°1′ W 162
Arthonnay, Fr. 47°55′ N, 4°13′ E 150
Arthur, Ill., U.S. 39°42′ N, 88°28′ W 102
Arthur, Nebr., U.S. 41°33′ N, 101°42′ W 90
Arthur, Lac, lake, Can. 51°6′ N, 62°48′ W 111
Arthur's Pass, N.Z. 42°57′ S, 171°33′ E 240
Arti, Russ. 56°25′ N, 58°37′ E 154
Artigas, Uru. 30°24′ S, 56°31′ W 139
Artigas, station, Antarctica 61°59′ S, 58°38′ W 134
Art'ik, Arm. 40°37′ N, 43°57′ E 195
Artix, Fr. 43°24′ N, 0°33′ E 150
Artois, region, Europe 50°17′ N, 1°58′ E 163
Artova, Turk. 40°2′ N, 36°16′ E 156
Artrutx, Cabo d', Sp. 39°56′ N, 3°27′ E 150
Arturo Prat, Chile, station, Antarctica 62°38′ S, 59°39′ W 134
Artux, China 39°45′ N, 76°6′ E 184
Artvin, Turk. 41°11′ N, 41°49′ E 195
Artyom, Azerb. 40°28′ N, 50°19′ E 195
Aru, Dem. Rep. of the Congo 2°48′ N, 30°50′ E 224
Aru, Kepulauan, islands, Arafura Sea 6°8′ S, 133°44′ E 192
Arua, Dem. Rep. of the Congo 3°4′ N, 30°56′ E 207
Aruajá, Braz. 5°0′ S, 66°51′ W 130
Aruanã, Braz. 14°58′ S, 51°8′ W 138
Aruba, island, Netherlands 13°0′ N, 70°0′ W 118
Arun Qi, China 48°8′ N, 123°34′ E 198
Arunachal Pradesh, adm. division, India 28°39′ N, 94°2′ E 188
Arundel, U.K. 50°51′ N, 0°34′ E 162
Arusha, Tanzania 3°22′ S, 36°42′ E 224
Arusha, adm. division, Tanzania 4°7′ S, 35°4′ E 218
Aruwimi, river, Dem. Rep. of the Congo 1°37′ N, 25°21′ E 224
Arvada, Colo., U.S. 39°47′ N, 105°6′ W 90
Arvayheer, Mongolia 46°12′ N, 102°50′ E 198
Arve, river, Fr. 46°3′ N, 6°36′ E 167
Arvi, India 20°59′ N, 78°13′ E 188
Arviat, Can. 61°5′ N, 94°10′ W 106
Arvika, Nor. 59°39′ N, 12°36′ E 152
Arvin, Calif., U.S. 35°12′ N, 118°50′ W 101
Arvon, Mount, Mich., U.S. 46°44′ N, 88°14′ W 94
Arxan, China 47°12′ N, 119°55′ E 198
Ary, Russ. 72°50′ N, 122°37′ E 173
Arya Köli, lake, Kaz. 45°55′ N, 66°3′ E 184
Aryqbayq, Kaz. 52°55′ N, 68°12′ E 184
Arys, Kaz. 42°25′ N, 68°47′ E 197
Arys, river, Kaz. 42°32′ N, 69°1′ E 197
Arzamas, Russ. 55°21′ N, 43°55′ E 154
Aržano, Croatia 43°35′ N, 16°58′ E 168
Arzew, Alg. 35°50′ N, 0°19′ E 150
Arzgir, Russ. 45°21′ N, 44°10′ E 158
Arzni, Arm. 40°19′ N, 44°36′ E 195
As Ela, Djibouti 10°59′ N, 42°12′ E 224
As Sabkhah, Syr. 35°46′ N, 39°19′ E 180
Aş Şāfī, Jordan 31°1′ N, 35°27′ E 194
As Salmān, Iraq 30°30′ N, 44°32′ E 180
As Salţ, Jordan 32°2′ N, 35°43′ E 194
As Salwá, Saudi Arabia 24°41′ N, 50°48′ E 196
As Samāwah (Samawah), Iraq 31°15′ N, 45°15′ E 180
As Sanām, Saudi Arabia 23°34′ N, 51°7′ E 196
Aş Şanamayn, Syr. 33°4′ N, 36°11′ E 194
Aş Şaqlabīyah, Syr. 35°21′ N, 36°22′ E 194
Aş Şarafand, Leb. 33°27′ N, 35°17′ E 194
As Sarfaia, spring, Lib. 23°38′ N, 17°11′ E 216
Aş Şawrah, Saudi Arabia 27°52′ N, 35°22′ E 180
As Sīb, Oman 23°41′ N, 58°11′ E 196
As Sidr, Lib. 30°39′ N, 18°18′ E 216
As Sidr, Saudi Arabia 23°24′ N, 39°44′ E 182
As Sikr, spring, Iraq 30°44′ N, 43°44′ E 180
As Sirḩān, Wādī, Jordan 31°9′ N, 36°42′ E 180
Aş Şufuq, spring, U.A.E. 23°43′ N, 51°48′ E 196
As Sulaymānīyah, Iraq 35°33′ N, 45°25′ E 180
As Sulaymānīyah, Saudi Arabia 24°6′ N, 47°16′ E 196
As Sulaymī, Saudi Arabia 26°15′ N, 41°23′ E 182
As Sulayyil, Saudi Arabia 20°27′ N, 45°34′ E 182
As Sulţān, Lib. 31°6′ N, 17°7′ E 216
Aş Şurrah, Yemen 13°56′ N, 46°11′ E 182
As Suwāqah, Jordan 31°21′ N, 36°6′ E 194
Aş Şuwār, Syr. 35°31′ N, 40°38′ E 180
As Suwaydā', Syr. 32°42′ N, 36°34′ E 194
As Suwayḩ, Oman 22°6′ N, 59°41′ E 182
Asa, river, Dem. Rep. of the Congo 4°55′ N, 25°15′ E 224
Asab, Namibia 25°27′ S, 17°54′ E 227
Asab, oil field, U.A.E. 23°12′ N, 54°8′ E 182
Asadābād, Gardaneh-ye, pass, Iran 34°48′ N, 48°10′ E 180
Aşaği Ağcakand, Azerb. 40°26′ N, 46°33′ E 195
Asahi, river, Japan 35°0′ N, 133°47′ E 201
Asahikawa, Japan 43°50′ N, 142°36′ E 190
Āsalē, Eth. 14°12′ N, 40°18′ E 182
Asansol, India 23°40′ N, 86°59′ E 197
Åsarna, Nor. 62°39′ N, 14°20′ E 152
Āsayita, Eth. 11°31′ N, 41°25′ E 182
Asbest, Russ. 57°2′ N, 61°28′ E 154
Asbestos, Can. 45°45′ N, 71°57′ W 94
Ascención, Bol. 15°43′ S, 63°8′ W 132
Ascensión, Mex. 24°18′ N, 99°55′ W 114
Ascensión, Mex. 31°5′ N, 108°0′ W 92
Ascensión, Bahía de la 19°30′ N, 88°2′ W 115
Ascension Fracture Zone, South Atlantic Ocean 6°36′ S, 11°59′ W 253
Aschaffenburg, Ger. 49°58′ N, 9°9′ E 167
Ascheberg, Ger. 51°48′ N, 7°36′ E 167
Aschendorf, Ger. 53°3′ N, 7°19′ E 163
Ascira, Somalia 10°19′ N, 50°56′ E 216
Ascó, Sp. 41°10′ N, 0°33′ E 164
Ascot, U.K. 51°24′ N, 0°40′ E 162
Ascotán, Chile 21°45′ S, 68°19′ W 137
Ascutney, Vt., U.S. 43°24′ N, 72°25′ W 104
Åseda, Nor. 57°10′ N, 15°20′ E 152
Asedjrad, Alg. 24°55′ N, 1°0′ E 214
Āsela, Eth. 7°51′ N, 39°2′ E 224
Åsele, Nor. 64°9′ N, 17°19′ E 152
Åseral, Nor. 58°36′ N, 7°25′ E 152
Asfeld, Fr. 49°27′ N, 4°7′ E 163
Asfûn el Maţâ'na, Egypt 25°25′ N, 32°28′ E 226
Aşgabat (Ashgabat), Turkm. 37°54′ N, 58°14′ E 180
Ash Fork, Ariz., U.S. 35°11′ N, 112°29′ W 82
Ash Grove, Mo., U.S. 37°18′ N, 93°34′ W 94
Ash Mountain, Can. 59°16′ N, 130°38′ W 108
Ash, river, Can. 50°27′ N, 84°56′ W 94
Ash Shabakah, Iraq 30°48′ N, 43°36′ E 180
Ash Sha'rā', Saudi Arabia 24°15′ N, 44°11′ E 182
Ash Sharawrah, Saudi Arabia 17°54′ N, 47°26′ E 182
Ash Sharqāţ, Iraq 35°26′ N, 43°15′ E 180
Ash Shaţrah, Iraq 31°25′ N, 46°6′ E 180
Ash Shawbak, Jordan 30°31′ N, 35°33′ E 194
Ash Shaykh Badr, Syr. 34°59′ N, 36°4′ E 194
Ash Shiḩr, Yemen 14°45′ N, 49°33′ E 182
Ash Shināfīyah, Iraq 31°37′ N, 44°39′ E 180
Ash Shişar, Oman 18°15′ N, 53°39′ E 182
Ash Shumlūl, Saudi Arabia 26°29′ N, 47°22′ E 196
Ash Shuqayq, Saudi Arabia 17°42′ N, 42°4′ E 182
Ash Shurayf, Saudi Arabia 25°42′ N, 39°12′ E 182
Ash Shuwayfāt, Leb. 33°48′ N, 35°30′ E 194
Ash Shuwayrif, Lib. 29°58′ N, 14°12′ E 216
Asha, Russ. 55°3′ N, 57°18′ E 154
Ashbourne, U.K. 53°0′ N, 1°45′ W 162
Ashburn, Ga., U.S. 31°42′ N, 83°39′ W 96
Ashburnham, Mass., U.S. 42°37′ N, 71°55′ W 104
Ashburton, N.Z. 43°55′ S, 171°47′ E 240
Ashby, Mass., U.S. 42°40′ N, 71°50′ W 104
Ashby de la Zouch, U.K. 52°44′ N, 1°29′ W 162
Ashchy Köl, lake, Kaz. 45°11′ N, 67°38′ E 184
Ashcroft, Can. 50°43′ N, 121°15′ W 90
Ashdod, Israel 31°47′ N, 34°39′ E 194
Ashdown, Ark., U.S. 33°40′ N, 94°8′ W 96
Ashdown Forest, region, Europe 50°57′ N, 0°12′ E 162
Ashern, Can. 51°11′ N, 98°21′ W 90
Asherton, Tex., U.S. 28°26′ N, 99°45′ W 92
Ashfield, Mass., U.S. 42°31′ N, 72°48′ W 104
Ashford, U.K. 51°9′ N, 0°52′ E 162
Ashford, Wash., U.S. 46°44′ N, 122°2′ W 100
Ashgabat see Aşgabat, Turkm. 37°54′ N, 58°14′ E 180
Ashikaga, Japan 36°20′ N, 139°27′ E 201
Ashikita, Japan 32°18′ N, 130°30′ E 201
Ashizuri Misaki, Japan 32°36′ N, 133°0′ E 201
Ashkadar, river, Russ. 53°2′ N, 55°16′ E 154
Ashkelon, ruin(s), Israel 31°39′ N, 34°30′ E 194
Ashkum, Ill., U.S. 40°51′ N, 87°57′ W 102
Ashland, Kans., U.S. 37°11′ N, 99°47′ W 92
Ashland, Ky., U.S. 38°27′ N, 82°39′ W 102
Ashland, La., U.S. 32°7′ N, 93°6′ W 103
Ashland, Me., U.S. 46°37′ N, 68°25′ W 94
Ashland, Mont., U.S. 45°34′ N, 106°16′ W 90
Ashland, Nebr., U.S. 41°1′ N, 96°21′ W 94
Ashland, N.H., U.S. 43°41′ N, 71°38′ W 104
Ashland, Ohio, U.S. 40°52′ N, 82°18′ W 102
Ashland, Pa., U.S. 40°46′ N, 76°22′ W 110
Ashland, Va., U.S. 37°45′ N, 77°29′ W 94
Ashland, Wis., U.S. 46°35′ N, 90°53′ W 94
Ashland, Mount, Oreg., U.S. 42°5′ N, 122°48′ W 90
Ashley, Ind., U.S. 41°30′ N, 85°5′ W 102
Ashley, N. Dak., U.S. 46°0′ N, 99°24′ W 94
Ashley, Ohio, U.S. 40°23′ N, 82°57′ W 102
Ashmont, Can. 54°7′ N, 111°35′ W 108
Ashmore Islands, Indian Ocean 12°34′ S, 122°16′ E 231
Ashmyany, Belarus 54°26′ N, 25°55′ E 166
Ashoknagar, India 24°32′ N, 77°44′ E 197
Ashqelon, Israel 31°40′ N, 34°34′ E 194
Ashtabula, Ohio, U.S. 41°51′ N, 80°48′ W 102
Ashtabula, Lake, N. Dak., U.S. 47°10′ N, 98°38′ W 90
Ashton, Idaho, U.S. 44°4′ N, 111°27′ W 90
Ashton, Ill., U.S. 41°51′ N, 89°14′ W 102
Ashton, Mich., U.S. 43°58′ N, 85°30′ W 102
Ashton, R.I., U.S. 41°56′ N, 71°26′ W 104
Ashton under Lyne, U.K. 53°29′ N, 2°6′ W 162
Ashuanipi, Can. 52°45′ N, 66°6′ W 111
Ashuanipi Lake, Can. 52°31′ N, 66°34′ W 111
Ashuapmushuan, Lac, lake, Can. 49°10′ N, 74°40′ W 94
Ashville, Can. 51°10′ N, 100°18′ W 90
Ashville, Ohio, U.S. 39°43′ N, 82°57′ W 102
Ashyrmy, Bichānāk, Arm. 39°33′ N, 45°7′ E 195
'Āşī (Orontes), river, Syr. 35°40′ N, 36°21′ E 194
Asia 3°0′ N, 103°0′ E 173
Asia, Kepulauan, islands, North Pacific Ocean 1°12′ N, 129°17′ E 192
Asia Minor see Anatolia, region, Asia 38°39′ N, 30°18′ E 180
Asiago, It. 45°52′ N, 11°30′ E 167
Asika, India 19°38′ N, 84°38′ E 188
Asikkala, Fin. 61°11′ N, 25°28′ E 166
Asilah, Mor. 35°28′ N, 6°2′ W 150
Asillo, Peru 14°50′ S, 70°21′ W 137
Asinara, Isola, island, It. 41°4′ N, 7°5′ E 214
Asino, Russ. 56°59′ N, 86°9′ E 169
Asipovichy, Belarus 53°17′ N, 28°45′ E 152
Asis, Ras, Sudan 18°17′ N, 37°36′ E 182
Ask, Nor. 60°28′ N, 5°10′ E 152
Aşkale, Turk. 39°56′ N, 40°41′ E 195
Askaniya Nova, Ukr. 46°27′ N, 33°53′ E 156
Asker, Nor. 59°50′ N, 10°26′ E 152
Askham, S. Af. 27°2′ S, 20°51′ E 227
Askī Mawşil, Iraq 36°31′ N, 42°37′ E 195
Åskilje, Nor. 64°53′ N, 17°51′ E 152
Askino, Russ. 56°6′ N, 56°35′ E 154
Askiz, Russ. 53°10′ N, 90°33′ E 184
Askole, Pak. 35°40′ N, 75°50′ E 188
Askrigg, U.K. 54°18′ N, 2°5′ W 162
Askvoll, Nor. 61°21′ N, 5°4′ E 152
Asler, spring, Mali 18°53′ N, 0°9′ E 222
Asmar, Afghan. 35°2′ N, 71°27′ E 186
Asmara, Eritrea 15°16′ N, 38°48′ E 182
Åsnes, Nor. 60°36′ N, 11°57′ E 152
Asni, Mor. 31°14′ N, 8°1′ W 214
Aso, peak, Japan 32°51′ N, 131°3′ E 201
Asola, It. 45°13′ N, 10°25′ E 167
Asopus, ruin(s), Gr. 36°41′ N, 22°45′ E 156
Āsosa, Eth. 10°2′ N, 34°29′ E 224
Asoteriba, Sudan 19°31′ N, 37°5′ E 182
Asoteriba, Jebel, peak, Sudan 21°49′ N, 36°24′ E 182
Aspang, Aust. 47°33′ N, 16°3′ E 168
Aspatria, U.K. 54°46′ N, 3°20′ W 162
Aspeå, Nor. 63°22′ N, 17°36′ E 152
Aspen, Colo., U.S. 39°11′ N, 106°50′ W 92
Aspen Butte, peak, Oreg., U.S. 42°18′ N, 122°11′ W 90
Aspen Range, Idaho, U.S. 42°42′ N, 111°34′ W 90
Aspermont, Tex., U.S. 33°8′ N, 100°14′ W 92
Aspiring, Mount, N.Z. 44°25′ S, 168°39′ E 240
Asprókavos, Ákra, Gr. 39°21′ N, 19°35′ E 156
Aspromonte, It. 38°1′ N, 15°50′ E 156
Aspy Bay 46°53′ N, 60°50′ W 111
Asquith, Can. 52°8′ N, 107°13′ W 90
Assa, Mor. 28°37′ N, 9°24′ W 214
Assab, Eritrea 12°59′ N, 42°41′ E 182
'Assâba, Mauritania 16°36′ N, 12°26′ W 222
Aşşafā, Syr. 33°13′ N, 36°48′ E 194
Assaikio, Nig. 8°34′ N, 8°53′ E 222
Assala, Congo 2°18′ S, 14°28′ E 218
Assam, adm. division, India 26°28′ N, 90°56′ E 188
Assaouas, spring, Niger 16°53′ N, 7°24′ E 222
Assateague Island National Seashore, Va., U.S. 38°4′ N, 75°9′ W 94
Assean Lake, lake, Can. 56°7′ N, 97°7′ W 108
Assebroek, Belg. 51°10′ N, 3°16′ E 163
Assen, Neth. 52°59′ N, 6°33′ E 163
Assiniboia, Can. 49°37′ N, 106°0′ W 90
Assiniboine, Mount, Can. 50°51′ N, 115°44′ W 90
Assiniboine, river, Can. 49°21′ N, 99°32′ W 80
Assinica, Lac, lake, Can. 50°30′ N, 75°45′ W 110
Assiou (Azéo), spring, Alg. 21°6′ N, 7°35′ E 222
Assis, Braz. 22°40′ S, 50°28′ W 138
Assis Brasil, Peru 10°56′ S, 69°41′ W 137
Asslar, Ger. 50°35′ N, 8°26′ E 167
Assodé, Niger 18°29′ N, 8°25′ E 222
Assok-Ngoum, Gabon 1°45′ N, 11°35′ E 218
Assos, ruin(s), Turk. 39°29′ N, 26°15′ E 156
Assoul, Mor. 32°2′ N, 5°17′ W 214
Assumption, Ill., U.S. 39°30′ N, 89°2′ W 102
Assumption Island, Seychelles 9°51′ S, 46°7′ E 218
Astana, Kaz. 51°7′ N, 71°14′ E 184
Astara, Azerb. 38°28′ N, 48°50′ E 195
Āstārā, Iran 38°25′ N, 48°48′ E 195
Asten, Neth. 51°24′ N, 5°44′ E 167
Asti, It. 44°54′ N, 8°12′ E 167
Astillero, Peru 13°24′ S, 69°38′ W 137
Astillero, Cerro del, peak, Mex. 20°16′ N, 99°39′ W 114
Asto, Mont, peak, Fr. 42°34′ N, 9°8′ E 156
Astola Island, Pak. 24°57′ N, 63°54′ E 182
Astorga, Sp. 42°26′ N, 6°4′ W 150
Astoria, Oreg., U.S. 46°10′ N, 123°48′ W 100
Astove Island, Seychelles 10°29′ S, 47°53′ E 220
Astrakhan', Russ. 46°19′ N, 48°4′ E 158
Astrakhan', adm. division, Russ. 47°9′ N, 46°39′ E 158
Åsträsk, Nor. 64°35′ N, 19°57′ E 152
Astravyets, Belarus 54°36′ N, 25°57′ E 166
Astryna, Belarus 53°44′ N, 24°34′ E 154
Asturias, adm. division, Sp. 43°24′ N, 7°1′ W 150
Asunción, Bol. 11°49′ S, 67°52′ W 137
Asunción, Parag. 25°19′ S, 57°49′ W 132
Asunción, Punta, Arg. 39°7′ S, 60°30′ W 139
Åsunden, lake, Nor. 57°53′ N, 15°25′ E 152
Asūne, Latv. 56°0′ N, 27°37′ E 166
Åsvær, island, Nor. 66°16′ N, 11°14′ E 152
Asvyeya, Belarus 56°1′ N, 28°5′ E 166
Asvyeyskaye, Vozyera, lake, Belarus 56°1′ N, 27°32′ E 166
Aswân, Egypt 24°4′ N, 32°54′ E 182
Asyûţ, Egypt 27°8′ N, 31°5′ E 180
Aszód, Hung. 47°39′ N, 19°28′ E 168
Aţ Ţafīlah, Jordan 30°50′ N, 35°36′ E 194
Aţ Ţā'if, Saudi Arabia 21°15′ N, 40°24′ E 182
At Tāj, Lib. 24°17′ N, 23°15′ E 216
At Tall, Syr. 33°35′ N, 36°18′ E 194
Aţ Ţayyibah, Jordan 31°3′ N, 35°36′ E 194
At Turbah, Yemen 12°45′ N, 43°29′ E 182
Aţ Ţuwayyah, spring, Saudi Arabia 27°41′ N, 40°50′ E 180
Ataa, Den. 69°46′ N, 51°1′ W 106
Atacama, adm. division, Chile 27°6′ S, 70°45′ W 132
Atacama, Desierto de, Chile 25°53′ S, 70°11′ W 132
Atacuari, river, Peru 3°25′ S, 71°16′ W 136
Atafu, island, N.Z. 8°29′ S, 172°40′ W 252
Atakora, Chaîne de l', Benin 10°7′ N, 1°12′ E 222
Atakpamé, Togo 7°33′ N, 1°8′ E 222
Atalaia do Norte, Braz. 4°19′ S, 70°7′ W 130
Atalaya, Peru 10°44′ S, 73°48′ W 137
Ataléia, Braz. 18°4′ S, 41°7′ W 138
Atami, Japan 35°4′ N, 139°3′ E 201
Atammik, Den. 64°51′ N, 52°9′ W 106
Atamyrat, Turkm. 37°52′ N, 65°11′ E 160
Atamyrat (Kerki), Turkm. 37°49′ N, 65°10′ E 197
Atar, Mauritania 20°31′ N, 13°3′ W 222
Atarfe, Sp. 37°13′ N, 3°41′ W 164
Atascadero, Calif., U.S. 35°29′ N, 120°41′ W 100
Atašiene, Latv. 56°32′ N, 26°21′ E 166
Atasta, ruin(s), Mex. 18°37′ N, 92°14′ W 115
Atasū, Kaz. 48°40′ N, 71°39′ E 184
Atauro, island, Indonesia 8°31′ S, 125°42′ E 192
Atáviros, peak, Gr. 36°11′ N, 27°47′ E 156
Atbara, Sudan 17°42′ N, 34°3′ E 182
Atbara, river, Sudan 14°10′ N, 35°57′ E 226
Atbasar, Kaz. 51°48′ N, 68°22′ E 184
At-Bashy, Kyrg. 41°7′ N, 75°47′ E 184
Atchafalaya Bay 29°27′ N, 91°38′ W 103
Atchison, Kans., U.S. 39°32′ N, 95°8′ W 94
Atea, Sp. 41°9′ N, 1°33′ W 164
Ateca, Sp. 41°19′ N, 1°49′ W 164
Ath, Belg. 50°37′ N, 3°47′ E 163
Ath Thumāmah, spring, Saudi Arabia 27°41′ N, 45°0′ E 180
Athabasca, Can. 54°41′ N, 113°15′ W 108
Athabasca, Lake, Can. 59°8′ N, 109°58′ W 108
Athabasca, Mount, Can. 52°10′ N, 117°17′ W 108
Athabasca, oil field, Can. 56°54′ N, 111°38′ W 108
Athabasca, river, Can. 53°26′ N, 117°6′ W 106
Athamánon, peak, Gr. 39°31′ N, 21°7′ E 156
Athenry, Ire. 53°17′ N, 8°46′ W 150
Athens, Ala., U.S. 34°48′ N, 86°58′ W 96
Athens, Ga., U.S. 33°57′ N, 83°24′ W 96
Athens, Ill., U.S. 39°57′ N, 89°44′ W 102
Athens, La., U.S. 32°38′ N, 93°2′ W 103
Athens, N.Y., U.S. 42°15′ N, 73°50′ W 104
Athens, Ohio, U.S. 39°19′ N, 82°6′ W 102
Athens, Pa., U.S. 41°57′ N, 76°32′ W 110
Athens, Tenn., U.S. 35°26′ N, 84°36′ W 96
Athens, Tex., U.S. 32°11′ N, 95°51′ W 96
Athens see Athína, Gr. 37°58′ N, 23°36′ E 156
Atherley, Can. 44°35′ N, 79°21′ W 110
Athi River, Kenya 1°28′ S, 36°59′ E 224
Athi, river, Kenya 2°31′ S, 38°21′ E 224
Athienou, Northern Cyprus, Cyprus 35°4′ N, 33°32′ E 194
Athína (Athens), Gr. 37°58′ N, 23°36′ E 156
Athlone, Ire. 53°25′ N, 7°58′ W 150
Athna, Cyprus 35°2′ N, 33°47′ E 156
Athol, Mass., U.S. 42°35′ N, 72°14′ W 104
Athol, N.Z. 45°30′ S, 168°35′ E 240
Atholl, Kap, Den. 76°6′ N, 73°24′ W 106
Atholville, Can. 47°58′ N, 66°44′ W 94
Áthos, Mount see Ágio Óros, peak, Gr. 40°8′ N, 24°15′ E 156
Athos, Mount see Ágio Óros, region, Gr. 40°14′ N, 23°2′ E 156
Athos Range, Antarctica 70°15′ S, 61°18′ E 248
Ati, Chad 13°15′ N, 18°22′ E 216
Ati Ardébé, Chad 12°45′ N, 17°41′ E 216
Atiak, Uganda 3°14′ N, 32°7′ E 224
Atiamuri, N.Z. 38°26′ S, 176°1′ E 240
Atico, Peru 16°12′ S, 73°38′ W 137
Atienza, Sp. 41°11′ N, 2°52′ W 164
Atik Lake, Can. 55°16′ N, 96°19′ W 108
Atikameg, Can. 55°54′ N, 115°41′ W 108
Atikameg Lake, Can. 53°57′ N, 100°58′ W 108
Atikameg, river, Can. 51°45′ N, 83°34′ W 110
Atiki, adm. division, Gr. 37°26′ N, 23°14′ E 156
Atikokan, Can. 48°44′ N, 91°37′ W 94
Atikonak Lake, Can. 52°30′ N, 65°11′ W 111
Atikwa Lake, lake, Can. 49°27′ N, 93°56′ W 90
Atiquipa, Peru 15°50′ S, 74°22′ W 137
Atka, Alas., U.S. 52°10′ N, 174°12′ W 160
Atka, Russ. 60°51′ N, 151°50′ E 160
Atka, island, Alas., U.S. 51°38′ N, 175°35′ W 160
Atkarsk, Russ. 51°53′ N, 45°2′ E 158
Atkinson, Nebr., U.S. 42°30′ N, 98°59′ W 90
Atkinson, N.H., U.S. 42°50′ N, 71°10′ W 104
Atkinson Lake, Can. 55°34′ N, 95°34′ W 108
Atkinson Point, Can. 69°54′ N, 134°2′ W 98
Atlacomulco, Mex. 19°47′ N, 99°55′ W 114
Atlanta, Ga., U.S. 33°44′ N, 84°29′ W 96

Atlanta, *Ill., U.S.* 40°15′ N, 89°14′ W **102**
Atlanta, *Mich., U.S.* 45°0′ N, 84°9′ W **94**
Atlanta, *Tex., U.S.* 33°6′ N, 94°10′ W **103**
Atlantic, *Iowa, U.S.* 41°22′ N, 95°1′ W **94**
Atlantic Beach, *Fla., U.S.* 30°19′ N, 81°25′ W **96**
Atlantic Beach, *N.C., U.S.* 34°42′ N, 76°46′ W **96**
Atlantic Ocean 38°49′ N, 72°7′ W **253**
Atlantic-Indian Ridge, *Indian Ocean* 53°30′ S, 21°10′ E **255**
Atlántico, adm. division, *Col.* 10°25′ N, 75°5′ W **136**
Atlántida, *Uru.* 34°46′ S, 55°43′ W **139**
Atlantis Fracture Zone, *North Atlantic Ocean* 29°7′ N, 40°8′ W **253**
Atlantis II Fracture Zone, *Indian Ocean* 34°58′ S, 57°3′ E **254**
Atlas Mountains, *Africa* 35°53′ N, 0°28′ E **164**
Atlas Saharien, mountains, *Alg.* 35°5′ N, 3°42′ E **150**
Atlin, *Can.* 59°35′ N, 133°44′ W **108**
'Atlit, *Israel* 32°41′ N, 34°56′ E **194**
Atlixco, *Mex.* 18°51′ N, 98°27′ W **114**
Atmakur, *India* 14°39′ N, 79°38′ E **188**
Atmakur, *India* 18°44′ N, 78°35′ E **188**
Atmautluak, *Alas., U.S.* 60°49′ N, 162°33′ W **98**
Atmore, *Ala., U.S.* 31°0′ N, 87°30′ W **103**
Atna Peak, *Can.* 53°55′ N, 128°10′ W **108**
Atocha, *Bol.* 21°0′ S, 66°20′ W **137**
Atoka, *N. Mex., U.S.* 32°46′ N, 104°24′ W **92**
Atoka, *Okla., U.S.* 34°21′ N, 96°7′ W **96**
Atokila, spring, *Mali* 22°46′ N, 5°56′ W **214**
Atome, *Angola* 11°54′ S, 14°37′ E **220**
Atotonilco, *Mex.* 24°14′ N, 102°50′ W **114**
Atotonilco el Alto, *Mex.* 20°32′ N, 102°32′ W **114**
Atoyac, *Mex.* 20°0′ N, 103°33′ W **114**
Atoyac, river, *Mex.* 17°58′ N, 98°42′ W **114**
Atqasuk, *Alas., U.S.* 70°28′ N, 157°34′ W **98**
Atrak, river, *Iran* 37°20′ N, 57°36′ E **180**
Atrato, river, *Col.* 7°29′ N, 77°11′ W **136**
Atsumi, *Japan* 38°38′ N, 139°37′ E **201**
Atsumi, *Japan* 34°37′ N, 137°7′ E **201**
Attachie, *Can.* 56°12′ N, 121°28′ W **108**
Attalla, *Ala., U.S.* 34°0′ N, 86°6′ W **96**
Attapu, *Laos* 14°55′ N, 106°46′ E **202**
Attawapiskat, *Can.* 52°58′ N, 82°31′ W **106**
Attawapiskat, river, *Can.* 52°3′ N, 87°31′ W **110**
Attendorn, *Ger.* 51°7′ N, 7°54′ E **167**
Attica, *Ind., U.S.* 40°16′ N, 87°15′ W **102**
Attica, *Kans., U.S.* 37°13′ N, 98°14′ W **92**
Attica, *Ohio, U.S.* 41°3′ N, 82°54′ W **102**
Attigny, *Fr.* 49°27′ N, 4°34′ E **163**
Attigu, *Sudan* 4°1′ N, 31°43′ E **224**
Attingal, *India* 8°40′ N, 76°48′ E **188**
Attleboro, *Mass., U.S.* 41°56′ N, 71°17′ W **104**
Attleborough, *U.K.* 52°30′ N, 1°1′ E **162**
Attoyac, river, *Tex., U.S.* 31°37′ N, 94°21′ W **103**
Attu, *Den.* 67°55′ N, 53°39′ W **106**
Attu, island, *Alas., U.S.* 52°47′ N, 171°26′ E **160**
Attur, *India* 11°35′ N, 78°36′ E **188**
Attwood Lake, *Can.* 51°11′ N, 89°9′ W **110**
Atuel, river, *Arg.* 35°38′ S, 67°47′ W **134**
Atura, *Uganda* 2°7′ N, 32°23′ E **224**
Atwater, *Calif., U.S.* 37°21′ N, 120°37′ W **100**
Atwood, *Kans., U.S.* 39°47′ N, 101°4′ W **90**
Atwood see Crooked Island, *Bahamas* 22°39′ N, 76°43′ W **81**
Atyashevo, *Russ.* 54°37′ N, 46°10′ E **154**
Atyraū, *Kaz.* 47°6′ N, 51°53′ E **158**
Atyrau, adm. division, *Kaz.* 47°28′ N, 50°45′ E **158**
Atzinging Lake, lake, *Can.* 60°9′ N, 103°50′ W **108**
Au Fer, Point, *La., U.S.* 29°11′ N, 91°28′ W **103**
Au Gres, *Mich., U.S.* 44°3′ N, 83°42′ W **102**
Au Gres, Point, *Mich., U.S.* 43°51′ N, 83°51′ W **102**
Au Sable, *Mich., U.S.* 44°25′ N, 83°21′ W **94**
Au Sable Forks, *N.Y., U.S.* 44°25′ N, 73°41′ W **104**
Au Sable Point, *Mich., U.S.* 46°21′ N, 86°10′ W **110**
Au Sable Point, *Mich., U.S.* 44°19′ N, 83°40′ W **110**
Au Sable, river, *Mich., U.S.* 44°41′ N, 84°44′ W **80**
Auas Mountains, *Namibia* 22°40′ S, 17°6′ E **227**
Aubarede Point, *Philippines* 17°17′ N, 122°28′ E **203**
Aúbe, *Mozambique* 16°22′ S, 39°46′ E **224**
Aube, river, *Fr.* 48°18′ N, 4°35′ E **163**
Aubenton, *Fr.* 49°49′ N, 4°12′ E **163**
Auberry, *Calif., U.S.* 37°4′ N, 119°30′ W **100**
Aubin, *Fr.* 44°31′ N, 2°13′ E **150**
Aubrac, Monts d', *Fr.* 44°47′ N, 2°47′ E **165**
Aubrey Cliffs, *Ariz., U.S.* 35°51′ N, 113°14′ W **92**
Aubrey Falls, *Can.* 46°44′ N, 83°14′ W **94**
Aubry Lake, *Can.* 67°31′ N, 127°14′ W **98**
Auburn, *Ala., U.S.* 32°36′ N, 85°29′ W **96**
Auburn, *Calif., U.S.* 38°53′ N, 121°6′ W **90**
Auburn, *Ill., U.S.* 39°34′ N, 89°44′ W **102**
Auburn, *Ind., U.S.* 41°21′ N, 85°4′ W **102**
Auburn, *Me., U.S.* 44°5′ N, 70°15′ W **104**
Auburn, *Mich., U.S.* 43°36′ N, 84°5′ W **102**
Auburn, *Miss., U.S.* 31°20′ N, 90°37′ W **103**
Auburn, *Mo., U.S.* 39°34′ N, 89°44′ W **94**
Auburn, *Nebr., U.S.* 40°22′ N, 95°51′ W **90**
Auburn, *N.H., U.S.* 43°0′ N, 71°21′ W **104**
Auburn, *N.Y., U.S.* 42°55′ N, 76°34′ W **94**
Auburn, *Wash., U.S.* 47°17′ N, 122°15′ W **100**
Auburn Range, *Austral.* 25°28′ S, 150°9′ E **230**
Auburndale, *Fla., U.S.* 28°4′ N, 81°48′ W **105**
Aucanquilcha, peak, *Chile* 21°15′ S, 68°34′ W **137**
Aucará, *Peru* 14°18′ S, 74°5′ W **137**
Auce, *Latv.* 56°28′ N, 22°52′ E **166**
Auch, *Fr.* 43°38′ N, 0°34′ E **150**
Auchi, *Nig.* 7°6′ N, 6°13′ E **222**
Auckland, *N.Z.* 36°53′ S, 174°48′ E **240**
Aude, river, *Fr.* 42°54′ N, 2°12′ E **165**
Auden, *Can.* 50°14′ N, 87°52′ W **94**
Auderville, *Fr.* 49°42′ N, 1°57′ W **150**
Audoin, Lac, lake, *Can.* 46°46′ N, 79°8′ W **94**
Audubon, *Iowa, U.S.* 41°41′ N, 94°55′ W **94**
Audun-le-Roman, *Fr.* 49°22′ N, 5°51′ E **163**
Aūezov, *Kaz.* 49°42′ N, 81°30′ E **184**
Auffay, *Fr.* 49°43′ N, 1°6′ E **163**
Aughty Mountains, Slieve, *Ire.* 52°54′ N, 9°21′ W **150**
Augrabies Falls National Park, *S. Af.* 28°38′ S, 20°6′ E **227**
Augsburg, *Ger.* 48°22′ N, 10°53′ E **152**
Augusta, *Austral.* 34°16′ S, 115°10′ E **231**
Augusta, *Ga., U.S.* 33°28′ N, 81°58′ W **96**
Augusta, *Kans., U.S.* 37°39′ N, 96°59′ W **92**
Augusta, *Ky., U.S.* 38°45′ N, 84°1′ W **102**
Augusta, *Me., U.S.* 44°18′ N, 69°49′ W **104**
Augusta, *Mont., U.S.* 47°28′ N, 112°24′ W **90**
Augusta, *Tex., U.S.* 31°30′ N, 95°19′ W **103**
Augusta, *Wis., U.S.* 44°40′ N, 91°7′ W **94**
Augusta, Mount, *Can.* 60°16′ N, 140°39′ W **98**
Augusta Victoria, *Chile* 24°7′ S, 69°6′ W **132**
Augusto Lima, *Braz.* 18°7′ S, 44°18′ W **138**
Augustów, *Pol.* 53°51′ N, 22°58′ E **166**
Augustus Island, *Austral.* 15°21′ S, 122°46′ E **230**
Augustus, Mount, *Austral.* 24°23′ S, 116°37′ E **230**
Auk, oil field, *North Sea* 56°23′ N, 1°57′ E **150**
Auke Bay, *Alas., U.S.* 58°24′ N, 134°41′ W **108**
Aukra, *Nor.* 62°46′ N, 6°54′ E **152**
Aukštaitija National Park, *Lith.* 55°22′ N, 25°37′ E **166**
Aul, *India* 20°40′ N, 86°39′ E **188**
Āūlīekōl, *Kaz.* 52°22′ N, 64°5′ E **184**
Aulis, ruin(s), *Gr.* 38°24′ N, 23°30′ E **156**
Aulla, *It.* 44°12′ N, 9°59′ E **167**
Aulneau Peninsula, *Can.* 49°22′ N, 94°42′ W **90**
Ault, *Fr.* 50°5′ N, 1°27′ E **163**
Aultbea, *U.K.* 57°50′ N, 5°35′ W **150**
Aulus-les-Bains, *Fr.* 42°46′ N, 1°20′ E **164**
Aumale, *Fr.* 49°45′ N, 1°45′ E **163**
Auna, *Nig.* 10°10′ N, 4°42′ E **222**
Auneau, *Fr.* 48°27′ N, 1°45′ E **163**
Auneuil, *Fr.* 49°22′ N, 1°59′ E **163**
Auno, *Nig.* 11°51′ N, 12°55′ E **216**
Aups, *Fr.* 43°37′ N, 6°12′ E **150**
Aur, island, *Malaysia* 2°20′ N, 104°22′ E **196**
Aura, *Fin.* 60°36′ N, 22°32′ E **166**
Aura, river, *Nor.* 62°19′ N, 8°10′ E **152**
Auraiya, *India* 26°26′ N, 79°29′ E **197**
Aurdal, *Nor.* 60°54′ N, 9°25′ E **152**
Aure, *Nor.* 63°15′ N, 8°34′ E **152**
Aurich, *Ger.* 53°28′ N, 7°28′ E **163**
Aurillac, *Fr.* 44°54′ N, 2°27′ E **150**
Aurisina, *It.* 45°45′ N, 13°40′ E **167**
Auritz (Burguete), *Sp.* 42°59′ N, 1°21′ W **164**
Auronzo di Cadore, *It.* 46°32′ N, 12°26′ E **167**
Aurora, *Can.* 43°59′ N, 79°28′ W **110**
Aurora, *Ill., U.S.* 41°45′ N, 88°18′ W **102**
Aurora, *Ind., U.S.* 39°2′ N, 84°56′ W **102**
Aurora, *Minn., U.S.* 47°31′ N, 92°16′ W **94**
Aurora, *Mo., U.S.* 41°45′ N, 88°18′ W **94**
Aurora, *Mo., U.S.* 36°57′ N, 93°43′ W **96**
Aurora, *Nebr., U.S.* 40°51′ N, 98°1′ W **90**
Aurora, *Ohio, U.S.* 41°18′ N, 81°21′ W **102**
Aurukun, *Austral.* 13°9′ S, 141°46′ E **238**
Aus, *Namibia* 26°41′ S, 16°16′ E **227**
Austevoll, *Nor.* 60°5′ N, 5°13′ E **152**
Austin, *Ind., U.S.* 38°45′ N, 85°48′ W **102**
Austin, *Minn., U.S.* 43°39′ N, 93°0′ W **94**
Austin, *Nev., U.S.* 39°30′ N, 117°5′ W **90**
Austin, *Pa., U.S.* 41°37′ N, 78°5′ W **94**
Austin, *Tex., U.S.* 30°14′ N, 97°50′ W **92**
Austral Islands (Tubuai Islands), *South Pacific Ocean* 21°30′ S, 152°33′ W **238**
Australia 24°25′ S, 128°31′ E **231**
Australia 22°0′ S, 133°0′ E **231**
Australian, *Can.* 52°43′ N, 122°26′ W **108**
Australian Alps, *Austral.* 37°20′ S, 145°56′ E **230**
Australian-Antarctic Basin, *Indian Ocean* 59°4′ S, 115°12′ E **255**
Australian Capital Territory, adm. division, *Austral.* 35°42′ S, 148°21′ E **231**
Austrått, *Nor.* 63°41′ N, 9°45′ E **152**
Austria 48°27′ N, 14°52′ E **152**
Autazes, *Braz.* 3°38′ S, 59°8′ W **130**
Auterive, *Fr.* 43°19′ N, 1°27′ E **164**
Authon-du-Perche, *Fr.* 48°11′ N, 0°53′ E **163**
Autlán, *Mex.* 19°46′ N, 104°22′ W **114**
Auve, *Fr.* 49°2′ N, 4°41′ E **163**
Auvergne, adm. division, *Fr.* 45°9′ N, 2°15′ E **150**
Auvergne, region, *Europe* 44°55′ N, 2°13′ E **165**
Auvillar, *Fr.* 44°3′ N, 0°53′ E **150**
Aux Sources, Mont, peak, *Lesotho* 28°56′ S, 28°42′ E **227**
Auxerre, *Fr.* 47°47′ N, 3°33′ E **150**
Auxonne, *Fr.* 47°11′ N, 5°23′ E **156**
Auyán Tepuí, peak, *Venez.* 5°48′ N, 62°42′ W **130**
Auyuittuq National Park, *Can.* 67°30′ N, 66°0′ W **106**
Ava, *Mo., U.S.* 36°57′ N, 92°39′ W **96**
Avakubi, *Dem. Rep. of the Congo* 1°21′ N, 27°39′ E **224**
Avala, peak, *Serb.* 44°42′ N, 20°29′ E **168**
Avallon, *Fr.* 47°28′ N, 3°54′ E **150**
Avalon, *Calif., U.S.* 33°19′ N, 118°20′ W **101**
Avalon Peninsula, *Can.* 47°20′ N, 53°50′ W **111**
Avaré, *Braz.* 23°6′ S, 48°57′ W **138**
Avarua, *New Zealand* 21°0′ S, 160°0′ W **241**
Avawatz Mountains, *Calif., U.S.* 35°36′ N, 116°30′ W **101**
Avawatz Pass, *Calif., U.S.* 35°31′ N, 116°27′ W **101**
Avay, *Kaz.* 49°34′ N, 72°52′ E **184**
Avebury, site, *U.K.* 51°26′ N, 1°53′ W **162**
Aveiro, *Braz.* 3°37′ S, 55°23′ W **130**
Aveiro, *Port.* 40°37′ N, 8°42′ W **214**
Aveiro, *Port.* 40°38′ N, 8°40′ W **150**
Aveiro, adm. division, *Port.* 40°37′ N, 8°58′ W **150**
Avellaneda, *Arg.* 34°42′ S, 58°20′ W **139**
Avenal, *Calif., U.S.* 36°0′ N, 120°9′ W **100**
Averias, *Arg.* 28°45′ S, 62°28′ W **139**
Aversa, *It.* 40°59′ N, 14°12′ E **156**
Avery, *Calif., U.S.* 38°12′ N, 120°23′ W **100**
Avery Island, *La., U.S.* 29°52′ N, 91°56′ W **103**
Aves, Islas de, islands, *Caribbean Sea* 12°7′ N, 67°29′ W **116**
Aves Ridge, *Caribbean Sea* 15°1′ N, 63°37′ W **253**
Avesnes, *Fr.* 50°7′ N, 3°55′ E **163**
Avesta, *Nor.* 60°7′ N, 16°7′ E **152**
Aveyron, river, *Fr.* 44°22′ N, 2°7′ E **165**
Avia Terai, *Arg.* 26°41′ S, 60°46′ W **139**
Aviano, *It.* 46°4′ N, 12°34′ E **167**
Avignon, *Fr.* 43°57′ N, 4°50′ E **214**
Ávila, *Sp.* 40°39′ N, 4°42′ W **150**
Avila Beach, *Calif., U.S.* 35°11′ N, 120°44′ W **100**
Ávila, Sierra de, *Sp.* 40°30′ N, 5°33′ W **150**
Avilla, *Ind., U.S.* 41°21′ N, 85°15′ W **102**
Avinger, *Tex., U.S.* 32°53′ N, 94°35′ W **103**
Avinurme, *Est.* 58°58′ N, 26°53′ E **166**
Avize, *Fr.* 48°57′ N, 4°0′ E **163**
Avoca, *Ind., U.S.* 38°54′ N, 86°34′ W **102**
Avoca, *Iowa, U.S.* 41°26′ N, 95°21′ W **90**
Avola, *It.* 36°54′ N, 15°7′ E **156**
Avon, *Mass., U.S.* 42°7′ N, 71°3′ W **104**
Avon, *N.C., U.S.* 35°21′ N, 75°31′ W **96**
Avon Park, *Fla., U.S.* 27°36′ N, 81°30′ W **105**
Avon, river, *U.K.* 51°27′ N, 2°43′ W **162**
Avonlea, *Can.* 50°0′ N, 105°5′ W **90**
Avonmouth, *U.K.* 51°30′ N, 2°42′ W **162**
Avontuur, *S. Af.* 33°44′ S, 23°11′ E **227**
Avraga, *Mongolia* 47°13′ N, 109°10′ E **198**
Avre, river, *Fr.* 48°41′ N, 0°53′ E **163**
Avsa, Gora, peak, *Russ.* 63°18′ N, 93°27′ E **169**
Avtovac, *Bosn. and Herzg.* 43°8′ N, 18°33′ E **168**
Awakino, *N.Z.* 38°42′ S, 174°39′ E **240**
Awali, oil field, *Bahrain* 25°55′ N, 50°29′ E **196**
Āwarē, *Eth.* 8°13′ N, 44°5′ E **218**
Awarua Bay 44°22′ S, 167°39′ E **240**
Āwasa, *Eth.* 6°57′ N, 38°26′ E **224**
Āwash, *Eth.* 8°59′ N, 40°10′ E **224**
Āwash National Park, *Eth.* 8°43′ N, 39°27′ E **224**
Awash, river, *Eth.* 9°38′ N, 40°17′ E **224**
Awaso, *Ghana* 6°13′ N, 2°16′ W **222**
Awat, *China* 40°38′ N, 80°22′ E **184**
Awbārī (Ubari), *Lib.* 26°37′ N, 12°45′ E **216**
Awdheegle, *Somalia* 1°57′ N, 44°50′ E **218**
Awe, *Nig.* 8°9′ N, 9°7′ E **222**
Aweil, *Sudan* 8°46′ N, 27°22′ E **224**
Awfist, *Western Sahara, Mor.* 25°45′ N, 14°38′ W **214**
Awgu, *Nig.* 6°4′ N, 7°26′ E **222**
Awio, *P.N.G.* 6°13′ S, 150°6′ E **192**
Awjilah, *Lib.* 29°9′ N, 21°14′ E **216**
Awka, *Nig.* 6°12′ N, 7°3′ E **222**
Awsard, *Western Sahara, Mor.* 22°39′ N, 14°19′ W **214**
Awwalī, river, *Leb.* 33°35′ N, 35°23′ E **194**
Axat, *Fr.* 42°48′ N, 2°12′ E **164**
Axbridge, *U.K.* 51°16′ N, 2°49′ W **162**
Axel Heiberg Island, *Can.* 80°42′ N, 95°47′ W **246**
Axim, *Ghana* 4°53′ N, 2°14′ W **222**
Axinim, *Braz.* 4°2′ S, 59°25′ W **130**
Axmarsbruk, *Nor.* 61°3′ N, 17°4′ E **152**
Axminster, *U.K.* 50°46′ N, 2°59′ W **162**
Axochiapan, *Mex.* 18°28′ N, 98°45′ W **114**
Axos, ruin(s), *Gr.* 35°17′ N, 24°44′ E **156**
Axtell, *Nebr., U.S.* 40°28′ N, 99°8′ W **90**
Ay, *Fr.* 49°3′ N, 4°0′ E **163**
Ay, *Kaz.* 47°29′ N, 80°35′ E **184**
Aya Bentih, *Eth.* 8°0′ N, 46°36′ E **218**
Ayabe, *Japan* 35°16′ N, 135°15′ E **201**
Ayacucho, *Arg.* 37°9′ S, 58°32′ W **139**
Ayacucho, *Bol.* 17°54′ S, 63°24′ W **137**
Ayacucho, *Col.* 8°35′ N, 73°34′ W **136**
Ayacucho, *Peru* 13°11′ S, 74°15′ W **137**
Ayacucho, adm. division, *Peru* 14°1′ S, 74°38′ W **137**
Ayad, oil field, *Yemen* 15°11′ N, 46°58′ E **182**
Ayakkum Hu, lake, *China* 37°38′ N, 88°29′ E **188**
Ayaköz, *Kaz.* 47°57′ N, 80°22′ E **184**
Ayaköz, river, *Kaz.* 46°55′ N, 79°28′ E **184**
Ayamonte, *Sp.* 37°12′ N, 7°24′ W **150**
Ayan, *Russ.* 56°27′ N, 137°54′ E **160**
Ayancık, *Turk.* 41°56′ N, 34°33′ E **156**
Ayanganna Mountain, *Guyana* 5°16′ N, 60°5′ W **130**
Ayangba, *Nig.* 7°29′ N, 7°8′ E **222**
Ayanka, *Russ.* 63°46′ N, 166°45′ E **160**
Ayapel, *Col.* 8°19′ N, 75°9′ W **136**
Ayapel, Serranía de, *Col.* 7°14′ N, 75°53′ W **136**
Ayaş, *Turk.* 40°1′ N, 32°20′ E **156**
Ayaviri, *Peru* 14°54′ S, 70°34′ W **137**
Aybak, *Afghan.* 36°13′ N, 68°5′ E **186**
Aydar Kŭl, lake, *Uzb.* 40°52′ N, 66°59′ E **197**
Ayde, Lac, lake, *Can.* 52°17′ N, 73°52′ W **111**
Aydın, *Turk.* 37°51′ N, 27°48′ E **156**
Aydıncık, *Turk.* 36°8′ N, 33°19′ E **156**
Aydyrlinskiy, *Russ.* 52°3′ N, 59°50′ E **154**
Āyelu Terara, peak, *Eth.* 10°3′ N, 40°37′ E **224**
Ayer, *Mass., U.S.* 42°33′ N, 71°36′ W **104**
Ayerbe, *Sp.* 42°16′ N, 0°41′ E **164**
Ayers Rock see Uluru, peak, *Austral.* 25°23′ S, 130°52′ E **230**
Ayersville, *Ohio, U.S.* 41°13′ N, 84°17′ W **102**
Ayeyarwady (Irrawady), river, *Myanmar* 21°54′ N, 95°42′ W **202**
Āykel, *Eth.* 12°30′ N, 37°3′ E **182**
Aykhal, *Russ.* 65°55′ N, 111°24′ E **160**
Aykino, *Russ.* 62°12′ N, 49°58′ E **154**
Aylesbury, *U.K.* 51°48′ N, 0°49′ E **162**
Ayllón, *Sp.* 41°24′ N, 3°22′ W **164**
Aylmer, *Can.* 42°46′ N, 80°58′ W **102**
Aylmer Lake, lake, *Can.* 63°39′ N, 108°52′ W **106**
Aylmer, Mount, *Can.* 51°19′ N, 115°31′ W **90**
Aylsham, *U.K.* 52°47′ N, 1°15′ E **162**
'Ayn al Ghazāl, spring, *Lib.* 21°50′ N, 24°52′ E **226**
'Ayn Dīwār, *Syr.* 37°16′ N, 42°9′ E **195**
'Ayn Sīdī Muḥammad, spring, *Lib.* 29°5′ N, 20°12′ E **216**
'Ayn Sifnī, *Iraq* 36°42′ N, 43°14′ E **195**
'Ayn Wabrah, spring, *Saudi Arabia* 27°25′ N, 47°20′ E **196**
'Ayn Zuwayyah, spring, *Lib.* 21°54′ N, 24°48′ E **226**
Ayna, *Peru* 12°43′ S, 73°53′ W **137**
Ayna, *Sp.* 38°32′ N, 2°4′ W **164**
Ayni, *Taj.* 39°22′ N, 68°32′ E **197**
'Aynūnah, *Saudi Arabia* 28°6′ N, 35°10′ E **180**
Ayod, *Sudan* 8°3′ N, 31°22′ E **224**
Ayon, Ostrov, island, *Russ.* 70°5′ N, 164°44′ E **160**
Ayora, *Sp.* 39°3′ N, 1°4′ W **164**
Ayorou, *Niger* 14°40′ N, 0°54′ E **222**
Ayos, *Cameroon* 3°57′ N, 12°31′ E **218**
'Ayoûn 'Abd el Mâlek, spring, *Mauritania* 24°55′ N, 7°28′ W **214**
'Ayoûnel el 'Atroûs, *Mauritania* 16°40′ N, 9°35′ W **222**
Aypolovo, *Russ.* 58°46′ N, 76°43′ E **169**
Ayr, *Austral.* 19°33′ S, 147°24′ E **231**
Ayr, *U.K.* 55°27′ N, 4°38′ W **150**
'Ayrah, *Syr.* 32°36′ N, 36°32′ E **194**
Ayrancı, *Turk.* 37°21′ N, 33°39′ E **156**
Ayribaba, Gora, peak, *Turkm.* 37°46′ N, 66°28′ E **197**
Āysha, *Eth.* 10°42′ N, 42°35′ E **224**
Āyteke Bī, *Kaz.* 45°52′ N, 62°8′ E **184**
Aytos, *Bulg.* 42°42′ N, 27°15′ E **156**
Ayu, Kepulauan, islands, *North Pacific Ocean* 0°44′ N, 128°54′ E **192**
Ayutla, *Mex.* 20°7′ N, 104°22′ W **114**
Ayutthaya, *Thai.* 14°21′ N, 100°32′ E **202**
Ayvaj, *Taj.* 36°59′ N, 68°0′ E **186**
Ayvalık, *Turk.* 39°17′ N, 26°43′ E **180**
Aywaille, *Belg.* 50°28′ N, 5°40′ E **167**
Az Zabadānī, *Syr.* 33°43′ N, 36°6′ E **194**
Az Zāhirīyah, *West Bank, Israel* 31°24′ N, 34°57′ E **194**
Az Zahrān (Dhahran), *Saudi Arabia* 26°15′ N, 50°1′ E **196**
Az Zarqā', *Jordan* 32°3′ N, 36°5′ E **194**
Az Zarqā', *Jordan* 32°3′ N, 36°7′ E **180**
Az Zawr, *Kuwait* 28°43′ N, 48°23′ E **196**
Az Zībār, *Iraq* 36°53′ N, 43°58′ E **195**
Az Zilfī, *Saudi Arabia* 26°17′ N, 44°49′ E **182**
Az Zubayr, *Iraq* 30°20′ N, 47°42′ E **180**
Āzād Shahr, *Iran* 37°11′ N, 55°19′ E **180**
Azamgarh, *India* 26°4′ N, 83°10′ E **197**
Azángaro, *Peru* 14°56′ S, 70°14′ W **137**
Azanja, *Serb.* 44°25′ N, 20°53′ E **168**
Azaouâd, region, *Africa* 17°57′ N, 3°35′ W **222**
Azaouagh, region, *Africa* 16°29′ N, 3°46′ E **222**
Azapa, *Chile* 18°35′ S, 70°14′ W **137**
Azapol'ye, *Russ.* 65°17′ N, 45°11′ E **154**
Azara, *Nig.* 8°20′ N, 9°12′ E **222**
Ā arān, *Iran* 37°30′ N, 47°3′ E **195**
Azare, *Nig.* 11°41′ N, 10°10′ E **222**
A'zāz, *Syr.* 36°35′ N, 37°2′ E **156**
Azdavay, *Turk.* 41°39′ N, 33°16′ E **156**
Azefal, *Mauritania* 20°51′ N, 15°9′ W **222**
Azeffoun, *Alg.* 36°53′ N, 4°25′ E **150**
Azélik, *Niger* 17°34′ N, 6°45′ E **222**
Azéo see Assiou, spring, *Alg.* 21°6′ N, 7°35′ E **222**
Azerbaijan 40°19′ N, 46°58′ E **195**
Azero, river, *Bol.* 19°42′ S, 64°7′ W **137**
Azerraf, spring, *Mali* 19°28′ N, 2°29′ E **222**
Azigui, spring, *Mali* 16°38′ N, 2°36′ E **222**
Azigzane, spring, *Mali* 22°20′ N, 3°18′ W **222**
Azilal, *Mor.* 31°58′ N, 6°33′ W **214**
Azlat, spring, *Mauritania* 16°49′ N, 14°5′ W **222**
Aznakayevo, *Russ.* 54°52′ N, 53°8′ E **154**
Aznalcóllar, *Sp.* 37°30′ N, 6°16′ W **164**
Azores (Açores), islands, *Port.* 39°29′ N, 27°35′ W **207**
Azov, *Russ.* 47°4′ N, 39°25′ E **158**
Azov, Sea of 45°58′ N, 35°0′ E **160**
Azovy, *Russ.* 64°50′ N, 65°11′ E **169**
Azraq ash Shīshān, *Jordan* 31°49′ N, 36°48′ E **194**
Azrou, *Mor.* 33°30′ N, 5°14′ W **214**
Azua, *Dom. Rep.* 18°28′ N, 70°43′ W **116**
Azuaga, *Sp.* 38°15′ N, 5°42′ W **164**
Azuara, *Sp.* 41°15′ N, 0°53′ E **164**
Azucena, *Arg.* 37°33′ S, 59°21′ W **139**
Azuer, river, *Sp.* 38°55′ N, 3°26′ W **164**
Azuero, Peninsula de, *Pan.* 7°36′ N, 80°51′ W **115**
Azufre Norte, Paso del, pass, *Arg.* 31°16′ S, 70°34′ W **134**
Azul, *Arg.* 36°46′ S, 59°50′ W **139**
Azul, river, *Mex.* 17°9′ N, 99°9′ W **114**
Azurduy, *Bol.* 20°0′ S, 64°28′ W **137**
Azure Lake, lake, *Can.* 52°22′ N, 120°23′ W **108**

B

Ba Dong, *Vietnam* 9°40′ N, 106°33′ E **202**
Ba Ria, *Vietnam* 10°29′ N, 107°10′ E **202**
Ba, river, *Vietnam* 13°25′ N, 108°29′ E **202**
Baabda, *Leb.* 33°50′ N, 35°31′ E **194**
Baalbeck, *Leb.* 34°0′ N, 36°12′ E **194**
Baarle-Hertog, *Belg.* 51°26′ N, 4°55′ E **167**
Baarn, *Neth.* 52°12′ N, 5°16′ E **163**
Ba'ashom, *Sudan* 13°25′ N, 31°22′ E **226**
Bab, oil field, *U.A.E.* 23°52′ N, 53°43′ E **196**
Bab Ozero, lake, *Russ.* 68°19′ N, 33°38′ E **152**
Baba Burnu, *Turk.* 39°30′ N, 25°37′ E **156**
Baba Dağ, peak, *Turk.* 36°29′ N, 29°6′ E **156**
Baba, peak, *Bulg.* 42°45′ N, 23°54′ E **156**
Babadag, *Rom.* 44°53′ N, 28°43′ E **158**
Babadag, peak, *Azerb.* 41°0′ N, 48°15′ E **195**
Babadaykhan, *Turkm.* 37°53′ N, 60°21′ E **180**
Babaeski, *Turk.* 41°25′ N, 27°4′ E **156**
Babak, *Philippines* 7°9′ N, 125°43′ E **203**
Babana, *Nig.* 10°27′ N, 3°49′ E **222**
Babanūsa, *Sudan* 11°15′ N, 27°46′ E **224**
Babar, island, *Indonesia* 8°21′ S, 129°10′ E **192**
Babati, *Tanzania* 4°12′ S, 35°44′ E **224**
Babayevo, *Russ.* 59°23′ N, 35°59′ E **154**
Babayurt, *Russ.* 43°34′ N, 46°44′ E **195**
Babb, *Mont., U.S.* 48°51′ N, 113°28′ W **90**
B'abdāt, *Leb.* 33°53′ N, 35°40′ E **194**
Babel, Mont de, peak, *Can.* 51°25′ N, 68°49′ W **111**
Babeldaob see Babelthuap, island, *Palau* 8°0′ N, 135°0′ E **242**
Babelthuap (Babeldaob), island, *Palau* 8°0′ N, 135°0′ E **242**
Baberu, *India* 25°34′ N, 80°44′ E **197**
Babi, island, *Indonesia* 2°3′ N, 96°40′ E **196**
Babia Góra, peak, *Slovakia* 49°33′ N, 19°28′ E **152**
Babian, river, *China* 23°31′ N, 101°16′ E **202**
Babilafuente, *Sp.* 40°58′ N, 5°27′ W **150**
Babin Nos, peak, *Bulg.* 43°41′ N, 22°22′ E **168**
Babine, *Can.* 55°19′ N, 126°36′ W **108**
Babine, river, *Can.* 55°41′ N, 127°32′ W **108**
Babino Polje, *Croatia* 42°43′ N, 17°31′ E **168**
Bābol, *Iran* 36°35′ N, 52°43′ E **180**
Babonã, river, *Braz.* 6°16′ S, 67°4′ W **130**
Baboquivari Peak, *Ariz., U.S.* 31°45′ N, 111°39′ W **92**
Babruysk, *Belarus* 53°5′ N, 29°17′ E **152**
Babson Park, *Fla., U.S.* 27°50′ N, 81°31′ W **105**
Babuna, *Maced.* 41°30′ N, 21°24′ E **168**
Babusar Pass, *Pak.* 35°8′ N, 74°2′ E **186**
Babushkina, *Russ.* 59°44′ N, 43°11′ E **154**
Babušnica, *Serb.* 43°4′ N, 22°25′ E **168**
Babuyan Channel 18°34′ N, 121°27′ E **203**
Babuyan, island, *Philippines* 19°34′ N, 122°1′ E **198**
Babuyan Islands, *South China Sea* 19°8′ N, 121°56′ E **203**
Babylon, *N.Y., U.S.* 40°41′ N, 73°19′ W **104**
Babylon, ruin(s), *Iraq* 32°30′ N, 44°16′ E **180**
Bač, *Serb.* 45°22′ N, 19°15′ E **168**
Bac Can, *Vietnam* 22°9′ N, 105°50′ E **198**
Bac Giang, *Vietnam* 21°16′ N, 106°13′ E **198**
Bac Lieu, *Vietnam* 9°18′ N, 105°42′ E **202**
Bac Ninh, *Vietnam* 21°11′ N, 106°2′ E **198**
Bacaadweyne, *Somalia* 7°10′ N, 47°34′ E **218**
Bacabal, *Braz.* 4°15′ S, 44°53′ W **132**
Bacadéhuachi, *Mex.* 29°41′ N, 109°9′ W **92**
Bacajá, river, *Braz.* 3°51′ S, 51°48′ W **130**
Bacan, island, *Indonesia* 0°38′ N, 126°26′ E **192**
Bacanora, *Mex.* 28°58′ N, 109°24′ W **92**
Bacarra, *Philippines* 18°16′ N, 120°37′ E **203**
Bacău, *Rom.* 46°33′ N, 26°55′ E **156**
Bacău, adm. division, *Rom.* 46°13′ N, 26°17′ E **156**
Baccarat, *Fr.* 48°27′ N, 6°45′ E **163**
Bæccegelhalde, peak, *Nor.* 69°31′ N, 21°45′ E **152**
Baceno, *It.* 46°16′ N, 8°18′ E **167**
Bacerac, *Mex.* 30°20′ N, 108°58′ W **92**
Băcești, *Rom.* 46°50′ N, 27°14′ E **156**
Bačevci, *Serb.* 44°11′ N, 19°55′ E **168**
Bach, *Mich., U.S.* 43°40′ N, 83°21′ W **102**
Bach Long Vi, Dao (Nightingale Island), *Vietnam* 19°46′ N, 107°30′ E **198**
Bach Ma National Park, *Vietnam* 16°12′ N, 108°7′ E **202**
Bach, Mynydd, peak, *U.K.* 52°17′ N, 4°4′ W **162**
Bacharach, *Ger.* 50°3′ N, 7°44′ E **167**
Bachelor, Mount, *Oreg., U.S.* 43°57′ N, 121°47′ W **90**
Bachíniva, *Mex.* 28°46′ N, 107°15′ W **92**
Bachu, *China* 39°44′ N, 78°34′ E **184**
Baciuty, *Pol.* 53°3′ N, 22°58′ E **152**
Back, river, *Can.* 64°47′ N, 105°2′ W **106**
Bačka Palanka, *Serb.* 45°14′ N, 19°23′ E **168**
Bačka, region, *Serb.* 45°44′ N, 18°55′ E **168**
Backbone Mountain, *Md., U.S.* 39°12′ N, 79°34′ W **94**
Backbone Ranges, *Can.* 61°28′ N, 124°16′ W **108**
Backe, *Nor.* 63°49′ N, 16°22′ E **152**
Bäckefors, *Nor.* 58°49′ N, 12°8′ E **152**
Bačko Gradište, *Serb.* 45°32′ N, 20°1′ E **168**
Bačko Petrovo Selo, *Serb.* 45°42′ N, 20°4′ E **168**
Bacnotan, *Philippines* 16°44′ N, 120°20′ E **203**
Baco, Mount, *Philippines* 12°49′ N, 121°6′ E **203**
Bacoachi, *Mex.* 30°38′ N, 109°59′ W **92**
Bacolod, *Philippines* 10°39′ N, 122°57′ E **203**
Bácsalmás, *Hung.* 46°7′ N, 19°20′ E **168**
Bács-Kiskun, adm. division, *Hung.* 46°31′ N, 19°2′ E **156**
Bad Axe, *Mich., U.S.* 43°47′ N, 83°0′ W **102**
Bad Bentheim, *Ger.* 52°18′ N, 7°10′ E **163**
Bad Bergzabern, *Ger.* 49°6′ N, 7°59′ E **163**
Bad Brückenau, *Ger.* 50°18′ N, 9°47′ E **167**
Bad Camberg, *Ger.* 50°18′ N, 8°16′ E **167**
Bad Driburg, *Ger.* 51°44′ N, 9°0′ E **167**
Bad Ems, *Ger.* 50°20′ N, 7°42′ E **167**
Bad Godesberg, *Ger.* 50°41′ N, 7°9′ E **167**
Bad Hersfeld, *Ger.* 50°51′ N, 9°42′ E **167**
Bad Homburg, *Ger.* 50°14′ N, 8°36′ E **167**
Bad Honnef, *Ger.* 50°38′ N, 7°13′ E **167**
Bad Hönningen, *Ger.* 50°30′ N, 7°19′ E **167**
Bad Iburg, *Ger.* 52°9′ N, 8°2′ E **163**
Bad Ischl, *Aust.* 47°42′ N, 13°38′ E **156**
Bad Karlshafen, *Ger.* 51°38′ N, 9°29′ E **167**
Bad Kissingen, *Ger.* 50°11′ N, 10°4′ E **167**
Bad Kreuznach, *Ger.* 49°50′ N, 7°52′ E **167**
Bad Laasphe, *Ger.* 50°55′ N, 8°24′ E **167**
Bad Lauterberg, *Ger.* 51°37′ N, 10°26′ E **167**
Bad Marienberg, *Ger.* 50°38′ N, 7°56′ E **167**
Bad Nauheim, *Ger.* 50°21′ N, 8°43′ E **167**
Bad Neuenahr-Ahrweiler, *Ger.* 50°33′ N, 7°7′ E **167**
Bad Neustadt, *Ger.* 50°19′ N, 10°11′ E **167**
Bad Orb, *Ger.* 50°13′ N, 9°21′ E **167**
Bad, river, *S. Dak., U.S.* 43°58′ N, 101°7′ W **90**
Bad Salzig, *Ger.* 50°12′ N, 7°37′ E **167**
Bad Soden-Salmünster, *Ger.* 50°16′ N, 9°21′ E **167**
Bad Sooden-Allendorf, *Ger.* 51°16′ N, 9°58′ E **167**
Bad Vilbel, *Ger.* 50°11′ N, 8°44′ E **167**
Bad Vöslau, *Aust.* 47°58′ N, 16°12′ E **168**
Bad Waldsee, *Ger.* 47°55′ N, 9°45′ E **152**
Bad Wildungen, *Ger.* 51°6′ N, 9°7′ E **167**
Badacsony, peak, *Hung.* 46°47′ N, 17°26′ E **168**
Badagri, *Nig.* 6°29′ N, 2°55′ E **222**
Badajoz, *Sp.* 38°51′ N, 6°58′ W **150**
Badalona, *Sp.* 41°26′ N, 2°14′ E **164**
Badalucco, *It.* 43°55′ N, 7°51′ E **167**

Badam, Kaz. 42°22′ N, 69°13′ E 197
Badamsha, Kaz. 50°33′ N, 58°16′ E 158
Badanah, Saudi Arabia 30°58′ N, 40°57′ E 180
Badaohe, China 43°11′ N, 126°32′ E 200
Baddeck, Can. 46°6′ N, 60°46′ W 111
Baddo, river, Pak. 28°5′ N, 64°35′ E 182
Baden, Aust. 48°0′ N, 16°14′ E 168
Baden, Eritrea 16°53′ N, 37°54′ E 182
Baden, Ger. 53°0′ N, 9°6′ E 150
Baden, Switz. 47°27′ N, 8°18′ E 150
Baden-Württemberg, adm. division, Ger. 47°47′ N, 7°43′ E 165
Badger, Minn., U.S. 48°45′ N, 96°3′ W 90
Badger Creek, river, Mont., U.S. 48°4′ N, 113°13′ W 108
Badia Polesine, It. 45°5′ N, 11°28′ E 167
Badiar National Park, Guinea 12°23′ N, 13°51′ W 222
Badin, Pak. 24°39′ N, 68°48′ E 186
Badjoki, Dem. Rep. of the Congo 2°53′ N, 22°21′ E 218
Badjoudé (Dompago), Benin 9°42′ N, 1°23′ E 222
Badlands, N. Dak., U.S. 47°2′ N, 104°19′ W 90
Badlands National Park, S. Dak., U.S. 43°15′ N, 102°43′ W 90
Badnjevac, Serb. 44°7′ N, 20°58′ E 168
Badogo, Mali 11°3′ N, 8°13′ W 222
Badong, China 30°58′ N, 110°23′ E 198
Badoumbé, Mali 13°41′ N, 10°15′ W 222
Badreïna, spring, Mauritania 17°47′ N, 11°6′ W 222
Baduein, Eth. 6°30′ N, 43°22′ E 218
Badupi, Myanmar 21°37′ N, 93°24′ E 188
Badvel, India 14°44′ N, 79°5′ E 188
Bad'ya, Russ. 60°29′ N, 53°22′ E 154
Baena, Sp. 37°37′ N, 4°21′ W 164
Baengnyeongdo, island, S. Korea 37°50′ N, 123°23′ E 198
Baeza, Sp. 37°59′ N, 3°28′ W 164
Bafang, Cameroon 5°8′ N, 10°10′ E 222
Bafarara, Mali 15°23′ N, 11°29′ W 222
Baffin Bay 73°51′ N, 73°33′ W 106
Bafia, Cameroon 4°42′ N, 11°14′ E 222
Bafing, river, Guinea 12°23′ N, 10°13′ W 222
Bafoulabé, Mali 13°49′ N, 10°52′ W 222
Bafousam, Cameroon 5°27′ N, 10°23′ E 222
Bāfq, Iran 31°32′ N, 55°22′ E 180
Bafra, Turk. 41°33′ N, 35°54′ E 156
Bafra Burnu, Turk. 41°45′ N, 35°24′ E 156
Bāft, Iran 29°16′ N, 56°39′ E 196
Bafuka, Dem. Rep. of the Congo 4°9′ N, 27°52′ E 224
Bafwabalinga, Dem. Rep. of the Congo 0°54′ N, 27°1′ E 224
Bafwaboli, Dem. Rep. of the Congo 0°42′ N, 26°7′ E 224
Bafwasende, Dem. Rep. of the Congo 1°8′ N, 27°11′ E 224
Bagabag, island, P.N.G. 4°48′ S, 146°17′ E 192
Bagadó, Col. 5°22′ N, 76°28′ W 136
Bagalkot, India 16°10′ N, 75°42′ E 188
Bagam, spring, Niger 15°40′ N, 6°34′ E 222
Bagamoyo, Tanzania 6°23′ S, 38°55′ E 224
Bagan, Russ. 54°3′ N, 77°45′ E 184
Bagan Datoh, Malaysia 3°58′ N, 100°47′ E 196
Bagan Serai, Malaysia 5°1′ N, 100°31′ E 196
Bagana, Nig. 7°58′ N, 7°34′ E 222
Baganga, Philippines 7°37′ N, 126°33′ E 203
Bagansiapiapi, Indonesia 2°12′ N, 100°49′ E 196
Bagan'yuvom, Russ. 66°5′ N, 58°2′ E 154
Bagaroua, Niger 14°30′ N, 4°25′ E 222
Bagata, Dem. Rep. of the Congo 3°49′ S, 17°56′ E 218
Bagatogo, Côte d'Ivoire 8°42′ N, 6°42′ W 222
Bagdad, Ariz., U.S. 34°34′ N, 113°12′ W 92
Bagdad, Fla., U.S. 30°53′ N, 87°2′ W 96
Bagdarin, Russ. 54°28′ N, 113°39′ E 190
Bagé, Braz. 31°21′ S, 54°8′ W 139
Bågede, Nor. 64°21′ N, 14°48′ E 152
Baggs, Wyo., U.S. 41°2′ N, 107°40′ W 90
Baghdād, Iraq 33°21′ N, 44°23′ E 180
Bagheria, It. 38°4′ N, 13°30′ E 156
Bāghīn, Iran 30°9′ N, 56°51′ E 196
Baghlan, Afghan. 36°11′ N, 68°48′ E 186
Baghran Khowleh, Afghan. 32°57′ N, 64°58′ E 186
Bağırpaşa Dağı, peak, Turk. 39°28′ N, 40°2′ E 195
Bağışlı, Turk. 37°51′ N, 44°0′ E 195
Bagley, Minn., U.S. 47°30′ N, 95°25′ W 90
Bagni del Masino, It. 46°15′ N, 9°35′ E 167
Bagno di Romagna, It. 43°50′ N, 11°56′ E 167
Bagnols-les-Bains, Fr. 44°31′ N, 3°40′ E 150
Bagnone, It. 44°19′ N, 9°59′ E 167
Bago, Myanmar 17°20′ N, 96°29′ E 202
Bagodar, India 24°4′ N, 85°49′ E 197
Bagoé, river, Mali 11°44′ N, 6°22′ W 222
Bagot, Mount, Can. 59°20′ N, 135°8′ W 108
Bagrationovsk, Russ. 54°22′ N, 20°31′ E 166
Bagrax see Bohu, China 41°56′ N, 86°40′ E 184
Bagrdan, Serb. 44°4′ N, 21°9′ E 168
Baguia, Timor-Leste 8°33′ S, 126°39′ E 238
Baguio, Philippines 16°23′ N, 120°34′ E 203
Baguio Point, Philippines 17°31′ N, 122°11′ E 203
Bagzane, Monts, Niger 17°49′ N, 8°37′ E 222
Bahabón de Esgueva, Sp. 41°51′ N, 3°44′ W 164
Bahama Islands, North Atlantic Ocean 23°51′ N, 76°7′ W 253
Bahamas 26°0′ N, 77°0′ W 118
Baharak, Afghan. 37°0′ N, 70°52′ E 186
Baharampur, India 24°3′ N, 88°16′ E 188
Baḥarîya, El Wâḥât el, Egypt 27°49′ N, 28°21′ E 180
Bahau, Malaysia 2°50′ N, 102°24′ E 196
Bahawalnagar, Pak. 30°2′ N, 73°16′ E 186
Bahawalpur, Pak. 29°24′ N, 71°40′ E 186
Bahçe, Turk. 37°14′ N, 36°35′ E 156
Bahçesaray, Turk. 38°4′ N, 42°47′ E 195
Bahdanaw, Belarus 54°10′ N, 26°8′ E 166
Bahdur Island, Sudan 17°59′ N, 37°52′ E 182
Bäherden, Turkm. 38°22′ N, 57°10′ E 160
Bahi, Tanzania 5°57′ S, 35°19′ E 224
Bahia, adm. division, Braz. 13°49′ S, 42°23′ W 138
Bahía Blanca, Arg. 38°43′ S, 62°17′ W 139
Bahía de CarŽaquez, Ecua. 0°42′ N, 80°19′ W 130
Bahía de Loreto National Park, Mex. 25°52′ N, 111°32′ W 238
Bahía de los Ángeles, Mex. 28°56′ N, 113°37′ W 92
Bahía, Islas de la, islands, Isla de RoatŽan 16°27′ N, 87°19′ W 115
Bahía Kino, Mex. 28°49′ N, 111°55′ W 92
Bahía Laura, Arg. 48°22′ S, 66°30′ W 134
Bahia see Salvador, Braz. 12°59′ S, 38°28′ W 132
Bahía Solano (Puerto Mutis), Col. 6°12′ N, 77°25′ W 136
Bahía Tortugas, Mex. 27°41′ N, 114°52′ W 112
Bahir Dar, Eth. 11°31′ N, 37°21′ E 182
Bahlah, Oman 22°57′ N, 57°15′ E 182
Bahr el 'Arab, river, Sudan 10°4′ N, 25°6′ E 224
Bahr ez Zaraf, river, Sudan 7°42′ N, 30°43′ E 224
Bahr Kéita (Doka), river, Chad 9°8′ N, 18°38′ E 218
Bahr Salamat, river, Chad 10°17′ N, 19°27′ E 216
Bahrah, oil field, Kuwait 29°39′ N, 47°49′ E 196
Bahraich, India 27°32′ N, 81°36′ E 197
Bahrain 26°0′ N, 51°0′ E 196
Bahrain, Gulf of 25°31′ N, 50°13′ E 196
Bāhū Kalāt, Iran 25°44′ N, 61°25′ E 182
Bahuaja-Sonene National Park, Peru 13°28′ S, 69°24′ W 137
Bai Bung, Mui, Vietnam 8°15′ N, 104°19′ E 202
Baia, Rom. 44°43′ N, 28°40′ E 156
Baia de Aramă, Rom. 44°59′ N, 22°49′ E 168
Baia de Arieş, Rom. 46°21′ N, 23°16′ E 168
Baía dos Tigres, Angola 16°38′ S, 11°40′ E 220
Baia Mare, Rom. 47°39′ N, 23°36′ E 168
Baibokoum, Chad 7°40′ N, 15°42′ E 218
Baicheng, China 45°35′ N, 122°50′ E 198
Baicheng, China 41°46′ N, 81°51′ E 184
Baidoa see Baydhabo, Somalia 3°5′ N, 43°41′ E 218
Baie-Comeau, Can. 49°13′ N, 68°10′ W 111
Baie-du-Poste see Mistassini, Can. 50°24′ N, 73°50′ W 110
Baie-Johan-Beetz, Can. 50°17′ N, 62°49′ W 111
Baie-Sainte-Catherine, Can. 48°6′ N, 69°44′ W 94
Baie-Sainte-Claire, site, Can. 49°52′ N, 64°35′ W 111
Baie-Saint-Paul, Can. 47°26′ N, 70°31′ W 94
Baihar, India 22°7′ N, 80°33′ E 197
Baihe, China 42°22′ N, 128°7′ E 198
Ba'ījī, Iraq 34°54′ N, 43°27′ E 180
Baijnath, India 29°57′ N, 79°37′ E 188
Baikal, Lake, Russ. 52°49′ N, 106°59′ E 238
Baikha, Russ. 64°54′ N, 88°0′ E 169
Baikonur Cosmodrome, spaceport, Kaz. 46°6′ N, 63°9′ E 184
Baile Átha Cliath see Dublin, Ire. 53°18′ N, 6°26′ W 150
Băile Herculane, Rom. 44°54′ N, 22°26′ E 168
Bailén, Sp. 38°5′ N, 3°46′ W 164
Bailey Island, Me., U.S. 43°43′ N, 70°0′ W 104
Bailingmiao see Darhan Muminggan Lianheqi, China 41°41′ N, 110°23′ E 198
Bailique, Braz. 1°0′ N, 50°3′ W 130
Bailique, Ilha, island, Braz. 1°4′ N, 49°56′ W 130
Bailleul, Fr. 50°43′ N, 2°44′ E 163
Baillie Islands, Beaufort Sea 70°39′ N, 129°39′ W 98
Baillieu Peak, Antarctica 67°57′ S, 60°27′ E 248
Bailong, river, China 33°26′ N, 104°17′ E 198
Bailundo, Angola 12°13′ S, 15°51′ E 220
Bainang, China 29°13′ N, 89°15′ E 197
Bainbridge, Ga., U.S. 30°53′ N, 84°34′ W 96
Bainbridge, Ind., U.S. 39°45′ N, 86°49′ W 102
Bainbridge, Ohio, U.S. 39°13′ N, 83°16′ W 102
Bainbridge Island, Wash., U.S. 47°37′ N, 122°32′ W 100
Baingoin, China 31°37′ N, 89°51′ E 188
Bainville, Mont., U.S. 48°7′ N, 104°15′ W 90
Baiona, Sp. 42°6′ N, 8°53′ W 150
Baiquan, China 47°37′ N, 126°4′ E 198
Bā'ir, Jordan 30°45′ N, 36°40′ E 194
Bairab Co, lake, China 34°55′ N, 82°29′ E 188
Baird, Miss., U.S. 33°23′ N, 90°36′ W 103
Baird, Tex., U.S. 32°23′ N, 99°24′ W 92
Baird Inlet 60°44′ N, 164°34′ W 98
Baird, Mount, Idaho, U.S. 43°21′ N, 111°11′ W 90
Baird Mountains, Alas., U.S. 67°24′ N, 161°29′ W 98
Bairiki see Tarawa, Kiribati 1°15′ N, 169°58′ E 242
Bairin Youqi, China 43°30′ N, 118°40′ E 198
Bairin Zuoqi, China 43°59′ N, 119°24′ E 198
Bairoil, Wyo., U.S. 42°15′ N, 107°33′ W 90
Baisha, China 29°31′ N, 119°15′ E 198
Baishan, China 42°38′ N, 127°12′ E 200
Baiso, It. 44°29′ N, 10°37′ E 167
Baitadi, Nepal 29°34′ N, 80°26′ E 197
Baixo Guandu, Braz. 19°32′ S, 40°59′ W 138
Baiyin, China 36°34′ N, 104°15′ E 198
Baiyuda, spring, Sudan 17°29′ N, 32°8′ E 182
Baja, Hung. 46°10′ N, 18°57′ E 168
Baja California, region, North America 31°27′ N, 115°59′ W 92
Baja California, adm. division, Mex. 30°0′ N, 115°0′ W 112
Baja California Sur, adm. division, Mex. 26°3′ N, 112°13′ W 112
Baja, Punta, Mex. 28°17′ N, 111°59′ W 92
Baja, Punta, Mex. 29°59′ N, 115°58′ W 92
Bajag, India 22°42′ N, 81°21′ E 197
Baján, Mex. 26°32′ N, 101°15′ W 114
Bājgīrān, Iran 37°37′ N, 58°24′ E 180
Bajiazi, China 42°41′ N, 129°9′ E 200
Bājil, Yemen 14°58′ N, 43°15′ E 182
Bajina Bašta, Serb. 43°58′ N, 19°35′ E 168
Bajitpur, Bangladesh 24°9′ N, 90°54′ E 197
Bajmok, Serb. 45°57′ N, 19°24′ E 168
Bajo Baudó, Col. 4°57′ N, 77°22′ W 136
Bajoga, Nig. 10°52′ N, 11°17′ E 222
Bajovo Polje, Mont. 43°0′ N, 18°53′ E 168
Bajram Curri, Alban. 42°21′ N, 20°3′ E 168
Bajzë, Alban. 42°16′ N, 19°26′ E 168
Bak, Hung. 46°43′ N, 16°51′ E 168
Bakaba, Chad 7°43′ N, 16°54′ E 218
Bakal, Russ. 54°59′ N, 58°51′ E 154
Bakala, Cen. Af. Rep. 6°9′ N, 20°21′ E 218
Bakałarzewo, Pol. 54°5′ N, 22°38′ E 166
Bakaly, Russ. 55°11′ N, 53°50′ E 154
Bakanas, Kaz. 44°49′ N, 76°17′ E 184
Bakaoré, Chad 15°17′ N, 21°47′ E 216
Bakchar, Russ. 56°59′ N, 82°4′ E 169
Bakel, Senegal 14°53′ N, 12°31′ W 222
Baker, Calif., U.S. 35°16′ N, 116°5′ W 101
Baker, La., U.S. 30°35′ N, 91°10′ W 103
Baker, Mont., U.S. 46°20′ N, 104°18′ W 90
Baker, Nev., U.S. 39°0′ N, 114°8′ W 92
Baker, Oreg., U.S. 44°46′ N, 117°52′ W 90
Baker Foreland, Can. 62°46′ N, 90°36′ W 106
Baker Island, U.S. 0°18′ N, 176°37′ W 238
Baker Lake, Can. 62°18′ N, 99°20′ W 106
Baker Lake, Can. 64°19′ N, 96°7′ W 73
Baker Lake, Wash., U.S. 48°42′ N, 121°52′ W 100
Baker, Mount, Wash., U.S. 48°46′ N, 121°51′ W 100
Bakersfield, Calif., U.S. 35°22′ N, 119°1′ W 101
Bakewell, U.K. 53°12′ N, 1°41′ W 162
Bakhanay, Russ. 66°16′ N, 123°37′ E 173
Bakhchysaray, Ukr. 44°45′ N, 33°51′ E 156
Bakhma Dam, Iraq 36°31′ N, 44°10′ E 195
Bakhmach, Ukr. 51°11′ N, 32°48′ E 158
Bakhta, Russ. 62°19′ N, 89°10′ E 160
Bakhta, river, Russ. 63°43′ N, 90°2′ E 169
Bakhtegān, Daryācheh-ye, lake, Iran 29°21′ N, 53°32′ E 196
Bakı (Baku), Azerb. 40°23′ N, 49°44′ E 195
Baki, spring, Chad 16°58′ N, 21°10′ E 216
Bakin Birji, Niger 14°10′ N, 8°52′ E 222
Bakırdağı, Turk. 38°12′ N, 35°47′ E 156
Bako, Côte d'Ivoire 9°7′ N, 7°36′ W 222
Bako, Eth. 5°50′ N, 36°37′ E 224
Bakony, Hung. 47°17′ N, 17°23′ E 168
Bakouma, Cen. Af. Rep. 5°42′ N, 22°50′ E 218
Bakoye, river, Africa 12°50′ N, 9°26′ W 222
Bakr Uzyak, Russ. 52°59′ N, 58°36′ E 154
Baktalórántháza, Hung. 48°0′ N, 22°3′ E 168
Baku see Bakı, Azerb. 40°23′ N, 49°44′ E 195
Bakundi, Nig. 8°1′ N, 10°45′ E 222
Bakungan, Indonesia 2°58′ N, 97°29′ E 196
Bakuriani, Ga. 41°44′ N, 43°31′ E 195
Bakutis Coast, Antarctica 75°0′ S, 115°49′ W 248
Bakwanga see Mbuji-Mayi, Dem. Rep. of the Congo 6°10′ S, 23°36′ E 224
Bala, Senegal 14°1′ N, 13°11′ W 222
Bâlâ, Turk. 39°32′ N, 33°7′ E 156
Bala, U.K. 52°54′ N, 3°37′ W 162
Balabac, Philippines 8°1′ N, 117°2′ E 203
Balabac, island, Philippines 7°49′ N, 115°56′ E 192
Balabac Strait 7°38′ N, 116°33′ E 203
Bălăciţa, Rom. 44°23′ N, 23°7′ E 168
Balaena Islands, Indian Ocean 65°59′ S, 112°14′ E 248
Balaghat, India 21°49′ N, 80°13′ E 197
Balaguer, Sp. 41°47′ N, 0°46′ E 164
Balaka, Malawi 14°54′ S, 34°56′ E 224
Balakän, Azerb. 41°43′ N, 46°25′ E 195
Balakété, Cen. Af. Rep. 6°54′ N, 19°57′ E 218
Balakhna, Russ. 56°25′ N, 43°37′ E 154
Balaki, Guinea 12°12′ N, 11°52′ W 222
Balaklava, Ukr. 44°30′ N, 33°34′ E 158
Balakliya, Ukr. 49°29′ N, 36°52′ E 158
Balakovo, Russ. 52°0′ N, 47°50′ E 158
Balama, Mozambique 13°15′ S, 38°38′ E 224
Balancán, Mex. 17°47′ N, 91°34′ W 115
Balangir, India 20°42′ N, 83°28′ E 188
Balanikha, Russ. 65°56′ N, 43°19′ E 154
Balao, Ecua. 3°2′ S, 79°48′ W 130
Balashivka, Ukr. 50°59′ N, 26°57′ E 152
Balashov, Russ. 51°29′ N, 43°10′ E 158
Balástya, Hung. 46°25′ N, 20°1′ E 168
Balâţ, Egypt 25°33′ N, 29°14′ E 226
Balatina, Mold. 47°41′ N, 27°20′ E 158
BalatonföldvŽar, Hung. 46°50′ N, 17°51′ E 168
Balatonfüred, Hung. 46°57′ N, 17°53′ E 168
Balavé, Burkina Faso 12°23′ N, 4°11′ W 222
Balazote, Sp. 38°53′ N, 2°9′ W 164
Balbina, Represa da, dam, Braz. 1°25′ S, 60°25′ W 130
Balcad, Somalia 2°18′ N, 45°26′ E 218
Balcarce, Arg. 37°51′ S, 58°17′ W 139
Balcarres, Can. 50°47′ N, 103°33′ W 90
Balchik, Bulg. 43°26′ N, 28°11′ E 156
Balclutha, N.Z. 46°15′ S, 169°42′ E 240
Bald Butte, peak, Oreg., U.S. 43°40′ N, 119°27′ W 90
Bald Eagle Mountain, Pa., U.S. 40°59′ N, 77°48′ W 94
Bald Knob, Ark., U.S. 35°17′ N, 91°35′ W 96
Bald Mountain, peak, Calif., U.S. 40°54′ N, 121°11′ W 90
Bald Mountain, peak, Can. 54°5′ N, 61°29′ W 111
Bald Mountain, peak, Idaho, U.S. 44°20′ N, 114°26′ W 90
Bald Mountain, peak, Nev., U.S. 38°34′ N, 117°8′ W 90
Bald Mountain, peak, Oreg., U.S. 44°33′ N, 118°0′ W 90
Bald Mountain, peak, Vt., U.S. 44°45′ N, 72°5′ W 94
Baldhill Dam, N. Dak., U.S. 47°19′ N, 98°45′ W 82
Baldock Lake, Can. 56°32′ N, 98°25′ W 108
Baldone, Latv. 56°44′ N, 24°23′ E 166
Baldwin, La., U.S. 29°49′ N, 91°33′ W 103
Baldwin, Mich., U.S. 43°53′ N, 85°52′ W 102
Baldwinville, Mass., U.S. 42°36′ N, 72°5′ W 104
Baldwyn, Miss., U.S. 34°30′ N, 88°38′ W 96
Baldy Mountain, peak, Can. 51°28′ N, 120°6′ W 90
Baldy Mountain, peak, Can. 51°27′ N, 100°49′ W 90
Baldy Mountain, peak, Can. 49°8′ N, 119°20′ W 90
Baldy Mountain, peak, Mont., U.S. 45°20′ N, 113°7′ W 90
Baldy Peak, Ariz., U.S. 33°53′ N, 109°37′ W 92
Bale Mountains National Park, Eth. 6°33′ N, 38°57′ E 224
Balearic Islands, Sp. 40°4′ N, 3°1′ E 164
Balearic Sea 40°47′ N, 1°23′ E 150
Baleia, Ponta da, Braz. 17°40′ S, 39°9′ W 132
Baleine, Rivière à la, river, Can. 57°24′ N, 67°59′ W 106
Balen, Belg. 51°9′ N, 5°9′ E 167
Baler, Philippines 15°46′ N, 121°32′ E 203
Balerma, Sp. 36°43′ N, 2°54′ W 164
Baleshwar, India 21°29′ N, 86°53′ E 188
Baley, Russ. 51°36′ N, 116°35′ E 238
Baléya, Mali 12°16′ N, 9°58′ W 222
Baleyara, Niger 13°56′ N, 2°50′ E 222
Balezino, Russ. 57°57′ N, 53°5′ E 154
Balguntay, China 42°46′ N, 86°18′ E 184
Bal'āf, Yemen 14°1′ N, 48°10′ E 182
Balḥo, Djibouti 12°2′ N, 42°12′ E 182
Bali, India 25°13′ N, 73°16′ E 186
Bali, island, Indonesia 9°21′ S, 114°38′ E 192
Bali Sea 7°47′ S, 114°55′ E 192
Baliangao, Philippines 8°40′ N, 123°37′ E 203
Balige, Indonesia 2°21′ N, 99°3′ E 196
Balık Göl, lake, Turk. 41°34′ N, 35°44′ E 156
Balıkesir, Turk. 39°38′ N, 27°51′ E 156
Balikpapan, Indonesia 1°12′ S, 116°46′ E 192
Baling, Malaysia 5°40′ N, 100°54′ E 196
Balinţ, Rom. 45°49′ N, 21°51′ E 168
Balintang Channel 19°44′ N, 121°25′ E 203
Balipara, India 26°48′ N, 92°43′ E 188
Baliza, Braz. 16°14′ S, 52°25′ W 138
Balkan Mountains, Bulg. 43°16′ N, 22°39′ E 168
Balkanabat (Nebitdag), Turkm. 39°31′ N, 54°21′ E 180
Balkány, Hung. 47°46′ N, 21°49′ E 168
Balkany, Russ. 53°29′ N, 59°34′ E 154
Balkashīno, Kaz. 52°27′ N, 68°40′ E 184
Balkh, Afghan. 36°46′ N, 66°58′ E 186
Balkhash, Lake, Kaz. 46°0′ N, 69°44′ E 173
Ball Lake, lake, Can. 50°13′ N, 94°17′ W 90
Ballâna, Egypt 24°17′ N, 32°58′ E 182
Ballantine, Mont., U.S. 45°55′ N, 108°9′ W 90
Ballarat, Austral. 37°34′ S, 143°55′ E 231
Ballé, Mali 15°21′ N, 8°36′ W 222
Ballenas, Canal de 29°14′ N, 114°0′ W 92
Balleny Islands, South Pacific Ocean 66°21′ S, 162°20′ E 255
Balleza, Mex. 26°57′ N, 106°22′ W 112
Ballinger, Tex., U.S. 31°43′ N, 99°57′ W 92
Ballobar, Sp. 41°36′ N, 0°11′ E 164
Ball's Pyramid, island, Austral. 32°15′ S, 157°57′ E 230
Ballstad, Nor. 68°4′ N, 13°28′ E 152
Ballston Spa, N.Y., U.S. 43°0′ N, 73°52′ W 104
Balmaceda, Chile 45°59′ S, 71°48′ W 123
Balmertown, Can. 51°3′ N, 93°45′ W 90
Balmoral Castle, site, U.K. 57°0′ N, 3°20′ W 150
Balmorhea, Tex., U.S. 30°57′ N, 103°45′ W 92
Balnearia, Arg. 31°0′ S, 62°40′ W 139
Balneario de los Novillos see I, Mex. 29°22′ N, 101°19′ W 112
Balod, India 20°44′ N, 81°12′ E 188
Balombo, Angola 12°22′ S, 14°47′ E 220
Balonne, river, Austral. 28°41′ S, 147°59′ E 230
Balotra, India 25°51′ N, 72°14′ E 186
Balqash, Kaz. 46°52′ N, 74°58′ E 184
Balqash Köli, lake, Kaz. 45°35′ N, 73°9′ E 190
Balş, Rom. 44°22′ N, 24°4′ E 156
Balsas, Braz. 7°32′ S, 46°3′ W 130
Balsas, Mex. 17°59′ N, 99°46′ W 114
Balsas, river, Braz. 8°24′ S, 46°19′ W 130
Balsas, river, Braz. 10°47′ S, 47°39′ W 130
Balsas, river, Mex. 18°29′ N, 100°56′ W 114
Balta, N. Dak., U.S. 48°9′ N, 100°3′ W 90
Balta, Rom. 44°52′ N, 22°39′ E 168
Balta, Ukr. 47°55′ N, 29°38′ E 156
Balta Albă, Rom. 45°18′ N, 27°16′ E 156
Baltasar Brum, Uru. 30°43′ S, 57°20′ W 139
Bălţi, Mold. 47°45′ N, 27°57′ E 152
Baltic Sea 59°13′ N, 17°48′ E 152
Balţîm, Egypt 31°34′ N, 31°4′ E 180
Baltimore, Md., U.S. 39°17′ N, 76°38′ W 94
Baltimore, Ohio, U.S. 39°50′ N, 82°36′ W 102
Baltit, Pak. 36°19′ N, 74°41′ E 186
Baltiysk, Russ. 54°39′ N, 19°54′ E 166
Baltrum, island, Ger. 53°41′ N, 7°26′ E 163
Balumbal, Eth. 8°33′ N, 45°10′ E 218
Balurghat, India 25°12′ N, 88°47′ E 197
Balvi, Latv. 57°6′ N, 27°14′ E 166
Balya, Turk. 39°43′ N, 27°34′ E 156
Balykcha, Russ. 51°18′ N, 87°43′ E 184
Balykchy, Kyrg. 42°26′ N, 76°10′ E 184
Balyksa, Russ. 53°23′ N, 89°8′ E 184
Balyqshy, Kaz. 47°2′ N, 51°52′ E 158
Balzola, It. 45°11′ N, 8°24′ E 167
Bam, Iran 29°2′ N, 58°23′ E 196
Bam Co, lake, China 31°29′ N, 90°37′ E 188
Bama, Nig. 11°32′ N, 13°41′ E 216
Bamako, Mali 12°37′ N, 8°10′ W 222
Bamba, Mali 17°2′ N, 1°26′ W 222
Bambafouga, Guinea 10°11′ N, 11°53′ W 222
Bambamarca, Peru 6°35′ S, 78°34′ W 130
Bambara, Chad 8°54′ N, 18°34′ E 218
Bambara, Mali 13°25′ N, 4°11′ W 222
Bambari, Cen. Af. Rep. 5°45′ N, 20°39′ E 218
Bambesa, Dem. Rep. of the Congo 3°24′ N, 25°43′ E 224
Bambey, Senegal 14°44′ N, 16°19′ W 222
Bambili, Dem. Rep. of the Congo 3°36′ N, 26°7′ E 224
Bambinga, Dem. Rep. of the Congo 3°45′ S, 18°51′ E 218
Bambio, Cen. Af. Rep. 3°59′ N, 16°58′ E 218
Bambouti, Cen. Af. Rep. 5°23′ N, 27°11′ E 224
Bambuí, Braz. 20°2′ S, 45°57′ W 138
Bambuyka, Russ. 55°46′ N, 115°33′ E 190
Bamenda, Cameroon 5°53′ N, 10°9′ E 222
Bamfield, Can. 48°47′ N, 125°8′ W 100
Bamian, Afghan. 34°51′ N, 67°51′ E 186
Bamingui, Cen. Af. Rep. 7°30′ N, 20°12′ E 218
Bampton, U.K. 51°44′ N, 1°33′ W 162
Bampton, U.K. 50°59′ N, 3°29′ W 162
Bamy, Turkm. 38°43′ N, 56°49′ E 180
Ban Bang Hin, Thai. 9°32′ N, 98°35′ E 202
Ban Don, Vietnam 12°54′ N, 107°47′ E 202
Ban Don, Ao 9°17′ N, 99°0′ E 202
Ban Don see Surat Thani, Thai. 9°7′ N, 99°20′ E 202
Ban Dong, Thai. 19°33′ N, 100°57′ E 202
Ban Hinboun, Laos 17°37′ N, 104°37′ E 202
Ban Khai, Thai. 12°47′ N, 101°20′ E 202
Ban Nam-Om, Laos 20°43′ N, 101°4′ E 202
Ban Napè, Laos 18°19′ N, 105°6′ E 202
Ban Phai, Thai. 16°6′ N, 102°41′ E 202
Ban Sanam Chai, Thai. 7°34′ N, 100°25′ E 196
Ban Taphan, Laos 15°56′ N, 105°25′ E 202
Ban Xénô, Laos 16°41′ N, 105°0′ E 202
Bañados de Otuquis, marsh, Braz. 20°54′ S, 60°29′ W 132
Bañados del Izozog, marsh, Bol. 18°55′ S, 62°31′ W 132
Banak, Nor. 70°2′ N, 25°1′ E 152
Banalia, Dem. Rep. of the Congo 1°33′ N, 25°25′ E 224
Banam, Cambodia 11°19′ N, 105°16′ E 202
Banamba, Mali 13°34′ N, 7°26′ W 222
Banana Islands, North Atlantic Ocean 7°56′ N, 13°50′ W 222
Bananfara, Guinea 11°19′ N, 8°56′ W 222
Bananga, India 6°56′ N, 93°58′ E 188
Banankoro, Guinea 9°10′ N, 9°18′ W 222
Banaras see Varanasi, India 25°18′ N, 82°57′ E 197
Banâs, Râs, Egypt 23°52′ N, 35°49′ E 182
Banas, river, India 25°5′ N, 74°2′ E 186
Banatsko Novo Selo, Serb. 44°59′ N, 20°46′ E 168
Banaz, Turk. 38°44′ N, 29°45′ E 156
Banbalah, Tun. 35°42′ N, 10°48′ E 156
Banbān, Saudi Arabia 24°58′ N, 46°36′ E 196
Banbar, China 31°4′ N, 94°46′ E 188
Banbury, U.K. 52°3′ N, 1°21′ W 162
Banco, Punta, C.R. 8°17′ N, 83°54′ W 115
Bancroft, Can. 45°3′ N, 77°52′ W 94
Bancroft, Iowa, U.S. 43°17′ N, 94°14′ W 94
Bancroft, Mich., U.S. 42°51′ N, 84°4′ W 102
Banda, Dem. Rep. of the Congo 4°8′ N, 27°4′ E 224
Banda, India 24°3′ N, 78°57′ E 197
Banda, India 25°27′ N, 80°19′ E 197
Banda Aceh, Indonesia 5°30′ N, 95°20′ E 196
Banda, Kepulauan, islands, Banda Sea 5°8′ S, 129°26′ E 192
Banda Nkwanta, Ghana 8°22′ N, 2°8′ W 222
Banda, Pointe, Gabon 3°46′ S, 10°57′ E 218
Banda Sea 5°42′ S, 127°27′ E 254
Banda Sea 5°13′ S, 123°58′ E 173
Bandai-Asahi National Park, Japan 38°17′ N, 139°38′ E 201
Bandajuma, Sierra Leone 7°35′ N, 11°39′ W 222
Bandān, Iran 31°23′ N, 60°42′ E 186
Bandar 'Abbās, Iran 27°11′ N, 56°13′ E 196
Bandar Lampung, Indonesia 5°28′ S, 105°7′ E 192
Bandar Murcaayo, Somalia 11°36′ N, 50°26′ E 182
Bandar see Machilipatnam, India 16°11′ N, 81°10′ E 188
Bandar Seri Begawan, Brunei 4°52′ N, 114°50′ E 203
Bandarban, Bangladesh 22°12′ N, 92°11′ E 188
Bandarbeyla, Somalia 9°25′ N, 50°48′ E 216
Bandar-e Anzalī, Iran 37°30′ N, 49°20′ E 195
Bandar-e Chārak, Iran 26°46′ N, 54°17′ E 196
Bandar-e Deylam, Iran 30°2′ N, 50°13′ E 196
Bandar-e Eman Khomeynī, Iran 30°27′ N, 49°3′ E 180
Bandar-e Genāveh, Iran 29°36′ N, 50°29′ E 196
Bandar-e Khoemir, Iran 26°57′ N, 55°34′ E 196
Bandar-e Lengeh, Iran 26°37′ N, 54°54′ E 196
Bandar-e Māh Shahr, Iran 30°38′ N, 49°12′ E 180
Bandar-e Maqām, Iran 26°58′ N, 53°29′ E 196
Bandar-e Rīg, Iran 29°29′ N, 50°39′ E 196
Bandar-e Torkaman, Iran 36°54′ N, 54°3′ E 180
Bandau, Malaysia 6°33′ N, 116°46′ E 203
Bandeira, peak, Braz. 20°30′ S, 41°53′ W 138
Bandeirante, Braz. 13°43′ S, 50°51′ W 138
Bandéko, Congo 1°56′ N, 17°27′ E 218
Bandelierkop, S. Af. 23°21′ S, 29°49′ E 227
Bandera, Arg. 28°52′ S, 62°17′ W 139
Bandera, Tex., U.S. 29°43′ N, 99°5′ W 92
Bandiagara, Mali 14°20′ N, 3°38′ W 222
Bandikui, India 27°2′ N, 76°35′ E 197
Bandırma, Turk. 40°19′ N, 27°57′ E 156
Bandon, Oreg., U.S. 43°6′ N, 124°24′ W 90
Bändovan Burnu, Azerb. 39°34′ N, 49°20′ E 195
Bandundu, Dem. Rep. of the Congo 3°24′ S, 17°23′ E 218
Bandundu, adm. division, Dem. Rep. of the Congo 4°38′ S, 16°30′ E 218
Bandung, Indonesia 7°1′ S, 107°32′ E 192
Băneasa, Rom. 45°57′ N, 27°55′ E 156
Bañeres, Sp. 38°43′ N, 0°40′ E 164
Banes, Cuba 20°58′ N, 75°44′ W 116
Banff, Can. 51°11′ N, 115°33′ W 108
Banff National Park, Can. 51°29′ N, 116°37′ W 238
Banfora, Burkina Faso 10°38′ N, 4°47′ W 222
Bang Mun Nak, Thai. 16°1′ N, 100°21′ E 202
Bang Saphan, Thai. 11°14′ N, 99°31′ E 202
Bangalore (Bengaluru), India 12°59′ N, 77°35′ E 188
Bangar, Philippines 16°54′ N, 120°25′ E 203
Bangassou, Cen. Af. Rep. 4°38′ N, 22°48′ E 207
Banggai, Kepulauan, islands, Banda Sea 2°42′ S, 123°39′ E 192
Banggi, island, Malaysia 7°2′ N, 117°21′ E 192
Banghāzī (Benghazi), Lib. 32°6′ N, 20°4′ E 216
Banghiang, river, Laos 16°17′ N, 105°14′ E 202
Bangka, island, Indonesia 2°24′ S, 106°18′ E 192
Bangkaru, island, Indonesia 1°52′ N, 97°4′ E 196
Bangkinang, Indonesia 0°21′ N, 101°1′ E 196

Bangkok see Krung Thep, *Thai.* 13°44′ N, 100°24′ E **202**
Bangladesh 24°0′ N, 90°0′ E **188**
Bangor, *Me., U.S.* 44°48′ N, 68°47′ W **111**
Bangor, *Mich., U.S.* 42°18′ N, 86°7′ W **102**
Bangor, *U.K.* 53°13′ N, 4°7′ W **162**
Bangs, *Tex., U.S.* 31°41′ N, 99°8′ W **92**
Bangs, Mount, *Ariz., U.S.* 36°46′ N, 113°54′ W **101**
Bangu, *Dem. Rep. of the Congo* 9°5′ S, 23°43′ E **224**
Bangué, *Cameroon* 3°12′ N, 15°9′ E **218**
Bangued, *Philippines* 17°37′ N, 120°38′ E **203**
Bangui, *Cen. Af. Rep.* 4°21′ N, 18°22′ E **218**
Bangui-Motoba, *Congo* 2°28′ N, 17°16′ E **218**
Bangui, *Philippines* 18°32′ N, 120°46′ E **203**
Banguru, *Dem. Rep. of the Congo* 0°28′ N, 27°6′ E **224**
Bangwade, *Dem. Rep. of the Congo* 1°0′ N, 25°14′ E **224**
Banh, *Burkina Faso* 14°4′ N, 2°27′ W **222**
Banhine National Park, *Mozambique* 22°54′ S, 32°6′ E **227**
Bani, *Cen. Af. Rep.* 7°7′ N, 22°54′ E **218**
Baní, *Dom. Rep.* 18°16′ N, 70°20′ W **116**
Bani, Jebel, *Mor.* 29°44′ N, 7°57′ W **214**
Bani, river, *Mali* 13°31′ N, 4°52′ W **222**
Banī Sharfā, *Saudi Arabia* 19°38′ N, 41°30′ E **182**
Banī Walīd, *Lib.* 31°46′ N, 14°0′ E **216**
Bania, *Cen. Af. Rep.* 4°6′ N, 16°6′ E **218**
Bania, *Côte d'Ivoire* 9°0′ N, 3°10′ W **222**
Banihal Pass, *India* 33°30′ N, 75°12′ E **186**
Banikoara, *Benin* 11°19′ N, 2°27′ E **222**
Baniou, *Alg.* 35°24′ N, 4°20′ E **150**
Banissa, *Kenya* 3°47′ N, 40°16′ E **224**
Bāniyās, *Syr.* 35°11′ N, 35°57′ E **194**
Banja, *Serb.* 43°33′ N, 19°33′ E **168**
Banja Koviljača, *Serb.* 44°30′ N, 19°9′ E **168**
Banja Luka, *Bosn. and Herzg.* 44°46′ N, 17°10′ E **168**
Banjarmasin, *Indonesia* 3°24′ S, 114°29′ E **192**
Banjul, *Gambia* 13°23′ N, 16°38′ W **222**
Bankä, *Azerb.* 39°25′ N, 49°15′ E **195**
Bankas, *Mali* 14°4′ N, 3°33′ W **222**
Banket, *Zimb.* 17°25′ S, 30°24′ E **224**
Bankilare, *Niger* 14°27′ N, 0°44′ E **222**
Bankim, *Cameroon* 6°4′ N, 11°29′ E **222**
Bankor, *Mali* 16°51′ N, 3°47′ W **222**
Banks Island, *Can.* 53°3′ N, 131°0′ W **98**
Banks Island, *Can.* 73°31′ N, 129°47′ W **106**
Banks Islands, *Coral Sea* 14°34′ S, 168°7′ E **238**
Banks Peninsula, *N.Z.* 43°50′ S, 172°37′ E **240**
Bankura, *India* 23°12′ N, 87°4′ E **197**
Bankya, *Bulg.* 42°42′ N, 23°8′ E **168**
Bannalec, *Fr.* 47°55′ N, 3°42′ W **150**
Banner, *Wyo., U.S.* 44°36′ N, 106°52′ W **90**
Banning, *Calif., U.S.* 33°56′ N, 116°54′ W **101**
Bannock Peak, *Idaho, U.S.* 42°36′ N, 112°46′ W **90**
Bannock Range, *Idaho, U.S.* 42°34′ N, 112°36′ W **90**
Bannu, *Pak.* 32°57′ N, 70°38′ E **186**
Banova Jaruga, *Croatia* 45°26′ N, 16°55′ E **168**
Banovići, *Bosn. and Herzg.* 44°24′ N, 18°28′ E **168**
Banow, *Afghan.* 35°36′ N, 69°20′ E **186**
Bánréve, *Slovakia* 48°18′ N, 20°21′ E **156**
Bansang, *Gambia* 13°25′ N, 14°41′ W **222**
Banská Bystrica, *Slovakia* 48°44′ N, 19°8′ E **152**
BanskobystrickŽy, adm. division, *Slovakia* 48°28′ N, 18°34′ E **152**
Bantaeng, *Indonesia* 5°31′ S, 119°52′ E **192**
Bantala, *Ghana* 9°51′ N, 1°49′ W **222**
Bantam, *Conn., U.S.* 41°43′ N, 73°14′ W **104**
Banyak, Kepulauan, islands, *Indian Ocean* 1°45′ N, 96°30′ E **196**
Banyas, *Israel* 33°14′ N, 35°41′ E **194**
Banyo, *Cameroon* 6°42′ N, 11°48′ E **218**
Banyos, Cap de, *Sp.* 39°51′ N, 3°36′ E **164**
Banyuwangi, *Indonesia* 8°10′ S, 114°21′ E **192**
Banzare Coast, *Antarctica* 68°40′ S, 129°50′ E **248**
Bao Bilia, spring, *Chad* 16°27′ N, 22°56′ E **226**
Bao Flala, *Mali* 12°12′ N, 6°35′ W **222**
Bao Ha, *Vietnam* 22°13′ N, 104°20′ E **202**
Bao Lac, *Vietnam* 22°58′ N, 105°39′ E **198**
Baode, *China* 38°57′ N, 111°2′ E **198**
Baoding, *China* 38°51′ N, 115°28′ E **198**
Baofeng, *China* 33°52′ N, 113°5′ E **198**
Baogarada, *Chad* 12°9′ N, 16°19′ E **216**
Baoji, *China* 34°25′ N, 107°9′ E **198**
Baojing, *China* 28°41′ N, 109°41′ E **198**
Baoro, *Cen. Af. Rep.* 5°39′ N, 15°57′ E **218**
Baoshan, *China* 25°8′ N, 99°8′ E **190**
Baoting, *China* 18°36′ N, 109°39′ E **198**
Baotou, *China* 40°36′ N, 110°0′ E **198**
Baoulé, *Mali* 12°56′ N, 8°36′ W **222**
Baoulé, river, *Mali* 13°57′ N, 9°27′ W **222**
Baoying, *China* 33°16′ N, 119°22′ E **198**
Bapaume, *Fr.* 50°5′ N, 2°50′ E **163**
Bapia, *Dem. Rep. of the Congo* 4°24′ N, 24°57′ E **224**
Baqên, *China* 31°54′ N, 93°59′ E **188**
Baqty, *Kaz.* 46°41′ N, 82°48′ E **184**
Ba'qūbah, *Iraq* 33°43′ N, 44°40′ E **180**
Bar, *Mont.* 42°5′ N, 19°5′ E **168**
Bar, *Ukr.* 49°4′ N, 27°44′ E **152**
Bar Harbor, *Me., U.S.* 44°23′ N, 68°12′ W **82**
Bar Mills, *Me., U.S.* 43°36′ N, 70°33′ W **104**
Bara, *Sudan* 13°41′ N, 30°20′ E **226**
Bara Banki, *India* 26°54′ N, 81°11′ E **197**
Bara Simbil, Jebel, peak, *Sudan* 13°27′ N, 24°10′ E **226**
Baraawe, *Somalia* 1°3′ N, 44°2′ E **218**
Barabinsk, *Russ.* 55°17′ N, 78°23′ E **184**
Baraboo, *Wis., U.S.* 43°28′ N, 89°44′ W **94**
Baraboo, river, *Wis., U.S.* 43°30′ N, 90°5′ W **102**
Baraboulé, *Burkina Faso* 14°13′ N, 1°52′ W **222**
Baracoa, *Cuba* 20°20′ N, 74°30′ W **116**
Baradá, river, *Syr.* 33°36′ N, 36°1′ E **194**
Baradero, *Arg.* 33°51′ S, 59°30′ W **139**
Baraga, *Mich., U.S.* 46°47′ N, 88°31′ W **94**
Bărăganul, *Rom.* 44°15′ N, 26°55′ E **156**
Baragoi, *Kenya* 1°44′ N, 36°47′ E **224**
Barahona, *Dom. Rep.* 18°11′ N, 71°5′ W **116**
Barakat, *Sudan* 14°13′ N, 33°35′ E **182**
Baram, river, *Malaysia* 3°55′ N, 113°58′ E **192**
Baramandougou, *Mali* 13°37′ N, 4°38′ W **222**
Baramula, *India* 34°10′ N, 74°23′ E **186**
Baran', *Belarus* 54°29′ N, 28°40′ E **166**
Baran, *India* 25°5′ N, 76°31′ E **197**
Baranama, *Guinea* 10°11′ N, 8°46′ W **222**
Baranavichy, *Belarus* 53°6′ N, 26°1′ E **152**
Baranoa, *Col.* 10°47′ N, 74°57′ W **136**
Baranof Island, *Alas., U.S.* 56°3′ N, 135°55′ W **98**
Baranovka, *Russ.* 49°55′ N, 46°2′ E **158**
Baranya, adm. division, *Hung.* 45°55′ N, 17°41′ E **156**
Barão de Grajaú, *Braz.* 6°43′ S, 43°3′ W **132**
Barão de Melgaço, *Braz.* 16°15′ S, 55°57′ W **132**
Barassoli, spring, *Eritrea* 13°36′ N, 42°5′ E **182**
Barat Daya, Kepulauan, islands, *Banda Sea* 6°36′ S, 126°45′ E **192**
Barataria, *La., U.S.* 29°43′ N, 90°8′ W **103**
Barataria Bay 29°22′ N, 90°11′ W **103**
Barbacena, *Braz.* 21°13′ S, 43°46′ W **138**
Barbacoas, *Col.* 1°38′ N, 78°13′ W **136**
Barbadillo, *Sp.* 40°55′ N, 5°52′ W **150**
Barbadillo del Mercado, *Sp.* 42°2′ N, 3°22′ W **164**
Barbados 13°0′ N, 60°0′ W **116**
Barbaria, Cap de, *Sp.* 38°19′ N, 1°24′ E **150**
Barbas, Cap, *Western Sahara, Mor.* 21°56′ N, 16°47′ W **214**
Barbastro, *Sp.* 42°2′ N, 0°7′ E **164**
Barbate, *Sp.* 36°11′ N, 5°57′ W **164**
Barbazan, *Fr.* 43°2′ N, 0°36′ E **164**
Bārbele, *Latv.* 56°26′ N, 24°35′ E **166**
Barberton, *Ohio, U.S.* 41°0′ N, 81°37′ W **110**
Barberton, *S. Af.* 25°50′ S, 31°0′ E **227**
Barberville, *Fla., U.S.* 29°11′ N, 81°26′ W **105**
Barbosa, *Col.* 5°56′ N, 73°39′ W **136**
Barbourville, *Ky., U.S.* 36°52′ N, 83°54′ W **96**
Barbuda, island, *Antigua and Barbuda* 17°45′ N, 61°51′ W **116**
Barcarrota, *Sp.* 38°31′ N, 6°52′ W **164**
Barce see Al Marj, *Lib.* 32°30′ N, 20°53′ E **216**
Barcelona, *Sp.* 41°23′ N, 2°10′ E **164**
Barcelona, *Venez.* 10°5′ N, 64°44′ W **136**
Barcelonnette, *Fr.* 44°23′ N, 6°38′ E **167**
Barcelos, *Braz.* 1°0′ N, 62°58′ W **130**
Barco, *N.C., U.S.* 36°23′ N, 76°0′ W **96**
Barcs, *Hung.* 45°57′ N, 17°28′ E **168**
Barczewo, *Pol.* 53°50′ N, 20°40′ E **166**
Bard, *Calif., U.S.* 32°47′ N, 114°34′ W **101**
Bärdä, *Azerb.* 40°23′ N, 47°6′ E **195**
Barda, *Russ.* 56°56′ N, 55°39′ E **154**
Barda Hills, *India* 21°50′ N, 69°41′ E **186**
Bardaale, *Somalia* 7°0′ N, 47°54′ E **218**
Bardaï, *Chad* 21°20′ N, 17°1′ E **216**
Bardas Blancas, *Arg.* 35°52′ S, 69°50′ W **134**
Bardawīl, Sabkhet el 31°7′ N, 33°2′ E **194**
Barddhaman, *India* 23°13′ N, 87°52′ E **197**
Bardoli, *India* 21°8′ N, 73°7′ E **186**
Bardon Hill, peak, *U.K.* 52°42′ N, 1°21′ W **162**
Bardonecchia, *It.* 45°5′ N, 6°42′ E **167**
Bardstown, *Ky., U.S.* 37°47′ N, 85°29′ W **94**
Bardwell, *Ky., U.S.* 36°51′ N, 89°1′ W **96**
Bare Mountain, *Nev., U.S.* 36°50′ N, 116°43′ W **101**
Barèges, *Fr.* 42°53′ N, 6°357′ E **164**
Bareilly, *India* 28°20′ N, 79°24′ E **197**
Barents Plain, *Arctic Ocean* 83°46′ N, 15°37′ E **255**
Barents Sea 71°12′ N, 27°58′ E **152**
Barentsburg, *Nor.* 77°58′ N, 14°33′ E **160**
Barentsøya, island, *Nor.* 78°41′ N, 22°17′ E **246**
Barentu, *Eritrea* 15°6′ N, 37°35′ E **182**
Barevo, *Bosn. and Herzg.* 44°25′ N, 17°14′ E **168**
Barfleur, Pointe de, *Fr.* 49°39′ N, 1°54′ W **150**
Barga, *China* 30°52′ N, 81°19′ E **197**
Barga, *It.* 44°5′ N, 10°29′ E **167**
Bargaal, *Somalia* 11°13′ N, 51°3′ E **216**
Bargarh, *India* 21°19′ N, 83°35′ E **188**
Bargē, *Eth.* 6°13′ N, 36°53′ E **224**
Bårgo, peak, *Nor.* 66°16′ N, 18°7′ E **152**
Barguzin, *Russ.* 53°41′ N, 109°32′ E **190**
Barham, Mount, *Can.* 59°44′ N, 133°36′ W **98**
Barharwa, *India* 24°51′ N, 87°47′ E **197**
Barhi, *India* 24°14′ N, 85°23′ E **197**
Barhi, *India* 23°56′ N, 80°51′ E **197**
Bari, *Dem. Rep. of the Congo* 3°22′ N, 19°24′ E **218**
Bari, *India* 26°37′ N, 77°36′ E **197**
Bari, *It.* 41°7′ N, 16°51′ E **156**
Barika, *Alg.* 35°21′ N, 5°22′ E **150**
Barikowt, *Afghan.* 35°17′ N, 71°32′ E **186**
Baril Lake, *Can.* 58°45′ N, 111°57′ W **108**
Barīm (Perim), island, *Yemen* 12°36′ N, 42°32′ E **182**
Barinas, *Venez.* 8°38′ N, 70°15′ W **136**
Barinas, adm. division, *Venez.* 8°23′ N, 70°58′ W **136**
Baringa, *Dem. Rep. of the Congo* 0°42′ N, 20°53′ E **218**
Baripada, *India* 21°57′ N, 86°43′ E **197**
Bariri, *Braz.* 22°5′ S, 48°41′ W **138**
Bârîs, *Egypt* 24°40′ N, 30°30′ E **182**
Barisal, *Bangladesh* 22°42′ N, 90°17′ E **197**
Barisan, Pegunungan, *Indonesia* 1°4′ S, 100°23′ E **196**
Barito, river, *Indonesia* 2°13′ S, 114°39′ E **192**
Baritú National Park, *Arg.* 22°25′ S, 64°46′ W **132**
Bark Lake, *Can.* 46°50′ N, 82°54′ W **94**
Bark Point, *Wis., U.S.* 46°40′ N, 91°13′ W **94**
Barkā', *Oman* 23°40′ N, 57°54′ E **196**
Barkald, *Nor.* 61°59′ N, 10°54′ E **152**
Barkley, Lake, *Ky., U.S.* 36°20′ N, 88°40′ W **81**
Barkley Sound 48°50′ N, 125°50′ W **108**
Barkly East, *S. Af.* 30°58′ S, 27°33′ E **227**
Barkly Tableland, *Austral.* 19°43′ S, 136°41′ E **230**
Barkly West, *S. Af.* 28°33′ S, 24°31′ E **227**
Barkol, *China* 43°31′ N, 92°51′ E **190**
Barksdale, *Tex., U.S.* 29°44′ N, 100°2′ W **92**
Barksdale Air Force Base, *La., U.S.* 32°27′ N, 93°42′ W **103**
Barla Dağı, peak, *Turk.* 38°2′ N, 30°37′ E **156**
Bar-le-Duc, *Fr.* 48°46′ N, 5°10′ E **163**
Barlee Range Nature Reserve, *Austral.* 23°21′ S, 115°39′ E **238**
Barlow Pass, *Oreg., U.S.* 45°16′ N, 121°42′ W **90**
Barmer, *India* 25°43′ N, 71°23′ E **186**
Barmou, *Niger* 15°8′ N, 5°27′ E **222**
Barmouth, *U.K.* 52°43′ N, 4°3′ W **162**
Barnard, *Vt., U.S.* 43°43′ N, 72°38′ W **104**
Barnaul, *Russ.* 53°23′ N, 83°48′ E **184**
Barnegat, *N.J., U.S.* 39°45′ N, 74°14′ W **94**
Barnegat Light, *N.J., U.S.* 39°44′ N, 74°7′ W **94**
Barnes Ice Cap, *Can.* 68°46′ N, 73°57′ W **106**
Barnes Sound 25°13′ N, 80°35′ W **105**
Barnesville, *Minn., U.S.* 46°37′ N, 96°26′ W **90**
Barnesville, *Ohio, U.S.* 39°58′ N, 81°11′ W **102**
Barnet, *Vt., U.S.* 44°17′ N, 72°4′ W **104**
Barnhart, *Tex., U.S.* 31°6′ N, 101°10′ W **92**
Barnoldswick, *U.K.* 53°55′ N, 2°12′ W **162**
Barnsley, *U.K.* 53°32′ N, 1°28′ W **162**
Barnstaple, *U.K.* 51°5′ N, 4°3′ W **162**
Barnum, *Minn., U.S.* 46°29′ N, 92°44′ W **94**
Baro, *Nig.* 8°33′ N, 6°22′ E **222**
Barons, *Can.* 49°59′ N, 113°5′ W **90**
Barouéli, *Mali* 13°4′ N, 6°50′ W **222**
Barpeta, *India* 26°19′ N, 90°57′ E **197**
Barques, Pointe aux, *Mich., U.S.* 44°4′ N, 82°55′ W **102**
Barquisimeto, *Venez.* 10°0′ N, 69°19′ W **136**
Barr, *Fr.* 48°24′ N, 7°26′ E **163**
Barra, *Braz.* 10°58′ S, 43°8′ W **123**
Barra, *Braz.* 11°6′ S, 43°11′ W **132**
Barra da Estiva, *Braz.* 13°39′ S, 41°20′ W **138**
Barra de Navidad, *Mex.* 19°12′ N, 104°43′ W **114**
Barra de São João, *Braz.* 22°34′ S, 42°0′ W **138**
Barra del Tordo, *Mex.* 23°0′ N, 97°47′ W **114**
Barra do Bugres, *Braz.* 15°4′ S, 57°13′ W **132**
Barra do Corda, *Braz.* 5°33′ S, 45°15′ W **132**
Barra do Cuanza, *Angola* 9°18′ S, 13°7′ E **220**
Barra do Dande, *Angola* 8°29′ S, 13°21′ E **218**
Barra do Garças, *Braz.* 15°53′ S, 52°16′ W **138**
Barra do Piraí, *Braz.* 22°30′ S, 43°46′ W **138**
Barra do Quaraí, *Uru.* 30°15′ S, 57°34′ W **139**
Barra do São Manuel, *Braz.* 7°19′ S, 58°2′ W **130**
Barra Head, *U.K.* 56°38′ N, 8°2′ W **150**
Barra Mansa, *Braz.* 22°34′ S, 44°9′ W **138**
Barra Patuca, *Hond.* 15°48′ N, 84°18′ W **115**
Barra, Ponta da, *Mozambique* 23°42′ S, 35°29′ E **227**
Barracão do Barreto, *Braz.* 8°50′ S, 58°25′ W **130**
Barrage Daniel-Johnson, dam, *Can.* 50°23′ N, 69°12′ W **111**
Barrage Gouin, dam, *Can.* 48°7′ N, 74°5′ W **94**
Barragem, *Mozambique* 24°24′ S, 32°53′ E **227**
Barrancabermeja, *Col.* 7°3′ N, 73°50′ W **136**
Barrancas, *Venez.* 8°43′ N, 62°14′ W **116**
Barranco Branco, *Braz.* 19°35′ S, 56°8′ W **132**
Barranco Branco, *Braz.* 21°7′ S, 57°51′ W **134**
Barrancos de Guadalupe, *Mex.* 29°57′ N, 104°45′ W **92**
Barranqueras, *Arg.* 27°30′ S, 58°57′ W **139**
Barranquilla, *Col.* 10°57′ N, 74°50′ W **136**
Barras, *Braz.* 4°17′ S, 42°19′ W **132**
Barras, *Col.* 1°46′ S, 73°13′ W **136**
Barraute, *Can.* 48°26′ N, 77°40′ W **94**
Barrax, *Sp.* 39°2′ N, 2°13′ W **164**
Barre, *Mass., U.S.* 42°25′ N, 72°7′ W **104**
Barre, *Vt., U.S.* 44°12′ N, 72°31′ W **104**
Barreiras, *Braz.* 12°10′ S, 44°58′ W **132**
Barreirinha, *Braz.* 2°49′ S, 57°5′ W **130**
Barreiro, *Port.* 38°36′ N, 9°8′ W **214**
Barrême, *Fr.* 43°57′ N, 6°21′ E **167**
Barren Island, *U.S.* 52°44′ S, 60°8′ W **134**
Barretos, *Braz.* 20°35′ S, 48°36′ W **138**
Barrhead, *Can.* 54°8′ N, 114°25′ W **108**
Barrie, *Can.* 44°23′ N, 79°42′ W **94**
Barrier Bay 67°42′ S, 78°28′ E **248**
Barrier Range, *Austral.* 31°5′ S, 140°54′ E **230**
Barriles, ruin(s), *Pan.* 8°42′ N, 82°50′ W **115**
Barrington, *Ill., U.S.* 42°9′ N, 88°8′ W **102**
Barrington, *N.H., U.S.* 43°13′ N, 71°3′ W **104**
Barrington, *R.I., U.S.* 41°44′ N, 71°19′ W **104**
Barro Alto, *Braz.* 15°6′ S, 48°58′ W **138**
Barrocão, *Braz.* 16°24′ S, 43°16′ W **138**
Barron, *Wis., U.S.* 45°23′ N, 91°52′ W **94**
Barrow, *Alas., U.S.* 71°8′ N, 156°35′ W **98**
Barrow Canyon, *Arctic Ocean* 72°4′ N, 151°21′ W **255**
Barrow Creek, *Austral.* 21°33′ S, 133°54′ E **231**
Barrow in Furness, *U.K.* 54°7′ N, 3°13′ W **162**
Barrow Island, *Austral.* 20°51′ S, 114°19′ E **230**
Barrow, Point, *Alas., U.S.* 71°40′ N, 155°42′ W **246**
Barrow Strait 74°8′ N, 97°17′ W **106**
Barrows, *Can.* 52°49′ N, 101°27′ W **108**
Barry, *U.K.* 51°23′ N, 3°17′ W **162**
Barry, Lac, lake, *Can.* 48°59′ N, 75°59′ W **94**
Barry's Bay, *Can.* 45°28′ N, 77°41′ W **94**
Barryton, *Mich., U.S.* 43°44′ N, 85°9′ W **102**
Barrytown, *N.Z.* 42°15′ S, 171°20′ E **240**
Barshatas, *Kaz.* 48°4′ N, 78°32′ E **184**
Barshyn, *Kaz.* 49°37′ N, 69°30′ E **184**
Barsi, *India* 18°14′ N, 75°41′ E **188**
Barstow, *Calif., U.S.* 34°53′ N, 117°2′ W **101**
Bar-sur-Aube, *Fr.* 48°13′ N, 4°43′ E **163**
Bārta, *Latv.* 56°21′ N, 21°8′ E **166**
Bārta, river, *Latv.* 56°18′ N, 21°2′ E **166**
Barter Island, *Alas., U.S.* 70°11′ N, 145°51′ W **106**
Barthelemy Pass, *Laos* 19°31′ N, 104°1′ E **202**
Bartica, *Guyana* 6°19′ N, 58°41′ W **130**
Bartın, *Turk.* 41°38′ N, 32°20′ E **156**
Bartlesville, *Okla., U.S.* 36°43′ N, 95°59′ W **96**
Bartlett, *Nebr., U.S.* 41°51′ N, 98°33′ W **90**
Bartlett, *N.H., U.S.* 44°4′ N, 71°18′ W **104**
Bartlett, *Tex., U.S.* 30°46′ N, 97°26′ W **92**
Bartolomeu Dias, *Mozambique* 21°12′ S, 35°6′ E **227**
Barton, *N. Dak., U.S.* 48°29′ N, 100°12′ W **94**
Barton upon Humber, *U.K.* 53°40′ N, 0°27′ E **162**
Bartoszyce, *Pol.* 54°14′ N, 20°48′ E **166**
Bartow, *Fla., U.S.* 27°50′ N, 81°51′ W **112**
Bartow, *Ger.* 53°49′ N, 13°20′ E **152**
Barú, VolcŽan, *Pan.* 8°47′ N, 82°41′ W **115**
Barus, *Indonesia* 2°3′ N, 98°22′ E **196**
Baruth, *Ger.* 52°4′ N, 13°29′ E **152**
Baruun Urt, *Mongolia* 46°40′ N, 113°16′ E **198**
Baruunharaa, *Mongolia* 48°58′ N, 106°3′ E **198**
Baruunsuu, *Mongolia* 43°45′ N, 105°31′ E **198**
Barvinkove, *Ukr.* 48°56′ N, 37°6′ E **158**
Barysaw, *Belarus* 54°13′ N, 28°29′ E **166**
Barysh, *Russ.* 53°39′ N, 47°13′ E **154**
Barzas, *Russ.* 55°45′ N, 86°29′ E **169**
Bāsa'īdū, *Iran* 26°37′ N, 55°17′ E **196**
Basail, *Arg.* 27°51′ S, 59°18′ W **139**
Basal, *Pak.* 33°32′ N, 72°19′ E **186**
Basankusu, *Dem. Rep. of the Congo* 1°7′ N, 19°50′ E **207**
Basargech'ar, *Arm.* 40°12′ N, 45°42′ E **195**
Basaseachic, *Mex.* 28°10′ N, 108°11′ W **92**
Basavilbaso, *Arg.* 32°23′ S, 58°51′ W **139**
Basco, *Philippines* 20°25′ N, 121°58′ E **203**
Bas-Congo, adm. division, *Dem. Rep. of the Congo* 5°10′ S, 13°44′ E **218**
Bascuñán, Cabo, *Chile* 28°48′ S, 72°52′ W **134**
Basekpio, *Dem. Rep. of the Congo* 4°45′ N, 24°38′ E **224**
Basel, *Switz.* 47°33′ N, 7°35′ E **150**
Basey, *Philippines* 11°18′ N, 125°3′ E **203**
Bashaw, *Can.* 52°35′ N, 112°59′ W **108**
Bashi, *Ala., U.S.* 31°57′ N, 87°51′ W **103**
Bashi Channel 21°28′ N, 120°30′ E **198**
Bashkortostan, adm. division, *Russ.* 54°0′ N, 55°48′ E **154**
Basilan, island, *Philippines* 6°14′ N, 122°25′ E **192**
Basile, *La., U.S.* 30°28′ N, 92°37′ W **103**
Basiliano, *It.* 46°1′ N, 13°5′ E **167**
Basilicata, adm. division, *It.* 40°59′ N, 15°38′ E **156**
Basílio, *Braz.* 31°53′ S, 53°2′ W **139**
Basin, *Wyo., U.S.* 44°21′ N, 108°3′ W **90**
Basin Harbor, *Vt., U.S.* 44°11′ N, 73°22′ W **104**
Basinger, *Fla., U.S.* 27°23′ N, 81°2′ W **105**
Basingstoke, *U.K.* 51°16′ N, 1°6′ W **162**
Basirhat, *India* 22°40′ N, 88°48′ E **197**
Baška, *Croatia* 44°58′ N, 14°44′ E **156**
Başkale, *Turk.* 38°2′ N, 43°56′ E **195**
Baskin, *La., U.S.* 32°14′ N, 91°44′ W **103**
Baskomutan National Park, *Turk.* 38°51′ N, 30°15′ E **156**
Baslow, *U.K.* 53°15′ N, 1°37′ W **162**
Basoda, *India* 23°51′ N, 77°56′ E **197**
Basoko, *Dem. Rep. of the Congo* 1°17′ N, 23°35′ E **224**
Basongo, *Dem. Rep. of the Congo* 4°23′ S, 20°22′ E **218**
Basque Country, adm. division, *Sp.* 43°10′ N, 3°2′ W **164**
Basra see Al Başrah, *Iraq* 30°30′ N, 47°48′ E **207**
Bass Islands, *Lake Erie* 41°36′ N, 83°0′ W **102**
Bass Lake, *Calif., U.S.* 37°20′ N, 119°34′ W **100**
Bass Strait 39°32′ S, 143°59′ E **231**
Bassae, ruin(s), *Gr.* 37°25′ N, 21°42′ E **156**
Bassano, *Can.* 50°47′ N, 112°29′ W **90**
Bassano del Grappa, *It.* 45°46′ N, 11°44′ E **167**
Bassar, *Togo* 9°14′ N, 0°46′ E **222**
Bassas da India, adm. division, *Fr.* 21°15′ S, 39°13′ E **220**
Basse Santa Su, *Gambia* 13°17′ N, 14°15′ W **222**
Basse-Normandie, adm. division, *Fr.* 49°7′ N, 1°9′ W **150**
Basse-Terre, *Fr.* 16°0′ N, 61°44′ W **116**
Basseterre, *Saint Kitts and Nevis* 17°0′ N, 63°0′ W **118**
Basse-Terre, island, *Fr.* 16°10′ N, 62°34′ W **116**
Bassett, *Nebr., U.S.* 42°33′ N, 99°33′ W **90**
Bassfield, *Miss., U.S.* 31°28′ N, 89°45′ W **103**
Bassigbiri, *Cen. Af. Rep.* 5°18′ N, 26°54′ E **224**
Bassikounou, *Mauritania* 15°52′ N, 5°58′ W **222**
Bastak, *Iran* 27°11′ N, 54°25′ E **196**
Bastar, *India* 19°14′ N, 81°58′ E **188**
Bastevarre, peak, *Nor.* 68°57′ N, 22°12′ E **152**
Basti, *India* 26°46′ N, 82°44′ E **197**
Bastia, *Fr.* 42°40′ N, 9°23′ E **214**
Bastimentos, Isla, island, *Pan.* 9°23′ N, 82°9′ W **115**
Bastrop, *La., U.S.* 32°46′ N, 91°55′ W **103**
Bastrop, *Tex., U.S.* 30°6′ N, 97°19′ W **92**
Bastuträsk, *Nor.* 64°46′ N, 20°1′ E **152**
Bastyn', *Belarus* 52°23′ N, 26°44′ E **152**
Basuo see Dongfang, *China* 19°3′ N, 108°38′ E **198**
Bat Yam, *Israel* 32°1′ N, 34°44′ E **194**
Bata, *Equatorial Guinea* 2°1′ N, 9°47′ E **207**
Bata, *Rom.* 46°1′ N, 22°2′ E **168**
Batac, *Philippines* 18°4′ N, 120°33′ E **203**
Batagay, *Russ.* 67°42′ N, 134°52′ E **160**
Batagay Alyta, *Russ.* 67°47′ N, 130°22′ E **160**
Batajnica, *Serb.* 44°53′ N, 20°17′ E **168**
Batala, *India* 31°47′ N, 75°13′ E **186**
Batam, island, *Indonesia* 0°53′ N, 103°40′ E **196**
Batama, *Dem. Rep. of the Congo* 0°53′ N, 26°35′ E **224**
Batamay, *Russ.* 63°30′ N, 129°24′ E **160**
Batamorghab, *Afghan.* 35°37′ N, 63°20′ E **186**
Batan, island, *Philippines* 20°30′ N, 122°3′ E **198**
Batan Islands, *Philippine Sea* 20°36′ N, 122°2′ E **203**
Batang, *China* 30°6′ N, 98°58′ E **190**
Batang Ai National Park, *Malaysia* 1°14′ N, 111°42′ E **238**
Batang Berjuntai, *Malaysia* 3°22′ N, 101°25′ E **196**
Batanga, *Gabon* 0°19′ N, 9°21′ E **218**
Batangafo, *Cen. Af. Rep.* 7°15′ N, 18°18′ E **218**
Batangas, *Philippines* 13°48′ N, 121°2′ E **203**
Batangtoru, *Indonesia* 1°30′ N, 99°4′ E **196**
Batara, *Cen. Af. Rep.* 5°50′ N, 16°8′ E **218**
Bátaszék, *Hung.* 46°11′ N, 18°42′ E **168**
Batatais, *Braz.* 20°55′ S, 47°36′ W **138**
Batavia, *N.Y., U.S.* 42°59′ N, 78°11′ W **94**
Bataysk, *Russ.* 47°6′ N, 39°46′ E **156**
Batchawana Bay, *Can.* 46°56′ N, 84°36′ W **94**
Batchawana Mountain, *Can.* 47°5′ N, 84°29′ W **94**
Batesville, *Ark., U.S.* 35°45′ N, 91°42′ W **96**
Batesville, *Miss., U.S.* 34°17′ N, 89°57′ W **96**
Batesville, *Tex., U.S.* 28°56′ N, 99°38′ W **92**
Batetskaya, *Russ.* 58°38′ N, 30°22′ E **166**
Bath, *Me., U.S.* 43°54′ N, 69°50′ W **104**
Bath, *N.H., U.S.* 44°9′ N, 71°58′ W **104**
Bath, *N.Y., U.S.* 42°20′ N, 77°20′ W **94**
Bath, *U.K.* 51°23′ N, 2°23′ W **162**
Bathurst, *Can.* 47°32′ N, 65°44′ W **106**
Bathurst, *S. Af.* 33°32′ S, 26°48′ E **227**
Bathurst, Cape, *Can.* 70°19′ N, 130°47′ W **98**
Bathurst Inlet 67°37′ N, 111°0′ W **106**
Bathurst Inlet, *Can.* 66°24′ N, 107°24′ W **73**
Bathurst Island, *Austral.* 12°5′ S, 128°51′ E **230**
Bathurst Island, *Can.* 74°41′ N, 102°4′ W **106**
Batī, *Eth.* 11°12′ N, 40°1′ E **224**
Batié, *Burkina Faso* 9°54′ N, 2°58′ W **222**
Batina, *Croatia* 45°49′ N, 18°48′ E **168**
Batista, Serra da, *Braz.* 6°40′ S, 41°49′ W **132**
Batkanu, *Sierra Leone* 9°3′ N, 12°25′ W **222**
Batlava, *Serb.* 42°50′ N, 21°14′ E **168**
Batley, *U.K.* 53°43′ N, 1°38′ W **162**
Batman, *Turk.* 37°53′ N, 41°10′ E **195**
Batna, *Alg.* 35°31′ N, 6°8′ E **150**
Batoche National Historic Site, *Can.* 52°42′ N, 106°10′ W **108**
Batočina, *Serb.* 44°9′ N, 21°3′ E **168**
Baton Rouge, *La., U.S.* 30°25′ N, 91°13′ W **103**
Batopilas, *Mex.* 27°1′ N, 107°46′ W **112**
Batouri, *Cameroon* 4°25′ N, 14°20′ E **218**
Batovi see Tamitatoala, river, *Braz.* 14°11′ S, 53°58′ W **132**
Batrina, *Croatia* 45°11′ N, 17°39′ E **168**
Bătrîna, *Rom.* 45°48′ N, 22°35′ E **168**
Batroun, *Leb.* 34°16′ N, 35°40′ E **194**
Batsí, *Gr.* 37°51′ N, 24°46′ E **156**
Batson, *Tex., U.S.* 30°13′ N, 94°37′ W **103**
Battambang, *Cambodia* 13°7′ N, 103°11′ E **202**
Battenberg, *Ger.* 51°0′ N, 8°39′ E **167**
Batticaloa, *Sri Lanka* 7°44′ N, 81°43′ E **188**
Battle, *U.K.* 50°54′ N, 0°29′ E **162**
Battle Creek, *Mich., U.S.* 42°18′ N, 85°12′ W **102**
Battle Creek, river, *Mont., U.S.* 49°3′ N, 109°32′ W **108**
Battle Ground, *Ind., U.S.* 40°30′ N, 86°50′ W **102**
Battle Ground, *Wash., U.S.* 45°46′ N, 122°33′ W **100**
Battle Harbour, *Can.* 52°15′ N, 55°38′ W **111**
Battle Mountain, *Nev., U.S.* 40°43′ N, 117°19′ W **90**
Battle, river, *Can.* 52°17′ N, 112°10′ W **80**
Battleford, *Can.* 52°43′ N, 108°20′ W **108**
Battonya, *Hung.* 46°17′ N, 21°2′ E **168**
Batu, Kepulauan, islands, *Tanahmasa* 5°297′ N, 98°10′ E **196**
Batu Pahat, *Malaysia* 1°52′ N, 102°56′ E **196**
Batu, peak, *Eth.* 6°53′ N, 39°39′ E **224**
Bat'umi, *Ga.* 41°38′ N, 41°38′ E **195**
Batupanjang, *Indonesia* 1°45′ N, 101°33′ E **196**
Baturaja, *Indonesia* 4°10′ S, 104°9′ E **192**
Baturino, *Russ.* 57°42′ N, 85°17′ E **169**
Baturité, *Braz.* 4°20′ S, 38°54′ W **132**
Baturité, Serra de, *Braz.* 4°45′ S, 39°36′ W **132**
Batys Qazaqstan, adm. division, *Kaz.* 49°52′ N, 49°51′ E **158**
Bau, *Sudan* 11°22′ N, 34°6′ E **216**
Baú, river, *Braz.* 6°41′ S, 52°57′ W **130**
Baubau, *Indonesia* 5°36′ S, 122°41′ E **192**
Bauchi, *Nig.* 10°19′ N, 9°50′ E **222**
Baudeau, Lac, lake, *Can.* 51°37′ N, 73°44′ W **110**
Baudette, *Minn., U.S.* 48°41′ N, 94°39′ W **90**
Baudó, *Col.* 5°1′ N, 77°7′ W **136**
Baudó, Serranía de, *Col.* 5°31′ N, 78°6′ W **115**
Bauges, *Fr.* 45°34′ N, 5°59′ E **165**
Bauld, Cape, *Can.* 51°40′ N, 55°58′ W **111**
Baunatal, *Ger.* 51°15′ N, 9°26′ E **167**
Baunei, *It.* 40°2′ N, 9°39′ E **156**
Baunt, *Russ.* 55°20′ N, 113°12′ E **190**
Baure, *Nig.* 12°50′ N, 8°44′ E **222**
Baures, *Bol.* 13°39′ S, 63°36′ W **137**
Baures, river, *Bol.* 12°43′ S, 64°5′ W **137**
Bauru, *Braz.* 22°21′ S, 49°5′ W **138**
Baús, *Braz.* 18°27′ S, 53°0′ W **138**
Bauska, *Latv.* 56°24′ N, 24°11′ E **166**
Bautīno, *Kaz.* 44°33′ N, 50°16′ E **158**
Bauya, *Sierra Leone* 8°10′ N, 12°37′ W **222**
Baūyrzhan Momyshuly, *Kaz.* 42°37′ N, 70°45′ E **197**
Bavanište, *Serb.* 44°48′ N, 20°52′ E **168**
Bavaria, adm. division, *Ger.* 49°12′ N, 11°22′ E **167**
Bavay, *Fr.* 50°16′ N, 3°48′ E **163**
Baviácora, *Mex.* 29°43′ N, 110°11′ W **92**
Bavispe, river, *Mex.* 30°27′ N, 109°6′ W **92**
Bavly, *Russ.* 54°21′ N, 53°24′ E **154**
Bawītī, *Egypt* 28°21′ N, 28°50′ E **180**
Bawku, *Ghana* 11°3′ N, 0°16′ E **222**
Bawlake, *Myanmar* 19°11′ N, 97°17′ E **202**
Bawlf, *Can.* 52°54′ N, 112°28′ W **108**
Bawmi, *Myanmar* 17°20′ N, 94°36′ E **202**
Bawtry, *U.K.* 53°26′ N, 1°1′ W **162**
Baxaya, peak, *Somalia* 11°17′ N, 49°35′ E **218**
Baxdo, *Somalia* 5°48′ N, 47°17′ E **218**
Baxley, *Ga., U.S.* 31°46′ N, 82°22′ W **96**
Baxoi, *China* 30°2′ N, 96°57′ E **188**
Baxter, *Minn., U.S.* 46°21′ N, 94°18′ W **94**
Baxter Peak, *Colo., U.S.* 39°39′ N, 107°24′ W **90**
Baxterville, *Miss., U.S.* 31°4′ N, 89°37′ W **103**
Bay City, *Mich., U.S.* 43°35′ N, 83°53′ W **102**
Bay City, *Tex., U.S.* 28°58′ N, 95°58′ W **96**
Bay City, *Wis., U.S.* 44°35′ N, 92°27′ W **94**
Bay de Verde, *Can.* 48°6′ N, 52°54′ W **111**
Bay Minette, *Ala., U.S.* 30°51′ N, 87°46′ W **103**
Bay Port, *Mich., U.S.* 43°50′ N, 83°23′ W **102**
Bay Roberts, *Can.* 47°35′ N, 53°16′ W **111**
Bay Saint Louis, *Miss., U.S.* 30°18′ N, 89°20′ W **103**
Bay Shore, *N.Y., U.S.* 40°43′ N, 73°16′ W **104**
Bay Springs, *Miss., U.S.* 31°58′ N, 89°17′ W **103**

Baya, Dem. Rep. of the Congo 2°31' N, 20°17' E 218
Bay'ah, Oman 25°45' N, 56°18' E 196
Bayamo, Cuba 20°21' N, 76°38' W 115
Bayan, China 46°3' N, 127°25' E 198
Bayan, Mongolia 47°11' N, 107°33' E 198
Bayan, Mongolia 48°27' N, 111°0' E 198
Bayan Har Shan, China 34°35' N, 95°13' E 188
Bayan Har Shankou, pass, China 34°10' N, 97°41' E 188
Bayan Huxu see Horqin Youyi Zhongqi, China 45°5' N, 121°25' E 198
Bayan Mod, China 40°45' N, 104°31' E 198
Bayan Obo, China 41°46' N, 109°58' E 198
Bayan Ovoo, Mongolia 47°49' N, 112°4' E 198
Bayan Uul, Mongolia 49°5' N, 112°45' E 198
Bayana, India 26°53' N, 77°14' E 197
Bayanaūyl, Kaz. 50°45' N, 75°42' E 184
Bayanhongor, Mongolia 46°37' N, 100°8' E 190
Bayano, Lago, lake, Pan. 9°0' N, 79°0' W 116
Bayan-Ölgiy, adm. division, Mongolia 48°37' N, 89°55' E 184
Bayan-Ovoo, Mongolia 48°57' N, 111°25' E 198
Bayard, Nebr., U.S. 41°45' N, 103°21' W 92
Bayard, N. Mex., U.S. 32°44' N, 108°8' W 92
Bayasgalant, Mongolia 46°57' N, 112°2' E 198
Bayat, Turk. 38°58' N, 30°55' E 156
Bayawan, Philippines 9°23' N, 122°48' E 203
Baybay, Philippines 10°40' N, 124°50' E 203
Bayboro, N.C., U.S. 35°9' N, 76°47' W 96
Bayburt, Turk. 40°16' N, 40°14' E 195
Baydhabo (Baidoa), Somalia 3°5' N, 43°41' E 218
Bayerischer Wald, Ger. 48°59' N, 12°19' E 152
Bayfield, Can. 43°32' N, 81°41' W 102
Bayfield, Wis., U.S. 46°49' N, 90°50' W 94
Bayghanīn, Kaz. 48°42' N, 55°53' E 158
Bayḩan al Qişāb, Yemen 14°49' N, 45°46' E 182
Baykal, Ozero, lake, Russ. 53°48' N, 103°44' E 190
Baykalovo, Russ. 57°26' N, 63°42' E 154
Baykalovo, Russ. 57°45' N, 67°40' E 169
Baykan, Turk. 38°8' N, 41°47' E 195
Baykonur see Bayqongyr, Kaz. 47°47' N, 66°0' E 184
Baykurt, China 39°56' N, 75°32' E 184
Bayliss, Mount, Antarctica 73°30' S, 62°4' E 248
Baymak, Russ. 52°38' N, 58°11' E 154
Baynū, Leb. 34°32' N, 36°10' E 194
Bayombong, Philippines 16°29' N, 121°8' E 203
Bayon, Fr. 48°28' N, 6°19' E 163
Bayonet Point, Fla., U.S. 28°19' N, 82°43' W 105
Bayonne, Fr. 43°29' N, 1°30' W 164
Bayonne, N.J., U.S. 40°40' N, 74°8' W 104
Bayou La Batre, Ala., U.S. 30°23' N, 88°16' W 103
Bayou Macon, river, La., U.S. 32°6' N, 91°32' W 103
Bayovar, Peru 5°47' S, 81°4' W 130
Bayport, Minn., U.S. 45°0' N, 92°48' W 94
Bayqongyr (Leninsk, Baykonur), Kaz. 47°47' N, 66°0' E 184
Bayqongyr, adm. division, Kaz. 46°3' N, 62°27' E 184
Bayramaly, Turkm. 37°36' N, 62°10' E 184
Bayramiç, Turk. 39°48' N, 26°35' E 156
Bayreuth, Ger. 49°56' N, 11°34' E 152
Bays, Lake of, Can. 45°15' N, 79°35' W 94
Bayshint, Mongolia 49°40' N, 90°20' E 184
Bayshonas, Kaz. 47°18' N, 53°0' E 158
Bayt al Faqīh, Yemen 14°29' N, 43°16' E 182
Bayt Lahiyah, Gaza Strip, Israel 31°33' N, 34°30' E 194
Bayt La'm (Bethlehem), West Bank, Israel 31°41' N, 35°12' E 194
Baytīn, West Bank, Israel 31°55' N, 35°14' E 194
Baytown, Tex., U.S. 29°43' N, 94°58' W 103
Bayville, N.Y., U.S. 40°54' N, 73°34' W 104
Bayyrqum, Kaz. 41°54' N, 68°5' E 184
Bayzo, Niger 13°52' N, 4°45' E 222
Baza, Sp. 37°29' N, 2°48' W 164
Baza'i Gonbad, Afghan. 37°13' N, 74°5' E 186
Bazar-Kurgan, Kyrg. 41°1' N, 72°46' E 197
Bazarnyy Karabulak, Russ. 52°15' N, 46°27' E 158
Bazarsholan, Kaz. 48°58' N, 51°55' E 158
Bazartöbe, Kaz. 49°23' N, 51°53' E 158
Bazaruto, Ilha do, island, Mozambique 21°44' S, 34°29' E 227
Bazber, Eth. 10°36' N, 35°7' E 224
Bazhong, China 31°53' N, 106°39' E 198
Baziaş, Rom. 44°48' N, 21°22' E 168
Bazin, river, Can. 47°29' N, 75°0' W 94
Bazkovskaya, Russ. 49°33' N, 41°35' E 158
Bazmān, Kūh-e, peak, Iran 27°51' N, 60°2' E 182
Bazzano, It. 44°30' N, 11°4' E 167
Bcharre, Leb. 34°14' N, 36°0' E 194
Be, Nosy, island, Madagascar 13°24' S, 47°23' E 220
Beach, N. Dak., U.S. 46°53' N, 104°1' W 90
Beach Haven, N.J., U.S. 39°33' N, 74°16' W 94
Beacon, N.Y., U.S. 41°29' N, 73°59' W 104
Beaconsfield, U.K. 51°36' N, 0°39' E 162
Beade, Sp. 42°19' N, 8°10' W 150
Beale Air Force Base, Calif., U.S. 39°8' N, 121°30' W 90
Beale, Cape, Can. 48°37' N, 125°31' W 90
Beaminster, U.K. 50°48' N, 2°44' W 162
Beampingaratra, peak, Madagascar 24°36' S, 46°39' E 220
Bear Bay 75°23' N, 88°10' W 106
Bear Creek, river, Colo., U.S. 37°26' N, 102°48' W 80
Bear Island see Bjørnøya, Nor. 73°46' N, 15°27' E 160
Bear Islands see Medvezh'i Ostrova, islands, East Siberian Sea 71°5' N, 151°1' E 160
Bear Lake, Can. 55°2' N, 96°49' W 108
Bear Lake, Can. 56°6' N, 127°4' W 108
Bear Lake, Mich., U.S. 44°24' N, 86°9' W 94
Bear Lodge Mountains, Wyo., U.S. 44°39' N, 104°42' W 90
Bear Peninsula, Antarctica 74°18' S, 106°40' W 248
Bear River, Utah, U.S. 41°37' N, 112°8' W 90
Bear, river, Idaho, U.S. 42°27' N, 111°48' W 90
Bear River Range, Utah, U.S. 41°18' N, 111°34' W 90
Beardmore, Can. 49°37' N, 87°57' W 94
Beardstown, Mo., U.S. 40°0' N, 90°25' W 94
Béarn, region, Europe 42°57' N, 0°52' E 164
Bears Paw Mountains, Mont., U.S. 48°18' N, 109°52' W 90
Beas, Sp. 37°25' N, 6°48' W 164
Beas de Segura, Sp. 38°14' N, 2°52' W 164
Beasain, Sp. 43°2' N, 2°13' W 164
Beata, Cabo, Dom. Rep. 17°30' N, 71°22' W 116
Beata, Isla, island, Dom. Rep. 17°16' N, 71°33' W 116
Beatrice, Nebr., U.S. 40°15' N, 96°45' W 90
Beatton River, Can. 57°22' N, 121°27' W 108
Beatton, river, Can. 57°18' N, 121°27' W 108
Beatty, Nev., U.S. 36°54' N, 116°47' W 101
Beattyville, Can. 48°51' N, 77°10' W 94
Beatys Butte, peak, Oreg., U.S. 42°23' N, 119°25' W 90
Beaucamps, Fr. 49°49' N, 1°47' E 163
Beauceville, Can. 46°13' N, 70°46' W 111
Beauchêne Island, U.K. 52°56' S, 61°53' W 134
Beaufort, Malaysia 5°22' N, 115°46' E 203
Beaufort, S.C., U.S. 32°24' N, 80°53' W 112
Beaufort Marine Corps Air Station, S.C., U.S. 32°29' N, 80°48' W 96
Beaufort Sea 69°54' N, 141°54' W 106
Beaufort Sea 72°45' N, 137°20' W 255
Beaufort see Belfort, ruin(s), Leb. 33°19' N, 35°30' E 194
Beaufort Shelf, Beaufort Sea 70°4' N, 142°6' W 255
Beaufort Slope, Beaufort Sea 70°37' N, 141°34' W 255
Beaufort West, S. Af. 32°21' S, 22°35' E 227
Beaugency, Fr. 47°47' N, 1°37' E 150
Beaumaris, U.K. 53°15' N, 4°5' W 162
Beaumetz-lès-Loges, Fr. 50°13' N, 2°38' E 163
Beaumont, Belg. 50°14' N, 4°14' E 163
Beaumont, Calif., U.S. 33°56' N, 116°59' W 101
Beaumont, Fr. 49°8' N, 2°16' E 163
Beaumont, Miss., U.S. 31°8' N, 88°54' W 103
Beaumont, Tex., U.S. 30°4' N, 94°7' W 103
Beaumont-le-Roger, Fr. 49°5' N, 0°47' E 163
Beaupré, Can. 47°2' N, 70°54' W 94
Beauraing, Belg. 50°6' N, 4°56' E 167
Beauregard, Miss., U.S. 31°43' N, 90°24' W 103
Beausejour, Can. 50°3' N, 96°31' W 108
Beauvais, Fr. 49°26' N, 2°5' E 163
Beauval, Can. 55°9' N, 107°39' W 108
Beauval, Fr. 50°5' N, 2°20' E 163
Beauvezer, Fr. 44°8' N, 6°34' E 167
Beaver, Alas., U.S. 66°14' N, 147°28' W 98
Beaver, Ohio, U.S. 39°1' N, 82°49' W 102
Beaver, Okla., U.S. 36°47' N, 100°32' W 96
Beaver, Oreg., U.S. 45°16' N, 123°50' W 90
Beaver, Pa., U.S. 40°41' N, 80°19' W 94
Beaver, Utah, U.S. 38°16' N, 112°38' W 90
Beaver, Wash., U.S. 48°2' N, 124°20' W 100
Beaver Bay, Minn., U.S. 47°14' N, 91°20' W 94
Beaver City, Nebr., U.S. 40°7' N, 99°50' W 90
Beaver Creek, Can. 62°24' N, 140°52' W 98
Beaver Dam, Ky., U.S. 37°24' N, 86°53' W 96
Beaver Dam, Wis., U.S. 43°27' N, 88°50' W 102
Beaver Falls, Pa., U.S. 40°44' N, 80°20' W 94
Beaver Hill Lake, Can. 54°14' N, 95°24' W 108
Beaver Island, Mich., U.S. 45°20' N, 85°49' W 81
Beaver Lake, N. Dak., U.S. 46°20' N, 100°7' W 90
Beaver, river, Can. 60°29' N, 126°29' W 108
Beaver, river, Can. 54°40' N, 112°3' W 108
Beaver, river, Can. 53°43' N, 61°38' W 111
Beaverdell, Can. 49°25' N, 119°4' W 90
Beaverhead Mountains, Mont., U.S. 45°36' N, 113°50' W 90
Beaverlodge, Can. 55°12' N, 119°27' W 108
Beaverton, Can. 44°25' N, 79°9' W 94
Beaverton, Mich., U.S. 43°51' N, 84°30' W 102
Beawar, India 26°4' N, 74°18' E 186
Bebedouro, Braz. 20°57' S, 48°30' W 138
Bebeji, Nig. 11°39' N, 8°16' E 222
Bebington, U.K. 53°22' N, 3°0' W 162
Béboto, Chad 8°17' N, 16°55' E 218
Bebra, Ger. 50°58' N, 9°46' E 167
Becán, ruin(s), Mex. 18°33' N, 89°39' W 115
Bécancour, Can. 46°21' N, 72°25' W 94
Beccles, U.K. 52°26' N, 1°33' E 163
Bečej, Serb. 45°37' N, 20°2' E 168
Béchar, Alg. 31°39' N, 2°13' W 214
Becharof Lake, Alas., U.S. 58°4' N, 159°33' W 106
Bechater, Tun. 37°18' N, 9°45' E 156
Bechem, Ghana 7°7' N, 2°3' W 222
Bechetu, Rom. 43°46' N, 23°57' E 156
Becker, Mount, Antarctica 75°9' S, 72°53' W 248
Becket, Mass., U.S. 42°19' N, 73°6' W 104
Beckley, W. Va., U.S. 37°46' N, 81°12' W 94
Beckum, Ger. 51°45' N, 8°1' E 167
Beckville, Tex., U.S. 32°14' N, 94°28' W 103
Beckwourth Pass, Calif., U.S. 39°47' N, 120°8' W 90
Beda, oil field, Lib. 28°14' N, 18°44' E 216
Bedale, U.K. 54°17' N, 1°36' W 162
Beddgelert, U.K. 53°0' N, 4°6' W 162
Beddouza, Cap, Mor. 32°37' N, 10°38' W 214
Bedēsa, Eth. 8°51' N, 40°45' E 224
Bedford, Can. 44°43' N, 63°41' W 111
Bedford, Ind., U.S. 38°52' N, 86°29' W 102
Bedford, Iowa, U.S. 40°39' N, 94°43' W 94
Bedford, N.H., U.S. 42°56' N, 71°32' W 104
Bedford, Pa., U.S. 40°0' N, 78°31' W 94
Bedford, S. Af. 32°41' S, 26°4' E 227
Bedford, U.K. 52°8' N, 0°28' E 162
Bedi, India 22°32' N, 70°0' E 186
Bednesti, Can. 53°51' N, 123°8' W 108
Bednodem'yanovsk, Russ. 53°53' N, 43°10' E 154
Bedonia, It. 44°30' N, 9°38' E 167
Bédouaram, Niger 15°44' N, 13°8' E 216
Bedous, Fr. 43°0' N, 0°36' E 164
Bee Ridge, Fla., U.S. 27°18' N, 82°27' W 105
Beebe, Ark., U.S. 35°3' N, 91°53' W 96
Beebe River, N.H., U.S. 43°49' N, 71°40' W 104
Beech Grove, Ind., U.S. 39°43' N, 86°5' W 102
Beecher City, Ill., U.S. 39°10' N, 88°47' W 102
Beechy, Can. 50°53' N, 107°25' W 90
Beer, Somalia 9°21' N, 45°48' E 216
Be'ér 'Ada, spring, Israel 30°19' N, 34°54' E 194
Be'ér Ḥafir, spring, Israel 30°43' N, 34°35' E 194
Be'ér Sheva, Israel 31°13' N, 34°50' E 180
Be'ér Sheva' (Beersheba), Israel 31°14' N, 34°47' E 194
Beerberg, Grosser, peak, Ger. 50°38' N, 10°38' E 152
Beersheba see Be'Żer Sheva', Israel 31°14' N, 34°47' E 194
Beestekraal, S. Af. 25°24' S, 27°35' E 227
Beeston, U.K. 52°55' N, 1°14' W 162
Beetz, Lac, lake, Can. 50°30' N, 63°11' W 111
Beeville, Tex., U.S. 28°23' N, 97°45' W 92
Befale, Dem. Rep. of the Congo 0°26' N, 20°58' E 218
Befandriana, Madagascar 15°15' S, 48°35' E 220
Befandriana Atsimo, Madagascar 22°7' S, 43°51' E 220
Befori, Dem. Rep. of the Congo 0°9' N, 22°17' E 218
Befotaka, Madagascar 23°48' S, 47°1' E 220
Bega, river, Rom. 45°51' N, 21°56' E 168
Begaly, Kaz. 49°55' N, 55°17' E 158
Begejski Kanal, canal, Serb. 45°31' N, 20°28' E 168
Bēgī, Eth. 9°20' N, 34°32' E 224
Begonte, Sp. 43°8' N, 7°42' W 150
Béguégué, Chad 8°53' N, 18°52' E 218
Begunitsy, Russ. 59°33' N, 29°16' E 152
Behagle see Laï, Chad 9°23' N, 16°20' E 216
Béhague, Pointe, Fr. 4°43' N, 51°56' W 130
Behan, Can. 55°14' N, 111°28' W 108
Behara, Madagascar 24°57' S, 46°25' E 220
Behbehān, Iran 30°34' N, 50°15' E 180
Behm Canal 55°45' N, 132°3' W 108
Beho, Belg. 50°14' N, 5°58' E 167
Behring Point, Bahamas 24°30' N, 77°46' W 96
Behshahr, Iran 36°43' N, 53°33' E 180
Bei'an, China 48°16' N, 126°32' E 198
Beiarn, Nor. 67°0' N, 14°35' E 152
Beida, river, China 39°9' N, 97°39' E 188
Beigang, China 42°23' N, 127°28' E 200
Beihai, China 21°26' N, 109°8' E 198
Beijing, adm. division, China 40°32' N, 116°8' E 198
Beijing (Peking), China 39°52' N, 116°9' E 198
Beila, Jebel, peak, Sudan 13°41' N, 34°46' E 182
Beilen, Neth. 52°51' N, 6°31' E 163
Beiliu, China 22°42' N, 110°19' E 198
Beilrode, Ger. 51°33' N, 13°4' E 152
Beilu, river, China 34°47' N, 93°23' E 188
Beilul, Eritrea 13°9' N, 42°22' E 182
Beinn Bhreagh, site, Can. 46°4' N, 60°48' W 111
Beipiao, China 41°52' N, 120°47' E 198
Beira, Mozambique 19°50' S, 34°53' E 224
Beirut see Beyrouth, Leb. 33°53' N, 35°26' E 194
Beitbridge, Zimb. 22°10' S, 29°58' E 227
Beitun, China 47°19' N, 87°48' E 184
Beiuş, Rom. 46°40' N, 22°23' E 168
Beizhen, China 41°37' N, 121°50' E 198
Beja, Port. 38°1' N, 7°52' W 150
Beja, Tun. 36°43' N, 9°11' E 156
Beja, adm. division, Port. 37°41' N, 8°36' W 150
Bejaïa (Bougie), Alg. 36°46' N, 5°2' E 150
Béjar, Sp. 40°23' N, 5°47' W 150
Bek, river, Cameroon 3°1' N, 14°23' E 218
Bekaa Valley see Al Biqā', region, Leb. 33°43' N, 35°51' E 194
Bekaie, Dem. Rep. of the Congo 2°29' S, 18°17' E 218
Bekdash see Karabogaz, Turkm. 41°32' N, 52°35' E 158
Békés, Hung. 46°46' N, 21°8' E 168
Békés, adm. division, Hung. 46°50' N, 20°45' E 156
Békéscsaba, Hung. 46°40' N, 21°5' E 168
Bekily, Madagascar 24°11' S, 45°17' E 220
Bekobod, Uzb. 40°12' N, 69°15' E 197
Bekodoka, Madagascar 17°1' S, 45°7' E 220
Bekoropoka-Antongo, Madagascar 21°27' S, 43°32' E 220
Bekwai, Ghana 6°29' N, 1°34' W 222
Bela, India 25°53' N, 81°58' E 197
Bela, Pak. 26°14' N, 66°20' E 186
Bela Crkva, Serb. 44°53' N, 21°26' E 168
Bela Vista, Mozambique 26°18' S, 32°40' E 227
Bela Vista de GoiŽas, Braz. 17°1' S, 48°59' W 138
Bela-Bela (Warmbaths), S. Af. 24°55' S, 28°16' E 227
Bélabo, Cameroon 4°49' N, 13°16' E 218
Belalcázar, Sp. 38°34' N, 5°10' W 164
Belanger, river, Can. 53°14' N, 97°28' W 108
Belarus 53°57' N, 27°35' E 154
Belasica, Gr. 41°23' N, 23°1' E 168
Belawan, Indonesia 3°46' N, 98°42' E 196
Belaya Glina, Russ. 46°5' N, 40°52' E 158
Belaya Gora, Russ. 68°8' N, 146°6' E 160
Belaya Kalitva, Russ. 48°10' N, 40°50' E 158
Belaya Kholunitsa, Russ. 58°50' N, 50°52' E 154
Belaya, peak, Eth. 11°23' N, 36°4' E 182
Belaya, river, Russ. 52°52' N, 56°57' E 154
Belcaire, Fr. 42°48' N, 1°56' E 164
Belcher, La., U.S. 32°44' N, 93°51' W 103
Belcher Channel 76°55' N, 100°16' W 106
Belcher Islands, Hudson Bay 56°1' N, 80°5' W 106
Belcheragh, Afghan. 35°46' N, 65°13' E 186
Belchertown, Mass., U.S. 42°16' N, 72°25' W 104
Belchite, Sp. 41°17' N, 0°46' E 164
Belding, Mich., U.S. 43°6' N, 85°14' W 102
Belebey, Russ. 54°6' N, 54°12' E 154
Belecke, Ger. 51°28' N, 8°20' E 167
Beled, Hung. 47°27' N, 17°5' E 168
Beledweyne, Somalia 4°43' N, 45°10' E 218
Belej, Croatia 44°47' N, 14°24' E 156
Belém, Braz. 1°24' S, 48°28' W 130
Belén, Arg. 27°39' S, 67°3' W 134
Belén, Chile 18°30' S, 69°34' W 137
Belén, Col. 1°25' N, 75°57' W 136
Belen, N. Mex., U.S. 34°39' N, 106°46' W 92
Belén, Parag. 23°29' S, 57°18' W 132
Belén, Uru. 30°49' S, 57°45' W 139
Beles, river, Eth. 11°1' N, 36°15' E 182
Bélesta, Fr. 42°54' N, 1°54' E 164
Belev, Russ. 53°47' N, 36°5' E 154
Beleza, river, Braz. 10°11' S, 51°13' W 132
Belfair, Wash., U.S. 47°26' N, 122°49' W 100
Belfast, Me., U.S. 44°25' N, 69°2' W 94
Belfast, N.Z. 43°28' S, 172°36' E 240
Belfast, S. Af. 25°42' S, 30°2' E 227
Belfast, U.K. 54°34' N, 6°5' W 150
Belfield, N. Dak., U.S. 46°52' N, 103°13' W 90
Bēlfodiyo, Eth. 10°29' N, 34°48' E 224
Belford, U.K. 55°35' N, 1°50' W 150
Belfort, Fr. 47°38' N, 6°50' E 150
Belfort (Beaufort), ruin(s), Leb. 33°19' N, 35°30' E 194
Belgaum, India 15°49' N, 74°31' E 188
Belgica Bank, Greenland Sea 78°11' N, 13°45' W 255
Belgioioso, It. 45°9' N, 9°19' E 167
Belgium 50°41' N, 4°16' E 163
Belgorod, Russ. 50°37' N, 36°32' E 158
Belgorod, adm. division, Russ. 50°59' N, 36°52' E 158
Belgrade, Me., U.S. 44°26' N, 69°51' W 104
Belgrade, Mont., U.S. 45°45' N, 111°11' W 90
Belgrade see Beograd, Serb. 44°47' N, 20°24' E 168
Belgrano II, station, Antarctica 77°55' S, 34°4' W 248
Belhaven, N.C., U.S. 35°33' N, 76°38' W 96
Belhedan, oil field, Lib. 27°53' N, 19°10' E 216
Beli, Nig. 7°49' N, 10°58' E 222
Beli Manastir, Croatia 45°44' N, 18°36' E 168
Beli Potok, Serb. 43°30' N, 22°4' E 168
Belica, Alban. 41°14' N, 20°23' E 156
Belica, Croatia 46°25' N, 16°31' E 168
Belidzhi, Russ. 41°50' N, 48°28' E 195
Beliliou see Peleliu, island, Palau 7°0' N, 134°15' E 242
Belinskiy, Russ. 52°57' N, 43°23' E 154
Beliş, Rom. 46°39' N, 23°2' E 168
Belitung (Billiton), island, Indonesia 3°41' S, 107°3' E 192
Beliu, Rom. 46°29' N, 21°59' E 168
Belize 16°58' N, 89°1' W 115
Belize City, Belize 17°30' N, 88°13' W 115
Beljanica, Serb. 44°10' N, 21°30' E 168
Bel'kovskiy, Ostrov, island, Russ. 75°28' N, 126°33' E 160
Bell Lake, lake, Can. 49°47' N, 91°13' W 94
Bell Peninsula, Can. 63°28' N, 84°36' W 106
Bell, river, Can. 49°40' N, 77°37' W 94
Bell Rock, Can. 60°0' N, 112°5' W 108
Bell Ville, Arg. 32°40' S, 62°38' W 139
Bella Bella, Can. 52°8' N, 128°3' W 108
Bella Flor, Bol. 11°8' S, 67°49' W 137
Bella Unión, Uru. 30°17' S, 57°37' W 139
Bella Vista, Arg. 28°31' S, 59°2' W 132
Bella Vista, Braz. 22°8' S, 56°24' W 132
Bellac, Fr. 46°6' N, 1°3' E 150
Bellagio, It. 45°58' N, 9°14' E 167
Bellaire, Mich., U.S. 44°58' N, 85°12' W 94
Bellaire, Tex., U.S. 29°41' N, 95°29' W 96
Bellamy, Ala., U.S. 32°26' N, 88°9' W 103
Bellary, India 15°8' N, 76°53' E 188
Bellavista, Peru 5°33' S, 78°43' W 130
Bellavista, Peru 1°35' S, 75°33' W 136
Belle Fourche, S. Dak., U.S. 44°38' N, 103°52' W 82
Belle Fourche, river, Wyo., U.S. 43°45' N, 105°45' W 80
Belle Glade, Fla., U.S. 26°40' N, 80°41' W 105
Belle Isle, island, Can. 52°4' N, 55°26' W 106
Belle Isle, Strait of 51°28' N, 56°49' W 111
Belle Plaine, Iowa, U.S. 41°53' N, 92°17' W 94
Belle Plaine, Minn., U.S. 44°36' N, 93°46' W 94
Belle Yella, Liberia 7°13' N, 10°2' W 222
Belledonne, Chaîne de, Fr. 45°10' N, 5°50' E 165
Bellefontaine, Ohio, U.S. 40°21' N, 83°45' W 102
Bellefonte, Pa., U.S. 40°53' N, 77°47' W 94
Bellenden Ker National Park, Austral. 17°25' S, 145°31' E 238
Belleoram, Can. 47°30' N, 55°25' W 111
Belleview, Fla., U.S. 29°3' N, 82°3' W 105
Belleville, Can. 44°9' N, 77°22' W 94
Belleville, Fr. 46°5' N, 4°43' E 150
Belleville, Ill., U.S. 38°30' N, 89°58' W 102
Belleville, Kans., U.S. 39°48' N, 97°38' W 90
Belleville, Mo., U.S. 38°30' N, 89°58' W 94
Belleville, Wis., U.S. 42°50' N, 89°32' W 102
Bellevue, Congo 2°5' N, 13°51' E 218
Bellevue, Idaho, U.S. 43°28' N, 114°16' W 90
Bellevue, Iowa, U.S. 42°15' N, 90°26' W 94
Bellevue, Mich., U.S. 42°27' N, 85°1' W 102
Bellevue, Nebr., U.S. 41°8' N, 95°54' W 90
Bellevue, Ohio, U.S. 41°16' N, 82°50' W 102
Bellevue, Tex., U.S. 33°36' N, 98°1' W 96
Bellevue, Wash., U.S. 47°35' N, 122°13' W 100
Bellflower, Ill., U.S. 40°19' N, 88°32' W 102
Bellinger, Lac, lake, Can. 51°10' N, 75°0' W 110
Bellingham, Wash., U.S. 48°46' N, 122°29' W 100
Bellingrath Gardens, site, Ala., U.S. 30°24' N, 88°11' W 103
Bellingshausen Plain, South Pacific Ocean 65°21' S, 112°43' W 255
Bellingshausen Sea 70°32' S, 88°38' W 248
Bellingshausen, station, Antarctica 62°17' S, 58°44' W 248
Bellinzona, Switz. 46°11' N, 9°1' E 167
Bellmore, Ind., U.S. 39°45' N, 87°6' W 102
Bello, Col. 6°20' N, 75°35' W 136
Bello Islands, Monte, Indian Ocean 20°10' S, 113°11' E 230
Bellona Island, Solomon Islands 11°0' S, 160°0' E 242
Bellows Falls, Vt., U.S. 43°7' N, 72°28' W 104
Bellpat, Pak. 29°1' N, 68°5' E 186
Belluno, It. 46°8' N, 12°12' E 167
Bellville, Ohio, U.S. 40°36' N, 82°31' W 102
Bellville, Tex., U.S. 29°55' N, 96°16' W 96
Bellvís, Sp. 41°39' N, 0°49' E 164
Bellwood, La., U.S. 31°29' N, 93°12' W 103
Belmar, N.J., U.S. 40°10' N, 74°2' W 94
BŽelmez, Sp. 38°15' N, 5°12' W 164
Belmond, Iowa, U.S. 42°49' N, 93°36' W 94
Belmont, N.H., U.S. 43°26' N, 71°29' W 104
Belmont, S. Af. 29°27' S, 24°20' E 227
Belmont, Vt., U.S. 43°24' N, 72°50' W 104
Belmonte, Braz. 15°56' S, 38°56' W 132
Belmonte, Sp. 39°33' N, 2°43' W 150
Belmopan, Belize 17°10' N, 88°56' W 115
Belo, Madagascar 20°48' S, 44°1' E 220
Belo Horizonte, Braz. 19°55' S, 43°55' W 138
Belo Horizonte, Braz. 5°18' S, 52°50' W 130
Beloci, Mold. 47°52' N, 28°56' E 156
Belogorsk, Russ. 51°2' N, 128°27' E 190
Belogorsk, Russ. 54°59' N, 88°33' E 169
Belogorskiy, Kaz. 49°26' N, 83°9' E 184
Beloha, Madagascar 25°9' S, 45°2' E 220
Beloit, Kans., U.S. 39°27' N, 98°7' W 90
Beloit, Wis., U.S. 42°31' N, 89°2' W 102
Beloljin, Serb. 43°13' N, 21°23' E 168
Belomorsk, Russ. 64°28' N, 34°38' E 154
Belonia, India 23°12' N, 91°28' E 197
Belorado, Sp. 42°24' N, 3°12' W 164
Belorechensk, Russ. 44°46' N, 39°52' E 158
Beloretsk, Russ. 53°58' N, 58°23' E 154
Beloshchel'ye, Russ. 64°56' N, 46°48' E 154
Belot'i, Ga. 42°17' N, 44°7' E 195
Belo-Tsiribihina, Madagascar 19°41' S, 44°31' E 220
Belovo, Russ. 54°22' N, 86°22' E 184
Beloyarskiy, Russ. 63°42' N, 66°58' E 169
Beloye More (White Sea) 63°17' N, 35°24' E 160
Beloye Ozero, lake, Russ. 59°33' N, 37°43' E 154
Belozersk, Russ. 59°57' N, 37°50' E 154
Belpre, Ohio, U.S. 39°16' N, 81°35' W 102
Belt, Mont., U.S. 47°22' N, 110°56' W 90
Belterra, Braz. 2°38' S, 54°59' W 130
Belton, S.C., U.S. 34°30' N, 82°31' W 96
Belton, Tex., U.S. 31°2' N, 97°27' W 92
Belukha, Gora, peak, Russ. 49°46' N, 86°31' E 184
Belush'ya Guba, Russ. 71°28' N, 52°29' E 160
Belush'ye, Russ. 66°52' N, 47°37' E 154
Belušić, Serb. 43°47' N, 21°8' E 168
Belvidere, Ill., U.S. 42°14' N, 88°51' W 102
Belvidere, S. Dak., U.S. 43°49' N, 101°17' W 90
Belvidere Mountain, Vt., U.S. 44°45' N, 72°39' W 94
Belvoir, U.K. 52°53' N, 0°48' E 162
Belyayevka, Russ. 51°23' N, 56°23' E 158
Belyy, Russ. 55°48' N, 33°1' E 154
Belyy, Ostrov, island, Russ. 73°28' N, 65°53' E 160
Belyy, Ostrov, island, Russ. 73°26' N, 70°30' E 160
Belyy Yar, Russ. 58°25' N, 85°8' E 169
Belz, Ukr. 50°23' N, 24°1' E 152
Belzoni, Miss., U.S. 33°9' N, 90°31' W 103
Bemaraha, Madagascar 20°44' S, 44°42' E 220
Bembe, Angola 7°2' S, 14°18' E 218
Bembéréké, Benin 10°12' N, 2°40' E 222
Bement, Ill., U.S. 39°54' N, 88°34' W 102
Bemetara, India 21°44' N, 81°31' E 188
Bemidji, Minn., U.S. 47°28' N, 94°55' W 90
Bemis, Tenn., U.S. 35°33' N, 88°49' W 96
Ben Gardane, Tun. 33°9' N, 11°12' E 214
Ben Lomond, Calif., U.S. 37°5' N, 122°6' W 100
Ben S'Rour, Alg. 35°3' N, 4°34' E 150
Ben Zohra, spring, Alg. 28°37' N, 3°50' W 214
Bena Dibele, Dem. Rep. of the Congo 4°8' S, 22°48' E 218
Bena Makima, Dem. Rep. of the Congo 5°2' S, 21°7' E 218
Benabarre, Sp. 42°6' N, 0°28' E 164
Benalup, Sp. 36°21' N, 5°50' W 164
Benamaurel, Sp. 37°35' N, 2°41' W 164
Benamejí, Sp. 37°16' N, 4°33' W 164
Benasque, Sp. 42°35' N, 0°32' E 164
Bénat, Cap, Fr. 43°1' N, 6°11' E 165
Benavente, Sp. 42°0' N, 5°43' W 150
Benavides, Tex., U.S. 27°35' N, 98°24' W 92
Benbow, Calif., U.S. 40°3' N, 123°47' W 90
Benbulbin, peak, Ire. 54°20' N, 8°36' W 150
Bende, Nig. 5°35' N, 7°38' E 222
Bender, Mold. 46°48' N, 29°28' E 156
Bendorf, Ger. 50°25' N, 7°34' E 167
Bēne, Latv. 56°28' N, 23°1' E 166
Bené Beraq, Israel 32°5' N, 34°50' E 194
Benedito Leite, Braz. 7°13' S, 44°36' W 132
Bénéna, Mali 13°7' N, 4°24' W 222
Benenitra, Madagascar 23°24' S, 45°3' E 220
Beneraird, peak, U.K. 55°3' N, 5°2' W 150
Bénestroff, Fr. 48°54' N, 6°45' E 163
Benfeld, Fr. 48°22' N, 7°34' E 163
Bengal, adm. division, India 21°51' N, 88°25' E 197
Bengal, Bay of 13°12' N, 85°28' E 188
Bengaluru see Bangalore, India 12°59' N, 77°35' E 188
Bengbu, China 32°53' N, 117°21' E 198
Benghazi see Banghāzī, Lib. 32°6' N, 20°4' E 216
Bengkalis, Indonesia 1°30' N, 102°7' E 196
Bengkalis, island, Indonesia 1°38' N, 102°5' E 196
Bengkayang, Indonesia 0°51' N, 109°27' E 196
Bengkulu, Indonesia 3°49' S, 102°18' E 192
Bengo, adm. division, Angola 8°8' S, 13°15' E 220
Bengough, Can. 49°23' N, 105°8' W 90
Benguela, Angola 12°38' S, 13°23' E 220
Benguela, adm. division, Angola 13°17' S, 12°57' E 220
Benguérua, Ilha, island, Mozambique 22°11' S, 34°56' E 227
Benha, Egypt 30°25' N, 31°12' E 180

Beni, Dem. Rep. of the Congo 0°24' N, 29°26' E 224
Beni Abbes, Alg. 30°8' N, 2°10' W 214
Beni, adm. division, Bol. 13°40' S, 65°45' W 137
Beni Mazâr, Egypt 28°27' N, 30°46' E 180
Beni Mellal, Mor. 32°24' N, 6°22' W 214
Beni, river, Bol. 12°25' S, 66°55' W 137
Beni Saf, Alg. 35°17' N, 1°23' W 150
Beni Suef, Egypt 29°4' N, 31°3' E 180
Beni Tajit, Mor. 32°21' N, 3°28' W 214
Benicarló, Sp. 40°24' N, 0°25' E 164
Benicasim, Sp. 40°3' N, 7°416' E 164
Benicia, Calif., U.S. 38°3' N, 122°10' W 100
Benidorm, Sp. 38°31' N, 0°8' E 164
Benifaió, Sp. 39°16' N, 0°26' E 164
Benin 10°4' N, 1°52' E 214
Benin, Bight of 4°25' N, 1°49' E 222
Benin City, Nig. 6°23' N, 5°38' E 222
Benissa, Sp. 38°42' N, 5°297' E 164
Benito, Can. 51°54' N, 101°33' W 108
Benito Juárez, Mex. 32°34' N, 115°0' W 101
Benito Juárez, Mex. 17°49' N, 92°33' W 115
Benito Juárez National Park see 2, Mex. 17°15' N, 96°46' W 112
Benjamin, Tex., U.S. 33°34' N, 99°48' W 92
Benjamin Constant, Braz. 4°25' S, 70°4' W 132
Benjamín Hill, Mex. 30°11' N, 111°8' W 92
Benkelman, Nebr., U.S. 40°3' N, 101°33' W 90
Benld, Ill., U.S. 39°5' N, 89°49' W 102
Bennane Head, U.K. 55°10' N, 5°15' W 150
Bennett, Can. 59°51' N, 134°56' W 108
Bennett Island, Russ. 77°0' N, 149°0' E 255
Bennett Lake, lake, Can. 53°23' N, 96°35' W 108
Benneydale, N.Z. 38°31' S, 175°20' E 240
Bennington, N.H., U.S. 43°0' N, 71°56' W 104
Bennington, Vt., U.S. 42°52' N, 73°12' W 104
Bénnsané, Guinea 11°26' N, 14°1' W 222
Benom, peak, Malaysia 3°50' N, 102°0' E 196
Benoud, Alg. 32°20' N, 0°15' E 214
Benoy, Chad 8°57' N, 16°20' E 216
Bensberg, Ger. 50°58' N, 7°8' E 167
Benson, Ariz., U.S. 31°57' N, 110°20' W 112
Benson, Minn., U.S. 45°18' N, 95°37' W 90
Benson, N.C., U.S. 35°22' N, 78°34' W 96
Benson, Vt., U.S. 43°42' N, 73°19' W 104
Bent Jbail, Leb. 33°7' N, 35°25' E 194
Benta, Malaysia 4°1' N, 101°58' E 196
Bentiaba, Angola 14°18' S, 12°22' E 220
Bentinck Island, Austral. 17°25' S, 137°54' E 230
Bentinck, island, Myanmar 11°30' N, 97°26' E 202
Bentinck Point, Can. 46°26' N, 61°17' W 111
Bentiu, Sudan 9°9' N, 29°47' E 224
Bentley, Mich., U.S. 43°56' N, 84°9' W 102
Bento Gonçalves, Braz. 29°10' S, 51°30' W 139
Benton, Ark., U.S. 34°32' N, 92°36' W 96
Benton, Ky., U.S. 36°51' N, 88°21' W 94
Benton, La., U.S. 32°40' N, 93°45' W 103
Benton, Me., U.S. 44°34' N, 69°34' W 94
Benton, Miss., U.S. 32°48' N, 90°16' W 103
Benton, N.H., U.S. 44°5' N, 71°55' W 104
Benton Harbor, Mich., U.S. 42°6' N, 86°27' W 102
Bentong, Malaysia 3°34' N, 101°55' E 196
Bentonia, Miss., U.S. 32°37' N, 90°23' W 103
Bentonville, Ark., U.S. 36°21' N, 94°13' W 94
Benty, Guinea 9°8' N, 13°13' W 222
Benue, river, Nig. 8°0' N, 7°50' E 222
Benwee Head, Ire. 54°21' N, 10°10' W 150
Benxi, China 41°16' N, 123°47' E 200
Benzdorp, Suriname 3°42' N, 54°7' W 130
Benzú, Mor. 35°54' N, 5°23' W 150
Beo, Indonesia 4°15' N, 126°52' E 192
Beograd (Belgrade), Serb. 44°47' N, 20°24' E 168
Beohari, India 24°2' N, 81°22' E 197
Beolgyo, S. Korea 34°48' N, 127°21' E 200
Beowawe, Nev., U.S. 40°35' N, 116°30' W 90
Beppu, Japan 36°7' N, 133°4' E 201
Beppu, Japan 33°16' N, 131°29' E 201
Bequia, island, Saint Vincent and The Grenadines 13°0' N, 61°11' W 116
Bera Ndjoko, Congo 3°15' N, 16°58' E 218
Berau, Teluk 2°35' S, 131°10' E 192
Berber, Sudan 18°0' N, 34°2' E 182
Berbérati, Cen. Af. Rep. 4°18' N, 15°47' E 218
Bercedo, Sp. 43°4' N, 3°27' W 164
Berceto, It. 44°30' N, 9°59' E 167
Berck, Fr. 50°25' N, 1°35' E 163
Berdigestyakh, Russ. 62°8' N, 127°5' E 160
Berdoba, Chad 16°0' N, 22°53' E 216
Berdsk, Russ. 54°46' N, 83°11' E 184
Berdún, Sp. 42°36' N, 0°52' E 164
Berdyans'k, Ukr. 46°46' N, 36°46' E 156
Berdyaush, Russ. 55°11' N, 59°12' E 154
Berdychiv, Ukr. 49°53' N, 28°41' E 152
Berdyuzh'ye, Russ. 55°48' N, 68°20' E 184
Berea, Ky., U.S. 37°33' N, 84°18' W 96
Berea, Ohio, U.S. 41°21' N, 81°51' W 102
Bérébi, Côte d'Ivoire 4°40' N, 7°2' W 222
Bereeda, Somalia 11°44' N, 51°3' E 182
Bereku, Tanzania 4°27' S, 35°46' E 224
Berekum, Ghana 7°29' N, 2°35' W 222
Beremend, Hung. 45°46' N, 18°25' E 168
Beren, Liman, lake, Russ. 46°52' N, 44°37' E 158
Berenda, Calif., U.S. 37°2' N, 120°10' W 100
Berenice, Egypt 23°54' N, 35°25' E 182
Berens River, Can. 52°21' N, 96°59' W 82
Berens, river, Can. 51°49' N, 93°43' W 110
Berens, river, Can. 52°5' N, 96°53' W 80
Berestechko, Ukr. 50°20' N, 25°6' E 158
Bereşti, Rom. 46°5' N, 27°51' E 156
Berettyó, river, Rom. 47°15' N, 21°39' E 168
Berettyóújfalu, Hung. 47°14' N, 21°32' E 168
Berevo, Madagascar 19°46' S, 44°58' E 220
Berezivka, Ukr. 47°16' N, 30°54' E 156
Bereznik, Russ. 62°49' N, 42°49' E 154
Berezniki, Russ. 59°24' N, 56°48' E 154
Berezovka, Russ. 57°38' N, 57°22' E 154
Berezovka, Russ. 59°20' N, 82°47' E 169
Berezovka, Russ. 65°0' N, 56°38' E 154
Berezovo, Russ. 63°58' N, 65°5' E 169
Berezovskaya, Russ. 50°14' N, 43°59' E 158
Berezovskiy, Russ. 55°34' N, 86°18' E 169
Berga, Nor. 57°14' N, 16°0' E 152
Berga, Sp. 42°6' N, 1°50' E 164
Bergama, Turk. 39°4' N, 27°11' E 180
Bergamo, It. 45°42' N, 9°39' E 167
Bergedorf, Ger. 53°29' N, 10°12' E 150
Bergen, Ger. 54°25' N, 13°26' E 152
Bergen, Nor. 60°23' N, 5°19' E 152
Bergen aan Zee, Neth. 52°40' N, 4°38' E 163
Bergen op Zoom, Neth. 51°29' N, 4°17' E 163
Bergerac, Fr. 44°51' N, 0°28' E 150
Bergersen, Mount, Antarctica 72°6' S, 25°32' E 248
Bergheim, Ger. 50°57' N, 6°39' E 167
Bergisch Gladbach, Ger. 50°59' N, 7°7' E 167
Bergkamen, Ger. 51°37' N, 7°39' E 167
Bergland, Namibia 23°0' S, 17°5' E 227
Bergö, Fin. 62°56' N, 21°9' E 152
Bergsfjord, Nor. 70°15' N, 21°49' E 152
Bergshamra, Sw. 59°37' N, 18°35' E 166
Bergsjö, Nor. 61°58' N, 17°1' E 152
Berguent, Mor. 34°1' N, 2°0' W 214
Bergues, Fr. 50°57' N, 2°26' E 163
Bergum, Neth. 53°11' N, 5°58' E 163
Bergville, S. Af. 28°44' S, 29°20' E 227
Berh, Mongolia 47°44' N, 111°8' E 198
Berhala, Selat 0°50' N, 103°54' E 196
Berikei, oil field, Russ. 42°20' N, 47°58' E 195
Bering Sea 65°53' N, 166°10' W 246
Bering Strait 65°53' N, 168°36' W 255
Beringil, Sudan 12°8' N, 25°43' E 216
Beringovskiy, Russ. 63°8' N, 179°6' E 160
Berja, Sp. 36°50' N, 2°57' W 164
Berkåk, Nor. 62°49' N, 10°1' E 152
Berkeley, Calif., U.S. 37°52' N, 122°16' W 100
Berkner Island, Antarctica 78°9' S, 43°53' W 248
Berkovići, Bosn. and Herzg. 43°4' N, 18°10' E 168
Berkshire, Mass., U.S. 42°30' N, 73°12' W 104
Berkshires, The, Mass., U.S. 42°27' N, 73°8' W 104
Berland, river, Can. 53°40' N, 118°10' W 108
Berlikum, Neth. 53°14' N, 5°38' E 163
Berlin, Ger. 52°29' N, 13°14' E 152
Berlin, Md., U.S. 38°19' N, 75°14' W 94
Berlin, N.H., U.S. 44°28' N, 71°12' W 104
Berlin, N.Y., U.S. 42°41' N, 73°23' W 104
Berlin, Wis., U.S. 43°57' N, 88°56' W 94
Berlin, Mount, Antarctica 75°56' S, 135°13' W 248
Bermeja, Punta, Arg. 41°21' S, 63°11' W 134
Bermeja, Sierra, Sp. 36°33' N, 5°16' W 164
Bermejillo, Mex. 25°52' N, 103°39' W 114
Bermejo, river, Arg. 25°37' S, 60°8' W 134
Bermeo, Sp. 43°23' N, 2°45' W 164
Bermuda Islands, U.K. 32°0' N, 65°0' W 118
Bermuda Rise, North Atlantic Ocean 32°2' N, 64°35' W 253
Bern, Switz. 46°55' N, 7°21' E 165
Bernalillo, N. Mex., U.S. 35°17' N, 106°34' W 82
Bernard Lake, lake, Can. 45°41' N, 79°50' W 110
Bernardo de Irigoyen, Arg. 32°11' S, 61°8' W 139
Bernardo de Irigoyen, Arg. 26°15' S, 53°41' W 139
Bernardston, Mass., U.S. 42°40' N, 72°34' W 104
Bernasconi, Arg. 37°57' S, 63°42' W 139
Bernay, Fr. 49°5' N, 0°35' E 150
Berne, Ind., U.S. 40°38' N, 84°57' W 102
Berner Alpen, Switz. 46°20' N, 6°59' E 165
Berneval, Fr. 49°57' N, 1°10' E 163
Bernice, La., U.S. 32°48' N, 92°40' W 103
Bernie, Mo., U.S. 36°40' N, 89°58' W 96
Bernier Bay 70°59' N, 90°44' W 106
Bernier Island, Austral. 24°41' S, 111°44' E 230
Bernina Pass, Switz. 46°26' N, 10°0' E 167
Bernina, Piz, peak, Switz. 46°23' N, 9°52' E 167
Bernkastel-Kues, Ger. 49°55' N, 7°5' E 167
Bernterode, Ger. 51°24' N, 10°29' E 167
Bero, river, Angola 15°3' S, 12°9' E 220
Berón de Astrada, Arg. 27°33' S, 57°32' W 139
Beroroha, Madagascar 21°37' S, 45°9' E 220
Bérouboauy, Benin 10°32' N, 2°41' E 222
Beroun, Czech Rep. 49°58' N, 14°4' E 152
Berovo, Maced. 41°43' N, 22°52' E 168
Berri, oil field, Saudi Arabia 27°5' N, 49°29' E 196
Berriane, Alg. 32°51' N, 3°45' E 214
Berrien Springs, Mich., U.S. 41°56' N, 86°21' W 102
Berrouaghia, Alg. 36°7' N, 2°54' E 150
Berry, Ky., U.S. 38°30' N, 84°23' W 102
Berry Creek, river, Can. 51°34' N, 111°39' W 90
Berry Islands, Atlantic Ocean 25°23' N, 77°42' W 96
Berry, region, Europe 46°51' N, 1°18' E 165
Berryville, Ark., U.S. 36°21' N, 93°35' W 96
Berseba, Namibia 26°0' S, 17°46' E 227
Bersenbrück, Ger. 52°33' N, 7°57' E 163
Bershad', Ukr. 48°24' N, 29°38' E 156
Bertam, Malaysia 5°11' N, 102°1' E 196
Berthierville, Can. 46°5' N, 73°11' W 110
Berthold, N. Dak., U.S. 48°18' N, 101°45' W 90
Berthoud, Colo., U.S. 40°18' N, 105°6' W 90
Berthoud Pass, Colo., U.S. 39°47' N, 105°47' W 90
Bertincourt, Fr. 50°4' N, 2°56' E 163
Bertoua, Cameroon 4°32' N, 13°40' E 218
Bertrab Nunatak, peak, Antarctica 78°26' S, 36°22' W 248
Bertrand, Nebr., U.S. 40°31' N, 99°39' W 92
Bertwell, Can. 52°35' N, 102°36' W 108
Beru, island, Kiribati 1°12' S, 175°57' E 252
Beruniy, Uzb. 41°43' N, 60°43' E 180
Beruri, Braz. 3°53' S, 61°23' W 130
Berutti, Arg. 35°50' S, 62°29' W 139
Berveni, Rom. 47°45' N, 22°28' E 168
Berwick, La., U.S. 29°41' N, 91°15' W 103
Berwick, Me., U.S. 43°16' N, 70°52' W 104
Berwick upon Tweed, U.K. 55°45' N, 2°1' W 150
Berwyn, Can. 56°9' N, 117°44' W 108
Berwyn, U.K. 52°51' N, 3°26' W 162
Beryslav, Ukr. 46°53' N, 33°19' E 156
Bērzaune, Latv. 56°48' N, 26°2' E 166
Bērze, river, Latv. 56°37' N, 23°18' E 166
Berzosilla, Sp. 42°46' N, 4°3' W 164
Berzovia, Rom. 45°25' N, 21°36' E 168
Besançon, Fr. 47°14' N, 6°1' E 150
Beserah, Malaysia 3°54' N, 103°20' E 196
Beshanq, Uzb. 40°25' N, 70°33' E 197
Beshkent, Uzb. 38°47' N, 65°37' E 197
Beşiri, Turk. 37°54' N, 41°20' E 195
Beška, Serb. 45°7' N, 20°4' E 168
Besko, Pol. 49°34' N, 21°56' E 152
Besköl, Kaz. 54°45' N, 69°4' E 184
Beslan, Russ. 43°9' N, 44°32' E 195
Beslet, peak, Bulg. 41°47' N, 23°48' E 156
Besna Kobila, peak, Serb. 42°31' N, 22°11' E 168
Besnard Lake, lake, Can. 55°25' N, 106°33' W 108
Besni Fok, Serb. 44°58' N, 20°24' E 168
Beşparmak Dağı, peak, Turk. 37°29' N, 27°30' E 156
Bessaker, Nor. 64°14' N, 10°20' E 152
Bessemer, Ala., U.S. 33°23' N, 86°56' W 96
Betsöbe, Kaz. 52°29' N, 73°8' E 184
Bestuzhevo, Russ. 61°37' N, 44°1' E 154
Bet Guvrin, Israel 31°36' N, 34°53' E 194
Bét ha Shitta, Israel 32°33' N, 35°26' E 194
Bét She'an (Beth-shan), Israel 32°29' N, 35°30' E 194
Bét She'arim, ruin(s), Israel 32°41' N, 35°5' E 194
Bét Shemesh, Israel 31°44' N, 34°59' E 194
Betafo, Madagascar 19°52' S, 46°51' E 220
Betamba, Dem. Rep. of the Congo 2°16' S, 21°25' E 218
Betanty (Faux Cap), Madagascar 25°34' S, 45°31' E 220
Betanzos, Bol. 19°33' S, 65°23' W 137
Betanzos, Sp. 43°15' N, 8°14' W 150
Bétaré Oya, Cameroon 5°31' N, 14°5' E 218
Betbeder, Peninsula, Arg. 44°43' S, 65°19' W 134
Bete Hor, Eth. 11°33' N, 38°58' E 182
Bétera, Sp. 39°35' N, 0°28' E 164
Bétérou, Benin 9°12' N, 2°13' E 222
Bethal, S. Af. 26°26' S, 29°25' E 227
Bethanie, Namibia 26°31' S, 17°9' E 227
Bethany, Ill., U.S. 39°38' N, 88°45' W 102
Bethany, Mo., U.S. 40°15' N, 94°1' W 94
Bethany Beach, Del., U.S. 38°31' N, 75°4' W 94
Bethel, Alas., U.S. 60°45' N, 161°52' W 98
Bethel, Conn., U.S. 41°22' N, 73°25' W 104
Bethel, Ohio, U.S. 38°57' N, 84°5' W 102
Bethel, Vt., U.S. 43°49' N, 72°38' W 104
Bethesda, U.K. 53°11' N, 4°3' W 162
Bethlehem, N.H., U.S. 44°16' N, 71°42' W 104
Bethlehem, S. Af. 28°15' S, 28°15' E 227
Bethlehem see Bayt La'm, West Bank, Israel 31°41' N, 35°12' E 194
Bethpage, N.Y., U.S. 40°44' N, 73°30' W 104
Beth-shan see Bét She'an, Israel 32°29' N, 35°30' E 194
Bethulie, S. Af. 30°27' S, 25°59' E 227
Béthune, Fr. 50°31' N, 2°38' E 163
Betijoque, Venez. 9°22' N, 70°44' W 136
Betioky, Madagascar 23°43' S, 44°19' E 220
Betong, Thai. 5°47' N, 101°4' E 196
Bétou, Congo 3°5' N, 18°30' E 218
Betpaqdala, Asia 45°34' N, 64°32' E 184
Betroka, Madagascar 23°13' S, 46°8' E 220
Betsiamites, Can. 48°56' N, 68°39' W 94
Betsiamites, river, Can. 49°24' N, 69°51' W 94
Bettendorf, Iowa, U.S. 41°33' N, 90°30' W 94
Bettie, Tex., U.S. 32°48' N, 94°58' W 103
Bettioua, Alg. 35°47' N, 0°16' E 150
Bettola, It. 44°46' N, 9°36' E 167
Bettsville, Ohio, U.S. 41°14' N, 83°13' W 102
Betul, India 21°55' N, 77°54' E 197
Betws-y-Coed, U.K. 53°5' N, 3°48' W 162
Betzdorf, Ger. 50°47' N, 7°52' E 167
Béu, Angola 6°14' S, 15°27' E 218
Beuil, Fr. 44°5' N, 6°57' E 167
Beulah, Colo., U.S. 38°5' N, 105°0' W 90
Beulah, N. Dak., U.S. 47°15' N, 101°48' W 90
Beurfou, spring, Chad 15°54' N, 14°58' E 216
Beverley, U.K. 53°50' N, 0°26' E 162
Beverley Head, Can. 49°11' N, 59°4' W 111
Beverly, Mass., U.S. 42°32' N, 70°53' W 104
Beverly, Ohio, U.S. 39°32' N, 81°38' W 102
Beverly Hills, Fla., U.S. 28°56' N, 82°27' W 105
Beverungen, Ger. 51°40' N, 9°22' E 167
Beverwijk, Neth. 52°30' N, 4°37' E 163
Bewdley, U.K. 52°21' N, 2°20' W 162
Bex, Switz. 46°15' N, 7°0' E 167
Bexhill, U.K. 50°50' N, 0°28' E 162
Bey Dağları, Turk. 36°36' N, 29°46' E 156
Bey Dağı, peak, Turk. 39°41' N, 37°47' E 156
Bey Dağı, peak, Turk. 38°16' N, 35°59' E 156
Beycesultan, ruin(s), Turk. 38°14' N, 29°33' E 156
Beyla, Guinea 8°39' N, 8°39' W 222
Beyneu, Kaz. 45°18' N, 55°13' E 158
Beypazarı, Turk. 40°9' N, 31°54' E 156
Beyra, Somalia 6°55' N, 47°25' E 218
Beyrouth (Beirut), Leb. 33°53' N, 35°26' E 194
Beyşehir, Turk. 37°41' N, 31°44' E 156
Beyşehir Gölü, lake, Turk. 37°43' N, 31°9' E 180
Beysug, river, Russ. 45°53' N, 39°3' E 156
Beytüşşebap, Turk. 37°33' N, 43°3' E 195
Bezdan, Serb. 45°50' N, 18°55' E 168
Bezerra, river, Braz. 13°14' S, 47°29' W 138
Bezhanitsy, Russ. 56°57' N, 29°52' E 166
Bezhetsk, Russ. 57°44' N, 36°44' E 154
Béziers, Fr. 43°20' N, 3°13' E 164
Bhadarwah, India 32°57' N, 75°45' E 186
Bhadra, India 29°7' N, 75°10' E 186
Bhadrakh, India 21°5' N, 86°31' E 188
Bhadravati, India 13°52' N, 75°44' E 188
Bhagalpur, India 25°13' N, 87°0' E 197
Bhairahawa, Nepal 27°32' N, 83°23' E 197
Bhakkar, Pak. 31°37' N, 71°7' E 186
Bhaktapur, Nepal 27°41' N, 85°26' E 197
Bhamo, Myanmar 24°17' N, 97°16' E 190
Bhandara, India 21°2' N, 79°38' E 190
Bhanpura, India 24°31' N, 75°46' E 197
Bharatpur, India 27°13' N, 77°28' E 197
Bharatpur, India 23°46' N, 81°47' E 197
Bharthana, India 26°43' N, 79°14' E 197
Bharuch, India 21°42' N, 72°57' E 186
Bhatapara, India 21°44' N, 81°56' E 188
Bhatinda, India 30°13' N, 74°57' E 186
Bhatkal, India 14°0' N, 74°32' E 188
Bhatpara, India 22°51' N, 88°25' E 197
Bhavnagar, India 21°46' N, 72°7' E 186
Bheigeir, Beinn, peak, U.K. 55°43' N, 6°12' W 150
Bhera, Pak. 32°27' N, 72°58' E 186
Bhikangaon, India 21°53' N, 75°58' E 197
Bhilai, India 21°13' N, 81°21' E 188
Bhilsa see Vidisha, India 23°32' N, 77°51' E 197
Bhind, India 26°32' N, 78°46' E 197
Bhinmal, India 24°59' N, 72°16' E 186
Bhisho, S. Af. 32°49' S, 27°31' E 227
Bhiwani, India 28°46' N, 76°9' E 197
Bhojpur, Nepal 27°9' N, 87°4' E 197
Bhopal, India 23°16' N, 77°25' E 197
Bhubaneshwar, India 20°17' N, 85°48' E 188
Bhumibol Dam, Thai. 17°9' N, 98°57' E 202
Bhusawal, India 21°2' N, 75°46' E 188
Bhutan 27°24' N, 89°54' E 188
Bia, Monts, Dem. Rep. of the Congo 9°32' S, 26°9' E 224
Biá, river, Braz. 3°24' S, 67°24' W 136
Bia, river, Ghana 6°27' N, 2°49' W 222
Biak, Indonesia 1°4' S, 136°1' E 192
Biak, island, Indonesia 0°45' N, 135°57' E 192
Biała Góra, peak, Pol. 50°15' N, 23°16' E 152
Biała Podlaska, Pol. 52°2' N, 23°6' E 158
Białogard, Pol. 54°0' N, 15°59' E 152
Białowieża, Pol. 52°2' N, 23°6' E 152
Biały Bór, Pol. 53°54' N, 16°49' E 152
Białystok, Pol. 53°8' N, 23°9' E 152
Bianco, It. 38°6' N, 16°8' E 156
Biankouma, Côte d'Ivoire 7°38' N, 7°36' W 222
Biaora, India 23°56' N, 76°55' E 197
Biar, Sp. 38°37' N, 0°46' E 164
Biar Zahr, spring, Tun. 31°29' N, 10°6' E 214
Bīārjomand, Iran 36°2' N, 55°57' E 180
Biarritz, Fr. 43°25' N, 1°39' W 214
Bias, Fr. 44°8' N, 1°15' W 150
Biasca, Switz. 46°21' N, 8°58' E 167
Biaza, Russ. 56°34' N, 78°18' E 169
Biba, Egypt 28°55' N, 30°57' E 180
Bibai, Japan 43°18' N, 141°52' E 190
Bibala, Angola 14°44' S, 13°18' E 220
Bibémi, Cameroon 9°18' N, 13°52' E 216
Bibiani, Ghana 6°28' N, 2°18' W 222
Bibile, Sri Lanka 7°9' N, 81°15' E 188
Bibione, It. 45°38' N, 13°1' E 167
Bibury, U.K. 51°45' N, 1°50' W 162
Bicaj, Alban. 41°59' N, 20°25' E 168
Bicas, Braz. 21°43' S, 43°6' W 138
Bicaz, Rom. 46°54' N, 26°4' E 156
Bicester, U.K. 51°53' N, 1°9' W 162
Biche, Lac la, lake, Can. 54°53' N, 112°30' W 108
Bichena, Eth. 10°23' N, 38°14' E 224
Bichi, Nig. 12°12' N, 8°13' E 222
Bichvint'a, Ga. 43°9' N, 40°20' E 195
Bickerdike, Can. 53°32' N, 116°39' W 108
Bickerton Island, Austral. 13°39' S, 134°25' E 230
Bicknell, Ind., U.S. 38°46' N, 87°18' W 102
Bicknell, Utah, U.S. 38°20' N, 111°33' W 90
Bicske, Hung. 47°28' N, 18°39' E 168
Bida, Nig. 9°3' N, 5°59' E 222
Bidar, India 17°54' N, 77°32' E 188
Bidarray, Fr. 43°16' N, 1°21' W 164
Biddeford, Me., U.S. 43°29' N, 70°28' W 104
Bidwell, Mount, Calif., U.S. 41°57' N, 120°15' W 90
Bié, adm. division, Angola 12°56' S, 16°44' E 220
Bié Plateau, Angola 11°41' S, 15°45' E 220
Biele Karpaty, Czech Rep. 49°5' N, 17°49' E 152
Bieler See, lake, Switz. 47°5' N, 7°4' E 165
Biella, It. 45°34' N, 8°2' E 167
Bielsa, Sp. 42°37' N, 0°13' E 164
Bielsk, Pol. 52°39' N, 19°48' E 152
Bielsk Podlaski, Pol. 52°46' N, 23°10' E 152
Bielsko-Biała, Pol. 49°49' N, 19°2' E 152
Bien Hoa, Vietnam 10°58' N, 106°49' E 202
Bienvenida, Sp. 38°18' N, 6°13' W 164
Bienville, Lac, lake, Can. 54°59' N, 74°39' W 106
Biescas, Sp. 42°37' N, 0°19' E 164
Bieżuń, Pol. 52°57' N, 19°52' E 152
Bifoum, Gabon 0°20' N, 10°24' E 218
Big Baldy Mountain, Mont., U.S. 46°56' N, 110°41' W 90
Big Baldy, peak, Idaho, U.S. 44°45' N, 115°18' W 90
Big Bay, Mich., U.S. 46°48' N, 87°44' W 94
Big Bear Lake, Calif., U.S. 34°14' N, 116°57' W 101
Big Beaver House, Can. 52°55' N, 89°52' W 82
Big Belt Mountains, Mont., U.S. 46°58' N, 111°39' W 90
Big Bend National Park, Tex., U.S. 29°9' N, 103°44' W 72
Big Black, river, Miss., U.S. 32°43' N, 90°14' W 103
Big Blue, river, Nebr., U.S. 41°1' N, 97°55' W 80
Big Bog, marsh, Minn., U.S. 48°18' N, 94°29' W 90
Big Creek, Calif., U.S. 37°12' N, 119°15' W 100
Big Cypress National Preserve, Fla., U.S. 26°5' N, 81°11' W 105
Big Cypress Swamp, marsh, Fla., U.S. 26°1' N, 81°12' W 105
Big Delta, Alas., U.S. 64°1' N, 145°49' W 98
Big Elk Mountain, Idaho, U.S. 43°12' N, 111°21' W 90
Big Falls, Minn., U.S. 48°9' N, 93°50' W 90
Big Fork, river, Minn., U.S. 48°4' N, 94°0' W 90
Big Horn Peak, Ariz., U.S. 33°36' N, 113°13' W 92
Big Interior Mountain, Can. 49°27' N, 125°36' W 90
Big Lake, Minn., U.S. 45°18' N, 93°45' W 94
Big Lake, Tex., U.S. 31°11' N, 101°28' W 92
Big Lake Ranch, Can. 52°23' N, 121°52' W 108
Big Lookout Mountain, Oreg., U.S. 44°35' N, 117°23' W 90
Big Maria Mountains, Calif., U.S. 33°54' N, 114°56' W 101
Big Mountain, Nev., U.S. 41°16' N, 119°9' W 90
Big Pine, Calif., U.S. 37°10' N, 118°19' W 101
Big Pine Key, Fla., U.S. 24°39' N, 81°22' W 105
Big Pine Mountain, Calif., U.S. 34°41' N, 119°42' W 100
Big Piney, Wyo., U.S. 42°32' N, 110°6' W 90
Big Piskwanish Point, Can. 51°44' N, 80°27' W 110
Big Port Walter, Alas., U.S. 56°23' N, 134°45' W 108
Big Rapids, Mich., U.S. 43°42' N, 85°30' W 102
Big River, Can. 53°50' N, 107°1' W 108
Big, river, Mo., U.S. 38°16' N, 90°40' W 80
Big Sable Point, Mich., U.S. 44°2' N, 86°40' W 102
Big Salmon, river, Can. 61°46' N, 134°30' W 98
Big Sand Lake, Can. 57°33' N, 100°35' W 108
Big Sandy, Mont., U.S. 48°9' N, 110°6' W 90
Big Sandy, Tex., U.S. 32°34' N, 95°7' W 103
Big Sandy Lake, lake, Can. 54°22' N, 104°45' W 108
Big Sandy Reservoir, Wyo., U.S. 42°17' N, 109°49' W 90
Big Sioux, river, S. Dak., U.S. 45°17' N, 97°38' W 80
Big Smoky Valley, Nev., U.S. 38°13' N, 117°46' W 90
Big Snowy Mountains, Mont., U.S. 46°51' N, 109°39' W 90
Big Southern Butte, Idaho, U.S. 43°23' N, 113°6' W 90
Big Spring, Tex., U.S. 32°13' N, 101°28' W 92
Big Springs, Nebr., U.S. 41°3' N, 102°6' W 90
Big Squaw Mountain, Me., U.S. 45°28' N, 69°48' W 94
Big Stone City, S. Dak., U.S. 45°16' N, 96°30' W 90
Big Sur, Calif., U.S. 36°16' N, 121°49' W 100
Big Thicket National Preserve, Tex., U.S. 30°26' N, 94°41' W 103
Big Timber, Mont., U.S. 45°48' N, 109°58' W 90
Big Trout Lake, Can. 53°51' N, 92°1' W 106
Big Trout Lake, Can. 53°43' N, 89°55' W 106
Big Valley, Can. 52°2' N, 112°46' W 90
Big Valley Mountains, Calif., U.S. 41°10' N, 121°33' W 90
Big Wells, Tex., U.S. 28°33' N, 99°35' W 92
Big White Mountain, Can. 49°43' N, 119°2' W 90
Big Wood Cay, island, Bahamas 24°25' N, 77°40' W 116
Biga, Turk. 40°13' N, 27°12' E 156
Bigadiç, Turk. 39°23' N, 28°7' E 156
Bigelow Mountain, Me., U.S. 45°8' N, 70°22' W 94
Bigfork, Minn., U.S. 47°42' N, 93°40' W 90
Bigfork, Mont., U.S. 48°2' N, 114°7' W 90
Biggar, Can. 52°3' N, 107°59' W 90
Bigge Island, Austral. 14°23' S, 124°2' E 230
Biggeluobbal, Nor. 69°22' N, 23°22' E 152
Biggleswade, U.K. 52°4' N, 0°16' E 162
Biggs, Calif., U.S. 39°24' N, 121°43' W 90
Bighorn Mountains, Wyo., U.S. 43°48' N, 107°26' W 90
Bignasco, Switz. 46°21' N, 8°36' E 167
Bigniba, river, Can. 49°2' N, 77°43' W 94
Bignona, Senegal 12°48' N, 16°10' W 222
Bigobo, Dem. Rep. of the Congo 5°27' S, 27°34' E 224
Bigstick Lake, Can. 50°16' N, 109°40' W 90
Bigstone Lake, lake, Can. 53°36' N, 96°20' W 108
Bigstone, river, Can. 55°28' N, 95°12' W 108
Bihać, Bosn. and Herzg. 44°49' N, 15°53' E 168
Bihar, adm. division, India 25°9' N, 84°25' E 188
Bihar Sharif, India 25°10' N, 85°30' E 197
Biharamulo, Tanzania 2°40' S, 31°21' E 224
Biharkeresztes, Hung. 47°7' N, 21°42' E 168
Bihor, adm. division, Rom. 46°51' N, 21°40' E 156
Bihor, Munţii, Rom. 46°42' N, 22°25' E 168
Bihosava, Belarus 55°50' N, 27°42' E 166
Bīīkzhal, Kaz. 46°51' N, 54°48' E 158
Bijagós, ArquipŽelago dos, North Atlantic Ocean 10°37' N, 16°42' W 222
Bijapur, India 18°46' N, 80°49' E 188
Bijapur, India 16°49' N, 75°42' E 188
Bījār, Iran 35°50' N, 47°32' E 180
Bijauri, Nepal 28°6' N, 82°28' E 197
Bijawar, India 24°37' N, 79°30' E 197
Bijeljina, Bosn. and Herzg. 44°45' N, 19°14' E 168
Bijelo Polje, Mont. 43°1' N, 19°44' E 168
Bijie, China 27°18' N, 105°19' E 198
Bikaner, India 28°1' N, 73°20' E 186
Bikava, Latv. 56°44' N, 27°2' E 166
Bikin, Russ. 46°53' N, 134°22' E 190
Bikita, Zimb. 20°6' S, 31°37' E 227
Bīkkū Bīttī, peak, Lib. 22°8' N, 19°11' E 216
Bikoro, Dem. Rep. of the Congo 0°45' N, 18°6' E 218
Bikovo, Serb. 46°0' N, 19°45' E 168
Bila, river, China 49°9' N, 122°19' E 198
Bila, Tanjung, Indonesia 1°8' N, 108°39' E 196
Bila Tserkva, Ukr. 49°47' N, 30°14' E 158
Biläcäri, Azerb. 40°27' N, 49°47' E 195
Bilād Banī Bū 'Alī, Oman 22°4' N, 59°18' E 182
Bilanga, Burkina Faso 12°32' N, 5°296' W 222
Bilaspur, India 22°4' N, 82°8' E 197
Biläsuvar, Azerb. 39°26' N, 48°31' E 195
Bilati, Dem. Rep. of the Congo 0°36' N, 28°47' E 224
Bilati, river, Dem. Rep. of the Congo 0°53' N, 28°12' E 224
Bilbao, Sp. 43°14' N, 2°58' W 150
Bile, Ukr. 51°38' N, 26°4' E 152
Bileća, Bosn. and Herzg. 42°52' N, 18°24' E 168
Bilecik, Turk. 39°58' N, 29°58' E 156
Bilhorod-Dnistrovs'kyy, Ukr. 46°11' N, 30°17' E 156
Bili, Dem. Rep. of the Congo 4°7' N, 25°3' E 224
Bili, river, Dem. Rep. of the Congo 4°4' N, 24°28' E 224
Bilibino, Russ. 67°54' N, 166°13' E 160
Bilican Dağları, peak, Turk. 38°56' N, 42°6' E 195

285

Bouca, Cen. Af. Rep. 6°29′ N, 18°18′ E 218
Boucau, Fr. 43°31′ N, 1°30′ W 150
Bouchier, Lac, lake, Can. 50°2′ N, 78°23′ W 110
Boucle Du Baoulé National Park, Mali 13°39′ N, 9°25′ W 222
Boudenib, Mor. 32°1′ N, 3°36′ W 214
Boudjellil, Alg. 36°19′ N, 4°20′ E 150
Bouga, Chad 8°8′ N, 15°34′ E 218
Bougainville, Cape, Austral. 13°49′ S, 126°3′ E 231
Bougainville, island, P.N.G. 5°54′ S, 153°10′ E 192
Bougar'oûn, Cap, Alg. 37°7′ N, 6°26′ E 150
Boughzoul, Alg. 35°44′ N, 2°50′ E 150
Bougie see Bejaïa, Alg. 36°46′ N, 5°2′ E 150
Bougouni, Mali 11°26′ N, 7°30′ W 222
Bouilly, Fr. 48°10′ N, 4°0′ E 163
Bouira, Alg. 36°21′ N, 3°54′ E 150
Boujad, Mor. 32°50′ N, 6°25′ W 214
Boujdour, Western Sahara, Mor. 26°8′ N, 14°29′ W 214
Boujdour, Cap, Western Sahara, Mor. 26°7′ N, 16°1′ W 214
Boukombé, Benin 10°11′ N, 1°6′ E 222
Boukoula, Cameroon 10°9′ N, 13°29′ E 216
Boukra, Western Sahara, Mor. 26°22′ N, 12°53′ W 214
Boula, Mali 15°4′ N, 8°27′ W 222
Boulder, Colo., U.S. 40°2′ N, 105°17′ W 90
Boulder, Mont., U.S. 46°13′ N, 112°7′ W 90
Boulder City, Nev., U.S. 35°55′ N, 114°50′ W 82
Boulder Creek, Calif., U.S. 37°7′ N, 122°9′ W 100
Boulder Peak, Calif., U.S. 41°34′ N, 123°11′ W 90
Boulogne, Fr. 43°17′ N, 0°37′ E 164
Boulogne-sur-Mer, Fr. 50°44′ N, 1°36′ E 163
Boulouli, Mali 15°36′ N, 9°20′ W 222
Boulsa, Burkina Faso 12°39′ N, 0°37′ E 222
Boultoum, Niger 14°41′ N, 10°18′ E 222
Boumdeït, spring, Mauritania 17°27′ N, 11°22′ W 222
Boumerdas, Alg. 36°45′ N, 3°29′ E 150
Boun Nua, Laos 21°40′ N, 101°54′ E 202
Boun Tai, Laos 21°25′ N, 101°58′ E 202
Bouna, Côte d'Ivoire 9°16′ N, 3°0′ W 222
Boundary, Can. 49°0′ N, 109°22′ W 90
Boundary Bald Mountain, Me., U.S. 45°45′ N, 70°18′ W 94
Boundary Peak, Nev., U.S. 37°50′ N, 118°26′ W 90
Boundiali, Côte d'Ivoire 9°31′ N, 6°29′ W 222
Boundji, Congo 1°2′ S, 15°22′ E 218
Bountiful Islands, Gulf of Carpentaria 17°3′ S, 140°1′ E 230
Bounty Trough, South Pacific Ocean 47°2′ S, 178°29′ W 252
Bourbon, Ind., U.S. 41°17′ N, 86°7′ W 102
Bourbonnais, Ill., U.S. 41°9′ N, 87°54′ W 102
Bourbonnais, region, Europe 46°45′ N, 2°23′ E 165
Bourbourg, Fr. 50°56′ N, 2°12′ E 163
Bouré Siké, spring, Mali 15°50′ N, 5°18′ W 222
Bourem, Mali 16°58′ N, 0°20′ E 222
Bouressa, Mali 19°58′ N, 2°13′ E 222
Bourg, La., U.S. 29°33′ N, 90°38′ W 103
Bourges, Fr. 47°4′ N, 2°24′ E 150
Bourg-Madame, Fr. 42°25′ N, 1°56′ E 164
Bourgneuf, Fr. 47°2′ N, 1°57′ W 150
Bourgogne, adm. division, Fr. 47°19′ N, 2°55′ E 150
Bourke, Austral. 30°8′ S, 145°56′ E 231
Bourlier, Alg. 35°23′ N, 1°38′ E 150
Bourne, U.K. 52°46′ N, 0°22′ E 162
Bournemouth, U.K. 50°43′ N, 1°54′ W 162
Bouroum, Burkina Faso 13°38′ N, 0°39′ E 222
Bourscheid, Lux. 49°53′ N, 6°4′ E 167
Bourtoutou, Chad 11°14′ N, 22°50′ E 218
Bouse, Ariz., U.S. 33°56′ N, 114°1′ W 101
Boussens, Fr. 43°10′ N, 0°57′ E 164
Bousso, Chad 10°32′ N, 16°43′ E 216
Bouszibé Aneyda, spring, Mali 16°14′ N, 5°16′ W 222
Boutilimit, Mauritania 17°32′ N, 14°44′ W 222
Bouvet Island, Norway 54°28′ S, 3°23′ E 255
Bouza, Niger 14°22′ N, 5°55′ E 222
Bovec, Slov. 46°20′ N, 13°34′ E 167
Bovenden, Ger. 51°35′ N, 9°56′ E 167
Boves, Fr. 49°49′ N, 2°22′ E 163
Bovill, Idaho, U.S. 46°50′ N, 116°24′ W 90
Bovina, Tex., U.S. 34°30′ N, 102°53′ W 92
Bovril, Arg. 31°19′ S, 59°25′ W 139
Bow, N.H., U.S. 43°9′ N, 71°33′ W 104
Bow Island, Can. 49°51′ N, 111°23′ W 90
Bow, river, Can. 51°6′ N, 114°34′ W 90
Bowbells, N. Dak., U.S. 48°48′ N, 102°15′ W 90
Bowdle, S. Dak., U.S. 45°26′ N, 99°41′ W 90
Bowdoin Canyon, Can. 53°34′ N, 65°28′ W 111
Bowen, Austral. 20°0′ S, 148°15′ E 231
Bowen Island, Can. 49°22′ N, 123°21′ W 100
Bowes, U.K. 54°31′ N, 2°1′ W 162
Bowie, Ariz., U.S. 32°19′ N, 109°28′ W 92
Bowie, Tex., U.S. 33°32′ N, 97°51′ W 92
Bowling Green, Fla., U.S. 27°38′ N, 81°49′ W 105
Bowling Green, Ind., U.S. 39°22′ N, 87°1′ W 102
Bowling Green, Ky., U.S. 36°59′ N, 86°27′ W 96
Bowling Green, Ohio, U.S. 41°22′ N, 83°39′ W 102
Bowling Green, Va., U.S. 38°2′ N, 77°21′ W 94
Bowling Green Bay National Park, Austral. 19°34′ S, 146°39′ E 238
Bowman, N. Dak., U.S. 46°10′ N, 103°26′ W 90
Bowman Bay 65°33′ N, 77°12′ W 106
Bowman Island, Antarctica 64°34′ S, 104°9′ E 248
Bowman, Mount, Can. 51°11′ N, 121°52′ W 90
Bowness, U.K. 54°21′ N, 2°55′ W 162
Bowo see Bomi, China 29°53′ N, 95°40′ E 188
Bowser, Can. 49°25′ N, 124°41′ W 100
Bowser Lake, Can. 56°24′ N, 129°52′ W 108
Bowsman, Can. 52°14′ N, 101°13′ W 108
Bowwood, Zambia 17°7′ S, 26°16′ E 224
Boxing, China 37°9′ N, 118°7′ E 198
Boxtel, Neth. 51°35′ N, 5°19′ E 167
Boyabat, Turk. 41°27′ N, 34°45′ E 156
Boyacá, adm. division, Col. 5°17′ N, 73°33′ W 136
Boyang, China 29°0′ N, 116°38′ E 198
Boyarka, Russ. 70°43′ N, 97°24′ E 160
Boyce, La., U.S. 31°22′ N, 92°40′ W 103
Boyd, Can. 55°53′ N, 96°27′ W 108
Boyd Lake, Can. 61°22′ N, 104°4′ W 108
Boyer, river, Can. 57°54′ N, 117°43′ W 108
Boyes Hot Springs, Calif., U.S. 38°19′ N, 122°29′ W 100
Boykétté, Cen. Af. Rep. 5°24′ N, 20°49′ E 218
Boyle, Can. 54°35′ N, 112°48′ W 108
Boyle, Ire. 53°58′ N, 8°20′ W 150
Boyne City, Mich., U.S. 45°12′ N, 85°1′ W 94
Boynitsa, Bulg. 43°57′ N, 22°31′ E 168
Boynton Beach, Fla., U.S. 26°32′ N, 80°5′ W 105
Boyoma Falls, Dem. Rep. of the Congo 1°23′ N, 21°41′ E 206
Boyoma Falls (Stanley Falls), Dem. Rep. of the Congo 0°14′ N, 25°9′ E 224
Boyson, Uzb. 38°12′ N, 67°12′ E 197
Boyuibe, Bol. 20°28′ S, 63°16′ W 137
Boz Burun, Turk. 40°17′ N, 28°50′ E 156
Boz Dağ, peak, Turk. 37°18′ N, 29°7′ E 156
Bozalan Burun, Turk. 38°12′ N, 26°27′ E 156
Bozashchy Tübegi, Kaz. 45°9′ N, 51°36′ E 158
Bozburun, Turk. 36°41′ N, 28°4′ E 156
Bozburun Dağı, peak, Turk. 37°16′ N, 31°0′ E 156
Bozdoğan, Turk. 37°39′ N, 28°18′ E 156
Bozeman, Mont., U.S. 45°38′ N, 111°3′ W 90
Bozene, Dem. Rep. of the Congo 2°58′ N, 19°13′ E 218
Boževac, Serb. 44°32′ N, 21°23′ E 168
Bozhou, China 33°49′ N, 115°44′ E 198
Božica, Serb. 42°36′ N, 22°24′ E 168
Bozkır, Turk. 37°11′ N, 32°13′ E 156
Bozkurt, Turk. 41°58′ N, 34°1′ E 158
Bozoum, Cen. Af. Rep. 6°15′ N, 16°23′ E 218
Bozoy, Kaz. 46°10′ N, 58°45′ E 158
Bozüyük, Turk. 39°55′ N, 30°1′ E 156
Bozzolo, It. 45°5′ N, 10°28′ E 167
Bra, It. 44°41′ N, 7°51′ E 167
Brabant Island, Antarctica 64°4′ S, 64°38′ W 134
Brabant Lake, lake, Can. 56°0′ N, 104°18′ W 108
Brač, island, Croatia 43°15′ N, 16°54′ E 168
Bracebridge, Can. 45°2′ N, 79°20′ W 94
Bräcke, Nor. 62°45′ N, 15°26′ E 152
Bracken Lake, lake, Can. 53°35′ N, 100°14′ W 108
Brackendale, Can. 49°45′ N, 123°8′ W 100
Brackettville, Tex., U.S. 29°18′ N, 100°25′ W 92
Brackley, U.K. 52°2′ N, 1°9′ W 162
Bracknell, U.K. 51°22′ N, 0°46′ E 162
Brackwede, Ger. 51°59′ N, 8°29′ E 167
Brad, Rom. 46°7′ N, 22°49′ E 168
Bradenton, Fla., U.S. 27°29′ N, 82°35′ W 105
Bradenton Beach, Fla., U.S. 27°28′ N, 82°41′ W 105
Bradford, Ill., U.S. 41°10′ N, 89°41′ W 102
Bradford, Ohio, U.S. 40°7′ N, 84°26′ W 102
Bradford, Pa., U.S. 41°57′ N, 78°40′ W 94
Bradford, U.K. 53°47′ N, 1°46′ W 162
Bradford, Vt., U.S. 43°59′ N, 72°9′ W 104
Bradford on Avon, U.K. 51°21′ N, 2°15′ W 162
Bradley, Ark., U.S. 33°5′ N, 93°41′ W 103
Bradley, Calif., U.S. 35°52′ N, 120°49′ W 100
Bradley, Ill., U.S. 41°9′ N, 87°51′ W 102
Bradley, S. Dak., U.S. 45°4′ N, 97°40′ W 90
Bradley Junction, Fla., U.S. 27°47′ N, 81°59′ W 105
Bradninch, U.K. 50°49′ N, 3°26′ W 162
Brador, Collines de, peak, Can. 51°33′ N, 57°18′ W 111
Bradwell on Sea, U.K. 51°43′ N, 0°54′ E 162
Brady, Nebr., U.S. 41°2′ N, 100°21′ W 90
Brady, Tex., U.S. 31°7′ N, 99°20′ W 92
Brașov, adm. division, Rom. 45°42′ N, 24°42′ E 156
Braeside, Can. 45°27′ N, 76°26′ W 94
Braga, Port. 41°32′ N, 8°27′ W 150
Braga, adm. division, Port. 41°24′ N, 8°40′ W 150
Bragado, Arg. 35°7′ S, 60°30′ W 139
Bragança, Braz. 1°4′ S, 46°48′ W 130
Bragança, Port. 41°46′ N, 6°48′ W 214
Bragança, Port. 41°49′ N, 6°47′ W 150
Bragança, adm. division, Port. 41°28′ N, 7°16′ W 150
Braham, Minn., U.S. 45°42′ N, 93°10′ W 94
Brahestad see Raahe, Fin. 64°41′ N, 24°27′ E 152
Brahmapur, India 19°19′ N, 84°47′ E 188
Brahmaputra, river, India 26°18′ N, 92°11′ E 190
Brăila, Rom. 45°16′ N, 27°57′ E 156
Brăila, adm. division, Rom. 44°57′ N, 27°19′ E 156
Braine, Fr. 49°20′ N, 3°30′ E 163
Braine l'Alleud, Belg. 50°41′ N, 4°21′ E 163
Brainerd, Minn., U.S. 46°20′ N, 94°11′ W 90
Braintree, Mass., U.S. 42°12′ N, 71°1′ W 104
Braintree, U.K. 51°53′ N, 0°32′ E 162
Brakel, Ger. 51°43′ N, 9°11′ E 167
Bräkne-Hoby, Nor. 56°14′ N, 15°8′ E 152
Bralorne, Can. 50°47′ N, 122°48′ W 90
Bramber, U.K. 50°51′ N, 0°18′ E 162
Brampton, Can. 43°41′ N, 79°46′ W 94
Bramsche, Ger. 52°24′ N, 7°58′ E 163
Branchville, S.C., U.S. 33°14′ N, 80°49′ W 96
Branco, river, Braz. 13°41′ S, 60°24′ W 130
Brandberg, peak, Namibia 21°10′ S, 14°27′ E 220
Brandbu, Nor. 60°24′ N, 10°31′ E 152
Brandenburg, adm. division, Ger. 52°36′ N, 12°16′ E 152
Brandfort, S. Af. 28°43′ S, 26°25′ E 227
Brändö, Fin. 60°24′ N, 21°2′ E 166
Brandon, Can. 49°49′ N, 99°57′ W 90
Brandon, Fla., U.S. 27°57′ N, 82°16′ W 105
Brandon, Miss., U.S. 32°15′ N, 90°0′ W 103
Brandon, U.K. 52°26′ N, 0°37′ E 162
Brandon, Vt., U.S. 43°47′ N, 73°7′ W 104
Brandon, Wis., U.S. 43°43′ N, 88°47′ W 102
Brandon Mountain, Ire. 52°13′ N, 10°20′ W 150
Brandsen, Arg. 35°9′ S, 58°16′ W 139
Brandvlei, S. Af. 30°26′ S, 20°26′ E 227
Brandy Peak, Oreg., U.S. 42°35′ N, 123°58′ W 90
Branford, Conn., U.S. 41°16′ N, 72°50′ W 104
Branford, Fla., U.S. 29°58′ N, 82°56′ W 96
Braniewo, Pol. 54°21′ N, 19°48′ E 166
Brankovina, Serb. 44°21′ N, 19°52′ E 168
Bransfield Island, Antarctica 63°28′ S, 58°57′ W 134
Branson, Mo., U.S. 36°38′ N, 93°14′ W 96
Brant, N.Y., U.S. 42°34′ N, 79°2′ W 110
Brant Lake, N.Y., U.S. 43°40′ N, 73°45′ W 104
Brantford, Can. 43°7′ N, 80°16′ W 110
Bras Coupé, Lac du, lake, Can. 49°33′ N, 75°43′ W 94
Bras d'Or Lake, Can. 45°55′ N, 61°18′ W 111
Brasileia, Braz. 10°57′ S, 68°44′ W 137
Brasileiro, Planalto, South America 17°41′ S, 44°49′ W 138
Brasília, Braz. 15°49′ S, 48°0′ W 138
Brasília de Minas, Braz. 16°13′ S, 44°28′ W 138
Brasília Legal, Braz. 3°52′ S, 55°39′ W 130
Braslaw, Belarus 55°38′ N, 27°3′ E 166
Brașov, Rom. 45°38′ N, 25°35′ E 156
Brass, Nig. 4°17′ N, 6°15′ E 222
Brasschaat, Belg. 51°17′ N, 4°28′ E 167
Brasstown Bald, peak, Ga., U.S. 34°51′ N, 83°53′ W 96
Bratan, peak, Bulg. 42°29′ N, 25°4′ E 156
Bratca, Rom. 46°54′ N, 22°39′ E 168
Bratislava (Pressburg), Slovakia 48°7′ N, 16°57′ E 152
Bratislavský, adm. division, Slovakia 47°40′ N, 10°52′ E 156
Bratiya, peak, Bulg. 42°34′ N, 24°5′ E 156
Bratsk, Russ. 56°24′ N, 101°23′ E 160
Brattleboro, Vt., U.S. 42°50′ N, 72°34′ W 104
Bratunac, Bosn. and Herzg. 44°12′ N, 19°20′ E 168
Brauron, ruin(s), Gr. 37°54′ N, 23°52′ E 156
Braux, Fr. 49°50′ N, 4°45′ E 163
Brawley, Calif., U.S. 32°59′ N, 115°33′ W 101
Bray, Fr. 49°56′ N, 2°42′ E 163
Brazeau, Mount, Can. 52°31′ N, 117°27′ W 108
Brazeau, river, Can. 52°46′ N, 116°22′ W 108
Brazeau see Nordegg, Can. 52°28′ N, 116°7′ W 108
Brazil 10°11′ S, 55°28′ W 132
Brazil, Ind., U.S. 39°31′ N, 87°7′ W 102
Brazoria, Tex., U.S. 29°2′ N, 95°34′ W 96
Brazos Peak, N. Mex., U.S. 36°48′ N, 106°30′ W 92
Brazzaville, Congo 4°13′ S, 15°0′ E 218
Brčko, Bosn. and Herzg. 44°52′ N, 18°47′ E 168
Brea, Calif., U.S. 33°55′ N, 117°55′ W 101
Brea, Cerros de la, Peru 4°32′ S, 80°56′ W 130
Breakenridge, Mount, Can. 49°42′ N, 121°58′ W 100
Breaux Bridge, La., U.S. 30°15′ N, 91°55′ W 103
Breaza, Rom. 45°11′ N, 25°38′ E 158
Breckenridge, Mich., U.S. 43°23′ N, 84°29′ W 102
Breckenridge, Minn., U.S. 46°14′ N, 96°35′ W 90
Breckenridge, Tex., U.S. 32°45′ N, 98°55′ W 112
Brecknock, Peninsula, Chile 54°36′ S, 74°29′ W 134
Břeclav, Czech Rep. 48°45′ N, 16°53′ E 152
Brecon, U.K. 51°56′ N, 3°23′ W 162
Brecon Beacons, peak, U.K. 51°53′ N, 3°28′ W 162
Brecon Beacons National Park, U.K. 51°53′ N, 3°26′ W 162
Breda, Neth. 51°34′ N, 4°45′ E 167
Bredasdorp, S. Af. 34°32′ S, 20°2′ E 227
Bredbyn, Nor. 63°26′ N, 18°6′ E 152
Bredene, Belg. 51°13′ N, 2°57′ E 150
Bredon Hill, U.K. 52°3′ N, 2°5′ W 162
Bredy, Russ. 52°25′ N, 60°17′ E 154
Breezewood, Pa., U.S. 39°59′ N, 78°15′ W 94
Bregovo, Bulg. 44°9′ N, 22°38′ E 168
Breil-sur-Roya, Fr. 43°56′ N, 7°29′ E 167
Breitenworbis, Ger. 51°25′ N, 10°25′ E 167
Breitungen, Ger. 50°45′ N, 10°18′ E 167
Brejo, Braz. 3°41′ S, 42°50′ W 132
Brejolândia, Braz. 12°30′ S, 43°58′ W 132
Brekovica, Bosn. and Herzg. 44°51′ N, 15°51′ E 168
Breloh, Ger. 53°1′ N, 10°5′ E 150
Bremangerpollen, Nor. 61°51′ N, 4°58′ E 152
Bremen, Ga., U.S. 33°41′ N, 85°8′ W 96
Bremen, Ger. 53°5′ N, 8°47′ E 163
Bremen, Ind., U.S. 41°26′ N, 86°9′ W 102
Bremen, Ohio, U.S. 39°41′ N, 82°26′ W 102
Bremen, adm. division, Ger. 53°4′ N, 8°27′ E 150
Bremer Bay 34°47′ S, 119°6′ E 230
Bremerhaven, Ger. 53°32′ N, 8°36′ E 150
Bremerton, Wash., U.S. 47°32′ N, 122°40′ W 100
Bremnes, Nor. 59°46′ N, 5°9′ E 152
Bremsnes, Nor. 63°4′ N, 7°39′ E 152
Brenes, Sp. 37°32′ N, 5°53′ W 164
Brenham, Tex., U.S. 30°9′ N, 96°24′ W 96
Brenner Pass, It. 47°0′ N, 11°30′ E 167
Breno, It. 45°57′ N, 10°18′ E 167
Brenton Bay 11°34′ S, 130°45′ E 230
Brentwood, Calif., U.S. 37°55′ N, 121°43′ W 100
Brentwood, N.Y., U.S. 40°47′ N, 73°14′ W 104
Brentwood, U.K. 51°37′ N, 0°17′ E 162
Brescia, It. 45°32′ N, 10°13′ E 167
Breskens, Neth. 51°23′ N, 3°33′ E 163
Bresles, Fr. 49°24′ N, 2°15′ E 163
Bressanone, It. 46°44′ N, 11°38′ E 167
Brest, Belarus 52°5′ N, 23°41′ E 152
Brest, Fr. 48°23′ N, 4°30′ W 150
Brest, Pol. 52°4′ N, 23°42′ E 160
Brestovac, Serb. 43°9′ N, 21°52′ E 168
Bretagne, adm. division, Fr. 48°10′ N, 4°8′ W 150
Breteuil, Fr. 49°37′ N, 2°17′ E 163
Breteuil, Fr. 48°49′ N, 0°54′ E 163
Breton, Can. 53°5′ N, 114°29′ W 108
Breton, Cape, Can. 45°56′ N, 59°46′ W 111
Bretón, Cayo, island, Cuba 21°7′ N, 80°16′ W 116
Breton Island, Cape, Can. 45°19′ N, 63°50′ W 81
Breton Sound 29°28′ N, 89°22′ W 103
Brett, Cape, N.Z. 35°11′ S, 174°16′ E 240
Breu, river, Braz. 3°45′ S, 66°39′ W 136
Breu, river, South America 9°25′ S, 72°31′ W 137
Breueh, island, Indonesia 5°47′ N, 94°35′ E 196
Breuil-Cervinia, It. 45°56′ N, 7°38′ E 167
Breves, Braz. 1°39′ S, 50°31′ W 130
Brevik, Nor. 59°3′ N, 9°41′ E 152
Brevoort Island, Can. 63°4′ N, 63°59′ W 106
Brevoort Lake, lake, Mich., U.S. 45°58′ N, 85°25′ W 110
Brew, Mount, Can. 50°34′ N, 122°2′ W 90
Brewer, Me., U.S. 44°47′ N, 68°46′ W 94
Brewerville, Liberia 6°20′ N, 10°47′ W 222
Brewster, Kans., U.S. 39°22′ N, 101°24′ W 90
Brewster, Mass., U.S. 41°45′ N, 70°5′ W 104
Brewster, Nebr., U.S. 41°54′ N, 99°52′ W 90
Brewster, N.Y., U.S. 41°23′ N, 73°39′ W 104
Brewster, Ohio, U.S. 40°42′ N, 81°36′ W 102
Brewster, Wash., U.S. 48°5′ N, 119°49′ W 90
Brewster, Mount, Antarctica 72°54′ S, 169°59′ E 248
Brewton, Ala., U.S. 31°6′ N, 87°4′ W 96
Breza, Bosn. and Herzg. 44°1′ N, 18°15′ E 168
Brezičani, Bosn. and Herzg. 45°0′ N, 16°40′ E 168
Brezina, Alg. 33°7′ N, 1°14′ E 214
Brezno, Slovakia 48°48′ N, 19°39′ E 156
Brezolles, Fr. 48°41′ N, 1°4′ E 163
Brezovo Polje, Bosn. and Herzg. 44°50′ N, 18°57′ E 168
Bria, Cen. Af. Rep. 6°29′ N, 22°2′ E 218
Brian Head, peak, Utah, U.S. 37°40′ N, 112°54′ W 92
Briançon, Fr. 44°53′ N, 6°38′ E 167
Briare, Fr. 47°38′ N, 2°43′ E 150
Bribie Island, Austral. 27°17′ S, 151°4′ E 230
Bridge City, Tex., U.S. 30°0′ N, 93°52′ W 103
Bridgehampton, N.Y., U.S. 40°56′ N, 72°19′ W 104
Bridgend, U.K. 51°30′ N, 3°34′ W 162
Bridgeport, Ala., U.S. 34°56′ N, 85°43′ W 96
Bridgeport, Calif., U.S. 38°15′ N, 119°16′ W 100
Bridgeport, Conn., U.S. 41°10′ N, 73°12′ W 104
Bridgeport, Nebr., U.S. 41°39′ N, 103°8′ W 90
Bridgeport, Tex., U.S. 33°11′ N, 97°45′ W 92
Bridgeport, Lake, Tex., U.S. 33°17′ N, 98°40′ W 81
Bridger Peak, Wyo., U.S. 41°10′ N, 107°7′ W 90
Bridgeton, N.C., U.S. 35°7′ N, 77°2′ W 96
Bridgetown, Barbados 13°3′ N, 59°43′ W 116
Bridgetown, Ohio, U.S. 39°8′ N, 84°39′ W 102
Bridgewater, Can. 44°22′ N, 64°33′ W 111
Bridgewater, Mass., U.S. 41°59′ N, 70°59′ W 104
Bridgnorth, U.K. 52°31′ N, 2°26′ W 162
Bridgton, Me., U.S. 44°3′ N, 70°43′ W 104
Bridgwater, U.K. 51°7′ N, 3°1′ W 162
Bridlington, U.K. 54°4′ N, 0°14′ E 162
Bridport, Vt., U.S. 43°58′ N, 73°20′ W 104
Brienne-le-Château, Fr. 48°23′ N, 4°31′ E 163
Brienz, Switz. 46°45′ N, 8°0′ E 167
Brienzer See, lake, Switz. 46°41′ N, 7°42′ E 167
Brig, Switz. 46°20′ N, 8°0′ E 167
Brigantine, N.J., U.S. 39°23′ N, 74°24′ W 94
Brigden, Can. 42°48′ N, 82°18′ W 102
Brigg, U.K. 53°32′ N, 0°29′ E 162
Brigham City, Utah, U.S. 41°30′ N, 112°0′ W 90
Brighouse, U.K. 53°42′ N, 1°47′ W 162
Brightlingsea, U.K. 51°48′ N, 1°1′ E 162
Brighton, Can. 44°1′ N, 77°43′ W 110
Brighton, Colo., U.S. 39°58′ N, 104°49′ W 90
Brighton, Mich., U.S. 42°30′ N, 83°47′ W 102
Brighton, U.K. 50°50′ N, 0°9′ E 162
Brijuni Otoci (Brioni Islands), Gulf of Venice 44°51′ N, 13°23′ E 167
Brikama, Gambia 13°17′ N, 16°33′ W 222
Brilon, Ger. 51°24′ N, 8°32′ E 167
Brimfield, Ill., U.S. 40°49′ N, 89°54′ W 102
Brinkburn Priory, site, U.K. 55°16′ N, 1°55′ W 150
Brinkley, Ark., U.S. 34°51′ N, 91°12′ W 96
Brinnon, Wash., U.S. 47°39′ N, 122°55′ W 100
Brion, Île, island, Can. 47°28′ N, 61°18′ W 81
Brioni Islands see Brijuni Otoci, Gulf of Venice 44°51′ N, 13°23′ E 167
Brioude, Fr. 45°17′ N, 3°21′ E 150
Briouze, Fr. 48°41′ N, 0°23′ E 150
Brisbane, Austral. 27°28′ S, 152°53′ E 230
Bristol, Conn., U.S. 41°40′ N, 72°56′ W 104
Bristol, Ind., U.S. 41°42′ N, 85°50′ W 102
Bristol, N.H., U.S. 43°35′ N, 71°45′ W 104
Bristol, R.I., U.S. 41°40′ N, 71°17′ W 104
Bristol, S. Dak., U.S. 45°19′ N, 97°47′ W 90
Bristol, Tenn., U.S. 36°35′ N, 82°12′ W 96
Bristol, U.K. 51°26′ N, 2°35′ W 162
Bristol, Vt., U.S. 44°8′ N, 73°5′ W 104
Bristol Bay 56°13′ N, 160°33′ W 106
Bristol Channel 51°25′ N, 4°42′ W 150
Bristol Mountains, Calif., U.S. 34°58′ N, 116°11′ W 101
Bristow, Okla., U.S. 35°47′ N, 96°23′ W 94
Britannia Beach, Can. 49°36′ N, 123°12′ W 100
British Channel 80°37′ N, 47°37′ E 160
British Columbia, adm. division, Can. 54°39′ N, 126°22′ W 106
British Indian Ocean Territory, United Kingdom 7°0′ S, 72°0′ E 188
British Mountains, Can. 69°15′ N, 141°7′ W 98
British Virgin Islands, United Kingdom 18°31′ N, 64°41′ W 116
Brits, S. Af. 25°40′ S, 27°46′ E 227
Britstown, S. Af. 30°36′ S, 23°31′ E 227
Britt, Can. 45°47′ N, 80°32′ W 94
Britt, Iowa, U.S. 43°4′ N, 93°47′ W 94
Britton, S. Dak., U.S. 45°46′ N, 97°46′ W 94
Brive, Fr. 45°8′ N, 1°31′ E 150
Briviesca, Sp. 42°32′ N, 3°21′ W 150
Brnaze, Croatia 43°40′ N, 16°39′ E 168
Brno, Czech Rep. 49°11′ N, 16°37′ E 152
Broadback, river, Can. 51°13′ N, 78°42′ W 110
Broaddus, Tex., U.S. 31°17′ N, 94°17′ W 103
Broadstairs, U.K. 51°21′ N, 1°25′ E 163
Broadus, Mont., U.S. 45°25′ N, 105°26′ W 90
Broadview, Can. 50°22′ N, 102°35′ W 108
Broadwater, Nebr., U.S. 41°36′ N, 102°52′ W 90
Broceni, Latv. 56°41′ N, 22°33′ E 166
Brochet, Can. 57°54′ N, 101°39′ W 108
Brochet, Lac au, lake, Can. 49°40′ N, 70°15′ W 94
Brochet, Lac, lake, Can. 58°38′ N, 101°52′ W 108
Brock Island, Can. 78°23′ N, 115°4′ W 246
Brock, river, Can. 50°5′ N, 75°5′ W 110
Brocken, peak, Ger. 51°47′ N, 10°30′ E 152
Brockport, N.Y., U.S. 43°12′ N, 77°58′ W 94
Brockport, Pa., U.S. 41°15′ N, 78°45′ W 94
Brockton, Mass., U.S. 42°4′ N, 71°2′ W 104
Brockville, Can. 44°36′ N, 75°42′ W 110
Brockway, Mont., U.S. 47°16′ N, 105°46′ W 90
Brockway, Pa., U.S. 41°14′ N, 78°48′ W 94
Brocton, Ill., U.S. 39°43′ N, 87°56′ W 102
Brod, Maced. 41°31′ N, 21°12′ E 168
Brodarevo, Serb. 43°13′ N, 19°42′ E 168
Brodec, Maced. 41°46′ N, 20°41′ E 168
Brodeur Peninsula, Can. 71°43′ N, 89°33′ W 106
Brodhead, Wis., U.S. 42°37′ N, 89°23′ W 102
Brodica, Serb. 44°29′ N, 21°49′ E 168
Brodick, U.K. 55°34′ N, 5°9′ W 150
Brodilovo, Bulg. 42°5′ N, 27°51′ E 156
Brodnytsya, Ukr. 51°45′ N, 26°16′ E 152
Brodokalmak, Russ. 55°33′ N, 61°59′ E 154
Brody, Ukr. 50°4′ N, 25°8′ E 152
Brogan, Oreg., U.S. 44°14′ N, 117°32′ W 90
Broken Arrow, Okla., U.S. 36°2′ N, 95°47′ W 96
Broken Bow, Nebr., U.S. 41°24′ N, 99°39′ W 90
Broken Bow, Okla., U.S. 34°1′ N, 94°45′ W 96
Broken Bow Lake, lake, Okla., U.S. 34°10′ N, 94°57′ W 96
Broken Hill see Kabwe, Zambia 14°29′ S, 28°25′ E 224
Broken Ridge, Indian Ocean 31°50′ S, 95°31′ E 254
Brokind, Nor. 58°12′ N, 15°40′ E 152
Brokopondo, Suriname 5°4′ N, 55°2′ W 130
Bromarv, Fin. 59°58′ N, 23°0′ E 166
Bromley Mountain, Vt., U.S. 43°13′ N, 72°58′ W 104
Bromyard, U.K. 52°10′ N, 2°31′ W 162
Brønderslev, Den. 57°15′ N, 9°56′ E 150
Broni, It. 45°4′ N, 9°15′ E 167
Brønnøysund, Nor. 65°26′ N, 12°12′ E 152
Bronson, Fla., U.S. 29°26′ N, 82°40′ W 105
Bronson, Tex., U.S. 31°19′ N, 94°1′ W 103
Bronte, Tex., U.S. 31°52′ N, 100°18′ W 92
Bronyts'ka Huta, Ukr. 50°54′ N, 27°18′ E 152
Brook, Ind., U.S. 40°51′ N, 87°22′ W 102
Brookeland, Tex., U.S. 31°7′ N, 93°59′ W 103
Brooker, Fla., U.S. 29°53′ N, 82°21′ W 105
Brooke's Point, Philippines 8°48′ N, 117°50′ E 203
Brookfield, Conn., U.S. 41°28′ N, 73°25′ W 104
Brookfield, Mo., U.S. 39°46′ N, 93°3′ W 94
Brookfield, Wis., U.S. 43°4′ N, 88°7′ W 102
Brookhaven, Miss., U.S. 31°34′ N, 90°26′ W 103
Brookhaven National Laboratory, N.Y., U.S. 40°52′ N, 72°54′ W 104
Brookings, Oreg., U.S. 42°3′ N, 124°16′ W 82
Brookline, Mass., U.S. 42°19′ N, 71°8′ W 104
Brooklyn, Conn., U.S. 41°47′ N, 71°58′ W 104
Brooklyn, Ind., U.S. 39°32′ N, 86°24′ W 102
Brooklyn, Mich., U.S. 42°5′ N, 84°15′ W 102
Brooklyn, Miss., U.S. 31°2′ N, 89°10′ W 103
Brookmere, Can. 49°48′ N, 120°51′ W 100
Brookport, Mo., U.S. 37°7′ N, 88°37′ W 96
Brooks, Can. 50°33′ N, 111°55′ W 90
Brooks Bay 50°11′ N, 128°1′ W 108
Brooks Brook, Can. 60°25′ N, 133°10′ W 108
Brooks, Cape, Antarctica 73°53′ S, 60°24′ W 248
Brooks Range, Alas., U.S. 67°30′ N, 153°45′ W 106
Brookston, Ind., U.S. 40°35′ N, 86°52′ W 102
Brooksville, Fla., U.S. 28°34′ N, 82°24′ W 105
Brooksville, Ky., U.S. 38°39′ N, 84°5′ W 102
Brooksville, Miss., U.S. 33°12′ N, 88°35′ W 103
Brookville, Ind., U.S. 39°25′ N, 85°1′ W 102
Brookville, Pa., U.S. 41°9′ N, 79°5′ W 94
Brookville Lake, Ind., U.S. 39°31′ N, 85°11′ W 102
Brookwood, Ala., U.S. 33°16′ N, 87°19′ W 103
Broome, Austral. 17°58′ S, 122°20′ E 238
Broqueles, Punta, Col. 9°13′ N, 76°36′ W 136
Brøstrud, Nor. 60°18′ N, 8°30′ E 152
Brothers, The, islands, North Atlantic Ocean 21°50′ N, 75°43′ W 116
Brothers, The, islands, Red Sea 26°35′ N, 34°31′ E 180
Brou, Fr. 48°12′ N, 1°10′ E 163
Brough, U.K. 54°31′ N, 2°19′ W 162
Broughton in Furness, U.K. 54°17′ N, 3°13′ W 162
Broughton Island see Qikiqtarjuaq, Can. 67°30′ N, 63°52′ W 73
Broulkou, spring, Chad 16°39′ N, 18°11′ E 216
Brouwershaven, Neth. 51°43′ N, 3°53′ E 163
Brovary, Ukr. 50°30′ N, 30°52′ E 158
Browerville, Minn., U.S. 46°4′ N, 94°53′ W 90
Brown City, Mich., U.S. 43°13′ N, 82°59′ W 102
Brown Willy, peak, U.K. 50°34′ N, 4°41′ W 150
Browne Bay 72°57′ N, 100°30′ W 106
Brownfield, Me., U.S. 43°56′ N, 70°56′ W 104
Brownfield, Tex., U.S. 33°9′ N, 102°17′ W 92
Brownhills, U.K. 52°39′ N, 1°56′ W 162
Browning, Mont., U.S. 48°31′ N, 113°2′ W 90
Browns, Ala., U.S. 32°26′ N, 87°22′ W 103
Browns, N.Z. 46°10′ S, 168°25′ E 240
Brown's Cay, island, Bahamas 25°19′ N, 79°26′ W 105
Browns Town, Jam. 18°23′ N, 77°23′ W 115
Browns Valley, Minn., U.S. 45°35′ N, 96°50′ W 90
Brownsboro, Tex., U.S. 32°17′ N, 95°37′ W 103
Brownson Islands, Amundsen Sea 73°56′ S, 104°11′ W 248
Brownstown, Ind., U.S. 38°53′ N, 86°3′ W 102
Brownsville, Tenn., U.S. 35°34′ N, 89°16′ W 96
Brownsville, Tex., U.S. 25°57′ N, 97°28′ W 114
Brownsville, Vt., U.S. 43°28′ N, 72°29′ W 104
Brownsweg, Suriname 4°59′ N, 55°11′ W 130
Brownwood, Tex., U.S. 31°41′ N, 98°58′ W 92
Brownwood, Lake, Tex., U.S. 31°52′ N, 99°50′ W 81
Bršečine, Croatia 42°43′ N, 17°57′ E 168
Bru, Nor. 61°32′ N, 5°12′ E 152
Bruce Mines, Can. 46°18′ N, 83°48′ W 94
Bruce, Mount, Austral. 22°39′ S, 117°57′ E 230

Bruce Peninsula, North America 44°50′ N, 81°23′ W 110
Bruck, Aust. 48°1′ N, 16°47′ E 168
Brugg, Switz. 47°28′ N, 8°13′ E 156
Brugge, Belg. 51°12′ N, 3°13′ E 163
Brüggen, Ger. 51°14′ N, 6°10′ E 167
Brühl, Ger. 50°49′ N, 6°53′ E 167
Bruini, India 29°10′ N, 96°8′ E 188
Brûlé, Lac, lake, Can. 46°54′ N, 77°32′ W 94
Brumado, Braz. 14°15′ S, 41°38′ W 138
Brumath, Fr. 48°44′ N, 7°41′ E 163
Brundidge, Ala., U.S. 31°42′ N, 85°49′ W 96
Bruneau, Idaho, U.S. 42°53′ N, 115°48′ W 90
Bruneau, river, Idaho, U.S. 42°57′ N, 115°48′ W 90
Brunei 5°0′ N, 115°0′ E 192
Brunico, It. 46°47′ N, 11°56′ E 167
Bruno, Can. 52°15′ N, 105°32′ W 108
Bruno, It. 44°46′ N, 8°26′ E 167
Brunson, S.C., U.S. 32°55′ N, 81°12′ W 96
Brunssum, Neth. 50°57′ N, 5°58′ E 167
Brunswick, Ga., U.S. 31°8′ N, 81°30′ W 96
Brunswick, Me., U.S. 43°54′ N, 69°59′ W 104
Brunswick, Ohio, U.S. 41°13′ N, 81°51′ W 102
Brunswick Lake, lake, Can. 48°56′ N, 83°57′ W 94
Brunswick Naval Air Station, Me., U.S. 43°53′ N, 69°58′ W 104
Brunswick, Peninsula de, Chile 53°26′ S, 73°18′ W 134
Brunt Ice Shelf, Antarctica 76°2′ S, 31°32′ W 248
Brus, Serb. 43°22′ N, 21°1′ E 168
Brus Laguna, Hond. 15°44′ N, 84°32′ W 115
Brusartsi, Bulg. 43°39′ N, 23°4′ E 168
Brush, Colo., U.S. 40°15′ N, 103°38′ W 90
Brusnik, Serb. 44°6′ N, 22°27′ E 168
Brusovo, Russ. 60°30′ N, 87°24′ E 169
Brusque, Braz. 27°6′ S, 48°55′ W 138
Brussels (Bruxelles), Belg. 50°50′ N, 4°17′ E 163
Brussels Capital, adm. division, Belg. 50°53′ N, 3°56′ E 150
Brusturi, Rom. 47°9′ N, 22°16′ E 168
Brusy, Pol. 53°53′ N, 17°43′ E 152
Bruxelles see Brussels, Belg. 50°50′ N, 4°17′ E 163
Bruyères, Fr. 48°12′ N, 6°42′ E 163
Bruzgi, Belarus 53°34′ N, 23°42′ E 152
Bruzual, Venez. 8°1′ N, 69°21′ W 136
Bryan, Ohio, U.S. 41°27′ N, 84°33′ W 102
Bryan, Tex., U.S. 30°39′ N, 96°22′ W 96
Bryansk, Russ. 53°12′ N, 34°25′ E 154
Bryansk, Russ. 44°19′ N, 46°58′ E 158
Bryansk, adm. division, Russ. 52°59′ N, 32°4′ E 154
Bryant, Ark., U.S. 34°34′ N, 92°30′ W 96
Bryant, Fla., U.S. 26°49′ N, 80°35′ W 105
Bryant, S. Dak., U.S. 44°33′ N, 97°30′ W 90
Bryant, Cape, Antarctica 71°34′ S, 60°10′ W 248
Bryant Pond, Me., U.S. 44°22′ N, 70°39′ W 104
Bryce Canyon National Park, Utah, U.S. 37°22′ N, 112°11′ W 92
Bryceland, La., U.S. 32°27′ N, 92°59′ W 103
Brykalansk, Russ. 65°28′ N, 54°14′ E 154
Bryne, Nor. 58°44′ N, 5°38′ E 152
Bryson City, N.C., U.S. 35°25′ N, 83°26′ W 96
Bryukhovetskaya, Russ. 45°50′ N, 38°56′ E 156
Brza Palanka, Serb. 44°28′ N, 22°25′ E 168
Brzeg, Pol. 50°50′ N, 17°28′ E 152
Bu Hasa, oil field, U.A.E. 23°27′ N, 53°7′ E 182
Bū Sunbul, Jabal, peak, Lib. 23°8′ N, 22°12′ E 216
Bua, river, Malawi 13°43′ S, 33°25′ E 224
Bua Yai, Thai. 15°35′ N, 102°24′ E 202
Bu'aale, Somalia 1°1′ N, 42°38′ E 224
Buan, S. Korea 35°43′ N, 126°45′ E 200
Buatan, Indonesia 0°44′ N, 101°47′ E 196
Buatyrma, river, Kaz. 49°39′ N, 84°23′ E 184
Bu'ayrāt al Ḩasūn, Lib. 31°23′ N, 15°41′ E 216
Buba, Guinea-Bissau 11°34′ N, 15°2′ W 222
Buberos, Sp. 41°38′ N, 2°12′ W 164
Būbīyān, island, Kuwait 29°40′ N, 48°23′ E 180
Bucak, Turk. 37°26′ N, 30°36′ E 180
Bucakkışla, Turk. 36°56′ N, 33°1′ E 156
Bucaramanga, Col. 7°7′ N, 73°6′ W 136
Buccaneer Archipelago, Indian Ocean 15°46′ S, 122°50′ E 230
Buchach, Ukr. 49°2′ N, 25°24′ E 152
Buchan Gulf 71°43′ N, 76°50′ W 106
Buchanan, Liberia 5°49′ N, 10°3′ W 222
Buchanan, Mich., U.S. 41°48′ N, 86°22′ W 102
Buchanan Bay 78°53′ N, 82°59′ W 246
Buchanan, Lake, Tex., U.S. 30°47′ N, 98°54′ W 92
Buchans, Can. 48°48′ N, 56°52′ W 111
Buchardo, Arg. 34°44′ S, 63°26′ W 139
Bucharest see Bucureşti, Rom. 44°27′ N, 25°57′ E 156
Buchon, Point, U.S. 35°10′ N, 121°14′ W 100
Buchy, Fr. 49°34′ N, 1°21′ E 163
Buciumi, Rom. 47°2′ N, 23°3′ E 168
Buck Point, Can. 52°52′ N, 132°58′ W 108
Buckatunna, Miss., U.S. 31°33′ N, 88°32′ W 103
Buckeye Lake, Ohio, U.S. 39°55′ N, 82°30′ W 102
Buckfield, Me., U.S. 44°16′ N, 70°23′ W 104
Buckingham, Can. 45°35′ N, 75°24′ W 94
Buckingham, U.K. 51°59′ N, 1°0′ E 162
Buckley, Ill., U.S. 40°35′ N, 88°3′ W 102
Buckley, Wash., U.S. 47°8′ N, 122°2′ W 100
Bucklin, Kans., U.S. 37°32′ N, 99°39′ W 90
Buckner, Ark., U.S. 33°21′ N, 93°27′ W 103
Buckner, Mo., U.S. 37°58′ N, 89°1′ W 96
Bucks, Ala., U.S. 31°0′ N, 88°1′ W 103
Buckskin Mountains, Ariz., U.S. 34°7′ N, 114°4′ W 101
Bucksport, Me., U.S. 44°34′ N, 68°48′ W 111
Buco Zau, Angola 4°44′ S, 12°30′ E 218
Bucoda, Wash., U.S. 46°47′ N, 122°53′ W 100
Bucovăţ, Mold. 47°11′ N, 28°28′ E 158
Bucureşti, adm. division, Rom. 44°32′ N, 25°44′ E 156
Bucureşti (Bucharest), Rom. 44°27′ N, 25°57′ E 156
Bucyrus, Ohio, U.S. 40°47′ N, 82°58′ W 102
Bud, Nor. 62°54′ N, 6°55′ E 152
Bud Bud, Somalia 4°12′ N, 46°30′ E 218
Buda, Tex., U.S. 30°3′ N, 97°50′ W 92
Buda, Ukr. 51°14′ N, 27°16′ E 152
Budac, peak, Rom. 47°5′ N, 25°35′ E 156
Budăi, Mold. 45°51′ N, 28°28′ E 156
Budalin, Myanmar 22°24′ N, 95°8′ E 202
Buđanovci, Serb. 44°53′ N, 19°51′ E 168
Budapest, Hung. 47°28′ N, 19°1′ E 168
Budapest, adm. division, Hung. 47°25′ N, 18°44′ E 156
Budaun, India 28°1′ N, 79°8′ E 197
Budd Coast, Antarctica 67°41′ S, 114°55′ E 248
Bude, Miss., U.S. 31°27′ N, 90°51′ W 103
Budennovsk, Russ. 44°44′ N, 44°2′ E 158
Budennovskaya, Russ. 46°51′ N, 41°33′ E 158
Buđevo, Serb. 43°7′ N, 20°3′ E 168
Büdingen, Ger. 50°17′ N, 9°7′ E 167
Budogoshch', Russ. 59°18′ N, 32°30′ E 154
Budrio, It. 44°32′ N, 11°33′ E 167
Budva, Mont. 42°16′ N, 18°50′ E 168
Buech, river, Fr. 44°28′ N, 5°39′ E 165
Bueil, Lac, lake, Can. 50°46′ N, 74°38′ W 110
Buellton, Calif., U.S. 34°37′ N, 120°13′ W 100
Buen Tiempo, Cabo, Arg. 51°29′ S, 68°57′ W 134
Buena Vista, Bol. 17°29′ S, 63°39′ W 137
Buena Vista, Mex. 23°37′ N, 109°39′ W 112
Buena Vista, Venez. 6°11′ N, 68°34′ W 136
Buena Vista, Va., U.S. 37°44′ N, 79°22′ W 96
Buenaventura, Col. 3°49′ N, 77°4′ W 136
Buenaventura, Mex. 29°50′ N, 107°30′ W 92
Buenavista, Philippines 9°0′ N, 125°25′ E 203
BuenŽopolis, Braz. 17°53′ S, 44°12′ W 138
Buenos Aires, Arg. 34°37′ S, 58°34′ W 139
Buenos Aires, Col. 3°13′ S, 70°2′ W 136
Buenos Aires, adm. division, Arg. 36°12′ S, 61°3′ W 139
Buenos Aires, Punta, Arg. 42°12′ S, 66°20′ W 134
Buey, Cabeza de, peak, Sp. 38°37′ N, 3°15′ W 164
Buffalo, Minn., U.S. 45°9′ N, 93°53′ W 94
Buffalo, Mo., U.S. 37°37′ N, 93°5′ W 96
Buffalo, N.Y., U.S. 42°53′ N, 78°54′ W 94
Buffalo, Ohio, U.S. 39°55′ N, 81°29′ W 102
Buffalo, Okla., U.S. 36°48′ N, 99°38′ W 92
Buffalo, S. Dak., U.S. 45°34′ N, 103°34′ W 90
Buffalo, Tex., U.S. 31°27′ N, 96°4′ W 96
Buffalo, W. Va., U.S. 38°36′ N, 82°0′ W 102
Buffalo, Wyo., U.S. 44°20′ N, 106°42′ W 90
Buffalo Head Prairie, Can. 58°2′ N, 116°21′ W 108
Buffalo Hump, peak, Idaho, U.S. 45°35′ N, 115°46′ W 90
Buffalo Lake, Can. 60°18′ N, 115°54′ W 108
Buffalo Mountain, Nev., U.S. 40°12′ N, 118°13′ W 90
Buffalo Narrows, Can. 55°52′ N, 108°30′ W 108
Buffalo, river, Can. 59°23′ N, 114°33′ W 108
Buford, Ga., U.S. 34°6′ N, 84°1′ W 96
Bug, peninsula, Ger. 54°30′ N, 13°11′ E 152
Buga, Col. 3°54′ N, 76°21′ W 136
Buganda, region, Africa 1°2′ N, 31°15′ E 224
Bugdayly, Turkm. 38°27′ N, 54°23′ E 180
Bugge Islands, Bellingshausen Sea 69°2′ S, 69°44′ W 248
Bugojno, Bosn. and Herzg. 44°2′ N, 17°26′ E 168
Bugrino, Russ. 68°48′ N, 49°11′ E 169
Bugt, China 48°44′ N, 121°57′ E 198
Buguey, Philippines 18°16′ N, 121°49′ E 203
Bugul'ma, Russ. 54°33′ N, 52°52′ E 154
Buguruslan, Russ. 53°38′ N, 52°26′ E 154
Buhăeşti, Rom. 46°46′ N, 27°33′ E 156
Bu'ayrat al-'Utaybah, lake, Syr. 33°30′ N, 36°22′ E 194
Buhen, ruin(s), Sudan 21°46′ N, 30°51′ E 182
Buhera, Zimb. 19°21′ S, 31°26′ E 224
Buhl, Idaho, U.S. 42°37′ N, 114°46′ W 90
Buhl, Minn., U.S. 47°29′ N, 92°48′ W 110
Buhuşi, Rom. 46°43′ N, 26°41′ E 158
Bui National Park, Ghana 8°39′ N, 3°8′ W 222
Builth Wells, U.K. 52°8′ N, 3°24′ W 162
Buinsk, Russ. 54°58′ N, 48°17′ E 154
Buitepos, Namibia 22°17′ S, 19°56′ E 227
Bujalance, Sp. 37°53′ N, 4°23′ W 164
Bujanovac, Serb. 42°28′ N, 21°46′ E 168
Bujaraloz, Sp. 41°29′ N, 0°10′ E 164
Bujumbura, Burundi 3°25′ S, 29°11′ E 224
Bük, Hung. 47°22′ N, 16°46′ E 168
Buk, Pol. 52°21′ N, 16°31′ E 152
Buka, island, P.N.G. 5°15′ S, 153°51′ E 192
Bukachivtsi, Ukr. 49°14′ N, 24°30′ E 152
Bukadaban Feng, peak, China 36°12′ N, 90°26′ E 188
Bukama, Dem. Rep. of the Congo 9°15′ S, 25°50′ E 224
Bukanik, Maja, peak, Alban. 41°0′ N, 20°10′ E 156
Bukavu, Dem. Rep. of the Congo 2°32′ S, 28°48′ E 224
Bukcha, Belarus 51°45′ N, 27°38′ E 152
Bukene, Tanzania 4°15′ S, 32°52′ E 224
Bukhara see Buxoro, Uzb. 39°47′ N, 64°25′ E 197
Bukit Baka-Bukit Raya National Park, Indonesia 0°53′ N, 112°3′ E 238
Bukit Tawau National Park, Malaysia 4°28′ N, 117°35′ E 238
Bukit Tigah Puluh National Park, Indonesia 0°58′ N, 102°38′ E 196
Bukittinggi, Indonesia 0°17′ N, 100°22′ E 196
Bükk, Hung. 47°58′ N, 20°23′ E 168
Bükkösd, Hung. 46°6′ N, 17°59′ E 168
Bukmuiža, Latv. 56°10′ N, 27°40′ E 166
Bukoba, Tanzania 1°22′ S, 31°47′ E 224
Bukowiec, Pol. 52°16′ N, 16°14′ E 152
Bukukun, Russ. 49°24′ N, 111°9′ E 198
Bukwiumi, Nig. 12°5′ N, 5°26′ E 222
Bula, Indonesia 3°5′ S, 130°24′ E 192
Bula, Nig. 10°1′ N, 9°36′ E 222
Bülach, Switz. 47°31′ N, 8°32′ E 150
Bulacle, Somalia 5°20′ N, 46°32′ E 218
Bülaevo, Kaz. 54°55′ N, 70°26′ E 184
Bulag, Mongolia 48°12′ N, 108°30′ E 198
Bulan, Ky., U.S. 37°17′ N, 83°10′ W 96
Bulan, Philippines 12°42′ N, 123°53′ E 203
Bulanash, Russ. 57°17′ N, 61°59′ E 154
Bulancak, Turk. 40°57′ N, 38°12′ E 156
Bulandshahr, India 28°24′ N, 77°52′ E 197
Bulanık, Turk. 39°5′ N, 42°14′ E 195
Bulawayo, Zimb. 20°9′ S, 28°36′ E 227
Buldan, Turk. 38°2′ N, 28°49′ E 156
Bulgan, Mongolia 48°49′ N, 103°38′ E 198
Bulgan, Mongolia 44°6′ N, 103°34′ E 198
Bulgan, adm. division, Mongolia 48°20′ N, 102°20′ E 198
Bulgar, Russ. 54°59′ N, 49°17′ E 154
Bulgaria 42°38′ N, 24°1′ E 156
Bulgnéville, Fr. 48°12′ N, 5°49′ E 163
Buliluyan, Cape, Philippines 8°21′ N, 116°45′ E 203
Bull Mountains, Mont., U.S. 46°9′ N, 108°41′ W 90
Bulla Régia, ruin(s), Tun. 36°33′ N, 8°38′ E 156
Bullard, Tex., U.S. 32°7′ N, 95°19′ W 103
Bullas, Sp. 38°2′ N, 1°41′ W 164
Bullaxaar, Somalia 10°20′ N, 44°22′ E 216
Bulle, Switz. 46°37′ N, 7°3′ E 167
Bullhead City, Ariz., U.S. 35°8′ N, 114°34′ W 101
Bullion Mountains, Calif., U.S. 34°28′ N, 116°14′ W 101
Bullmoose Mountain, Can. 55°0′ N, 121°39′ W 108
Bulls, N.Z. 40°11′ S, 175°23′ E 240
Bulls Head, peak, Can. 49°36′ N, 110°55′ W 90
Bully Choop Mountain, Calif., U.S. 40°32′ N, 122°52′ W 90
Bultfontein, S. Af. 28°20′ S, 26°8′ E 227
Buluan, Philippines 6°43′ N, 124°47′ E 203
Bulukumba, Indonesia 5°34′ S, 120°3′ E 192
Bulungkol, China 38°40′ N, 74°55′ E 184
Bulungu, Dem. Rep. of the Congo 4°35′ S, 18°33′ E 218
Bulung'ur, Uzb. 39°45′ N, 67°15′ E 197
Bum La, pass, China 27°49′ N, 91°54′ E 197
Bumba, Dem. Rep. of the Congo 6°56′ S, 19°16′ E 218
Bumba, Dem. Rep. of the Congo 2°11′ N, 22°25′ E 218
Bumbah, Khalīj al 32°18′ N, 22°3′ E 216
Bumbat, Mongolia 46°29′ N, 104°3′ E 198
Bumbuli, Dem. Rep. of the Congo 3°25′ S, 20°29′ E 218
Buna, Bosn. and Herzg. 43°14′ N, 17°49′ E 168
Buna, Dem. Rep. of the Congo 3°18′ S, 18°56′ E 218
Buna, Kenya 2°44′ N, 39°31′ E 224
Buna, Tex., U.S. 30°24′ N, 93°58′ W 103
Bunazi, Tanzania 1°15′ S, 31°25′ E 224
Bunbury, Austral. 33°21′ S, 115°40′ E 231
Bunda, Tanzania 2°0′ S, 33°55′ E 224
Bunde, Ger. 53°10′ N, 7°17′ E 163
Bundi, India 25°25′ N, 75°38′ E 197
Bundoran, Ire. 54°27′ N, 8°18′ W 150
Bundyur, Russ. 57°33′ N, 81°58′ E 169
Bunga, Nig. 11°2′ N, 9°40′ E 222
Bungay, U.K. 52°27′ N, 1°26′ E 163
Bunger Hills, Antarctica 65°28′ S, 101°11′ E 248
Bungle Bungle Range, site, Austral. 17°26′ S, 128°18′ E 230
Bungo, Angola 7°28′ S, 15°22′ E 218
Bungo Suidō 33°1′ N, 132°0′ E 201
Bungoma, Kenya 0°32′ N, 34°34′ E 224
Bungotakada, Japan 33°33′ N, 131°26′ E 201
Bunia, Dem. Rep. of the Congo 1°31′ N, 30°11′ E 224
Bunker, Mo., U.S. 37°27′ N, 91°13′ W 94
Bunker Group, islands, Coral Sea 23°51′ S, 152°40′ E 230
Bunker Hill, Ind., U.S. 40°38′ N, 86°6′ W 102
Bunker Hill, Nev., U.S. 39°15′ N, 117°13′ W 90
Bunkerville, Nev., U.S. 36°46′ N, 114°8′ W 101
Bunkeya, Dem. Rep. of the Congo 10°25′ S, 26°56′ E 224
Bunkie, La., U.S. 30°56′ N, 92°11′ W 103
Bunnell, Fla., U.S. 29°27′ N, 81°17′ W 105
Bunnell Mountain, peak, N.H., U.S. 44°46′ N, 71°34′ W 94
Buñol, Sp. 39°25′ N, 0°48′ E 164
Bünyan, Turk. 38°50′ N, 35°51′ E 156
Bunza, Nig. 12°4′ N, 3°59′ E 222
Bunzoqa, Sudan 12°28′ N, 34°13′ E 182
Buol, Indonesia 1°7′ N, 121°19′ E 192
Buon Me Thuot, Vietnam 12°41′ N, 108°2′ E 202
Buor Khaya, Mys, Russ. 71°47′ N, 131°9′ E 172
Buq'ata, Israel 33°12′ N, 35°46′ E 194
Buqayq, Saudi Arabia 25°56′ N, 49°40′ E 196
Buqbuq, Egypt 31°31′ N, 25°33′ E 226
Bur, Russ. 58°48′ N, 107°4′ E 160
Bûr Fu'ad, Egypt 31°14′ N, 32°19′ E 194
Bur, river, Russ. 70°58′ N, 120°22′ E 160
Bûr Safâga, Egypt 26°44′ N, 33°54′ E 180
Bûr Sa'îd (Port Said), Egypt 31°15′ N, 32°18′ E 194
Bûr Taufîq, Egypt 29°56′ N, 32°30′ E 180
Bura, Kenya 1°6′ S, 39°58′ E 224
Buraan, Somalia 10°10′ N, 48°43′ E 216
Buram, Sudan 10°50′ N, 25°11′ E 224
Buranhém, river, Braz. 16°30′ S, 40°4′ W 138
Burannoye, Russ. 50°59′ N, 54°29′ E 158
Burao (Burco), Somalia 9°34′ N, 45°36′ E 207
Burāq, Syr. 33°10′ N, 36°29′ E 194
Buras, La., U.S. 29°20′ N, 89°32′ W 103
Buratai, Nig. 10°54′ N, 12°4′ E 216
Buraydah, Saudi Arabia 26°21′ N, 44°0′ E 180
Burbach, Ger. 50°44′ N, 8°4′ E 163
Burbank, Calif., U.S. 34°10′ N, 118°18′ W 101
Burco see Burao, Somalia 9°34′ N, 45°36′ E 207
Burdalyk, Turkm. 38°24′ N, 64°22′ E 197
Burden, Mount, Can. 56°9′ N, 123°33′ W 108
Burdesi, Eth. 6°32′ N, 37°13′ E 224
Burditt Lake, lake, Can. 48°53′ N, 94°13′ W 90
Burdur, Turk. 37°42′ N, 30°17′ E 156
Burduy, Russ. 65°39′ N, 48°5′ E 154
Burē, Eth. 8°18′ N, 35°7′ E 224
Burē, Eth. 10°42′ N, 37°3′ E 224
Bure, river, U.K. 52°50′ N, 1°9′ E 162
Büren, Ger. 51°32′ N, 8°33′ E 167
Bürenhayrhan, Mongolia 46°13′ N, 91°34′ E 190
Burford, U.K. 51°48′ N, 1°38′ W 162
Burg, Ger. 54°26′ N, 11°12′ E 152
Burg, Ger. 53°59′ N, 9°16′ E 152
Burg el 'Arab, Egypt 30°54′ N, 29°30′ E 180
Burgan, oil field, Kuwait 28°53′ N, 47°51′ E 196
Burgas, Bulg. 42°30′ N, 27°28′ E 156
Burgas, adm. division, Bulg. 42°44′ N, 26°44′ E 156
Burgaw, N.C., U.S. 34°33′ N, 77°56′ W 96
Burgdorf, Switz. 47°2′ N, 7°37′ E 150
Burgersdorp, S. Af. 31°0′ S, 26°17′ E 227
Burgess Hill, U.K. 50°57′ N, 0°9′ E 162
Burgess, Mount, Can. 66°4′ N, 139°58′ W 98
Burgos, Mex. 24°55′ N, 98°47′ W 114
Burgos, Sp. 42°18′ N, 3°43′ W 164
Burgsinn, Ger. 50°8′ N, 9°38′ E 167
Burgsvik, Sw. 57°2′ N, 18°16′ E 166
Burguete see Auritz, Sp. 42°59′ N, 1°21′ W 164
Burgui, Sp. 42°43′ N, 1°2′ W 164
Burgundy, region, Europe 47°10′ N, 4°11′ E 165
Burhaniye, Turk. 39°30′ N, 26°57′ E 156
Burhanpur, India 21°18′ N, 76°12′ E 188
Burhave, Ger. 53°34′ N, 8°22′ E 163
Buribay, Russ. 51°57′ N, 58°11′ E 154
Burica, Punta, C.R. 7°56′ N, 83°32′ W 115
Burigi, Lake, Tanzania 2°5′ S, 30°45′ E 224
Burin, Can. 47°2′ N, 55°10′ W 111
Buritis, Braz. 15°38′ S, 46°27′ W 138
Burkburnett, Tex., U.S. 34°4′ N, 98°34′ W 92
Burke, S. Dak., U.S. 43°9′ N, 99°18′ W 90
Burke, Tex., U.S. 31°13′ N, 94°47′ W 103
Burke Island, Antarctica 72°57′ S, 105°21′ W 248
Burketown, Austral. 17°46′ S, 139°40′ E 238
Burkett, Mount, Can. 57°9′ N, 132°27′ W 108
Burkeville, Tex., U.S. 30°58′ N, 93°40′ W 103
Burkina Faso 12°40′ N, 1°39′ W 214
Burk's Falls, Can. 45°37′ N, 79°24′ W 94
Burla, Russ. 53°16′ N, 78°23′ E 184
Burleson, Tex., U.S. 32°32′ N, 97°19′ W 96
Burlingame, Kans., U.S. 38°43′ N, 95°50′ W 90
Burlington, Can. 43°19′ N, 79°47′ W 94
Burlington, Colo., U.S. 39°17′ N, 102°16′ W 90
Burlington, N.J., U.S. 40°3′ N, 74°52′ W 94
Burlington, Vt., U.S. 44°28′ N, 73°13′ W 104
Burlington, Wash., U.S. 48°28′ N, 122°20′ W 100
Burlington, Wis., U.S. 42°40′ N, 88°17′ W 102
Burma see Myanmar 21°5′ N, 95°9′ E 192
Burmantovo, Russ. 61°17′ N, 60°29′ E 154
Burnaby, Can. 49°16′ N, 122°57′ W 100
Burnet, Tex., U.S. 30°44′ N, 98°13′ W 96
Burnett Bay 73°53′ N, 127°36′ W 106
Burnett Lake, lake, Can. 59°1′ N, 102°51′ W 108
Burney, Calif., U.S. 40°53′ N, 121°40′ W 90
Burney Mountain, Calif., U.S. 40°47′ N, 121°43′ W 90
Burnham Market, U.K. 52°56′ N, 0°44′ E 162
Burnham on Crouch, U.K. 51°37′ N, 0°49′ E 162
Burnham on Sea, U.K. 51°14′ N, 2°59′ W 162
Burnie, Austral. 41°3′ S, 145°55′ E 231
Burnley, U.K. 53°47′ N, 2°14′ W 162
Burnmouth, U.K. 55°50′ N, 2°5′ W 150
Burns, Miss., U.S. 32°6′ N, 89°33′ W 103
Burns, Oreg., U.S. 43°35′ N, 119°4′ W 90
Burns, Wyo., U.S. 41°11′ N, 104°22′ W 90
Burns Lake, Can. 54°13′ N, 125°46′ W 108
Burnt Peak, Calif., U.S. 34°40′ N, 118°38′ W 101
Burnt, river, Oreg., U.S. 44°33′ N, 118°8′ W 80
Burqin, China 47°44′ N, 86°53′ E 184
Burr, Mount, Austral. 37°40′ S, 140°15′ E 230
Burra, Nig. 11°1′ N, 8°59′ E 222
Burrel, Alban. 41°36′ N, 20°0′ E 168
Burren, region, Europe 52°59′ N, 9°22′ W 150
Burriana, Sp. 39°54′ N, 0°4′ W 164
Burrinjuck Reservoir, lake, Austral. 34°54′ S, 147°35′ E 230
Burro Peak, N. Mex., U.S. 32°34′ N, 108°30′ W 92
Burro, Serranías del, Mex. 29°31′ N, 102°42′ W 112
Burrow Head, U.K. 54°42′ N, 4°22′ W 150
Burrton, Kans., U.S. 38°1′ N, 97°41′ W 90
Burrwood, La., U.S. 28°58′ N, 89°23′ W 103
Bursa, Turk. 40°12′ N, 29°2′ E 156
Burscheid, Ger. 51°5′ N, 7°6′ E 167
Bursey, Mount, Antarctica 75°54′ S, 131°52′ W 248
Burt Lake, lake, Mich., U.S. 45°25′ N, 84°58′ W 94
Burtnieku Ezers, lake, Latv. 57°45′ N, 24°55′ E 166
Burton, Mich., U.S. 42°57′ N, 83°36′ W 102
Burton, Nebr., U.S. 42°53′ N, 99°36′ W 90
Burton Agnes, U.K. 54°2′ N, 0°20′ E 162
Burton upon Trent, U.K. 52°48′ N, 1°39′ W 162
Buru, island, Indonesia 3°2′ S, 126°2′ E 192
Burûn, Râs, Egypt 31°13′ N, 32°58′ E 194
Burun Shibertuy, Gora, peak, Russ. 49°36′ N, 109°46′ E 198
Burundi 3°0′ S, 30°0′ E 224
Bururi, Burundi 3°57′ S, 29°38′ E 224
Burutu, Nig. 5°23′ N, 5°31′ E 222
Burwash Landing, Can. 61°26′ N, 139°1′ W 98
Burwell, Nebr., U.S. 41°45′ N, 99°9′ W 90
Bury Saint Edmunds, U.K. 52°14′ N, 0°42′ E 162
Buryatiya, adm. division, Russ. 53°21′ N, 108°28′ E 160
Bürylbaytal, Kaz. 44°52′ N, 74°3′ E 184
Burzil Pass, Pak. 34°52′ N, 75°4′ E 186
Busan (Pusan), S. Korea 35°6′ N, 129°3′ E 200
Busan City, adm. division, S. Korea 35°8′ N, 129°3′ E 200
Busanga, Dem. Rep. of the Congo 10°13′ S, 25°19′ E 224
Busanga Swamp, marsh, Zambia 14°24′ S, 25°16′ E 224
Busangu, Dem. Rep. of the Congo 8°32′ S, 25°27′ E 224
Buşayrā, Jordan 30°44′ N, 35°36′ E 194
Busca, It. 44°31′ N, 7°28′ E 167
Buseck, Ger. 50°36′ N, 8°47′ E 167
Būshehr, Iran 28°54′ N, 50°52′ E 196
Bushgan, oil field, Iran 28°56′ N, 51°53′ E 196
Bushmanland, region, Africa 29°42′ S, 19°4′ E 227
Bushnell, Fla., U.S. 28°40′ N, 82°7′ W 105
Bushnell, Mo., U.S. 40°32′ N, 90°31′ W 94
Bushnell, Nebr., U.S. 41°13′ N, 103°54′ W 90
Bushtricë, Alban. 41°52′ N, 20°25′ E 168
Businga, Dem. Rep. of the Congo 3°17′ N, 20°56′ E 218
Busira, river, Dem. Rep. of the Congo 0°26′ N, 19°3′ E 218
Buslē, Eth. 5°23′ N, 44°20′ E 218
Busovača, Bosn. and Herzg. 44°6′ N, 17°51′ E 168
Buşrá al Ḩarīrī, Syr. 32°50′ N, 36°20′ E 194
Buşrá ash Shām, Syr. 32°31′ N, 36°28′ E 194
Busseri, Sudan 7°31′ N, 27°57′ E 224
Busseri, river, Sudan 6°38′ N, 26°33′ E 224
Bussoleno, It. 45°8′ N, 7°8′ E 167
Bussum, Neth. 52°16′ N, 5°9′ E 163
Bustamante, Mex. 26°30′ N, 100°32′ W 114
Bustard Islands, North America 45°37′ N, 81°16′ W 94
Bustarviejo, Sp. 40°51′ N, 3°42′ W 164
Buştenari, oil field, Rom. 45°7′ N, 25°44′ E 156
Bustillos, Laguna, lake, Mex. 28°34′ N, 107°21′ W 92
Busto, Cabo, Sp. 43°34′ N, 6°28′ W 150
Buston, Taj. 40°30′ N, 69°17′ E 197
Busu Mandji, Dem. Rep. of the Congo 2°51′ N, 21°15′ E 218
Busu-Djanoa, Dem. Rep. of the Congo 1°39′ N, 21°20′ E 218
Bususulu, Dem. Rep. of the Congo 0°49′ N, 20°44′ E 218
But e Koritës, peak, Alban. 40°45′ N, 20°47′ E 156
Buta, Dem. Rep. of the Congo 2°44′ N, 24°44′ E 224
Butare, Rwanda 2°37′ S, 29°42′ E 224
Bute Helu, Kenya 2°40′ N, 39°51′ E 224
Bute Inlet 50°34′ N, 125°22′ W 90
Butembo, Dem. Rep. of the Congo 0°6′ N, 29°15′ E 224
Buteni, Rom. 46°20′ N, 22°8′ E 168
Buthidaung, Myanmar 20°54′ N, 92°28′ E 188
Butiá, Braz. 30°8′ S, 51°56′ W 139
Butiaba, Uganda 1°47′ N, 31°19′ E 224
Butler, Ala., U.S. 32°5′ N, 88°13′ W 103
Butler, Ga., U.S. 32°33′ N, 84°14′ W 96
Butler, Ky., U.S. 38°46′ N, 84°22′ W 102
Butler, Mo., U.S. 38°14′ N, 94°20′ W 94
Butler, Ohio, U.S. 40°34′ N, 82°26′ W 102
Butler, Pa., U.S. 40°51′ N, 79°54′ W 94
Butler Island, Antarctica 72°6′ S, 60°8′ W 248
Butļeri, Latv. 57°3′ N, 25°49′ E 166
Butlerville, Ind., U.S. 39°1′ N, 85°31′ W 102
Buţmah, oil field, Iraq 36°40′ N, 42°36′ E 195
Buton, island, Indonesia 4°47′ S, 123°16′ E 192
Butte, Mont., U.S. 45°59′ N, 112°32′ W 82
Butte, Nebr., U.S. 42°53′ N, 98°52′ W 90
Butte Mountains, Nev., U.S. 39°43′ N, 115°26′ W 90
Butterwick, U.K. 52°58′ N, 7°416′ E 162
Butterworth, Malaysia 5°24′ N, 100°23′ E 196
Buttes, Sierra, peak, Calif., U.S. 39°34′ N, 120°44′ W 90
Buttle Lake, lake, Can. 49°33′ N, 125°56′ W 90
Button Islands, Labrador Sea 60°23′ N, 64°18′ W 106
Buttonwillow, Calif., U.S. 35°24′ N, 119°30′ W 100
Butuan, Philippines 8°59′ N, 125°32′ E 203
Buturlinovka, Russ. 50°50′ N, 40°36′ E 158
Butwal, Nepal 27°41′ N, 83°30′ E 197
Butyaalo, Somalia 11°26′ N, 49°57′ E 216
Butzbach, Ger. 50°26′ N, 8°40′ E 167
Buuhoodle, Somalia 8°14′ N, 46°22′ E 218
Buulobarde, Somalia 3°48′ N, 45°37′ E 218
Buur Gaabo, Somalia 1°13′ S, 41°51′ E 224
Buurhakaba, Somalia 2°45′ N, 44°7′ E 218
Buwayḑān, Syr. 33°11′ N, 36°26′ E 194
Buxar, India 25°32′ N, 83°56′ E 197
Buxoro (Bukhara), Uzb. 39°47′ N, 64°25′ E 197
Buxton, Guyana 6°39′ N, 58°3′ W 130
Buxton, Me., U.S. 43°38′ N, 70°32′ W 104
Buxton, N.C., U.S. 35°16′ N, 75°34′ W 96
Buxton, U.K. 53°15′ N, 1°55′ W 162
Buy, Russ. 58°29′ N, 41°36′ E 154
Buyant, Mongolia 46°12′ N, 110°49′ E 198
Buyant Ovoo, Mongolia 44°56′ N, 107°12′ E 198
Buyant-Uhaa see Saynshand, Mongolia 44°51′ N, 110°9′ E 190
Buynaksk, Russ. 42°48′ N, 47°7′ E 195
Buyo, Côte d'Ivoire 6°11′ N, 7°1′ W 222
Buyr Nuur, lake, Mongolia 47°49′ N, 117°29′ E 198
Buyun Shan, peak, China 40°4′ N, 122°41′ E 200
Buzancy, Fr. 49°25′ N, 4°57′ E 163
Buzău, adm. division, Rom. 45°36′ N, 26°10′ E 156
Buzău, Pasul, pass, Rom. 45°35′ N, 26°9′ E 156
Buzaymah, Lib. 24°55′ N, 22°1′ E 216
Buzlove, Ukr. 48°19′ N, 22°23′ E 152
Büzmey'in, Turkm. 38°1′ N, 58°16′ E 180
Buzul Daği, peak, Turk. 37°27′ N, 43°50′ E 195
Buzuluk, Russ. 52°46′ N, 52°13′ E 154
Buzzards Bay, Mass., U.S. 41°44′ N, 70°38′ W 104
Bwendi, Dem. Rep. of the Congo 4°1′ N, 26°42′ E 224
Bwere, river, Dem. Rep. of the Congo 3°44′ N, 27°19′ E 224
Byahoml', Belarus 54°43′ N, 28°3′ E 166
Byala, Bulg. 43°28′ N, 25°44′ E 156
Byala, Bulg. 42°52′ N, 27°53′ E 156
Byalynichy, Belarus 54°0′ N, 29°43′ E 166
Byam Channel 75°15′ N, 109°24′ W 106
Byam Martin, Cape, Can. 73°20′ N, 77°1′ W 106
Byam Martin Island, Can. 74°29′ N, 104°57′ W 106
Byarezina, river, Belarus 53°24′ N, 29°5′ E 152
Byarezina, river, Belarus 54°13′ N, 26°34′ E 166

Byaroza, *Belarus* 52°31′ N, 24°58′ E **152**
Byblos see Jbail, *Leb.* 34°7′ N, 35°39′ E **194**
Bychikha, *Belarus* 55°40′ N, 30°3′ E **166**
Bydalen, *Nor.* 63°5′ N, 13°45′ E **152**
Bydgoszcz, *Pol.* 53°8′ N, 18°1′ E **152**
Byer, *Ohio, U.S.* 39°9′ N, 82°38′ W **102**
Byerazino, *Belarus* 53°53′ N, 29°1′ E **166**
Byers, *Colo., U.S.* 39°42′ N, 104°14′ W **90**
Byesville, *Ohio, U.S.* 39°57′ N, 81°33′ W **102**
Bygdeå, *Nor.* 64°3′ N, 20°51′ E **152**
Bygstad, *Nor.* 61°22′ N, 5°41′ E **152**
Bykhaw, *Belarus* 53°30′ N, 30°18′ E **154**
Bykovo, *Russ.* 49°37′ N, 45°21′ E **158**
Bykovskiy, *Russ.* 71°43′ N, 129°19′ E **160**
Bylas, *Ariz., U.S.* 33°7′ N, 110°7′ W **92**
Bylot Island, *Can.* 73°51′ N, 81°13′ W **106**
Bylot, island, *Can.* 72°49′ N, 75°55′ W **106**
Byng Inlet, *Can.* 45°44′ N, 80°33′ W **94**
Bynguano Range, *Austral.* 31°8′ S, 142°42′ E **230**
Byram, *Miss., U.S.* 32°10′ N, 90°16′ W **103**
Byrd, Cape, *Antarctica* 69°52′ S, 79°21′ W **248**
Byrd, Lac, lake, *Can.* 47°1′ N, 77°12′ W **110**
Byron, *Calif., U.S.* 37°51′ N, 121°39′ W **100**
Byron, *Ill., U.S.* 42°7′ N, 89°16′ W **102**
Byron, Cape, *Austral.* 28°38′ S, 153°45′ E **230**
Byron, Isla, island, *Chile* 47°44′ S, 76°33′ W **134**
Byrum, *Den.* 57°14′ N, 10°59′ E **150**
Byske, *Nor.* 64°57′ N, 21°10′ E **152**
Bytów, *Pol.* 54°9′ N, 17°29′ E **152**
Byumba, *Rwanda* 1°39′ S, 30°2′ E **224**
Bzip'i, river, *Europe* 43°22′ N, 40°37′ E **195**

C

Ca Mau, *Vietnam* 9°12′ N, 105°7′ E **202**
Ca Na, *Vietnam* 11°22′ N, 108°51′ E **202**
Ca Na, Mui, *Vietnam* 10°56′ N, 109°0′ E **202**
Ca, river, *Vietnam* 19°12′ N, 104°44′ E **202**
C.A. Rosetti, *Rom.* 45°17′ N, 29°33′ E **156**
Caaguazú, *Parag.* 25°27′ S, 56°1′ W **132**
Caamaño Sound 52°48′ N, 129°56′ W **108**
Caapucú, *Parag.* 26°15′ S, 57°11′ W **139**
Caatinga, *Braz.* 17°8′ S, 45°58′ W **138**
Caazapá, *Parag.* 26°9′ S, 56°23′ W **139**
Cabaiguán, *Cuba* 22°5′ N, 79°31′ W **116**
Caballococha, *Peru* 3°58′ S, 70°30′ W **130**
Caballos Mesteños, Llano de los, *Mex.* 28°36′ N, 104°37′ W **112**
Cabana, *Peru* 8°25′ S, 78°1′ W **130**
Cabanaconde, *Peru* 15°40′ S, 71°58′ W **137**
Cabanatuan, *Philippines* 15°28′ N, 120°58′ E **203**
Cabañeros National Park, *Sp.* 39°14′ N, 4°33′ W **164**
Cabanes, *Sp.* 40°9′ N, 0°3′ E **164**
Cabano, *Can.* 47°39′ N, 68°55′ W **94**
Cabedelo, *Braz.* 7°4′ S, 34°52′ W **132**
Cabery, *Ill., U.S.* 40°59′ N, 88°13′ W **102**
Cabeza de Lagarto, Punta, *Peru* 10°15′ S, 80°8′ W **130**
Cabeza de Pava, *Col.* 2°47′ N, 69°13′ W **136**
Cabeza del Buey, *Sp.* 38°43′ N, 5°14′ W **164**
Cabezas, *Bol.* 18°49′ S, 63°26′ W **137**
Cabildo, *Arg.* 38°30′ S, 61°57′ W **139**
Cabimas, *Venez.* 10°24′ N, 71°29′ W **136**
Cabinda, *Angola* 5°35′ S, 12°10′ E **218**
Cabinet Mountains, *Mont., U.S.* 48°20′ N, 116°13′ W **90**
Cabiri, *Angola* 8°53′ S, 13°40′ E **220**
Cable, *Wis., U.S.* 46°12′ N, 91°17′ W **94**
Cabo Blanco, *Arg.* 47°12′ S, 65°47′ W **134**
Cabo Delgado, adm. division, *Mozambique* 12°22′ S, 38°34′ E **220**
Cabo Frio, *Braz.* 22°51′ S, 42°1′ W **138**
Cabo Gracias a Dios, *Nicar.* 14°58′ N, 83°14′ W **115**
Cabo Raso, *Arg.* 44°21′ S, 65°17′ W **134**
Cabo San Lucas, *Mex.* 22°51′ N, 109°56′ W **112**
Cabonga, Réservoir, lake, *Can.* 47°6′ N, 78°13′ W **81**
Cabonga, Réservoir, lake, *Can.* 47°14′ N, 78°10′ W **106**
Cabool, *Mo., U.S.* 37°6′ N, 92°6′ W **96**
Caborca, *Mex.* 30°42′ N, 112°11′ W **92**
Cabot, *Vt., U.S.* 44°23′ N, 72°20′ W **104**
Cabot Head, *Can.* 45°15′ N, 81°17′ W **94**
Cabot, Mount, *N.H., U.S.* 44°29′ N, 71°26′ W **104**
Cabra de Santo Cristo, *Sp.* 37°42′ N, 3°16′ W **164**
Cabral, *Dom. Rep.* 18°14′ N, 71°12′ W **116**
Cabrera Baja, Sierra de la, *Sp.* 42°3′ N, 7°8′ W **150**
Cabrera, island, *Sp.* 38°52′ N, 2°54′ E **214**
Cabri, *Can.* 50°37′ N, 108°28′ W **90**
Cabri Lake, lake, *Can.* 51°4′ N, 110°5′ W **90**
Cabriel, river, *Sp.* 39°23′ N, 1°27′ W **164**
Cabrillo National Monument, *Calif., U.S.* 32°40′ N, 117°17′ W **101**
Cabrobó, *Braz.* 8°31′ S, 39°21′ W **132**
Cabrón, Cabo, *Dom. Rep.* 19°22′ N, 69°11′ W **116**
Cabruta, *Venez.* 7°40′ N, 66°16′ W **136**
Cabugao, *Philippines* 17°49′ N, 120°27′ E **203**
Cabure, *Venez.* 11°9′ N, 69°38′ W **136**
Cabuyaro, *Col.* 4°16′ N, 72°48′ W **136**
Caçador, *Braz.* 26°47′ S, 51°0′ W **139**
Cacahuamilpa, *Mex.* 18°40′ N, 99°33′ W **114**
Cacahuatepec, *Mex.* 16°14′ N, 98°11′ W **112**
Cacahuatique, peak, *El Salv.* 13°45′ N, 88°20′ W **115**
Čačak, *Serb.* 43°52′ N, 20°20′ E **168**
Cacalotán, *Mex.* 23°4′ N, 105°50′ W **114**
Cacaoui, Lac, lake, *Can.* 50°52′ N, 67°26′ W **111**
Caçapava do Sul, *Braz.* 30°30′ S, 53°30′ W **139**
Caccia, Capo, *It.* 40°34′ N, 7°24′ E **156**
Cacequi, *Braz.* 29°55′ S, 54°51′ W **139**
Cáceres, *Braz.* 16°7′ S, 57°39′ W **132**
Cáceres, *Col.* 7°35′ N, 75°19′ W **136**
Cáceres, *Sp.* 39°28′ N, 6°23′ W **164**
Cachari, *Arg.* 36°23′ S, 59°31′ W **139**
Cache Bay, *Can.* 46°22′ N, 79°59′ W **94**
Cache Peak, *Idaho, U.S.* 42°11′ N, 113°43′ W **90**
Cacheu, *Guinea-Bissau* 12°14′ N, 16°7′ W **222**
Cachimbo, *Braz.* 9°19′ S, 54°51′ W **130**
Cachimbo, Serra do, *Braz.* 7°52′ S, 56°39′ W **130**
Cachingues, *Angola* 13°7′ S, 16°43′ E **220**
Cachisca, Lac, lake, *Can.* 50°24′ N, 75°36′ W **110**
Cachoeira, *Braz.* 14°23′ S, 55°34′ W **132**
Cachoeira Alta, *Braz.* 18°51′ S, 50°56′ W **138**
Cachoeira do Sul, *Braz.* 30°2′ S, 52°56′ W **139**
Cachoeira Ipadu, fall(s), *Braz.* 0°15′ N, 67°20′ W **136**
Cachoeira Ipanoré, fall(s), *Braz.* 0°13′ N, 68°29′ W **136**
Cachoeiro do Itapemirim, *Braz.* 20°54′ S, 41°9′ W **138**
Cachos, Punta, *Chile* 27°41′ S, 72°17′ W **134**
Cachuela Esperanza, *Bol.* 10°36′ S, 65°34′ W **137**
Cacine, *Guinea-Bissau* 11°6′ N, 15°2′ W **222**
Cacolo, *Angola* 10°11′ S, 19°13′ E **207**
Caconda, *Angola* 13°44′ S, 15°4′ E **220**
Cacongo, *Angola* 5°15′ S, 12°7′ E **218**
Cactus, *Tex., U.S.* 36°0′ N, 101°59′ W **92**
Cactus Flat, *Nev., U.S.* 37°52′ N, 116°55′ W **90**
Cactus Range, *Nev., U.S.* 37°54′ N, 117°6′ W **90**
Caçu, *Braz.* 18°35′ S, 51°12′ W **138**
Caculé, *Braz.* 14°34′ S, 42°12′ W **138**
Cacuri, *Venez.* 4°48′ N, 65°20′ W **136**
Cacuso, *Angola* 9°27′ S, 15°44′ E **218**
Cadaadley, *Somalia* 9°44′ N, 44°40′ E **218**
Cadair Idris, peak, *U.K.* 52°41′ N, 3°57′ W **162**
Cadale, *Somalia* 2°44′ N, 46°27′ E **218**
Cadaqués, *Sp.* 42°16′ N, 3°16′ E **164**
Čađavica, *Croatia* 45°45′ N, 17°50′ E **168**
Caddo, *Okla., U.S.* 34°6′ N, 96°16′ W **96**
Caddo Lake, *Tex., U.S.* 32°44′ N, 94°30′ W **81**
Cade, *La., U.S.* 30°2′ N, 91°54′ W **103**
Cadereyta, *Mex.* 25°34′ N, 99°59′ W **114**
Cadí, Serra del, *Sp.* 42°16′ N, 1°28′ E **164**
Cadillac, *Can.* 49°43′ N, 107°45′ W **90**
Cadillac Mountain, *Me., U.S.* 44°20′ N, 68°19′ W **94**
Çadır Dağı, peak, *Turk.* 38°12′ N, 43°3′ E **195**
Cadiz, *Ky., U.S.* 36°52′ N, 87°50′ W **96**
Cadiz, *Ohio, U.S.* 40°15′ N, 81°0′ W **102**
Cadiz, *Philippines* 10°56′ N, 123°16′ E **203**
Cádiz, *Sp.* 36°31′ N, 6°18′ W **164**
Cadomin, *Can.* 53°0′ N, 117°20′ W **108**
Cady Mountains, *Calif., U.S.* 34°57′ N, 116°20′ W **101**
Caen, *Fr.* 49°11′ N, 0°22′ E **150**
Caerdydd see Cardiff, *U.K.* 51°28′ N, 3°12′ W **162**
Caerlaverock Castle, site, *U.K.* 54°58′ N, 3°38′ W **150**
Caerleon, *U.K.* 51°36′ N, 2°57′ W **162**
Caernarfon, *U.K.* 53°9′ N, 4°14′ W **162**
Caerphilly, *U.K.* 51°35′ N, 3°13′ W **162**
Caesarea, ruin(s), *Israel* 32°29′ N, 34°51′ E **194**
Caeté, *Braz.* 19°54′ S, 43°35′ W **138**
Caeté, river, *Braz.* 9°29′ S, 69°35′ W **130**
Caetité, *Braz.* 14°5′ S, 42°31′ W **138**
Cafayate, *Arg.* 26°4′ S, 65°58′ W **132**
Cafuini, river, *Braz.* 1°12′ N, 58°27′ W **130**
Cagayan de Oro, *Philippines* 8°31′ N, 124°36′ E **203**
Cagayan Islands, *Sulu Sea* 9°6′ N, 121°20′ E **203**
Cagayan, river, *Philippines* 18°5′ N, 121°37′ E **203**
Cagayan Sulu Island, *Philippines* 6°52′ N, 118°36′ E **192**
Cagliari, *It.* 39°13′ N, 9°6′ E **156**
Cagnano Varano, *It.* 41°49′ N, 15°46′ E **156**
Caguán, river, *Col.* 1°9′ N, 74°44′ W **136**
Cahama, *Angola* 16°15′ S, 14°12′ E **220**
Cahora Bassa, *Mozambique* 15°38′ S, 32°46′ E **224**
Cahora Bassa Dam, *Mozambique* 15°46′ S, 32°3′ E **224**
Cahore Point, *Ire.* 52°34′ N, 6°9′ W **150**
Cahors, *Fr.* 44°31′ N, 1°18′ E **214**
Cahuinari National Park, *Col.* 1°18′ S, 71°54′ W **136**
Cahuinari, river, *Col.* 1°22′ S, 71°29′ W **136**
Cahuita National Park, *C.R.* 9°42′ N, 82°55′ W **115**
Cahul, *Mold.* 45°54′ N, 28°10′ E **156**
Cai Bau, *Vietnam* 21°8′ N, 107°28′ E **198**
Caia, *Mozambique* 17°49′ S, 35°18′ E **224**
Caiabis, Serra dos, *Braz.* 12°29′ S, 56°51′ W **130**
Caianda, *Angola* 11°4′ S, 23°30′ E **224**
Caiapó, river, *Braz.* 16°33′ S, 51°17′ W **138**
Caiapó, Serra do, *Braz.* 17°38′ S, 53°25′ W **132**
Caiapônia, *Braz.* 16°59′ S, 51°49′ W **138**
Caibarién, *Cuba* 22°29′ N, 79°28′ W **116**
Caicara, *Venez.* 7°36′ N, 66°10′ W **136**
Caicó, *Braz.* 6°30′ S, 37°7′ W **132**
Caicos Islands, *North Atlantic Ocean* 21°25′ N, 71°58′ W **116**
Caijiapo, *China* 34°19′ N, 107°33′ E **198**
Cailloma, *Peru* 15°13′ S, 71°45′ W **137**
Caimito, *Col.* 8°49′ N, 75°8′ W **136**
Cainde, *Angola* 15°34′ S, 13°20′ E **220**
Cains, river, *Can.* 46°20′ N, 66°23′ W **94**
Cainsville, *Mo., U.S.* 40°25′ N, 93°46′ W **94**
Caird Coast, *Antarctica* 76°29′ S, 32°29′ W **248**
Cairngorm Mountains, *U.K.* 57°3′ N, 4°35′ W **150**
Cairns, *Austral.* 16°56′ S, 145°45′ E **231**
Cairnwell Pass, *U.K.* 56°52′ N, 3°25′ W **150**
Cairo, *Ga., U.S.* 30°52′ N, 84°13′ W **96**
Cairo, *Mo., U.S.* 37°0′ N, 89°10′ W **96**
Cairo, *N.Y., U.S.* 42°17′ N, 74°1′ W **104**
Cairo see El Qâhira, *Egypt* 30°3′ N, 31°8′ E **180**
Cairo Montenotte, *It.* 44°23′ N, 8°16′ E **167**
Caistor, *U.K.* 53°29′ N, 0°19′ E **162**
Caithness, Ord of, peak, *U.K.* 58°8′ N, 3°41′ W **150**
Caitou, *Angola* 14°31′ S, 13°4′ E **220**
Caiundo, *Angola* 15°44′ S, 17°26′ E **220**
Caiza, *Bol.* 20°4′ S, 65°45′ W **137**
Caiza see Villa Ingavi, *Bol.* 21°47′ S, 63°33′ W **137**
Cajamarca, *Peru* 7°8′ S, 78°32′ W **130**
Cajamarca, adm. division, *Peru* 4°58′ S, 79°20′ W **130**
Cajatambo, *Peru* 10°30′ S, 77°1′ W **130**
Cajàzeiras, *Braz.* 6°54′ S, 38°32′ W **132**
Čajniče, *Bosn. and Herzg.* 43°33′ N, 19°4′ E **168**
Cajon Pass, *Calif., U.S.* 34°20′ N, 117°27′ W **101**
Caju, Ilha do, island, *Braz.* 2°56′ S, 42°35′ W **132**
Çakırgöl Dağı, peak, *Turk.* 40°33′ N, 39°38′ E **195**
Çakmak, *Turk.* 39°10′ N, 31°52′ E **156**
Çakmak Dağı, peak, *Turk.* 39°45′ N, 42°9′ E **195**
Çal, *Turk.* 38°4′ N, 29°23′ E **156**
Cal Madow, Buuraha, peak, *Somalia* 10°56′ N, 48°7′ E **218**
Cala, *Sp.* 37°57′ N, 6°19′ W **164**
Cala Rajada, *Sp.* 39°41′ N, 3°27′ E **150**
Cala see Doğruyol, *Turk.* 41°3′ N, 43°20′ E **195**
Calabar, *Nig.* 4°57′ N, 8°20′ E **222**
Calabozo, *Venez.* 8°55′ N, 67°28′ W **136**
Calabria, adm. division, *It.* 39°5′ N, 16°5′ E **156**
Calaburras, Punta de, *Sp.* 36°20′ N, 4°39′ W **164**
Calacoto, *Bol.* 17°22′ S, 68°43′ W **137**
Calaf, *Sp.* 41°43′ N, 1°30′ E **164**
Calafat, *Rom.* 43°59′ N, 22°56′ E **168**
Calahorra, *Sp.* 42°18′ N, 1°58′ W **164**
Calais, *Fr.* 50°57′ N, 1°51′ E **163**
Calais, *Me., U.S.* 45°10′ N, 67°17′ W **94**
Calakmul, ruin(s), *Mex.* 18°4′ N, 89°57′ W **115**
Calalaste, Sierra de, *Arg.* 25°16′ S, 67°50′ W **132**
Calalzo, *It.* 46°27′ N, 12°21′ E **167**
Calama, *Braz.* 8°3′ S, 62°51′ W **130**
Calama, *Chile* 22°28′ S, 68°58′ W **137**
Calamar, *Col.* 10°13′ N, 74°58′ W **136**
Calamar, *Col.* 1°57′ N, 72°34′ W **136**
Calamarca, *Bol.* 16°59′ S, 68°8′ W **137**
Calamian Group, islands, *Sulu Sea* 11°37′ N, 119°18′ E **203**
Calamocha, *Sp.* 40°54′ N, 1°18′ W **164**
Calamonte, *Sp.* 38°53′ N, 6°23′ W **164**
Calamus, river, *Nebr., U.S.* 42°18′ N, 100°3′ W **90**
Calañas, *Sp.* 37°39′ N, 6°54′ W **150**
Calanda, *Sp.* 40°55′ N, 0°15′ E **164**
Calandula, *Angola* 9°6′ S, 15°58′ E **218**
Calang, *Indonesia* 4°39′ N, 95°35′ E **196**
Calanscio, oil field, *Lib.* 28°1′ N, 21°18′ E **216**
Calapan, *Philippines* 13°24′ N, 121°10′ E **203**
Călăraşi, adm. division, *Rom.* 44°23′ N, 26°25′ E **156**
Călăraşi, *Mold.* 47°16′ N, 28°18′ E **156**
Călăraşi, *Rom.* 44°11′ N, 27°19′ E **156**
Calasparra, *Sp.* 38°13′ N, 1°43′ W **164**
Calatayud, *Sp.* 41°21′ N, 1°40′ W **164**
Călăţele, *Rom.* 46°45′ N, 23°1′ E **168**
Calatorao, *Sp.* 41°31′ N, 1°21′ W **164**
Calavà, Capo, *It.* 38°12′ N, 14°19′ E **156**
Calayan, island, *Philippines* 19°26′ N, 120°55′ E **198**
Calbayog, *Philippines* 12°4′ N, 124°35′ E **203**
Calbiga, *Philippines* 11°37′ N, 125°1′ E **203**
Calca, *Peru* 13°19′ S, 71°59′ W **137**
Calcanhar, Ponta do, *Braz.* 5°8′ S, 35°29′ W **132**
Calcasieu Lake, *La., U.S.* 29°52′ N, 93°33′ W **103**
Calcasieu, river, *La., U.S.* 30°22′ N, 93°8′ W **103**
Calceta, *Venez.* 7°4′ N, 62°30′ W **130**
Calchaquí, *Arg.* 29°50′ S, 60°18′ W **139**
Calcutta see Kolkata, *India* 22°33′ N, 88°21′ E **197**
Caldas, adm. division, *Col.* 5°10′ N, 75°51′ W **136**
Caldas da Rainha, *Port.* 39°23′ N, 9°9′ W **150**
Caldas Novas, *Braz.* 17°48′ S, 48°40′ W **138**
Caldbeck, *U.K.* 54°45′ N, 3°3′ W **162**
Caldera, *Chile* 27°6′ S, 70°52′ W **132**
Calderitas, *Mex.* 18°34′ N, 88°17′ W **115**
Caldes de Malavella, *Sp.* 41°50′ N, 2°49′ E **164**
Çaldıran, *Turk.* 39°6′ N, 43°50′ E **195**
Caldonazzo, *It.* 45°59′ N, 11°14′ E **167**
Caldron Snout, lake, *U.K.* 54°40′ N, 2°32′ W **162**
Caldwell, *Idaho, U.S.* 43°39′ N, 116°40′ W **82**
Caldwell, *Kans., U.S.* 37°0′ N, 97°37′ W **92**
Caldwell, *Ohio, U.S.* 39°44′ N, 81°31′ W **102**
Caldwell, *Tex., U.S.* 30°31′ N, 96°42′ W **96**
Caledon, *S. Af.* 34°13′ S, 19°26′ E **227**
Caledonia, *Minn., U.S.* 43°38′ N, 91°29′ W **94**
Calella, *Sp.* 41°36′ N, 2°39′ E **164**
Caleta Buena, *Chile* 19°53′ S, 70°10′ W **137**
Caleta Pabellón de Pica, *Chile* 20°56′ S, 70°10′ W **137**
Calexico, *Calif., U.S.* 32°40′ N, 115°30′ W **101**
Calf, The, peak, *U.K.* 54°22′ N, 2°33′ W **162**
Calgary, *Can.* 51°3′ N, 114°5′ W **90**
Calhoun Falls, *S.C., U.S.* 34°5′ N, 82°36′ W **96**
Cali, *Col.* 3°24′ N, 76°33′ W **136**
Calico Peak, *Nev., U.S.* 41°49′ N, 117°22′ W **90**
Calico Rock, *Ark., U.S.* 36°6′ N, 92°10′ W **96**
Caliente, *Calif., U.S.* 35°18′ N, 118°38′ W **101**
Caliente, *Nev., U.S.* 37°35′ N, 114°30′ W **82**
Caliente Range, *Calif., U.S.* 35°0′ N, 119°45′ W **100**
California, *Mo., U.S.* 38°37′ N, 92°33′ W **94**
California, adm. division, *Calif., U.S.* 36°52′ N, 120°58′ W **92**
California City, *Calif., U.S.* 35°7′ N, 117°59′ W **101**
California Coastal National Monument, *Pacific Ocean* 37°19′ N, 122°49′ W **100**
California, Golfo de (Mar de CortŽes) 30°47′ N, 114°31′ W **112**
California, Gulf of (Sea of Cortez),31°12′ N, 114°47′ W **73**
California Hot Springs, *Calif., U.S.* 35°53′ N, 118°41′ W **101**
California Spaceport, *Calif., U.S.* 34°35′ N, 120°39′ W **100**
California Valley, *Calif., U.S.* 35°19′ N, 120°1′ W **100**
Cālig, *Sp.* 40°26′ N, 0°20′ E **164**
Calilegua, *Arg.* 23°45′ S, 64°46′ W **132**
Cälilibad, *Azerb.* 39°12′ N, 48°28′ E **195**
Călimani, Munţii, *Rom.* 47°0′ N, 24°32′ E **156**
Calion, *Ark., U.S.* 33°18′ N, 92°33′ W **103**
Calipatria, *Calif., U.S.* 33°7′ N, 115°31′ W **101**
Calispell Peak, *Wash., U.S.* 48°24′ N, 117°36′ W **90**
Calkini, *Mex.* 20°23′ N, 90°4′ W **115**
Callaghan, Mount, *Nev., U.S.* 39°42′ N, 117°2′ W **90**
Callamura, spring, *Austral.* 27°39′ S, 140°53′ E **230**
Callander, *Can.* 46°13′ N, 79°22′ W **94**
Callao, *Peru* 12°4′ S, 77°9′ W **130**
Callaway, *Nebr., U.S.* 41°15′ N, 99°55′ W **90**
Calling Lake, *Can.* 55°8′ N, 113°47′ W **108**
Calling Lake, *Can.* 55°15′ N, 113°12′ W **108**
Callirhoe, ruin(s), *Jordan* 31°35′ N, 35°32′ E **194**
Calmar, *Can.* 53°15′ N, 113°49′ W **108**
Calnali, *Mex.* 20°52′ N, 98°35′ W **114**
Calne, *U.K.* 51°25′ N, 2°1′ W **162**
Calonga, *Angola* 16°1′ S, 15°13′ E **220**
Caloosahatchee, canal, *Fla., U.S.* 26°45′ N, 81°29′ W **105**
Calotmul, *Mex.* 21°0′ N, 88°12′ W **112**
Caloto, *Col.* 3°3′ N, 76°24′ W **136**
Calpe (Calp), *Sp.* 38°39′ N, 0°3′ E **164**
Calpulalpan de MŽendez, *Mex.* 17°19′ N, 96°25′ W **114**
Çaltı Burnu, *Turk.* 41°17′ N, 37°0′ E **156**
Caluango, *Angola* 8°21′ S, 19°36′ E **218**
Calulo, *Angola* 10°0′ S, 14°54′ E **220**
Calunda, *Angola* 12°8′ S, 23°33′ E **220**
Caluso, *It.* 45°18′ N, 7°52′ E **167**
Caluula, *Somalia* 11°52′ N, 50°43′ E **182**
Calvados Chain, islands, *Solomon Sea* 11°41′ S, 150°22′ E **192**
Calvert, *Ala., U.S.* 31°9′ N, 88°0′ W **103**
Calvert, *Tex., U.S.* 30°57′ N, 96°40′ W **96**
Calvin, *La., U.S.* 31°56′ N, 92°47′ W **103**
Calvinia, *S. Af.* 31°28′ S, 19°46′ E **227**
Calwa, *Calif., U.S.* 36°42′ N, 119°45′ W **100**
Calydon, ruin(s), *Gr.* 38°21′ N, 21°25′ E **156**
Çam Burnu, *Turk.* 41°9′ N, 37°45′ E **156**
Cam Pha, *Vietnam* 21°2′ N, 107°18′ E **198**
Cam Ranh, *Vietnam* 11°53′ N, 109°14′ E **202**
Cam Ranh, Vung 11°37′ N, 109°3′ E **202**
Cam Xuyen, *Vietnam* 18°15′ N, 106°2′ E **198**
Camabatela, *Angola* 8°11′ S, 15°22′ E **218**
Camacã, *Braz.* 15°26′ S, 39°29′ W **138**
Camachigama, Lac, lake, *Can.* 47°48′ N, 77°5′ W **94**
Camacho, *Mex.* 24°25′ N, 102°22′ W **114**
Camacupa, *Angola* 12°2′ S, 17°28′ E **220**
Camaguán, *Venez.* 8°6′ N, 67°34′ W **136**
Camagüey, *Cuba* 21°23′ N, 77°54′ W **116**
Camagüey, adm. division, *Cuba* 21°27′ N, 78°32′ W **116**
Camagüey, ArchipiŽelago de, *North Atlantic Ocean* 22°40′ N, 78°24′ W **116**
Camaleão, Ilha, island, *Braz.* 0°8′ N, 48°50′ W **130**
Camaná, *Peru* 16°38′ S, 72°43′ W **137**
Camanche Reservoir, lake, *Calif., U.S.* 38°13′ N, 121°8′ W **100**
Camanongue, *Angola* 11°26′ S, 20°11′ E **220**
Camapuã, *Braz.* 19°32′ S, 54°6′ W **132**
Camaquã, *Braz.* 30°52′ S, 51°51′ W **139**
Camaquã, river, *Braz.* 31°3′ S, 53°4′ W **139**
Camăr, *Rom.* 47°17′ N, 22°38′ E **168**
Camarat, Cap, *Fr.* 43°7′ N, 6°40′ E **165**
Çamardı, *Turk.* 37°50′ N, 34°58′ E **156**
Camargo, *Bol.* 20°40′ S, 65°16′ W **137**
Camargo, *Okla., U.S.* 36°0′ N, 99°18′ W **92**
Camargue, Île de la, islands, *Golfe Dulion* 43°28′ N, 4°23′ E **165**
Camarón, Cabo, *Hond.* 15°59′ N, 85°0′ W **115**
Camarones, *Arg.* 44°46′ S, 65°45′ W **134**
Camarones, *Chile* 19°3′ S, 69°56′ W **137**
Camas, *Sp.* 37°24′ N, 6°3′ W **164**
Camas, *Wash., U.S.* 45°34′ N, 122°26′ W **90**
Camas Valley, *Oreg., U.S.* 43°1′ N, 123°41′ W **90**
Camatindi, *Bol.* 21°0′ S, 63°31′ W **137**
Cambeak, point, *U.K.* 50°45′ N, 5°11′ W **150**
Camblaya, river, *Bol.* 20°57′ S, 65°16′ W **137**
Cambodia 12°37′ N, 103°48′ E **192**
Cambona, *Mozambique* 11°47′ S, 36°33′ E **224**
Camborne, *U.K.* 50°13′ N, 5°19′ W **150**
Cambrai, *Fr.* 50°9′ N, 3°15′ E **163**
Cambria, *Calif., U.S.* 35°34′ N, 121°7′ W **100**
Cambria Icefield, *Can.* 55°51′ N, 129°25′ W **108**
Cambrian Mountains, *U.K.* 52°2′ N, 3°33′ W **162**
Cambridge, *Idaho, U.S.* 44°34′ N, 116°41′ W **90**
Cambridge, *Nebr., U.S.* 40°16′ N, 100°11′ W **90**
Cambridge, *N.Z.* 37°54′ S, 175°29′ E **240**
Cambridge, *Ohio, U.S.* 40°1′ N, 81°35′ W **102**
Cambridge, *U.K.* 52°11′ N, 0°9′ E **162**
Cambridge Bay, *Can.* 69°6′ N, 105°2′ W **106**
Cambridge City, *Ind., U.S.* 39°48′ N, 85°11′ W **102**
Cambridge Gulf 15°11′ S, 127°52′ E **230**
Cambrils de Mar, *Sp.* 41°4′ N, 1°3′ E **164**
Cambulo, *Angola* 7°44′ S, 21°14′ E **218**
Cambundi-Catembo, *Angola* 10°4′ S, 17°31′ E **220**
Cambutal, Cerro, peak, *Pan.* 7°18′ N, 80°38′ W **115**
Camden, *Ala., U.S.* 31°59′ N, 87°17′ W **96**
Camden, *Ark., U.S.* 33°33′ N, 92°51′ W **96**
Camden, *Ind., U.S.* 40°36′ N, 86°32′ W **102**
Camden, *Me., U.S.* 44°13′ N, 69°4′ W **94**
Camden, *Miss., U.S.* 32°46′ N, 89°51′ W **103**
Camden, *N.J., U.S.* 39°56′ N, 75°8′ W **94**
Camden, *N.Y., U.S.* 43°20′ N, 75°46′ W **94**
Camden, *N.C., U.S.* 36°19′ N, 76°11′ W **96**
Camden, *Tex., U.S.* 30°53′ N, 94°45′ W **103**
Camden Bay 69°56′ N, 147°43′ W **98**
Camdenton, *Mo., U.S.* 37°59′ N, 92°44′ W **94**
Camelgooda Hill, *Austral.* 18°31′ S, 123°43′ E **230**
Çameli, *Turk.* 37°4′ N, 29°19′ E **156**
Camels Hump, peak, *Austral.* 23°51′ S, 131°27′ E **230**
Camels Hump, peak, *Vt., U.S.* 44°18′ N, 72°55′ W **104**
Camenca, *Transdniestria, Mold.* 48°2′ N, 28°44′ E **156**
Cameron, *Ariz., U.S.* 35°51′ N, 111°25′ W **92**
Cameron, *La., U.S.* 29°47′ N, 93°20′ W **103**
Cameron, *Tex., U.S.* 30°50′ N, 96°58′ W **96**
Cameron Falls, *Can.* 49°8′ N, 88°19′ W **94**
Cameron Lake, lake, *Can.* 48°59′ N, 84°45′ W **110**
Cameroon 4°33′ N, 11°3′ E **218**
Cameroon Mountain, *Cameroon* 4°15′ N, 9°4′ E **222**
Cametá, *Braz.* 2°14′ S, 49°31′ W **130**
Camiguin, island, *Philippines* 18°49′ N, 122°1′ E **198**
Camilla, *Ga., U.S.* 31°13′ N, 84°13′ W **96**
Camiña, *Chile* 19°18′ S, 69°27′ W **137**
Caminha, *Port.* 41°52′ N, 8°51′ W **150**
Camiranga, *Braz.* 1°51′ S, 46°18′ W **130**
Camiri, *Bol.* 20°7′ S, 63°34′ W **137**
Camirus, ruin(s), *Gr.* 36°18′ N, 27°48′ E **156**
Camisea, *Peru* 11°43′ S, 73°2′ W **137**
Camisea, river, *Peru* 11°57′ S, 72°59′ W **137**
Camissombo, *Angola* 8°11′ S, 20°40′ E **218**
Camocim, *Braz.* 2°57′ S, 40°52′ W **132**
Camooweal, *Austral.* 19°56′ S, 138°8′ E **231**
Camopi, *Fr.* 3°11′ N, 52°20′ W **130**
Camopi, river, *Braz.* 2°28′ N, 53°20′ W **130**
Camorta Island, *India* 7°38′ N, 93°39′ E **188**
Camoruco, *Col.* 6°27′ N, 70°31′ W **136**
Camousitchouane, Lac, lake, *Can.* 51°2′ N, 76°24′ W **110**
Camp Crook, *S. Dak., U.S.* 45°32′ N, 104°0′ W **90**
Camp David, site, *Md., U.S.* 39°39′ N, 77°32′ W **94**
Camp Douglas, *Wis., U.S.* 43°54′ N, 90°16′ W **102**
Camp Nelson, *Calif., U.S.* 36°9′ N, 118°38′ W **101**
Camp Pendleton Marine Corps Base, *Calif., U.S.* 33°20′ N, 117°29′ W **101**
Camp Point, *Mo., U.S.* 40°1′ N, 91°4′ W **94**
Camp Wood, *Tex., U.S.* 29°39′ N, 100°1′ W **92**
Campagne-lès-Hesdin, *Fr.* 50°23′ N, 1°52′ E **163**
Campamento, *Col.* 4°30′ N, 70°24′ W **136**
Campana, *Arg.* 34°11′ S, 58°56′ W **139**
Campana, Isla, island, *Chile* 48°13′ S, 77°9′ W **134**
Campanario, *Sp.* 38°51′ N, 5°37′ W **164**
Campania, adm. division, *It.* 41°12′ N, 13°54′ E **156**
Campbell, *Calif., U.S.* 37°17′ N, 121°57′ W **100**
Campbell, Cape, *N.Z.* 41°44′ S, 174°12′ E **240**
Campbell Hill, *Ohio, U.S.* 40°21′ N, 83°45′ W **102**
Campbell Island, *N.Z.* 52°37′ S, 169°0′ E **252**
Campbell Plateau, *South Pacific Ocean* 50°28′ S, 171°45′ E **252**
Campbell River, *Can.* 50°1′ N, 125°15′ W **90**
Campbell's Bay, *Can.* 45°43′ N, 76°36′ W **94**
Campbellsburg, *Ind., U.S.* 38°38′ N, 86°16′ W **102**
Campbellsburg, *Ky., U.S.* 38°30′ N, 85°13′ W **102**
Campbellsville, *Ky., U.S.* 37°19′ N, 85°21′ W **96**
Campbellton, *Can.* 47°58′ N, 66°41′ W **94**
Campeche, *Mex.* 19°48′ N, 90°40′ W **115**
Campeche, adm. division, *Mex.* 18°56′ N, 91°2′ W **112**
Campeche Bank, *Gulf of Mexico* 21°58′ N, 90°5′ W **253**
Camperville, *Can.* 52°1′ N, 100°12′ W **108**
Campidano, *It.* 39°44′ N, 8°33′ E **156**
Campina Grande, *Braz.* 7°11′ S, 35°53′ W **123**
Campina Verde, *Braz.* 19°33′ S, 49°29′ W **138**
Campinas, *Braz.* 22°56′ S, 47°5′ W **138**
Campo, *Calif., U.S.* 32°36′ N, 116°29′ W **101**
Campo, *Colo., U.S.* 37°6′ N, 102°35′ W **92**
Campo, *Mozambique* 17°46′ S, 36°22′ E **224**
Campo, *Sp.* 42°24′ N, 0°24′ E **164**
Campo Belo, *Braz.* 20°53′ S, 45°15′ W **138**
Campo Corral, *Col.* 5°3′ N, 70°43′ W **136**
Campo de Criptana, *Sp.* 39°24′ N, 3°7′ W **164**
Campo Durán, oil field, *Arg.* 22°15′ S, 63°46′ W **137**
Campo Erê, *Braz.* 26°24′ S, 53°1′ W **139**
Campo Esperanza, *Parag.* 22°19′ S, 59°38′ W **132**
Campo Florido, *Braz.* 19°48′ S, 48°36′ W **138**
Campo Gallo, *Arg.* 26°35′ S, 62°50′ W **139**
Campo Grande, *Braz.* 20°28′ S, 54°36′ W **132**
Campo Largo, *Arg.* 26°47′ S, 60°51′ W **139**
Campo Largo, *Braz.* 25°30′ S, 49°34′ W **138**
Campo Maior, *Braz.* 4°52′ S, 42°13′ W **132**
Campo Mourão, *Braz.* 24°4′ S, 52°24′ W **138**
Campo, Punta, *Equatorial Guinea* 2°18′ N, 9°14′ E **218**
Campo Troco, *Col.* 4°52′ N, 68°9′ W **136**
Campoalegre, *Col.* 2°41′ N, 75°21′ W **136**
Campobasso, *It.* 41°34′ N, 14°39′ E **156**
Campobello, *S.C., U.S.* 35°6′ N, 82°10′ W **96**
Campodolcino, *It.* 46°24′ N, 9°20′ E **167**
Campos, *Braz.* 21°48′ S, 41°23′ W **138**
Campos Altos, *Braz.* 19°43′ S, 46°12′ W **138**
Campos Belos, *Braz.* 13°4′ S, 46°55′ W **138**
Campos Novos, *Braz.* 27°25′ S, 51°14′ W **139**
Campos, Punta, *Mex.* 18°53′ N, 104°40′ W **114**
Camposampiero, *It.* 45°34′ N, 11°55′ E **167**
Camprodon, *Sp.* 42°17′ N, 2°22′ E **164**
Campti, *La., U.S.* 31°52′ N, 93°7′ W **103**
Campton, *N.H., U.S.* 43°51′ N, 71°39′ W **104**
Campuya, *Peru* 1°46′ S, 73°31′ W **136**
Camrose, *Can.* 53°0′ N, 112°51′ W **108**
Camsell Portage, *Can.* 59°37′ N, 109°14′ W **108**
Camucuio, *Angola* 14°8′ S, 13°17′ E **220**
Çan, *Turk.* 40°1′ N, 27°1′ E **156**
Can Tho, *Vietnam* 10°2′ N, 105°44′ E **202**
Cana Brava, *Braz.* 17°22′ S, 45°52′ W **138**
Canaan, *Conn., U.S.* 42°1′ N, 73°20′ W **104**
Canaan, *N.H., U.S.* 43°39′ N, 72°1′ W **104**
Canaan, *Trinidad and Tobago* 11°8′ N, 60°49′ W **116**
Canada 58°59′ N, 99°52′ W **106**
Canada Basin, *Arctic Ocean* 77°38′ N, 139°23′ W **255**
Canada Bay 50°40′ N, 56°41′ W **111**
Cañada de Gómez, *Arg.* 32°50′ S, 61°21′ W **139**
Cañada Honda, *Arg.* 31°59′ S, 68°33′ W **134**
Cañada Ombú, *Arg.* 28°19′ S, 60°2′ W **139**
Canada Plain, *Arctic Ocean* 76°14′ N, 148°23′ W **255**
Cañada Seca, *Arg.* 34°25′ S, 62°57′ W **139**
Canadian, *Tex., U.S.* 35°53′ N, 100°24′ W **92**

Casilda, Arg. 33°3′ S, 61°9′ W 139
Casiquiare, river, Venez. 2°27′ N, 66°40′ W 136
Casma, Peru 9°28′ S, 78°18′ W 130
Casmalia, Calif., U.S. 34°50′ N, 120°33′ W 100
Caspar, Calif., U.S. 39°21′ N, 123°49′ W 90
Caspe, Sp. 41°14′ N, 3°177′ W 164
Casper, Wyo., U.S. 42°50′ N, 106°19′ W 90
Caspian Depression, Kaz. 43°48′ N, 46°17′ E 195
Caspian Sea 38°26′ N, 49°1′ E 160
Caspiana, La., U.S. 32°16′ N, 93°36′ W 103
Cass, W. Va., U.S. 38°24′ N, 79°56′ W 94
Cass City, Mich., U.S. 43°35′ N, 83°10′ W 102
Cass Lake, Minn., U.S. 47°21′ N, 94°38′ W 90
Cass, river, Mich., U.S. 43°28′ N, 83°16′ W 102
Cassai, Angola 10°37′ S, 21°59′ E 220
Cassai, river, Angola 11°13′ S, 20°20′ E 220
Cassamba, Angola 13°7′ S, 20°20′ E 220
Cassel, Fr. 50°48′ N, 2°28′ E 163
Casselberry, Fla., U.S. 28°40′ N, 81°22′ W 105
Casselton, N. Dak., U.S. 46°53′ N, 97°14′ W 90
Cássia, Braz. 20°34′ S, 46°58′ W 138
Cassiar, Can. 59°17′ N, 129°50′ W 108
Cassiar Mountains, Can. 58°18′ N, 129°24′ W 108
Cassidy, Can. 49°2′ N, 123°52′ W 100
Cassilândia, Braz. 19°7′ S, 51°48′ W 138
Cassinga, Angola 15°9′ S, 16°5′ E 220
Cassino, Braz. 32°10′ S, 52°13′ W 139
Cassiporé, Cabo, Braz. 3°46′ N, 51°3′ W 130
Cassou, Burkina Faso 11°34′ N, 2°5′ W 222
Cassumbe, Angola 11°6′ S, 16°41′ E 220
Cassville, Mo., U.S. 36°40′ N, 93°53′ W 94
Cassville, Wis., U.S. 42°42′ N, 90°59′ W 94
Castaic, Calif., U.S. 34°30′ N, 118°38′ W 101
Castalla, Sp. 38°35′ N, 0°41′ E 164
Castanhal, Braz. 1°18′ S, 47°58′ W 130
Castaño Nuevo, Arg. 31°2′ S, 69°36′ W 134
Castaños, Mex. 26°46′ N, 101°27′ W 96
Casteggio, It. 45°0′ N, 9°7′ E 167
Castel Bolognese, It. 44°19′ N, 11°46′ E 167
Castel San Giovanni, It. 45°3′ N, 9°26′ E 167
Castelfranco Veneto, It. 45°40′ N, 11°55′ E 156
Castelli, Arg. 36°6′ S, 57°49′ W 139
Castelló de la Plana see Castellón de la Plana, Sp. 39°59′ N, 0°2′ W 164
Castellón de la Plana (Castelló de la Plana), Sp. 39°59′ N, 0°2′ W 164
Castellote, Sp. 40°47′ N, 0°20′ E 164
Castelnovo ne' Monti, It. 44°25′ N, 10°23′ E 167
Castelo Branco, Port. 39°49′ N, 7°31′ W 150
Castelo Branco, adm. division, Port. 39°50′ N, 7°58′ W 150
Casterton, U.K. 54°12′ N, 2°34′ W 162
Castets, Fr. 43°53′ N, 1°10′ W 150
Castiglione delle Stiviere, It. 45°22′ N, 10°29′ E 167
Castile and Leon, adm. division, Sp. 41°56′ N, 3°33′ W 164
Castile La Mancha, adm. division, Sp. 40°28′ N, 2°58′ W 164
Castilla, Playa de, Sp. 37°3′ N, 6°45′ W 164
Castillo de San Marcos National Monument, Fla., U.S. 29°53′ N, 81°22′ W 105
Castillo de Teayo, ruin(s), Mex. 20°39′ N, 97°45′ W 114
Castillo, Pampa del, Arg. 46°18′ S, 68°44′ W 134
Castillos, Uru. 34°14′ S, 53°53′ W 139
Castle Acre, U.K. 52°42′ N, 0°41′ E 162
Castle Dale, Utah, U.S. 39°12′ N, 111°1′ W 90
Castle Hedingham, U.K. 51°59′ N, 0°36′ E 162
Castle Mountain, peak, Alas., U.S. 56°51′ N, 132°16′ W 108
Castle Mountain, peak, Calif., U.S. 35°56′ N, 120°23′ W 100
Castle Mountain, peak, Can. 51°19′ N, 116°0′ W 90
Castle Mountain, peak, Tex., U.S. 31°15′ N, 102°22′ W 92
Castle Peak, Colo., U.S. 38°59′ N, 106°57′ W 90
Castle Peak, Idaho, U.S. 44°1′ N, 114°40′ W 90
Castle Rising, U.K. 52°47′ N, 0°29′ E 162
Castle Rock, Colo., U.S. 39°22′ N, 104°52′ W 90
Castle Rock, Wash., U.S. 46°16′ N, 122°54′ W 100
Castle Rock, peak, Oreg., U.S. 44°0′ N, 118°16′ W 90
Castle Sinclair, site, U.K. 58°26′ N, 3°12′ W 150
Castlebar, Ire. 53°51′ N, 9°19′ W 150
Castlebay, U.K. 56°57′ N, 7°29′ W 150
Castlecliff, N.Z. 39°57′ S, 174°58′ E 240
Castleford, U.K. 53°43′ N, 1°21′ W 162
Castlegar, Can. 49°18′ N, 117°41′ W 90
Castlepoint, N.Z. 40°55′ S, 176°12′ E 240
Castleton, U.K. 54°27′ N, 0°57′ E 162
Castleton, Vt., U.S. 43°36′ N, 73°11′ W 104
Castleton-on-Hudson, N.Y., U.S. 42°31′ N, 73°46′ W 104
Castlewood, S. Dak., U.S. 44°42′ N, 97°3′ W 90
Castor, Can. 52°12′ N, 111°55′ W 90
Castor, La., U.S. 32°14′ N, 93°10′ W 103
Castries, Saint Lucia 13°59′ N, 61°8′ W 116
Castril, Sp. 37°47′ N, 2°46′ W 164
Castro, Braz. 24°46′ S, 50°1′ W 138
Castro, Chile 42°27′ S, 73°51′ W 134
Castronuño, Sp. 41°22′ N, 5°17′ W 150
Castropol, Sp. 43°30′ N, 7°2′ W 150
Castroville, Calif., U.S. 36°46′ N, 121°45′ W 100
Castuera, Sp. 38°43′ N, 5°34′ W 164
Casuala, Mozambique 15°23′ S, 33°37′ E 224
Casummit Lake, Can. 51°28′ N, 92°22′ W 110
Çat, Turk. 39°37′ N, 41°1′ E 195
Cat Island, Bahamas 24°30′ N, 75°28′ W 116
Cat Island, Miss., U.S. 30°17′ N, 89°7′ W 103
Cat Lake, Can. 51°43′ N, 91°48′ W 110
Cat Tien National Park, Vietnam 11°20′ N, 106°58′ E 202
Catacaos, Peru 5°11′ S, 80°44′ W 130
Cataguases, Braz. 21°23′ S, 42°40′ W 138
Catahoula Lake, La., U.S. 31°25′ N, 92°27′ W 103
Cataingan, Philippines 12°1′ N, 123°58′ E 203
Çatak, Turk. 38°0′ N, 43°2′ E 195
Catalão, Braz. 18°12′ S, 47°57′ W 138
Catalina, Chile 25°14′ S, 69°47′ W 132
Catalina, Punta, Chile 52°44′ S, 68°43′ W 134
Catalonia, adm. division, Sp. 41°46′ N, 1°7′ E 164
Catamarca, Arg. 28°30′ S, 65°47′ W 132
Catamarca, adm. division, Arg. 28°47′ S, 68°39′ W 134
Catán Lil, Arg. 39°43′ S, 70°37′ W 134
Catandica, Mozambique 18°4′ S, 33°10′ E 220
Catanduanes, island, Philippines 13°52′ N, 124°26′ E 192
Catanduva, Braz. 21°6′ S, 48°58′ W 138
Catania, It. 37°30′ N, 15°4′ E 156
Catania, Piana di, It. 37°17′ N, 14°26′ E 156
Catanzaro, It. 38°53′ N, 16°35′ E 156
Catarina, Tex., U.S. 28°20′ N, 99°37′ W 92
Catarman, Philippines 12°29′ N, 124°38′ E 203
Catarroja, Sp. 39°24′ N, 0°24′ E 164
Catatumbo-Bari National Park, Col. 9°0′ N, 73°30′ W 136
Catauara, Braz. 3°19′ S, 56°26′ W 130
Cataviña, Mex. 29°45′ N, 114°49′ W 92
Catawba Island, Ohio, U.S. 41°34′ N, 82°50′ W 102
Catbalogan, Philippines 11°46′ N, 124°55′ E 203
Cateel, Philippines 7°51′ N, 126°25′ E 203
Catemaco, Mex. 18°25′ N, 95°7′ W 114
Catete, Angola 9°8′ S, 13°40′ E 218
Catete, river, Braz. 6°22′ S, 54°14′ W 130
Cathedral Mountain, Tex., U.S. 30°8′ N, 103°43′ W 92
Catherine, Ala., U.S. 32°10′ N, 87°29′ W 103
Catheys Valley, Calif., U.S. 37°25′ N, 120°8′ W 100
Cathlamet, Wash., U.S. 46°11′ N, 123°22′ W 100
Catinaccio, peak, It. 46°28′ N, 11°36′ E 167
Catió, Guinea-Bissau 11°16′ N, 15°15′ W 222
Catirina, Punta, peak, It. 40°28′ N, 9°27′ E 156
Catlow Valley, Oreg., U.S. 42°45′ N, 119°7′ W 90
Catnip Mountain, Nev., U.S. 41°50′ N, 119°28′ W 90
Catoche, Cabo, Mex. 21°28′ N, 87°10′ W 116
Catoctin Mountain, Md., U.S. 39°50′ N, 77°35′ W 94
Catoctin Mountain Park, Md., U.S. 39°37′ N, 77°33′ W 94
Catorce, Mex. 23°39′ N, 100°53′ W 114
Catota, Angola 14°2′ S, 17°23′ E 220
Catria, Monte, peak, It. 43°26′ N, 12°37′ E 156
Catriló, Arg. 36°25′ S, 63°27′ W 139
Catskill, N.Y., U.S. 42°13′ N, 73°53′ W 104
Catskill Mountains, N.Y., U.S. 42°26′ N, 74°10′ W 104
Catterick, U.K. 54°22′ N, 1°38′ W 162
Cattolica, It. 43°58′ N, 12°44′ E 167
Catuane, Mozambique 26°44′ S, 32°15′ E 227
Catur, Mozambique 13°45′ S, 35°37′ E 224
Cau Giat, Vietnam 19°9′ N, 105°38′ E 202
Cauaburi, river, Braz. 4°238′ N, 66°19′ W 136
Cauayan, Philippines 9°58′ N, 122°36′ E 203
Cauca, adm. division, Col. 2°29′ N, 77°31′ W 136
Cauca, river, Col. 6°18′ N, 75°46′ W 136
Caucaia, Braz. 3°44′ S, 38°40′ W 132
Caucasia, Col. 7°57′ N, 75°14′ W 136
Caucasus Mountains, Asia-Europe 42°3′ N, 44°7′ E 158
Caucete, Arg. 31°40′ S, 68°18′ W 134
Cauchon Lake, Can. 55°28′ N, 97°4′ W 108
Caudéran, Fr. 44°51′ N, 0°38′ E 150
Caudete, Sp. 38°42′ N, 0°59′ E 164
Caudry, Fr. 50°7′ N, 3°23′ E 163
Caungula, Angola 8°27′ S, 18°38′ E 218
Cauquenes, Chile 35°59′ S, 72°21′ W 134
Caura, river, Venez. 6°56′ N, 64°51′ W 130
Caurés, river, Braz. 1°16′ S, 63°17′ W 130
Cauro, Fr. 41°54′ N, 8°54′ E 156
Causapscal, Can. 48°20′ N, 67°13′ W 94
Căuşeni, Mold. 46°37′ N, 29°23′ E 156
Cautário, river, Braz. 11°47′ S, 63°55′ W 137
Caution, Cape, Can. 50°58′ N, 128°14′ W 108
Cauto, river, Cuba 20°39′ N, 76°41′ W 116
Cavalaire, Fr. 43°10′ N, 6°30′ E 150
Cavalcante, Braz. 13°48′ S, 47°31′ W 138
Cavalese, It. 46°17′ N, 11°27′ E 167
Cavalier, N. Dak., U.S. 48°45′ N, 97°39′ W 90
Cavalla, river, Africa 6°18′ N, 7°56′ W 222
Cavalleria, Cap de, Sp. 40°3′ N, 3°48′ E 164
Cavallermaggiore, It. 44°42′ N, 7°41′ E 167
Cavallo Pass, U.S. 28°17′ N, 96°20′ W 96
Cavally, river, Côte d'Ivoire 6°19′ N, 8°14′ W 222
Cavan, Ire. 53°58′ N, 7°22′ W 150
Cavarzere, It. 45°7′ N, 12°4′ E 167
Cave, N.Z. 44°19′ S, 170°59′ E 240
Cave Creek, Ariz., U.S. 33°49′ N, 111°56′ W 92
Cave Mountain, Calif., U.S. 35°3′ N, 116°22′ W 101
Cave Point, U.S. 44°45′ N, 87°9′ W 94
Cavendish, Vt., U.S. 43°23′ N, 72°37′ W 104
Caviana, Ilha, island, Braz. 0°22′ N, 49°54′ W 130
Cavignac, Fr. 45°5′ N, 0°24′ E 150
Cavinas, Bol. 12°34′ S, 66°50′ W 137
Cavite, Philippines 14°29′ N, 120°53′ E 203
Cavo, Monte, peak, It. 41°44′ N, 12°37′ E 156
Cavour, It. 44°46′ N, 7°23′ E 167
Cavtat (Epidaurum), Croatia 42°34′ N, 18°13′ E 168
Çavuş Burnu, Turk. 36°19′ N, 30°32′ E 156
Çavuşçu Gölü, lake, Turk. 38°25′ N, 31°35′ E 156
Cawker City, Kans., U.S. 39°29′ N, 98°27′ W 92
Cawood, U.K. 53°50′ N, 1°8′ W 162
Cawston, U.K. 52°45′ N, 1°9′ E 162
Caxambu, Braz. 22°0′ S, 44°56′ W 138
Caxias, Braz. 4°29′ S, 71°26′ W 130
Caxias, Braz. 4°47′ S, 43°19′ W 132
Caxias do Sul, Braz. 29°11′ S, 51°10′ W 139
Caxito, Angola 8°35′ S, 13°41′ E 218
Çay, Turk. 38°35′ N, 31°1′ E 156
Cayacal, Punta, Mex. 17°44′ N, 102°12′ W 114
Çaycuma, Turk. 41°25′ N, 32°2′ E 156
Çayeli, Turk. 41°5′ N, 40°43′ E 195
Cayenne, Fr. Guiana, Fr. 4°58′ N, 52°19′ W 130
Cayeux-sur-Mer, Fr. 50°10′ N, 1°30′ E 163
Cayey, U.S. 18°7′ N, 66°11′ W 116
Çayıralan, Turk. 39°18′ N, 35°38′ E 156
Cayman Trench, Caribbean Sea 17°52′ N, 80°50′ W 253
Caynaba, Somalia 8°56′ N, 46°25′ E 216
Cayo Agua, Isla, island, Pan. 9°2′ N, 82°0′ W 115
Cayucos, Calif., U.S. 35°27′ N, 120°55′ W 100
Cayuga, Ind., U.S. 39°56′ N, 87°28′ W 102
Cayuga Lake, N.Y., U.S. 42°41′ N, 77°13′ W 94
Cazage, Angola 11°3′ S, 20°44′ E 220
Cazalla de la Sierra, Sp. 37°55′ N, 5°47′ W 164
Cazères, Fr. 43°12′ N, 1°3′ E 164
Cazombo, Angola 11°55′ S, 22°58′ E 220
Cazones, river, Mex. 20°14′ N, 98°10′ W 114
Cazorla, Sp. 37°54′ N, 3°2′ W 164
Cazorla, Venez. 8°0′ N, 67°0′ W 136
Ceadîr-Lunga, Mold. 46°2′ N, 28°50′ E 156
Ceará, adm. division, Braz. 5°20′ S, 40°29′ W 132
Ceará Mirim, Braz. 5°38′ S, 35°26′ W 132
Ceara Plain, South Atlantic Ocean 0°23′ N, 37°43′ W 253
Cébaco, Isla de, island, Pan. 7°22′ N, 81°30′ W 115
Ceballos, Mex. 26°31′ N, 104°9′ W 114
Cebollar, Arg. 29°6′ S, 66°32′ W 134
Cebollatí, Uru. 33°15′ S, 53°51′ W 139
Céboruco, VolcŽan, Mex. 21°7′ N, 104°32′ W 114
Cebu, Philippines 10°20′ N, 123°54′ E 203
Cebu, island, Philippines 11°11′ N, 123°27′ E 192
Cece, Hung. 46°45′ N, 18°38′ E 168
Cecil Lake, Can. 56°17′ N, 120°35′ W 108
Cecil Rhodes, Mount, Austral. 25°28′ S, 121°15′ E 230
Cecina, It. 43°18′ N, 10°31′ E 156
Cedar Creek Peak, Idaho, U.S. 42°26′ N, 113°8′ W 90
Cedar Creek Reservoir, lake, Tex., U.S. 32°20′ N, 96°47′ W 96
Cedar Falls, Iowa, U.S. 42°30′ N, 92°28′ W 94
Cedar Grove, Calif., U.S. 36°48′ N, 118°41′ W 101
Cedar Grove, Wis., U.S. 43°34′ N, 87°49′ W 102
Cedar Key, Fla., U.S. 29°8′ N, 83°3′ W 105
Cedar Lake, Can. 53°1′ N, 101°7′ W 81
Cedar Lake, Can. 50°7′ N, 93°38′ W 90
Cedar Lake, Ind., U.S. 41°20′ N, 87°28′ W 102
Cedar Lake, lake, Can. 45°58′ N, 78°50′ W 94
Cedar Mountains, Utah, U.S. 40°35′ N, 113°9′ W 90
Cedar Pass, Calif., U.S. 41°33′ N, 120°17′ W 90
Cedar Pass, S. Dak., U.S. 43°45′ N, 101°56′ W 90
Cedar Rapids, Iowa, U.S. 41°57′ N, 91°39′ W 94
Cedar Ridge, Calif., U.S. 39°11′ N, 121°2′ W 90
Cedar, river, Iowa, U.S. 42°9′ N, 92°21′ W 80
Cedar Vale, Kans., U.S. 37°4′ N, 96°30′ W 92
Cedarburg, Wis., U.S. 43°17′ N, 87°59′ W 102
Cedars of Lebanon, site, Leb. 34°14′ N, 36°2′ E 194
Cedarvale, Can. 55°0′ N, 128°19′ W 108
Cedarville, Calif., U.S. 41°31′ N, 120°11′ W 90
Cedral, Mex. 23°47′ N, 100°43′ W 114
Cedros, Mex. 24°39′ N, 101°48′ W 114
Cedros, Isla, island, Mex. 27°56′ N, 115°10′ W 112
Cedros Trench, North Pacific Ocean 24°2′ N, 112°32′ W 252
Ceek, Somalia 8°55′ N, 45°19′ E 216
Ceel Afweyn, Somalia 9°52′ N, 47°15′ E 216
Ceel Buur, Somalia 4°44′ N, 46°35′ E 218
Ceel Dhaab, Somalia 8°49′ N, 46°34′ E 216
Ceel Huur, Somalia 5°0′ N, 48°20′ E 218
Ceeldheere, Somalia 3°52′ N, 47°13′ E 218
Ceepeecee, Can. 49°53′ N, 126°44′ W 90
Ceerigaabo (Erigavo), Somalia 10°34′ N, 47°24′ E 218
Cefa, Rom. 46°54′ N, 21°42′ E 168
Cegléd, Hung. 47°10′ N, 19°49′ E 168
Cehegín, Sp. 38°5′ N, 1°48′ W 164
Ceheng, China 24°58′ N, 105°49′ E 198
Cehotina, river, Europe 43°30′ N, 18°48′ E 168
Cehu Silvaniei, Rom. 47°24′ N, 23°12′ E 168
Ceiba Grande, ruin(s), Mex. 17°22′ N, 93°51′ W 115
Ceica, Rom. 46°51′ N, 22°10′ E 168
Cejal, Col. 2°42′ N, 67°55′ W 136
Cejolao, Arg. 27°28′ S, 62°20′ W 139
Çekerek, Turk. 40°5′ N, 35°29′ E 156
Çekerek, river, Turk. 40°25′ N, 35°18′ E 156
Celarain, Punta, Mex. 20°10′ N, 86°59′ W 115
Celaya, Mex. 20°30′ N, 100°49′ W 114
Celebes see Sulawesi, island, Indonesia 2°0′ S, 121°0′ E 192
Celebes Basin, Celebes Sea 3°27′ N, 121°47′ E 254
Celebes Sea 3°49′ N, 119°35′ E 192
Çeleken, Turkm. 39°26′ N, 53°8′ E 180
Celić, Bosn. and Herzg. 44°43′ N, 18°47′ E 168
Celina, Ohio, U.S. 40°32′ N, 84°35′ W 102
Celje, Slov. 46°14′ N, 15°14′ E 156
Cella, Sp. 40°27′ N, 1°18′ W 164
Cellar Head, U.K. 58°25′ N, 6°8′ W 150
Celldömölk, Hung. 47°15′ N, 17°10′ E 168
Celle, Ger. 52°36′ N, 10°5′ E 150
Celtic Sea 50°32′ N, 8°3′ W 150
Cement, Okla., U.S. 34°54′ N, 98°8′ W 92
Cemerno, Serb. 43°38′ N, 20°13′ E 168
Çemişgezek, Turk. 39°4′ N, 38°54′ E 195
Cempoala see Zempoala, ruin(s), Mex. 19°23′ N, 96°28′ W 114
Cenchreae, ruin(s), Gr. 37°53′ N, 22°55′ E 156
Cencia see Ch'ench'a, Eth. 6°15′ N, 37°38′ E 224
Cenderawasih, Teluk 3°0′ S, 133°34′ E 192
Cenicero, Sp. 42°28′ N, 2°39′ W 164
Centenario, Mex. 18°39′ N, 90°17′ W 115
Centennial Mountains, Idaho, U.S. 44°29′ N, 112°28′ W 90
Center, Colo., U.S. 37°44′ N, 106°6′ W 92
Center, N. Dak., U.S. 47°5′ N, 101°17′ W 90
Center, Tex., U.S. 31°46′ N, 94°11′ W 103
Center Barnstead, N.H., U.S. 43°20′ N, 71°17′ W 104
Center Conway, N.H., U.S. 43°59′ N, 71°4′ W 104
Center Harbor, N.H., U.S. 43°42′ N, 71°28′ W 104
Center Hill, Fla., U.S. 28°38′ N, 82°0′ W 105
Center Lovell, Me., U.S. 44°10′ N, 70°54′ W 104
Center Moriches, N.Y., U.S. 40°48′ N, 72°48′ W 104
Center Ossipee, N.H., U.S. 43°45′ N, 71°10′ W 104
Center Peak, Calif., U.S. 36°12′ N, 120°40′ W 100
Center Point, Tex., U.S. 29°54′ N, 99°2′ W 92
Centerburg, Ohio, U.S. 40°17′ N, 82°41′ W 102
Centerfield, Utah, U.S. 39°7′ N, 111°48′ W 92
Centerville, Calif., U.S. 36°43′ N, 119°30′ W 100
Centerville, Iowa, U.S. 40°43′ N, 92°53′ W 94
Centerville, Mass., U.S. 41°38′ N, 70°22′ W 104
Centerville, S. Dak., U.S. 43°5′ N, 96°58′ W 94
Centerville, Tex., U.S. 31°14′ N, 95°58′ W 96
Centerville, Utah, U.S. 40°55′ N, 111°52′ W 90
Centinela, Picacho del, peak, Mex. 29°3′ N, 102°42′ W 92
Cento, It. 44°43′ N, 11°17′ E 167
Central, Alas., U.S. 65°33′ N, 144°52′ W 98
Central, Ariz., U.S. 32°52′ N, 109°47′ W 92
Central, adm. division, Mongolia 46°58′ N, 105°11′ E 198
Central African Republic 7°1′ N, 21°10′ E 218
Central Butte, Can. 50°48′ N, 106°32′ W 90
Central City, Ill., U.S. 38°32′ N, 89°8′ W 102
Central City, Ky., U.S. 37°17′ N, 87°7′ W 96
Central City, Nebr., U.S. 41°6′ N, 98°1′ W 92
Central City, S. Dak., U.S. 44°22′ N, 103°46′ W 90
Central, Cordillera, Dom. Rep. 19°16′ N, 71°38′ W 116
Central, Cordillera, Peru 6°52′ S, 77°30′ W 130
Central Islip, N.Y., U.S. 40°47′ N, 73°12′ W 104
Central Kalahari Game Reserve, Botswana 22°34′ S, 23°16′ E 227
Central, Massif, Europe 44°5′ N, 1°58′ E 214
Central Mount Wedge, peak, Austral. 22°57′ S, 131°37′ E 230
Central Pacific Basin, North Pacific Ocean 7°5′ N, 176°34′ W 252
Central Range, P.N.G. 5°6′ S, 141°26′ E 192
Centralia, Ill., U.S. 38°31′ N, 89°8′ W 102
Centralia, Mo., U.S. 39°11′ N, 92°8′ W 94
Centralia, Wash., U.S. 46°41′ N, 122°58′ W 100
Centre, Ala., U.S. 34°8′ N, 85°41′ W 96
Centre, adm. division, Fr. 47°39′ N, 0°50′ E 150
Centre de Marcoule, site, Fr. 44°8′ N, 4°40′ E 165
Centre Island, Austral. 16°25′ S, 136°48′ E 230
Centreville, Mich., U.S. 41°54′ N, 85°31′ W 102
Centreville, Miss., U.S. 31°4′ N, 91°4′ W 103
Cenxi, China 22°56′ N, 111°1′ E 198
Çepan, Alban. 40°25′ N, 20°15′ E 156
Cephalonia see Kefaloniá, adm. division, Gr. 38°22′ N, 20°3′ E 156
Cepin, Croatia 45°30′ N, 18°32′ E 168
Ceprano, It. 41°32′ N, 13°31′ E 156
Cer, peak, Serb. 44°35′ N, 19°27′ E 168
Ceram, island, Indonesia 3°48′ S, 129°2′ E 192
Ceram Sea 2°26′ S, 128°3′ E 192
Cerbat Mountains, Ariz., U.S. 35°29′ N, 114°7′ W 101
Cerbatana, Serranía de la, Venez. 6°31′ N, 66°45′ W 130
Cerbère, Fr. 42°26′ N, 3°8′ E 164
Cerbicales, Îles, islands, Tyrrhenian Sea 41°24′ N, 9°24′ E 156
Cère, river, Fr. 44°50′ N, 2°21′ E 165
Cerea, It. 45°12′ N, 11°12′ E 167
Cereal, Can. 51°26′ N, 110°48′ W 90
Cereales, Arg. 36°52′ S, 63°51′ W 139
Ceres, Arg. 29°53′ S, 61°57′ W 139
Ceres, Braz. 15°21′ S, 49°37′ W 138
Ceres, Calif., U.S. 37°35′ N, 120°58′ W 100
Ceres, S. Af. 33°21′ S, 19°18′ E 227
Cerf Island, Seychelles 9°36′ S, 49°54′ E 218
Cerigo see Kithira, island, Gr. 36°17′ N, 23°3′ E 180
Cermei, Rom. 46°33′ N, 21°50′ E 168
Çermik, Turk. 38°8′ N, 39°27′ E 195
Cerna, Croatia 45°11′ N, 18°41′ E 168
Cerne Abbas, U.K. 50°48′ N, 2°29′ W 162
Cernik, Croatia 45°17′ N, 17°23′ E 168
Cerovljani, Bosn. and Herzg. 45°3′ N, 17°14′ E 168
Cerralvo, Mex. 26°5′ N, 99°37′ W 114
Cerralvo, Isla, island, Mex. 23°58′ N, 109°49′ W 112
Cerrillos, ruin(s), Mex. 18°33′ N, 92°10′ W 115
Cerritos, Mex. 22°24′ N, 100°16′ W 114
Cerro Azul, Mex. 21°12′ N, 97°44′ W 114
Cerro Azul, Peru 13°2′ S, 76°31′ W 130
Cerro Chato, Uru. 33°5′ S, 55°10′ W 139
Cerro de Garnica National Park, Mex. 19°39′ N, 101°5′ W 112
Cerro de la Estrella National Park (8), Mex. 19°11′ N, 99°10′ W 112
Cerro de las Mesas, ruin(s), Mex. 18°41′ N, 96°7′ W 114
Cerro de Pasco, Peru 10°42′ S, 76°16′ W 130
Cerro Gordo, Ill., U.S. 39°52′ N, 88°44′ W 102
Cerro Jána, Meseta del, Venez. 5°36′ N, 65°51′ W 136
Cerrón, peak, Venez. 10°17′ N, 70°44′ W 136
Cervales, peak, Sp. 39°32′ N, 5°21′ W 164
Cervera, Sp. 41°39′ N, 1°16′ E 164
Cervia, It. 44°15′ N, 12°19′ E 167
Cervione, Fr. 42°26′ N, 9°29′ E 156
Cervignano, It. 45°49′ N, 13°19′ E 167
Cervo, Sp. 43°39′ N, 7°26′ W 150
Cesana Torinese, It. 44°57′ N, 6°49′ E 167
César, adm. division, Col. 9°23′ N, 73°54′ W 136
Cesena, It. 44°8′ N, 12°14′ E 167
Cesenatico, It. 44°11′ N, 12°24′ E 167
Cesiomaggiore, It. 46°5′ N, 11°58′ E 167
Cēsis, Latv. 57°17′ N, 25°15′ E 166
České Budějovice, Czech Rep. 48°59′ N, 14°27′ E 152
Ceský Les, Czech Rep. 49°28′ N, 12°41′ E 152
Çeşme, Turk. 38°16′ N, 26°18′ E 156
Cesney, Cape, Antarctica 66°10′ S, 136°15′ E 248
Cess, river, Liberia 5°40′ N, 8°58′ W 222
Cessnock, Austral. 32°48′ S, 151°22′ E 231
Cesvaine, Latv. 56°57′ N, 26°18′ E 166
Cetate, Rom. 44°6′ N, 23°4′ E 168
Cetina, Sp. 41°16′ N, 1°59′ W 164
Cetinje, Mont. 42°23′ N, 18°54′ E 168
Ceuta, Sp. 35°53′ N, 5°20′ W 150
Cévennes, region, Europe 45°7′ N, 4°13′ E 165
Cevio, Switz. 46°19′ N, 8°35′ E 167
Ceyhan, Turk. 37°1′ N, 35°49′ E 156
Ceyhan, river, Turk. 37°21′ N, 36°16′ E 180
Ceylanpınar, Turk. 36°50′ N, 40°5′ E 195
Ceylon, Can. 49°27′ N, 104°36′ W 90
Chaadayevka, Russ. 53°8′ N, 45°58′ E 154
Chābahār, Iran 25°18′ N, 60°39′ E 182
Chaboullié, Lac, lake, Can. 50°52′ N, 78°32′ W 110
Chac, oil field, Mex. 19°14′ N, 92°33′ W 115
Chacabuco, Arg. 34°40′ S, 60°28′ W 139
Chacalluta, Chile 18°25′ S, 70°20′ W 137
Chacarilla, Chile 20°39′ S, 69°8′ W 137
Chachani, Nevado, peak, Peru 16°14′ S, 71°35′ W 137
Chachapoyas, Peru 6°9′ S, 77°51′ W 130
Chachersk, Belarus 52°50′ N, 30°57′ E 154
Chachoengsao, Thai. 13°43′ N, 101°4′ E 202
Chachora, India 24°10′ N, 77°0′ E 197
Chachro, Pak. 25°7′ N, 70°17′ E 186
Chaco, adm. division, Arg. 27°11′ S, 60°49′ W 139
Chaco Culture National Historic Park, N. Mex., U.S. 36°6′ N, 108°26′ W 92
Chaco National Park, Arg. 26°54′ S, 59°45′ W 139
Chacon, Cape, Alas., U.S. 54°29′ N, 132°5′ W 108
Chad 15°25′ N, 17°21′ E 216
Chad Basain National Park, Nig. 12°10′ N, 13°45′ E 218
Chad, Lake, Chad 13°48′ N, 13°22′ E 216
Chadan, Russ. 51°19′ N, 91°41′ E 184
Chadron, Nebr., U.S. 42°49′ N, 103°0′ W 90
Chadwick, Mo., U.S. 36°55′ N, 93°3′ W 96
Chaedong, N. Korea 39°28′ N, 126°12′ E 200
Chaeronea, ruin(s), Gr. 38°28′ N, 22°43′ E 156
Chaeryŏng, N. Korea 38°24′ N, 125°38′ E 200
Chafarinas, Islas, islands, Alboran Sea 35°13′ N, 2°52′ W 150
Chafe, Nig. 11°54′ N, 6°55′ E 222
Chaffee, Mo., U.S. 37°10′ N, 89°40′ W 96
Chafurray, Col. 3°9′ N, 73°16′ W 136
Chagai, Pak. 29°19′ N, 64°39′ E 182
Chagang, adm. division, N. Korea 40°45′ N, 126°30′ E 200
Chagda, Russ. 58°44′ N, 130°49′ E 160
Chagdo Kangri, peak, China 34°10′ N, 84°4′ E 188
Chaghcharan, Afghan. 34°28′ N, 65°13′ E 186
Chagoda, Russ. 59°7′ N, 35°18′ E 154
Chagos Archipelago (Oil Islands), Indian Ocean 6°42′ S, 71°25′ E 188
Chagos Trench, Indian Ocean 10°25′ S, 72°50′ E 254
Chagos-Laccadive Ridge, Arabian Sea 2°17′ N, 72°13′ E 254
Chaguaramas, Venez. 9°20′ N, 66°17′ W 136
Chagyl, Turkm. 40°49′ N, 55°17′ E 158
Chahar Borj, Afghan. 34°20′ N, 62°12′ E 186
Chahbounia, Alg. 35°31′ N, 2°36′ E 150
Chah-e Ab, Afghan. 37°25′ N, 69°50′ E 186
Ch'aho, N. Korea 40°12′ N, 128°41′ E 200
Chaibasa, India 22°32′ N, 85°49′ E 197
Chaïmane, spring, Mauritania 21°4′ N, 13°6′ W 222
Chain Fracture Zone, South Atlantic Ocean 1°56′ S, 16°17′ W 253
Chaîne de Mitumba, Dem. Rep. of the Congo 8°5′ S, 27°22′ E 224
Chai-Nat, Thai. 15°14′ N, 100°10′ E 202
Chaira, Laguna, lake, Col. 1°13′ N, 75°21′ W 136
Chaitén, Chile 42°54′ S, 72°45′ W 134
Chaiya, Thai. 9°23′ N, 99°10′ E 202
Chajarí, Arg. 30°44′ S, 57°57′ W 139
Chak Chak, Sudan 8°36′ N, 26°57′ E 224
Chakar, river, Pak. 29°24′ N, 68°7′ E 186
Chakaran, Afghan. 36°54′ N, 71°9′ E 186
Chakaria, Bangladesh 21°47′ N, 92°4′ E 188
Chake Chake, Tanzania 5°12′ S, 39°46′ E 218
Chakhansur, Afghan. 31°10′ N, 62°6′ E 186
Chakia, India 25°2′ N, 83°11′ E 188
Chakkarat, Thai. 15°2′ N, 102°25′ E 202
Chakmak-Suu, Kyrg. 41°59′ N, 71°26′ E 197
Chakola, Russ. 64°17′ N, 44°14′ E 154
Chakradharpur, India 22°41′ N, 85°38′ E 197
Chakrata, India 30°42′ N, 77°53′ E 197
Chakwal, Pak. 32°55′ N, 72°53′ E 186
Chala, Peru 15°54′ S, 74°16′ W 137
Chala, Tanzania 7°37′ S, 31°17′ E 224
Chalabesa, Zambia 11°23′ S, 30°59′ E 224
Chalatenango, El Salv. 14°1′ N, 88°55′ W 115
Chalaua, Mozambique 16°5′ S, 39°13′ E 224
Chalbi Desert, Kenya 3°33′ N, 36°48′ E 224
Chalchihuites, Mex. 23°27′ N, 103°54′ W 114
Ch'alchīs Terara, peak, Eth. 9°6′ N, 36°37′ E 224
Chalengkou, China 38°1′ N, 93°55′ E 188
Chaleur Bay 47°51′ N, 66°0′ W 111
Chalhuanca, Peru 14°19′ S, 73°15′ W 137
Chaling, China 26°51′ N, 113°31′ E 198
Chalkyitsik, Alas., U.S. 66°38′ N, 143°44′ W 98
Challacollo, Chile 20°59′ S, 69°24′ W 137
Challans, Fr. 46°51′ N, 1°54′ W 150
Challapata, Bol. 18°55′ S, 66°45′ W 137
Challenger Deep, North Pacific Ocean 10°16′ N, 142°13′ E 252
Challenger Point, peak, Colo., U.S. 37°57′ N, 105°40′ W 90
Challis, Idaho, U.S. 44°30′ N, 114°14′ W 90
Chālmeh, Iran 39°29′ N, 48°3′ E 195
Chalon, Fr. 46°47′ N, 4°50′ E 150
Châlons-en-Champagne, Fr. 48°57′ N, 4°22′ E 163
Chaloyuk, Turkm. 37°26′ N, 54°13′ E 180
Chālūs, Iran 36°41′ N, 51°19′ E 180
Cham, Ger. 49°12′ N, 12°40′ E 152
Chama, Ghana 8°49′ N, 0°58′ E 222
Chama, N. Mex., U.S. 36°53′ N, 106°36′ W 92
Chamah, peak, Malaysia 5°12′ N, 101°29′ E 196
Chaman, Pak. 30°53′ N, 66°33′ E 186

CHA-CHI

Chaman Bid, Iran 37°28' N, 56°39' E 180
Chamba, Nepal 32°34' N, 76°9' E 188
Chamba, Tanzania 11°32' S, 37°1' E 224
Chambak, Cambodia 11°14' N, 104°47' E 202
Chambeaux, Lac, lake, Can. 53°39' N, 69°17' W 111
Chamberlain, S. Dak., U.S. 43°47' N, 99°19' W 90
Chamberlain Lake, Me., U.S. 46°8' N, 70°3' W 94
Chambers, Ariz., U.S. 35°12' N, 109°26' W 92
Chambeshi, river, Zambia 11°2' S, 31°11' E 224
Chambira, river, Peru 3°58' S, 75°57' W 130
Chambishi, Zambia 12°40' S, 28°4' E 224
Chambless, Calif., U.S. 34°33' N, 115°33' W 101
Chambley, Fr. 49°3' N, 5°53' E 163
Chambord, Can. 48°24' N, 72°4' W 94
Chame, Punta, Pan. 8°32' N, 79°41' W 115
Chamela, Mex. 19°32' N, 105°5' W 114
Chamical, Arg. 30°23' S, 66°19' W 134
Chamiss Bay, Can. 50°5' N, 127°20' W 90
Chamizal National Memorial, Tex., U.S. 31°44' N, 106°30' W 92
Chamonix, Fr. 45°55' N, 6°51' E 167
Champa, India 22°2' N, 82°40' E 197
Champagne, region, Europe 49°46' N, 4°21' E 167
Champagne-Ardenne, adm. division, Fr. 48°18' N, 3°36' E 150
Champaign, Ill., U.S. 40°6' N, 88°15' W 102
Champasak, Laos 14°56' N, 105°50' E 202
Champion, Can. 50°14' N, 113°10' W 90
Champion, Ohio, U.S. 41°18' N, 80°51' W 102
Champlain, N.Y., U.S. 44°59' N, 73°28' W 94
Champotón, Mex. 19°21' N, 90°44' W 115
Champotón, river, Mex. 19°29' N, 90°38' W 115
Chamzinka, Russ. 54°25' N, 45°48' E 154
Chanac, Fr. 44°27' N, 3°20' E 150
Chañaral, Chile 26°23' S, 70°39' W 132
Chenārān, Iran 36°39' N, 59°5' E 180
Chanaro, Cerro, peak, Venez. 5°28' N, 64°0' W 130
Chancamayo, Peru 12°36' S, 72°26' W 137
Chancay, Peru 11°34' S, 77°17' W 130
Chanco, Chile 35°44' S, 72°34' W 134
Chandalar, river, Alas., U.S. 66°56' N, 149°16' W 98
Chandausi, India 28°26' N, 78°46' E 197
Chandeleur Islands, Gulf of Mexico 29°39' N, 88°48' W 103
Chandeleur Sound 29°48' N, 89°15' W 103
Chandigarh, India 30°43' N, 76°51' E 197
Chandigarh, adm. division, India 30°45' N, 76°18' E 188
Chandler, Ariz., U.S. 33°18' N, 111°50' W 92
Chandler, Can. 48°20' N, 64°40' W 111
Chandler, Okla., U.S. 35°40' N, 96°52' W 92
Chandler, Mount, Antarctica 75°19' S, 73°25' W 248
Chandless, river, Braz. 10°2' S, 70°12' W 137
Chandpur, Bangladesh 23°13' N, 90°41' E 197
Chandpur, India 29°7' N, 78°15' E 197
Chandrapur, India 20°3' N, 79°17' E 190
Chang, Ko, island, Thai. 11°52' N, 101°42' E 202
Chang La, pass, India 34°2' N, 77°55' E 188
Changalane, Mozambique 26°14' S, 32°14' E 227
Changane, river, Mozambique 24°3' S, 34°3' E 227
Changara, Mozambique 16°50' S, 33°16' E 224
Changbai, China 41°27' N, 128°12' E 200
Changchun, China 43°52' N, 125°16' E 198
Changde, China 29°5' N, 111°43' E 198
Changhua, Taiwan, China 23°59' N, 120°31' E 198
Changhŭng, N. Korea 40°24' N, 128°20' E 200
Changji, China 44°3' N, 87°19' E 184
Changjiang (Shiliu), China 19°13' N, 109°2' E 198
Changjin, N. Korea 40°21' N, 127°15' E 200
Changjin Reservoir, lake, N. Korea 40°29' N, 126°46' E 200
Changjin, river, N. Korea 40°55' N, 127°15' E 200
Changle, China 25°58' N, 119°33' E 198
Changli, China 39°43' N, 119°11' E 198
Changling, China 44°16' N, 124°1' E 198
Changma, China 39°52' N, 96°43' E 188
Changmar, China 34°27' N, 79°57' E 188
Changni, S. Korea 37°19' N, 128°31' E 200
Changning, China 26°23' N, 112°24' E 198
Changping, China 40°12' N, 116°13' E 198
Changsha, China 28°13' N, 113°1' E 198
Changshou, China 29°51' N, 107°4' E 198
Changshu, China 31°36' N, 120°40' E 198
Changting, China 25°50' N, 116°16' E 198
Changtu, China 42°43' N, 124°8' E 200
Changwon, S. Korea 35°16' N, 128°45' E 200
Changxi, China 31°48' N, 105°59' E 198
Changxing Dao, island, China 39°29' N, 120°1' E 198
Changyŏn, N. Korea 38°14' N, 125°5' E 200
Changzheng, China 36°41' N, 105°2' E 198
Changzhi, China 36°10' N, 113°6' E 198
Changzhou, China 31°50' N, 120°0' E 198
Channapatna, India 12°40' N, 77°11' E 188
Channel Country, Austral. 25°2' S, 138°35' E 230
Channel Islands, adm. division, U.K. 49°26' N, 2°48' W 150
Channel Islands National Park, Calif., U.S. 34°5' N, 120°34' W 101
Channel-Port aux Basques, Can. 47°34' N, 59°9' W 111
Chanthaburi, Thai. 12°36' N, 102°9' E 202
Chantilly, Fr. 49°11' N, 2°28' E 163
Chantrey Inlet 67°23' N, 98°31' W 106
Chanute, Kans., U.S. 37°39' N, 95°28' W 94
Chany, Russ. 55°16' N, 76°54' E 184
Chany, Ozero, lake, Russ. 54°57' N, 76°49' E 184
Chany, Ozero, lake, Russ. 54°39' N, 75°46' E 160
Chaor, river, China 47°14' N, 121°38' E 198
Chaoyang, China 41°35' N, 120°24' E 198
Chaoyang, China 23°13' N, 116°33' E 198
Chaoyang see Huinan, China 42°42' N, 126°4' E 200
Chaoyangchuan, China 42°51' N, 129°19' E 200
Chaozhou, China 23°37' N, 116°33' E 198
Chapada dos Guimarães, Braz. 15°25' S, 55°47' W 132
Chapada Dos Veadeiros National Park, Braz. 14°10' S, 47°50' W 138
Chapadinha, Braz. 3°46' S, 43°20' W 132
Chapaev, Kaz. 50°11' N, 51°8' E 158
Chapais, Can. 49°48' N, 74°54' W 94
Chapala, Mex. 20°18' N, 103°12' W 112
Chapala, Lago de, lake, Mex. 20°2' N, 103°30' W 114
Chapare, river, Bol. 16°21' S, 65°2' W 137
Chaparral, Col. 3°41' N, 75°26' W 136
Chapayevsk, Russ. 52°58' N, 49°48' E 154
Chapeau, Can. 45°55' N, 77°4' W 94
Chapeauroux, Fr. 44°49' N, 3°44' E 150
Chapecó, Braz. 27°4' S, 52°36' W 139
Chapimarca, Peru 13°59' S, 73°3' W 137
Chapleau, Can. 47°49' N, 83°24' W 94
Chaplin Lake, Can. 50°13' N, 107°8' W 108
Chapman, Ala., U.S. 31°40' N, 86°43' W 96
Chapman, Kans., U.S. 38°57' N, 97°2' W 90
Chapman, Mount, Antarctica 82°25' S, 104°25' W 248
Chapman, Mount, Can. 51°56' N, 118°24' W 90
Chapoma, Russ. 66°8' N, 38°44' E 154
Chappaquiddick Island, Mass., U.S. 41°23' N, 70°27' W 104
Chappell, Nebr., U.S. 41°4' N, 102°28' W 90
Chaput Hughes, Can. 48°8' N, 80°4' W 94
Chaqui, Bol. 19°35' S, 65°28' W 137
Char, Mauritania 21°32' N, 12°50' W 222
Chara, Russ. 56°48' N, 118°10' E 160
Chara, river, Russ. 59°0' N, 118°31' E 160
Charadai, Arg. 27°37' S, 59°54' W 139
Charagua, Bol. 19°48' S, 63°18' W 137
Charalá, Col. 6°15' N, 73°7' W 136
Charambirá, Punta, Col. 4°8' N, 78°10' W 136
Charaña, Bol. 17°40' S, 69°27' W 137
Charanwala, India 27°51' N, 72°11' E 186
Charata, Arg. 27°13' S, 61°12' W 139
Charay, Mex. 26°0' N, 108°50' W 112
Charcoal Lake, Can. 58°44' N, 103°14' W 108
Charcot Bay 63°49' S, 61°4' W 134
Charcot Island, Antarctica 70°11' S, 79°50' W 248
Chard, Can. 55°50' N, 110°54' W 108
Chard, U.K. 50°52' N, 2°58' W 162
Charenton, La., U.S. 29°52' N, 91°32' W 103
Chari, river, Africa 13°9' N, 14°33' E 216
Charikar, Afghan. 35°1' N, 69°10' E 186
Chariton, Iowa, U.S. 41°1' N, 93°19' W 94
Chariton, river, Mo., U.S. 40°44' N, 93°9' W 80
Charity, Guyana 7°21' N, 58°37' W 130
Charity Island, Mich., U.S. 43°59' N, 83°25' W 102
Chärjew see Türkmenabat, Turkm. 39°4' N, 63°35' E 184
Charkayuvom, Russ. 65°48' N, 54°51' E 154
Charlemont, Mass., U.S. 42°37' N, 72°53' W 104
Charleroi, Belg. 50°25' N, 4°26' E 167
Charles, Cape, Va., U.S. 37°1' N, 75°57' W 96
Charles Fuhr, Arg. 50°13' S, 71°53' W 134
Charles Island, Can. 62°36' N, 77°12' W 106
Charles Lake, lake, Can. 59°45' N, 111°12' W 108
Charles Mound, Ill., U.S. 42°28' N, 90°17' W 102
Charles, Mount, Austral. 27°46' S, 117°13' E 230
Charlesbourg, Can. 46°51' N, 71°17' W 94
Charleston, Ill., U.S. 39°29' N, 88°11' W 102
Charleston, N.Z. 41°56' S, 171°27' E 240
Charleston, S.C., U.S. 32°47' N, 79°57' W 96
Charleston, W. Va., U.S. 38°19' N, 81°43' W 94
Charleston Peak, Nev., U.S. 36°15' N, 115°45' W 101
Charlestown, N.H., U.S. 43°13' N, 72°26' W 104
Charleville-Mézières, Fr. 49°46' N, 4°43' E 163
Charlevoix, Mich., U.S. 45°18' N, 85°16' W 94
Charlie Lake, Can. 56°15' N, 120°59' W 108
Charlie-Gibbs Fracture Zone, North Atlantic Ocean 51°53' N, 33°3' W 253
Charlotte, Mich., U.S. 42°33' N, 84°51' W 102
Charlotte, N.C., U.S. 35°12' N, 80°51' W 96
Charlotte, Tex., U.S. 28°51' N, 98°43' W 96
Charlotte, Vt., U.S. 44°18' N, 73°16' W 104
Charlotte Amalie, Virgin Islands, U.S. 18°0' N, 65°0' W 118
Charlotte Harbor 26°42' N, 83°11' W 80
Charlotte Harbor, Fla., U.S. 26°58' N, 82°4' W 105
Charlotte Lake, lake, Can. 52°6' N, 125°48' W 108
Charlottetown, Can. 46°13' N, 63°16' W 111
Charlotteville, Trinidad and Tobago 11°16' N, 60°33' W 116
Charlton City, Mass., U.S. 42°8' N, 72°0' W 104
Charlton Island, Can. 52°5' N, 80°29' W 81
Charly, Fr. 48°58' N, 3°16' E 163
Charmes, Fr. 48°21' N, 6°17' E 163
Charny, Can. 46°43' N, 71°16' W 94
Charouine, Alg. 29°2' N, 0°15' E 214
Charron Lake, lake, Can. 52°39' N, 95°47' W 108
Charters Towers, Austral. 20°7' S, 146°17' E 231
Chartres, Fr. 48°27' N, 1°28' E 163
Charyshskoye, Russ. 51°26' N, 83°43' E 184
Chascomús, Arg. 35°34' S, 58°1' W 139
Chase, Alas., U.S. 62°27' N, 150°6' W 98
Chase, Can. 50°49' N, 119°40' W 90
Chase, Mich., U.S. 43°53' N, 85°38' W 102
Chase City, Va., U.S. 36°47' N, 78°28' W 96
Chase, Mount, Me., U.S. 46°5' N, 68°34' W 94
Chase Mountain, Can. 56°32' N, 125°22' W 108
Chasel'ka, Russ. 65°7' N, 81°26' E 169
Chashniki, Belarus 54°51' N, 29°13' E 166
Chaska, Minn., U.S. 44°46' N, 93°38' W 94
Chasŏng, N. Korea 41°26' N, 126°38' E 200
Chasovo, Russ. 62°2' N, 50°40' E 154
Chassahowitzka, Fla., U.S. 28°41' N, 82°35' W 105
Chastyye, Russ. 57°16' N, 55°4' E 154
Chataignier, La., U.S. 30°32' N, 92°20' W 103
Chatawa, Miss., U.S. 31°2' N, 90°29' W 103
Châteaumeillant, Fr. 46°34' N, 2°11' E 150
Châteauneuf-en-Thymerais, Fr. 48°34' N, 1°14' E 163
Château-Porcien, Fr. 49°32' N, 4°14' E 163
Châteauroux, Fr. 46°49' N, 1°41' E 150
Château-Salins, Fr. 48°49' N, 6°30' E 163
Châteauvert, Lac, lake, Can. 47°34' N, 74°36' W 110
Chateh, Can. 58°41' N, 118°48' W 108
Châtel, Fr. 46°16' N, 6°49' E 167
Châtelet, Belg. 50°24' N, 4°32' E 167
Châtellerault, Fr. 46°48' N, 0°31' E 150
Châtel-Saint-Denis, Switz. 46°33' N, 6°55' E 167
Châtel-sur-Moselle, Fr. 48°18' N, 6°24' E 163
Châtenois, Fr. 48°17' N, 5°49' E 163
Chatfield, Minn., U.S. 43°50' N, 92°12' W 110
Chatham, Can. 47°1' N, 65°28' W 94
Chatham, Can. 42°23' N, 82°11' W 102
Chatham, Ill., U.S. 39°39' N, 89°42' W 102
Chatham, La., U.S. 32°18' N, 92°29' W 103
Chatham, Mass., U.S. 41°40' N, 69°58' W 104
Chatham, Miss., U.S. 33°4' N, 91°7' W 103
Chatham, Mo., U.S. 39°39' N, 89°42' W 94
Chatham, N.H., U.S. 44°9' N, 71°1' W 104
Chatham, N.Y., U.S. 42°21' N, 73°37' W 104
Chatham, U.K. 51°21' N, 0°30' E 162
Chatham, Va., U.S. 36°48' N, 79°25' W 96
Chatham, Isla, island, Chile 51°9' S, 74°8' W 134
Chatham Rise, South Pacific Ocean 43°29' S, 178°25' W 252
Châtillon, Fr. 49°6' N, 3°46' E 163
Chatom, Ala., U.S. 31°27' N, 88°15' W 103
Chatra, India 24°11' N, 84°51' E 197
Chatsu, India 26°35' N, 75°57' E 197
Chatsworth, Ill., U.S. 40°45' N, 88°19' W 102
Chattahoochee, Fla., U.S. 30°40' N, 84°54' W 112
Chattahoochee, river, U.S. 32°4' N, 85°8' W 80
Chattanooga, Tenn., U.S. 35°1' N, 85°19' W 96
Chattaroy, W. Va., U.S. 37°42' N, 82°18' W 96
Chatteris, U.K. 52°27' N, 5°297' E 162
Chatyr-Tash, Kyrg. 40°54' N, 76°26' E 184
Chau Doc, Vietnam 10°41' N, 105°7' E 202
Chauk, Myanmar 20°53' N, 94°50' E 202
Chaullay, Peru 13°1' S, 72°39' W 137
Chaulnes, Fr. 49°48' N, 2°47' E 163
Chaumont, Fr. 48°6' N, 5°8' E 150
Chaumont-en-Vexin, Fr. 49°16' N, 1°53' E 163
Chaumu, India 27°10' N, 75°42' E 197
Chauncey, Ohio, U.S. 39°24' N, 82°8' W 102
Chaunskaya Guba 69°10' N, 165°0' E 160
Chauny, Fr. 49°37' N, 3°14' E 163
Chauvin, Can. 52°41' N, 110°9' W 108
Chauvin, La., U.S. 29°26' N, 90°36' W 103
Chavan'ga, Russ. 66°8' N, 37°40' E 154
Chaves, Braz. 0°24' N, 49°48' W 123
Chaves, Port. 41°44' N, 7°30' W 150
Chaveslândia, Braz. 18°58' S, 50°36' W 138
Cháviva, Col. 4°18' N, 72°18' W 136
Chavuma, Zambia 13°5' S, 22°43' E 220
Chavusy, Belarus 53°46' N, 31°0' E 154
Chawang, Thai. 8°26' N, 99°31' E 202
Chayanta, Bol. 18°28' S, 66°28' W 137
Chaykovskiy, Russ. 56°48' N, 54°9' E 154
Cheadle, U.K. 52°59' N, 2°0' W 162
Cheaha Mountain, Ala., U.S. 33°27' N, 85°53' W 96
Cheapside, Va., U.S. 37°12' N, 75°59' W 96
Cheb, Czech Rep. 50°4' N, 12°22' E 152
Chebanse, Ill., U.S. 41°0' N, 87°55' W 102
Chebarkul', Russ. 55°0' N, 60°19' E 154
Chebeague Island, Me., U.S. 43°44' N, 70°8' W 104
Cheboksary, Russ. 56°5' N, 47°11' E 154
Cheboygan, Mich., U.S. 45°38' N, 84°30' W 94
Chebsara, Russ. 59°10' N, 38°49' E 154
Checa, Sp. 40°34' N, 1°47' W 164
Chech, Erg, Alg. 23°26' N, 4°20' W 206
Chechnya, adm. division, Russ. 43°33' N, 44°59' E 158
Checotah, Okla., U.S. 35°27' N, 95°32' W 96
Cheddar, U.K. 51°16' N, 2°47' W 162
Cheduba Island, Myanmar 18°29' N, 92°36' E 188
Chedworth, U.K. 51°48' N, 1°55' W 162
Cheecham, Can. 56°16' N, 110°53' W 108
Cheepash, river, Can. 50°42' N, 82°33' W 110
Cheepay, river, Can. 51°7' N, 83°35' W 110
Cheetham, Cape, Antarctica 69°54' S, 167°30' E 248
Chefornak, Alas., U.S. 60°12' N, 164°14' W 98
Chegdomyn, Russ. 51°6' N, 133°12' E 238
Chegga, spring, Mauritania 25°22' N, 5°47' W 214
Chegutu, Zimb. 18°9' S, 30°10' E 224
Chehalis, Wash., U.S. 46°39' N, 122°58' W 100
Chehalis, river, Wash., U.S. 46°59' N, 123°25' W 100
Chehar Borjak, Afghan. 30°17' N, 62°7' E 186
Cheïkria, spring, Alg. 25°29' N, 5°28' W 214
Cheju see Jeju, S. Korea 33°29' N, 126°32' E 200
Chela, Serra da, Angola 16°7' S, 12°39' E 220
Ch'elago, Eth. 4°9' N, 40°3' E 224
Chelak, Uzb. 39°58' N, 66°51' E 197
Chelan, Wash., U.S. 47°50' N, 120°1' W 90
Chelan Falls, Wash., U.S. 47°47' N, 119°59' W 108
Chelem, Mex. 21°15' N, 89°44' W 116
Chelforó, Arg. 39°6' S, 66°31' W 134
Chellal, Alg. 35°30' N, 4°23' E 150
Chełm, Pol. 51°7' N, 23°27' E 152
Chełmża, Pol. 53°21' N, 18°26' E 152
Chelmsford, Mass., U.S. 42°35' N, 71°22' W 104
Chelmsford, U.K. 51°44' N, 0°29' E 162
Chelmuzhi, Russ. 62°32' N, 35°43' E 154
Chelsea, Mich., U.S. 42°18' N, 84°2' W 102
Chelsea, Okla., U.S. 36°31' N, 95°26' W 96
Chelsea, Vt., U.S. 43°59' N, 72°27' W 104
Cheltenham, U.K. 51°53' N, 2°5' W 162
Chelva, Sp. 39°44' N, 1°0' E 150
Chelyabinsk, Russ. 55°9' N, 61°25' E 154
Chelyabinsk, adm. division, Russ. 53°58' N, 59°14' E 154
Chelyuskin, Mys, Russ. 76°44' N, 103°34' E 172
Chemaïa, Mor. 32°5' N, 8°40' W 214
Chemba, Mozambique 17°11' S, 34°50' E 224
Chemehuevi Peak, Calif., U.S. 34°32' N, 114°36' W 101
Chémery, Fr. 49°35' N, 4°50' E 163
Chemnitz, Ger. 50°48' N, 12°55' E 160
Chemtou, ruin(s), Tun. 36°28' N, 8°29' E 156
Chemult, Oreg., U.S. 43°13' N, 121°48' W 90
Chen Barag Qi, China 49°17' N, 119°24' E 198
Chenab, river, Pak. 31°18' N, 72°22' E 186
Chenachane, Alg. 26°3' N, 4°14' W 214
Chenango Bridge, N.Y., U.S. 42°10' N, 75°53' W 94
Chenārān, Iran 36°39' N, 59°5' E 180
Ch'ench'a (Cencia), Eth. 6°15' N, 37°38' E 224
Chénérailles, Fr. 46°7' N, 2°10' E 150
Cheney, Wash., U.S. 47°28' N, 117°36' W 90
Cheneyville, La., U.S. 30°59' N, 92°18' W 103
Chengbu, China 26°22' N, 110°19' E 198
Chengchow see Zhengzhou, China 34°46' N, 113°36' E 198
Chengde, China 41°0' N, 117°55' E 198
Chengdu, China 30°43' N, 104°2' E 198
Chengele, India 28°47' N, 96°17' E 188
Chenggu, China 33°8' N, 107°19' E 198
Chenghai, China 23°29' N, 116°48' E 198
Chengkou, China 31°54' N, 108°39' E 198
Ch'engkung, Taiwan, China 23°8' N, 121°24' E 198
Chengshan Jiao, China 37°24' N, 122°45' E 198
Chengxian, China 33°44' N, 105°40' E 198
Chennai (Madras), India 13°5' N, 80°16' E 188
Chenoa, Ill., U.S. 40°44' N, 88°43' W 102
Chenxi, China 28°2' N, 110°12' E 198
Chenxiangtun, China 41°33' N, 123°29' E 200
Chenzhou, China 25°48' N, 113°2' E 198
Cheo Reo, Vietnam 13°23' N, 108°25' E 202
Cheom Ksan, Cambodia 14°16' N, 104°56' E 202
Cheonan, S. Korea 36°47' N, 127°8' E 200
Cheongeong, S. Korea 36°26' N, 129°6' E 200
Cheongju, S. Korea 36°37' N, 127°30' E 200
Cheongyang, S. Korea 36°26' N, 126°48' E 200
Cheorwon, S. Korea 38°14' N, 127°13' E 200
Chepachet, R.I., U.S. 41°54' N, 71°41' W 104
Chepes, Arg. 31°20' S, 66°35' W 134
Chepstow, U.K. 51°38' N, 2°41' W 162
Cheptsa, river, Russ. 58°8' N, 52°54' E 154
Cher, river, Fr. 46°54' N, 2°17' E 165
Cherán, Mex. 19°40' N, 101°57' W 114
Cherangany Hills, Kenya 1°32' N, 35°1' E 224
Cherari, Eth. 9°55' N, 35°52' E 224
Cheraw, S.C., U.S. 34°40' N, 79°55' W 96
Cherchell, Alg. 36°35' N, 2°12' E 150
Cherdyn', Russ. 60°24' N, 56°25' E 154
Cheremkhovo, Russ. 53°16' N, 102°55' E 190
Cheremukhovo, Russ. 60°21' N, 59°59' E 154
Cherepanovo, Russ. 54°14' N, 83°29' E 184
Chereponi, Ghana 10°7' N, 0°17' E 222
Cherepovets, Russ. 59°7' N, 37°55' E 154
Cherevkovo, Russ. 61°46' N, 45°17' E 154
Chereya, Belarus 54°36' N, 29°20' E 166
Chéri, Niger 13°25' N, 11°21' E 222
Cheriton, Va., U.S. 37°17' N, 75°58' W 96
Cherkasy, Ukr. 49°26' N, 32°3' E 158
Cherkessk, Russ. 44°14' N, 42°3' E 158
Cherla, India 18°4' N, 80°50' E 188
Cherlak, Russ. 54°9' N, 74°53' E 184
Chermenino, Russ. 59°2' N, 43°59' E 154
Chermoz, Russ. 58°46' N, 56°5' E 154
Chern', Russ. 53°25' N, 36°57' E 154
Chernaya Kholunitsa, Russ. 58°52' N, 51°46' E 154
Chernevichi, Belarus 54°1' N, 28°49' E 166
Chernevo, Russ. 58°39' N, 28°12' E 166
Cherni Vrŭkh, peak, Bulg. 42°32' N, 23°12' E 156
Chernihiv, Ukr. 51°27' N, 31°20' E 158
Chernivtsi, Ukr. 48°17' N, 25°57' E 152
Chernoborskaya, Russ. 52°8' N, 53°38' E 154
Chernofski, Alas., U.S. 53°22' N, 167°34' W 98
Chernogorsk, Russ. 53°49' N, 91°16' E 184
Chernorechenskiy, Russ. 60°42' N, 52°15' E 154
Chernovka, Russ. 54°12' N, 80°5' E 184
Chernushka, Russ. 56°30' N, 56°1' E 154
Chernyakhovsk, Russ. 54°36' N, 21°49' E 152
Chernyanka, Russ. 50°55' N, 37°48' E 158
Chernyshevskiy, Russ. 62°52' N, 112°40' E 160
Chernyy Otrog, Russ. 51°51' N, 56°0' E 158
Chernyy Yar, Russ. 48°2' N, 46°4' E 158
Cherokee, Okla., U.S. 36°44' N, 98°21' W 92
Cherokee Sound, Bahamas 26°16' N, 77°3' W 96
Cherokees, Lake O' The, Okla., U.S. 36°42' N, 95°40' W 80
Cherrapunji, India 25°15' N, 91°42' E 197
Cherry Creek Range, Nev., U.S. 39°59' N, 115°6' W 90
Cherry Creek, river, S. Dak., U.S. 44°42' N, 102°31' W 90
Cherskaya, Russ. 57°39' N, 28°17' E 166
Cherskiy, Russ. 68°39' N, 161°29' E 160
Cherskogo, Khrebet, Russ. 66°20' N, 138°20' E 160
Chersonesus, ruin(s), Gr. 35°18' N, 25°17' E 156
Chertkovo, Russ. 49°27' N, 40°8' E 158
Cherva, Russ. 62°16' N, 48°41' E 154
Chervonohrad, Ukr. 50°22' N, 24°15' E 152
Chervyanka, Russ. 57°39' N, 99°28' E 160
Cherykaw, Belarus 53°32' N, 31°23' E 154
Chesaning, Mich., U.S. 43°10' N, 84°7' W 102
Chesapeake, Va., U.S. 36°49' N, 76°17' W 96
Chesapeake, W. Va., U.S. 38°12' N, 81°34' W 94
Chesham, U.K. 51°42' N, 0°38' E 162
Cheshire, Conn., U.S. 41°29' N, 72°54' W 104
Cheshire, Mass., U.S. 42°33' N, 73°10' W 104
Cheshskaya Guba 67°9' N, 44°36' E 169
Cheshunt, U.K. 51°41' N, 0°3' E 162
Cheslatta Lake, lake, Can. 53°38' N, 125°40' W 108
Chesley, Can. 44°17' N, 81°6' W 110
Chesma, Russ. 53°51' N, 60°32' E 154
Cheste, Sp. 39°29' N, 0°42' E 164
Chester, Mo., U.S. 37°54' N, 89°49' W 96
Chester, Mont., U.S. 48°28' N, 110°59' W 90
Chester, N.H., U.S. 42°57' N, 71°16' W 104
Chester, S.C., U.S. 34°42' N, 81°13' W 96
Chester, U.K. 53°12' N, 2°51' W 162
Chester, Vt., U.S. 43°15' N, 72°36' W 104
Chester le Street, U.K. 54°51' N, 1°36' W 162
Chesterfield, Ind., U.S. 40°6' N, 85°36' W 102
Chesterfield, U.K. 53°14' N, 1°27' W 162
Chesterfield, Îles, islands, Coral Sea 18°54' S, 154°49' E 238
Chesterfield Inlet, Can. 63°19' N, 90°50' W 106
Chesterhill, Ohio, U.S. 39°28' N, 81°51' W 102
Chesterton Range, Austral. 26°17' S, 147°27' E 230
Chestertown, N.Y., U.S. 43°38' N, 73°49' W 104
Chestnut Ridge, Pa., U.S. 40°29' N, 79°22' W 94
Chetamale, India 10°44' N, 92°41' E 188
Chete Safari Area, Zimb. 17°30' S, 27°12' E 224
Chetek, Wis., U.S. 45°18' N, 91°40' W 94
Chéticamp, Can. 46°36' N, 61°1' W 111
Chetumal, Mex. 18°30' N, 88°27' W 115
Chetwynd, Can. 55°41' N, 121°39' W 108
Chevillon, Fr. 48°31' N, 5°7' E 163
Cheviot, N.Z. 42°50' S, 173°16' E 240
Cheviot Hills, U.K. 55°10' N, 2°47' W 150
Cheviot, The, peak, U.K. 55°27' N, 2°16' W 150
Ch'ew Bahir, lake, Eth. 4°40' N, 36°40' E 224
Chewelah, Wash., U.S. 48°15' N, 117°45' W 90
Chewore Safari Area, Zimb. 15°58' S, 29°52' E 224
Cheyenne, Okla., U.S. 35°35' N, 99°40' W 92
Cheyenne, Wyo., U.S. 41°6' N, 104°55' W 90
Cheyenne, river, S. Dak., U.S. 44°24' N, 102°2' W 90
Cheyenne, river, Wyo., U.S. 42°53' N, 104°36' W 80
Cheyenne Wells, Colo., U.S. 38°48' N, 102°21' W 90
Chezacut, Can. 52°25' N, 124°2' W 108
Chhad Bet, site, Pak. 24°13' N, 69°54' E 186
Chhapra, India 25°46' N, 84°43' E 197
Chhatarpur, India 24°54' N, 79°35' E 197
Chhattīsgarh, adm. division, India 19°11' N, 81°20' E 188
Chhep, Cambodia 13°46' N, 105°27' E 202
Chhindwara, India 22°4' N, 78°56' E 197
Chhlong, Cambodia 12°14' N, 105°57' E 202
Chhukha, Bhutan 27°10' N, 89°30' E 197
Chi, river, Thai. 15°56' N, 102°18' E 202
Chia, Sp. 42°31' N, 0°27' E 164
Chiai, Taiwan, China 23°28' N, 120°25' E 198
Chiang Dao, Thai. 19°23' N, 98°57' E 202
Chiang Khan, Thai. 17°53' N, 101°37' E 202
Chiang Mai, Thai. 18°48' N, 98°58' E 202
Chiang Rai, Thai. 19°55' N, 99°48' E 202
Chiang Saen, Laos 20°18' N, 100°3' E 202
Chiange, Angola 15°43' S, 13°54' E 220
Chiapa, Chile 19°33' S, 69°14' W 137
Chiapas, adm. division, Mex. 16°28' N, 93°24' W 112
Chiari, It. 45°32' N, 9°54' E 167
Chiasso, Switz. 45°51' N, 9°1' E 167
Chiat'aisi, Ga. 42°14' N, 43°17' E 195
Chiautla, Mex. 18°15' N, 98°36' W 114
Chiavari, It. 44°19' N, 9°20' E 167
Chiavenna, It. 46°19' N, 9°23' E 167
Chiba, Japan 35°34' N, 140°9' E 201
Chiba, adm. division, Japan 35°44' N, 139°54' E 201
Chibabava, Mozambique 20°17' S, 33°41' E 227
Chibi, Zimb. 20°19' S, 30°29' E 227
Chibia, Angola 15°14' S, 13°40' E 220
Chibougamau, Can. 49°54' N, 74°22' W 94
Chibougamau, Lac, lake, Can. 49°49' N, 75°44' W 81
Chibuto, Mozambique 24°42' S, 33°34' E 227
Chibwe, Zambia 14°12' S, 28°29' E 224
Chic Chocs Mountains, Can. 48°42' N, 67°1' W 94
Chicago, Ill., U.S. 41°51' N, 87°37' W 102
Chicamba, Angola 4°59' S, 12°2' E 218
Chichagof, Alas., U.S. 57°41' N, 136°8' W 108
Chichagof Island, Alas., U.S. 58°3' N, 138°7' W 98
Chichaoua, Mor. 31°31' N, 8°47' W 214
Chichas, Cordillera de, Bol. 20°47' S, 66°25' W 132
Chiché, river, Braz. 8°54' S, 54°6' W 130
Chichén Itzá, ruin(s), Mex. 20°40' N, 88°42' W 115
Chichester, N.H., U.S. 43°14' N, 71°25' W 104
Chichester, U.K. 50°50' N, 0°47' E 162
Chichi Jima Rettō, islands, Philippine Sea 26°41' N, 142°19' E 190
Chichibu, Japan 35°58' N, 139°6' E 201
Chichibu-Tama National Park, Japan 35°50' N, 138°11' E 201
Chichihualco, Mex. 17°40' N, 99°41' W 114
Chichiriviche, Venez. 10°56' N, 68°17' W 136
Chickaloon, Alas., U.S. 61°48' N, 148°28' W 98
Chickasaw, Ala., U.S. 30°45' N, 88°3' W 103
Chickasha, Okla., U.S. 35°2' N, 97°57' W 92
Chiclana de la Frontera, Sp. 36°25' N, 6°9' W 164
Chiclayo, Peru 6°44' S, 79°51' W 130
Chico, Calif., U.S. 39°43' N, 121°51' W 90
Chico, river, Arg. 48°23' S, 71°58' W 134
Chico, river, Arg. 45°2' S, 67°5' W 134
Chicomo, Mozambique 24°31' S, 34°19' E 227
Chicontepec, Mex. 20°57' N, 98°10' W 114
Chicopee, Ga., U.S. 34°14' N, 83°51' W 96
Chicopee, Mass., U.S. 42°8' N, 72°37' W 104
Chicot Island, La., U.S. 29°39' N, 89°22' W 103
Chicoutai, Point, Can. 50°5' N, 61°8' W 111
Chicoutimi-Nord, Can. 48°26' N, 71°6' W 94
Chicualacuala, Mozambique 22°4' S, 31°43' E 227
Chicuma, Angola 13°26' S, 14°49' E 220
Chidenguele, Mozambique 24°54' S, 34°10' E 227
Chiefland, Fla., U.S. 29°28' N, 82°51' W 105
Chiengi, Zambia 8°41' S, 29°10' E 224
Chietla, Mex. 18°29' N, 98°34' W 114
Chifeng, China 42°15' N, 118°59' E 198
Chifre, Serra do, Braz. 17°46' S, 42°41' W 132
Chignahuapan, Mex. 19°48' N, 98°2' W 114
Chignecto Bay 45°35' N, 64°44' W 111
Chignecto, Cape, Can. 45°15' N, 65°39' W 111
Chignik, Alas., U.S. 56°8' N, 158°13' W 106
Chiguana, Bol. 21°7' S, 67°58' W 137
Chiguaza, Ecua. 2°2' S, 77°52' W 136
Chigubo, Mozambique 22°49' S, 33°30' E 227

D

Daman and Diu, adm. division, India 20°18′ N, 71°51′ E 188
Daman (Damão), India 20°25′ N, 72°52′ E 186
Damanava, Belarus 52°49′ N, 25°30′ E 152
Damane, spring, Mauritania 19°20′ N, 14°33′ W 222
Damanhûr, Egypt 31°1′ N, 30°22′ E 180
Damão see Daman, India 20°25′ N, 72°52′ E 186
Damar, island, Indonesia 7°28′ S, 127°44′ E 192
Damara, Cen. Af. Rep. 4°57′ N, 18°43′ E 218
Damaraland, region, Africa 21°4′ S, 15°26′ E 227
Damas Cays, North Atlantic Ocean 23°23′ N, 80°1′ W 116
Damasak, Nig. 13°8′ N, 12°33′ E 216
Damascus see Dimashq, Syr. 33°30′ N, 36°14′ E 194
Damaturu, Nig. 11°44′ N, 11°55′ E 222
Damāvand, Qolleh-ye, peak, Iran 35°58′ N, 52°0′ E 180
Damba, Angola 6°41′ S, 15°7′ E 218
Dambarta, Nig. 12°26′ N, 8°31′ E 222
Damboa, Nig. 11°10′ N, 12°49′ E 216
Damergou, region, Africa 14°49′ N, 9°0′ E 222
Dāmghān, Iran 36°11′ N, 54°19′ E 180
Damietta see Dumyât, Egypt 31°25′ N, 31°49′ E 180
Daming, China 36°15′ N, 115°8′ E 198
Damingzhen, China 42°32′ N, 123°40′ E 200
Damīr Qābū, Syr. 36°57′ N, 41°52′ E 195
Dāmiyā, Jordan 32°6′ N, 35°33′ E 194
Dammarie, Fr. 48°20′ N, 1°29′ E 163
Dammartin-en-Goële, Fr. 49°2′ N, 2°40′ E 163
Damme, Ger. 52°31′ N, 8°12′ E 163
Damongo, Ghana 9°4′ N, 1°49′ W 222
Damour, Leb. 33°43′ N, 35°27′ E 194
Damous, Alg. 36°32′ N, 1°43′ E 150
Dampier, Austral. 20°40′ S, 116°43′ E 231
Dampier Archipelago, Indian Ocean 20°18′ S, 117°11′ E 230
Dampier Land, Austral. 17°35′ S, 122°12′ E 230
Dampierre, Fr. 48°32′ N, 4°21′ E 163
Damqawt, Yemen 16°35′ N, 52°49′ E 182
Damsarkhū, Syr. 35°32′ N, 35°46′ E 194
Damvillers, Fr. 49°20′ N, 5°23′ E 163
Damxung, China 30°35′ N, 91°9′ E 197
Damyang, S. Korea 35°18′ N, 126°59′ E 200
Dan, Israel 33°13′ N, 35°38′ E 194
Dan Gulbi, Nig. 11°35′ N, 6°16′ E 222
Dan, river, N.C., U.S. 36°35′ N, 79°20′ W 80
Dana, Ind., U.S. 39°48′ N, 87°30′ W 102
Ḑānā, Jordan 30°40′ N, 35°36′ E 194
Dana, Mount, Calif., U.S. 37°53′ N, 119°16′ W 100
Dana Point, Calif., U.S. 33°28′ N, 117°43′ W 101
Danané, Côte d'Ivoire 7°8′ N, 8°9′ W 222
Danbury, Conn., U.S. 41°23′ N, 73°28′ W 104
Danbury, Iowa, U.S. 42°13′ N, 95°44′ W 90
Danbury, N.H., U.S. 43°31′ N, 71°53′ W 104
Danbury, Tex., U.S. 29°13′ N, 95°21′ W 103
Danby, Vt., U.S. 43°20′ N, 73°0′ W 104
Dancheng, China 33°37′ N, 115°14′ E 198
Danco Coast, Antarctica 64°6′ S, 61°55′ W 134
Dandéla, Guinea 10°55′ N, 8°24′ W 222
Dandeldhura, Nepal 29°16′ N, 80°34′ E 197
Dandong, China 40°10′ N, 124°24′ E 200
Dandurand, Lac, lake, Can. 47°48′ N, 75°9′ W 94
Dane, Can. 48°5′ N, 80°1′ W 94
Danfa, Mali 14°9′ N, 7°30′ W 222
Danfeng, China 33°42′ N, 110°24′ E 198
Danfina, Mali 11°2′ N, 7°9′ W 222
Danfort Hills, Colo., U.S. 40°20′ N, 108°25′ W 90
Danforth, Me., U.S. 45°39′ N, 67°52′ W 94
Dangara, Taj. 38°15′ N, 69°16′ E 197
Dangchang, China 33°55′ N, 104°25′ E 198
Dange, Angola 7°58′ S, 15°1′ E 218
Danger Islands, Weddell Sea 63°57′ S, 54°20′ W 134
Danger Islands see Pukapuka Atoll, South Pacific Ocean 10°35′ S, 167°12′ W 238
Danger Point, S. Af. 34°53′ S, 19°1′ E 227
Dangé-Saint-Romain, Fr. 46°56′ N, 0°37′ E 150
Dangila, Eth. 11°15′ N, 36°52′ E 182
Dangjin Shankou, pass, China 39°17′ N, 94°15′ E 188
Dango, Sudan 9°58′ N, 24°43′ E 224
Dango, Qoz, Sudan 10°29′ N, 24°11′ E 224
Dangrek Range, Thai. 14°34′ N, 103°21′ E 202
Dangriga, Belize 16°57′ N, 88°15′ W 115
Dangshan, China 34°27′ N, 116°21′ E 198
Dangtu, China 31°34′ N, 118°28′ E 198
Danguya, Cen. Af. Rep. 6°27′ N, 22°41′ E 218
Daniel, Wyo., U.S. 42°52′ N, 110°4′ W 90
Daniel, oil field, Arg. 52°17′ S, 68°54′ W 134
Daniel's Harbour, Can. 50°14′ N, 57°35′ W 111
Danilov, Russ. 58°11′ N, 40°8′ E 154
Danilovgrad, Mont. 42°32′ N, 19°7′ E 168
Danilovka, Russ. 64°42′ N, 57°47′ E 154
Danjiangkou, China 32°34′ N, 111°31′ E 198
Ḑank, Oman 23°32′ N, 56°17′ E 196
Dankov, Russ. 53°14′ N, 39°1′ E 154
Danlí, Hond. 14°1′ N, 86°31′ W 112
Danmark Havn, Den. 76°46′ N, 18°35′ W 246
Dannemora, N.Y., U.S. 44°42′ N, 73°44′ W 94
Dañoso, Cabo, Arg. 49°2′ S, 67°13′ W 134
Dansheha, Eth. 13°30′ N, 36°54′ E 182
Dansville, N.Y., U.S. 42°33′ N, 77°43′ W 94
Danu, Mold. 47°51′ N, 27°30′ E 152
Danube, river, Europe 44°29′ N, 21°15′ E 143
Danvers, Ill., U.S. 40°30′ N, 89°11′ W 102
Danvers, Mass., U.S. 42°33′ N, 70°57′ W 104
Danville, Ill., U.S. 40°9′ N, 87°37′ W 102
Danville, Ind., U.S. 39°45′ N, 86°32′ W 102
Danville, Ky., U.S. 37°38′ N, 84°46′ W 94
Danville, N.H., U.S. 42°54′ N, 71°8′ W 104
Danville, Ohio, U.S. 40°26′ N, 82°16′ W 102
Danville, Va., U.S. 36°34′ N, 79°25′ W 96
Danxian (Nada), China 19°28′ N, 109°34′ E 198
Danzhai, China 26°11′ N, 107°47′ E 198
Dao, Philippines 10°30′ N, 121°57′ E 203
Dao Timmi, Niger 20°33′ N, 13°31′ E 216
Daoxian, China 25°32′ N, 111°34′ E 198
Daozhen, China 28°52′ N, 107°40′ E 198
Dapa, Philippines 9°47′ N, 126°3′ E 203
Dapaong, Togo 10°50′ N, 0°11′ E 222
Dapchi, Nig. 12°29′ N, 11°31′ E 222
Daphne, Ala., U.S. 30°35′ N, 87°54′ W 103
Dapp, Can. 54°20′ N, 113°56′ W 108
Dapuchaihe, China 42°50′ N, 128°1′ E 200
Daqing, China 46°33′ N, 125°6′ E 198
Daqqaq, Sudan 12°57′ N, 26°53′ E 216
Dār B'ishtār, Leb. 34°15′ N, 35°47′ E 194
Dar es Salaam, Tanzania 6°49′ S, 39°6′ E 224
Dar et Touibia, Tun. 35°19′ N, 10°12′ E 156
Dar Rounga, region, Africa 10°24′ N, 23°37′ E 224
Dar'ā (Edrei), Syr. 32°37′ N, 36°6′ E 194
Dārāb, Iran 28°45′ N, 54°33′ E 196
Daraban, Pak. 31°42′ N, 70°22′ E 186
Daraina, Madagascar 13°17′ S, 49°38′ E 220
Darakhiv, Ukr. 49°17′ N, 25°33′ E 152
Darakht-e Yahya, Pak. 31°48′ N, 68°10′ E 186
Darány, Hung. 45°59′ N, 17°34′ E 168
Darâw, Egypt 24°22′ N, 32°54′ E 182
Darazo, Nig. 10°58′ N, 10°25′ E 222
Darbandi Khan Dam, Iraq 34°44′ N, 45°3′ E 180
Darbėnai, Lith. 56°1′ N, 21°12′ E 166
Darbhanga, India 26°10′ N, 85°53′ E 197
D'Arcole Islands, Indian Ocean 15°0′ S, 122°41′ E 230
Darda, Croatia 45°37′ N, 18°40′ E 168
Dardanelle, Ark., U.S. 35°12′ N, 93°10′ W 96
Dardanelle, Calif., U.S. 38°20′ N, 119°52′ W 100
Dardanelles see Çanakkale Boğazı, Turk. 40°9′ N, 24°58′ E 157
Darende, Turk. 38°33′ N, 37°28′ E 156
Darero, river, Somalia 9°15′ N, 47°47′ E 218
Darfur, region, Africa 11°6′ N, 23°28′ E 224
Darganata, Turkm. 40°27′ N, 62°9′ E 180
Dargaz, Iran 37°27′ N, 59°6′ E 180
Dargeçit, Turk. 37°33′ N, 41°46′ E 195
Dargol, Niger 13°54′ N, 1°12′ E 222
Darhan, Mongolia 46°43′ N, 109°15′ E 198
Darhan, Mongolia 49°31′ N, 105°58′ E 198
Darhan Muminggan Lianheqi (Bailingmiao), China 41°41′ N, 110°23′ E 198
Darhan-Uul, adm. division, Mongolia 49°29′ N, 105°55′ E 198
Darien, Conn., U.S. 41°4′ N, 73°28′ W 104
Darien, Ga., U.S. 31°21′ N, 81°27′ W 96
Darién National Park, Pan. 7°23′ N, 78°0′ W 136
Darién, Serranía del, Pan. 8°31′ N, 77°58′ W 136
Darjiling, India 26°58′ N, 88°14′ E 197
Dark Canyon, Utah, U.S. 37°48′ N, 110°0′ W 92
Darley Hills, Antarctica 80°41′ S, 172°40′ E 248
Darling, S. Af. 33°22′ S, 18°19′ E 227
Darling Downs, Austral. 27°20′ S, 149°55′ E 230
Darling, river, Austral. 31°16′ S, 144°40′ E 230
Darlington, U.K. 54°31′ N, 1°34′ W 162
Darlington, Wis., U.S. 42°40′ N, 90°6′ W 102
Darmstadt, Ger. 49°52′ N, 8°38′ E 167
Darnah (Derna), Lib. 32°44′ N, 22°38′ E 216
Darney, Fr. 48°5′ N, 6°1′ E 150
Darnley Bay 69°23′ N, 124°25′ W 106
Daroca, Sp. 41°6′ N, 1°25′ W 164
Daroot-Korgon, Kyrg. 39°32′ N, 72°3′ E 197
Daror, Eth. 8°12′ N, 44°30′ E 218
Darou Khoudos, Senegal 15°7′ N, 16°40′ W 222
Darovskoy, Russ. 58°43′ N, 47°56′ E 154
Darregueira, Arg. 37°45′ S, 63°9′ W 139
Darreh Gaz, Iran 37°26′ N, 59°4′ E 180
Darrington, Wash., U.S. 48°13′ N, 121°38′ W 100
Darrouzett, Tex., U.S. 36°25′ N, 100°21′ W 92
Darss, Ger. 54°18′ N, 12°27′ E 152
Dartmoor, region, Europe 50°45′ N, 4°7′ W 162
Dartmouth, Can. 44°40′ N, 63°35′ W 111
Dartmouth, Mass., U.S. 41°34′ N, 71°1′ W 104
Daru, P.N.G. 9°9′ S, 143°11′ E 192
Daruvar, Croatia 45°35′ N, 17°12′ E 168
Darvaza, Turkm. 40°5′ N, 58°30′ E 180
Darvel Bay 4°50′ N, 117°51′ E 203
Darwen, U.K. 53°42′ N, 2°28′ W 162
Darwendale, Zimb. 17°45′ S, 30°32′ E 224
Darwin, Austral. 12°30′ S, 130°37′ E 230
Darwin, Calif., U.S. 36°15′ N, 117°37′ W 101
Darwin, Isla, island, Ecua. 1°8′ N, 92°28′ W 130
Darwin, Mount, Calif., U.S. 37°10′ N, 118°43′ W 101
Darya Khan, Pak. 31°47′ N, 71°11′ E 186
Dārzīn, Iran 29°6′ N, 58°8′ E 196
Das, Pak. 35°6′ N, 75°5′ E 186
D'Asagny National Park, Côte d'Ivoire 5°11′ N, 4°56′ W 222
Dasburg, Ger. 50°2′ N, 6°8′ E 167
Dashbalbar, Mongolia 49°31′ N, 114°22′ E 198
Dashkäsän, Azerb. 40°30′ N, 46°3′ E 195
Dashkuduk, Turkm. 40°37′ N, 52°53′ E 158
Dasht, river, Pak. 25°37′ N, 61°59′ E 182
Dasht-e Navar, marsh, Afghan. 33°40′ N, 67°7′ E 186
Daşköpri, Turkm. 36°18′ N, 62°36′ E 186
Daşoguz, Turkm. 41°51′ N, 59°58′ E 180
Dassa-Zoume, Benin 7°44′ N, 2°12′ E 222
Dassel, Ger. 51°47′ N, 9°40′ E 167
Datça, Turk. 36°44′ N, 27°39′ E 156
Dateland, Ariz., U.S. 32°47′ N, 113°32′ W 101
Datia, India 25°38′ N, 78°26′ E 197
Datian, China 25°40′ N, 117°51′ E 198
Datong, China 40°7′ N, 113°14′ E 198
Datteln, Ger. 51°39′ N, 7°20′ E 167
Datu Piang, Philippines 7°2′ N, 124°28′ E 203
Datu, Tanjong, Malaysia 2°8′ N, 109°23′ E 196
Datuk, island, Indonesia 0°12′ N, 108°14′ E 196
Daud Khel, Pak. 32°52′ N, 71°40′ E 186
Daudnagar, India 25°0′ N, 84°23′ E 197
Daugaard-Jensen Land, Den. 80°8′ N, 63°33′ W 246
Daugai, Lith. 54°22′ N, 24°20′ E 166
Daugava, river, Latv. 56°17′ N, 26°13′ E 166
Daugava, river, Latv. 56°46′ N, 24°10′ E 166
Daugavpils, Latv. 55°51′ N, 26°30′ E 166
Dauli, Somalia 8°48′ N, 50°26′ E 216
Daun, Ger. 50°11′ N, 6°49′ E 167
D'Aunay Bugt 68°49′ N, 28°49′ W 246
Daung Kyun, island, Myanmar 12°6′ N, 98°7′ E 202
Dauphin, Can. 51°8′ N, 100°3′ W 90
Dauphin Island, Ala., U.S. 30°6′ N, 88°18′ W 103
Dauphin Lake, Can. 51°16′ N, 100°32′ W 81
Dauphin, Péninsule du, Can. 51°18′ N, 72°54′ W 110
Dauphiné, region, Europe 44°22′ N, 4°50′ E 165
Däväçi, Azerb. 41°11′ N, 48°59′ E 195
Davangere, India 14°27′ N, 75°55′ E 188
Davant, La., U.S. 29°36′ N, 89°53′ W 103
Davao, Philippines 7°7′ N, 125°36′ E 203
Dāvar Panāh, Iran 27°18′ N, 62°21′ E 182
Davegoriale, Somalia 8°43′ N, 44°52′ E 218
Davenport, Calif., U.S. 37°0′ N, 122°12′ W 100
Davenport, Fla., U.S. 28°9′ N, 81°37′ W 105
Davenport, Iowa, U.S. 41°32′ N, 90°37′ W 110
Davenport, Mount, Austral. 22°28′ S, 130°38′ E 230
Daventry, U.K. 52°15′ N, 1°10′ W 162
David, Pan. 8°22′ N, 82°19′ W 123
Davidson, Can. 51°16′ N, 106°0′ W 90
Davie, Fla., U.S. 26°3′ N, 80°15′ W 105
Davies, Cape, Antarctica 71°35′ S, 100°20′ W 248
Davis, Calif., U.S. 38°32′ N, 121°46′ W 90
Davis, Okla., U.S. 34°29′ N, 97°7′ W 92
Davis Dam, Ariz., U.S. 35°10′ N, 114°34′ W 101
Davis Dam, Nev., U.S. 35°12′ N, 114°37′ W 101
Davis Inlet, Can. 55°53′ N, 60°48′ W 106
Davis Islands, Indian Ocean 66°35′ S, 108°0′ E 248
Davis, Mount, Pa., U.S. 39°46′ N, 79°16′ W 94
Davis Mountains, Tex., U.S. 30°44′ N, 104°13′ W 92
Davis Sea 66°31′ S, 89°40′ E 248
Davis, station, Antarctica 68°30′ S, 78°25′ E 248
Davis Strait 70°31′ N, 60°40′ W 73
Davison, Mich., U.S. 43°1′ N, 83°30′ W 102
Davlekanovo, Russ. 54°14′ N, 54°58′ E 154
Davlos, Northern Cyprus, Cyprus 35°24′ N, 33°54′ E 194
Davor, Croatia 45°7′ N, 17°29′ E 168
Davos, Switz. 46°47′ N, 9°47′ E 167
Davy Lake, Can. 58°51′ N, 108°49′ W 108
Dawa, river, Eth. 4°42′ N, 39°44′ E 224
Dawadawa, Ghana 8°21′ N, 1°35′ W 222
Dawei, Myanmar 14°5′ N, 98°13′ E 202
Dawhinava, Belarus 54°39′ N, 27°26′ E 166
Dawkah, Oman 18°41′ N, 53°58′ E 182
Dawmat al Jandal, Saudi Arabia 29°47′ N, 39°53′ E 180
Dawna Range, Myanmar 16°49′ N, 98°1′ E 202
Dawqah, Saudi Arabia 19°35′ N, 40°55′ E 182
Dawra, Western Sahara, Mor. 27°27′ N, 13°0′ W 214
Dawros Head, Ire. 54°48′ N, 8°57′ W 150
Dawson, Can. 64°5′ N, 139°18′ W 98
Dawson City see Dawson, Can. 64°5′ N, 139°18′ W 98
Dawson, Ga., U.S. 31°45′ N, 84°27′ W 96
Dawson, Minn., U.S. 44°55′ N, 96°4′ W 90
Dawson, N. Dak., U.S. 46°51′ N, 99°46′ W 90
Dawson, Tex., U.S. 31°52′ N, 96°41′ W 96
Dawson Bay 52°50′ N, 101°22′ W 108
Dawson Creek, Can. 55°44′ N, 120°16′ W 108
Dawson, Isla, island, Chile 54°10′ S, 70°9′ W 134
Dawson, Mount, Can. 51°8′ N, 117°32′ W 90
Dawson Springs, Ky., U.S. 37°9′ N, 87°41′ W 96
Dawu, China 31°30′ N, 114°4′ E 198
Dawukou see Shizuishan, China 39°4′ N, 106°25′ E 198
Dawwah, Oman 20°39′ N, 58°53′ E 182
Dax, Fr. 43°42′ N, 1°3′ W 150
Daxian, China 31°15′ N, 107°24′ E 198
Daxing, China 39°44′ N, 116°19′ E 198
Dayang, river, China 40°15′ N, 123°18′ E 200
Dayet el Khadra, spring, Alg. 27°25′ N, 8°30′ W 214
Daying, China 42°8′ N, 127°17′ E 200
Daylight Pass, Calif., U.S. 36°46′ N, 116°57′ W 101
Daymán, river, Uru. 31°34′ S, 57°40′ W 139
Dayong, China 29°8′ N, 110°35′ E 198
Dayr Abū Sa'īd, Jordan 32°29′ N, 35°41′ E 194
Dayr al A'nar, Leb. 34°7′ N, 36°7′ E 194
Dayr al Balaḩ, Gaza Strip, Israel 31°25′ N, 34°21′ E 194
Dayr 'Aţīyah, Syr. 34°5′ N, 36°46′ E 194
Dayr az Zawr, Syr. 35°19′ N, 40°5′ E 180
Daysland, Can. 52°51′ N, 112°17′ W 108
Dayton, Nev., U.S. 39°15′ N, 119°37′ W 90
Dayton, Ohio, U.S. 39°44′ N, 84°11′ W 102
Dayton, Tenn., U.S. 35°29′ N, 85°1′ W 96
Dayton, Tex., U.S. 30°1′ N, 94°54′ W 103
Dayton, Wash., U.S. 46°18′ N, 117°58′ W 82
Dayton, Wyo., U.S. 44°50′ N, 107°16′ W 90
Daytona Beach, Fla., U.S. 29°13′ N, 81°3′ W 105
Dayu, China 25°24′ N, 114°19′ E 198
Dayville, Conn., U.S. 41°50′ N, 71°54′ W 104
Dazhu, China 30°46′ N, 107°15′ E 198
Dazkırı, Turk. 37°54′ N, 29°51′ E 156
Dazu, China 29°46′ N, 105°44′ E 198
Dchira, Western Sahara, Mor. 27°1′ N, 13°3′ W 214
De Aar, S. Af. 30°39′ S, 23°59′ E 227
De Beque, Colo., U.S. 39°20′ N, 108°13′ W 90
De Berry, Tex., U.S. 32°17′ N, 94°11′ W 103
De Cocksdorp, Neth. 53°9′ N, 4°51′ E 163
De Forest, Wis., U.S. 43°15′ N, 89°21′ W 102
De Graff, Ohio, U.S. 40°18′ N, 83°55′ W 102
De Kalb, Miss., U.S. 32°44′ N, 88°39′ W 103
De Kalb, Tex., U.S. 33°30′ N, 94°38′ W 96
De Kastri, Russ. 51°38′ N, 140°35′ E 190
De la Garma, Arg. 37°58′ S, 60°25′ W 139
De Land, Fla., U.S. 29°1′ N, 81°19′ W 105
De Land, Ill., U.S. 40°6′ N, 88°39′ W 102
De Leon Springs, Fla., U.S. 29°6′ N, 81°22′ W 105
De Long Mountains, Alas., U.S. 68°7′ N, 164°15′ W 98
De Long, Ostrova, islands, East Siberian Sea 75°48′ N, 158°9′ E 160
De Queen, Ark., U.S. 34°0′ N, 94°21′ W 96
De Quincy, La., U.S. 30°26′ N, 93°27′ W 103
De Ridder, La., U.S. 30°49′ N, 93°18′ W 103
De Smet, S. Dak., U.S. 44°22′ N, 97°35′ W 90
De Soto, Miss., U.S. 31°58′ N, 88°43′ W 103
De Soto, Mo., U.S. 38°7′ N, 90°34′ W 94
De Soto, Wis., U.S. 43°25′ N, 91°12′ W 94
De Tour Village, Mich., U.S. 45°59′ N, 83°55′ W 94
De Witt, Ark., U.S. 34°16′ N, 91°21′ W 96
De Witt, Iowa, U.S. 41°49′ N, 90°32′ W 94
Dead Horse Point, site, Utah, U.S. 38°30′ N, 109°47′ W 90
Dead Indian Peak, Wyo., U.S. 44°35′ N, 109°42′ W 90
Dead Mountains, Calif., U.S. 35°6′ N, 114°50′ W 101
Dead Sea, lake, Jordan 31°28′ N, 35°24′ E 194
Deadmans Cay, Bahamas 23°7′ N, 75°4′ W 116
Deadman's Cays, North Atlantic Ocean 24°6′ N, 80°37′ W 116
Deadmen Valley, Can. 61°2′ N, 124°23′ W 108
Deadwood, Can. 56°44′ N, 117°30′ W 108
Deadwood, S. Dak., U.S. 44°22′ N, 103°42′ W 82
Deadwood Lake, Can. 59°0′ N, 129°12′ W 108
Deadwood Reservoir, Idaho, U.S. 44°19′ N, 116°4′ W 90
Deakin, Austral. 30°46′ S, 128°57′ E 231
Deal, U.K. 51°13′ N, 1°23′ E 163
De'an, China 29°18′ N, 115°45′ E 198
Dean Channel 52°33′ N, 127°44′ W 108
Deán Funes, Arg. 30°25′ S, 64°21′ W 134
Dean Island, Antarctica 74°22′ S, 126°8′ W 248
Dean, river, Can. 52°53′ N, 126°11′ W 108
Dearborn, Mich., U.S. 42°18′ N, 83°13′ W 102
Dearg, Beinn, peak, U.K. 56°51′ N, 4°0′ W 150
Dearg, Beinn, peak, U.K. 57°45′ N, 5°3′ W 150
Dease Arm 66°42′ N, 120°16′ W 98
Dease Inlet 70°56′ N, 156°54′ W 98
Dease Lake, Can. 58°27′ N, 130°4′ W 108
Dease, river, Can. 58°54′ N, 130°11′ W 108
Dease Strait 69°0′ N, 106°42′ W 246
Death Valley, Calif., U.S. 36°27′ N, 116°53′ W 101
Death Valley Junction, Calif., U.S. 36°17′ N, 116°26′ W 101
Death Valley National Park (Devils Hole), Nev., U.S. 36°25′ N, 116°19′ W 101
Deatley Island, Antarctica 73°45′ S, 73°41′ W 248
Debao, China 23°16′ N, 106°34′ E 198
Debar, Maced. 41°31′ N, 20°32′ E 168
Debark', Eth. 13°12′ N, 37°51′ E 182
Debary, Fla., U.S. 28°53′ N, 81°19′ W 105
Debden, Can. 53°31′ N, 106°52′ W 108
Debdou, Mor. 34°0′ N, 3°2′ W 214
Dębek, Pol. 54°48′ N, 18°5′ E 152
Debelica, Serb. 43°39′ N, 22°15′ E 168
Debenham, U.K. 52°13′ N, 1°10′ E 162
Débéré, Mali 15°5′ N, 3°1′ W 222
Debikut, India 25°21′ N, 88°32′ E 197
Debin, Russ. 62°18′ N, 150°29′ E 160
Debir, ruin(s), Israel 31°27′ N, 34°51′ E 194
Dęblin, Pol. 51°33′ N, 21°50′ E 152
Débo, Lake, Mali 15°13′ N, 4°26′ W 222
Debrc, Serb. 44°36′ N, 19°53′ E 168
Debre Birhan, Eth. 9°39′ N, 39°31′ E 224
Debre Mark'os, Eth. 10°19′ N, 37°42′ E 224
Debre Tabor, Eth. 11°50′ N, 38°0′ E 182
Debre Zebīt, Eth. 11°48′ N, 38°35′ E 182
Debre Zeyit, Eth. 10°36′ N, 35°42′ E 224
Debrecen, Hung. 47°31′ N, 21°38′ E 168
Debrzno, Pol. 53°32′ N, 17°14′ E 152
Decamere, Eritrea 15°4′ N, 39°4′ E 182
Deçan (Dečani), Kosovo 42°31′ N, 20°18′ E 168
Dečani see Deçan, Kosovo 42°31′ N, 20°18′ E 168
Decatur, Ill., U.S. 39°50′ N, 88°57′ W 102
Decatur, Ind., U.S. 40°49′ N, 84°56′ W 102
Decatur, Mich., U.S. 42°6′ N, 85°58′ W 102
Decatur, Miss., U.S. 32°25′ N, 89°7′ W 103
Decatur, Mo., U.S. 39°50′ N, 88°57′ W 94
Decatur, Tex., U.S. 33°13′ N, 97°35′ W 92
Deception Island, Antarctica 63°16′ S, 60°43′ W 134
Dechu, India 26°47′ N, 72°19′ E 186
Deckerville, Mich., U.S. 43°31′ N, 82°44′ W 102
Decorah, Iowa, U.S. 43°17′ N, 91°48′ W 94
Deddington, U.K. 51°58′ N, 1°20′ W 162
Dededo, Guam, U.S. 14°0′ N, 147°0′ E 242
Dedegöl Dağı, peak, Turk. 37°37′ N, 31°12′ E 156
Deder, Eth. 9°17′ N, 41°26′ E 224
Dedham, Mass., U.S. 42°14′ N, 71°11′ W 104
Dedino, Maced. 41°34′ N, 22°25′ E 168
Dédougou, Burkina Faso 12°27′ N, 3°28′ W 222
Dedovichi, Russ. 57°32′ N, 30°0′ E 166
Dedu, China 48°30′ N, 126°9′ E 198
Dedza, Malawi 14°23′ S, 34°16′ E 224
Dee, river, Ire. 53°51′ N, 6°42′ W 150
Dee, river, U.K. 53°5′ N, 2°53′ W 162
Deep Bay 61°13′ N, 117°11′ W 108
Deep Bay see Chilumba, Malawi 10°24′ S, 34°13′ E 224
Deep Crater, Calif., U.S. 41°26′ N, 121°38′ W 90
Deep Creek, Bahamas 24°49′ N, 76°17′ W 96
Deep Creek Peak, Idaho, U.S. 42°28′ N, 112°43′ W 90
Deep Creek Range, Utah, U.S. 39°36′ N, 114°20′ W 90
Deep River, Can. 46°6′ N, 77°31′ W 94
Deep River, Conn., U.S. 41°23′ N, 72°27′ W 104
Deer Creek, Ill., U.S. 40°37′ N, 89°20′ W 102
Deer Lake, Can. 52°40′ N, 94°59′ W 81
Deer Lake, Can. 49°1′ N, 57°22′ W 111
Deer Lodge, Mont., U.S. 46°23′ N, 112°44′ W 90
Deer Park, Ala., U.S. 31°12′ N, 88°19′ W 103
Deer River, Minn., U.S. 47°19′ N, 93°49′ W 94
Deer, river, Can. 57°36′ N, 94°32′ W 108
Deer Trail, Colo., U.S. 39°36′ N, 104°3′ W 90
Deerfield, Ill., U.S. 42°10′ N, 87°52′ W 102
Deerfield, Mass., U.S. 42°32′ N, 72°37′ W 104
Deerfield, N.H., U.S. 43°8′ N, 71°14′ W 104
Deerfield Beach, Fla., U.S. 26°18′ N, 80°7′ W 105
Deerhurst, U.K. 51°57′ N, 2°11′ W 162
Deering, Alas., U.S. 65°54′ N, 162°50′ W 98
Deeth, Nev., U.S. 41°4′ N, 115°17′ W 90
Defa, oil field, Lib. 27°45′ N, 19°46′ E 216
Defensores del Chaco National Park, Parag. 20°12′ S, 62°1′ W 132
Defiance, Ohio, U.S. 41°15′ N, 84°23′ W 102
Défirou, spring, Niger 20°33′ N, 15°3′ E 216
Dég, Hung. 46°51′ N, 18°27′ E 168
Degana, India 26°53′ N, 74°19′ E 186
Deganya, Israel 32°41′ N, 35°34′ E 194
Dêgê, China 31°51′ N, 98°37′ E 190
Degeh Bur, Eth. 8°10′ N, 43°30′ E 218
Degelen, peak, Kaz. 49°52′ N, 77°51′ E 184
Degerby, Fin. 60°4′ N, 24°9′ E 166
Degerfors, Nor. 59°14′ N, 14°22′ E 152
Degerhamn, Sw. 56°21′ N, 16°23′ E 152
Dego, It. 44°26′ N, 8°19′ E 167
Deh Bīd, Iran 30°36′ N, 53°11′ E 180
Deh Khavak, Afghan. 35°39′ N, 69°55′ E 186
Deh Mollā, Iran 30°33′ N, 49°38′ E 186
Deh Shu, Afghan. 30°23′ N, 63°19′ E 186
Dehgam, India 23°9′ N, 72°48′ E 186
Dehibat, Tun. 32°2′ N, 10°41′ E 214
Dehqonobod, Uzb. 38°21′ N, 66°30′ E 197
Dehra Dun, India 30°20′ N, 78°2′ E 197
Dehui, China 44°30′ N, 125°40′ E 198
Deim Zubeir, Sudan 7°42′ N, 26°13′ E 224
Deinze, Belg. 50°58′ N, 3°31′ E 163
Deir Mawâs, Egypt 27°40′ N, 30°46′ E 180
Dej, Rom. 47°8′ N, 23°55′ E 156
Dejë, Mal, peak, Alban. 41°41′ N, 20°7′ E 168
Dejen, Ras, peak, Eth. 13°11′ N, 38°19′ E 182
Dejiang, China 28°16′ N, 108°6′ E 198
Dekalb, Ill., U.S. 41°55′ N, 88°44′ W 102
Dekese, Dem. Rep. of the Congo 3°29′ S, 21°24′ E 218
Dekhisor, Taj. 39°27′ N, 69°32′ E 197
Dekina, Nig. 7°38′ N, 7°0′ E 222
Dekle Beach, Fla., U.S. 29°51′ N, 83°37′ W 105
Dekoa, Cen. Af. Rep. 6°14′ N, 19°3′ E 218
Del Rio, Tex., U.S. 29°21′ N, 100°55′ W 112
Del Verme Falls, Eth. 5°9′ N, 40°15′ E 224
Delacroix, La., U.S. 29°45′ N, 89°48′ W 103
Delamar Mountains, Nev., U.S. 37°8′ N, 114°58′ W 101
Delami, Sudan 11°50′ N, 30°28′ E 218
Delano, Calif., U.S. 35°46′ N, 119°14′ W 100
Delano Peak, Utah, U.S. 38°21′ N, 112°26′ W 90
Delanson, N.Y., U.S. 42°44′ N, 74°12′ W 104
Delaram, Afghan. 32°14′ N, 63°26′ E 186
Delareyville, S. Af. 26°42′ S, 25°25′ E 220
Delavan, Ill., U.S. 40°21′ N, 89°33′ W 102
Delaware, Ohio, U.S. 40°17′ N, 83°5′ W 102
Delaware, adm. division, Del., U.S. 39°36′ N, 75°46′ W 94
Delaware Bay 38°16′ N, 76°18′ W 94
Delaware Mountains, Tex., U.S. 31°54′ N, 104°55′ W 92
Delbrück, Ger. 51°45′ N, 8°32′ E 167
Delcambre, La., U.S. 29°56′ N, 92°0′ W 103
Delčevo, Maced. 41°57′ N, 22°46′ E 168
Delémont, Switz. 47°22′ N, 7°19′ E 156
Delesseps Lake, lake, Can. 50°41′ N, 91°15′ W 110
Delft, Neth. 52°1′ N, 4°21′ E 163
Delfzijl, Neth. 53°20′ N, 6°55′ E 163
Delgada, Point, Calif., U.S. 39°51′ N, 124°30′ W 90
Delgado, Cabo, Mozambique 10°43′ S, 40°42′ E 224
Delgerhet, Mongolia 45°50′ N, 110°29′ E 198
Delgo, Sudan 20°6′ N, 30°36′ E 226
Delhi, Calif., U.S. 37°25′ N, 120°47′ W 100
Delhi, India 28°41′ N, 77°10′ E 197
Delhi, La., U.S. 32°26′ N, 91°30′ W 103
Delhi, N.Y., U.S. 42°16′ N, 74°56′ W 94
Delhi, adm. division, India 28°37′ N, 76°44′ E 188
Deli Jovan, Serb. 44°21′ N, 22°12′ E 168
Delia, Can. 51°39′ N, 112°23′ W 90
Délices, Fr. 4°43′ N, 53°47′ W 130
Delicias, Mex. 28°9′ N, 105°29′ W 92
Deligrad, Serb. 43°36′ N, 21°35′ E 168
Deljān, Iran 34°0′ N, 50°40′ E 180
Deliktaş, Turk. 39°19′ N, 37°12′ E 156
Délįne, Can. 65°13′ N, 123°26′ W 98
Delingha, China 37°22′ N, 97°29′ E 188
Delisle, Can. 51°55′ N, 107°8′ W 90
Delisle, Can. 48°37′ N, 71°42′ W 94
Delium, battle, Gr. 38°19′ N, 23°32′ E 156
Dell, U.K. 58°28′ N, 6°20′ W 150
Dell Rapids, S. Dak., U.S. 43°48′ N, 96°43′ W 90
Delle, Fr. 47°30′ N, 6°59′ E 150
Dellenbaugh, Mount, Ariz., U.S. 36°6′ N, 113°34′ W 101
Dellys, Alg. 36°54′ N, 3°54′ E 150
Delmar, Md., U.S. 38°27′ N, 75°35′ W 94
Delmar, N.Y., U.S. 42°37′ N, 73°51′ W 104
Deloraine, Can. 49°11′ N, 100°30′ W 90
Delos, ruin(s), Gr. 37°22′ N, 25°10′ E 156
Delphi, ruin(s), Gr. 38°28′ N, 22°24′ E 156
Delphos, Ohio, U.S. 40°50′ N, 84°21′ W 102
Delray Beach, Fla., U.S. 26°28′ N, 80°6′ W 105
Delta, Colo., U.S. 38°44′ N, 108°4′ W 90
Delta, La., U.S. 32°18′ N, 90°56′ W 103
Delta, Utah, U.S. 39°20′ N, 112°34′ W 90
Delta Amacuro, adm. division, Venez. 8°57′ N, 61°48′ W 130
Delta du Saloum National Park, Senegal 13°39′ N, 16°27′ W 222
Deltona, Fla., U.S. 28°53′ N, 81°15′ W 105
Dema, river, Russ. 54°28′ N, 55°29′ E 154
Demanda, Sierra de la, Sp. 42°19′ N, 3°14′ W 164
Demange-aux-Eaux, Fr. 48°34′ N, 5°27′ E 163
Demarcation Point, Can. 69°34′ N, 143°59′ W 98
Demba, Dem. Rep. of the Congo 5°30′ S, 22°13′ E 218
Dembech'a, Eth. 10°31′ N, 37°28′ E 224
Dembī Dolo, Eth. 8°31′ N, 34°47′ E 224
Dembia, Dem. Rep. of the Congo 3°29′ N, 25°51′ E 224
Demerara Plain, North Atlantic Ocean 9°25′ N, 48°41′ W 253
Demetrias, ruin(s), Gr. 39°20′ N, 22°52′ E 156
Demidov, Russ. 55°14′ N, 31°31′ E 154
Demidovo, Russ. 56°45′ N, 29°33′ E 166
Deming, N. Mex., U.S. 32°15′ N, 107°45′ W 92

Deming, *Wash., U.S.* 48°49′ N, 122°13′ W **100**
Demini, river, *Braz.* 1°24′ N, 63°13′ W **130**
Demirci, *Turk.* 39°3′ N, 28°38′ E **156**
Demirköprü Barajı, dam, *Turk.* 38°48′ N, 28°0′ E **156**
Demirtaş, *Turk.* 36°25′ N, 32°10′ E **156**
Demiti, river, *Braz.* 0°51′ N, 67°4′ W **136**
Demmitt, *Can.* 55°25′ N, 119°55′ W **108**
Democratic Republic of the Congo 1°57′ S, 17°24′ E **218**
Demon, *Ghana* 9°29′ N, 0°11′ E **222**
Demonte, *It.* 44°18′ N, 7°17′ E **167**
Demopolis, *Ala., U.S.* 32°32′ N, 87°50′ W **103**
Demotte, *Ind., U.S.* 41°11′ N, 87°13′ W **102**
Demşuş, *Rom.* 45°34′ N, 22°48′ E **168**
Demta, *Indonesia* 2°23′ S, 140°10′ E **192**
Dem'yanka, river, *Russ.* 58°52′ N, 71°21′ E **169**
Demyansk, *Russ.* 57°37′ N, 32°28′ E **154**
Dem'yanskoye, *Russ.* 59°32′ N, 69°25′ E **169**
Demydivka, *Ukr.* 50°24′ N, 25°20′ E **152**
Den Burg, *Neth.* 53°3′ N, 4°46′ E **163**
Den Chai, *Thai.* 17°59′ N, 100°3′ E **202**
Den Helder, *Neth.* 52°57′ N, 4°45′ E **163**
Den Oever, *Neth.* 52°55′ N, 5°1′ E **163**
Denain, *Fr.* 50°19′ N, 3°23′ E **163**
Denair, *Calif., U.S.* 37°31′ N, 120°49′ W **100**
Denakil, region, *Africa* 12°35′ N, 40°8′ E **182**
Denali see McKinley, Mount, *Alas., U.S.* 62°54′ N, 151°17′ W **98**
Denan, *Eth.* 6°27′ N, 43°29′ E **218**
Denare Beach, *Can.* 54°40′ N, 102°4′ W **108**
Denbigh, *U.K.* 53°11′ N, 3°24′ W **162**
Dendtler Island, *Antarctica* 72°46′ S, 90°30′ W **248**
Denekamp, *Neth.* 52°23′ N, 7°0′ E **163**
Deng Deng, *Cameroon* 5°8′ N, 13°28′ E **218**
Dengkou, *China* 40°18′ N, 106°54′ E **198**
Dêngqên, *China* 31°33′ N, 95°35′ E **188**
Dengu, river, *Dem. Rep. of the Congo* 4°30′ N, 24°14′ E **224**
Dengzhou, *China* 32°39′ N, 112°5′ E **198**
Denham Springs, *La., U.S.* 30°28′ N, 90°58′ W **96**
Denholm, *Can.* 52°39′ N, 108°2′ W **108**
Denia, *Sp.* 38°51′ N, 0°7′ E **164**
Deniliquin, *Austral.* 35°31′ S, 144°55′ E **231**
Denio, *Nev., U.S.* 41°59′ N, 118°39′ W **90**
Denis, *Gabon* 0°17′ N, 9°22′ E **218**
Denison, *Iowa, U.S.* 41°59′ N, 95°21′ W **90**
Denison, *Tex., U.S.* 33°44′ N, 96°32′ W **96**
Denisovka, *Russ.* 66°14′ N, 55°19′ E **154**
Denisovskaya, *Russ.* 60°18′ N, 41°34′ E **154**
Denizli, *Turk.* 37°45′ N, 29°5′ E **156**
Denman Island, *Can.* 49°32′ N, 124°49′ W **100**
Denmark 56°12′ N, 8°45′ E **152**
Denmark, *Me., U.S.* 43°58′ N, 70°49′ W **104**
Denmark, *S.C., U.S.* 33°18′ N, 81°9′ W **96**
Denmark Strait 64°13′ N, 38°21′ W **246**
Dennis, *Mass., U.S.* 41°44′ N, 70°12′ W **104**
Dennison, *Ohio, U.S.* 40°23′ N, 81°20′ W **102**
Denov, *Uzb.* 38°17′ N, 67°54′ E **197**
Denpasar, *Indonesia* 8°44′ S, 115°1′ E **192**
Denso, *Mali* 10°27′ N, 8°5′ W **222**
Denton, *Md., U.S.* 38°52′ N, 75°50′ W **94**
Denton, *Tex., U.S.* 33°12′ N, 97°8′ W **92**
D'Entrecasteaux Islands, *Solomon Sea* 9°50′ S, 151°24′ E **231**
Denver, *Colo., U.S.* 39°43′ N, 105°6′ W **90**
Denver, *Ind., U.S.* 40°51′ N, 86°5′ W **102**
Denver City, *Tex., U.S.* 32°56′ N, 102°50′ W **92**
Denzil, *Can.* 52°13′ N, 109°38′ W **108**
Deoband, *India* 29°40′ N, 77°41′ E **197**
Deobhog, *India* 19°56′ N, 82°39′ E **188**
Deoghar, *India* 24°27′ N, 86°42′ E **197**
Deoria, *India* 26°29′ N, 83°47′ E **197**
Departure Bay, *Can.* 49°11′ N, 123°58′ W **100**
Deposit, *N.Y., U.S.* 42°3′ N, 75°26′ W **110**
Depot Harbour, *Can.* 45°18′ N, 80°5′ W **94**
Depot Peak, *Antarctica* 69°6′ S, 64°14′ E **248**
Deputatskiy, *Russ.* 69°16′ N, 139°52′ E **173**
Deqing, *China* 30°33′ N, 120°4′ E **198**
Deqing, *China* 23°10′ N, 111°46′ E **198**
Dera Ghazi Khan, *Pak.* 30°3′ N, 70°41′ E **186**
Dera Ismail Khan, *Pak.* 31°47′ N, 70°55′ E **186**
Deraheib, *Sudan* 21°55′ N, 35°8′ E **182**
Derati, spring, *Kenya* 3°47′ N, 36°23′ E **224**
Derbent, *Russ.* 42°0′ N, 48°20′ E **195**
Derbisaka, *Cen. Af. Rep.* 5°43′ N, 24°52′ E **224**
Derby, *Austral.* 17°23′ S, 123°43′ E **238**
Derby, *Conn., U.S.* 41°19′ N, 73°6′ W **104**
Derby, *Kans., U.S.* 37°31′ N, 97°16′ W **90**
Derby, *Miss., U.S.* 30°45′ N, 89°35′ W **103**
Derby, *U.K.* 52°55′ N, 1°29′ W **162**
Derby Acres, *Calif., U.S.* 35°15′ N, 119°37′ W **101**
Derdara, *Mor.* 35°7′ N, 5°18′ W **150**
Derdepoort, *S. Af.* 24°41′ S, 26°21′ E **227**
Derecske, *Hung.* 47°21′ N, 21°34′ E **168**
Dérégoué, *Burkina Faso* 10°46′ N, 4°9′ W **222**
Dereisa, *Sudan* 12°43′ N, 22°47′ E **216**
Derevyansk, *Russ.* 61°44′ N, 53°23′ E **154**
Dergachi, *Russ.* 51°12′ N, 48°48′ E **158**
Derhachi, *Ukr.* 50°7′ N, 36°7′ E **158**
Derik, *Turk.* 37°20′ N, 40°19′ E **195**
Derm, *Namibia* 23°40′ S, 18°13′ E **227**
Dermbach, *Ger.* 50°42′ N, 10°6′ E **167**
Dermott, *Ark., U.S.* 33°30′ N, 91°27′ W **96**
Derna see Darnah, *Lib.* 32°44′ N, 22°38′ E **216**
Dernberg, Cape, *Namibia* 27°44′ S, 15°33′ E **227**
Dernieres, Isles, *Gulf of Mexico* 29°3′ N, 90°55′ W **103**
Derom, Mount, *Antarctica* 71°36′ S, 35°22′ E **248**
Derri, *Somalia* 4°21′ N, 46°38′ E **218**
Derry, *La., U.S.* 31°30′ N, 92°58′ W **103**
Derry, *N.H., U.S.* 42°52′ N, 71°20′ W **104**
Derudeb, *Sudan* 17°29′ N, 36°4′ E **182**
Derust, *S. Af.* 33°27′ S, 22°32′ E **227**
Derval, *Fr.* 47°39′ N, 1°41′ W **150**
Derventa, *Bosn. and Herzg.* 44°58′ N, 17°53′ E **168**
Derwent, *Can.* 53°38′ N, 110°58′ W **108**
Derwent, river, *U.K.* 54°11′ N, 0°44′ E **162**
Derwent Water, lake, *U.K.* 54°33′ N, 3°22′ W **162**
Deryneia, *Northern Cyprus, Cyprus* 35°3′ N, 33°57′ E **194**
Derzhavino, *Russ.* 53°14′ N, 52°19′ E **154**
Derzhavīnsk, *Kaz.* 51°6′ N, 66°18′ E **184**
Des Allemands, *La., U.S.* 29°50′ N, 90°29′ W **103**
Des Moines, *Iowa, U.S.* 41°33′ N, 93°40′ W **94**
Des Moines, *N. Mex., U.S.* 36°44′ N, 103°50′ W **92**
Des Moines, river, *Iowa, U.S.* 43°26′ N, 95°10′ W **80**
Des Plaines, *Ill., U.S.* 42°2′ N, 87°54′ W **102**
Desa, *Rom.* 43°53′ N, 23°1′ E **168**
Desaguadero, *Peru* 16°39′ S, 69°5′ W **137**
Desatoya Mountains, *Nev., U.S.* 39°31′ N, 117°53′ W **90**
Desbiens, *Can.* 48°24′ N, 71°57′ W **94**
Descalvado, *Braz.* 21°57′ S, 47°38′ W **138**
Descanso, *Calif., U.S.* 32°51′ N, 116°37′ W **101**
Deschutes, river, *Oreg., U.S.* 44°13′ N, 121°5′ W **80**
Desē, *Eth.* 11°5′ N, 39°36′ E **224**
Deseada, *Chile* 22°53′ S, 69°51′ W **137**
Deseado, river, *Arg.* 46°54′ S, 69°39′ W **134**
Desemboque, *Mex.* 30°34′ N, 113°3′ W **92**
Desengaño, Punta, *Arg.* 49°15′ S, 67°33′ W **134**
Deseret, *Utah, U.S.* 39°16′ N, 112°39′ W **90**
Deseret Peak, *Utah, U.S.* 40°26′ N, 112°41′ W **90**
Deseronto, *Can.* 44°12′ N, 77°3′ W **94**
Desert Center, *Calif., U.S.* 33°43′ N, 115°25′ W **101**
Desert Hot Springs, *Calif., U.S.* 33°57′ N, 116°31′ W **101**
Desert Island, Mount, *Me., U.S.* 43°48′ N, 68°16′ W **81**
Désert, Lac, lake, *Can.* 46°34′ N, 76°44′ W **94**
Desert National Park, *India* 26°16′ N, 70°18′ E **186**
Desert Peak, *Utah, U.S.* 41°10′ N, 113°26′ W **90**
Desert Range, *Nev., U.S.* 36°51′ N, 115°27′ W **101**
Desert Shores, *Calif., U.S.* 33°24′ N, 116°3′ W **101**
Desert Valley, *Nev., U.S.* 41°12′ N, 118°30′ W **90**
Desertas, Ilhas, islands, *North Atlantic Ocean* 33°17′ N, 17°23′ W **214**
Deserters Peak, *Can.* 56°56′ N, 125°0′ W **108**
Deshler, *Nebr., U.S.* 40°6′ N, 97°45′ W **90**
Deshler, *Ohio, U.S.* 41°12′ N, 83°54′ W **102**
Deshnoke, *India* 27°48′ N, 73°21′ E **186**
Desierto del Carmen National Park see 13, *Mex.* 18°52′ N, 99°38′ W **112**
Désirade, La, island, *Fr.* 16°15′ N, 60°59′ W **116**
Deskenatlata Lake, *Can.* 60°55′ N, 113°9′ W **108**
Desloge, *Mo., U.S.* 37°51′ N, 90°31′ W **94**
Desmarais, Point, *Can.* 60°50′ N, 117°6′ W **108**
Desmaraisville, *Can.* 49°30′ N, 76°12′ W **94**
Desmochado, *Parag.* 27°7′ S, 58°5′ W **139**
Desna, river, *Russ.* 54°20′ N, 32°53′ E **154**
Desna, river, *Ukr.* 51°6′ N, 31°7′ E **158**
Desnogorsk, *Russ.* 54°8′ N, 33°13′ E **154**
Desnudez, Punta, *Arg.* 38°59′ S, 59°37′ W **139**
Desolación, Isla, island, *Chile* 53°2′ S, 76°38′ W **134**
Desolation Canyon, *Utah, U.S.* 39°42′ N, 110°18′ W **90**
Desordem, Serra da, *Braz.* 3°15′ S, 47°0′ W **130**
Despotovac, *Serb.* 44°5′ N, 21°25′ E **168**
Desroches, islands, *Indian Ocean* 6°36′ S, 51°11′ E **218**
Dessalines, *Haiti* 19°17′ N, 72°32′ W **116**
Dessau, *Ger.* 51°50′ N, 12°15′ E **152**
Destruction Island, *Wash., U.S.* 47°34′ N, 124°36′ W **100**
Destruction, Mount, *Austral.* 24°35′ S, 127°45′ E **230**
Desvres, *Fr.* 50°39′ N, 1°50′ E **163**
Deta, *Rom.* 45°24′ N, 21°13′ E **168**
Dete, *Zimb.* 18°38′ S, 26°50′ E **224**
Detour, Point, *U.S.* 45°27′ N, 86°34′ W **94**
Detroit, *Me., U.S.* 44°47′ N, 69°19′ W **94**
Detroit, *Mich., U.S.* 42°20′ N, 83°3′ W **102**
Dettelbach, *Ger.* 49°47′ N, 10°8′ E **167**
Deurne, *Neth.* 51°28′ N, 5°46′ E **167**
Deux Balé National Park, *Burkina Faso* 11°34′ N, 3°2′ W **222**
Deux Décharges, Lac aux, lake, *Can.* 51°58′ N, 71°19′ W **111**
Deva, *Rom.* 45°53′ N, 22°55′ E **168**
Devarkonda, *India* 16°41′ N, 78°57′ E **188**
Dévaványa, *Hung.* 47°1′ N, 20°58′ E **168**
Deveci Dağı, peak, *Turk.* 40°5′ N, 35°51′ E **156**
Devecser, *Hung.* 47°5′ N, 17°26′ E **168**
Develi, *Turk.* 38°22′ N, 35°31′ E **156**
Deventer, *Neth.* 52°15′ N, 6°8′ E **163**
Devenyns, Lac, lake, *Can.* 47°3′ N, 74°25′ W **94**
Devers, *Tex., U.S.* 30°0′ N, 94°36′ W **103**
Devgarh, *India* 25°30′ N, 73°59′ E **186**
Devi, river, *India* 20°33′ N, 85°53′ E **188**
Devil's Bridge, *U.K.* 52°21′ N, 3°51′ W **162**
Devils Cataract see Raudal Yupurari, fall(s), *Col.* 0°58′ N, 71°28′ W **136**
Devils Gate, pass, *Calif., U.S.* 38°21′ N, 119°23′ W **100**
Devils Hole see Death Valley National Park, *Nev., U.S.* 36°25′ N, 116°19′ W **101**
Devils Lake, *N. Dak., U.S.* 48°5′ N, 98°52′ W **90**
Devils Paw, mountain, *Can.–U.S.* 58°42′ N, 134°2′ W **108**
Devils Playground, *Calif., U.S.* 35°1′ N, 115°54′ W **101**
Devils Postpile National Monument, *Calif., U.S.* 37°36′ N, 119°11′ W **92**
Devils, river, *Tex., U.S.* 29°58′ N, 101°18′ W **92**
Devilsbit Mountain, *Ire.* 52°48′ N, 8°1′ W **150**
Devine, *Tex., U.S.* 29°7′ N, 98°55′ W **96**
Devine, Mount, *Ariz., U.S.* 32°7′ N, 111°52′ W **92**
Devizes, *U.K.* 51°21′ N, 2°0′ W **162**
Devli, *India* 25°45′ N, 75°23′ E **197**
Devola, *Ohio, U.S.* 39°27′ N, 81°28′ W **102**
Devon Island, *Can.* 75°13′ N, 79°17′ W **106**
Devoto, *Arg.* 31°27′ S, 62°19′ W **139**
Devrek, *Turk.* 41°13′ N, 31°54′ E **156**
Devrekâni, *Turk.* 41°36′ N, 33°49′ E **156**
Đevrske, *Croatia* 43°56′ N, 15°50′ E **156**
Dewa, Ujung, *Indonesia* 2°58′ N, 95°46′ E **196**
Dewar, *Okla., U.S.* 35°26′ N, 95°57′ W **96**
Dewas, *India* 22°58′ N, 76°3′ E **197**
Dewetsdorp, *S. Af.* 29°37′ S, 26°36′ E **227**
Dewey, *Okla., U.S.* 36°46′ N, 95°57′ W **96**
Dewey Lake, *Ky., U.S.* 37°27′ N, 83°21′ W **81**
Deweyville, *Tex., U.S.* 30°16′ N, 93°45′ W **103**
Dewitt, *Mich., U.S.* 42°50′ N, 84°34′ W **102**
Dewsbury, *U.K.* 53°41′ N, 1°38′ W **162**
Dexter, *Me., U.S.* 45°1′ N, 69°18′ W **94**
Dexter, *Mich., U.S.* 42°19′ N, 83°54′ W **102**
Dexter, *Mo., U.S.* 36°47′ N, 89°57′ W **96**
Deyhūk, *Iran* 33°16′ N, 57°31′ E **180**
Deyyer, *Iran* 27°49′ N, 51°56′ E **196**
Dez, river, *Iran* 33°0′ N, 48°44′ E **180**
Dezfūl, *Iran* 32°23′ N, 48°23′ E **180**
Dezhneva, Mys (East Cape), *Russ.* 65°45′ N, 169°46′ W **98**
Dezhou, *China* 37°28′ N, 116°18′ E **198**
Dgūqara, *Kaz.* 46°1′ N, 55°58′ E **158**
Dhahabān, *Saudi Arabia* 21°56′ N, 39°5′ E **182**
Dhahran see Az Zahrān, *Saudi Arabia* 26°15′ N, 50°1′ E **196**
Dhaka, *Bangladesh* 23°38′ N, 90°17′ E **197**
Dhamār, *Yemen* 14°30′ N, 44°27′ E **182**
Dhanbad, *India* 23°47′ N, 86°24′ E **197**
Dhandhuka, *India* 22°16′ N, 71°58′ E **186**
Dhangadhi, *Nepal* 28°40′ N, 80°39′ E **197**
D'Hanis, *Tex., U.S.* 29°19′ N, 99°16′ W **92**
Dhankuta, *Nepal* 26°57′ N, 87°19′ E **197**
Dhanora, *India* 20°15′ N, 80°20′ E **188**
Dharan Bazar, *Nepal* 26°45′ N, 87°11′ E **197**
Dharmjaygarh, *India* 22°29′ N, 83°13′ E **197**
Dhasan, river, *India* 24°11′ N, 78°46′ E **197**
Dhāt Ra's, *Jordan* 30°59′ N, 35°44′ E **194**
Dhaulagiri, peak, *Nepal* 28°41′ N, 83°29′ E **197**
Dhebar Lake, *India* 24°16′ N, 73°41′ E **186**
Dhërmi, *Alban.* 40°9′ N, 19°38′ E **156**
Dhībān (Dibon), *Jordan* 31°29′ N, 35°46′ E **194**
Dhone, *India* 15°24′ N, 77°52′ E **188**
Dhorain, Beinn, peak, *U.K.* 58°6′ N, 3°57′ W **150**
Dhule, *India* 20°52′ N, 74°45′ E **188**
Dhupgarh, peak, *India* 22°25′ N, 78°19′ E **197**
Dhuusamarreeb (Dusa Marreb), *Somalia* 5°31′ N, 46°24′ E **218**
Di Linh, *Vietnam* 11°35′ N, 108°4′ E **202**
Dia, *Mali* 14°53′ N, 3°17′ W **222**
Diablo, Cerro, peak, *Tex., U.S.* 31°51′ N, 105°28′ W **92**
Diablo, El Picacho del, peak, *Mex.* 30°56′ N, 115°27′ W **92**
Diablo, Mount, *Calif., U.S.* 37°52′ N, 121°57′ W **100**
Diablo Peak, *Oreg., U.S.* 42°57′ N, 120°40′ W **90**
Diablo Range, *Calif., U.S.* 37°13′ N, 121°39′ W **100**
Diablo, Sierra, *Tex., U.S.* 31°3′ N, 105°0′ W **92**
Diadé, *Mauritania* 16°15′ N, 7°33′ W **222**
Diafarabé, *Mali* 14°11′ N, 5°0′ W **222**
Diala, *Mali* 14°13′ N, 10°10′ W **222**
Dialafara, *Mali* 13°28′ N, 11°25′ W **222**
Dialakoto, *Senegal* 13°18′ N, 13°20′ W **222**
Diamante, *Arg.* 32°3′ S, 60°34′ W **139**
Diamantina, *Braz.* 18°16′ S, 43°35′ W **138**
Diamantina, Chapada, *Braz.* 12°50′ S, 42°58′ W **138**
Diamantina Fracture Zone, *Indian Ocean* 36°3′ S, 105°25′ E **254**
Diamantino, *Braz.* 16°32′ S, 53°14′ W **138**
Diamantino, *Braz.* 14°28′ S, 56°29′ W **132**
Diamond Craters, *Oreg., U.S.* 43°8′ N, 119°2′ W **90**
Diamond Harbour, *India* 22°11′ N, 88°12′ E **197**
Diamond Head, peak, *Hawai'i, U.S.* 21°14′ N, 157°51′ W **99**
Diamond Island, *Myanmar* 15°35′ N, 94°16′ E **202**
Diamond Mountains, *Calif., U.S.* 40°7′ N, 120°34′ W **90**
Diamond Mountains, *Nev., U.S.* 39°43′ N, 116°5′ W **90**
Diamond Peak, *Colo., U.S.* 40°56′ N, 108°57′ W **90**
Diamond Peak, *Oreg., U.S.* 43°30′ N, 122°14′ W **90**
Diamond Peak, *Wash., U.S.* 46°5′ N, 117°38′ W **90**
Diamond Point, *N.Y., U.S.* 43°28′ N, 73°43′ W **104**
Diamond Valley, *Nev., U.S.* 39°56′ N, 116°12′ W **90**
Diamondville, *Wyo., U.S.* 41°45′ N, 110°32′ W **90**
Diamou, *Mali* 14°6′ N, 11°17′ W **222**
Diana, *Tex., U.S.* 32°41′ N, 94°46′ W **103**
Dianbai, *China* 21°32′ N, 110°59′ E **198**
Diandioumé, *Mali* 15°27′ N, 9°21′ W **222**
Dianguina, *Mauritania* 15°19′ N, 10°56′ W **222**
Dianjiang, *China* 30°18′ N, 107°23′ E **198**
Diano d'Alba, *It.* 44°38′ N, 8°2′ E **167**
Diapaga, *Burkina Faso* 12°4′ N, 1°46′ E **222**
Diar el Haj Hassan, *Tun.* 35°17′ N, 11°3′ E **156**
Diarville, *Fr.* 48°22′ N, 6°7′ E **163**
Diavolo, Mount, *India* 12°41′ N, 92°54′ E **188**
Dībā al Ḩiṣn, *U.A.E.* 25°38′ N, 56°12′ E **196**
Dibaya, *Dem. Rep. of the Congo* 6°34′ S, 22°55′ E **218**
Dibaya Lubue, *Dem. Rep. of the Congo* 4°14′ S, 19°50′ E **218**
Dibbis, *Sudan* 12°33′ N, 24°12′ E **216**
Dibella, spring, *Niger* 17°23′ N, 13°13′ E **222**
Dibo, *Eth.* 10°46′ N, 38°19′ E **224**
Diboll, *Tex., U.S.* 31°9′ N, 94°48′ W **103**
Dibon see Dhībān, *Jordan* 31°29′ N, 35°46′ E **194**
Dibrugarh, *India* 27°27′ N, 94°56′ E **188**
Dibulla, *Col.* 11°14′ N, 73°20′ W **136**
Dickens, *Tex., U.S.* 33°35′ N, 100°51′ W **92**
Dickey Peak, *Idaho, U.S.* 44°13′ N, 113°57′ W **90**
Dickinson, *Tex., U.S.* 29°26′ N, 95°3′ W **103**
Dickson, *Russ.* 73°19′ N, 81°0′ E **160**
Dickson, *Tenn., U.S.* 36°4′ N, 87°23′ W **96**
Dicle, *Turk.* 38°22′ N, 40°5′ E **195**
Dicle see Tigris, river, *Turk.* 37°41′ N, 41°7′ E **195**
Dicomano, *It.* 43°54′ N, 11°31′ E **167**
Didibiran, *Russ.* 52°4′ N, 139°13′ E **190**
Didcot, *U.K.* 51°36′ N, 1°15′ W **162**
Dider, *Alg.* 25°12′ N, 8°26′ E **214**
Dīdēsa, river, *Eth.* 9°31′ N, 35°52′ E **224**
Didhav, *Eth.* 12°35′ N, 40°54′ E **182**
Didi Abuli, Mt'a, peak, *Ga.* 41°26′ N, 43°35′ E **195**
Didia, *Tanzania* 3°50′ S, 33°3′ E **224**
Didiéni, *Mali* 13°54′ N, 8°5′ W **222**
Dīdīmtu, *Eth.* 8°45′ N, 42°9′ E **224**
Didoko, *Côte d'Ivoire* 5°58′ N, 5°19′ W **222**
Didsbury, *Can.* 51°41′ N, 114°8′ W **90**
Didwana, *India* 27°23′ N, 74°35′ E **186**
Diébougou, *Burkina Faso* 10°57′ N, 3°16′ W **222**
Diecke, *Guinea* 7°15′ N, 8°59′ W **222**
Diefenbaker, Lake, *Can.* 51°15′ N, 107°39′ W **90**
Diego de Almagro, *Chile* 26°23′ S, 70°5′ W **134**
Diego de Almagro, Isla, island, *Chile* 51°19′ S, 78°10′ W **134**
Diego Garcia, island, *U.K.* 7°53′ S, 72°18′ E **188**
Diego Garcia, island, *U.K.* 7°17′ S, 72°25′ E **254**
Diekirch, *Lux.* 49°52′ N, 6°9′ E **167**
Diélé, *Congo* 1°56′ S, 14°37′ E **218**
Diéma, *Mali* 14°35′ N, 9°12′ W **222**
Diemel, river, *Ger.* 51°30′ N, 9°24′ E **167**
Dien Bien, *Vietnam* 21°21′ N, 103°0′ E **202**
Dien Chou, *Vietnam* 18°59′ N, 105°35′ E **202**
Dien Khanh, *Vietnam* 12°14′ N, 109°6′ E **202**
Diepholz, *Ger.* 52°36′ N, 8°22′ E **150**
Dieppe, *Fr.* 49°54′ N, 1°3′ E **163**
Dieppe Lake, lake, *Can.* 61°37′ N, 116°55′ W **108**
Dierdorf, *Ger.* 50°32′ N, 7°39′ E **163**
Dieren, *Neth.* 52°3′ N, 6°5′ E **167**
Diest, *Belg.* 50°59′ N, 5°2′ E **167**
Dieterich, *Ill., U.S.* 39°3′ N, 88°24′ W **102**
Dieulouard, *Fr.* 48°50′ N, 6°4′ E **163**
Dieuze, *Fr.* 48°49′ N, 6°43′ E **163**
Dieveniškės, *Lith.* 54°12′ N, 25°37′ E **166**
Diez, *Ger.* 50°22′ N, 8°0′ E **167**
Dif, *Kenya* 0°55′ N, 40°55′ E **224**
Diffa, *Niger* 13°21′ N, 12°37′ E **216**
Differdange, *Lux.* 49°32′ N, 5°53′ E **163**
Difnein, island, *Eritrea* 16°29′ N, 38°48′ E **182**
Digba, *Dem. Rep. of the Congo* 4°20′ N, 25°47′ E **224**
Digboi, *India* 27°23′ N, 95°38′ E **188**
Digby, *Can.* 44°37′ N, 65°46′ W **111**
Dighton, *Kans., U.S.* 38°29′ N, 100°28′ W **90**
Dighton, *Mass., U.S.* 41°48′ N, 71°8′ W **104**
Dighton, *Mich., U.S.* 44°5′ N, 85°21′ W **102**
Digne, *Fr.* 44°5′ N, 6°14′ E **167**
Digny, *Fr.* 48°32′ N, 1°8′ E **163**
Digor, *Turk.* 40°22′ N, 43°24′ E **195**
Digos, *Philippines* 6°47′ N, 125°20′ E **203**
Digri, *Pak.* 25°10′ N, 69°7′ E **186**
Digul, river, *Indonesia* 7°13′ S, 139°20′ E **192**
Digya National Park, *Ghana* 7°10′ N, 0°48′ E **222**
Dihōk, *Iraq* 36°52′ N, 42°52′ E **195**
Diinsoor, *Somalia* 2°25′ N, 42°57′ E **218**
Dijlah see Tigris, river, *Iraq* 32°8′ N, 46°36′ E **180**
Dijon, *Fr.* 47°19′ N, 5°2′ E **150**
Dik, *Chad* 9°57′ N, 17°30′ E **216**
Dika, Mys, *Russ.* 75°37′ N, 114°26′ E **172**
Dikhil, *Djibouti* 11°12′ N, 42°22′ E **224**
Dikili, *Turk.* 39°2′ N, 26°53′ E **156**
Diksmuide, *Belg.* 51°2′ N, 2°51′ E **163**
Dikwa, *Nig.* 12°3′ N, 13°56′ E **216**
Dīla, *Eth.* 6°28′ N, 38°18′ E **224**
Dildarde Burnu, *Turk.* 36°26′ N, 31°17′ E **156**
Dili, *Dem. Rep. of the Congo* 3°25′ N, 26°44′ E **224**
Dili, *Timor-Leste* 8°47′ S, 125°17′ E **230**
Dilijan, *Arm.* 40°44′ N, 44°50′ E **195**
Dilj Planina, *Croatia* 45°16′ N, 17°52′ E **168**
Dillenburg, *Ger.* 50°44′ N, 8°16′ E **167**
Dilley, *Tex., U.S.* 28°39′ N, 99°10′ W **92**
Dilling, *Sudan* 12°1′ N, 29°40′ E **216**
Dillingen, *Ger.* 49°21′ N, 6°44′ E **163**
Dillingham, *Alas., U.S.* 58°57′ N, 158°36′ W **73**
Dillon, *Can.* 55°54′ N, 108°55′ W **108**
Dillon, *Mont., U.S.* 45°11′ N, 112°38′ W **90**
Dillon, *S.C., U.S.* 34°25′ N, 79°23′ W **96**
Dillon, river, *Can.* 55°31′ N, 110°13′ W **108**
Dillsboro, *Ind., U.S.* 39°0′ N, 85°3′ W **102**
Dilolo, *Dem. Rep. of the Congo* 10°44′ S, 22°22′ E **220**
Dilworth, *Minn., U.S.* 46°51′ N, 96°41′ W **90**
Dima, *Dem. Rep. of the Congo* 3°29′ S, 17°24′ E **218**
Dimapur, *India* 25°52′ N, 93°47′ E **188**
Dimas, *Mex.* 23°40′ N, 106°47′ W **114**
Dimashq (Damascus), *Syr.* 33°30′ N, 36°14′ E **194**
Dimbelenge, *Dem. Rep. of the Congo* 5°32′ S, 23°3′ E **218**
Dimbokro, *Côte d'Ivoire* 6°34′ N, 4°42′ W **222**
Dimitrovgrad, *Bulg.* 42°3′ N, 25°35′ E **156**
Dimitrovgrad, *Russ.* 54°15′ N, 49°34′ E **154**
Dimitrovgrad, *Serb.* 43°0′ N, 22°46′ E **168**
Dimmitt, *Tex., U.S.* 34°31′ N, 102°19′ W **92**
Dimock, *S. Dak., U.S.* 43°26′ N, 97°59′ W **90**
Dimona, *Israel* 31°3′ N, 35°0′ E **194**
Dīmtu, *Eth.* 5°8′ N, 41°57′ E **224**
Dinajpur, *Bangladesh* 25°36′ N, 88°36′ E **197**
Dinan, *Fr.* 48°27′ N, 2°4′ W **150**
Dinant, *Belg.* 50°16′ N, 4°55′ E **167**
Dinar, *Turk.* 38°3′ N, 30°10′ E **156**
Dīnār, Kūh-e, peak, *Iran* 30°45′ N, 51°30′ E **180**
Dinara, *Bosn. and Herzg.* 43°50′ N, 16°33′ E **168**
Dinas Mawddwy, *U.K.* 52°42′ N, 3°42′ W **162**
Dinde, *Angola* 14°14′ S, 13°41′ E **220**
Dinder National Park, *Sudan* 12°32′ N, 35°8′ E **182**
Dinder, river, *Sudan* 12°26′ N, 35°4′ E **182**
Dinga, *Dem. Rep. of the Congo* 5°17′ S, 16°39′ E **218**
Ding'an, *China* 19°39′ N, 110°19′ E **198**
Dingbian, *China* 37°36′ N, 107°36′ E **198**
Dinggyê, *China* 28°26′ N, 87°46′ E **197**
Dingnan, *China* 24°44′ N, 115°0′ E **198**
Dingtao, *China* 35°3′ N, 115°36′ E **198**
Dinguiraye, *Guinea* 11°17′ N, 10°44′ W **222**
Dingxi, *China* 35°33′ N, 104°32′ E **198**
Dingxiang, *China* 38°28′ N, 112°58′ E **198**
Dingxing, *China* 39°17′ N, 115°49′ E **198**
Dingzhou, *China* 38°31′ N, 114°59′ E **198**
Dingzi Gang 36°21′ N, 120°50′ E **198**
Dinkey Creek, *Calif., U.S.* 37°5′ N, 119°11′ W **101**
Dinklage, *Ger.* 52°39′ N, 8°8′ E **163**
Dinorwic, *Can.* 49°41′ N, 92°30′ W **94**
Dinorwic Lake, lake, *Can.* 49°31′ N, 93°7′ W **94**
Dinosaur, *Colo., U.S.* 40°14′ N, 109°1′ W **90**
Dinslaken, *Ger.* 51°33′ N, 6°44′ E **167**
Dinuba, *Calif., U.S.* 36°32′ N, 119°24′ W **100**
Dioïla, *Mali* 12°29′ N, 6°48′ W **222**
Dioka, *Mali* 14°54′ N, 10°7′ W **222**
Diona, spring, *Chad* 17°52′ N, 22°37′ E **216**
Diongoï, *Mali* 14°53′ N, 9°35′ W **222**
Dionísio Cerqueira, *Arg.* 26°17′ S, 53°37′ W **139**
Diorbivol, *Senegal* 16°5′ N, 13°48′ W **222**
Dios, Cayos de, *Caribbean Sea* 21°16′ N, 81°16′ W **116**
Diosig, *Rom.* 47°17′ N, 22°1′ E **168**
Dioulouloü, *Senegal* 13°1′ N, 16°31′ W **222**
Dioumdiouréré, *Mali* 14°51′ N, 2°0′ W **222**
Dioundiou, *Niger* 12°35′ N, 3°30′ E **222**
Dioura, *Mali* 14°52′ N, 5°15′ W **222**
Diourbel, *Senegal* 14°39′ N, 16°7′ W **222**
Diphu Pass, *India* 28°14′ N, 97°21′ E **188**
Dipkarpaz see Rizokarpaso, *Cyprus* 35°36′ N, 34°22′ E **194**
Diplo, *Pak.* 24°28′ N, 69°36′ E **186**
Dipolog, *Philippines* 8°36′ N, 123°21′ E **203**
Dipton, *N.Z.* 45°55′ S, 168°23′ E **240**
Dir, *Pak.* 35°11′ N, 71°53′ E **186**
Dira, Djebel, peak, *Alg.* 36°4′ N, 3°34′ E **150**
Dirdal, *Nor.* 58°49′ N, 6°9′ E **152**
Dirē, *Eth.* 10°9′ N, 38°41′ E **224**
Diré, *Mali* 16°17′ N, 3°24′ W **222**
Dirē Dawa, *Eth.* 9°34′ N, 41°51′ E **224**
Dírfis, Óros, *Gr.* 38°32′ N, 23°38′ E **156**
Dirico, *Angola* 17°56′ S, 20°43′ E **220**
Dirj, *Lib.* 30°9′ N, 10°26′ E **214**
Dirk Hartog Island, *Austral.* 26°19′ S, 110°56′ E **230**
Dirkou, *Niger* 19°4′ N, 12°50′ E **216**
Dirra, *Sudan* 13°35′ N, 26°5′ E **226**
Dirranbandi, *Austral.* 28°36′ S, 148°19′ E **231**
Disa, *India* 24°15′ N, 72°11′ E **186**
Disappointment, Cape, *Wash., U.S.* 46°13′ N, 124°26′ W **100**
Disaster Bay 37°41′ S, 149°37′ E **231**
Discovery Bay 38°20′ S, 139°30′ E **230**
Discovery Tablemount, *South Atlantic Ocean* 42°9′ S, 0°31′ E **253**
Disentis-Mustér, *Switz.* 46°42′ N, 8°50′ E **167**
Dishna, *Egypt* 26°10′ N, 32°25′ E **180**
Disko see Qeqertarsuaq, island, *Den.* 69°31′ N, 62°11′ W **106**
Dismal Mountains, *Antarctica* 68°45′ S, 53°53′ E **248**
Dismal, river, *Nebr., U.S.* 41°45′ N, 101°4′ W **90**
Dispur, *India* 26°6′ N, 91°44′ E **197**
Disraëli, *Can.* 45°53′ N, 71°21′ W **94**
Diss, *U.K.* 52°22′ N, 1°6′ E **162**
Disteghil Sar, peak, *Pak.* 36°16′ N, 75°4′ E **186**
District, Lake, region, *Europe* 54°15′ N, 3°22′ W **162**
District of Columbia, adm. division, *D.C., U.S.* 38°55′ N, 77°12′ W **94**
District, Peak, region, *Europe* 53°17′ N, 1°57′ W **162**
Distrito Federal, adm. division, *Braz.* 15°42′ S, 48°13′ W **138**
Distrito Federal, adm. division, *Mex.* 19°9′ N, 99°21′ W **114**
Disūq, *Egypt* 31°7′ N, 30°39′ E **180**
Ditaranto, Golfo 39°48′ N, 16°53′ E **156**
Ditinn, *Guinea* 10°53′ N, 12°13′ W **222**
Diu, *India* 20°41′ N, 70°56′ E **188**
Dium, ruin(s), *Gr.* 40°9′ N, 22°23′ E **156**
Dīvāndarreh, *Iran* 36°0′ N, 46°58′ E **180**
Divénié, *Congo* 2°39′ S, 12°3′ E **218**
Divernon, *Ill., U.S.* 39°32′ N, 89°41′ W **102**
Divinhe, *Mozambique* 20°42′ S, 34°48′ E **227**
Divinópolis, *Braz.* 20°10′ S, 44°55′ W **138**
Divisadero Barrancas, *Mex.* 27°32′ N, 107°48′ W **112**
Diviso, *Col.* 1°22′ N, 78°27′ W **136**
Divisor, Serra do, *Braz.* 8°10′ S, 73°52′ W **130**
Divjakë, *Alban.* 40°59′ N, 19°31′ E **156**
Divnoye, *Russ.* 45°52′ N, 43°10′ E **158**
Divo, *Côte d'Ivoire* 5°47′ N, 5°21′ W **222**
Divonne, *Fr.* 46°21′ N, 6°8′ E **167**
Divriği, *Turk.* 39°20′ N, 38°7′ E **180**
Diwal Qol, *Afghan.* 34°20′ N, 67°57′ E **186**
Diwana, *Pak.* 26°5′ N, 67°19′ E **186**
Dixfield, *Me., U.S.* 44°31′ N, 70°27′ W **104**
Dixie Butte, peak, *Oreg., U.S.* 44°34′ N, 118°42′ W **90**
Dixon, *Calif., U.S.* 38°26′ N, 121°50′ W **90**
Dixon, *Ill., U.S.* 41°49′ N, 89°29′ W **102**
Dixon, *Ky., U.S.* 37°30′ N, 87°42′ W **94**
Dixon, *Mo., U.S.* 37°58′ N, 92°6′ W **94**
Dixon, *Mont., U.S.* 47°17′ N, 114°20′ W **90**
Dixon Entrance 54°17′ N, 133°50′ W **108**
Dixons Mills, *Ala., U.S.* 32°3′ N, 87°48′ W **103**
Dixonville, *Can.* 56°32′ N, 117°41′ W **108**
Diyadin, *Turk.* 39°32′ N, 43°41′ E **195**
Diyālá, river, *Iraq* 34°20′ N, 45°5′ E **186**
Diyarbakır, *Turk.* 37°54′ N, 40°17′ E **195**
Diz, *Pak.* 26°36′ N, 63°27′ E **182**
Dizy, *Fr.* 49°3′ N, 3°57′ E **163**
Dja, river, *Cameroon* 3°14′ N, 12°30′ E **218**
Dja, river, *Cameroon* 3°1′ N, 14°6′ E **218**
Djado, *Niger* 21°1′ N, 12°18′ E **222**
Djado, Plateau du, *Niger* 21°41′ N, 11°25′ E **222**
Djako, *Cen. Af. Rep.* 8°18′ N, 22°29′ E **218**
Djamaa, *Alg.* 33°31′ N, 5°57′ E **214**
Djambala, *Congo* 2°32′ S, 14°45′ E **218**
Djanet, *Alg.* 24°23′ N, 9°22′ E **207**
Djaul, island, *P.N.G.* 3°10′ S, 150°7′ E **192**
Djebel Onk, *Alg.* 34°41′ N, 8°2′ E **214**
Djédaa, *Chad* 13°31′ N, 18°36′ E **216**
Djelfa, *Alg.* 34°41′ N, 3°15′ E **214**
Djéli Mahé, *Mali* 15°25′ N, 10°37′ W **222**
Djema, *Cen. Af. Rep.* 5°58′ N, 25°18′ E **224**
Djember, *Chad* 10°26′ N, 17°50′ E **216**

Duda, river, Col. 2°58' N, 74°15' W 136
Dudelange, Lux. 49°28' N, 6°4' E 163
Duderstadt, Ger. 51°31' N, 10°14' E 167
Dudhi, India 24°12' N, 83°13' E 197
Dudhnai, India 25°58' N, 90°45' E 197
Dudinka, Russ. 69°25' N, 86°24' E 169
Dudley, Mass., U.S. 42°2' N, 71°56' W 104
Dudley, U.K. 52°30' N, 2°6' W 162
Dudleyville, Ariz., U.S. 32°56' N, 110°44' W 92
Dudo, Somalia 9°16' N, 50°11' E 216
Dudub, Eth. 6°54' N, 46°44' E 218
Dudypta, river, Russ. 71°10' N, 91°51' E 160
Duékoué, Côte d'Ivoire 6°39' N, 7°20' W 222
Dueodde, Den. 54°53' N, 14°30' E 152
Duero, river, Sp. 41°17' N, 2°56' W 214
Dufek Coast, Antarctica 84°41' S, 154°15' W 248
Dufek Massif, peak, Antarctica 82°41' S, 54°13' W 248
Duff Islands, South Pacific Ocean 9°30' S, 167°28' E 238
Dugo Selo, Croatia 45°48' N, 16°13' E 168
Dugulle, spring, Somalia 2°14' N, 44°30' E 218
Dugway, Utah, U.S. 40°13' N, 112°45' W 90
Duida-Marahuaca National Park, Venez. 3°36' N, 65°58' W 136
Duisburg, Ger. 51°25' N, 6°45' E 167
Duitama, Col. 5°49' N, 73°3' W 136
Duiwelskloof, S. Af. 23°42' S, 30°9' E 227
Dujuuma, Somalia 1°10' N, 42°34' E 224
Duk Fadiat, Sudan 7°42' N, 31°25' E 224
Duk Faiwil, Sudan 7°30' N, 31°26' E 224
Dukafulu, Eth. 5°7' N, 39°7' E 224
Dukambia, Eritrea 14°44' N, 37°29' E 182
Dukhān, Qatar 25°20' N, 50°47' E 196
Dukku, Nig. 10°47' N, 10°46' E 222
Dūkštas, Lith. 55°31' N, 26°18' E 166
Dula, Dem. Rep. of the Congo 4°41' N, 20°17' E 218
Dulan, China 36°19' N, 98°8' E 188
Dulce, river, Arg. 29°58' S, 62°44' W 139
Dulion, Golfe 43°2' N, 3°49' E 150
Dülmen, Ger. 51°50' N, 7°16' E 167
Dulovka, Russ. 57°30' N, 28°20' E 166
Duluth, Minn., U.S. 46°47' N, 92°8' W 94
Dulverton, U.K. 51°2' N, 3°33' W 162
Dūmā, Syr. 33°34' N, 36°24' E 194
Duma, river, Dem. Rep. of the Congo 4°32' N, 26°35' E 224
Dumaguete, Philippines 9°18' N, 123°14' E 203
Dumai, Indonesia 1°41' N, 101°27' E 196
Dumaran, island, Philippines 10°19' N, 119°57' E 192
Dumas, Ark., U.S. 33°52' N, 91°30' W 96
Dumas, Tex., U.S. 35°50' N, 101°59' W 92
Dumas, Peninsula, Chile 55°4' S, 68°22' W 134
Ḑumayr, Syr. 33°38' N, 36°41' E 194
Dume, river, Dem. Rep. of the Congo 5°3' N, 24°48' E 224
Dumfries, U.K. 55°4' N, 3°36' W 150
Dumka, India 24°14' N, 87°15' E 197
Dummett, Mount, Antarctica 73°16' S, 63°25' E 248
Dumoine, Lac, lake, Can. 46°51' N, 78°28' W 94
Dumont d'Urville, station, Antarctica 66°39' S, 139°39' E 248
Dümpelfeld, Ger. 50°26' N, 6°57' E 167
Dumra, India 26°33' N, 85°30' E 197
Dumshaf Plain, Norwegian Sea 69°58' N, 1°51' E 255
Dumyāţ (Damietta), Egypt 31°25' N, 31°49' E 180
Dun, Fr. 49°23' N, 5°12' E 163
Dun Aengus, ruin(s), Ire. 53°7' N, 9°55' W 150
Dún Dealgan see Dundalk, Ire. 53°59' N, 6°24' W 150
Duna, river, Europe 47°44' N, 17°37' E 168
Dunaff Head, Ire. 55°17' N, 7°53' W 150
Dunaharaszti, Hung. 47°21' N, 19°6' E 168
Dunakeszi, Hung. 47°37' N, 19°9' E 168
Dunapataj, Hung. 46°38' N, 19°0' E 168
Dunărea, river, Europe 43°42' N, 22°49' E 180
Dunaszekcső, Hung. 46°4' N, 18°44' E 168
Dunaújváros, Hung. 46°58' N, 18°55' E 168
Dunavecse, Hung. 46°54' N, 18°58' E 168
Dunay, Russ. 42°53' N, 132°20' E 200
Dunayivtsi, Ukr. 48°52' N, 26°51' E 152
Dunbar, W. Va., U.S. 38°21' N, 81°45' W 94
Dunblane, Can. 51°12' N, 106°55' W 90
Duncan, Ariz., U.S. 32°42' N, 109°6' W 92
Duncan, Can. 48°46' N, 123°41' W 100
Duncan, Okla., U.S. 34°28' N, 97°58' W 96
Duncan Passage 10°58' N, 91°46' E 188
Dundaga, Latv. 57°30' N, 22°19' E 166
Dundalk (Dún Dealgan), Ire. 53°59' N, 6°24' W 150
Dundas, Ill., U.S. 38°50' N, 88°6' W 102
Dundas Islands, North Pacific Ocean 54°35' N, 130°38' W 98
Dundas Peninsula, Can. 74°29' N, 116°39' W 106
Dundbürd, Mongolia 47°57' N, 111°29' E 198
Dundee, Fla., U.S. 28°1' N, 81°38' W 105
Dundee, Mich., U.S. 41°57' N, 83°39' W 102
Dundee, S. Af. 28°10' S, 30°9' E 227
Dundee, U.K. 56°36' N, 3°10' W 143
Dundee Island, Antarctica 63°49' S, 58°1' W 134
Dundo, Angola 7°24' S, 20°47' E 218
Dundrennan, U.K. 54°49' N, 3°57' W 162
Dundret, peak, Nor. 67°5' N, 20°23' E 152
Dund-Urt, Mongolia 47°56' N, 106°12' E 198
Dund-Us see Hovd, Mongolia 48°2' N, 91°40' E 190
Dune Sandy Hook, Can. 47°11' N, 61°45' W 111
Dunedin, Fla., U.S. 28°1' N, 82°46' W 105
Dunedin, N.Z. 45°52' S, 170°28' E 240
Dunedin, river, Can. 58°56' N, 124°29' W 108
Dunes City, Oreg., U.S. 43°52' N, 124°8' W 90
Dunfermline, U.K. 56°4' N, 3°28' W 150
Dungannon, Can. 43°50' N, 81°37' W 102
Dungarpur, India 23°50' N, 73°43' E 186
Dungas, Niger 13°4' N, 9°19' E 222
Dungeness, U.K. 50°54' N, 0°58' E 162
Dungeness, Punta, Arg. 52°31' S, 68°22' W 134
Dungu, Dem. Rep. of the Congo 3°33' N, 28°34' E 224
Dungu, river, Dem. Rep. of the Congo 3°40' N, 28°34' E 224
Dungunab, Sudan 21°5' N, 37°4' E 182
Dunhua, China 43°23' N, 128°7' E 198
Dunhuang, China 40°10' N, 94°42' E 188
Dunilavichy, Belarus 55°4' N, 27°13' E 166
Dunk Island, Austral. 18°2' S, 146°15' E 230
Dunkassa, Benin 10°19' N, 3°7' E 222
Dunkerque (Dunkirk), Fr. 51°1' N, 2°21' E 163
Dunkery Beacon, peak, U.K. 51°9' N, 3°37' W 162
Dunkirk, Ind., U.S. 40°22' N, 85°12' W 94
Dunkirk, N.Y., U.S. 42°28' N, 79°21' W 94
Dunkirk, river, Can. 57°8' N, 113°2' W 108
Dunkirk see Dunkerque, Fr. 51°1' N, 2°21' E 163
Dunkur, Eth. 11°54' N, 35°56' E 182
Dunkwa, Ghana 5°56' N, 1°48' W 222
Dunlap, Iowa, U.S. 41°50' N, 95°35' W 90
Dunlop, Can. 54°44' N, 98°51' W 108
Dunluce Castle, site, U.K. 55°11' N, 6°41' W 150
Dunmore Town, Bahamas 25°30' N, 76°38' W 96
Dunn, N.C., U.S. 35°18' N, 78°37' W 96
Dunnellon, Fla., U.S. 29°3' N, 82°28' W 105
Dunning, Nebr., U.S. 41°48' N, 100°7' W 90
Dunnottar Castle, site, U.K. 56°55' N, 2°19' W 150
Dunqul, spring, Egypt 23°23' N, 31°39' E 182
Dunrobin Castle, site, U.K. 57°58' N, 4°5' W 150
Dunseith, N. Dak., U.S. 48°47' N, 100°4' W 90
Dunsmuir, Calif., U.S. 41°12' N, 122°18' W 90
Dunstable, U.K. 51°53' N, 0°32' E 162
Dunstanburgh Castle, site, U.K. 55°28' N, 1°42' W 150
Dunster, Can. 53°6' N, 119°53' W 108
Dunster, U.K. 51°11' N, 3°26' W 162
Dunte, Latv. 57°25' N, 24°25' E 166
Duntroon, N.Z. 44°53' S, 170°38' E 240
Dunvegan, Can. 55°57' N, 118°37' W 108
Dunvegan Lake, Can. 60°10' N, 107°45' W 108
Duolun, China 42°10' N, 116°30' E 198
Duparquet, Lac, lake, Can. 48°27' N, 79°52' W 110
Dupont, Ind., U.S. 38°53' N, 85°31' W 102
Dupree, S. Dak., U.S. 45°2' N, 101°37' W 90
Dupuyer, Mont., U.S. 48°9' N, 112°31' W 90
Duqm, Oman 19°37' N, 57°41' E 182
Duque de Caxias, Braz. 22°44' S, 43°18' W 138
Duque de York, Isla, island, Chile 50°51' S, 77°57' W 134
Dur Sharrukin, ruin(s), Iraq 36°30' N, 43°3' E 195
Durack Range, Austral. 16°42' S, 127°6' E 230
Durance, river, Fr. 43°50' N, 5°55' E 165
Durance, river, Fr. 44°41' N, 6°35' E 165
Durand, Ill., U.S. 42°25' N, 89°21' W 102
Durand, Mich., U.S. 42°53' N, 83°59' W 102
Durand, Wis., U.S. 44°37' N, 91°58' W 94
Duranes, peak, Sp. 38°50' N, 4°42' W 164
Durango, Colo., U.S. 37°15' N, 107°52' W 92
Durango, Mex. 24°0' N, 104°43' W 114
Durango, adm. division, Mex. 24°46' N, 105°26' W 114
Durant, Miss., U.S. 33°3' N, 89°52' W 103
Durant, Okla., U.S. 33°58' N, 96°23' W 96
Duraykīsh, Syr. 34°54' N, 36°7' E 194
Durazno, Uru. 33°22' S, 56°30' W 139
Durban, S. Af. 29°52' S, 30°57' E 227
Durbe, Latv. 56°35' N, 21°22' E 166
Durbuy, Belg. 50°21' N, 5°25' E 167
Dúrcal, Sp. 36°59' N, 3°34' W 164
Đurđevac, Croatia 46°2' N, 17°4' E 168
Đurđevik, Bosn. and Herzg. 44°26' N, 18°38' E 168
Durduri, Somalia 11°14' N, 48°35' E 216
Düren, Ger. 50°48' N, 6°29' E 167
Durham, Can. 44°9' N, 80°49' W 102
Durham, Conn., U.S. 41°28' N, 72°41' W 104
Durham, N.H., U.S. 43°8' N, 70°57' W 104
Durham, N.C., U.S. 35°58' N, 78°55' W 96
Durham, U.K. 54°47' N, 1°35' W 162
Duri, oil field, Indonesia 1°22' N, 101°5' E 196
Durlston Head, U.K. 50°23' N, 1°57' W 150
Ḑurmā, Saudi Arabia 24°35' N, 46°7' E 182
Durmitor, mountains, Mont. 43°10' N, 18°54' E 168
Durmitor National Park, Mont. 43°10' N, 19°21' E 168
Durov Dag, oil field, Azerb. 39°30' N, 49°4' E 195
Dursley, U.K. 51°40' N, 2°21' W 162
Dursunbey, Turk. 39°36' N, 28°37' E 156
Duru, Dem. Rep. of the Congo 4°15' N, 28°49' E 224
Duru, river, Dem. Rep. of the Congo 3°39' N, 28°11' E 224
Dūru', Iran 32°17' N, 60°33' E 180
D'Urville Island, Antarctica 63°0' S, 57°29' W 134
Durwalē, Eth. 8°47' N, 43°4' E 218
Dusa Marreb see Dhuusamarreeb, Somalia 5°31' N, 46°24' E 218
Duşak, Turkm. 37°12' N, 60°2' E 180
Dusetos, Lith. 55°44' N, 25°52' E 166
Dusey, river, Can. 51°10' N, 87°15' W 110
Dūsh, Egypt 24°34' N, 30°37' E 182
Dushan, China 25°48' N, 107°31' E 198
Dushanbe, Taj. 38°34' N, 68°40' E 197
Dushanzi (Maytag), China 44°17' N, 84°53' E 184
Dushet'i, Ga. 42°3' N, 44°41' E 195
Dŭskotna, Bulg. 42°52' N, 27°11' E 156
Dusky Sound 45°49' S, 165°58' E 240
Duson, La., U.S. 30°13' N, 92°11' W 103
Düsseldorf, Ger. 51°14' N, 6°47' E 167
Dustin Island, Antarctica 71°52' S, 94°44' W 248
Dutch John, Utah, U.S. 40°55' N, 109°24' W 90
Dutch Mountain, Utah, U.S. 40°12' N, 113°55' W 90
Dutlwe, Botswana 23°56' S, 23°50' E 227
Dutovo, Russ. 63°49' N, 56°42' E 154
Dutse, Nig. 11°43' N, 9°19' E 222
Dutsin Ma, Nig. 12°27' N, 7°29' E 222
Dutton, Can. 42°38' N, 81°30' W 102
Dutton, Mount, Utah, U.S. 38°0' N, 112°17' W 90
Duvan, Russ. 55°42' N, 57°51' E 154
Duvergé, Dom. Rep. 18°22' N, 71°33' W 116
Duvno, Bosn. and Herzg. 43°43' N, 17°13' E 168
Duwayhin, Khawr 24°14' N, 51°0' E 196
Duxbury, Mass., U.S. 42°2' N, 70°41' W 104
Duxford, U.K. 52°5' N, 0°9' E 162
Duy Xuyen, Vietnam 15°53' N, 108°15' E 202
Duyun, China 26°16' N, 107°34' E 198
Duz Dag, oil field, Azerb. 39°22' N, 49°6' E 195
Düzce, Turk. 40°50' N, 31°10' E 156
Dvarets, Belarus 53°24' N, 25°35' E 152
Dvina, river, Russ. 61°15' N, 46°22' E 160
Dvinskaya Guba 64°31' N, 38°23' E 143
Dvinskoy, Russ. 62°11' N, 45°8' E 154
Dvor, Croatia 45°3' N, 16°22' E 168
Dvukh Pilotov, Kosa, Russ. 68°5' N, 178°33' E 98
Dwarfie Stane, ruin(s), U.K. 58°51' N, 3°28' W 150
Dwarka, India 22°15' N, 68°59' E 186
Dwight, Ill., U.S. 41°5' N, 88°25' W 102
Dwikozy, Pol. 50°43' N, 21°48' E 152
Dyalakoro, Mali 12°3' N, 7°51' W 222
Dyat'kovo, Russ. 53°32' N, 34°21' E 154
Dyce, Can. 54°21' N, 100°11' W 108
Dyer, Cape, Can. 66°20' N, 61°26' W 106
Dyero, Mali 12°50' N, 6°30' W 222
Dyersburg, Tenn., U.S. 36°2' N, 89°23' W 96
Dymchurch, U.K. 51°1' N, 1°0' E 162
Dyment, Can. 49°37' N, 92°20' W 94
Dyrøy, Nor. 69°3' N, 17°30' E 152
Dytikí ElŽada, adm. division, Gr. 38°2' N, 21°22' E 156
Dytikí Makedonía, adm. division, Gr. 40°26' N, 21°7' E 156
Dyupkun, Ozero, lake, Russ. 67°58' N, 96°30' E 169
Dyurtyuli, Russ. 55°28' N, 54°55' E 154
Dzanga-Ndoki National Park, Cen. Af. Rep. 2°30' N, 15°16' E 218
Dzavhan, river, Mongolia 47°49' N, 93°37' E 190
Dzerzhinsk, Russ. 56°14' N, 43°31' E 154
Dzerzhīnskoe, Kaz. 45°48' N, 81°4' E 184
Dzhagdy, Khrebet, Russ. 53°42' N, 130°43' E 190
Dzhalinda, Russ. 53°35' N, 123°57' E 190
Dzhankoy, Ukr. 45°41' N, 34°20' E 156
Dzhugdzhur, Khrebet, Russ. 57°47' N, 136°52' E 160
Działdowo, Pol. 53°13' N, 20°10' E 152
Dzibalchén, Mex. 19°27' N, 89°45' W 115
Dzibilchaltún, ruin(s), Mex. 21°5' N, 89°42' W 116
Džigolj, Serb. 43°20' N, 21°35' E 168
Dzilam de Bravo, Mex. 21°22' N, 88°55' W 116
Dzioua, Alg. 33°14' N, 5°16' E 214
Dzisna, Belarus 55°34' N, 28°9' E 166
Dzisna, river, Belarus 55°26' N, 27°41' E 166
Dzivin, Belarus 51°56' N, 24°35' E 152
Dzodze, Ghana 6°14' N, 0°57' E 222
Dzogsool, Mongolia 46°47' N, 107°7' E 198
Dzonot Carretero, Mex. 21°24' N, 87°53' W 116
Dzotol, Mongolia 45°52' N, 115°5' E 198
Dzuiché, Mex. 19°53' N, 88°51' W 115
Dzūkija National Park, Lith. 53°56' N, 24°10' E 166
Dzūkste, Latv. 56°47' N, 23°13' E 166
Dzungarian Basin, China 45°51' N, 82°34' E 172
Dzungarian Gate, Kaz. 45°8' N, 73°45' E 172
Dzüünbayan, Mongolia 44°30' N, 110°7' E 198
Dzüünbulag, Mongolia 47°8' N, 115°40' E 198
Dzüünharaa, Mongolia 48°55' N, 106°28' E 198
Dzuunmod, Mongolia 47°41' N, 107°0' E 198
Dzvina Zakh, river, Belarus 55°34' N, 28°34' E 166
Dzyalyatsichy, Belarus 53°46' N, 25°59' E 158

E

Eabamet Lake, Can. 51°31' N, 89°14' W 81
Eads, Colo., U.S. 38°28' N, 102°48' W 90
Eagle, Alas., U.S. 64°43' N, 141°21' W 98
Eagle, Colo., U.S. 39°38' N, 106°49' W 90
Eagle Butte, S. Dak., U.S. 44°56' N, 101°15' W 90
Eagle Cap, peak, Oreg., U.S. 45°8' N, 117°23' W 90
Eagle Crags, peak, Calif., U.S. 35°23' N, 117°6' W 101
Eagle Creek, river, Can. 52°12' N, 109°23' W 80
Eagle Grove, Iowa, U.S. 42°39' N, 93°53' W 94
Eagle Islands, Indian Ocean 6°13' S, 69°38' E 188
Eagle Lake, Calif., U.S. 40°34' N, 121°33' W 81
Eagle Lake, Can. 49°32' N, 93°29' W 110
Eagle Lake, Fla., U.S. 27°58' N, 81°47' W 105
Eagle Mountain, Minn., U.S. 47°52' N, 90°40' W 94
Eagle Mountains, Calif., U.S. 33°50' N, 115°41' W 101
Eagle Peak, Calif., U.S. 41°16' N, 120°18' W 90
Eagle Peak, Calif., U.S. 38°10' N, 119°27' W 100
Eagle Peak, Mont., U.S. 47°14' N, 115°28' W 90
Eagle Peak, N. Mex., U.S. 33°39' N, 108°38' W 92
Eagle Peak, Tex., U.S. 30°53' N, 105°9' W 92
Eagle River, Mich., U.S. 47°24' N, 88°18' W 94
Eagle, river, Can. 52°46' N, 58°44' W 111
Eaglesham, Can. 55°46' N, 117°54' W 108
Eagletail Mountains, Ariz., U.S. 33°40' N, 113°43' W 101
Ear Falls, Can. 50°38' N, 93°14' W 90
Earl Park, Ind., U.S. 40°40' N, 87°24' W 102
Earlimart, Calif., U.S. 35°52' N, 119°17' W 100
Earlington, Ky., U.S. 37°15' N, 87°31' W 96
Earlton, Can. 47°42' N, 79°49' W 94
Earlville, Ill., U.S. 41°34' N, 88°56' W 102
Earnscleugh, N.Z. 45°14' S, 169°18' E 240
Earp, Calif., U.S. 34°9' N, 114°19' W 101
Earth, Tex., U.S. 34°12' N, 102°25' W 92
Easingwold, U.K. 54°7' N, 1°11' W 162
Easley, S.C., U.S. 34°49' N, 82°37' W 96
East Anglia, region, Europe 52°26' N, 0°22' E 162
East Anglian Heights, U.K. 52°23' N, 0°27' E 162
East Angus, Can. 45°28' N, 71°40' W 94
East Antarctica, region, Antarctica 75°20' S, 113°12' E 248
East Arlington, Vt., U.S. 43°3' N, 73°9' W 104
East Aurora, N.Y., U.S. 42°45' N, 78°38' W 94
East Barnet, Vt., U.S. 44°19' N, 72°3' W 104
East Barre, Vt., U.S. 44°9' N, 72°28' W 104
East Base, station, Antarctica 68°4' S, 67°16' W 248
East Bay 28°57' N, 89°18' W 103
East Bay 29°31' N, 94°43' W 103
East Bergholt, U.K. 51°58' N, 1°1' E 162
East Beskids, Pol. 49°28' N, 20°46' E 152
East Brewton, Ala., U.S. 31°4' N, 87°3' W 96
East Bridgewater, Mass., U.S. 42°1' N, 70°58' W 104
East Burke, Vt., U.S. 44°35' N, 71°57' W 104
East Butte, peak, Idaho, U.S. 43°29' N, 112°44' W 90
East Butte, peak, Mont., U.S. 48°50' N, 111°14' W 90
East Caicos, island, U.K. 21°45' N, 71°27' W 116
East Cape, N.Z. 37°42' S, 178°33' E 240
East Cape see Dezhneva, Mys, Russ. 65°45' N, 169°46' W 98
East Caroline Basin, North Pacific Ocean 2°2' N, 146°50' E 252
East Chicago, Ind., U.S. 41°37' N, 87°26' W 102
East China Sea 30°53' N, 125°13' E 190
East Coast Bays, N.Z. 36°45' S, 174°45' E 240
East Corinth, Vt., U.S. 44°3' N, 72°14' W 104
East Cote Blanche Bay 29°31' N, 91°39' W 103
East Coulee, Can. 51°22' N, 112°31' W 90
East Dereham, U.K. 52°40' N, 0°56' E 162
East Dubuque, Mo., U.S. 42°29' N, 90°37' W 94
East Fairview, N. Dak., U.S. 47°50' N, 104°2' W 108
East Falkland, island, Falk. Is., U.K. 51°14' S, 58°25' W 134
East Freetown, Mass., U.S. 41°45' N, 70°58' W 104
East Frisan Islands, North Sea 53°46' N, 7°12' E 163
East Glacier Park, Mont., U.S. 48°25' N, 113°14' W 90
East Govç, adm. division, Mongolia 44°17' N, 108°52' E 198
East Grand Forks, Minn., U.S. 47°55' N, 97°2' W 108
East Greenbush, N.Y., U.S. 42°34' N, 73°43' W 104
East Greenwich, R.I., U.S. 41°39' N, 71°28' W 104
East Grinstead, U.K. 51°7' N, 1°58' W 162
East Hampton, N.Y., U.S. 40°57' N, 72°12' W 104
East Hardwick, Vt., U.S. 44°30' N, 72°19' W 104
East Hartford, Conn., U.S. 41°45' N, 72°39' W 104
East Hartland, Conn., U.S. 41°59' N, 72°55' W 104
East Hebron, N.H., U.S. 43°41' N, 71°47' W 104
East Isaac, island, Bahamas 25°51' N, 78°53' W 105
East Jordan, Mich., U.S. 45°9' N, 85°7' W 94
East Lake, Mich., U.S. 44°14' N, 86°17' W 102
East Lansing, Mich., U.S. 42°44' N, 84°28' W 102
East Las Vegas, Nev., U.S. 36°5' N, 115°3' W 101
East Lempster, N.H., U.S. 43°13' N, 72°11' W 104
East London, S. Af. 32°59' S, 27°52' E 227
East Machias, Me., U.S. 44°44' N, 67°25' W 94
East Mariana Basin, North Pacific Ocean 12°38' N, 151°56' E 252
East Marion, N.Y., U.S. 41°7' N, 72°21' W 104
East Montpelier, Vt., U.S. 44°16' N, 72°30' W 104
East Mountain, Oreg., U.S. 44°59' N, 122°14' W 90
East Mountain, Vt., U.S. 44°38' N, 71°51' W 94
East Naples, Fla., U.S. 26°6' N, 81°46' W 105
East Pacific Rise, South Pacific Ocean 25°9' S, 113°45' W 252
East Palatka, Fla., U.S. 29°38' N, 81°36' W 105
East Pepperell, Mass., U.S. 42°39' N, 71°35' W 104
East Pine, Can. 55°42' N, 121°12' W 108
East Point, Can. 44°2' N, 60°9' W 111
East Point, Can. 51°21' N, 80°2' W 110
East Point, Can. 46°29' N, 62°3' W 111
East Prairie, Mo., U.S. 36°46' N, 89°23' W 94
East Providence, R.I., U.S. 41°49' N, 71°23' W 104
East Quogue, N.Y., U.S. 40°50' N, 72°36' W 104
East Range, Nev., U.S. 40°40' N, 118°1' W 90
East Retford, U.K. 53°19' N, 0°57' E 162
East Ridge, Tenn., U.S. 34°59' N, 85°14' W 96
East Saint Johnsbury, Vt., U.S. 44°26' N, 71°58' W 104
East Saint Louis, Mo., U.S. 38°36' N, 90°8' W 94
East Sea see Japan, Sea of 39°9' N, 128°12' E 200
East Sebago, Me., U.S. 43°50' N, 70°39' W 104
East Siberian Sea 72°23' N, 162°36' E 246
East Springfield, Pa., U.S. 41°57' N, 80°25' W 94
East Stoneham, Me., U.S. 44°15' N, 70°50' W 104
East Sullivan, N.H., U.S. 42°59' N, 72°13' W 104
East Tasman Plateau, Tasman Sea 43°59' S, 150°40' E 252
East Tavaputs Plateau, Utah, U.S. 39°28' N, 110°1' W 90
East Templeton, Mass., U.S. 42°33' N, 72°3' W 104
East Thetford, Vt., U.S. 43°48' N, 72°12' W 104
East Timor see Timor-Leste 9°0' S, 125°0' E 192
East Topsham, Vt., U.S. 44°7' N, 72°15' W 104
East Troy, Wis., U.S. 42°47' N, 88°24' W 102
East Wallingford, Vt., U.S. 43°26' N, 72°54' W 104
Eastbourne, U.K. 50°46' N, 0°16' E 162
Eastend, Can. 49°29' N, 108°50' W 90
Easter Fracture Zone, South Pacific Ocean 22°42' S, 111°2' W 252
Easter Group, islands, Indian Ocean 28°53' S, 111°18' E 230
Easter Island (Pascua, Isla de), Chile 27°0' S, 109°0' W 241
Eastern, adm. division, Mongolia 47°33' N, 114°13' E 198
Eastern Cape, adm. division, S. Af. 31°43' S, 25°38' E 227
Eastern Desert, Africa 30°44' N, 32°4' E 194
Eastern Equatoria, adm. division, Sudan 5°14' N, 32°41' E 218
Eastern Ghats, Asia 20°12' N, 83°44' E 188
Eastern Group, islands, Great Australian Bight 34°17' S, 124°9' E 230
Eastern Point, Mass., U.S. 42°31' N, 70°41' W 104
Easterville, Can. 53°3' N, 99°40' W 108
Eastford, Conn., U.S. 41°53' N, 72°5' W 104
Eastham, Mass., U.S. 41°50' N, 69°59' W 104
Easthampton, Mass., U.S. 42°15' N, 72°41' W 104
Eastlake, Ohio, U.S. 41°38' N, 81°27' W 102
Eastleigh, U.K. 50°58' N, 1°22' W 162
Eastmain, Can. 52°10' N, 78°33' W 106
Eastmain, river, Can. 51°58' N, 73°51' W 110
Eastmain Un, Réservoir de, lake, Can. 51°56' N, 77°4' W 110
Eastman, Ga., U.S. 32°11' N, 83°11' W 96
Easton, Calif., U.S. 36°38' N, 119°48' W 100
Easton, Conn., U.S. 41°14' N, 73°19' W 104
Easton, Ill., U.S. 40°13' N, 89°51' W 102
Easton, Md., U.S. 38°46' N, 76°4' W 94
Easton, Pa., U.S. 40°41' N, 75°14' W 94
Easton, Wash., U.S. 47°12' N, 121°12' W 100
Eastpoint, Fla., U.S. 29°45' N, 84°52' W 96
Eastport, Me., U.S. 44°54' N, 67°0' W 94
Eastport, N.Y., U.S. 40°49' N, 72°44' W 104
Eastsound, Wash., U.S. 48°41' N, 122°55' W 100
Eaton, Colo., U.S. 40°31' N, 104°44' W 90
Eaton, Ohio, U.S. 39°44' N, 84°38' W 102
Eaton Rapids, Mich., U.S. 42°31' N, 84°40' W 102
Eatonia, Can. 51°13' N, 109°23' W 90
Eatonton, Ga., U.S. 33°18' N, 83°24' W 96
Eatonville, Wash., U.S. 46°50' N, 122°17' W 100
Eau Claire, Wis., U.S. 44°48' N, 91°29' W 94
Eau Claire, Lac à l', lake, Can. 55°52' N, 76°46' W 106
Eau Froide, Lac à l', lake, Can. 50°49' N, 73°17' W 110
Eau Jaune, Lac à l', lake, Can. 49°39' N, 75°29' W 94
Eauripik Atoll, F.S.M. 6°41' N, 140°4' E 192
Eauze, Fr. 43°51' N, 0°5' E 150
Eaval, peak, U.K. 57°30' N, 7°16' W 150
Ébano, Mex. 22°11' N, 98°23' W 114
Ebbetts Pass, Calif., U.S. 38°33' N, 119°49' W 100
Ebbw Vale, U.K. 51°46' N, 3°13' W 162
Ebenezer, Miss., U.S. 32°57' N, 90°6' W 103
Ebeyti, Kaz. 48°9' N, 55°24' E 158
Ebino, Japan 32°3' N, 130°49' E 201
Ebinur Hu, lake, China 44°41' N, 82°37' E 184
Eboda see 'Abda, ruin(s), Israel 30°47' N, 34°43' E 194
Ebola, river, Dem. Rep. of the Congo 3°31' N, 21°25' E 218
Ebolowa, Cameroon 2°57' N, 11°7' E 218
Ebro, Embalse del, lake, Sp. 43°2' N, 4°7' W 164
Ebro, river, Sp. 42°42' N, 3°23' W 164
Ebruchorr, Gora, Russ. 67°43' N, 31°55' E 152
Ecbatana see Hamadān, Iran 34°48' N, 48°27' E 180
Eccleshall, U.K. 52°50' N, 2°15' W 162
Eceabat, Turk. 40°11' N, 26°19' E 156
Echallens, Switz. 46°38' N, 6°38' E 167
Echarate, Peru 12°46' S, 72°35' W 137
Echizen Misaki, Japan 35°53' N, 135°42' E 201
Echkill-Tash, Kyrg. 42°20' N, 79°25' E 184
Echo Bay, Can. 66°5' N, 117°54' W 106
Echo Bay, Can. 46°29' N, 84°4' W 94
Echo Cliffs, Ariz., U.S. 36°28' N, 111°36' W 92
Echo Summit, pass, Calif., U.S. 38°48' N, 120°3' W 90
Echternach, Lux. 49°48' N, 6°25' E 167
Echuca, Austral. 36°8' S, 144°48' E 231
Écija, Sp. 37°32' N, 5°5' W 164
Eckerö, Fin. 60°12' N, 19°36' E 166
Écommoy, Fr. 47°49' N, 0°16' E 150
Ecoporanga, Braz. 18°25' S, 40°53' W 138
Écorce, Lac de l', lake, Can. 47°0' N, 77°17' W 94
Ecrins National Park, Fr. 44°44' N, 6°21' E 167
Ecuador 1°33' S, 78°58' W 130
Ecueillé, Fr. 47°4' N, 1°20' E 150
Ed, Nor. 58°54' N, 11°54' E 152
Ed Da'ein, Sudan 11°25' N, 26°7' E 216
Ed Damazin, Sudan 11°49' N, 34°18' E 182
Ed Damer, Sudan 17°31' N, 34°0' E 182
Ed Debba, Sudan 18°0' N, 30°57' E 226
Ed Dueim, Sudan 13°56' N, 32°18' E 182
Edam, Can. 53°11' N, 108°45' W 108
Edberg, Can. 52°46' N, 112°47' W 108
Edd, Eritrea 13°55' N, 41°36' E 182
Eddiceton, Miss., U.S. 31°30' N, 90°48' W 103
Eddontenajon, Can. 57°47' N, 129°56' W 108
Eddy, Mount, Calif., U.S. 41°18' N, 122°35' W 90
Eddystone Rocks, islands, English Channel 50°15' N, 5°13' W 150
Eddyville, Ky., U.S. 37°5' N, 88°6' W 96
Ede, Neth. 52°2' N, 5°39' E 167
Edéa, Cameroon 3°47' N, 10°9' E 222
Edehon Lake, Can. 60°25' N, 97°45' W 108
Eden, Can. 42°46' N, 80°44' W 102
Eden, Miss., U.S. 32°58' N, 90°21' W 103
Eden, N.C., U.S. 36°30' N, 79°47' W 96

Eden, *Tex., U.S.* 31°11' N, 99°51' W **92**
Eden, *Wyo., U.S.* 42°3' N, 109°26' W **90**
Eden, river, *U.K.* 54°47' N, 2°49' W **162**
Edenburg, *S. Af.* 29°46' S, 25°55' E **227**
Edenton, *N.C., U.S.* 36°3' N, 76°38' W **96**
Edessa see Şanlıurfa, *Turk.* 37°6' N, 38°45' E **180**
Edewecht, *Ger.* 53°7' N, 7°59' E **163**
Edgar, *Nebr., U.S.* 40°21' N, 97°59' W **90**
Edgecomb, *Me., U.S.* 43°57' N, 69°38' W **104**
Edgeley, *N. Dak., U.S.* 46°20' N, 98°44' W **90**
Edgell Island, *Can.* 61°45' N, 64°46' W **106**
Edgemont, *S. Dak., U.S.* 43°18' N, 103°49' W **90**
Edgeøya, island, *Nor.* 77°32' N, 25°31' E **160**
Edgerly, *La., U.S.* 30°13' N, 93°31' W **103**
Edgerton, *Can.* 52°43' N, 110°27' W **108**
Edgerton, *Minn., U.S.* 43°51' N, 96°8' W **90**
Edgerton, *Wis., U.S.* 42°49' N, 89°5' W **110**
Edgerton, *Wyo., U.S.* 43°24' N, 106°13' W **90**
Edgewater, *Fla., U.S.* 28°58' N, 80°54' W **105**
Edgewood, *Ill., U.S.* 38°55' N, 88°40' W **102**
Edgeworthstown see Mostrim, *Ire.* 53°41' N, 7°38' W **150**
Edievale, *N.Z.* 45°48' S, 169°23' E **240**
Edigueri, spring, *Chad* 19°54' N, 15°54' E **216**
Edina, *Mo., U.S.* 40°9' N, 92°10' W **94**
Edinburg, *Miss., U.S.* 32°47' N, 89°21' W **103**
Edinburgh, *Ind., U.S.* 39°21' N, 85°58' W **102**
Edinburgh, *U.K.* 55°55' N, 3°22' W **150**
Edirne (Adrianople), *Turk.* 41°39' N, 26°34' E **156**
Edison, *Calif., U.S.* 35°21' N, 118°53' W **101**
Edison, *Ga., U.S.* 31°32' N, 84°44' W **96**
Edison, *N.J., U.S.* 40°30' N, 74°26' W **94**
Edison, *Wash., U.S.* 48°32' N, 122°27' W **100**
Edith Cavell, Mount, *Can.* 52°39' N, 118°8' W **108**
Edith, Mount, *Mont., U.S.* 46°23' N, 111°15' W **90**
Edjeleh, oil field, *Alg.* 27°49' N, 9°44' E **214**
Edmond, *Okla., U.S.* 35°37' N, 97°29' W **96**
Edmonds, *Wash., U.S.* 47°47' N, 122°22' W **100**
Edmonton, *Can.* 53°33' N, 113°39' W **108**
Edmore, *Mich., U.S.* 43°24' N, 85°3' W **102**
Edmore, *N. Dak., U.S.* 48°23' N, 98°28' W **90**
Edmundston, *Can.* 47°22' N, 68°19' W **94**
Edna, *Tex., U.S.* 28°58' N, 96°38' W **96**
Edna Bay, *Alas., U.S.* 55°57' N, 133°40' W **108**
Edolo, *It.* 46°11' N, 10°20' E **167**
Edough, Djebel, *Alg.* 36°57' N, 6°55' E **150**
Edøy, *Nor.* 63°19' N, 8°2' E **152**
Edrei see Dar'ā, *Syr.* 32°37' N, 36°6' E **194**
Edremit, *Turk.* 39°34' N, 27°0' E **156**
Edrengiyn Nuruu, *Mongolia* 44°49' N, 97°6' E **190**
Edson, *Can.* 53°35' N, 116°27' W **108**
Edsvalla, *Nor.* 59°26' N, 13°8' E **152**
Eduardo Castex, *Arg.* 35°54' S, 64°18' W **134**
Edward, Mount, *Antarctica* 75°6' S, 70°29' W **248**
Edwards, *Calif., U.S.* 34°56' N, 117°56' W **101**
Edwards, *Miss., U.S.* 32°18' N, 90°36' W **103**
Edwards Air Force Base, *Calif., U.S.* 34°54' N, 117°56' W **101**
Edwards Plateau, *Tex., U.S.* 30°39' N, 101°4' W **92**
Edwardsport, *Ind., U.S.* 38°48' N, 87°16' W **102**
Edwardsville, *Ill., U.S.* 38°48' N, 89°58' W **102**
Edziza, Mount, *Can.* 57°41' N, 130°45' W **108**
Edzná, ruin(s), *Mex.* 19°33' N, 90°23' W **115**
Eede, *Neth.* 51°15' N, 3°27' E **163**
Eeklo, *Belg.* 51°11' N, 3°33' E **163**
Eel, river, *Ind., U.S.* 39°21' N, 87°6' W **102**
Effie, *La., U.S.* 31°11' N, 92°10' W **103**
Effingham, *Ill., U.S.* 39°6' N, 88°32' W **102**
Eflâni, *Turk.* 41°25' N, 32°57' E **156**
Eg, *Mongolia* 48°49' N, 110°5' E **198**
Egadi, Isole, islands, *Tyrrhenian Sea* 37°48' N, 11°13' E **156**
Egalah, Adrar, peak, *Niger* 18°9' N, 8°32' E **222**
Egan Range, *Nev., U.S.* 39°49' N, 115°8' W **90**
Eganville, *Can.* 45°32' N, 77°6' W **94**
Egedesminde see Aasiaat, *Den.* 68°45' N, 52°53' W **106**
Egenolf Lake, *Can.* 59°2' N, 100°32' W **108**
Eger, *Hung.* 47°53' N, 20°22' E **168**
Egeria Fracture Zone, *Indian Ocean* 19°30' S, 68°2' E **254**
Egersund, *Nor.* 58°26' N, 6°0' E **150**
Egg Lake, *Can.* 54°58' N, 106°50' W **108**
Egg, river, *Can.* 59°58' N, 95°33' W **108**
Eggan, *Nig.* 8°39' N, 6°13' E **222**
Eggebek, *Ger.* 54°38' N, 9°22' E **150**
Eggenburg, *Aust.* 48°38' N, 15°49' E **152**
Éghezée, *Belg.* 50°35' N, 4°53' E **167**
Eğil, *Turk.* 38°15' N, 40°5' E **195**
Egindibulaq, *Kaz.* 49°49' N, 76°26' E **184**
Egindiköl, *Kaz.* 51°3' N, 69°31' E **184**
Égio, *Gr.* 38°12' N, 22°6' E **180**
Eglinton Island, *Can.* 75°24' N, 126°46' W **106**
Eglon, ruin(s), *Israel* 31°31' N, 34°41' E **194**
Egmont Islands, *Indian Ocean* 7°21' S, 70°31' E **188**
Egmont, Mount see Taranaki, Mount, peak, *N.Z.* 39°20' S, 173°58' E **240**
Egremont, *U.K.* 54°28' N, 3°32' W **162**
Eğridir, *Turk.* 37°50' N, 30°49' E **156**
Eğridir Gölü, lake, *Turk.* 38°5' N, 30°11' E **180**
Eğrigöz Dağı, peak, *Turk.* 39°23' N, 29°2' E **156**
Éguas (Correntina), river, *Braz.* 13°42' S, 45°43' W **138**
Egvekinot, *Russ.* 66°17' N, 179°1' W **160**
Egyek, *Hung.* 47°38' N, 20°52' E **168**
Egypt 26°46' N, 27°58' E **216**
Ehime, adm. division, *Japan* 33°37' N, 132°38' E **201**
Ehingen, *Ger.* 48°16' N, 9°44' E **152**
Ehrang, *Ger.* 49°48' N, 6°41' E **167**
Ehrenberg, *Ger.* 50°30' N, 9°59' E **167**
Ei, *Japan* 31°12' N, 130°30' E **201**
Eide, *Nor.* 62°53' N, 7°26' E **152**
Eiderdamm, *Ger.* 54°14' N, 7°58' E **150**
Eidsbugarden, *Nor.* 61°22' N, 8°15' E **152**
Eidskog, *Nor.* 60°1' N, 12°6' E **152**
Eidsvoll, *Nor.* 60°19' N, 11°12' E **152**
Eifel, region, *Europe* 50°38' N, 7°3' E **167**
Eige, Càrn, peak, *U.K.* 57°16' N, 5°13' W **150**
Eigerøy, region, *North Sea* 58°25' N, 5°35' E **150**
Eight Degree Channel 7°30' N, 71°39' E **188**
Eight Mile Rock, *Bahamas* 26°31' N, 78°47' W **105**
Eighty Mile Beach, *Austral.* 20°6' S, 119°49' E **231**
Eil Malk see Mecherchar, island, *Palau* 7°7' N, 134°22' E **242**
Eilendorf, *Ger.* 50°46' N, 6°10' E **167**
Eiler Rasmussen, Cape, *Den.* 81°2' N, 11°2' W **246**
Eiler Rasmussen, Kap, *Den.* 82°38' N, 19°35' W **246**
Eilerts de Haan Gebergte, *Suriname* 2°50' N, 56°17' W **130**
Eina, *Nor.* 60°38' N, 10°35' E **152**
Eindhoven, *Neth.* 51°26' N, 5°28' E **167**
Eion, ruin(s), *Gr.* 40°46' N, 23°46' E **156**
Eirik Ridge, *North Atlantic Ocean* 57°47' N, 44°35' W **253**
Eirunepé, *Braz.* 6°40' S, 69°55' W **130**
Eisenach, *Ger.* 50°58' N, 10°19' E **167**
Eisenstadt, *Aust.* 47°50' N, 16°31' E **168**
Eišiškės, *Lith.* 54°10' N, 24°58' E **166**
Eitorf, *Ger.* 50°45' N, 7°27' E **167**
Eivissa, *Sp.* 38°53' N, 1°25' E **150**
Eixe, Sierra do, *Sp.* 42°16' N, 7°23' W **150**
Ejea de los Caballeros, *Sp.* 42°7' N, 1°10' W **164**
Ejeda, *Madagascar* 24°20' S, 44°30' E **220**
Ejin Horo Qi (Altan Xiret), *China* 39°33' N, 109°44' E **198**
Ejin Qi, *China* 42°1' N, 101°30' E **190**
Ejouj, spring, *Mauritania* 17°1' N, 9°23' W **222**
Ejura, *Ghana* 7°25' N, 1°24' W **222**
Ekalaka, *Mont., U.S.* 45°52' N, 104°34' W **90**
Ekenäs (Tammisaari), *Fin.* 59°58' N, 23°26' E **166**
Ekerem, *Turkm.* 38°5' N, 53°50' E **180**
Ekeren, *Belg.* 51°16' N, 4°25' E **163**
Eket, *Nig.* 4°39' N, 7°56' E **222**
Ekibastuz, *Kaz.* 51°44' N, 75°19' E **184**
Ekkerøy, *Nor.* 70°4' N, 30°8' E **152**
Eklund Islands, *Bellingshausen Sea* 73°25' S, 70°57' W **248**
Ekoli, *Dem. Rep. of the Congo* 0°25' N, 24°16' E **224**
Ekombe, *Dem. Rep. of the Congo* 1°8' N, 21°32' E **218**
Ekonda, *Russ.* 66°5' N, 103°55' E **160**
Ekrafane, *Niger* 15°21' N, 3°43' E **222**
Ekukola, *Dem. Rep. of the Congo* 0°30' N, 18°53' E **218**
Ekwan, river, *Can.* 53°36' N, 84°16' W **106**
Ekwendeni, *Malawi* 11°23' S, 33°48' E **224**
El Abiadh, Ras, *Tun.* 37°16' N, 9°8' E **156**
Ēl Ābrēd, *Eth.* 5°30' N, 45°14' E **218**
El Adeb Larache, oil field, *Alg.* 27°23' N, 8°44' E **214**
El Agreb, oil field, *Alg.* 30°37' N, 5°30' E **214**
El Aïoun, *Mor.* 34°35' N, 2°29' W **214**
El 'Aiyaẓ, *Egypt* 29°37' N, 31°12' E **180**
El 'Alamein, *Egypt* 30°49' N, 28°52' E **180**
El Álamo, *Mex.* 31°32' N, 116°1' W **92**
El 'Âmirîya, *Egypt* 31°1' N, 29°48' E **180**
El Angel, *Ecua.* 0°36' N, 78°7' W **136**
El 'Arag, spring, *Egypt* 28°53' N, 26°27' E **180**
El Aricha, *Alg.* 34°13' N, 1°16' W **214**
El 'Arîsh (Rhinocolura), *Egypt* 31°6' N, 33°46' E **194**
El Arneb, spring, *Mali* 16°19' N, 4°55' W **222**
El Atimine, spring, *Alg.* 28°51' N, 3°9' W **214**
El Badâri, *Egypt* 27°1' N, 31°23' E **180**
El Bagre, *Col.* 7°36' N, 74°47' W **136**
El Bah, *Eth.* 9°44' N, 41°47' E **224**
El Bahrein, spring, *Egypt* 28°41' N, 26°30' E **180**
El Ballâh, *Egypt* 30°45' N, 32°17' E **194**
El Ballestero, *Sp.* 38°50' N, 2°28' W **164**
El Balyana, *Egypt* 26°14' N, 31°55' E **180**
El Banco, *Col.* 9°1' N, 73°58' W **136**
El Bauga, *Sudan* 18°13' N, 33°52' E **182**
El Baúl, *Venez.* 8°56' N, 68°20' W **136**
El Bayadh, *Alg.* 33°42' N, 1°0' E **214**
El Béoua, spring, *Mali* 15°6' N, 6°25' W **222**
El Berié, spring, *Mauritania* 16°11' N, 9°57' W **222**
El Beru Hagia, *Somalia* 2°47' N, 41°3' E **224**
El Beyed, spring, *Mauritania* 16°55' N, 10°3' W **222**
El Bher, spring, *Mauritania* 15°59' N, 8°42' W **222**
El Biar, *Alg.* 36°44' N, 3°1' E **150**
El Bonillo, *Sp.* 38°57' N, 2°33' W **164**
El Borma, oil field, *Tun.* 31°36' N, 9°9' E **214**
El Bosque, *Sp.* 36°45' N, 5°31' W **164**
El Burgo de Osma, *Sp.* 41°35' N, 3°4' W **164**
El Cabo de Gata, *Sp.* 36°46' N, 2°15' W **164**
El Caburé, *Arg.* 26°2' S, 62°21' W **139**
El Caín, *Arg.* 41°37' S, 68°16' W **134**
El Calafate (Lago Argentino), *Arg.* 50°26' S, 72°13' W **123**
El Callao, *Venez.* 7°22' N, 61°49' W **130**
El Calvario, *Venez.* 9°0' N, 66°59' W **136**
El Campello, *Sp.* 38°25' N, 0°24' E **164**
El Campillo de la Jara, *Sp.* 39°35' N, 5°3' W **164**
El Campo, *Tex., U.S.* 29°11' N, 96°17' W **96**
El Cap, *Egypt* 30°56' N, 32°17' E **194**
El Capitan, peak, *Mont., U.S.* 45°59' N, 114°29' W **90**
El Carmen, *Arg.* 24°24' S, 65°18' W **132**
El Carmen, *Bol.* 18°49' S, 58°35' W **132**
El Carmen, *Bol.* 14°0' S, 63°41' W **137**
El Carmen, *Col.* 5°55' N, 76°14' W **136**
El Carmen, *Venez.* 1°15' N, 66°50' W **136**
El Carpio, *Sp.* 37°56' N, 4°31' W **164**
El Castillo de Las Concepción, *Nicar.* 10°58' N, 84°24' W **115**
El Ceibo, *Guatemala* 17°16' N, 90°55' W **115**
El Centro, *Calif., U.S.* 32°47' N, 115°34' W **101**
El Chichón, peak, *Mex.* 17°21' N, 93°23' W **115**
El Chico, *Mex.* 20°8' N, 98°54' W **112**
El Choro, *Bol.* 18°24' S, 67°9' W **137**
El Cimaterio, *Mex.* 20°29' N, 100°27' W **112**
El Claro, *Mex.* 30°28' N, 111°11' W **92**
El Cocuy, *Col.* 6°24' N, 72°28' W **136**
El Cocuy National Park, *Col.* 6°35' N, 72°43' W **136**
El Cogoi, *Arg.* 24°48' S, 59°12' W **132**
El Colorado, *Arg.* 26°18' S, 59°23' W **139**
El Corcovado, *Arg.* 43°30' S, 71°32' W **134**
El Cuyo, *Mex.* 21°32' N, 87°42' W **116**
El 'Dab'a, *Egypt* 31°1' N, 28°23' E **180**
El Dakka, ruin(s), *Egypt* 23°4' N, 32°32' E **182**
El Deir, *Egypt* 25°19' N, 32°33' E **182**
El Descanso, *Mex.* 32°12' N, 116°54' W **92**
El Desemboque, *Mex.* 29°33' N, 112°26' W **92**
El Desmonte, *Arg.* 22°42' S, 62°17' W **132**
El Djouf, *Mauritania* 19°53' N, 10°5' W **222**
El Dorado, *Ark., U.S.* 33°11' N, 92°41' W **103**
El Dorado, *Kans., U.S.* 37°47' N, 96°52' W **92**
El Dorado, *Venez.* 6°43' N, 61°36' W **130**
El Dorado Springs, *Mo., U.S.* 37°51' N, 94°2' W **94**
El Egder, spring, *Eth.* 3°51' N, 38°54' E **224**
El Eglab, region, *Africa* 25°45' N, 5°58' W **214**
El Encanto, *Col.* 1°38' S, 73°14' W **136**
El Esfuerzo, *Mex.* 25°23' N, 103°15' W **114**
El Faiyûm, *Egypt* 29°16' N, 30°48' E **180**
El Farâid, Gebel, peak, *Egypt* 23°31' N, 35°19' E **182**
El Fasher, *Sudan* 13°37' N, 25°19' E **226**
El Fashn, *Egypt* 28°48' N, 30°50' E **180**
El Fifi, *Sudan* 10°3' N, 25°1' E **224**
El Fuerte, *Mex.* 23°49' N, 103°8' W **114**
El Fula, *Sudan* 11°46' N, 28°20' E **216**
El Gâga, *Egypt* 24°48' N, 30°30' E **226**
El Gallego, *Mex.* 29°48' N, 106°23' W **92**
El Galpón, *Arg.* 25°24' S, 64°39' W **134**
El Gassi, oil field, *Alg.* 30°53' N, 5°37' E **214**
El Geili, *Sudan* 16°0' N, 32°37' E **182**
El Gezira, region, *Africa* 14°22' N, 32°15' E **182**
El Ghobena, *Tun.* 35°29' N, 9°38' E **156**
El Gîza, *Egypt* 30°1' N, 31°8' E **180**
El Golea, *Alg.* 30°33' N, 2°43' E **207**
El Goled Bahri, *Sudan* 18°27' N, 30°40' E **226**
El Golfo de Santa Clara, *Mex.* 31°41' N, 114°32' W **92**
El Grau, *Sp.* 38°59' N, 0°10' E **164**
El Grau de Castelló, *Sp.* 39°58' N, 2°0' E **164**
El Grullo, *Mex.* 19°48' N, 104°14' W **114**
El Guapo, *Venez.* 10°8' N, 66°2' W **136**
El Hadjira, *Alg.* 32°37' N, 5°31' E **214**
El Hajeb, *Mor.* 33°41' N, 5°25' W **214**
El Hamma, *Tun.* 33°55' N, 9°48' E **216**
El Ḥammâm, *Egypt* 30°51' N, 29°19' E **180**
El Hank, region, *Africa* 24°58' N, 6°26' W **214**
El Haouaria, *Tun.* 37°3' N, 11°0' E **156**
El Haraïg, *Tun.* 35°47' N, 9°13' E **156**
El Harrach, *Alg.* 36°48' N, 3°9' E **214**
El Hasaheisa, *Sudan* 14°41' N, 33°17' E **182**
El Hawata, *Sudan* 13°24' N, 34°36' E **182**
El Ḥeiz, *Egypt* 28°2' N, 28°37' E **180**
El Hiaïda, *Mor.* 35°5' N, 6°11' W **150**
El Higo, *Mex.* 21°45' N, 98°27' W **114**
El Hilla, *Sudan* 13°24' N, 27°5' E **226**
El Hobra, *Alg.* 32°10' N, 4°43' E **214**
El Homeur, *Alg.* 29°52' N, 1°36' E **214**
El Huariche, *Mex.* 24°49' N, 103°9' W **114**
El Iskandarîya (Alexandria), *Egypt* 31°10' N, 29°55' E **180**
El Jabha (Puerto Capaz), *Mor.* 35°12' N, 4°40' W **150**
El Jadida (Mazagan), *Mor.* 33°15' N, 8°33' W **214**
El Jardín, *Sp.* 38°48' N, 2°19' W **164**
El Jebelein, *Sudan* 12°34' N, 32°52' E **182**
El Jemm, *Tun.* 35°18' N, 10°43' E **156**
El Kanâyis, spring, *Egypt* 25°0' N, 33°16' E **182**
El Karaba, *Sudan* 18°29' N, 33°44' E **182**
El Karnak, ruin(s), *Egypt* 25°44' N, 32°37' E **182**
El Katulo, spring, *Kenya* 2°26' N, 40°35' E **224**
El Kawa, *Sudan* 13°42' N, 32°31' E **182**
El Kef, *Tun.* 36°11' N, 8°42' E **156**
El Kelaa des Srarhna, *Mor.* 32°5' N, 7°25' W **214**
Ēl Kerē, *Eth.* 5°48' N, 42°9' E **224**
El Khandaq, *Sudan* 18°36' N, 30°34' E **226**
El Khârga, *Egypt* 25°28' N, 30°29' E **182**
El Kharrouba, *Tun.* 35°23' N, 9°59' E **156**
El Khnâchîch, *Mali* 21°6' N, 5°26' W **222**
El Kodab, *Sudan* 16°12' N, 32°30' E **182**
El Koin, *Sudan* 19°18' N, 30°33' E **216**
El Kseïbat, *Alg.* 27°58' N, 0°30' E **214**
El Kseur, *Alg.* 36°40' N, 4°51' E **150**
El Ksiba, *Mor.* 32°38' N, 6°3' W **214**
El Kuntilla, *Egypt* 29°58' N, 34°41' E **180**
El Lagowa, *Sudan* 11°25' N, 29°8' E **216**
El Lein, spring, *Kenya* 0°26' N, 40°30' E **224**
El Leiya, *Sudan* 16°15' N, 35°26' E **182**
El Limón, *Mex.* 22°48' N, 99°1' W **114**
El Lucero, *Mex.* 25°56' N, 103°26' W **114**
El Macao, *Dom. Rep.* 18°45' N, 68°31' W **116**
El Mahalla el Kubra, *Egypt* 30°59' N, 31°8' E **226**
El Mahârîq, *Egypt* 25°39' N, 30°36' E **226**
El Mahfoura, spring, *Alg.* 32°34' N, 2°12' E **214**
El Maitén, *Arg.* 42°3' S, 71°11' W **134**
El Maïz, *Alg.* 28°25' N, 0°15' E **214**
El Malpais National Monument, *N. Mex., U.S.* 34°36' N, 110°21' W **92**
El Manaqil, *Sudan* 14°12' N, 33°0' E **182**
El Mango, *Venez.* 1°54' N, 66°33' W **136**
El Manshâh, *Egypt* 26°29' N, 31°42' E **180**
El Mansour, *Alg.* 27°38' N, 0°19' E **214**
El Manṣûra, *Egypt* 30°58' N, 31°24' E **180**
El Maqdaba, spring, *Egypt* 30°53' N, 34°0' E **194**
El Mazâr, *Egypt* 31°1' N, 33°23' E **194**
El Medda, *Mauritania* 19°56' N, 13°20' W **222**
El Meghaïer, *Alg.* 33°56' N, 5°54' E **214**
El Melemm, *Sudan* 9°55' N, 28°43' E **224**
El Messir, spring, *Chad* 15°43' N, 16°59' E **216**
El Mhabes, spring, *Mauritania* 23°43' N, 8°53' W **214**
El Milagro, *Arg.* 31°1' S, 65°59' W **134**
El Milhas, spring, *Mauritania* 25°25' N, 6°55' W **214**
El Milia, *Alg.* 36°48' N, 6°16' E **150**
El Mina, *Leb.* 34°27' N, 35°49' E **194**
El Mîna, *Leb.* 34°27' N, 35°49' E **156**
El Minya, *Egypt* 28°7' N, 30°41' E **180**
El Mirador, ruin(s), *Guatemala* 17°43' N, 90°3' W **115**
El Mirage, *Ariz., U.S.* 33°37' N, 112°19' W **92**
El Moale, spring, *Sudan* 10°20' N, 23°46' E **224**
El Moïnane, spring, *Mauritania* 19°10' N, 11°29' W **222**
El Morro National Monument, *N. Mex., U.S.* 35°1' N, 108°26' W **92**
El Moueïla, *Mauritania* 21°38' N, 10°36' W **222**
El Mouilha, spring, *Mali* 16°40' N, 5°6' W **222**
El Mraïti, spring, *Mali* 19°12' N, 2°19' W **222**
El Mrâyer, spring, *Mauritania* 21°28' N, 8°12' W **222**
El Mreïti, spring, *Mauritania* 23°29' N, 7°56' W **214**
El Mreyyé, region, *Africa* 18°48' N, 8°16' W **222**
El Mughâzî, *Gaza Strip, Israel* 31°23' N, 34°22' E **194**
El Mulato, *Mex.* 29°22' N, 104°11' W **92**
El Mzereb, spring, *Mali* 24°46' N, 6°23' W **214**
El Nasser, *Egypt* 24°34' N, 33°2' E **182**
El Nayar, *Mex.* 23°55' N, 104°41' W **114**
El Nido, *Philippines* 11°10' N, 119°24' E **203**
El Niybo, *Eth.* 4°31' N, 39°54' E **224**
El Obeid, *Sudan* 13°8' N, 30°11' E **226**
El Oro, *Mex.* 19°46' N, 100°8' W **114**
El Oualadji, *Mali* 16°13' N, 3°28' W **214**
El Palmito, *Mex.* 25°35' N, 104°59' W **114**
El Pao, *Venez.* 8°1' N, 62°38' W **130**
El Pao, *Venez.* 8°46' N, 64°39' W **116**
El Paso, *Ill., U.S.* 40°43' N, 89°1' W **102**
El Paso, *Tex., U.S.* 31°45' N, 106°29' W **92**
El Paso Mountains, *Calif., U.S.* 35°23' N, 117°59' W **101**
El Payo, *Sp.* 40°18' N, 6°45' W **150**
El Perelló, *Sp.* 40°52' N, 0°43' E **164**
El Perú, *Venez.* 7°18' N, 61°50' W **130**
El Pescadero, *Mex.* 23°20' N, 110°11' W **112**
El Picazo, *Sp.* 39°26' N, 2°7' W **164**
El Piñal, *Venez.* 7°26' N, 68°41' W **136**
El Plomo, *Mex.* 31°14' N, 112°4' W **92**
El Pobo de Dueñas, *Sp.* 40°45' N, 1°39' W **164**
El Pont de Suert, *Sp.* 42°23' N, 0°44' E **164**
El Portal, *Calif., U.S.* 37°41' N, 119°48' W **100**
El Portezuelo, *Arg.* 46°2' S, 71°38' W **134**
El Porvenir, *Col.* 4°42' N, 71°23' W **136**
El Porvenir, *Pan.* 9°34' N, 78°59' W **115**
El Porvenir, *Venez.* 6°56' N, 68°43' W **136**
El Potosí, *Mex.* 24°50' N, 100°20' W **114**
El Potosí National Park, *Mex.* 21°58' N, 100°4' W **112**
El Pozo, *Mex.* 30°55' N, 109°16' W **92**
El Pozo, *Mex.* 24°54' N, 107°15' W **112**
El Progreso, *Hond.* 15°21' N, 87°48' W **115**
El Pueblito, *Mex.* 29°5' N, 105°8' W **92**
El Puente, *Bol.* 21°14' S, 65°19' W **137**
El Qâhira (Cairo), *Egypt* 30°3' N, 31°8' E **180**
El Qanṭara, *Egypt* 30°51' N, 32°19' E **194**
El Qaṣr, *Egypt* 25°42' N, 28°50' E **180**
El Quseima, *Egypt* 30°39' N, 34°22' E **194**
El Râshda, *Egypt* 25°33' N, 28°54' E **226**
El Real, *Pan.* 8°6' N, 77°45' W **115**
El Reno, *Okla., U.S.* 35°30' N, 97°57' W **92**
El Rhaïlassiya Oumm Amoura, spring, *Mauritania* 16°26' N, 9°24' W **222**
El Rio, *Calif., U.S.* 34°14' N, 119°11' W **101**
El Rito, *N. Mex., U.S.* 36°21' N, 106°12' W **92**
El Roble, *Mex.* 23°13' N, 106°14' W **114**
El Ronquillo, *Sp.* 37°43' N, 6°11' W **164**
El Rosario, *Mex.* 30°4' N, 115°46' W **92**
El Ruâfa, spring, *Egypt* 30°49' N, 34°7' E **194**
El Rubio, *Sp.* 37°21' N, 5°0' W **164**
El Rucio, *Mex.* 23°23' N, 102°4' W **114**
El Rusbayo, *Mex.* 31°1' N, 109°15' W **92**
El Sabinal National Park, *Mex.* 26°3' N, 99°47' W **112**
El Salado, *Mex.* 24°15' N, 100°51' W **114**
El Salto, *Mex.* 20°31' N, 103°11' W **114**
El Salto, *Mex.* 23°44' N, 105°22' W **114**
El Salvador 14°0' N, 89°0' W **115**
El Salvador, *Mex.* 24°28' N, 100°53' W **114**
El Samán de Apure, *Venez.* 7°52' N, 68°43' W **136**
El Sasabe, *Mex.* 31°28' N, 111°33' W **92**
El Sauz, *Mex.* 29°0' N, 106°15' W **92**
El Sauzal, *Mex.* 31°53' N, 116°41' W **92**
El Seco, *Mex.* 19°6' N, 97°39' W **114**
El Shab, spring, *Egypt* 22°18' N, 29°45' E **226**
El Sibû', ruin(s), *Egypt* 22°44' N, 32°22' E **182**
El Soberbio, *Arg.* 27°21' S, 54°15' W **139**
El Socorro, *Venez.* 8°59' N, 65°45' W **136**
El Sombrero, *Venez.* 9°23' N, 67°4' W **136**
El Sueco, *Mex.* 29°51' N, 106°23' W **92**
El Suweis (Suez), *Egypt* 30°1' N, 32°26' E **180**
El Tajín, ruin(s), *Mex.* 20°24' N, 97°28' W **114**
El Tama National Park, *Venez.* 7°10' N, 72°14' W **136**
El Tecuan, *Mex.* 19°21' N, 104°58' W **114**
El Teleno, peak, *Sp.* 42°19' N, 6°28' W **150**
El Tell el Ahmar, *Egypt* 30°53' N, 32°24' E **194**
El Tigre, *Col.* 6°45' N, 71°46' W **136**
El Tîna, *Egypt* 31°2' N, 32°17' E **194**
El Toboso, *Sp.* 39°31' N, 3°2' W **164**
El Tocuyo, *Venez.* 9°45' N, 69°49' W **136**
El Tomatal, *Mex.* 28°26' N, 114°6' W **92**
El Toro, peak, *Sp.* 39°58' N, 4°5' E **164**
El Trébol, *Arg.* 32°13' S, 61°42' W **139**
El Triunfo, Pirámide, peak, *Arg.* 25°45' S, 61°51' W **132**
El Tuito, *Mex.* 20°19' N, 105°25' W **114**
El Tuparro National Park, *Col.* 5°10' N, 67°0' W **136**
El Tûr, *Egypt* 28°14' N, 33°37' E **180**
El Turbio, *Arg.* 51°42' S, 72°8' W **134**
El Valle, *Col.* 6°5' N, 77°26' W **136**
El Veladero National Park, *Mex.* 16°53' N, 100°0' W **112**
El Vendrell, *Sp.* 41°13' N, 1°32' E **164**
El Vergel, *Mex.* 26°26' N, 106°24' W **114**
El Wak, *Kenya* 2°44' N, 40°53' E **224**
El Walamo, *Mex.* 23°6' N, 106°13' W **114**
El Wasifîya, *Egypt* 30°33' N, 32°8' E **194**
El Wâsṭa, *Egypt* 29°20' N, 31°10' E **180**
El Wuz, *Sudan* 15°1' N, 30°12' E **226**
El Yagual, *Venez.* 7°29' N, 68°26' W **136**
El Zape, *Mex.* 25°46' N, 105°45' W **114**
Elaho, river, *Can.* 50°14' N, 123°38' W **100**
Elaia, Cape, *Northern Cyprus, Cyprus* 35°16' N, 34°4' E **194**
Elan', *Russ.* 57°38' N, 63°38' E **154**
Elat, *Israel* 29°35' N, 34°59' E **180**
Elato Atoll, *F.S.M.* 6°59' N, 145°34' E **192**
El'Atrun, spring, *Sudan* 18°6' N, 26°36' E **226**
El'Auja see Nizzana, *Israel* 30°52' N, 34°25' E **194**
Elâzığ, *Turk.* 38°39' N, 39°12' E **195**
Elba, *Ala., U.S.* 31°24' N, 86°4' W **96**
Elba, Cape see Hadarba, Ras, *Egypt* 21°49' N, 36°55' E **182**
Elba, island, *It.* 42°54' N, 9°57' E **214**
Elbe, *Wash., U.S.* 46°45' N, 122°12' W **100**
Elbe, river, *Ger.* 53°7' N, 10°4' E **143**
Elbert, Mount, *Colo., U.S.* 39°6' N, 106°31' W **90**
Elberta, *Mich., U.S.* 44°35' N, 86°13' W **94**
Elbeuf, *Fr.* 49°17' N, 1°0' E **163**
Elbistan, *Turk.* 38°11' N, 37°10' E **156**
Elbląg, *Pol.* 54°9' N, 19°25' E **166**
Elbow, *Can.* 51°8' N, 106°38' W **90**
Elbow Cays, *North Atlantic Ocean* 23°56' N, 81°24' W **116**
Elbow Lake, *Minn., U.S.* 45°59' N, 95°59' W **90**
El'brus, peak, *Russ.* 43°18' N, 42°24' E **195**
Elburg, *Neth.* 52°26' N, 5°49' E **163**
Elburz, *Iran* 36°26' N, 52°39' E **207**
Elburz Mountains see Alborz, Reshteh-ye, *Iran* 36°43' N, 49°25' E **195**
Elche de la Sierra, *Sp.* 38°26' N, 2°3' W **164**
Elche (Elx), *Sp.* 38°15' N, 0°42' E **164**
Elcho Island, *Austral.* 11°51' S, 135°35' E **192**
Elda, *Sp.* 38°28' N, 0°49' E **150**
Eldama Ravine, *Kenya* 4°238' N, 35°43' E **224**
El'dikan, *Russ.* 60°48' N, 135°14' E **160**
Eldon, *Iowa, U.S.* 40°55' N, 92°13' W **94**
Eldon, *Mo., U.S.* 38°19' N, 92°35' W **94**
Eldorado, *Arg.* 26°29' S, 54°42' W **139**
Eldorado, *Mex.* 24°18' N, 107°23' W **112**
Eldorado, *Mo., U.S.* 37°47' N, 88°26' W **96**
Eldorado, *Okla., U.S.* 34°26' N, 99°39' W **96**
Eldorado, *Tex., U.S.* 30°51' N, 100°36' W **92**
Eldorado Mountains, *Nev., U.S.* 35°49' N, 114°58' W **101**
Eldorado Pass, *Oreg., U.S.* 44°20' N, 118°7' W **90**
Eldorado Paulista, *Braz.* 24°35' S, 48°9' W **138**
Eldoret, *Kenya* 0°28' N, 35°18' E **224**
Electra, *Tex., U.S.* 34°0' N, 98°55' W **92**
Electric Mills, *Miss., U.S.* 32°44' N, 88°28' W **103**
Electric Peak, *Mont., U.S.* 44°59' N, 110°56' W **90**
El'Ein, spring, *Sudan* 16°34' N, 29°17' E **226**
Eleja, *Latv.* 56°24' N, 23°41' E **166**
Elek, *Hung.* 46°32' N, 21°14' E **168**
Elektrostal', *Russ.* 55°45' N, 38°30' E **154**
Elephant Island, *Antarctica* 61°4' S, 55°14' W **134**
Elephant Mountain, *Tex., U.S.* 29°59' N, 103°36' W **92**
Elephant Point, *U.S.* 66°15' N, 161°24' W **98**
Eleşkirt, *Turk.* 39°47' N, 42°39' E **195**
Eleuthera Island, *Bahamas* 25°12' N, 76°7' W **116**
Eleutherae, ruin(s), *Gr.* 38°10' N, 23°17' E **156**
Eleutherna, ruin(s), *Gr.* 35°18' N, 24°34' E **156**
Elfers, *Fla., U.S.* 28°13' N, 82°42' W **105**
Elfin Cove, *U.S.* 58°11' N, 136°20' W **98**
Elfrida, *Ariz., U.S.* 31°41' N, 109°40' W **92**
Elgå, *Nor.* 62°9' N, 11°56' E **152**
Elgin, *Ill., U.S.* 42°2' N, 88°16' W **102**
Elgin, *Nebr., U.S.* 41°57' N, 98°6' W **90**
Elgin, *N. Dak., U.S.* 46°23' N, 101°52' W **90**
Elgin, *Oreg., U.S.* 45°33' N, 117°56' W **90**
Elgin, *Tex., U.S.* 30°20' N, 97°22' W **92**
El'ginskiy, *Russ.* 64°42' N, 142°12' E **173**
Elgon, Mount, *Uganda* 1°4' N, 34°29' E **224**
Elgoras, Gora, peak, *Russ.* 68°5' N, 31°24' E **152**
Elias Garcia, *Angola* 9°3' S, 20°14' E **218**
Elida, *N. Mex., U.S.* 33°56' N, 103°40' W **92**
Elida, *Ohio, U.S.* 40°46' N, 84°12' W **102**
Eliki Gounda, *Niger* 15°3' N, 8°36' E **222**
Elikónas (Helicon), peak, *Gr.* 38°17' N, 22°47' E **156**
Elila, river, *Dem. Rep. of the Congo* 3°26' S, 27°52' E **224**
Elila, river, *Dem. Rep. of the Congo* 2°55' S, 26°23' E **224**
Eliot, *Me., U.S.* 43°9' N, 70°48' W **104**
Elipa, *Dem. Rep. of the Congo* 1°4' S, 24°19' E **224**
Elis, ruin(s), *Gr.* 37°52' N, 21°18' E **156**
Élisabethville see Lubumbashi, *Dem. Rep. of the Congo* 11°43' S, 27°26' E **224**
Elisenvaara, *Russ.* 61°23' N, 29°45' E **166**
Eliseu Martins, *Braz.* 8°11' S, 43°43' W **132**
Elista, *Russ.* 46°16' N, 44°9' E **158**
Elizabeth, *La., U.S.* 30°51' N, 92°48' W **103**
Elizabeth, *Miss., U.S.* 33°24' N, 90°53' W **103**
Elizabeth, *N.J., U.S.* 40°39' N, 74°14' W **94**
Elizabeth, *W. Va., U.S.* 39°3' N, 81°25' W **102**
Elizabeth City, *N.C., U.S.* 36°18' N, 76°16' W **96**
Elizabeth Falls, *Can.* 59°20' N, 105°49' W **108**
Elizabeth Islands, *Atlantic Ocean* 41°21' N, 71°2' W **104**
Elizabeth Mountain, *Utah, U.S.* 40°57' N, 110°48' W **90**
Elizabethton, *Tenn., U.S.* 36°20' N, 82°14' W **96**
Elizabethtown, *Ind., U.S.* 39°7' N, 85°49' W **102**
Elizabethtown, *Ky., U.S.* 37°40' N, 85°52' W **96**
Elizabethtown, *Mo., U.S.* 37°27' N, 88°18' W **96**
Elizabethtown, *N.Y., U.S.* 44°13' N, 73°37' W **104**
Elizondo, *Sp.* 43°8' N, 1°31' W **150**
Elk, *Pol.* 53°50' N, 22°21' E **152**
Elk, *Calif., U.S.* 39°8' N, 123°43' W **90**
Elk City, *Okla., U.S.* 35°23' N, 99°26' W **92**
Elk Creek, river, *S. Dak., U.S.* 44°13' N, 102°53' W **90**
Elk Grove, *Calif., U.S.* 38°24' N, 121°23' W **100**
Elk Hills, *Calif., U.S.* 35°20' N, 119°31' W **100**
Elk Island National Park, *Can.* 53°32' N, 113°12' W **238**

Elk Lake, Can. 47°43' N, 80°21' W 94
Elk Lake, Mich., U.S. 44°47' N, 85°37' W 94
Elk Mountain, Wyo., U.S. 41°37' N, 106°36' W 90
Elk Peak, Mont., U.S. 46°25' N, 110°50' W 90
Elk Point, Can. 53°53' N, 110°55' W 108
Elk Point, S. Dak., U.S. 42°39' N, 96°41' W 90
Elk River, Idaho, U.S. 46°45' N, 116°13' W 90
Elk River, Minn., U.S. 45°17' N, 93°34' W 94
Elk, river, Can. 49°23' N, 114°53' W 108
Elk, river, Colo., U.S. 40°34' N, 106°58' W 90
Elk, river, W. Va., U.S. 38°22' N, 80°55' W 80
Elkhart, Ind., U.S. 41°40' N, 85°59' W 82
Elkhart, Kans., U.S. 37°0' N, 101°54' W 92
Elkhart, Tex., U.S. 31°36' N, 95°35' W 103
Elkhart Lake, Wis., U.S. 43°49' N, 88°1' W 102
Elkhead Mountains, Colo., U.S. 40°40' N, 107°46' W 90
Elkhorn, Can. 49°59' N, 101°15' W 90
Elkhorn, Wis., U.S. 42°40' N, 88°33' W 102
Elkhorn City, Ky., U.S. 37°18' N, 82°22' W 94
Elkhorn Mountain, Can. 49°47' N, 125°55' W 90
Elkhorn, river, Nebr., U.S. 42°21' N, 99°26' W 80
Elkhovo, Bulg. 42°10' N, 26°34' E 158
Elkin, N.C., U.S. 36°14' N, 80°53' W 96
Elkins, N. Mex., U.S. 33°41' N, 104°4' W 92
Elkins, W. Va., U.S. 38°55' N, 79°51' W 94
Elkland, Pa., U.S. 41°59' N, 77°20' W 94
Elko, Can. 49°18' N, 115°7' W 90
Elko, Nev., U.S. 40°53' N, 115°51' W 106
Elkton, Fla., U.S. 29°46' N, 81°27' W 105
Elkton, Ky., U.S. 36°48' N, 87°10' W 96
Elkton, Md., U.S. 39°36' N, 75°51' W 94
Elkton, Mich., U.S. 43°48' N, 83°11' W 102
Elkview, W. Va., U.S. 38°26' N, 81°30' W 102
Ellef Ringnes Island, Can. 77°11' N, 103°31' W 106
Elleh Creek, river, Can. 58°32' N, 122°26' W 108
Ellen, Mount, Utah, U.S. 38°5' N, 110°53' W 90
Ellenboro, W. Va., U.S. 39°16' N, 81°4' W 102
Ellendale, N. Dak., U.S. 46°0' N, 98°32' W 90
Ellensburg, Wash., U.S. 46°58' N, 120°35' W 90
Ellenton, Fla., U.S. 27°32' N, 82°30' W 105
Ellesmere Island, Can. 76°28' N, 77°40' W 106
Ellesmere Port, U.K. 53°17' N, 2°54' W 162
Ellettsville, Ind., U.S. 39°13' N, 86°38' W 102
Ellila, spring, Chad 16°42' N, 20°20' E 216
Ellington, Conn., U.S. 41°53' N, 72°29' W 104
Ellinwood, Kans., U.S. 38°20' N, 98°35' W 82
Elliot, S. Af. 31°21' S, 27°49' E 227
Elliot Lake, Can. 46°23' N, 82°40' W 110
Elliott, Cape, Antarctica 65°39' S, 106°26' E 248
Elliott Lake, Can. 61°1' N, 100°2' W 108
Ellis, Idaho, U.S. 44°41' N, 114°2' W 90
Ellis, Kans., U.S. 38°55' N, 99°34' W 90
Ellis, Mount, Mont., U.S. 45°32' N, 111°1' W 90
Ellisburg, N.Y., U.S. 43°43' N, 76°9' W 110
Ellisland, site, U.K. 55°6' N, 3°46' W 150
Ellisras see Lephalale, S. Af. 23°40' S, 27°42' E 227
Elliston, Austral. 33°40' S, 134°54' E 231
Ellisville, Miss., U.S. 31°35' N, 89°13' W 103
Ełk, Pol. 53°50' N, 22°20' E 152
Ellore see Eluru, India 16°46' N, 81°7' E 188
Ells, river, Can. 56°59' N, 112°21' W 108
Ellsworth, Kans., U.S. 38°43' N, 98°14' W 90
Ellsworth, Me., U.S. 44°31' N, 68°24' W 82
Ellsworth Land, region, Antarctica 73°44' S, 96°14' W 248
Ellsworth, Mount, Utah, U.S. 37°44' N, 110°42' W 92
Ellsworth Mountains, Antarctica 76°23' S, 90°19' W 248
Elm Creek, Nebr., U.S. 40°42' N, 99°23' W 90
Elma, Wash., U.S. 47°0' N, 123°24' W 100
Elmadağı, Turk. 39°55' N, 33°14' E 156
Elmalı, Turk. 36°43' N, 29°55' E 156
Elmer City, Wash., U.S. 47°59' N, 118°56' W 90
Elmira, N.Y., U.S. 42°5' N, 76°50' W 94
Elmo, Wyo., U.S. 41°53' N, 106°31' W 90
Elmsta, Sw. 59°58' N, 18°42' E 166
Elmwood, Ill., U.S. 40°45' N, 89°58' W 102
Elnora, Ind., U.S. 38°52' N, 87°5' W 102
Elortondo, Arg. 33°43' S, 61°38' W 139
Elorza, Venez. 7°1' N, 69°31' W 136
Elos, ruin(s), Gr. 36°47' N, 22°40' E 156
Elota, Mex. 23°56' N, 106°42' W 114
Eloy, Ariz., U.S. 32°44' N, 111°34' W 112
Eloy Alfaro, Ecua. 2°16' S, 79°51' W 130
Elrose, Can. 51°12' N, 108°4' W 90
Elroy, Wis., U.S. 43°44' N, 90°17' W 102
Elsa, Tex., U.S. 26°17' N, 97°59' W 114
Elsas, Can. 48°32' N, 82°55' W 94
Elsberry, Mo., U.S. 39°9' N, 90°47' W 94
Elsdorf, Ger. 53°14' N, 9°22' E 152
Elsen Nur, lake, China 35°14' N, 91°46' E 188
Elsie, Mich., U.S. 43°4' N, 84°24' W 102
Elst, Neth. 51°55' N, 5°50' E 167
Elstow, U.K. 52°7' N, 0°28' E 162
Eltanin Fracture Zone System, South Pacific Ocean 52°39' S, 138°6' W 252
Elten, Ger. 51°51' N, 6°10' E 167
Eltham, N.Z. 39°27' S, 174°18' E 240
Elton, La., U.S. 30°28' N, 92°42' W 103
El'ton, Russ. 49°9' N, 46°47' E 158
Eltopia, Wash., U.S. 46°26' N, 119°1' W 90
Eltville, Ger. 50°1' N, 8°6' E 167
Eluru (Ellore), India 16°46' N, 81°7' E 188
Elva, Est. 58°10' N, 26°22' E 166
Elvas, Port. 38°52' N, 7°10' W 150
Elvenes, Nor. 69°40' N, 30°8' E 152
Elvins, Mo., U.S. 37°49' N, 90°33' W 96
Elwell, Lake, Mont., U.S. 48°20' N, 111°36' W 90
Elwood, Ill., U.S. 41°24' N, 88°7' W 102
Elwood, Ind., U.S. 40°16' N, 85°50' W 102
Elwood, Kans., U.S. 39°43' N, 94°53' W 94
Elwood, Nebr., U.S. 40°34' N, 99°52' W 90
Elx see Elche, Sp. 38°15' N, 0°42' E 164
Ely, Minn., U.S. 47°53' N, 91°53' W 94
Ely, Nev., U.S. 39°17' N, 114°48' W 238
Ely, U.K. 52°23' N, 0°15' E 162
Ely, Isle of, U.K. 52°24' N, 0°11' E 162
Elyria, Ohio, U.S. 41°21' N, 82°5' W 102
Elyrus, ruin(s), Gr. 35°15' N, 23°42' E 156
Emådalen, Nor. 61°19' N, 14°42' E 152
Emajõgi, river, Est. 58°24' N, 26°7' E 166
Emām Taqī, Iran 35°59' N, 59°23' E 180
Emas National Park, Braz. 18°19' S, 53°5' W 138
Embari, river, Braz. 0°48' N, 67°0' W 136
Embarras Portage, Can. 58°24' N, 111°26' W 108
Embi, Kaz. 48°50' N, 58°6' E 158
Embira, river, Braz. 9°17' S, 70°51' W 137
Embu, Kenya 0°33' N, 37°27' E 224
Emden, Ger. 53°21' N, 7°12' E 163
Emel'dzhak, Russ. 58°19' N, 126°40' E 160
Emerald Island, Can. 76°42' N, 113°8' W 106
Emero, river, Bol. 13°38' S, 68°3' W 137
Emerson, Ark., U.S. 33°5' N, 93°12' W 103
Emerson, Can. 49°0' N, 97°11' W 90
Emerson Peak, Calif., U.S. 41°13' N, 120°15' W 90
Emery, Utah, U.S. 38°55' N, 111°14' W 90
Emery Mills, Me., U.S. 43°30' N, 70°51' W 104
Emet, Turk. 39°21' N, 29°14' E 156
Emgayet, oil field, Lib. 28°57' N, 12°45' E 143
Emigrant Pass, Nev., U.S. 40°40' N, 116°14' W 90
Emigrant Peak, Mont., U.S. 45°14' N, 110°47' W 90
Emilia-Romagna, adm. division, It. 44°40' N, 10°18' E 167
Emilius, Mount, It. 45°39' N, 7°24' E 165
Emily, Minn., U.S. 46°43' N, 93°58' W 94
Emily, Mount, Oreg., U.S. 45°24' N, 118°11' W 90
Emin, China 46°29' N, 83°38' E 184
Emin, river, China 46°24' N, 83°0' E 184
Emin, river, Kaz. 46°16' N, 81°53' E 184
Emir Dağları, peak, Turk. 38°50' N, 31°9' E 156
Emirdağ, Turk. 39°0' N, 31°9' E 156
Emisou, Tarso, peak, Chad 21°23' N, 18°32' E 216
Emlichheim, Ger. 52°36' N, 6°51' E 163
Emma, Mount, Ariz., U.S. 36°15' N, 113°14' W 92
Emmaboda, Nor. 56°37' N, 15°31' E 152
Emmaste, Est. 58°43' N, 22°33' E 166
Emmaus, Pa., U.S. 40°31' N, 75°30' W 94
Emmeloord, Neth. 52°42' N, 5°44' E 163
Emmen, Neth. 52°47' N, 6°53' E 163
Emmen, Switz. 47°3' N, 8°18' E 150
Emmerich, Ger. 51°49' N, 6°15' E 167
Emmetsburg, Iowa, U.S. 43°5' N, 94°41' W 90
Emmett, Idaho, U.S. 43°51' N, 116°30' W 90
Emmonak, Alas., U.S. 62°42' N, 164°42' W 98
Emmons, Mount, Utah, U.S. 40°41' N, 110°23' W 90
Emo, Can. 48°38' N, 93°50' W 90
Emory Peak, Tex., U.S. 29°12' N, 103°21' W 92
Empangeni, S. Af. 28°44' S, 31°51' E 227
Empedrado, Arg. 27°55' S, 58°48' W 139
Emperor Seamounts, North Pacific Ocean 43°13' N, 170°0' E 252
Emperor Trough, North Pacific Ocean 44°20' N, 174°43' E 252
Empire, La., U.S. 29°22' N, 89°36' W 103
Empire, Mich., U.S. 44°48' N, 86°3' W 94
Empoli, It. 43°43' N, 10°57' E 156
Emporia, Kans., U.S. 38°23' N, 96°11' W 90
Emporia, Va., U.S. 36°41' N, 77°32' W 96
Emporio, ruin(s), Gr. 38°11' N, 25°55' E 156
Emporium, Pa., U.S. 41°30' N, 78°15' W 94
Empress, Can. 50°57' N, 110°1' W 90
Empty Quarter see Ar Rub' al Khālī, Saudi Arabia 18°28' N, 46°3' E 182
Ems, river, Ger. 52°1' N, 7°43' E 167
Emsdetten, Ger. 52°10' N, 7°32' E 163
En Amakane, spring, Mali 16°35' N, 0°59' E 222
'En Boqeq, Israel 31°11' N, 35°21' E 194
'En Gedi, Israel 31°27' N, 35°22' E 194
'En Gev, Israel 32°46' N, 35°38' E 194
En Nahud, Sudan 12°40' N, 28°26' E 226
'En Yahav, Israel 30°37' N, 35°11' E 194
Ena, Japan 35°25' N, 137°24' E 201
Ena Lake, Can. 59°57' N, 108°27' W 108
Enånger, Nor. 61°32' N, 16°58' E 152
Encantadas, Serra das, Braz. 30°51' S, 53°28' W 139
Encantado, Cerro, peak, Mex. 27°2' N, 112°38' W 112
Encanto, Cape, Philippines 15°29' N, 121°37' E 203
Encarnación, Parag. 27°20' S, 55°50' W 139
Encarnación de Díaz, Mex. 21°30' N, 102°15' W 114
Enchi, Ghana 5°49' N, 2°50' W 222
Encinal, Tex., U.S. 28°2' N, 99°21' W 92
Encinillas, Mex. 29°13' N, 106°17' W 92
Encinillas, Laguna de, lake, Mex. 29°24' N, 107°45' W 81
Encinitas, Calif., U.S. 33°2' N, 117°18' W 101
Encino, Tex., U.S. 26°56' N, 98°8' W 96
Encontrados, Venez. 9°2' N, 72°15' W 136
Encruzilhada, Braz. 15°33' S, 40°55' W 138
Encruzilhada do Sul, Braz. 30°33' S, 52°34' W 139
Endako, Can. 54°5' N, 125°1' W 108
Endau, Kenya 1°19' S, 38°34' E 224
Endeavour, Can. 52°10' N, 102°40' W 108
Enderby, Can. 50°33' N, 119°9' W 90
Enderby Land, region, Antarctica 69°55' S, 39°37' E 248
Enderby Plain, Indian Ocean 58°55' S, 44°16' E 255
Enderlin, N. Dak., U.S. 46°36' N, 97°37' W 90
Endicott Mountains, Alas., U.S. 67°34' N, 155°1' W 98
Endrőd, Hung. 46°56' N, 20°46' E 168
Endwell, N.Y., U.S. 42°6' N, 76°1' W 94
Energetik, Russ. 51°44' N, 58°56' E 154
Enez, Turk. 40°42' N, 26°3' E 156
Enfer, Pointe d', Fr. 14°17' N, 61°38' W 116
Enfida, Tun. 36°7' N, 10°23' E 156
Enfield, Conn., U.S. 41°57' N, 72°36' W 104
Enfield, N.Z. 45°3' S, 170°50' E 240
Enfield, U.K. 51°39' N, 7°415' W 162
Enfield Center, N.H., U.S. 43°35' N, 72°7' W 104
Engaño, Cabo, Dom. Rep. 18°35' N, 68°15' W 116
'En-Gedi, ruin(s), Israel 31°27' N, 35°21' E 194
Engelberg, Switz. 46°48' N, 8°24' E 167
Engelhard, N.C., U.S. 35°31' N, 76°1' W 96
Engels, Russ. 51°25' N, 46°9' E 158
Engemann Lake, Can. 57°49' N, 107°49' W 108
Engen, Can. 54°1' N, 124°17' W 108
Engerdal, Nor. 61°45' N, 11°56' E 152
Engershand, Mongolia 47°44' N, 107°21' E 198
Enggano, island, Indonesia 5°46' S, 101°5' E 192
Enghien, Belg. 50°41' N, 4°2' E 163
Engizek Dağı, Turk. 37°46' N, 36°29' E 156
England, adm. division, U.K. 52°25' N, 2°59' W 143
Englehart, Can. 47°50' N, 79°52' W 94
Englewood, Fla., U.S. 26°58' N, 82°21' W 105
Englewood, Kans., U.S. 37°1' N, 100°0' W 92
Englewood, Ohio, U.S. 39°52' N, 84°19' W 102
English Channel (La Manche) 49°57' N, 3°16' W 150
English River, Can. 49°13' N, 90°58' W 94
English, river, Can. 50°30' N, 95°13' W 80
English, river, Can. 49°50' N, 92°1' W 94
Engure, Latv. 57°8' N, 23°12' E 166
Engures Ezers, lake, Latv. 57°14' N, 22°50' E 166
Enid, Okla., U.S. 36°22' N, 97°52' W 92
Enid, Mount, Austral. 21°46' S, 116°12' E 230
Enilda, Can. 55°24' N, 116°18' W 108
Enken, Mys, Russ. 56°57' N, 139°57' E 172
Enkirch, Ger. 49°58' N, 7°8' E 167
Enköping, Nor. 59°37' N, 17°3' E 152
Enmelen, Russ. 65°1' N, 175°51' W 98
Enna, It. 37°34' N, 14°16' E 156
Ennadai, Can. 61°7' N, 100°53' W 108
Ennadai Lake, Can. 60°42' N, 102°23' W 108
Ennigerloh, Ger. 51°49' N, 8°0' E 167
Enning, S. Dak., U.S. 44°33' N, 102°34' W 90
Ennis, Ire. 52°50' N, 9°0' W 150
Ennis, Tex., U.S. 32°18' N, 96°38' W 96
Enniskillen, U.K. 54°20' N, 7°38' W 150
Enns, Aust. 48°13' N, 14°28' E 156
Eno, Fin. 62°45' N, 30°8' E 152
Eno, river, Japan 34°33' N, 132°40' E 201
Enonkoski, Fin. 62°4' N, 28°55' E 152
Enontekiö, Fin. 68°23' N, 23°35' E 152
Énos, Óros, peak, Gr. 38°7' N, 20°35' E 156
Enrique Urien, Arg. 27°33' S, 60°37' W 139
Enschede, Neth. 52°13' N, 6°53' E 163
Ensenada, Mex. 31°51' N, 116°38' W 92
Enshi, China 30°14' N, 109°24' E 198
Entebbe, Uganda 6°357' N, 32°27' E 224
Enterprise, Ala., U.S. 31°18' N, 85°51' W 96
Enterprise, Can. 60°40' N, 116°4' W 108
Enterprise, Miss., U.S. 32°10' N, 88°48' W 103
Enterprise, Utah, U.S. 37°34' N, 113°43' W 92
Entinas, Punta, Sp. 36°31' N, 2°44' W 150
Entrada, Punta, Arg. 50°22' S, 68°28' W 134
Entrance, Can. 53°21' N, 117°42' W 108
Entraunes, Fr. 44°10' N, 6°45' E 167
Entre Ríos, Bol. 21°33' S, 64°13' W 137
Entre Ríos, adm. division, Arg. 31°43' S, 59°58' W 139
Entre-Rios, Mozambique 14°58' S, 37°24' E 224
Entwistle, Can. 53°33' N, 114°56' W 108
Enugu, Nig. 6°26' N, 7°29' E 222
Enumclaw, Wash., U.S. 47°10' N, 121°59' W 100
Enurmino, Russ. 66°55' N, 171°46' W 98
Envigado, Col. 6°8' N, 75°37' W 130
Envira, Braz. 7°23' S, 70°14' W 130
Enyellé, Congo 2°51' N, 18°4' E 218
Enying, Hung. 46°56' N, 18°15' E 168
Enzan, Japan 35°41' N, 138°44' E 201
Eola, La., U.S. 30°53' N, 92°14' W 103
Eolie see Lipari, Isole, islands, Mediterranean Sea 38°39' N, 13°46' E 156
Eonyang, S. Korea 35°33' N, 129°10' E 200
Epe, Neth. 52°21' N, 5°58' E 163
Epembe, spring, Namibia 17°35' S, 13°34' E 220
Epéna, Congo 1°23' N, 17°27' E 218
Épernay, Fr. 49°2' N, 3°56' E 163
Épernon, Fr. 48°35' N, 1°40' E 163
Epes, Ala., U.S. 32°41' N, 88°8' W 103
Ephesus, ruin(s), Turk. 37°55' N, 27°12' E 156
Ephraim, Utah, U.S. 39°21' N, 111°35' W 90
Ephrata, Wash., U.S. 47°18' N, 119°34' W 90
Epidaurum see Cavtat, Croatia 42°34' N, 18°13' E 168
Epidaurus Limerás, ruin(s), Gr. 36°43' N, 22°56' E 156
Épilá, Sp. 41°37' N, 1°17' W 164
Épinal, Fr. 48°10' N, 6°26' E 163
Epini, Dem. Rep. of the Congo 1°26' N, 28°21' E 224
Epirus, region, Europe 40°27' N, 19°28' E 156
Episkopi, Cyprus 34°40' N, 32°54' E 194
Epping Forest, U.K. 51°38' N, 2°119' E 162
Eps, La., U.S. 32°35' N, 91°29' W 103
Epsom, U.K. 51°20' N, 0°17' E 162
Epu Pel, Arg. 37°36' S, 64°16' W 139
Epukiro, Namibia 21°45' S, 19°8' E 227
Epulu, river, Dem. Rep. of the Congo 1°29' N, 28°42' E 224
Equator, adm. division, Dem. Rep. of the Congo 9°535' N, 18°55' E 218
Equatorial Channel 0°14' N, 72°8' E 188
Equatorial Guinea 1°38' N, 10°28' E 218
Er Rachidia, Mor. 31°58' N, 4°21' W 143
Er Rahad, Sudan 12°43' N, 30°36' E 216
Er Rif, Mor. 35°15' N, 5°28' W 150
Er Roseires, Sudan 11°52' N, 34°24' E 182
Er Rout Sanihida, spring, Niger 21°53' N, 11°52' E 222
Eraclea, It. 45°34' N, 12°40' E 167
Erath, La., U.S. 29°56' N, 92°2' W 103
Erbaa, Turk. 40°40' N, 36°34' E 156
Erbab, Jebel, peak, Sudan 18°40' N, 36°59' E 182
Erçek, Turk. 38°37' N, 43°34' E 195
Erçek Gölü, lake, Turk. 38°39' N, 43°23' E 195
Erciş, Turk. 38°59' N, 43°18' E 195
Erciyeş Dağı, peak, Turk. 38°30' N, 35°22' E 156
Ercsi, Hung. 47°14' N, 18°53' E 168
Érd, Hung. 47°22' N, 18°55' E 168
Erdao, river, China 42°44' N, 127°38' E 200
Erdaobaihe, China 42°26' N, 128°7' E 200
Erdébé, Plateau d', Chad 17°17' N, 21°23' E 216
Erdek, Turk. 40°24' N, 27°45' E 156
Erdemli, Turk. 36°36' N, 34°18' E 156
Erdenet, Mongolia 48°57' N, 104°17' E 198
Erdut, Croatia 45°31' N, 19°2' E 168
Erebus, Mount, Antarctica 77°26' S, 167°55' E 248
Erechim, Braz. 27°39' S, 52°18' W 139
Ereğli, Turk. 41°17' N, 31°25' E 156
Ereğli, Turk. 37°29' N, 34°2' E 156
Erego, Mozambique 16°3' S, 37°11' E 224
Erei, Monti, It. 37°23' N, 14°3' E 156
Eremiya, Bulg. 42°12' N, 22°50' E 168
Erenhot, China 43°39' N, 111°57' E 198
Eresus, ruin(s), Gr. 39°7' N, 25°50' E 156
Erétria, ruin(s), Gr. 38°23' N, 23°42' E 156
Ereymentaū, Kaz. 51°41' N, 73°22' E 184
Erfoud, Mor. 31°29' N, 4°15' W 214
Erft, river, Ger. 51°2' N, 6°29' E 167
Erftstadt, Ger. 50°47' N, 6°44' E 167
Erfurt, Ger. 50°59' N, 11°2' E 152
'Erg Chech, Alg. 25°13' N, 3°16' W 214
'Erg el Ahmar, Mali 24°14' N, 4°55' W 214
'Erg Iguidi, Alg. 24°15' N, 8°24' W 214
'Erg I-n-Sâkâne, Mali 20°43' N, 0°54' E 222
Ergani, Turk. 38°17' N, 39°45' E 195
Ergel, Mongolia 43°13' N, 109°8' E 198
Ērgļi, Latv. 56°53' N, 25°39' E 166
Erg-n-Ataram, Alg. 23°45' N, 1°6' E 214
Ergun, river, Asia 50°18' N, 119°1' E 190
Eriba, Sudan 16°37' N, 36°3' E 182
Éric, Lac, lake, Can. 51°50' N, 65°59' W 111
Erice, It. 38°2' N, 12°35' E 156
Erick, Okla., U.S. 35°11' N, 99°53' W 92
Erickson, Can. 50°30' N, 99°54' W 90
Erie, Ill., U.S. 41°38' N, 90°5' W 102
Erie, Pa., U.S. 42°6' N, 80°5' W 94
Erie, Lake 42°11' N, 83°6' W 73
Erieau, Can. 42°15' N, 81°56' W 102
Erigavo see Ceerigaabo, Somalia 10°34' N, 47°24' E 218
Eriksdale, Can. 50°51' N, 98°6' W 90
Erímanthos, Óros, peak, Gr. 37°58' N, 21°45' E 156
Erimi, Cyprus 34°40' N, 32°55' E 194
Eritrea 15°32' N, 37°35' E 218
Erits, river, Kaz. 51°34' N, 77°33' E 184
Erkelenz, Ger. 51°4' N, 6°19' E 167
Erkilet, Turk. 38°48' N, 35°27' E 156
Erkner, Ger. 52°24' N, 13°45' E 152
Erkowit, Sudan 18°45' N, 37°3' E 182
Erla, Sp. 42°6' N, 0°57' E 164
Erlangen, Ger. 49°35' N, 11°0' E 152
Ermelo, S. Af. 26°32' S, 29°58' E 227
Ermenek, Turk. 36°36' N, 32°55' E 156
Ermidas-Sado, Port. 37°59' N, 8°25' W 150
Ermil, Sudan 13°33' N, 27°38' E 226
Ermoúpoli, Gr. 37°26' N, 24°56' E 156
Ernakulam, India 9°59' N, 76°17' E 188
Erndtebrück, Ger. 50°59' N, 8°15' E 167
Ernstberg, peak, Ger. 50°13' N, 6°44' E 167
Eromanga, Austral. 26°39' S, 143°17' E 231
Erongo Mountains, Namibia 21°44' S, 15°27' E 227
Eros, La., U.S. 32°22' N, 92°25' W 103
Eroug, spring, Mali 18°20' N, 2°4' W 222
Erpengdianzi, China 41°10' N, 125°33' E 200
Er-Remla, Tun. 34°46' N, 11°14' E 156
Errigal Mountain, Ire. 55°0' N, 8°13' W 150
Error Tablemount, Arabian Sea 9°58' N, 56°3' E 254
Erskine, Minn., U.S. 47°38' N, 96°2' W 90
Erstein, Fr. 48°25' N, 7°39' E 163
Ertai, China 46°8' N, 90°7' E 190
Ertis, Kaz. 53°19' N, 75°27' E 184
Ertis, river, Kaz. 54°12' N, 74°56' E 160
Ertix, river, China 48°2' N, 85°34' E 184
Eruh, Turk. 37°44' N, 42°9' E 195
Erundu, Namibia 20°41' S, 16°23' E 227
Ervenik, Croatia 44°5' N, 15°55' E 168
Erwin, N.C., U.S. 35°19' N, 78°42' W 96
Erwitte, Ger. 51°36' N, 8°21' E 167
Erzgebirge, Czech Rep. 50°18' N, 12°34' E 152
Erzin, Russ. 50°14' N, 95°18' E 190
Erzincan, Turk. 39°44' N, 39°28' E 195
Erzurum, Turk. 39°54' N, 41°17' E 195
Es Bordes, Sp. 42°43' N, 0°42' E 164
Es Mercadal, Sp. 39°59' N, 4°4' E 150
Es Safiya, Sudan 15°31' N, 30°6' E 226
Es Salam, Sudan 18°5' N, 33°53' E 182
Es Sufeiya, Sudan 15°27' N, 34°40' E 182
Esa, river, Belarus 54°43' N, 28°30' E 166
Esbjerg, Den. 55°27' N, 8°36' E 160
Esbo see Espoo, Fin. 60°11' N, 24°34' E 166
Escalante, Utah, U.S. 37°46' N, 111°37' W 92
Escanaba, Mich., U.S. 45°48' N, 87°7' W 106
Escárcega, Mex. 18°36' N, 90°46' W 115
Escatawpa, river, Ala., U.S. 30°27' N, 88°27' W 103
Escatrón, Sp. 41°16' N, 0°20' E 164
Eschenburg, Ger. 50°48' N, 8°20' E 167
Schweiler, Ger. 50°48' N, 6°15' E 167
Escobedo, Mex. 27°11' N, 101°22' W 96
Escondido, Calif., U.S. 33°7' N, 117°6' W 101
Escudero, station, Antarctica 62°5' S, 58°48' W 134
Escudilla Mountain, Ariz., U.S. 33°56' N, 109°11' W 92
Escuela de Caza de MorŽon, Sp. 37°9' N, 5°37' W 164
Escuinapa, Mex. 22°50' N, 105°47' W 114
Escuintla, Guatemala 14°16' N, 90°47' W 115
Escuintla, Mex. 15°18' N, 92°40' W 115
Escuminac, Point, Can. 47°6' N, 64°49' W 111
Ese Khayya, Russ. 67°28' N, 134°38' E 160
Eséka, Cameroon 3°41' N, 10°47' E 222
Esenguly, Turkm. 37°27' N, 53°57' E 180
Esens, Ger. 53°39' N, 7°36' E 163
Esfahan (Isfahan), Iran 32°40' N, 51°38' E 180
Esfandak, Iran 27°5' N, 62°51' E 182
Eshkamesh, Afghan. 36°27' N, 69°16' E 186
Eshkashem, Taj. 36°44' N, 71°34' E 186
Eshowe, S. Af. 28°54' S, 31°24' E 227
Esiama, Ghana 4°58' N, 2°21' W 222
Esik, Kaz. 43°21' N, 77°25' E 184
Esil, Kaz. 51°57' N, 66°27' E 184
Esil, river, Kaz. 53°18' N, 66°55' E 184
Esimi, Gr. 41°1' N, 25°57' E 156
Esira, Madagascar 24°21' S, 46°47' E 220
Esk, river, U.K. 55°14' N, 3°17' W 150
Esk, river, U.K. 54°28' N, 0°54' E 162
Eskdale, N.Z. 39°25' S, 176°49' E 240
Eskene, Kaz. 47°20' N, 52°52' E 158
Esker, Can. 54°0' N, 66°33' W 106
Eskimo Point, Can. 58°49' N, 94°20' W 108
Eskipazar, Turk. 40°58' N, 32°32' E 156
Eskişehir, Turk. 39°46' N, 30°31' E 156
Eslāmābād, Iran 34°9' N, 46°32' E 180
Eşler Dağı, peak, Turk. 37°39' N, 29°12' E 156
Eşme, Turk. 38°24' N, 28°57' E 156
Esmeralda, river, Bol. 13°28' S, 67°59' W 137
Esmeraldas, Ecua. 0°55' N, 79°48' W 130
Esmoraca, Bol. 21°41' S, 66°19' W 137
Esnagi Lake, Can. 48°40' N, 84°49' W 94
Espa, Nor. 60°34' N, 11°16' E 152
Espada, Punta, Col. 12°4' N, 71°8' W 136
Espakeh, Iran 26°46' N, 60°12' E 182
Espanola, Can. 46°15' N, 81°46' W 94
Espanola, N. Mex., U.S. 35°59' N, 106°6' W 92
Esparza, C.R. 9°58' N, 84°40' W 116
Esperanza, Arg. 31°27' S, 60°54' W 139
Esperanza, Arg. 51°5' S, 70°38' W 134
Esperanza, Peru 9°49' S, 70°44' W 137
Esperanza Inlet 49°45' N, 127°40' W 90
Esperanza, station, Antarctica 63°34' S, 57°4' W 248
Espichel, Cabo, Port. 38°11' N, 9°37' W 150
Espiel, Sp. 38°11' N, 5°1' W 164
Espigão Mestre, Braz. 14°41' S, 46°14' W 138
Espinal, Bol. 17°13' S, 58°28' W 132
Espinar see Yauri, Peru 14°51' S, 71°24' W 137
Espinazo, Mex. 26°16' N, 101°6' W 114
Espino, Venez. 8°32' N, 66°1' W 136
Espinosa, Braz. 14°59' S, 42°50' W 138
Espírito Santo, adm. division, Braz. 19°55' S, 41°11' W 138
Espírito Santo see Vila Velha, Braz. 20°25' S, 40°21' W 138
Espiritu, Philippines 17°59' N, 120°39' E 203
Espita, Mex. 21°0' N, 88°20' W 116
Espoo (Esbo), Fin. 60°11' N, 24°34' E 166
Esposende, Port. 41°31' N, 8°48' W 150
Espuña, peak, Sp. 37°51' N, 1°37' W 164
Espungabera, Mozambique 20°30' S, 32°47' E 227
Espy, Pa., U.S. 41°0' N, 76°25' W 110
Esqueda, Mex. 30°41' N, 109°35' W 92
Esquel, Arg. 42°58' S, 71°19' W 123
Esquimalt, Can. 48°25' N, 123°24' W 100
Esquina, Arg. 30°0' S, 59°33' W 139
Essaouira, Mor. 31°35' N, 9°39' W 143
Essé, Cameroon 4°6' N, 11°50' E 218
Essen, Belg. 51°27' N, 4°29' E 167
Essen, Ger. 51°27' N, 7°0' E 167
Essen, Ger. 52°44' N, 7°56' E 163
Essendon, Mount, Austral. 25°2' S, 120°18' E 230
Essex, Calif., U.S. 34°44' N, 115°15' W 101
Essex, Conn., U.S. 41°21' N, 72°24' W 104
Essex, Mass., U.S. 42°37' N, 70°48' W 104
Essex, N.Y., U.S. 44°18' N, 73°23' W 104
Essex Junction, Vt., U.S. 44°29' N, 73°7' W 104
Essexville, Mich., U.S. 43°36' N, 83°50' W 102
Esson, Gabon 1°14' N, 11°34' E 218
Essoûk, Mali 18°46' N, 1°5' E 222
Est, Cap, Madagascar 15°13' S, 50°28' E 220
Est, Pointe de l', Can. 49°5' N, 61°39' W 111
Estacado, Llano, North America 34°53' N, 103°50' W 92
Estación Maritima Antártica, station, Chile, Antarctica 62°12' S, 58°57' E 248
Estados, Isla de los (Staten Island), Arg. 55°28' S, 64°48' W 134
Estahbān, Iran 29°5' N, 54°3' E 196
Estância, Braz. 11°15' S, 37°28' W 132
Estancia Rojas Silva, Parag. 22°33' S, 59°5' W 132
Estancias, peak, Sp. 37°34' N, 2°6' W 164
Estavayer-le-Lac, Switz. 46°50' N, 6°51' E 167
Estcourt, S. Af. 29°2' S, 29°51' E 220
Este, It. 45°14' N, 11°39' E 167
Estelí, Nicar. 13°5' N, 86°21' W 115
Estella (Lizarra), Sp. 42°39' N, 2°2' W 164
Estelline, S. Dak., U.S. 44°33' N, 96°55' W 90
Estelline, Tex., U.S. 34°31' N, 100°27' W 92
Estepa, Sp. 37°17' N, 4°54' W 164
Estepona, Sp. 36°25' N, 5°9' W 164
Estérel, Fr. 43°28' N, 6°35' E 165
Esterfeld, Ger. 52°41' N, 7°15' E 163
Esterhazy, Can. 50°38' N, 102°8' W 90
Esternay, Fr. 48°43' N, 3°32' E 163
Estero, Point, Calif., U.S. 35°23' N, 121°7' W 100
Esteros del Iberá, marsh, Arg. 28°15' S, 58°7' W 139
Esterwegen, Ger. 52°59' N, 7°37' E 163
Estes Park, Colo., U.S. 40°22' N, 105°32' W 90
Estevan, Can. 49°7' N, 103°2' W 90
Estherville, Iowa, U.S. 43°23' N, 94°49' W 94
Estherwood, La., U.S. 30°10' N, 92°28' W 103
Estill, S.C., U.S. 32°45' N, 81°15' W 96
Estissac, Fr. 48°15' N, 3°48' E 163
Eston, Can. 51°9' N, 108°45' W 90
Estonia 58°38' N, 25°30' E 166
Estreito, Braz. 31°49' S, 51°45' W 139
Estreito, Serra do, Braz. 10°32' S, 43°49' W 132
Estrela do Norte, Braz. 13°50' S, 49°6' W 138
Estrela, Serra da, Port. 39°59' N, 8°2' W 150
Estrella, peak, Sp. 38°23' N, 3°39' W 164
Estrella, Punta, Mex. 30°55' N, 114°43' W 92
Estrondo, Serra do, Braz. 9°16' S, 49°36' W 130
Etah, site, Den. 78°18' N, 73°12' W 246
Étain, Fr. 49°12' N, 5°38' E 163
Etal Atoll, F.S.M. 5°46' N, 154°5' E 192
Étampes, Fr. 48°25' N, 2°9' E 163
Étaples, Fr. 50°31' N, 1°38' E 163
Etawah, India 26°45' N, 79°0' E 197
Etawney Lake, Can. 57°50' N, 97°31' W 108
Etéké, Gabon 1°30' S, 11°33' E 218

F

Fika, Nig. 11°17′ N, 11°17′ E 222
Filabres, Sierra de los, Sp. 37°12′ N, 2°32′ W 164
Filabusi, Zimb. 20°31′ S, 29°17′ E 227
Filadelfia, Bol. 11°24′ S, 68°49′ W 137
Filadélfia, Braz. 7°22′ S, 47°32′ W 130
Filadelfia, Parag. 22°19′ S, 60°4′ W 132
Fil'akovo, Slovakia 48°15′ N, 19°50′ E 152
Filattiera, It. 44°19′ N, 9°56′ E 167
Filchner Mountains, Antarctica 72°42′ S, 4°23′ E 248
File Axe, Lac, lake, Can. 50°15′ N, 74°7′ W 110
File Lake, Can. 54°50′ N, 100°42′ W 108
Filer, Idaho, U.S. 42°34′ N, 114°37′ W 90
Filer City, Mich., U.S. 44°12′ N, 86°18′ W 102
Filey, U.K. 54°12′ N, 0°18′ E 162
Filia, Gr. 39°15′ N, 26°8′ E 156
Filiaşi, Rom. 44°33′ N, 23°31′ E 156
Filimon Sîrbu, Rom. 45°5′ N, 27°15′ E 156
Filingué, Niger 14°23′ N, 3°17′ E 222
Filipów, Pol. 54°10′ N, 22°36′ E 152
Filisur, Switz. 46°40′ N, 9°40′ E 167
Fillmore, Calif., U.S. 34°24′ N, 118°55′ W 101
Fillmore, Utah, U.S. 38°57′ N, 112°19′ W 90
Fils, Lac du, lake, Can. 46°38′ N, 78°36′ W 94
Filton, U.K. 51°30′ N, 2°35′ W 162
Filtu, Eth. 5°8′ N, 40°39′ E 224
Filyos, river, Turk. 41°28′ N, 31°53′ E 180
Fimbul Ice Shelf, Antarctica 70°45′ S, 0°21′ E 248
Finale Emilia, It. 44°50′ N, 11°17′ E 167
Fiñana, Sp. 37°9′ N, 2°51′ W 164
Finarwa, Eth. 13°4′ N, 38°59′ E 182
Fındıklı, Turk. 41°16′ N, 41°7′ E 195
Findlay, Ill., U.S. 39°31′ N, 88°45′ W 102
Findlay, Ohio, U.S. 41°1′ N, 83°38′ W 102
Findlay, Mount, Can. 50°4′ N, 116°35′ W 90
Fingoè, Mozambique 15°12′ S, 31°51′ E 224
Finike, Turk. 36°17′ N, 30°7′ E 156
Finiq, Alban. 39°54′ N, 20°3′ E 156
Finke, Austral. 25°37′ S, 134°36′ E 231
Finland 63°28′ N, 25°46′ E 152
Finland, Minn., U.S. 47°24′ N, 91°16′ W 94
Finland, Gulf of 60°11′ N, 25°58′ E 152
Finlay, river, Can. 57°38′ N, 126°26′ W 108
Finley, Calif., U.S. 39°0′ N, 122°53′ W 90
Finley, N. Dak., U.S. 47°29′ N, 97°51′ W 90
Finmoore, Can. 53°56′ N, 123°37′ W 108
Finne, region, Europe 51°7′ N, 11°16′ E 152
Finnentrop, Ger. 51°11′ N, 7°58′ E 167
Finnmarks-vidda, Nor. 69°2′ N, 22°6′ E 152
Finnskog, Nor. 60°42′ N, 12°22′ E 152
Finnsnes, Nor. 69°14′ N, 18°0′ E 152
Finse, Nor. 60°36′ N, 7°23′ E 152
Finspång, Nor. 58°41′ N, 15°44′ E 152
Finsteraarhorn, peak, Switz. 46°32′ N, 8°5′ E 167
Finström, Fin. 60°15′ N, 19°54′ E 166
Fiordland National Park, N.Z. 45°0′ S, 165°54′ E 240
Fîrdea, Rom. 45°45′ N, 22°10′ E 168
Fire Island National Seashore, Atlantic Ocean 40°35′ N, 73°26′ W 104
Firebag, river, Can. 57°27′ N, 110°59′ W 108
Firedrake Lake, Can. 61°15′ N, 105°31′ W 108
Firenze (Florence), It. 43°47′ N, 11°14′ E 167
Firenzuola, It. 44°7′ N, 11°22′ E 167
Firmat, Arg. 33°28′ S, 61°30′ W 139
Firozabad, India 27°7′ N, 78°22′ E 197
Firozpur, India 30°57′ N, 74°38′ E 186
First Sugar Mill, site, Hawai'i, U.S. 21°53′ N, 159°30′ W 99
Firūzābād, Iran 28°48′ N, 52°38′ E 196
Fīrūzkūh, Iran 35°46′ N, 52°44′ E 180
Fish Camp, Calif., U.S. 37°28′ N, 119°39′ W 100
Fish Cove Point, Can. 54°4′ N, 57°19′ W 111
Fish Haven, Idaho, U.S. 42°3′ N, 111°24′ W 92
Fish River Canyon Nature Reserve, Namibia 28°4′ S, 17°32′ E 227
Fisher, Ill., U.S. 40°18′ N, 88°21′ W 102
Fisher, La., U.S. 31°28′ N, 93°29′ W 103
Fisher Branch, Can. 51°5′ N, 97°38′ W 90
Fisher Strait 62°55′ N, 84°37′ W 106
Fishers Island, N.Y., U.S. 41°15′ N, 72°12′ W 104
Fishers Peak, Colo., U.S. 37°4′ N, 104°33′ W 92
Fishing Lake, Can. 52°8′ N, 95°50′ W 108
Fiskdale, Mass., U.S. 42°6′ N, 72°8′ W 104
Fiske, Cape, Antarctica 74°15′ S, 60°22′ W 248
Fiskenæsset see Qeqertarsuatsiaat, Den. 63°6′ N, 50°43′ W 106
Fismes, Fr. 49°18′ N, 3°41′ E 163
Fisterra, Cabo, Sp. 42°51′ N, 9°43′ W 150
Fitchburg, Mass., U.S. 42°34′ N, 71°48′ W 104
Fitchville, Conn., U.S. 41°33′ N, 72°9′ W 104
Fitero, Sp. 42°3′ N, 1°52′ W 164
Fitri, Lac, lake, Chad 12°53′ N, 16°54′ E 216
Fitz Roy, Monte, peak, Arg. 49°18′ S, 73°23′ W 134
Fitzcarrald, Peru 11°48′ S, 72°22′ W 137
Fitzgerald, Can. 59°51′ N, 111°41′ W 108
Fitzgerald, Ga., U.S. 31°42′ N, 83°15′ W 96
Fitzpatrick, Can. 47°28′ N, 72°46′ W 94
Fitzroy Crossing, Austral. 18°15′ S, 125°32′ E 238
Fiume see Rijeka, Croatia 45°20′ N, 14°26′ E 156
Fiumicino, It. 41°46′ N, 12°13′ E 156
Fivizzano, It. 44°14′ N, 10°8′ E 167
Fizi, Dem. Rep. of the Congo 4°21′ S, 28°54′ E 224
Fjällåsen, Nor. 67°30′ N, 20°4′ E 152
Flå, Nor. 63°11′ N, 10°19′ E 152
Fladerer Bay 73°19′ S, 84°19′ W 248
Fladungen, Ger. 50°31′ N, 10°7′ E 167
Flagler, Colo., U.S. 39°17′ N, 103°4′ W 90
Flagler Beach, Fla., U.S. 29°28′ N, 81°9′ W 105
Flagstaff, Ariz., U.S. 35°19′ N, 111°35′ W 238
Flåm, Nor. 60°50′ N, 7°7′ E 152
Flamand, Lac, lake, Can. 47°40′ N, 73°50′ W 94
Flamborough, U.K. 54°6′ N, 0°7′ E 162
Flamborough Head, U.K. 54°6′ N, 8°475′ W 162
Flamenco, Isla, island, Arg. 40°29′ S, 62°7′ W 134
Flamingo, Fla., U.S. 25°8′ N, 80°56′ W 105
Flamingo Point, Bahamas 24°43′ N, 76°15′ W 96
Flanagan, Ill., U.S. 40°52′ N, 88°52′ W 102
Flandreau, S. Dak., U.S. 44°1′ N, 96°37′ W 90
Flannan Isles, Atlantic Ocean 58°7′ N, 8°10′ W 150
Flat, Alas., U.S. 62°20′ N, 158°7′ W 98
Flat River, Mo., U.S. 37°50′ N, 90°31′ W 96
Flat, river, Mich., U.S. 43°16′ N, 85°17′ W 102
Flat Rock, Ill., U.S. 38°54′ N, 87°40′ W 102
Flat Top Mountain, Va., U.S. 37°25′ N, 79°39′ W 96
Flatbush, Can. 54°41′ N, 114°9′ W 108
Flateland, Nor. 59°16′ N, 7°29′ E 152
Flathead Lake, Mont., U.S. 47°49′ N, 114°45′ W 90
Flathead Range, Mont., U.S. 48°18′ N, 114°3′ W 90
Flattery, Cape, Wash., U.S. 48°22′ N, 124°53′ W 100
Flavigny-sur-Ozerain, Fr. 47°30′ N, 4°31′ E 150
Flavy-le-Martel, Fr. 49°42′ N, 3°12′ E 163
Flaxton, N. Dak., U.S. 48°53′ N, 102°24′ W 90
Fleeton, Va., U.S. 37°48′ N, 76°17′ W 94
Fleetwood, U.K. 53°55′ N, 3°1′ W 162
Flekkefjord, Nor. 58°13′ N, 6°40′ E 160
Flemingsburg, Ky., U.S. 38°24′ N, 83°45′ W 94
Flemish Cap, North Atlantic Ocean 47°7′ N, 44°36′ W 253
Flen, Nor. 59°3′ N, 16°33′ E 152
Flensburg, Ger. 54°47′ N, 9°25′ E 152
Flers, Fr. 48°44′ N, 0°35′ E 150
Flesberg, Nor. 59°51′ N, 9°25′ E 152
Fletcher, Cape, Antarctica 67°38′ S, 61°20′ E 248
Fletcher Lake, Can. 58°11′ N, 94°38′ W 108
Fletcher Plain, Arctic Ocean 86°43′ N, 162°1′ E 255
Flett Lake, Can. 60°27′ N, 104°25′ W 108
Fleurance, Fr. 43°50′ N, 0°39′ E 150
Fleurier, Switz. 46°54′ N, 6°35′ E 167
Flevoland, adm. division, Neth. 52°18′ N, 4°50′ E 150
Flieden, Ger. 50°25′ N, 9°35′ E 167
Flims, Switz. 46°50′ N, 9°18′ E 167
Flin Flon, Can. 54°47′ N, 101°52′ W 108
Flinders Entrance 9°52′ S, 143°32′ E 230
Flinders Group, islands, Coral Sea 14°38′ S, 144°11′ E 230
Flinders Island, Austral. 40°15′ S, 146°5′ E 230
Flinders Island, Austral. 33°35′ S, 132°48′ E 230
Flinders Passage 19°4′ S, 147°16′ E 230
Flinders Ranges, Austral. 30°14′ S, 138°14′ E 230
Flint, Mich., U.S. 43°0′ N, 83°41′ W 102
Flint, U.K. 53°14′ N, 3°8′ W 162
Flint Creek Range, Mont., U.S. 46°20′ N, 113°15′ W 90
Flint Hills, Kans., U.S. 38°28′ N, 96°36′ W 90
Flint Island, Kiribati 11°27′ S, 151°51′ W 252
Flint Lake, Can. 49°50′ N, 86°11′ W 94
Flint, river, Ala., U.S. 35°3′ N, 86°30′ W 96
Flint, river, Ga., U.S. 30°58′ N, 84°31′ W 112
Flix, Sp. 41°12′ N, 0°32′ E 164
Flixecourt, Fr. 50°0′ N, 2°5′ E 163
Flize, Fr. 49°41′ N, 4°47′ E 163
Flodden, battle, U.K. 55°37′ N, 2°21′ W 150
Flomaton, Ala., U.S. 30°59′ N, 87°17′ W 96
Floodwood, Minn., U.S. 46°55′ N, 92°57′ W 94
Flor de Agosto, Peru 2°24′ S, 73°8′ W 136
Flora, Ill., U.S. 38°39′ N, 88°29′ W 102
Flora, Ind., U.S. 40°32′ N, 86°31′ W 102
Flora, Miss., U.S. 32°31′ N, 90°19′ W 103
Flora, Mo., U.S. 38°39′ N, 88°29′ W 94
Flora, Oreg., U.S. 45°53′ N, 117°20′ W 90
Floral City, Fla., U.S. 28°45′ N, 82°18′ W 105
Florange, Fr. 49°20′ N, 6°8′ E 163
Florence, Ala., U.S. 34°48′ N, 87°43′ W 112
Florence, Ariz., U.S. 33°1′ N, 111°23′ W 92
Florence, Colo., U.S. 38°23′ N, 105°7′ W 90
Florence, Kans., U.S. 38°13′ N, 96°56′ W 90
Florence, Ky., U.S. 38°59′ N, 84°37′ W 102
Florence, Miss., U.S. 32°9′ N, 90°7′ W 103
Florence, Oreg., U.S. 43°58′ N, 124°6′ W 90
Florence, S.C., U.S. 34°11′ N, 79°47′ W 96
Florence, Vt., U.S. 43°42′ N, 73°5′ W 104
Florence, Wis., U.S. 45°55′ N, 88°15′ W 94
Florence Peak, Calif., U.S. 36°24′ N, 118°36′ W 101
Florence see Firenze, It. 43°47′ N, 11°14′ E 167
Florencia, Col. 1°37′ N, 75°38′ W 136
Florennes, Belg. 50°15′ N, 4°36′ E 167
Florenville, Belg. 49°41′ N, 5°19′ E 163
Flores, Braz. 7°53′ S, 37°59′ W 132
Flores, Guatemala 16°57′ N, 89°53′ W 116
Flores, island, Indonesia 9°22′ S, 120°40′ E 192
Flores Sea 7°54′ S, 118°8′ E 192
Florescência, Braz. 9°39′ S, 68°45′ W 137
Floriano, Braz. 6°49′ S, 43°3′ W 132
Florianópolis, Braz. 27°35′ S, 48°30′ W 138
Florida, Bol. 18°32′ S, 63°31′ W 137
Florida, N. Mex., U.S. 34°5′ N, 106°54′ W 92
Florida, Uru. 34°6′ S, 56°14′ W 139
Florida, adm. division, Fla., U.S. 26°39′ N, 82°22′ W 96
Florida Bay 24°55′ N, 80°49′ W 116
Florida Bay 25°4′ N, 80°55′ W 105
Florida City, Fla., U.S. 25°26′ N, 80°30′ W 105
Florida Islands, Solomon Sea 9°0′ S, 160°0′ E 242
Florida Keys, Atlantic Ocean 24°52′ N, 80°55′ W 105
Florida Negra, Arg. 48°18′ S, 67°21′ W 134
Florida Ridge, Fla., U.S. 27°34′ N, 80°22′ W 105
Florida, Straits of 25°7′ N, 79°48′ W 105
Florida's Turnpike, Fla., U.S. 27°49′ N, 81°4′ W 105
Florido, river, Mex. 26°41′ N, 105°4′ W 80
Florien, La., U.S. 31°25′ N, 93°29′ W 103
Florissant, Mo., U.S. 38°47′ N, 90°20′ W 94
Florø, Nor. 61°33′ N, 5°1′ E 160
Flötningen, Nor. 61°51′ N, 12°12′ E 152
Flower Garden Banks National Marine Sanctuary, Gulf of Mexico 28°1′ N, 94°27′ W 103
Flower's Cove, Can. 51°18′ N, 56°43′ W 111
Floyd, La., U.S. 32°39′ N, 91°25′ W 103
Floyd, N. Mex., U.S. 34°12′ N, 103°35′ W 92
Floyd, Mount, Ariz., U.S. 35°22′ N, 112°47′ W 92
Floyd, river, Iowa, U.S. 42°21′ N, 96°36′ W 80
Floydada, Tex., U.S. 33°58′ N, 101°20′ W 92
Flumet, Fr. 45°49′ N, 6°30′ E 167
Flushing, Mich., U.S. 43°4′ N, 83°50′ W 102
Flushing, Ohio, U.S. 40°8′ N, 81°3′ W 102
Flushing see Vlissingen, Neth. 51°27′ N, 3°34′ E 163
Fly Lake, oil field, Austral. 27°35′ S, 139°26′ E 230
Flying Fish, Cape, Antarctica 71°55′ S, 102°43′ W 248
Foam Lake, Can. 51°39′ N, 103°32′ W 90
Foča, Bosn. and Herzg. 43°29′ N, 18°46′ E 168
Fochi, spring, Chad 18°57′ N, 15°56′ E 216
Focşani, Rom. 45°42′ N, 27°10′ E 143
Foga, Sudan 13°37′ N, 27°59′ E 226
Fogang, China 23°48′ N, 113°32′ E 198
Foggaret el Arab, Alg. 27°11′ N, 2°48′ E 214
Foggia, It. 41°29′ N, 15°33′ E 143
Föglö, Fin. 60°0′ N, 20°25′ E 166
Fogo Island, Can. 49°43′ N, 54°0′ W 106
Foinaven, peak, U.K. 58°23′ N, 5°0′ W 150
Foix, Fr. 42°57′ N, 1°37′ E 164
Foix, region, Europe 42°58′ N, 1°22′ E 165
Fojnica, Bosn. and Herzg. 43°56′ N, 17°53′ E 168
Fokino, Russ. 53°23′ N, 34°26′ E 154
Fokku, Nig. 11°41′ N, 4°29′ E 222
Földeák, Hung. 46°20′ N, 20°30′ E 168
Folégandros, island, Gr. 36°28′ N, 24°13′ E 180
Foley, Ala., U.S. 30°24′ N, 87°41′ W 103
Foley, Minn., U.S. 45°38′ N, 93°56′ W 94
Foley Island, Can. 68°24′ N, 77°53′ W 106
Foleyet, Can. 48°14′ N, 82°26′ W 94
Foligno, It. 42°56′ N, 12°43′ E 156
Folkestone, U.K. 51°5′ N, 1°10′ E 163
Folkingham, U.K. 52°53′ N, 0°24′ E 162
Follett, Tex., U.S. 36°25′ N, 100°8′ W 92
Föllinge, Nor. 63°39′ N, 14°37′ E 152
Follonica, It. 42°55′ N, 10°45′ E 156
Folsom, Calif., U.S. 38°40′ N, 121°11′ W 90
Folsom, La., U.S. 30°38′ N, 90°12′ W 103
Folteşti, Rom. 45°44′ N, 28°2′ E 158
Fond du Lac, Wis., U.S. 43°47′ N, 88°26′ W 102
Fond-du-Lac, Can. 59°19′ N, 107°11′ W 108
Fonelas, Sp. 37°24′ N, 3°11′ W 164
Fongafale see Funafuti, Tuvalu 9°0′ S, 179°0′ E 241
Fongen, peak, Nor. 63°9′ N, 11°30′ E 152
Fonseca, Col. 10°52′ N, 72°52′ W 136
Fonseca, Golfo de 13°9′ N, 88°27′ W 112
Fontaine Lake, Can. 59°38′ N, 107°7′ W 108
Fontainebleau, Fr. 48°23′ N, 2°42′ E 163
Fontana, Calif., U.S. 34°5′ N, 117°27′ W 101
Fontas, Can. 58°17′ N, 121°44′ W 108
Fontas, river, Can. 58°10′ N, 121°53′ W 108
Fonte Boa, Braz. 2°33′ S, 66°6′ W 136
Fonteneau, Lac, lake, Can. 51°54′ N, 62°11′ W 111
Fonyód, Hung. 46°43′ N, 17°32′ E 168
Foothills, Can. 53°3′ N, 116°49′ W 108
Foping, China 33°32′ N, 108°1′ E 198
Foppolo, It. 46°3′ N, 9°44′ E 167
Forbes, Mount, Austral. 23°44′ S, 130°22′ E 230
Forbes, Mount, Can. 51°51′ N, 117°3′ W 90
Forcados, Nig. 5°23′ N, 5°26′ E 222
Ford, U.K. 56°10′ N, 5°27′ W 150
Ford City, Calif., U.S. 35°9′ N, 119°29′ W 100
Ford City, Pa., U.S. 40°45′ N, 79°32′ W 94
Ford, Mount, Antarctica 70°50′ S, 163°28′ E 248
Førde, Nor. 61°26′ N, 5°51′ E 152
Fordingbridge, U.K. 50°55′ N, 1°48′ W 162
Fordyce, Ark., U.S. 33°47′ N, 92°24′ W 96
Fore, Nor. 66°55′ N, 13°38′ E 152
Forécariah, Guinea 9°24′ N, 13°7′ W 222
Forel, Mont, peak, Den. 66°56′ N, 37°16′ W 106
Foreman, Ark., U.S. 33°42′ N, 94°25′ W 96
Foremost, Can. 49°28′ N, 111°27′ W 90
Forest, Can. 43°4′ N, 82°0′ W 102
Forest, Miss., U.S. 32°21′ N, 89°30′ W 112
Forest, Ohio, U.S. 40°47′ N, 83°31′ W 102
Forest City, Iowa, U.S. 43°14′ N, 93°39′ W 94
Forest Dale, Vt., U.S. 43°49′ N, 73°4′ W 104
Forest Grove, Oreg., U.S. 45°30′ N, 123°7′ W 90
Forest Hill, La., U.S. 31°1′ N, 92°33′ W 103
Forest Park, Ohio, U.S. 39°16′ N, 84°30′ W 102
Forester Pass, Calif., U.S. 36°42′ N, 118°23′ W 101
Forestville, Can. 48°44′ N, 69°5′ W 94
Forestville, Mich., U.S. 43°39′ N, 82°37′ W 102
Forez, Monts du, Fr. 45°55′ N, 3°30′ E 165
Forgan, Okla., U.S. 36°53′ N, 100°32′ W 92
Forges-les-Eaux, Fr. 49°36′ N, 1°32′ E 163
Forillon National Park, Can. 48°51′ N, 63°58′ W 111
Forks, Wash., U.S. 47°55′ N, 124°24′ W 100
Forlì, It. 44°13′ N, 12°1′ E 167
Forlimpopoli, It. 44°11′ N, 12°6′ E 167
Forman, N. Dak., U.S. 46°5′ N, 97°39′ W 90
Formentera, island, Sp. 38°27′ N, 1°37′ E 214
Formentor, Cap de, Sp. 40°5′ N, 3°19′ E 164
Formerie, Fr. 49°38′ N, 1°44′ E 163
Formiga, Braz. 20°30′ S, 45°26′ W 138
Formosa, Arg. 26°11′ S, 58°11′ W 139
Formosa, Braz. 15°34′ S, 47°20′ W 138
Formosa, adm. division, Arg. 25°6′ S, 59°40′ W 139
Formosa do Rio Prêto, Braz. 11°3′ S, 45°13′ W 130
Formosa, island, Guinea-Bissau 11°37′ N, 16°30′ W 222
Formosa, Serra, Braz. 12°8′ S, 55°27′ W 130
Formoso, Braz. 15°0′ S, 46°15′ W 138
Formoso, Braz. 13°38′ S, 48°55′ W 138
Formoso, river, Braz. 12°45′ S, 49°34′ W 138
Formoso, river, Braz. 14°27′ S, 45°28′ W 138
Forno di Zoldo, It. 46°20′ N, 12°9′ E 167
Fornovo di Taro, It. 44°40′ N, 10°5′ E 167
Føroyar see Faroe Islands, North Atlantic Ocean 62°34′ N, 11°40′ W 143
Forozan, oil field, Kuwait 28°44′ N, 49°43′ E 196
Forrest, Ill., U.S. 40°44′ N, 88°25′ W 102
Forrest City, Ark., U.S. 34°59′ N, 90°48′ W 96
Forrest Lake, Can. 57°31′ N, 109°57′ W 108
Forreston, Ill., U.S. 42°7′ N, 89°35′ W 102
Fors, Nor. 62°59′ N, 16°41′ E 152
Forsand, Nor. 58°53′ N, 6°7′ E 152
Forsayth, Austral. 18°35′ S, 143°34′ E 231
Forsby, Fin. 60°30′ N, 25°57′ E 166
Forse, Nor. 63°8′ N, 17°0′ E 154
Forsmark, Nor. 65°29′ N, 15°49′ E 152
Forsnäs, Nor. 66°14′ N, 18°37′ E 152
Forssa, Fin. 60°49′ N, 23°37′ E 166
Forst, Ger. 51°44′ N, 14°38′ E 152
Forsyth, Mo., U.S. 36°40′ N, 93°7′ W 96
Forsyth, Mont., U.S. 46°14′ N, 106°40′ W 90
Forsyth Island, Austral. 16°59′ S, 137°1′ E 230
Forsyth Lake, Can. 59°31′ N, 107°59′ W 108
Fort Abbas, Pak. 29°13′ N, 72°54′ E 186
Fort Adams, Miss., U.S. 31°4′ N, 91°34′ W 103
Fort Albany, Can. 52°13′ N, 81°39′ W 110
Fort Assiniboine, Can. 54°21′ N, 114°47′ W 108
Fort Atkinson, Wis., U.S. 42°55′ N, 88°51′ W 102
Fort Belvoir, Va., U.S. 38°40′ N, 77°13′ W 94
Fort Benjamin Harrison, Ind., U.S. 39°51′ N, 86°4′ W 102
Fort Benning, Ga., U.S. 32°19′ N, 85°2′ W 96
Fort Benton, Mont., U.S. 47°48′ N, 110°40′ W 90
Fort Black, Can. 55°24′ N, 107°45′ W 108
Fort Bragg, Calif., U.S. 39°26′ N, 123°49′ W 90
Fort Caroline National Memorial, Fla., U.S. 30°20′ N, 81°34′ W 96
Fort Chipewyan, Can. 58°43′ N, 111°7′ W 108
Fort Clatsop National Memorial, Oreg., U.S. 46°6′ N, 123°55′ W 100
Fort Collins, Colo., U.S. 40°34′ N, 105°6′ W 90
Fort Collinson, site, Can. 71°36′ N, 118°5′ W 106
Fort Conger, site, Can. 81°49′ N, 65°57′ W 246
Fort Defiance, Ariz., U.S. 35°43′ N, 109°6′ W 82
Fort Deposit, Ala., U.S. 31°59′ N, 86°34′ W 96
Fort Detrick, Md., U.S. 39°25′ N, 77°31′ W 94
Fort Devens, Mass., U.S. 42°31′ N, 71°38′ W 104
Fort Dick, Calif., U.S. 41°51′ N, 124°10′ W 90
Fort Dodge, Iowa, U.S. 42°29′ N, 94°11′ W 94
Fort Dorval, Péninsule du, Can. 50°56′ N, 73°21′ W 111
Fort Edward, N.Y., U.S. 43°15′ N, 73°36′ W 104
Fort Frances, Can. 48°40′ N, 93°33′ W 106
Fort Fraser, Can. 54°3′ N, 124°31′ W 108
Fort Gay, W. Va., U.S. 38°6′ N, 82°37′ W 94
Fort Gibson, Okla., U.S. 35°46′ N, 95°15′ W 96
Fort Good Hope, Can. 66°14′ N, 128°29′ W 106
Fort Gordon, Ga., U.S. 33°22′ N, 82°16′ W 96
Fort Gouraud see Fdérik, Mauritania 22°41′ N, 12°43′ W 214
Fort Hall, Idaho, U.S. 43°3′ N, 112°26′ W 90
Fort Hill see Chitipa, Malawi 9°43′ S, 33°14′ E 224
Fort Hope, Can. 51°33′ N, 88°1′ W 110
Fort Irwin, Calif., U.S. 35°15′ N, 116°42′ W 101
Fort Kent, Me., U.S. 47°15′ N, 68°35′ W 111
Fort Laramie, Wyo., U.S. 42°12′ N, 104°31′ W 90
Fort Laramie National Historic Site, Wyo., U.S. 42°10′ N, 104°38′ W 90
Fort Lauderdale, Fla., U.S. 26°7′ N, 80°10′ W 105
Fort Lewis, Wash., U.S. 47°2′ N, 122°36′ W 100
Fort Liard, Can. 60°14′ N, 123°26′ W 108
Fort Lupton, Colo., U.S. 40°4′ N, 104°49′ W 90
Fort MacKay, Can. 57°12′ N, 111°42′ W 108
Fort Macleod, Can. 49°42′ N, 113°24′ W 90
Fort Madison, Iowa, U.S. 40°38′ N, 91°20′ W 94
Fort Matanzas National Monument, Fla., U.S. 29°43′ N, 81°19′ W 105
Fort McKinley, Ohio, U.S. 39°47′ N, 84°16′ W 102
Fort McMurray, Can. 56°40′ N, 111°23′ W 108
Fort McPherson, Can. 67°27′ N, 134°44′ W 98
Fort Mill, S.C., U.S. 35°0′ N, 80°56′ W 96
Fort Miribel, Alg. 29°26′ N, 3°1′ E 214
Fort Morgan, Ala., U.S. 30°13′ N, 88°3′ W 103
Fort Morgan, Colo., U.S. 40°15′ N, 103°49′ W 90
Fort Motylinski see Tarhaouhaout, Alg. 22°38′ N, 5°55′ E 214
Fort Myers, Fla., U.S. 26°38′ N, 81°52′ W 105
Fort Myers Beach, Fla., U.S. 26°27′ N, 81°57′ W 105
Fort Necessity National Battlefield, Pa., U.S. 39°47′ N, 79°42′ W 94
Fort Nelson, Can. 58°42′ N, 122°42′ W 106
Fort Nelson, river, Can. 59°20′ N, 123°45′ W 108
Fort Niagara, site, N.Y., U.S. 43°14′ N, 79°8′ W 94
Fort Ogden, Fla., U.S. 27°5′ N, 81°57′ W 105
Fort Payne, Ala., U.S. 34°25′ N, 85°44′ W 96
Fort Peck, Mont., U.S. 47°59′ N, 106°28′ W 90
Fort Peck Dam, Mont., U.S. 47°43′ N, 106°34′ W 90
Fort Peck Lake, Mont., U.S. 47°40′ N, 107°29′ W 90
Fort Pierce, Fla., U.S. 27°26′ N, 80°20′ W 105
Fort Pierre, S. Dak., U.S. 44°21′ N, 100°23′ W 90
Fort Pierre Bordes see Ti-n-Zaouâtene, Alg. 19°58′ N, 2°57′ E 222
Fort Polk, La., U.S. 31°0′ N, 93°15′ W 103
Fort Portal, Uganda 0°38′ N, 30°16′ E 224
Fort Prince of Wales National Historical Park, Can. 58°44′ N, 94°24′ W 108
Fort Providence, Can. 61°24′ N, 117°36′ W 108
Fort Qu' Appelle, Can. 50°43′ N, 103°50′ W 90
Fort Quitman, site, Tex., U.S. 31°3′ N, 105°40′ W 92
Fort Recovery, Ohio, U.S. 40°23′ N, 84°46′ W 102
Fort Resolution, Can. 61°10′ N, 113°39′ W 108
Fort Ritchie, Md., U.S. 39°41′ N, 77°35′ W 94
Fort Rock, Oreg., U.S. 43°20′ N, 121°4′ W 90
Fort Saint, Tun. 30°16′ N, 9°36′ E 214
Fort Saint James, Can. 54°25′ N, 124°12′ W 108
Fort Saint John, Can. 56°13′ N, 120°52′ W 108
Fort Sam Houston, Tex., U.S. 29°26′ N, 98°31′ W 92
Fort Saskatchewan, Can. 53°41′ N, 113°14′ W 108
Fort Scott, Kans., U.S. 37°48′ N, 94°42′ W 96
Fort Severn, Can. 56°0′ N, 87°42′ W 106
Fort Shafter, Hawai'i, U.S. 21°19′ N, 157°56′ W 99
Fort Shawnee, Ohio, U.S. 40°40′ N, 84°8′ W 102
Fort Shevchenko, Kaz. 44°30′ N, 50°16′ E 158
Fort Sill, Okla., U.S. 34°38′ N, 98°29′ W 92
Fort Simcoe, site, Wash., U.S. 46°18′ N, 120°57′ W 90
Fort Simpson, Can. 61°49′ N, 121°23′ W 106
Fort Smith, Ark., U.S. 35°20′ N, 94°25′ W 96
Fort Smith, Can. 60°2′ N, 112°11′ W 106
Fort St. John, Can. 56°13′ N, 120°53′ W 246
Fort Stockton, Tex., U.S. 30°52′ N, 102°53′ W 92
Fort Sumner, N. Mex., U.S. 34°28′ N, 104°14′ W 92
Fort Supply, Okla., U.S. 36°33′ N, 99°34′ W 92
Fort Supply Lake, Okla., U.S. 36°21′ N, 100°49′ W 81
Fort Ternan, Kenya 0°13′ N, 35°22′ E 224
Fort Thompson, S. Dak., U.S. 44°4′ N, 99°28′ W 90
Fort Trinquet see Bir Mogreïn, Mauritania 25°13′ N, 11°37′ W 214
Fort Union National Monument, N. Mex., U.S. 35°53′ N, 105°6′ W 92
Fort Valley, Ga., U.S. 32°32′ N, 83°53′ W 96
Fort Vermilion, Can. 58°22′ N, 115°58′ W 108
Fort Wayne, Ind., U.S. 41°3′ N, 85°8′ W 102
Fort White, Fla., U.S. 29°55′ N, 82°43′ W 105
Fort Worth, Tex., U.S. 32°43′ N, 97°19′ W 92
Fort Yates, N. Dak., U.S. 46°4′ N, 100°40′ W 90
Fort Yukon, Alas., U.S. 66°32′ N, 145°5′ W 106
Fortaleza, Bol. 12°6′ S, 66°51′ W 137
Fortaleza, Bol. 9°49′ S, 65°30′ W 137
Fortaleza, Braz. 3°46′ S, 38°32′ W 132
Fort-Coulonge, Can. 45°50′ N, 76°44′ W 94
Fort-de-France, Fr. 14°36′ N, 61°4′ W 116
Forteau, Can. 51°26′ N, 56°59′ W 111
Fortezza, It. 46°47′ N, 11°35′ E 167
Fortim, Braz. 4°30′ S, 37°49′ W 132
Fortín, Mex. 18°54′ N, 97°1′ W 114
Fortín Carlos A. LŽopez, Parag. 21°19′ S, 59°42′ W 132
Fortín General Díaz, Parag. 23°31′ S, 60°35′ W 132
Fortín Infante Rivarola, Parag. 21°38′ S, 62°25′ W 132
Fortín Madrejón, Parag. 20°37′ S, 59°52′ W 132
Fortín Presidente Ayala, Parag. 23°29′ S, 59°43′ W 132
Fortín Suárez Arana, Bol. 18°39′ S, 60°9′ W 132
Fortín Teniente Américo Picco, Parag. 19°39′ S, 59°47′ W 132
Fortress Mountain, Wyo., U.S. 44°18′ N, 109°53′ W 90
Fortress of Louisbourg National Historic Site, Can. 45°52′ N, 60°7′ W 111
Fortun, Nor. 61°30′ N, 7°39′ E 152
Fortuna, N. Dak., U.S. 48°53′ N, 103°47′ W 90
Fortune Island see Long Cay, Bahamas 22°35′ N, 76°5′ W 116
Fortville, Ind., U.S. 39°55′ N, 85°51′ W 102
Forūr, island, Iran 26°8′ N, 54°22′ E 180
Foshan, China 23°3′ N, 113°6′ E 198
Fosheim Peninsula, Can. 79°5′ N, 90°14′ W 246
Fosna, Nor. 63°36′ N, 9°53′ E 152
Fosnes, Nor. 64°39′ N, 11°17′ E 152
Foso, Ghana 5°42′ N, 1°18′ W 222
Fossacesia, It. 42°14′ N, 14°28′ E 156
Fossano, It. 44°33′ N, 7°42′ E 167
Fossil, Oreg., U.S. 44°59′ N, 120°13′ W 82
Fosston, Minn., U.S. 47°33′ N, 95°47′ W 90
Foster, Austral. 38°38′ S, 146°11′ E 231
Foster Bugt 72°24′ N, 28°4′ W 73
Foster Center, R.I., U.S. 41°47′ N, 71°44′ W 104
Foster, Mount, Can. 59°45′ N, 135°37′ W 108
Foster Peak, Can. 51°3′ N, 116°15′ W 90
Foster, river, Can. 56°21′ N, 105°54′ W 108
Fostoria, Ohio, U.S. 41°9′ N, 83°24′ W 102
Fota Terara, peak, Eth. 9°8′ N, 38°24′ E 224
Fotokol, Cameroon 12°26′ N, 14°16′ E 216
Fouke, Ark., U.S. 33°15′ N, 93°54′ W 103
Foulweather, Cape, Oreg., U.S. 44°47′ N, 124°44′ W 90
Foulwind, Cape, N.Z. 41°48′ S, 171°0′ E 240
Foum Tataouine, Tun. 32°57′ N, 10°26′ E 216
Foum Zguid, Mor. 30°6′ N, 6°55′ W 214
Foumban, Cameroon 5°42′ N, 10°52′ E 222
Fountain, Colo., U.S. 38°41′ N, 104°42′ W 92
Fountain, Mich., U.S. 44°3′ N, 86°11′ W 102
Fountain City, Ind., U.S. 39°57′ N, 84°55′ W 102
Fountain City, Wis., U.S. 44°8′ N, 91°42′ W 110
Fountain Hill, Ark., U.S. 33°20′ N, 91°52′ W 103
Four Corners Monument, U.S. 36°59′ N, 109°6′ W 92
Four, spring, Mauritania 16°3′ N, 8°50′ W 222
Fourcroy, Cape, Austral. 11°36′ S, 128°59′ E 230
Fourmies, Fr. 50°1′ N, 4°2′ E 163
Foúrni, Gr. 37°34′ N, 26°29′ E 156
Fournier, Lac, lake, Can. 51°28′ N, 66°0′ W 111
Fouta Djallon, region, Africa 12°3′ N, 12°50′ W 222
Fowler, Calif., U.S. 36°38′ N, 119°42′ W 100
Fowler, Colo., U.S. 38°7′ N, 104°2′ W 90
Fowler, Ind., U.S. 40°36′ N, 87°19′ W 102
Fowler, Kans., U.S. 37°22′ N, 100°12′ W 92
Fowler, Mich., U.S. 42°59′ N, 84°45′ W 102
Fowlers Bay 32°11′ S, 131°19′ E 230
Fowlerville, Mich., U.S. 42°39′ N, 84°4′ W 102
Fox Creek, Can. 54°23′ N, 116°48′ W 108
Fox Glacier, N.Z. 43°30′ S, 170°0′ E 240
Fox Islands, Anadyrskiy Zaliv 52°57′ N, 168°37′ W 98
Fox Lake, Can. 58°26′ N, 114°31′ W 108
Fox Lake, Wis., U.S. 43°32′ N, 88°54′ W 102
Fox Mountain, Nev., U.S. 41°0′ N, 119°39′ W 90
Fox Point, Wis., U.S. 43°9′ N, 87°54′ W 102
Fox, river, Can. 55°57′ N, 93°55′ W 108
Fox, river, Wis., U.S. 43°56′ N, 89°2′ W 102
Fox Valley, Can. 50°28′ N, 109°29′ W 90
Foxboro, Mass., U.S. 42°3′ N, 71°16′ W 104
Foxe Basin 67°2′ N, 80°27′ W 106
Foxe Channel 64°14′ N, 82°12′ W 106
Foxe Peninsula, Can. 64°50′ N, 80°3′ W 106
Foxton, N.Z. 40°29′ S, 175°19′ E 240
Foxworth, Miss., U.S. 31°13′ N, 89°53′ W 103
Foyé, Guinea 11°17′ N, 13°31′ W 222

G

Gambia Plain, North Atlantic Ocean 12°33′ N, 27°53′ W 253
Gambie, river, Senegal 12°54′ N, 13°7′ W 222
Gambier, Ohio, U.S. 40°22′ N, 82°23′ W 102
Gambier, Îles, islands, South Pacific Ocean 22°42′ S, 138°12′ W 238
Gambier Island, Can. 49°32′ N, 123°36′ W 100
Gambier Islands, Great Australian Bight 35°21′ S, 136°39′ E 230
Gamboma, Congo 1°54′ S, 15°51′ E 218
Gamboula, Cen. Af. Rep. 4°10′ N, 15°12′ E 218
Gamdou, Niger 13°27′ N, 10°3′ E 222
Gamlakarleby see Kokkola, Fin. 63°49′ N, 23°5′ E 152
Gamleby, Nor. 57°54′ N, 16°23′ E 152
Gamma, oil field, Azerb. 39°43′ N, 49°19′ E 195
Gammelstad, Nor. 65°37′ N, 22°1′ E 152
Gamoep, S. Af. 29°55′ S, 18°23′ E 227
Gamova, Mys, Russ. 42°24′ N, 131°12′ E 200
Gamph, Slieve (Ox Mountains, The), Ire. 54°2′ N, 9°28′ W 150
Gampo, S. Korea 35°47′ N, 129°32′ E 200
Gamsby, river, Can. 53°5′ N, 127°21′ W 108
Gamud, peak, Eth. 4°1′ N, 38°3′ E 224
Gamyshlyja, Turkm. 38°21′ N, 54°0′ E 180
Gan, Fr. 43°14′ N, 0°23′ E 164
Gan Gan, Arg. 42°29′ S, 68°11′ W 134
Gan, island, Maldives 0°2′ N, 73°22′ E 188
Gan, river, China 26°29′ N, 114°32′ E 198
Gan, river, China 49°20′ N, 124°41′ E 198
Ganado, Ariz., U.S. 35°42′ N, 109°32′ W 92
Ganado, Tex., U.S. 29°2′ N, 96°31′ W 96
Gäncä, Azerb. 40°41′ N, 46°20′ E 195
Gandajika, Dem. Rep. of the Congo 6°46′ S, 23°58′ E 224
Gander, Can. 48°56′ N, 54°29′ W 106
Gander, river, Can. 48°55′ N, 54°53′ W 111
Gandhidham, India 23°5′ N, 70°8′ E 186
Gandhinagar, India 23°19′ N, 72°38′ E 186
Gandi, Nig. 13°2′ N, 4°51′ E 222
Gandia, Sp. 38°57′ N, 0°11′ E 164
Gandino, It. 45°49′ N, 9°54′ E 167
Gandole, Nig. 8°24′ N, 11°37′ E 222
Gandu, Braz. 13°46′ S, 39°30′ W 138
Gang, island, Maldives 1°34′ N, 73°29′ E 188
Ganga (Ganges), river, India 26°9′ N, 81°17′ E 190
Gangala na Bodio, Dem. Rep. of the Congo 3°38′ N, 29°9′ E 224
Ganganagar, India 29°56′ N, 73°54′ E 186
Gangdaba, Tchabal, Cameroon 7°23′ N, 11°49′ E 218
Gangdisê Shan, China 30°58′ N, 83°13′ E 197
Gangelt, Ger. 50°59′ N, 5°59′ E 167
Ganges Fan, Bay of Bengal 14°34′ N, 84°35′ E 254
Ganges, river, India 25°40′ N, 81°12′ E 197
Ganges see Ganga, river, India 26°9′ N, 81°17′ E 190
Ganggyeong, S. Korea 36°9′ N, 127°3′ E 200
Ganghwa, S. Korea 37°44′ N, 126°29′ E 200
Gangi, It. 37°47′ N, 14°12′ E 156
Gangjin, S. Korea 34°37′ N, 126°47′ E 200
Gangneung, S. Korea 37°45′ N, 128°53′ E 200
Gangtok, India 27°23′ N, 88°35′ E 197
Gangu, China 34°43′ N, 105°18′ E 198
Gangwon, adm. division, S. Korea 37°45′ N, 128°15′ E 200
Ganhe, China 50°43′ N, 123°14′ E 238
Gania, Guinea 11°1′ N, 10°21′ W 222
Ganjam, India 19°25′ N, 85°3′ E 188
Gannan, China 47°53′ N, 123°31′ E 198
Gannat, Fr. 46°5′ N, 3°12′ E 150
Gannett Peak, Wyo., U.S. 43°10′ N, 109°45′ W 90
Ganongga see Ranongga, island, Solomon Islands 8°5′ S, 156°30′ E 242
Ganquan, China 36°19′ N, 109°25′ E 198
Ganseong, S. Korea 38°22′ N, 128°27′ E 200
Gansu, adm. division, China 38°17′ N, 101°53′ E 188
Ganta, Liberia 7°5′ N, 9°0′ W 222
Gantgaw, Myanmar 22°12′ N, 94°9′ E 188
Ganwo, Nig. 11°11′ N, 4°37′ E 222
Ganyushkino, Kaz. 46°36′ N, 49°16′ E 158
Ganzhou, China 25°56′ N, 114°57′ E 198
Gao, Mali 16°16′ N, 1°59′ W 222
Gaolan, China 36°22′ N, 103°56′ E 198
Gaoping, China 35°46′ N, 112°53′ E 198
Gaoua, Burkina Faso 10°19′ N, 3°12′ W 222
Gaoual, Guinea 11°46′ N, 13°16′ W 222
Gaoyang, China 38°42′ N, 115°49′ E 198
Gaoyou Hu, lake, China 32°42′ N, 118°40′ E 198
Gap, Fr. 44°32′ N, 6°4′ E 150
Gapan, Philippines 15°19′ N, 120°56′ E 203
Gapyeong, S. Korea 37°49′ N, 127°31′ E 200
Gar, China 32°11′ N, 79°57′ E 188
Gara, Hung. 46°1′ N, 19°3′ E 168
Garabogaz Aylagy, lake, Turkm. 41°4′ N, 51°40′ E 160
Garabogazköl, Turkm. 41°2′ N, 52°55′ E 158
Garacad, Somalia 6°55′ N, 49°23′ E 218
Garachiné, Pan. 8°3′ N, 78°23′ W 115
Garadag, Somalia 9°26′ N, 46°55′ E 216
Garadase, Eth. 5°4′ N, 38°9′ E 224
Garagum, Turkm. 37°50′ N, 63°24′ E 197
Garamba National Park, Dem. Rep. of the Congo 4°27′ N, 28°50′ E 224
Garamba, river, Dem. Rep. of the Congo 3°44′ N, 29°17′ E 224
Garanhuns, Braz. 8°52′ S, 36°31′ W 132
Garapuava, Braz. 16°6′ S, 46°37′ W 138
Garavuti, Taj. 37°31′ N, 68°25′ E 184
Garawe, Liberia 4°37′ N, 7°53′ W 222
Garba Tula, Kenya 0°29′ N, 38°32′ E 224
Garbahaarrey, Somalia 3°7′ N, 42°11′ E 224
Garberville, Calif., U.S. 40°6′ N, 123°48′ W 82
Garbyang, India 30°9′ N, 80°49′ E 197
Garça, Braz. 22°14′ S, 49°43′ W 138
Garças, river, Braz. 8°40′ S, 40°29′ W 132
García de la Cadena, Mex. 21°9′ N, 103°28′ W 114
Garcias, Braz. 20°36′ S, 52°14′ W 138
Garden City, Kans., U.S. 37°58′ N, 100°53′ W 90
Garden City, N.Y., U.S. 40°43′ N, 73°38′ W 104
Garden Creek, Can. 58°43′ N, 113°56′ W 108
Garden Lake, Can. 49°28′ N, 90°15′ W 94
Garden of the Gods, site, Hawai'i, U.S. 20°52′ N, 157°2′ W 99
Garden Peninsula, Mich., U.S. 45°49′ N, 86°42′ W 94
Garden, river, Can. 46°37′ N, 84°5′ W 94
Gardiner, Me., U.S. 44°12′ N, 69°47′ W 104
Gardiner, Mont., U.S. 45°2′ N, 110°42′ W 90
Gardiner, Oreg., U.S. 43°43′ N, 124°6′ W 90
Gardiner Dam, Can. 51°2′ N, 107°12′ W 90
Gardiner, Mount, Austral. 22°15′ S, 132°27′ E 230
Gardiners Island, N.Y., U.S. 41°4′ N, 72°5′ W 104
Gardiz, Afghan. 33°35′ N, 69°12′ E 186
Gardner, Ill., U.S. 41°11′ N, 88°18′ W 102
Gardner, Mass., U.S. 42°34′ N, 72°0′ W 104
Gardner Canal 53°19′ N, 128°44′ W 108
Gardner Pinnacles, Hawai'i, U.S. 24°57′ N, 169°23′ W 99
Gárdony, Hung. 47°12′ N, 18°38′ E 168
Gares see Puente la Reina, Sp. 42°39′ N, 1°49′ W 164
Garešnica, Croatia 45°33′ N, 16°56′ E 168
Garf Husein, ruin(s), Egypt 23°12′ N, 32°42′ E 182
Garfield Mountain, Mont., U.S. 44°29′ N, 112°40′ W 90
Garfield Peak, Wyo., U.S. 42°42′ N, 107°21′ W 90
Gargan, Mont, peak, Fr. 45°36′ N, 1°37′ E 165
Gargano, Promontorio del, It. 41°45′ N, 15°55′ E 168
Gargano, Testa del, It. 41°48′ N, 16°12′ E 168
Gargantua, Cape, Can. 47°34′ N, 85°38′ W 94
Gargouna, Mali 15°59′ N, 0°14′ E 222
Gargždai, Lith. 55°43′ N, 21°23′ E 166
Garhakota, India 23°45′ N, 79°10′ E 197
Gari, Russ. 59°26′ N, 62°21′ E 154
Garibaldi, Braz. 29°16′ S, 51°32′ W 139
Garibaldi, Can. 49°57′ N, 123°9′ W 100
Garibaldi, Mount, Can. 49°49′ N, 123°2′ W 100
Garibaldi, Paso, pass, Arg. 54°35′ S, 67°38′ W 134
Garies, S. Af. 30°34′ S, 17°58′ E 227
Garissa, Kenya 0°30′ N, 39°39′ E 224
Garitz, Ger. 50°11′ N, 10°2′ E 167
Garko, Nig. 11°37′ N, 8°48′ E 222
Garland, Ark., U.S. 33°20′ N, 93°44′ W 103
Garland, Tex., U.S. 32°52′ N, 96°39′ W 96
Garlasco, It. 45°11′ N, 8°54′ E 167
Garliava, Lith. 54°49′ N, 23°51′ E 166
Garlin, Fr. 43°33′ N, 0°17′ E 150
Garmsār, Iran 35°13′ N, 52°15′ E 180
Garner, Iowa, U.S. 43°5′ N, 93°35′ W 94
Garnet Range, Mont., U.S. 46°51′ N, 113°35′ W 90
Garnett, Kans., U.S. 38°15′ N, 95°14′ W 94
Garonne, river, Fr. 44°36′ N, 1°0′ E 143
Garopaba, Braz. 28°4′ S, 48°40′ W 138
Garou, Lac, lake, Mali 16°2′ N, 3°4′ W 222
Garoua, Cameroon 9°18′ N, 13°22′ E 216
Garoua, Niger 13°53′ N, 13°9′ E 216
Garoua Boulaï, Cameroon 5°48′ N, 14°34′ E 218
Garré, Arg. 36°34′ S, 62°35′ W 139
Garrett, Ind., U.S. 41°20′ N, 85°9′ W 102
Garrettsville, Ohio, U.S. 41°16′ N, 81°6′ W 102
Garrison, Ky., U.S. 38°35′ N, 83°10′ W 102
Garrison, N. Dak., U.S. 47°38′ N, 101°26′ W 90
Garrison, Tex., U.S. 31°49′ N, 94°30′ W 103
Garrison, Utah, U.S. 38°55′ N, 114°2′ W 92
Garrucha, Sp. 37°10′ N, 1°50′ W 164
Garruchos, Braz. 28°16′ S, 55°41′ W 139
Garry Lake, Can. 65°58′ N, 102°24′ W 106
Garrygala, Turkm. 38°27′ N, 56°17′ E 180
Garsen, Kenya 2°18′ S, 40°5′ E 224
Garsila, Sudan 12°21′ N, 23°7′ E 216
Garson Lake, Can. 56°14′ N, 110°41′ W 108
Garssen, Ger. 52°39′ N, 10°7′ E 150
Garstang, U.K. 53°54′ N, 2°47′ W 162
Gartow, Ger. 53°1′ N, 11°27′ E 152
Garub, Namibia 26°38′ S, 16°5′ E 227
Garvão, Port. 37°42′ N, 8°21′ W 150
Garwa, India 24°9′ N, 83°48′ E 197
Gary, Ind., U.S. 41°34′ N, 87°22′ W 102
Gary, Tex., U.S. 32°1′ N, 94°23′ W 103
Garyarsa, China 31°36′ N, 80°31′ E 188
Garyville, La., U.S. 30°3′ N, 90°37′ W 103
Garza, Arg. 28°10′ S, 63°34′ W 139
Garzan, oil field, Turk. 37°53′ N, 41°38′ E 195
Garzê, China 31°42′ N, 99°51′ E 190
Garzón, Col. 2°11′ N, 75°40′ W 136
Garzón, Uru. 34°37′ S, 54°34′ W 139
Gas, Kans., U.S. 37°53′ N, 95°21′ W 94
Gas City, Ind., U.S. 40°28′ N, 85°37′ W 102
Gasa, Bhutan 27°54′ N, 89°35′ E 197
Gascony, region, Europe 42°47′ N, 1°18′ E 165
Gascueña, Sp. 40°17′ N, 2°31′ W 164
Gåsefjord 69°54′ N, 29°46′ W 246
Gåseland, Den. 70°12′ N, 32°55′ W 246
Gashagar, Nig. 13°20′ N, 12°46′ E 216
Gashaka, Nig. 7°19′ N, 11°29′ E 222
Gashua, Nig. 12°52′ N, 11°5′ E 222
Gąski, Pol. 53°56′ N, 22°25′ E 166
Gąsocin, Pol. 52°43′ N, 20°41′ E 152
Gasparilla Island, Fla., U.S. 26°43′ N, 82°25′ W 105
Gaspé, Cap, Can. 48°41′ N, 64°8′ W 111
Gaspé Peninsula, Can. 48°18′ N, 67°57′ W 80
Gass Peak, Nev., U.S. 36°22′ N, 115°14′ W 101
Gassol, Nig. 8°31′ N, 10°29′ E 222
Gassville, Ark., U.S. 36°16′ N, 92°30′ W 96
Gastilovtsy, Belarus 53°44′ N, 24°57′ E 152
Gaston, N.C., U.S. 36°30′ N, 77°39′ W 96
Gaston, Lake, Va., U.S. 36°30′ N, 78°23′ W 96
Gastonia, N.C., U.S. 35°15′ N, 81°12′ W 96
Gastre, Arg. 42°19′ S, 69°18′ W 134
Gåsvær, islands, Norwegian Sea 66°1′ N, 10°55′ E 152
Gata, Cabo de, Sp. 36°32′ N, 2°12′ W 164
Gata, Cape, Cyprus 34°29′ N, 32°59′ E 194
Gata de Gorgos, Sp. 38°46′ N, 0°5′ E 164
Gata, Sierra de, Sp. 40°8′ N, 6°50′ W 150
Gataga, river, Can. 58°25′ N, 126°18′ W 108
Gătaia, Rom. 45°26′ N, 21°26′ E 168
Gatchina, Russ. 59°32′ N, 30°5′ E 152
Gate, Okla., U.S. 36°49′ N, 100°2′ W 92
Gate City, Va., U.S. 36°38′ N, 82°36′ W 96
Gatelo, Eth. 5°59′ N, 38°11′ E 224
Gates of the Rocky Mountains, pass, Mont., U.S. 46°51′ N, 111°56′ W 90
Gateshead, U.K. 54°56′ N, 1°37′ W 150
Gateway, Colo., U.S. 38°42′ N, 108°58′ W 90
Gatico, Chile 22°32′ S, 70°17′ W 137
Gâtine, Hauteurs de, Fr. 47°1′ N, 1°14′ W 150
Gatineau, Can. 45°28′ N, 75°40′ W 82
Gatineau, river, Can. 45°55′ N, 76°8′ W 94
Gaṭrūyeh, Iran 29°13′ N, 54°40′ E 196
Gattinara, It. 45°37′ N, 8°21′ E 167
Gatwick, U.K. 51°8′ N, 0°10′ E 162
Gaucín, Sp. 36°30′ N, 5°20′ W 164
Gauer Lake, Can. 57°1′ N, 98°6′ W 108
Gauja, river, Latv. 57°13′ N, 24°50′ E 166
Gaujiena, Latv. 57°30′ N, 26°23′ E 166
Gauré, Lith. 55°14′ N, 22°28′ E 166
Gausta, peak, Nor. 59°50′ N, 8°31′ E 152
Gauteng, adm. division, S. Af. 26°24′ S, 27°21′ E 227
Gauya National Park, Latv. 57°19′ N, 24°42′ E 166
Gavà, Sp. 41°17′ N, 2°1′ E 164
Gavāter, Iran 25°7′ N, 61°29′ E 182
Gāvbandī, Iran 27°8′ N, 53°5′ E 196
Gávdos, island, Gr. 34°37′ N, 23°48′ E 180
Gavião, Port. 39°26′ N, 7°57′ W 150
Gavião, river, Braz. 14°42′ S, 41°0′ W 138
Gaviota, Calif., U.S. 34°28′ N, 120°14′ W 100
Gaviotas, Col. 4°26′ N, 70°47′ W 136
Gavirate, It. 45°51′ N, 8°42′ E 167
Gävle, Sw. 60°40′ N, 16°57′ E 160
Gavrilov Yam, Russ. 57°16′ N, 39°51′ E 154
Gavrilovo, Russ. 69°12′ N, 35°51′ E 152
Gávrovon, peak, Gr. 39°8′ N, 21°15′ E 156
Gavry, Russ. 56°54′ N, 27°52′ E 166
Gawachab, Namibia 27°4′ S, 17°50′ E 227
Gawler, Austral. 34°35′ S, 138°45′ E 231
Gawler Ranges, Austral. 32°9′ S, 135°22′ E 230
Gay, Russ. 51°25′ N, 58°25′ E 158
Gay Head, Mass., U.S. 41°17′ N, 70°55′ W 104
Gaya, India 24°48′ N, 84°59′ E 197
Gaya, Nig. 11°51′ N, 9°1′ E 222
Gaya, Niger 11°55′ N, 3°26′ E 222
Gayaza, Uganda 0°50′ N, 30°47′ E 224
Gaylor Mountain, Ark., U.S. 35°43′ N, 94°11′ W 96
Gaylord, Mich., U.S. 45°1′ N, 84°41′ W 94
Gaylord, Minn., U.S. 44°32′ N, 94°15′ W 90
Gayny, Russ. 60°19′ N, 54°19′ E 154
Gaza, adm. division, Mozambique 23°14′ S, 31°51′ E 220
Gaza City see Ghazzah, Gaza Strip, Israel 31°29′ N, 34°28′ E 194
Gaza Strip, special sovereignity, Israel 31°21′ N, 33°57′ E 194
Gazak, Iran 27°37′ N, 59°57′ E 182
G'azalkent, Uzb. 41°33′ N, 69°44′ E 197
Gazamni, Niger 14°20′ N, 10°31′ E 222
Gazanjyk, Turkm. 39°10′ N, 55°47′ E 180
Gazaoua, Niger 13°35′ N, 7°55′ E 222
Gazelle Peninsula, P.N.G. 4°33′ S, 151°15′ E 192
Gazi, Dem. Rep. of the Congo 1°3′ N, 24°28′ E 224
Gazi, Kenya 4°27′ S, 39°29′ E 224
Gaziantep, Turk. 37°2′ N, 37°25′ E 180
Gazimagusa see Ammochostos, Northern Cyprus, Cyprus 35°7′ N, 33°56′ E 194
Gazipaşa, Turk. 36°17′ N, 32°18′ E 156
Gazli, Uzb. 40°8′ N, 63°28′ E 197
Gazojak, Turkm. 41°10′ N, 61°22′ E 180
Gazū, Kūh-e, peak, Iran 28°16′ N, 61°30′ E 182
Gbadolite, Dem. Rep. of the Congo 4°18′ N, 21°3′ E 218
Gbarnga, Liberia 6°51′ N, 9°33′ W 222
Gberia Fotombu, Sierra Leone 9°51′ N, 11°12′ W 222
Gboko, Nig. 7°19′ N, 8°57′ E 222
Gcuwa, S. Af. 32°21′ S, 28°7′ E 227
Gdańsk, Pol. 54°21′ N, 18°38′ E 166
Gdanskaya Guba 71°3′ N, 74°49′ E 160
Gdov, Russ. 58°44′ N, 27°48′ E 166
Gdynia, Pol. 54°29′ N, 18°31′ E 166
Gearhart, Oreg., U.S. 46°1′ N, 123°54′ W 100
Gearhart Mountain, Oreg., U.S. 42°30′ N, 120°57′ W 90
Gêba, river, Senegal 12°38′ N, 14°29′ W 222
Gebe, island, Indonesia 0°6′ N, 129°13′ E 192
Gebeit, Sudan 18°57′ N, 36°46′ E 182
Gebeit, Sudan 21°4′ N, 36°19′ E 182
Gebel Adda, ruin(s), Egypt 22°12′ N, 31°32′ E 182
Gebiley, Somalia 9°38′ N, 43°36′ E 216
Gebra, Ger. 51°25′ N, 10°37′ E 152
Gebze, Turk. 40°48′ N, 29°26′ E 156
Gech'a, Eth. 7°26′ N, 35°21′ E 224
Gedaref, Sudan 14°0′ N, 35°24′ E 182
Gedaref, adm. division, Sudan 14°5′ N, 34°13′ E 182
Geddes, S. Dak., U.S. 43°14′ N, 98°42′ W 90
Gedern, Ger. 50°25′ N, 9°12′ E 167
Gedid Ras el Fil, Sudan 12°41′ N, 25°43′ E 216
Gediz, Turk. 39°3′ N, 29°24′ E 156
Gedlegubē, Eth. 6°50′ N, 45°2′ E 218
Gēdo, Eth. 8°58′ N, 37°26′ E 224
Gèdre, Fr. 42°48′ N, 0°1′ E 164
Gedser, Den. 54°35′ N, 11°56′ E 152
Geel, Belg. 51°9′ N, 4°58′ E 167
Geelong, Austral. 38°11′ S, 144°23′ E 231
Geelvink Channel 28°34′ S, 112°19′ E 230
Geeste, Ger. 52°36′ N, 7°16′ E 163
Geeveston, Austral. 43°5′ S, 146°56′ E 231
Gê'gyai, China 32°29′ N, 80°58′ E 188
Geidam, Nig. 12°53′ N, 11°56′ E 222
Geikie, river, Can. 57°28′ N, 104°9′ W 108
Geilenkirchen, Ger. 50°58′ N, 6°7′ E 167
Geilo Hills, Kenya 3°12′ N, 40°49′ E 224
Geisa, Ger. 50°43′ N, 9°56′ E 167
Geisenheim, Ger. 49°58′ N, 7°57′ E 167
Geita, Tanzania 2°56′ S, 32°9′ E 224
Gejiu, China 23°18′ N, 103°6′ E 202
Gel, river, Sudan 6°59′ N, 29°3′ E 224
Gela, It. 37°4′ N, 14°14′ E 156
Geladaintong, peak, China 33°6′ N, 90°38′ E 188
Geladī, Eth. 6°57′ N, 46°28′ E 218
Gelahun, Liberia 7°43′ N, 10°28′ W 222
Gelai, peak, Tanzania 2°37′ S, 36°2′ E 224
Gelasa, Selat 3°8′ S, 106°41′ E 192
Geldermalsen, Neth. 51°53′ N, 5°16′ E 167
Geldern, Ger. 51°29′ N, 6°20′ E 167
Geldrop, Neth. 51°25′ N, 5°33′ E 167
Geleen, Neth. 50°58′ N, 5°49′ E 167
Gelendzhik, Russ. 44°34′ N, 38°6′ E 156
Gélengdeng, Chad 10°54′ N, 15°31′ E 216
Gelgaudiškis, Lith. 55°4′ N, 22°57′ E 166
Gelhak, Sudan 11°3′ N, 32°40′ E 182
Gelibolu (Gallipoli), Turk. 40°25′ N, 26°38′ E 156
Gellinsoor, Somalia 6°20′ N, 46°42′ E 218
Gelnhausen, Ger. 50°12′ N, 9°11′ E 167
Gelse, Hung. 46°35′ N, 16°59′ E 168
Gelsenkirchen, Ger. 51°30′ N, 7°5′ E 167
Gemas, Malaysia 2°37′ N, 102°36′ E 196
Gembloux, Belg. 50°34′ N, 4°41′ E 167
Gemena, Dem. Rep. of the Congo 3°12′ N, 19°54′ E 207
Gemerek, Turk. 39°10′ N, 36°3′ E 156
Gemert, Neth. 51°33′ N, 5°40′ E 167
Gemlik, Turk. 40°25′ N, 29°9′ E 156
Gemona del Friuli, It. 46°16′ N, 13°8′ E 167
Gemsa, Egypt 27°40′ N, 33°36′ E 180
Gemsbok National Park, Botswana 25°25′ S, 20°49′ E 227
Gemünden, Ger. 50°58′ N, 8°57′ E 167
Gen, river, China 50°24′ N, 121°3′ E 190
Genalē, river, Eth. 4°55′ N, 41°17′ E 224
Genalē, river, Eth. 6°8′ N, 39°1′ E 224
Genç, Turk. 38°44′ N, 40°32′ E 195
Geneina, Sudan 13°20′ N, 22°29′ E 216
General Alvear, Arg. 36°3′ S, 60°3′ W 139
General Alvear, Arg. 34°57′ S, 67°41′ W 134
General Arenales, Arg. 34°18′ S, 61°17′ W 139
General Artigas, Parag. 26°51′ S, 56°13′ W 139
General Belgrano, Arg. 35°45′ S, 58°30′ W 139
General Bernardo O'Higgins, station, Antarctica 63°26′ S, 57°47′ W 134
General Bravo, Mex. 25°47′ N, 99°10′ W 114
General Cabrera, Arg. 32°49′ S, 63°52′ W 139
General Cepeda, Mex. 25°21′ N, 101°29′ W 114
General Conesa, Arg. 36°29′ S, 57°19′ W 139
General D. Cerri, Arg. 38°44′ S, 62°24′ W 139
General Enrique Martínez, Uru. 33°13′ S, 53°51′ W 139
General Eugenio A. Garay, Parag. 20°33′ S, 62°10′ W 134
General Galarza, Arg. 32°43′ S, 59°22′ W 139
General Galeana, Mex. 25°27′ N, 105°13′ W 114
General Güemes, Arg. 24°40′ S, 65°4′ W 132
General Guido, Arg. 36°38′ S, 57°46′ W 139
General José de San Martín, Arg. 26°33′ S, 59°21′ W 139
General Juan Madariaga, Arg. 37°0′ S, 57°7′ W 139
General La Madrid, Arg. 37°15′ S, 61°17′ W 139
General Lavalle, Arg. 36°25′ S, 56°56′ W 139
General Leonidas Plaza GutiŽerrez, Ecua. 3°4′ S, 78°25′ W 136
General Levalle, Arg. 34°3′ S, 63°53′ W 134
General Lorenzo Vintter, Arg. 40°44′ S, 64°28′ W 134
General MacArthur, Philippines 11°16′ N, 125°33′ E 203
General Paz, Arg. 35°31′ S, 58°20′ W 139
General Paz, Arg. 27°45′ S, 57°38′ W 139
General Pico, Arg. 35°39′ S, 63°44′ W 139
General Pinedo, Arg. 27°19′ S, 61°18′ W 139
General Pinto, Arg. 34°46′ S, 61°52′ W 139
General Pirán, Arg. 37°17′ S, 57°49′ W 139
General Saavedra, Bol. 17°15′ S, 63°14′ W 137
General San Martín, Arg. 38°2′ S, 63°34′ W 139
General San Martín, Arg. 34°33′ S, 58°33′ W 139
General San Martín, Arg. 44°5′ S, 70°28′ W 134
General Santos, Philippines 6°9′ N, 125°13′ E 203
General Terán, Mex. 25°15′ N, 99°42′ W 114
General Treviño, Mex. 26°12′ N, 99°29′ W 114
General Trías, Mex. 28°19′ N, 106°23′ W 92
General Viamonte, Arg. 34°59′ S, 61°4′ W 139
General Villegas, Arg. 35°1′ S, 63°1′ W 139
Genesee, Idaho, U.S. 46°32′ N, 116°57′ W 90
Genesee, river, N.Y., U.S. 42°15′ N, 78°17′ W 80
Geneseo, Ill., U.S. 41°27′ N, 90°10′ W 102
Geneseo, N.Y., U.S. 42°47′ N, 77°50′ W 94
Geneva, Ala., U.S. 31°1′ N, 85°53′ W 96
Geneva, Ill., U.S. 41°52′ N, 88°19′ W 102
Geneva, Nebr., U.S. 40°30′ N, 97°37′ W 94
Geneva, N.Y., U.S. 42°52′ N, 76°59′ W 94
Geneva, Ohio, U.S. 41°47′ N, 80°58′ W 102
Genève, Switz. 46°11′ N, 6°9′ E 167
Gengma, China 23°33′ N, 99°22′ E 202
Geni, river, Sudan 7°22′ N, 32°53′ E 224
Genk, Belg. 50°56′ N, 5°30′ E 167
Gennargentu, Monti del, It. 39°48′ N, 8°39′ E 156
Genoa, Ill., U.S. 42°4′ N, 88°42′ W 102
Genoa, Nebr., U.S. 41°26′ N, 97°45′ W 90
Genoa, Ohio, U.S. 41°30′ N, 83°21′ W 102
Genoa see Genova, It. 44°24′ N, 8°57′ E 167
Génolhac, Fr. 44°21′ N, 3°56′ E 150
Génoto, Senegal 13°35′ N, 13°53′ W 222
Genova (Genoa), It. 44°24′ N, 8°57′ E 167
Genova, Golfo di 44°4′ N, 7°33′ E 150
Gent, Belg. 51°3′ N, 3°44′ E 163
Genthin, Ger. 52°24′ N, 12°9′ E 152
Genyem, Indonesia 2°33′ S, 140°9′ E 192
Geoagiu, Rom. 45°55′ N, 23°12′ E 168
Geochang, S. Korea 35°41′ N, 127°55′ E 200
Geographical Society Ø, island, Den. 72°30′ N, 21°29′ W 246
Geoje, S. Korea 34°51′ N, 128°37′ E 200
George, S. Af. 33°58′ S, 22°26′ E 227
George, Lake, Fla., U.S. 29°15′ N, 81°41′ W 105
George, Lake, N.Y., U.S. 43°36′ N, 74°9′ W 81
George, river, Can. 57°32′ N, 66°1′ W 106
George Sound 44°59′ S, 167°7′ E 240
George Town, Malaysia 5°25′ N, 100°17′ E 196
George Town, U.K. 19°18′ N, 81°24′ W 115
George Town, United Kingdom 19°0′ N, 81°0′ W 118
George V Coast, Antarctica 69°8′ S, 153°28′ E 248
George Washington Birthplace National Monument, Va., U.S. 38°10′ N, 77°0′ W 94
George West, Tex., U.S. 28°19′ N, 98°7′ W 92
George, Zemlya, island, Russ. 79°13′ N, 47°22′ E 160
Georgetown, Austral. 18°17′ S, 143°32′ E 238
Georgetown, Fla., U.S. 29°23′ N, 81°38′ W 105
Georgetown, Gambia 13°29′ N, 14°48′ W 222
Georgetown, Guyana 6°40′ N, 58°21′ W 130
Georgetown, Ill., U.S. 39°58′ N, 87°38′ W 102
Georgetown, La., U.S. 31°45′ N, 92°23′ W 103
Georgetown, Me., U.S. 43°48′ N, 69°46′ W 104
Georgetown, Miss., U.S. 31°52′ N, 90°11′ W 103
Georgetown, Ohio, U.S. 38°51′ N, 83°54′ W 102
Georgetown, S.C., U.S. 33°22′ N, 79°19′ W 96
Georgetown, Tex., U.S. 30°37′ N, 97°40′ W 92
Georgia 42°0′ N, 44°0′ E 195
Georgia, adm. division, Ga., U.S. 32°40′ N, 84°11′ W 96
Georgia, Strait of 49°53′ N, 124°58′ W 90
Georgian Bay 45°4′ N, 81°13′ W 80
Georgīevka, Kaz. 49°19′ N, 81°33′ E 184
Georgiyevsk, Russ. 44°9′ N, 43°28′ E 158
Georgiyevskoye, Russ. 58°41′ N, 45°6′ E 154
Gera, Ger. 50°53′ N, 12°5′ E 152
Geraardsbergen, Belg. 50°47′ N, 3°54′ E 163
Geral de Goiás, Serra, Braz. 12°46′ S, 46°59′ W 130
Geral, Serra, Braz. 25°36′ S, 51°43′ W 132
Geraldine, Mont., U.S. 47°34′ N, 110°17′ W 90
Geraldine, N.Z. 44°6′ S, 171°14′ E 240
Geraldton, Can. 49°44′ N, 86°57′ W 94
Gerar, ruin(s), Israel 31°21′ N, 34°33′ E 194
Gerasa see Jarash, Jordan 32°17′ N, 35°53′ E 194
Gerbéviller, Fr. 48°30′ N, 6°30′ E 163
Gercüş, Turk. 37°33′ N, 41°25′ E 195
Gerdine, Mount, Alas., U.S. 61°25′ N, 152°42′ W 98
Gerede, Turk. 40°48′ N, 32°11′ E 156
Gereshk, Afghan. 31°48′ N, 64°34′ E 186
Gérgal, Sp. 37°6′ N, 2°33′ W 164
Gerik, Malaysia 5°25′ N, 101°6′ E 196
Gering, Nebr., U.S. 41°49′ N, 103°40′ W 90
Gerlachovský Štít, peak, Slovakia 49°8′ N, 20°3′ E 152
Germain, Grand lac, lake, Can. 51°11′ N, 67°11′ W 111
Germaine, Lac, lake, Can. 52°59′ N, 68°16′ W 111
Germânia, Braz. 10°36′ S, 70°5′ W 137
Germania Land, Den. 76°52′ N, 17°54′ W 246
Germansen Landing, Can. 55°43′ N, 124°43′ W 108
Germantown, Ill., U.S. 38°32′ N, 89°32′ W 102
Germantown, N.Y., U.S. 42°8′ N, 73°54′ W 104
Germantown, Tenn., U.S. 35°4′ N, 89°49′ W 96
Germany 51°17′ N, 7°48′ E 150
Germfask, Mich., U.S. 46°16′ N, 85°56′ W 110
Germī, Iran 39°3′ N, 48°6′ E 195
Gernsbach, Ger. 48°45′ N, 8°19′ E 152
Gerolakkos, Cyprus 35°10′ N, 33°15′ E 194
Gerolstein, Ger. 50°13′ N, 6°40′ E 163
Gerrard, Can. 50°30′ N, 117°18′ W 90
Gersfeld, Ger. 50°27′ N, 9°55′ E 167
Gerstungen, Ger. 50°58′ N, 10°3′ E 167
Gêrzê, China 32°29′ N, 84°3′ E 188
Gerze, Turk. 41°48′ N, 35°11′ E 156
Gescher, Ger. 51°57′ N, 7°0′ E 167
Geseke, Ger. 51°38′ N, 8°29′ E 167
Geser, Indonesia 3°57′ S, 130°51′ E 192
Geta, Fin. 60°21′ N, 19°50′ E 166
Getafe, Sp. 40°18′ N, 3°44′ W 164
Geteina, Sudan 14°49′ N, 32°23′ E 182
Gettysburg, S. Dak., U.S. 44°59′ N, 99°59′ W 90
Getúlio Vargas, Braz. 27°54′ S, 52°13′ W 139
Gety, Dem. Rep. of the Congo 1°11′ N, 30°11′ E 224
Geumpang, Indonesia 4°56′ N, 96°6′ E 196
Geumsan, S. Korea 36°5′ N, 127°29′ E 200
Gevaş, Turk. 38°16′ N, 43°4′ E 195
Gevelsberg, Ger. 51°18′ N, 7°20′ E 163
Gewanē, Eth. 10°7′ N, 40°36′ E 224
Gex, Fr. 46°19′ N, 6°3′ E 167
Geylegphug, Bhutan 26°49′ N, 90°37′ E 197
Geyve, Turk. 40°30′ N, 30°19′ E 156
Gézenti, Chad 21°39′ N, 18°19′ E 216
Gezer, ruin(s), Israel 31°51′ N, 34°52′ E 194
Gezira, adm. division, Sudan 14°30′ N, 32°33′ E 182
Ghaba North, oil field, Oman 21°24′ N, 57°15′ E 182
Ghabāghib, Syr. 33°11′ N, 36°12′ E 194
Ghabeish, Sudan 12°9′ N, 27°18′ E 216
Ghadāmis (Ghadames), Lib. 30°7′ N, 9°28′ E 214
Ghaddūwah, Lib. 26°27′ N, 14°18′ E 216
Ghagghar, river, India 29°40′ N, 75°1′ E 197
Ghana 7°51′ N, 1°42′ W 214
Ghanzi, Botswana 21°41′ S, 21°44′ E 227
Gharbi Island, Tun. 34°27′ N, 10°39′ E 214
Ghardaïa, Alg. 32°17′ N, 3°34′ E 207
Ghārib, Gebel, peak, Egypt 28°6′ N, 32°47′ E 180
Gharm, Taj. 39°4′ N, 70°25′ E 197
Gharo, Pak. 24°44′ N, 67°37′ E 186
Gharyān, Lib. 32°9′ N, 13°0′ E 216
Ghāt, Lib. 24°57′ N, 10°10′ E 214
Ghatampur, India 26°9′ N, 80°9′ E 188
Ghawar Oil Field, Saudi Arabia 25°5′ N, 49°15′ E 196
Ghaziabad, India 28°40′ N, 77°25′ E 197
Ghazipur, India 25°35′ N, 83°34′ E 197
Ghazīr, Leb. 34°1′ N, 35°40′ E 194
Ghazni, Afghan. 33°34′ N, 68°33′ E 186
Ghazzah (Gaza City), Gaza Strip, Israel 31°29′ N, 34°28′ E 194
Ghelar, Rom. 45°42′ N, 22°47′ E 168
Ghent, Ky., U.S. 38°43′ N, 85°3′ W 102
Ghent, N.Y., U.S. 42°19′ N, 73°38′ W 104

Ghilarza, *It.* 40°8′ N, 8°50′ E 156
Ghilvaci, *Rom.* 47°41′ N, 22°41′ E 168
Ghisonaccia, *Fr.* 42°0′ N, 9°25′ E 156
Ghlo, Beinn a', peak, *U.K.* 56°49′ N, 3°48′ W 150
Ghost River, *Can.* 50°9′ N, 91°27′ W 94
Ghoumrassen, *Tun.* 33°1′ N, 10°15′ E 214
Ghraiba, *Tun.* 34°31′ N, 10°12′ E 156
Ghunthur, *Syr.* 34°23′ N, 37°8′ E 194
Ghurian, *Afghan.* 34°27′ N, 61°30′ E 186
Gia Nghia, *Vietnam* 12°15′ N, 107°37′ E 202
Gia Rai, *Vietnam* 9°13′ N, 105°28′ E 202
Gialo, oil field, *Lib.* 28°30′ N, 21°21′ E 216
Giant Forest, *Calif., U.S.* 36°34′ N, 118°47′ W 101
Giant's Ring, ruin(s), *U.K.* 54°31′ N, 6°5′ W 150
Giarso, *Eth.* 5°14′ N, 37°33′ E 224
Gibara, *Cuba* 21°7′ N, 76°11′ W 116
Gibbon, *Nebr., U.S.* 40°44′ N, 98°51′ W 90
Gibbs Island, *Antarctica* 61°44′ S, 55°25′ W 134
Gibeah, ruin(s), *Israel* 31°48′ N, 35°11′ E 194
Gibeon, *Namibia* 25°8′ S, 17°46′ E 227
Gibraltar, adm. division, *U.K.* 36°7′ N, 5°35′ W 164
Gibraltar, Strait of 36°2′ N, 6°40′ W 150
Gibsland, *La., U.S.* 32°31′ N, 93°3′ W 96
Gibson City, *Ill., U.S.* 40°27′ N, 88°22′ W 102
Gibson Desert, *Austral.* 23°7′ S, 121°58′ E 230
Gibsonburg, *Ohio, U.S.* 41°22′ N, 83°19′ W 102
Gibsons, *Can.* 49°24′ N, 123°31′ W 100
Gibsonton, *Fla., U.S.* 27°50′ N, 82°22′ W 105
Gīdamī, *Eth.* 8°56′ N, 34°33′ E 224
Giddalur, *India* 15°22′ N, 78°56′ E 188
Giddings, *Tex., U.S.* 30°10′ N, 96°56′ W 96
Gīdolē, *Eth.* 5°37′ N, 37°27′ E 224
Giel, *Sudan* 11°20′ N, 32°44′ E 182
Gien, *Fr.* 47°41′ N, 2°38′ E 150
Giera, *Rom.* 45°25′ N, 20°59′ E 168
Giessen, *Ger.* 50°34′ N, 8°39′ E 167
Gieten, *Neth.* 53°0′ N, 6°45′ E 163
Giffard, Lac, lake, *Can.* 51°7′ N, 77°25′ W 110
Gifford, *Fla., U.S.* 27°40′ N, 80°25′ W 105
Gifford, river, *Can.* 70°40′ N, 84°39′ W 106
Gift Lake, *Can.* 55°53′ N, 115°54′ W 108
Gifu, *Japan* 35°24′ N, 136°46′ E 201
Gifu, adm. division, *Japan* 35°48′ N, 136°49′ E 201
Gig Harbor, *Wash., U.S.* 47°18′ N, 122°36′ W 100
Gigant, *Russ.* 46°30′ N, 41°14′ E 158
Giganta, Sierra de la, *Mex.* 25°57′ N, 111°37′ W 112
Gijón, *Sp.* 43°30′ N, 5°42′ W 150
Gikongoro, *Rwanda* 2°31′ S, 29°33′ E 224
Gila, *N. Mex., U.S.* 32°57′ N, 108°34′ W 92
Gila Bend, *Ariz., U.S.* 32°56′ N, 112°43′ W 92
Gila Bend Mountains, *Ariz., U.S.* 33°24′ N, 113°42′ W 101
Gila Cliff Dwellings National Monument, *N. Mex., U.S.* 33°13′ N, 108°21′ W 92
Gila Mountains, *Ariz., U.S.* 33°9′ N, 109°59′ W 92
Gila, river, *Ariz., U.S.* 33°12′ N, 110°9′ W 80
Gilbâna, *Egypt* 30°55′ N, 32°28′ E 194
Gilbert, *La., U.S.* 32°3′ N, 91°40′ W 103
Gilbert, *Minn., U.S.* 47°29′ N, 92°29′ W 94
Gilbert Islands, *North Pacific Ocean* 0°46′ N, 173°11′ E 238
Gilbert, Islas, *Drake Passage* 55°7′ S, 73°15′ W 134
Gilbert, Mount, *Can.* 50°51′ N, 124°21′ W 90
Gilbert Peak, *Utah, U.S.* 40°47′ N, 110°25′ W 90
Gilbert Peak, *Wash., U.S.* 46°27′ N, 121°26′ W 100
Gilbert Plains, *Can.* 51°7′ N, 100°30′ W 90
Gilbertville, *Mass., U.S.* 42°18′ N, 72°13′ W 104
Gilbués, *Braz.* 9°51′ S, 45°23′ W 130
Gildeskål, *Nor.* 67°3′ N, 14°2′ E 152
Gildford, *Mont., U.S.* 48°33′ N, 110°17′ W 90
Gilead, *Me., U.S.* 44°23′ N, 70°59′ W 104
Giles Meteorological Station, site, *Austral.* 25°7′ S, 128°4′ E 230
Giles, Mount, *Antarctica* 75°2′ S, 137°1′ W 248
Gilford, *N.H., U.S.* 43°32′ N, 71°25′ W 104
Gilgal, *West Bank, Israel* 31°58′ N, 35°26′ E 194
Gilgil, *Kenya* 0°30′ N, 36°19′ E 224
Gilgit, *Pak.* 35°52′ N, 74°19′ E 186
Gilgit-Baltistan, adm. division, *Pak.* 36°0′ N, 75°0′ E 186
Giljeva Planina, *Mont.* 43°3′ N, 19°50′ E 168
Gillam, *Can.* 56°20′ N, 94°44′ W 108
Gilleleje, *Den.* 56°6′ N, 12°18′ E 152
Gillespie, *Ill., U.S.* 39°7′ N, 89°50′ W 102
Gillett, *Ark., U.S.* 34°5′ N, 91°23′ W 96
Gillette, *Wyo., U.S.* 44°16′ N, 105°30′ W 90
Gillies Islands, *Davis Sea* 66°37′ S, 98°44′ E 248
Gillingham, *U.K.* 51°22′ N, 0°32′ E 162
Gillis Range, *Nev., U.S.* 38°43′ N, 118°40′ W 90
Gillock Island, *Antarctica* 70°22′ S, 72°12′ E 248
Gills Rock, *Wis., U.S.* 45°16′ N, 87°1′ W 94
Gilman, *Ill., U.S.* 40°45′ N, 88°0′ W 102
Gilman, *Vt., U.S.* 44°24′ N, 71°44′ W 104
Gilmer, *Tex., U.S.* 32°43′ N, 94°58′ W 103
Gīlo Wenz, river, *Eth.* 7°40′ N, 33°38′ E 224
Gilroy, *Calif., U.S.* 37°0′ N, 121°35′ W 100
Gīmbī, *Eth.* 9°8′ N, 35°49′ E 224
Gimcheon, *S. Korea* 36°5′ N, 128°8′ E 200
Gimhae, *S. Korea* 35°12′ N, 128°54′ E 200
Gimhwa, *S. Korea* 38°17′ N, 127°28′ E 200
Gimje, *S. Korea* 35°48′ N, 126°54′ E 200
Gimli, *Can.* 50°37′ N, 97°2′ W 90
Gimo, *Sw.* 60°10′ N, 18°8′ E 166
Ginâḥ, *Egypt* 25°21′ N, 30°28′ E 226
Gingdindlovu, *S. Af.* 29°2′ S, 31°32′ E 227
Gingoog, *Philippines* 8°48′ N, 125°7′ E 203
Gīnīr, *Eth.* 7°12′ N, 40°43′ E 224
Ginostra, *It.* 38°47′ N, 15°11′ E 156
Giohar see Jawhar, *Somalia* 2°47′ N, 45°34′ E 218
Gióna, Óros, peak, *Gr.* 38°38′ N, 22°10′ E 156
Giovinazzo, *It.* 41°11′ N, 16°40′ E 156
Ģipka, *Latv.* 57°34′ N, 22°36′ E 166
Gir National Park, *India* 21°15′ N, 70°30′ E 186
Girard, *Ill., U.S.* 39°26′ N, 89°47′ W 102
Girard, *Kans., U.S.* 37°28′ N, 94°50′ W 94
Girard, *Ohio, U.S.* 41°9′ N, 80°42′ W 94
Girardot, *Col.* 4°19′ N, 74°48′ W 136
Girawa, *Eth.* 9°7′ N, 41°51′ E 224
Girbanat, *Sudan* 12°0′ N, 33°9′ E 182
Gîrbou, *Rom.* 47°10′ N, 23°24′ E 168
Gîrbovi, *Rom.* 44°48′ N, 26°45′ E 156
Giresun, *Turk.* 40°55′ N, 38°22′ E 158
Girga, *Egypt* 26°19′ N, 31°49′ E 180
Giridih, *India* 24°9′ N, 86°19′ E 197
Gîrla Mare, *Rom.* 44°12′ N, 22°46′ E 168
Gîrlişte, *Rom.* 45°10′ N, 21°48′ E 168
Girne see Kyrenia, *Northern Cyprus, Cyprus* 35°20′ N, 33°18′ E 194
Giroc, *Rom.* 45°42′ N, 21°15′ E 168
Girolata, *Fr.* 42°21′ N, 8°37′ E 156
Girona, *Sp.* 41°58′ N, 2°50′ E 164
Giruá, *Braz.* 28°5′ S, 54°21′ W 139
Giruliai, *Lith.* 55°46′ N, 21°6′ E 166
Girvas, *Russ.* 62°28′ N, 33°44′ E 154
Gisborne, *N.Z.* 38°40′ S, 178°0′ E 240
Giscome, *Can.* 54°3′ N, 122°23′ W 108
Gisors, *Fr.* 49°16′ N, 1°45′ E 163
Gisselberg, *Ger.* 50°45′ N, 8°44′ E 167
Gitega, *Burundi* 3°27′ S, 29°55′ E 224
Giuba, Isole, islands, *Indian Ocean* 0°45′ N, 41°29′ E 224
Giulianova, *It.* 42°44′ N, 13°56′ E 156
Giuncarico, *It.* 42°55′ N, 10°58′ E 156
Giurgeni, *Rom.* 44°44′ N, 27°51′ E 158
Giurgiu, *Rom.* 43°53′ N, 25°56′ E 156
Giurgiu, adm. division, *Rom.* 44°8′ N, 25°43′ E 156
Give, *Den.* 55°49′ N, 9°13′ E 150
Givet, *Fr.* 50°7′ N, 4°48′ E 167
Giyani, *S. Af.* 23°17′ S, 30°44′ E 227
Giyon, *Eth.* 8°34′ N, 38°1′ E 224
Gizab, *Afghan.* 33°27′ N, 66°0′ E 186
Gizhiga, *Russ.* 62°8′ N, 160°11′ E 160
Gizhuduvan, *Uzb.* 40°6′ N, 64°42′ E 197
Giżycko, *Pol.* 54°1′ N, 21°45′ E 166
Gjakova (Dakovica), *Kosovo* 42°23′ N, 20°26′ E 168
Gjalicë e Lumës, Mal, peak, *Alban.* 42°0′ N, 20°25′ E 168
Gjegjan, *Alban.* 41°56′ N, 20°0′ E 168
Gjelsvik Mountains, *Antarctica* 72°8′ S, 4°59′ W 248
Gjerstad, *Nor.* 58°52′ N, 9°0′ E 152
Gjilan (Gnjilane), *Kosovo* 42°27′ N, 21°27′ E 168
Gjinar, *Alban.* 41°2′ N, 20°12′ E 156
Gjoa Haven, *Can.* 68°36′ N, 96°0′ W 106
Gjøvdal, *Nor.* 58°51′ N, 8°17′ E 152
Gjuhëzës, Kepi i, *Alban.* 40°27′ N, 18°34′ E 156
Gjuvikfjell, peak, *Nor.* 59°57′ N, 7°55′ E 152
Gkreko, Cape, *Cyprus* 34°53′ N, 33°55′ E 194
Gla, ruin(s), *Gr.* 38°23′ N, 23°10′ E 156
Glace Bay, *Can.* 46°11′ N, 59°58′ W 111
Glacier, *Wash., U.S.* 48°52′ N, 121°58′ W 100
Glacier Bay 58°40′ N, 136°50′ W 108
Glacier Bay National Park and Preserve, *Alas., U.S.* 58°40′ N, 137°23′ W 73
Glacier Peak, *Wash., U.S.* 48°5′ N, 121°10′ W 100
Glacier Strait 75°57′ N, 80°39′ W 106
Gladstone, *Can.* 50°13′ N, 98°58′ W 90
Gladstone, *Mich., U.S.* 45°50′ N, 87°2′ W 94
Gladstone, *Oreg., U.S.* 45°23′ N, 122°37′ W 90
Gladwin, *Mich., U.S.* 43°58′ N, 84°29′ W 102
Gladys Lake, *Can.* 59°52′ N, 133°39′ W 108
Glamoč, *Bosn. and Herzg.* 44°2′ N, 16°50′ E 168
Glan, *Philippines* 5°50′ N, 125°11′ E 203
Glandore, *Ire.* 51°34′ N, 9°7′ W 150
Glandorf, *Ger.* 52°4′ N, 8°0′ E 163
Glarus, *Switz.* 47°2′ N, 9°4′ E 156
Glas, Lac du, lake, *Can.* 51°49′ N, 75°47′ W 110
Glasco, *Kans., U.S.* 39°20′ N, 97°51′ W 90
Glasco, *N.Y., U.S.* 42°1′ N, 73°58′ W 104
Glasford, *Ill., U.S.* 40°33′ N, 89°48′ W 102
Glasgow, *Ky., U.S.* 37°0′ N, 85°55′ W 96
Glasgow, *Mont., U.S.* 48°11′ N, 106°39′ W 90
Glasgow, *U.K.* 55°51′ N, 4°27′ W 143
Glaslyn, *Can.* 53°21′ N, 108°22′ W 108
Glass Buttes, peak, *Oreg., U.S.* 43°32′ N, 120°10′ W 90
Glass Mountain, *Calif., U.S.* 37°45′ N, 118°47′ W 90
Glass Mountain, *Calif., U.S.* 41°35′ N, 121°35′ W 90
Glass Mountains, *Tex., U.S.* 30°30′ N, 103°11′ W 92
Glastonbury, *Conn., U.S.* 41°42′ N, 72°37′ W 104
Glastonbury, *U.K.* 51°8′ N, 2°43′ W 162
Glavičice, *Bosn. and Herzg.* 44°35′ N, 19°12′ E 168
Glazachevo, *Russ.* 57°12′ N, 30°13′ E 166
Glazov, *Russ.* 58°6′ N, 52°43′ E 154
Gleichberg, Grosser, peak, *Ger.* 50°22′ N, 10°29′ E 152
Gleichen, *Can.* 50°52′ N, 113°4′ W 90
Gleisdorf, *Aust.* 47°6′ N, 15°42′ E 168
Glen, *N.H., U.S.* 44°6′ N, 71°11′ W 104
Glen Allan, *Miss., U.S.* 33°0′ N, 91°2′ W 103
Glen Arbor, *Mich., U.S.* 44°53′ N, 85°59′ W 94
Glen Cove, *N.Y., U.S.* 40°52′ N, 73°38′ W 104
Glen Park, *N.Y., U.S.* 44°0′ N, 75°58′ W 94
Glen, river, *U.K.* 52°47′ N, 0°34′ E 162
Glen Rose, *Tex., U.S.* 32°14′ N, 97°45′ W 92
Glen Ullin, *N. Dak., U.S.* 46°47′ N, 101°51′ W 90
Glenada, *Oreg., U.S.* 43°56′ N, 124°6′ W 90
Glenavy, *N.Z.* 44°54′ S, 171°5′ E 240
Glenboro, *Can.* 49°32′ N, 99°18′ W 90
Glencliff, *N.H., U.S.* 43°58′ N, 71°54′ W 104
Glencoe, *Can.* 42°44′ N, 81°42′ W 102
Glencoe, *Minn., U.S.* 44°45′ N, 94°10′ W 94
Glendale, *Ariz., U.S.* 33°32′ N, 112°10′ W 92
Glendale, *Calif., U.S.* 34°8′ N, 118°16′ W 101
Glendive, *Mont., U.S.* 47°4′ N, 104°44′ W 90
Glendo, *Wyo., U.S.* 42°29′ N, 105°1′ W 90
Glendon, *Can.* 54°14′ N, 111°10′ W 108
Glenfield, *U.K.* 52°38′ N, 1°14′ W 162
Glenmora, *La., U.S.* 30°57′ N, 92°36′ W 103
Glenn, Mount, *Ariz., U.S.* 31°56′ N, 110°3′ W 92
Glenns Ferry, *Idaho, U.S.* 42°58′ N, 115°19′ W 90
Glennville, *Calif., U.S.* 35°44′ N, 118°43′ W 101
Glennville, *Ga., U.S.* 31°55′ N, 81°56′ W 96
Glenora, *Can.* 57°52′ N, 131°26′ W 108
Glenorchy, *N.Z.* 44°52′ S, 168°26′ E 240
Glenrock, *Wyo., U.S.* 42°51′ N, 105°53′ W 90
Glens Falls, *N.Y., U.S.* 43°18′ N, 73°39′ W 104
Glenwood, *Minn., U.S.* 45°38′ N, 95°24′ W 94
Glenwood, *N. Mex., U.S.* 33°18′ N, 108°52′ W 92
Glenwood, *Oreg., U.S.* 45°38′ N, 123°16′ W 100
Glenwood, *Va., U.S.* 36°35′ N, 79°23′ W 96
Glenwood, *Wash., U.S.* 46°0′ N, 121°18′ W 100
Glenwood, *W. Va., U.S.* 38°34′ N, 82°12′ W 102
Glidden, *Wis., U.S.* 46°8′ N, 90°36′ W 94
Glina, *Croatia* 45°20′ N, 16°6′ E 168
Glīthion, *Gr.* 36°43′ N, 22°32′ E 216
Glittertind, peak, *Nor.* 61°38′ N, 8°24′ E 152
Gliwice, *Pol.* 50°17′ N, 18°38′ E 152
Głogów, *Pol.* 51°39′ N, 16°5′ E 152
Głomno, *Pol.* 54°18′ N, 20°44′ E 152
Globe, *Ariz., U.S.* 33°24′ N, 110°47′ W 92
Gloggnitz, *Aust.* 47°40′ N, 15°56′ E 168
Glommersträsk, *Nor.* 65°14′ N, 19°40′ E 152
Glorenza, *It.* 46°40′ N, 10°33′ E 167
Glória, *Braz.* 9°13′ S, 38°20′ W 132
Gloria Ridge, *North Atlantic Ocean* 54°34′ N, 45°3′ W 253
Glorieuses, Îles, islands, *Indian Ocean* 11°10′ S, 47°2′ E 220
Glorioso Islands, *Indian Ocean* 11°19′ S, 44°49′ E 207
Gloster, *Miss., U.S.* 31°11′ N, 91°2′ W 103
Gloucester, *Can.* 45°24′ N, 75°35′ W 94
Gloucester, *Mass., U.S.* 42°36′ N, 70°40′ W 104
Gloucester, *U.K.* 51°51′ N, 2°14′ W 162
Glouster, *Ohio, U.S.* 39°29′ N, 82°4′ W 102
Glubokiy, *Russ.* 46°58′ N, 42°38′ E 158
Glubokiy, *Russ.* 48°32′ N, 40°20′ E 158
Glübokoe, *Kaz.* 50°8′ N, 82°18′ E 184
Glubokoye, *Russ.* 56°38′ N, 28°59′ E 166
Glusk, *Belarus* 52°52′ N, 28°47′ E 152
Glyncorrwg, *U.K.* 51°41′ N, 3°37′ W 162
Glyndon, *Minn., U.S.* 46°52′ N, 96°37′ W 94
Gmelinka, *Russ.* 50°21′ N, 46°52′ E 158
Gmünd, *Aust.* 48°45′ N, 14°58′ E 152
Gmunden, *Aust.* 47°55′ N, 13°47′ E 156
Gnadenhutten, *Ohio, U.S.* 40°20′ N, 81°25′ W 102
Gnarp, *Nor.* 62°4′ N, 17°12′ E 152
Gnas, *Aust.* 46°52′ N, 15°51′ E 168
Gnesta, *Nor.* 59°2′ N, 17°18′ E 152
Gnetalovo, *Russ.* 56°52′ N, 29°37′ E 166
Gnjilane see Gjilan, *Kosovo* 42°27′ N, 21°27′ E 168
Go Cong, *Vietnam* 10°22′ N, 106°41′ E 202
Goa, adm. division, *India* 14°59′ N, 74°13′ E 188
Goageb, *Namibia* 26°45′ S, 17°12′ E 227
Goalpara, *India* 26°7′ N, 90°34′ E 197
Goaso, *Ghana* 6°49′ N, 2°32′ W 222
Goat Mountain, *Mont., U.S.* 47°17′ N, 113°26′ W 90
Goat, river, *Can.* 49°10′ N, 116°12′ W 90
Goathland, *U.K.* 54°24′ N, 0°44′ E 162
Goba, *Eth.* 6°58′ N, 39°55′ E 224
Gobabis, *Namibia* 22°27′ S, 18°58′ E 227
Gobernador Crespo, *Arg.* 30°21′ S, 60°24′ W 139
Gobernador Duval, *Arg.* 38°42′ S, 66°26′ W 134
Gobernador Gregores, *Arg.* 48°45′ S, 70°16′ W 134
Gobernador Ingeniero Valentín Virasoro, *Arg.* 28°3′ S, 56°3′ W 139
Gobi, *Asia* 41°49′ N, 103°50′ E 198
Gobles, *Mich., U.S.* 42°20′ N, 85°52′ W 102
Gobō, *Japan* 33°53′ N, 135°9′ E 201
Goch, *Ger.* 51°40′ N, 6°10′ E 167
Gochang, *S. Korea* 35°26′ N, 126°42′ E 200
Gochas, *Namibia* 24°51′ S, 18°44′ E 227
Godalming, *U.K.* 51°11′ N, 0°37′ E 162
Godbout, *Can.* 49°19′ N, 67°38′ W 82
Godda, *India* 24°49′ N, 87°13′ E 197
Goddard, *Can.* 56°50′ N, 135°19′ W 108
Godeanu, peak, *Rom.* 45°16′ N, 22°38′ E 168
Godech, *Bulg.* 43°0′ N, 23°4′ E 168
Godere, *Eth.* 5°2′ N, 43°59′ E 218
Goderich, *Can.* 43°43′ N, 81°42′ W 102
Godfrey, *Mo., U.S.* 38°57′ N, 90°12′ W 94
Godfrey Tank, spring, *Austral.* 20°15′ S, 126°34′ E 230
Godhavn see Qeqertarsuaq, *Den.* 69°15′ N, 53°30′ W 106
Godhra, *India* 22°46′ N, 73°35′ E 186
Gödöll o, *Hung.* 47°35′ N, 19°21′ E 168
Gods Lake, *Can.* 54°38′ N, 94°12′ W 108
Gods, river, *Can.* 55°18′ N, 93°23′ W 108
Godthåb see Nuuk, *Greenland, Den.* 64°14′ N, 51°38′ W 106
Godwin Austen see K2, peak, *Pak.* 35°51′ N, 76°25′ E 186
Godzikowice, *Pol.* 50°54′ N, 17°19′ E 152
Goéland, Lac au, lake, *Can.* 49°36′ N, 78°10′ W 81
Goélands, Lac aux, lake, *Can.* 55°13′ N, 66°38′ W 106
Goes, *Neth.* 51°30′ N, 3°52′ E 163
Goffstown, *N.H., U.S.* 43°1′ N, 71°37′ W 104
Gog Magog Hills, *U.K.* 52°4′ N, 0°10′ E 162
Gogama, *Can.* 47°40′ N, 81°43′ W 94
Gogebic Range, *Mich., U.S.* 46°32′ N, 90°10′ W 94
Göggingen, *Ger.* 48°20′ N, 10°52′ E 152
Gogland, island, *Russ.* 60°6′ N, 26°43′ E 166
Gogói, *Mozambique* 20°19′ S, 33°8′ E 227
Gogounou, *Benin* 10°46′ N, 2°47′ E 222
Gogrial, *Sudan* 8°29′ N, 28°7′ E 224
Goha, *Eth.* 10°19′ N, 34°33′ E 224
Gohad, *India* 26°24′ N, 78°26′ E 197
Goheung, *S. Korea* 34°35′ N, 127°18′ E 200
Goiandira, *Braz.* 18°10′ S, 48°7′ W 138
Goianésia, *Braz.* 15°22′ S, 49°9′ W 138
Goiânia, *Braz.* 16°43′ S, 49°17′ W 138
Goianinha, *Braz.* 6°17′ S, 35°11′ W 132
Goiás, *Braz.* 15°55′ S, 50°6′ W 138
Goiás, adm. division, *Braz.* 16°18′ S, 50°32′ W 138
Goiatuba, *Braz.* 18°5′ S, 49°24′ W 138
Goio Erê, *Braz.* 24°12′ S, 53°3′ W 138
Goioxim, *Braz.* 25°13′ S, 52°2′ W 138
Goito, *It.* 45°15′ N, 10°40′ E 167
Gojeb, river, *Eth.* 7°10′ N, 36°58′ E 224
Gök, river, *Turk.* 41°38′ N, 34°30′ E 156
Goka, *Japan* 36°18′ N, 133°14′ E 201
Gokase, river, *Japan* 32°38′ N, 131°16′ E 201
Gökçeada, island, *Turk.* 39°55′ N, 25°30′ E 180
Gökdepe, *Turkm.* 38°9′ N, 57°58′ E 180
Göksu, river, *Turk.* 37°3′ N, 32°40′ E 156
Göksu, river, *Turk.* 37°56′ N, 36°21′ E 156
Göksun, *Turk.* 38°2′ N, 36°29′ E 156
Gokwe, *Zimb.* 18°13′ S, 28°57′ E 224
Gol, *Nor.* 60°42′ N, 8°53′ E 152
Gol Bax, *Somalia* 0°19′ N, 41°36′ E 224
Golaghat, *India* 26°34′ N, 93°55′ E 188
Golan Heights, region, *Asia* 32°56′ N, 35°38′ E 194
Gölbaşı, *Turk.* 39°47′ N, 32°48′ E 156
Golconda, *Nev., U.S.* 40°57′ N, 117°30′ W 90
Gölcük, *Turk.* 40°43′ N, 29°48′ E 158
Gold Bar, *Wash., U.S.* 47°50′ N, 121°41′ W 100
Gold Beach, *Oreg., U.S.* 42°24′ N, 124°26′ W 82
Gold Coast, *Austral.* 27°58′ S, 153°23′ E 231
Gold Coast, region, *Africa* 5°10′ N, 2°17′ W 222
Gold Hill, *Nev., U.S.* 39°17′ N, 119°40′ W 92
Gold Mines, site, *Egypt* 22°37′ N, 33°13′ E 182
Gold Rock, *Can.* 49°27′ N, 92°42′ W 90
Gołdap, *Pol.* 54°17′ N, 22°17′ E 154
Golden, *Can.* 51°18′ N, 116°58′ W 108
Golden Hinde, peak, *Can.* 49°38′ N, 125°50′ W 90
Golden Meadow, *La., U.S.* 29°22′ N, 90°17′ W 103
Goldendale, *Wash., U.S.* 45°48′ N, 120°49′ W 90
Goldfield, *Iowa, U.S.* 42°43′ N, 93°55′ W 94
Goldfield, *Nev., U.S.* 37°40′ N, 117°14′ W 82
Goldonna, *La., U.S.* 32°0′ N, 92°55′ W 103
Goldpines, *Can.* 50°39′ N, 93°11′ W 90
Goldsboro, *N.C., U.S.* 35°23′ N, 78°1′ W 96
Goldsmith, *Tex., U.S.* 31°57′ N, 102°37′ W 92
Goldsmith Channel 73°5′ N, 111°1′ W 106
Goldthwaite, *Tex., U.S.* 31°26′ N, 98°34′ W 92
Göle, *Turk.* 40°47′ N, 42°35′ E 195
Golela, *Swaziland* 27°16′ S, 31°55′ E 227
Goleta, *Calif., U.S.* 34°26′ N, 119°51′ W 100
Golfito, *C.R.* 8°39′ N, 83°11′ W 115
Goliad, *Tex., U.S.* 28°39′ N, 97°23′ W 96
Gölköy, *Turk.* 40°42′ N, 37°37′ E 156
Golmud, *China* 36°19′ N, 94°52′ E 190
Golmud, river, *China* 35°44′ N, 95°6′ E 188
Golondrina, *Arg.* 28°32′ S, 60°4′ W 139
Gölören, *Turk.* 37°52′ N, 33°51′ E 156
Golovin, *Alas., U.S.* 64°27′ N, 162°59′ W 98
Golpāyegān, *Iran* 33°28′ N, 50°14′ E 180
Gölpazarı, *Turk.* 40°16′ N, 30°18′ E 158
Golran, *Afghan.* 35°7′ N, 61°41′ E 186
Golubac, *Serb.* 44°38′ N, 21°37′ E 168
Golubovci, *Mont.* 42°21′ N, 19°13′ E 168
Golūboyka, *Kaz.* 53°7′ N, 74°12′ E 184
Golyam Perelik, peak, *Bulg.* 41°35′ N, 24°29′ E 156
Golyshmanovo, *Russ.* 56°22′ N, 68°24′ E 184
Goma, *Dem. Rep. of the Congo* 1°41′ S, 29°11′ E 224
Gómara, *Sp.* 41°36′ N, 2°14′ W 164
Gombari, *Dem. Rep. of the Congo* 2°43′ N, 29°5′ E 224
Gombe, *Nig.* 10°15′ N, 11°7′ E 222
Gombe National Park, *Tanzania* 4°47′ S, 29°34′ E 224
Gomera, island, *Sp.* 28°6′ N, 18°13′ W 214
Gómez Farías, *Mex.* 24°56′ N, 101°2′ W 114
Gómez Palacio, *Mex.* 25°34′ N, 103°31′ W 114
Gomīshān, *Iran* 37°4′ N, 53°59′ E 180
Gomo, *China* 33°57′ N, 85°19′ E 188
Gomo Co, lake, *China* 34°1′ N, 84°47′ E 188
Gomoh, *India* 23°51′ N, 86°9′ E 197
Gomotartsi, *Bulg.* 44°4′ N, 22°58′ E 168
Gomphi, ruin(s), *Gr.* 39°24′ N, 21°30′ E 156
Gomshasar, Mt. (Gyamish), peak, *Azerb.* 40°17′ N, 46°19′ E 195
Gonam, *Russ.* 57°15′ N, 130°53′ E 160
Gonarezhou National Park, *Zimb.* 21°50′ S, 31°35′ E 227
Gonâve, Île de la, island, *Haiti* 19°1′ N, 74°5′ W 116
Gonbad-e Kāvūs, *Iran* 37°22′ N, 55°18′ E 180
Gonda, *India* 27°7′ N, 81°58′ E 197
Gondal, *India* 21°57′ N, 70°47′ E 186
Gonder, *Eth.* 12°34′ N, 37°25′ E 182
Gondey, *Chad* 9°4′ N, 19°21′ E 218
Gondia, *India* 21°27′ N, 80°10′ E 188
Gondola, *Mozambique* 19°10′ S, 33°38′ E 224
Gondrecourt, *Fr.* 48°30′ N, 5°31′ E 163
Gönen, *Turk.* 40°6′ N, 27°38′ E 156
Gong'an, *China* 30°1′ N, 112°11′ E 198
Gongbo'gyamda, *China* 29°55′ N, 93°0′ E 190
Gongcheng, *China* 24°52′ N, 110°45′ E 198
Gongga Shan, peak, *China* 29°38′ N, 101°36′ E 190
Gonggar, *China* 29°17′ N, 90°48′ E 197
Gongju, *S. Korea* 36°25′ N, 127°9′ E 200
Gonglee, *Liberia* 5°43′ N, 9°27′ W 222
Gongliu, *China* 43°25′ N, 82°18′ E 184
Gongola, river, *Nig.* 11°5′ N, 11°29′ E 222
Gongoûe, *Gabon* 0°33′ N, 9°15′ E 218
Gongxi, *China* 27°38′ N, 115°51′ E 198
Gongzhuling, *China* 43°30′ N, 124°52′ E 198
Goniądz, *Pol.* 53°28′ N, 22°43′ E 158
Gonja, *Tanzania* 4°21′ S, 38°5′ E 224
Gonjo, *China* 30°52′ N, 98°16′ E 188
Gōno, river, *Japan* 34°53′ N, 132°27′ E 201
Gōnoura, *Japan* 33°44′ N, 129°41′ E 201
Gonzales, *Calif., U.S.* 36°30′ N, 121°28′ W 100
Gonzales, *La., U.S.* 30°13′ N, 90°56′ W 103
Gonzales, *Tex., U.S.* 29°29′ N, 97°27′ W 96
González, *Mex.* 22°48′ N, 98°26′ W 114
González Chaves, *Arg.* 38°4′ S, 60°6′ W 139
González Moreno, *Arg.* 35°32′ S, 63°20′ W 139
Good Hope, Cape of, *S. Af.* 34°25′ S, 18°30′ E 253
Good Hope, Cape of, *S. Af.* 34°33′ S, 12°22′ E 206
Good Hope Mountain, *Can.* 51°9′ N, 124°15′ W 90
Good Pine, *La., U.S.* 31°40′ N, 92°11′ W 103
Goodenough, Cape, *Antarctica* 65°58′ S, 126°13′ E 248
Goodenough Island, *P.N.G.* 9°15′ S, 149°59′ E 192
Goodenough, Mount, *Can.* 67°56′ N, 135°41′ W 98
Goodhouse, *S. Af.* 28°57′ S, 18°14′ E 227
Gooding, *Idaho, U.S.* 42°57′ N, 114°43′ W 90
Goodland, *Fla., U.S.* 25°55′ N, 81°41′ W 105
Goodland, *Ind., U.S.* 40°45′ N, 87°18′ W 102
Goodland, *Kans., U.S.* 39°20′ N, 101°42′ W 82
Goodman, *Miss., U.S.* 32°56′ N, 89°56′ W 103
Goodman, *Wis., U.S.* 45°37′ N, 88°22′ W 94
Goodnews Bay, *Alas., U.S.* 59°8′ N, 161°31′ W 106
Goodrich, *Tex., U.S.* 30°35′ N, 94°57′ W 103
Goodridge, *Minn., U.S.* 48°8′ N, 95°50′ W 90
Goodsir, Mount, *Can.* 51°11′ N, 116°28′ W 90
Goodsoil, *Can.* 54°22′ N, 109°15′ W 108
Goodsprings, *Nev., U.S.* 35°49′ N, 115°27′ W 101
Goodwell, *Okla., U.S.* 36°34′ N, 101°39′ W 92
Goole, *U.K.* 53°42′ N, 0°54′ E 162
Goondiwindi, *Austral.* 28°30′ S, 150°21′ E 231
Goonhilly Downs, site, *U.K.* 50°0′ N, 5°18′ W 150
Goor, *Neth.* 52°14′ N, 6°35′ E 163
Goose, Lac, lake, *Can.* 53°3′ N, 74°38′ W 111
Goose Lake, *Calif., U.S.* 41°58′ N, 121°18′ W 81
Goose Lake, *Can.* 51°43′ N, 107°47′ W 90
Goose, river, *Can.* 54°54′ N, 117°3′ W 108
Goose Rocks Beach, *Me., U.S.* 43°24′ N, 70°25′ W 104
Goosenest, peak, *Calif., U.S.* 41°42′ N, 122°19′ W 90
Gooseprairie, *Wash., U.S.* 46°53′ N, 121°17′ W 100
Gooty, *India* 15°6′ N, 77°40′ E 188
Gop, *India* 22°3′ N, 69°54′ E 186
Gor, *Sp.* 37°21′ N, 2°58′ W 164
Gorakhpur, *India* 26°43′ N, 83°21′ E 197
Goranci, *Bosn. and Herzg.* 43°25′ N, 17°43′ E 168
Goransko, *Mont.* 43°7′ N, 18°50′ E 168
Goražde, *Bosn. and Herzg.* 43°40′ N, 18°58′ E 168
Gorbukova, *Russ.* 59°31′ N, 89°33′ E 169
Gorda, Punta, *Calif., U.S.* 40°5′ N, 124°41′ W 90
Gorda, Punta, *Nicar.* 14°13′ N, 83°2′ W 115
Gördalen, *Nor.* 61°35′ N, 12°28′ E 152
Gordion, ruin(s), *Turk.* 39°35′ N, 31°52′ E 156
Gordo, *Ala., U.S.* 33°17′ N, 87°54′ W 103
Gordon, *Nebr., U.S.* 42°47′ N, 102°13′ W 90
Gordon, *Wis., U.S.* 46°13′ N, 91°49′ W 94
Gordon Horne Peak, *Can.* 51°47′ N, 118°55′ W 90
Gordon Lake, *Can.* 56°23′ N, 111°4′ W 108
Gordondale, *Can.* 55°50′ N, 119°34′ W 108
Gordon's, *Bahamas* 22°52′ N, 74°52′ W 116
Goré, *Chad* 7°54′ N, 16°38′ E 218
Gorē, *Eth.* 8°10′ N, 35°31′ E 224
Gore, *N.Z.* 46°7′ S, 168°56′ E 240
Gore Bay, *Can.* 45°55′ N, 82°29′ W 94
Gore Mountain, *Vt., U.S.* 44°54′ N, 71°53′ W 94
Gore Range, *Colo., U.S.* 40°5′ N, 106°44′ W 90
Gorecki, Mount, *Antarctica* 83°23′ S, 59°14′ W 248
Goree, *Tex., U.S.* 33°27′ N, 99°32′ W 92
Görele, *Turk.* 41°2′ N, 38°59′ E 158
Gorey, *Ire.* 49°11′ N, 2°3′ W 150
Gorgān, *Iran* 36°50′ N, 54°25′ E 180
Gorgonta, *Arg.* 33°48′ S, 66°45′ W 134
Gorgora, *Eth.* 12°13′ N, 37°17′ E 182
Gorgova, *Rom.* 45°10′ N, 29°10′ E 156
Gorguz, *Mex.* 28°53′ N, 111°10′ W 92
Gorham, *Me., U.S.* 43°40′ N, 70°27′ W 104
Gori, *Ga.* 41°57′ N, 44°8′ E 195
Gori Rit, *Somalia* 8°0′ N, 48°8′ E 218
Gorinchem, *Neth.* 51°49′ N, 4°59′ E 167
Goris, *Arm.* 39°30′ N, 46°20′ E 195
Gorizia, *It.* 45°56′ N, 13°36′ E 167
Gorj, adm. division, *Rom.* 44°42′ N, 23°8′ E 156
Gorjani, *Croatia* 45°23′ N, 18°21′ E 168
Gorkha, *Nepal* 28°2′ N, 84°40′ E 197
Gorki, *Russ.* 65°4′ N, 65°29′ E 169
Gorleston, *U.K.* 52°34′ N, 1°42′ E 163
Görlitz, *Ger.* 51°8′ N, 14°58′ E 152
Gorman, *Calif., U.S.* 34°45′ N, 118°49′ W 101
Gorman, *Tex., U.S.* 32°12′ N, 98°41′ W 92
Gornja Tuzla, *Bosn. and Herzg.* 44°34′ N, 18°44′ E 168
Gornji Muć, *Croatia* 43°41′ N, 16°25′ E 168
Gornji Vakuf (Uskoplje), *Bosn. and Herzg.* 43°55′ N, 17°33′ E 168
Gorno Altaysk, *Russ.* 51°57′ N, 86°2′ E 184
Gorno-Altay, adm. division, *Russ.* 50°43′ N, 85°39′ E 184
Gornozavodsk, *Russ.* 46°32′ N, 141°52′ E 190
Gornyak, *Russ.* 51°0′ N, 81°30′ E 184
Gornyatskiy, *Russ.* 67°31′ N, 64°13′ E 169
Gornyy, *Russ.* 51°43′ N, 48°36′ E 158
Gornyy Balykley, *Russ.* 49°35′ N, 45°0′ E 158
Goro, river, *Cen. Af. Rep.* 9°13′ N, 21°36′ E 218
Gorodets, *Russ.* 58°30′ N, 29°47′ E 166
Gorodets, *Russ.* 56°37′ N, 43°35′ E 154
Gorodishche, *Russ.* 53°16′ N, 45°45′ E 154
Gorodishche, *Russ.* 58°14′ N, 29°53′ E 166
Gorodovikovsk, *Russ.* 46°4′ N, 41°48′ E 158
Gorom Gorom, *Burkina Faso* 14°27′ N, 0°15′ E 222
Gorong, Kepulauan, islands, *Banda Sea* 4°39′ S, 130°39′ E 192
Gorongosa National Park, *Mozambique* 19°13′ S, 34°35′ E 224
Gorongosa, Serra da, peak, *Mozambique* 18°27′ S, 34°0′ E 224
Gorontalo, *Indonesia* 0°38′ N, 123°2′ E 192
Gortyn, ruin(s), *Gr.* 35°3′ N, 24°50′ E 156
Gorutuba, river, *Braz.* 15°10′ S, 43°32′ W 138
Goryachiy Klyuch, *Russ.* 44°37′ N, 39°6′ E 156
Gorzów Wielkopolski, *Pol.* 52°44′ N, 15°15′ E 152
Górzyca, *Pol.* 52°29′ N, 14°40′ E 152
Goschen Strait 10°40′ S, 150°46′ E 192
Gosen, *Japan* 37°43′ N, 139°10′ E 201
Goseong, *S. Korea* 34°58′ N, 128°19′ E 200
Gosford, *Austral.* 33°23′ S, 151°20′ E 231
Gosforth, *U.K.* 54°25′ N, 3°26′ W 162
Goshen, *Calif., U.S.* 36°21′ N, 119°26′ W 100
Goshen, *N.H., U.S.* 43°18′ N, 72°9′ W 104
Goshen, *Utah, U.S.* 39°56′ N, 111°54′ W 90
Goshute Mountains, *Nev., U.S.* 40°27′ N, 114°29′ W 90
Gospić, *Croatia* 44°32′ N, 15°21′ E 156

Gosport, Ind., U.S. 39°20′ N, 86°40′ W 102
Goss, Miss., U.S. 31°20′ N, 89°54′ W 103
Gosselies, Belg. 50°28′ N, 4°26′ E 167
Gossinga, Sudan 8°38′ N, 25°57′ E 224
Gostilje, Serb. 43°39′ N, 19°50′ E 168
Gostiņi, Latv. 56°36′ N, 25°46′ E 166
Gostivar, Maced. 41°47′ N, 20°54′ E 168
Gota, Eth. 9°31′ N, 41°21′ E 224
Götaland, region, Europe 58°8′ N, 10°51′ E 150
Göteborg, Nor. 57°41′ N, 11°57′ E 152
Gotha, Ger. 50°57′ N, 10°42′ E 152
Gothenburg, Nebr., U.S. 40°56′ N, 100°11′ W 92
Gothèye, Niger 13°49′ N, 1°31′ E 222
Gotland, island, Sw. 57°33′ N, 18°49′ E 166
Gotska Sandön, island, Sw. 58°24′ N, 19°12′ E 166
Gotska Sandön National Park, Sw. 58°12′ N, 19°28′ E 166
Gōtsu, Japan 35°0′ N, 132°13′ E 200
Göttingen, Ger. 51°32′ N, 9°55′ E 167
Goubéré, Cen. Af. Rep. 5°50′ N, 26°43′ E 224
Gouda, Neth. 52°0′ N, 4°42′ E 167
Goudiry, Senegal 14°10′ N, 12°45′ W 222
Goudoumaria, Niger 13°43′ N, 11°8′ E 222
Gouéké, Guinea 7°57′ N, 8°43′ W 222
Gouin, Réservoir, lake, Can. 48°18′ N, 76°31′ W 106
Gouin, Réservoir, lake, Can. 48°18′ N, 76°42′ W 81
Goulais, river, Can. 46°44′ N, 84°41′ W 110
Goulburn, Austral. 34°46′ S, 149°45′ E 231
Goulburn Islands, Arafura Sea 11°36′ S, 133°38′ E 192
Gould, Ark., U.S. 33°58′ N, 91°35′ W 96
Gould Bay 77°46′ S, 49°17′ W 248
Gould Coast, Antarctica 84°15′ S, 127°3′ W 248
Gouldsboro, Me., U.S. 44°28′ N, 68°3′ W 111
Goulimine, Mor. 28°57′ N, 10°5′ W 143
Goulmima, Mor. 31°43′ N, 4°57′ W 214
Goumbou, Mali 14°58′ N, 7°27′ W 222
Gouméré, Côte d'Ivoire 7°55′ N, 3°0′ W 222
Gounarou, Benin 10°51′ N, 2°49′ E 222
Goundam, Mali 16°24′ N, 3°41′ W 222
Goundi, Chad 9°20′ N, 17°21′ E 216
Gounou Gaya, Chad 9°39′ N, 15°28′ E 216
Gouradi, spring, Chad 16°24′ N, 17°11′ E 216
Gouré, Niger 14°0′ N, 10°15′ E 222
Gouring, spring, Chad 18°44′ N, 19°8′ E 216
Gourlay Lake, Can. 48°51′ N, 85°29′ W 94
Gourma, region, Africa 12°15′ N, 2°118′ W 222
Gourma Rharous, Mali 16°52′ N, 1°55′ W 222
Gournay, Fr. 49°28′ N, 1°43′ E 163
Gournia, ruin(s), Gr. 35°5′ N, 25°42′ E 156
Gouro, Chad 19°32′ N, 19°33′ E 216
Gove, Kans., U.S. 38°58′ N, 100°29′ W 90
Govena, Mys, Russ. 59°34′ N, 165°28′ E 160
Governador Valadares, Braz. 18°51′ S, 41°55′ W 138
Governor's Harbour, adm. division, Bahamas 25°18′ N, 77°33′ W 116
Govĭsümber, adm. division, Mongolia 46°22′ N, 108°22′ E 198
Gowanda, N.Y., U.S. 42°27′ N, 78°57′ W 94
Gowen, Okla., U.S. 34°51′ N, 95°29′ W 96
Gower Peninsula, U.K. 51°36′ N, 4°6′ W 162
Gowganda, Can. 47°38′ N, 80°45′ W 110
Gowmal Kalay, Afghan. 32°28′ N, 69°0′ E 186
Goya, Arg. 29°10′ S, 59°16′ W 139
Göyçay, Azerb. 40°38′ N, 47°44′ E 195
Goyeau, Pointe, Can. 51°37′ N, 78°58′ W 110
Goyelle, Lac, lake, Can. 50°43′ N, 61°15′ W 111
Göynük, Turk. 40°24′ N, 30°48′ E 156
Goz Beïda, Chad 12°13′ N, 21°25′ E 216
Goz Pass, Can. 64°31′ N, 132°24′ W 98
Goz Regeb, Sudan 16°1′ N, 35°34′ E 182
Gozo, island, Malta 36°4′ N, 13°38′ E 216
Graaff-Reinet, S. Af. 32°17′ S, 24°27′ E 227
Graafwater, S. Af. 32°9′ S, 18°34′ E 227
Grabo, Côte d'Ivoire 4°55′ N, 7°30′ W 214
Grabovac, Serb. 44°35′ N, 20°5′ E 168
Gračanica, Bosn. and Herzg. 44°42′ N, 18°17′ E 168
Grace, Mount, Mass., U.S. 42°41′ N, 72°23′ W 104
Gracefield, Can. 46°6′ N, 76°3′ W 94
Graceville, Minn., U.S. 45°33′ N, 96°28′ W 90
Grachevka, Russ. 52°54′ N, 52°54′ E 158
Gracias a Dios, Cabo, Nicar. 14°51′ N, 83°10′ W 115
Gradac, Mont. 43°22′ N, 19°9′ E 168
Gradačac, Bosn. and Herzg. 44°53′ N, 18°25′ E 168
Gradaús, Braz. 7°41′ S, 51°11′ W 130
Gradaús, Serra dos, Braz. 8°20′ S, 51°0′ W 130
Gradisca d'Isonzo, It. 45°54′ N, 13°30′ E 167
Gradište, Croatia 45°8′ N, 18°42′ E 168
Grado, It. 45°41′ N, 13°23′ E 167
Gradsko, Maced. 41°34′ N, 21°57′ E 168
Gräfenhainichen, Ger. 51°44′ N, 12°27′ E 152
Grafing, Ger. 48°2′ N, 11°58′ E 152
Graford, Tex., U.S. 32°55′ N, 98°15′ W 92
Grafton, N. Dak., U.S. 48°23′ N, 97°27′ W 90
Grafton, Vt., U.S. 43°10′ N, 72°37′ W 104
Grafton, W. Va., U.S. 39°20′ N, 80°2′ W 94
Grafton, Wis., U.S. 43°18′ N, 87°58′ W 102
Grafton, Mount, Nev., U.S. 38°40′ N, 114°50′ W 90
Grafton Notch, pass, Me., U.S. 44°35′ N, 70°56′ W 104
Graham, Can. 49°15′ N, 90°34′ W 94
Graham, Tex., U.S. 33°5′ N, 98°34′ W 92
Graham Bell, Ostrov, island, Russ. 81°26′ N, 63°57′ E 160
Graham Island, Can. 54°11′ N, 133°54′ W 98
Graham Lake, Can. 56°30′ N, 115°16′ W 108
Graham, Mount, Ariz., U.S. 32°41′ N, 109°56′ W 92
Graham, river, Can. 56°23′ N, 123°5′ W 108
Grahamstown, S. Af. 33°18′ S, 26°29′ E 227
Grahovo, Mont. 42°38′ N, 18°40′ E 168
Graian Alps, It. 45°31′ N, 6°43′ E 165
Grain Coast, region, Africa 5°23′ N, 9°22′ W 222
Grajal de Campos, Sp. 42°18′ N, 5°3′ W 150
Grajaú, river, Braz. 5°19′ S, 46°2′ W 130
Gramada, Bulg. 43°50′ N, 22°39′ E 168
Gramado, Braz. 29°20′ S, 50°50′ W 139
Gramercy, La., U.S. 30°3′ N, 90°42′ W 103
Grámos, Óros, Gr. 40°11′ N, 20°38′ E 156
Grampian Mountains, U.K. 56°38′ N, 5°6′ W 150
Gran, Nor. 60°21′ N, 10°34′ E 152
Gran Bajo de San Julián, Arg. 49°23′ S, 70°59′ W 134
Gran Canaria, island, Sp. 27°21′ N, 15°22′ W 214
Gran Chaco, region, Parag. 21°5′ S, 61°33′ W 134
Gran Morelos, Mex. 28°14′ N, 106°33′ W 92
Gran Pajonal, region, South America 10°40′ S, 74°28′ W 130
Gran Paradiso, peak, It. 45°31′ N, 7°13′ E 165
Gran Sabana, La, Venez. 5°4′ N, 62°25′ W 130
Gran Sasso d'Italia, It. 42°24′ N, 13°13′ E 156
Gran Tarajal, Sp. 28°14′ N, 14°3′ W 214
Granada, Col. 3°31′ N, 73°44′ W 136
Granada, Colo., U.S. 38°3′ N, 102°19′ W 90
Granada, Nicar. 11°55′ N, 85°59′ W 115
Granada, Sp. 37°13′ N, 3°39′ W 143
Granada, Sp. 37°11′ N, 3°36′ W 164
Granadero Gatica, Arg. 26°52′ S, 62°42′ W 139
Granados, Mex. 29°51′ N, 109°21′ W 92
Granbori, Suriname 3°48′ N, 54°54′ W 130
Granbury, Tex., U.S. 32°26′ N, 97°46′ W 92
Granby, Colo., U.S. 40°4′ N, 105°56′ W 90
Granby, Mass., U.S. 42°15′ N, 72°31′ W 104
Granby, Vt., U.S. 44°34′ N, 71°46′ W 104
Grand Bahama, island, Bahamas 27°0′ N, 78°0′ W 118
Grand Bank, Can. 47°4′ N, 55°48′ W 111
Grand Banks of Newfoundland, North Atlantic Ocean 45°14′ N, 52°41′ W 253
Grand Bend, Can. 43°18′ N, 81°44′ W 102
Grand Blanc, Mich., U.S. 42°55′ N, 83°37′ W 102
Grand Cane, La., U.S. 32°4′ N, 93°49′ W 103
Grand Canyon, Ariz., U.S. 36°4′ N, 113°37′ W 101
Grand Canyon National Park, Ariz., U.S. 35°50′ N, 114°11′ W 101
Grand Cayman, island, U.K. 19°0′ N, 81°0′ W 118
Grand Centre, Can. 54°23′ N, 110°14′ W 108
Grand Cess, Liberia 4°40′ N, 8°11′ W 214
Grand Chenier, La., U.S. 29°45′ N, 92°58′ W 103
Grand Coteau, La., U.S. 30°24′ N, 92°2′ W 103
Grand Coulee, Wash., U.S. 47°48′ N, 119°24′ W 90
Grand Coulee, Wash., U.S. 47°55′ N, 119°1′ W 90
Grand Falls, Can. 47°1′ N, 67°47′ W 94
Grand Falls-Windsor, Can. 48°53′ N, 55°42′ W 106
Grand Forks, Can. 49°1′ N, 118°28′ W 108
Grand Forks, N. Dak., U.S. 47°53′ N, 97°3′ W 90
Grand Forks Air Force Base, N. Dak., U.S. 47°56′ N, 97°31′ W 90
Grand Haven, Mich., U.S. 43°2′ N, 86°14′ W 102
Grand Island, Nebr., U.S. 40°54′ N, 98°22′ W 90
Grand Isle, La., U.S. 29°15′ N, 90°0′ W 103
Grand Junction, Colo., U.S. 39°4′ N, 108°34′ W 90
Grand Junction, Mich., U.S. 42°23′ N, 86°4′ W 102
Grand Lake, Can. 46°3′ N, 66°25′ W 94
Grand Lake, La., U.S. 29°46′ N, 91°28′ W 103
Grand Lake, La., U.S. 30°0′ N, 93°16′ W 103
Grand Ledge, Mich., U.S. 42°44′ N, 84°46′ W 102
Grand Manan Island, island, Can. 44°42′ N, 66°47′ W 111
Grand Marais, Can. 50°31′ N, 96°34′ W 90
Grand Marais, Mich., U.S. 46°39′ N, 86°0′ W 94
Grand Marais, Minn., U.S. 47°45′ N, 90°23′ W 94
Grand Mesa, Colo., U.S. 38°57′ N, 108°22′ W 90
Grand Popo, Benin 6°17′ N, 1°51′ E 222
Grand Portage, Minn., U.S. 47°57′ N, 89°45′ W 82
Grand Portal Point, Mich., U.S. 46°14′ N, 86°30′ W 94
Grand Prairie, Tex., U.S. 32°43′ N, 96°58′ W 92
Grand Rapids, Can. 53°10′ N, 99°20′ W 108
Grand Rapids, Mich., U.S. 42°56′ N, 85°40′ W 102
Grand Rapids, Minn., U.S. 47°13′ N, 93°32′ W 90
Grand Ridge, Ill., U.S. 41°14′ N, 88°50′ W 102
Grand, river, Mich., U.S. 42°57′ N, 85°46′ W 80
Grand, river, Mo., U.S. 40°15′ N, 94°24′ W 80
Grand, river, S. Dak., U.S. 45°40′ N, 101°46′ W 90
Grand Saline, Tex., U.S. 32°39′ N, 95°43′ W 96
Grand-Santi, Fr. 4°20′ N, 54°23′ W 130
Grand Teton, peak, Wyo., U.S. 43°42′ N, 110°53′ W 90
Grand Traverse Bay 44°59′ N, 86°0′ W 110
Grandas, Sp. 43°12′ N, 6°54′ W 150
Grand-Bassam, Côte d'Ivoire 5°13′ N, 3°46′ W 222
Grande, Bahía 51°3′ S, 70°13′ W 134
Grande, Baía, lake, Bol. 15°28′ S, 60°41′ W 132
Grande Cache, Can. 53°53′ N, 119°10′ W 108
Grande Cayemite, island, Haiti 18°33′ N, 73°42′ W 116
Grande, Cayo, island, Cuba 20°40′ N, 79°37′ W 116
Grande, Cayo, island, Venez. 11°32′ N, 66°37′ W 116
Grande, Corno, peak, It. 42°27′ N, 13°29′ E 156
Grande, Cuchilla, Uru. 33°58′ S, 56°15′ W 139
Grande de Lípez, river, Bol. 22°0′ S, 67°21′ W 137
Grande Prairie, Can. 55°10′ N, 118°49′ W 108
Grande, Punta, Chile 25°7′ S, 70°31′ W 132
Grande, river, Braz. 20°30′ S, 48°51′ W 138
Grande, river, Braz. 13°5′ S, 45°35′ W 138
Grande, river, Can. 48°40′ N, 65°15′ W 111
Grande, Serra, Braz. 10°11′ S, 61°36′ W 130
Grande, Serra (Caruana), peak, Braz. 2°34′ N, 60°46′ W 130
Grande Sertão Veredas National Park, Braz. 15°32′ S, 46°6′ W 138
Grande, Sierra, Mex. 29°42′ N, 105°8′ W 112
Grande-Terre, island, Fr. 16°32′ N, 61°28′ W 116
Grandfalls, Tex., U.S. 31°19′ N, 102°51′ W 92
Grandfather Mountain, N.C., U.S. 36°5′ N, 81°54′ W 96
Grandfield, Okla., U.S. 34°12′ N, 98°41′ W 92
Grand-Fort-Philippe, Fr. 50°59′ N, 2°5′ E 163
Grand-Lahou, Côte d'Ivoire 5°8′ N, 5°2′ W 222
Grand-Mère, Can. 46°36′ N, 72°43′ W 94
Grandpré, Fr. 49°20′ N, 4°51′ E 163
Grandview, Can. 51°9′ N, 100°43′ W 90
Grandview, Wash., U.S. 46°14′ N, 119°55′ W 90
Grandvilliers, Fr. 49°39′ N, 1°56′ E 163
Grañén, Sp. 41°56′ N, 0°22′ E 164
Grange, U.K. 54°10′ N, 2°56′ W 162
Granger, Ind., U.S. 41°44′ N, 86°7′ W 102
Granger, Tex., U.S. 30°41′ N, 97°27′ W 92
Granger, Wyo., U.S. 41°36′ N, 109°58′ W 90
Granges, Fr. 48°8′ N, 6°47′ E 163
Grangeville, Idaho, U.S. 45°53′ N, 116°7′ W 82
Granisle, Can. 54°54′ N, 126°18′ W 108
Granite, Okla., U.S. 34°56′ N, 99°24′ W 92
Granite Falls, Minn., U.S. 44°46′ N, 95°34′ W 90
Granite Falls, Wash., U.S. 48°4′ N, 121°58′ W 100
Granite Mountain, Nev., U.S. 40°16′ N, 117°54′ W 90
Granite Mountains, Wyo., U.S. 42°44′ N, 108°1′ W 90
Granite Pass, Calif., U.S. 35°25′ N, 116°35′ W 101
Granite Peak, Mont., U.S. 45°8′ N, 109°53′ W 90
Granite Peak, Nev., U.S. 41°38′ N, 117°41′ W 90
Granite Peak, Nev., U.S. 40°46′ N, 119°31′ W 90
Granite Peak, Utah, U.S. 40°6′ N, 113°20′ W 90
Granite Peak, Wyo., U.S. 42°32′ N, 108°57′ W 90
Granity, N.Z. 41°40′ S, 171°51′ E 240
Granja, Braz. 3°9′ S, 40°51′ W 132
Granja de Torrehermosa, Sp. 38°18′ N, 5°37′ W 164
Grankulla (Kauniainen), Fin. 60°11′ N, 24°43′ E 152
Granma, Cuba 19°51′ N, 77°33′ W 116
Gränna, Nor. 58°1′ N, 14°28′ E 152
Grannd Erg Oriental, Alg. 33°50′ N, 7°52′ E 156
Gransee, Ger. 53°1′ N, 13°8′ E 152
Grant, Mich., U.S. 43°19′ N, 85°49′ W 102
Grant, Nebr., U.S. 40°50′ N, 101°44′ W 90
Grant City, Mo., U.S. 40°27′ N, 94°25′ W 94
Grant Island, Antarctica 73°36′ S, 131°2′ W 248
Grant, Mount, Nev., U.S. 38°33′ N, 118°53′ W 90
Grant Range, Nev., U.S. 38°35′ N, 115°34′ W 90
Grantham, N.H., U.S. 43°29′ N, 72°8′ W 104
Grantham, U.K. 52°54′ N, 0°39′ E 162
Grant-Kohrs Ranch National Historic Site, Mont., U.S. 46°22′ N, 112°52′ W 90
Grants, N. Mex., U.S. 35°8′ N, 107°51′ W 112
Grants Pass, Oreg., U.S. 42°26′ N, 123°21′ W 90
Grantsburg, Wis., U.S. 45°45′ N, 92°41′ W 110
Grantsville, W. Va., U.S. 38°55′ N, 81°6′ W 102
Grantville, Ga., U.S. 33°13′ N, 84°51′ W 96
Granum, Can. 49°52′ N, 113°31′ W 90
Granville, Fr. 48°50′ N, 1°36′ W 150
Granville, N. Dak., U.S. 48°14′ N, 100°51′ W 90
Granville, Vt., U.S. 43°58′ N, 72°51′ W 104
Granville, W. Va., U.S. 39°38′ N, 80°0′ W 94
Granville Lake, Can. 56°16′ N, 101°37′ W 108
Granvin, Nor. 60°34′ N, 6°41′ E 152
Grão Mogol, Braz. 16°35′ S, 42°57′ W 138
Grapeland, Tex., U.S. 31°28′ N, 95°29′ W 103
Grapevine Mountains, Calif., U.S. 36°56′ N, 117°13′ W 101
Grapevine Peak, Nev., U.S. 36°57′ N, 117°11′ W 101
Graphite Peak, Antarctica 85°15′ S, 167°50′ E 248
Grapska Donja, Bosn. and Herzg. 44°47′ N, 18°4′ E 168
Graskop, S. Af. 24°58′ S, 30°50′ E 227
Grasmere, U.K. 54°27′ N, 3°1′ W 162
Gräsö, island, Sw. 60°26′ N, 18°25′ E 166
Grass, river, Can. 55°6′ N, 98°33′ W 108
Grass Valley, Calif., U.S. 39°12′ N, 121°5′ W 90
Grasset, Lac, lake, Can. 49°55′ N, 78°40′ W 94
Grassington, U.K. 54°4′ N, 1°59′ W 162
Grassland, Can. 54°48′ N, 112°42′ W 108
Grasslands National Park, Can. 48°54′ N, 108°0′ W 90
Grassrange, Mont., U.S. 47°0′ N, 108°48′ W 90
Grassy Butte, N. Dak., U.S. 47°22′ N, 103°17′ W 90
Grassy Island Lake, Can. 51°51′ N, 110°51′ W 90
Grassy Key, island, Fla., U.S. 24°43′ N, 80°55′ W 105
Grassy Mountain, Oreg., U.S. 42°37′ N, 117°25′ W 90
Grästorp, Nor. 58°19′ N, 12°39′ E 152
Grates Point, Can. 48°11′ N, 53°9′ W 111
Graton, Calif., U.S. 38°26′ N, 122°53′ W 92
Gråträsk, Nor. 65°28′ N, 19°45′ E 152
Graus, Sp. 42°10′ N, 0°19′ E 164
Grave, Neth. 51°45′ N, 5°43′ E 167
Grave Peak, Idaho, U.S. 46°22′ N, 114°49′ W 90
Gravedona, It. 46°9′ N, 9°17′ E 167
Gravelbourg, Can. 49°52′ N, 106°34′ W 90
Gravelines, Fr. 50°59′ N, 2°8′ E 163
Gravelotte, S. Af. 23°56′ S, 30°36′ E 227
Gravenhurst, Can. 44°54′ N, 79°22′ W 94
Gravesend, U.K. 51°25′ N, 0°21′ E 162
Gravette, Ark., U.S. 36°23′ N, 94°28′ W 96
Gravvik, Nor. 64°59′ N, 11°48′ E 152
Gray, Me., U.S. 43°53′ N, 70°20′ W 104
Gray, Mount, Antarctica 74°53′ S, 136°11′ W 248
Grayland, Wash., U.S. 46°47′ N, 124°6′ W 100
Grayling, Alas., U.S. 62°57′ N, 160°9′ W 98
Grayling, Mich., U.S. 44°40′ N, 84°43′ W 94
Grays, U.K. 51°29′ N, 0°20′ E 162
Grays Harbor 46°49′ N, 125°15′ W 80
Grays Peak, Colo., U.S. 39°36′ N, 105°54′ W 90
Grayslake, Ill., U.S. 42°20′ N, 88°3′ W 102
Grayson, Ky., U.S. 38°19′ N, 82°57′ W 94
Grayson, La., U.S. 32°2′ N, 92°7′ W 103
Grayville, Mo., U.S. 38°14′ N, 88°0′ W 94
Grayvoron, Russ. 50°28′ N, 35°39′ E 158
Graz, Aust. 47°4′ N, 15°26′ E 156
Grazie, Monte le, peak, It. 42°10′ N, 11°50′ E 156
Grdelica, Serb. 42°53′ N, 22°4′ E 168
Grea de Albarracín, Sp. 40°24′ N, 1°22′ W 164
Great Artesian Basin, Australia 22°45′ S, 142°18′ E 230
Great Australian Bight 37°7′ S, 130°17′ E 231
Great Badminton, U.K. 51°32′ N, 2°17′ W 162
Great Barrier Reef, Coral Sea 16°34′ S, 147°16′ E 252
Great Barrier Reef Marine Park, Coral Sea 19°12′ S, 147°53′ E 238
Great Barrington, Mass., U.S. 42°11′ N, 73°23′ W 104
Great Basalt Wall National Park, Austral. 20°7′ S, 144°57′ E 238
Great Basin, North America 36°22′ N, 114°27′ W 101
Great Basin National Park, Nev., U.S. 38°36′ N, 114°29′ W 90
Great Bear Lake, Can. 65°31′ N, 121°54′ W 106
Great Britain, island, U.K. 52°5′ N, 1°42′ W 143
Great Channel 6°12′ N, 93°33′ E 188
Great Corn Island see Maíz Grande, Isla del, Nicar. 11°44′ N, 83°2′ W 115
Great Crater, Israel 30°55′ N, 34°59′ E 194
Great Divide Basin, Wyo., U.S. 41°58′ N, 108°11′ W 90
Great Dividing Range, Australia 11°52′ S, 142°8′ E 192
Great Driffield, U.K. 54°0′ N, 0°26′ E 162
Great Exuma, island, Bahamas 23°23′ N, 76°30′ W 116
Great Eastern Erg, Alg. 30°0′ N, 7°0′ E 156
Great Falls, Can. 50°23′ N, 96°4′ W 90
Great Falls, Mont., U.S. 47°28′ N, 111°18′ W 90
Great Falls, S.C., U.S. 34°33′ N, 80°54′ W 96
Great Fish, river, S. Af. 33°1′ S, 25°53′ E 227
Great Guana Cay, island, Bahamas 23°53′ N, 76°37′ W 116
Great Harbour Cay, island, Bahamas 25°39′ N, 77°45′ W 81
Great Harbour Deep, Can. 50°22′ N, 56°33′ W 111
Great Inagua Island, Bahamas 21°14′ N, 73°53′ W 116
Great Indian Desert, India 26°55′ N, 68°30′ E 186
Great Isaac, island, Bahamas 26°0′ N, 79°20′ W 105
Great Island, peak, Can. 58°59′ N, 96°42′ W 108
Great Islets Harbour 51°7′ N, 56°40′ W 111
Great Kei, river, S. Af. 32°20′ S, 27°54′ E 227
Great Lakes Naval Training Center, Ill., U.S. 42°17′ N, 87°54′ W 102
Great Namaland, region, Africa 26°5′ S, 14°59′ E 227
Great Nicobar, island, India 6°29′ N, 93°53′ E 188
Great Orme's Head, U.K. 53°20′ N, 4°0′ W 162
Great Ouse, river, U.K. 52°36′ N, 0°17′ E 162
Great Pedro Bluff, Jam. 17°45′ N, 78°41′ W 115
Great Point, Mass., U.S. 41°23′ N, 70°8′ W 104
Great Pond, lake, Me., U.S. 44°29′ N, 70°3′ W 104
Great Ruaha, river, Tanzania 7°21′ S, 35°14′ E 224
Great Sacandaga Lake, N.Y., U.S. 43°17′ N, 74°11′ W 104
Great Salt Lake, Utah, U.S. 41°16′ N, 113°26′ W 106
Great Salt Lake Desert, Utah, U.S. 40°26′ N, 113°47′ W 90
Great Salt Plains Lake, Okla., U.S. 36°45′ N, 99°5′ W 81
Great Sandy Desert, Australia 20°22′ S, 122°54′ E 230
Great Sitkin, island, Alas., U.S. 52°12′ N, 177°22′ W 160
Great Slave Lake, Can. 61°13′ N, 117°25′ W 73
Great Smoky Mountains, N.C., U.S. 35°44′ N, 83°34′ W 96
Great Snow Mountain, Can. 57°25′ N, 124°12′ W 108
Great Victoria Desert, Austral. 28°18′ S, 126°42′ E 230
Great Wall, China 39°15′ N, 110°33′ E 198
Great Wall, station, Antarctica 62°12′ S, 58°57′ W 134
Great Western Erg, Alg. 30°20′ N, 0°0′ W 156
Great Yarmouth, U.K. 52°36′ N, 1°42′ E 163
Great Zab, river, Turk. 37°27′ N, 43°41′ E 195
Great Zab see Zāb al Kabīr, river, Iraq 36°32′ N, 43°40′ E 195
Great Zimbabwe, ruin(s), Zimb. 20°24′ S, 30°58′ E 227
Greater Antilles, Caribbean Sea 17°49′ N, 73°28′ W 116
Greater Khingan Range, China 52°0′ N, 122°48′ E 172
Grebbestad, Nor. 58°41′ N, 11°15′ E 152
Grebenau, Ger. 50°44′ N, 9°27′ E 167
Grebenstein, Ger. 51°27′ N, 9°25′ E 167
Gréboun, peak, Niger 19°55′ N, 8°29′ E 222
Greco, Monte, peak, It. 41°47′ N, 13°54′ E 156
Gredos, Sierra de, Sp. 40°16′ N, 5°43′ W 150
Greece 39°6′ N, 21°44′ E 156
Greeley, Colo., U.S. 40°25′ N, 104°43′ W 90
Greeley, Nebr., U.S. 41°32′ N, 98°33′ W 90
Green Bay 44°38′ N, 87°59′ W 94
Green Island, N.Z. 45°53′ S, 170°24′ E 240
Green Islands, South Pacific Ocean 3°45′ S, 153°35′ E 192
Green Islands, South Pacific Ocean 4°1′ S, 154°11′ E 238
Green Lake, Can. 54°18′ N, 107°47′ W 108
Green Lake, Wis., U.S. 43°49′ N, 88°57′ W 102
Green Mountains, Vt., U.S. 44°2′ N, 73°0′ W 104
Green Mountains, Wyo., U.S. 42°27′ N, 107°57′ W 90
Green River, Utah, U.S. 38°59′ N, 110°10′ W 92
Green River, Wyo., U.S. 41°32′ N, 109°28′ W 90
Green, river, Ky., U.S. 37°37′ N, 87°33′ W 94
Green, river, U.S. 39°51′ N, 109°57′ W 90
Greenacres, Calif., U.S. 35°23′ N, 119°8′ W 101
Greenbush, Minn., U.S. 48°40′ N, 96°13′ W 90
Greenbush Lake, Can. 50°55′ N, 90°38′ W 110
Greencastle, Ind., U.S. 39°38′ N, 86°52′ W 102
Greene, Me., U.S. 44°11′ N, 70°8′ W 104
Greeneville, Tenn., U.S. 36°9′ N, 82°51′ W 96
Greenfield, Calif., U.S. 36°19′ N, 121°15′ W 100
Greenfield, Ind., U.S. 39°47′ N, 85°46′ W 102
Greenfield, Iowa, U.S. 41°18′ N, 94°27′ W 94
Greenfield, Mo., U.S. 37°24′ N, 93°51′ W 96
Greenfield, N.H., U.S. 42°56′ N, 71°53′ W 104
Greenfield, N. Mex., U.S. 33°9′ N, 104°21′ W 92
Greenfield, Ohio, U.S. 39°21′ N, 83°24′ W 102
Greenhorn Mountain, Colo., U.S. 37°52′ N, 105°6′ W 90
Greenhorn Mountains, Calif., U.S. 35°41′ N, 118°54′ W 92
Greenland (Kalaallit Nunaat), Den. 67°11′ N, 50°25′ W 106
Greenland, N.H., U.S. 43°1′ N, 70°51′ W 104
Greenland Fracture Zone, Greenland Sea 74°53′ N, 2°12′ E 255
Greenland Sea 74°52′ N, 4°29′ E 160
Greenland Sea 68°26′ N, 25°49′ W 246
Greenland Sea 73°24′ N, 12°53′ W 255
Greenough, Mount, Alas., U.S. 69°6′ N, 141°54′ W 98
Greenport, N.Y., U.S. 41°6′ N, 72°23′ W 104
Greensboro, Ala., U.S. 32°42′ N, 87°36′ W 103
Greensboro, Ga., U.S. 33°33′ N, 83°11′ W 96
Greensboro, N.C., U.S. 36°3′ N, 79°49′ W 96
Greensboro Bend, Vt., U.S. 44°32′ N, 72°16′ W 104
Greensburg, Ind., U.S. 39°19′ N, 85°29′ W 102
Greensburg, Kans., U.S. 37°35′ N, 99°18′ W 92
Greensburg, La., U.S. 30°49′ N, 90°41′ W 103
Greensburg, Pa., U.S. 40°17′ N, 79°34′ W 94
Greentown, Ind., U.S. 40°28′ N, 85°58′ W 102
Greenup, Ill., U.S. 39°13′ N, 88°10′ W 102
Greenup, Ky., U.S. 38°33′ N, 82°50′ W 102
Greenview, Ill., U.S. 40°4′ N, 89°45′ W 102
Greenville, Ala., U.S. 31°49′ N, 86°37′ W 96
Greenville, Can. 55°3′ N, 129°36′ W 108
Greenville, Fla., U.S. 30°26′ N, 83°38′ W 96
Greenville, Ill., U.S. 38°53′ N, 89°24′ W 102
Greenville, Ky., U.S. 37°12′ N, 87°11′ W 94
Greenville, Liberia 5°0′ N, 9°3′ W 222
Greenville, Me., U.S. 45°27′ N, 69°36′ W 94
Greenville, Mich., U.S. 43°10′ N, 85°16′ W 102
Greenville, Miss., U.S. 33°23′ N, 91°4′ W 103
Greenville, N.H., U.S. 42°46′ N, 71°50′ W 104
Greenville, Ohio, U.S. 40°5′ N, 84°38′ W 102
Greenville, Pa., U.S. 41°24′ N, 80°23′ W 94
Greenville, S.C., U.S. 34°50′ N, 82°25′ W 96
Greenville, Tex., U.S. 33°6′ N, 96°6′ W 96
Greenwich, Conn., U.S. 41°1′ N, 73°38′ W 104
Greenwich, N.Y., U.S. 43°5′ N, 73°31′ W 104
Greenwich, Ohio, U.S. 41°1′ N, 82°31′ W 102
Greenwich, U.K. 51°27′ N, 3°180′ E 162
Greenwich Island, Antarctica 62°45′ S, 59°27′ W 134
Greenwood, Ark., U.S. 35°11′ N, 94°16′ W 96
Greenwood, Can. 49°5′ N, 118°41′ W 90
Greenwood, Ind., U.S. 39°37′ N, 86°6′ W 102
Greenwood, Me., U.S. 44°18′ N, 70°39′ W 104
Greenwood, Miss., U.S. 33°29′ N, 90°11′ W 96
Greenwood, S.C., U.S. 34°11′ N, 82°11′ W 112
Greenwood, Mount, Austral. 13°47′ S, 129°52′ E 230
Greer, Ariz., U.S. 34°1′ N, 109°27′ W 92
Greetsiel, Ger. 53°30′ N, 7°5′ E 163
Gregoire Lake, Can. 56°27′ N, 111°36′ W 108
Gregório, river, Braz. 7°39′ S, 71°13′ W 130
Gregory, S. Dak., U.S. 43°12′ N, 99°27′ W 90
Gregory National Park, Austral. 16°23′ S, 129°58′ E 238
Gregory Range, Austral. 18°43′ S, 142°20′ E 230
Greiffenberg, Ger. 53°5′ N, 13°56′ E 152
Greifswald, Ger. 54°6′ N, 13°22′ E 152
Gremikha, Russ. 68°0′ N, 39°23′ E 169
Gremyachinsk, Russ. 58°35′ N, 57°52′ E 154
Grenå, Den. 56°25′ N, 10°51′ E 150
Grenada 12°0′ N, 62°0′ W 116
Grenada, Calif., U.S. 41°39′ N, 122°32′ W 92
Grenada, Miss., U.S. 33°43′ N, 89°49′ W 96
Grenchen, Switz. 47°11′ N, 7°22′ E 150
Grenfell, Can. 50°24′ N, 102°56′ W 90
Grenoble, Fr. 45°11′ N, 5°43′ E 150
Grenora, N. Dak., U.S. 48°36′ N, 103°57′ W 90
Grenville, Can. 45°37′ N, 74°37′ W 94
Grenville Channel 53°42′ N, 130°45′ W 108
Grenville, Mount, Can. 50°58′ N, 124°36′ W 90
Grenville, Point, Wash., U.S. 47°13′ N, 124°31′ W 100
Gresford, U.K. 53°5′ N, 2°59′ W 162
Gressåmoen National Park, Nor. 64°18′ N, 12°52′ E 152
Gretna, La., U.S. 29°54′ N, 90°4′ W 103
Greven, Ger. 52°5′ N, 7°37′ E 163
Grevenbroich, Ger. 51°5′ N, 6°35′ E 167
Grevenmacher, Lux. 49°40′ N, 6°25′ E 163
Grevesmühlen, Ger. 53°51′ N, 11°12′ E 152
Grey Islands, Labrador Sea 50°26′ N, 55°8′ W 106
Grey Range, Austral. 28°39′ S, 142°4′ E 230
Greybull, Wyo., U.S. 44°28′ N, 108°4′ W 90
Greylock, Mount, Mass., U.S. 42°37′ N, 73°12′ W 104
Greymouth, N.Z. 42°30′ S, 171°13′ E 240
Greytown, N.Z. 41°6′ S, 175°29′ E 240
Grezzana, It. 45°30′ N, 11°0′ E 167
Griam More, Ben, peak, U.K. 58°18′ N, 4°9′ W 150
Gribanovskiy, Russ. 51°27′ N, 41°53′ E 158
Gribe, Mal, Alban. 40°15′ N, 19°29′ E 156
Grico, oil field, Venez. 8°55′ N, 66°40′ W 136
Gridino, Russ. 65°53′ N, 34°28′ E 152
Gridley, Ill., U.S. 40°44′ N, 88°53′ W 102
Grieskirchen, Aust. 48°13′ N, 13°50′ E 152
Griffin, Ga., U.S. 33°13′ N, 84°16′ W 96
Grigorevka, Kyrg. 42°44′ N, 77°48′ E 184
Grigoriopol, Mold. 47°9′ N, 29°17′ E 158
Grimari, Cen. Af. Rep. 5°43′ N, 20°5′ E 218
Grimsby, Can. 43°10′ N, 79°34′ W 94

Grimsby, *U.K.* 53°34′ N, 0°5′ E **162**
Grimshaw, *Can.* 56°11′ N, 117°37′ W **108**
Grimstad, *Nor.* 58°20′ N, 8°34′ E **150**
Grindelwald, *Switz.* 46°37′ N, 8°2′ E **167**
Grinnell, *Iowa, U.S.* 41°44′ N, 92°43′ W **94**
Grinnell Peninsula, *Can.* 76°38′ N, 95°22′ W **106**
Griñón, *Sp.* 40°12′ N, 3°51′ W **164**
Grintavec, peak, *Slov.* 46°21′ N, 14°28′ E **156**
Gripsholm, site, *Nor.* 59°14′ N, 17°5′ E **152**
Griquatown, *S. Af.* 28°51′ S, 23°15′ E **227**
Grise Fiord, *Can.* 76°21′ N, 82°51′ W **106**
Grishkino, *Russ.* 57°57′ N, 82°44′ E **169**
Grisslehamn, *Sw.* 60°4′ N, 18°44′ E **166**
Griswoldville, *Mass., U.S.* 42°39′ N, 72°43′ W **104**
Griva, *Latv.* 55°49′ N, 26°31′ E **166**
Griva, *Russ.* 60°34′ N, 50°55′ E **154**
Grizim, spring, *Alg.* 25°25′ N, 3°4′ W **214**
Grizzly Bear Hills, *Can.* 55°35′ N, 109°42′ W **108**
Grizzly Mountain, *Can.* 51°42′ N, 120°20′ W **90**
Grmeic, *Bosn. and Herzg.* 44°21′ N, 16°29′ E **168**
Grobiņa, *Latv.* 56°32′ N, 21°9′ E **166**
Grocka, *Serb.* 44°39′ N, 20°42′ E **168**
Groenlo, *Neth.* 52°2′ N, 6°36′ E **167**
Grombalia, *Tun.* 36°35′ N, 10°31′ E **214**
Gromovo, *Russ.* 60°41′ N, 30°16′ E **166**
Grong, *Nor.* 64°27′ N, 12°20′ E **152**
Groningen, *Neth.* 53°12′ N, 6°33′ E **163**
Gronlid, *Can.* 53°5′ N, 104°28′ W **108**
Grønøy, *Nor.* 66°47′ N, 13°25′ E **152**
Groom, *Tex., U.S.* 35°13′ N, 101°5′ W **92**
Groot Karasberge, peak, *Namibia* 27°12′ S, 18°37′ E **227**
Groote Eylandt, island, *Austral.* 14°27′ S, 137°3′ E **230**
Grootfontein, *Namibia* 19°32′ S, 18°7′ E **220**
Gros Mécatina, Cap du, *Can.* 50°38′ N, 59°8′ W **111**
Gros Morne National Park, *Can.* 49°46′ N, 58°30′ W **111**
Gros Morne, peak, *Can.* 49°34′ N, 57°52′ W **111**
Gros Ventre, *Wyo., U.S.* 43°24′ N, 111°16′ W **80**
Gros Ventre Range, *Wyo., U.S.* 43°28′ N, 110°52′ W **90**
Grosio, *It.* 46°17′ N, 10°14′ E **167**
Grosne, river, *Fr.* 46°32′ N, 4°38′ E **165**
Grossa, Ponta, *Braz.* 1°14′ N, 49°54′ W **130**
Grossa, Punta, *Sp.* 39°5′ N, 1°16′ E **150**
Grossalmerode, *Ger.* 51°15′ N, 9°46′ E **167**
Grossefehn, *Ger.* 53°24′ N, 7°36′ E **163**
Grossenkneten, *Ger.* 52°56′ N, 8°16′ E **163**
Grossenlüder, *Ger.* 50°36′ N, 9°32′ E **167**
Grosseto, *It.* 42°45′ N, 11°5′ E **156**
Grossglockner, peak, *Aust.* 47°4′ N, 12°37′ E **156**
Gross-Umstadt, *Ger.* 49°52′ N, 8°54′ E **167**
Grostenquin, *Fr.* 48°57′ N, 6°43′ E **163**
Grosvenor Seamount, *North Pacific Ocean* 28°4′ N, 166°46′ E **252**
Groton, *Mass., U.S.* 42°36′ N, 71°35′ W **104**
Groton, *S. Dak., U.S.* 45°26′ N, 98°7′ W **90**
Groton, *Vt., U.S.* 44°12′ N, 72°12′ W **104**
Grøtøy, *Nor.* 67°49′ N, 14°42′ E **152**
Grottammare, *It.* 42°59′ N, 13°51′ E **156**
Grotte de Lascaux, site, *Fr.* 45°2′ N, 1°9′ E **165**
Grouard, *Can.* 55°31′ N, 116°8′ W **108**
Groundhog, river, *Can.* 49°22′ N, 82°15′ W **94**
Grouse Creek, *Utah, U.S.* 41°42′ N, 113°54′ W **92**
Grouse Creek Mountain, *Idaho, U.S.* 44°21′ N, 113°59′ W **90**
Grouse Creek Mountains, *Utah, U.S.* 41°29′ N, 114°8′ W **90**
Grovane, *Nor.* 58°17′ N, 7°58′ E **152**
Grove Hill, *Ala., U.S.* 31°42′ N, 87°46′ W **103**
Groveland, *Calif., U.S.* 37°49′ N, 120°15′ W **100**
Groveland, *Fla., U.S.* 28°33′ N, 81°51′ W **105**
Groveport, *Ohio, U.S.* 39°51′ N, 82°53′ W **102**
Grover, *Colo., U.S.* 40°52′ N, 104°15′ W **90**
Grover, *Pa., U.S.* 41°36′ N, 76°53′ W **94**
Grover Beach, *Calif., U.S.* 35°7′ N, 120°38′ W **92**
Groves, *Tex., U.S.* 29°55′ N, 93°56′ W **103**
Groveton, *N.H., U.S.* 44°36′ N, 71°32′ W **94**
Groveton, *Tex., U.S.* 31°2′ N, 95°7′ W **103**
Growler Pass, *Ariz., U.S.* 32°10′ N, 112°55′ W **92**
Groznyy, *Russ.* 43°18′ N, 45°39′ E **195**
Grubišno Polje, *Croatia* 45°41′ N, 17°10′ E **168**
Gruda, *Croatia* 42°30′ N, 18°22′ E **168**
Grudopole, *Belarus* 52°53′ N, 25°42′ E **152**
Grudovo, *Bulg.* 42°20′ N, 27°10′ E **156**
Grue, *Nor.* 60°26′ N, 12°2′ E **152**
Gruemirë, *Alban.* 42°9′ N, 19°31′ E **168**
Gruesa, Punta, *Chile* 20°23′ S, 70°36′ W **137**
Grulla, *Tex., U.S.* 26°17′ N, 98°39′ W **114**
Grums, *Nor.* 59°21′ N, 13°4′ E **152**
Grünau, *Namibia* 27°44′ S, 18°21′ E **227**
Grünberg, *Ger.* 50°35′ N, 8°57′ E **167**
Grundforsen, *Nor.* 61°17′ N, 12°52′ E **152**
Gruver, *Tex., U.S.* 36°14′ N, 101°25′ W **92**
Gruža, *Serb.* 43°54′ N, 20°46′ E **168**
Gryazi, *Russ.* 52°28′ N, 39°48′ E **158**
Gryazovets, *Russ.* 58°52′ N, 40°14′ E **154**
Grygla, *Minn., U.S.* 48°16′ N, 95°39′ W **90**
Gryźliny, *Pol.* 53°37′ N, 20°20′ E **152**
Gstaad, *Switz.* 46°27′ N, 7°18′ E **167**
Gua Musang, *Malaysia* 4°52′ N, 101°58′ E **196**
Guabito, *Pan.* 9°29′ N, 82°36′ W **115**
Guaca, *Col.* 6°50′ N, 72°50′ W **136**
Guacamaya, *Col.* 2°15′ N, 75°1′ W **136**
Guachara, *Venez.* 7°16′ N, 68°23′ W **136**
Guachochi, *Mex.* 26°50′ N, 107°5′ W **112**
Guaçui, *Braz.* 20°49′ S, 41°44′ W **138**
Guadalajara, *Mex.* 20°39′ N, 103°26′ W **114**
Guadalajara, *Sp.* 40°36′ N, 3°10′ W **164**
Guadalajara, *Sp.* 40°37′ N, 3°10′ W **214**
Guadalcanal, *Sp.* 38°5′ N, 5°50′ W **164**
Guadalcanal, island, *Solomon Islands* 10°0′ S, 160°0′ E **242**
Guadalquivir, river, *Sp.* 37°52′ N, 6°2′ W **143**
Guadalupe, *Braz.* 6°49′ S, 43°35′ W **132**
Guadalupe, *Calif., U.S.* 34°57′ N, 120°35′ W **100**
Guadalupe, *Mex.* 25°40′ N, 100°15′ W **114**
Guadalupe, *Mex.* 32°1′ N, 116°40′ W **112**
Guadalupe, *Mex.* 29°22′ N, 110°27′ W **92**
Guadalupe, *Mex.* 22°44′ N, 102°29′ W **114**
Guadalupe, *Sp.* 39°27′ N, 5°19′ W **164**
Guadalupe Bravos, *Mex.* 31°22′ N, 106°7′ W **92**
Guadalupe, Isla de, island, *Fr.* 28°27′ N, 118°49′ W **112**
Guadalupe Mountains, *N. Mex., U.S.* 32°16′ N, 105°7′ W **92**
Guadalupe Peak, *Tex., U.S.* 31°51′ N, 104°56′ W **92**
Guadalupe, Sierra de, *Sp.* 39°15′ N, 5°52′ W **164**
Guadarrama, Sierra de, *Sp.* 41°18′ N, 3°18′ W **164**
Guadeloupe, islands, *Fr.* 16°23′ N, 61°59′ W **116**
Guadiana, river, *Sp.* 38°15′ N, 7°35′ W **143**
Guadix, *Sp.* 37°18′ N, 3°9′ W **164**
Guafo, Isla, island, *Chile* 43°32′ S, 75°41′ W **134**
Guaíba, *Braz.* 30°10′ S, 51°21′ W **139**
Guaicuí, *Braz.* 17°12′ S, 44°51′ W **138**
Guáimaro, *Cuba* 21°3′ N, 77°24′ W **116**
Guainía, adm. division, *Col.* 2°47′ N, 69°53′ W **136**
Guainía, river, *Col.* 2°8′ N, 69°29′ W **136**
Guaira, *Braz.* 24°7′ S, 54°15′ W **132**
Guaitecas, Islas, islands, *South Pacific Ocean* 43°59′ S, 76°28′ W **134**
Guajaba, Cayo, island, *Cuba* 21°51′ N, 77°26′ W **116**
Guajará-Mirim, *Braz.* 10°49′ S, 65°20′ W **137**
Guajarraã, *Braz.* 7°46′ S, 66°57′ W **130**
Guaje, Llano del, *Mex.* 27°50′ N, 103°43′ W **112**
Guajira, adm. division, *Col.* 11°6′ N, 73°23′ W **136**
Guajira, Península de la, *Col.* 11°58′ N, 72°6′ W **136**
Gualaca, *Pan.* 8°31′ N, 82°18′ W **115**
Gualaguala, Punta, *Chile* 22°47′ S, 70°56′ W **137**
Gualala, *Calif., U.S.* 38°46′ N, 123°32′ W **90**
Gualán, *Guatemala* 15°7′ N, 89°24′ W **115**
Gualeguay, *Arg.* 33°7′ S, 59°18′ W **139**
Gualeguaychú, *Arg.* 33°3′ S, 58°29′ W **139**
Gualicho, Gran Bajo del, *Arg.* 40°15′ S, 67°12′ W **134**
Gualjaina, *Arg.* 42°42′ S, 70°33′ W **134**
Guam, *U.S.* 13°18′ N, 144°15′ E **242**
Guamareyes, *Col.* 0°30′ N, 73°1′ W **136**
Guamblin, Isla, island, *Chile* 45°1′ S, 76°41′ W **134**
Guamini, *Arg.* 37°2′ S, 62°23′ W **139**
Guamo, *Col.* 3°59′ N, 75°1′ W **136**
Guamúchil, *Mex.* 25°27′ N, 108°5′ W **112**
Guanabacoa, *Cuba* 23°7′ N, 82°18′ W **96**
Guanabara, *Braz.* 10°41′ S, 70°8′ W **137**
Guanacevi, *Mex.* 25°58′ N, 105°57′ W **114**
Guanaco, *Arg.* 35°42′ S, 61°40′ W **139**
Guanaco, Paso del, pass, *Chile* 36°1′ S, 70°23′ W **134**
Guanaja, Isla de, island, *Hond.* 16°31′ N, 85°49′ W **115**
Guanajuato, *Mex.* 20°58′ N, 101°20′ W **114**
Guanajuato, adm. division, *Mex.* 21°2′ N, 101°49′ W **114**
Guanambi, *Braz.* 14°14′ S, 42°46′ W **138**
Guanare, *Venez.* 9°2′ N, 69°47′ W **136**
Guanare, river, *Venez.* 8°44′ N, 69°30′ W **136**
Guanay, *Bol.* 15°28′ S, 67°53′ W **137**
Guandacol, *Arg.* 29°32′ S, 68°32′ W **134**
Guangchang, *China* 26°50′ N, 116°11′ E **198**
Guangdong, adm. division, *China* 23°48′ N, 112°55′ E **198**
Guangfeng, *China* 28°27′ N, 118°13′ E **198**
Guanghai, *China* 21°55′ N, 112°46′ E **198**
Guangrao, *China* 37°6′ N, 118°25′ E **198**
Guangshan, *China* 32°0′ N, 114°52′ E **198**
Guangshui, *China* 31°37′ N, 114°3′ E **198**
Guangxi Zhuang, adm. division, *China* 23°49′ N, 107°53′ E **198**
Guangyuan, *China* 32°23′ N, 105°52′ E **173**
Guangzhou (Canton), *China* 23°6′ N, 113°17′ E **198**
Guanhaes, *Braz.* 18°48′ S, 43°1′ W **138**
Guanshui, *China* 40°52′ N, 124°33′ E **200**
Guanta, *Venez.* 10°14′ N, 64°35′ W **116**
Guantánamo, *Cuba* 20°8′ N, 75°14′ W **116**
Guantánamo, adm. division, *Cuba* 20°8′ N, 75°31′ W **116**
Guanyan, *China* 34°16′ N, 119°14′ E **198**
Guanyang, *China* 25°29′ N, 111°6′ E **198**
Guapé, *Braz.* 20°47′ S, 45°56′ W **138**
Guapí, *Col.* 2°33′ N, 77°57′ W **136**
Guaporé, *Braz.* 28°58′ S, 51°57′ W **139**
Guaporé Iténez, river, *South America* 11°49′ S, 65°5′ W **137**
Guaporé, river, *Braz.* 15°29′ S, 58°50′ W **132**
Guaqui, *Bol.* 16°40′ S, 68°51′ W **137**
Guará, river, *Braz.* 13°26′ S, 45°34′ W **132**
Guara, Sierra de, *Sp.* 42°23′ N, 0°26′ E **164**
Guarabira, *Braz.* 6°52′ S, 35°32′ W **132**
Guaraci, *Braz.* 20°33′ S, 48°56′ W **138**
Guaraí, *Braz.* 8°59′ S, 48°13′ W **130**
Guarapari, *Braz.* 20°41′ S, 40°31′ W **138**
Guarapuava, *Braz.* 25°23′ S, 51°29′ W **138**
Guaraqueçaba, *Braz.* 25°18′ S, 48°20′ W **138**
Guaratinguetá, *Braz.* 22°51′ S, 45°10′ W **138**
Guaratuba, *Braz.* 25°55′ S, 48°35′ W **138**
Guarda, *Port.* 40°32′ N, 7°17′ W **150**
Guarda, adm. division, *Port.* 40°43′ N, 7°34′ W **150**
Guarda Mor, *Braz.* 17°48′ S, 47°7′ W **138**
Guardatinajas, *Venez.* 9°1′ N, 67°38′ W **136**
Guardia Escolta, *Arg.* 28°57′ S, 62°11′ W **139**
Guaribe, river, *Braz.* 8°2′ S, 60°33′ W **130**
Guárico, adm. division, *Venez.* 8°47′ N, 67°29′ W **136**
Guarico, Punta, *Cuba* 20°40′ N, 74°44′ W **116**
Guarromán, *Sp.* 38°10′ N, 3°41′ W **164**
Guasave, *Mex.* 25°33′ N, 108°29′ W **82**
Guascama, Punta, *Col.* 2°21′ N, 78°28′ W **136**
Guasipati, *Venez.* 7°27′ N, 61°56′ W **130**
Guastalla, *It.* 44°55′ N, 10°38′ E **167**
Guatemala 15°4′ N, 91°3′ W **115**
Guatemala City, *Guatemala* 14°34′ N, 90°40′ W **115**
Guatemala Basin, *North Pacific Ocean* 6°59′ N, 94°28′ W **252**
Guateque, *Col.* 5°0′ N, 73°28′ W **136**
Guatraché, *Arg.* 37°42′ S, 63°29′ W **139**
Guaviare, adm. division, *Col.* 1°43′ N, 73°27′ W **136**
Guaviare, river, *Col.* 3°12′ N, 70°17′ W **136**
Guaxupé, *Braz.* 21°18′ S, 46°43′ W **138**
Guayabal, *Cuba* 20°42′ N, 77°39′ W **116**
Guayabal, *Venez.* 7°58′ N, 67°23′ W **136**
Guayabero, river, *Col.* 2°13′ N, 73°43′ W **136**
Guayalejo, river, *Mex.* 23°24′ N, 99°4′ W **114**
Guayaquil, *Ecua.* 2°17′ S, 79°57′ W **130**
Guaymas, *Mex.* 28°4′ N, 110°50′ W **238**
Guaymas, Cerro, peak, *Mex.* 28°10′ N, 111°14′ W **92**
Guaymas, Valle de, *Mex.* 28°16′ N, 110°51′ W **112**
Guaynabo, *P.R., U.S.* 18°0′ N, 66°0′ W **118**
Guba, *Dem. Rep. of the Congo* 10°38′ S, 26°24′ E **224**
Guba, *Eth.* 11°14′ N, 35°18′ E **182**
Guba Dolgaya, *Russ.* 70°17′ N, 58°45′ E **169**
Gubakha, *Russ.* 58°50′ N, 57°34′ E **169**
Guban, region, *Africa* 10°31′ N, 42°50′ E **216**
Gubat, *Philippines* 12°55′ N, 124°7′ E **203**
Gubdor, *Russ.* 60°13′ N, 56°34′ E **154**
Guben, *Pol.* 51°57′ N, 14°41′ E **152**
Gubio, *Nig.* 12°27′ N, 12°45′ E **216**
Gubkin, *Russ.* 51°15′ N, 37°32′ E **158**
Guča, *Serb.* 43°46′ N, 20°12′ E **168**
Gucheng, *China* 32°15′ N, 111°33′ E **198**
Gudaut'a, *Ga.* 43°6′ N, 40°40′ E **195**
Gudbrandsdalen, *Nor.* 61°58′ N, 9°10′ E **152**
Guddu Barrage, dam, *Pak.* 28°31′ N, 69°35′ E **186**
Gudensberg, *Ger.* 51°11′ N, 9°23′ E **167**
Gudivada, *India* 16°23′ N, 81°1′ E **188**
Gudžiūnai, *Lith.* 55°31′ N, 23°45′ E **166**
Guéckédo, *Guinea* 8°33′ N, 10°9′ W **222**
Guedon Dong, oil field, *Indonesia* 4°51′ N, 97°45′ E **196**
Guelph, *Can.* 43°33′ N, 80°14′ W **94**
Guelta Mouri Idié, spring, *Chad* 23°3′ N, 15°14′ E **216**
Guemar, *Alg.* 33°29′ N, 6°48′ E **214**
Guéné, *Benin* 11°45′ N, 3°14′ E **222**
Güeppí, *Peru* 0°8′ N, 75°13′ W **136**
Güepsa, *Col.* 6°2′ N, 73°37′ W **136**
Guer, *Fr.* 47°54′ N, 2°9′ W **150**
Güer Aike, *Arg.* 51°36′ S, 69°37′ W **134**
Guéra, Massif de, peak, *Chad* 11°55′ N, 18°5′ E **218**
Guerara, *Alg.* 32°47′ N, 4°29′ E **214**
Guercif, *Mor.* 34°16′ N, 3°19′ W **214**
Guéréda, *Chad* 14°29′ N, 22°2′ E **216**
Guernsey, island, *U.K.* 49°27′ N, 2°36′ W **150**
Guernsey, *Wyo., U.S.* 42°16′ N, 104°43′ W **90**
Guerrero, adm. division, *Mex.* 17°45′ N, 100°51′ W **114**
Guerzim, *Alg.* 29°40′ N, 1°40′ W **214**
Guest Peninsula, *Antarctica* 76°20′ S, 149°54′ W **248**
Gueydan, *La., U.S.* 30°1′ N, 92°31′ W **103**
Guézaoua, *Niger* 16°29′ N, 8°47′ E **222**
Gugu, peak, *Eth.* 8°11′ N, 39°50′ E **224**
Guguan, island, *U.S.* 17°22′ N, 146°1′ E **192**
Gui, river, *China* 24°0′ N, 110°41′ E **198**
Guia Lopes da Laguna, *Braz.* 21°28′ S, 56°2′ W **132**
Guichen Bay 37°15′ S, 138°16′ E **230**
Guichi, *China* 30°40′ N, 117°27′ E **198**
Güicho, *Kyrg.* 40°18′ N, 73°29′ E **197**
Guidan Roumji, *Niger* 13°41′ N, 6°33′ E **222**
Guide, *China* 35°52′ N, 101°36′ E **190**
Guider, *Cameroon* 9°55′ N, 13°56′ E **218**
Guidiguir, *Niger* 13°41′ N, 9°49′ E **222**
Guidimouni, *Niger* 13°42′ N, 9°26′ E **222**
Guiding, *China* 26°33′ N, 107°14′ E **198**
Guidouma, *Gabon* 1°38′ S, 10°42′ E **218**
Guienne, region, *Europe* 44°10′ N, 1°7′ E **165**
Guiglo, *Côte d'Ivoire* 6°26′ N, 7°30′ W **222**
Guijá, *Mozambique* 24°27′ S, 33°3′ E **227**
Guildford, *U.K.* 51°14′ N, 0°36′ E **162**
Guildhall, *Vt., U.S.* 44°34′ N, 71°35′ W **104**
Guilford, *Conn., U.S.* 41°16′ N, 72°41′ W **104**
Guilford, *Me., U.S.* 45°10′ N, 69°24′ W **94**
Guilford, *Vt., U.S.* 42°48′ N, 72°35′ W **104**
Guilin, *China* 25°17′ N, 110°13′ E **198**
Guillaume-Delisle, Lac, lake, *Can.* 56°7′ N, 79°17′ W **106**
Guillaumes, *Fr.* 44°5′ N, 6°51′ E **167**
Guillestre, *Fr.* 44°39′ N, 6°38′ E **167**
Guilvinec, *Fr.* 47°47′ N, 4°18′ W **150**
Guimarães, *Braz.* 2°6′ S, 44°36′ W **132**
Guimarães, *Port.* 41°26′ N, 8°20′ W **214**
Guimi, spring, *Mauritania* 17°29′ N, 13°18′ W **222**
Guin, *Ala., U.S.* 33°59′ N, 87°55′ W **96**
Guindulman, *Philippines* 9°47′ N, 124°28′ E **203**
Guinea 10°20′ N, 10°36′ W **214**
Guinea, Gulf of 4°29′ N, 0°6′ E **222**
Guinea-Bissau 12°7′ N, 15°13′ W **214**
Guines, *Cuba* 22°50′ N, 82°3′ W **112**
Guînes, *Fr.* 50°51′ N, 1°52′ E **163**
Guinguinéo, *Senegal* 14°16′ N, 15°54′ W **222**
Guiones, Punta, *C.R.* 9°51′ N, 86°34′ W **115**
Guiping, *China* 23°21′ N, 110°1′ E **198**
Guir, Hamada du, *Alg.* 31°41′ N, 3°42′ W **214**
Guir, spring, *Mali* 18°52′ N, 2°51′ W **222**
Guiratinga, *Braz.* 16°23′ S, 53°47′ W **132**
Guisborough, *U.K.* 54°32′ N, 1°3′ W **162**
Guise, *Fr.* 49°54′ N, 3°39′ E **163**
Guita Koulouba, *Cen. Af. Rep.* 5°55′ N, 23°22′ E **218**
Guitiriz, *Sp.* 43°9′ N, 7°57′ W **150**
Guitri, *Côte d'Ivoire* 5°30′ N, 5°14′ W **222**
Guiuan, *Philippines* 11°4′ N, 125°43′ E **203**
Guixi, *China* 28°18′ N, 116°59′ E **198**
Guixian, *China* 23°8′ N, 109°35′ E **198**
Guiyang, *China* 26°36′ N, 106°41′ E **198**
Guiyang, *China* 25°46′ N, 112°43′ E **198**
Guizhou, adm. division, *China* 27°34′ N, 106°15′ E **198**
Gujar Khan, *Pak.* 33°12′ N, 73°18′ E **186**
Gujarat, adm. division, *India* 22°12′ N, 69°57′ E **188**
Gujba, *Nig.* 11°29′ N, 11°52′ E **222**
Gujranwala, *Pak.* 32°8′ N, 74°9′ E **186**
Gujrat, *Pak.* 32°32′ N, 74°6′ E **186**
Gulbarga, *India* 17°19′ N, 76°50′ E **188**
Gulbene, *Latv.* 57°10′ N, 26°45′ E **166**
Gulen, *Nor.* 60°59′ N, 5°5′ E **152**
Gulf Hammock, *Fla., U.S.* 29°14′ N, 82°44′ W **105**
Gulf Shores, *Ala., U.S.* 30°14′ N, 87°42′ W **103**
Gulfport, *Fla., U.S.* 27°45′ N, 82°42′ W **105**
Gulfport, *Miss., U.S.* 30°21′ N, 89°5′ W **103**
Gulfport, *Mo., U.S.* 40°48′ N, 91°4′ W **94**
Gulin, *China* 28°5′ N, 105°52′ E **198**
Guling, *China* 29°36′ N, 115°52′ E **198**
Guliston, *Uzb.* 40°29′ N, 68°47′ E **197**
Guliya Shan, peak, *China* 49°48′ N, 122°21′ E **198**
Gulkana, *Alas., U.S.* 62°18′ N, 145°20′ W **106**
Gull Islands, *Lake Superior* 48°11′ N, 88°12′ W **94**
Gull Lake, *Can.* 50°4′ N, 108°29′ W **90**
Gull Lake, *Can.* 52°30′ N, 114°20′ W **108**
Gull Lake, *Can.* 51°13′ N, 92°16′ W **110**
Gull Lake, *Mich., U.S.* 42°24′ N, 85°30′ W **102**
Gullion, Slieve, peak, *U.K.* 54°6′ N, 6°32′ W **150**
Güllük, *Turk.* 37°13′ N, 27°35′ E **156**
Gulma, *Nig.* 12°37′ N, 4°20′ E **222**
Gülnar, *Turk.* 36°20′ N, 33°24′ E **156**
Gülşehir, *Turk.* 38°44′ N, 34°37′ E **156**
Gülshat, *Kaz.* 46°39′ N, 74°23′ E **184**
Gulsvik, *Nor.* 60°22′ N, 9°36′ E **152**
Gulu, *Uganda* 2°45′ N, 32°17′ E **224**
Gulwe, *Tanzania* 6°26′ S, 36°23′ E **224**
Gulyayevo, *Russ.* 64°30′ N, 40°33′ E **154**
Guma see Pishan, *China* 37°39′ N, 78°22′ E **184**
Gumal, river, *Pak.* 31°45′ N, 69°17′ E **186**
Gumare, *Botswana* 19°21′ S, 22°11′ E **220**
Gumban, *Eth.* 7°37′ N, 43°15′ E **218**
Gumdag, *Turkm.* 39°16′ N, 54°35′ E **180**
Gumel, *Nig.* 12°36′ N, 9°23′ E **222**
Gumiel de Hizán, *Sp.* 41°46′ N, 3°42′ W **164**
Gumla, *India* 23°2′ N, 84°33′ E **197**
Gumma, adm. division, *Japan* 36°32′ N, 138°28′ E **201**
Gummersbach, *Ger.* 51°1′ N, 7°33′ E **167**
Gummi, *Nig.* 12°2′ N, 5°9′ E **222**
Gumuru, *Sudan* 6°36′ N, 32°54′ E **224**
Gümüşdere, *Turk.* 38°22′ N, 43°12′ E **195**
Gümüşhane, *Turk.* 40°26′ N, 39°26′ E **195**
Gümüşören, *Turk.* 38°14′ N, 35°37′ E **156**
Gun Cay, island, *Bahamas* 25°33′ N, 79°29′ W **105**
Guna, *Eth.* 8°17′ N, 39°51′ E **224**
Guna, *India* 24°37′ N, 77°19′ E **197**
Guna Terara, peak, *Eth.* 11°42′ N, 38°7′ E **182**
Gundlupet, *India* 11°49′ N, 76°40′ E **188**
Gungu, *Dem. Rep. of the Congo* 5°46′ S, 19°14′ E **218**
Gunib, *Russ.* 42°20′ N, 46°52′ E **195**
Gunisao Lake, *Can.* 53°30′ N, 96°43′ W **108**
Gunnbjørn Fjeld, peak, *Den.* 68°41′ N, 30°44′ W **73**
Gunnison, *Utah, U.S.* 39°9′ N, 111°48′ W **90**
Gunsan, *S. Korea* 35°57′ N, 126°44′ E **200**
Guntersville, *Ala., U.S.* 34°19′ N, 86°21′ W **112**
Guntur, *India* 16°17′ N, 80°26′ E **190**
Gunung Bentuang National Park, *Indonesia* 1°14′ N, 112°46′ E **238**
Gunung Leuser National Park, *Indonesia* 3°50′ N, 96°48′ E **196**
Gunung Lorentz National Park, *Indonesia* 4°32′ S, 137°12′ E **238**
Gunung Mulu National Park, *Malaysia* 4°2′ N, 114°34′ E **238**
Gunung Palung National Park, *Indonesia* 1°14′ S, 109°51′ E **238**
Gunungsitoli, *Indonesia* 1°20′ N, 97°31′ E **196**
Guoyang, *China* 33°29′ N, 116°11′ E **198**
Gupis, *Pak.* 36°12′ N, 73°25′ E **186**
Gura Văii, *Rom.* 44°40′ N, 22°33′ E **168**
Guragē, peak, *Eth.* 8°14′ N, 38°17′ E **224**
Gurahonţ, *Rom.* 46°16′ N, 22°21′ E **168**
Gurais, *India* 34°35′ N, 74°52′ E **186**
Gurba, river, *Dem. Rep. of the Congo* 4°0′ N, 27°27′ E **224**
Gurbis, peak, *Nor.* 68°57′ N, 24°55′ E **152**
Gurdaspur, *India* 32°3′ N, 75°25′ E **186**
Gurdon, *Ark., U.S.* 33°54′ N, 93°9′ W **96**
Güre, *Turk.* 38°38′ N, 29°7′ E **156**
Gurgaon, *India* 28°26′ N, 77°2′ E **197**
Gurgei, Jebel, peak, *Sudan* 13°49′ N, 24°13′ E **226**
Gurghiu, Munţii, *Rom.* 46°52′ N, 24°42′ E **156**
Gurha, *India* 25°9′ N, 71°39′ E **186**
Gurī, *Eth.* 7°30′ N, 40°35′ E **224**
Guri Dam, *Venez.* 7°24′ N, 63°16′ W **130**
Guri i Topit, peak, *Alban.* 40°46′ N, 20°23′ E **156**
Gurig National Park, *Austral.* 11°34′ S, 131°52′ E **238**
Gurinhatã, *Braz.* 19°14′ S, 49°49′ W **138**
Gurktaler Alpen, *Aust.* 46°50′ N, 13°31′ E **167**
Gurnet Point, *Mass., U.S.* 42°0′ N, 70°37′ W **104**
Gurrea del GŽallego, *Sp.* 42°0′ N, 0°46′ E **164**
Gürün, *Turk.* 38°42′ N, 37°15′ E **156**
Gurupá, *Braz.* 1°27′ S, 51°38′ W **132**
Gurupi, *Braz.* 11°47′ S, 49°6′ W **130**
Gurupi, Cabo, *Braz.* 0°54′ N, 46°18′ W **130**
Gurupi, river, *Braz.* 2°55′ S, 46°25′ W **130**
Gurupi, Serra do, *Braz.* 5°4′ S, 48°1′ W **130**
Guruve, *Zimb.* 16°40′ S, 30°42′ E **224**
Gur'yevsk, *Russ.* 54°47′ N, 20°34′ E **166**
Gur'yevsk, *Russ.* 54°17′ N, 86°4′ E **184**
Gus' Khrustal'nyy, *Russ.* 55°35′ N, 40°39′ E **154**
Gusau, *Nig.* 12°10′ N, 6°42′ E **222**
Güsen, *Ger.* 52°21′ N, 11°59′ E **152**
Gusev, *Russ.* 54°36′ N, 22°13′ E **166**
Guşgy, *Turkm.* 35°18′ N, 62°25′ E **186**
Guşgy, river, *Turkm.* 37°12′ N, 62°30′ E **186**
Gushan, *China* 39°53′ N, 123°33′ E **200**
Gushi, *China* 32°10′ N, 115°38′ E **198**
Gusinaya, Guba 71°25′ N, 145°37′ E **160**
Güssing, *Aust.* 47°2′ N, 16°19′ E **168**
Gustav Bull Mountains, *Antarctica* 67°41′ S, 65°17′ E **248**
Gustav Holm, Kap, *Den.* 66°28′ N, 34°2′ W **106**
Gustavia, *Fr.* 17°53′ N, 62°51′ W **116**
Gustavo Díaz Ordaz, *Mex.* 26°13′ N, 98°36′ W **114**
Gustavus, *Alas., U.S.* 58°25′ N, 135°44′ W **108**
Gustine, *Calif., U.S.* 37°15′ N, 121°2′ W **100**
Guta, *Tanzania* 2°8′ S, 33°41′ E **224**
Gutâiu, peak, *Rom.* 47°41′ N, 23°47′ E **156**
Gutenstein, *Aust.* 47°53′ N, 15°53′ E **168**
Gütersloh, *Ger.* 51°54′ N, 8°22′ E **167**
Guthrie, *Ky., U.S.* 36°38′ N, 87°10′ W **96**
Guthrie, *Okla., U.S.* 35°51′ N, 97°24′ W **96**
Guthrie, *Tex., U.S.* 33°36′ N, 100°20′ W **92**
Gutian, *China* 26°36′ N, 118°42′ E **198**
Gutiérrez, *Bol.* 19°28′ S, 63°36′ W **137**
Gutiérrez Zamora, *Mex.* 20°27′ N, 97°6′ W **114**
Guttenberg, *Iowa, U.S.* 42°46′ N, 91°7′ W **94**
Gutu, *Zimb.* 19°41′ S, 31°9′ E **224**
Güvem, *Turk.* 40°35′ N, 32°40′ E **156**
Guwahati, *India* 26°11′ N, 91°42′ E **197**
Guyana 5°35′ N, 59°12′ W **130**
Guyanais Space Center, *Fr.* 5°9′ N, 52°52′ W **130**
Guyang, *China* 41°1′ N, 110°5′ E **198**
Guymon, *Okla., U.S.* 36°40′ N, 101°30′ W **92**
Guyuan, *China* 41°40′ N, 115°38′ E **198**
Guyuan, *China* 35°59′ N, 106°14′ E **198**
Güzeloluk, *Turk.* 36°45′ N, 34°5′ E **156**
Güzelyurt see Morphou, *Turk.* 38°15′ N, 34°22′ E **156**
Guzhang, *China* 28°35′ N, 109°57′ E **198**
Guzmán, *Mex.* 31°11′ N, 107°27′ W **92**
G'uzor, *Uzb.* 38°36′ N, 66°15′ E **197**
Gwa, *Myanmar* 17°36′ N, 94°36′ E **202**
Gwadabawa, *Nig.* 13°21′ N, 5°12′ E **222**
Gwadar, *Pak.* 25°8′ N, 62°23′ E **182**
Gwagwada, *Nig.* 10°14′ N, 7°12′ E **222**
Gwai, *Zimb.* 19°19′ S, 27°42′ E **224**
Gwaii Haanas National Park Reserve and Haida Heritage Site, *Can.* 52°10′ N, 130°59′ W **108**
Gwalangu, *Dem. Rep. of the Congo* 2°17′ N, 18°14′ E **218**
Gwalior, *India* 26°14′ N, 78°8′ E **197**
Gwanda, *Zimb.* 20°56′ S, 28°58′ E **227**
Gwandu, *Nig.* 12°31′ N, 4°38′ E **222**
Gwane, *Dem. Rep. of the Congo* 4°41′ N, 25°54′ E **224**
Gwane, river, *Dem. Rep. of the Congo* 4°53′ N, 25°25′ E **218**
Gwangju (Kwangju), *S. Korea* 35°8′ N, 126°56′ E **200**
Gwanju City, adm. division, *S. Korea* 35°10′ N, 126°55′ E **200**
Gwangyang, *S. Korea* 34°56′ N, 127°36′ E **200**
Gwardafuy, Cape, *Somalia* 11°38′ N, 51°18′ E **182**
Gwayi River, *Zimb.* 18°37′ S, 27°11′ E **224**
Gwayi, river, *Zimb.* 18°50′ S, 27°10′ E **224**
Gwembe, *Zambia* 16°30′ S, 27°36′ E **224**
Gweru, *Zimb.* 19°30′ S, 29°47′ E **224**
Gweta, *Botswana* 20°10′ S, 25°15′ E **227**
Gwinn, *Mich., U.S.* 46°17′ N, 87°27′ W **94**
Gwinner, *N. Dak., U.S.* 46°13′ N, 97°41′ W **90**
Gwoza, *Nig.* 11°7′ N, 13°43′ E **216**
Gwydir, river, *Austral.* 29°22′ S, 148°51′ E **230**
Gya La Pass, *China* 28°46′ N, 84°32′ E **197**
Gyaca, *China* 29°7′ N, 92°30′ E **188**
Gyamish see Gomshasar, Mt., peak, *Azerb.* 40°17′ N, 46°19′ E **195**
Gyangzê, *China* 28°57′ N, 89°39′ E **197**
Gyaring Hu, lake, *China* 34°55′ N, 96°23′ E **188**
Gyarmat, *Hung.* 47°27′ N, 17°29′ E **168**
Gyda, *Russ.* 70°50′ N, 78°36′ E **169**
Gydanskiy Poluostrov, *Russ.* 69°23′ N, 74°30′ E **169**
Gyékényes, *Hung.* 46°13′ N, 17°0′ E **168**
Gyeonggi, adm. division, *S. Korea* 37°15′ N, 127°3′ E **200**
Gyeongju (Kyŏngju), *S. Korea* 35°48′ N, 129°15′ E **200**
Gyeongsang, *S. Korea* 35°47′ N, 128°46′ E **200**
Gyeongsang, North, adm. division, *S. Korea* 36°20′ N, 128°45′ E **200**
Gyeongsang, South, adm. division, *S. Korea* 35°15′ N, 128°15′ E **200**
Gyirong (Zongga), *China* 28°59′ N, 85°16′ E **197**
Gyldenløve Fjord 64°6′ N, 43°28′ W **106**
Gylgen, *Nor.* 66°21′ N, 22°41′ E **152**
Gympie, *Austral.* 26°9′ S, 152°41′ E **231**
Gyōda, *Japan* 36°7′ N, 139°28′ E **201**
Gyoga, *S. Korea* 37°22′ N, 129°15′ E **200**
Gyoga, *S. Korea* 37°28′ N, 127°59′ E **200**
Gyoha, *S. Korea* 37°45′ N, 126°46′ E **200**
Gyoma, *Hung.* 46°56′ N, 20°50′ E **168**
Gyönk, *Hung.* 46°34′ N, 18°28′ E **168**
Gyopáros, *Hung.* 46°34′ N, 20°38′ E **168**
Győr, *Hung.* 47°39′ N, 17°39′ E **168**
Győr-Moson-Sopron, adm. division, *Hung.* 47°29′ N, 16°47′ E **156**
Gypsumville, *Can.* 51°46′ N, 98°39′ W **108**
Gyueshevo, *Bulg.* 42°13′ N, 22°29′ E **168**
Gyula, *Hung.* 46°39′ N, 21°17′ E **168**
Gyumri, *Arm.* 40°46′ N, 43°50′ E **195**
Gyzylarbat, *Turkm.* 38°58′ N, 56°14′ E **180**
Gyzyletrek, *Turkm.* 37°41′ N, 54°44′ E **180**
Gyzylgaya, *Turkm.* 40°36′ N, 55°27′ E **158**
Gyzylsuw, *Turkm.* 39°46′ N, 53°1′ E **180**

H

Ha Coi, *Vietnam* 21°27′ N, 107°43′ E **202**
Ha Giang, *Vietnam* 22°48′ N, 104°59′ E **202**
Ha On, *Israel* 32°43′ N, 35°37′ E **194**
Ha Tien, *Vietnam* 10°26′ N, 104°27′ E **202**
Ha Tinh, *Vietnam* 18°21′ N, 105°53′ E **202**
Ha Trung, *Vietnam* 20°0′ N, 105°48′ E **198**
Häädemeeste, *Est.* 58°4′ N, 24°28′ E **166**
Haag, *Aust.* 48°5′ N, 14°35′ E **156**
Haamstede, *Neth.* 51°42′ N, 3°44′ E **163**
Ha'apai Group, islands, *South Pacific Ocean* 19°16′ S, 177°22′ W **238**

Haapajärvi, Fin. 63°44′ N, 25°18′ E 152
Haapamäki, Fin. 62°14′ N, 24°37′ E 152
Haapasaari, Fin. 60°16′ N, 27°12′ E 166
Haapavesi, Fin. 64°7′ N, 25°19′ E 152
Haapsalu, Est. 58°55′ N, 23°30′ E 166
Haar, Ger. 48°6′ N, 11°44′ E 152
Haarlem, Neth. 52°23′ N, 4°37′ E 163
Haast, N.Z. 43°54′ S, 169°0′ E 240
Haaway, Somalia 1°7′ N, 43°45′ E 218
Hab, river, Pak. 25°7′ N, 66°55′ E 186
Habahe (Kaba), China 48°4′ N, 86°21′ E 184
Ḩabarūt, Oman 17°15′ N, 52°48′ E 182
Habaswein, Kenya 0°59′ N, 39°30′ E 224
Habay, Can. 58°51′ N, 118°47′ W 108
Ḩabbūsh, Leb. 33°25′ N, 35°28′ E 194
Habermehl Peak, Antarctica 71°54′ S, 6°7′ E 248
Habibas, Îles, islands, Mediterranean Sea 35°46′ N, 1°30′ W 150
Habiganj, Bangladesh 24°20′ N, 91°20′ E 197
Habomai Islands, North Pacific Ocean 42°31′ N, 145°36′ E 190
Ḩabshān, U.A.E. 23°51′ N, 53°37′ E 196
Hacha, Col. 7°420′ N, 75°31′ W 136
Hachenburg, Ger. 50°39′ N, 7°48′ E 167
Hachi, India 27°49′ N, 94°1′ E 188
Hachijō Jima, island, Japan 33°6′ N, 137°49′ E 190
Hachiman, Japan 35°44′ N, 136°57′ E 201
Hachinohe, Japan 40°26′ N, 141°30′ E 190
Hachiōji, Japan 35°38′ N, 139°20′ E 201
Hachita, N. Mex., U.S. 31°55′ N, 108°19′ W 92
Hacıbektaş, Turk. 38°56′ N, 34°34′ E 156
Hackås, Nor. 62°55′ N, 14°31′ E 152
Hackberry, Ariz., U.S. 35°21′ N, 113°44′ W 101
Hackberry, La., U.S. 29°59′ N, 93°21′ W 103
Hackness, U.K. 54°17′ N, 0°31′ E 162
Hadabat el Gîlf el Kebîr, Egypt 24°6′ N, 25°40′ E 226
Hadada, Jebel, peak, Sudan 20°46′ N, 28°33′ E 226
Hadamar, Ger. 50°26′ N, 8°2′ E 167
Hadarba, Ras (Elba, Cape), Egypt 21°49′ N, 36°55′ E 182
Ḩaddā', Saudi Arabia 21°27′ N, 39°32′ E 182
Haddo House, site, U.K. 57°22′ N, 2°21′ W 150
Haddummati Atoll, Maldives 1°47′ N, 72°32′ E 188
Hadejia, Nig. 12°30′ N, 10°5′ E 222
Ḩadera, Israel 32°26′ N, 34°55′ E 194
Haderslev, Den. 55°15′ N, 9°29′ E 150
Hadībоh, Yemen 12°37′ N, 53°57′ E 182
Hadid, Cap, Mor. 31°45′ N, 10°42′ W 214
Ḩadīd, Jabal, peak, Lib. 20°21′ N, 22°11′ E 216
Hadilik, China 37°52′ N, 86°6′ E 184
Hadım, Turk. 36°59′ N, 32°26′ E 156
Hadīyah, Saudi Arabia 25°32′ N, 38°37′ E 182
Hadjadj, Alg. 36°5′ N, 0°19′ E 164
Hadleigh, U.K. 52°2′ N, 0°56′ E 162
Hadley, Mass., U.S. 42°19′ N, 72°36′ W 104
Hadley Bay 72°10′ N, 110°44′ W 106
Hadong, S. Korea 35°4′ N, 127°46′ E 200
Ḩaḑramawt, region, Asia 16°17′ N, 49°26′ E 182
Hadrut (Gadrut), Azerb. 39°30′ N, 47°0′ E 195
Hadsten, Den. 56°19′ N, 10°2′ E 152
Hadsund, Den. 56°43′ N, 10°7′ E 150
Hadyach, Ukr. 50°20′ N, 33°54′ E 158
Haedo, Cuchilla de, Uru. 31°29′ S, 56°45′ W 139
Haeju, N. Korea 38°2′ N, 125°42′ E 200
Haeju-man 37°47′ N, 125°42′ E 200
Haemi, S. Korea 36°41′ N, 126°33′ E 200
Haenam, S. Korea 34°32′ N, 126°37′ E 200
Ḩafar al Bāţin, Saudi Arabia 28°24′ N, 46°0′ E 180
Haffkrug, Ger. 54°3′ N, 10°45′ E 150
Hafford, Can. 52°44′ N, 107°22′ W 108
Hafik, Turk. 39°51′ N, 37°23′ E 156
Ḩafīt, Jabal, peak, U.A.E. 24°3′ N, 55°41′ E 196
Hafizabad, Pak. 32°3′ N, 73°39′ E 186
Haflong, India 25°10′ N, 92°59′ E 188
Haft Gel, Iran 31°28′ N, 49°34′ E 180
Hag 'Abdullah, Sudan 13°55′ N, 33°34′ E 182
Hagadera, Kenya 2°119′ N, 40°23′ E 224
Hagåtña (Agana), Guam, U.S. 13°0′ N, 145°0′ E 242
Hagemeister Island, Alas., U.S. 58°9′ N, 161°42′ W 98
Hagen, Ger. 51°22′ N, 7°28′ E 167
Hagen Fjord 81°30′ N, 28°8′ W 246
Hagenower Heide, Ger. 53°24′ N, 11°13′ E 150
Hagensborg, Can. 52°22′ N, 126°33′ W 108
Hägere Hiywet, Eth. 8°56′ N, 37°54′ E 224
Hagerhill, Ky., U.S. 37°46′ N, 82°48′ W 96
Hagerman, N. Mex., U.S. 33°6′ N, 104°20′ W 92
Hagerman Fossil Beds National Monument, Idaho, U.S. 42°47′ N, 115°2′ W 90
Hagerstown, Md., U.S. 39°38′ N, 77°43′ W 94
Hagfors, Nor. 60°2′ N, 13°41′ E 152
Häggenås, Nor. 63°23′ N, 14°53′ E 152
Häggsjön, Nor. 63°54′ N, 14°11′ E 152
Hagi, Japan 34°24′ N, 131°25′ E 200
Hagia Triada, ruin(s), Gr. 35°2′ N, 24°41′ E 156
Hags Head, Ire. 52°46′ N, 9°50′ W 150
Hague, N.Y., U.S. 43°44′ N, 73°31′ W 104
Hague, Cap de la, Fr. 49°41′ N, 2°29′ W 150
Haguenau, Fr. 48°48′ N, 7°47′ E 163
Haha Jima Rettō, islands, North Pacific Ocean 26°35′ N, 139°20′ E 190
Hahn, Ger. 50°31′ N, 7°53′ E 167
Hahót, Hung. 46°38′ N, 16°54′ E 168
Hai'an, China 32°32′ N, 120°25′ E 198
Haicheng, China 40°52′ N, 122°44′ E 200
Haidargarh, India 26°35′ N, 81°20′ E 197
Haifa, Israel 32°46′ N, 35°0′ E 180
Haifa see Ḩefa, Israel 32°47′ N, 35°0′ E 194
Haifeng, China 22°57′ N, 115°20′ E 198
Haig, Austral. 31°1′ S, 126°4′ E 231
Haiger, Ger. 50°44′ N, 8°12′ E 167
Haikang, China 20°50′ N, 110°2′ E 198
Haikou, China 20°1′ N, 110°19′ E 198
Ha'iku, Hawai'i, U.S. 20°55′ N, 156°20′ W 99
Ḩā'il, Saudi Arabia 27°30′ N, 41°43′ E 180
Hailar, China 49°9′ N, 119°38′ E 198
Hailar, river, China 49°32′ N, 121°17′ E 198
Hailesboro, N.Y., U.S. 44°17′ N, 75°28′ W 110
Haileybury, Can. 47°27′ N, 79°38′ W 94
Hailong, China 42°39′ N, 125°50′ E 200
Hails, China 41°25′ N, 106°25′ E 198
Hailun, China 47°28′ N, 126°58′ E 198
Hailuoto, Fin. 65°0′ N, 24°42′ E 152
Hainan, adm. division, China 19°22′ N, 108°59′ E 198
Hainan, island, China 19°47′ N, 108°42′ E 198
Haines, Alas., U.S. 59°14′ N, 135°31′ W 108
Haines City, Fla., U.S. 28°6′ N, 81°38′ W 105
Haines Junction, Can. 60°53′ N, 137°27′ W 98
Haiphong, Vietnam 20°52′ N, 106°39′ E 198
Haitan Dao, island, China 25°30′ N, 119°55′ E 198
Haiti 19°8′ N, 72°17′ W 116
Haiwee Reservoir, lake, Calif., U.S. 36°9′ N, 118°6′ W 101
Haiya, Sudan 18°17′ N, 36°19′ E 182
Haiyan, China 30°31′ N, 120°52′ E 198
Haiyuan, China 36°35′ N, 105°36′ E 198
Hajdú-Bihar, adm. division, Hung. 47°17′ N, 21°10′ E 156
Hajdúhadház, Hung. 47°40′ N, 21°40′ E 168
Hajdúnánás, Hung. 47°50′ N, 21°26′ E 168
Hajdúszoboszló, Hung. 47°26′ N, 21°26′ E 168
Haji Pir Pass, Pak. 33°55′ N, 74°4′ E 186
Hajinbu, S. Korea 37°37′ N, 128°32′ E 200
Ḩajjah, Yemen 15°40′ N, 43°33′ E 182
Ḩājjīābād, Iran 28°18′ N, 55°50′ E 196
Hajnówka, Pol. 52°44′ N, 23°35′ E 158
Hajós, Hung. 46°23′ N, 19°7′ E 168
Hakai Passage 51°41′ N, 128°43′ W 108
Hakansonmonts, Dem. Rep. of the Congo 8°49′ S, 25°38′ E 224
Hakari (Akera), river, Azerb. 39°28′ N, 46°37′ E 195
Hakataramea, N.Z. 44°44′ S, 170°31′ E 240
Hakkâri, Turk. 37°33′ N, 43°38′ E 195
Hakkas, Nor. 66°54′ N, 21°34′ E 152
Hakken San, peak, Japan 34°10′ N, 135°50′ E 201
Hakodate, Japan 41°55′ N, 140°33′ E 190
Hakui, Japan 36°53′ N, 136°47′ E 201
Hakusan National Park, Japan 36°6′ N, 136°33′ E 201
Ḩalab (Aleppo), Syr. 36°11′ N, 37°9′ E 156
Ḩalab (Aleppo), Syr. 36°11′ N, 37°9′ E 180
Ḩalabjah, Iraq 35°10′ N, 45°59′ E 180
Halâl, Gebel el, Egypt 30°34′ N, 33°53′ E 194
Halali, Namibia 19°1′ S, 16°30′ E 220
Halastó, lake, Hung. 47°35′ N, 20°48′ E 168
Halayeb, Egypt 22°11′ N, 36°35′ E 182
Halba, Leb. 34°32′ N, 36°4′ E 194
Halba Desēt, island, Eritrea 12°43′ N, 42°12′ E 182
Halbturn, Aust. 47°52′ N, 16°58′ E 168
Ḩalbūn, Syr. 33°39′ N, 36°14′ E 194
Halcon, Mount, Philippines 13°15′ N, 120°55′ E 203
Halden, Nor. 59°6′ N, 11°22′ E 152
Haldia, India 22°3′ N, 88°4′ E 197
Haldwani, India 29°14′ N, 79°30′ E 197
Hale, Mich., U.S. 44°22′ N, 83°49′ W 110
Hale Eddy, N.Y., U.S. 42°0′ N, 75°24′ W 94
Haleakalā Observatories, site, Hawai'i, U.S. 20°41′ N, 156°19′ W 99
Haleki'i-Pihana Heiaus, site, Hawai'i, U.S. 20°54′ N, 156°33′ W 99
Halesowen, U.K. 52°27′ N, 2°3′ W 162
Halesworth, U.K. 52°20′ N, 1°29′ E 163
Haleyville, Ala., U.S. 34°13′ N, 87°38′ W 96
Half Assini, Ghana 5°4′ N, 2°53′ W 214
Half Moon Bay, Calif., U.S. 37°27′ N, 122°27′ W 100
Half Moon Cay Natural Monument Reserve, Belize 17°6′ N, 87°41′ W 115
Halfmoon Bay, N.Z. 46°55′ S, 168°7′ E 240
Halfway, Oreg., U.S. 44°51′ N, 117°8′ W 90
Halfway Point, Can. 51°40′ N, 81°4′ W 110
Halfway, river, Can. 56°52′ N, 122°50′ W 108
Haliartus, battle, Gr. 38°22′ N, 22°56′ E 156
Halibut, oil field, Austral. 38°33′ S, 148°18′ E 230
Halibut Point, Mass., U.S. 42°41′ N, 70°39′ W 104
Halicz, peak, Pol. 49°4′ N, 22°40′ E 152
Halifax, Can. 44°37′ N, 63°43′ W 111
Halifax, Mass., U.S. 41°59′ N, 70°53′ W 104
Halifax, N.C., U.S. 36°19′ N, 77°37′ W 96
Halifax, Va., U.S. 36°45′ N, 78°56′ W 96
Halkett, Cape, Alas., U.S. 70°44′ N, 152°18′ W 98
Halkida, Gr. 38°30′ N, 23°37′ E 180
Halkidiki, Gr. 40°35′ N, 22°57′ E 156
Halkirk, Can. 52°16′ N, 112°10′ W 108
Hall Beach, Can. 68°46′ N, 81°21′ W 73
Hall Islands, North Pacific Ocean 8°9′ N, 152°10′ E 192
Hall Peninsula, Can. 63°28′ N, 66°19′ W 106
Hall Summit, La., U.S. 32°9′ N, 93°18′ W 103
Hälla, Nor. 63°55′ N, 17°16′ E 152
Hallam Peak, Can. 52°10′ N, 118°53′ W 108
Hallandale, Fla., U.S. 25°59′ N, 80°10′ W 105
Halle, Belg. 50°44′ N, 4°13′ E 163
Halle, Ger. 52°3′ N, 8°22′ E 167
Halle, Ger. 51°27′ N, 11°58′ E 152
Hallenberg, Ger. 51°6′ N, 8°36′ E 150
Hallendorf, Ger. 52°9′ N, 10°21′ E 167
Hallettsville, Tex., U.S. 29°25′ N, 96°56′ W 96
Halley, station, Antarctica 75°38′ S, 26°34′ W 248
Hallgren, Mount, Antarctica 73°26′ S, 3°58′ W 248
Halliday, N. Dak., U.S. 47°19′ N, 102°22′ W 90
Halliday Lake, Can. 61°19′ N, 109°42′ W 108
Halligen, islands, North Sea 54°44′ N, 7°33′ E 152
Hallim, S. Korea 33°23′ N, 126°15′ E 198
Hallingdal, Nor. 60°26′ N, 8°49′ E 152
Hallingskarvet, peak, Nor. 60°35′ N, 7°40′ E 152
Halliste, river, Est. 58°27′ N, 24°58′ E 166
Hällnäs, Nor. 64°18′ N, 19°37′ E 152
Hallock, Minn., U.S. 48°45′ N, 96°59′ W 90
Halloran Springs, Calif., U.S. 35°21′ N, 115°54′ W 101
Hallowell, Me., U.S. 44°16′ N, 69°49′ W 104
Halls Creek, Austral. 18°17′ S, 127°44′ E 238
Hallschlag, Ger. 50°21′ N, 6°27′ E 167
Hallsville, Tex., U.S. 32°29′ N, 94°35′ W 103
Hălmagiu, Rom. 46°16′ N, 22°38′ E 168
Halmahera, island, Indonesia 1°32′ N, 128°44′ E 192
Halmeu, Rom. 47°58′ N, 23°1′ E 168
Halmstad, Sw. 56°42′ N, 12°52′ E 160
Hal'shany, Belarus 54°15′ N, 26°1′ E 166
Halstead, Kans., U.S. 37°59′ N, 97°31′ W 90
Halstead, U.K. 51°56′ N, 0°39′ E 162
Halten Bank, Norwegian Sea 65°1′ N, 6°31′ E 253
Haltern, Ger. 51°45′ N, 7°10′ E 167
Halulu Heiau, site, Hawai'i, U.S. 20°44′ N, 157°1′ W 99
Halus, ruin(s), Gr. 39°7′ N, 22°45′ E 156
Ḩaluẕa, Ḩolot, Israel 31°7′ N, 34°16′ E 194
Ham, Chad 10°1′ N, 15°42′ E 216
Ham, Fr. 49°44′ N, 3°2′ E 163
Hamada, Japan 34°53′ N, 132°5′ E 200
Hamadade Tinrhert, Alg.-Lib. 28°40′ N, 6°46′ E 214
Hamadān (Ecbatana), Iran 34°48′ N, 48°27′ E 180
Hamaguir, Alg. 30°51′ N, 3°4′ W 214
Ḩamāh (Hamath), Syr. 35°7′ N, 36°45′ E 194
Hamajima, Japan 34°18′ N, 136°46′ E 201
Hāmākua, region, Oceania 19°34′ N, 155°33′ W 99
Hamamatsu, Japan 34°42′ N, 137°45′ E 201
Haman, S. Korea 35°13′ N, 128°25′ E 200
Hamar, Nor. 60°47′ N, 11°4′ E 152
Hamarøy, Nor. 68°3′ N, 15°38′ E 152
Hamasaka, Japan 35°36′ N, 134°27′ E 201
Ḩamâta, Gebel, peak, Egypt 24°10′ N, 34°56′ E 182
Hamath see Ḩamāh, Syr. 35°7′ N, 36°45′ E 194
Hamburg, Ark., U.S. 33°12′ N, 91°48′ W 103
Hamburg, Ger. 53°33′ N, 10°1′ E 150
Hamburg, Iowa, U.S. 40°36′ N, 95°39′ W 90
Hamburg, N.Y., U.S. 42°43′ N, 78°50′ W 94
Hamburg, adm. division, Ger. 53°34′ N, 9°31′ E 150
Hambuti, spring, Sudan 16°50′ N, 32°26′ E 182
Hamchang, S. Korea 36°32′ N, 128°11′ E 200
Ḩamḑah, Saudi Arabia 18°57′ N, 43°40′ E 182
Ḩamdānah, Saudi Arabia 19°57′ N, 40°35′ E 182
Hamden, Conn., U.S. 41°22′ N, 72°55′ W 104
Hamden, Ohio, U.S. 39°8′ N, 82°32′ W 102
Hämeenkyrö, Fin. 61°37′ N, 23°8′ E 166
Hämeenlinna, Fin. 61°0′ N, 24°22′ E 166
Hamelin Pool 26°29′ S, 113°37′ E 230
Hameln, Ger. 52°6′ N, 9°22′ E 150
Hamer Koke, Eth. 5°11′ N, 36°46′ E 224
Hamersley Range, Austral. 21°46′ S, 116°17′ E 230
Hamgyong, North, adm. division, N. Korea 41°54′ N, 129°24′ E 200
Hamgyong, South, adm. division, N. Korea 40°14′ N, 127°31′ E 200
Hamhŭng, N. Korea 39°53′ N, 127°32′ E 200
Hami, China 42°48′ N, 93°23′ E 190
Hamid, Dar, Sudan 13°44′ N, 31°24′ E 182
Hamilton, Ala., U.S. 34°8′ N, 87°59′ W 96
Hamilton, Bermuda Islands, U.K. 32°0′ N, 65°0′ W 118
Hamilton, Can. 43°14′ N, 79°51′ W 110
Hamilton, Mo., U.S. 39°43′ N, 94°0′ W 94
Hamilton, Mo., U.S. 40°23′ N, 91°21′ W 94
Hamilton, N.Y., U.S. 42°49′ N, 75°33′ W 94
Hamilton, N.Z. 37°48′ S, 175°15′ E 240
Hamilton, Ohio, U.S. 39°23′ N, 84°33′ W 102
Hamilton, Tex., U.S. 31°41′ N, 98°7′ W 92
Hamilton, U.K. 55°45′ N, 4°3′ W 150
Hamilton Inlet 54°3′ N, 61°22′ W 73
Hamilton, Mount, Antarctica 80°38′ S, 159°7′ E 248
Hamilton, Mount, Nev., U.S. 39°13′ N, 115°37′ W 90
Hamilton Sound 49°31′ N, 55°5′ W 111
Hamina, Fin. 60°34′ N, 27°11′ E 166
Hamiota, Can. 50°11′ N, 100°36′ W 90
Hamirpur, India 25°54′ N, 80°9′ E 197
Hamjun, N. Korea 39°32′ N, 127°13′ E 200
Hamlet, Ind., U.S. 41°22′ N, 86°35′ W 102
Hamlet, N.C., U.S. 34°52′ N, 79°43′ W 96
Hamlin, Me., U.S. 47°3′ N, 67°49′ W 111
Hamlin, N.Y., U.S. 43°18′ N, 77°56′ W 94
Hamlin, Tex., U.S. 32°52′ N, 100°8′ W 92
Hamm, Ger. 51°40′ N, 7°48′ E 167
Hammam Lif, Tun. 36°41′ N, 10°19′ E 214
Hammarland, Fin. 60°12′ N, 19°43′ E 154
Hammerdal, Nor. 63°35′ N, 15°19′ E 152
Hammeren, Den. 55°17′ N, 14°49′ E 152
Hammerfest, Nor. 70°37′ N, 24°3′ E 160
Hamminkeln, Ger. 51°43′ N, 6°35′ E 167
Hammond, Ill., U.S. 39°47′ N, 88°36′ W 102
Hammond, Ind., U.S. 41°35′ N, 87°29′ W 102
Hammond, La., U.S. 30°29′ N, 90°27′ W 103
Hammond, Mont., U.S. 45°11′ N, 104°55′ W 90
Hammond, Oreg., U.S. 46°10′ N, 123°57′ W 100
Hammonton, N.J., U.S. 39°37′ N, 74°49′ W 94
Hamningberg, Nor. 70°30′ N, 30°36′ E 152
Hamont, Belg. 51°14′ N, 5°32′ E 167
Hampden, N.Z. 45°21′ S, 170°47′ E 240
Hampton, Ark., U.S. 33°30′ N, 92°29′ W 96
Hampton, Fla., U.S. 29°51′ N, 82°9′ W 105
Hampton, Iowa, U.S. 42°44′ N, 93°12′ W 94
Hampton, N.H., U.S. 42°56′ N, 70°50′ W 104
Hampton, S.C., U.S. 32°51′ N, 81°7′ W 96
Hampton, Va., U.S. 37°1′ N, 76°22′ W 96
Hampton Bays, N.Y., U.S. 40°52′ N, 72°32′ W 104
Hampton Beach, N.H., U.S. 42°54′ N, 70°50′ W 104
Hampton Butte, peak, Oreg., U.S. 43°45′ N, 120°22′ W 90
Hampton, Mount, Antarctica 76°22′ S, 125°11′ W 248
Hampyeong, S. Korea 35°2′ N, 126°30′ E 200
Hamrånge, Nor. 60°55′ N, 17°1′ E 152
Hamrat esh Sheikh, Sudan 14°32′ N, 27°57′ E 226
Hamyang, S. Korea 35°30′ N, 127°44′ E 200
Han, Ghana 10°41′ N, 2°28′ W 222
Han Pijesak, Bosn. and Herzg. 44°4′ N, 18°58′ E 168
Han, river, China 23°54′ N, 116°25′ E 198
Han, river, China 32°44′ N, 109°0′ E 198
Han, river, S. Korea 37°33′ N, 128°29′ E 200
Han sur Lesse, Belg. 50°6′ N, 5°12′ E 167
Han Uul, Mongolia 47°58′ N, 114°40′ E 198
Hanamalo Point, U.S. 19°6′ N, 156°15′ W 99
Hanang, peak, Tanzania 4°28′ S, 35°21′ E 224
Hanau, Ger. 50°7′ N, 8°55′ E 167
Hancheng, China 35°30′ N, 110°25′ E 198
Hanchuan, China 30°36′ N, 113°47′ E 198
Hancock, Mich., U.S. 47°8′ N, 88°36′ W 94
Hancock, Minn., U.S. 45°28′ N, 95°49′ W 90
Hancock, Vt., U.S. 43°55′ N, 72°52′ W 104
Handa, Japan 34°52′ N, 136°56′ E 201
Handan, China 36°37′ N, 114°27′ E 198
Handen, Sw. 59°9′ N, 18°9′ E 166
Handies Peak, Colo., U.S. 37°53′ N, 107°35′ W 90
Haneti, Tanzania 5°29′ S, 35°54′ E 224
Hanford, Calif., U.S. 36°20′ N, 119°40′ W 100
Hangatiki, N.Z. 38°17′ S, 175°9′ E 240
Hanggin Houqi, China 40°51′ N, 107°5′ E 198
Hanggin Qi, China 39°51′ N, 108°43′ E 198
Hangklip, Cape, S. Af. 34°38′ S, 18°11′ E 227
Hangö (Hanko), Fin. 59°49′ N, 22°57′ E 166
Hangu, China 39°13′ N, 117°43′ E 198
Hangzhou, China 30°21′ N, 120°13′ E 198
Hanhöhiy, Mongolia 47°39′ N, 112°7′ E 198
Hani, Turk. 38°24′ N, 40°24′ E 195
Haniá (Canea), Gr. 35°25′ N, 23°59′ E 180
Ḩanīsh al Kabīr, island, Yemen 13°25′ N, 42°45′ E 182
Hankinson, N. Dak., U.S. 46°3′ N, 96°55′ W 90
Hanko see Hangö, Fin. 59°49′ N, 22°57′ E 166
Hanksville, Utah, U.S. 38°21′ N, 110°42′ W 90
Hanle, India 32°45′ N, 78°57′ E 188
Hanley, U.K. 53°1′ N, 2°11′ W 162
Hanmer Springs, N.Z. 42°32′ S, 172°50′ E 240
Hann, Mount, Austral. 15°55′ S, 125°35′ E 230
Hanna, Can. 51°39′ N, 111°56′ W 90
Hanna, Ind., U.S. 41°24′ N, 86°47′ W 102
Hanna, Wyo., U.S. 41°52′ N, 106°33′ W 90
Hannibal, Mo., U.S. 39°42′ N, 91°23′ W 94
Hannibal, Ohio, U.S. 39°39′ N, 80°53′ W 94
Hannover (Hanover), Ger. 52°22′ N, 9°45′ E 150
Hanoi, Vietnam 21°0′ N, 105°40′ E 198
Hanover, Can. 44°8′ N, 81°0′ W 102
Hanover, Conn., U.S. 41°38′ N, 72°5′ W 104
Hanover, Ill., U.S. 42°14′ N, 90°16′ W 102
Hanover, Ind., U.S. 38°42′ N, 85°28′ W 102
Hanover, Kans., U.S. 39°52′ N, 96°53′ W 90
Hanover, Mich., U.S. 42°5′ N, 84°34′ W 102
Hanover, N.H., U.S. 43°42′ N, 72°18′ W 104
Hanover, N. Mex., U.S. 32°48′ N, 108°5′ W 92
Hanover, Pa., U.S. 39°48′ N, 76°59′ W 94
Hanover, S. Af. 31°4′ S, 24°26′ E 227
Hanover, Isla, island, Chile 51°9′ S, 76°32′ W 134
Hanover see Hannover, Ger. 52°22′ N, 9°45′ E 150
Hanp'o, N. Korea 38°12′ N, 126°29′ E 200
Hansard, Can. 54°4′ N, 121°55′ W 108
Hansen, Idaho, U.S. 42°32′ N, 114°18′ W 90
Hansen Inlet 75°20′ S, 67°43′ W 248
Hansjö, Nor. 61°9′ N, 14°34′ E 152
Hantsavichy, Belarus 52°45′ N, 26°26′ E 152
Hanumangarh, India 29°36′ N, 74°17′ E 186
Hanuy, river, Mongolia 48°41′ N, 102°6′ E 198
Hanyang, China 30°32′ N, 114°4′ E 198
Hanyin, China 32°53′ N, 108°31′ E 198
Hanzhong, China 33°6′ N, 107°3′ E 198
Haparanda, Nor. 65°49′ N, 24°5′ E 152
Happisburgh, U.K. 52°49′ N, 1°31′ E 163
Happy, Tex., U.S. 34°43′ N, 101°52′ W 92
Happy Valley-Goose Bay, Can. 53°19′ N, 60°22′ W 106
Hapur, India 28°42′ N, 77°47′ E 197
Ḩaql, Saudi Arabia 29°13′ N, 34°56′ E 180
Har Ayrag, Mongolia 45°41′ N, 109°15′ E 198
Har Horin (Karakorum), ruin(s), Mongolia 47°14′ N, 102°43′ E 198
Ḩaraḑ, Saudi Arabia 24°7′ N, 49°5′ E 196
Haradnaya, Belarus 51°51′ N, 26°30′ E 152
Haradok, Belarus 55°28′ N, 30°0′ E 166
Harads, Nor. 66°4′ N, 20°57′ E 152
Haradzyeya, Belarus 53°18′ N, 26°32′ E 152
Haranomachi, Japan 37°38′ N, 140°57′ E 201
Harappa, ruin(s), Pak. 30°40′ N, 72°45′ E 186
Harare, Zimb. 17°53′ S, 30°56′ E 224
Harat, island, Eritrea 15°53′ N, 39°5′ E 182
Haraz, Chad 13°57′ N, 19°25′ E 216
Haraza, Jebel, peak, Sudan 15°3′ N, 30°19′ E 226
Harazé Mangueigne, Chad 9°54′ N, 20°47′ E 216
Harbin, China 45°43′ N, 126°42′ E 198
Harbor Beach, Mich., U.S. 43°50′ N, 82°41′ W 102
Harbour Breton, Can. 47°28′ N, 55°50′ W 111
Harcuvar Mountains, Ariz., U.S. 33°56′ N, 113°45′ W 101
Harda, India 22°22′ N, 77°5′ E 197
Hardangervidda, Nor. 60°13′ N, 7°19′ E 152
Hardenberg, Neth. 52°34′ N, 6°38′ E 163
Harderwijk, Neth. 52°20′ N, 5°36′ E 163
Hardin, Mo., U.S. 39°8′ N, 90°39′ W 94
Hardin, Mont., U.S. 45°43′ N, 107°37′ W 90
Hardin, Tex., U.S. 30°8′ N, 94°44′ W 103
Harding Lake, Can. 56°7′ N, 98°59′ W 108
Hardisty, Can. 52°39′ N, 111°18′ W 108
Hardman, Oreg., U.S. 45°10′ N, 119°44′ W 90
Hardwick, Mass., U.S. 42°20′ N, 72°13′ W 104
Hardwick, Vt., U.S. 44°29′ N, 72°23′ W 104
Hardwood Point, Mich., U.S. 43°54′ N, 82°41′ W 102
Hardy, Ark., U.S. 36°18′ N, 91°29′ W 96
Hardy, Peninsula, Chile 55°49′ S, 67°37′ W 248
Hardy, river, Mex. 32°26′ N, 115°17′ W 101
Hareid, Nor. 62°21′ N, 6°0′ E 152
Haren, Ger. 52°48′ N, 7°14′ E 163
Hārer, Eth. 9°15′ N, 42°7′ E 224
Harewa, Eth. 9°55′ N, 42°1′ E 224
Harg, Nor. 58°45′ N, 16°56′ E 152
Hargeysa, Somalia 9°29′ N, 44°2′ E 216
Harghita, adm. division, Rom. 46°25′ N, 25°1′ E 156
Harghita, Munţii, Rom. 46°8′ N, 25°13′ E 156
Hargla, Est. 57°37′ N, 26°22′ E 166
Hargshamn, Nor. 60°9′ N, 18°23′ E 152
Hari, river, Indonesia 1°15′ S, 101°51′ E 196
Haría, Sp. 29°10′ N, 13°29′ W 214
Hariat, spring, Mali 16°10′ N, 2°24′ E 222
Haricha, Hamâda el, Mali 22°44′ N, 3°50′ W 214
Haridwar, India 29°58′ N, 78°8′ E 197
Harihari, N.Z. 43°11′ S, 170°32′ E 240
Harirud, river, Afghan. 34°35′ N, 65°7′ E 186
Harīrūd, river, Asia 35°46′ N, 61°16′ E 180
Hariyo, Somalia 5°1′ N, 47°26′ E 218
Harjavalta, Fin. 61°16′ N, 22°6′ E 166
Harkány, Hung. 45°51′ N, 18°13′ E 168
Harlan, Iowa, U.S. 41°38′ N, 95°20′ W 90
Harlandsville, Liberia 5°49′ N, 9°58′ W 222
Harlem, Mont., U.S. 48°31′ N, 108°47′ W 90
Harleston, U.K. 52°24′ N, 1°17′ E 162
Harlingen, Neth. 53°10′ N, 5°25′ E 163
Harlowton, Mont., U.S. 46°25′ N, 109°49′ W 82
Harmaliyah, oil field, Saudi Arabia 24°11′ N, 49°37′ E 196
Harmancık, Turk. 39°41′ N, 29°7′ E 156
Harmil, island, Eritrea 16°26′ N, 40°13′ E 182
Harmony, Minn., U.S. 43°33′ N, 92°1′ W 94
Harnai, India 17°51′ N, 73°8′ E 188
Harney Basin, Oreg., U.S. 43°35′ N, 119°50′ W 90
Harney, Lake, Fla., U.S. 28°44′ N, 81°14′ W 105
Harney Lake, Oreg., U.S. 43°13′ N, 119°42′ W 81
Harney Peak, S. Dak., U.S. 43°50′ N, 103°37′ W 90
Härnösand, Nor. 62°37′ N, 17°54′ E 152
Haro, Sp. 42°31′ N, 2°52′ W 164
Haro, Cabo, Mex. 27°44′ N, 111°40′ W 112
Harold Byrd Mountains, Antarctica 85°15′ S, 138°26′ W 248
Haro-Shiikh, Somalia 9°17′ N, 44°48′ E 218
Harpanahalli, India 14°49′ N, 75°58′ E 188
Harper, Liberia 4°32′ N, 7°43′ W 222
Harper Creek, river, Can. 58°0′ N, 114°56′ W 108
Harperville, Miss., U.S. 32°28′ N, 89°30′ W 103
Harpster, Ohio, U.S. 40°43′ N, 83°14′ W 102
Harput, Turk. 38°42′ N, 39°13′ E 195
Harqin, China 41°8′ N, 119°45′ E 198
Harqin Qi, China 41°56′ N, 118°39′ E 198
Harquahala Mountains, Ariz., U.S. 33°44′ N, 115°23′ W 112
Ḩarrah, Yemen 14°59′ N, 50°18′ E 182
Ḩarrākah, Syr. 34°43′ N, 37°2′ E 194
Harran, Nor. 64°34′ N, 12°27′ E 152
Harrell, Ark., U.S. 33°29′ N, 92°25′ W 103
Harricana, river, Can. 50°50′ N, 79°33′ W 80
Harriet, Mount, Austral. 26°36′ S, 130°52′ E 230
Harrington, U.K. 54°36′ N, 3°35′ W 162
Harrington, Wash., U.S. 47°27′ N, 118°16′ W 90
Harriott Lake, Can. 56°7′ N, 103°22′ W 108
Harris, Mount, Can. 59°12′ N, 136°39′ W 108
Harris Park, region, Europe 58°2′ N, 6°56′ W 150
Harrisburg, Ark., U.S. 35°33′ N, 90°44′ W 96
Harrisburg, Mo., U.S. 37°43′ N, 88°32′ W 94
Harrisburg, Nebr., U.S. 41°33′ N, 103°46′ W 90
Harrisburg, Oreg., U.S. 44°15′ N, 123°9′ W 90
Harrisburg, Pa., U.S. 40°14′ N, 77°0′ W 94
Harrislee, Ger. 54°48′ N, 9°23′ E 150
Harrismith, S. Af. 28°17′ S, 29°7′ E 227
Harrison, Ark., U.S. 36°13′ N, 93°7′ W 96
Harrison, Idaho, U.S. 47°26′ N, 116°47′ W 90
Harrison, Me., U.S. 44°6′ N, 70°41′ W 104
Harrison, Mich., U.S. 44°1′ N, 84°48′ W 102
Harrison, Nebr., U.S. 42°41′ N, 103°54′ W 90
Harrison Bay 70°18′ N, 152°41′ W 98
Harrison, Cape, Can. 54°48′ N, 58°3′ W 106
Harrison Hot Springs, Can. 49°17′ N, 121°47′ W 100
Harrison Lake, Can. 49°34′ N, 122°16′ W 100
Harrison Pass, Nev., U.S. 40°19′ N, 115°31′ W 90
Harrisonburg, La., U.S. 31°46′ N, 91°50′ W 103
Harrisonburg, Va., U.S. 38°26′ N, 78°53′ W 94
Harriston, Can. 43°53′ N, 80°51′ W 102
Harriston, Miss., U.S. 31°43′ N, 91°1′ W 103
Harrisville, Mich., U.S. 44°39′ N, 83°19′ W 94
Harrisville, R.I., U.S. 41°57′ N, 71°41′ W 104
Harrisville, W. Va., U.S. 39°12′ N, 81°4′ W 102
Harrodsburg, Ind., U.S. 39°0′ N, 86°33′ W 102
Harrogate, U.K. 53°59′ N, 1°33′ W 162
Harrow, Can. 42°2′ N, 82°55′ W 102
Harry S. Truman Reservoir, lake, Mo., U.S. 38°18′ N, 94°56′ W 81
Harsewinkel, Ger. 51°57′ N, 8°13′ E 167
Harşit, river, Turk. 40°42′ N, 38°53′ E 195
Harsud, India 22°5′ N, 76°45′ E 197
Hart, Mich., U.S. 43°41′ N, 86°22′ W 102
Hart, Tex., U.S. 34°23′ N, 102°8′ W 92
Hart Fell, peak, U.K. 55°23′ N, 3°31′ W 150
Hart Hills, Antarctica 84°21′ S, 89°48′ W 248
Hart Mountain, Oreg., U.S. 42°27′ N, 119°49′ W 90
Hart, river, Can. 64°56′ N, 137°28′ W 98
Harta, Hung. 46°42′ N, 19°1′ E 168
Hartberg, Aust. 47°16′ N, 15°56′ E 168
Hårteigen, peak, Nor. 60°10′ N, 6°56′ E 152
Hartford, Ala., U.S. 31°5′ N, 85°42′ W 96
Hartford, Conn., U.S. 41°45′ N, 72°43′ W 104
Hartford, Liberia 5°56′ N, 10°2′ W 222
Hartford, Me., U.S. 44°21′ N, 70°21′ W 104
Hartford, Mich., U.S. 42°11′ N, 86°10′ W 102
Hartford, S. Dak., U.S. 43°36′ N, 96°57′ W 90
Hartford, Vt., U.S. 43°39′ N, 72°21′ W 104
Hartford, Wis., U.S. 43°18′ N, 88°23′ W 102
Hartford City, Ind., U.S. 40°27′ N, 85°22′ W 102
Hartigan, Mount, Antarctica 76°48′ S, 125°29′ W 248
Hartland, Can. 46°16′ N, 67°32′ W 94
Hartland, U.K. 50°59′ N, 4°29′ W 150
Hartland, Vt., U.S. 43°32′ N, 72°25′ W 104
Hartlepool, U.K. 54°41′ N, 1°13′ W 162
Hartley, Iowa, U.S. 43°10′ N, 95°29′ W 94

I

J

Jamalpur, *Bangladesh* 24°53′ N, 89°54′ E **197**
Jaman Pass, *Taj.* 37°25′ N, 74°41′ E **197**
Jamanari, river, *Braz.* 2°26′ S, 69°13′ W **136**
Jamari, river, *Braz.* 8°52′ S, 63°30′ W **130**
Jambes, *Belg.* 50°27′ N, 4°53′ E **167**
Jambi, *Indonesia* 1°41′ S, 103°33′ E **192**
Jambur, oil field, *Iraq* 35°1′ N, 44°31′ E **180**
Jambusar, *India* 22°3′ N, 72°48′ E **186**
James Bay 52°12′ N, 81°23′ W **110**
James City, *Pa., U.S.* 41°36′ N, 78°50′ W **94**
James Lake, *Can.* 57°15′ N, 100°15′ W **108**
James, river, *Can.* 51°47′ N, 115°9′ W **90**
James, river, *N. Dak., U.S.* 46°39′ N, 98°34′ W **90**
James, river, *S. Dak., U.S.* 45°3′ N, 98°16′ W **94**
James, river, *Va., U.S.* 37°54′ N, 78°33′ W **94**
James Ross Island, *Antarctica* 64°13′ S, 57°4′ W **134**
Jameson Land, *Den.* 70°56′ N, 23°8′ W **246**
Jamesport, *N.Y., U.S.* 40°56′ N, 72°35′ W **104**
Jamestown, *Calif., U.S.* 37°56′ N, 120°26′ W **100**
Jamestown, *Ind., U.S.* 39°55′ N, 86°38′ W **102**
Jamestown, *N.Y., U.S.* 42°6′ N, 79°15′ W **94**
Jamestown, *N.C., U.S.* 35°59′ N, 79°57′ W **96**
Jamestown, *R.I., U.S.* 41°29′ N, 71°23′ W **104**
Jamestown, *S. Af.* 31°7′ S, 26°47′ E **227**
Jämijärvi, *Fin.* 61°48′ N, 22°40′ E **166**
Jamkhandi, *India* 16°30′ N, 75°16′ E **188**
Jammu, *India* 32°44′ N, 74°51′ E **186**
Jammu and Kashmir, adm. division, *India* 33°48′ N, 76°20′ E **188**
Jamnagar, *India* 22°26′ N, 70°4′ E **186**
Jamno, *Pol.* 54°14′ N, 16°11′ E **152**
Jampur, *Pak.* 29°33′ N, 70°35′ E **186**
Jämsä, *Fin.* 61°51′ N, 25°10′ E **166**
Jämsänkoski, *Fin.* 61°54′ N, 25°8′ E **166**
Jamshedpur, *India* 22°46′ N, 86°13′ E **197**
Jämtlands Sikås, *Nor.* 63°37′ N, 15°13′ E **152**
Jamui, *India* 24°54′ N, 86°12′ E **197**
Jan Mayen, island, *Nor.* 71°0′ N, 8°0′ W **246**
Jan Mayen Fracture Zone, *Norwegian Sea* 70°55′ N, 6°54′ W **255**
Jan Mayen Ridge, *Norwegian Sea* 69°26′ N, 8°15′ W **255**
Jana, oil field, *Saudi Arabia* 27°23′ N, 49°48′ E **196**
Janakkala, *Fin.* 60°53′ N, 24°33′ E **166**
Janakpur, *Nepal* 26°40′ N, 85°55′ E **197**
Janaúba, *Braz.* 15°47′ S, 43°20′ W **138**
Janaucu, Ilha, island, *Braz.* 0°27′ N, 51°15′ W **130**
Jandaq, *Iran* 34°2′ N, 54°28′ E **180**
Janesville, *Wis., U.S.* 42°42′ N, 89°0′ W **102**
Jangamo, *Mozambique* 24°4′ S, 35°18′ E **227**
Janghang, *S. Korea* 36°1′ N, 126°44′ E **200**
Jangheung, *S. Korea* 34°38′ N, 126°54′ E **200**
Janghowon, *S. Korea* 37°6′ N, 127°37′ E **200**
Jangpyeong, *S. Korea* 37°35′ N, 128°24′ E **200**
Jangseong, *S. Korea* 35°17′ N, 126°51′ E **200**
Janikowo, *Pol.* 52°45′ N, 18°7′ E **152**
Janīn, *West Bank, Israel* 32°27′ N, 35°18′ E **194**
Janja, *Bosn. and Herzg.* 44°40′ N, 19°16′ E **168**
Janjina, *Croatia* 42°54′ N, 17°25′ E **168**
Jannaale, *Somalia* 1°45′ N, 44°41′ E **218**
Janos, *Mex.* 30°51′ N, 108°10′ W **92**
Jánossomorja, *Hung.* 47°46′ N, 17°8′ E **168**
Jansen, *Colo., U.S.* 37°10′ N, 104°33′ W **92**
Jansenville, *S. Af.* 32°54′ S, 24°44′ E **227**
Januária, *Braz.* 15°27′ S, 44°26′ W **138**
Janville, *Fr.* 48°11′ N, 1°52′ E **163**
Jaora, *India* 23°37′ N, 75°9′ E **188**
Japan 36°0′ N, 137°35′ E **190**
Japan, Sea of (East Sea) 39°9′ N, 128°12′ E **200**
Japan Trench, *North Pacific Ocean* 35°43′ N, 143°30′ E **252**
Japurá, *Braz.* 1°52′ S, 66°41′ W **136**
Jaqué, *Pan.* 7°30′ N, 78°9′ W **136**
Jaquí, *Peru* 15°31′ S, 74°27′ W **137**
Jarābulus, *Syr.* 36°47′ N, 37°58′ E **180**
Jarafuel, *Sp.* 39°8′ N, 1°5′ W **164**
Jaraguá, *Braz.* 15°49′ S, 49°23′ W **138**
Jaraguá do Sul, *Braz.* 26°29′ S, 49°3′ W **138**
Jaraicejo, *Sp.* 39°39′ N, 5°49′ W **150**
Jarales, *N. Mex., U.S.* 34°36′ N, 106°46′ W **92**
Jaramillo, *Arg.* 47°9′ S, 67°8′ W **134**
Jarash (Gerasa), *Jordan* 32°17′ N, 35°53′ E **194**
Jarauçu, river, *Braz.* 2°47′ S, 53°6′ W **130**
Jaray, *Sp.* 41°41′ N, 2°8′ W **164**
Jarbidge, *Nev., U.S.* 41°53′ N, 115°25′ W **90**
Jarbidge, river, *Idaho, U.S.* 42°24′ N, 115°39′ W **90**
Järbo, *Nor.* 60°41′ N, 16°35′ E **152**
Jardim, *Braz.* 21°30′ S, 56°5′ W **132**
Jardim do Seridó, *Braz.* 6°38′ S, 36°47′ W **132**
Jardine River National Park, *Austral.* 11°20′ S, 142°18′ E **238**
Jardinésia, *Braz.* 19°17′ S, 48°44′ W **138**
Jæren, region, *Europe* 58°33′ N, 5°32′ E **150**
Jargalant, *Mongolia* 46°57′ N, 115°15′ E **198**
Jari, river, *Braz.* 1°49′ N, 54°28′ W **130**
Jari, river, *Braz.* 0°15′ N, 53°7′ W **130**
Jarkovac, *Serb.* 45°16′ N, 20°46′ E **168**
Jarny, *Fr.* 49°10′ N, 5°53′ E **163**
Jarocin, *Pol.* 51°57′ N, 17°30′ E **152**
Järpen, *Nor.* 63°21′ N, 13°28′ E **152**
Jars, Plain of, *Laos* 19°24′ N, 103°2′ E **202**
Jartai, *China* 39°45′ N, 105°47′ E **198**
Jaru, *Braz.* 10°25′ S, 62°30′ W **130**
Jaru, river, *Braz.* 10°38′ S, 62°25′ W **132**
Jarud Qi, *China* 44°35′ N, 120°55′ E **198**
Järva Jaani, *Est.* 59°0′ N, 25°51′ E **166**
Järvakandi, *Est.* 58°46′ N, 24°47′ E **166**
Järvenpää, *Fin.* 69°27′ N, 28°47′ E **152**
Järvenpää, *Fin.* 60°27′ N, 25°4′ E **166**
Jarvie, *Can.* 54°26′ N, 113°59′ W **108**
Järvsö, *Nor.* 61°42′ N, 16°6′ E **152**
Jarwa, *India* 27°38′ N, 82°30′ E **197**
Jaša Tomić, *Serb.* 45°27′ N, 20°50′ E **168**
Jasdan, *India* 22°1′ N, 71°12′ E **186**
Jasenjani, *Bosn. and Herzg.* 43°29′ N, 17°49′ E **168**
Jasenovac, *Croatia* 45°16′ N, 16°54′ E **168**
Jasenovo Polje, *Mont.* 42°52′ N, 18°58′ E **168**
Jashpurnagar, *India* 22°53′ N, 84°8′ E **197**
Jasikan, *Ghana* 7°25′ N, 0°28′ E **222**
Jašiūnai, *Lith.* 54°27′ N, 25°18′ E **166**
Jāsk, *Iran* 25°40′ N, 57°50′ E **196**
Jasło, *Pol.* 49°44′ N, 21°28′ E **152**
Jasmund National Park, *Ger.* 54°32′ N, 13°33′ E **152**
Jason Islands, *South Atlantic Ocean* 51°19′ S, 63°21′ W **134**
Jasonville, *Ind., U.S.* 39°9′ N, 87°12′ W **102**
Jasper, *Ala., U.S.* 33°48′ N, 87°16′ W **96**
Jasper, *Ark., U.S.* 35°59′ N, 93°13′ W **96**
Jasper, *Can.* 52°53′ N, 118°8′ W **106**
Jasper, *Fla., U.S.* 30°30′ N, 82°58′ W **96**
Jasper, *Ga., U.S.* 34°27′ N, 84°26′ W **96**
Jasper, *Mich., U.S.* 41°47′ N, 84°2′ W **102**
Jasper, *Tex., U.S.* 30°54′ N, 94°0′ W **103**
Jasper National Park, *Can.* 53°16′ N, 119°17′ W **108**
Jastarnia, *Pol.* 54°42′ N, 18°38′ E **166**
Jastrebac, *Serb.* 43°31′ N, 21°5′ E **168**
Jastrebarsko, *Croatia* 45°39′ N, 15°39′ E **156**
Jastrowie, *Pol.* 53°25′ N, 16°49′ E **152**
Jászapáti, *Hung.* 47°30′ N, 20°9′ E **168**
Jászberény, *Hung.* 47°29′ N, 19°55′ E **168**
Jászfényszaru, *Hung.* 47°34′ N, 19°44′ E **168**
Jász-Nagykún-Szolnok, adm. division, *Hung.* 47°26′ N, 19°47′ E **156**
Jászszentandrás, *Hung.* 47°34′ N, 20°10′ E **168**
Jataí, *Braz.* 17°54′ S, 51°43′ W **138**
Jatapu, river, *Braz.* 0°49′ N, 58°59′ W **130**
Jath, *India* 17°2′ N, 75°11′ E **188**
Jati, *Pak.* 24°21′ N, 68°16′ E **186**
Jatobá, river, *Braz.* 13°59′ S, 54°21′ W **130**
Jatobal, *Braz.* 4°36′ S, 49°45′ W **130**
Jau, *Angola* 15°16′ S, 13°27′ E **220**
Jaú, *Braz.* 22°20′ S, 48°36′ W **138**
Jaú National Park, *Braz.* 2°36′ S, 62°56′ W **130**
Jaú, river, *Braz.* 2°36′ S, 63°25′ W **130**
Jauaperi, river, *Braz.* 0°20′ N, 61°1′ W **130**
Jaumave, *Mex.* 23°23′ N, 99°23′ W **114**
Jaunciems, *Latv.* 57°2′ N, 24°11′ E **166**
Jaungulbene, *Latv.* 57°3′ N, 26°34′ E **166**
Jaunjelgava, *Latv.* 56°35′ N, 25°4′ E **166**
Jaunpiebalga, *Latv.* 57°9′ N, 26°1′ E **166**
Jaunpur, *India* 25°43′ N, 82°40′ E **197**
Jauru, river, *Braz.* 15°53′ S, 58°17′ W **132**
Jauru, river, *Braz.* 18°42′ S, 54°12′ W **132**
Java, island, *Indonesia* 8°16′ S, 109°10′ E **192**
Java Ridge, *Indian Ocean* 9°48′ S, 112°28′ E **254**
Java Sea 4°53′ S, 109°50′ E **192**
Java Trench (Sunda Trench), *Indian Ocean* 10°30′ S, 110°0′ E **254**
Javari, river, *South America* 6°25′ S, 73°12′ W **130**
Jávea (Xàbia), *Sp.* 38°47′ N, 0°9′ E **164**
Javier, Isla, island, *Chile* 47°17′ S, 75°35′ W **134**
Javor, *Serb.* 43°27′ N, 19°57′ E **168**
Jawan, oil field, *Iraq* 35°54′ N, 42°51′ E **180**
Jawhar (Giohar), *Somalia* 2°47′ N, 45°34′ E **218**
Jawi, *Indonesia* 0°48′ N, 109°14′ E **196**
Jay, *Me., U.S.* 44°30′ N, 70°14′ W **104**
Jay, *N.Y., U.S.* 44°22′ N, 73°45′ W **104**
Jay, *Okla., U.S.* 36°24′ N, 94°48′ W **94**
Jay Em, *Wyo., U.S.* 42°28′ N, 104°22′ W **90**
Jay Peak, *Vt., U.S.* 44°54′ N, 72°37′ W **94**
Jaya, Puncak, peak, *Indonesia* 4°1′ S, 137°0′ E **192**
Jayanti, *India* 26°41′ N, 89°32′ E **197**
Jayapura, *Indonesia* 2°39′ S, 140°44′ E **192**
Jayrūd, *Syr.* 33°48′ N, 36°44′ E **194**
Jayton, *Tex., U.S.* 33°14′ N, 100°35′ W **92**
Jaz Mūrīān, Hāmūn-e, lake, *Iran* 27°27′ N, 58°26′ E **180**
Jazā'ir az Zubayr, island, *Yemen* 14°58′ N, 41°3′ E **182**
Jazā'ir Farasān, islands, *Red Sea* 17°8′ N, 41°25′ E **182**
Jbail (Byblos), *Leb.* 34°7′ N, 35°39′ E **194**
Jbinate, *Mor.* 35°7′ N, 5°58′ W **150**
Jdiriya, *Western Sahara, Mor.* 27°17′ N, 10°27′ W **214**
Jean, *Nev., U.S.* 35°46′ N, 115°20′ W **101**
Jean Lafitte National Historical Park and Preserve, *La., U.S.* 29°55′ N, 90°2′ W **103**
Jean Marie River, *Can.* 61°31′ N, 120°39′ W **108**
Jeannette Island, *Russ.* 76°39′ N, 159°13′ E **255**
Jean-Rabel, *Haiti* 19°52′ N, 73°12′ W **116**
Jebāl Bārez, Kūh-e, peak, *Iran* 28°46′ N, 58°7′ E **196**
Jebarna, *Tun.* 34°49′ N, 10°28′ E **156**
Jebba, *Nig.* 9°7′ N, 4°48′ E **222**
Jebel, *Rom.* 45°34′ N, 21°14′ E **168**
Jebel Aulia, *Sudan* 15°15′ N, 32°30′ E **182**
Jebel, Bahr al, adm. division, *Sudan* 4°21′ N, 30°14′ E **224**
Jebel, oil field, *Lib.* 28°32′ N, 19°47′ E **216**
Jebibina, *Tun.* 36°7′ N, 10°5′ E **156**
Jecheon, *S. Korea* 37°7′ N, 128°13′ E **200**
Jeddah, *Saudi Arabia* 21°31′ N, 39°12′ E **182**
Jędrzejów, *Pol.* 50°38′ N, 20°19′ E **152**
Jef Jef el Kebir, peak, *Chad* 20°30′ N, 21°13′ E **216**
Jefferson, *Ala., U.S.* 32°23′ N, 87°54′ W **103**
Jefferson, *N.H., U.S.* 44°24′ N, 71°29′ W **104**
Jefferson, *N.Y., U.S.* 42°28′ N, 74°37′ W **94**
Jefferson, *Tex., U.S.* 32°46′ N, 94°23′ W **103**
Jefferson, *Wis., U.S.* 43°0′ N, 88°47′ W **102**
Jefferson City, *Mo., U.S.* 38°31′ N, 92°17′ W **94**
Jefferson City, *Tenn., U.S.* 36°7′ N, 83°30′ W **96**
Jefferson, Mount, *Nev., U.S.* 38°44′ N, 117°1′ W **90**
Jefferson, Mount, *Oreg., U.S.* 44°39′ N, 121°53′ W **90**
Jeffersonville, *Ind., U.S.* 38°17′ N, 85°44′ W **94**
Jeffersonville, *Ohio, U.S.* 39°39′ N, 83°33′ W **102**
Jega, *Nig.* 12°13′ N, 4°23′ E **222**
Jeju (Cheju), *S. Korea* 33°29′ N, 126°32′ E **200**
Jeju, adm. division, *S. Korea* 35°25′ N, 126°30′ E **200**
Jeju-Do, island, *S. Korea* 33°34′ N, 125°54′ E **198**
Jēkabpils, *Latv.* 56°30′ N, 25°53′ E **166**
Jelbart Ice Shelf, *Antarctica* 70°24′ S, 6°22′ W **248**
Jeldēsa, *Eth.* 9°41′ N, 42°9′ E **224**
Jelenia Góra, *Pol.* 50°53′ N, 15°44′ E **152**
Jelgava, *Latv.* 56°38′ N, 23°40′ E **160**
Jelgava (Mitau), *Latv.* 56°38′ N, 23°40′ E **166**
Jellico, *Tenn., U.S.* 36°34′ N, 84°8′ W **96**
Jellicoe, *Can.* 49°42′ N, 87°32′ W **94**
Jelnica, *Pol.* 51°57′ N, 22°40′ E **154**
Jelsa, *Croatia* 43°8′ N, 16°41′ E **168**
Jema, river, *Eth.* 10°2′ N, 38°32′ E **224**
Jemaja, island, *Indonesia* 3°7′ N, 105°17′ E **196**
Jember, *Indonesia* 8°8′ S, 113°41′ E **238**
Jemez Pueblo, *N. Mex., U.S.* 35°37′ N, 106°43′ W **92**
Jeminay, *China* 47°29′ N, 85°52′ E **184**
Jena, *Fla., U.S.* 29°39′ N, 83°23′ W **105**
Jena, *La., U.S.* 31°40′ N, 92°9′ W **96**
Jenaien, *Tun.* 31°44′ N, 10°8′ E **216**
Jengish Chokusu see Pobedy Peak, *China* 42°2′ N, 80°3′ E **184**
Jenkins, *Ky., U.S.* 37°10′ N, 82°38′ W **96**
Jenner, peak, *Ger.* 47°32′ N, 12°56′ E **156**
Jennie, *Ark., U.S.* 33°14′ N, 91°17′ W **103**
Jennings, *La., U.S.* 30°12′ N, 92°40′ W **103**
Jennings, river, *Can.* 59°29′ N, 132°0′ W **108**
Jenpeg, *Can.* 54°30′ N, 98°6′ W **108**
Jensen, *Utah, U.S.* 40°22′ N, 109°20′ W **82**
Jensen Beach, *Fla., U.S.* 27°14′ N, 80°14′ W **105**
Jenu, *Indonesia* 0°36′ N, 109°50′ E **196**
Jeogu, *S. Korea* 34°44′ N, 128°38′ E **200**
Jeolla, North, adm. division, *S. Korea* 35°45′ N, 127°15′ E **200**
Jeolla, South, adm. division, *S. Korea* 34°45′ N, 127°0′ E **200**
Jeongeup, *S. Korea* 35°33′ N, 126°52′ E **200**
Jeongseon, *S. Korea* 37°23′ N, 128°40′ E **200**
Jeonju, *S. Korea* 35°48′ N, 127°9′ E **200**
Jequié, *Braz.* 13°50′ S, 40°6′ W **138**
Jequitaí, *Braz.* 17°15′ S, 44°30′ W **138**
Jequitaí, river, *Braz.* 17°22′ S, 44°7′ W **138**
Jequitinhonha, *Braz.* 16°27′ S, 41°3′ W **138**
Jerantut, *Malaysia* 3°57′ N, 102°21′ E **196**
Jerba Island, *Tun.* 34°0′ N, 10°25′ E **214**
Jeremoabo, *Braz.* 10°4′ S, 38°21′ W **132**
Jeremy, Cape, *Antarctica* 69°24′ S, 72°52′ W **248**
Jerez de García Salinas, *Mex.* 22°38′ N, 103°1′ W **114**
Jerez de la Frontera, *Sp.* 36°41′ N, 6°9′ W **164**
Jeréz de los Caballeros, *Sp.* 38°18′ N, 6°47′ W **164**
Jerez, Punta, *Mex.* 22°53′ N, 97°42′ W **114**
Jérica, *Sp.* 39°55′ N, 0°34′ E **164**
Jericho, *Vt., U.S.* 44°30′ N, 73°0′ W **104**
Jericho see Arīḩā, *West Bank, Israel* 31°51′ N, 35°27′ E **194**
Jericó, *Col.* 5°46′ N, 75°48′ W **136**
Jermyn, *Pa., U.S.* 41°31′ N, 75°34′ W **110**
Jerome, *Ariz., U.S.* 34°45′ N, 112°5′ W **112**
Jerome, *Ark., U.S.* 33°23′ N, 91°28′ W **103**
Jersey, island, *U.K.* 49°13′ N, 2°7′ W **150**
Jersey City, *N.J., U.S.* 40°43′ N, 74°4′ W **104**
Jerseyside, *Can.* 47°15′ N, 53°57′ W **111**
Jerseyville, *Mo., U.S.* 39°6′ N, 90°20′ W **94**
Jerusalem (Yerushalayim, Al-Quds), *Israel* 31°46′ N, 35°9′ E **194**
Jervis Bay Territory 35°11′ S, 149°35′ E **230**
Jervis Inlet 50°0′ N, 124°8′ W **100**
Jeseník, *Czech Rep.* 49°45′ N, 17°9′ E **152**
Jessen, *Ger.* 51°47′ N, 12°56′ E **152**
Jessnitz, *Ger.* 51°41′ N, 12°17′ E **152**
Jessore, *Bangladesh* 23°9′ N, 89°9′ E **197**
Jesup, *Ga., U.S.* 31°35′ N, 81°54′ W **96**
Jesús Carranza, *Mex.* 17°26′ N, 95°1′ W **114**
Jesús María, *Arg.* 31°0′ S, 64°8′ W **134**
Jesús María, *Mex.* 21°58′ N, 102°21′ W **114**
Jesús María, Boca de 24°30′ N, 98°13′ W **114**
Jetait, *Can.* 56°3′ N, 101°20′ W **108**
Jetmore, *Kans., U.S.* 38°5′ N, 99°55′ W **90**
Jetpur, *India* 21°44′ N, 70°36′ E **186**
Jeumont, *Fr.* 50°17′ N, 4°5′ E **163**
Jeungpyeong, *S. Korea* 36°46′ N, 127°34′ E **200**
Jever, *Ger.* 53°34′ N, 7°54′ E **163**
Jewell, *Iowa, U.S.* 42°17′ N, 93°38′ W **94**
Jewett, *Ill., U.S.* 39°11′ N, 88°15′ W **102**
Jewett, *Tex., U.S.* 31°20′ N, 96°8′ W **96**
Jewett City, *Conn., U.S.* 41°36′ N, 72°0′ W **104**
Jewish Autonomous Region, *Russ.* 49°5′ N, 131°14′ E **160**
Jeypore, *India* 18°55′ N, 82°30′ E **190**
Jez. Kopań, lake, *Pol.* 54°37′ N, 16°4′ E **152**
Jezercë, Maja, peak, *Alban.* 42°26′ N, 19°46′ E **168**
Ježevica, *Serb.* 43°56′ N, 20°5′ E **168**
Jeżewo, *Pol.* 53°30′ N, 18°28′ E **152**
Jezzine, *Leb.* 33°33′ N, 35°34′ E **194**
J.F.K. International Airport, *N.Y., U.S.* 40°36′ N, 73°57′ W **94**
Jhalawar, *India* 24°34′ N, 76°10′ E **197**
Jhang Sadr, *Pak.* 31°15′ N, 72°20′ E **186**
Jhansi, *India* 25°25′ N, 78°32′ E **197**
Jharkhand, adm. division, *India* 23°44′ N, 85°22′ E **188**
Jharsuguda, *India* 21°52′ N, 84°3′ E **188**
Jhatpat, *Pak.* 28°25′ N, 68°20′ E **186**
Jhelum, *Pak.* 32°54′ N, 73°45′ E **186**
Jhelum, river, *Pak.* 32°16′ N, 72°35′ E **186**
Jhunjhunun, *India* 28°6′ N, 75°24′ E **197**
Jiahe, *China* 25°34′ N, 112°19′ E **198**
Jiamusi, *China* 46°53′ N, 130°18′ E **190**
Ji'an, *China* 27°8′ N, 114°56′ E **198**
Ji'an, *China* 41°8′ N, 126°10′ E **200**
Jianchang, *China* 40°50′ N, 119°45′ E **198**
Jiang'an, *China* 28°38′ N, 105°2′ E **198**
Jiangcheng, *China* 22°34′ N, 101°50′ E **202**
Jianghua, *China* 24°55′ N, 111°44′ E **198**
Jiangle, *China* 26°48′ N, 117°25′ E **198**
Jiangling, *China* 30°23′ N, 112°9′ E **198**
Jiangmen, *China* 22°33′ N, 113°1′ E **198**
Jiangshan, *China* 28°45′ N, 118°37′ E **198**
Jiangsu, adm. division, *China* 33°41′ N, 118°13′ E **198**
Jiangxi, adm. division, *China* 27°28′ N, 115°30′ E **198**
Jiangyou, *China* 31°47′ N, 104°34′ E **198**
Jianli, *China* 29°50′ N, 112°51′ E **198**
Jianning, *China* 26°50′ N, 116°45′ E **198**
Jianping, *China* 41°23′ N, 119°40′ E **198**
Jianshui, *China* 23°33′ N, 102°46′ E **202**
Jianyang, *China* 27°18′ N, 118°5′ E **198**
Jiaohe, *China* 43°44′ N, 127°25′ E **198**
Jiaokou, *China* 36°58′ N, 111°13′ E **198**
Jiaonan, *China* 35°53′ N, 119°59′ E **198**
Jiaozhou, *China* 36°20′ N, 120°3′ E **198**
Jiaozuo, *China* 35°12′ N, 113°11′ E **198**
Jiashi, *China* 39°28′ N, 76°37′ E **184**
Jiawang, *China* 34°28′ N, 117°23′ E **198**
Jiaxian, *China* 38°3′ N, 110°26′ E **198**
Jiaxing, *China* 30°44′ N, 120°42′ E **198**
Jiayu, *China* 29°58′ N, 113°57′ E **198**
Jiayuguan, *China* 39°50′ N, 98°18′ E **188**
Jibal, oil field, *Oman* 22°14′ N, 56°1′ E **182**
Jibóia, *Braz.* 1°13′ N, 69°34′ W **136**
Jibou, *Rom.* 47°15′ N, 23°17′ E **168**
Jicarón, Isla, island, *Pan.* 7°10′ N, 82°31′ W **115**
Jicatuyo, river, *Hond.* 14°59′ N, 88°43′ W **116**
Jičín, *Czech Rep.* 50°26′ N, 15°21′ E **152**
Jidali, *Somalia* 10°40′ N, 47°39′ E **216**
Jiddat al Ḩarāsīs, *Oman* 19°19′ N, 55°56′ E **182**
Jieshou, *China* 33°21′ N, 115°20′ E **198**
Jiexiu, *China* 37°1′ N, 111°54′ E **198**
Jieyang, *China* 23°31′ N, 116°17′ E **198**
Jieznas, *Lith.* 54°36′ N, 24°10′ E **166**
Jigme Dorji National Park, *Bhutan* 27°52′ N, 89°53′ E **197**
Jihlava, *Czech Rep.* 49°23′ N, 15°35′ E **152**
Jihočeský, adm. division, *Czech Rep.* 49°4′ N, 13°42′ E **152**
Jihomoravský, adm. division, *Czech Rep.* 48°53′ N, 15°51′ E **152**
Jijel, *Alg.* 36°48′ N, 5°45′ E **150**
Jijiga, *Eth.* 9°18′ N, 42°44′ E **218**
Jilava, *Rom.* 44°21′ N, 26°5′ E **156**
Jilib, *Somalia* 0°26′ N, 42°48′ E **218**
Jilin, *China* 43°50′ N, 126°35′ E **198**
Jilin, adm. division, *China* 43°43′ N, 126°4′ E **198**
Jiloy, *Azerb.* 40°19′ N, 50°34′ E **195**
Jīma, *Eth.* 7°37′ N, 36°47′ E **224**
Jimbolia, *Rom.* 45°47′ N, 20°43′ E **168**
Jimena de la Frontera, *Sp.* 36°26′ N, 5°28′ W **164**
Jiménez, *Mex.* 27°6′ N, 104°55′ W **112**
Jiménez, *Mex.* 29°2′ N, 100°41′ W **92**
Jiménez del Teul, *Mex.* 23°8′ N, 104°5′ W **114**
Jimo, *China* 36°26′ N, 120°30′ E **198**
Jin, river, *China* 28°9′ N, 114°59′ E **198**
Jinan, *China* 36°39′ N, 116°58′ E **198**
Jinan, *S. Korea* 36°32′ N, 129°3′ E **200**
Jinan, *S. Korea* 35°46′ N, 127°26′ E **200**
Jincheng, *China* 35°30′ N, 112°49′ E **198**
Jindo, *S. Korea* 34°26′ N, 126°15′ E **200**
Jing see Jinghe, *China* 44°35′ N, 82°58′ E **184**
Jingbian, *China* 37°35′ N, 108°47′ E **198**
Jingde, *China* 30°18′ N, 118°33′ E **198**
Jingdezhen, *China* 29°19′ N, 117°16′ E **198**
Jinggu, *China* 23°30′ N, 100°41′ E **202**
Jinghai, *China* 38°57′ N, 117°3′ E **198**
Jinghe (Jing), *China* 44°35′ N, 82°58′ E **184**
Jinghong, *China* 22°0′ N, 100°45′ E **202**
Jingle, *China* 38°20′ N, 111°57′ E **198**
Jingmen, *China* 31°0′ N, 112°10′ E **198**
Jingpeng see Hexigten Qi, *China* 43°16′ N, 117°28′ E **198**
Jingtai, *China* 37°9′ N, 104°7′ E **198**
Jingxi, *China* 23°6′ N, 106°27′ E **198**
Jingxing, *China* 38°3′ N, 113°58′ E **198**
Jingyu, *China* 42°23′ N, 126°49′ E **200**
Jingyuan, *China* 36°32′ N, 104°41′ E **198**
Jingyuan, *China* 35°27′ N, 106°21′ E **198**
Jingzhou, *China* 26°35′ N, 109°39′ E **198**
Jinhae, *S. Korea* 35°9′ N, 128°40′ E **200**
Jinhua, *China* 29°11′ N, 119°41′ E **198**
Jining, *China* 41°4′ N, 113°5′ E **198**
Jining, *China* 35°23′ N, 116°38′ E **198**
Jinja, *Uganda* 0°24′ N, 33°12′ E **224**
Jinjiang, *China* 24°46′ N, 118°35′ E **198**
Jinotega, *Nicar.* 13°5′ N, 85°58′ W **115**
Jinping, *China* 26°43′ N, 109°10′ E **198**
Jinping, *China* 22°48′ N, 103°11′ E **202**
Jinsha, *China* 27°23′ N, 106°13′ E **198**
Jinsha (Yangtze), river, *China* 25°47′ N, 103°15′ E **190**
Jinshan, *China* 30°52′ N, 121°6′ E **198**
Jinshi, *China* 29°39′ N, 111°53′ E **198**
Jinta, *China* 39°59′ N, 98°58′ E **188**
Jinxiang, *China* 35°5′ N, 116°21′ E **198**
Jinzhai, *China* 31°43′ N, 115°47′ E **198**
Jinzhou, *China* 39°8′ N, 121°47′ E **198**
Jinzhou, *China* 41°10′ N, 121°10′ E **198**
Ji-Paraná, *Braz.* 10°53′ S, 61°58′ W **130**
Jiquilpan, *Mex.* 19°59′ N, 102°44′ W **114**
Jirgatol, *Taj.* 39°13′ N, 71°13′ E **197**
Jirisan, peak, *S. Korea* 35°19′ N, 127°42′ E **200**
Jīroft, *Iran* 28°41′ N, 57°47′ E **196**
Jishou, *China* 28°15′ N, 109°43′ E **198**
Jishui, *China* 27°15′ N, 115°7′ E **198**
Jisr ash Shughūr, *Syr.* 35°48′ N, 36°17′ E **156**
Jitra, *Malaysia* 6°15′ N, 100°25′ E **196**
Jiu, river, *Rom.* 45°16′ N, 23°19′ E **168**
Jiujiang, *China* 29°40′ N, 115°57′ E **198**
Jiuquan Space Launch Center, *China* 40°42′ N, 99°37′ E **188**
Jiutai, *China* 44°9′ N, 125°48′ E **198**
Jiwani, *Pak.* 25°2′ N, 61°48′ E **182**
Jixi, *China* 30°4′ N, 118°38′ E **198**
Jixi, *China* 45°7′ N, 130°54′ E **190**
Jixian, *China* 36°6′ N, 110°40′ E **198**
Jixian, *China* 40°2′ N, 117°21′ E **198**
Jiyuan, *China* 35°6′ N, 112°32′ E **198**
Jīzān, *Saudi Arabia* 16°52′ N, 42°35′ E **182**
Jizzax, *Uzb.* 40°6′ N, 67°50′ E **197**
Joaçaba, *Braz.* 27°10′ S, 51°32′ W **139**
Joaíma, *Braz.* 16°40′ S, 41°4′ W **138**
Joal-Fadiot, *Senegal* 14°12′ N, 16°37′ W **222**
João Monlevade, *Braz.* 19°52′ S, 43°8′ W **138**
João Pessoa, *Braz.* 7°7′ S, 34°53′ W **132**
João Pinheiro, *Braz.* 17°43′ S, 46°12′ W **138**
Joaquim Távora, *Braz.* 23°29′ S, 49°59′ W **138**
Joaquin, *Tex., U.S.* 31°57′ N, 94°3′ W **103**
Joaquín V. GonzZalez, *Arg.* 25°8′ S, 64°9′ W **132**
Job Peak, *Nev., U.S.* 39°34′ N, 118°20′ W **90**
Jōban, *Japan* 36°59′ N, 140°49′ E **201**
Jochiwon, *S. Korea* 36°34′ N, 127°17′ E **200**
Joconoxtle, *Mex.* 23°12′ N, 104°26′ W **114**
Jocotepec, *Mex.* 20°17′ N, 103°28′ W **114**
Jocotepec, *Mex.* 17°32′ N, 95°57′ W **114**
Jodar, *Sp.* 37°50′ N, 3°21′ W **164**
Jodhpur, *India* 26°15′ N, 73°1′ E **188**
Jodoigne, *Belg.* 50°43′ N, 4°51′ E **167**
Joensuu, *Fin.* 62°36′ N, 29°43′ E **152**
Joerg Peninsula, *Antarctica* 68°21′ S, 64°22′ W **248**
Joesjö, *Nor.* 65°43′ N, 14°36′ E **152**
Jōetsu, *Japan* 37°8′ N, 138°13′ E **201**
Joeuf, *Fr.* 49°13′ N, 6°0′ E **163**
Joffre, Mount, *Can.* 50°31′ N, 115°17′ W **90**
Jõgeva, *Est.* 58°44′ N, 26°22′ E **166**
Johannesburg, *Calif., U.S.* 35°22′ N, 117°39′ W **101**
Johannesburg, *S. Af.* 26°12′ S, 28°2′ E **227**
John, Cape, *Can.* 45°49′ N, 63°14′ W **111**
John Day, *Oreg., U.S.* 44°24′ N, 118°58′ W **90**
John Day, river, *Oreg., U.S.* 45°7′ N, 120°3′ W **106**
John D'Or Prairie, *Can.* 58°30′ N, 115°8′ W **108**
John F. Kennedy Space Center, *Fla., U.S.* 28°30′ N, 80°44′ W **105**
John Jay, Mount, *Alas., U.S.* 56°8′ N, 130°36′ W **108**
John Long Mountains, *Mont., U.S.* 46°34′ N, 113°48′ W **90**
John Muir National Historic Site, *Calif., U.S.* 37°59′ N, 122°9′ W **100**
John o'Groats, site, *U.K.* 58°37′ N, 3°11′ W **150**
Johnsburg, *N.Y., U.S.* 43°36′ N, 74°0′ W **104**
Johnson, *Kans., U.S.* 37°33′ N, 101°46′ W **92**
Johnson City, *Tenn., U.S.* 36°18′ N, 82°22′ W **96**
Johnson City, *Tex., U.S.* 30°15′ N, 98°25′ W **92**
Johnson, Pico de, peak, *Mex.* 29°7′ N, 112°16′ W **92**
Johnson Space Center, *Tex., U.S.* 29°30′ N, 95°8′ W **103**
Johnsonburg, *Pa., U.S.* 41°28′ N, 78°40′ W **94**
Johnsondale, *Calif., U.S.* 35°58′ N, 118°33′ W **101**
Johnsons Crossing, *Can.* 60°30′ N, 133°18′ W **108**
Johnsons Pass, *Utah, U.S.* 40°19′ N, 112°35′ W **90**
Johnsons Station, *Miss., U.S.* 31°20′ N, 90°28′ W **103**
Johnston, *R.I., U.S.* 41°49′ N, 71°30′ W **104**
Johnston Atoll, *United States* 17°0′ N, 170°0′ W **99**
Johnston Falls, *Zambia* 10°39′ S, 28°9′ E **224**
Johnston, Mount, *Antarctica* 71°37′ S, 66°55′ E **248**
Johnstone Hill, *Austral.* 23°41′ S, 129°48′ E **230**
Johnstown, *N.Y., U.S.* 43°0′ N, 74°24′ W **94**
Johnstown, *Ohio, U.S.* 40°8′ N, 82°41′ W **102**
Johor Bahru, *Malaysia* 1°30′ N, 103°44′ E **196**
Johovac, *Bosn. and Herzg.* 44°50′ N, 18°1′ E **168**
Jõhvi, *Est.* 59°21′ N, 27°24′ E **166**
Joinville, *Braz.* 26°18′ S, 48°50′ W **138**
Joinville, *Fr.* 48°26′ N, 5°6′ E **163**
Joinville Island, *Antarctica* 63°11′ S, 55°28′ W **134**
Jojutla, *Mex.* 18°35′ N, 99°11′ W **114**
Jokau, *Sudan* 8°21′ N, 33°50′ E **224**
Jokijärvi, *Fin.* 65°28′ N, 28°35′ E **152**
Jokioinen, *Fin.* 60°47′ N, 23°26′ E **166**
Jokkmokk, *Nor.* 66°36′ N, 19°50′ E **152**
Joliet, *Ill., U.S.* 41°31′ N, 88°4′ W **102**
Joliette, *Can.* 46°1′ N, 73°27′ W **94**
Jolliet, Lac, lake, *Can.* 51°30′ N, 77°25′ W **110**
Jolo, *Philippines* 6°3′ N, 120°59′ E **203**
Jomboy, *Uzb.* 39°42′ N, 67°4′ E **197**
Jomda, *China* 31°29′ N, 98°11′ E **188**
Jomppala, *Fin.* 69°46′ N, 26°58′ E **152**
Jomu (Tinde), *Tanzania* 3°53′ S, 33°11′ E **224**
Jonathan Point, *Belize* 16°35′ N, 88°18′ W **115**
Jonava, *Lith.* 55°5′ N, 24°16′ E **166**
Jonesboro, *Ark., U.S.* 35°50′ N, 90°42′ W **96**
Jonesboro, *Ind., U.S.* 40°28′ N, 85°38′ W **102**
Jonesboro, *La., U.S.* 32°13′ N, 92°43′ W **103**
Jonesboro, *Mo., U.S.* 37°26′ N, 89°16′ W **96**
Jonesville, *Ind., U.S.* 39°5′ N, 85°54′ W **102**
Jonesville, *La., U.S.* 31°36′ N, 91°50′ W **103**
Jonesville, *N.C., U.S.* 36°13′ N, 80°51′ W **96**
Jonesville, *S.C., U.S.* 34°49′ N, 81°42′ W **96**
Jonglei, *Sudan* 6°48′ N, 31°15′ E **224**
Jongli, adm. division, *Sudan* 7°18′ N, 31°5′ E **218**
Joniškėlis, *Lith.* 56°2′ N, 24°9′ E **166**
Joniškis, *Lith.* 56°13′ N, 23°35′ E **166**
Jönköping, *Nor.* 57°45′ N, 14°8′ E **152**
Jonuta, *Mex.* 18°5′ N, 92°9′ W **115**
Joplin, *Mont., U.S.* 48°31′ N, 110°47′ W **90**
Jora, *India* 26°19′ N, 77°48′ E **197**
Jordan 30°42′ N, 36°5′ E **180**
Jordan, *Ala., U.S.* 31°29′ N, 88°15′ W **103**
Jordan, *Minn., U.S.* 44°39′ N, 93°38′ W **94**
Jordan, *Mont., U.S.* 47°18′ N, 106°55′ W **90**
Jordan, river, *Asia* 32°0′ N, 36°0′ E **194**
Jordânia, *Braz.* 15°56′ S, 40°12′ W **138**
Jordet, *Nor.* 61°25′ N, 12°8′ E **152**
Jorge Montt, Isla, island, *Chile* 51°22′ S, 74°31′ W **134**
Jörn, *Nor.* 65°3′ N, 20°1′ E **152**
Jornada del Muerto, *N. Mex., U.S.* 33°10′ N, 106°46′ W **112**
Jørpeland, *Nor.* 59°1′ N, 6°2′ E **152**
Jos, *Nig.* 9°53′ N, 8°53′ E **222**
Jošanička Banja, *Serb.* 43°23′ N, 20°45′ E **168**
Jose Abad Santos, *Philippines* 5°55′ N, 125°36′ E **203**
José Batlle y-Ordóñez, *Uru.* 33°28′ S, 55°10′ W **139**
José Enrique Rodó, *Uru.* 33°43′ S, 57°31′ W **139**
José María, *Col.* 2°11′ N, 68°5′ W **136**
Jose Panganiban, *Philippines* 14°17′ N, 122°42′ E **203**

José Pedro Varela, *Uru.* 33°28' S, 54°32' W **139**
Joseph, *Oreg., U.S.* 45°21' N, 117°14' W **90**
Joseph Bonaparte Gulf 13°4' S, 127°7' E **231**
Joseph City, *Ariz., U.S.* 34°57' N, 110°20' W **92**
Joseph, Lac, lake, *Can.* 52°49' N, 65°47' W **111**
Josephine, Mount, *Antarctica* 77°25' S, 152°0' W **248**
Joshimath, *India* 30°30' N, 79°34' E **197**
Joshua Tree, *Calif., U.S.* 34°8' N, 116°20' W **101**
Joshua Tree National Park, *Calif., U.S.* 33°47' N, 116°0' W **101**
Josipdol, *Croatia* 45°11' N, 15°17' E **156**
Jøssund, *Nor.* 63°50' N, 9°47' E **152**
Jotunheimen, *Nor.* 61°27' N, 7°38' E **152**
Joulter Cays, *Atlantic Ocean* 25°15' N, 78°52' W **96**
Jounie, *Leb.* 33°58' N, 35°37' E **194**
Jourdanton, *Tex., U.S.* 28°53' N, 98°33' W **92**
Joure, *Neth.* 52°58' N, 5°48' E **163**
Joussard, *Can.* 55°22' N, 115°59' W **108**
Joutsa, *Fin.* 61°44' N, 26°6' E **166**
Joutseno, *Fin.* 61°5' N, 28°28' E **166**
Jowai, *India* 25°24' N, 92°11' E **188**
Joya, *Mex.* 26°27' N, 101°13' W **114**
Joyce, *Wash., U.S.* 48°7' N, 123°44' W **100**
Joyce, Mount, *Antarctica* 75°32' S, 161°28' E **248**
Ju, river, *China* 31°26' N, 111°15' E **198**
Juami, river, *Braz.* 2°13' S, 68°13' W **136**
Juan Aldama, *Mex.* 24°15' N, 103°25' W **114**
Juan Cousté, *Arg.* 38°55' S, 63°8' W **139**
Juan de Fuca Ridge, *North Pacific Ocean* 46°49' N, 129°21' W **252**
Juan de Fuca, Strait of 48°17' N, 124°1' W **90**
Juan de Nova, Île, island, *France* 17°7' S, 41°34' E **224**
Juan E. Barra, *Arg.* 37°50' S, 60°31' W **139**
Juan Fernández, Archipiélago, *South Pacific Ocean* 33°15' S, 82°48' W **123**
Juan Fernández Islands, *South Pacific Ocean* 33°38' S, 80°1' W **253**
Juan José Castelli, *Arg.* 25°58' S, 60°37' W **139**
Juan Lacaze, *Uru.* 34°25' S, 57°25' W **139**
Juan N. Fernández, *Arg.* 38°1' S, 59°16' W **139**
Juan Perez Sound 52°30' N, 132°27' W **108**
Juan Stuven, Isla, island, *Chile* 47°57' S, 77°11' W **134**
Juan Viego, *Col.* 3°24' N, 68°18' W **136**
Juankoski, *Fin.* 63°3' N, 28°18' E **152**
Juárez, *Arg.* 37°42' S, 59°49' W **139**
Juárez, *Mex.* 30°19' N, 108°8' W **92**
Juárez, *Mex.* 27°36' N, 100°44' W **96**
Juárez, Sierra de, *Mex.* 31°47' N, 116°1' W **112**
Juazeiro, *Braz.* 9°28' S, 40°32' W **132**
Juazeiro do Norte, *Braz.* 7°13' S, 39°21' W **132**
Juba, *Sudan* 4°50' N, 31°34' E **224**
Jubany, station, *Antarctica* 62°18' S, 58°29' W **134**
Jubayl, *Leb.* 34°6' N, 35°40' E **216**
Jubb Jannīn, *Leb.* 33°37' N, 35°47' E **194**
Jubba, river, *Somalia* 1°26' N, 42°22' E **206**
Jubbah, *Saudi Arabia* 28°0' N, 40°55' E **180**
Jubilee Pass, *Calif., U.S.* 35°54' N, 116°36' W **101**
Juby, Cap, *Mor.* 27°48' N, 13°57' W **214**
Jucás, *Braz.* 6°31' S, 39°34' W **132**
Juchitán, *Mex.* 16°26' N, 95°5' W **112**
Juchitlán, *Mex.* 20°4' N, 104°7' W **114**
Judas, Punta, *C.R.* 9°23' N, 85°5' W **115**
Judayyidat 'Ar'ar, *Saudi Arabia* 31°14' N, 41°21' E **180**
Judge Howay, Mount, *Can.* 49°28' N, 122°22' W **100**
Judith Basin, *Mont., U.S.* 47°2' N, 110°10' W **90**
Judith Gap, *Mont., U.S.* 46°39' N, 109°46' W **90**
Judith Mountains, *Mont., U.S.* 47°17' N, 109°16' W **90**
Judsonia, *Ark., U.S.* 35°16' N, 91°39' W **96**
Jufari, river, *Braz.* 0°20' N, 62°36' W **130**
Juhaym, spring, *Iraq* 29°37' N, 45°23' E **196**
Juhor, *Serb.* 43°53' N, 20°59' E **168**
Juifang, *Taiwan, China* 25°5' N, 121°51' E **198**
Juigalpa, *Nicar.* 12°6' N, 85°23' W **115**
Juist, island, *Ger.* 53°40' N, 6°44' E **163**
Juiz de Fora, *Braz.* 21°44' S, 43°21' W **138**
Jujuy, adm. division, *Arg.* 22°42' S, 66°40' W **137**
Jukbyeon, *S. Korea* 37°3' N, 129°25' E **200**
Jukkasjärvi, *Nor.* 67°50' N, 20°36' E **152**
Jukuniemi, *Fin.* 61°46' N, 29°58' E **166**
Julaca, *Bol.* 20°57' S, 67°33' W **137**
Juli, *Peru* 16°17' S, 69°27' W **137**
Juliaca, *Peru* 15°31' S, 70°8' W **137**
Julian, *Calif., U.S.* 33°4' N, 116°37' W **101**
Julian Alps, *Slov.* 46°26' N, 13°33' E **167**
Julian Peak, *Can.* 50°27' N, 124°23' W **90**
Julianehåb see Qaqortoq, *Den.* 60°47' N, 46°7' W **106**
Jülich, *Ger.* 50°55' N, 6°21' E **167**
Julimes, *Mex.* 28°24' N, 105°27' W **92**
Júlio de Castilhos, *Braz.* 29°15' S, 53°42' W **139**
Jullundur, *India* 31°19' N, 75°35' E **186**
Julpo, *S. Korea* 35°35' N, 126°41' E **200**
Julu, *China* 37°13' N, 115°0' E **198**
Julu Rayeu, oil field, *Indonesia* 4°58' N, 97°36' E **196**
Juma, *Uzb.* 39°41' N, 66°38' E **197**
Juma, river, *Braz.* 5°31' S, 65°2' W **132**
Jumba, *Somalia* 0°18' N, 42°38' E **218**
Jumbilla, *Peru* 5°49' S, 77°47' W **130**
Jumbo Peak, *Nev., U.S.* 36°10' N, 114°15' W **101**
Jumilla, *Sp.* 38°28' N, 1°21' W **164**
Jumla, *Nepal* 29°17' N, 82°12' E **197**
Jumunjin, *S. Korea* 37°53' N, 128°49' E **200**
Junagadh, *India* 21°32' N, 70°26' E **186**
Junan, *China* 35°13' N, 118°52' E **198**
Junction, *Tex., U.S.* 30°28' N, 99°46' W **92**
Junction, *Utah, U.S.* 38°14' N, 112°13' W **90**
Junction City, *Ark., U.S.* 33°1' N, 92°44' W **103**
Junction City, *Kans., U.S.* 39°0' N, 96°51' W **90**
Jundiaí, *Braz.* 23°10' S, 46°54' W **138**
Juneau, *Alas., U.S.* 58°19' N, 134°31' W **108**
Juneau, *Wis., U.S.* 43°24' N, 88°42' W **102**
Juneda, *Sp.* 41°32' N, 0°48' E **164**
Jungar Qi, *China* 39°39' N, 110°54' E **198**
Jungfrau, peak, *Switz.* 46°32' N, 7°56' E **167**
Junggar Pendi, *China* 45°57' N, 84°44' E **184**
Junín, *Arg.* 34°37' S, 60°55' W **139**
Junín, *Col.* 1°19' N, 78°17' W **136**
Junín, adm. division, *Peru* 11°26' S, 74°42' W **137**
Junín de los Andes, *Arg.* 39°55' S, 71°6' W **134**
Juniper Mountain, peak, *Oreg., U.S.* 42°55' N, 120°1' W **90**
Juniper Peak, *Nev., U.S.* 39°46' N, 119°17' W **90**
Junipero Serra Peak, *Calif., U.S.* 36°8' N, 121°28' W **100**
Juniville, *Fr.* 49°23' N, 4°22' E **163**
Junnar, *India* 19°12' N, 73°53' E **188**
Juno Beach, *Fla., U.S.* 26°52' N, 80°4' W **105**
Junosuando, *Nor.* 67°25' N, 22°28' E **152**
Junsele, *Nor.* 63°41' N, 16°56' E **152**
Juntura, *Oreg., U.S.* 43°44' N, 118°5' W **90**
Juntusranta, *Fin.* 65°12' N, 29°27' E **152**
Juodkrantė, *Russ.* 55°34' N, 21°6' E **166**
Jupaguá, *Braz.* 11°50' S, 44°20' W **132**
Jupiter, *Fla., U.S.* 26°56' N, 80°6' W **105**
Jupiter, river, *Can.* 49°40' N, 63°36' W **111**
Jupiter Well, spring, *Austral.* 22°59' S, 126°42' E **230**
Juquiá, *Braz.* 24°19' S, 47°37' W **138**
Jur, river, *Sudan* 8°34' N, 28°35' E **224**
Jura Mountains, *Switz.* 46°58' N, 6°23' E **165**
Jura, Paps of, mountain, *U.K.* 55°53' N, 6°7' W **150**
Juradó, *Col.* 7°7' N, 77°47' W **136**
Juramento, *Braz.* 16°50' S, 43°36' W **138**
Juramento see Pasaje, river, *Arg.* 28°44' S, 62°58' W **139**
Jurbarkas, *Lith.* 55°4' N, 22°45' E **166**
Jurf ad Darāwīsh, *Jordan* 30°41' N, 35°51' E **194**
Jurien Bay 30°46' S, 114°35' E **230**
Jūrmala, *Latv.* 56°57' N, 23°48' E **166**
Jūrmalciems, *Latv.* 56°18' N, 21°0' E **166**
Jurmo, *Fin.* 59°49' N, 21°34' E **166**
Juruá, *Braz.* 3°28' S, 66°9' W **136**
Juruá, river, *Braz.* 3°1' S, 66°9' W **132**
Jurumirim Dam, *Braz.* 23°24' S, 49°18' W **138**
Juruti, *Braz.* 2°10' S, 56°8' W **130**
Jussey, *Fr.* 47°49' N, 5°53' E **150**
Justo Daract, *Arg.* 33°53' S, 65°10' W **134**
Jutaí, *Braz.* 5°11' S, 68°52' W **130**
Jutaí, Ilha Grande de, islands, *South America* 3°21' S, 49°31' W **130**
Jutaí, river, *Braz.* 3°21' S, 67°32' W **136**
Jutiapa, *Guatemala* 14°17' N, 89°52' W **115**
Jutica, *Braz.* 1°4' N, 69°31' W **136**
Juticalpa, *Hond.* 14°43' N, 86°12' W **115**
Jutland, peninsula, *Ger.-Den.* 55°35' N, 8°29' E **150**
Juuru, *Est.* 59°2' N, 24°56' E **166**
Juva, *Fin.* 61°53' N, 27°47' E **166**
Juventino Rosas, *Mex.* 20°37' N, 101°0' W **114**
Juventud, Isla de La, adm. division, *Cuba* 21°24' N, 83°32' W **116**
Juxian, *China* 35°36' N, 118°50' E **198**
Juxtlahuaca, *Mex.* 17°19' N, 98°2' W **114**
Juye, *China* 35°22' N, 116°6' E **198**
Jūymand, *Iran* 34°20' N, 58°41' E **180**
Jūyom, *Iran* 28°5' N, 53°49' E **196**
Juzennecourt, *Fr.* 48°10' N, 4°58' E **163**
Jwaneng, *Botswana* 24°34' S, 24°35' E **227**
Jyderup, *Den.* 55°39' N, 11°24' E **152**
Jyrgalang, *Kyrg.* 42°38' N, 78°58' E **184**
Jyväskylä, *Fin.* 62°12' N, 25°42' E **152**

K

K2 (Qoghir, Godwin Austen), peak, *Pak.* 35°51' N, 76°25' E **186**
Ka, river, *Nig.* 11°38' N, 5°19' E **222**
Ka' Ū, region, *Oceania* 19°15' N, 155°39' W **99**
Kaabong, *Uganda* 3°30' N, 34°6' E **224**
Kaa-Iya National Park, *Bol.* 19°25' S, 61°49' W **132**
Kaamanen, *Fin.* 69°6' N, 27°12' E **152**
Kaambooni, *Somalia* 1°38' S, 41°36' E **224**
Kaambooni, Raas, *Somalia* 1°36' S, 40°53' E **224**
Kaaresuvanto, *Fin.* 68°27' N, 22°27' E **152**
Kaba, *Hung.* 47°22' N, 21°16' E **168**
Kaba see Habahe, *China* 48°4' N, 86°21' E **184**
Kabaena, island, *Indonesia* 5°48' S, 121°7' E **192**
Kabala, *Sierra Leone* 9°34' N, 11°34' W **222**
Kabale, *Uganda* 1°19' S, 29°59' E **224**
Kabalo, *Dem. Rep. of the Congo* 6°4' S, 26°55' E **224**
Kabambare, *Dem. Rep. of the Congo* 4°44' S, 27°38' E **224**
Kabanga, *Zambia* 17°30' S, 26°47' E **224**
Kabangoué, *Côte d'Ivoire* 10°10' N, 7°33' W **222**
Kabanjahe, *Indonesia* 3°8' N, 98°29' E **196**
Kabara, *Mali* 16°40' N, 3°0' W **222**
Kabardino-Balkariya, adm. division, *Russ.* 43°33' N, 42°31' E **195**
Kabare, *Dem. Rep. of the Congo* 2°32' S, 28°42' E **224**
Kabarnet, *Kenya* 0°28' N, 35°45' E **224**
Kabasalan, *Philippines* 7°50' N, 122°45' E **203**
Kabasha, *Dem. Rep. of the Congo* 0°43' N, 29°12' E **224**
Kabba, *Nig.* 7°52' N, 6°3' E **222**
Kåbdalis, *Nor.* 66°8' N, 19°56' E **152**
Kabenung Lake, *Can.* 48°15' N, 85°30' W **94**
Kabinakagami Lake, *Can.* 48°47' N, 86°7' W **81**
Kabinda, *Dem. Rep. of the Congo* 6°11' S, 24°27' E **224**
Kabīr, river, *Asia* 34°35' N, 36°7' E **194**
Kabo, *Cen. Af. Rep.* 7°36' N, 18°36' E **218**
Kabol (Kabul), *Afghan.* 34°34' N, 69°2' E **186**
Kabompo, *Zambia* 13°37' S, 24°10' E **224**
Kabompo, river, *Zambia* 13°34' S, 24°16' E **224**
Kabongo, *Dem. Rep. of the Congo* 7°21' S, 25°34' E **224**
Kabore-Tambi National Park, *Burkina Faso* 11°10' N, 1°50' W **222**
Kabosa Island, *Myanmar* 12°51' N, 97°24' E **202**
Kaboudia, Ras, *Tun.* 35°10' N, 11°9' E **156**
Kabūd Gombad, *Iran* 37°1' N, 59°48' E **180**
Kabugao, *Philippines* 18°3' N, 121°8' E **203**
Kabul see Kabol, *Afghan.* 34°34' N, 69°2' E **186**
Kabunda, *Dem. Rep. of the Congo* 12°29' S, 29°20' E **224**
Kabushiya, *Sudan* 16°51' N, 33°42' E **182**
Kabwe (Broken Hill), *Zambia* 14°29' S, 28°25' E **224**
Kabylie, region, *Africa* 36°31' N, 4°4' E **150**
Kać, *Serb.* 45°18' N, 19°56' E **168**
Kaçanik, *Kosovo* 42°14' N, 21°15' E **168**
Kachanovo, *Russ.* 57°27' N, 27°46' E **166**
Kachia, *Nig.* 9°52' N, 7°57' E **222**
Kachikau, *Botswana* 18°10' S, 24°28' E **224**
Kachīry, *Kaz.* 53°4' N, 76°7' E **184**
Kachkanar, *Russ.* 58°44' N, 59°30' E **154**
Kachreti, *Ga.* 41°39' N, 45°40' E **195**
Kachug, *Russ.* 54°3' N, 105°59' E **190**
Kachung, *Uganda* 1°54' N, 32°56' E **224**
Kaçkar Dağı, peak, *Turk.* 40°50' N, 41°6' E **195**
Kada, spring, *Chad* 19°21' N, 19°36' E **216**
Kadaingti, *Myanmar* 17°37' N, 97°30' E **202**
Kadam, peak, *Uganda* 1°45' N, 34°37' E **224**
Kadan Kyun, island, *Myanmar* 12°33' N, 98°29' E **202**
Kadarkút, *Hung.* 46°14' N, 17°37' E **168**
Kade, *Ghana* 6°6' N, 0°52' E **222**
Kadé, *Guinea* 12°10' N, 13°53' W **222**
Kadéï, river, *Cen. Af. Rep.* 3°48' N, 15°32' E **218**
Kadesh, battle, *Syr.* 34°34' N, 36°25' E **194**
Kadesh-Barnea see 'Ain el Qideirât, spring, *Egypt* 30°39' N, 34°25' E **194**
Kadiana, *Mali* 10°44' N, 6°31' W **222**
Kadıköy, *Turk.* 40°39' N, 26°52' E **158**
Kadıköy, *Turk.* 40°58' N, 29°2' E **158**
Kading, river, *Laos* 18°19' N, 104°10' E **202**
Kadınhanı, *Turk.* 38°13' N, 32°13' E **156**
Kadiolo, *Mali* 10°33' N, 5°46' W **222**
Kadiria, *Alg.* 36°31' N, 3°41' E **150**
Kadirli, *Turk.* 37°21' N, 36°5' E **156**
Kadivka, *Ukr.* 48°31' N, 38°36' E **158**
Kadnikov, *Russ.* 59°30' N, 40°21' E **154**
Kado, *Nig.* 7°37' N, 9°40' E **222**
Kadom, *Russ.* 54°32' N, 42°30' E **154**
Kadoma, *Zimb.* 18°21' S, 29°56' E **224**
Kadrifakovo, *Maced.* 41°48' N, 22°3' E **168**
Kadugli, *Sudan* 10°59' N, 29°40' E **224**
Kaduna, *Nig.* 10°30' N, 7°24' E **222**
Kaduy, *Russ.* 59°10' N, 37°12' E **154**
Kadyy, *Russ.* 57°47' N, 43°10' E **154**
Kadzherom, *Russ.* 64°40' N, 55°48' E **154**
Kaech'ŏn, *N. Korea* 39°42' N, 125°52' E **200**
Kaédi, *Mauritania* 16°8' N, 13°36' W **222**
Kaélé, *Cameroon* 10°6' N, 14°26' E **216**
Ka'ena Point, *Hawai'i, U.S.* 21°34' N, 158°40' W **99**
Kaeng Krachan National Park, *Thai.* 12°44' N, 98°58' E **202**
Kaeo, *N.Z.* 35°6' S, 173°47' E **240**
Ka'eo, peak, *Hawai'i, U.S.* 21°53' N, 160°12' W **99**
Kaesŏng, *N. Korea* 37°58' N, 126°32' E **200**
Kafakumba, *Dem. Rep. of the Congo* 9°41' S, 23°45' E **224**
Kafanchan, *Nig.* 9°36' N, 8°18' E **222**
Kaffrine, *Senegal* 14°6' N, 15°32' W **222**
Kafia Kingi, *Sudan* 9°15' N, 24°24' E **224**
Kafin, *Nig.* 9°29' N, 7°5' E **222**
Kåfjord, *Nor.* 69°56' N, 23°0' E **152**
Kåfjord, *Nor.* 69°31' N, 20°51' E **152**
Kafr Buhum, *Syr.* 35°3' N, 36°41' E **194**
Kafu, river, *Uganda* 1°8' N, 31°26' E **224**
Kafue, *Zambia* 15°47' S, 28°10' E **224**
Kafue National Park, *Zambia* 14°52' S, 25°40' E **224**
Kafue, river, *Zambia* 14°31' S, 26°26' E **224**
Kafue, river, *Zambia* 15°41' S, 26°27' E **224**
Kafufu, river, *Tanzania* 7°5' S, 31°31' E **224**
Kafulwe, *Zambia* 9°0' S, 29°1' E **224**
Kaga, *Japan* 36°18' N, 136°17' E **201**
Kaga Bandoro, *Cen. Af. Rep.* 6°54' N, 19°11' E **218**
Kagan, *Pak.* 34°45' N, 73°34' E **186**
Kagawa, adm. division, *Japan* 34°11' N, 133°41' E **201**
Kåge, *Nor.* 64°49' N, 20°56' E **152**
Kagera, adm. division, *Tanzania* 2°38' S, 30°33' E **218**
Kagera, river, *Africa* 1°8' S, 30°42' E **224**
Kagianagami Lake, *Can.* 50°58' N, 88°38' W **110**
Kağızman, *Turk.* 40°8' N, 43°6' E **195**
Kagmar, *Sudan* 14°25' N, 30°23' E **226**
Kagopal, *Chad* 8°15' N, 16°26' E **218**
Kagoshima, *Japan* 31°34' N, 130°32' E **201**
Kagoshima, adm. division, *Japan* 31°15' N, 130°34' E **201**
Kagoshima Space Center, *Japan* 31°16' N, 131°0' E **201**
Kaguyak, *Alas., U.S.* 56°51' N, 153°51' W **98**
Kahama, *Tanzania* 3°49' S, 32°35' E **224**
Kahan, *Pak.* 29°18' N, 68°57' E **186**
Kahemba, *Dem. Rep. of the Congo* 7°20' S, 18°59' E **218**
Kāhili, peak, *Hawai'i, U.S.* 21°58' N, 159°33' W **99**
Kahler Asten, peak, *Ger.* 51°10' N, 8°26' E **167**
Kahlotus, *Wash., U.S.* 46°37' N, 118°33' W **90**
Kahntah, *Can.* 58°19' N, 120°55' W **108**
Kahntah, river, *Can.* 57°50' N, 120°51' W **108**
Kahnūj, *Iran* 27°54' N, 57°45' E **196**
Kahoku, *Japan* 38°26' N, 140°18' E **201**
Kaho'olawe, island, *Hawai'i, U.S.* 20°21' N, 157°18' W **99**
Kahperusvaara, peak, *Fin.* 69°8' N, 21°1' E **152**
Kahramanmaraş, *Turk.* 37°35' N, 36°55' E **156**
Kahtla, *Est.* 58°24' N, 22°59' E **166**
Kahuku Point, *Hawai'i, U.S.* 21°44' N, 158°21' W **99**
Kahurangi National Park, *N.Z.* 41°11' S, 171°19' E **240**
Kahuzi-Biega National Park, *Dem. Rep. of the Congo* 2°0' S, 27°14' E **224**
Kai Iwi, *N.Z.* 39°53' S, 174°54' E **240**
Kai, Kepulauan, islands, *Banda Sea* 5°58' S, 130°47' E **192**
Kaiama, *Nig.* 9°35' N, 4°0' E **222**
Kaibara, *Japan* 35°7' N, 135°3' E **201**
Kā'id, spring, *Iraq* 32°2' N, 40°57' E **180**
Kaifeng, *China* 34°48' N, 114°19' E **198**
Kaifu, *Japan* 33°36' N, 134°20' E **201**
Kaiholena, peak, *Hawai'i, U.S.* 19°10' N, 155°38' W **99**
Kaihu, *N.Z.* 35°45' S, 173°42' E **240**
Kaikoura, *N.Z.* 42°25' S, 173°39' E **240**
Kailahun, *Sierra Leone* 8°14' N, 10°35' W **222**
Kaili, *China* 26°34' N, 107°59' E **198**
Kailu, *China* 43°39' N, 121°16' E **198**
Kaimana, *Indonesia* 3°39' S, 133°45' E **192**
Käina, *Est.* 58°49' N, 22°46' E **166**
Kainan, *Japan* 34°9' N, 135°13' E **201**
Kainji Dam, *Nig.* 9°40' N, 4°19' E **222**
Kainji Lake National Park, *Nig.* 9°45' N, 5°4' E **222**
Kainuunkylä, *Fin.* 66°13' N, 23°47' E **152**
Kairala, *Fin.* 67°10' N, 27°23' E **152**
Kaisersesch, *Ger.* 50°13' N, 7°8' E **167**
Kaiserslautern, *Ger.* 49°26' N, 7°45' E **163**
Kaishantun, *China* 42°42' N, 129°44' E **200**
Kaišiadorys, *Lith.* 54°52' N, 24°26' E **166**
Kaitangata, *N.Z.* 46°17' S, 169°50' E **240**
Kaithal, *India* 29°47' N, 76°25' E **197**
Ka'iwaloa Heiau and Olowalu Petroglyphs, site, *Hawai'i, U.S.* 20°49' N, 156°40' W **99**
Kaixian, *China* 31°11' N, 108°20' E **198**
Kaiyang, *China* 27°4' N, 107°0' E **198**
Kaiyuan, *China* 42°32' N, 124°3' E **200**
Kaiyuan, *China* 23°40' N, 103°9' E **202**
Kajaani, *Fin.* 64°12' N, 27°39' E **152**
Kajaki, *Afghan.* 32°12' N, 65°5' E **186**
Kajaki Dam, *Afghan.* 32°1' N, 64°29' E **186**
Kajang, *Malaysia* 3°0' N, 101°45' E **196**
Kajiado, *Kenya* 1°52' S, 36°48' E **224**
Kajiki, *Japan* 31°43' N, 130°40' E **201**
Kajo Kaji, *Sudan* 3°48' N, 31°36' E **224**
Kajok, *Sudan* 8°16' N, 27°58' E **224**
Kajuru, *Nig.* 10°19' N, 7°38' E **222**
Kaka, *Sudan* 10°37' N, 32°7' E **224**
Kaka, *Turkm.* 37°21' N, 59°36' E **180**
Kakada, spring, *Chad* 16°8' N, 15°29' E **216**
Kakadu National Park, *Austral.* 13°22' S, 132°5' E **238**
Kakahi, *N.Z.* 38°59' S, 175°21' E **240**
Kakamas, *S. Af.* 28°47' S, 20°35' E **227**
Kakamega, *Kenya* 0°15' N, 34°46' E **224**
Kakana, *India* 9°9' N, 92°55' E **188**
Kakanj, *Bosn. and Herzg.* 44°9' N, 18°5' E **168**
Kakanui, *N.Z.* 45°12' S, 170°53' E **240**
Kakaramea, *N.Z.* 39°43' S, 174°25' E **240**
Kakasszék, *Hung.* 46°32' N, 20°36' E **168**
Kakata, *Liberia* 6°25' N, 10°21' W **222**
Kakatahi, *N.Z.* 39°41' S, 175°21' E **240**
Kake, *Alas., U.S.* 56°58' N, 133°57' W **108**
Kake, *Japan* 34°36' N, 132°20' E **201**
Kaketsa Mountain, *Can.* 58°10' N, 131°59' W **108**
Kakhib, *Russ.* 42°23' N, 46°36' E **195**
Kākhk, *Iran* 34°7' N, 58°38' E **180**
Kakhovka, *Ukr.* 46°48' N, 33°29' E **156**
Kakhovs'ke Vodoskhovyshche, lake, *Ukr.* 46°59' N, 32°23' E **156**
Kakinada (Cocanada), *India* 16°59' N, 82°15' E **188**
Kakisa, *Can.* 60°54' N, 117°21' W **108**
Kakisa Lake, *Can.* 60°57' N, 118°37' W **108**
Kakisa, river, *Can.* 60°44' N, 119°16' W **108**
Kakogawa, *Japan* 34°46' N, 134°51' E **201**
Kakshaal Range see Kök Shal Tau, *Kyrg.* 41°22' N, 77°33' E **184**
Kakskerta, *Fin.* 60°20' N, 22°13' E **166**
Kaktovik, *Alas., U.S.* 69°59' N, 143°40' W **98**
Kakuda, *Japan* 37°58' N, 140°45' E **201**
Kakuma, *Kenya* 3°40' N, 34°50' E **224**
Kakwa, river, *Can.* 54°13' N, 118°43' W **108**
Kál, *Hung.* 47°43' N, 20°17' E **168**
Kala, *Azerb.* 40°27' N, 50°10' E **195**
Kala, *Tanzania* 8°8' S, 31°0' E **224**
Kalaallit Nunaat see Greenland, *Den.* 67°11' N, 50°25' W **106**
Kalabagh, *Pak.* 32°59' N, 71°35' E **186**
Kalabo, *Zambia* 14°59' S, 22°40' E **220**
Kalābsha and Beit el Wāli, ruin(s), *Egypt* 23°32' N, 32°42' E **182**
Kalach, *Russ.* 50°25' N, 40°58' E **158**
Kalach na Donu, *Russ.* 48°43' N, 43°32' E **158**
Kalachinsk, *Russ.* 54°59' N, 74°36' E **184**
Kalae (South Point), *Hawai'i, U.S.* 18°40' N, 155°43' W **99**
Kalahari Desert, *Africa* 19°27' S, 24°2' E **224**
Kalahari Gemsbok National Park, *S. Af.* 26°6' S, 19°47' E **227**
Kalaikhum, *Taj.* 38°28' N, 70°47' E **197**
Kalajoki, *Fin.* 64°12' N, 23°55' E **152**
Kalakamate, *Botswana* 20°39' S, 27°18' E **227**
Kalakan, *Russ.* 55°11' N, 116°45' E **190**
Kalakepen, *Indonesia* 2°47' N, 97°48' E **196**
Kalalua, peak, *Hawai'i, U.S.* 19°23' N, 155°7' W **99**
Kalam, *Pak.* 35°31' N, 72°36' E **186**
Kalama, *Wash., U.S.* 46°0' N, 122°50' W **100**
Kalama, river, *Wash., U.S.* 46°1' N, 122°45' W **100**
Kalamalka Lake, *Can.* 50°5' N, 119°57' W **108**
Kalamáta, *Gr.* 37°2' N, 22°7' E **216**
Kalamazoo, *Mich., U.S.* 42°17' N, 85°36' W **102**
Kalambo Falls, *Zambia* 8°51' S, 31°17' E **224**
Kalana, *Mali* 10°47' N, 8°13' W **222**
Kalangala, *Uganda* 0°23' N, 32°16' E **224**
Kalangali, *Tanzania* 6°6' S, 33°55' E **224**
Kalanshiyū ar Ramlī al Kabīr, Sarīr (Sand Sea of Calanscio), *Lib.* 28°52' N, 23°25' E **180**
Kalanshiyū, Sarīr, *Lib.* 26°35' N, 20°7' E **216**
Kalao, island, *Indonesia* 7°27' S, 119°55' E **192**
Kalaotoa, island, *Indonesia* 7°28' S, 121°50' E **192**
Kälarne, *Nor.* 62°59' N, 16°4' E **152**
Kalasin, *Thai.* 16°28' N, 103°31' E **202**
Kalat, *Pak.* 29°2' N, 66°33' E **186**
Kalaupapa National Historic Park, *Hawai'i, U.S.* 20°42' N, 158°0' W **99**
Kalaus, river, *Russ.* 45°50' N, 43°15' E **158**
Kalawao, site, *Hawai'i, U.S.* 21°10' N, 157°0' W **99**
Kalay'mor, *Turkm.* 35°41' N, 62°33' E **186**
Kalay-wa, *Myanmar* 23°10' N, 94°13' E **202**
Kalbā, *U.A.E.* 25°4' N, 56°17' E **196**
Kälbäcär see Karvachar, *Azerb.* 40°8' N, 46°1' E **195**
Kalbān, *Oman* 20°17' N, 58°41' E **182**
Kaldrma, *Bosn. and Herzg.* 44°18' N, 16°11' E **168**
Kale Burnu, *Turk.* 41°4' N, 38°54' E **195**
Kale (Myra), *Turk.* 36°13' N, 29°57' E **156**
Kalecik, *Turk.* 40°6' N, 33°25' E **156**
Kalehe, *Dem. Rep. of the Congo* 2°7' S, 28°50' E **224**
Kalemie, *Dem. Rep. of the Congo* 5°57' S, 29°11' E **224**
Kalemyo, *Myanmar* 23°10' N, 94°1' E **202**
Kalene Hill, *Zambia* 11°13' S, 24°10' E **224**
Kalenyy, *Kaz.* 49°32' N, 51°35' E **158**
Kalesija, *Bosn. and Herzg.* 44°27' N, 18°55' E **168**
Kaletnik, *Pol.* 54°10' N, 23°5' E **152**
Kalevala, *Russ.* 65°12' N, 31°12' E **152**
Kaleybar, *Iran* 38°56' N, 47°3' E **195**
Kalgachikha, *Russ.* 63°20' N, 36°48' E **154**
Kalí Límni, peak, *Gr.* 35°34' N, 27°4' E **156**
Kali Sindh, river, *India* 24°28' N, 76°7' E **197**
Kaliakoúda, peak, *Gr.* 38°47' N, 21°40' E **156**
Kaliakra, Nos, *Bulg.* 43°17' N, 28°17' E **156**
Kalibo, *Philippines* 11°40' N, 122°22' E **203**
Kalida, *Ohio, U.S.* 40°58' N, 84°12' W **102**
Kalima, *Dem. Rep. of the Congo* 2°39' S, 26°35' E **218**
Kalimantan see Borneo, island, *Indonesia* 4°28' S, 111°26' E **192**
Kalimash, *Alban.* 42°5' N, 20°18' E **168**
Kálimnos, *Gr.* 36°57' N, 26°59' E **156**
Kalimpang, *India* 27°4' N, 88°26' E **197**
Kaliningrad, *Russ.* 54°42' N, 20°27' E **166**
Kaliningrad Oblast, adm. division, *Russ.* 54°47' N, 20°9' E **166**
Kalinino, *Arm.* 41°7' N, 44°15' E **195**
Kalinino, *Russ.* 45°9' N, 39°1' E **156**
Kalinino, *Russ.* 57°18' N, 56°23' E **154**
Kalininsk, *Russ.* 51°29' N, 44°28' E **158**
Kalinivka, *Ukr.* 49°28' N, 28°42' E **152**
Kalinkavichy, *Belarus* 52°5' N, 29°26' E **152**
Kalino, *Russ.* 58°14' N, 57°38' E **154**
Kalinovik, *Bosn. and Herzg.* 43°30' N, 18°26' E **168**
Kaliro, *Uganda* 0°52' N, 33°29' E **224**
Kalis, *Somalia* 8°23' N, 49°3' E **216**
Kalispell, *Mont., U.S.* 48°12' N, 114°21' W **106**
Kalisz, *Pol.* 51°45' N, 18°5' E **152**
Kaliua, *Tanzania* 5°4' S, 31°46' E **224**
Kalix, *Nor.* 65°51' N, 23°7' E **154**
Kalixälven, river, *Nor.* 67°41' N, 19°45' E **152**
Kalkan, *Turk.* 36°15' N, 29°25' E **156**
Kalkar, *Ger.* 51°42' N, 6°17' E **167**
Kalkaska, *Mich., U.S.* 44°43' N, 85°11' W **94**
Kalkfeld, *Namibia* 20°55' S, 16°12' E **227**
Kalkkinen, *Fin.* 61°17' N, 25°41' E **166**
Kalkrand, *Namibia* 24°5' S, 17°35' E **227**
Kallam, *India* 18°32' N, 76°1' E **188**
Kallaste, *Est.* 58°38' N, 27°7' E **166**
Kallithéa, *Gr.* 37°57' N, 23°42' E **156**
Kałuszyn, *Pol.* 52°12' N, 21°47' E **152**
Kallmet, *Alban.* 41°50' N, 19°41' E **168**
Kallo, *Fin.* 67°25' N, 24°27' E **152**
Kallunki, *Fin.* 66°38' N, 28°54' E **152**
Kalmar, *Nor.* 56°39' N, 16°20' E **152**
Kalmthout, *Belg.* 51°23' N, 4°28' E **167**
Kalmykiya, adm. division, *Russ.* 46°7' N, 43°37' E **158**
Kalnai, *India* 22°47' N, 83°29' E **197**
Kalnik, peak, *Croatia* 46°7' N, 16°26' E **168**
Kalo Chorio, *Cyprus* 34°50' N, 33°2' E **194**
Kalocsa, *Hung.* 46°31' N, 18°58' E **168**
Kaloko-Honokōhau National Historical Park, *Hawai'i, U.S.* 19°40' N, 156°5' W **99**
Kaloli Point, *U.S.* 19°34' N, 154°56' W **99**
Kalomo, *Zambia* 17°3' S, 26°28' E **224**
Kalotina, *Bulg.* 42°59' N, 22°51' E **168**
Kalpi, *India* 26°6' N, 79°43' E **197**
Kalpin, *China* 40°34' N, 78°54' E **184**
Kalsubai, peak, *India* 19°34' N, 73°34' E **188**
Kaltag, *Alas., U.S.* 64°11' N, 158°53' W **98**
Kaltay, *Russ.* 56°14' N, 84°54' E **169**
Kalterherberg, *Ger.* 50°31' N, 6°12' E **167**
Kaltungo, *Nig.* 9°48' N, 11°18' E **222**
Kaluga, *Russ.* 54°34' N, 36°20' E **154**
Kaluga, adm. division, *Russ.* 54°14' N, 34°5' E **154**
Kalulushi, *Zambia* 12°52' S, 28°5' E **224**
Kalundu, *Zambia* 10°17' S, 29°22' E **224**
Kalungwishi, river, *Zambia* 9°40' S, 29°0' E **220**
Kalush, *Ukr.* 49°0' N, 24°21' E **158**
Kalvåg, *Nor.* 61°46' N, 4°51' E **152**
Kalvarija, *Lith.* 54°26' N, 23°11' E **166**
Kälviä, *Fin.* 63°51' N, 23°24' E **152**
Kalvitsa, *Fin.* 61°53' N, 27°15' E **166**
Kalvola, *Fin.* 61°5' N, 24°7' E **166**
Kalwang, *Aust.* 47°26' N, 14°46' E **156**
Kalweyn, Ghubbet, *Somalia* 11°7' N, 46°28' E **216**
Kal'ya, *Russ.* 60°17' N, 59°54' E **154**
Kalyan, *India* 19°14' N, 73°8' E **188**
Kalyazin, *Russ.* 57°12' N, 37°50' E **154**
Kám, *Hung.* 47°5' N, 16°53' E **168**
Kam, river, *Nig.* 8°10' N, 11°4' E **222**
Kama, *Dem. Rep. of the Congo* 3°38' S, 27°7' E **224**
Kama, *Myanmar* 19°3' N, 95°4' E **202**
Kama, *Russ.* 60°8' N, 62°1' E **154**
Kama, river, *Dem. Rep. of the Congo* 3°30' S, 26°55' E **218**
Kama, river, *Russ.* 60°10' N, 55°25' E **154**
Kamae, *Japan* 32°47' N, 131°55' E **201**
Kamaing, *Myanmar* 25°29' N, 96°40' E **188**
Kamaishi, *Japan* 39°17' N, 141°42' E **190**

Kit Carson, *Colo., U.S.* 38°45′ N, 102°48′ W **90**
Kita, *Mali* 13°2′ N, 9°30′ W **222**
Kitaibaraki, *Japan* 36°46′ N, 140°43′ E **201**
Kitakata, *Japan* 37°39′ N, 139°51′ E **201**
Kitakyūshū, *Japan* 33°52′ N, 130°53′ E **200**
Kitale, *Kenya* 1°0′ N, 34°58′ E **224**
Kitchener, *Can.* 43°26′ N, 80°29′ W **94**
Kitchener Lake, *Can.* 56°59′ N, 128°11′ W **108**
Kitchigama, river, *Can.* 50°58′ N, 79°24′ W **80**
Kitee, *Fin.* 62°4′ N, 30°6′ E **152**
Kitenda, *Dem. Rep. of the Congo* 6°49′ S, 17°26′ E **218**
Kitgum, *Uganda* 3°14′ N, 32°53′ E **224**
Kithaírnas, Óros, peak, *Gr.* 38°10′ N, 23°10′ E **156**
Kithira (Cerigo), island, *Gr.* 36°17′ N, 23°3′ E **180**
Kithira, island, *Gr.* 36°22′ N, 23°6′ E **143**
Kiti, Cape, *Cyprus* 34°44′ N, 33°34′ E **194**
Kitimat, *Can.* 54°4′ N, 128°42′ W **108**
Kitlope, river, *Can.* 53°14′ N, 128°8′ W **108**
Kitob, *Uzb.* 39°8′ N, 66°53′ E **197**
Kitombe, *Dem. Rep. of the Congo* 5°23′ S, 18°57′ E **218**
Kitsa, *Russ.* 68°30′ N, 33°11′ E **152**
Kitscoty, *Can.* 53°19′ N, 110°20′ W **108**
Kitsuki, *Japan* 33°25′ N, 131°36′ E **201**
Kittery, *Me., U.S.* 43°5′ N, 70°45′ W **104**
Kittery Point, *Me., U.S.* 43°5′ N, 70°42′ W **104**
Kittilä, *Fin.* 67°39′ N, 24°51′ E **152**
Kittitas, *Wash., U.S.* 46°57′ N, 120°26′ W **90**
Kitty Hawk, *N.C., U.S.* 36°2′ N, 75°41′ W **82**
Kitui, *Kenya* 1°23′ S, 38°1′ E **224**
Kitwanga, *Can.* 55°5′ N, 128°4′ W **108**
Kitwe, *Zambia* 12°50′ S, 28°11′ E **224**
Kitzbühel, *Aust.* 47°26′ N, 12°23′ E **156**
Kitzbüheler Alpen, *Aust.* 47°22′ N, 11°45′ E **156**
Kitzingen, *Ger.* 49°44′ N, 10°8′ E **152**
Kiukainen, *Fin.* 61°12′ N, 22°5′ E **166**
Kiuruvesi, *Fin.* 63°38′ N, 26°34′ E **154**
Kiuyu, Ras, *Tanzania* 4°55′ S, 39°53′ E **224**
Kivalina, *Alas., U.S.* 67°40′ N, 164°30′ W **98**
Kivalo, *Fin.* 65°43′ N, 25°0′ E **152**
Kivertsi, *Ukr.* 50°49′ N, 25°26′ E **152**
Kivijärvi, *Fin.* 63°7′ N, 25°5′ E **152**
Kivik, *Nor.* 55°40′ N, 14°14′ E **152**
Kiviõli, *Est.* 59°20′ N, 26°55′ E **166**
Kivivaara, *Fin.* 63°36′ N, 30°10′ E **152**
Kivumba, *Tanzania* 4°38′ S, 30°40′ E **224**
Kiwai, island, *P.N.G.* 8°51′ S, 143°38′ E **192**
Kiwalik, *U.S.* 66°1′ N, 161°55′ W **98**
Kiya, *Russ.* 67°36′ N, 44°11′ E **169**
Kiyāt, *Saudi Arabia* 18°41′ N, 41°26′ E **182**
Kıyıköy, *Turk.* 41°36′ N, 28°5′ E **156**
Kiyiu Lake, *Can.* 51°35′ N, 109°24′ W **90**
Kiyuk Lake, *Can.* 60°27′ N, 100°55′ W **108**
Kizel, *Russ.* 59°0′ N, 57°42′ E **154**
Kizema, *Russ.* 61°7′ N, 44°56′ E **154**
Kızılcahamam, *Turk.* 40°27′ N, 32°37′ E **156**
Kızılırmak, *Turk.* 40°21′ N, 33°58′ E **156**
Kızılırmak, river, *Turk.* 40°33′ N, 34°43′ E **180**
Kızılliman Burnu, *Turk.* 35°58′ N, 32°26′ E **156**
Kizil'skoye, *Russ.* 52°43′ N, 58°49′ E **154**
Kızıltepe, *Turk.* 37°11′ N, 40°36′ E **195**
Kizimkazi, Ras, *Tanzania* 6°39′ S, 39°0′ E **224**
Kizlyar, *Russ.* 43°49′ N, 46°40′ E **195**
Kizlyarskiy Zaliv 44°24′ N, 46°34′ E **158**
Kizner, *Russ.* 56°16′ N, 51°34′ E **154**
Kizreka, *Russ.* 65°32′ N, 31°54′ E **152**
Kjelvik, *Nor.* 70°58′ N, 26°7′ E **152**
Kjøpsvik, *Nor.* 68°5′ N, 16°21′ E **152**
Kjya, islands, *Norwegian Sea* 64°33′ N, 9°43′ E **152**
Klabat, peak, *Indonesia* 1°34′ N, 124°51′ E **192**
Kladanj, *Bosn. and Herzg.* 44°13′ N, 18°40′ E **168**
Kladnica, *Serb.* 43°22′ N, 20°2′ E **168**
Klafeld, *Ger.* 50°55′ N, 8°0′ E **167**
Klaipėda, *Lith.* 55°42′ N, 21°10′ E **166**
Klamath, *Calif., U.S.* 41°31′ N, 124°2′ W **90**
Klamath, *Calif., U.S.* 40°45′ N, 123°5′ W **90**
Klamath Falls, *Oreg., U.S.* 42°13′ N, 121°46′ W **82**
Klamath Mountains Mountains, *Calif., U.S.* 42°1′ N, 125°19′ W **80**
Klamono, *Indonesia* 1°4′ S, 131°25′ E **192**
Klarabro, *Nor.* 60°46′ N, 12°46′ E **152**
Klawer, *S. Af.* 31°50′ S, 18°36′ E **227**
Kle, *Liberia* 6°37′ N, 10°54′ W **222**
Kleczkowski, Lac, lake, *Can.* 50°47′ N, 64°6′ W **111**
Klein Karas, *Namibia* 27°35′ S, 18°3′ E **227**
Klekovača, peak, *Bosn. and Herzg.* 44°25′ N, 16°27′ E **168**
Kléla, *Mali* 11°43′ N, 5°40′ W **222**
Klemtu, *Can.* 52°34′ N, 128°33′ W **108**
Klenike, *Serb.* 42°23′ N, 21°54′ E **168**
Klenje, *Serb.* 44°48′ N, 19°26′ E **168**
Klerksdorp, *S. Af.* 26°53′ S, 26°39′ E **227**
Klery Creek, *Alas., U.S.* 67°10′ N, 160°25′ W **98**
Kleshchevo, *Russ.* 63°16′ N, 39°11′ E **154**
Klesiv, *Ukr.* 51°18′ N, 26°52′ E **152**
Kleszczele, *Pol.* 52°36′ N, 23°19′ E **154**
Kletnya, *Russ.* 53°19′ N, 33°12′ E **154**
Kletskiy, *Russ.* 49°18′ N, 43°3′ E **158**
Klevan', *Ukr.* 50°44′ N, 25°57′ E **152**
Kleve, *Ger.* 51°47′ N, 6°8′ E **167**
Klibreck, Ben, peak, *U.K.* 58°13′ N, 4°31′ W **150**
Kličevac, *Serb.* 44°45′ N, 21°17′ E **168**
Klichaw, *Belarus* 53°27′ N, 29°23′ E **152**
Klickitat, *Wash., U.S.* 45°48′ N, 121°9′ W **100**
Klickitat, river, *Wash., U.S.* 46°9′ N, 121°14′ W **100**
Klimovsk, *Russ.* 55°17′ N, 37°28′ E **154**
Klin, *Russ.* 56°20′ N, 36°42′ E **154**
Klinaklini, river, *Can.* 51°15′ N, 125°47′ W **108**
Klingenbach, *Aust.* 47°45′ N, 16°32′ E **168**
Klingenberg, *Ger.* 49°45′ N, 9°12′ E **167**
Klintehamn, *Sw.* 57°23′ N, 18°11′ E **166**
Klintsovka, *Russ.* 51°40′ N, 49°15′ E **158**
Klintsy, *Russ.* 52°44′ N, 32°14′ E **154**
Klipplaat, *S. Af.* 33°0′ S, 24°19′ E **227**
Klisura, *Serb.* 42°45′ N, 22°23′ E **168**
Ključ, *Bosn. and Herzg.* 44°32′ N, 16°45′ E **168**
Kłodzko, *Pol.* 50°25′ N, 16°40′ E **152**
Kłomnice, *Pol.* 50°55′ N, 19°21′ E **152**
Klos, *Alban.* 41°29′ N, 20°8′ E **168**
Kloster, *Ger.* 54°35′ N, 13°7′ E **152**
Klosters, *Switz.* 46°52′ N, 9°52′ E **167**
Klövsjö, *Nor.* 62°31′ N, 14°8′ E **152**
Klukshu, *Can.* 60°17′ N, 137°2′ W **98**
Klukwan, *Alas., U.S.* 59°25′ N, 135°48′ W **108**
Klyastitsa, *Russ.* 55°47′ N, 29°36′ E **166**
Klyastitsy, *Belarus* 55°52′ N, 28°37′ E **166**
Klyavlino, *Russ.* 54°15′ N, 52°2′ E **154**
Klyetsk, *Belarus* 53°3′ N, 26°40′ E **154**
Klyuchevoye, *Russ.* 60°26′ N, 28°44′ E **166**
Klyuchi, *Russ.* 52°6′ N, 79°16′ E **184**
Klyukvenka, *Russ.* 58°31′ N, 85°57′ E **169**
Knaresborough, *U.K.* 54°1′ N, 1°28′ W **162**
Knee Lake, *Can.* 55°9′ N, 94°45′ W **108**
Knee Lake, *Can.* 55°50′ N, 107°20′ W **108**
Kneippbyn, *Sw.* 57°35′ N, 18°13′ E **166**
Knesebeck, *Ger.* 52°41′ N, 10°42′ E **150**
Knife Delta 58°50′ N, 95°0′ W **108**
Knife, river, *N. Dak., U.S.* 47°3′ N, 102°59′ W **80**
Knighton, *U.K.* 52°19′ N, 3°3′ W **162**
Knightsville, *Ind., U.S.* 39°31′ N, 87°5′ W **102**
Knin, *Croatia* 44°2′ N, 16°11′ E **168**
Knittelfeld, *Aust.* 47°14′ N, 14°48′ E **156**
Knjaževac, *Serb.* 43°33′ N, 22°15′ E **168**
Knock Farril, ruin(s), *U.K.* 57°34′ N, 4°38′ W **150**
Knockadoon Head, *Ire.* 51°40′ N, 7°53′ W **150**
Knockboy, peak, *Ire.* 51°47′ N, 9°32′ W **150**
Knockmealdown Mountains, *Ire.* 52°13′ N, 8°1′ W **150**
Knokke-Heist, *Belg.* 51°20′ N, 3°18′ E **163**
Knosós see Cnossus, ruin(s), *Gr.* 35°16′ N, 25°4′ E **156**
Knottingley, *U.K.* 53°42′ N, 1°14′ W **162**
Knox, *Ind., U.S.* 41°16′ N, 86°37′ W **102**
Knox, Cape, *Can.* 53°59′ N, 133°31′ W **108**
Knox City, *Tex., U.S.* 33°24′ N, 99°49′ W **92**
Knox Coast, *Antarctica* 68°16′ S, 107°4′ E **248**
Knoxville, *Iowa, U.S.* 41°18′ N, 93°5′ W **94**
Knoxville, *Tenn., U.S.* 35°58′ N, 83°56′ W **96**
Knucklas, *U.K.* 52°21′ N, 3°6′ W **162**
Knud Rasmussen Land, region, *Arctic Ocean* 77°1′ N, 66°28′ W **106**
Knüllwald, *Ger.* 51°0′ N, 9°28′ E **167**
Knysna, *S. Af.* 34°1′ S, 23°3′ E **227**
Kō Saki, *Japan* 33°58′ N, 129°1′ E **200**
Koal, spring, *Chad* 14°26′ N, 16°26′ E **216**
Koala, *Burkina Faso* 13°24′ N, 0°8′ E **222**
Koani, *Tanzania* 6°0′ S, 39°20′ E **218**
Kobayashi, *Japan* 31°59′ N, 130°58′ E **201**
Kōbe, *Japan* 34°41′ N, 135°9′ E **201**
Kobelyaky, *Ukr.* 49°11′ N, 34°8′ E **158**
København (Copenhagen), *Den.* 55°40′ N, 12°23′ E **152**
Kobern-Gondorf, *Ger.* 50°18′ N, 7°27′ E **167**
Kobi-ri, *N. Korea* 39°5′ N, 126°1′ E **200**
Koblenz, *Ger.* 50°20′ N, 7°34′ E **167**
K'obo, *Eth.* 12°7′ N, 39°37′ E **182**
Kobowen Swamp, marsh, *Sudan* 5°23′ N, 33°14′ E **224**
Kobozha, *Russ.* 58°48′ N, 35°0′ E **154**
Kobroor, island, *Indonesia* 6°31′ S, 134°40′ E **192**
Kobryn, *Belarus* 52°14′ N, 24°21′ E **152**
Kobu, *Azerb.* 40°24′ N, 49°42′ E **195**
Kobuk, *Alas., U.S.* 66°49′ N, 156°58′ W **98**
Kobuk, river, *Alas., U.S.* 66°55′ N, 159°28′ W **98**
K'obulet'i, *Ga.* 41°49′ N, 41°47′ E **195**
Kobyay, *Russ.* 63°29′ N, 127°1′ E **160**
Kocaeli (İzmit), *Turk.* 40°47′ N, 29°46′ E **180**
Kočani, *Maced.* 41°55′ N, 22°24′ E **168**
Koçbaşı Tepe, peak, *Turk.* 39°24′ N, 43°18′ E **195**
Koceljevo, *Serb.* 44°28′ N, 19°50′ E **168**
Koch Bihar, *India* 26°18′ N, 89°23′ E **197**
Kochi (Cochin), *India* 9°50′ N, 76°24′ E **173**
Koch Peak, *Mont., U.S.* 45°0′ N, 111°32′ W **90**
Kochas, *India* 25°13′ N, 83°53′ E **188**
Kochechum, river, *Russ.* 67°10′ N, 98°19′ E **160**
Kochen'ga, *Russ.* 60°9′ N, 43°33′ E **154**
Kocherinovo, *Bulg.* 42°5′ N, 23°4′ E **168**
Kochevo, *Russ.* 59°36′ N, 54°20′ E **154**
Kōchi, *Japan* 33°34′ N, 133°31′ E **201**
Kōchi, adm. division, *Japan* 33°13′ N, 132°48′ E **201**
Kochkor, *Kyrg.* 42°8′ N, 75°41′ E **184**
Kochubey, *Russ.* 44°23′ N, 46°31′ E **158**
Kochumdek, *Russ.* 64°24′ N, 93°11′ E **169**
Kocie, Góry, *Pol.* 51°24′ N, 16°2′ E **152**
Kock, *Pol.* 51°38′ N, 22°26′ E **152**
Kocs, *Hung.* 47°35′ N, 18°11′ E **168**
Kocsola, *Hung.* 46°31′ N, 18°10′ E **168**
Kodesjärvi, *Fin.* 62°2′ N, 22°4′ E **166**
Kodiak, *Alas., U.S.* 57°43′ N, 152°30′ W **98**
Kodiak Island, *Alas., U.S.* 56°52′ N, 152°48′ W **98**
Kodinar, *India* 20°46′ N, 70°42′ E **188**
Kodino, *Russ.* 63°42′ N, 39°43′ E **154**
Kodinskiy, *Russ.* 58°34′ N, 99°5′ E **160**
Kodok, *Sudan* 9°55′ N, 32°7′ E **224**
Kōes, *Namibia* 26°0′ S, 19°7′ E **227**
Kofa Mountains, *Ariz., U.S.* 33°19′ N, 113°59′ W **101**
Kofarnihon see Vahdat, *Taj.* 38°32′ N, 69°1′ E **197**
Koffiefontein, *S. Af.* 29°25′ S, 25°0′ E **227**
Kofili, *Mali* 15°15′ N, 8°46′ W **222**
Koforidua, *Ghana* 6°6′ N, 0°16′ E **222**
Kōfu, *Japan* 35°39′ N, 138°35′ E **201**
Koga, *Japan* 36°11′ N, 139°44′ E **201**
Køge Bugt 55°23′ N, 12°3′ E **152**
Kogolym, *Russ.* 62°20′ N, 74°49′ E **169**
Kogon, *Uzb.* 39°43′ N, 64°34′ E **197**
Kogon, river, *Guinea* 11°26′ N, 14°29′ W **222**
Kohala, region, *Oceania* 20°10′ N, 155°53′ W **99**
Kohat, *Pak.* 33°34′ N, 71°29′ E **186**
Kohila, *Est.* 59°9′ N, 24°43′ E **166**
Kohima, *India* 25°43′ N, 94°9′ E **188**
Kohler, *Wis., U.S.* 43°44′ N, 87°47′ W **102**
Kohlu, *Pak.* 29°55′ N, 69°16′ E **186**
Kohnieh, *Cambodia* 13°6′ N, 107°3′ E **202**
Kohtla-Järve, *Est.* 59°22′ N, 27°14′ E **166**
Kohunlich, ruin(s), *Mex.* 18°21′ N, 89°4′ W **115**
Koide, *Japan* 37°13′ N, 138°58′ E **201**
Koidern, *Can.* 61°57′ N, 140°33′ W **98**
Koidu, *Sierra Leone* 8°38′ N, 10°59′ W **222**
Koilani, *Cyprus* 34°49′ N, 32°51′ E **194**
Koin, *N. Korea* 40°29′ N, 126°23′ E **200**
Koivu, *Fin.* 66°9′ N, 25°11′ E **152**
Kojā, river, *Iran* 25°30′ N, 61°18′ E **182**
Kok, river, *Asia* 20°6′ N, 99°28′ E **202**
Kök Shal Tau (Kakshaal Range), *Kyrg.* 41°22′ N, 77°33′ E **184**
Kokanee Peak, *Can.* 49°42′ N, 117°14′ W **90**
Kökar, *Fin.* 59°56′ N, 20°52′ E **166**
Kokas, *Indonesia* 2°47′ S, 132°19′ E **192**
Kök-Aygyr, *Kyrg.* 40°43′ N, 75°39′ E **184**
Kōke'e Lodge, site, *Hawai'i, U.S.* 22°7′ N, 159°43′ W **99**
Kokemäki, *Fin.* 61°13′ N, 22°16′ E **166**
Kokenau, *Indonesia* 4°37′ S, 136°13′ E **192**
Kokickny, adm. division, *Slovakia* 48°34′ N, 20°35′ E **152**
Kokin Brod, *Serb.* 43°29′ N, 19°49′ E **168**
Kokka, *Sudan* 20°1′ N, 30°33′ E **226**
Kokkina, *Northern Cyprus, Cyprus* 35°10′ N, 32°36′ E **194**
Kokkola (Gamlakarleby), *Fin.* 63°49′ N, 23°5′ E **152**
Koko, *Eth.* 10°20′ N, 36°3′ E **224**
Koko, *Nig.* 11°26′ N, 4°31′ E **222**
Koko Head, peak, *Hawai'i, U.S.* 21°14′ N, 157°44′ W **99**
Kokomo, *Ind., U.S.* 40°29′ N, 86°8′ W **102**
Kokomo, *Miss., U.S.* 31°11′ N, 90°1′ W **103**
Kokong, *Botswana* 24°20′ S, 23°4′ E **227**
Kokoro, *Nig.* 8°54′ N, 3°9′ E **222**
Kökpekti, *Kaz.* 48°44′ N, 82°23′ E **184**
Kokrines, *Alas., U.S.* 64°56′ N, 154°41′ W **98**
Koksan, *N. Korea* 38°45′ N, 126°40′ E **200**
Kökshetaū, *Kaz.* 53°17′ N, 69°25′ E **184**
Koksovyy, *Russ.* 48°14′ N, 40°37′ E **158**
Kokstad, *S. Af.* 30°35′ S, 29°25′ E **227**
Köktal, *Kaz.* 44°6′ N, 79°47′ E **184**
Köktöbe, *Kaz.* 51°37′ N, 77°23′ E **184**
Kokubu, *Japan* 31°42′ N, 130°45′ E **201**
Kola, *Bosn. and Herzg.* 44°42′ N, 17°4′ E **168**
Kola, *Russ.* 68°49′ N, 33°14′ E **160**
Kola Peninsula, *Russ.* 67°40′ N, 28°12′ E **172**
Kolahun, *Liberia* 8°17′ N, 10°6′ W **222**
Kolaka, *Indonesia* 4°2′ S, 121°30′ E **192**
Kolar, *India* 13°9′ N, 78°8′ E **188**
Kolari, *Fin.* 67°21′ N, 23°46′ E **152**
Kolarovgrad see Shumen, *Bulg.* 43°16′ N, 26°55′ E **156**
Kolárovo, *Slovakia* 47°54′ N, 17°59′ E **168**
Kolåsen, *Nor.* 63°45′ N, 12°58′ E **152**
Kolayat, *India* 27°50′ N, 72°57′ E **186**
Kolbio, *Kenya* 1°11′ S, 41°7′ E **224**
Kol'chugino, *Russ.* 56°18′ N, 39°18′ E **154**
Kolda, *Senegal* 12°54′ N, 14°58′ W **222**
Koldewey, Store, island, *Den.* 75°50′ N, 17°54′ W **246**
Kolding, *Den.* 55°28′ N, 9°27′ E **150**
Költuk, *Kyrg.* 39°56′ N, 73°30′ E **197**
Kole, *Dem. Rep. of the Congo* 2°4′ N, 25°26′ E **224**
Kole, *Dem. Rep. of the Congo* 3°33′ S, 22°27′ E **218**
Kolé, *Mali* 12°6′ N, 8°21′ W **222**
Koler, *Nor.* 65°28′ N, 20°27′ E **152**
Kolezhma, *Russ.* 64°14′ N, 35°45′ E **154**
Kolga Laht 59°28′ N, 25°13′ E **166**
Kolguyev, Ostrov, island, *Russ.* 69°29′ N, 48°57′ E **169**
Kolhapur, *India* 16°41′ N, 74°14′ E **188**
Kolī, *Eth.* 10°19′ N, 36°45′ E **224**
Koli, *Fin.* 63°6′ N, 29°45′ E **152**
Koliganek, *Alas., U.S.* 59°45′ N, 157°20′ W **98**
Kolik'yegan, *Russ.* 61°42′ N, 79°8′ E **169**
Kolik'yegan, river, *Russ.* 61°31′ N, 79°14′ E **169**
Kolimbiné, river, *Mali* 14°49′ N, 12°8′ W **222**
Kolka, *Latv.* 57°43′ N, 22°32′ E **166**
Kolkas Rags, *Latv.* 57°44′ N, 22°36′ E **166**
Kolkata (Calcutta), *India* 22°33′ N, 88°21′ E **197**
Kolky, *Ukr.* 51°5′ N, 25°39′ E **152**
Kollegal, *India* 12°9′ N, 77°9′ E **188**
Kolliоura, *Gabon* 0°11′ N, 12°8′ E **218**
Kolmanskop, *Namibia* 26°44′ S, 15°14′ E **227**
Kolmogorovo, *Russ.* 59°14′ N, 91°15′ E **169**
Köln (Cologne), *Ger.* 50°56′ N, 6°57′ E **167**
Kolo, *Niger* 13°19′ N, 2°23′ E **222**
Kołobrzeg, *Pol.* 54°9′ N, 15°33′ E **152**
Kolodishchi, *Belarus* 53°56′ N, 27°46′ E **166**
Kolodnya, *Russ.* 54°47′ N, 32°16′ E **154**
Kologi, *Sudan* 10°51′ N, 31°0′ E **224**
Kologriv, *Russ.* 58°49′ N, 44°22′ E **154**
Kolokani, *Mali* 13°36′ N, 8°2′ W **222**
Kololo, *Eth.* 7°27′ N, 42°0′ E **224**
Kolomna, *Russ.* 55°4′ N, 38°41′ E **154**
Kolomyya, *Ukr.* 48°31′ N, 25°2′ E **152**
Kolosib, *India* 24°13′ N, 92°38′ E **188**
Kolosovka, *Russ.* 56°31′ N, 73°37′ E **169**
Kolosovykh, Ostrov, island, *Russ.* 74°9′ N, 87°14′ E **160**
Kolozhno, Ozero, lake, *Russ.* 67°44′ N, 30°18′ E **152**
Kolpakovskiy, *Russ.* 54°31′ N, 155°58′ E **160**
Kolpashevo, *Russ.* 58°19′ N, 82°57′ E **169**
Kolpino, *Russ.* 59°44′ N, 30°36′ E **166**
Kolpny, *Russ.* 52°13′ N, 37°3′ E **158**
Kol'skiy Poluostrov, *Russ.* 67°17′ N, 38°11′ E **169**
Koluszki, *Pol.* 51°44′ N, 19°48′ E **152**
Kolva, river, *Russ.* 60°47′ N, 56°50′ E **154**
Kolva, river, *Russ.* 66°19′ N, 56°53′ E **154**
Kolvereid, *Nor.* 64°52′ N, 11°38′ E **152**
Kolvitsa, *Russ.* 67°4′ N, 33°0′ E **152**
Kolwezi, *Dem. Rep. of the Congo* 10°46′ S, 25°26′ E **224**
Kolyma, river, *Russ.* 67°7′ N, 152°3′ E **160**
Kolyma, river, *Russ.* 65°53′ N, 152°45′ E **172**
Kolymskoye, *Russ.* 68°47′ N, 158°38′ E **160**
Kolymskoye Nagor'ye, *Russ.* 61°35′ N, 155°21′ E **160**
Kolyuchin, Ostrov, island, *Russ.* 67°21′ N, 174°33′ W **98**
Kolyuchinskaya Guba 66°38′ N, 178°0′ W **98**
Kolyvan', *Russ.* 51°19′ N, 82°42′ E **184**
Kôm Dafana, ruin(s), *Egypt* 30°50′ N, 32°7′ E **194**
Kôm Ombo, *Egypt* 24°27′ N, 32°55′ E **182**
Kom, peak, *Bulg.* 43°9′ N, 23°1′ E **168**
Komádi, *Hung.* 47°0′ N, 21°30′ E **168**
Komagane, *Japan* 35°44′ N, 137°56′ E **201**
Komagvær, *Nor.* 70°14′ N, 30°36′ E **152**
Komandorskiye Ostrova (Commander Islands), *Bering Sea* 53°42′ N, 162°31′ E **160**
Komarne, *Ukr.* 49°37′ N, 23°41′ E **152**
Komárno, *Slovakia* 47°46′ N, 18°7′ E **168**
Komárom, *Hung.* 47°44′ N, 18°7′ E **168**
Komárom-Esztergom, adm. division, *Hung.* 47°45′ N, 17°55′ E **156**
Komarovo, *Russ.* 59°33′ N, 50°18′ E **154**
Komatipoort, *S. Af.* 25°26′ S, 31°56′ E **227**
Komatsu, *Japan* 36°24′ N, 136°28′ E **201**
Komatsushima, *Japan* 33°59′ N, 134°34′ E **201**
Komba, *Dem. Rep. of the Congo* 2°52′ N, 24°3′ E **224**
Komenotsu, *Japan* 32°6′ N, 130°20′ E **201**
Komi, adm. division, *Russ.* 63°40′ N, 52°9′ E **154**
Komi-Permyak, adm. division, *Russ.* 60°27′ N, 52°55′ E **169**
Komiža, *Croatia* 43°2′ N, 16°5′ E **168**
Komló, *Hung.* 46°10′ N, 18°16′ E **168**
Komodo, island, *Indonesia* 9°13′ S, 119°17′ E **230**
Komoé, river, *Africa* 9°15′ N, 4°13′ W **222**
Komoé, river, *Côte d'Ivoire* 5°40′ N, 3°23′ W **222**
Komoro, *Japan* 36°19′ N, 138°26′ E **201**
Komotini, *Gr.* 41°7′ N, 25°24′ E **156**
Komovi, peak, *Mont.* 42°40′ N, 19°37′ E **168**
Kompong Chhnang, *Cambodia* 12°15′ N, 104°39′ E **202**
Kompong Speu, *Cambodia* 11°24′ N, 104°29′ E **202**
Kompong Sralao, *Cambodia* 14°5′ N, 105°45′ E **202**
Kompong Trach, *Cambodia* 10°34′ N, 104°27′ E **202**
Komsa, *Russ.* 61°45′ N, 89°19′ E **169**
Komses'yegan, *Russ.* 61°16′ N, 83°32′ E **169**
Komsomol, *Kaz.* 47°26′ N, 53°40′ E **158**
Komsomolets, *Kaz.* 53°47′ N, 62°3′ E **154**
Komsomolets, Ostrov, island, *Russ.* 81°49′ N, 109°24′ E **246**
Komsomolets Shyghanaghy 45°19′ N, 52°3′ E **158**
Komsomol'sk, *Russ.* 57°2′ N, 40°16′ E **154**
Komsomol'sk na Amure, *Russ.* 50°30′ N, 136°57′ E **190**
Komsomol'skiy, *Russ.* 69°5′ N, 172°43′ E **173**
Komsomol'skoe, *Kaz.* 50°26′ N, 60°27′ E **158**
Komsomol'skoy Pravdy, Ostrova, islands, *Laptev Sea* 76°50′ N, 108°45′ E **160**
Komsomol'skoye, *Russ.* 50°45′ N, 46°59′ E **158**
Komu, *Fin.* 63°40′ N, 26°8′ E **152**
Komusan, *N. Korea* 42°7′ N, 129°41′ E **200**
Kon Tum, *Vietnam* 14°21′ N, 107°59′ E **202**
Kona, *Mali* 14°56′ N, 3°55′ W **222**
Kona, region, *Oceania* 19°25′ N, 155°54′ W **99**
Konakovo, *Russ.* 56°40′ N, 36°47′ E **154**
Konakpınar, *Turk.* 38°54′ N, 37°17′ E **156**
Konarak, *India* 19°53′ N, 86°4′ E **188**
Konawa, *Okla., U.S.* 34°56′ N, 96°44′ W **96**
Konch, *India* 25°58′ N, 79°8′ E **197**
Konda, river, *Russ.* 60°42′ N, 63°22′ E **169**
Kondiás, *Gr.* 39°51′ N, 25°9′ E **156**
Kondoa, *Tanzania* 4°55′ S, 35°48′ E **224**
Kondol', *Russ.* 52°47′ N, 45°5′ E **158**
Kondolole, *Dem. Rep. of the Congo* 1°20′ N, 26°0′ E **224**
Kondopoga, *Russ.* 62°11′ N, 34°22′ E **154**
Kondoz, *Afghan.* 36°47′ N, 68°54′ E **186**
Kondrovo, *Russ.* 54°49′ N, 35°57′ E **154**
Konduga, *Nig.* 11°38′ N, 13°25′ E **216**
Kondukur, *India* 15°11′ N, 79°55′ E **188**
Konergino, *Russ.* 65°57′ N, 178°47′ W **98**
Konetsbor, *Russ.* 64°51′ N, 57°42′ E **154**
Köneürgench, *Turkm.* 42°18′ N, 59°10′ E **180**
Konevo, *Russ.* 62°6′ N, 39°19′ E **154**
Konfara, *Guinea* 11°55′ N, 8°52′ W **222**
Kong, *Côte d'Ivoire* 9°9′ N, 4°38′ W **222**
Kong Christian IX Land, *Den.* 68°38′ N, 33°55′ W **106**
Kong Christian X Land, *Den.* 73°44′ N, 52°49′ W **246**
Kong Frederik VI Kyst, *Den.* 61°32′ N, 52°50′ W **106**
Kong Frederik VIII Land, *Den.* 79°7′ N, 62°48′ W **246**
Kong Karls Land, islands, *Barents Sea* 78°20′ N, 30°46′ E **160**
Kong Kemul, peak, *Indonesia* 1°54′ N, 115°51′ E **192**
Kong, Koh, island, *Cambodia* 11°20′ N, 102°19′ E **202**
Kong, river, *Laos* 15°33′ N, 106°51′ E **202**
Köngäs, *Fin.* 67°52′ N, 24°51′ E **152**
Kongelai, *Kenya* 1°22′ N, 35°1′ E **224**
Konginkangas, *Fin.* 62°45′ N, 25°44′ E **154**
Konglu, *Myanmar* 27°17′ N, 97°56′ E **188**
Kongolo, *Dem. Rep. of the Congo* 5°25′ S, 26°56′ E **224**
Kongor, *Sudan* 7°8′ N, 31°21′ E **224**
Kongsfjord, *Nor.* 70°41′ N, 29°20′ E **152**
Kongsmoen, *Nor.* 64°52′ N, 12°25′ E **152**
Kongur Shan, peak, *China* 38°36′ N, 75°14′ E **184**
Kongwa, *Tanzania* 6°9′ S, 36°26′ E **224**
Konibodom, *Taj.* 40°18′ N, 70°27′ E **197**
Königswinter, *Ger.* 50°40′ N, 7°11′ E **167**
Konin, *Pol.* 52°12′ N, 18°14′ E **152**
Köniz, *Switz.* 46°54′ N, 7°25′ E **167**
Konjic, *Bosn. and Herzg.* 43°38′ N, 17°58′ E **168**
Konjuh, peak, *Bosn. and Herzg.* 44°17′ N, 18°30′ E **168**
Konkouré, river, *Guinea* 10°17′ N, 13°31′ W **222**
Konnur, *India* 16°10′ N, 74°44′ E **188**
Konosha, *Russ.* 60°59′ N, 40°12′ E **154**
Konotop, *Ukr.* 51°12′ N, 33°16′ E **158**
Kon'ovo, *Bulg.* 42°32′ N, 26°10′ E **156**
Konta, *India* 17°48′ N, 81°22′ E **188**
Kontagora, *Nig.* 10°21′ N, 5°29′ E **222**
Kontcha, *Cameroon* 7°54′ N, 12°13′ E **218**
Kontiomäki, *Fin.* 64°20′ N, 28°4′ E **152**
Konya (Iconium), *Turk.* 37°51′ N, 32°29′ E **156**
Konz, *Ger.* 49°41′ N, 6°36′ E **163**
Konza, *Kenya* 1°47′ S, 37°7′ E **224**
Koocanusa, Lake, *Can.* 49°4′ N, 115°56′ W **108**
Ko'oko'olau, peak, *Hawai'i, U.S.* 19°36′ N, 155°37′ W **99**
Koopmansfontein, *S. Af.* 28°15′ S, 24°3′ E **227**
Koosa, *Est.* 58°30′ N, 27°2′ E **166**
Koostatak, *Can.* 51°25′ N, 97°22′ W **90**
Kootenai, *Idaho, U.S.* 48°17′ N, 116°33′ W **108**
Kootenay Lake, *Can.* 49°44′ N, 116°47′ W **108**
Kow, *Mauritania* 15°54′ N, 12°47′ W **222**
Kopaonik, mountains, *Kos.* 43°15′ N, 20°50′ E **156**
Kópasker, *Ice.* 66°21′ N, 16°31′ W **246**
Köpbirlik, *Kaz.* 46°27′ N, 77°12′ E **184**
Köpekkayası Burnu, *Turk.* 41°56′ N, 31°52′ E **156**
Köpenick, *Ger.* 52°27′ N, 13°33′ E **152**
Kopetdag Mountains, *Iran* 38°27′ N, 55°37′ E **180**
Kopeysk, *Russ.* 55°5′ N, 61°36′ E **154**
Köping, *Nor.* 59°29′ N, 15°58′ E **152**
Kopište, island, *Croatia* 42°41′ N, 16°33′ E **168**
Koplik, *Alban.* 42°12′ N, 19°26′ E **168**
Koporskiy Zaliv 59°47′ N, 28°26′ E **166**
Koppang, *Nor.* 61°33′ N, 11°3′ E **152**
Kopparberg, *Nor.* 59°52′ N, 15°0′ E **152**
Kopperå, *Nor.* 63°23′ N, 11°53′ E **152**
Koprivnica, *Croatia* 46°10′ N, 16°50′ E **168**
Kõpu, *Est.* 58°54′ N, 22°11′ E **166**
Kop'ung, *N. Korea* 40°35′ N, 125°55′ E **200**
Kopylovka, *Russ.* 58°39′ N, 82°19′ E **169**
Kora National Park, *Kenya* 0°29′ N, 38°18′ E **224**
Korab, Mal, *Alban.* 41°43′ N, 20°27′ E **168**
K'orahē, *Eth.* 6°35′ N, 44°11′ E **218**
Korba, *India* 22°22′ N, 82°44′ E **197**
Korba, *Tun.* 36°35′ N, 10°51′ E **156**
Korbach, *Ger.* 51°16′ N, 8°51′ E **167**
Korbevac, *Serb.* 42°34′ N, 22°2′ E **168**
Korbol, *Chad* 10°1′ N, 17°42′ E **216**
Korbovo, *Serb.* 44°31′ N, 22°42′ E **168**
Korçë, *Alban.* 40°37′ N, 20°47′ E **143**
Korčula, *Croatia* 42°56′ N, 17°7′ E **156**
Korčula, island, *Croatia* 42°52′ N, 16°25′ E **168**
Korčulanski Kanal 42°59′ N, 16°23′ E **168**
Korday, *Kaz.* 43°3′ N, 74°42′ E **184**
Koré Mayroua, *Niger* 13°23′ N, 3°53′ E **222**
Korea, North 40°12′ N, 126°16′ E **200**
Korea, South 36°43′ N, 127°7′ E **200**
Korea Strait (Tsushima Strait) 34°9′ N, 125°22′ E **190**
Korem, *Eth.* 12°28′ N, 39°31′ E **182**
Korenevo, *Russ.* 51°23′ N, 34°59′ E **158**
Korenovsk, *Russ.* 45°31′ N, 39°27′ E **156**
Korepino, *Russ.* 61°4′ N, 57°5′ E **154**
Korets', *Ukr.* 50°37′ N, 27°7′ E **152**
Korf, *Russ.* 60°20′ N, 165°42′ E **173**
Korgon, *Kyrg.* 39°51′ N, 70°5′ E **197**
Korhogo, *Côte d'Ivoire* 9°26′ N, 5°39′ W **222**
Korinthiakós Kólpos 38°23′ N, 21°36′ E **156**
Kórinthos, *Gr.* 37°52′ N, 22°55′ E **180**
Kőris Hegy, peak, *Hung.* 47°16′ N, 17°43′ E **168**
Korita, *Bosn. and Herzg.* 43°2′ N, 18°29′ E **168**
Kōriyama, *Japan* 37°23′ N, 140°22′ E **201**
Korkino, *Russ.* 54°53′ N, 61°27′ E **154**
Korkuteli, *Turk.* 37°4′ N, 30°12′ E **156**
Korla, *China* 41°41′ N, 86°14′ E **184**
Korliki, *Russ.* 61°30′ N, 82°27′ E **169**
Kormakitis, *Northern Cyprus, Cyprus* 35°20′ N, 33°0′ E **194**
Kormakitis, Cape, *Northern Cyprus, Cyprus* 35°22′ N, 32°42′ E **194**
Körmend, *Hung.* 47°0′ N, 16°37′ E **168**
Kornaka, *Niger* 14°8′ N, 6°55′ E **222**
Kornilovo, *Russ.* 53°31′ N, 81°13′ E **184**
Koro, *Côte d'Ivoire* 8°29′ N, 7°26′ W **222**
Koro Kidinga, spring, *Chad* 16°58′ N, 16°56′ E **216**
Korocha, *Russ.* 50°48′ N, 37°12′ E **158**
Korogwe, *Tanzania* 5°8′ S, 38°29′ E **224**
Koronadal, *Philippines* 6°21′ N, 124°46′ E **203**
Koronga, *Mali* 15°21′ N, 7°37′ W **222**
Koronga, Mont, peak, *Togo* 9°2′ N, 1°10′ E **222**
Korónos, *Gr.* 37°7′ N, 25°33′ E **156**
Koror, *Palau* 7°20′ N, 134°30′ E **242**
Körösladany, *Hung.* 46°58′ N, 21°4′ E **168**
Korosozero, *Russ.* 63°41′ N, 35°21′ E **154**
Korosten', *Ukr.* 50°55′ N, 28°45′ E **152**
Korotoyak, *Russ.* 50°59′ N, 39°10′ E **158**
Korpela, *Russ.* 66°14′ N, 30°1′ E **152**
Korpilahti, *Fin.* 62°0′ N, 25°31′ E **166**
Korpilombolo, *Nor.* 66°51′ N, 23°1′ E **152**
Korpisalmi, *Fin.* 63°57′ N, 29°37′ E **152**
Korpisel'kya, *Russ.* 62°19′ N, 30°58′ E **152**
Korpo, *Fin.* 60°9′ N, 21°32′ E **166**
Korsakov, *Russ.* 46°44′ N, 142°58′ E **190**
Korshiv, *Ukr.* 48°37′ N, 24°59′ E **152**
Korsnäs, *Fin.* 62°46′ N, 21°9′ E **152**
Korsnes, *Nor.* 70°12′ N, 23°15′ E **152**
Korsnes, *Nor.* 68°14′ N, 16°1′ E **152**
Korsør, *Den.* 55°18′ N, 11°11′ E **152**
Korsze, *Pol.* 54°9′ N, 21°8′ E **166**
Korti, *Sudan* 18°1′ N, 31°35′ E **182**
Kortkeros, *Russ.* 61°49′ N, 51°38′ E **154**
Kortrijk, *Belg.* 50°49′ N, 3°17′ E **163**
Korup National Park, *Cameroon* 5°10′ N, 9°15′ E **222**
Korvatunturi, peak, *Fin.* 68°3′ N, 29°10′ E **152**
Koryakskiy, *Russia* 60°0′ N, 165°0′ E **160**
Koryakskoye Nagor'ye, *Russ.* 60°46′ N, 165°33′ E **160**
Koryazhma, *Russ.* 61°16′ N, 47°15′ E **154**
Korytnitsi, *Belarus* 53°52′ N, 29°26′ E **166**
Kos, *Gr.* 36°53′ N, 27°17′ E **156**
Kosa, *Eth.* 7°50′ N, 36°49′ E **218**
Kosa, *Russ.* 59°57′ N, 55°1′ E **154**
Kosan, *N. Korea* 38°50′ N, 127°25′ E **200**
Kosaya Gora, *Russ.* 54°5′ N, 37°29′ E **154**
Kosciusko, *Miss., U.S.* 33°2′ N, 89°35′ W **103**
Kosciuszko, Mount, *Austral.* 36°30′ S, 148°2′ E **230**

Log Lane Village, Colo., U.S. 40°15′ N, 103°52′ W 90
Loga, Niger 13°33′ N, 3°21′ E 222
Logan, Iowa, U.S. 41°38′ N, 95°48′ W 90
Logan, Kans., U.S. 39°39′ N, 99°34′ W 90
Logan, N. Mex., U.S. 35°21′ N, 103°25′ W 92
Logan, Ohio, U.S. 39°32′ N, 82°24′ W 102
Logan, Utah, U.S. 41°44′ N, 111°48′ W 82
Logan, Mount, peak, Ariz., U.S. 36°20′ N, 113°16′ W 92
Logan, Mount, peak, Can. 60°37′ N, 140°32′ W 98
Logan, Mount, peak, Can. 48°52′ N, 66°44′ W 111
Logan, Mount, peak, Wash., U.S. 48°31′ N, 120°59′ W 100
Logan Pass, Mont., U.S. 48°41′ N, 113°42′ W 90
Logandale, Nev., U.S. 36°35′ N, 114°30′ W 101
Logăneşti, Mold. 46°55′ N, 28°32′ E 158
Logansport, Ind., U.S. 40°44′ N, 86°21′ W 102
Logansport, La., U.S. 31°57′ N, 94°1′ W 103
Logashkino, Russ. 70°49′ N, 153°44′ E 173
Loge, river, Angola 7°44′ S, 13°12′ E 220
Logone Birni, Cameroon 11°46′ N, 15°2′ E 216
Logoniégué, Burkina Faso 9°54′ N, 4°33′ W 222
Logoualé, Côte d'Ivoire 7°3′ N, 7°33′ W 222
Logroño, Sp. 42°26′ N, 2°27′ W 164
Logrosán, Sp. 39°20′ N, 5°30′ W 164
Løgstør, Den. 56°56′ N, 9°14′ E 150
Loharano, Madagascar 21°45′ S, 48°9′ E 220
Lohardaga, India 23°24′ N, 84°41′ E 197
Loharghat, India 25°57′ N, 91°26′ E 197
Loharu, India 28°26′ N, 75°49′ E 197
Lohatlha, S. Af. 28°3′ S, 23°2′ E 227
Lohikoski, Fin. 61°36′ N, 28°42′ E 166
Lohiniva, Fin. 67°9′ N, 24°58′ E 152
Lohja (Lojo), Fin. 60°14′ N, 24°1′ E 166
Lôho, Côte d'Ivoire 8°38′ N, 5°9′ W 222
Lohr, Ger. 49°59′ N, 9°33′ E 167
Lohusuu, Est. 58°55′ N, 27°0′ E 166
Loi Mwe, Myanmar 21°9′ N, 99°46′ E 202
Loi, Phou, peak, Laos 20°17′ N, 103°5′ E 202
Loiano, It. 44°16′ N, 11°18′ E 167
Loikaw, Myanmar 19°42′ N, 97°10′ E 202
Loile, river, Dem. Rep. of the Congo 1°11′ S, 20°17′ E 218
Loimaa, Fin. 60°49′ N, 23°1′ E 166
Loir, river, Fr. 48°13′ N, 1°17′ E 163
Loire, river, Fr. 46°26′ N, 3°56′ E 165
Loire, river, Fr. 46°48′ N, 1°52′ W 142
Loire, river, Fr. 45°9′ N, 3°58′ E 165
Loire, river, Fr. 48°16′ N, 2°37′ E 165
Loja, Ecua. 4°1′ S, 79°13′ W 130
Loja, Sp. 37°9′ N, 4°9′ W 164
Lojo see Lohja, Fin. 60°14′ N, 24°1′ E 166
Loka, Sudan 4°15′ N, 30°57′ E 224
Lokachi, Ukr. 50°44′ N, 24°38′ E 152
Lokalahti, Fin. 60°40′ N, 21°28′ E 166
Lokandu, Dem. Rep. of the Congo 2°34′ S, 25°45′ E 224
Lokchim, river, Russ. 61°36′ N, 51°43′ E 154
Lokeren, Belg. 51°5′ N, 4°0′ E 163
Lokhwabe, Botswana 24°9′ S, 21°50′ E 227
Lokichokio, Kenya 4°13′ N, 34°20′ E 224
Lokila, Sudan 4°38′ N, 32°26′ E 224
Lokitaung, Kenya 4°12′ N, 35°45′ E 224
Lokka, Fin. 67°47′ N, 27°40′ E 152
Løkken, Nor. 63°5′ N, 9°42′ E 152
Loknya, Russ. 56°50′ N, 30°10′ E 166
Lokoja, Nig. 7°45′ N, 6°41′ E 222
Lokolama, Dem. Rep. of the Congo 2°36′ S, 19°51′ E 218
Lokolenge, Dem. Rep. of the Congo 1°9′ N, 22°36′ E 218
Lokomo, Cameroon 2°52′ N, 15°17′ E 218
Lökösháza, Hung. 46°25′ N, 21°14′ E 168
Lokossa, Benin 6°39′ N, 1°40′ E 222
Loks Land, island, Can. 62°9′ N, 64°30′ W 106
Loksa, Est. 59°33′ N, 25°45′ E 166
Lokutu, Dem. Rep. of the Congo 1°5′ N, 23°36′ E 224
Lokwakangole, Kenya 3°26′ N, 35°50′ E 224
Lol, river, Sudan 8°56′ N, 26°15′ E 224
Lol, river, Sudan 8°48′ N, 28°36′ E 224
Loleta, Calif., U.S. 40°38′ N, 124°14′ W 90
Lolgorien, Kenya 1°14′ S, 34°48′ E 224
Lolimi, Sudan 4°34′ N, 34°2′ E 224
Loliondo, Tanzania 2°3′ S, 35°39′ E 224
Lollar, Ger. 50°38′ N, 8°43′ E 167
Lolo, Mount, peak, Can. 50°48′ N, 120°12′ W 90
Lolo Pass, Idaho, U.S. 46°37′ N, 114°36′ W 90
Lolobau, island, P.N.G. 4°51′ S, 150°14′ E 192
Lolowau, Indonesia 0°57′ N, 97°33′ E 196
Lom, Bulg. 43°49′ N, 23°13′ E 168
Lom, Nor. 61°50′ N, 8°31′ E 152
Lom Sak, Thai. 16°47′ N, 101°7′ E 202
Loma Mountains, Sierra Leone 9°5′ N, 11°27′ W 222
Lomami, river, Dem. Rep. of the Congo 0°47′ N, 24°17′ E 224
Lomami, river, Dem. Rep. of the Congo 4°35′ S, 24°49′ E 224
Lomami, river, Dem. Rep. of the Congo 7°19′ S, 25°26′ E 224
Lomas del Real, Mex. 22°30′ N, 97°55′ W 114
Lombarda, Serra, Braz. 3°17′ N, 51°55′ W 130
Lombardy, adm. division, It. 45°33′ N, 9°3′ E 167
Lombez, Fr. 43°28′ N, 0°52′ E 164
Lomblen, island, Indonesia 8°58′ S, 123°36′ E 192
Lombok, island, Indonesia 9°26′ S, 115°17′ E 192
Lomé, Togo 6°10′ N, 1°7′ E 222
Lomela, Dem. Rep. of the Congo 2°19′ S, 23°17′ E 218
Lomela, river, Dem. Rep. of the Congo 0°35′ N, 21°5′ E 218
Lometa, Tex., U.S. 31°12′ N, 98°24′ W 92
Lomié, Cameroon 3°21′ N, 13°37′ E 218
Lomira, Wis., U.S. 43°35′ N, 88°27′ W 102
Lommel, Belg. 51°13′ N, 5°18′ E 167
Lomond, Ben, peak, U.K. 56°10′ N, 4°44′ W 150
Lomonosov, Russ. 59°51′ N, 29°42′ E 166
Lomonosov Ridge, Arctic Ocean 88°59′ N, 116°17′ W 255
Lomovoye, Russ. 64°2′ N, 40°38′ E 154
Lomphat, Cambodia 13°39′ N, 106°57′ E 202
Lompoc, Calif., U.S. 34°39′ N, 120°28′ W 100
Łomża, Pol. 53°10′ N, 22°5′ E 152
Lon, Hon, island, Vietnam 12°32′ N, 109°26′ E 202
Lonauli, India 18°43′ N, 73°24′ E 188
Londinières, Fr. 49°50′ N, 1°24′ E 163
London, Can. 42°59′ N, 81°13′ W 102
London, Ohio, U.S. 39°52′ N, 83°27′ W 102
London, U.K. 51°31′ N, 0°9′ E 162
Londonderry, U.K. 54°58′ N, 7°16′ W 143
Londonderry, Vt., U.S. 43°13′ N, 72°49′ W 104
Londonderry, Isla, island, Chile 55°33′ S, 72°31′ W 248
Londres, Arg. 27°43′ S, 67°9′ W 132
Londrina, Braz. 23°18′ S, 51°11′ W 138
Lone Pine, Calif., U.S. 36°36′ N, 118°5′ W 101
Lone Star, Tex., U.S. 32°55′ N, 94°44′ W 103
Lonely Bay 61°39′ N, 115°31′ W 108
Lonepine, Mont., U.S. 47°40′ N, 114°40′ W 90
Long Barn, Calif., U.S. 38°5′ N, 120°9′ W 100
Long Bay Cays, islands, North Atlantic Ocean 23°49′ N, 77°0′ W 116
Long Beach, Calif., U.S. 33°46′ N, 118°12′ W 101
Long Beach, Miss., U.S. 30°20′ N, 89°10′ W 103
Long Beach, N.Y., U.S. 40°35′ N, 73°40′ W 104
Long Beach, Wash., U.S. 46°20′ N, 124°3′ W 100
Long Branch, N.J., U.S. 40°18′ N, 74°1′ W 94
Long Branch, Tex., U.S. 32°4′ N, 94°35′ W 103
Long Cay (Fortune Island), Bahamas 22°35′ N, 76°5′ W 116
Long Creek, Oreg., U.S. 44°41′ N, 119°7′ W 90
Long Creek, river, North America 49°3′ N, 103°40′ W 90
Long Eaton, U.K. 52°53′ N, 1°17′ W 162
Long Island, Austral. 22°4′ S, 148°43′ E 230
Long Island, Bahamas 23°4′ N, 74°52′ W 116
Long Island, Can. 44°23′ N, 81°10′ W 106
Long Island, Can. 44°20′ N, 67°13′ W 80
Long Island, N.Y., U.S. 40°58′ N, 73°14′ W 104
Long Island, P.N.G. 5°35′ S, 146°13′ E 192
Long Island Sound 41°5′ N, 73°6′ W 104
Long Key, island, Fla., U.S. 24°47′ N, 80°49′ W 105
Long Lake, Can. 49°20′ N, 87°26′ W 110
Long Meg, ruin(s), U.K. 54°43′ N, 2°42′ W 162
Long Melford, U.K. 52°4′ N, 0°43′ E 162
Long Point, Can. 42°30′ N, 80°6′ W 94
Long Point, Can. 54°13′ N, 58°6′ W 111
Long Point, Can. 48°45′ N, 59°26′ W 111
Long Point, Can. 53°2′ N, 98°26′ W 108
Long Pond, lake, Mass., U.S. 41°47′ N, 71°5′ W 104
Long Prairie, Minn., U.S. 45°57′ N, 94°52′ W 90
Long Sutton, U.K. 52°46′ N, 0°7′ E 162
Long Xuyen, Vietnam 10°19′ N, 105°18′ E 192
Longa, Angola 14°43′ S, 18°30′ E 220
Longa, Proliv 70°18′ N, 174°28′ E 160
Long'an, China 23°7′ N, 107°39′ E 198
Longares, Sp. 41°23′ N, 1°10′ W 164
Longarone, It. 46°16′ N, 12°17′ E 167
Longboat Key, Fla., U.S. 27°26′ N, 82°40′ W 105
Longbranch, Wash., U.S. 47°11′ N, 122°46′ W 100
Longchuan, China 24°4′ N, 115°17′ E 198
Longde, China 35°37′ N, 106°6′ E 198
Longfellow Mountains, Me., U.S. 44°27′ N, 71°10′ W 104
Longford, Ire. 53°43′ N, 7°49′ W 150
Longhai, China 24°19′ N, 117°51′ E 198
Longhua, China 41°21′ N, 117°47′ E 198
Longhurst, N.C., U.S. 36°25′ N, 78°59′ W 96
Longhurst, Mount, peak, Antarctica 79°19′ S, 158°10′ E 248
Longjiang, China 47°23′ N, 123°13′ E 198
Longjing see Yanji, China 42°46′ N, 129°24′ E 200
Longju, India 28°38′ N, 93°31′ E 188
Longkou, China 37°42′ N, 120°25′ E 198
Longlac, Can. 49°47′ N, 86°32′ W 110
Longleaf, La., U.S. 30°59′ N, 92°34′ W 103
Longli, China 26°30′ N, 106°57′ E 198
Longlin, China 24°47′ N, 105°19′ E 198
Longmeadow, Mass., U.S. 42°3′ N, 72°35′ W 104
Longmen, China 23°43′ N, 114°15′ E 198
Longmont, Colo., U.S. 40°10′ N, 105°2′ W 106
Longnan, China 24°49′ N, 114°49′ E 198
Longobucco, It. 39°27′ N, 16°37′ E 156
Longonot, peak, Kenya 0°54′ N, 36°22′ E 224
Longquan, China 28°6′ N, 119°7′ E 198
Longrais, Lac, lake, Can. 54°10′ N, 68°48′ W 111
Longs Peak, Colo., U.S. 40°14′ N, 105°41′ W 90
Longshan, China 29°28′ N, 109°28′ E 198
Longstreet, La., U.S. 32°4′ N, 93°57′ W 103
Longtam, Sudan 8°55′ N, 30°44′ E 224
Longueuil, Can. 45°31′ N, 73°30′ W 94
Longuyon, Fr. 49°26′ N, 5°35′ E 163
Longview, N.C., U.S. 35°44′ N, 81°23′ W 96
Longview, Tex., U.S. 32°29′ N, 94°44′ W 103
Longview, Wash., U.S. 46°7′ N, 122°57′ W 100
Longville, La., U.S. 30°35′ N, 93°15′ W 103
Longwy, Fr. 49°31′ N, 5°45′ E 163
Longxi, China 35°1′ N, 104°36′ E 198
Longxian, China 34°53′ N, 106°48′ E 198
Longyan, China 25°4′ N, 117°0′ E 198
Longyearbyen, Nor. 78°10′ N, 15°34′ E 160
Long"yugan, Russ. 64°54′ N, 71°25′ E 169
Longzhen, China 48°41′ N, 126°49′ E 198
Longzhou, China 22°23′ N, 106°48′ E 198
Löningen, Ger. 52°44′ N, 7°45′ E 163
Łoniów, Pol. 50°32′ N, 21°31′ E 152
Lonjica, Croatia 45°50′ N, 16°20′ E 168
Lonkala, Dem. Rep. of the Congo 4°38′ S, 23°15′ E 218
Lonquimay, Arg. 36°30′ S, 63°37′ W 139
Lønsdal, Nor. 66°44′ N, 15°25′ E 152
Lons-le-Saunier, Fr. 46°40′ N, 5°32′ E 150
Loogootee, Ind., U.S. 38°40′ N, 86°54′ W 102
Lookeba, Okla., U.S. 35°20′ N, 98°22′ W 92
Lookout, Cape, Alas., U.S. 54°54′ N, 133°53′ W 108
Lookout, Cape, Antarctica 62°6′ S, 55°18′ W 248
Lookout, Cape, N.C., U.S. 34°30′ N, 76°32′ W 96
Lookout, Cape, U.S. 45°8′ N, 124°8′ W 90
Lookout Mountain, peak, Can. 53°35′ N, 64°13′ W 111
Lookout Mountain, peak, N. Mex., U.S. 35°12′ N, 108°21′ W 92
Lookout Mountain, peak, Oreg., U.S. 45°19′ N, 121°37′ W 90
Lookout, Point, Mich., U.S. 44°3′ N, 83°35′ W 102
Loolmalasin, peak, Tanzania 3°3′ S, 35°45′ E 224
Loon Lake, Can. 54°2′ N, 109°9′ W 108
Loon Lake, N.Y., U.S. 44°32′ N, 74°4′ W 104
Loon, Pointe, Can. 51°52′ N, 78°39′ W 110
Loon, river, Can. 56°33′ N, 115°24′ W 108
Lop, China 37°6′ N, 80°6′ E 184
Lop Buri, Thai. 14°49′ N, 100°36′ E 202
Lop Nur, lake, China 40°35′ N, 89°42′ E 188
Lopare, Bosn. and Herzg. 44°38′ N, 18°48′ E 168
Lopatin, Russ. 43°50′ N, 47°40′ E 195
Lopatino, Russ. 52°36′ N, 45°49′ E 158
Lopatka, Mys, Russ. 51°8′ N, 156°37′ E 160
Lopatyn, Ukr. 50°11′ N, 24°48′ E 152
Lope Reserve, Gabon 0°38′ N, 11°20′ E 206
Lopera, Sp. 37°57′ N, 4°13′ W 164
Loperot, Kenya 2°17′ N, 35°51′ E 224
Lopez, Wash., U.S. 48°30′ N, 122°54′ W 100
López Collada, Mex. 31°40′ N, 113°59′ W 92
Lopez Lake, Calif., U.S. 35°12′ N, 120°34′ W 101
Lopez Point, Calif., U.S. 35°57′ N, 121°42′ W 100
Lopi, Congo 2°55′ N, 16°39′ E 218
Loppa, Nor. 70°19′ N, 21°26′ E 152
Lopphavet 70°9′ N, 18°9′ E 160
Loppi, Fin. 60°41′ N, 24°24′ E 166
Lopshen'ga, Russ. 64°59′ N, 37°25′ E 154
Lopud, island, Croatia 42°37′ N, 17°49′ E 168
Lopydino, Russ. 61°8′ N, 52°8′ E 154
Lora del Río, Sp. 37°39′ N, 5°33′ W 164
Lorain, Ohio, U.S. 41°26′ N, 82°11′ W 102
Loralai, Pak. 30°21′ N, 68°39′ E 186
Lorca, Sp. 37°40′ N, 1°42′ W 164
Lorch, Ger. 50°2′ N, 7°48′ E 167
Lord Howe Island, Austral. 31°31′ S, 156°53′ E 230
Lord Howe Rise, Tasman Sea 33°48′ S, 163°25′ E 252
Lord Loughborough, island, Myanmar 10°28′ N, 96°37′ E 202
Lord Mayor Bay 69°41′ N, 94°10′ W 106
Lord, river, Can. 50°52′ N, 123°36′ W 90
Lordsburg, N. Mex., U.S. 32°21′ N, 108°42′ W 92
Lore Lindu National Park, Indonesia 1°40′ S, 119°48′ E 238
Loreauville, La., U.S. 30°2′ N, 91°45′ W 103
Lorena, Braz. 22°46′ S, 45°6′ W 138
Lorengau, P.N.G. 2°6′ S, 147°14′ E 192
Lorenzo, Idaho, U.S. 43°43′ N, 111°53′ W 90
Lorenzo, Tex., U.S. 33°38′ N, 101°32′ W 92
Lorenzo Geyres, Uru. 32°2′ S, 57°51′ W 139
Loreo, It. 45°3′ N, 12°10′ E 167
Loreto, Bol. 15°16′ S, 64°39′ W 137
Loreto, Braz. 7°5′ S, 45°9′ W 132
Loreto, Ecua. 0°44′ N, 77°21′ W 136
Loreto, Mex. 22°16′ N, 101°58′ W 114
Loreto, Philippines 10°22′ N, 125°35′ E 203
Loreto, adm. division, Peru 3°3′ S, 74°42′ W 136
Loretto, Tenn., U.S. 35°3′ N, 87°26′ W 96
Lorian Swamp, marsh, Kenya 0°52′ N, 39°6′ E 224
Lorica, Col. 9°14′ N, 75°50′ W 136
Lőrinci, Hung. 47°44′ N, 19°41′ E 168
Loriol, Fr. 44°45′ N, 4°49′ E 150
Loris, S.C., U.S. 34°3′ N, 78°54′ W 96
Loriu Plateau, Kenya 1°51′ N, 36°13′ E 224
Lorman, Miss., U.S. 31°48′ N, 91°3′ W 103
Lormi, India 22°17′ N, 81°40′ E 197
Lornel, Pointe de, Fr. 50°34′ N, 1°24′ E 163
Loro, Col. 2°11′ N, 69°33′ W 136
Lorraine, adm. division, Fr. 48°37′ N, 5°1′ E 150
Lorraine, region, Fr. 49°50′ N, 4°47′ E 167
Lorukumu, Kenya 2°50′ N, 35°12′ E 224
Lorup, Ger. 52°55′ N, 7°38′ E 163
Los, Nor. 61°43′ N, 15°8′ E 152
Los Alamos, Calif., U.S. 34°44′ N, 120°18′ W 100
Los Alamos, N. Mex., U.S. 35°52′ N, 106°19′ W 92
Los Alerces National Park, Arg. 42°54′ S, 72°10′ W 122
Los Altos, Calif., U.S. 37°21′ N, 122°9′ W 100
Los Amores, Arg. 28°6′ S, 60°0′ W 139
Los Angeles, Calif., U.S. 34°3′ N, 118°16′ W 101
Los Ángeles, Chile 37°28′ S, 72°22′ W 134
Los Banos, Calif., U.S. 37°3′ N, 120°52′ W 100
Los Barrios, Sp. 36°11′ N, 5°30′ W 164
Los Blancos, Arg. 23°34′ S, 62°38′ W 132
Los Dolores, Sp. 37°38′ N, 1°1′ W 150
Los Frentones, Arg. 26°24′ S, 61°27′ W 139
Los Glaciares National Park, Arg. 50°6′ S, 73°33′ W 122
Los Hermanos, islands, Caribbean Sea 11°55′ N, 64°25′ W 116
Los, Îles de, islands, North Atlantic Ocean 9°5′ N, 13°56′ W 222
Los Juries, Arg. 28°27′ S, 62°7′ W 139
Los Katios National Park, Col. 7°35′ N, 77°6′ W 136
Los Lagos, adm. division, Chile 41°7′ S, 73°59′ W 134
Los Lavaderos, Mex. 23°27′ N, 98°3′ W 114
Los Loros, Chile 27°51′ S, 70°10′ W 132
Los Mármoles National Park, Mex. 20°47′ N, 99°35′ W 72
Los Mochis, Mex. 25°45′ N, 109°0′ W 112
Los Monjes, Islas, islands, Caribbean Sea 12°0′ N, 71°6′ W 116
Los Monos, ruin(s), Mex. 18°9′ N, 100°30′ W 114
Los Ojos, N. Mex., U.S. 36°43′ N, 106°34′ W 92
Los Olivos, Calif., U.S. 34°40′ N, 120°8′ W 100
Los Organos, Mex. 23°43′ N, 103°51′ W 114
Los Osos, Calif., U.S. 35°18′ N, 120°51′ W 100
Los Palacios, Cuba 22°35′ N, 83°15′ W 116
Los Pirpintos, Arg. 26°10′ S, 62°4′ W 139
Los Remedios, Mex. 24°34′ N, 106°25′ W 114
Los Remedios National Park, Mex. 19°28′ N, 99°23′ W 112
Los Reyes, Mex. 19°34′ N, 102°29′ W 114
Los Reyes Islands, South Pacific Ocean 1°51′ S, 147°45′ E 192
Los Ríos, adm. division, Chile 40°14′ S, 72°40′ W 134
Los Roques, Islas, islands, Caribbean Sea 12°4′ N, 66°32′ W 116
Los Santos de Maimona, Sp. 38°27′ N, 6°24′ W 164
Los Telares, Arg. 29°1′ S, 63°27′ W 139
Los Teques, Venez. 10°21′ N, 67°3′ W 136
Los Vilos, Chile 31°55′ S, 71°31′ W 134
Los Yébenes, Sp. 39°34′ N, 3°53′ W 164
Losada, river, Col. 2°19′ N, 74°30′ W 136
Losap Atoll 6°37′ N, 153°19′ E 192
Losha, Belarus 53°26′ N, 27°23′ E 152
Łosice, Pol. 52°11′ N, 22°43′ E 158
Losinoborskaya, Russ. 58°24′ N, 89°23′ E 169
Łoski, Pol. 53°55′ N, 23°24′ E 166
Lost Hills, Calif., U.S. 35°36′ N, 119°42′ W 100
Lost River Range, Idaho, U.S. 44°20′ N, 113°53′ W 90
Lost Springs, Wyo., U.S. 42°45′ N, 104°57′ W 90
Lost Trail Pass, Mont., U.S. 45°39′ N, 113°57′ W 90
Lost World Caverns, site, W. Va., U.S. 37°49′ N, 80°32′ W 96
Lostmans River, Fla., U.S. 25°25′ N, 81°21′ W 105
Lot, river, Fr. 44°28′ N, 3°3′ E 165
Lota, Chile 37°8′ S, 73°9′ W 134
Lotagipi Swamp, marsh, Kenya 4°51′ N, 34°29′ E 224
Lothair, S. Af. 26°24′ S, 30°25′ E 227
Lotilla, river, Sudan 5°40′ N, 32°46′ E 224
Lotmozero, Russ. 68°7′ N, 30°11′ E 152
Loto, Dem. Rep. of the Congo 2°50′ S, 22°29′ E 218
Lott, Tex., U.S. 31°11′ N, 97°2′ W 96
Lotte, Ger. 52°16′ N, 7°56′ E 163
Lou, island, P.N.G. 2°42′ S, 146°53′ E 192
Louangphrabang, Laos 19°51′ N, 102°6′ E 202
Louann, Ark., U.S. 33°22′ N, 92°48′ W 103
Loubet Coast, Antarctica 67°22′ S, 66°45′ W 248
Loudon, Malawi 12°9′ S, 33°27′ E 224
Loudon, N.H., U.S. 43°17′ N, 71°28′ W 104
Loudonville, Ohio, U.S. 40°37′ N, 82°14′ W 102
Loue, river, Fr. 47°1′ N, 5°29′ E 165
Loufan, China 38°3′ N, 111°46′ E 198
Louga, Côte d'Ivoire 5°4′ N, 6°14′ W 222
Louga, Senegal 15°37′ N, 16°14′ W 222
Louge, Arg. 36°54′ S, 61°39′ W 139
Loughborough, U.K. 52°46′ N, 1°13′ W 162
Lougheed Island, Can. 76°50′ N, 107°36′ W 106
Louin, Miss., U.S. 32°3′ N, 89°16′ W 103
Louis Trichardt (Makhado), S. Af. 23°3′ S, 29°53′ E 227
Louis Ussing, Kap 67°2′ N, 33°5′ W 246
Louisa, Ky., U.S. 38°5′ N, 82°37′ W 94
Louisburg, N.C., U.S. 36°6′ N, 78°18′ W 96
Louise, Miss., U.S. 32°58′ N, 90°36′ W 103
Louise Falls, Can. 60°15′ N, 116°34′ W 108
Louisiade Archipelago, islands, Solomon Sea 12°43′ S, 154°40′ E 238
Louisiade Archipelago, islands, Solomon Sea 12°7′ S, 149°11′ E 192
Louisiana, Mo., U.S. 39°26′ N, 91°4′ W 94
Louisiana, adm. division, La., U.S. 31°7′ N, 93°7′ W 103
Louisiana Point, La., U.S. 29°43′ N, 93°52′ W 103
Louisville, Ill., U.S. 38°45′ N, 88°30′ W 102
Louisville, Ky., U.S. 38°14′ N, 85°46′ W 94
Louisville, Miss., U.S. 33°6′ N, 89°3′ W 103
Louisville, Ohio, U.S. 40°49′ N, 81°16′ W 102
Louisville Ridge, South Pacific Ocean 31°0′ S, 172°30′ W 252
Louis-Xiv, Pointe, Can. 54°27′ N, 79°40′ W 106
Loukhi, Russ. 66°4′ N, 33°0′ E 152
Loukouo, Congo 3°37′ S, 14°39′ E 218
Loulan Yiji, ruin(s), China 40°25′ N, 89°43′ E 188
Loulay, Fr. 46°2′ N, 0°32′ E 150
Loulouni, Mali 10°54′ N, 5°38′ W 222
Loum, Cameroon 4°41′ N, 9°46′ E 222
Lount Lake, Can. 50°6′ N, 94°40′ W 90
Louny, Czech Rep. 50°20′ N, 13°47′ E 152
Loup City, Nebr., U.S. 41°15′ N, 98°59′ W 90
Loup, river, Nebr., U.S. 41°14′ N, 97°58′ W 90
Lourdes, Fr. 43°6′ N, 4°237′ W 164
Lourdes-de-Blanc-Sablon, Can. 51°26′ N, 57°17′ W 106
Louth, U.K. 53°21′ N, 3°179′ W 162
Louviers, Fr. 49°12′ N, 1°9′ E 163
Louza, Tun. 35°3′ N, 10°58′ E 156
Lov Ozero, lake, Russ. 67°55′ N, 35°28′ E 152
Lövånger, Nor. 64°21′ N, 21°17′ E 152
Lovat', river, Russ. 57°29′ N, 31°34′ E 154
Lövberga, Nor. 63°57′ N, 15°49′ E 152
Lovea, Cambodia 13°21′ N, 102°55′ E 202
Lovech, Bulg. 43°8′ N, 24°42′ E 156
Lovech, adm. division, Bulg. 42°53′ N, 24°11′ E 156
Lovelady, Tex., U.S. 31°6′ N, 95°27′ W 103
Loveland Pass, Colo., U.S. 39°39′ N, 105°52′ W 90
Lovell, Me., U.S. 44°7′ N, 70°55′ W 104
Lovell, Wyo., U.S. 44°49′ N, 108°24′ W 90
Lovelock, Nev., U.S. 40°11′ N, 118°29′ W 90
Lovere, It. 45°49′ N, 10°4′ E 167
Loverna, Can. 51°40′ N, 109°58′ W 90
Loves Park, Ill., U.S. 42°18′ N, 89°4′ W 102
Lovilsa see Lovisa, Fin. 60°26′ N, 26°12′ E 166
Loving, N. Mex., U.S. 32°17′ N, 104°6′ W 92
Lovington, N. Mex., U.S. 32°56′ N, 103°21′ W 92
Lovisa (Loviisa), Fin. 60°26′ N, 26°12′ E 166
Lovlya, Russ. 59°55′ N, 49°22′ E 154
Lövő, Hung. 47°29′ N, 16°47′ E 168
Lovozero, Russ. 68°0′ N, 35°2′ E 152
Lovran, Croatia 45°17′ N, 14°15′ E 156
Lovreč, Croatia 43°29′ N, 16°58′ E 168
Lovrin, Rom. 45°58′ N, 20°47′ E 168
Lóvua, Angola 11°38′ S, 23°41′ E 220
Lóvua, Angola 7°19′ S, 20°10′ E 218
Low Bush River, Can. 48°56′ N, 80°10′ W 94
Low, Cape, Can. 62°51′ N, 87°4′ W 106
Low Island, Antarctica 63°21′ S, 61°57′ W 134
Lowa, Dem. Rep. of the Congo 1°25′ S, 25°50′ E 224
Lowa, river, Dem. Rep. of the Congo 1°23′ S, 26°55′ E 224
Lowell, Ind., U.S. 41°16′ N, 87°25′ W 102
Lowell, Mass., U.S. 42°38′ N, 71°20′ W 104
Lowell, Mich., U.S. 42°56′ N, 85°21′ W 102
Lower Arrow Lake, Can. 49°29′ N, 118°56′ W 90
Lower Hutt, N.Z. 41°13′ S, 174°57′ E 240
Lower Matecumbe Key, island, Fla., U.S. 24°50′ N, 80°42′ W 105
Lower Post, Can. 59°57′ N, 128°27′ W 108
Lower Red Lake, Minn., U.S. 48°0′ N, 95°35′ W 94
Lower Saxony, adm. division, Ger. 51°47′ N, 9°27′ E 167
Lower Zambezi National Park, Zambia 15°25′ S, 28°48′ E 224
Lowestoft, U.K. 52°28′ N, 1°43′ E 163
Łowicz, Pol. 52°5′ N, 19°54′ E 152
Lowland, N.C., U.S. 35°18′ N, 76°36′ W 96
Lowry, Minn., U.S. 45°41′ N, 95°32′ W 90
Lowry, Îles, islands, Indian Ocean 12°35′ S, 49°42′ E 220
Lowville, N.Y., U.S. 43°47′ N, 75°30′ W 110
Loxley, Ala., U.S. 30°36′ N, 87°45′ W 103
Loxton, S. Af. 31°30′ S, 22°19′ E 227
Loya, river, Dem. Rep. of the Congo 8°475′ N, 27°45′ E 224
Loyal, Ben, peak, U.K. 58°23′ N, 4°33′ W 150
Loyall, Ky., U.S. 36°50′ N, 83°21′ W 96
Loyalty Islands 20°7′ S, 166°47′ E 238
Loyew, Belarus 51°55′ N, 30°53′ E 158
Loyola, Punta, Arg. 51°48′ S, 68°54′ W 134
Loyoro, Uganda 3°19′ N, 34°13′ E 224
Lozenets, Bulg. 42°12′ N, 27°48′ E 156
Loznica, Serb. 44°31′ N, 19°12′ E 168
Lozova, Ukr. 48°54′ N, 36°19′ E 158
Lozovik, Serb. 44°28′ N, 21°4′ E 168
Loz'va, river, Russ. 61°47′ N, 59°54′ E 154
Lü Tao, island, Taiwan, China 22°30′ N, 121°31′ E 198
Lua Dekere, river, Dem. Rep. of the Congo 3°53′ N, 19°30′ E 218
Lua, river, Dem. Rep. of the Congo 2°49′ N, 18°31′ E 218
Luabo, Mozambique 18°24′ S, 36°8′ E 224
Luacano, Angola 11°11′ S, 21°39′ E 220
Luaha-sibuha, Indonesia 0°30′ N, 98°27′ E 196
Luahiwa Petroglyphs, site, Hawai'i, U.S. 20°47′ N, 156°57′ W 99
Lualaba (Congo), river, Dem. Rep. of the Congo 5°35′ S, 27°7′ E 224
Luama, river, Dem. Rep. of the Congo 4°41′ S, 27°17′ E 224
Luambe National Park, Zambia 12°37′ S, 31°37′ E 224
Luampa, river, Zambia 15°16′ S, 24°38′ E 224
Lu'an, China 31°44′ N, 116°31′ E 198
Luan, river, China 41°27′ N, 117°5′ E 198
Luanda, Angola 8°54′ S, 13°3′ E 218
Luanda, adm. division, Angola 9°17′ S, 12°39′ E 218
Luando, Angola 11°43′ S, 18°33′ E 220
Luando Integral Nature Reserve, Angola 11°24′ S, 16°28′ E 220
Luang, Thale, lake, Thai. 7°24′ N, 99°51′ E 196
Luangundo, river, Angola 16°17′ S, 19°35′ E 220
Luangwa, Zambia 15°37′ S, 30°20′ E 224
Luangwa, river, Zambia 12°14′ S, 32°10′ E 224
Luanping, China 40°54′ N, 117°18′ E 198
Luanshya, Zambia 13°8′ S, 28°22′ E 224
Luanxian, China 39°46′ N, 118°41′ E 198
Luanza, Dem. Rep. of the Congo 8°42′ S, 28°39′ E 224
Luarca, Sp. 43°31′ N, 6°34′ W 150
Luashi, Dem. Rep. of the Congo 10°56′ S, 23°34′ E 224
Luau, Angola 10°44′ S, 22°14′ E 220
Lubaantun, ruin(s), Belize 16°15′ N, 89°7′ W 115
Lubamiti, Dem. Rep. of the Congo 2°32′ S, 17°46′ E 218
Lubāna, Latv. 56°53′ N, 26°42′ E 166
Lubānas Ezers, lake, Latv. 56°45′ N, 26°36′ E 166
Lubanda, Dem. Rep. of the Congo 5°13′ S, 26°38′ E 224
Lubango, Angola 14°57′ S, 13°28′ E 220
Lubao, Dem. Rep. of the Congo 5°20′ S, 25°43′ E 224
Lubba Gerih, spring, Somalia 10°21′ N, 44°38′ E 216
Lübben, Ger. 51°56′ N, 13°53′ E 152
Lubbock, Tex., U.S. 33°32′ N, 101°50′ W 92
Lubec, Me., U.S. 44°50′ N, 67°0′ W 94
Lübeck, Ger. 53°51′ N, 10°42′ E 152
Lubefu, Dem. Rep. of the Congo 4°44′ S, 24°24′ E 224
Lubelskie, adm. division, Pol. 51°2′ N, 21°49′ E 152
Lübenka, Kaz. 50°27′ N, 54°6′ E 158
Lubero, Dem. Rep. of the Congo 0°12′ N, 29°11′ E 224
Lubéron, Montagne du, Fr. 43°42′ N, 5°16′ E 165
Lubi, river, Dem. Rep. of the Congo 5°49′ S, 23°28′ E 224
Lubicon Lake, Can. 56°22′ N, 116°23′ W 108
Lubilash, river, Dem. Rep. of the Congo 8°21′ S, 24°7′ E 224
Lubine, Île, island, U.K. 6°46′ S, 70°20′ E 188
Lublin, Pol. 51°15′ N, 22°33′ E 152
Lubliniec, Pol. 50°40′ N, 18°41′ E 152
Lubnica, Serb. 43°51′ N, 22°12′ E 168
Lubny, Ukr. 50°1′ N, 32°56′ E 158
Lubongola, Dem. Rep. of the Congo 2°39′ S, 27°52′ E 218
Lubosalma, Russ. 63°4′ N, 31°45′ E 152
Lubuagan, Philippines 17°21′ N, 121°10′ E 203
Lubudi, Dem. Rep. of the Congo 9°58′ S, 25°58′ E 224

M

MAR-MAY

Marir, Gezaîr (Mirear), islands, Egypt 23°5' N, 35°51' E 182
Mariscal Estigarribia, Parag. 22°2' S, 60°37' W 132
Maristova, Nor. 61°6' N, 8°1' E 152
Maritime Alps, Fr. 44°2' N, 6°45' E 165
Maritime Territory, adm. division, Russ. 45°20' N, 135°8' E 190
Mariupol', Ukr. 47°5' N, 37°28' E 156
Mariusa National Park, Venez. 9°23' N, 61°33' W 116
Marīvān, Iran 35°31' N, 46°11' E 180
Mariy-El, adm. division, Russ. 56°19' N, 46°11' E 154
Mariyets, Russ. 56°30' N, 49°53' E 154
Marj 'Uyūn, Leb. 33°21' N, 35°35' E 194
Märjamaa, Est. 58°54' N, 24°23' E 166
Marjonbuloq, Uzb. 39°59' N, 67°21' E 197
Marka see Merca, Somalia 1°41' N, 44°53' E 207
Markala, Mali 13°40' N, 6°4' W 222
Markansu, Taj. 39°19' N, 73°21' E 197
Markapur, India 15°42' N, 79°17' E 188
Markaryd, Nor. 56°28' N, 13°35' E 152
Markdale, Can. 44°18' N, 80°39' W 110
Markelsdorfer Huk, Kattegat 54°37' N, 10°49' E 152
Markesan, Wis., U.S. 43°42' N, 88°59' W 102
Market Drayton, U.K. 52°53' N, 2°30' W 162
Market Harborough, U.K. 52°28' N, 0°55' E 162
Market Rasen, U.K. 53°22' N, 0°21' E 162
Market Weighton, U.K. 53°51' N, 0°41' E 162
Markha, river, Russ. 64°57' N, 116°6' E 160
Markham, Can. 43°51' N, 79°17' W 94
Markham Bay 63°24' N, 74°18' W 106
Markham, Mount, peak, Antarctica 82°47' S, 162°59' E 248
Markit, China 38°57' N, 77°37' E 184
Markkina, Fin. 68°29' N, 22°16' E 152
Markle, Ind., U.S. 40°49' N, 85°20' W 102
Markounda, Cen. Af. Rep. 7°33' N, 16°57' E 218
Markovac, Serb. 44°13' N, 21°5' E 168
Markovo, Russ. 64°41' N, 170°4' E 160
Marks Butte, peak, Colo., U.S. 40°48' N, 102°36' W 90
Marksville, La., U.S. 31°6' N, 92°5' W 103
Markušica, Croatia 45°22' N, 18°41' E 168
Marl, Ger. 51°39' N, 7°6' E 167
Marlboro, Vt., U.S. 42°51' N, 72°44' W 104
Marlborough, N.H., U.S. 42°53' N, 72°13' W 104
Marlborough, U.K. 51°24' N, 1°44' W 162
Marle, Fr. 49°44' N, 3°47' E 163
Marles, Fr. 50°30' N, 2°30' E 150
Marlette, Mich., U.S. 43°19' N, 83°5' W 102
Marlin, Tex., U.S. 31°17' N, 96°53' W 96
Marlin, oil field, Bass Strait 38°17' S, 148°12' E 230
Marlow, N.H., U.S. 43°6' N, 72°13' W 104
Marlow, Okla., U.S. 34°38' N, 97°58' W 92
Marlow, U.K. 51°34' N, 0°47' E 162
Marmagao, India 15°23' N, 73°48' E 173
Marmara Denizi, Turkey 40°37' N, 27°43' E 156
Marmaris, Turk. 36°51' N, 28°14' E 156
Marmarth, N. Dak., U.S. 46°16' N, 103°54' W 90
Marmolada, peak, It. 46°26' N, 11°47' E 167
Marmolejo, Sp. 38°2' N, 4°11' W 164
Marmul, oil field, Oman 18°10' N, 55°23' E 182
Marne, river, Fr. 48°49' N, 2°37' E 163
Maroa, Ill., U.S. 40°1' N, 88°57' W 102
Maroa, Venez. 2°45' N, 67°33' W 136
Maroantsetra, Madagascar 15°25' S, 49°41' E 220
Marol, Pak. 34°45' N, 76°16' E 186
Marolambo, Madagascar 20°4' S, 48°8' E 220
Maromandia, Madagascar 14°9' S, 48°5' E 220
Maromokotro, peak, Madagascar 14°4' S, 48°50' E 220
Marondera, Zimb. 18°14' S, 31°30' E 224
Marone, It. 45°44' N, 10°5' E 167
Marónia, Gr. 40°54' N, 25°31' E 156
Maronne, river, Fr. 45°1' N, 1°59' E 165
Maros, Indonesia 4°58' S, 119°32' E 192
Marotandrano, Madagascar 16°11' S, 48°48' E 220
Marotiri, island, Fr. 27°49' S, 143°42' W 252
Maroua, Cameroon 10°36' N, 14°20' E 216
Marouini, river, South America 2°10' N, 53°57' W 130
Marovoay, Madagascar 16°8' S, 46°39' E 220
Marqaköl, lake, Kaz. 48°42' N, 85°14' E 184
Marquard, S. Af. 28°41' S, 27°23' E 227
Marquesas Fracture Zone, South Pacific Ocean 10°40' S, 131°47' W 252
Marquesas Islands, South Pacific Ocean 11°28' S, 141°48' W 238
Marquesas Keys, islands, Gulf of Mexico 24°26' N, 82°20' W 105
Marquette, Mich., U.S. 46°32' N, 87°24' W 94
Marquette, Lac, lake, Can. 48°54' N, 74°33' W 94
Marquise, Fr. 50°49' N, 1°42' E 163
Marra, Jebel, peak, Sudan 12°50' N, 23°50' E 206
Marrakech, Mor. 31°39' N, 8°1' W 214
Marrasjärvi, Fin. 66°25' N, 25°6' E 152
Marrecas, Serra das, Braz. 9°33' S, 41°40' W 132
Marromeu, Mozambique 18°19' S, 35°55' E 224
Marrupa, Mozambique 13°12' S, 37°30' E 224
Mars Hill, peak, Me., U.S. 46°30' N, 67°54' W 94
Marsá al 'Uwayjā', Lib. 30°54' N, 17°51' E 216
Marsa 'Alam, spring, Egypt 25°4' N, 34°51' E 182
Marsa Fatma, Eritrea 14°51' N, 40°20' E 182
Marsa Sha'ab, Egypt 22°49' N, 35°45' E 182
Marsabit, Kenya 2°18' N, 38°0' E 224
Marsabit Nature Reserve, Kenya 1°54' N, 37°47' E 224
Marsala, It. 37°48' N, 12°26' E 156
Marsberg, Ger. 51°27' N, 8°52' E 167
Marsden Point, N.Z. 35°53' S, 174°28' E 240
Marseillan, Fr. 43°21' N, 3°30' E 164
Marseille, Fr. 43°17' N, 5°22' E 150
Marsfjället, peak, Nor. 65°5' N, 15°13' E 152
Marsh Island, La., U.S. 29°24' N, 92°2' W 103
Marsh Pass, Ariz., U.S. 36°38' N, 110°25' W 92
Marsh Peak, Utah, U.S. 40°41' N, 109°54' W 90
Marsh Point, Can. 57°5' N, 92°20' W 108
Marshall, Alas., U.S. 61°52' N, 162°4' W 98
Marshall, Ark., U.S. 35°53' N, 92°39' W 96
Marshall, Ill., U.S. 39°23' N, 87°41' W 102
Marshall, Liberia 6°4' N, 10°23' W 222
Marshall, Mich., U.S. 42°16' N, 84°57' W 102
Marshall, Minn., U.S. 44°26' N, 95°48' W 90
Marshall, Mo., U.S. 39°6' N, 93°16' W 82
Marshall, Tex., U.S. 32°32' N, 94°23' W 103
Marshall Bennett Islands, Solomon Sea 8°46' S, 152°2' E 230
Marshall Islands, Marshall Islands 9°2' N, 170°3' E 238
Marshalltown, Iowa, U.S. 42°4' N, 92°53' W 82
Marshfield, Mo., U.S. 37°19' N, 92°54' W 94
Marshfield, Vt., U.S. 44°21' N, 72°22' W 104
Marshfield, Wis., U.S. 44°39' N, 90°11' W 94
Marsland, Nebr., U.S. 42°26' N, 103°18' W 90
Mars-la-Tour, Fr. 49°6' N, 5°53' E 163
Marston Moor, battle, U.K. 53°58' N, 1°16' W 162
Marstrand, Sw. 57°53' N, 11°33' E 150
Marsyaty, Russ. 60°4' N, 60°25' E 154
Mart, Tex., U.S. 31°31' N, 96°49' W 96
Martaban, Myanmar 16°34' N, 97°35' E 202
Martaban, Gulf of 15°50' N, 96°1' E 192
Martakert (Ağdara), Asia 40°12' N, 46°47' E 195
Martap, Cameroon 6°50' N, 13°3' E 218
Martapura, Indonesia 3°30' S, 114°45' E 192
Marte R. Gómez, Presa, lake, Mex. 26°12' N, 100°24' W 80
Martem'yanovskaya, Russ. 61°58' N, 39°11' E 154
Marten Mountain, peak, Can. 55°28' N, 114°50' W 108
Martés, peak, Sp. 39°18' N, 1°0' E 164
Martfű, Hung. 47°0' N, 20°17' E 168
Martha's Vineyard, island, Mass., U.S. 41°14' N, 70°47' W 104
Marthaville, La., U.S. 31°43' N, 93°25' W 103
Martigny, Switz. 46°6' N, 7°3' E 167
Martigues, Fr. 43°23' N, 5°3' E 150
Martil, Mor. 35°37' N, 5°17' W 150
Martin, Mich., U.S. 42°32' N, 85°39' W 102
Martin, S. Dak., U.S. 43°10' N, 101°44' W 90
Martin, Lake, Ala., U.S. 32°51' N, 86°22' W 80
Martin, river, Can. 61°31' N, 122°26' W 108
Martin Vaz Islands, South Atlantic Ocean 20°29' S, 28°57' W 253
Martinborough, N.Z. 41°15' S, 175°29' E 240
Martinez, Calif., U.S. 38°1' N, 122°9' W 100
Martinez, Ga., U.S. 33°30' N, 82°6' W 96
Martinez Lake, Ariz., U.S. 32°58' N, 114°28' W 101
Martinique, Fr. 14°26' N, 61°27' W 116
Martinique Passage 15°1' N, 62°3' W 116
Martinsburg, N.Y., U.S. 43°44' N, 75°29' W 94
Martinsville, Ill., U.S. 39°19' N, 87°53' W 102
Martinsville, Ind., U.S. 39°25' N, 86°26' W 102
Martinsville, Va., U.S. 36°40' N, 79°53' W 96
Martna, Est. 58°50' N, 23°47' E 166
Marton, N.Z. 40°6' S, 175°24' E 240
Martorell, Sp. 41°27' N, 1°54' E 164
Martos, Sp. 37°43' N, 3°59' W 164
Martti, Fin. 67°28' N, 28°21' E 152
Martuni, Arm. 40°8' N, 45°16' E 195
Martuni (Xocavand), Azerb. 39°48' N, 47°5' E 195
Martyn, Mount, peak, Antarctica 69°19' S, 157°39' E 248
Ma'ruf, Afghan. 31°29' N, 67°3' E 186
Maruia, N.Z. 42°12' S, 172°14' E 240
Marumori, Japan 37°55' N, 140°46' E 201
Marungu, Dem. Rep. of the Congo 8°10' S, 29°36' E 224
Maruoka, Japan 36°8' N, 136°16' E 201
Marv Dasht, Iran 29°55' N, 52°56' E 196
Marvin Spur, Arctic Ocean 86°15' N, 118°55' W 255
Marvine, Mount, peak, Utah, U.S. 38°39' N, 111°42' W 90
Marwar, India 25°43' N, 73°37' E 186
Marx, Russ. 51°36' N, 46°42' E 158
Mary, Turkm. 37°36' N, 61°50' E 180
Mary, river, Austral. 25°36' S, 152°13' E 230
Mar'yanovka, Russ. 54°55' N, 72°44' E 184
Marydale, S. Af. 29°28' S, 22°7' E 227
Maryland, adm. division, Md., U.S. 39°33' N, 77°50' W 94
Maryport, U.K. 54°42' N, 3°30' W 162
Mary's Harbour, Can. 52°24' N, 55°58' W 73
Marystown, Can. 47°10' N, 55°9' W 111
Marysvale, Utah, U.S. 38°26' N, 112°13' W 90
Marysville, Calif., U.S. 39°9' N, 121°37' W 92
Marysville, Can. 45°58' N, 66°37' W 94
Marysville, Kans., U.S. 39°49' N, 96°39' W 92
Marysville, Mich., U.S. 42°53' N, 82°30' W 102
Marysville, Ohio, U.S. 40°13' N, 83°22' W 102
Marysville, Wash., U.S. 48°2' N, 122°11' W 100
Maryville, Mo., U.S. 40°20' N, 94°53' W 82
Maryville, Tenn., U.S. 35°45' N, 83°58' W 96
Marzafal, Mali 17°56' N, 0°59' E 222
Marzo, Cabo, Col. 6°41' N, 78°6' W 136
Marzūq, Lib. 25°55' N, 13°53' E 216
Mas de las Matas, Sp. 40°51' N, 0°15' E 164
Masada, ruin(s), Israel 31°18' N, 35°19' E 194
Masai Mara National Reserve, Kenya 1°27' S, 35°5' E 224
Masai Steppe, Tanzania 5°43' S, 37°1' E 224
Masaka, Uganda 0°22' N, 31°43' E 224
Masalasef, Chad 11°45' N, 17°10' E 216
Masallı, Azerb. 39°1' N, 48°39' E 195
Masalembu, Kepulauan, islands, Java Sea 5°56' S, 113°19' E 192
Masan, S. Korea 35°11' N, 128°33' E 200
Masasi, Tanzania 10°43' S, 38°47' E 224
Masavi, Bol. 19°24' S, 63°18' W 137
Masaya, Nicar. 11°57' N, 86°6' W 115
Masayama, Sierra Leone 8°14' N, 10°49' W 222
Masbate, Philippines 12°20' N, 123°36' E 203
Masbate, island, Philippines 11°55' N, 122°11' E 192
Mascara, Alg. 35°23' N, 0°7' E 150
Mascarene Basin, Indian Ocean 13°57' S, 55°8' E 254
Mascarene Plain, Indian Ocean 21°15' S, 51°32' E 254
Mascart, Cape, Antarctica 66°35' S, 71°50' W 248
Mascota, Mex. 20°31' N, 104°48' W 114
Mascoutah, Ill., U.S. 38°28' N, 89°47' W 102
Masein, Myanmar 23°22' N, 94°21' E 202
Maseru, Lesotho 29°19' S, 27°24' E 227
Masfjorden, Nor. 60°47' N, 5°19' E 152
Mash'abbé Sade, Israel 30°59' N, 34°46' E 194
Mashābih, island, Saudi Arabia 25°35' N, 35°47' E 182
Masham, U.K. 54°13' N, 1°40' W 162
Mashan, China 23°40' N, 108°10' E 198
Mashhad, Iran 36°19' N, 59°35' E 180
Mashigina, Guba 74°4' N, 47°51' E 160
Mashkai, river, Pak. 26°44' N, 65°14' E 182
Mashuray, Afghan. 32°8' N, 68°20' E 186
Masi, Nor. 69°26' N, 23°38' E 152
Masindi, Uganda 1°38' N, 31°42' E 224
Masindi Port, Uganda 1°39' N, 32°4' E 224
Masinloc, Philippines 15°34' N, 119°58' E 203
Maşīrah, Jazīrat (Masira), island, Oman 20°43' N, 58°55' E 182
Masisea, Peru 8°40' S, 74°21' W 130
Masisi, Dem. Rep. of the Congo 1°24' S, 28°47' E 224
Māsiyah, Tall al, peak, Syr. 32°47' N, 36°39' E 194
Masjed Soleymān, Iran 31°54' N, 49°20' E 180
Maska, Nig. 11°17' N, 7°19' E 222
Maskan, Raas, Somalia 11°9' N, 43°34' E 216
Maskūtān, Iran 26°51' N, 59°53' E 182
Maslen Nos, Bulg. 42°20' N, 27°46' E 156
Maslovare, Bosn. and Herzg. 44°33' N, 17°31' E 168
Maslovo, Russ. 60°9' N, 60°31' E 154
Masoala, Presqu'île de, Madagascar 16°16' S, 50°11' E 220
Masoller, Uru. 31°7' S, 55°59' W 139
Masomeloka, Madagascar 20°17' S, 48°37' E 220
Mason, Ill., U.S. 38°57' N, 88°38' W 102
Mason, Mich., U.S. 42°34' N, 84°26' W 102
Mason, Ohio, U.S. 39°21' N, 84°19' W 102
Mason, Tex., U.S. 30°43' N, 99°13' W 92
Mason Bay 47°3' S, 167°36' E 240
Mason City, Ill., U.S. 40°12' N, 89°42' W 102
Mason City, Iowa, U.S. 43°7' N, 93°12' W 94
Masqaţ (Muscat), Oman 23°30' N, 58°32' E 196
Massa, Congo 3°46' S, 15°27' E 218
Massa, It. 44°1' N, 10°8' E 167
Massa Lombarda, It. 44°26' N, 11°49' E 167
Massachusetts, adm. division, Mass., U.S. 42°14' N, 72°39' W 104
Massachusetts Bay 42°11' N, 70°43' W 104
Massafra, It. 40°35' N, 17°7' E 156
Massaguet, Chad 12°31' N, 15°25' E 216
Massakory, Chad 13°0' N, 15°42' E 216
Massambara, Braz. 29°7' S, 56°4' W 139
Massangena, Mozambique 21°33' S, 33°2' E 227
Massat, Fr. 42°52' N, 1°20' E 164
Massava, Russ. 60°38' N, 62°5' E 154
Massawa, Eritrea 15°37' N, 39°23' E 182
Massenya, Chad 11°27' N, 16°9' E 216
Masset, Can. 53°59' N, 132°2' W 98
Masseube, Fr. 43°25' N, 0°33' E 164
Massillon, Ohio, U.S. 40°47' N, 81°31' W 102
Massinga, Mozambique 23°16' S, 35°20' E 227
Massingir, Mozambique 23°47' S, 32°7' E 227
Masson Island, Antarctica 66°3' S, 96°8' E 248
Masson Range, Antarctica 68°32' S, 59°23' E 248
Mastābah, Saudi Arabia 20°49' N, 39°26' E 182
Maştağa, Azerb. 40°33' N, 49°59' E 195
Mastic Beach, N.Y., U.S. 40°45' N, 72°51' W 104
Mastic Point, Bahamas 25°4' N, 78°0' W 96
Mastuj, Pak. 36°15' N, 72°33' E 186
Mastūrah, Saudi Arabia 23°7' N, 38°51' E 182
Masty, Belarus 53°25' N, 24°33' E 152
Masuda, Japan 34°39' N, 131°51' E 200
Masuria, region, Pol. 54°12' N, 19°41' E 166
Masvingo, Zimb. 20°6' S, 30°47' E 227
Maşyāf, Syr. 35°3' N, 36°20' E 194
Mat, river, Alban. 41°38' N, 19°38' E 168
Mata, Dem. Rep. of the Congo 7°55' S, 21°56' E 218
Mata Mata, S. Af. 25°50' S, 20°3' E 227
Mata Ortíz, Mex. 30°7' N, 108°4' W 92
Matachewan, Can. 47°56' N, 80°38' W 94
Matachic, Mex. 28°50' N, 107°44' W 92
Matadi, Dem. Rep. of the Congo 5°49' S, 13°27' E 218
Matador, Tex., U.S. 33°59' N, 100°50' W 92
Matagalpa, Nicar. 12°54' N, 85°54' W 115
Matagami, Can. 49°47' N, 77°39' W 94
Matagami, Lac, lake, Can. 50°0' N, 78°4' W 94
Matagorda, Tex., U.S. 28°41' N, 95°58' W 96
Matagorda Bay 28°28' N, 97°19' W 80
Matagorda Peninsula, Tex., U.S. 28°31' N, 96°26' W 96
Matak, island, Indonesia 3°25' N, 106°17' E 196
Matakana, N.Z. 36°23' S, 174°42' E 240
Matala, Angola 14°47' S, 14°59' E 220
Matala, ruin(s), Gr. 34°58' N, 24°39' E 156
Matam, Senegal 15°39' N, 13°21' W 222
Matameye, Niger 13°23' N, 8°26' E 222
Matamoros, Mex. 18°34' N, 98°29' W 114
Matamoros, Mex. 25°31' N, 103°15' W 114
Matamoros, Mex. 25°53' N, 97°31' W 114
Ma'ţan al Ḩusayyāt, spring, Lib. 30°21' N, 20°33' E 216
Ma'ţan as Sarra, spring, Lib. 21°35' N, 21°52' E 216
Ma'ţan Bishrah, spring, Lib. 23°0' N, 22°41' E 226
Ma'ţan Shārib, spring, Egypt 30°16' N, 28°26' E 180
Matandu, river, Tanzania 8°52' S, 38°38' E 224
Matane, Can. 48°49' N, 67°33' W 94
Matanzas, Cuba 23°4' N, 81°36' W 96
Matanzas, adm. division, Cuba 22°59' N, 81°44' W 116
Matanzas, island, Cuba 22°5' N, 82°46' W 116
Matão, Serra do, Braz. 9°38' S, 51°31' W 130
Mataojo, Uru. 31°11' S, 56°23' W 139
Matapás see Akrotírio Ténaro, Gr. 36°13' N, 21°38' E 156
Matapi, Suriname 4°59' N, 57°21' W 130
Mataporquera, Sp. 42°52' N, 4°11' W 150
Matapwa, Tanzania 9°42' S, 39°24' E 224
Matara, Sri Lanka 5°58' N, 80°32' E 188
Mataram, Indonesia 8°36' S, 116°6' E 192
Matarani, Peru 17°0' S, 72°7' W 137
Matarka, Mor. 33°21' N, 2°42' W 214
Mataró, Sp. 41°32' N, 2°26' E 164
Matassi, spring, Sudan 18°49' N, 29°47' E 226
Mätäsvaara, Fin. 63°25' N, 29°32' E 152
Matata, N.Z. 37°55' S, 176°46' E 240
Matatiele, S. Af. 30°22' S, 28°46' E 227
Mataurá, river, Braz. 6°15' S, 60°59' W 130
Matawai, N.Z. 38°22' S, 177°33' E 240
Matay, Kaz. 45°31' N, 57°6' E 158
Matay, Kaz. 45°52' N, 78°41' E 184
Mateguá, Bol. 13°3' S, 62°49' W 130
Matehuala, Mex. 23°37' N, 100°39' W 96
Matemo, Ilha, island, Mozambique 12°11' S, 40°39' E 224
Matera, It. 40°39' N, 16°36' E 156
Matese, It. 41°26' N, 14°7' E 156
Mátészalka, Hung. 47°56' N, 22°21' E 168
Matetsi, Zimb. 18°19' S, 25°56' E 224
Matfors, Nor. 62°20' N, 17°0' E 152
Matguia, Tun. 34°40' N, 10°20' E 156
Mather, Calif., U.S. 37°52' N, 119°52' W 100
Mather, Mount, peak, Antarctica 73°32' S, 60°30' E 248
Matheson, Can. 48°32' N, 80°29' W 94
Matheson Island, Can. 51°43' N, 96°57' W 108
Mathews, Va., U.S. 37°25' N, 76°20' W 96
Mathews Peak, Kenya 1°13' N, 37°14' E 224
Mathis, Tex., U.S. 28°5' N, 97°49' W 92
Mathura, India 27°27' N, 77°38' E 197
Mati, Philippines 6°59' N, 126°12' E 203
Matiakoali, Burkina Faso 12°21' N, 1°3' E 222
Matias Cardoso, Braz. 14°56' S, 43°55' W 138
Matin, India 22°46' N, 82°25' E 197
Matkasel'kya, Russ. 61°57' N, 30°30' E 152
Matlabas, S. Af. 24°15' S, 27°30' E 227
Matli, Pak. 25°4' N, 68°47' E 186
Matlock, U.K. 53°8' N, 1°33' W 162
Mato, Dem. Rep. of the Congo 8°1' S, 24°54' E 224
Mato, Cerro, peak, Venez. 7°12' N, 65°23' W 136
Mato Grosso, adm. division, Braz. 14°29' S, 52°39' W 138
Mato Grosso do Sul, adm. division, Braz. 20°12' S, 53°26' W 138
Mato Grosso, Planalto do, South America 14°13' S, 58°51' W 123
Mato Verde, Braz. 15°25' S, 42°55' W 138
Matobo National Park, Zimb. 20°38' S, 28°11' E 206
Matochkin Shar, Russ. 73°21' N, 56°33' E 160
Matochkin Shar, Proliv 72°52' N, 49°46' E 160
Matoio, Angola 7°28' S, 14°37' E 220
Matola, Malawi 13°39' S, 34°55' E 224
Matombo, Tanzania 7°2' S, 37°47' E 224
Matope, Malawi 15°21' S, 34°58' E 224
Matopos, Zimb. 20°25' S, 28°28' E 227
Matos, river, Bol. 14°30' S, 66°0' W 137
Matosinhos, Port. 41°10' N, 8°43' W 150
Mátra, Hung. 47°3' N, 19°43' E 168
Matraca, Col. 3°1' N, 69°7' W 136
Mátrafüred, Hung. 47°48' N, 19°58' E 168
Maţra', Oman 23°36' N, 58°32' E 182
Maţrūḩ, Egypt 31°20' N, 27°12' E 180
Matsena, Nig. 13°8' N, 10°3' E 222
Matsu, island, Taiwan, China 26°16' N, 120°3' E 198
Matsubase, Japan 32°37' N, 130°41' E 201
Matsue, Japan 35°27' N, 133°3' E 201
Matsumoto, Japan 36°13' N, 137°59' E 201
Matsunaga, Japan 34°27' N, 133°16' E 201
Matsusaka, Japan 34°33' N, 136°33' E 201
Matsushiro, Japan 36°34' N, 138°13' E 201
Matsutō, Japan 36°30' N, 136°33' E 201
Matsuura, Japan 33°20' N, 129°42' E 201
Matsuyama, Japan 33°49' N, 132°46' E 201
Mattagami Lake, lake, Can. 47°47' N, 82°6' W 110
Mattagami, river, Can. 50°10' N, 82°17' W 110
Mattapoisett, Mass., U.S. 41°39' N, 70°50' W 104
Mattawa, Can. 46°18' N, 78°41' W 94
Matterhorn Peak, Calif., U.S. 38°5' N, 119°25' W 100
Matterhorn, peak, Nev., U.S. 41°48' N, 115°28' W 90
Matterhorn, peak, Switz. 45°59' N, 7°37' E 165
Mattersburg, Aust. 47°43' N, 16°24' E 168
Matthews Peak, Ariz., U.S. 36°21' N, 109°13' W 92
Matthew's Ridge, Guyana 7°27' N, 60°6' W 130
Mattili, India 18°32' N, 82°13' E 188
Mattinata, It. 41°42' N, 16°2' E 168
Mattituck, N.Y., U.S. 40°59' N, 72°32' W 104
Mattoon, Ill., U.S. 39°29' N, 88°22' W 102
Matugama, Sri Lanka 6°30' N, 80°7' E 188
Matunuck, R.I., U.S. 41°22' N, 71°33' W 104
Maturango Peak, Calif., U.S. 36°6' N, 117°35' W 92
Maturín, Venez. 9°42' N, 63°12' W 116
Matusadona National Park, Zimb. 17°10' S, 28°4' E 224
Matveyevka, Russ. 53°29' N, 53°35' E 154
Matxitxako, Cabo, Sp. 43°19' N, 2°48' W 164
Matyl'ka, Russ. 63°20' N, 85°34' E 169
Matzen, oil field, Aust. 48°21' N, 16°35' E 152
Mau, India 25°54' N, 83°31' E 197
Mau Ranipur, India 25°13' N, 79°8' E 197
Mauá, Mozambique 13°52' S, 37°10' E 224
Maubeuge, Fr. 50°16' N, 3°58' E 163
Ma-ubin, Myanmar 16°43' N, 95°36' E 202
Maubourguet, Fr. 43°27' N, 3°178' E 164
Maud, Tex., U.S. 33°19' N, 94°22' W 103
Maud Rise, South Atlantic Ocean 65°26' S, 4°0' E 255
Maude, Cape, Antarctica 82°34' S, 179°24' E 248
Maués, Braz. 3°23' S, 57°43' W 130
Maués, river, Braz. 4°23' S, 57°25' W 130
Maug Islands, Maug Islands 20°2' N, 145°20' E 192
Mauganj, India 24°42' N, 81°52' E 197
Maugerville, Can. 45°53' N, 66°28' W 94
Maui, island, Hawai'i, U.S. 20°39' N, 156°2' W 99
Maukme, Myanmar 20°13' N, 97°42' E 202
Maule, adm. division, Chile 35°44' S, 72°37' W 134
Mauléon, Fr. 43°12' N, 0°53' E 164
Maullín, Chile 41°38' S, 73°37' W 134
Maumakeogh, peak, Ire. 54°15' N, 9°36' W 150
Maumee, Ohio, U.S. 41°33' N, 83°40' W 102
Maumelle, Lake, Ark., U.S. 34°50' N, 93°1' W 96
Maumere, Indonesia 8°47' S, 122°13' E 192
Maun, Botswana 19°59' S, 23°23' E 220
Mauna Kea Observatories, site, Hawai'i, U.S. 19°49' N, 155°32' W 99
Mauna Loa Observatory, site, Hawai'i, U.S. 19°31' N, 155°38' W 99
Maungaturoto, N.Z. 36°7' S, 174°21' E 240
Maungdaw, Myanmar 20°52' N, 92°22' E 188
Maungmagan Islands, Andaman Sea 13°58' N, 97°13' E 202
Maunoir, Lac, lake, Can. 67°36' N, 118°28' W 246
Maurepas, Lake, La., U.S. 30°11' N, 90°56' W 96
Maurepas, Lake, La., U.S. 30°14' N, 90°46' W 103
Maures, Monts des, Fr. 43°19' N, 5°52' E 165
Maurice, La., U.S. 30°5' N, 92°8' W 103
Mauriceville, N.Z. 40°47' S, 175°42' E 240
Mauriceville, Tex., U.S. 30°10' N, 93°53' W 103
Mauritania 20°5' N, 14°29' W 214
Mauritius 20°18' S, 57°35' E 254
Mauritius Trench, Indian Ocean 22°23' S, 56°10' E 254
Maurs, Fr. 44°42' N, 2°11' E 150
Maury Bay 66°27' S, 127°0' E 248
Maury Mountains, peak, Oreg., U.S. 44°1' N, 120°27' W 90
Maury Seachannel, North Atlantic Ocean 56°23' N, 24°27' W 253
Mauston, Wis., U.S. 43°46' N, 90°4' W 102
Mauthen, Aust. 46°39' N, 13°0' E 167
Mavago, Mozambique 12°27' S, 36°13' E 224
Maverick, Ariz., U.S. 33°44' N, 109°33' W 92
Mavinga, Angola 15°47' S, 20°11' E 207
Mavonde, Mozambique 18°33' S, 33°3' E 224
Mavroli, Cyprus 35°3' N, 32°27' E 194
Mavrovo, Maced. 41°40' N, 20°45' E 168
Mavrovo National Park, Maced. 41°13' N, 20°50' E 180
Mavrovouni Mine, site, Cyprus 35°5' N, 32°47' E 194
Mavrovoúni, peak, Gr. 39°26' N, 22°31' E 156
Mawlá Maţar, Yemen 14°48' N, 48°38' E 182
Mawlamyine, Myanmar 16°24' N, 97°41' E 192
Mawlite, Myanmar 23°36' N, 94°19' E 202
Mawlu, Myanmar 24°26' N, 96°13' E 188
Mawqaq, Saudi Arabia 27°25' N, 41°9' E 180
Mawshij, Yemen 13°43' N, 43°19' E 182
Mawson, Australia, station, Antarctica 67°38' S, 63°5' E 248
Mawson, Cape, Antarctica 70°29' S, 77°38' W 248
Mawson Coast, Antarctica 67°50' S, 61°7' E 248
Max, N. Dak., U.S. 47°48' N, 101°19' W 90
Maxaas, Somalia 4°23' N, 46°8' E 218
Maxcanú, Mex. 20°33' N, 90°0' W 115
Maxhamish Lake, Can. 59°48' N, 124°19' W 108
Maxixe, Mozambique 23°45' S, 35°18' E 227
Maxton, N.C., U.S. 34°43' N, 79°22' W 96
Maxwell, N. Mex., U.S. 36°31' N, 104°34' W 92
Maxwell Bay 74°19' N, 89°56' W 106
Maxwelton House, site, U.K. 55°11' N, 3°57' W 150
May, Cape 81°35' S, 173°55' E 248
May Point, Cape, N.J., U.S. 38°38' N, 75°1' W 94
Maya, island, Indonesia 1°39' S, 109°16' E 192
Maya, Mesa de, Colo., U.S. 37°1' N, 103°46' W 92
Maya Mountains, Belize 16°41' N, 89°8' W 115
Maya, river, Russ. 55°23' N, 132°42' E 160
Maya, river, Russ. 58°9' N, 137°20' E 160
Mayabandar, India 12°52' N, 92°59' E 188
Mayaguana, adm. division, Bahamas 22°15' N, 73°18' W 116
Mayaguana Island, Bahamas 22°31' N, 73°18' W 116
Mayagüez, P.R., U.S. 18°11' N, 67°10' W 116
Mayahi, Niger 13°52' N, 7°31' E 222
Mayāmey, Iran 36°30' N, 55°46' E 180
Mayang, China 27°54' N, 109°48' E 198
Mayapán, ruin(s), Mex. 20°35' N, 89°35' W 115
Mayarí, Cuba 20°40' N, 75°42' W 116
Maybeury, W. Va., U.S. 37°21' N, 81°23' W 96
Maych'ew, Eth. 12°47' N, 39°32' E 182
Mayda, Russ. 66°20' N, 41°53' E 154
Maydān Ikbiz, Syr. 36°48' N, 36°39' E 156
Maydelle, Tex., U.S. 31°46' N, 95°18' W 103
Maydh, Somalia 10°53' N, 47°4' E 216
Maydh, island, Somalia 11°21' N, 46°49' E 216
Maydī, Yemen 16°18' N, 42°52' E 182
Mayen, Ger. 50°19' N, 7°13' E 167
Mayersville, Miss., U.S. 32°52' N, 91°3' W 103
Mayerthorpe, Can. 53°56' N, 115°11' W 108
Mayevo, Russ. 56°22' N, 29°51' E 166
Mayfa'ah, Yemen 14°19' N, 47°31' E 182
Mayfield, Ky., U.S. 36°44' N, 88°40' W 82
Mayfield, N.Z. 43°51' S, 171°25' E 240
Mayfield Peak, Idaho, U.S. 44°29' N, 114°50' W 90
Mayhill, N. Mex., U.S. 32°53' N, 105°29' W 92
Maykop, Russ. 44°38' N, 40°3' E 156
Maymecha, river, Russ. 71°36' N, 97°42' E 160
Maymont, Can. 52°32' N, 107°42' W 108

Musgrave Land, Can. 53°36' N, 56°12' W 111
Musgrave, Port 12°9' S, 141°2' E 230
Musgrave Ranges, Austral. 25°59' S, 131°49' E 230
Mushandike Sanctuary, Zimb. 20°13' S, 30°18' E 206
Mushâsh el Sirr, spring, Egypt 30°37' N, 33°46' E 194
Mushenge, Dem. Rep. of the Congo 4°29' S, 21°18' E 218
Mushie, Dem. Rep. of the Congo 3°2' S, 16°51' E 218
Mushorah, oil field, Iraq 36°55' N, 42°14' E 195
Mushu, island, P.N.G. 3°39' S, 142°39' E 192
Music Mountains, peak, Ariz., U.S. 35°31' N, 113°43' W 101
Musina (Messina), S. Af. 22°21' S, 30°1' E 227
Musiri, India 10°58' N, 78°29' E 188
Muskeg, river, Can. 60°16' N, 123°9' W 108
Muskeget Channel 41°19' N, 70°29' W 104
Muskeget Island, Mass., U.S. 41°19' N, 70°18' W 104
Muskegon, Mich., U.S. 43°13' N, 86°16' W 102
Muskegon Heights, Mich., U.S. 43°11' N, 86°15' W 102
Muskegon, river, Mich., U.S. 43°50' N, 85°18' W 102
Muskogee, Okla., U.S. 35°44' N, 95°22' W 96
Muskwa, Can. 58°44' N, 122°43' W 108
Muskwa, river, Can. 56°8' N, 114°38' W 108
Musmar, Sudan 18°11' N, 35°35' E 182
Musoma, Tanzania 1°31' S, 33°49' E 224
Musquaro, Lac, lake, Can. 50°29' N, 61°41' W 111
Mussau, island, P.N.G. 1°31' S, 149°47' E 192
Mussau Islands, P.N.G. 1°17' S, 149°36' E 192
Musselshell, Mont., U.S. 46°28' N, 108°6' W 90
Musselshell, river, Mont., U.S. 46°28' N, 109°57' W 90
Mussende, Angola 10°33' S, 16°2' E 220
Mussuma, Angola 14°17' S, 21°57' E 220
Mustafakemalpaşa, Turk. 40°4' N, 28°23' E 180
Mustahīl, Eth. 5°14' N, 44°42' E 218
Mustang, Nepal 29°12' N, 83°58' E 197
Mustayevo, Russ. 51°47' N, 53°27' E 158
Mustio see Svarta, Fin. 60°8' N, 23°51' E 166
Mustjala, Est. 58°27' N, 22°14' E 166
Mustla, Est. 58°13' N, 25°50' E 166
Mustvee, Est. 58°50' N, 26°53' E 166
Musudan Missile Launch Site, N. Korea 40°46' N, 129°44' E 200
Musún, Cerro, peak, Nicar. 12°58' N, 85°18' W 115
Musungu, Dem. Rep. of the Congo 2°45' N, 28°22' E 224
Muswabik, river, Can. 51°56' N, 85°31' W 110
Mûţ, Egypt 25°28' N, 28°57' E 226
Mut, Turk. 36°38' N, 33°26' E 156
Mutá, Ponta do, Braz. 14°23' S, 38°50' W 132
Mu'tah, Jordan 31°5' N, 35°41' E 194
Mutalahti, Fin. 62°25' N, 31°4' E 152
Mutanda, Zambia 12°23' S, 26°14' E 224
Mutarara, Mozambique 17°27' S, 35°8' E 224
Mutare, Zimb. 18°58' S, 32°39' E 224
Mutatá, Col. 7°16' N, 76°32' W 136
Mutha, Kenya 1°49' S, 38°24' E 224
Muting, Indonesia 7°21' S, 140°14' E 192
Mutki, Turk. 38°24' N, 41°54' E 195
Mutnyy Materik, Russ. 65°55' N, 55°0' E 154
Mutoko, Zimb. 17°26' S, 32°13' E 224
Mutombo Mukulu, Dem. Rep. of the Congo 7°58' S, 23°59' E 224
Mutoray, Russ. 61°27' N, 100°26' E 160
Mutriba, oil field, Kuwait 29°46' N, 47°14' E 196
Mutshatsha, Dem. Rep. of the Congo 10°40' S, 24°26' E 224
Mutumbo, Angola 13°15' S, 17°18' E 220
Mutum-Paraná, Braz. 9°40' S, 65°0' W 137
Mutunópolis, Braz. 13°41' S, 49°17' W 138
Muurla, Fin. 60°20' N, 23°14' E 166
Muuruvesi, Fin. 63°0' N, 28°10' E 152
Muxia, Sp. 43°5' N, 9°14' W 150
Muyinga, Burundi 2°52' S, 30°19' E 224
Mŭynoq, Uzb. 43°49' N, 58°56' E 160
Muyumba, Dem. Rep. of the Congo 7°15' S, 27°1' E 224
Muzaffarabad, Pak. 34°23' N, 73°33' E 186
Muzaffargarh, Pak. 30°4' N, 71°12' E 186
Muzaffarnagar, India 29°29' N, 77°40' E 197
Muzaffarpur, India 26°5' N, 85°23' E 197
Muzhi, Russ. 65°21' N, 64°36' E 169
Muzon, Cape, Alas., U.S. 54°29' N, 132°42' W 108
Múzquiz, Mex. 27°52' N, 101°31' W 92
Muztag, peak, China 36°24' N, 87°20' E 188
Muztag, peak, China 35°59' N, 80°10' E 188
Muztagata, peak, China 38°17' N, 75°2' E 184
Muztagh Pass, China 35°53' N, 76°12' E 186
Mvadhi-Ousyé, Gabon 1°12' N, 13°11' E 218
Mvolo, Sudan 6°3' N, 29°55' E 224
Mvomero, Tanzania 6°17' S, 37°26' E 224
Mvouti, Congo 4°16' S, 12°26' E 218
Mvuma, Zimb. 19°19' S, 30°29' E 224
Mwadingusha, Dem. Rep. of the Congo 10°45' S, 27°10' E 224
Mwadui, Tanzania 3°35' S, 33°39' E 224
Mwakete, Tanzania 9°20' S, 34°14' E 224
Mwali, island, Comoros 12°34' S, 43°15' E 220
Mwami, Zimb. 16°41' S, 29°46' E 224
Mwanza, Dem. Rep. of the Congo 7°51' S, 26°39' E 224
Mwanza, Tanzania 2°32' S, 32°55' E 224
Mwanza, adm. division, Tanzania 2°57' S, 31°56' E 224
Mwatate, Kenya 3°32' S, 38°21' E 218
Mwaya, Tanzania 9°32' S, 33°55' E 224
Mweelrea, peak, Ire. 53°36' N, 9°56' W 150
Mweka, Dem. Rep. of the Congo 4°52' S, 21°31' E 218
Mwene-Ditu, Dem. Rep. of the Congo 7°1' S, 23°24' E 224
Mwenezi, Zimb. 21°25' S, 30°45' E 227
Mwenezi, river, Zimb. 21°45' S, 31°8' E 227
Mwenga, Dem. Rep. of the Congo 3°4' S, 28°26' E 224
Mwenzo, Zambia 9°21' S, 32°41' E 224
Mweru, Lake, Dem. Rep. of the Congo 9°16' S, 26°39' E 207
Mweru Wantipa National Park, Zambia 9°9' S, 29°20' E 224
Mwimba, Dem. Rep. of the Congo 9°12' S, 22°46' E 218
Mwingi, Kenya 0°57' N, 38°4' E 224
Mwinilunga, Zambia 11°44' S, 24°25' E 224
Mwitikira, Tanzania 6°30' S, 35°39' E 224
Mwombezhi, river, Zambia 12°41' S, 25°43' E 224
My Tho, Vietnam 10°21' N, 106°21' E 202
Myadzyel, Belarus 54°51' N, 26°56' E 166
Myakit, Russ. 61°29' N, 151°59' E 160
Myakka City, Fla., U.S. 27°21' N, 82°9' W 105
Myakka, river, Fla., U.S. 27°13' N, 82°22' W 105
Myaksa, Russ. 58°52' N, 38°15' E 154
Myanaung, Myanmar 18°20' N, 95°13' E 202
Myanmar (Burma) 21°5' N, 95°9' E 192
Myeik, Myanmar 12°35' N, 98°38' E 192
Myingyan, Myanmar 21°28' N, 95°25' E 202
Myitkyinā, Myanmar 25°29' N, 97°20' E 190
Myitta, Myanmar 14°10' N, 98°30' E 202
Myken, islands, Norwegian Sea 66°43' N, 11°26' E 152
Mykhaylivka, Ukr. 47°14' N, 35°15' E 156
Mykolayiv, Ukr. 49°31' N, 23°57' E 158
Mykolayiv, Ukr. 46°59' N, 32°2' E 156
Myla, Russ. 65°25' N, 50°42' E 154
Mylius Erichsen Land 80°43' N, 42°2' W 246
Myllykoski, Fin. 60°46' N, 26°46' E 166
Mymensingh, Bangladesh 24°53' N, 90°40' E 197
Mynämäki, Fin. 60°40' N, 21°56' E 166
Mynbulaq, Uzb. 42°12' N, 62°55' E 180
Myohaung, Myanmar 20°38' N, 93°10' E 188
Myohyang Sanmaek, N. Korea 39°58' N, 126°24' E 200
Myōkō, Japan 36°55' N, 138°12' E 201
Myoungmya, Myanmar 16°34' N, 94°55' E 202
Myra see Kale, Turk. 36°13' N, 29°57' E 156
Mýrdalsjökull, glacier, Ice. 63°11' N, 18°33' W 142
Myrhorod, Ukr. 49°57' N, 33°31' E 158
Myrskylä, Fin. 60°39' N, 25°48' E 166
Myrtle Beach, S.C., U.S. 33°39' N, 78°54' W 82
Myrtle Creek, Oreg., U.S. 43°1' N, 123°17' W 90
Myrtle Point, Oreg., U.S. 43°3' N, 124°8' W 90
Mys Kamennyy, Russ. 68°29' N, 73°26' E 169
Mys Shmidta, Russ. 68°54' N, 179°31' W 98
Mys Zhelaniya, Russ. 76°50' N, 68°29' E 160
Mysen, Nor. 59°34' N, 11°19' E 152
Myshkino, Russ. 57°46' N, 38°26' E 154
Myślice, Pol. 53°54' N, 19°30' E 166
Mysovaya, Russ. 67°44' N, 155°59' E 160
Mystic, Conn., U.S. 41°21' N, 71°58' W 104
Mystic, Iowa, U.S. 40°46' N, 92°57' W 94
Mysy, Russ. 60°36' N, 54°4' E 154
Mytilene see Mitilíni, Gr. 39°6' N, 26°33' E 156
Myton, Utah, U.S. 40°11' N, 110°3' W 90
Myyeldino, Russ. 61°48' N, 54°46' E 154
Mzima Springs, Kenya 2°59' S, 38°4' E 224
Mzimba, Malawi 11°52' S, 33°32' E 224
Mzuzu, Malawi 11°27' S, 33°54' E 224

N

Nā'ālehu, Hawai'i, U.S. 19°3' N, 155°36' W 99
Naachtún Dos Lagunas Biotope, Guatemala 17°35' N, 90°14' W 115
Naama, Alg. 33°16' N, 0°21' E 214
Naandi, Sudan 4°58' N, 27°49' E 224
Naantali, Fin. 60°28' N, 22°2' E 166
Naas, Ire. 53°12' N, 6°40' W 150
Nabā, Jabal (Nebo, Mount), peak, Jordan 31°45' N, 35°43' E 194
Nababiep, S. Af. 29°36' S, 17°47' E 227
Nabas, Philippines 11°49' N, 122°6' E 203
Naberera, Tanzania 4°12' S, 36°56' E 224
Naberezhnyye Chelny, Russ. 55°40' N, 52°22' E 154
Nabeul, Tun. 36°27' N, 10°44' E 156
Nabilatuk, Uganda 2°3' N, 34°35' E 224
Nabire, Indonesia 3°21' S, 135°28' E 238
Nablus see Nābulus, West Bank, Israel 32°12' N, 35°17' E 194
Naboomspruit see Mookgophong, S. Af. 24°31' S, 28°44' E 227
Nabordo, Nig. 10°11' N, 9°25' E 222
Naborton, La., U.S. 32°1' N, 93°35' W 103
Nabq, Egypt 28°7' N, 34°23' E 180
Nābulus (Nablus), West Bank, Israel 32°12' N, 35°17' E 194
Nabúri, Mozambique 16°57' S, 39°0' E 224
Nacala, Mozambique 14°33' S, 40°43' E 224
Nacaome, Hond. 13°31' N, 87°29' W 115
Nacaroa, Mozambique 14°18' S, 39°49' E 224
Nacebe, Bol. 10°58' S, 67°27' W 137
Naches, Wash., U.S. 46°42' N, 120°42' W 90
Nachikatsuura, Japan 33°35' N, 135°54' E 201
Nachingwea, Tanzania 10°25' S, 38°46' E 224
Nachna, India 27°31' N, 71°44' E 186
Náchod, Czech Rep. 50°24' N, 16°10' E 152
Nachuge, India 10°44' N, 92°31' E 188
Nacimiento, Mex. 28°3' N, 101°45' W 92
Nacimiento, Lake, Calif., U.S. 35°44' N, 121°17' W 100
Naciria, Alg. 36°44' N, 3°50' E 150
Nacka, Sw. 59°17' N, 18°7' E 166
Nackhörn, Ger. 54°18' N, 7°50' E 152
Naco, Mex. 31°17' N, 109°58' W 92
Nacogdoches, Tex., U.S. 31°34' N, 94°39' W 103
Nácori Chico, Mex. 29°39' N, 109°5' W 92
Nacozari, river, Mex. 29°23' N, 109°44' W 80
Nacozari Viejo, Mex. 30°21' N, 109°39' W 92
Ñacunday, Parag. 26°4' S, 54°35' W 139
Nada see Danxian, China 19°28' N, 109°34' E 198
Nadale, island, Maldives 0°16' N, 72°12' E 188
Nadanbo, China 43°9' N, 125°27' E 200
Nadap, Hung. 47°15' N, 18°36' E 168
Nadiad, India 22°41' N, 72°51' E 186
Nădlac, Rom. 46°10' N, 20°47' E 168
Nădrag, Rom. 45°40' N, 22°13' E 168
Nadu, adm. division, India 11°19' N, 79°30' E 188
Nádudvar, Hung. 47°25' N, 21°9' E 168
Nadvoitsy, Russ. 63°53' N, 34°13' E 152
Nadym, Russ. 65°35' N, 72°33' E 169
Nadym, river, Russ. 63°43' N, 72°30' E 169
Nafūsah, Jabal, Lib. 31°17' N, 10°13' E 214
Nafada, Nig. 11°2' N, 11°19' E 222
Nafana, Côte d'Ivoire 9°11' N, 4°48' W 222
Naft Khaneh Naft-e-Shāh, oil field, Iraq 34°6' N, 45°18' E 180
Naft-e Safīd, oil field, Iran 31°41' N, 49°12' E 180
Nafuce, Nig. 12°19' N, 6°30' E 222
Nag, Pak. 27°21' N, 65°4' E 186
Nag 'Hammâdi, Egypt 26°3' N, 32°9' E 180
Naga, Philippines 13°38' N, 123°10' E 203
Naga Hills, Myanmar 25°34' N, 94°35' E 188
Nagagami Lake, Can. 49°21' N, 85°32' W 94
Nagagami, river, Can. 49°45' N, 84°34' W 94
Nagagamisis Lake, Can. 49°27' N, 85°16' W 94
Nagahama, Japan 35°22' N, 136°16' E 201
Nagahama, Japan 33°36' N, 132°29' E 201
Nagai, Japan 38°6' N, 140°1' E 201
Nagano, Japan 36°40' N, 138°12' E 201
Nagano, adm. division, Japan 35°59' N, 137°38' E 201
Naganuma, Japan 37°17' N, 140°12' E 201
Nagaoka, Japan 37°26' N, 138°51' E 201
Nagar, India 32°5' N, 77°13' E 188
Nagar Parkar, Pak. 24°23' N, 70°47' E 186
Nagarzê, China 28°58' N, 90°21' E 197
Nagas Point, Can. 52°1' N, 131°45' W 108
Nagasaki, Japan 32°45' N, 129°52' E 201
Nagasaki, adm. division, Japan 32°47' N, 129°50' E 201
Nagashima, Japan 34°12' N, 136°20' E 201
Nagato, Japan 34°21' N, 131°11' E 200
Nagaur, India 27°10' N, 73°45' E 186
Nagda, India 23°26' N, 75°27' E 197
Nagēlē, Eth. 5°20' N, 39°36' E 224
Nagercoil, India 8°10' N, 77°25' E 188
Nagina, India 29°26' N, 78°24' E 197
Nagishot, Sudan 4°15' N, 33°33' E 224
Nagorno-Karabakh, special sovereignty, Azerb. 39°45' N, 46°34' E 195
Nagornyy, Russ. 55°58' N, 124°54' E 160
Nagorsk, Russ. 59°19' N, 50°49' E 154
Nagoya, Japan 35°8' N, 136°55' E 201
Nagpur, India 21°8' N, 79°5' E 197
Nagqu, China 31°27' N, 92°0' E 188
Nagyatád, Hung. 46°13' N, 17°22' E 168
Nagybajom, Hung. 46°23' N, 17°30' E 168
Nagybátony, Hung. 47°58' N, 19°49' E 168
Nagycenk, Hung. 47°36' N, 16°41' E 168
Nagydorog, Hung. 46°37' N, 18°39' E 168
Nagykereki, Hung. 47°11' N, 21°47' E 168
Nagykőros, Hung. 47°1' N, 19°46' E 168
Nagymányok, Hung. 46°16' N, 18°28' E 168
Nagyszénás, Hung. 46°41' N, 20°40' E 168
Naha, Japan 26°13' N, 127°38' E 190
Nahal Hever, ruin(s), Israel 31°25' N, 35°17' E 194
Nahal 'Oz, Israel 31°27' N, 34°29' E 194
Nahanni Butte, Can. 61°2' N, 123°23' W 108
Nahanni National Park Reserve, Can. 61°8' N, 125°57' W 108
Nahant, Mass., U.S. 42°25' N, 70°55' W 104
Nahari, Japan 33°25' N, 134°1' E 201
Nahariyya, Israel 33°0' N, 35°5' E 194
Nahāvand, Iran 34°12' N, 48°21' E 180
Nahlin, river, Can. 58°48' N, 131°26' W 108
Nahrin, Afghan. 36°2' N, 69°8' E 186
Nahuel Huapí National Park, Arg. 41°4' S, 71°53' W 122
Naicam, Can. 52°25' N, 104°29' W 108
Naij Gol, river, China 35°52' N, 92°56' E 188
Nailsworth, U.K. 51°41' N, 2°13' W 162
Na'ima, Sudan 14°36' N, 32°15' E 182
Naiman Qi, China 42°48' N, 120°38' E 198
Nain, Can. 56°29' N, 61°49' W 106
Nā'īn, Iran 32°50' N, 53°7' E 180
Nainpur, India 22°25' N, 80°7' E 197
Nainwa, India 25°47' N, 75°53' E 197
Nairn, La., U.S. 29°25' N, 89°37' W 103
Nairn, U.K. 57°35' N, 3°53' W 150
Nairobi, Kenya 1°20' S, 36°39' E 224
Nairobi National Park, Kenya 1°28' S, 36°31' E 206
Nairôto, Mozambique 12°24' S, 39°6' E 224
Nais Saar, island, Est. 59°32' N, 23°57' E 166
Naivasha, Kenya 0°45' N, 36°27' E 224
Naj Tunich, site, Guatemala 16°18' N, 89°22' W 115
Najaf see An Najaf, Iraq 31°58' N, 44°19' E 180
Najafābād, Iran 32°38' N, 51°25' E 180
Najd, region, Saudi Arabia 26°8' N, 42°8' E 182
Najrān, Saudi Arabia 17°44' N, 44°27' E 182
Naju, S. Korea 35°0' N, 126°44' E 200
Naka, river, Japan 33°44' N, 134°17' E 201
Nakajō, Japan 38°3' N, 139°24' E 201
Nakaminato, Japan 36°20' N, 140°36' E 201
Nakamura, Japan 32°58' N, 132°55' E 201
Nakanno, Russ. 62°57' N, 108°15' E 160
Nakano, Japan 36°44' N, 138°22' E 201
Nakanojō, Japan 36°35' N, 138°50' E 201
Nakatosa, Japan 33°18' N, 133°12' E 201
Nakatsu, Japan 33°35' N, 131°12' E 201
Nakatsugawa, Japan 35°28' N, 137°31' E 201
Nakfa, Eritrea 16°38' N, 38°25' E 182
Nakhl, Egypt 29°52' N, 33°47' E 180
Nakhodka, Russ. 67°40' N, 77°44' E 169
Nakhodka, Russ. 42°51' N, 132°48' E 190
Nakhon Nayok, Thai. 14°13' N, 101°12' E 202
Nakhon Phanom, Thai. 17°23' N, 104°44' E 202
Nakhon Ratchasima (Khorat), Thai. 14°58' N, 102°7' E 202
Nakhon Sawan, Thai. 15°41' N, 100°5' E 202
Nakhon Si Thammarat, Thai. 8°26' N, 99°57' E 202
Nakina, Can. 50°11' N, 86°38' W 82
Nakina, river, Can. 58°51' N, 133°3' W 108
Näkkälä, Fin. 68°36' N, 23°31' E 152
Naknek, Alas., U.S. 58°41' N, 157°5' W 98
Nako, Burkina Faso 10°39' N, 3°3' W 222
Nakonde, Zambia 9°23' S, 32°45' E 224
Nakop, Namibia 28°6' S, 19°59' E 227
Nakovo, Serb. 45°52' N, 20°32' E 168
Nakuru, Kenya 0°18' N, 36°5' E 224
Nakusp, Can. 50°14' N, 117°49' W 90
Nal'chik, Russ. 43°30' N, 43°38' E 195
Nallihan, Turk. 40°11' N, 31°21' E 156
Nālūt, Lib. 31°54' N, 10°58' E 214
Nam Can, Vietnam 8°48' N, 105°1' E 202
Nam Co, lake, China 30°45' N, 89°50' E 188
Nam Dinh, Vietnam 20°26' N, 106°8' E 198
Nam Nao National Park, Thai. 16°25' N, 101°24' E 202
Nam Ngum Dam, Laos 18°42' N, 102°29' E 202
Nam Phong Dam, Thai. 16°34' N, 102°8' E 202
Nam Phung Dam, Thai. 16°49' N, 102°59' E 202
Nam, river, S. Korea 35°17' N, 128°16' E 200
Nam Tok, Thai. 14°23' N, 98°57' E 202
Namaacha, Mozambique 25°57' S, 32°1' E 227
Namacunde, Angola 17°19' S, 15°49' E 220
Namacurra, Mozambique 17°29' S, 37°2' E 224
Namak, S. Korea 36°34' N, 127°46' E 200
Namanga, Kenya 2°33' S, 36°49' E 224
Namangan, Uzb. 40°59' N, 71°38' E 197
Namanyere, Tanzania 7°31' S, 31°2' E 224
Namapa, Mozambique 13°44' S, 39°51' E 224
Namaponda, Mozambique 15°51' S, 39°53' E 224
Namaqualand, region, S. Af. 30°11' S, 17°12' E 227
Namarrói, Mozambique 15°58' S, 36°49' E 224
Namasagali, Uganda 0°59' N, 32°58' E 224
Namatanai, P.N.G. 3°41' S, 152°25' E 238
Nambinda, Tanzania 9°37' S, 37°37' E 224
Nambu, Japan 35°16' N, 138°26' E 201
Namdae, river, N. Korea 41°8' N, 129°4' E 200
Namdapha National Park, India 27°30' N, 96°34' E 188
Nameigos Lake, Can. 48°45' N, 85°12' W 94
Namerikawa, Japan 36°45' N, 137°19' E 201
Nametil, Mozambique 15°44' S, 39°24' E 224
Namgia, India 31°46' N, 78°41' E 188
Namib Desert, Angola 15°54' S, 12°10' E 220
Namibe, Angola 15°14' S, 12°10' E 220
Namibe, adm. division, Angola 16°24' S, 11°50' E 220
Namibia 21°53' S, 15°16' E 220
Namib-Naukluft Park, Namibia 25°49' S, 15°21' E 227
Namies, S. Af. 29°17' S, 19°11' E 227
Namīn, Iran 38°29' N, 48°30' E 195
Namiquipa, Mex. 29°14' N, 107°25' W 92
Namjagbarwa Feng, peak, China 29°37' N, 94°55' E 188
Namji, S. Korea 35°23' N, 128°29' E 200
Namlea, Indonesia 3°16' S, 127°1' E 192
Namling, China 29°42' N, 89°3' E 197
Namoi, river, Austral. 30°32' S, 147°10' E 231
Nāmolokama Mountain, peak, Hawai'i, U.S. 22°7' N, 159°33' W 99
Namoluk Atoll 5°35' N, 150°28' E 192
Namonuito Atoll, North Pacific Ocean 8°43' N, 149°21' E 192
Nampa, Can. 56°3' N, 117°9' W 108
Nampa, Idaho, U.S. 43°32' N, 116°34' W 82
Nampala, Mali 15°15' N, 5°34' W 222
Namp'o, N. Korea 38°43' N, 125°25' E 200
Nampō Shotō, islands, North Pacific Ocean 30°47' N, 138°20' E 190
Nampula, Mozambique 15°8' S, 39°17' E 224
Nampula, adm. division, Mozambique 15°0' S, 37°41' E 224
Namsos, Nor. 64°29' N, 11°41' E 160
Namsskogan, Nor. 64°55' N, 13°12' E 152
Namtsy, Russ. 62°41' N, 129°32' E 160
Namtu, Myanmar 23°1' N, 97°27' E 202
Namu, Can. 51°50' N, 127°49' W 108
Namuli, peak, Mozambique 15°26' S, 36°59' E 224
Namuno, Mozambique 13°31' S, 38°52' E 224
Namur, Belg. 50°28' N, 4°51' E 167
Namur Lake, Can. 57°18' N, 113°21' W 108
Namuruputh, Kenya 4°31' N, 35°54' E 224
Namutoni, Namibia 18°51' S, 16°57' E 220
Namwala, Zambia 15°46' S, 26°25' E 224
Namwon, S. Korea 35°23' N, 127°23' E 200
Namyang, N. Korea 40°44' N, 129°17' E 200
Nan, Thai. 18°48' N, 100°45' E 202
Nan Hulsan Hu, lake, China 36°42' N, 94°42' E 188
Nan, river, Thai. 18°37' N, 100°46' E 202
Nana, river, Cen. Af. Rep. 5°48' N, 15°21' E 218
Nanaimo, Can. 49°9' N, 123°57' W 100
Nanakru, Liberia 4°52' N, 8°45' W 222
Nanam, Korea 41°41' N, 129°39' E 200
Nan'an, China 24°55' N, 118°22' E 198
Nanao, Japan 37°2' N, 136°56' E 201
Nanbu, China 31°20' N, 106°0' E 198
Nancheng, China 28°41' N, 115°54' E 198
Nancheng, China 27°33' N, 116°37' E 198
Nanchong, China 30°49' N, 106°2' E 198
Nanchuan, China 29°11' N, 107°3' E 198
Ñancorainza, Bol. 20°41' S, 63°28' W 137
Nancy, Fr. 48°41' N, 6°11' E 163
Nanda Devi, peak, India 30°22' N, 79°52' E 197
Nandan, China 24°57' N, 107°30' E 198
Nanded, India 19°11' N, 77°19' E 188
Nanfen, China 41°8' N, 123°48' E 200
Nanfeng, China 27°13' N, 116°25' E 198
Nang, China 29°5' N, 93°6' E 188
Nanga Parbat, peak, Pak. 35°13' N, 74°28' E 186
Nangade, Mozambique 11°6' S, 39°43' E 224
Nangapinoh, Indonesia 0°21' N, 111°38' E 192
Nangin, Myanmar 10°32' N, 98°29' E 202
Nangis, Fr. 48°33' N, 3°0' E 163
Nangnim, N. Korea 40°57' N, 127°8' E 200
Nangong, China 37°18' N, 115°23' E 198
Nangqên, China 32°15' N, 96°28' E 188
Nangtud, Mount, peak, Philippines 11°16' N, 122°6' E 203
Nanika Lake, lake, Can. 53°45' N, 128°5' W 108
Nanjiang, China 32°24' N, 106°46' E 198
Nanjing, China 32°5' N, 118°48' E 198
Nanjing, China 24°22' N, 117°16' E 198
Nankang, China 25°39' N, 114°41' E 198
Nankoku, Japan 33°34' N, 133°38' E 201
Nanle, China 36°3' N, 115°11' E 198
Nanning, China 22°49' N, 108°19' E 198
Nanortalik 60°13' N, 45°14' W 106
Nanpara, India 27°50' N, 81°30' E 197
Nanping, China 42°18' N, 129°12' E 200
Nanping, China 26°37' N, 118°4' E 198
Nanri Dao, island, China 24°53' N, 119°22' E 198
Nansan Dao, island, China 21°1' N, 110°37' E 198
Nansei Shotō (Ryukyu Islands), East China Sea 25°0' N, 125°56' E 190
Nansen Basin, Arctic Ocean 85°0' N, 78°46' E 255
Nansen Land 82°0' N, 43°58' W 246
Nansen Sound 80°31' N, 104°17' W 72
Nansio, Tanzania 2°7' S, 33°4' E 224
Nantais, Lac, lake, Can. 61°33' N, 76°5' W 246
Nantes, Fr. 47°12' N, 1°36' W 150
Nanteuil-le-Haudouin, Fr. 49°8' N, 2°48' E 163
Nanticoke, Pa., U.S. 41°11' N, 76°1' W 110
Nanton, Can. 50°20' N, 113°47' W 108
Nantong, China 32°2' N, 120°54' E 198
Nantucket, Mass., U.S. 41°16' N, 70°7' W 104
Nantucket Inlet 74°39' S, 66°32' W 248
Nantucket Island, Mass., U.S. 41°22' N, 70°2' W 104
Nantucket Sound 41°26' N, 70°19' W 104
Nantulo, Mozambique 12°30' S, 39°1' E 224
Nantwich, U.K. 53°3' N, 2°31' W 162
Nanuque, Braz. 17°49' S, 40°21' W 138
Nanusa, Kepulauan, islands, Philippine Sea 4°57' N, 126°54' E 203
Nanxi, China 28°51' N, 104°56' E 198
Nanxian, China 29°23' N, 112°23' E 198
Nanxiong, China 25°6' N, 114°15' E 198
Nanyang, China 33°1' N, 112°34' E 198
Nanyuki, Kenya 1°58' S, 37°4' E 224
Nanzhang, China 31°47' N, 111°50' E 198
Nanzhila, Zambia 16°6' S, 26°1' E 224
Nao, Cabo de La, Sp. 38°30' N, 0°10' E 214
Naococane, Lac, lake, Can. 52°47' N, 71°20' W 111
Naozhou Dao, island, China 20°51' N, 110°39' E 198
Napa, Calif., U.S. 38°18' N, 122°19' W 100
Napá, Mozambique 13°17' S, 39°3' E 224
Napaimiut, Alas., U.S. 61°32' N, 158°41' W 98
Napaleofú, Arg. 37°38' S, 58°46' W 139
Napalkovo, Russ. 70°3' N, 73°54' E 169
Napanee, Can. 44°14' N, 76°59' W 82
Napas, Russ. 59°48' N, 81°57' E 169
Napasoq 65°4' N, 52°21' W 106
Napenay, Arg. 26°44' S, 60°38' W 139
Naperville, Ill., U.S. 41°46' N, 88°9' W 102
Napier, N.Z. 39°30' S, 176°54' E 240
Napier Bay 11°54' S, 131°12' E 231
Naples, Fla., U.S. 26°9' N, 81°48' W 105
Naples, Me., U.S. 43°57' N, 70°37' W 104
Naples, Tex., U.S. 33°11' N, 94°41' W 103
Naples see Napoli, It. 40°51' N, 14°15' E 156
Napo, China 23°21' N, 105°50' E 198
Napo, river, Ecua. 1°14' S, 77°33' W 136
Napo, river, Peru 2°38' S, 74°29' W 122
Napoleon, N. Dak., U.S. 46°29' N, 99°47' W 90
Napoleon, Ohio, U.S. 41°22' N, 84°8' W 102
Napoleonville, La., U.S. 29°55' N, 91°3' W 103
Napoli (Naples), It. 40°51' N, 14°15' E 156
Nappanee, Ind., U.S. 41°26' N, 86°1' W 102
Nāpu'ukūlua, peak, Hawai'i, U.S. 19°42' N, 155°40' W 99
Naqoura, Leb. 33°7' N, 35°8' E 194
Nara, Japan 34°42' N, 135°50' E 201
Nara, Mali 15°10' N, 7°18' W 222
Nara, adm. division, Japan 34°17' N, 135°40' E 201
Nara, river, Pak. 24°46' N, 69°35' E 186
Nara Visa, N. Mex., U.S. 35°36' N, 103°6' W 92
Narach, Belarus 54°55' N, 26°41' E 166
Narach, Vozyera, lake, Belarus 54°52' N, 26°17' E 166
Na'rān, Israel 33°2' N, 35°42' E 194
Naranbulag, Mongolia 49°14' N, 113°19' E 198
Narang, Afghan. 34°44' N, 70°57' E 186
Narasannapeta, India 18°24' N, 84°5' E 188
Narasapur, India 16°27' N, 81°40' E 188
Narathiwat, Thai. 6°26' N, 101°49' E 196
Narayanganj, Bangladesh 23°26' N, 90°40' E 197
Nærbø, Nor. 58°40' N, 5°38' E 152
Narbonne, Fr. 43°10' N, 2°59' E 164
Narcondam Island, India 13°28' N, 94°19' E 188
Nardīn, Iran 37°0' N, 55°57' E 180
Naré, Arg. 30°58' S, 60°28' W 139
Nares Land 81°45' N, 46°0' W 72
Nares Plain, North Atlantic Ocean 22°43' N, 63°8' W 253
Narib, Namibia 24°12' S, 17°46' E 227
Naricual, Venez. 10°2' N, 64°37' W 116
Narimanabad, Azerb. 38°51' N, 48°50' E 195
Narin, river, China 36°20' N, 92°32' E 188
Nariño, adm. division, Col. 1°27' N, 78°30' W 136
Narlı, Turk. 37°25' N, 37°8' E 156
Narmada, river, India 22°56' N, 78°26' E 197
Narodnaya, Gora, peak, Russ. 65°6' N, 59°49' E 154
Narok, Kenya 1°6' S, 35°50' E 224
Narowlya, Belarus 51°44' N, 29°38' E 158
Nærøy, Nor. 64°48' N, 11°16' E 152
Närpiö see Närpes, Fin. 62°27' N, 21°18' E 152
Narragansett Pier, R.I., U.S. 41°25' N, 71°28' W 104

New Holstein, Wis., U.S. 43°56' N, 88°6' W 102
New Iberia, La., U.S. 29°58' N, 91°49' W 103
New Ipswich, N.H., U.S. 42°45' N, 71°52' W 104
New Ireland, island, P.N.G. 3°27' S, 149°43' E 192
New Island, New Island 51°50' S, 62°10' W 134
New Jersey, adm. division, N.J., U.S. 41°2' N, 74°51' W 94
New Lebanon, N.Y., U.S. 42°27' N, 73°25' W 104
New Lenox, Ill., U.S. 41°29' N, 87°58' W 102
New Lexington, Ohio, U.S. 39°41' N, 82°12' W 102
New Lisbon, Wis., U.S. 43°51' N, 90°11' W 102
New Liskeard, Can. 47°30' N, 79°41' W 94
New London, Conn., U.S. 41°20' N, 72°7' W 104
New London, N.H., U.S. 43°24' N, 71°59' W 104
New London, Ohio, U.S. 41°4' N, 82°24' W 102
New London, Tex., U.S. 32°14' N, 94°57' W 103
New London, Wis., U.S. 44°23' N, 88°46' W 110
New Madrid, Mo., U.S. 36°35' N, 89°31' W 96
New Market, Ind., U.S. 39°57' N, 86°56' W 102
New Matamoras, Ohio, U.S. 39°31' N, 81°4' W 102
New Meadows, Idaho, U.S. 44°57' N, 116°16' W 90
New Mexico, adm. division, N. Mex., U.S. 34°43' N, 106°25' W 92
New Miami, Ohio, U.S. 39°25' N, 84°32' W 102
New Milford, Conn., U.S. 41°34' N, 73°25' W 104
New Orleans, La., U.S. 29°56' N, 90°5' W 103
New Osnaburgh, Can. 51°12' N, 90°12' W 110
New Paltz, N.Y., U.S. 41°44' N, 74°5' W 104
New Paris, Ohio, U.S. 39°51' N, 84°47' W 102
New Philadelphia, Ohio, U.S. 40°28' N, 81°26' W 102
New Plymouth, Idaho, U.S. 43°57' N, 116°50' W 90
New Plymouth, N.Z. 39°6' S, 174°6' E 240
New Point, Ind., U.S. 39°17' N, 85°20' W 102
New Port Richey, Fla., U.S. 28°15' N, 82°43' W 105
New Prague, Minn., U.S. 44°31' N, 93°36' W 94
New Providence, island, Bahamas 25°1' N, 77°26' W 118
New Radnor, U.K. 52°14' N, 3°9' W 162
New Richmond, Can. 48°10' N, 65°53' W 94
New Richmond, Ohio, U.S. 38°56' N, 84°16' W 102
New Richmond, Wis., U.S. 45°7' N, 92°33' W 94
New, river, Calif., U.S. 33°5' N, 115°43' W 101
New, river, W. Va., U.S. 37°51' N, 81°3' W 94
New Roads, La., U.S. 30°41' N, 91°27' W 103
New Rochelle, N.Y., U.S. 40°55' N, 73°48' W 104
New Rockford, N. Dak., U.S. 47°39' N, 99°10' W 90
New Romney, U.K. 50°59' N, 0°56' E 162
New Salem, Mass., U.S. 42°30' N, 72°20' W 104
New Salem, N. Dak., U.S. 46°49' N, 101°27' W 90
New Schwabenland, region, Antarctica 73°46' S, 13°38' W 248
New Shoreham, R.I., U.S. 41°10' N, 71°34' W 104
New Siberian Islands see Novosi Birskiye Ostrova, Russ. 76°14' N, 142°6' E 160
New Smyrna Beach, Fla., U.S. 29°0' N, 80°56' W 105
New South Wales, adm. division, Austral. 32°28' S, 147°11' E 231
New Summerfield, Tex., U.S. 31°57' N, 95°5' W 103
New Town, N. Dak., U.S. 47°57' N, 102°30' W 90
New Ulm, Minn., U.S. 44°18' N, 94°29' W 90
New Washington, Ind., U.S. 38°33' N, 85°33' W 102
New Waterford, Can. 46°14' N, 60°6' W 111
New Waverly, Tex., U.S. 30°31' N, 95°29' W 103
New Willard, Tex., U.S. 30°46' N, 94°53' W 103
New Windsor, N.Y., U.S. 41°28' N, 74°3' W 104
New York, N.Y., U.S. 40°43' N, 74°1' W 104
New York, adm. division, N.Y., U.S. 42°56' N, 76°33' W 94
New York Mountains, Calif., U.S. 35°22' N, 115°20' W 101
New York Mountains, Calif., U.S. 35°22' N, 115°26' W 80
New Zealand 42°2' S, 173°5' E 240
Newala, Tanzania 10°58' S, 39°16' E 224
Newark, Ark., U.S. 35°41' N, 91°26' W 96
Newark, Ill., U.S. 41°32' N, 88°35' W 102
Newark, N.J., U.S. 40°43' N, 74°12' W 94
Newark, N.Y., U.S. 43°2' N, 77°6' W 94
Newark, Ohio, U.S. 40°3' N, 82°25' W 102
Newark, U.K. 53°4' N, 0°49' E 162
Newaygo, Mich., U.S. 43°24' N, 85°48' W 102
Newbald, U.K. 53°49' N, 0°38' E 162
Newbern, Ala., U.S. 32°35' N, 87°32' W 103
Newbern, Tenn., U.S. 36°6' N, 89°17' W 96
Newberry, Fla., U.S. 29°38' N, 82°37' W 105
Newberry, Mich., U.S. 46°21' N, 85°31' W 94
Newberry Springs, Calif., U.S. 34°49' N, 116°42' W 101
Newbrook, Can. 54°18' N, 112°58' W 108
Newburgh, N.Y., U.S. 41°30' N, 74°2' W 104
Newbury, U.K. 51°23' N, 1°20' W 162
Newbury, Vt., U.S. 44°4' N, 72°4' W 104
Newburyport, Mass., U.S. 42°48' N, 70°53' W 104
Newcastle, Can. 47°0' N, 65°35' W 94
Newcastle, S. Af. 27°46' S, 29°55' E 227
Newcastle, Tex., U.S. 33°10' N, 98°44' W 92
Newcastle, U.K. 54°12' N, 5°55' W 150
Newcastle, U.K. 54°58' N, 1°38' W 162
Newcastle, Wyo., U.S. 43°49' N, 104°12' W 90
Newcastle Bay 10°58' S, 141°25' E 230
Newcastle under Lyme, U.K. 53°0' N, 2°15' W 162
Newcastle Waters, Austral. 17°23' S, 133°23' E 231
Newcomb, N.Y., U.S. 43°57' N, 74°11' W 104
Newcomb, Tenn., U.S. 36°32' N, 84°10' W 96
Newcomerstown, Ohio, U.S. 40°16' N, 81°36' W 102
Newell, Ark., U.S. 33°8' N, 92°45' W 103
Newell, S. Dak., U.S. 44°42' N, 103°25' W 90
Newell, Lake, Can. 50°19' N, 112°29' W 90
Newellton, La., U.S. 32°3' N, 91°16' W 103
Newenham, Cape, Alas., U.S. 58°18' N, 162°19' W 106
Newenham, Cape, Alas., U.S. 58°38' N, 164°32' W 98
Newfields, N.H., U.S. 43°2' N, 70°57' W 104
Newfoundland and Labrador, adm. division, Can. 48°5' N, 58°29' W 111
Newfoundland, Island of, Can. 48°58' N, 53°21' W 106
Newgrange Mound, ruin(s), Ire. 53°40' N, 6°36' W 150
Newhalem, Wash., U.S. 48°40' N, 121°17' W 100
Newhalen, Alas., U.S. 59°39' N, 155°1' W 98
Newhaven, U.K. 50°47' N, 4°238' E 162
Newington, Conn., U.S. 41°41' N, 72°44' W 104
Newkirk, N. Mex., U.S. 35°4' N, 104°16' W 92
Newkirk, Okla., U.S. 36°52' N, 97°3' W 92
Newllano, La., U.S. 31°5' N, 93°17' W 103
Newman, Calif., U.S. 37°18' N, 121°3' W 100
Newman, Ill., U.S. 39°47' N, 88°0' W 102
Newman Island, island, Antarctica 75°13' S, 146°2' W 248
Newman, Mount, peak, Austral. 23°17' S, 119°19' E 230
Newmarket, Can. 44°2' N, 79°28' W 94
Newmarket, N.H., U.S. 43°4' N, 70°57' W 104
Newmarket, U.K. 52°14' N, 0°24' E 162
Newnan, Ga., U.S. 33°22' N, 84°48' W 112
Newport, Ark., U.S. 35°34' N, 91°18' W 82
Newport, Ind., U.S. 39°51' N, 87°25' W 102
Newport, Mich., U.S. 41°59' N, 83°18' W 102
Newport, N.H., U.S. 43°22' N, 72°11' W 104
Newport, Oreg., U.S. 44°38' N, 124°5' W 82
Newport, R.I., U.S. 41°29' N, 71°19' W 104
Newport, Tenn., U.S. 35°57' N, 83°12' W 96
Newport, U.K. 50°41' N, 1°18' W 162
Newport, U.K. 51°35' N, 3°0' W 162
Newport, U.K. 52°45' N, 2°23' W 162
Newport, Vt., U.S. 44°56' N, 72°13' W 82
Newport, Wash., U.S. 48°10' N, 117°4' W 108
Newport Beach, Calif., U.S. 33°38' N, 117°57' W 101
Newport News, Va., U.S. 36°58' N, 76°26' W 94
Newport Pagnell, U.K. 52°4' N, 0°44' E 162
Newry, Me., U.S. 44°29' N, 70°48' W 104
Newry, S.C., U.S. 34°43' N, 82°56' W 96
Newsome, Tex., U.S. 32°57' N, 95°8' W 103
Newtok, Alas., U.S. 60°57' N, 164°37' W 98
Newton, Ill., U.S. 38°58' N, 88°11' W 102
Newton, Iowa, U.S. 41°41' N, 93°3' W 94
Newton, Kans., U.S. 38°2' N, 97°21' W 90
Newton, Mass., U.S. 42°19' N, 71°15' W 104
Newton, Miss., U.S. 32°18' N, 89°9' W 103
Newton, Mo., U.S. 38°58' N, 88°11' W 94
Newton, Tex., U.S. 30°49' N, 93°46' W 103
Newton Falls, Ohio, U.S. 41°10' N, 80°58' W 102
Newtown, Conn., U.S. 41°24' N, 73°19' W 104
Newtown, U.K. 52°30' N, 3°18' W 162
New-Wes-Valley, Can. 49°9' N, 53°35' W 111
Nexpa, river, Mex. 18°7' N, 102°40' W 114
Neya, Russ. 58°17' N, 43°52' E 154
Neyrīz, Iran 29°12' N, 54°18' E 196
Neyshābūr, Iran 36°12' N, 58°51' E 180
Neyto, Ozero, lake, Russ. 69°51' N, 68°36' E 169
Neyvo Shaytanskiy, Russ. 57°46' N, 61°14' E 154
Nez Perce Pass, Mont., U.S. 45°42' N, 114°31' W 90
Nezperce, Idaho, U.S. 46°13' N, 116°14' W 90
N'Gabé, Congo 3°14' S, 16°8' E 218
Ngahere, N.Z. 42°25' S, 171°27' E 240
Ngambé, Cameroon 4°15' N, 10°39' E 222
Ngamda, China 31°5' N, 96°37' E 188
Ngamring, China 29°17' N, 87°11' E 197
Ngangla Ringco, lake, China 31°40' N, 82°35' E 188
Nganglong Kangri, peak, China 32°50' N, 80°41' E 188
Ngangzê Co, lake, China 30°56' N, 86°20' E 197
N'Gao, Congo 2°30' S, 15°45' E 218
Ngao, Thai. 18°46' N, 99°57' E 202
Ngaoundal, Cameroon 6°26' N, 13°25' E 218
Ngaoundéré, Cameroon 7°16' N, 13°34' E 218
Ngaputaw, Myanmar 16°31' N, 94°42' E 188
Ngara, Tanzania 2°31' S, 30°39' E 224
Ngaruawahia, N.Z. 37°43' S, 175°10' E 240
Ngauruhoe, Mount, peak, N.Z. 39°12' S, 175°32' E 240
Ngayu, river, Dem. Rep. of the Congo 1°53' N, 27°25' E 224
Ngcheangel, island, Palau 8°4' N, 134°43' E 242
Ngeaur see Angaur, island, Palau 7°0' N, 134°0' E 242
Ngerengere, Tanzania 6°42' S, 38°7' E 224
Ngeruktabel (Urukthapel), island, Palau 7°13' N, 134°24' E 242
Nggatokae, island, Solomon Islands 8°45' S, 158°10' E 242
Nghia Lo, Vietnam 21°37' N, 104°28' E 202
Ngoïla, Cameroon 2°45' N, 14°0' E 218
Ngoko, Congo 0°35' N, 15°21' E 218
Ngola Shankou, pass, China 35°30' N, 99°28' E 188
Ngomba, Tanzania 8°25' S, 32°54' E 224
Ngomeni, Ras, Kenya 2°59' S, 40°14' E 224
Ngong, Kenya 1°23' S, 36°40' E 224
Ngop, Sudan 6°13' N, 30°10' E 224
Ngoqumaima, China 32°30' N, 86°51' E 188
Ngorno-Karabakh, special sovereignty, Asia 39°59' N, 46°23' E 195
Ngorongoro Crater, peak, Tanzania 3°15' S, 35°31' E 224
Ngote, Dem. Rep. of the Congo 2°12' N, 30°48' E 224
Ngoto, Cen. Af. Rep. 4°4' N, 17°18' E 218
Ngouo, Mont, peak, Cen. Af. Rep. 7°55' N, 24°32' E 224
Ngouri, Chad 13°39' N, 15°23' E 216
Ngourti, Niger 15°19' N, 13°11' E 216
Ngoywa, Tanzania 5°55' S, 32°47' E 224
Ngozi, Burundi 2°56' S, 29°47' E 224
Ngudu, Tanzania 2°56' S, 33°21' E 224
Nguigmi, Niger 14°17' N, 13°6' E 216
Ngukurr, Austral. 14°44' S, 134°46' E 238
Ngulu Atoll, F.S.M. 8°42' N, 134°55' E 192
Ngum, river, Laos 18°47' N, 102°47' E 202
N'gungo, Angola 11°47' S, 14°9' E 220
Nguni, Kenya 0°49' N, 38°17' E 224
Nguru, Nig. 12°53' N, 10°28' E 222
Ngurumahiga, Tanzania 10°18' S, 37°57' E 224
Nha Trang, Vietnam 12°15' N, 109°10' E 202
Nhamundá, Braz. 2°13' S, 56°44' W 130
Nhamundá, river, Braz. 1°33' S, 58°0' W 132
Nhecolândia, Braz. 19°15' S, 57°1' W 132
Nho Quan, Vietnam 20°20' N, 105°45' E 202
Nhulunbuy, Austral. 12°18' S, 136°48' E 238
Nia Nia, Dem. Rep. of the Congo 1°29' N, 27°40' E 224
Niabembe, Dem. Rep. of the Congo 2°11' S, 27°40' E 224
Niadi, Dem. Rep. of the Congo 4°25' S, 18°50' E 218
Niafounké, Mali 15°56' N, 4°1' W 222
Niagassola, Guinea 12°20' N, 9°8' W 222
Niamey, Niger 13°29' N, 2°0' E 222
Niandan Koro, Guinea 11°6' N, 9°14' W 222
Niangara, Dem. Rep. of the Congo 3°41' N, 27°53' E 224
Niangay, Lac, lake, Mali 15°54' N, 3°22' W 222
Niangoloko, Burkina Faso 10°17' N, 4°56' W 222
Niantic, Conn., U.S. 41°19' N, 72°12' W 104
Niantic, Ill., U.S. 39°50' N, 89°10' W 102
Nianzishan, China 47°33' N, 122°54' E 198
Niapidou, Côte d'Ivoire 5°18' N, 6°3' W 222
Niapu, Dem. Rep. of the Congo 2°24' N, 26°32' E 224
Niari, river, Congo 3°33' S, 12°45' E 218
Nias, island, Indonesia 0°26' N, 97°33' E 196
Niassa, adm. division, Mozambique 12°52' S, 35°24' E 224
Niaza, spring, Mauritania 18°13' N, 11°0' W 222
Nīca, Latv. 56°21' N, 21°1' E 166
Nicaragua 12°38' N, 85°49' W 115
Nicaragua, Lago de, Nicar. 11°30' N, 85°30' W 116
Nice, Fr. 43°42' N, 7°15' E 167
Nichihara, Japan 34°31' N, 131°51' E 201
Nichinan, Japan 31°36' N, 131°21' E 201
Nicholasville, Ky., U.S. 37°52' N, 84°34' W 96
Nicholls' Town, Bahamas 25°7' N, 78°2' W 96
Nichollstown and Berry Islands, adm. division, Bahamas 25°47' N, 78°22' W 96
Nicholson, Can. 47°58' N, 83°46' W 94
Nickel Centre, Can. 46°33' N, 80°52' W 94
Nickelsdorf, Aust. 47°56' N, 17°4' E 168
Nickerson, Kans., U.S. 38°8' N, 98°6' W 90
Nickol Bay 20°40' S, 115°56' E 230
Nicobar Islands, Andaman Sea 8°59' N, 93°39' E 192
Nicolás Bravo, Mex. 24°21' N, 104°44' W 114
Nicolet, Can. 46°13' N, 72°37' W 94
Nicopolis, ruin(s), Gr. 38°59' N, 20°37' E 156
Nicopolis see Suşehri, Turk. 40°8' N, 38°5' E 180
Nicosia see Lefkosia, Cyprus 35°9' N, 33°18' E 194
Nicotera, It. 38°34' N, 15°55' E 156
Nicoya, C.R. 10°8' N, 85°26' W 115
Nicuadala, Mozambique 17°38' S, 36°48' E 224
Nida, Russ. 55°19' N, 21°2' E 166
Nidda, Ger. 50°24' N, 9°1' E 167
Niddatal, Ger. 50°17' N, 8°48' E 167
Nidder, river, Ger. 50°22' N, 9°3' E 167
Nidže, Maced. 41°1' N, 21°41' E 156
Nidzh, Azerb. 40°57' N, 47°39' E 195
Niebla, Sp. 37°21' N, 6°42' W 164
Niechorze, Pol. 54°5' N, 15°4' E 152
Nied, river, Fr. 49°5' N, 6°20' E 163
Nieddu, Monte, peak, It. 40°44' N, 9°30' E 156
Niederaula, Ger. 50°48' N, 9°35' E 167
Niederbronn, Fr. 48°57' N, 7°38' E 163
Niedere Tauern, Aust. 47°11' N, 13°24' E 156
Niedoradz, Pol. 51°52' N, 15°40' E 152
Niéjirane, spring, Mauritania 17°32' N, 9°51' W 222
Niem, Cen. Af. Rep. 6°5' N, 15°15' E 218
Niemba, Dem. Rep. of the Congo 5°59' S, 28°24' E 224
Niéna, Mali 11°26' N, 6°21' W 222
Niers, river, Ger. 51°41' N, 5°58' E 167
Nierstein, Ger. 49°52' N, 8°20' E 167
Nieuw Amsterdam, Suriname 5°50' N, 55°6' W 130
Nieuwe Pekela, Neth. 53°4' N, 6°56' E 163
Nieuwpoort, Belg. 51°7' N, 2°44' E 163
Nieves, Bol. 14°5' S, 65°54' W 137
Nieves, Mex. 24°0' N, 103°2' W 114
Nif, Indonesia 3°19' S, 130°34' E 192
Niğde, Turk. 37°58' N, 34°42' E 180
Niger 17°56' N, 8°41' E 216
Niger Delta, Nig. 5°29' N, 6°7' E 222
Niger, river, Africa 5°54' N, 6°33' E 222
Nigeria 9°25' N, 6°46' E 218
Nightingale Island see Bach Long Vi, Dao, Vietnam 19°46' N, 107°30' E 198
Nihonmatsu, Japan 37°35' N, 140°26' E 201
Niigata, Japan 37°55' N, 139°5' E 201
Niigata, adm. division, Japan 37°27' N, 138°42' E 201
Niihama, Japan 33°56' N, 133°17' E 201
Ni'ihau, island, Hawai'i, U.S. 21°36' N, 160°11' W 99
Niimi, Japan 35°0' N, 133°28' E 201
Niitsu, Japan 37°47' N, 139°8' E 201
Nijar, Sp. 36°57' N, 2°13' W 164
Nijmegen, Neth. 51°50' N, 5°51' E 167
Nikel', Russ. 69°24' N, 30°10' E 152
Nikiniki, Indonesia 9°49' S, 124°28' E 192
Nikiski, Gulf of Alaska 60°43' N, 151°18' W 98
Nikitin Seamount, Indian Ocean 3°48' S, 82°58' E 254
Nikki, Benin 9°56' N, 3°9' E 222
Nikkō, Japan 36°43' N, 139°37' E 201
Nikkō National Park, Japan 37°3' N, 139°40' E 201
Nikolai, Alas., U.S. 63°0' N, 154°11' W 98
Nikolayevo, Russ. 58°15' N, 29°28' E 166
Nikolayevsk, Russ. 50°3' N, 45°33' E 158
Nikolayevsk na Amure, Russ. 53°14' N, 140°36' E 190
Nikolo Berezovka, Russ. 56°6' N, 54°18' E 154
Nikol'sk, Russ. 53°41' N, 46°7' E 154
Nikol'sk, Russ. 59°30' N, 45°32' E 154
Nikol'skoye, Russ. 52°4' N, 55°42' E 154
Nikol'skoye, Russ. 47°43' N, 46°21' E 158
Nikol'skoye, Russ. 55°13' N, 165°54' E 160
Nikonga, river, Tanzania 4°2' S, 31°30' E 224
Nikopol', Ukr. 47°34' N, 34°24' E 156
Nikpey, Iran 36°52' N, 48°12' E 195
Niksar, Turk. 40°35' N, 36°57' E 156
Nīkshahr, Iran 26°13' N, 60°13' E 182
Nikšić, Mont. 42°46' N, 18°56' E 168
Nikulino, Russ. 60°21' N, 90°1' E 169
Niland, Calif., U.S. 33°14' N, 115°32' W 101
Nilandu Atoll, Maldives 2°56' N, 72°6' E 188
Nilandu, island, Maldives 0°27' N, 73°24' E 188
Nile, river, Africa 27°17' N, 31°18' E 206
Niles, Mich., U.S. 41°48' N, 86°15' W 102
Niles, Ohio, U.S. 41°10' N, 80°45' W 94
Nili, Alg. 33°24' N, 3°2' E 214
Nilka, China 43°47' N, 82°38' E 184
Nilsen, Mount, peak, Antarctica 77°54' S, 154°11' W 248
Nilsen Plateau, Antarctica 86°27' S, 180°0' E 248
Nilsiä, Fin. 63°10' N, 28°0' E 152
Nimach, India 24°27' N, 74°51' E 188
Nimba Mountains, Guinea 8°22' N, 9°5' W 222
Nimbahera, India 24°38' N, 74°40' E 188
Nimberra Well, spring, Austral. 23°6' S, 123°18' E 230
Nîmes, Fr. 43°49' N, 4°22' E 214
Nímfai, Gr. 39°45' N, 19°47' E 156
Nimule, Sudan 3°34' N, 32°5' E 224
Nin, Croatia 44°14' N, 15°9' E 156
Ninayeri, Nicar. 14°27' N, 83°18' W 115
Ninda, Angola 14°54' S, 21°25' E 220
Nine Degree Channel 8°40' N, 71°55' E 188
Ninemile Peak, Nev., U.S. 39°8' N, 116°20' W 90
Ninety East Ridge, Indian Ocean 8°11' S, 88°50' E 254
Ninety Mile Beach, N.Z. 35°3' S, 172°43' E 240
Nineveh, ruin(s), Iraq 36°21' N, 42°59' E 195
Ninfas, Punta, Arg. 43°10' S, 64°20' W 134
Ning'an, China 44°20' N, 129°32' E 190
Ningbo, China 29°54' N, 121°29' E 198
Ningcheng, China 41°34' N, 119°20' E 198
Ningde, China 26°40' N, 119°31' E 198
Ningdu, China 26°26' N, 115°55' E 198
Ningguo, China 30°34' N, 119°1' E 198
Ningi, Nig. 11°3' N, 9°32' E 222
Ningming, China 22°5' N, 107°1' E 198
Ningshan, China 33°20' N, 108°19' E 198
Ningwu, China 39°0' N, 112°13' E 198
Ningxia, adm. division, China 36°46' N, 105°17' E 198
Ningyuan, China 25°36' N, 111°56' E 198
Ninh Binh, Vietnam 20°14' N, 105°56' E 198
Ninh Hoa, Vietnam 12°30' N, 109°8' E 202
Ninigo Group, islands, South Pacific Ocean 0°49' N, 142°30' E 192
Ninigo Islands, islands, South Pacific Ocean 1°10' S, 142°49' E 192
Ninilchik, Gulf of Alaska 60°3' N, 151°39' W 98
Nioaque, Braz. 21°9' S, 55°50' W 132
Niobrara, river, Nebr., U.S. 42°37' N, 102°2' W 90
Nioka, Dem. Rep. of the Congo 2°8' N, 30°39' E 224
Nioki, Dem. Rep. of the Congo 2°44' S, 17°38' E 218
Niokolo-Koba National Park, Senegal 13°2' N, 13°30' W 222
Niono, Mali 14°16' N, 6°0' W 222
Nioro du Sahel, Mali 15°14' N, 9°38' W 222
Niort, Fr. 46°19' N, 0°28' E 150
Niout, spring, Mauritania 16°3' N, 6°52' W 222
Nipa, oil field, Venez. 9°6' N, 64°8' W 116
Nipani, India 16°24' N, 74°23' E 188
Nipawin, Can. 53°21' N, 104°1' W 108
Nipigon, Can. 49°1' N, 88°16' W 94
Nipigon Bay 48°50' N, 89°13' W 80
Nipigon, Lake, Can. 50°12' N, 88°35' W 94
Nipin, river, Can. 55°24' N, 109°25' W 108
Nipissing, Lake, Can. 46°21' N, 80°13' W 80
Nipomo, Calif., U.S. 35°2' N, 120°29' W 100
Nipple, The, peak, Can. 49°56' N, 121°38' W 100
Nipton, Calif., U.S. 35°27' N, 115°17' W 101
Niquelândia, Braz. 14°33' S, 48°30' W 138
Niquero, Cuba 20°2' N, 77°34' W 115
Nīr, Iran 38°3' N, 47°59' E 195
Nir Yiẕhaq, Israel 31°14' N, 34°21' E 194
Nir'am, Israel 31°30' N, 34°34' E 194
Nirasaki, Japan 35°41' N, 138°27' E 201
Ñire Có, Arg. 37°0' S, 68°28' W 134
Nirji see Morin Dawa, China 48°27' N, 124°30' E 198
Nirmal, India 19°6' N, 78°20' E 188
Nirmali, India 26°18' N, 86°34' E 197
Niš, Serb. 43°18' N, 21°54' E 168
Niṣāb, Saudi Arabia 29°8' N, 44°44' E 180
Niṣāb, Yemen 14°31' N, 46°33' E 182
Nišava, river, Serb. 43°18' N, 22°7' E 168
Nishi Nasuno, Japan 36°52' N, 139°58' E 201
Nishikō, Japan 32°36' N, 130°27' E 201
Nishinomiya, Japan 34°44' N, 135°18' E 201
Nishio, Japan 34°50' N, 137°4' E 201
Nishiwaki, Japan 34°58' N, 134°57' E 201
Nishtūn, Yemen 15°48' N, 52°10' E 182
Niska, Fin. 64°35' N, 26°33' E 152
Niskayuna, N.Y., U.S. 42°45' N, 73°51' W 104
Nissedal, Nor. 59°9' N, 8°30' E 152
Nissi, Est. 59°4' N, 24°17' E 166
Nissilä, Fin. 63°56' N, 26°48' E 152
Nisswa, Minn., U.S. 46°30' N, 94°18' W 90
Niṭā', Saudi Arabia 27°10' N, 48°23' E 196
Nītaure, Latv. 57°3' N, 25°7' E 166
Nitchequon, Can. 53°12' N, 70°53' W 111
Niterói, Braz. 22°56' S, 43°3' W 138
Nitmiluk National Park, Austral. 14°16' S, 132°7' E 238
Nitra, Slovakia 48°18' N, 18°6' E 168
Nitransky, adm. division, Slovakia 48°10' N, 17°51' E 152
Nitro, W. Va., U.S. 38°25' N, 81°51' W 94
Nitsa, river, Russ. 57°45' N, 63°3' E 154
Niue, island, N.Z. 18°58' S, 169°55' W 238
Niut, peak, Indonesia 0°59' N, 109°50' E 196
Niutou Shan, island, China 28°54' N, 121°49' E 198
Niuxintai, China 41°20' N, 123°55' E 200
Niva, Fin. 65°9' N, 28°21' E 152
Niva, Russ. 61°36' N, 30°14' E 166
Nivala, Fin. 63°54' N, 24°55' E 152
Nivelles, Belg. 50°35' N, 4°19' E 163
Nivernais, region, Fr. 47°30' N, 3°17' E 165
Nivshera, Russ. 62°24' N, 53°1' E 154
Nixon, Tex., U.S. 29°15' N, 97°45' W 92
Nizamabad, India 18°40' N, 78°5' E 188
Nizamghat, India 28°14' N, 95°43' E 188
Nizao, Dom. Rep. 18°14' N, 70°13' W 116
Nizhnekamsk, Russ. 55°33' N, 51°53' E 154
Nizhneshadrino, Russ. 59°53' N, 90°38' E 169
Nizhneudinsk, Russ. 54°53' N, 99°14' E 190
Nizhnevartovsk, Russ. 60°54' N, 76°35' E 169
Nizhniy Baskunchak, Russ. 48°11' N, 46°42' E 158
Nizhniy Lomov, Russ. 53°30' N, 43°40' E 154
Nizhniy Novgorod, Russ. 56°15' N, 44°0' E 154
Nizhniy Novgorod, adm. division, Russ. 56°0' N, 43°9' E 154
Nizhniy Tagil, Russ. 57°56' N, 59°59' E 154
Nizhniy Ufaley, Russ. 55°56' N, 60°3' E 154
Nizhniye Nikulyasy, Russ. 60°27' N, 30°44' E 152
Nizhniye Sergi, Russ. 56°40' N, 59°16' E 154
Nizhnyaya Mgla, Russ. 66°29' N, 44°27' E 154
Nizhnyaya Omra, Russ. 62°46' N, 55°51' E 154
Nizhnyaya Pesha, Russ. 66°46' N, 47°38' E 154
Nizhnyaya Salda, Russ. 58°5' N, 60°44' E 154
Nizhnyaya Tunguska, river, Russ. 64°30' N, 90°34' E 169
Nizhnyaya Tura, Russ. 58°41' N, 59°49' E 154
Nizhnyaya Voch', Russ. 61°12' N, 54°11' E 154
Nizhyn, Ukr. 51°2' N, 31°53' E 158
Nizi, Dem. Rep. of the Congo 1°44' N, 30°17' E 224
Nizip, Turk. 36°58' N, 37°50' E 180
Nízke Tatry, Slovakia 48°51' N, 19°24' E 152
Nizwá, Oman 22°55' N, 57°31' E 182
Nizza Monferrato, It. 44°46' N, 8°21' E 167
Nizzana (El'Auja), Israel 30°52' N, 34°25' E 194
Njazidja, island, Comoros 11°46' S, 43°35' E 220
Njegoš, peak, Mont. 42°54' N, 18°43' E 168
Njegoševo, Serb. 45°45' N, 19°44' E 168
Njombe, Tanzania 9°22' S, 34°45' E 224
Njombe, river, Tanzania 7°22' S, 34°8' E 224
Njunnesvarre, peak, Nor. 68°45' N, 19°17' E 152
Njurunda, Nor. 62°14' N, 17°20' E 152
Nkambe, Cameroon 6°29' N, 10°43' E 222
Nkawkaw, Ghana 6°33' N, 0°46' E 222
Nkayi, Zimb. 19°3' S, 28°55' E 224
Nkhata Bay, Malawi 11°35' S, 34°17' E 224
Nkhotakota, Malawi 12°56' S, 34°15' E 224
Nkhunga, Malawi 12°29' S, 34°3' E 224
Nkongsamba, Cameroon 4°53' N, 9°56' E 222
Nkoul, Cameroon 3°30' N, 13°33' E 218
Nkululu, river, Tanzania 6°19' S, 32°39' E 224
Nkundi, Tanzania 7°50' S, 31°25' E 224
Nkurenkuru, Namibia 17°39' S, 18°36' E 220
Nkusi, river, Uganda 1°8' N, 30°56' E 224
No, Lake, Sudan 9°22' N, 30°7' E 224
Noamundi, India 22°11' N, 85°31' E 197
Noarvas, peak, Nor. 68°47' N, 24°35' E 152
Noatak, Alas., U.S. 67°29' N, 163°5' W 98
Noatak, river, Alas., U.S. 68°4' N, 159°51' W 98
Nobeoka, Japan 32°35' N, 131°39' E 201
Noble, Ill., U.S. 38°41' N, 88°14' W 102
Noble, La., U.S. 31°40' N, 93°42' W 103
Noblesville, Ind., U.S. 40°2' N, 86°0' W 102
Nobska Point, Mass., U.S. 41°28' N, 70°40' W 104
Nocatee, Fla., U.S. 27°10' N, 81°53' W 105
Noce, river, It. 46°16' N, 10°59' E 167
Noceto, It. 44°48' N, 10°10' E 167
Nochistlán, Mex. 21°20' N, 102°52' W 114
Nochixtlán, Mex. 17°26' N, 97°14' W 114
Nocona, Tex., U.S. 33°46' N, 97°42' W 92
Nodales, Bahía de los 48°5' S, 67°43' W 134
Nodaway, river, Iowa, U.S. 40°1' N, 95°9' W 80
Noel Kempff Mercado National Park, Bol. 14°31' S, 62°11' W 132
Noel, Mount, peak, Can. 50°43' N, 122°56' W 90
Noelville, Can. 46°7' N, 80°26' W 94
Nofre, Peña, peak, Sp. 42°0' N, 7°26' W 150
Nogales, Ariz., U.S. 31°21' N, 110°57' W 112
Nogales, Mex. 31°17' N, 110°57' W 92
Nogara, It. 45°10' N, 11°3' E 167
Nōgata, Japan 33°43' N, 130°42' E 200
Nogayskaya Step', Russ. 44°29' N, 46°3' E 180
Nogayty, Kaz. 45°17' N, 55°55' E 158
Nogent-le-Roi, Fr. 48°38' N, 1°32' E 163
Nogent-le-Rotrou, Fr. 48°19' N, 0°49' E 163
Nogent-sur-Seine, Fr. 48°29' N, 3°30' E 163
Noginsk, Russ. 64°25' N, 91°16' E 169
Nogliki, Russ. 51°47' N, 143°4' E 190
Nógrád, adm. division, Hung. 47°58' N, 19°1' E 156
Nohar, India 29°11' N, 74°47' E 186
Nohfelden, Ger. 49°34' N, 7°8' E 163
Nohona o Hae, peak, Hawai'i, U.S. 19°54' N, 155°44' W 99
Noia, Sp. 42°47' N, 8°55' W 150
Noir, Isla, island, Chile 54°23' S, 74°10' W 134
Noire, Montagne, peak, Fr. 43°25' N, 2°25' E 165
Noire, river, Can. 46°46' N, 77°41' W 94
Noires, Montagnes, Fr. 48°2' N, 4°9' W 150
Nojima Zaki, Japan 34°45' N, 139°53' E 201

Nok Kundi, Pak. 28°49' N, 62°47' E 182
Nokaneng, Botswana 19°41' S, 22°11' E 220
Nokara, Mali 15°10' N, 2°24' W 222
Nokia, Fin. 61°28' N, 23°31' E 166
Nokola, Russ. 61°10' N, 38°51' E 154
Nokomis, Can. 51°30' N, 105°2' W 90
Nokomis, Ill., U.S. 39°17' N, 89°17' W 102
Nokou, Chad 14°35' N, 14°45' E 216
Nola, Cen. Af. Rep. 3°42' N, 16°5' E 218
Noli, It. 44°12' N, 8°25' E 167
Nolinsk, Russ. 57°33' N, 49°57' E 154
Noma Misaki, Japan 31°16' N, 129°55' E 201
Nomans Land, island, Mass., U.S. 41°11' N, 70°52' W 104
Nomansland Point, Can. 52°1' N, 81°2' W 110
Nombre de Dios, Mex. 23°49' N, 104°14' W 114
Nombre de Dios, Mex. 28°42' N, 106°7' W 92
Nome, Alas., U.S. 64°25' N, 165°28' W 98
Nome, Tex., U.S. 30°1' N, 94°26' W 103
Nome Lake, Can. 59°38' N, 131°35' W 108
Nomgon, Mongolia 42°52' N, 104°53' E 198
Nomhon, China 36°22' N, 96°26' E 188
Nomhon, river, China 36°31' N, 96°27' E 188
Nomo Saki, Japan 32°28' N, 129°35' E 201
Nomoneas, island, F.S.M. 7°25' N, 151°52' E 242
Nomwin Atoll, F.S.M. 9°13' N, 150°41' E 192
Nonancourt, Fr. 48°46' N, 1°12' E 163
Nonburg, Russ. 65°33' N, 50°32' E 154
Nondalton, Alas., U.S. 59°56' N, 155°0' W 98
Nong Khai, Thai. 17°52' N, 102°44' E 202
Nong'an, China 44°27' N, 125°11' E 198
Nongoma, S. Af. 27°54' S, 31°37' E 227
Nongpoh, India 25°51' N, 91°51' E 197
Nono, Eth. 8°30' N, 37°22' E 224
Nonoava, Mex. 27°28' N, 106°44' W 112
Nonsan, S. Korea 36°11' N, 127°6' E 200
Nonthaburi, Thai. 13°53' N, 100°31' E 202
Noonan, N. Dak., U.S. 48°52' N, 103°1' W 108
Noord Beveland, Neth. 51°33' N, 3°42' E 163
Noordoewer, Namibia 28°44' S, 17°37' E 227
Noormarkku, Fin. 61°35' N, 21°51' E 166
Nootka, Can. 49°37' N, 126°39' W 90
Nopah Range, Calif., U.S. 36°4' N, 116°10' W 101
Nóqui, Angola 5°55' S, 13°28' E 218
Nora, Ill., U.S. 42°26' N, 89°57' W 102
Nora, Nor. 59°30' N, 14°59' E 152
Nora, island, Eritrea 16°4' N, 39°43' E 182
Nora, ruin(s), It. 38°59' N, 8°55' E 156
Norak, Taj. 38°23' N, 69°21' E 197
Norberg, Nor. 60°3' N, 15°54' E 152
Norco, La., U.S. 29°59' N, 90°25' W 103
Nord 81°43' N, 17°32' W 246
Nord Frøya, Nor. 63°45' N, 8°47' E 152
Nord, Petit lac du, lake, Can. 50°46' N, 67°57' W 111
Nordaustlandet, island, Nor. 80°34' N, 5°48' E 160
Norddalsfjord, Nor. 61°39' N, 5°22' E 152
Norddeich, Ger. 53°37' N, 7°10' E 163
Nordegg (Brazeau), Can. 52°28' N, 116°7' W 108
Norden, Ger. 53°36' N, 7°11' E 163
Norderney, Ger. 53°42' N, 7°9' E 163
Nordfold, Nor. 67°45' N, 15°11' E 152
Nordhordland, region, North Sea 60°50' N, 4°39' E 152
Nordhorn, Ger. 52°26' N, 7°3' E 163
Nordkapp (North Cape), Nor. 71°6' N, 25°55' E 152
Nordkinnhalvøya, Nor. 70°45' N, 26°37' E 152
Nord-Kivu, adm. division, Dem. Rep. of the Congo 0°10' N, 28°8' E 224
Nordli, Nor. 64°28' N, 13°36' E 152
Nordmaling, Nor. 63°33' N, 19°30' E 152
Nordøstrundingen 80°22' N, 30°36' W 72
Nordøyan, islands, Norwegian Sea 64°47' N, 9°13' E 152
Nordøyane, islands, Nor. 62°38' N, 4°46' E 152
Nordoyar, islands, Norwegian Sea 62°30' N, 9°12' W 72
Nord-Pas-De-Calais, adm. division, Fr. 50°24' N, 1°57' E 150
Nordreisa, Nor. 69°46' N, 21°2' E 152
Nordvik, Nor. 66°7' N, 12°31' E 152
Nordvik, Russ. 73°59' N, 111°16' E 160
Norfolk, Conn., U.S. 41°59' N, 73°12' W 104
Norfolk, Nebr., U.S. 42°0' N, 97°26' W 90
Norfolk, Va., U.S. 36°51' N, 76°17' W 96
Norfolk Island, Australia 29°0' S, 168°0' E
Norfolk Ridge, South Pacific Ocean 27°44' S, 167°48' E 252
Norfork Lake, Ark., U.S. 36°16' N, 93°15' W 80
Nori, Russ. 66°11' N, 72°31' E 169
Noril'sk, Russ. 69°20' N, 88°8' E 169
Normal, Ill., U.S. 40°30' N, 88°59' W 102
Norman, Okla., U.S. 35°11' N, 97°27' W 92
Norman Wells, Can. 65°18' N, 126°44' W 98
Normanby Island, P.N.G. 9°58' S, 151°19' E 192
Normandin, Can. 48°49' N, 72°31' W 94
Normandy, Tex., U.S. 28°53' N, 100°35' W 96
Normandy, region, Fr. 48°57' N, 0°46' E 163
Normanton, Austral. 17°46' S, 141°10' E 238
Normétal, Can. 49°0' N, 79°23' W 94
Norphlet, Ark., U.S. 33°17' N, 92°40' W 103
Ñorquincó, Arg. 41°50' S, 70°51' W 134
Norra Storfjället, peak, Nor. 65°51' N, 15°10' E 152
Norrby, Nor. 64°25' N, 15°37' E 152
Nørresundby, Den. 57°3' N, 9°55' E 150
Norrfors, Nor. 63°46' N, 18°59' E 152
Norrhult, Nor. 57°7' N, 15°9' E 152
Norris Lake, lake, Tenn., U.S. 36°18' N, 84°3' W 94
Norrköping, Nor. 58°33' N, 16°9' E 152
Norrland, region, Sw. 61°29' N, 17°15' E 166
Norrtälje, Sw. 59°45' N, 18°39' E 166
Norseman, Austral. 32°12' S, 121°47' E 231
Norske Øer, islands, Norske Øer 78°33' N, 16°48' W 246
Norte, adm. division, Braz. 4°51' S, 37°14' W 132
Norte, Cabo, Braz. 1°44' N, 49°56' W 130
Norte, Cayo 18°50' N, 87°32' W 115
Norte de Santander, adm. division, Col. 8°18' N, 73°17' W 136
Norte, Punta, Arg. 36°18' S, 56°43' W 139
Norte, Punta, Arg. 50°51' S, 69°6' W 134
Norte, Serra do, Braz. 10°18' S, 59°11' W 130
Nortelândia, Braz. 14°29' S, 56°48' W 132
Nörten-Hardenberg, Ger. 51°37' N, 9°57' E 167
North Adams, Mass., U.S. 42°41' N, 73°7' W 104
North Albanian Alps, Alban. 42°31' N, 19°47' E 168
North America 25°0' N, 112°0' W 73
North Amherst, Mass., U.S. 42°24' N, 72°32' W 104
North Andaman, island, India 13°28' N, 91°39' E 188
North Andover, Mass., U.S. 42°41' N, 71°9' W 104
North Anson, Me., U.S. 44°51' N, 69°55' W 94
North Atlantic Ocean 20°33' N, 74°33' W 253
North Augusta, S.C., U.S. 33°30' N, 81°59' W 96
North Aulatsivik Island, Can. 59°49' N, 63°58' W 106
North Australian Basin, Indian Ocean 14°56' S, 117°17' E 254
North Baldy, peak, Wash., U.S. 48°31' N, 117°14' W 90
North Baltimore, Ohio, U.S. 41°10' N, 83°40' W 102
North Barrule, peak 54°16' N, 4°29' W 150
North Battleford, Can. 52°47' N, 108°19' W 108
North Bay, Can. 46°18' N, 79°27' W 94
North Belcher Islands, islands, Hudson Bay 56°39' N, 83°25' W 106
North Bend, Can. 49°52' N, 121°27' W 100
North Bend, Wash., U.S. 47°28' N, 121°47' W 100
North Bennington, Vt., U.S. 42°55' N, 73°15' W 104
North Berwick, Me., U.S. 43°18' N, 70°44' W 104
North Bimini, island, Bahamas 25°46' N, 79°29' W 105
North Bonneville, Wash., U.S. 45°38' N, 121°58' W 100
North Boston, N.Y., U.S. 42°40' N, 78°48' W 110
North Bradley, Mich., U.S. 43°41' N, 84°29' W 102
North Branch, Mich., U.S. 43°13' N, 83°9' W 102
North Branch, Minn., U.S. 45°30' N, 92°59' W 94
North Branford, Conn., U.S. 41°19' N, 72°47' W 104
North Bridgton, Me., U.S. 44°6' N, 70°43' W 104
North Caicos, island, North Caicos 22°1' N, 72°1' W 80
North Canton, Ohio, U.S. 40°52' N, 81°24' W 102
North, Cape, Antarctica 70°15' S, 169°9' E 248
North Cape, Can. 47°2' N, 60°54' W 111
North Cape, Can. 46°59' N, 64°47' W 111
North Cape, N.Z. 34°24' S, 172°51' E 240
North Cape May, N.J., U.S. 38°58' N, 74°58' W 94
North Cape see Horn, Ice. 66°30' N, 26°3' W 246
North Cape see Nordkapp, Nor. 71°10' N, 25°50' E 152
North Carolina, adm. division, N.C., U.S. 35°44' N, 80°14' W 96
North Carver, Mass., U.S. 41°55' N, 70°49' W 104
North Cascades National Park, Wash., U.S. 48°34' N, 121°27' W 100
North Cat Cay, island, Bahamas 25°32' N, 79°16' W 105
North Channel 45°49' N, 83°42' W 80
North Channel 54°35' N, 5°17' W 150
North Clarendon, Vt., U.S. 43°34' N, 72°59' W 104
North College Hill, Ohio, U.S. 39°12' N, 84°34' W 102
North Conway, N.H., U.S. 44°2' N, 71°8' W 104
North Cowichan, Can. 48°51' N, 123°42' W 100
North Creek, N.Y., U.S. 43°41' N, 74°0' W 104
North Dakota, adm. division, N. Dak., U.S. 47°45' N, 101°21' W 90
North Dartmouth, Mass., U.S. 41°37' N, 71°0' W 104
North Downs, region, U.K. 51°8' N, 0°49' E 162
North Eagle Butte, S. Dak., U.S. 44°59' N, 101°15' W 90
North East Land, island, Nor. 79°53' N, 23°37' E 255
North Edgecomb, Me., U.S. 43°59' N, 69°39' W 104
North Edwards, Calif., U.S. 35°2' N, 117°50' W 101
North Egremont, Mass., U.S. 42°11' N, 73°27' W 104
North Fiji Basin, South Pacific Ocean 17°30' S, 173°11' E 252
North Fond du Lac, Wis., U.S. 43°48' N, 88°30' W 102
North Foreland, Drake Passage 61°14' S, 61°24' W 248
North Foreland, U.K. 51°22' N, 1°25' E 163
North Fork, Calif., U.S. 37°13' N, 119°32' W 100
North Fork, river, Kans., U.S. 39°29' N, 100°4' W 90
North Fort Myers, Fla., U.S. 26°40' N, 81°53' W 105
North Fryeburg, Me., U.S. 44°7' N, 70°59' W 104
North Grosvenor Dale, Conn., U.S. 41°58' N, 71°55' W 104
North Hampton, N.H., U.S. 42°58' N, 70°51' W 104
North Hartland, Vt., U.S. 43°35' N, 72°22' W 104
North Haven, N.Y., U.S. 41°1' N, 72°19' W 104
North Head, Can. 53°43' N, 56°24' W 111
North Head, N.Z. 36°36' S, 173°49' E 240
North Hodge, La., U.S. 32°18' N, 92°43' W 96
North Holland, adm. division, Neth. 53°6' N, 4°6' E 150
North Horr, Kenya 3°18' N, 37°4' E 224
North Hudson, N.Y., U.S. 43°57' N, 73°44' W 104
North Industry, Ohio, U.S. 40°44' N, 81°22' W 102
North Island, Austral. 15°27' S, 136°40' E 230
North Jay, Me., U.S. 44°32' N, 70°15' W 104
North Judson, Ind., U.S. 41°12' N, 86°46' W 102
North Kingstown (Wickford), R.I., U.S. 41°34' N, 71°28' W 104
North Knife Lake, Can. 58°2' N, 97°42' W 108
North La Veta Pass, Colo., U.S. 37°36' N, 105°13' W 90
North Land see Severnaya Zemlya, islands, Russ. 80°22' N, 102°0' E 160
North Las Vegas, Nev., U.S. 36°11' N, 115°9' W 101
North Liberty, Ind., U.S. 41°31' N, 86°26' W 102
North Little Rock, Ark., U.S. 34°47' N, 92°16' W 82
North Loup, river, Nebr., U.S. 42°25' N, 101°5' W 80
North Luangwa National Park, Zambia 11°43' S, 32°2' E 224
North Mamm Peak, Colo., U.S. 39°22' N, 107°57' W 90
North Manchester, Ind., U.S. 40°59' N, 85°46' W 102
North Miami, Fla., U.S. 25°54' N, 80°12' W 105
North Montpelier, Vt., U.S. 44°17' N, 72°28' W 104
North Moose Lake, Can. 54°10' N, 100°33' W 108
North Muskegon, Mich., U.S. 43°15' N, 86°17' W 102
North Myrtle Beach, S.C., U.S. 33°48' N, 78°42' W 96
North Naples, Fla., U.S. 26°13' N, 81°48' W 105
North Negril Point, Jam. 18°23' N, 79°33' W 116
North Orange, Mass., U.S. 42°37' N, 72°17' W 104
North Oxford, Mass., U.S. 42°9' N, 71°53' W 104
North Pacific Ocean 22°12' N, 118°57' W 252
North Palisade, peak, Calif., U.S. 37°5' N, 118°34' W 101
North Palmetto Point, Bahamas 25°10' N, 76°10' W 96
North Pass, Colo., U.S. 38°11' N, 106°35' W 90
North Peak, Nev., U.S. 40°39' N, 117°13' W 90
North Pine, Can. 56°24' N, 120°48' W 108
North Platte, Nebr., U.S. 41°10' N, 100°44' W 106
North Platte, river, Wyo., U.S. 42°50' N, 105°34' W 106
North Point, Mich., U.S. 44°49' N, 83°16' W 94
North Port, Fla., U.S. 27°4' N, 82°15' W 105
North Powder, Oreg., U.S. 45°1' N, 117°56' W 90
North Pownal, Vt., U.S. 42°47' N, 73°16' W 104
North Rhine-Westphalia, adm. division, Ger. 51°18' N, 6°44' E 167
North River, Can. 59°0' N, 94°54' W 73
North, river, Can. 53°53' N, 58°14' W 111
North, river, Wash., U.S. 46°48' N, 123°42' W 100
North Salem, N.H., U.S. 42°50' N, 71°15' W 104
North Saskatchewan, river, Can. 52°15' N, 116°35' W 108
North Scituate, Mass., U.S. 42°13' N, 70°48' W 104
North Sea 55°38' N, 2°30' E 150
North Sentinel Island, India 11°29' N, 91°2' E 188
North Shapleigh, Me., U.S. 43°36' N, 70°54' W 104
North Shore, Calif., U.S. 33°31' N, 115°56' W 101
North Shoshone Peak, Nev., U.S. 39°8' N, 117°34' W 90
North Slope, Alas., U.S. 69°31' N, 155°32' W 98
North Springfield, Pa., U.S. 41°59' N, 80°27' W 94
North Springfield, Vt., U.S. 43°19' N, 72°32' W 104
North Star, Can. 56°51' N, 117°39' W 108
North Stradbroke Island, Austral. 28°5' S, 150°57' E 230
North Tawton, U.K. 50°48' N, 3°54' W 162
North Thetford, Vt., U.S. 43°50' N, 72°12' W 104
North Truro, Mass., U.S. 42°2' N, 70°6' W 104
North Turner, Me., U.S. 44°20' N, 70°15' W 104
North Vancouver, Can. 49°19' N, 123°3' W 100
North Vassalboro, Me., U.S. 44°29' N, 69°38' W 104
North Vernon, Ind., U.S. 39°0' N, 85°38' W 102
North Wabasca Lake, Can. 56°2' N, 114°57' W 108
North Walpole, N.H., U.S. 43°8' N, 72°27' W 104
North Walsham, U.K. 52°49' N, 1°22' E 163
North Warren, Pa., U.S. 41°52' N, 79°10' W 110
North Waterford, Me., U.S. 44°13' N, 70°46' W 104
North Webster, Ind., U.S. 41°19' N, 85°42' W 102
North Weddell Ridge see America-Antarctic Ridge, South Atlantic Ocean 59°5' S, 16°0' W 255
North West Cape, Austral. 21°48' S, 114°19' E 230
North West Point, Can. 53°25' N, 60°2' W 111
North West River, Can. 53°34' N, 60°8' W 111
North West Rocks, islands, Caribbean Sea 14°31' N, 80°34' W 115
North Wildwood, N.J., U.S. 39°0' N, 74°48' W 94
North Yolla Bolly Mountains, peak, Calif., U.S. 40°11' N, 123°4' W 90
North York Moors, National Park, U.K. 54°20' N, 1°2' W 162
Northallerton, U.K. 54°20' N, 1°27' W 162
Northam, Austral. 31°41' S, 116°41' E 231
Northam, S. Af. 24°58' S, 27°15' E 227
Northampton, Mass., U.S. 42°18' N, 72°38' W 104
Northampton, U.K. 52°14' N, 0°54' E 162
Northampton, Mount, peak, Antarctica 72°37' S, 169°35' E 248
Northbluff Point, Can. 51°27' N, 80°24' W 110
Northeast Cape, Alas., U.S. 63°5' N, 167°44' W 160
Northeast Greenland National Park, Greenland, Den. 77°0' N, 33°0' W 246
Northeast Pacific Basin, North Pacific Ocean 26°5' N, 145°35' W 252
Northeast Point, Bahamas 22°48' N, 74°14' W 80
Northeast Point, Can. 51°54' N, 55°18' W 111
Northeast Point, Jam. 18°12' N, 76°20' W 115
Northeim, Ger. 51°42' N, 9°59' E 167
Northern, adm. division, Sudan 20°14' N, 31°0' E 182
Northern Bahr Al Ghazal, adm. division, Sudan 9°11' N, 26°10' E 224
Northern Cape, adm. division, S. Af. 30°2' S, 19°39' E 227
Northern Cay, island, Belize 17°21' N, 87°29' W 116
Northern Cyprus, special sovereignty, Cyprus 35°16' N, 32°56' E 194
Northern Darfur, adm. division, Sudan 16°39' N, 23°59' E 226
Northern Head, Can. 46°4' N, 59°46' W 111
Northern Ireland, adm. division, U.K. 54°35' N, 7°41' W 150
Northern Mariana Islands, U.S. 20°7' N, 141°10' E 192
Northern Sierra Madre National Park, Philippines 16°48' N, 121°37' E 203
Northern Territory, adm. division, Austral. 19°14' S, 130°35' E 231
Northfield, Minn., U.S. 44°26' N, 93°8' W 94
Northfield, N.H., U.S. 43°25' N, 71°36' W 104
Northfield, Vt., U.S. 44°8' N, 72°40' W 104
Northfield Falls, Vt., U.S. 44°9' N, 72°39' W 104
Northford, Conn., U.S. 41°23' N, 72°48' W 104
Northport, Ala., U.S. 33°13' N, 87°35' W 103
Northport, Nebr., U.S. 41°41' N, 103°6' W 92
Northport, Wash., U.S. 48°53' N, 117°48' W 90
Northridge, Ohio, U.S. 39°59' N, 83°46' W 102
Northumberland, N.H., U.S. 44°33' N, 71°34' W 104
Northumberland Islands, Coral Sea 22°8' S, 150°56' E 230
Northville, N.Y., U.S. 43°13' N, 74°11' W 104
Northway, Alas., U.S. 62°51' N, 141°59' W 98
North-West, adm. division, S. Af. 26°44' S, 24°15' E 227
Northwest Angle, Minn., U.S. 49°4' N, 95°20' W 90
Northwest Atlantic Mid-Ocean Canyon, North Atlantic Ocean 52°31' N, 45°36' W 253
Northwest Miscou Point, Can. 48°11' N, 65°14' W 94
Northwest Pacific Basin, North Pacific Ocean 39°52' N, 157°39' E 252
Northwest Passages 70°33' N, 125°19' W 72
Northwest Territories, adm. division, Can. 60°25' N, 115°14' W 108
Northwestern Hawaiian Islands, North Pacific Ocean 23°42' N, 165°44' W 99
Northwich, U.K. 53°15' N, 2°31' W 162
Northwind Escarpment, Arctic Ocean 75°55' N, 153°20' W 255
Northwind Ridge, Arctic Ocean 76°13' N, 156°12' W 255
Northwood, N.H., U.S. 43°11' N, 71°10' W 104
Northwood, N. Dak., U.S. 47°43' N, 97°35' W 90
Northwood, Ohio, U.S. 41°35' N, 83°27' W 102
Norton, Kans., U.S. 39°49' N, 99°54' W 90
Norton, Va., U.S. 36°55' N, 82°39' W 94
Norton, Zimb. 17°56' S, 30°40' E 224
Norton Bay 64°20' N, 162°6' W 98
Norton Shores, Mich., U.S. 43°9' N, 86°16' W 102
Norton Sound 63°37' N, 165°6' W 98
Norvalspont, S. Af. 30°38' S, 25°24' E 227
Norvegia, Cape, Antarctica 71°16' S, 18°23' W 248
Norwalk, Calif., U.S. 33°55' N, 118°4' W 101
Norwalk, Conn., U.S. 41°7' N, 73°25' W 104
Norwalk, Ohio, U.S. 41°13' N, 82°37' W 102
Norway, Me., U.S. 44°12' N, 70°33' W 104
Norway, Mich., U.S. 45°47' N, 87°55' W 94
Norway 63°25' N, 10°58' E 152
Norway House, Can. 53°56' N, 97°52' W 108
Norwegian Basin, Norwegian Sea 68°5' N, 1°43' E 255
Norwegian Sea 68°1' N, 5°35' E 152
Norwich, Conn., U.S. 41°31' N, 72°5' W 104
Norwich, N.Y., U.S. 42°31' N, 75°33' W 94
Norwich, U.K. 52°37' N, 1°16' E 162
Norwich, Vt., U.S. 43°42' N, 72°19' W 104
Norwood, Colo., U.S. 38°7' N, 108°17' W 90
Norwood, La., U.S. 30°57' N, 91°7' W 103
Norwood, Mass., U.S. 42°11' N, 71°13' W 104
Norwood, Ohio, U.S. 39°9' N, 84°27' W 94
Noshul', Russ. 60°8' N, 49°35' E 154
Nosivka, Ukr. 50°54' N, 31°38' E 158
Nosok, Russ. 70°8' N, 82°12' E 169
Nosovshchina, Russ. 62°57' N, 37°3' E 154
Noşratābād, Iran 29°51' N, 59°56' E 180
Nosy-Varika, Madagascar 20°33' S, 48°31' E 220
Noszlop, Hung. 47°10' N, 17°26' E 168
Not Ozero, lake, Russ. 66°26' N, 30°49' E 152
Notch Peak, Utah, U.S. 39°7' N, 113°29' W 90
Notikewin, Can. 56°58' N, 117°38' W 108
Notikewin, river, Can. 56°55' N, 119°2' W 108
Nótio Egéo, adm. division, Gr. 37°12' N, 25°30' E 156
Nötö, Fin. 59°57' N, 21°45' E 166
Noto, It. 36°53' N, 15°4' E 156
Noto, Japan 37°19' N, 137°8' E 201
Notodden, Nor. 59°33' N, 9°17' E 152
Notre Dame Bay 49°29' N, 55°32' W 111
Notre Dame de Lourdes, Can. 49°31' N, 98°34' W 90
Notre-Dame-du-Nord, Can. 47°36' N, 79°29' W 94
Notsé, Togo 6°57' N, 1°9' E 222
Nottaway, river, Can. 51°13' N, 78°54' W 80
Nottingham, N.H., U.S. 43°6' N, 71°7' W 104
Nottingham, U.K. 52°57' N, 1°9' W 162
Nottingham Island, Can. 63°12' N, 82°17' W 106
Nottuln, Ger. 51°55' N, 7°21' E 167
Nouabalé-Ndoki National Park, Congo 2°10' N, 16°11' E 218
Nouadhibou (Port Étienne), Mauritania 20°56' N, 17°2' W 222
Nouakchott, Mauritania 18°6' N, 16°11' W 222
Nouamrhar, Mauritania 19°22' N, 16°32' W 222
Nouaoudar, Mauritania 16°46' N, 7°18' W 222
Nouart, Fr. 49°26' N, 5°3' E 163
Nouasser, Mor. 33°22' N, 7°39' W 214
Nouméa, New Caledonia, Fr. 22°11' S, 166°42' E 238
Nouna, Burkina Faso 12°43' N, 3°53' W 222
Noupoort, S. Af. 31°10' S, 24°55' E 227
Nourounba, Mali 12°31' N, 9°8' W 222
Nousu, Fin. 67°10' N, 28°36' E 152
Nouzonville, Fr. 49°47' N, 4°44' E 163
Nova América, Braz. 15°3' S, 50°0' W 138
Nova Andradina, Braz. 22°15' S, 53°21' W 138
Nova Esperança, Braz. 23°10' S, 52°17' W 138
Nova Esperança, Braz. 16°34' S, 43°56' W 138
Nova Friburgo, Braz. 22°18' S, 42°31' W 138
Nova Gorica, Slov. 45°57' N, 13°38' E 167
Nova Gradiška, Croatia 45°15' N, 17°22' E 168
Nova Granada, Braz. 20°32' S, 49°21' W 138
Nova Iguaçu, Braz. 22°45' S, 43°28' W 138
Nova Kakhovka, Ukr. 46°45' N, 33°17' E 156
Nova Kapela, Croatia 45°12' N, 17°36' E 168
Nova Kasaba, Bosn. and Herzg. 44°13' N, 19°7' E 168
Nova Lamego, Guinea-Bissau 12°17' N, 14°16' W 222
Nova Lima, Braz. 19°58' S, 43°51' W 138
Nova Mambone, Mozambique 21°1' S, 34°57' E 227
Nova Nabúri, Mozambique 16°50' S, 38°55' E 224
Nova Odesa, Ukr. 47°21' N, 31°45' E 156
Nova Olinda do Norte, Braz. 3°49' S, 59°2' W 130
Nova Prata, Braz. 28°50' S, 51°35' W 139
Nova Roma, Braz. 13°53' S, 46°59' W 138
Nova Scotia, adm. division, Can. 44°50' N, 65°14' W 111
Nova Sofala, Mozambique 20°10' S, 34°43' E 227
Nova Trento, Braz. 27°20' S, 48°56' W 138
Nova Varoš, Serb. 43°27' N, 19°48' E 168
Nova Venécia, Braz. 18°46' S, 40°26' W 138
Nova Viçosa, Braz. 17°54' S, 39°24' W 138
Novafeltria, It. 43°53' N, 12°17' E 167
Novalukoml', Belarus 54°42' N, 29°11' E 166
Novara, It. 45°26' N, 8°36' E 167
Novato, Calif., U.S. 38°7' N, 122°35' W 100
Novaya Lyalya, Russ. 59°1' N, 60°39' E 154
Novaya Shul'ba, Kaz. 50°32' N, 81°19' E 184
Novaya Sibir', Ostrov, island, Russ. 75°1' N, 151°6' E 160
Novaya Vodolaga, Ukr. 49°44' N, 35°53' E 158
Novaya Zemlya, island, Russ. 70°43' N, 57°35' E 169
Nové Zámky, Slovakia 47°59' N, 18°10' E 168
Novelda, Sp. 38°22' N, 0°47' E 164
Novgorod, adm. division, Russ. 58°2' N, 30°16' E 166
Novgorodka, Russ. 57°2' N, 28°33' E 166
Novhorod-Sivers'kyy, Ukr. 51°58' N, 33°18' E 158
Novi Bečej, Serb. 45°35' N, 20°8' E 168
Novi Kneževac, Serb. 46°2' N, 20°6' E 168
Novi Ligure, It. 44°45' N, 8°47' E 167
Novi Pazar, Bulg. 43°20' N, 27°11' E 158
Novi Pazar, Serb. 43°8' N, 20°31' E 168
Novi Sad, Serb. 45°14' N, 19°46' E 168
Novigrad, Croatia 45°20' N, 13°34' E 167
Novikovo, Russ. 58°9' N, 80°35' E 169
Novilara, It. 43°51' N, 12°55' E 167
Noville Peninsula, Antarctica 71°26' S, 95°25' W 248
Novillero, Mex. 22°21' N, 105°40' W 114
Novinka, Russ. 59°10' N, 30°20' E 166
Novo Acordo, Braz. 10°9' S, 47°20' W 130
Novo Aripuanã, Braz. 5°9' S, 60°21' W 130
Novo Cruzeiro, Braz. 17°29' S, 41°53' W 138
Novo Hamburgo, Braz. 29°42' S, 51°7' W 139
Novo Horizonte, Braz. 21°29' S, 49°15' W 138
Novo Izborsk, Russ. 57°47' N, 27°55' E 166
Novo Paraíso, Braz. 1°15' N, 60°18' W 123
Novo, river, Braz. 4°47' S, 53°49' W 130
Novoagansk, Russ. 61°57' N, 76°26' E 169
Novoaleksandrovsk, Russ. 45°31' N, 41°6' E 158
Novoaltaysk, Russ. 53°27' N, 84°6' E 184
Novoanninskiy, Russ. 50°28' N, 42°42' E 158
Novobogatinskoe, Kaz. 47°21' N, 51°11' E 158
Novocheremshansk, Russ. 54°21' N, 50°5' E 154
Novodvinsk, Russ. 64°25' N, 40°48' E 154
Novohrad-Volyns'kyy, Ukr. 50°34' N, 27°35' E 152
Novoishimskiy, Kaz. 53°13' N, 66°48' E 184
Novokhovansk, Russ. 55°55' N, 29°43' E 166
Novokuybyshevsk, Russ. 53°6' N, 50°0' E 154
Novokuznetsk, Russ. 53°48' N, 87°8' E 184
Novolazarevskaya, Russia, station, Antarctica 70°47' S, 11°39' E 248
Novomalykla, Russ. 54°10' N, 49°50' E 154
Novomichurinsk, Russ. 53°59' N, 39°49' E 154
Novomikhaylovskoye, Russ. 44°15' N, 38°55' E 156
Novomoskovsk, Russ. 54°3' N, 38°12' E 154
Novomoskovs'k, Ukr. 48°40' N, 35°18' E 158
Novonikolayevskiy, Russ. 50°56' N, 42°20' E 158
Novonikol'skoye, Russ. 49°5' N, 45°4' E 158
Novonikol'skoye, Russ. 59°43' N, 79°17' E 169
Novooleksiyivka, Ukr. 46°15' N, 34°37' E 156
Novoorsk, Russ. 51°23' N, 58°57' E 158
Novopokrovskaya, Russ. 45°58' N, 40°37' E 158
Novopskov, Ukr. 49°34' N, 39°9' E 158
Novorepnoye, Russ. 51°3' N, 48°21' E 158
Novorossiysk, Russ. 44°46' N, 37°41' E 156
Novorybnoye, Russ. 72°45' N, 105°56' E 160
Novorzhev, Russ. 57°1' N, 29°18' E 166
Novosel'ye, Russ. 58°5' N, 28°52' E 166
Novosergiyevka, Russ. 52°3' N, 53°36' E 158

Novoshakhtinsk, *Russ.* 47°43′ N, 39°57′ E **158**
Novosi Birskiye Ostrova (New Siberian Islands), *Russ.* 76°14′ N, 142°6′ E **160**
Novosibirsk, *Russ.* 55°3′ N, 83°2′ E **184**
Novosibirsk, adm. division, *Russ.* 54°25′ N, 77°40′ E **184**
Novosil′, *Russ.* 52°57′ N, 37°1′ E **154**
Novosil′skiy, Cape, *Antarctica* 68°20′ S, 159°52′ E **248**
Novosokol′niki, *Russ.* 56°20′ N, 30°13′ E **154**
Novotitarovskaya, *Russ.* 45°16′ N, 39°1′ E **156**
Novotroitsk, *Russ.* 51°13′ N, 58°16′ E **158**
Novoukrayinka, *Ukr.* 48°21′ N, 31°36′ E **156**
Novouzensk, *Russ.* 50°29′ N, 48°7′ E **158**
Novovyatsk, *Russ.* 58°28′ N, 49°41′ E **154**
Novozhilovskaya, *Russ.* 64°49′ N, 51°24′ E **154**
Novozybkov, *Russ.* 52°30′ N, 31°58′ E **154**
Novska, *Croatia* 45°19′ N, 16°59′ E **168**
Novyy Oskol, *Russ.* 50°46′ N, 37°53′ E **158**
Novyy Bor, *Russ.* 66°43′ N, 52°16′ E **154**
Novyy Buh, *Ukr.* 47°41′ N, 32°25′ E **156**
Novyy Buyan, *Russ.* 53°40′ N, 50°5′ E **154**
Novyy Port, *Russ.* 67°40′ N, 72°54′ E **169**
Novyy Uoyan, *Russ.* 56°5′ N, 111°38′ E **173**
Novyy Urengoy, *Russ.* 65°53′ N, 77°10′ E **169**
Novyy Vasyugan, *Russ.* 58°34′ N, 76°25′ E **169**
Now Zad, *Afghan.* 32°23′ N, 64°30′ E **186**
Nowa Sól, *Pol.* 51°47′ N, 15°43′ E **152**
Nowata, *Okla., U.S.* 36°41′ N, 95°39′ W **96**
Nowbarān, *Iran* 35°12′ N, 49°40′ E **180**
Nowgong, *India* 25°4′ N, 79°26′ E **197**
Nowra, *Austral.* 34°49′ S, 150°36′ E **231**
Nowshera, *Pak.* 33°57′ N, 72°0′ E **186**
Nowy Sącz, *Pol.* 49°40′ N, 20°47′ E **160**
Noxapater, *Miss., U.S.* 32°58′ N, 89°4′ W **103**
Noxon, *Mont., U.S.* 47°57′ N, 115°47′ W **90**
Noxubee, river, *Ala., U.S.* 33°11′ N, 88°47′ W **103**
Noy, river, *Laos* 17°6′ N, 105°20′ E **202**
Noyabr′sk, *Russ.* 63°12′ N, 75°24′ E **169**
Noyes, *Minn., U.S.* 48°57′ N, 97°13′ W **94**
Noyo, *Calif., U.S.* 39°25′ N, 123°49′ W **90**
Noyo, river, *Calif., U.S.* 39°20′ N, 123°46′ W **90**
Noyon, *Fr.* 49°34′ N, 3°0′ E **163**
Nsanje (Port Herald), *Malawi* 16°56′ S, 35°13′ E **224**
Nsawam, *Ghana* 5°50′ N, 0°21′ E **222**
Nsélé, *Gabon* 6°357′ N, 10°10′ E **218**
Nsoc, *Equatorial Guinea* 1°13′ N, 11°14′ E **218**
Nsontin, *Dem. Rep. of the Congo* 3°9′ S, 17°54′ E **218**
Nsukka, *Nig.* 6°51′ N, 7°23′ E **222**
Nsumbu National Park, *Zambia* 8°52′ S, 30°7′ E **206**
Ntakat, spring, *Mauritania* 16°49′ N, 11°45′ W **222**
N′Tima, *Congo* 3°47′ S, 12°3′ E **218**
Ntui, *Cameroon* 4°25′ N, 11°36′ E **222**
Nu (Salween), river, *Asia* 31°21′ N, 93°34′ E **190**
Nu′aymah, *Syr.* 32°38′ N, 36°10′ E **194**
Nuba Mountains, *Sudan* 10°45′ N, 30°5′ E **224**
Nubia, Lake, *Sudan* 21°56′ N, 30°53′ E **182**
Nubian Desert, *Sudan* 20°50′ N, 30°59′ E **182**
Nucet, *Rom.* 46°30′ N, 22°35′ E **168**
Nucla, *Colo., U.S.* 38°16′ N, 108°33′ W **90**
Nüden, *Mongolia* 43°58′ N, 110°37′ E **198**
Nueces, river, *Tex., U.S.* 28°12′ N, 98°46′ W **92**
Nueltin Lake, *Can.* 59°37′ N, 102°11′ W **106**
Nueva Esparta, adm. division, *Venez.* 10°57′ N, 64°24′ W **130**
Nueva Galia, *Arg.* 35°6′ S, 65°13′ W **134**
Nueva Gerona, *Cuba* 21°53′ N, 82°49′ W **116**
Nueva, Isla, island, *Chile* 55°13′ S, 66°24′ W **134**
Nueva Palmira, *Uru.* 33°54′ S, 58°20′ W **139**
Nueva Rosita, *Mex.* 27°55′ N, 101°12′ W **92**
Nuevo Berlín, *Uru.* 32°59′ S, 57°59′ W **139**
Nuevo Casas Grandes, *Mex.* 30°24′ N, 107°55′ W **92**
Nuevo Delicias, *Mex.* 26°16′ N, 102°48′ W **114**
Nuevo Ideal, *Mex.* 24°51′ N, 105°4′ W **114**
Nuevo Laredo, *Mex.* 27°28′ N, 99°32′ W **96**
Nuevo León, *Mex.* 32°25′ N, 115°14′ W **101**
Nuevo León, adm. division, *Mex.* 25°9′ N, 100°14′ W **114**
Nuevo Morelos, *Mex.* 22°30′ N, 99°13′ W **114**
Nuevo Rocafuerte, *Ecua.* 1°0′ N, 75°27′ W **136**
Nuevo Rodriguez, *Mex.* 27°8′ N, 100°4′ W **96**
Nugaaleed, Dooxo, *Somalia* 8°39′ N, 47°24′ E **216**
Nugrus, Gebel, peak, *Egypt* 24°47′ N, 34°29′ E **182**
Nuh, Ras, *Pak.* 24°55′ N, 62°25′ E **182**
Nuia, *Est.* 58°5′ N, 25°30′ E **166**
Nuijamaa, *Fin.* 60°58′ N, 28°34′ E **166**
Nuiqsut, *Alas., U.S.* 70°12′ N, 151°2′ W **98**
Nuits, *Fr.* 47°43′ N, 4°11′ E **150**
Nukhayb, *Iraq* 32°3′ N, 42°15′ E **180**
Nukheila (Merga), spring, *Sudan* 19°3′ N, 26°20′ E **226**
Nuku′alofa, *Tonga* 21°8′ S, 175°12′ W **241**
Nukumanu Atoll, *South Pacific Ocean* 4°52′ S, 159°33′ E **238**
Nukus, *Uzb.* 42°26′ N, 59°39′ E **180**
Nulato, *Alas., U.S.* 64°36′ N, 158°12′ W **98**
Nules, *Sp.* 39°51′ N, 0°10′ E **164**
Nullarbor Plain, *Austral.* 30°43′ S, 125°29′ E **230**
Numan, *Nig.* 9°29′ N, 12°5′ E **216**
Numata, *Japan* 36°38′ N, 139°2′ E **201**
Numazu, *Japan* 35°5′ N, 138°53′ E **201**
Numedal, region, *Nor.* 60°8′ N, 8°56′ E **152**
Numfoor, island, *Indonesia* 1°23′ S, 134°21′ E **192**
Nummi, *Fin.* 60°23′ N, 23°52′ E **166**
Numto, *Russ.* 63°30′ N, 71°20′ E **169**
Nunap Isua (Kap Farvel) 59°20′ N, 43°43′ W **106**
Nunavik 71°32′ N, 56°33′ W **106**
Nunavut, adm. division, *Can.* 65°9′ N, 74°23′ W **106**
Nunchía, *Col.* 5°35′ N, 72°14′ W **136**
Nuneaton, *U.K.* 52°31′ N, 1°27′ W **162**
Nuñes, island, *Chile* 53°38′ S, 74°58′ W **134**
Nungesser Lake, *Can.* 51°31′ N, 94°27′ W **80**
Nungnain Sum, *China* 45°42′ N, 119°0′ E **198**
Nungo, *Mozambique* 13°23′ S, 37°46′ E **224**
Nunim Lake, lake, *Can.* 59°28′ N, 102°54′ W **108**
Nunivak Island, *Alas., U.S.* 59°24′ N, 166°59′ W **98**
Nunkiní, *Mex.* 20°21′ N, 90°13′ W **112**
Nunligran, *Russ.* 64°51′ N, 175°16′ W **98**
Nuñoa, *Peru* 14°31′ S, 70°37′ W **137**
Nuoro, *It.* 40°19′ N, 9°19′ E **156**
Nuqayr, spring, *Saudi Arabia* 27°50′ N, 48°17′ E **196**
Nuquí, *Col.* 5°41′ N, 77°16′ W **136**
Nura, river, *Kaz.* 50°28′ N, 71°12′ E **184**
Nurki, Mys, *Russ.* 56°29′ N, 138°30′ E **160**
Nurlat, *Russ.* 54°26′ N, 50°41′ E **154**
Nurmes, *Fin.* 63°31′ N, 29°7′ E **152**
Nurmo, *Fin.* 62°49′ N, 22°50′ E **154**
Nürnberg, *Ger.* 49°26′ N, 11°0′ E **143**
Nurobod, *Uzb.* 39°34′ N, 66°17′ E **197**
Nurota, *Uzb.* 40°33′ N, 65°41′ E **197**
Nurri, Mount, peak, *Austral.* 31°45′ S, 145°48′ E **230**
Nushagak Peninsula, *Alas., U.S.* 58°17′ N, 160°46′ W **98**
Nushki, *Pak.* 29°31′ N, 66°3′ E **182**
Nut Mountain, *Can.* 52°8′ N, 103°23′ W **108**
Nuttby Mountain, peak, *Can.* 45°32′ N, 63°18′ W **111**
Nu′uanu Pali Overlook, site, *Hawai′i, U.S.* 21°20′ N, 157°50′ W **99**
Nuugaatsiaq 71°35′ N, 53°13′ W **106**
Nuuk (Godthåb), *Greenland, Den.* 64°14′ N, 51°38′ W **106**
Nuupas, *Fin.* 66°0′ N, 26°19′ E **154**
Nuussuaq 70°6′ N, 51°42′ W **106**
Nuussuaq (Kraulshavn) 74°9′ N, 57°1′ W **106**
Nuwara Eliya, *Sri Lanka* 6°56′ N, 80°47′ E **188**
Nuwerus, *S. Af.* 31°8′ S, 18°20′ E **227**
Nuyno, *Ukr.* 51°31′ N, 24°53′ E **158**
Nuyts Archipelago, islands, *Great Australian Bight* 32°45′ S, 130°56′ E **230**
Nwayfadh, *Africa* 24°53′ N, 14°50′ W **214**
Nxai Pan National Park, *Botswana* 20°3′ S, 24°40′ E **224**
Ny Ålesund, *Nor.* 78°50′ N, 12°1′ E **160**
Nyaake, *Liberia* 4°50′ N, 7°36′ W **222**
Nyac, *Alas., U.S.* 60°53′ N, 160°7′ W **98**
Nyagan′, *Russ.* 62°19′ N, 65°34′ E **169**
Nyahanga, *Tanzania* 2°22′ S, 33°34′ E **224**
Nyainqêntanglha Shan, peak, *China* 30°23′ N, 90°32′ E **197**
Nyainrong, *China* 32°2′ N, 92°14′ E **188**
Nyakabindi, *Tanzania* 2°37′ S, 33°55′ E **224**
Nyakanazi, *Tanzania* 3°6′ S, 31°15′ E **224**
Nyåker, *Nor.* 63°47′ N, 19°19′ E **152**
Nyakrom, *Ghana* 5°37′ N, 0°48′ E **222**
Nyaksimvol′, *Russ.* 62°29′ N, 60°51′ E **169**
Nyala, *Sudan* 12°2′ N, 24°55′ E **224**
Nyalam, *China* 28°11′ N, 85°57′ E **197**
Nyamandhlovu, *Zimb.* 19°53′ S, 28°16′ E **224**
Nyamapanda, *Zimb.* 16°56′ S, 32°48′ E **224**
Nyambiti, *Tanzania* 2°49′ S, 33°24′ E **218**
Nyamirembe, *Tanzania* 2°33′ S, 31°42′ E **224**
Nyamtumbo, *Tanzania* 10°31′ S, 36°6′ E **224**
Nyanding, river, *Sudan* 8°8′ N, 32°18′ E **224**
Nyandoma, *Russ.* 61°39′ N, 40°10′ E **154**
Nyanga, *Zimb.* 18°11′ S, 32°42′ E **224**
Nyanga Nature Reserve, *Congo* 3°2′ S, 11°27′ E **206**
Nyangwe, *Dem. Rep. of the Congo* 4°12′ S, 26°11′ E **218**
Nyanje, *Zambia* 14°24′ S, 31°47′ E **224**
Nyanza Lac, *Burundi* 4°20′ S, 29°36′ E **224**
Nyarling, river, *Can.* 60°20′ N, 114°23′ W **108**
Nyasa, Lake see Malawi, Lake, *Malawi* 34°30′ S, 12°0′ E **21**
Nyashabozh, *Russ.* 65°28′ N, 53°52′ E **154**
Nyaunglebin, *Myanmar* 17°58′ N, 96°42′ E **202**
Nyazepetrovsk, *Russ.* 56°3′ N, 59°39′ E **154**
Nyborg, *Den.* 55°17′ N, 10°47′ E **150**
Nyborg, *Nor.* 70°10′ N, 28°36′ E **152**
Nybro, *Nor.* 56°45′ N, 15°53′ E **152**
Nyda, *Russ.* 66°34′ N, 73°2′ E **169**
Nye Mountains, *Antarctica* 68°4′ S, 48°39′ E **248**
Nyeboe Land 81°28′ N, 53°44′ W **246**
Nyeharelaye, *Belarus* 53°33′ N, 27°4′ E **152**
Nyékládháza, *Hung.* 47°59′ N, 20°48′ E **168**
Nyeri, *Kenya* 0°26′ N, 36°57′ E **224**
Nyerol, *Sudan* 8°40′ N, 32°2′ E **224**
Nyika National Park, *Malawi* 11°6′ S, 34°9′ E **224**
Nyika Plateau, *Malawi* 10°39′ S, 33°28′ E **224**
Nyima, *China* 31°55′ N, 87°49′ E **188**
Nyimba, *Zambia* 14°35′ S, 30°50′ E **224**
Nyingchi, *China* 29°36′ N, 94°24′ E **188**
Nyírábrány, *Hung.* 47°33′ N, 22°3′ E **168**
Nyírbátor, *Hung.* 47°49′ N, 22°8′ E **168**
Nyíregyháza, *Hung.* 47°56′ N, 21°44′ E **168**
Nyiri Desert, *Kenya* 2°23′ S, 37°10′ E **224**
Nyiru, Mount, peak, *Kenya* 2°16′ N, 36°42′ E **224**
Nykarleby (Uusikaarlepyy), *Fin.* 63°31′ N, 22°32′ E **152**
Nykøbing, *Den.* 54°46′ N, 11°53′ E **152**
Nykøbing, *Den.* 56°47′ N, 8°49′ E **150**
Nykøbing, *Den.* 55°55′ N, 11°39′ E **152**
Nyköping, *Nor.* 58°44′ N, 16°59′ E **152**
Nylstroom see Modimolle, *S. Af.* 24°44′ S, 28°24′ E **227**
Nynäshamn, *Sw.* 58°53′ N, 17°53′ E **166**
Nyoma Rap, *India* 33°9′ N, 78°39′ E **188**
Nyoman, river, *Belarus* 53°52′ N, 25°34′ E **166**
Nyon, *Switz.* 46°25′ N, 6°16′ E **167**
Nyrob, *Russ.* 60°44′ N, 56°43′ E **154**
Nyrud, *Nor.* 69°9′ N, 29°12′ E **152**
Nyrza, *Russ.* 63°27′ N, 43°37′ E **154**
Nysa, *Pol.* 50°29′ N, 17°20′ E **152**
Nyssa, *Oreg., U.S.* 43°52′ N, 117°1′ W **90**
Nytva, *Russ.* 57°56′ N, 55°21′ E **154**
Nyukhcha, *Russ.* 63°27′ N, 46°28′ E **154**
Nyukka, *Russ.* 66°3′ N, 32°41′ E **152**
Nyuksenitsa, *Russ.* 60°24′ N, 44°18′ E **154**
Nyunzu, *Dem. Rep. of the Congo* 5°58′ S, 27°57′ E **224**
Nyurba, *Russ.* 63°22′ N, 118°13′ E **160**
Nyuvchim, *Russ.* 61°22′ N, 50°50′ E **154**
Nyzhn′ohirs′kyy, *Ukr.* 45°26′ N, 34°41′ E **156**
Nzara, *Sudan* 4°41′ N, 28°14′ E **224**
Nzega, *Tanzania* 4°14′ S, 33°11′ E **224**
Nzérékoré, *Guinea* 7°38′ N, 8°50′ W **222**
N′zeto, *Angola* 7°19′ S, 12°52′ E **218**
Nzi, river, *Côte d′Ivoire* 6°6′ N, 4°51′ W **222**
Nzo, *Guinea* 7°35′ N, 8°20′ W **222**
Nzo, river, *Côte d′Ivoire* 6°49′ N, 7°36′ W **222**
Nzoro, *Dem. Rep. of the Congo* 3°14′ N, 29°31′ E **224**
Nzoro, river, *Dem. Rep. of the Congo* 3°25′ N, 30°25′ E **224**
Nzwani, island, *Comoros* 12°36′ S, 44°15′ E **220**

O

Oacoma, *S. Dak., U.S.* 43°47′ N, 99°24′ W **90**
Oahe Dam, *S. Dak., U.S.* 44°39′ N, 101°32′ W **82**
Oahe, Lake, *N. Dak., U.S.* 45°33′ N, 100°54′ W **80**
O′ahu, island, *Hawai′i, U.S.* 21°43′ N, 158°0′ W **99**
Oak Bluffs, *Mass., U.S.* 41°27′ N, 70°35′ W **104**
Oak Creek, *Colo., U.S.* 40°17′ N, 106°57′ W **90**
Oak Grove, *La., U.S.* 32°50′ N, 91°23′ W **103**
Oak Harbor, *Ohio, U.S.* 41°30′ N, 83°9′ W **102**
Oak Harbor, *Wash., U.S.* 48°17′ N, 122°38′ W **100**
Oak Hill, *Fla., U.S.* 28°51′ N, 80°52′ W **105**
Oak Hill, *W. Va., U.S.* 37°58′ N, 81°9′ W **94**
Oak Lake, *Can.* 49°45′ N, 100°39′ W **90**
Oak Lawn, *Ill., U.S.* 41°43′ N, 87°45′ W **102**
Oak Park, *Ill., U.S.* 41°53′ N, 87°48′ W **102**
Oak Ridge, *La., U.S.* 32°36′ N, 91°46′ W **103**
Oak Ridge, *Tenn., U.S.* 36°0′ N, 84°15′ W **96**
Oak View, *Calif., U.S.* 34°24′ N, 119°19′ W **100**
Oakdale, *Calif., U.S.* 37°45′ N, 120°52′ W **100**
Oakdale, *La., U.S.* 30°47′ N, 92°40′ W **103**
Oakdale, *Mass., U.S.* 42°23′ N, 71°48′ W **104**
Oakengates, *U.K.* 52°41′ N, 2°26′ W **162**
Oakes, *N. Dak., U.S.* 46°7′ N, 98°6′ W **90**
Oakesdale, *Wash., U.S.* 47°7′ N, 117°15′ W **90**
Oakham, *U.K.* 52°39′ N, 0°44′ E **162**
Oakhurst, *Calif., U.S.* 37°20′ N, 119°40′ W **100**
Oakland, *Calif., U.S.* 37°48′ N, 122°16′ W **100**
Oakland, *Ill., U.S.* 39°38′ N, 88°2′ W **102**
Oakland, *Iowa, U.S.* 41°17′ N, 95°22′ W **90**
Oakland, *Me., U.S.* 44°32′ N, 69°44′ W **104**
Oakland, *Nebr., U.S.* 41°48′ N, 96°28′ W **90**
Oakland, *Oreg., U.S.* 43°24′ N, 123°18′ W **90**
Oakland, *Pa., U.S.* 41°56′ N, 75°38′ W **94**
Oakland Park, *Fla., U.S.* 26°10′ N, 80°9′ W **105**
Oakley, *Calif., U.S.* 37°59′ N, 121°44′ W **100**
Oakley, *Kans., U.S.* 39°7′ N, 100°52′ W **90**
Oakridge, *Oreg., U.S.* 43°44′ N, 122°28′ W **90**
Oaktown, *Ind., U.S.* 38°51′ N, 87°27′ W **102**
Oakura, *N.Z.* 39°10′ S, 173°57′ E **240**
Oakville, *Conn., U.S.* 41°35′ N, 73°5′ W **104**
Oakville, *Wash., U.S.* 46°48′ N, 123°14′ W **100**
Oamaru, *N.Z.* 45°6′ S, 170°57′ E **240**
Oaro, *N.Z.* 42°33′ S, 173°28′ E **240**
Ōasa, *Japan* 34°45′ N, 132°28′ E **201**
Oates Coast, *Antarctica* 69°56′ S, 159°4′ E **248**
Oatman, *Ariz., U.S.* 35°0′ N, 114°23′ W **101**
Oaxaca, *Mex.* 17°2′ N, 96°46′ W **114**
Oaxaca, adm. division, *Mex.* 17°32′ N, 97°22′ W **114**
Ob′, *Russ.* 54°59′ N, 82°50′ E **184**
Ob′ Bank, *Greenland Sea* 80°34′ N, 10°39′ W **255**
Ob′, river, *Russ.* 51°41′ N, 83°0′ E **172**
Ob′ Tablemount, *Indian Ocean* 52°22′ S, 41°12′ E **255**
Oba, *Can.* 49°5′ N, 84°6′ W **94**
Oba Lake, *Can.* 48°34′ N, 84°44′ W **94**
Obabika Lake, lake, *Can.* 47°3′ N, 80°43′ W **94**
Obak, spring, *Sudan* 18°10′ N, 34°51′ E **182**
Obala, *Cameroon* 4°12′ N, 11°31′ E **222**
Obalj, *Bosn. and Herzg.* 43°27′ N, 18°20′ E **168**
Obama, *Japan* 32°44′ N, 130°13′ E **201**
Obama, *Japan* 35°28′ N, 135°44′ E **201**
Obamsca, Lac, lake, *Can.* 50°23′ N, 78°51′ W **110**
Obamsca, river, *Can.* 50°51′ N, 78°50′ W **110**
Oban, *U.K.* 56°25′ N, 5°28′ W **150**
Obanazawa, *Japan* 38°36′ N, 140°25′ E **201**
Obando, *Col.* 3°48′ N, 67°51′ W **136**
Obed, *Can.* 53°34′ N, 117°14′ W **108**
Obed Wild and Scenic River, *Tenn., U.S.* 35°51′ N, 87°55′ W **80**
Oberá, *Arg.* 27°29′ S, 55°10′ W **139**
Oberdrauburg, *Aust.* 46°45′ N, 12°58′ E **167**
Oberhausen, *Ger.* 51°28′ N, 6°51′ E **167**
Oberlin, *Kans., U.S.* 39°49′ N, 100°33′ W **90**
Oberlin, *La., U.S.* 30°36′ N, 92°47′ W **103**
Oberlin, *Ohio, U.S.* 41°16′ N, 82°13′ W **102**
Obernai, *Fr.* 48°27′ N, 7°28′ E **163**
Obernburg, *Ger.* 49°50′ N, 9°9′ E **167**
Oberpullendorf, *Aust.* 47°30′ N, 16°31′ E **168**
Obersuhl, *Ger.* 50°57′ N, 10°1′ E **167**
Oberursel, *Ger.* 50°12′ N, 8°33′ E **167**
Oberwesel, *Ger.* 50°6′ N, 7°42′ E **167**
Obi, *Nig.* 8°20′ N, 8°45′ E **222**
Obi, island, *Indonesia* 1°21′ S, 127°18′ E **192**
Obi, Kepulauan, islands, *Indonesia* 2°17′ S, 126°42′ E **192**
Óbidos, *Braz.* 1°53′ S, 55°32′ W **130**
Óbidos, *Port.* 39°21′ N, 9°11′ W **150**
Obigarm, *Taj.* 38°43′ N, 69°45′ E **197**
Obihiro, *Japan* 42°55′ N, 143°9′ E **190**
Obili, *Gabon* 0°42′ N, 14°22′ E **218**
Obil′noye, *Russ.* 47°29′ N, 44°20′ E **158**
Obion, *Tenn., U.S.* 36°15′ N, 89°12′ W **96**
Obispo, Punta, *Chile* 26°45′ S, 71°27′ W **132**
Obispo Trejo, *Arg.* 30°47′ S, 63°26′ W **139**
Obispos, *Venez.* 8°37′ N, 70°8′ W **136**
Oblivskaya, *Russ.* 48°31′ N, 42°25′ E **158**
Oblong, *Ill., U.S.* 39°0′ N, 87°54′ W **102**
Obluch′ye, *Russ.* 49°6′ N, 131°5′ E **190**
Obninsk, *Russ.* 55°4′ N, 36°40′ E **154**
Obo, *Cen. Af. Rep.* 5°21′ N, 26°30′ E **224**
Obo Liang, *China* 38°48′ N, 92°39′ E **188**
Obock, *Djibouti* 11°55′ N, 43°20′ E **182**
Obokote, *Dem. Rep. of the Congo* 0°52′ N, 26°19′ E **224**
Obol′, *Belarus* 55°23′ N, 29°22′ E **166**
Obonga Lake, *Can.* 49°58′ N, 89°45′ W **94**
Obot, *Alban.* 41°59′ N, 19°25′ E **168**
Obouya, *Congo* 0°57′ N, 15°43′ E **218**
Oboyan′, *Russ.* 51°12′ N, 36°21′ E **158**
Obozerskiy, *Russ.* 63°27′ N, 40°24′ E **154**
Obra, river, *Pol.* 52°31′ N, 15°33′ E **152**
Obre Lake, lake, *Can.* 60°19′ N, 103°25′ W **108**
Obreja, *Rom.* 45°28′ N, 22°16′ E **168**
Obrenovac, *Serb.* 44°38′ N, 20°10′ E **168**
Obrian Peak see Trident Peak, *Nev., U.S.* 41°53′ N, 118°30′ W **90**
O′Brien, *Can.* 47°40′ N, 80°45′ W **110**
Obruk, *Turk.* 38°8′ N, 33°11′ E **156**
Observation Peak, *Calif., U.S.* 40°45′ N, 120°16′ W **90**
Obskaya Guba 67°26′ N, 71°48′ E **169**
Obuasi, *Ghana* 6°15′ N, 1°40′ W **222**
Obubra, *Nig.* 6°2′ N, 8°19′ E **222**
Ob′yachevo, *Russ.* 60°21′ N, 49°39′ E **154**
Obzor, *Bulg.* 42°49′ N, 27°52′ E **158**
Oca, Montes de, *Sp.* 42°24′ N, 3°38′ W **164**
Ocala, *Fla., U.S.* 29°11′ N, 82°8′ W **105**
Ocampo, *Mex.* 22°49′ N, 99°19′ W **114**
Ocampo, *Mex.* 26°36′ N, 101°29′ W **114**
Ocaña, *Col.* 8°12′ N, 73°20′ W **136**
Ocaña, *Sp.* 39°57′ N, 3°30′ W **164**
Occidental, Cordillera, *South America* 4°36′ N, 76°51′ W **122**
Occidental, Grand Erg, *Alg.* 30°22′ N, 0°26′ E **214**
Ocean Cay, island, *Bahamas* 25°25′ N, 79°26′ W **105**
Ocean City, *Md., U.S.* 38°20′ N, 75°6′ W **94**
Ocean City, *Wash., U.S.* 47°3′ N, 124°10′ W **100**
Ocean Falls, *Can.* 52°22′ N, 127°43′ W **108**
Ocean Grove, *Mass., U.S.* 41°43′ N, 71°13′ W **104**
Ocean Island see Kure Atoll, *Hawai′i, U.S.* 28°6′ N, 179°12′ W **99**
Ocean Lake, lake, *Wyo., U.S.* 43°9′ N, 108°57′ W **90**
Ocean Park, *Wash., U.S.* 46°28′ N, 124°3′ W **100**
Ocean Springs, *Miss., U.S.* 30°24′ N, 88°50′ W **96**
Oceano, *Calif., U.S.* 35°6′ N, 120°37′ W **100**
Oceanographer Fracture Zone, *North Atlantic Ocean* 34°28′ N, 33°24′ W **253**
Oceanside, *Calif., U.S.* 33°11′ N, 117°23′ W **101**
Ochakiv, *Ukr.* 46°41′ N, 31°29′ E **156**
Och′amch′ire, *Asia* 42°42′ N, 41°31′ E **195**
Ocher, *Russ.* 57°52′ N, 54°49′ E **154**
Ōchi, *Japan* 35°4′ N, 132°36′ E **201**
Ochobo, *Nig.* 7°10′ N, 7°59′ E **222**
Ochogavía, *Sp.* 42°55′ N, 1°6′ W **164**
Ochopee, *Fla., U.S.* 25°53′ N, 81°18′ W **105**
Ochre River, *Can.* 51°4′ N, 99°48′ W **90**
Ochtrup, *Ger.* 52°12′ N, 7°12′ E **163**
Ocilla, *Ga., U.S.* 31°35′ N, 83°16′ W **96**
Ockelbo, *Nor.* 60°53′ N, 16°42′ E **152**
Ocmulgee, river, *Ga., U.S.* 32°46′ N, 83°37′ W **80**
Ocnele Mari, *Rom.* 45°5′ N, 24°17′ E **156**
Ocniţa, *Mold.* 48°23′ N, 27°26′ E **156**
Ocoee, *Fla., U.S.* 28°34′ N, 81°33′ W **105**
Ocoña, *Peru* 16°27′ S, 73°6′ W **137**
Ocoña, river, *Peru* 16°2′ S, 73°19′ W **137**
Oconee, Lake, *Ga., U.S.* 33°21′ N, 83°39′ W **96**
Oconee, river, *Ga., U.S.* 32°41′ N, 83°14′ W **80**
Oconomowoc, *Wis., U.S.* 43°6′ N, 88°30′ W **102**
Oconto, *Wis., U.S.* 44°54′ N, 87°52′ W **94**
Oconto Falls, *Wis., U.S.* 44°52′ N, 88°8′ W **94**
Ocoruro, *Peru* 15°4′ S, 71°8′ W **137**
Ocós, *Guatemala* 14°32′ N, 92°12′ W **115**
Ocotillo, *Calif., U.S.* 32°44′ N, 116°2′ W **101**
Ocotillo Wells, *Calif., U.S.* 33°8′ N, 116°9′ W **101**
Ocotlán, *Mex.* 20°21′ N, 102°46′ W **114**
Ocoyo, *Peru* 14°3′ S, 75°1′ W **137**
Ocracoke, *N.C., U.S.* 35°6′ N, 76°0′ W **96**
Ocracoke Inlet 34°49′ N, 75°39′ W **80**
Ócsa, *Hung.* 47°17′ N, 19°14′ E **168**
Octave, river, *Can.* 48°52′ N, 78°35′ W **94**
Ocumare del Tuy, *Venez.* 10°5′ N, 66°47′ W **136**
Ocurí, *Bol.* 18°55′ S, 65°52′ W **137**
Oda, *Eth.* 6°41′ N, 41°10′ E **224**
Oda, *Ghana* 5°55′ N, 1°0′ E **222**
Ōda, *Japan* 35°11′ N, 132°30′ E **201**
Oda, Jebel, peak, *Sudan* 20°17′ N, 36°32′ E **182**
Ŏdaejin, *N. Korea* 41°21′ N, 129°47′ E **200**
Odanovce, *Serb.* 42°32′ N, 21°41′ E **168**
Odawara, *Japan* 35°15′ N, 139°9′ E **201**
Odda, *Nor.* 60°5′ N, 6°31′ E **152**
Oddur see Xuddur, *Somalia* 4°6′ N, 43°55′ E **218**
Odebolt, *Iowa, U.S.* 42°18′ N, 95°15′ W **90**
Odei, river, *Can.* 56°18′ N, 98°57′ W **108**
Odell, *Ill., U.S.* 41°0′ N, 88°31′ W **102**
Odell, *Oreg., U.S.* 45°36′ N, 121°33′ W **100**
Ödemiş, *Turk.* 38°13′ N, 27°56′ E **156**
Odendaalsrus, *S. Af.* 27°53′ S, 26°39′ E **227**
Odense, *Den.* 55°23′ N, 10°23′ E **150**
Odenwald, *Ger.* 49°45′ N, 8°35′ E **167**
Odesa, *Ukr.* 46°28′ N, 30°43′ E **156**
Odesdino, *Russ.* 63°28′ N, 54°25′ E **154**
Odessa, *Tex., U.S.* 31°49′ N, 102°22′ W **92**
Odessa, *Wash., U.S.* 47°18′ N, 118°42′ W **90**
Odiel, river, *Sp.* 37°34′ N, 6°47′ W **164**
Odienné, *Côte d′Ivoire* 9°31′ N, 7°34′ W **222**
Odin, Mount, peak, *Can.* 50°32′ N, 118°14′ W **90**
Odolanów, *Pol.* 51°35′ N, 17°41′ E **152**
Odon, *Ind., U.S.* 38°50′ N, 87°0′ W **102**
O′Donnell, *Tex., U.S.* 32°57′ N, 101°49′ W **92**
Odra, river, *Pol.* 51°37′ N, 16°16′ E **160**
Odra, river, *Sp.* 42°29′ N, 4°3′ W **164**
Odžaci, *Serb.* 45°29′ N, 19°16′ E **168**
Odžak, *Bosn. and Herzg.* 45°0′ N, 18°18′ E **168**
Odzala, *Congo* 0°32′ N, 14°34′ E **218**
Odzala National Park, *Congo* 0°45′ N, 14°35′ E **206**
Odzi, river, *Zimb.* 19°11′ S, 32°22′ E **224**
Oecusse see Pante Makasar, *Indonesia* 9°21′ S, 124°20′ E **192**
Oederan, *Ger.* 50°51′ N, 13°10′ E **152**
Oeiras, *Braz.* 7°0′ S, 42°10′ W **132**
Oelde, *Ger.* 51°49′ N, 8°7′ E **167**
Oelrichs, *S. Dak., U.S.* 43°10′ N, 103°15′ W **90**
Oelwein, *Iowa, U.S.* 42°40′ N, 91°55′ W **94**
Oeniadae, ruin(s), *Gr.* 38°23′ N, 21°5′ E **156**
Oenpelli, *Austral.* 12°22′ S, 133°6′ E **238**
Oerlenbach, *Ger.* 50°9′ N, 10°7′ E **167**
Oeta, Mount see Oíti, Óros, peak, *Gr.* 38°47′ N, 22°10′ E **156**
Of, *Turk.* 40°57′ N, 40°17′ E **195**
O′Fallon, *Ill., U.S.* 38°34′ N, 89°55′ W **102**
O′Fallon Creek, river, *Mont., U.S.* 46°49′ N, 105°31′ W **90**
Ofaqim, *Israel* 31°19′ N, 34°37′ E **194**
Ofen Pass, *Switz.* 46°38′ N, 10°17′ E **167**
Offa, *Nig.* 8°12′ N, 4°43′ E **222**
Offenbach, *Ger.* 50°5′ N, 8°46′ E **167**
Offutt Air Force Base, *Nebr., U.S.* 41°5′ N, 96°0′ W **90**
Oficina Dominador, *Chile* 24°23′ S, 69°34′ W **132**
Oficina, oil field, *Venez.* 8°43′ N, 64°27′ W **116**
Oficina Santa Fe, *Chile* 21°52′ S, 69°37′ W **137**
Ofin, river, *Ghana* 6°26′ N, 2°2′ W **222**
Ofu, island, *United States* 14°11′ S, 169°38′ W **241**
Ogadēn, region, *Eth.* 6°45′ N, 42°8′ E **224**
Ōgaki, *Japan* 35°21′ N, 136°37′ E **201**
Ogallala, *Nebr., U.S.* 41°7′ N, 101°44′ W **92**
Ogasawara Guntō see Bonin Islands, *North Pacific Ocean* 25°25′ N, 143°8′ E **238**
Ogbomosho, *Nig.* 8°10′ N, 4°16′ E **222**
Ogden, *Iowa, U.S.* 42°0′ N, 94°2′ W **94**
Ogden, *Utah, U.S.* 41°13′ N, 111°58′ W **90**
Ogden, Mount, peak, *Can.* 58°25′ N, 133°32′ W **108**
Ogema, *Can.* 49°33′ N, 104°56′ W **90**
Oggiono, *It.* 45°46′ N, 9°19′ E **167**
Ogi, *Japan* 37°49′ N, 138°16′ E **201**
Ogilvie Mountains, *Can.* 64°46′ N, 139°9′ W **106**
Oglanly, *Turkm.* 39°52′ N, 54°22′ E **180**
Oglat Beraber, spring, *Alg.* 30°24′ N, 3°34′ W **214**
Oglat d′Admamlalmat, spring, *Mauritania* 23°25′ N, 11°48′ W **214**
′Oglât ed Daoud, spring, *Mauritania* 23°31′ N, 6°57′ W **214**
′Oglât el Fersig, spring, *Mauritania* 21°49′ N, 6°21′ W **222**
′Oglat el Khnâchîch, spring, *Mali* 21°51′ N, 3°59′ W **222**
Oglats de Mkhaïzira, spring, *Mauritania* 22°44′ N, 10°18′ W **214**
Oglesby, *Ill., U.S.* 41°17′ N, 89°5′ W **102**
Oglethorpe, *Ga., U.S.* 32°17′ N, 84°4′ W **96**
Oglethorpe, Mount, peak, *Ga., U.S.* 34°28′ N, 84°24′ W **96**
Ogna, *Nor.* 58°31′ N, 5°48′ E **150**
Ognev Yar, *Russ.* 58°21′ N, 76°30′ E **169**
Ognon, river, *Fr.* 47°17′ N, 5°59′ E **165**
Ogoja, *Nig.* 6°38′ N, 8°42′ E **222**
Ogoki, *Can.* 51°40′ N, 85°52′ W **82**
Ogoki Reservoir, lake, *Can.* 50°50′ N, 89°14′ W **80**
Ogoki, river, *Can.* 51°5′ N, 86°10′ W **110**
Ögöömör, *Mongolia* 46°47′ N, 107°50′ E **198**
Ogōri, *Japan* 34°6′ N, 131°24′ E **200**
Ogou, river, *Togo* 8°48′ N, 1°25′ E **222**
Ogr, *Sudan* 12°2′ N, 27°1′ E **218**
Ograźden, *Maced.* 41°25′ N, 22°52′ E **168**
Ogre, *Latv.* 56°49′ N, 24°33′ E **166**
Ogre, river, *Latv.* 56°46′ N, 25°27′ E **166**
′Oguëilet en Nmâdi, spring, *Mauritania* 19°45′ N, 11°1′ W **222**
Oguma, *Nig.* 7°51′ N, 7°2′ E **222**
Ogunquit, *Me., U.S.* 43°14′ N, 70°37′ W **104**
Ogwashi Uku, *Nig.* 6°17′ N, 6°28′ E **222**
Ohanet, oil field, *Alg.* 28°46′ N, 8°49′ E **214**
Ohangoron, *Uzb.* 40°56′ N, 69°35′ E **197**
Ohau, *N.Z.* 40°41′ S, 175°15′ E **240**
Óhi, Óros, peak, *Gr.* 38°3′ N, 24°23′ E **156**
Ohio, *Ill., U.S.* 41°33′ N, 89°28′ W **102**
Ohio, adm. division, *Ohio, U.S.* 40°15′ N, 83°3′ W **102**
Ohio City, *Ohio, U.S.* 40°45′ N, 84°37′ W **102**
Ohio Range, *Antarctica* 85°4′ S, 101°32′ W **248**
Ohio, river, *U.S.* 37°37′ N, 87°7′ W **80**
Ōi, river, *Japan* 35°9′ N, 138°8′ E **201**
Oiapoque, *Braz.* 3°50′ N, 51°48′ W **130**
Oijärvi, *Fin.* 65°38′ N, 25°48′ E **152**
Oil City, *La., U.S.* 32°44′ N, 93°58′ W **103**
Oil City, *Pa., U.S.* 41°24′ N, 79°43′ W **94**
Oil Islands see Chagos Archipelago, *Indian Ocean* 6°42′ S, 71°25′ E **188**
Oildale, *Calif., U.S.* 35°25′ N, 119°2′ W **101**
Oilton, *Okla., U.S.* 36°3′ N, 96°35′ W **92**
Oilton, *Tex., U.S.* 27°27′ N, 98°58′ W **92**
Oise, river, *Fr.* 49°51′ N, 3°39′ E **163**
Ōita, *Japan* 33°13′ N, 131°37′ E **201**
Ōita, adm. division, *Japan* 33°42′ N, 131°34′ E **200**
Oíti, Óros (Oeta, Mount), peak, *Gr.* 38°47′ N, 22°10′ E **156**
Oiticica, *South America* 5°2′ S, 41°6′ W **132**
Oituz, *Rom.* 46°6′ N, 26°23′ E **156**
Ojai, *Calif., U.S.* 34°26′ N, 119°15′ W **101**
Öje, *Nor.* 60°48′ N, 13°49′ E **152**
Ojeda, *Arg.* 35°18′ S, 63°59′ W **139**
Ojinaga, *Mex.* 29°33′ N, 104°27′ W **92**
Ojiya, *Japan* 37°17′ N, 138°47′ E **201**
Ojo Caliente, *Mex.* 22°33′ N, 102°16′ W **114**
Ojo de Laguna, *Mex.* 29°26′ N, 106°25′ W **92**
Ojós, *Sp.* 38°8′ N, 1°22′ W **164**
Ojos del Salado, Cerro, peak, *Chile* 27°6′ S, 68°45′ W **132**
Ojuelos de Jalisco, *Mex.* 21°51′ N, 101°35′ W **114**

Oka, river, Russ. 55°43′ N, 42°12′ E 154
Oka, river, Russ. 53°14′ N, 36°17′ E 154
Okaba, Indonesia 8°7′ S, 139°37′ E 192
Okahandja, Namibia 21°59′ S, 16°53′ E 227
Okahukura, N.Z. 38°49′ S, 175°14′ E 240
Okak Islands, Can. 57°32′ N, 65°21′ W 106
Okakarara, Namibia 20°36′ S, 17°30′ E 227
Okaloacoochee Slough, marsh, Fla., U.S. 26°26′ N, 80°42′ W 105
Okanagan Lake, Can. 49°50′ N, 120°51′ W 80
Okanogan, Wash., U.S. 48°21′ N, 119°37′ W 90
Okanogan Range, Wash., U.S. 48°48′ N, 120°27′ W 90
Okány, Hung. 46°53′ N, 21°21′ E 168
Okaputa, Namibia 20°7′ S, 16°58′ E 227
Okara, Pak. 30°49′ N, 73°27′ E 186
Okatjoruu, Namibia 19°38′ S, 18°34′ E 220
Okaukuejo, Namibia 19°9′ S, 15°57′ E 220
Okavango Delta, Botswana 19°33′ S, 23°16′ E 224
Ōkawa, Japan 33°12′ N, 130°22′ E 201
Okawville, Ill., U.S. 38°25′ N, 89°33′ W 102
Okaya, Japan 36°4′ N, 138°2′ E 201
Okayama, Japan 34°38′ N, 133°53′ E 201
Okayama, adm. division, Japan 34°54′ N, 133°20′ E 201
Okazaki, Japan 34°56′ N, 137°10′ E 201
Okcheon, S. Korea 36°18′ N, 127°34′ E 200
Okeechobee, Fla., U.S. 27°15′ N, 80°50′ W 105
Okeechobee, Lake, Fla., U.S. 26°57′ N, 80°59′ W 105
Okeene, Okla., U.S. 36°6′ N, 98°20′ W 92
Okefenokee Swamp, marsh, Ga., U.S. 30°35′ N, 83°9′ W 80
Okene, Nig. 7°34′ N, 6°14′ E 222
Okha, India 22°26′ N, 69°3′ E 186
Okha, Russ. 53°33′ N, 142°43′ E 160
Okhaldhunga, Nepal 27°20′ N, 86°30′ E 197
Okhansk, Russ. 57°42′ N, 55°19′ E 154
Okhotsk, Russ. 59°26′ N, 143°20′ E 160
Okhotsk, Sea of 57°51′ N, 141°45′ E 160
Okhotskiy Perevoz, Russ. 61°52′ N, 135°38′ E 160
Okhtyrka, Ukr. 50°19′ N, 34°55′ E 158
Oki Guntō, islands, Sea of Japan 35°59′ N, 133°6′ E 201
Okiep, S. Af. 29°36′ S, 17°52′ E 227
Okinawa, island, Japan 26°22′ N, 128°16′ E 190
Okino Erabu Shima, island, Japan 27°2′ N, 128°25′ E 190
Okitipupa, Nig. 6°40′ N, 4°43′ E 222
Okkang, N. Korea 40°18′ N, 124°46′ E 200
Oklahoma, adm. division, Okla., U.S. 35°37′ N, 98°23′ W 96
Oklahoma City, Okla., U.S. 35°25′ N, 97°36′ W 92
Oklawaha, Fla., U.S. 29°2′ N, 81°56′ W 105
Okletac, Serb. 44°5′ N, 19°34′ E 168
Okmulgee, Okla., U.S. 35°36′ N, 95°58′ W 94
Okolona, Miss., U.S. 33°59′ N, 88°45′ W 96
Okotoks, Can. 50°44′ N, 113°59′ W 90
Okounfo, Benin 8°20′ N, 2°37′ E 222
Okoyo, Congo 1°27′ S, 15°1′ E 218
Okpara, river, Africa 7°44′ N, 2°37′ E 222
Okp'yŏng, N. Korea 39°16′ N, 127°20′ E 200
Oksino, Russ. 67°34′ N, 52°20′ E 169
Oksovskiy, Russ. 62°36′ N, 39°56′ E 154
Okstindan, peak, Nor. 65°59′ N, 14°11′ E 152
Oktyabr'sk, Kaz. 49°26′ N, 57°25′ E 158
Oktyabr'skiy, Kaz. 49°39′ N, 83°37′ E 184
Oktyabr'skiy, Russ. 55°5′ N, 60°10′ E 154
Oktyabr'skiy, Russ. 47°55′ N, 43°34′ E 158
Oktyabr'skiy, Russ. 54°27′ N, 53°35′ E 154
Oktyabr'skoe, Kaz. 52°8′ N, 65°40′ E 184
Oktyabr'skoye, Russ. 62°34′ N, 66°2′ E 169
Oktyabr'skoye, Russ. 52°23′ N, 55°37′ E 154
Oktyabr'skoye, Russ. 52°21′ N, 55°32′ E 184
Okučani, Croatia 45°15′ N, 17°12′ E 168
Ōkuchi, Japan 32°3′ N, 130°37′ E 201
Okulovka, Russ. 58°24′ N, 33°19′ E 154
Okunev Nos, Russ. 66°16′ N, 52°39′ E 154
Okushiri Tō, island, Japan 41°45′ N, 138°29′ E 190
Okuta, Nig. 9°12′ N, 3°15′ E 222
Ola, Ark., U.S. 35°1′ N, 93°14′ W 96
Ola, Russ. 59°37′ N, 151°11′ E 160
Ólafsvík, Ice. 64°53′ N, 23°45′ W 246
Olaine, Latv. 56°48′ N, 23°57′ E 166
Olancha, Calif., U.S. 36°17′ N, 118°2′ W 101
Olancha Peak, Calif., U.S. 36°15′ N, 118°10′ W 101
Olanchito, Hond. 15°28′ N, 86°35′ W 115
Ölands Norra Udde, Sw. 57°23′ N, 16°58′ E 152
Ölands Södra Udde, Sw. 55°54′ N, 16°3′ E 152
Olanga, Russ. 66°9′ N, 30°35′ E 152
Olary, Austral. 32°16′ S, 140°20′ E 231
Olasan, spring, Eth. 5°17′ N, 45°4′ E 218
Olascoaga, Arg. 35°15′ S, 60°39′ W 139
Olathe, Kans., U.S. 38°51′ N, 94°49′ W 94
Olavarría, Arg. 36°55′ S, 60°17′ W 139
Oława, Pol. 50°57′ N, 17°17′ E 152
Olbia, It. 40°55′ N, 9°28′ E 214
Old Cove Fort, site, Utah, U.S. 38°39′ N, 112°38′ W 90
Old Crow, Can. 67°32′ N, 139°56′ W 73
Old Dongola, ruin(s), Sudan 18°12′ N, 30°42′ E 226
Old Fort, Can. 55°4′ N, 126°20′ W 108
Old Man of the Mountain, site, N.H., U.S. 44°10′ N, 71°44′ W 104
Old Mkushi, Zambia 14°22′ S, 29°20′ E 224
Old Orchard Beach, Me., U.S. 43°30′ N, 70°24′ W 104
Old Rhodes Key, island, Fla., U.S. 25°22′ N, 80°14′ W 105
Old Sarum, ruin(s), U.K. 51°5′ N, 1°50′ W 162
Old Saybrook, Conn., U.S. 41°17′ N, 72°23′ W 104
Old Slains Castle, site, U.K. 57°20′ N, 2°1′ W 150
Old Speck Mountain, peak, Me., U.S. 44°33′ N, 71°0′ W 104
Old Sturbridge, site, Mass., U.S. 42°5′ N, 72°8′ W 104
Old Sugar Mill, site, Hawai'i, U.S. 21°30′ N, 157°53′ W 99
Old Town, Fla., U.S. 29°36′ N, 83°0′ W 105
Old Wives Lake, Can. 50°3′ N, 106°39′ W 90
Old Woman Mountains, Calif., U.S. 34°26′ N, 115°25′ W 101
Oldbury, U.K. 52°29′ N, 2°1′ W 162
Oldeani, Tanzania 3°20′ S, 35°34′ E 224
Olden, Nor. 61°50′ N, 6°49′ E 152
Oldenburg, Ger. 53°8′ N, 8°13′ E 163
Oldenzaal, Neth. 52°18′ N, 6°55′ E 163
Oldham, U.K. 53°32′ N, 2°7′ W 162
Olds, Can. 51°49′ N, 114°6′ W 90
Olduvai Gorge, site, Tanzania 2°57′ S, 35°14′ E 224
Öldzeyte Suma, Mongolia 44°33′ N, 106°10′ E 198
Öldziyt, Mongolia 44°39′ N, 109°3′ E 198
Olean, N.Y., U.S. 42°4′ N, 78°27′ W 94
Olecko, Pol. 54°1′ N, 22°31′ E 166
Olekma, river, Russ. 59°23′ N, 120°19′ E 160
Olekminsk, Russ. 60°23′ N, 120°16′ E 160
Oleksandriya, Ukr. 50°44′ N, 26°20′ E 152
Olema, Russ. 64°28′ N, 46°2′ E 154
Ølen, Nor. 59°35′ N, 5°47′ E 152
Olenegorsk, Russ. 68°8′ N, 33°15′ E 152
Olenek, Russ. 68°30′ N, 112°22′ E 160
Olenek, river, Russ. 66°59′ N, 107°5′ E 160
Olenekskiy Zaliv 72°54′ N, 114°57′ E 160
Olenino, Russ. 56°12′ N, 33°37′ E 154
Olenitsa, Russ. 66°26′ N, 35°13′ E 152
Oleniy, Ostrov, island, Russ. 72°2′ N, 72°25′ E 160
Olesno, Pol. 50°52′ N, 18°25′ E 152
Olevs'k, Ukr. 51°13′ N, 27°40′ E 152
Ølfjellet, peak, Nor. 66°46′ N, 15°4′ E 152
Olga, Lac, lake, Can. 49°45′ N, 77°35′ W 94
Olga, Mount see Kata Tjuta, peak, Austral. 25°21′ S, 130°31′ E 230
Olgastretet 78°6′ N, 20°12′ E 160
Ölgiy, Mongolia 48°57′ N, 89°50′ E 184
Ølgod, Den. 55°48′ N, 8°35′ E 150
Olhava, Fin. 65°28′ N, 25°22′ E 152
Oli Qoltyq Sory, marsh, Kaz. 45°20′ N, 53°31′ E 158
Oli, river, Nig. 9°46′ N, 4°0′ E 222
Oliete, Sp. 40°59′ N, 0°41′ E 164
Olifants, river, S. Af. 24°36′ S, 30°29′ E 227
Olifantshoek, S. Af. 27°58′ S, 22°42′ E 227
Olimarao Atoll 7°48′ N, 143°3′ E 192
Ólimbos, Gr. 35°44′ N, 27°11′ E 156
Ólimbos, Óros (Olympus), peak, Gr. 40°3′ N, 22°17′ E 156
Olímpia, Braz. 20°43′ S, 48°55′ W 138
Olinalá, Mex. 17°48′ N, 98°51′ W 114
Olinda, Braz. 8°0′ S, 34°55′ W 132
Olinda Entrance 11°17′ S, 142°53′ E 192
Olite, Sp. 42°28′ N, 1°39′ W 164
Oliva, Arg. 32°3′ S, 63°33′ W 139
Oliva, Sp. 38°55′ N, 0°8′ E 164
Oliva de la Frontera, Sp. 38°16′ N, 6°56′ W 150
Oliveira, Braz. 20°40′ S, 44°51′ W 138
Oliver, Can. 49°10′ N, 119°34′ W 90
Oliver Lake, lake, Can. 56°50′ N, 103°50′ W 108
Olivet, Mich., U.S. 42°27′ N, 84°55′ W 102
Olivia, Minn., U.S. 44°46′ N, 95°0′ W 90
Ol'khovka, Russ. 49°51′ N, 44°31′ E 158
Olla, La., U.S. 31°53′ N, 92°15′ W 103
Ollachea, Peru 13°49′ S, 70°32′ W 137
Ollagüe (Oyahue), Chile 21°14′ S, 68°18′ W 137
Ollagüe, Volcan, peak, Chile 21°19′ S, 68°20′ W 137
Ollanta, Peru 9°45′ S, 74°2′ W 137
Ollerton, U.K. 53°11′ N, 1°2′ W 162
Olmaliq, Uzb. 40°50′ N, 69°35′ E 197
Olnes, Alas., U.S. 65°5′ N, 147°40′ W 98
Olney, Ill., U.S. 38°42′ N, 88°1′ W 82
Olney, Tex., U.S. 33°21′ N, 98°46′ W 92
Olney, U.K. 52°9′ N, 0°42′ E 162
Oloibiri, oil field, Nig. 4°39′ N, 6°16′ E 222
Olomouc, Czech Rep. 49°35′ N, 17°16′ E 152
Olomoucký, adm. division, Czech Rep. 49°35′ N, 17°16′ E 152
Olonets, Russ. 60°56′ N, 33°2′ E 154
Olongapo, Philippines 14°50′ N, 120°17′ E 203
Olonzac, Fr. 43°16′ N, 2°42′ E 164
Oloron, Fr. 43°12′ N, 0°36′ E 164
Oloru, Nig. 8°39′ N, 4°35′ E 222
Olosega, island, United States 14°11′ S, 169°36′ W 241
Olot, Sp. 42°11′ N, 2°28′ E 164
Olovo, Bosn. and Herzg. 44°7′ N, 18°34′ E 168
Olovyannaya, Russ. 50°54′ N, 115°24′ E 190
Olovyannaya, Russ. 66°13′ N, 178°56′ W 98
Oloy, river, Russ. 66°12′ N, 160°20′ E 160
Olpe, Ger. 51°1′ N, 7°50′ E 167
Olshammar, Nor. 58°45′ N, 14°45′ E 152
Olsztyn, Pol. 53°46′ N, 20°28′ E 166
Olt, adm. division, Rom. 44°11′ N, 24°12′ E 156
Olt, river, Rom. 45°46′ N, 24°19′ E 156
Olten, Switz. 47°21′ N, 7°53′ E 156
Olteni, Rom. 44°11′ N, 25°18′ E 156
Olteniţa, Rom. 44°6′ N, 26°39′ E 156
Olton, Tex., U.S. 34°9′ N, 102°8′ W 92
Oltu, Turk. 40°34′ N, 41°57′ E 195
Oltu, river, Turk. 40°43′ N, 41°41′ E 195
Oluan Pi, Taiwan, China 21°39′ N, 120°53′ E 198
Olukonda, Namibia 18°6′ S, 16°4′ E 220
Ólvega, Sp. 41°45′ N, 1°59′ W 164
Olvera, Sp. 36°55′ N, 5°17′ W 164
Olympia, Wash., U.S. 47°1′ N, 122°56′ W 100
Olympia, ruin(s), Gr. 37°38′ N, 21°32′ E 156
Olympic Mountains, Wash., U.S. 47°16′ N, 123°50′ W 100
Olympic National Park, Wash., U.S. 48°0′ N, 125°7′ W 100
Olympos, peak, Cyprus 34°55′ N, 32°50′ E 194
Olympus, Mount, peak, Wash., U.S. 47°47′ N, 123°45′ W 100
Olympus, Mount see Ulu Dağ, peak, Turk. 40°4′ N, 29°7′ E 156
Olympus see Ólimbos, Óros, peak, Gr. 40°3′ N, 22°17′ E 156
Olynthus, ruin(s), Gr. 40°16′ N, 23°17′ E 156
Olyutorskiy, Mys, Russ. 59°44′ N, 170°18′ E 160
Om', river, Russ. 55°17′ N, 77°33′ E 184
Oma, China 32°26′ N, 83°17′ E 188
Oma, Miss., U.S. 31°43′ N, 90°9′ W 103
Oma, river, Russ. 66°23′ N, 46°47′ E 154
Ōmachi, Japan 36°30′ N, 137°51′ E 201
Omae Zaki, Japan 34°29′ N, 138°14′ E 201
Omaha, Nebr., U.S. 41°15′ N, 95°58′ W 90
Omaha, Tex., U.S. 33°10′ N, 94°45′ W 103
Omaha Beach, Fr. 49°17′ N, 1°13′ W 150
Omak, Wash., U.S. 48°24′ N, 119°33′ W 90
Omakau, N.Z. 45°5′ S, 169°38′ E 240
Omakere, N.Z. 40°3′ S, 176°49′ E 240
Oman 21°52′ N, 57°32′ E 182
Oman, Gulf of 24°46′ N, 57°23′ E 172
Oman, Gulf of 24°30′ N, 58°46′ E 254
Omarama, N.Z. 44°31′ S, 169°58′ E 240
Omaruru, Namibia 21°27′ S, 15°55′ E 227
Ombabika, Can. 50°14′ N, 87°54′ W 94
Ombaïa, Congo 2°24′ S, 13°10′ E 218
Ombombo, spring, Namibia 18°44′ S, 13°55′ E 220
Ombwe, Dem. Rep. of the Congo 4°23′ S, 25°32′ E 224
Omchali, Mys, Turkm. 40°54′ N, 53°5′ E 158
Omdurman, Sudan 15°36′ N, 32°27′ E 182
Omegna, It. 45°52′ N, 8°24′ E 167
Omer, Mich., U.S. 44°3′ N, 83°51′ W 102
Ometepec, Mex. 16°30′ N, 98°28′ W 73
Ōmihachiman, Japan 35°6′ N, 136°5′ E 201
Omihi, N.Z. 43°2′ S, 172°52′ E 240
Omineca, river, Can. 55°54′ N, 126°9′ W 108
Omiš, Croatia 43°26′ N, 16°42′ E 168
Ōmiya, Japan 35°54′ N, 139°38′ E 201
Ommaney, Cape, Alas., U.S. 56°0′ N, 135°20′ W 108
Ommen, Neth. 52°31′ N, 6°24′ E 163
Omo National Park, Eth. 5°39′ N, 35°20′ E 224
Omo, river, Eth. 5°54′ N, 35°55′ E 224
Omolon, Russ. 65°10′ N, 160°34′ E 173
Omolon, river, Russ. 69°30′ N, 155°38′ E 172
Omoloy, river, Russ. 69°50′ N, 132°42′ E 160
Omont, Fr. 49°35′ N, 4°42′ E 163
Omro, Wis., U.S. 44°1′ N, 88°45′ W 102
Omsk, Russ. 54°58′ N, 73°26′ E 184
Omsk, adm. division, Russ. 54°44′ N, 72°20′ E 184
Omsukchan, Russ. 62°29′ N, 155°44′ E 173
Omu Aran, Nig. 8°9′ N, 5°6′ E 222
Omul, peak, Rom. 45°26′ N, 25°22′ E 156
Omullyakhskaya Guba 72°1′ N, 138°2′ E 160
Ōmura, Japan 32°54′ N, 129°58′ E 201
Ōmuta, Japan 33°1′ N, 130°26′ E 201
Omutninsk, Russ. 58°40′ N, 52°15′ E 154
Oña, Sp. 42°43′ N, 3°26′ W 164
Onaga, Kans., U.S. 39°28′ N, 96°10′ W 90
Onakawana, Can. 50°36′ N, 81°27′ W 110
Onalaska, Tex., U.S. 30°47′ N, 95°7′ W 103
Onaman Lake, Can. 50°0′ N, 87°59′ W 110
Onamia, Minn., U.S. 46°3′ N, 93°41′ W 94
Onaping Lake, Can. 46°56′ N, 82°3′ W 94
Onarga, Ill., U.S. 40°42′ N, 88°1′ W 102
Onatchiway, Lac, lake, Can. 48°59′ N, 71°46′ W 94
Oñati, Sp. 43°1′ N, 2°24′ W 164
Onavas, Mex. 28°27′ N, 109°32′ W 92
Onawa, Iowa, U.S. 42°0′ N, 96°6′ W 90
Oncativo, Arg. 31°55′ S, 63°41′ W 139
Onda, Sp. 39°58′ N, 0°17′ E 164
Ondangwa, Namibia 17°56′ S, 15°59′ E 220
Ondas, river, Braz. 12°42′ S, 46°4′ W 132
Ondjiva, Angola 17°6′ S, 15°39′ E 220
Ondo, Nig. 7°7′ N, 4°49′ E 222
Ondor Sum, China 42°30′ N, 112°50′ E 198
Öndörhaan, Mongolia 47°22′ N, 110°40′ E 198
Öndörhushuu, Mongolia 47°59′ N, 113°55′ E 198
One and Half Degree Channel 0°58′ N, 72°7′ E 188
Oneco, Conn., U.S. 41°41′ N, 71°49′ W 104
Oneco, Fla., U.S. 27°27′ N, 82°32′ W 105
Onega, Russ. 63°55′ N, 38°12′ E 154
Oneida, N.Y., U.S. 43°5′ N, 75°41′ W 94
Oneida, Tenn., U.S. 36°29′ N, 84°31′ W 96
Oneida Lake, N.Y., U.S. 43°14′ N, 76°34′ W 80
O'Neill, Nebr., U.S. 42°26′ N, 98°40′ W 90
Oneonta, Ala., U.S. 33°56′ N, 86°29′ W 96
Oneonta, N.Y., U.S. 42°27′ N, 75°5′ W 94
Onezhskaya Guba 64°4′ N, 36°13′ E 154
Onezhskoye Ozero, lake, Russ. 60°31′ N, 33°29′ E 160
Ongarue, N.Z. 38°43′ S, 175°17′ E 240
Ongcheon, S. Korea 36°41′ N, 128°42′ E 200
Ongi, Mongolia 45°28′ N, 103°56′ E 198
Ongjin, N. Korea 37°55′ N, 125°22′ E 200
Ongniud Qi, China 42°56′ N, 118°59′ E 198
Ongoka, Dem. Rep. of the Congo 1°24′ S, 26°2′ E 224
Ongole, India 15°30′ N, 80°4′ E 188
Ongtustik Qazaqstan, adm. division, Kaz. 42°4′ N, 67°24′ E 197
Ongwediva, Namibia 17°55′ S, 15°54′ E 220
Oni, Ga. 42°33′ N, 43°27′ E 195
Onib, Sudan 21°26′ N, 35°16′ E 182
Onitsha, Nig. 6°15′ N, 6°46′ E 222
Onizuka Center for International Astronomy, site, Hawai'i, U.S. 19°43′ N, 155°29′ W 99
Önjüül, Mongolia 46°46′ N, 105°32′ E 198
Onley, Va., U.S. 37°41′ N, 75°44′ W 94
Onnela, Fin. 69°54′ N, 26°59′ E 152
Ōno, Japan 35°58′ N, 136°29′ E 201
Onolimbu, Indonesia 1°3′ N, 97°51′ E 196
Onomichi, Japan 34°25′ N, 133°12′ E 201
Onon, Mongolia 49°9′ N, 112°41′ E 198
Onon, Mongolia 48°32′ N, 110°30′ E 198
Onon, river, Asia 49°19′ N, 112°28′ E 198
Onoto, Venez. 9°36′ N, 65°12′ W 136
Onoway, Can. 53°42′ N, 114°13′ W 108
Onsen, Japan 35°32′ N, 134°29′ E 201
Onslow, Austral. 21°39′ S, 115°7′ E 231
Onsŏng, N. Korea 42°57′ N, 129°59′ E 200
Onsugok, S. Korea 37°37′ N, 126°28′ E 200
Ontario, Calif., U.S. 34°3′ N, 117°40′ W 101
Ontario, Ohio, U.S. 40°44′ N, 82°38′ W 102
Ontario, Oreg., U.S. 43°58′ N, 116°58′ W 82
Ontario, adm. division, Can. 51°1′ N, 90°29′ W 106
Ontario, Lake 43°37′ N, 78°57′ W 80
Ontojärvi, lake, Fin. 64°19′ N, 26°24′ E 154
Ontong Java Atoll, islands, South Pacific Ocean 7°9′ S, 159°58′ E 238
Ontur, Sp. 38°36′ N, 1°30′ W 164
Onuškis, Lith. 54°27′ N, 24°36′ E 166
Onyx, Calif., U.S. 35°41′ N, 118°15′ W 101
Oodaaq Island, 83°32′ N, 30°53′ W 255
Oodnadatta, Austral. 27°34′ S, 135°27′ E 231
Oodweyne, Somalia 9°22′ N, 45°5′ E 216
Ooldea, Austral. 30°28′ S, 131°50′ E 231
Oolitic, Ind., U.S. 38°53′ N, 86°33′ W 102
Oona River, Can. 53°57′ N, 130°19′ W 108
Ooruk-Tam, Kyrg. 41°26′ N, 76°39′ E 184
Oost Vlieland, Neth. 53°17′ N, 5°2′ E 163
Oostburg, Wis., U.S. 43°37′ N, 87°48′ W 102
Oostende (Ostend), Belg. 51°13′ N, 2°55′ E 163
Oosterhout, Neth. 51°39′ N, 4°51′ E 167
Ootsa Lake, Can. 53°50′ N, 126°3′ W 108
Opachuanau Lake, lake, Can. 56°42′ N, 100°14′ W 108
Opal, Wyo., U.S. 41°47′ N, 110°19′ W 92
Opala, Dem. Rep. of the Congo 0°38′ N, 24°20′ E 224
Opari, Sudan 3°55′ N, 32°5′ E 224
Oparino, Russ. 59°52′ N, 48°14′ E 154
Opasatica, Lac, lake, Can. 48°1′ N, 79°53′ W 110
Opasatika Lake, lake, Can. 49°2′ N, 83°40′ W 94
Opasatika, river, Can. 49°32′ N, 82°56′ W 94
Opataca, Lac, lake, Can. 50°13′ N, 75°49′ W 94
Opataouaga, Lac, lake, Can. 50°19′ N, 77°24′ W 94
Opelika, Ala., U.S. 32°38′ N, 85°24′ W 96
Opelousas, La., U.S. 30°30′ N, 92°6′ W 103
Opheim, Mont., U.S. 48°50′ N, 106°25′ W 90
Ophir, peak, Indonesia 8°475′ N, 99°55′ E 196
Ophthalmia Range, Austral. 23°24′ S, 118°34′ E 230
Opienge, Dem. Rep. of the Congo 0°15′ N, 27°21′ E 224
Opinaca, Réservoir, lake, Can. 52°3′ N, 77°47′ W 110
Opinaca, river, Can. 52°14′ N, 78°18′ W 106
Opladen, Ger. 51°4′ N, 7°0′ E 167
Oploca, Bol. 21°22′ S, 65°48′ W 137
Opobo, Nig. 4°34′ N, 7°32′ E 222
Opochka, Russ. 56°41′ N, 28°40′ E 166
Opoczno, Pol. 51°23′ N, 20°15′ E 152
Opodepe, Mex. 29°55′ N, 110°38′ W 92
Opole, Pol. 50°39′ N, 17°57′ E 152
Opolskie, adm. division, Pol. 50°39′ N, 17°57′ E 152
Opornyy, Kaz. 46°3′ N, 54°37′ E 158
Oporto see Porto, Port. 41°8′ N, 8°38′ W 150
Opotiki, N.Z. 38°2′ S, 177°19′ E 240
Opp, Ala., U.S. 31°16′ N, 86°15′ W 96
Oppenheim, Ger. 49°50′ N, 8°21′ E 167
Oppola, Russ. 61°34′ N, 30°19′ E 166
Oprişoru, Rom. 44°16′ N, 23°6′ E 168
Opsa, Belarus 55°32′ N, 26°49′ E 166
Opua, N.Z. 35°21′ S, 174°5′ E 240
Opukhliki, Russ. 56°5′ N, 30°9′ E 166
Opunake, N.Z. 39°28′ S, 173°51′ E 240
Opuwo, Namibia 18°6′ S, 13°50′ E 220
Oqtosh, Uzb. 39°55′ N, 65°55′ E 197
Or, Les Îles d' see Hyères, Îles d', islands, Mediterranean Sea 42°57′ N, 6°33′ E 165
Or, river, Asia 49°38′ N, 58°38′ E 158
Ora, oil field, Lib. 28°26′ N, 19°15′ E 216
Oradea, Rom. 47°3′ N, 21°57′ E 168
Öræfajökull, glacier, Ice. 63°52′ N, 15°30′ W 142
Orahovica, Croatia 45°32′ N, 17°54′ E 168
Oral, Kaz. 51°12′ N, 51°24′ E 158
Oran, Alg. 35°39′ N, 0°38′ E 214
Orange, Fr. 44°8′ N, 4°47′ E 214
Orange, Mass., U.S. 42°35′ N, 72°19′ W 104
Orange, Tex., U.S. 30°5′ N, 93°45′ W 103
Orange, Va., U.S. 38°14′ N, 78°7′ W 94
Orange, Cabo, Braz. 4°26′ N, 51°35′ W 130
Orange City, Fla., U.S. 28°57′ N, 81°19′ W 105
Orange City, Iowa, U.S. 42°58′ N, 96°5′ W 90
Orange Cove, Calif., U.S. 36°37′ N, 119°20′ W 100
Orange Grove, Tex., U.S. 27°56′ N, 97°56′ W 96
Orange (Oranje), river, Africa 28°40′ S, 18°39′ E 227
Orange, river, S. Af. 30°46′ S, 26°51′ E 227
Orange Walk, Belize 18°5′ N, 88°35′ W 115
Orangeburg, S.C., U.S. 33°29′ N, 80°51′ W 96
Orangeville, Can. 43°55′ N, 80°6′ W 94
Orangeville, Ill., U.S. 42°27′ N, 89°39′ W 102
Orango, island, Guinea-Bissau 11°1′ N, 16°41′ W 222
Oranienburg, Ger. 52°45′ N, 13°14′ E 152
Oranje Gebergte, Suriname 3°12′ N, 56°2′ W 130
Oranje see Orange, river, Africa 28°40′ S, 18°39′ E 227
Oranjemund, Namibia 28°31′ S, 16°25′ E 227
Oranjestad, Aruba, Neth. 12°34′ N, 70°2′ W 118
Oranzherei, Russ. 45°49′ N, 47°35′ E 158
Orapa, Botswana 21°16′ S, 25°17′ E 227
Orari, N.Z. 44°9′ S, 171°17′ E 240
Oras, Philippines 12°10′ N, 125°26′ E 203
Orašac, Maced. 42°3′ N, 21°48′ E 168
Orašje, Bosn. and Herzg. 45°1′ N, 18°40′ E 168
Oravais (Oravainen), Fin. 63°16′ N, 22°21′ E 152
Orawia, N.Z. 46°4′ S, 167°46′ E 240
Orba Co, lake, China 34°28′ N, 80°29′ E 188
Örbyhus, Nor. 60°13′ N, 17°39′ E 152
Orcadas, station, Antarctica 60°46′ S, 44°52′ W 134
Orce, Sp. 37°42′ N, 2°29′ W 164
Orcera, Sp. 38°18′ N, 2°39′ W 164
Orchard City, Colo., U.S. 38°50′ N, 107°58′ W 92
Orchards, Wash., U.S. 45°39′ N, 122°34′ W 100
Orchies, Fr. 50°28′ N, 3°14′ E 163
Orchomenus, ruin(s), Gr. 38°29′ N, 22°50′ E 156
Orcières, Fr. 44°41′ N, 6°19′ E 167
Orco, river, It. 45°23′ N, 7°25′ E 167
Orcutt, Calif., U.S. 34°51′ N, 120°28′ W 100
Ord, Nebr., U.S. 41°35′ N, 98°57′ W 90
Ord, Mount, peak, Austral. 17°22′ S, 125°22′ E 230
Ord Mountains, Calif., U.S. 34°40′ N, 116°49′ W 101
Orda, Russ. 57°11′ N, 56°56′ E 154
Orderville, Utah, U.S. 37°16′ N, 112°38′ W 92
Ordu, Turk. 40°58′ N, 37°54′ E 156
Ordubad, Asia 38°53′ N, 46°0′ E 195
Orduña, Sp. 42°58′ N, 3°2′ W 164
Orduña, peak, Sp. 37°19′ N, 3°33′ W 164
Ordway, Colo., U.S. 38°13′ N, 103°46′ W 90
Ordzhonīkīdze, Kaz. 52°27′ N, 61°41′ E 184
Ordzhonikidze, Ukr. 47°41′ N, 34°5′ E 156
Ore City, Tex., U.S. 32°48′ N, 94°44′ W 103
Orea, Sp. 40°32′ N, 1°43′ W 164
Oreana, Ill., U.S. 39°56′ N, 88°52′ W 102
Orebić, Croatia 42°58′ N, 17°9′ E 168
Örebro, Nor. 59°16′ N, 15°10′ E 152
Oredezh, Russ. 58°49′ N, 30°20′ E 166
Oregon, Ohio, U.S. 41°38′ N, 83°29′ W 102
Oregon, Wis., U.S. 42°55′ N, 89°23′ W 102
Oregon, adm. division, Oreg., U.S. 43°43′ N, 121°32′ W 90
Oregon Caves National Monument, Oreg., U.S. 42°5′ N, 123°29′ W 90
Oregon Dunes National Recreation Area, Oreg., U.S. 43°59′ N, 129°37′ W 80
Öregrund, Sw. 60°18′ N, 18°22′ E 166
Orekhovo-Zuyevo, Russ. 55°49′ N, 38°56′ E 154
Orel, Russ. 52°55′ N, 36°4′ E 154
Orel, adm. division, Russ. 52°59′ N, 35°55′ E 154
Orellana, Peru 6°56′ S, 75°14′ W 130
Orellana la Vieja, Sp. 39°0′ N, 5°32′ W 164
Orem, Utah, U.S. 40°18′ N, 111°41′ W 90
Ören, Turk. 37°1′ N, 27°57′ E 156
Orenburg, Russ. 51°47′ N, 55°9′ E 154
Orenburg, adm. division, Russ. 52°50′ N, 51°59′ E 154
Orense, Arg. 38°41′ S, 59°45′ W 139
Örenşehir, Turk. 38°59′ N, 36°40′ E 156
Orford, N.H., U.S. 43°54′ N, 72°8′ W 104
Orford, U.K. 52°5′ N, 1°31′ E 163
Orford Ness, U.K. 52°0′ N, 1°35′ E 163
Orfordville, N.H., U.S. 43°52′ N, 72°7′ W 104
Orfordville, Wis., U.S. 42°38′ N, 89°15′ W 102
Organ Peak, N. Mex., U.S. 32°20′ N, 106°43′ W 82
Organ Pipe Cactus National Monument, Ariz., U.S. 32°2′ N, 112°37′ W 80
Organt, Kaz. 44°7′ N, 66°46′ E 184
Organyà, Sp. 42°12′ N, 1°18′ E 164
Órgiva, Sp. 36°53′ N, 3°26′ W 164
Orgon, Fr. 43°47′ N, 5°1′ E 150
Orgun, Afghan. 32°52′ N, 69°11′ E 186
Orhaneli, Turk. 39°54′ N, 28°57′ E 156
Orhangazi, Turk. 40°29′ N, 29°17′ E 158
Orhei, Mold. 47°22′ N, 28°50′ E 156
Orhi, peak, Fr. 42°58′ N, 1°3′ W 164
Orhon, adm. division, Mongolia 49°2′ N, 104°5′ E 198
Orhon, river, Mongolia 48°34′ N, 104°41′ E 190
Orhontuul, Mongolia 48°54′ N, 104°57′ E 198
Oria, Sp. 37°29′ N, 2°18′ W 164
Orick, Calif., U.S. 41°16′ N, 124°5′ W 92
Oricum see Orikon, ruin(s), Alban. 40°17′ N, 19°19′ E 156
Orient, N.Y., U.S. 41°8′ N, 72°18′ W 104
Orient, Wash., U.S. 48°51′ N, 118°14′ W 90
Orient Point, N.Y., U.S. 41°9′ N, 72°20′ W 104
Oriental, Cordillera, Peru 5°11′ S, 77°46′ W 130
Oriental, Grand Erg, Alg. 29°30′ N, 4°11′ E 214
Orientale, adm. division, Dem. Rep. of the Congo 2°6′ N, 26°40′ E 218
Oriente, Arg. 38°44′ S, 60°37′ W 139
Oriente, Braz. 10°1′ S, 64°7′ W 137
Origny-Sainte-Benoite, Fr. 49°50′ N, 3°29′ E 163
Orihuela, Sp. 38°4′ N, 0°57′ E 164
Orikhiv, Ukr. 47°32′ N, 35°47′ E 156
Orikon (Oricum), ruin(s), Alban. 40°17′ N, 19°19′ E 156
Orillia, Can. 44°36′ N, 79°25′ W 94
Orimattila, Fin. 60°47′ N, 25°42′ E 166
Orinoca, Bol. 18°59′ S, 67°15′ W 137
Orinoco, river, Venez. 3°9′ N, 65°14′ W 130
Orissa, adm. division, India 21°55′ N, 84°41′ E 197
Orissaare, Est. 58°32′ N, 23°3′ E 166
Oristano, It. 39°54′ N, 8°35′ E 214
Orivesi, Fin. 61°40′ N, 24°18′ E 166
Oriximiná, Braz. 1°44′ S, 55°54′ W 130
Orizaba, Mex. 18°50′ N, 97°6′ W 114
Orizaba, Pico de, peak, Mex. 18°59′ N, 97°20′ W 114
Orizona, Braz. 17°4′ S, 48°19′ W 138
Orjen, peak, Mont. 42°33′ N, 18°30′ E 168
Orkney, S. Af. 26°59′ S, 26°38′ E 227
Orkney Islands, North Atlantic Ocean 59°28′ N, 6°40′ W 142
Orland, Calif., U.S. 39°44′ N, 122°13′ W 90
Orland, Me., U.S. 44°34′ N, 68°45′ W 94
Orlando, Fla., U.S. 28°32′ N, 81°23′ W 105
Orlando, Capo d', It. 38°11′ N, 13°59′ E 156
Orléanais, region, Fr. 48°23′ N, 1°15′ E 163
Orléans, Fr. 47°54′ N, 1°54′ E 163
Orleans, Ind., U.S. 38°39′ N, 86°27′ W 102
Orleans, Mass., U.S. 41°46′ N, 70°0′ W 104
Orleans, Nebr., U.S. 40°6′ N, 99°27′ W 90
Orlik, Russ. 52°36′ N, 99°50′ E 190
Orlová, Czech Rep. 49°50′ N, 18°25′ E 152
Orlovat, Serb. 45°15′ N, 20°33′ E 168
Orlovka, Russ. 56°55′ N, 76°24′ E 169
Orlovskiy, Russ. 46°49′ N, 41°56′ E 158
Orlu, Nig. 5°45′ N, 7°10′ E 222
Ormara, Pak. 25°12′ N, 64°35′ E 182
Ormara, Ras, Pak. 25°2′ N, 64°39′ E 182
Ormea, It. 44°9′ N, 7°54′ E 167
Ormoc, Philippines 11°2′ N, 124°36′ E 203
Ormond, N.Z. 38°33′ S, 177°55′ E 240

Ormond Beach, *Fla., U.S.* 29°16′ N, 81°4′ W **105**
Ormond by the Sea, *Fla., U.S.* 29°19′ N, 81°4′ W **105**
Ormož, *Slov.* 46°24′ N, 16°7′ E **168**
Ormskirk, *U.K.* 53°34′ N, 2°53′ W **162**
Orne, river, *Fr.* 49°7′ N, 5°44′ E **163**
Orneta, *Pol.* 54°5′ N, 20°7′ E **166**
Ornö, island, *Sw.* 59°0′ N, 18°32′ E **166**
Orno Peak, *Colo., U.S.* 40°3′ N, 107°10′ W **90**
Örnsköldsvik, *Nor.* 63°16′ N, 18°43′ E **152**
Oro Blanco, *Peru* 3°11′ S, 73°14′ W **136**
Oro Grande, *Calif., U.S.* 34°36′ N, 117°21′ W **101**
Oro Ingenio, *Bol.* 21°16′ S, 66°1′ W **137**
Oro, river, *Mex.* 25°55′ N, 105°18′ W **80**
Orobie, Alpi, *It.* 46°18′ N, 9°48′ E **167**
Orocopia Mountains, *Calif., U.S.* 33°38′ N, 115°55′ W **101**
Orocué, *Col.* 4°47′ N, 71°21′ W **136**
Orodara, *Burkina Faso* 10°57′ N, 4°56′ W **222**
Orofino, *Idaho, U.S.* 46°29′ N, 116°15′ W **90**
Orokam, *Nig.* 7°1′ N, 7°33′ E **222**
Oromia, region, *Eth.* 5°54′ N, 38°39′ E **224**
Oron, *Israel* 30°54′ N, 35°0′ E **194**
Oron, *Nig.* 4°49′ N, 8°12′ E **222**
Orono, *Me., U.S.* 44°52′ N, 68°41′ W **111**
Oronoquekamp, *Guyana* 2°43′ N, 57°32′ W **130**
Orontes see 'Āṣī, river, *Syr.* 35°40′ N, 36°21′ E **194**
Oropesa del Mar (Orpesa), *Sp.* 40°5′ N, 0°7′ E **164**
Oroquieta, *Philippines* 8°31′ N, 123°46′ E **203**
Orós, *Braz.* 6°21′ S, 38°53′ W **132**
Oros Áskio, peak, *Gr.* 40°23′ N, 21°28′ E **156**
Orosháza, *Hung.* 46°33′ N, 20°40′ E **168**
Orosi, *Calif., U.S.* 36°33′ N, 119°18′ W **100**
Orotukan, *Russ.* 62°13′ N, 151°26′ E **160**
Oroville, *Calif., U.S.* 39°30′ N, 121°35′ W **90**
Oroyek, *Russ.* 64°52′ N, 153°22′ E **160**
Oroz Betelu, *Sp.* 42°54′ N, 1°19′ W **164**
Orqohan, *China* 49°29′ N, 121°22′ E **198**
Orr, *Minn., U.S.* 48°2′ N, 92°50′ W **94**
Orrs Island, *Me., U.S.* 43°45′ N, 69°59′ W **104**
Orrville, *Ohio, U.S.* 40°49′ N, 81°45′ W **102**
Orsa, *Nor.* 61°6′ N, 14°35′ E **152**
Orsha, *Belarus* 54°31′ N, 30°31′ E **154**
Orshanka, *Russ.* 56°54′ N, 47°55′ E **154**
Orsk, *Russ.* 51°11′ N, 58°36′ E **158**
Örskär, island, *Sw.* 60°31′ N, 18°12′ E **166**
Orta, *Turk.* 40°37′ N, 33°6′ E **156**
Ortaca, *Turk.* 36°50′ N, 28°45′ E **156**
Ortegal, Cabo, *Sp.* 43°46′ N, 7°54′ W **150**
Orthez, *Fr.* 43°29′ N, 0°46′ E **164**
Orting, *Wash., U.S.* 47°4′ N, 122°13′ W **100**
Ortisei, *It.* 46°36′ N, 11°39′ E **167**
Orţişoara, *Rom.* 45°58′ N, 21°12′ E **168**
Ortiz, *Mex.* 28°17′ N, 110°44′ W **92**
Ortiz, *Mex.* 28°14′ N, 105°33′ W **92**
Ortiz, *Venez.* 9°35′ N, 67°19′ W **136**
Ortles, *It.* 46°22′ N, 10°15′ E **167**
Orto Surt, *Russ.* 62°34′ N, 125°4′ E **173**
Ortón, river, *Bol.* 11°2′ S, 66°58′ W **137**
Ortona, *It.* 42°21′ N, 14°23′ E **156**
Ortonville, *Mich., U.S.* 42°51′ N, 83°28′ W **102**
Ortonville, *Minn., U.S.* 45°17′ N, 96°27′ W **90**
Örträsk, *Nor.* 64°8′ N, 18°59′ E **152**
Orūmīyeh, *Iran* 37°30′ N, 44°58′ E **143**
Orūmīyeh, Daryācheh-ye (Urmia, Lake), *Iran* 38°7′ N, 45°16′ E **195**
Orūmīyeh (Urmia), *Iran* 37°37′ N, 45°4′ E **195**
Orungo, *Uganda* 2°0′ N, 33°28′ E **224**
Oruro, *Bol.* 17°59′ S, 67°8′ W **137**
Oruro, adm. division, *Bol.* 18°53′ S, 68°19′ W **137**
Orwell, *Ohio, U.S.* 41°31′ N, 80°52′ W **102**
Orwell, *Vt., U.S.* 43°48′ N, 73°19′ W **104**
Orxon, river, *China* 48°16′ N, 117°47′ E **198**
Orynyn, *Ukr.* 48°44′ N, 26°25′ E **152**
Orzinuovi, *It.* 45°24′ N, 9°55′ E **167**
Os, *Nor.* 60°11′ N, 5°27′ E **152**
Osa, *Russ.* 57°15′ N, 55°32′ E **154**
Osage, *Iowa, U.S.* 43°15′ N, 92°49′ W **94**
Osage, *Wyo., U.S.* 43°57′ N, 104°25′ W **90**
Osage City, *Kans., U.S.* 38°36′ N, 95°50′ W **90**
Ōsaka, *Japan* 34°42′ N, 135°32′ E **190**
Ōsaka, *Japan* 35°57′ N, 137°17′ E **201**
Ōsaka, *Japan* 34°40′ N, 135°30′ E **201**
Ōsaka, adm. division, *Japan* 34°20′ N, 135°21′ E **201**
Osakarovka, *Kaz.* 50°34′ N, 72°35′ E **184**
Osakis, *Minn., U.S.* 45°50′ N, 95°11′ W **90**
Osan, *S. Korea* 37°8′ N, 127°4′ E **200**
Osawatomie, *Kans., U.S.* 38°28′ N, 94°57′ W **94**
Osborn Plateau, *Indian Ocean* 14°42′ S, 86°43′ E **254**
Osborne, *Kans., U.S.* 39°25′ N, 98°43′ W **90**
Osby, *Nor.* 56°23′ N, 13°57′ E **152**
Oscar II Coast, *Antarctica* 65°25′ S, 61°36′ W **134**
Osceola, *Iowa, U.S.* 41°2′ N, 93°45′ W **94**
Osečina, *Serb.* 44°22′ N, 19°35′ E **168**
Ösel see Saaremaa, island, *Est.* 58°32′ N, 21°21′ E **166**
Osel'ki, *Russ.* 60°14′ N, 30°26′ E **166**
Osen, *Nor.* 64°18′ N, 10°31′ E **152**
Osgood, *Ind., U.S.* 39°7′ N, 85°17′ W **102**
Osgood Mountains, *Nev., U.S.* 41°3′ N, 117°37′ W **90**
Osh, *Kyrg.* 40°31′ N, 72°49′ E **197**
Oshakati, *Namibia* 17°54′ S, 15°48′ E **220**
Oshawa, *Can.* 43°53′ N, 78°50′ W **94**
Oshikango, *Namibia* 17°28′ S, 15°52′ E **220**
Ōshima, *Japan* 34°44′ N, 139°21′ E **201**
Oshkosh, *Nebr., U.S.* 41°24′ N, 102°22′ W **90**
Oshkosh, *Wis., U.S.* 44°1′ N, 88°33′ W **102**
Oshkur'ya, *Russ.* 66°0′ N, 56°40′ E **154**
Oshogbo, *Nig.* 7°50′ N, 4°35′ E **222**
Oshta, *Russ.* 60°49′ N, 35°33′ E **154**
Oshwe, *Dem. Rep. of the Congo* 3°27′ S, 19°29′ E **218**
Osian, *India* 26°41′ N, 72°55′ E **186**
Osijek, *Croatia* 45°32′ N, 18°40′ E **168**
Osilinka, river, *Can.* 56°4′ N, 125°26′ W **108**
Osinovka, *Russ.* 56°33′ N, 102°1′ E **160**
Osinovo, *Russ.* 61°18′ N, 89°49′ E **169**
Oskaloosa, *Iowa, U.S.* 41°17′ N, 92°38′ W **94**
Öskemen (Ust' Kamenogorsk), *Kaz.* 49°59′ N, 82°38′ E **184**
Oskoba, *Russ.* 60°20′ N, 100°33′ E **160**
Oskol, river, *Russ.* 50°34′ N, 37°37′ E **158**
Oslo, *Minn., U.S.* 48°10′ N, 97°8′ W **90**
Oslo, *Nor.* 59°53′ N, 10°33′ E **152**
Oslob, *Philippines* 9°32′ N, 123°23′ E **203**
Osma, *Sp.* 41°34′ N, 3°6′ W **164**
Osmancık, *Turk.* 40°58′ N, 34°47′ E **156**
Osmaniye, *Turk.* 37°4′ N, 36°13′ E **156**
Os'mino, *Russ.* 59°1′ N, 29°7′ E **166**
Osmus Saar, island, *Est.* 59°9′ N, 23°14′ E **166**
Osnabrück, *Ger.* 52°16′ N, 8°2′ E **163**
Osnaburgh House, *Can.* 51°8′ N, 90°17′ W **110**
Oso, *Wash., U.S.* 48°16′ N, 121°56′ W **100**
Oso, river, *Dem. Rep. of the Congo* 1°0′ N, 27°43′ E **224**
Osogovske Planina, *Maced.* 42°2′ N, 22°2′ E **168**
Osor, *Croatia* 44°42′ N, 14°23′ E **156**
Osório, *Braz.* 29°54′ S, 50°17′ W **134**
Osorno, *Chile* 40°34′ S, 73°9′ W **134**
Osorno, *Sp.* 42°24′ N, 4°22′ W **150**
Osoyoos, *Can.* 49°1′ N, 119°30′ W **108**
Ospika, river, *Can.* 57°3′ N, 124°28′ W **108**
Osprey, *Fla., U.S.* 27°12′ N, 82°28′ W **105**
Oss, *Neth.* 51°45′ N, 5°31′ E **167**
Ossa, Mount, peak, *Austral.* 41°53′ S, 145°50′ E **230**
Óssa, Óros, peak, *Gr.* 39°47′ N, 22°36′ E **156**
Ossabaw Island, *Ga., U.S.* 31°36′ N, 81°3′ W **112**
Osse, river, *Nig.* 7°44′ N, 5°58′ E **222**
Ossélé, *Congo* 1°26′ S, 15°19′ E **218**
Osseo, *Wis., U.S.* 44°33′ N, 91°13′ W **94**
Ossian, *Ind., U.S.* 40°52′ N, 85°10′ W **102**
Ossining, *N.Y., U.S.* 41°9′ N, 73°52′ W **104**
Ossipee, *N.H., U.S.* 43°40′ N, 71°8′ W **104**
Ossjøen, lake, *Nor.* 61°10′ N, 11°24′ E **152**
Ossokmanuan Reservoir, lake, *Can.* 52°59′ N, 66°19′ W **111**
Ossora, *Russ.* 59°14′ N, 163°0′ E **160**
Ostaboningue, Lac, lake, *Can.* 47°7′ N, 79°36′ W **94**
Ostashkov, *Russ.* 57°7′ N, 33°12′ E **154**
Östavall, *Nor.* 62°25′ N, 15°29′ E **152**
Ostbevern, *Ger.* 52°2′ N, 7°50′ E **167**
Ostellato, *It.* 44°44′ N, 11°56′ E **167**
Ostend see Oostende, *Belg.* 51°13′ N, 2°55′ E **163**
Østerdalen, *Nor.* 61°50′ N, 10°47′ E **152**
Östergarnsholme, island, *Sw.* 57°25′ N, 19°1′ E **166**
Osterode, *Ger.* 51°44′ N, 10°13′ E **167**
Östersund, *Nor.* 63°10′ N, 14°40′ E **152**
Osterville, *Mass., U.S.* 41°37′ N, 70°24′ W **104**
Östhammar, *Sw.* 60°14′ N, 18°18′ E **166**
Ostheim, *Ger.* 50°27′ N, 10°13′ E **167**
Ostiglia, *It.* 45°3′ N, 11°8′ E **167**
Östra Kvarken 63°31′ N, 20°16′ E **152**
Ostrava, *Czech Rep.* 49°49′ N, 18°15′ E **152**
Ostro, *Pol.* 53°4′ N, 21°33′ E **152**
Ostróda, *Pol.* 53°41′ N, 19°58′ E **152**
Ostrov, *Russ.* 57°21′ N, 28°21′ E **166**
Ostrov, *Russ.* 58°28′ N, 28°37′ E **166**
Ostrov Russkiy, island, *Russ.* 76°38′ N, 89°18′ E **160**
Ostrovtsy, *Russ.* 58°23′ N, 27°42′ E **166**
Ostrožac, *Bosn. and Herzg.* 43°40′ N, 17°50′ E **168**
Ostuni, *It.* 40°43′ N, 17°35′ E **156**
O'sullivan Lake, lake, *Can.* 50°22′ N, 87°38′ W **110**
Osuna, *Sp.* 37°14′ N, 5°7′ W **164**
Osvaldo Cruz, *Braz.* 21°47′ S, 50°52′ W **138**
Oswego, *N.Y., U.S.* 43°26′ N, 76°32′ W **110**
Oswestry, *U.K.* 52°51′ N, 3°4′ W **162**
Osyka, *Miss., U.S.* 31°0′ N, 90°30′ W **103**
Ōta, *Japan* 35°56′ N, 136°3′ E **201**
Ōta, *Japan* 36°16′ N, 139°24′ E **201**
Ōta, river, *Japan* 34°29′ N, 132°11′ E **201**
Otaci, *Mold.* 48°25′ N, 27°47′ E **152**
Ōtake, *Japan* 34°12′ N, 132°13′ E **200**
Otaki, *N.Z.* 40°46′ S, 175°8′ E **240**
Otanmäki, *Fin.* 64°4′ N, 27°4′ E **152**
Otar, *Kaz.* 43°31′ N, 75°12′ E **184**
Otare, Cerro, peak, *Col.* 1°43′ N, 72°49′ W **136**
Otaru, *Japan* 43°12′ N, 140°49′ E **190**
Otatara, *N.Z.* 46°27′ S, 168°18′ E **240**
Otautau, *N.Z.* 46°11′ S, 167°58′ E **240**
Otava, *Fin.* 61°37′ N, 27°2′ E **166**
Otavalo, *Ecua.* 0°11′ N, 78°24′ W **136**
Otavi, *Namibia* 19°39′ S, 17°19′ E **220**
Otawara, *Japan* 36°49′ N, 140°1′ E **201**
Otay, *Calif., U.S.* 32°36′ N, 117°6′ W **101**
Otchinjau, *Angola* 16°30′ S, 13°56′ E **220**
Otelec, *Rom.* 45°36′ N, 20°50′ E **168**
Oţelu Roşu, *Rom.* 45°30′ N, 22°23′ E **168**
Otematata, *N.Z.* 44°37′ S, 170°11′ E **240**
Otepää, *Est.* 58°2′ N, 26°29′ E **166**
Oteros, river, *Mex.* 27°19′ N, 108°36′ W **80**
Othello, *Wash., U.S.* 46°48′ N, 119°11′ W **90**
Otherside, river, *Can.* 59°5′ N, 107°21′ W **108**
Óthris, Óros, *Gr.* 38°57′ N, 22°19′ E **156**
Oti, river, *Ghana* 8°32′ N, 8°476′ E **222**
Otinapa, *Mex.* 24°0′ N, 105°1′ W **114**
Otira, *N.Z.* 42°50′ S, 171°33′ E **240**
Otis, *Colo., U.S.* 40°9′ N, 102°58′ W **90**
Otis, *Mass., U.S.* 42°11′ N, 73°6′ W **104**
Otisco, *Ind., U.S.* 38°32′ N, 85°39′ W **102**
Otish, Monts, peak, *Can.* 52°17′ N, 70°36′ W **111**
Otjikondo, *Namibia* 19°52′ S, 15°29′ E **220**
Otjimbingwe, *Namibia* 22°19′ S, 16°7′ E **227**
Otjivero, *Namibia* 22°16′ S, 17°51′ E **227**
Otjiwarongo, *Namibia* 20°27′ S, 16°39′ E **227**
Otley, *U.K.* 53°54′ N, 1°41′ W **162**
Otmök, *Kyrg.* 42°11′ N, 73°16′ E **197**
Otog Qi, *China* 39°6′ N, 107°58′ E **198**
Otok, *Croatia* 45°8′ N, 18°51′ E **168**
Otok, *Croatia* 43°41′ N, 16°43′ E **168**
Otoka, *Bosn. and Herzg.* 44°57′ N, 16°8′ E **168**
Otorohanga, *N.Z.* 38°11′ S, 175°13′ E **240**
Otoskwin, river, *Can.* 51°48′ N, 90°58′ W **80**
Otosquen, *Can.* 53°16′ N, 102°1′ W **108**
Otradnaya, *Russ.* 44°22′ N, 41°27′ E **158**
Otradnoye, *Russ.* 51°59′ N, 156°39′ E **160**
Otradnoye, *Russ.* 56°13′ N, 30°3′ E **166**
Otradnyy, *Russ.* 53°24′ N, 51°26′ E **154**
Otranto, Capo d', *It.* 40°2′ N, 18°31′ E **156**
Otsego, *Mich., U.S.* 42°26′ N, 85°42′ W **102**
Ōtsu, *Japan* 35°1′ N, 135°51′ E **201**
Otta, *Nig.* 6°44′ N, 3°13′ E **222**
Ottawa, *Can.* 45°22′ N, 75°50′ W **94**
Ottawa, *Ill., U.S.* 41°20′ N, 88°51′ W **102**
Ottawa, *Kans., U.S.* 38°34′ N, 95°17′ W **94**
Ottawa, *Mo., U.S.* 41°20′ N, 88°51′ W **110**
Ottawa, *Ohio, U.S.* 41°1′ N, 84°3′ W **102**
Ottawa Islands, islands, *Can.* 59°8′ N, 83°8′ W **106**
Ottenby, *Sw.* 56°14′ N, 16°26′ E **152**
Otter Creek, *Fla., U.S.* 29°19′ N, 82°47′ W **105**
Otter Head, *Can.* 47°53′ N, 86°14′ W **94**
Otter Rapids, *Can.* 50°11′ N, 81°40′ W **94**
Otterbein, *Ind., U.S.* 40°29′ N, 87°6′ W **102**
Otterndorf, *Ger.* 53°48′ N, 8°54′ E **152**
Ottoville, *Ohio, U.S.* 40°55′ N, 84°20′ W **102**
Otú, *Col.* 6°55′ N, 74°45′ W **136**
Otukpa, *Nig.* 7°4′ N, 7°40′ E **222**
Otukpo, *Nig.* 7°12′ N, 8°9′ E **222**
Otumpa, *Arg.* 27°20′ S, 62°16′ W **139**
Otynya, *Ukr.* 48°43′ N, 24°49′ E **152**
Ötztal Alps, *Aust.* 46°46′ N, 10°36′ E **167**
Ou Nua, *Laos* 22°16′ N, 101°48′ E **202**
Ou, river, *Laos* 21°49′ N, 102°6′ E **202**
Ouachita, Lake, *Ark., U.S.* 34°41′ N, 93°59′ W **80**
Ouachita Mountains, *Ark., U.S.* 34°26′ N, 95°36′ W **96**
Ouachita, river, *La., U.S.* 32°16′ N, 92°10′ W **103**
Ouadane, *Mauritania* 20°57′ N, 11°37′ W **222**
Ouadda, *Cen. Af. Rep.* 8°4′ N, 22°24′ E **218**
Ouagadougou, *Burkina Faso* 12°19′ N, 1°43′ W **222**
Ouagama, Lac, lake, *Can.* 50°37′ N, 77°43′ W **110**
Ouahigouya, *Burkina Faso* 13°34′ N, 2°26′ W **222**
Ouaka, river, *Cen. Af. Rep.* 5°11′ N, 19°49′ E **218**
Oualâta, *Mauritania* 17°18′ N, 7°2′ W **222**
Oualâta, Dahr, *Mauritania* 17°41′ N, 8°22′ W **222**
Oualidia, *Mor.* 32°43′ N, 9°4′ W **214**
Ouallam, *Niger* 14°22′ N, 1°59′ E **222**
Ouan Taredert, oil field, *Alg.* 27°26′ N, 9°29′ E **214**
Oua-n-Ahaggar, Tassili, *Alg.* 21°14′ N, 4°57′ E **222**
Ouanda Djallé, *Cen. Af. Rep.* 8°52′ N, 22°48′ E **218**
Ouandjia, *Cen. Af. Rep.* 9°17′ N, 22°40′ E **218**
Ouando, *Cen. Af. Rep.* 5°58′ N, 25°45′ E **224**
Ouango, *Cen. Af. Rep.* 4°20′ N, 22°29′ E **218**
Ouaouizarht, *Mor.* 32°12′ N, 6°23′ W **214**
Ouarane, *Mauritania* 20°48′ N, 11°23′ W **222**
Ouargaye, *Burkina Faso* 11°31′ N, 2°119′ E **222**
Ouargla, *Alg.* 31°56′ N, 5°20′ E **214**
Ouarkoye, *Burkina Faso* 12°6′ N, 3°41′ W **222**
Ouarkziz, Jebel, *Mor.* 28°10′ N, 9°37′ W **214**
Ouarra, river, *Cen. Af. Rep.* 5°49′ N, 25°48′ E **224**
Ouarsenis, Djebel, peak, *Alg.* 35°52′ N, 1°34′ E **150**
Ouas Ouas, spring, *Mali* 16°6′ N, 1°20′ E **222**
Ouasiemsca, river, *Can.* 49°43′ N, 73°11′ W **111**
Ouassane, spring, *Mauritania* 17°56′ N, 13°13′ W **222**
Ouassou, *Guinea* 10°2′ N, 13°45′ W **222**
Ouche, river, *Fr.* 47°15′ N, 4°48′ E **165**
Ouchennane, spring, *Mali* 17°23′ N, 1°59′ E **222**
Ouddorp, *Neth.* 51°48′ N, 3°55′ E **163**
Oude Rijn, river, *Neth.* 52°12′ N, 4°26′ E **163**
Oudeïka, spring, *Mali* 17°27′ N, 1°42′ W **222**
Oudenaarde, *Belg.* 50°50′ N, 3°36′ E **163**
Oudeschild, *Neth.* 53°2′ N, 4°50′ E **163**
Oudon, *Fr.* 47°21′ N, 1°19′ W **150**
Oudtshoorn, *S. Af.* 33°35′ S, 22°11′ E **227**
Oued Laou, *Mor.* 35°26′ N, 5°6′ W **150**
Oued Lili, *Alg.* 35°30′ N, 1°16′ E **150**
Oued Rhiou, *Alg.* 35°57′ N, 0°55′ E **164**
Oued Taria, *Alg.* 35°6′ N, 9°535′ E **150**
Oued Tlelat, *Alg.* 35°32′ N, 0°28′ E **150**
Oueïba, spring, *Chad* 18°24′ N, 23°18′ E **226**
Oueïta, spring, *Chad* 17°43′ N, 20°42′ E **216**
Ouella, spring, *Niger* 14°39′ N, 3°53′ E **222**
Ouellé, *Côte d'Ivoire* 7°14′ N, 4°2′ W **222**
Ouémé, river, *Benin* 8°19′ N, 2°11′ E **222**
Ouescapis, Lac, lake, *Can.* 50°15′ N, 77°36′ W **94**
Ouessa, *Burkina Faso* 11°3′ N, 2°48′ W **222**
Ouesso, *Congo* 1°51′ N, 16°2′ E **218**
Ouest, Pointe, *Haiti* 18°51′ N, 74°1′ W **116**
Ouest, Pointe de l' (Coupé Cap), *Fr.* 46°48′ N, 57°0′ W **111**
Ouffet, *Belg.* 50°26′ N, 5°26′ E **167**
Oufrane, *Alg.* 28°31′ N, 0°10′ E **214**
Ougarta, *Alg.* 29°40′ N, 2°16′ W **214**
Ougrée, *Belg.* 50°35′ N, 5°33′ E **167**
Ouidah, *Benin* 6°23′ N, 2°5′ E **222**
Oujaf, spring, *Mauritania* 17°50′ N, 7°54′ W **222**
Oujda, *Mor.* 34°38′ N, 1°55′ W **214**
Oujeft, *Mauritania* 20°2′ N, 13°4′ W **222**
Oulad el Abed, *Tun.* 35°59′ N, 10°17′ E **156**
Oulad Hammou, *Mor.* 35°7′ N, 6°9′ W **150**
Oulad Saïd, *Alg.* 29°27′ N, 0°15′ E **214**
Oulainen, *Fin.* 64°15′ N, 24°44′ E **152**
Ould Mouloud, spring, *Alg.* 23°46′ N, 0°9′ E **214**
Ouled Amar, *Alg.* 35°27′ N, 5°8′ E **150**
Ouled Djellal, *Alg.* 34°23′ N, 5°3′ E **214**
Oulou, river, *Cen. Af. Rep.* 10°27′ N, 22°30′ E **218**
Oulton Broad, *U.K.* 52°27′ N, 1°41′ E **163**
Oulton Lake, lake, *Can.* 60°45′ N, 111°53′ W **108**
Oulu, *Fin.* 64°59′ N, 25°47′ E **160**
Oulu (Uleåborg), *Fin.* 65°0′ N, 25°25′ E **152**
Oulx, *It.* 45°1′ N, 6°51′ E **167**
Oum Chalouba, *Chad* 15°47′ N, 20°45′ E **216**
Oum er Rbia, Oued, river, *Mor.* 32°10′ N, 8°13′ W **142**
Oum Hadjer, *Chad* 13°15′ N, 19°40′ E **216**
Oum Mesgué, *Mauritania* 16°17′ N, 7°15′ W **222**
Oumache, *Alg.* 34°40′ N, 5°42′ E **214**
Oumé, *Côte d'Ivoire* 6°17′ N, 5°25′ W **222**
Oumm el A'sel, spring, *Mali* 23°32′ N, 4°46′ W **214**
Oumm el Khez, spring, *Mauritania* 17°7′ N, 11°3′ W **222**
Ounasselkä, *Fin.* 67°32′ N, 24°23′ E **152**
Oundle, *U.K.* 52°28′ N, 0°29′ E **162**
Ounianga Kébir, *Chad* 19°4′ N, 20°31′ E **216**
Ounianga Sérir, spring, *Chad* 18°54′ N, 20°54′ E **216**
Ounissouli, spring, *Niger* 17°33′ N, 12°3′ E **222**
Ouololo, *Mali* 13°13′ N, 7°55′ W **222**
Ourafane, *Niger* 14°2′ N, 8°8′ E **222**
Ouray, *Utah, U.S.* 40°5′ N, 109°41′ W **90**
Ouray, Mount, peak, *Colo., U.S.* 38°24′ N, 106°18′ W **90**
Ourense, *Sp.* 42°19′ N, 7°53′ W **150**
Ouri, *Chad* 21°35′ N, 19°13′ E **216**
Ourinhos, *Braz.* 22°58′ S, 49°52′ W **138**
Ouro, *Braz.* 8°13′ S, 46°14′ W **130**
Ouro Preto, *Braz.* 20°24′ S, 43°31′ W **138**
Ouro Prêto, river, *Braz.* 10°44′ S, 64°28′ W **137**
Ours, Cap de l', *Can.* 49°36′ N, 62°30′ W **111**
Oursi, *Burkina Faso* 14°40′ N, 4°238′ E **222**
Ourthe, river, *Belg.* 50°11′ N, 5°34′ E **167**
Ouse, river, *U.K.* 54°4′ N, 1°21′ W **162**
Oust, *Fr.* 42°51′ N, 1°12′ E **164**
Outardes Quatre, Réservoir, lake, *Can.* 49°34′ N, 70°50′ W **94**
Outat Oulad el Hajj, *Mor.* 33°25′ N, 3°44′ W **214**
Outeniqua Mountains, *S. Af.* 33°49′ S, 22°28′ E **227**
Outer Banks, islands, *North Atlantic Ocean* 35°28′ N, 75°25′ W **96**
Outer Santa Barbara Channel 33°9′ N, 118°41′ W **101**
Outjo, *Namibia* 20°7′ S, 16°10′ E **227**
Outlook, *Can.* 51°29′ N, 107°5′ W **90**
Outokumpu, *Fin.* 62°43′ N, 29°0′ E **152**
Outram Island, *India* 12°17′ N, 93°14′ E **188**
Outtaye, *Mali* 14°28′ N, 8°23′ W **222**
Ovacık, *Turk.* 39°21′ N, 39°12′ E **195**
Ovada, *It.* 44°38′ N, 8°39′ E **167**
Oval Peak, *Wash., U.S.* 48°15′ N, 120°31′ W **90**
Ovalle, *Chile* 30°35′ S, 71°14′ W **134**
Ovalo, *Tex., U.S.* 32°10′ N, 99°50′ W **92**
Ovamboland, region, *Namibia* 19°53′ S, 15°29′ E **227**
Ovana, Cerro, peak, *Venez.* 4°37′ N, 67°4′ W **136**
Ovar, *Port.* 40°51′ N, 8°40′ W **150**
Overath, *Ger.* 50°56′ N, 7°16′ E **167**
Øverbygd, *Nor.* 69°0′ N, 19°7′ E **152**
Overflowing River, *Can.* 53°6′ N, 101°10′ W **108**
Overland Park, *Kans., U.S.* 38°56′ N, 94°41′ W **94**
Overland Pass, *Nev., U.S.* 40°1′ N, 115°36′ W **90**
Övermark (Ylimarkku), *Fin.* 62°35′ N, 21°25′ E **152**
Overpelt, *Belg.* 51°11′ N, 5°24′ E **167**
Överstjuktan, lake, *Nor.* 65°39′ N, 15°22′ E **152**
Overstrand, *U.K.* 52°54′ N, 1°20′ E **162**
Overton, *Nev., U.S.* 36°32′ N, 114°27′ W **101**
Overton, *Tex., U.S.* 32°16′ N, 94°59′ W **103**
Overton, *U.K.* 52°57′ N, 2°55′ W **162**
Överum, *Nor.* 58°0′ N, 16°17′ E **152**
Ovett, *Miss., U.S.* 31°27′ N, 89°1′ W **103**
Ovid, *Colo., U.S.* 40°57′ N, 102°23′ W **90**
Ovid, *Mich., U.S.* 43°0′ N, 84°22′ W **102**
Oviedo, *Sp.* 43°21′ N, 5°51′ W **150**
Ovišī, *Latv.* 57°29′ N, 21°33′ E **166**
Ovoot, *Mongolia* 45°20′ N, 113°38′ E **198**
Övör-Ereen, *Mongolia* 49°16′ N, 112°25′ E **198**
Ovruch, *Ukr.* 51°19′ N, 28°52′ E **152**
Owaka, *N.Z.* 46°28′ S, 169°42′ E **240**
Owando, *Congo* 0°33′ N, 15°53′ E **218**
Owaneco, *Ill., U.S.* 39°28′ N, 89°12′ W **102**
Owase, *Japan* 34°3′ N, 136°12′ E **201**
Owbeh, *Afghan.* 34°26′ N, 63°10′ E **186**
Owego, *N.Y., U.S.* 42°6′ N, 76°17′ W **94**
Owen Falls Dam, *Uganda* 0°5′ N, 33°1′ E **224**
Owen Fracture Zone, *Arabian Sea* 11°9′ N, 57°40′ E **254**
Owen, Mount, peak, *N.Z.* 41°34′ S, 172°28′ E **240**
Owen River, *N.Z.* 41°42′ S, 172°27′ E **240**
Owen Sound, *Can.* 44°34′ N, 80°56′ W **94**
Owen Stanley Range, *P.N.G.* 8°34′ S, 147°0′ E **192**
Owens Peak, *Calif., U.S.* 35°44′ N, 118°2′ W **101**
Owensboro, *Ky., U.S.* 37°45′ N, 87°7′ W **96**
Owensburg, *Ind., U.S.* 38°55′ N, 86°44′ W **102**
Owensville, *Mo., U.S.* 38°20′ N, 91°30′ W **94**
Owenton, *Ky., U.S.* 38°31′ N, 84°50′ W **102**
Owerri, *Nig.* 5°30′ N, 7°0′ E **222**
Owickeno, *Can.* 51°41′ N, 127°16′ W **108**
Owl Creek Mountains, *Wyo., U.S.* 43°36′ N, 109°5′ W **90**
Owlshead Mountains, *Calif., U.S.* 35°46′ N, 116°46′ W **101**
Owo, *Nig.* 6°28′ N, 7°43′ E **222**
Owo, *Nig.* 7°15′ N, 5°36′ E **222**
Owosso, *Mich., U.S.* 43°0′ N, 84°8′ W **102**
Owschlag, *Ger.* 54°24′ N, 9°35′ E **150**
Owyhee, *Nev., U.S.* 41°57′ N, 116°6′ W **90**
Owyhee Mountains, *Idaho, U.S.* 43°10′ N, 116°45′ W **90**
Owyhee, river, *Idaho, U.S.* 42°25′ N, 117°4′ W **106**
Ox Mountains, the see Gamph, Slieve, *Ire.* 54°2′ N, 9°28′ W **150**
Öxarfjörður 66°6′ N, 20°0′ W **142**
Oxbow Dam, *U.S.* 45°1′ N, 116°55′ W **90**
Oxford, *Kans., U.S.* 37°15′ N, 97°11′ W **90**
Oxford, *Me., U.S.* 44°7′ N, 70°30′ W **104**
Oxford, *Mich., U.S.* 42°48′ N, 83°16′ W **102**
Oxford, *Miss., U.S.* 34°20′ N, 89°31′ W **96**
Oxford, *Nebr., U.S.* 40°14′ N, 99°39′ W **90**
Oxford, *N.Z.* 43°19′ S, 172°11′ E **240**
Oxford, *Ohio, U.S.* 39°30′ N, 84°45′ W **102**
Oxford, *U.K.* 51°44′ N, 1°16′ W **162**
Oxford, *Wis., U.S.* 43°46′ N, 89°33′ W **102**
Oxford House, *Can.* 54°54′ N, 95°17′ W **108**
Oxford Peak, *Idaho, U.S.* 42°17′ N, 112°10′ W **90**
Oxnard, *Calif., U.S.* 34°11′ N, 119°12′ W **101**
Oxus see Ab-e Vakhan, river, *Afghan.* 37°8′ N, 72°26′ E **186**
Oya, *Malaysia* 2°47′ N, 111°52′ E **192**
Oyahue see Ollagüe, *Chile* 21°14′ S, 68°18′ W **137**
Oyan, *Kaz.* 50°44′ N, 50°23′ E **158**
Øye, *Nor.* 62°11′ N, 6°39′ E **152**
Oyé Yeska, spring, *Chad* 18°36′ N, 19°31′ E **216**
Oyem, *Gabon* 1°35′ N, 11°36′ E **207**
Oyen, *Can.* 51°22′ N, 110°29′ W **90**
Øygarden Group, islands, *Indian Ocean* 66°53′ S, 57°43′ E **248**
Oymyakon, *Russ.* 63°25′ N, 142°41′ E **160**
Oyo, *Congo* 1°10′ S, 15°59′ E **218**
Oyo, *Nig.* 7°54′ N, 3°57′ E **222**
Oyo, *Sudan* 21°56′ N, 36°12′ E **182**
Oyonnax, *Fr.* 46°15′ N, 5°38′ E **150**
Oyster Bay, *N.Y., U.S.* 40°52′ N, 73°32′ W **104**
Oyster River, *Can.* 49°53′ N, 125°8′ W **100**
Oysterville, *Wash., U.S.* 46°32′ N, 124°2′ W **100**
Oyyl, *Kaz.* 49°4′ N, 54°38′ E **158**
Özalp, *Turk.* 38°38′ N, 43°57′ E **195**
Ozamis, *Philippines* 8°13′ N, 123°50′ E **203**
Ozark, *Ala., U.S.* 31°27′ N, 85°39′ W **96**
Ozark, *Ark., U.S.* 35°28′ N, 93°51′ W **96**
Ozark, *Mo., U.S.* 37°0′ N, 93°11′ W **96**
Ozark National Scenic Riverways, *Mo., U.S.* 37°0′ N, 96°4′ W **80**
Ozark Plateau, *Mo., U.S.* 35°31′ N, 93°28′ W **96**
Ozen, *Kaz.* 43°27′ N, 53°3′ E **158**
Ozernovskiy, *Russ.* 51°32′ N, 156°34′ E **160**
Ozernoy, Mys, *Russ.* 57°26′ N, 163°12′ E **160**
Ozernyy, *Russ.* 55°30′ N, 32°29′ E **154**
Ozernyy, *Russ.* 51°6′ N, 60°57′ E **158**
Ozernyy, *Russ.* 66°23′ N, 179°3′ W **98**
Ozersk, *Russ.* 54°25′ N, 21°58′ E **166**
Ozery, *Russ.* 54°52′ N, 38°30′ E **154**
Ozgon, *Kyrg.* 40°45′ N, 73°18′ E **197**
Ozhiski Lake, *Can.* 51°57′ N, 89°4′ W **110**
Ozhogino, *Russ.* 68°59′ N, 147°39′ E **160**
Ozieri, *It.* 40°35′ N, 9°1′ E **156**
Ozinki, *Russ.* 51°11′ N, 49°46′ E **158**
Ozoli, *Latv.* 57°38′ N, 24°55′ E **166**
Ozona, *Tex., U.S.* 30°41′ N, 101°12′ W **92**
Ozorków, *Pol.* 51°57′ N, 19°17′ E **152**
Ozrinići, *Mont.* 42°44′ N, 19°0′ E **168**
Ōzu, *Japan* 33°30′ N, 132°32′ E **201**
Ozurget'i, *Ga.* 41°54′ N, 42°0′ E **195**

P

Pa Kha, *Vietnam* 22°34′ N, 104°16′ E **202**
Pa Mong Dam, *Asia* 18°10′ N, 101°26′ E **202**
Pa Sak, river, *Thai.* 15°27′ N, 101°2′ E **202**
Paakkola, *Fin.* 66°0′ N, 24°40′ E **152**
Paamiut (Frederikshåb) 62°4′ N, 49°33′ W **106**
Paarl, *S. Af.* 33°45′ S, 18°55′ E **227**
Paavola, *Fin.* 64°35′ N, 25°9′ E **152**
Paberžė, *Lith.* 54°56′ N, 25°14′ E **166**
Pabo, *Uganda* 2°58′ N, 32°7′ E **224**
Pabradė, *Lith.* 54°59′ N, 25°43′ E **166**
Pac, *Alban.* 42°17′ N, 20°12′ E **168**
Pacaás Novos National Park, *Braz.* 11°14′ S, 63°35′ W **137**
Pacaás Novos, river, *Braz.* 11°13′ S, 65°5′ W **137**
Pacaás Novos, Serra dos, *Braz.* 10°27′ S, 64°29′ W **130**
Pacahuaras, river, *Bol.* 10°25′ S, 66°13′ W **137**
Pacajus, *Braz.* 4°14′ S, 38°30′ W **132**
Pacanów, *Pol.* 50°24′ N, 21°2′ E **152**
Pacaraima, Sierra, *Venez.* 4°3′ N, 63°19′ W **130**
Pacasmayo, *Peru* 7°23′ S, 79°35′ W **130**
Pacaya, *Peru* 10°9′ S, 74°7′ W **137**
Paceco, *It.* 37°58′ N, 12°32′ E **156**
Pacheco Pass, *Calif., U.S.* 37°4′ N, 121°14′ W **100**
Pachelma, *Russ.* 53°18′ N, 43°20′ E **154**
Pachena Point, *Can.* 48°44′ N, 125°5′ W **100**
Pachía, *Peru* 17°56′ S, 70°9′ W **137**
Pachuca, *Mex.* 20°6′ N, 98°48′ W **114**
Pachuta, *Miss., U.S.* 32°1′ N, 88°53′ W **103**
Pacific, *Can.* 54°44′ N, 128°20′ W **108**
Pacific Beach, *Wash., U.S.* 47°10′ N, 124°11′ W **100**
Pacific Crest Trail, *U.S.* 47°55′ N, 121°14′ W **100**
Pacific Grove, *Calif., U.S.* 36°36′ N, 121°56′ W **100**
Pacific Missile Test Center, *Calif., U.S.* 34°6′ N, 119°10′ W **101**
Pacific Ocean 35°4′ N, 122°0′ W **252**
Pacific Rim National Park Reserve, *Can.* 48°38′ N, 124°46′ W **100**
Pacifica, *Calif., U.S.* 37°37′ N, 122°30′ W **100**
Pacific-Antarctic Ridge, *South Pacific Ocean* 63°11′ S, 161°29′ W **255**
Pačir, *Serb.* 45°54′ N, 19°26′ E **168**
Packwood, *Wash., U.S.* 46°35′ N, 121°41′ W **100**
Pacov, *Czech Rep.* 49°27′ N, 14°59′ E **152**
Padada, *Philippines* 6°41′ N, 125°21′ E **203**
Padang, *Indonesia* 3°2′ N, 105°42′ E **196**
Padang, *Indonesia* 0°55′ N, 100°22′ E **196**
Padang Endau, *Malaysia* 2°39′ N, 103°38′ E **196**
Padang, island, *Indonesia* 0°55′ N, 101°49′ E **196**
Padangpanjang, *Indonesia* 0°28′ N, 100°23′ E **196**
Padangsidempuan, *Indonesia* 1°23′ N, 99°17′ E **196**
Padany, *Russ.* 63°17′ N, 33°24′ E **152**
Padas, river, *Malaysia* 4°40′ N, 115°43′ E **203**
Padasjoki, *Fin.* 61°20′ N, 25°15′ E **166**
Padauiri, river, *Braz.* 0°59′ N, 64°48′ W **130**
Padcaya, *Bol.* 21°52′ S, 64°48′ W **137**
Paddle Prairie, *Can.* 57°55′ N, 117°27′ W **108**
Paden City, *W. Va., U.S.* 39°35′ N, 80°56′ W **102**
Paderborn, *Ger.* 51°43′ N, 8°45′ E **167**
Padeş, peak, *Rom.* 45°39′ N, 22°18′ E **168**
Padilla, *Bol.* 19°17′ S, 64°21′ W **137**
Padina, *Serb.* 45°7′ N, 20°44′ E **168**
Padirac, site, *Fr.* 44°51′ N, 1°42′ E **165**
Padlei, *Can.* 61°56′ N, 96°42′ W **73**
Padloping Island, *Can.* 67°11′ N, 62°19′ W **246**
Padova (Padua), *It.* 45°24′ N, 11°52′ E **167**

Párnitha, Óros, peak, *Gr.* 38°10′ N, 23°38′ E **156**
Párnonas, Óros, *Gr.* 37°22′ N, 22°31′ E **156**
Pärnu, *Est.* 58°23′ N, 24°29′ E **166**
Pärnu Jaagupi, *Est.* 58°36′ N, 24°27′ E **166**
Pärnu Laht 58°18′ N, 24°7′ E **166**
Pärnu, river, *Est.* 58°45′ N, 25°16′ E **166**
Paroho, lake, *S. Korea* 38°8′ N, 127°41′ E **200**
Páros, *Gr.* 37°4′ N, 25°9′ E **156**
Páros, island, *Gr.* 36°50′ N, 24°52′ E **180**
Parowan, *Utah, U.S.* 37°50′ N, 112°49′ W **92**
Parr, Cape 81°8′ S, 171°43′ E **248**
Parral, *Chile* 36°7′ S, 71°52′ W **134**
Parras de la Fuente, *Mex.* 25°25′ N, 102°12′ W **114**
Parris Island, *S.C., U.S.* 32°5′ N, 80°27′ W **112**
Parrish, *Fla., U.S.* 27°35′ N, 82°25′ W **105**
Parrs Halt, *Botswana* 23°22′ S, 27°16′ E **227**
Parry, Cape, *Can.* 69°59′ N, 124°19′ W **106**
Parry, Cape, *Can.* 70°11′ N, 126°24′ W **98**
Parry Islands, *Foxe Basin* 74°19′ N, 107°51′ W **106**
Parry, Kap 76°58′ N, 75°51′ W **106**
Parry, Kap, *Traill Ø* 72°1′ N, 21°53′ W **246**
Parry Peninsula, *Can.* 69°48′ N, 125°21′ W **98**
Parry Sound, *Can.* 45°20′ N, 80°2′ W **94**
Parshall, *N. Dak., U.S.* 47°57′ N, 102°10′ W **90**
Parsi, oil field, *Iran* 31°0′ N, 49°54′ E **180**
Parsnip Peak, *Nev., U.S.* 38°8′ N, 114°25′ W **90**
Parsnip Peak, *Oreg., U.S.* 42°50′ N, 117°11′ W **90**
Parsnip, river, *Can.* 54°34′ N, 122°18′ W **108**
Parsons, *Kans., U.S.* 37°19′ N, 95°16′ W **96**
Pårtefjället, peak, *Nor.* 67°9′ N, 17°29′ E **152**
Partridge Bay 53°8′ N, 56°28′ W **111**
Partridge, river, *Can.* 50°50′ N, 80°23′ W **110**
Parú, river, *Venez.* 4°34′ N, 66°7′ W **136**
Parucito, river, *Venez.* 5°2′ N, 66°8′ W **136**
Paruro, *Peru* 13°48′ S, 71°51′ W **137**
P'arvani, Tba, lake, *Ga.* 41°23′ N, 43°28′ E **195**
Parvatipuram, *India* 18°45′ N, 83°26′ E **188**
Paryang, *China* 30°11′ N, 83°20′ E **197**
Parychy, *Belarus* 52°46′ N, 29°29′ E **152**
Parys, *S. Af.* 26°58′ S, 27°27′ E **227**
Pasadena, *Calif., U.S.* 34°8′ N, 118°11′ W **101**
Pasadena, *Tex., U.S.* 29°41′ N, 95°12′ W **103**
Pasado, Cabo, *Ecua.* 0°22′ N, 81°24′ W **130**
Pasaje, *Ecua.* 3°28′ S, 79°49′ W **130**
Pasaje (Juramento), river, *Arg.* 28°44′ S, 62°58′ W **139**
P'asanauri, *Ga.* 42°19′ N, 44°37′ E **195**
Pascagoula, *Miss., U.S.* 30°21′ N, 88°32′ W **103**
Paşcani, *Rom.* 47°14′ N, 26°42′ E **156**
Pasco, *Wash., U.S.* 46°13′ N, 119°5′ W **90**
Pasco, adm. division, *Peru* 10°15′ S, 74°55′ W **137**
Pascoag, *R.I., U.S.* 41°57′ N, 71°43′ W **104**
Pascoal, Monte, peak, *Braz.* 16°53′ S, 39°25′ W **138**
Pascua, Isla de see Easter Island, *Chile* 27°0′ S, 109°0′ W **241**
Pasewalk, *Ger.* 53°30′ N, 13°59′ E **152**
Pasfield Lake, *Can.* 58°24′ N, 105°44′ W **108**
Pasha, river, *Russ.* 59°46′ N, 34°4′ E **154**
Pashiya, *Russ.* 58°26′ N, 58°22′ E **154**
Pashskiy Perevoz, *Russ.* 60°23′ N, 33°8′ E **154**
Pasinler, *Turk.* 39°59′ N, 41°40′ E **195**
Pasir Mas, *Malaysia* 6°3′ N, 102°7′ E **196**
Pasir Puteh, *Malaysia* 5°50′ N, 102°23′ E **196**
Paskwachi Bay 57°14′ N, 102°46′ W **108**
Pasley, Cape, *Austral.* 34°26′ S, 123°41′ E **231**
Pasni, *Pak.* 25°15′ N, 63°28′ E **182**
Paso de los Libres, *Arg.* 29°40′ S, 57°9′ W **139**
Paso de los Toros, *Uru.* 32°46′ S, 56°31′ W **139**
Paso de Ovejas, *Mex.* 19°16′ N, 96°26′ W **114**
Paso Robles, *Calif., U.S.* 35°37′ N, 120°42′ W **100**
Pasorapa, *Bol.* 18°21′ S, 64°39′ W **137**
Pasque Island, *Mass., U.S.* 41°27′ N, 70°53′ W **104**
Pass Christian, *Miss., U.S.* 30°18′ N, 89°15′ W **103**
Passadumkeag Mountain, peak, *Me., U.S.* 45°6′ N, 68°28′ W **94**
Passat Nunatak, peak, *Antarctica* 71°25′ S, 4°12′ W **248**
Passau, *Ger.* 48°33′ N, 13°28′ E **152**
Passero, Capo, *It.* 36°39′ N, 15°9′ E **216**
Passo Fundo, *Braz.* 28°16′ S, 52°27′ W **139**
Passos, *Braz.* 20°43′ S, 46°37′ W **138**
Pastavy, *Belarus* 55°7′ N, 26°50′ E **166**
Pastaza, river, *Ecua.* 2°3′ S, 77°39′ W **130**
Pastaza, river, *Peru* 4°29′ S, 76°33′ W **130**
Pasteur, *Arg.* 35°7′ S, 62°14′ W **139**
Pasto, *Col.* 1°13′ N, 77°17′ W **136**
Pastora Peak, *Ariz., U.S.* 36°46′ N, 109°14′ W **92**
Pastos Bons, *Braz.* 6°38′ S, 44°5′ W **132**
Pastrana, *Sp.* 40°24′ N, 2°56′ W **150**
Pasvalys, *Lith.* 56°3′ N, 24°22′ E **166**
Pasvik, *Nor.* 69°47′ N, 30°32′ E **152**
Pašvitinys, *Lith.* 56°9′ N, 23°47′ E **166**
Pásztó, *Hung.* 47°54′ N, 19°43′ E **168**
Pata, *Cen. Af. Rep.* 8°2′ N, 21°28′ E **218**
Patagonia, *Ariz., U.S.* 31°31′ N, 110°45′ W **92**
Patamisk, Lac, lake, *Can.* 52°52′ N, 71°43′ W **111**
Patan, *India* 23°50′ N, 72°7′ E **186**
Patan, *India* 17°24′ N, 73°55′ E **188**
Patan, *India* 23°16′ N, 79°43′ E **197**
Patan see Lalitpur, *Nepal* 27°36′ N, 85°22′ E **197**
Patani, *Indonesia* 0°15′ N, 128°46′ E **192**
Patara Shiraki, *Ga.* 41°17′ N, 46°20′ E **195**
Patchogue, *N.Y., U.S.* 40°45′ N, 73°1′ W **104**
Pate Island, *Kenya* 2°16′ S, 41°4′ E **224**
Pategi, *Nig.* 8°43′ N, 5°44′ E **222**
Pateley Bridge, *U.K.* 54°5′ N, 1°45′ W **162**
Patensie, *S. Af.* 33°46′ S, 24°48′ E **227**
Paternion, *Aust.* 46°43′ N, 13°40′ E **167**
Paterson, *N.J., U.S.* 40°54′ N, 74°11′ W **82**
Paterson Range, *Austral.* 21°46′ S, 121°56′ E **230**
Pathankot, *India* 32°16′ N, 75°42′ E **186**
Pathein, *Myanmar* 16°44′ N, 94°45′ E **202**
Pathfinder Dam, *Wyo., U.S.* 42°28′ N, 106°49′ W **90**
Pathum Thani, *Thai.* 14°1′ N, 100°31′ E **202**
Pati, river, *Braz.* 3°40′ S, 67°54′ W **136**
Patiala, *India* 30°19′ N, 76°22′ E **197**
Pativilca, *Peru* 10°42′ S, 77°47′ W **130**
Pátmos, *Gr.* 37°18′ N, 26°33′ E **156**
Patna, *India* 25°33′ N, 85°5′ E **197**
Patnos, *Turk.* 39°13′ N, 42°52′ E **195**
Pató, *Col.* 7°27′ N, 74°55′ W **136**
Patoka, *Ill., U.S.* 38°44′ N, 89°6′ W **102**
Patoka, *Ind., U.S.* 38°24′ N, 87°36′ W **94**
Patos, *Braz.* 7°0′ S, 37°15′ W **132**
Patos de Minas, *Braz.* 18°36′ S, 46°30′ W **138**
Patos, Lagoa dos, lake, *Braz.* 31°15′ S, 51°35′ W **139**
Patos, Laguna de, lake, *Mex.* 30°41′ N, 107°3′ W **92**
Patos, Ponta dos, *Braz.* 2°59′ S, 39°40′ W **132**
Pátra, *Gr.* 38°12′ N, 21°47′ E **180**
Patrae see Pátra, *Gr.* 38°14′ N, 21°43′ E **156**
Patricio Lynch, Isla, island, *Chile* 48°27′ S, 77°53′ W **134**
Patrick Air Force Base, *Fla., U.S.* 28°14′ N, 80°39′ W **105**
Patrick, Croagh, peak, *Ire.* 53°44′ N, 9°46′ W **150**
Patrick Point, peak, *Antarctica* 73°36′ S, 66°6′ E **248**
Patrimonio, *Braz.* 19°30′ S, 48°31′ W **138**
Patrington, *U.K.* 53°40′ N, 7°419′ W **162**
Patriot, *Ind., U.S.* 38°50′ N, 84°49′ W **102**
Patrocínio, *Braz.* 18°57′ S, 46°58′ W **138**
Pattani, *Thai.* 6°50′ N, 101°16′ E **196**
Patten, *Me., U.S.* 45°59′ N, 68°27′ W **94**
Patterson, *Calif., U.S.* 37°28′ N, 121°9′ W **100**
Patterson Lake, lake, *Can.* 57°37′ N, 109°54′ W **108**
Patterson, Mount, peak, *Calif., U.S.* 38°25′ N, 119°24′ W **90**
Patterson Mountain, peak, *Calif., U.S.* 36°58′ N, 119°6′ W **101**
Patti, *India* 31°16′ N, 74°53′ E **186**
Pattison, *Miss., U.S.* 31°53′ N, 90°53′ W **103**
Patton Seamounts, *North Pacific Ocean* 54°12′ N, 150°21′ W **252**
Pattullo, Mount, peak, *Can.* 56°13′ N, 129°48′ W **108**
Patu, *Braz.* 6°8′ S, 37°38′ W **132**
Patuakhali, *Bangladesh* 22°18′ N, 90°19′ E **197**
Patuanak, *Can.* 55°55′ N, 107°44′ W **108**
Patuca National Park, *Hond.* 14°27′ N, 85°53′ W **115**
Patuca, river, *Hond.* 14°16′ N, 85°54′ W **115**
Pătulele, *Rom.* 44°20′ N, 22°47′ E **168**
Patutahi, *N.Z.* 38°38′ S, 177°52′ E **240**
Patuxent River Naval Air Test Center, *Md., U.S.* 38°16′ N, 76°29′ W **94**
Pátzcuaro, *Mex.* 19°28′ N, 101°37′ W **114**
Pátzcuaro, Laguna de, lake, *Mex.* 19°30′ N, 102°3′ W **114**
Pau, *Fr.* 43°18′ N, 0°22′ E **164**
Pau d'Arco, river, *Braz.* 8°20′ S, 50°41′ W **132**
Paucarbamba, *Peru* 12°27′ S, 74°37′ W **137**
Paucartambo, *Peru* 13°22′ S, 71°36′ W **137**
Pauillac, *Fr.* 45°12′ N, 0°46′ E **150**
Pauini, *Braz.* 7°45′ S, 67°2′ W **130**
Pauini, river, *Braz.* 2°33′ S, 63°52′ W **130**
Pauini, river, *Braz.* 7°42′ S, 67°48′ W **130**
Pauini, river, *Braz.* 8°5′ S, 69°34′ W **130**
Paulatuk, *Can.* 69°26′ N, 124°6′ W **98**
Paulding, *Miss., U.S.* 32°0′ N, 89°1′ W **103**
Paulding, *Ohio, U.S.* 41°7′ N, 84°35′ W **102**
Pauléoula, *Côte d'Ivoire* 5°45′ N, 7°24′ W **222**
Paulilatino, *It.* 40°5′ N, 8°47′ E **156**
Paulina Peak, *Oreg., U.S.* 43°40′ N, 121°21′ W **90**
Pauline, Mount, peak, *Can.* 53°31′ N, 119°59′ W **108**
Paulis see Isiro, *Dem. Rep. of the Congo* 2°43′ N, 27°39′ E **224**
Paulista, *Braz.* 7°56′ S, 34°59′ W **132**
Paulistana, *Braz.* 8°10′ S, 41°9′ W **132**
Paull Lake, lake, *Can.* 56°8′ N, 105°11′ W **108**
Paullo, *It.* 45°25′ N, 9°23′ E **167**
Paulo Afonso, *Braz.* 9°24′ S, 38°16′ W **132**
Pauls Valley, *Okla., U.S.* 34°43′ N, 97°13′ W **92**
Pauma Valley, *Calif., U.S.* 33°18′ N, 117°0′ W **101**
Paungde, *Myanmar* 18°30′ N, 95°29′ E **202**
Pauni, *India* 20°45′ N, 79°37′ E **188**
Pauri, *India* 30°9′ N, 78°48′ E **197**
Pausa, *Peru* 15°19′ S, 73°22′ W **137**
Pauto, river, *Col.* 5°21′ N, 71°31′ W **136**
Pavão, *Braz.* 17°25′ S, 41°5′ W **138**
Pavda, *Russ.* 59°17′ N, 59°29′ E **154**
Păveh, *Iran* 35°3′ N, 46°21′ E **180**
Pavia, *It.* 45°11′ N, 9°9′ E **167**
Pavia, *Port.* 38°52′ N, 8°2′ W **150**
Pavie, *Fr.* 43°36′ N, 0°35′ E **150**
Pavillion, *Wyo., U.S.* 43°14′ N, 108°42′ W **90**
Pavilly, *Fr.* 49°34′ N, 0°57′ E **163**
Pāvilosta, *Latv.* 56°53′ N, 21°11′ E **166**
Pavino, *Russ.* 59°7′ N, 46°9′ E **154**
Pavlica, *Serb.* 43°20′ N, 20°39′ E **168**
Pavlodar, *Kaz.* 52°17′ N, 76°57′ E **184**
Pavlodar, adm. division, *Kaz.* 52°5′ N, 74°35′ E **184**
Pavlof Volcano, peak, *Alas., U.S.* 55°23′ N, 162°4′ W **98**
Pavlohrad, *Ukr.* 48°32′ N, 35°52′ E **158**
Pavlovac, *Croatia* 45°43′ N, 17°1′ E **168**
Pavlovka, *Russ.* 53°5′ N, 51°17′ E **154**
Pavlovka, *Russ.* 52°39′ N, 47°13′ E **158**
Pavlovo, *Russ.* 55°55′ N, 43°8′ E **154**
Pavlovsk, *Russ.* 50°27′ N, 40°6′ E **158**
Pavlovskaya, *Russ.* 46°8′ N, 39°44′ E **158**
Pavullo nel Frignano, *It.* 44°20′ N, 10°49′ E **167**
Pavy, *Russ.* 58°2′ N, 29°30′ E **166**
Paw Paw, *Mich., U.S.* 42°13′ N, 85°53′ W **94**
Pawarenga, *N.Z.* 35°24′ S, 173°15′ E **240**
Pawcatuck, *Conn., U.S.* 41°22′ N, 71°51′ W **104**
Pawhuska, *Okla., U.S.* 36°39′ N, 96°20′ W **92**
Pawlet, *Vt., U.S.* 43°20′ N, 73°12′ W **104**
Pawleys Island, *S.C., U.S.* 33°25′ N, 79°8′ W **96**
Pawling, *N.Y., U.S.* 41°33′ N, 73°37′ W **104**
Pawnee, *Okla., U.S.* 36°18′ N, 96°48′ W **92**
Pawnee Buttes, peak, *Colo., U.S.* 40°49′ N, 104°4′ W **90**
Pawnee City, *Nebr., U.S.* 40°5′ N, 96°10′ W **90**
Pawnee Creek, river, *Colo., U.S.* 40°31′ N, 104°0′ W **90**
Pawonków, *Pol.* 50°41′ N, 18°35′ E **152**
Pawtucket, *R.I., U.S.* 41°52′ N, 71°24′ W **104**
Paxí, *Gr.* 39°11′ N, 20°10′ E **156**
Paxtakor, *Uzb.* 40°22′ N, 67°59′ E **197**
Paxton, *Ill., U.S.* 40°27′ N, 88°6′ W **102**
Paxton, *Mass., U.S.* 42°18′ N, 71°56′ W **104**
Paxton, *Mo., U.S.* 40°27′ N, 88°6′ W **94**
Paxton, *Nebr., U.S.* 41°7′ N, 101°23′ W **90**
Payakumbuh, *Indonesia* 0°13′ N, 100°37′ E **196**
Payar, *Senegal* 14°24′ N, 14°32′ W **222**
Payas, peak, *Hond.* 15°43′ N, 85°0′ W **115**
Payer Mountains, *Antarctica* 71°54′ S, 15°30′ E **248**
Payerne, *Switz.* 46°49′ N, 6°57′ E **167**
Payette, *Idaho, U.S.* 44°2′ N, 116°53′ W **82**
Payne, *Ohio, U.S.* 41°4′ N, 84°44′ W **102**
Payne, Lac, lake, *Can.* 59°34′ N, 75°34′ W **106**
Payne, Mount, peak, *Peru* 12°19′ S, 73°39′ W **137**
Paynesville, *Minn., U.S.* 45°20′ N, 94°44′ W **90**
Payo see Panganiban, *Philippines* 13°56′ N, 124°17′ E **203**
Pays de La Loire, adm. division, *Fr.* 47°34′ N, 1°59′ W **150**
Paysandú, *Uru.* 32°21′ S, 58°2′ W **139**
Payshanba, *Uzb.* 39°54′ N, 66°16′ E **197**
Payson, *Ariz., U.S.* 34°13′ N, 111°19′ W **92**
Payson, *Utah, U.S.* 40°1′ N, 111°43′ W **90**
Paz, *Braz.* 25°41′ S, 52°11′ W **138**
Paz de Ariporo, *Col.* 5°50′ N, 71°51′ W **136**
Paz de Río, *Col.* 5°59′ N, 72°46′ W **136**
Paz, river, *Braz.* 9°26′ S, 52°2′ W **130**
Pazar, *Turk.* 40°16′ N, 36°16′ E **156**
Pazar, *Turk.* 41°10′ N, 40°52′ E **195**
Pazar, *Turk.* 40°17′ N, 32°42′ E **156**
Pazarcık, *Turk.* 37°29′ N, 37°19′ E **156**
Pazardzhik, *Bulg.* 42°12′ N, 24°19′ E **156**
Pazña, *Bol.* 18°38′ S, 66°56′ W **137**
Pčinja, river, *Maced.* 41°46′ N, 21°48′ E **156**
Pe, *Myanmar* 13°27′ N, 98°30′ E **202**
Pe Ell, *Wash., U.S.* 46°32′ N, 123°18′ W **100**
Peabody, *Kans., U.S.* 38°9′ N, 97°7′ W **94**
Peabody, *Mass., U.S.* 42°31′ N, 70°56′ W **104**
Peace Dale, *R.I., U.S.* 41°27′ N, 71°31′ W **104**
Peace Garden, *N. Dak., U.S.* 48°58′ N, 100°9′ W **90**
Peace River, *Can.* 56°14′ N, 117°15′ W **108**
Peace, river, *Can.* 57°16′ N, 116°57′ W **108**
Peace, river, *Fla., U.S.* 27°11′ N, 81°54′ W **105**
Peach Springs, *Ariz., U.S.* 35°31′ N, 113°25′ W **101**
Peaima Falls, *Guyana* 6°23′ N, 61°16′ W **130**
Peak District National Park, *U.K.* 51°21′ N, 1°50′ W **150**
Peaked Mountain, *Me., U.S.* 46°33′ N, 68°54′ W **94**
Peale, Mount, peak, *Utah, U.S.* 38°25′ N, 109°18′ W **90**
Peard Bay 70°39′ N, 160°16′ W **98**
Pearisburg, *Va., U.S.* 37°18′ N, 80°44′ W **96**
Pearl and Hermes Atoll, islands, *North Pacific Ocean* 26°30′ N, 179°37′ E **238**
Pearl Peak, *Nev., U.S.* 40°13′ N, 115°37′ W **90**
Pearl River, *La., U.S.* 30°21′ N, 89°45′ W **103**
Pearl, river, *Miss., U.S.* 30°46′ N, 89°41′ W **103**
Pearland, *Tex., U.S.* 29°32′ N, 95°17′ W **103**
Pearsall, *Tex., U.S.* 28°53′ N, 99°6′ W **92**
Pearse Canal 54°48′ N, 130°40′ W **108**
Pearson, *Ga., U.S.* 31°17′ N, 82°51′ W **96**
Pearston, *S. Af.* 32°36′ S, 25°8′ E **227**
Peary Land 83°29′ N, 42°51′ W **72**
Pease, river, *Tex., U.S.* 34°21′ N, 100°39′ W **80**
Peawanuk, *Can.* 55°3′ N, 85°34′ W **106**
Pebane, *Mozambique* 17°16′ S, 38°11′ E **224**
Pebas, *Peru* 3°19′ S, 71°51′ W **136**
Pebble Beach, *Calif., U.S.* 36°34′ N, 121°58′ W **100**
Pebble Island, *Pebble Island* 51°9′ S, 60°3′ W **248**
Peć see Peja, *Kosovo* 42°40′ N, 20°17′ E **168**
Pecan Island, *La., U.S.* 29°38′ N, 92°26′ W **103**
Peçanha, *Braz.* 18°34′ S, 42°35′ W **138**
Pécel, *Hung.* 47°29′ N, 19°20′ E **168**
Pechenga, *Russ.* 69°32′ N, 31°11′ E **152**
Pechina, *Sp.* 36°54′ N, 2°26′ W **164**
Pechora, *Russ.* 65°8′ N, 57°11′ E **154**
Pechora, river, *Russ.* 65°40′ N, 56°56′ E **154**
Pechorskaya Guba 68°13′ N, 50°14′ E **246**
Pechorskaya Nizmennost', *Russ.* 64°53′ N, 51°55′ E **154**
Pechorskoye More 69°0′ N, 53°8′ E **246**
Pechory, *Russ.* 57°48′ N, 27°36′ E **166**
Pecica, *Rom.* 46°10′ N, 21°4′ E **168**
Peciu Nou, *Rom.* 45°36′ N, 21°4′ E **168**
Peck, Mount, peak, *Can.* 58°17′ N, 124°52′ W **108**
Pecka, *Serb.* 44°18′ N, 19°32′ E **168**
Peconic, *N.Y., U.S.* 41°2′ N, 72°28′ W **104**
Pecora, Capo, *It.* 39°23′ N, 7°46′ E **156**
Pecos, *N. Mex., U.S.* 35°34′ N, 105°41′ W **92**
Pecos, *Tex., U.S.* 31°24′ N, 103°30′ W **92**
Pecos, river, *U.S.* 35°7′ N, 105°5′ W **92**
Pécs, *Hung.* 46°4′ N, 18°13′ E **168**
Pécsvárad, *Hung.* 46°8′ N, 18°25′ E **168**
Peddapalli, *India* 18°36′ N, 79°23′ E **188**
Pededze, river, *Latv.* 57°11′ N, 27°6′ E **166**
Pedernales, *Venez.* 9°54′ N, 62°16′ W **116**
Pedja, river, *Est.* 58°28′ N, 26°13′ E **166**
Pêdo Pass, *China* 29°24′ N, 83°24′ E **197**
Pedra Azul, *Braz.* 16°3′ S, 41°16′ W **138**
Pedra de Amolar, *Braz.* 10°34′ S, 46°25′ W **130**
Pedras Altas, *Braz.* 31°44′ S, 53°32′ W **139**
Pedras Negras, *Braz.* 12°49′ S, 62°54′ W **130**
Pedregal, *Venez.* 11°2′ N, 70°8′ W **136**
Pedreiras, *Braz.* 4°34′ S, 44°41′ W **132**
Pedrera, *Sp.* 37°13′ N, 4°55′ W **164**
Pedriceña, *Mex.* 25°5′ N, 103°49′ W **114**
Pedro Afonso, *Braz.* 8°59′ S, 48°10′ W **130**
Pedro Bay, *Alas., U.S.* 59°47′ N, 154°7′ W **98**
Pedro Cays, islands, *Caribbean Sea* 16°52′ N, 77°47′ W **115**
Pedro de Valdivia, *Chile* 22°37′ S, 69°44′ W **137**
Pedro González, Isla, island, *Pan.* 8°23′ N, 80°13′ W **115**
Pedro Juan Caballero, *Parag.* 22°36′ S, 55°46′ W **132**
Pedro Luro, *Arg.* 39°31′ S, 62°42′ W **139**
Pedro Montoya, *Mex.* 21°38′ N, 99°49′ W **114**
Pedro Muñoz, *Sp.* 39°23′ N, 2°57′ W **164**
Pedro Osório, *Braz.* 31°52′ S, 52°48′ W **139**
Pedro R. Fernández, *Arg.* 28°44′ S, 58°39′ W **139**
Pedroso, Sierra del, *Sp.* 38°27′ N, 5°51′ W **164**
Pee Dee, river, *S.C., U.S.* 34°48′ N, 79°52′ W **80**
Peebles, *Ohio, U.S.* 38°56′ N, 83°25′ W **102**
Peekskill, *N.Y., U.S.* 41°16′ N, 73°56′ W **104**
Peel, river, *Can.* 65°54′ N, 137°18′ W **98**
Peene, *U.K.* 51°7′ N, 1°14′ E **162**
Peeples Valley, *Ariz., U.S.* 34°15′ N, 112°44′ W **92**
Peerless Lake, *Can.* 56°41′ N, 115°8′ W **108**
Peetz, *Colo., U.S.* 40°57′ N, 103°8′ W **90**
Pego, *Sp.* 38°49′ N, 0°7′ E **164**
Pegtymel', river, *Russ.* 69°51′ N, 173°25′ E **160**
Pegyshdor, *Russ.* 63°26′ N, 50°35′ E **154**
Pehčevo, *Maced.* 41°45′ N, 22°54′ E **168**
Pehuajó, *Arg.* 35°47′ S, 61°54′ W **139**
Peine, *Ger.* 52°19′ N, 10°13′ E **152**
Peixe, *Braz.* 12°5′ S, 48°35′ W **130**
Peixe, river, *Braz.* 27°25′ S, 51°52′ W **139**
Peixe, river, *Braz.* 14°42′ S, 50°46′ W **138**
Peja (Peć), *Kosovo* 42°40′ N, 20°17′ E **168**
Pek, river, *Serb.* 44°34′ N, 21°34′ E **168**
Pekalongan, *Indonesia* 7°1′ S, 109°38′ E **192**
Pekan, *Malaysia* 3°30′ N, 103°24′ E **196**
Pekanbaru, *Indonesia* 0°32′ N, 101°27′ E **196**
Pekin, *Ill., U.S.* 40°33′ N, 89°39′ W **102**
Peking see Beijing, *China* 39°52′ N, 116°9′ E **198**
Pekkala, *Fin.* 66°21′ N, 26°52′ E **152**
Pelado, peak, *Sp.* 39°44′ N, 1°27′ W **150**
Pelagie, Isole, islands, *Mediterranean Sea* 35°6′ N, 12°12′ E **156**
Pelagosa see Palagruža, island, *Croatia* 42°25′ N, 16°0′ E **168**
Pelahatchie, *Miss., U.S.* 32°18′ N, 89°48′ W **103**
Pelalawan, *Indonesia* 0°29′ N, 102°6′ E **196**
Pelat, Mont, peak, *Fr.* 44°16′ N, 6°39′ E **165**
Peldoaivi, peak, *Fin.* 69°10′ N, 26°25′ E **152**
Peleaga, peak, *Rom.* 45°21′ N, 22°52′ E **168**
Pelechuco, *Bol.* 14°52′ S, 69°4′ W **137**
Peleduy, *Russ.* 59°45′ N, 112°45′ E **160**
Pelee Island, *Can.* 41°44′ N, 82°40′ W **102**
Pelée, Montagne, peak, *Martinique* 14°47′ N, 61°15′ W **116**
Pelendria, *Cyprus* 34°53′ N, 32°58′ E **194**
Peleng, island, *Indonesia* 2°0′ S, 122°52′ E **192**
Pelham, *Ga., U.S.* 31°7′ N, 84°9′ W **96**
Pelham, *Mass., U.S.* 42°23′ N, 72°25′ W **104**
Pelican, *Alas., U.S.* 57°58′ N, 136°14′ W **98**
Pelican, *La., U.S.* 31°52′ N, 93°36′ W **103**
Pelican Lake, lake, *Can.* 52°24′ N, 100°48′ W **108**
Pelican Mountain, peak, *Can.* 55°36′ N, 113°53′ W **108**
Pelican Narrows, *Can.* 55°12′ N, 102°56′ W **108**
Pelican Point, *Namibia* 22°55′ S, 13°55′ E **220**
Pelican Portage, *Can.* 55°41′ N, 112°36′ W **108**
Pelican Rapids, *Can.* 52°43′ N, 100°44′ W **108**
Pelican Rapids, *Minn., U.S.* 46°32′ N, 96°5′ W **94**
Pelinéo, Óros, peak, *Gr.* 38°33′ N, 25°56′ E **156**
Pelister National Park, *Maced.* 40°29′ N, 21°15′ E **168**
Pelister, peak, *Maced.* 40°59′ N, 21°7′ E **156**
Pelješac, *Croatia* 42°58′ N, 17°6′ E **168**
Pella, *S. Af.* 29°3′ S, 19°9′ E **227**
Pellegrini, *Arg.* 36°18′ S, 63°9′ W **139**
Pello, *Fin.* 66°47′ N, 24°0′ E **152**
Pelly, *Can.* 51°50′ N, 101°56′ W **90**
Pelly Crossing, *Can.* 62°53′ N, 136°34′ W **98**
Pelly, river, *Can.* 61°45′ N, 131°16′ W **98**
Pelokehn, *Liberia* 5°34′ N, 8°8′ W **222**
Peloponnesus, *Gr.* 38°2′ N, 21°53′ E **180**
Peloponnisos, adm. division, *Gr.* 36°51′ N, 22°29′ E **156**
Peloritani, Monti, *It.* 38°0′ N, 14°49′ E **156**
Pelotas, *Braz.* 31°44′ S, 52°19′ W **139**
Pelotas, river, *Braz.* 27°42′ S, 51°25′ W **139**
Pelplin, *Pol.* 53°55′ N, 18°42′ E **166**
Pelsart Group, islands, *Indian Ocean* 29°25′ S, 112°14′ E **230**
Peltovuoma, *Fin.* 68°22′ N, 24°11′ E **152**
Pelusium, ruin(s), *Egypt* 31°0′ N, 32°29′ E **194**
Pelvoux, Massif du, *Fr.* 44°50′ N, 6°9′ E **165**
Pelyatka, *Russ.* 69°59′ N, 82°13′ E **169**
Pelym, *Russ.* 59°40′ N, 63°5′ E **154**
Pelym, river, *Russ.* 60°42′ N, 62°22′ E **154**
Pemache, river, *Can.* 47°29′ N, 83°50′ W **110**
Pemaquid Point, *Me., U.S.* 43°37′ N, 69°34′ W **94**
Pematang, *Indonesia* 0°10′ N, 102°6′ E **196**
Pematangsiantar, *Indonesia* 3°2′ N, 99°7′ E **196**
Pemba, *Mozambique* 13°2′ S, 40°33′ E **224**
Pemba, *Zambia* 16°32′ S, 27°20′ E **224**
Pemba Island, *Tanzania* 5°7′ S, 39°54′ E **224**
Pemberton, *Can.* 50°19′ N, 122°49′ W **100**
Pembina, *N. Dak., U.S.* 48°56′ N, 97°17′ W **90**
Pembina Hills, *Can.* 49°27′ N, 98°58′ W **90**
Pembina, oil field, *Can.* 53°6′ N, 115°14′ W **108**
Pembina, river, *North America* 53°4′ N, 116°13′ W **108**
Pembroke, *Can.* 45°50′ N, 77°7′ W **110**
Pembroke, *Ga., U.S.* 32°8′ N, 81°38′ W **96**
Pembroke, *N.H., U.S.* 43°8′ N, 71°28′ W **104**
Pembroke, Cape, *East Falkland* 51°49′ S, 57°42′ W **134**
Pembrokeshire Coast National Park, *U.K.* 51°50′ N, 5°5′ W **150**
Peña Blanca, Cerro, peak, *Pan.* 8°39′ N, 80°40′ W **115**
Peña de Francia, Sierra de, *Sp.* 40°32′ N, 6°47′ W **150**
Peña Grande, *Sp.* 40°28′ N, 3°45′ W **164**
Penã Negra, Paso de, pass, *Chile* 28°14′ S, 69°28′ W **132**
Peña, Sierra de, *Sp.* 42°27′ N, 1°0′ E **164**
Penalva, *Braz.* 3°18′ S, 45°13′ W **132**
Penápolis, *Braz.* 21°24′ S, 50°7′ W **138**
Peñarroya, peak, *Sp.* 40°22′ N, 0°43′ E **164**
Penarth, *U.K.* 51°26′ N, 3°10′ W **162**
Peñas Blancas, *Nicar.* 11°13′ N, 85°36′ W **115**
Peñas, Cabo de, *Sp.* 43°39′ N, 6°7′ W **150**
Peñas de San Pedro, *Sp.* 38°43′ N, 2°0′ W **150**
Pencarreg, *U.K.* 52°4′ N, 4°8′ W **162**
Pench National Park, *India* 21°40′ N, 79°30′ E **197**
Penck, Cape 66°6′ S, 84°17′ E **248**
Pendé, river, *Cen. Af. Rep.* 6°38′ N, 15°51′ E **218**
Pendéli, peak, *Gr.* 38°4′ N, 23°48′ E **156**
Pendembu, *Sierra Leone* 8°3′ N, 10°42′ W **222**
Pender, *Nebr., U.S.* 42°5′ N, 96°43′ W **90**
Pender Bay 17°0′ S, 122°19′ E **230**
Pendjari National Park, *Benin* 11°17′ N, 1°27′ E **222**
Pendleton, *Ind., U.S.* 39°59′ N, 85°44′ W **102**
Pendleton, *Oreg., U.S.* 45°38′ N, 118°48′ W **90**
Pendleton, Mount, peak, *Can.* 59°12′ N, 129°29′ W **108**
Pendroy, *Mont., U.S.* 48°2′ N, 112°19′ W **90**
Penebangan, island, *Indonesia* 1°7′ S, 108°41′ E **196**
Penedo, *Braz.* 10°15′ S, 36°36′ W **132**
Penetanguishene, *Can.* 44°45′ N, 79°56′ W **94**
Penge, *Dem. Rep. of the Congo* 5°32′ S, 24°36′ E **224**
Penghu (Pescadores), islands, *Taiwan, China* 23°30′ N, 119°30′ E **191**
Penglai, *China* 37°47′ N, 120°49′ E **198**
Pengshui, *China* 29°18′ N, 108°14′ E **198**
Pengxi, *China* 30°45′ N, 105°42′ E **198**
Penha do Tapaua, *Braz.* 5°48′ S, 64°29′ W **130**
Penhold, *Can.* 52°7′ N, 113°53′ W **90**
Peniche, *Port.* 39°20′ N, 9°23′ W **214**
Peninga, *Russ.* 63°33′ N, 31°35′ E **152**
Península de Paria National Park, *Caribbean Sea* 10°37′ N, 62°36′ W **122**
Peñíscola, *Sp.* 40°21′ N, 0°23′ E **164**
Penitente, Serra do, *Braz.* 9°3′ S, 46°49′ W **130**
Pénjamo, *Mex.* 20°25′ N, 101°44′ W **114**
Penmaenmawr, *U.K.* 53°16′ N, 3°55′ W **162**
Penmarc'h, Pointe de, *Fr.* 47°29′ N, 4°56′ W **150**
Penmon, *U.K.* 53°18′ N, 4°3′ W **162**
Penn Yan, *N.Y., U.S.* 42°40′ N, 77°4′ W **94**
Penna, Punta della, *It.* 42°11′ N, 14°44′ E **156**
Pennabilli, *It.* 43°49′ N, 12°15′ E **167**
Pennant Point, *Can.* 44°20′ N, 63°44′ W **111**
Pennask Lake, *Can.* 49°56′ N, 120°44′ W **90**
Pennask Mountain, peak, *Can.* 49°52′ N, 120°12′ W **90**
Pennell Coast, *Antarctica* 70°51′ S, 173°14′ E **248**
Pennine Alps, *Switz.* 46°13′ N, 7°29′ E **165**
Pennines, The, *U.K.* 54°14′ N, 2°15′ W **162**
Pennino, Monte, peak, *It.* 43°5′ N, 12°48′ E **156**
Pennsboro, *W. Va., U.S.* 39°16′ N, 80°58′ W **102**
Pennsylvania, adm. division, *Pa., U.S.* 41°46′ N, 79°36′ W **94**
Pennville, *Ind., U.S.* 40°29′ N, 85°9′ W **102**
Penny, *Can.* 53°50′ N, 121°17′ W **108**
Penny Point 80°25′ S, 170°23′ E **248**
Pennycutaway, river, *Can.* 56°7′ N, 94°14′ W **108**
Peno, *Russ.* 56°56′ N, 32°47′ E **154**
Penobscot Bay 44°8′ N, 69°6′ W **80**
Penong, *Austral.* 31°57′ S, 132°59′ E **231**
Penrith, *U.K.* 54°40′ N, 2°46′ W **162**
Penryn, *Calif., U.S.* 38°51′ N, 121°11′ W **90**
Pensacola, *Fla., U.S.* 30°24′ N, 87°13′ W **96**
Pensacola Mountains, *Antarctica* 85°14′ S, 76°52′ W **248**
Penticton, *Can.* 49°27′ N, 119°33′ W **106**
Pentland Hills, *U.K.* 55°48′ N, 3°57′ W **150**
Pentland Skerries, islands, *North Sea* 58°23′ N, 2°50′ W **150**
Pentwater, *Mich., U.S.* 43°46′ N, 86°25′ W **102**
Penunjok, Tanjong, *Malaysia* 4°1′ N, 103°30′ E **196**
Penwell, *Tex., U.S.* 31°43′ N, 102°36′ W **92**
Penza, *Russ.* 53°9′ N, 45°3′ E **154**
Penza, adm. division, *Russ.* 53°28′ N, 43°26′ E **154**
Penzance, *U.K.* 50°7′ N, 5°33′ W **150**
Peoples Creek, river, *Mont., U.S.* 48°5′ N, 109°10′ W **108**
Peoria, *Ariz., U.S.* 33°34′ N, 112°14′ W **92**
Peoria, *Ill., U.S.* 40°40′ N, 89°37′ W **102**
Peotillos, *Mex.* 22°28′ N, 100°37′ W **114**
Peotone, *Ill., U.S.* 41°19′ N, 87°47′ W **102**
Pepe'ekeo, *Hawai'i, U.S.* 19°50′ N, 155°7′ W **99**
Pepel, *Sierra Leone* 8°37′ N, 13°4′ W **222**
Pephnos, ruin(s), *Gr.* 36°47′ N, 22°13′ E **156**
Pequeña, Punta, *Mex.* 26°6′ N, 113°34′ W **112**
Pequop Mountains, *Nev., U.S.* 40°40′ N, 114°44′ W **90**
Pera, *Cyprus* 35°1′ N, 33°15′ E **194**
Perälä, *Fin.* 62°27′ N, 21°36′ E **152**
Peralada, *Sp.* 42°18′ N, 3°1′ E **164**
Perales de Alfambra, *Sp.* 40°37′ N, 1°0′ E **164**
Peramiho, *Tanzania* 10°38′ S, 35°28′ E **224**
Peranka, *Fin.* 65°21′ N, 29°1′ E **154**
Peräposio, *Fin.* 66°11′ N, 27°52′ E **154**
Perast, *Mont.* 42°29′ N, 18°42′ E **168**
Perati, ruin(s), *Aegean Sea* 37°54′ N, 23°56′ E **156**
Percé, *Can.* 48°30′ N, 64°15′ W **111**
Perce Point, *Antarctica* 72°48′ S, 78°20′ W **248**
Perch Bay 58°2′ N, 102°23′ W **108**
Perche, region, *Fr.* 48°50′ N, 0°46′ E **163**
Percy Isles, islands, *Coral Sea* 21°39′ S, 150°29′ E **230**
Perdido, *Ala., U.S.* 30°59′ N, 87°37′ W **103**
Perdido, Monte, peak, *Sp.* 42°39′ N, 1°59′ W **164**
Perdido, river, *U.S.* 30°45′ N, 87°38′ W **103**
Perdizes, *Braz.* 19°22′ S, 47°19′ W **138**
Perechitsy, *Russ.* 58°48′ N, 30°3′ E **166**
Perechyn, *Ukr.* 48°43′ N, 22°26′ E **152**
Pereira, *Col.* 4°45′ N, 75°42′ W **136**
Pereira Barreto, *Braz.* 20°38′ S, 51°6′ W **138**
Perelazovskiy, *Russ.* 49°8′ N, 42°25′ E **158**
Perelyub, *Russ.* 51°51′ N, 50°21′ E **158**
Peremennyy, Cape, *Antarctica* 65°57′ S, 109°36′ E **248**
Peremetnoe, *Kaz.* 51°11′ N, 50°53′ E **158**

PER-PIN

Pereslavl' Zalesskiy, Russ. 56°44' N, 38°50' E 154
Perevolotskiy, Russ. 51°51' N, 54°12' E 158
Pereyaslav-Khmel'nyts'kyy, Ukr. 50°3' N, 31°33' E 158
Pérez, Isla, island, Mex. 22°17' N, 89°57' W 116
Perga, ruin(s), Turk. 36°59' N, 30°44' E 156
Pergamino, Arg. 33°57' S, 60°34' W 139
Perham, Minn., U.S. 46°34' N, 95°35' W 90
Perhentian Besar, island, Malaysia 5°58' N, 102°37' E 196
Perho, Fin. 63°13' N, 24°21' E 152
Peri Mirim, Braz. 2°41' S, 44°53' W 132
Periam, Rom. 46°2' N, 20°54' E 168
Péribonka, Lac, lake, Can. 49°55' N, 71°53' W 94
Péribonka, river, Can. 48°50' N, 71°20' W 111
Perico, Arg. 24°24' S, 65°7' W 134
Peridot, Ariz., U.S. 33°19' N, 110°27' W 92
Perigoso, Canal 3°177' S, 50°35' W 130
Perijá National Park, Venez. 9°15' N, 73°18' W 136
Perijá, Sierra de, Venez. 10°10' N, 73°20' W 136
Perim see Barīm, island, Yemen 12°36' N, 42°32' E 182
Perissa, Gr. 36°20' N, 25°27' E 156
Perito Moreno, Arg. 46°35' S, 70°55' W 134
Perito Moreno National Park, Arg. 48°0' S, 72°42' W 122
Peritoró, Braz. 4°17' S, 44°21' W 132
Perkins, Okla., U.S. 35°57' N, 97°2' W 92
Perkinston, Miss., U.S. 30°45' N, 89°8' W 103
Perkinsville, Vt., U.S. 43°22' N, 72°32' W 104
Perković, Croatia 43°40' N, 16°5' E 168
Perky, Fla., U.S. 24°38' N, 81°34' W 105
Perl, Ger. 49°28' N, 6°23' E 163
Perla, Ark., U.S. 34°20' N, 92°47' W 96
Perlas, Laguna de 12°24' N, 83°56' W 115
Perlevka, Russ. 51°50' N, 38°47' E 158
Perm', Russ. 57°57' N, 56°14' E 154
Perm', adm. division, Russ. 58°50' N, 56°13' E 154
Permas, Russ. 59°19' N, 45°36' E 154
Pernaja see Pernå, Fin. 60°26' N, 26°2' E 166
Pernambuco, adm. division, Braz. 8°41' S, 38°59' W 132
Pernambuco Plain, South Atlantic Ocean 7°10' S, 25°50' W 253
Pernik, Bulg. 42°36' N, 23°2' E 168
Pernik, adm. division, Bulg. 42°31' N, 22°44' E 168
Perniö, Fin. 60°11' N, 23°6' E 166
Pernitz, Aust. 47°54' N, 15°57' E 168
Peron Islands, Joseph Bonaparte Gulf 13°19' S, 128°31' E 230
Peronit Burnu, Turk. 41°23' N, 41°2' E 195
Péronne, Fr. 49°55' N, 2°55' E 163
Peros Banhos, atoll, Indian Ocean 5°16' S, 71°8' E 188
Perosa Argentina, It. 44°57' N, 7°12' E 167
Perote, Mex. 19°31' N, 97°16' W 114
Perouse Strait, La 45°35' N, 139°41' E 160
Perow, Can. 54°31' N, 126°27' W 108
Perpignan, Fr. 42°41' N, 2°53' E 164
Perrault Falls, Can. 50°19' N, 93°10' W 90
Perrault Lake, lake, Can. 50°14' N, 93°36' W 90
Perrine, Fla., U.S. 25°36' N, 80°22' W 105
Perris, Calif., U.S. 33°47' N, 117°16' W 101
Perros-Guirec, Fr. 48°48' N, 3°28' W 150
Perry, Fla., U.S. 30°5' N, 83°34' W 96
Perry, Ga., U.S. 32°27' N, 83°44' W 96
Perry, Iowa, U.S. 41°49' N, 94°6' W 94
Perry, Mich., U.S. 42°49' N, 84°12' W 102
Perry, Ohio, U.S. 41°44' N, 81°7' W 102
Perry, Okla., U.S. 36°15' N, 97°17' W 92
Perry, Utah, U.S. 41°27' N, 112°1' W 90
Perry Island, Foxe Basin 67°49' N, 102°21' W 106
Perrysburg, Ohio, U.S. 41°32' N, 83°38' W 102
Perryton, Tex., U.S. 36°22' N, 100°49' W 92
Perşembe, Turk. 41°4' N, 37°45' E 156
Persepolis, ruin(s), Iran 30°2' N, 52°54' E 196
Pershore, U.K. 52°6' N, 2°5' W 162
Persian Gulf 26°40' N, 51°30' E 196
Pertek, Turk. 38°52' N, 39°19' E 195
Perth, Austral. 31°57' S, 115°32' E 230
Perth, Can. 44°54' N, 76°16' W 94
Perth-Andover, Can. 46°43' N, 67°42' W 94
Pertominsk, Russ. 64°47' N, 38°20' E 154
Pertunmaa, Fin. 61°30' N, 26°28' E 166
Peru, Ill., U.S. 41°19' N, 89°8' W 102
Peru, Ind., U.S. 40°45' N, 86°4' W 102
Peru, Me., U.S. 44°30' N, 70°26' W 104
Peru, Mo., U.S. 41°19' N, 89°8' W 94
Peru, Nebr., U.S. 40°28' N, 95°44' W 94
Peru, N.Y., U.S. 44°34' N, 73°34' W 104
Peru 8°44' S, 77°9' W 130
Peru, Vt., U.S. 43°14' N, 72°54' W 104
Peru Basin, South Pacific Ocean 11°59' S, 88°41' W 252
Peru-Chile Trench, South Pacific Ocean 18°8' S, 73°12' W 253
Perugia, It. 43°6' N, 12°23' E 156
Perugorría, Arg. 29°20' S, 58°34' W 139
Péruwelz, Belg. 50°29' N, 3°35' E 163
Pervari, Turk. 37°53' N, 42°32' E 195
Pervomaevka, Kaz. 42°5' N, 69°52' E 197
Pervomaysk, Russ. 54°49' N, 43°49' E 154
Pervomays'k, Ukr. 48°4' N, 30°58' E 156
Pervomayskīy, Kaz. 50°14' N, 81°58' E 184
Pervomayskiy, Russ. 53°15' N, 40°14' E 154
Pervomayskiy, Russ. 59°33' N, 61°23' E 154
Pervomayskiy, Russ. 51°29' N, 55°4' E 158
Pervomayskoye, Russ. 51°26' N, 47°40' E 158
Pervomayskoye, Russ. 57°4' N, 86°21' E 169
Pervoural'sk, Russ. 56°56' N, 59°57' E 154
Pervyy Kuril'skiy Proliv 50°43' N, 153°5' E 160
Pesaro, It. 43°54' N, 12°55' E 167
Pescadero, Calif., U.S. 37°14' N, 122°24' W 100
Pescadores see Penghu, islands, Taiwan, China 23°30' N, 119°30' E 191
Pescara, It. 42°27' N, 14°13' E 156
Peschanyy, Mys, Kaz. 43°2' N, 50°52' E 195
Peschici, It. 41°56' N, 16°1' E 168
Peschiera, It. 45°26' N, 10°40' E 167
Pesha, river, Russ. 66°28' N, 48°19' E 154
Peshawar, Pak. 34°0' N, 71°35' E 186
Peshawarun, ruin(s), Afghan. 31°29' N, 61°31' E 186
Peshtigo, Wis., U.S. 45°3' N, 87°47' W 94
Peski, Russ. 51°15' N, 42°29' E 158
Peskovka, Russ. 59°1' N, 52°25' E 154
Pesochnoye, Russ. 57°58' N, 39°7' E 154
Pesotum, Ill., U.S. 39°54' N, 88°17' W 102
Pest, adm. division, Hung. 47°13' N, 18°57' E 156
Peşteana Jiu, Rom. 44°50' N, 23°18' E 168
Pestovo, Russ. 58°37' N, 35°50' E 154
Pestravka, Russ. 52°24' N, 49°56' E 158
Petaḥ Tiqwa, Israel 32°5' N, 34°53' E 194
Petäjävesi, Fin. 62°14' N, 25°11' E 154
Petal, Miss., U.S. 31°19' N, 89°14' W 103
Petalax (Petolahti), Fin. 62°49' N, 21°24' E 154
Petaluma, Calif., U.S. 38°13' N, 122°39' W 100
Pétange, Lux. 49°32' N, 5°51' E 163
Petare, Venez. 10°27' N, 66°48' W 116
Petatlán, Mex. 17°29' N, 101°16' W 114
Petatlán, river, Mex. 26°14' N, 107°46' W 80
Petatlán, river, Mex. 17°20' N, 101°31' W 112
Petauke, Zambia 14°16' S, 31°16' E 224
Petén, region, Guatemala 16°4' N, 90°38' W 115
Petenwell Lake, Wis., U.S. 44°6' N, 90°16' W 102
Peter I Island, Antarctica 68°58' S, 90°43' W 248
Peter Lake, Can. 57°11' N, 104°29' W 108
Peter Pond Lake, Can. 55°58' N, 111°17' W 106
Peterbell, Can. 48°36' N, 83°22' W 94
Peterborough, Austral. 32°59' S, 138°49' E 231
Peterborough, Can. 44°18' N, 78°21' W 94
Peterborough, U.K. 52°34' N, 0°15' E 162
Petermann Bjerg, peak 73°3' N, 29°0' W 246
Petermann Gletscher, glacier 78°50' N, 62°8' W 72
Petersberg, Ger. 50°33' N, 9°42' E 167
Petersburg, Alas., U.S. 56°36' N, 132°51' W 106
Petersburg, Ill., U.S. 40°0' N, 89°51' W 102
Petersburg, Ind., U.S. 38°29' N, 87°16' W 102
Petersburg, Mich., U.S. 41°53' N, 83°42' W 102
Petersburg, Tex., U.S. 33°51' N, 101°36' W 96
Petersburg, Va., U.S. 37°11' N, 77°23' W 82
Petersburg, W. Va., U.S. 38°59' N, 79°8' W 94
Petersburg National Battlefield, Va., U.S. 37°12' N, 77°27' W 96
Petersfield, U.K. 51°0' N, 0°56' E 162
Petersham, Mass., U.S. 42°29' N, 72°12' W 104
Petit Port, Alg. 36°11' N, 0°23' E 164
Petit-Louango Faunal Reserve, Gabon 2°20' S, 9°17' E 206
Petitot, river, Can. 59°49' N, 123°28' W 106
Petitot, river, Can. 60°4' N, 122°43' W 108
Petkula, Fin. 67°40' N, 26°41' E 152
Petlad, India 22°27' N, 72°49' E 186
Petlalcingo, Mex. 18°4' N, 97°55' W 114
Peto, Mex. 20°6' N, 88°57' W 115
Petolahti see Petalax, Fin. 62°49' N, 21°24' E 154
Petoskey, Mich., U.S. 45°20' N, 85°0' W 82
Petra, Ostrova, islands, Laptev Sea 75°41' N, 108°52' E 160
Petra, ruin(s), Jordan 30°17' N, 35°23' E 180
Petra Velikogo, Zaliv 42°40' N, 131°45' E 200
Petras, Mount, peak, Antarctica 75°47' S, 127°55' W 248
Petre, Point, Can. 43°38' N, 77°26' W 94
Petriano, It. 43°46' N, 12°43' E 167
Petrich, Bulg. 41°24' N, 23°9' E 180
Petrified Forest National Park, Ariz., U.S. 34°44' N, 109°45' W 92
Petrinja, Croatia 45°26' N, 16°16' E 168
Petrodvorets, Russ. 59°49' N, 29°47' E 166
Petroglyphs, site, Hawai'i, U.S. 19°0' N, 155°50' W 99
Petrolândia, Braz. 9°1' S, 38°15' W 132
Petrólea, Col. 8°29' N, 72°40' W 136
Petrolia, Calif., U.S. 40°19' N, 124°18' W 90
Petrolia, Can. 42°52' N, 82°10' W 102
Petrolia, Tex., U.S. 33°59' N, 98°14' W 92
Petrolina, Braz. 9°20' S, 40°31' W 123
Petrolina de Goiás, Braz. 16°9' S, 49°21' W 138
Petropavlovsk, Kaz. 54°51' N, 69°7' E 184
Petropavlovsk Kamchatskiy, Russ. 53°10' N, 158°42' E 160
Petroşani, Rom. 45°24' N, 23°22' E 168
Petrovac, Mont. 42°11' N, 18°57' E 168
Petrovac, Serb. 44°23' N, 21°25' E 168
Petrovaradin, Serb. 45°14' N, 19°52' E 168
Petrovgrad see Zrenjanin, Serb. 45°23' N, 20°22' E 168
Petrovići, Mont. 42°46' N, 18°29' E 168
Petrovsk, Russ. 52°19' N, 45°26' E 158
Petrovsk Zabaykal'skiy, Russ. 51°25' N, 108°56' E 190
Petrovskoye, Russ. 57°0' N, 39°11' E 154
Petrozavodsk, Russ. 61°45' N, 34°23' E 154
Petrun', Russ. 66°27' N, 60°54' E 169
Petscapiskau Hill, peak, Can. 54°23' N, 64°34' W 111
Petten, Neth. 52°44' N, 4°39' E 163
Petukhovo, Russ. 55°5' N, 67°57' E 184
Peukankuala, Indonesia 4°6' N, 96°12' E 196
Peumo, Chile 34°22' S, 71°13' W 134
Peunasoe, island, Indonesia 5°31' N, 94°35' E 202
Peuplier, Pointe du, Can. 51°13' N, 79°32' W 110
Peurasuvanto, Fin. 67°48' N, 26°43' E 152
Peureulak, Indonesia 4°50' N, 97°53' E 196
Pevek, Russ. 69°40' N, 170°27' E 160
Pevensey, U.K. 50°49' N, 0°20' E 162
Pewsum, Ger. 53°26' N, 7°4' E 163
Peyia, Cyprus 34°53' N, 32°22' E 194
Peza, river, Russ. 65°37' N, 46°57' E 154
Pézenas, Fr. 43°27' N, 3°24' E 164
Pezmog, Russ. 61°53' N, 51°50' E 154
Pezu, Pak. 32°18' N, 70°47' E 186
Pfungstadt, Ger. 49°48' N, 8°35' E 167
Phaestus, ruin(s), Gr. 35°1' N, 24°42' E 156
Phalasarna, ruin(s), Gr. 35°29' N, 23°29' E 156
Phalodi, India 27°6' N, 72°21' E 186
Phalsbourg, Fr. 48°45' N, 7°14' E 163
Phan, Thai. 19°31' N, 99°43' E 202
Phan Ly, Vietnam 11°13' N, 108°34' E 202
Phan Rang, Vietnam 11°34' N, 108°58' E 202
Phan Thiet, Vietnam 10°56' N, 108°4' E 202
Phanae, ruin(s), Gr. 38°11' N, 25°49' E 156
Phangan, Ko, island, Thai. 9°49' N, 99°43' E 202
Phangnga, Thai. 8°30' N, 98°32' E 202
Pharus see Hvar, island, Croatia 43°3' N, 16°47' E 168
Phato, Thai. 9°47' N, 98°49' E 202
Phatthalung, Thai. 7°38' N, 100°6' E 196
Phayao, Thai. 19°13' N, 99°55' E 202
Phelps, Tex., U.S. 30°41' N, 95°26' W 103
Phelps Lake, lake, Can. 59°10' N, 103°45' W 108
Pheneus, ruin(s), Gr. 37°53' N, 22°14' E 156
Phenix City, Ala., U.S. 32°27' N, 85°1' W 96
Phetchabun, Thai. 16°25' N, 101°8' E 202
Phetchaburi, Thai. 13°7' N, 99°55' E 202
Phiafai, Laos 14°49' N, 105°58' E 202
Phibun Mangsaban, Thai. 15°15' N, 105°14' E 202
Phichai, Thai. 17°18' N, 100°6' E 202
Phichit, Thai. 16°25' N, 100°19' E 202
Philadelphia, Miss., U.S. 32°45' N, 89°7' W 103
Philadelphia, Pa., U.S. 39°57' N, 75°11' W 94
Philadelphia see 'Ammān, Jordan 31°56' N, 35°53' E 194
Philae, ruin(s), Egypt 23°56' N, 32°44' E 182
Philbin Inlet 74°5' S, 113°45' W 248
Philip, S. Dak., U.S. 44°2' N, 101°41' W 90
Philip Smith Mountains, Alas., U.S. 67°56' N, 149°31' W 98
Philippeville, Belg. 50°11' N, 4°32' E 167
Philippi, W. Va., U.S. 39°8' N, 80°3' W 94
Philippi, ruin(s), Gr. 41°0' N, 24°10' E 156
Philippine Basin, Philippine Sea 14°23' N, 128°46' E 254
Philippine Sea 15°8' N, 123°42' E 203
Philippine Trench, Philippine Sea 11°16' N, 127°0' E 254
Philippines 15°0' N, 121°0' E 203
Philippolis, S. Af. 30°16' S, 25°16' E 227
Philippopolis see Plovdiv, Bulg. 42°9' N, 24°45' E 156
Philippopolis see Shahbā', Syr. 32°51' N, 36°37' E 194
Philipstown, S. Af. 30°25' S, 24°27' E 227
Phillip Bay, Port 38°18' S, 143°6' E 230
Phillip Island, island, Austral. 38°56' S, 144°23' E 230
Phillips, Tex., U.S. 35°40' N, 101°22' W 92
Phillips, Wis., U.S. 45°41' N, 90°24' W 94
Phillips, Mount, peak, Austral. 24°29' S, 116°18' E 230
Phillipsburg, Kans., U.S. 39°44' N, 99°20' W 92
Phillipsburg, N.J., U.S. 40°41' N, 75°12' W 110
Philmont, N.Y., U.S. 42°14' N, 73°39' W 104
Philomath, Oreg., U.S. 44°31' N, 123°22' W 90
Philomena, Can. 55°9' N, 111°40' W 108
Phitsanulok, Thai. 16°52' N, 100°12' E 202
Phnom Bokor National Park, Cambodia 10°46' N, 103°34' E 172
Phnom Penh, Cambodia 11°32' N, 104°45' E 202
Pho, Laem, Thai. 6°54' N, 101°24' E 196
Phoenix, Ariz., U.S. 33°25' N, 112°8' W 92
Phoenix Islands, South Pacific Ocean 4°31' S, 173°41' W 238
Phon Phisai, Thai. 18°3' N, 103°6' E 202
Phong Tho, Vietnam 22°32' N, 103°21' E 202
Phôngsali, Laos 21°44' N, 102°5' E 202
Phra Thong, Ko, island, Thai. 8°47' N, 97°49' E 202
Phraaspa, ruin(s), Iran 36°44' N, 47°18' E 195
Phrae, Thai. 18°9' N, 100°9' E 202
Phran Kratai, Thai. 16°40' N, 99°37' E 202
Phrao, Thai. 18°7' N, 100°7' E 190
Phrao, Thai. 19°24' N, 99°11' E 202
Phrom Phiram, Thai. 17°3' N, 100°12' E 202
Phu Cat, Vietnam 14°1' N, 109°4' E 202
Phu Loc, Vietnam 16°17' N, 107°53' E 202
Phu Ly, Vietnam 20°33' N, 105°55' E 198
Phu My, Vietnam 14°12' N, 109°2' E 202
Phu Quoc, Dao, island, Vietnam 9°53' N, 103°33' E 202
Phu Rieng, Vietnam 11°42' N, 106°56' E 202
Phuket, Thai. 7°54' N, 98°23' E 202
Phuket, Ko, island, Thai. 7°38' N, 97°55' E 196
Phum Kompadou, Cambodia 13°48' N, 107°25' E 202
Phuntsholing, Bhutan 26°52' N, 89°20' E 197
Phuoc Long, Vietnam 9°27' N, 105°25' E 202
Phuthaditjhada, S. Af. 28°33' S, 28°47' E 227
Phutthaisong, Thai. 15°28' N, 102°56' E 202
Phyarpon, Myanmar 16°17' N, 95°39' E 202
Pi, Pol. 53°8' N, 16°44' E 152
Piacenza, It. 45°2' N, 9°40' E 167
Piacouadie, Lac, lake, Can. 51°13' N, 71°36' W 111
Piadena, It. 45°7' N, 10°21' E 167
Piana, Fr. 42°14' N, 8°38' E 156
Pianello Val Tidone, It. 44°56' N, 9°23' E 167
Pianguan, China 39°27' N, 111°29' E 198
Pianoro, It. 44°22' N, 11°20' E 167
Pianosa, It. 42°35' N, 10°5' E 156
Piapot, Can. 49°58' N, 109°7' W 90
Piaseczno, Pol. 52°4' N, 21°1' E 152
Piatã, Braz. 13°13' S, 41°45' W 138
Piatra, Rom. 43°48' N, 25°10' E 156
Piatra Neamţ, Rom. 46°56' N, 26°22' E 156
Piauí, adm. division, Braz. 10°24' S, 45°55' W 130
Piauí, Serra do, Braz. 9°52' S, 42°4' W 132
Piaxtla, river, Mex. 23°54' N, 106°6' W 114
Piazzi, Isla, island, Chile 51°36' S, 73°59' W 134
Pibor Post, Sudan 6°44' N, 33°6' E 224
Pic, river, Can. 48°51' N, 86°10' W 94
Pica, Chile 20°31' S, 69°22' W 137
Picacho, Ariz., U.S. 32°43' N, 111°28' W 92
Picacho Pass, Ariz., U.S. 32°37' N, 111°24' W 92
Picachos, Cerro dos, peak, Mex. 29°21' N, 114°12' W 92
Picardie, adm. division, Fr. 49°35' N, 1°44' E 150
Picardy, region, Fr. 49°58' N, 1°57' E 163
Picassent, Sp. 39°20' N, 0°29' E 164
Picayune, Miss., U.S. 30°31' N, 89°40' W 103
Picerno, It. 40°39' N, 15°38' E 156
Pichanal, Arg. 23°17' S, 64°13' W 134
Picher, Okla., U.S. 36°57' N, 94°51' W 96
Pichhor, India 25°56' N, 78°23' E 197
Pichilemu, Chile 34°25' S, 72°0' W 134
Pichilingue, Mex. 24°17' N, 110°20' W 112
Pickens, Miss., U.S. 32°53' N, 89°59' W 103
Pickerel Lake, Can. 48°33' N, 91°59' W 110
Pickering, U.K. 54°14' N, 0°47' E 162
Pickering Nunatak, peak, Antarctica 71°27' S, 70°58' E 248
Pickle Crow, Can. 51°29' N, 90°4' W 110
Pickle Lake, Can. 51°28' N, 90°11' W 110
Pickton, Tex., U.S. 33°1' N, 95°23' W 103
Pico da Neblina National Park, Braz. 0°7' N, 65°34' W 136
Pico de Orizaba National Park, Mex. 19°0' N, 97°34' W 72
Pico de Tancítaro National Park, Mex. 19°18' N, 102°43' W 72
Pico, island, Port. 38°21' N, 28°24' W 253
Pico Truncado, Arg. 46°45' S, 67°57' W 134
Picos, Braz. 7°6' S, 41°26' W 132
Picton, Can. 44°0' N, 77°9' W 94
Picton, N.Z. 41°19' S, 174°0' E 240
Pictou, Can. 45°41' N, 62°43' W 111
Picture Gorge, site, Oreg., U.S. 44°32' N, 119°43' W 90
Pictured Rocks, Mich., U.S. 46°30' N, 87°10' W 80
Pictured Rocks National Lakeshore, Mich., U.S. 46°12' N, 92°34' W 80
Picuris Peak, N. Mex., U.S. 36°13' N, 105°44' W 92
Pidurutalagala, peak, Sri Lanka 6°58' N, 80°41' E 188
Piedecuesta, Col. 6°58' N, 73°4' W 136
Piedmont, Mo., U.S. 37°9' N, 90°42' W 96
Piedmont, adm. division, It. 44°51' N, 6°58' E 165
Piedra, Calif., U.S. 36°49' N, 119°23' W 100
Piedra del Águila, Arg. 40°2' S, 70°6' W 134
Piedra Lais, Venez. 3°6' N, 65°56' W 136
Piedra Parada, ruin(s), Mex. 16°48' N, 93°33' W 115
Piedra Shotel, Arg. 44°23' S, 70°30' W 134
Piedra Sola, Uru. 32°4' S, 56°19' W 139
Piedrabuena, Sp. 39°2' N, 4°11' W 164
Piedras Blancas, Point, Calif., U.S. 35°41' N, 121°29' W 100
Piedras Negras, Mex. 28°40' N, 100°31' W 92
Piedras Negras, ruin(s), Guatemala 17°11' N, 91°23' W 115
Piedras, Punta, Arg. 35°25' S, 57°9' W 139
Piedras, river, Peru 11°22' S, 70°42' W 137
Piedritas, Arg. 34°47' S, 62°58' W 139
Piedruja, Latv. 55°47' N, 27°26' E 166
Pieksämäki, Fin. 62°16' N, 27°7' E 154
Piendamó, Col. 2°38' N, 76°33' W 136
Pieniężno, Pol. 54°13' N, 20°8' E 166
Pierce, Idaho, U.S. 46°28' N, 115°47' W 90
Pierce, Nebr., U.S. 42°11' N, 97°32' W 90
Piéria, Óros, Gr. 40°7' N, 22°3' E 156
Pierre, S. Dak., U.S. 44°21' N, 100°26' W 90
Pierre Lake, lake, Can. 49°28' N, 81°6' W 94
Pierrefonds, Fr. 49°20' N, 2°58' E 163
Pierrelatte, Fr. 44°22' N, 4°41' E 150
Pierson, Fla., U.S. 29°14' N, 81°28' W 105
Piet Retief, S. Af. 27°1' S, 30°45' E 227
Pietarsaari see Jakobstad, Fin. 63°39' N, 22°39' E 152
Pietermaritzburg, S. Af. 29°35' S, 30°21' E 227
Pietersburg see Polokwane, S. Af. 23°54' S, 29°26' E 227
Pietro Verri, Somalia 3°20' N, 45°39' E 218
Pietrosu, peak, Rom. 47°5' N, 25°4' E 156
Pietrosul, peak, Rom. 47°34' N, 24°32' E 156
Pieve d'Alpago, It. 46°9' N, 12°20' E 167
Pieve di Cadore, It. 46°25' N, 12°20' E 167
Pigailoe (West Fayu Atoll) 8°36' N, 146°3' E 192
Pigeon, Mich., U.S. 43°49' N, 83°16' W 102
Pigeon Cove, Mass., U.S. 42°40' N, 70°38' W 104
Pigeon Lake, Can. 53°2' N, 114°24' W 108
Pigeon Point, Lake Superior 47°46' N, 89°36' W 94
Pigeon, river, Can. 52°13' N, 96°58' W 108
Piggott, Ark., U.S. 36°22' N, 90°12' W 96
Pigüé, Arg. 37°37' S, 62°23' W 139
Pihlava, Fin. 61°32' N, 21°36' E 166
Pihtipudas, Fin. 63°21' N, 25°32' E 154
Pihuamo, Mex. 19°15' N, 103°22' W 114
Pihyŏn, N. Korea 40°0' N, 124°35' E 200
Pi'ilanihale Heiau, site, Hawai'i, U.S. 20°47' N, 156°6' W 99
Pijijiapan, Mex. 15°40' N, 93°15' W 115
Pikalevo, Russ. 59°33' N, 34°5' E 154
Pikangikum, Can. 51°48' N, 93°57' W 82
Pike, river, Wis., U.S. 45°31' N, 88°3' W 94
Pikelot, island, F.S.M. 8°17' N, 147°41' E 192
Pikes Peak, Colo., U.S. 38°49' N, 105°7' W 90
Piketberg, S. Af. 32°54' S, 18°43' E 227
Piketon, Ohio, U.S. 39°3' N, 83°1' W 102
Pikeville, Ky., U.S. 37°29' N, 82°32' W 96
Pikounda, Congo 0°30' N, 16°38' E 218
Pikwitonei, Can. 55°35' N, 97°12' W 108
Pila, Arg. 36°2' S, 58°10' W 139
Pila, peak, Sp. 38°15' N, 1°14' W 164
Pilani, India 28°21' N, 75°37' E 197
Pilão Arcado, Braz. 9°57' S, 42°32' W 132
Pilar, Arg. 31°26' S, 61°16' W 139
Pilar, Parag. 26°51' S, 58°16' W 139
Pilar, Cabo, Chile 52°46' S, 76°6' W 134
Pilatovica, peak, Europe 43°7' N, 20°54' E 168
Pilaya, river, Bol. 21°13' S, 64°29' W 137
Pilcaniyeu, Arg. 41°9' S, 70°41' W 134
Pilcomayo, river, Bol. 19°19' S, 65°2' W 137
Pil'dozero, Russ. 65°40' N, 33°27' E 152
Pil'gyn, Russ. 69°19' N, 179°3' E 98
Pilibhit, India 28°37' N, 79°47' E 197
Pilio, Gr. 38°45' N, 23°34' E 156
Pílio, Óros, peak, Gr. 39°25' N, 22°58' E 156
Pillcopata, Peru 13°5' S, 71°11' W 137
Pilling, U.K. 53°55' N, 2°55' W 162
Pilón, river, Mex. 25°15' N, 100°31' W 114
Pilón-Lajas National Park, Bol. 14°51' S, 66°41' W 137
Pílos, Gr. 36°54' N, 21°41' E 156
Pilot Butte, peak, Oreg., U.S. 44°3' N, 121°20' W 90
Pilot Knob, Mo., U.S. 37°37' N, 90°39' W 96
Pilot Knob, peak, Ark., U.S. 35°33' N, 93°20' W 96
Pilot Knob, peak, Idaho, U.S. 45°52' N, 115°47' W 90
Pilot Mound, Can. 49°12' N, 98°55' W 108
Pilot Peak, Nev., U.S. 38°20' N, 118°4' W 90
Pilot Peak, Nev., U.S. 41°0' N, 114°9' W 90
Pilot Peak, Wyo., U.S. 44°57' N, 109°59' W 90
Pilot Point, Alas., U.S. 57°31' N, 157°38' W 98
Pilottown, La., U.S. 29°11' N, 89°15' W 103
Pilsen see Plzeň, Czech Rep. 49°44' N, 13°23' E 152
Pil'skaya Guba, Russ. 66°47' N, 34°12' E 152
Piltene, Latv. 57°13' N, 21°40' E 166
Pil'tun, Zaliv 52°48' N, 141°39' E 160
Pim, river, Russ. 62°20' N, 71°29' E 169
Pimenta Bueno, Braz. 11°41' S, 61°15' W 130
Piña, Pan. 9°16' N, 80°2' W 130
Pinacate, Cerro del, peak, Mex. 31°44' N, 113°35' W 92
Pinang, island, Malaysia 5°14' N, 99°44' E 196
Pinangah, Malaysia 5°15' N, 116°48' E 203
Pinar del Río, Cuba 22°25' N, 83°43' W 116
Pinar del Río, adm. division, Cuba 22°33' N, 83°55' W 116
Pinar del Río, island, Cuba 23°1' N, 83°27' W 116
Pınarbaşı, Turk. 38°42' N, 36°24' E 156
Pinardville, N.H., U.S. 42°59' N, 71°31' W 104
Pinas, Arg. 31°9' S, 65°28' W 134
Pinatubo, Mount, peak, Philippines 15°5' N, 120°1' E 238
Pinawa, Can. 50°8' N, 95°52' W 90
Pincehely, Hung. 46°41' N, 18°25' E 168
Pincén, Arg. 34°51' S, 63°55' W 139
Pincher, Can. 49°31' N, 113°57' W 90
Pincher Creek, Can. 49°28' N, 113°56' W 90
Pinchi Lake, lake, Can. 54°32' N, 124°49' W 108
Pinckney, Mich., U.S. 42°26' N, 83°57' W 102
Pinconning, Mich., U.S. 43°50' N, 83°59' W 102
Pîncota, Rom. 46°20' N, 21°43' E 168
Pindamonhangaba, Braz. 22°57' S, 45°27' W 138
Pinders Point, Bahamas 26°27' N, 78°42' W 105
Pindi Bhattian, Pak. 31°54' N, 73°14' E 186
Pindi Gheb, Pak. 33°14' N, 72°17' E 186
Píndos, peak, Gr. 39°18' N, 21°28' E 156
Pindus Mountains, Gr. 39°54' N, 20°40' E 156
Pine Bluff, Ark., U.S. 34°12' N, 92°1' W 96
Pine Bluffs, Wyo., U.S. 41°11' N, 104°5' W 90
Pine, Cape, Can. 46°38' N, 54°6' W 111
Pine City, Minn., U.S. 45°47' N, 93°0' W 94
Pine Creek, Austral. 13°51' S, 131°51' E 231
Pine Falls, Can. 50°31' N, 96°17' W 108
Pine Flat, Calif., U.S. 35°52' N, 118°39' W 101
Pine Flat Lake, Calif., U.S. 36°50' N, 119°32' W 101
Pine Forest Range, Nev., U.S. 41°41' N, 119°7' W 90
Pine Hill, Ala., U.S. 31°58' N, 87°35' W 103
Pine Hills, Fla., U.S. 28°34' N, 81°28' W 105
Pine Island, Fla., U.S. 26°37' N, 82°25' W 105
Pine Island Bay 74°36' S, 97°34' W 248
Pine Mountain, Ky., U.S. 37°17' N, 82°36' W 96
Pine Mountain, peak, Calif., U.S. 35°41' N, 121°9' W 100
Pine Mountain, peak, Calif., U.S. 35°33' N, 118°49' W 101
Pine Pass, Can. 55°23' N, 122°41' W 108
Pine Plains, N.Y., U.S. 41°58' N, 73°40' W 104
Pine Point, Can. 60°46' N, 114°19' W 73
Pine Point, Can. 60°46' N, 114°22' W 108
Pine Point, Me., U.S. 43°32' N, 70°21' W 104
Pine River, Can. 51°46' N, 100°33' W 90
Pine River, Can. 55°55' N, 107°28' W 108
Pine River, Minn., U.S. 46°42' N, 94°25' W 90
Pine, river, Can. 55°52' N, 121°7' W 108
Pine, river, Mich., U.S. 44°1' N, 85°39' W 102
Pine Valley, Can. 55°38' N, 122°10' W 108
Pinecrest, Calif., U.S. 38°11' N, 120°1' W 100
Pinedale, Calif., U.S. 36°50' N, 119°48' W 92
Pinega, Russ. 64°43' N, 43°19' E 154
Pinega, river, Russ. 63°44' N, 45°11' E 154
Pinehouse Lake, Can. 55°33' N, 107°14' W 108
Pinehouse Lake, Can. 55°30' N, 106°37' W 108
Pinehurst, Ga., U.S. 32°11' N, 83°46' W 96
Pinehurst, N.C., U.S. 35°11' N, 79°29' W 96
Pineland, Tex., U.S. 31°14' N, 93°58' W 103
Pinellas Park, Fla., U.S. 27°51' N, 82°42' W 105
Pinerolo, It. 44°53' N, 7°20' E 167
Pinetown, S. Af. 29°49' S, 30°46' E 227
Pineville, Ky., U.S. 36°44' N, 83°43' W 96
Pineville, La., U.S. 31°18' N, 92°26' W 103
Piney, Fr. 48°22' N, 4°19' E 163
Piney Buttes, Mont., U.S. 47°27' N, 107°14' W 90
Piney Point, Fla., U.S. 29°46' N, 83°35' W 105
Piney Woods, Miss., U.S. 32°2' N, 89°59' W 103
Ping, river, Thai. 16°8' N, 99°46' E 202
Pingba, China 26°26' N, 106°14' E 198
Pingchang, China 31°35' N, 107°4' E 198
Pingdingshan, China 33°44' N, 113°19' E 198
Pingdu, China 36°49' N, 119°58' E 198
Pinggang, China 42°56' N, 124°50' E 200
Pingguo, China 23°18' N, 107°34' E 198
Pingjiang, China 28°45' N, 113°37' E 198
Pingle, China 24°35' N, 110°41' E 198
Pingli, China 32°29' N, 109°24' E 198
Pingliang, China 35°31' N, 106°39' E 198
Pinglu, China 39°31' N, 112°17' E 198
Pinglu, China 34°53' N, 111°12' E 198
Pingluo, China 38°57' N, 106°33' E 198
Pingnan, China 23°34' N, 110°23' E 198
Pingquan, China 41°2' N, 118°39' E 198
Pingsha, China 22°2' N, 113°12' E 198
Pingtan, China 25°28' N, 119°51' E 198
Pingtang, China 25°50' N, 107°17' E 198
Pingtung, Taiwan, China 22°43' N, 120°31' E 198
Pingwu, China 32°28' N, 104°34' E 198

Primrose Lake, *Can.* 54°46′ N, 110°37′ W **108**
Prince Albert, *Can.* 53°10′ N, 105°46′ W **108**
Prince Albert, *S. Af.* 33°15′ S, 22°2′ E **227**
Prince Albert Mountains, *Antarctica* 75°43′ S, 179°49′ E **248**
Prince Albert National Park, *Can.* 53°40′ N, 106°52′ W **108**
Prince Albert Peninsula, *Can.* 72°24′ N, 124°18′ W **106**
Prince Albert Sound 70°23′ N, 110°14′ W **246**
Prince Alfred, Cape, *Can.* 74°7′ N, 132°53′ W **106**
Prince Charles Island, *Can.* 67°18′ N, 84°1′ W **106**
Prince Charles's Cave, site 57°26′ N, 6°16′ W **150**
Prince Edward Fracture Zone, *Indian Ocean* 44°27′ S, 35°49′ E **254**
Prince Edward Island, *Can.* 46°35′ N, 62°1′ W **106**
Prince Edward Island, adm. division, *Can.* 46°18′ N, 63°31′ W **111**
Prince Edward Islands, *Indian Ocean* 46°47′ S, 37°53′ E **254**
Prince George, *Can.* 53°44′ N, 122°48′ W **106**
Prince Gustaf Adolf Sea 78°44′ N, 105°4′ W **246**
Prince of Wales Island, *Alas., U.S.* 55°18′ N, 135°26′ W **98**
Prince of Wales Island, *Austral.* 11°18′ S, 141°21′ E **192**
Prince of Wales Island, *Can.* 71°17′ N, 103°2′ W **106**
Prince of Wales Strait 72°19′ N, 120°33′ W **72**
Prince Patrick Island, *Can.* 75°38′ N, 126°11′ W **106**
Prince Regent Inlet 72°52′ N, 90°5′ W **246**
Prince Regent Nature Reserve, *Austral.* 15°39′ S, 124°56′ E **238**
Prince Rupert, *Can.* 54°17′ N, 130°19′ W **108**
Prince William Forest Park, *Va., U.S.* 38°34′ N, 77°27′ W **94**
Prince William Sound 60°4′ N, 147°27′ W **98**
Princess Anne, *Md., U.S.* 38°12′ N, 75°41′ W **94**
Princess Astrid Coast, *Antarctica* 71°37′ S, 4°26′ E **248**
Princess Martha Coast, *Antarctica* 75°5′ S, 27°22′ W **248**
Princess Ragnhild Coast, *Antarctica* 70°44′ S, 23°46′ E **248**
Princeton, *Can.* 49°25′ N, 120°32′ W **90**
Princeton, *Ill., U.S.* 41°22′ N, 89°27′ W **102**
Princeton, *Mo., U.S.* 40°23′ N, 93°35′ W **94**
Princeton, *N.J., U.S.* 40°20′ N, 74°40′ W **94**
Princeton, *Wis., U.S.* 43°51′ N, 89°8′ W **102**
Princeville, *Ill., U.S.* 40°55′ N, 89°45′ W **102**
Principe Channel 53°21′ N, 130°24′ W **108**
Príncipe da Beira, *Braz.* 12°28′ S, 64°24′ W **137**
Príncipe, island, *Sao Tome and Principe* 1°21′ N, 6°33′ E **214**
Prineville, *Oreg., U.S.* 44°17′ N, 120°50′ W **82**
Prins Karls Forland, island, *Nor.* 78°53′ N, 3°57′ W **246**
Prinzapolka, *Nicar.* 13°22′ N, 83°36′ W **115**
Prior, Cabo 43°31′ N, 8°38′ W **150**
Priozersk, *Russ.* 61°2′ N, 30°7′ E **166**
Priozerskoye, *Russ.* 45°15′ N, 44°49′ E **158**
Prisaca, *Rom.* 45°52′ N, 26°47′ E **158**
Prishtina (Priština), *Kos.* 42°40′ N, 21°10′ E **168**
Prislop, Pasul, pass, *Rom.* 47°36′ N, 24°53′ E **152**
Priština see Prishtina, *Kos.* 42°40′ N, 21°10′ E **168**
Pritchett, *Colo., U.S.* 37°22′ N, 102°52′ W **92**
Pritzwalk, *Ger.* 53°10′ N, 12°11′ E **152**
Privlaka, *Croatia* 44°15′ N, 15°6′ E **156**
Privodino, *Russ.* 61°4′ N, 46°34′ E **154**
Privolzhsk, *Russ.* 57°21′ N, 41°17′ E **154**
Privolzhskaya Vozvyshennost', *Russ.* 53°31′ N, 46°34′ E **154**
Privolzhskiy, *Russ.* 51°19′ N, 46°6′ E **158**
Privolzh'ye, *Russ.* 52°51′ N, 48°39′ E **154**
Priyutnoye, *Russ.* 46°3′ N, 43°20′ E **158**
Prizren, *Kos.* 42°13′ N, 20°43′ E **168**
Prizzi, *It.* 37°44′ N, 13°26′ E **156**
Prnjavor, *Bosn. and Herzg.* 44°51′ N, 17°39′ E **168**
Prnjavor, *Serb.* 44°41′ N, 19°23′ E **168**
Proberta, *Calif., U.S.* 40°5′ N, 122°11′ W **90**
Probizhna, *Ukr.* 49°0′ N, 25°58′ E **152**
Probstzella, *Ger.* 50°32′ N, 11°24′ E **152**
Proctor, *Minn., U.S.* 46°45′ N, 92°15′ W **94**
Proctor, *Vt., U.S.* 43°39′ N, 73°4′ W **104**
Proddatur, *India* 14°44′ N, 78°35′ E **188**
Prodromi, *Cyprus* 35°1′ N, 32°23′ E **194**
Progreso, *Mex.* 21°17′ N, 89°40′ W **116**
Progress, Russia, station, *Antarctica* 69°33′ S, 76°34′ E **248**
Progresso, *Braz.* 9°47′ S, 71°44′ W **137**
Prokhladnyy, *Russ.* 43°44′ N, 44°0′ E **195**
Prokhorkino, *Russ.* 59°30′ N, 79°28′ E **169**
Prokop'yevsk, *Russ.* 53°53′ N, 86°49′ E **184**
Prokuplje, *Serb.* 43°14′ N, 21°35′ E **168**
Proletarsk, *Russ.* 46°41′ N, 41°35′ E **158**
Proletarskiy, *Russ.* 50°46′ N, 35°49′ E **158**
Prolivy, *Russ.* 65°17′ N, 32°14′ E **152**
Prolog, *Bosn. and Herzg.* 43°46′ N, 16°49′ E **168**
Promissão, *Braz.* 18°18′ S, 55°40′ W **132**
Promyshlennyy, *Kaz.* 51°7′ N, 71°35′ E **184**
Pronsfeld, *Ger.* 50°9′ N, 6°20′ E **167**
Prophet River, *Can.* 58°5′ N, 122°45′ W **108**
Prophet, river, *Can.* 57°34′ N, 124°5′ W **108**
Prophetstown, *Ill., U.S.* 41°40′ N, 89°57′ W **102**
Propriá, *Braz.* 10°16′ S, 36°52′ W **132**
Prorva, *Kaz.* 45°56′ N, 53°17′ E **158**
Prosek, *Alban.* 41°44′ N, 19°56′ E **168**
Prosperity, *W. Va., U.S.* 37°49′ N, 81°13′ W **94**
Prosser, *Wash., U.S.* 46°10′ N, 119°47′ W **90**
Protection, *Kans., U.S.* 37°11′ N, 99°30′ W **92**
Protem, *S. Af.* 34°14′ S, 20°4′ E **227**
Prouts Neck, *Me., U.S.* 43°31′ N, 70°20′ W **104**
Provencal, *La., U.S.* 31°38′ N, 93°13′ W **103**
Provence, region, *Fr.* 43°11′ N, 5°35′ E **165**
Provence-Alpes-Côte D'Azur, adm. division, *Fr.* 43°54′ N, 4°52′ E **150**
Proves, *It.* 46°28′ N, 11°1′ E **167**
Providence, *Ky., U.S.* 37°23′ N, 87°46′ W **96**
Providence, *R.I., U.S.* 41°49′ N, 71°27′ W **104**
Providence Island, *Seychelles* 9°32′ S, 51°7′ E **218**
Providence Mountains, *Calif., U.S.* 35°1′ N, 115°35′ W **101**
Providencia, Isla de, island, *Col.* 13°4′ N, 82°8′ W **115**
Providência, Serra da, *Braz.* 10°43′ S, 61°36′ W **130**
Provideniya, *Russ.* 64°31′ N, 173°8′ W **98**
Provincetown, *Mass., U.S.* 42°2′ N, 70°12′ W **104**
Provins, *Fr.* 48°33′ N, 3°17′ E **163**
Provo, *Serb.* 44°40′ N, 19°54′ E **168**
Provo, *Utah, U.S.* 40°14′ N, 111°38′ W **90**
Provost, *Can.* 52°21′ N, 110°16′ W **108**
Prozor, *Bosn. and Herzg.* 43°47′ N, 17°36′ E **168**
Prudentópolis, *Braz.* 25°15′ S, 51°0′ W **138**
Prudhoe Bay, *Alas., U.S.* 70°12′ N, 148°22′ W **98**
Prud'homme, *Can.* 52°20′ N, 105°54′ W **108**
Prüm, *Ger.* 50°12′ N, 6°24′ E **167**
Prüm, river, *Ger.* 50°8′ N, 6°17′ E **167**
Pruna, *Sp.* 36°58′ N, 5°14′ W **164**
Prundeni, *Rom.* 44°45′ N, 24°14′ E **156**
Prusac, *Bosn. and Herzg.* 44°5′ N, 17°23′ E **168**
Prussia, region, *Pol.* 54°29′ N, 19°50′ E **166**
Pruszcz Gdański, *Pol.* 54°16′ N, 18°36′ E **166**
Prut, river, *Ukr.* 48°18′ N, 26°2′ E **158**
Pryazha, *Russ.* 61°41′ N, 33°41′ E **154**
Prydz Bay 69°36′ S, 73°49′ E **248**
Pryluky, *Ukr.* 50°34′ N, 32°26′ E **158**
Prymors'k, *Ukr.* 46°43′ N, 36°17′ E **156**
Prymors'ke, *Ukr.* 46°23′ N, 35°19′ E **156**
Pryor, *Okla., U.S.* 36°17′ N, 95°19′ W **94**
Pryor Mountains, *Mont., U.S.* 45°17′ N, 108°32′ W **90**
Prypyats', river, *Belarus* 51°39′ N, 29°36′ E **158**
Przemyśl, *Pol.* 49°45′ N, 22°47′ E **152**
Przeradz, *Pol.* 53°46′ N, 16°33′ E **152**
Przerośl, *Pol.* 54°14′ N, 22°38′ E **166**
Przeworsk, *Pol.* 50°3′ N, 22°32′ E **152**
Przytu, *Pol.* 53°22′ N, 22°17′ E **152**
Psará, *Gr.* 38°32′ N, 25°33′ E **156**
Psiloreítis see Ídi, Óros, peak, *Gr.* 35°12′ N, 24°41′ E **156**
Pskov, *Russ.* 57°49′ N, 28°22′ E **166**
Pskov, adm. division, *Russ.* 57°21′ N, 28°27′ E **166**
Ps'ol, river, *Ukr.* 49°17′ N, 33°25′ E **158**
Psunj, peak, *Croatia* 45°22′ N, 17°17′ E **168**
Ptsich, river, *Belarus* 53°51′ N, 27°4′ E **152**
Ptuj, *Slov.* 46°25′ N, 15°52′ E **168**
Pua, *Thai.* 19°14′ N, 100°53′ E **202**
Puán, *Arg.* 37°35′ S, 62°47′ W **139**
Puarent', Ozero, lake, *Russ.* 68°44′ N, 33°7′ E **152**
Pubei, *China* 22°15′ N, 109°31′ E **198**
Puca Barranca, *Peru* 2°43′ S, 73°32′ W **136**
Puca Urco, *Peru* 2°22′ S, 71°54′ W **136**
Pucacuro, river, *Peru* 2°55′ S, 75°18′ W **136**
Pucallpa, *Peru* 8°25′ S, 74°36′ W **137**
Pucará, *Bol.* 18°44′ S, 64°18′ W **137**
Pucará, *Peru* 15°6′ S, 70°24′ W **137**
Pucarani, *Bol.* 16°24′ S, 68°30′ W **137**
Pucheng, *China* 34°56′ N, 109°34′ E **198**
Pucheng, *China* 27°58′ N, 118°30′ E **198**
Puckett, *Miss., U.S.* 32°3′ N, 89°46′ W **103**
Pudasjärvi, *Fin.* 65°24′ N, 26°52′ E **152**
Pudem, *Russ.* 58°18′ N, 52°15′ E **154**
Pudimoe, *S. Af.* 27°26′ S, 24°42′ E **227**
Pudino, *Russ.* 57°35′ N, 79°26′ E **169**
Pudozh, *Russ.* 61°49′ N, 36°38′ E **154**
Pudu, *Indonesia* 0°25′ N, 102°16′ E **196**
Puducherry, adm. division, *India* 11°44′ N, 79°40′ E **188**
Puducherry (Pondicherry), *India* 11°56′ N, 79°47′ E **188**
Pudukkottai, *India* 10°25′ N, 78°48′ E **188**
Puebla, *Mex.* 18°59′ N, 98°16′ W **114**
Puebla, adm. division, *Mex.* 18°51′ N, 98°31′ W **114**
Puebla de Alcocer, *Sp.* 38°59′ N, 5°16′ W **150**
Puebla de Don Rodrigo, *Sp.* 39°4′ N, 4°38′ W **164**
Pueblo, *Colo., U.S.* 38°17′ N, 104°39′ W **90**
Pueblo Bonito, site, *N. Mex., U.S.* 36°3′ N, 108°2′ W **92**
Pueblo Mountains, *Oreg., U.S.* 42°14′ N, 118°57′ W **90**
Pueblo Nuevo, *Mex.* 23°23′ N, 105°21′ W **114**
Pueblo Nuevo, *Peru* 16°44′ S, 72°27′ W **137**
Pueblo Nuevo, *Venez.* 11°57′ N, 69°57′ W **136**
Pueblo Nuevo Tiquisate, *Guatemala* 14°15′ N, 91°22′ W **115**
Puelches, *Arg.* 38°9′ S, 65°56′ W **134**
Puente de Ixtla, *Mex.* 18°35′ N, 99°21′ W **114**
Puente la Reina (Gares), *Sp.* 42°39′ N, 1°49′ W **164**
Puente-Genil, *Sp.* 37°23′ N, 4°47′ W **164**
Pu'er, *China* 22°56′ N, 101°3′ E **202**
Puertecitos, *Mex.* 30°14′ N, 114°41′ W **92**
Puerto Acosta, *Bol.* 15°34′ S, 69°15′ W **137**
Puerto Aisén, *Chile* 45°25′ S, 72°59′ W **123**
Puerto Alegre, *Peru* 8°44′ S, 74°14′ W **130**
Puerto Alfonso, *Col.* 2°13′ S, 71°2′ W **136**
Puerto América, *Peru* 4°42′ S, 77°3′ W **130**
Puerto Ángel, *Mex.* 15°39′ N, 96°31′ W **112**
Puerto Arista, *Mex.* 15°58′ N, 93°50′ W **115**
Puerto Armuelles, *Pan.* 8°18′ N, 82°51′ W **115**
Puerto Asís, *Col.* 0°27′ N, 76°32′ W **136**
Puerto Aurora, *Peru* 2°12′ S, 74°18′ W **136**
Puerto Ayacucho, *Venez.* 5°37′ N, 67°32′ W **136**
Puerto Ayora, *Ecua.* 0°45′ N, 90°20′ W **130**
Puerto Bahía Negra, *Parag.* 20°12′ S, 58°14′ W **132**
Puerto Baquerizo Moreno, *Ecua.* 0°57′ N, 89°27′ W **130**
Puerto Barrios, *Guatemala* 15°42′ N, 88°36′ W **115**
Puerto Belgrano, *Arg.* 38°53′ S, 62°6′ W **139**
Puerto Bermúdez, *Peru* 10°19′ S, 74°54′ W **137**
Puerto Berrío, *Col.* 6°28′ N, 74°26′ W **136**
Puerto Boy, *Col.* 0°11′ N, 74°53′ W **136**
Puerto Cabello, *Venez.* 10°27′ N, 68°1′ W **136**
Puerto Cabezas, *Nicar.* 14°2′ N, 83°24′ W **115**
Puerto Cahuinari, *Col.* 1°26′ S, 70°44′ W **136**
Puerto Capaz see El Jabha, *Mor.* 35°12′ N, 4°40′ W **150**
Puerto Carabuco, *Bol.* 15°44′ S, 69°5′ W **137**
Puerto Carlos, *Col.* 1°41′ S, 71°52′ W **136**
Puerto Carlos, *Peru* 12°57′ S, 70°15′ W **137**
Puerto Carranza, *Col.* 2°38′ S, 70°11′ W **136**
Puerto Carreño, *Col.* 6°9′ N, 67°25′ W **136**
Puerto Chicama, *Peru* 7°43′ S, 79°26′ W **130**
Puerto Coig, *Arg.* 50°54′ S, 69°13′ W **134**
Puerto Colombia, *Col.* 10°57′ N, 74°57′ W **136**
Puerto Copal, *Peru* 3°1′ S, 74°46′ W **136**
Puerto Córdoba, *Col.* 1°20′ S, 69°53′ W **136**
Puerto Cortés, *Hond.* 15°49′ N, 87°56′ W **116**
Puerto Cumarebo, *Venez.* 11°27′ N, 69°22′ W **136**
Puerto Curaray, *Peru* 2°26′ S, 74°7′ W **136**
Puerto de Lomas, *Peru* 15°34′ S, 74°50′ W **137**
Puerto de Luna, *N. Mex., U.S.* 34°49′ N, 104°37′ W **92**
Puerto de Nutrias, *Venez.* 8°5′ N, 69°20′ W **136**
Puerto de Santa Cruz, *Sp.* 39°18′ N, 5°51′ W **164**
Puerto Deseado, *Arg.* 47°43′ S, 65°55′ W **134**
Puerto El Triunfo, *El Salv.* 13°16′ N, 88°34′ W **115**
Puerto Escondido, *Col.* 9°2′ N, 76°15′ W **136**
Puerto Escondido, *Mex.* 15°52′ N, 97°6′ W **112**
Puerto Estrella, *Col.* 12°19′ N, 71°20′ W **136**
Puerto Francisco de Orellana, *Ecua.* 0°30′ N, 77°2′ W **136**
Puerto Frey, *Bol.* 14°44′ S, 61°10′ W **132**
Puerto General Ovando, *Bol.* 9°51′ S, 65°39′ W **137**
Puerto Grether, *Bol.* 17°14′ S, 64°23′ W **137**
Puerto Heath, *Bol.* 12°33′ S, 68°39′ W **137**
Puerto Huitoto, *Col.* 0°16′ N, 74°3′ W **136**
Puerto Inírida, *Col.* 3°44′ N, 67°53′ W **136**
Puerto Iradier, *Equatorial Guinea* 1°6′ N, 9°43′ E **218**
Puerto Jiménez, *C.R.* 8°32′ N, 83°19′ W **115**
Puerto La Concordia, *Col.* 2°38′ N, 72°49′ W **136**
Puerto La Cruz, *Venez.* 10°12′ N, 64°39′ W **130**
Puerto La Esperanza, *Parag.* 22°0′ S, 58°3′ W **132**
Puerto La Paz, *Arg.* 22°29′ S, 62°24′ W **132**
Puerto La Victoria, *Parag.* 22°17′ S, 57°58′ W **132**
Puerto Lápice, *Sp.* 39°19′ N, 3°29′ W **164**
Puerto Leguízamo, *Col.* 0°11′ N, 74°47′ W **136**
Puerto Leigue, *Bol.* 14°19′ S, 64°53′ W **137**
Puerto Lempira, *Hond.* 15°10′ N, 83°47′ W **115**
Puerto Libertad, *Mex.* 29°55′ N, 112°41′ W **92**
Puerto Limón, *Col.* 1°0′ N, 76°32′ W **136**
Puerto Limón, *C.R.* 9°45′ N, 83°4′ W **123**
Puerto Limón, *C.R.* 9°59′ N, 83°2′ W **115**
Puerto Lobos, *Mex.* 30°16′ N, 112°51′ W **92**
Puerto Lobos (Arroyo Verde), *Arg.* 42°2′ S, 65°5′ W **134**
Puerto López, *Col.* 4°6′ N, 72°59′ W **136**
Puerto López (Tucacas), *Col.* 11°56′ N, 71°18′ W **136**
Puerto Lumbreras, *Sp.* 37°33′ N, 1°50′ W **164**
Puerto Macaco, *Col.* 2°0′ N, 71°5′ W **136**
Puerto Madryn, *Arg.* 42°53′ S, 64°59′ W **123**
Puerto Maldonado, *Peru* 12°39′ S, 69°13′ W **137**
Puerto Mamoré, *Bol.* 16°43′ S, 64°51′ W **137**
Puerto Miraña, *Col.* 1°21′ S, 70°20′ W **136**
Puerto Mirando, *Venez.* 10°46′ N, 71°34′ W **116**
Puerto Montt, *Chile* 41°29′ S, 72°58′ W **134**
Puerto Morazán, *Nicar.* 12°50′ N, 87°10′ W **115**
Puerto Morelos, *Mex.* 20°50′ N, 86°56′ W **116**
Puerto Mutis see Bahía Solano, *Col.* 6°12′ N, 77°25′ W **136**
Puerto Napo, *Ecua.* 1°7′ S, 77°52′ W **136**
Puerto Naré, *Col.* 6°9′ N, 74°37′ W **136**
Puerto Natales, *Chile* 51°39′ S, 72°29′ W **134**
Puerto Nuevo, *Col.* 5°43′ N, 70°1′ W **136**
Puerto Obaldía, *Col.* 8°40′ N, 77°25′ W **115**
Puerto Olaya, *Col.* 6°29′ N, 74°22′ W **136**
Puerto Páez, *Venez.* 6°14′ N, 67°23′ W **136**
Puerto Pardo, *Peru* 12°33′ S, 68°48′ W **137**
Puerto Patiño, *Bol.* 16°36′ S, 65°50′ W **137**
Puerto Peñasco, *Mex.* 31°18′ N, 113°33′ W **92**
Puerto Pinasco, *Parag.* 22°36′ S, 57°52′ W **132**
Puerto Piracuacito, *Arg.* 28°11′ S, 59°10′ W **139**
Puerto Píritu, *Venez.* 10°3′ N, 65°3′ W **116**
Puerto Pizarro, *Col.* 0°16′ N, 73°28′ W **136**
Puerto Plata, *Dom. Rep.* 19°46′ N, 70°41′ W **116**
Puerto Portillo, *Peru* 9°46′ S, 72°46′ W **137**
Puerto Prado, *Peru* 11°11′ S, 74°20′ W **137**
Puerto Princesa, *Philippines* 9°44′ N, 118°45′ E **203**
Puerto Principe, *Col.* 0°27′ N, 75°9′ W **136**
Puerto Real, *Sp.* 36°31′ N, 6°12′ W **164**
Puerto Rico, *Bol.* 11°8′ S, 67°35′ W **137**
Puerto Rico, *Col.* 2°33′ N, 74°14′ W **136**
Puerto Rico, adm. division, *U.S.* 18°13′ N, 66°29′ W **118**
Puerto Rico Trench, *North Atlantic Ocean* 19°41′ N, 63°30′ W **253**
Puerto Rondón, *Col.* 6°19′ N, 71°7′ W **136**
Puerto Salgar, *Col.* 5°28′ N, 74°38′ W **136**
Puerto Salvatierra, *Peru* 3°34′ S, 76°31′ W **136**
Puerto San Augustín, *Peru* 2°45′ S, 71°25′ W **136**
Puerto San Francisquito, *Mex.* 28°24′ N, 112°54′ W **92**
Puerto San José, *Guatemala* 13°56′ N, 90°50′ W **115**
Puerto San Julián, *Arg.* 49°17′ S, 67°46′ W **134**
Puerto Sandino, *Nicar.* 12°10′ N, 86°44′ W **115**
Puerto Santa Cruz, *Arg.* 50°0′ S, 68°33′ W **134**
Puerto Saucedo, *Bol.* 14°1′ S, 62°50′ W **130**
Puerto Siles, *Bol.* 12°47′ S, 65°7′ W **137**
Puerto Socorro, *Col.* 2°48′ S, 69°59′ W **136**
Puerto Tejada, *Col.* 3°14′ N, 76°25′ W **136**
Puerto Tirol, *Arg.* 27°22′ S, 59°6′ W **139**
Puerto Tres Palmas, *Parag.* 21°43′ S, 57°59′ W **132**
Puerto Umbría, *Col.* 0°47′ N, 76°35′ W **136**
Puerto Vallarta, *Mex.* 20°35′ N, 105°16′ W **114**
Puerto Velarde, *Bol.* 16°31′ S, 63°41′ W **137**
Puerto Velasco Ibarra, *Ecua.* 1°22′ S, 90°33′ W **130**
Puerto Villamil, *Ecua.* 0°55′ N, 90°57′ W **130**
Puerto Villarroel, *Bol.* 16°54′ S, 64°49′ W **137**
Puerto Villazón, *Bol.* 13°29′ S, 61°56′ W **130**
Puerto Wilches, *Col.* 7°20′ N, 73°52′ W **136**
Puertollano, *Sp.* 38°41′ N, 4°7′ W **164**
Pueşti, *Rom.* 46°24′ N, 27°30′ E **156**
Puesto Arturo, *Peru* 1°51′ S, 73°20′ W **136**
Pugachev, *Russ.* 52°1′ N, 48°48′ E **158**
Pugal, *India* 28°30′ N, 72°49′ E **186**
Puget Sound 47°46′ N, 123°32′ W **80**
Puget-Théniers, *Fr.* 43°57′ N, 6°52′ E **167**
Puglia, adm. division, *It.* 41°12′ N, 15°15′ E **156**
Pugŏ, *N. Korea* 42°2′ N, 129°58′ E **200**
Puhja, *Est.* 58°19′ N, 26°18′ E **166**
Pui, *Rom.* 45°31′ N, 23°6′ E **168**
Puig Major, peak, *Sp.* 39°47′ N, 2°45′ E **164**
Puigcerdà, *Fr.* 42°25′ N, 1°55′ E **164**
Puigmal d'Err, peak, *Sp.* 42°22′ N, 2°3′ E **164**
Puig-reig, *Sp.* 41°57′ N, 1°52′ E **164**
Puiseaux, *Fr.* 48°11′ N, 2°28′ E **163**
Pujehun, *Sierra Leone* 7°21′ N, 11°44′ W **222**
Pujiang, *China* 29°30′ N, 119°55′ E **198**
Pujŏn, *N. Korea* 40°26′ N, 127°37′ E **200**
Pujŏn, river, *N. Korea* 40°54′ N, 127°33′ E **200**
Puka, *Est.* 58°3′ N, 26°13′ E **166**
Puka see Pukë, *Alban.* 42°2′ N, 19°53′ E **168**
Pukaki, Lake, *N.Z.* 44°7′ S, 169°48′ E **240**
Pukapuka Atoll (Danger Islands), *South Pacific Ocean* 10°35′ S, 167°12′ W **238**
Pukapuka, island, *Fr.* 14°46′ S, 138°53′ W **252**
Pukari, *Russ.* 65°58′ N, 30°1′ E **152**
Pukaskwa National Park, *Can.* 48°16′ N, 88°31′ W **94**
Pukatawagan, *Can.* 55°45′ N, 101°17′ W **108**
Pukchin, *N. Korea* 40°12′ N, 125°44′ E **200**
Pukch'ŏng, *N. Korea* 40°14′ N, 128°21′ E **200**
Pukë (Puka), *Alban.* 42°2′ N, 19°53′ E **168**
Pukeashun Mountain, peak, *Can.* 51°12′ N, 119°19′ W **90**
Pukehou, *N.Z.* 39°51′ S, 176°38′ E **240**
Pukekohe, *N.Z.* 37°13′ S, 174°53′ E **240**
Pukemiro, *N.Z.* 37°38′ S, 175°0′ E **240**
Pukovac, *Serb.* 43°10′ N, 21°50′ E **168**
Puksa, *Russ.* 62°35′ N, 40°20′ E **154**
Puksoozero, *Russ.* 62°36′ N, 40°34′ E **154**
Pula, Capo di, *It.* 38°53′ N, 8°59′ E **156**
Pulacayo, *Bol.* 20°28′ S, 66°40′ W **137**
Pulaj, *Alban.* 41°53′ N, 19°23′ E **168**
Pulandian, *China* 39°25′ N, 122°2′ E **198**
Pulap Atoll 7°29′ N, 150°1′ E **192**
Pular, Cerro, peak, *Chile* 24°12′ S, 68°12′ W **132**
Pulaski, *N.Y., U.S.* 43°34′ N, 76°8′ W **94**
Pulaski, *Tenn., U.S.* 35°10′ N, 87°1′ W **96**
Pulaski, *Va., U.S.* 37°2′ N, 80°47′ W **96**
Pulaukijang, *Indonesia* 0°42′ N, 103°11′ E **196**
Pulheim, *Ger.* 51°0′ N, 6°47′ E **167**
Puli, *Taiwan, China* 23°52′ N, 120°57′ E **198**
Pulkkila, *Fin.* 64°16′ N, 25°50′ E **152**
Pullen Island, island, *Antarctica* 73°2′ S, 63°3′ W **248**
Pullman, *Mich., U.S.* 42°28′ N, 86°5′ W **102**
Pullman, *Wash., U.S.* 46°44′ N, 117°10′ W **90**
Pullo, *Peru* 15°15′ S, 73°50′ W **137**
Pulog, Mount, peak, *Philippines* 16°35′ N, 120°49′ E **203**
Pulozero, *Russ.* 68°21′ N, 33°18′ E **152**
Pulpí, *Sp.* 37°24′ N, 1°44′ W **164**
Púlpito, Punta, *Mex.* 26°33′ N, 111°32′ W **112**
Pülümür, *Turk.* 39°29′ N, 39°53′ E **195**
Puluwat Atoll 6°50′ N, 149°57′ E **192**
Puma Yumco, lake, *China* 28°40′ N, 90°6′ E **197**
Pummanki, *Russ.* 69°46′ N, 31°53′ E **152**
Pumpsaint, *U.K.* 52°1′ N, 3°56′ W **162**
Puna, *Arg.* 27°47′ S, 62°30′ W **139**
Puná, Isla, island, *Ecua.* 3°11′ S, 80°46′ W **130**
Puna, region, *Hawai'i, U.S.* 19°32′ N, 155°23′ W **99**
Punakha, *Bhutan* 27°37′ N, 89°51′ E **197**
Punata, *Bol.* 17°35′ S, 65°47′ W **137**
Punch, *India* 33°46′ N, 74°6′ E **186**
Punchaw, *Can.* 53°27′ N, 123°15′ W **108**
Pune, *India* 18°30′ N, 73°53′ E **188**
Pungan, *Uzb.* 40°47′ N, 70°55′ E **197**
P'ungch'ŏn see Kwail, *N. Korea* 38°25′ N, 125°1′ E **200**
Punggi, *S. Korea* 36°51′ N, 128°32′ E **200**
Punilla, Cordillera de la, *Chile* 29°37′ S, 71°36′ W **134**
Punitaqui, *Chile* 30°50′ S, 71°17′ W **134**
Punjab, adm. division, *India* 30°2′ N, 74°58′ E **197**
Punjab, adm. division, *Pak.* 30°51′ N, 71°22′ E **186**
Punkaharju, *Fin.* 61°47′ N, 29°18′ E **166**
Puno, *Peru* 15°53′ S, 70°1′ W **137**
Puno, adm. division, *Peru* 15°4′ S, 70°39′ W **137**
Punta Abreojos, *Mex.* 26°44′ N, 113°38′ W **112**
Punta Alta, *Arg.* 38°49′ S, 62°4′ W **139**
Punta Arenas, *Chile* 53°6′ S, 70°56′ W **134**
Punta Cardón, *Venez.* 11°38′ N, 70°13′ W **136**
Punta de Bombón, *Peru* 17°13′ S, 71°46′ W **137**
Punta de Díaz, *Chile* 28°3′ S, 70°38′ W **132**
Punta del Este, *Uru.* 34°58′ S, 54°58′ W **139**
Punta Gorda, *Fla., U.S.* 26°55′ N, 82°2′ W **105**
Punta Gorda, *Nicar.* 11°31′ N, 83°48′ W **115**
Punta Gorda, river, *Nicar.* 11°45′ N, 84°16′ W **115**
Punta Indio, *Arg.* 35°21′ S, 57°18′ W **139**
Punta La Marmora, peak, *It.* 39°58′ N, 9°14′ E **156**
Punta Maldonado, *Mex.* 16°19′ N, 98°33′ W **112**
Punta Prieta, *Mex.* 28°54′ N, 114°21′ W **92**
Punta Skala, *Croatia* 44°11′ N, 15°8′ E **156**
Puntarenas, *C.R.* 9°59′ N, 84°50′ W **115**
Punto Fijo, *Venez.* 11°41′ N, 70°14′ W **136**
Puntzi Lake, lake, *Can.* 52°10′ N, 124°26′ W **108**
Punxsutawney, *Pa., U.S.* 40°56′ N, 78°59′ W **94**
Puok, *Cambodia* 13°28′ N, 103°46′ E **202**
Puokio, *Fin.* 64°44′ N, 27°16′ E **152**
Puolanka, *Fin.* 64°50′ N, 27°36′ E **152**
Puqi, *China* 29°38′ N, 113°51′ E **198**
Puquina, *Peru* 16°40′ S, 71°11′ W **137**
Puquio, *Peru* 14°43′ S, 74°9′ W **137**
Puračić, *Bosn. and Herzg.* 44°33′ N, 18°28′ E **168**
Puranpur, *India* 28°31′ N, 80°7′ E **197**
Purari, river, *P.N.G.* 7°1′ S, 144°29′ E **192**
Purcell, *Okla., U.S.* 35°0′ N, 97°22′ W **92**
Purcell Mountains, *Can.* 48°59′ N, 116°12′ W **108**
Purchena, *Sp.* 37°19′ N, 2°22′ W **164**
Purdy Islands, *Bismarck Sea* 3°3′ S, 144°14′ E **192**
Purépero, *Mex.* 19°53′ N, 102°1′ W **114**
Puri, *Angola* 7°43′ S, 15°40′ E **218**
Puri, *India* 19°48′ N, 85°49′ E **188**
Purificación, *Mex.* 19°42′ N, 104°39′ W **114**
Purikari Neem, *Est.* 59°39′ N, 25°21′ E **166**
Purmerend, *Neth.* 52°30′ N, 4°56′ E **163**
Purnema, *Russ.* 64°24′ N, 37°21′ E **154**
Purnia, *India* 25°45′ N, 87°28′ E **197**
Purnululu National Park, *Austral.* 17°30′ S, 128°16′ E **238**
Pursat, *Cambodia* 12°35′ N, 103°48′ E **202**
Puruándiro, *Mex.* 20°4′ N, 101°31′ W **114**
Puruê, river, *Braz.* 2°12′ S, 68°30′ W **136**
Purukcahu, *Indonesia* 0°34′ N, 114°29′ E **192**
Purulia, *India* 23°20′ N, 86°21′ E **197**
Purus, river, *Braz.* 9°3′ S, 69°52′ W **132**
Purvis, *Miss., U.S.* 31°7′ N, 89°24′ W **103**
Puryŏng, *N. Korea* 42°3′ N, 129°41′ E **200**
Pusad, *India* 19°53′ N, 77°34′ E **188**
Pusan see Busan, *S. Korea* 35°6′ N, 129°3′ E **200**
Pushkin, *Russ.* 59°41′ N, 30°21′ E **152**
Pushkino, *Russ.* 51°12′ N, 46°55′ E **158**
Pushkinskiye Gory, *Russ.* 57°1′ N, 28°53′ E **166**
Pusi, *Peru* 15°30′ S, 69°58′ W **137**
Püspökladány, *Hung.* 47°18′ N, 21°7′ E **168**
Püssi, *Est.* 59°20′ N, 27°2′ E **166**
Pusticamica, Lac, lake, *Can.* 49°19′ N, 77°6′ W **110**
Pustoshka, *Russ.* 56°19′ N, 29°28′ E **166**
Pusztamérges, *Hung.* 46°19′ N, 19°41′ E **168**
Puta, *Azerb.* 40°19′ N, 49°38′ E **195**
Putahow Lake, lake, *Can.* 59°50′ N, 101°15′ W **108**
Putao, *Myanmar* 27°23′ N, 97°19′ E **190**
Putari, Lagoa, lake, *Braz.* 13°3′ S, 61°54′ W **130**
Putaruru, *N.Z.* 38°3′ S, 175°46′ E **240**
Putian, *China* 25°26′ N, 119°3′ E **198**
Putilovo, *Russ.* 59°22′ N, 44°35′ E **154**
Putina, *Peru* 14°57′ S, 69°54′ W **137**
Put-in-Bay, *Ohio, U.S.* 41°39′ N, 82°48′ W **102**
Putla, *Mex.* 17°0′ N, 97°56′ W **112**
Put'Lenina, *Russ.* 68°28′ N, 107°40′ E **173**
Putna, *Rom.* 47°52′ N, 25°37′ E **156**
Putnam, *Conn., U.S.* 41°54′ N, 71°55′ W **104**
Putnam, *Dem. Rep. of the Congo* 1°25′ N, 28°34′ E **224**
Putorana, Plato, *Russ.* 68°46′ N, 91°28′ E **169**
Putorino, *N.Z.* 39°8′ S, 177°1′ E **240**
Putre, *Chile* 18°14′ S, 69°37′ W **137**
Putsonderwater, *S. Af.* 29°12′ S, 21°50′ E **227**
Puttalam, *Sri Lanka* 8°2′ N, 79°51′ E **188**
Putten, *Neth.* 52°14′ N, 5°36′ E **163**
Puttur, *India* 12°44′ N, 75°12′ E **188**
Puttur, *India* 13°27′ N, 79°33′ E **188**
Putu Range, *Liberia* 5°32′ N, 7°50′ W **222**
Putumayo, *Ecua.* 9°535′ N, 75°53′ W **136**
Putumayo, adm. division, *Col.* 0°34′ N, 77°9′ W **136**
Putumayo, river, *South America* 2°52′ S, 73°10′ W **122**
Putussibau, *Indonesia* 0°52′ N, 112°51′ E **192**
Pu'u Kūlua, peak, *Hawai'i, U.S.* 19°31′ N, 155°29′ W **99**
Pu'u Lehua, peak, *Hawai'i, U.S.* 19°33′ N, 155°51′ W **99**
Pu'u Maka'ala, peak, *Hawai'i, U.S.* 19°31′ N, 155°17′ W **99**
Pu'u Mākanaka, peak, *Hawai'i, U.S.* 19°50′ N, 155°29′ W **99**
Pu'uhonua O Hōnaunau National Historical Park (City of Refuge National Historical Park), *Hawai'i, U.S.* 19°24′ N, 155°57′ W **99**
Pu'ukoholā Heiau National Historic Site, *Hawai'i, U.S.* 20°1′ N, 155°52′ W **99**
Puulavesi, lake, *Fin.* 61°41′ N, 26°26′ E **166**
Puumala, *Fin.* 61°31′ N, 28°9′ E **166**
Pu'uomahuka Heiau, site, *Hawai'i, U.S.* 21°38′ N, 158°6′ W **99**
Puvirnituq, *Can.* 60°5′ N, 77°15′ W **73**
Puxian, *China* 36°24′ N, 111°5′ E **198**
Puyallup, *Wash., U.S.* 47°9′ N, 122°18′ W **100**
Puyang, *China* 35°41′ N, 114°58′ E **198**
Puylaurens, *Fr.* 43°34′ N, 2°0′ E **150**
Puyo, *Ecua.* 1°36′ S, 78°4′ W **136**
Puyoô-Bellocq-Ramous, *Fr.* 43°32′ N, 0°55′ E **164**
Puysegur Point, *N.Z.* 46°21′ S, 166°20′ E **240**
Pwani, adm. division, *Tanzania* 7°19′ S, 38°26′ E **224**
Pweto, *Zambia* 8°29′ S, 28°52′ E **224**
Pwllheli, *U.K.* 52°53′ N, 4°25′ W **150**
Pyakupur, river, *Russ.* 63°23′ N, 73°59′ E **169**
Pyalitsa, *Russ.* 66°14′ N, 39°28′ E **154**
Pyal'ma, *Russ.* 62°24′ N, 35°58′ E **154**
P'yana, river, *Russ.* 55°26′ N, 44°27′ E **154**
Pyasina, river, *Russ.* 71°11′ N, 90°11′ E **160**
Pyasino, Ozero, lake, *Russ.* 69°58′ N, 86°36′ E **169**
Pyasinskiy Zaliv 73°39′ N, 78°4′ E **160**
Pyatigorsk, *Russ.* 44°4′ N, 43°6′ E **158**
Pyatimarskoe, *Kaz.* 49°31′ N, 50°28′ E **158**
P'yatykhatky, *Ukr.* 48°24′ N, 33°40′ E **156**
Pyay, *Myanmar* 18°51′ N, 95°14′ E **202**
Pydna 168 B.C., battle, *Gr.* 40°22′ N, 22°27′ E **156**
Pyeongchang, *S. Korea* 37°21′ N, 128°23′ E **200**
Pyeonghae, *S. Korea* 36°43′ N, 129°28′ E **200**
Pyeongtaek, *S. Korea* 36°57′ N, 127°7′ E **200**
Pyetrikaw, *Belarus* 52°8′ N, 28°34′ E **152**
Pyhäjärvi, lake, *Fin.* 60°59′ N, 21°55′ E **166**
Pyhäjoki, *Fin.* 64°27′ N, 24°13′ E **152**
Pyhämaa, *Fin.* 60°56′ N, 21°20′ E **166**
Pyhäntä, *Fin.* 64°5′ N, 26°18′ E **152**
Pyhäsalmi, *Fin.* 63°40′ N, 25°54′ E **152**
Pyhäselkä, *Fin.* 62°24′ N, 29°56′ E **152**
Pyhätunturi, peak, *Fin.* 66°59′ N, 26°56′ E **152**
Pyhtää (Pyttis), *Fin.* 60°29′ N, 26°33′ E **166**
Pyinkayaing, *Myanmar* 15°58′ N, 94°25′ E **202**
Pyinmanaa, *Myanmar* 19°46′ N, 96°10′ E **202**
Pyin-U-Lwin, *Myanmar* 22°1′ N, 96°27′ E **202**
Pylos, ruin(s), *Ionian Sea* 36°56′ N, 21°34′ E **156**
P'yŏngyang, *N. Korea* 39°1′ N, 125°45′ E **200**
P'yŏngsan, *N. Korea* 38°20′ N, 126°24′ E **200**

P'yŏngsan, *N. Korea* 40°36' N, 127°57' E **200**
P'yŏng-sŏng, *N. Korea* 39°13' N, 125°52' E **200**
P'yŏngwŏn, *N. Korea* 39°18' N, 125°37' E **200**
Pyote, *Tex., U.S.* 31°31' N, 103°8' W **92**
Pyramid Lake, *Nev., U.S.* 39°50' N, 120°31' W **80**
Pyramid Mountain, peak, *Can.* 58°52' N, 130°0' W **108**
Pyramid Peak, *Calif., U.S.* 36°22' N, 116°40' W **101**
Pyrds Bay 68°45' S, 74°19' E **255**
Pyrenees, *Sp.* 43°7' N, 1°10' E **165**
Pyrrha, ruin(s), *Gr.* 39°8' N, 26°12' E **156**
Pyryatyn, *Ukr.* 50°12' N, 32°30' E **158**
Pyshchug, *Russ.* 58°52' N, 45°43' E **154**
Pyshma, *Russ.* 56°58' N, 63°13' E **154**
Pytalovo, *Russ.* 57°3' N, 27°52' E **166**
Pýthion, *Gr.* 41°22' N, 26°36' E **156**
Pytteggja, peak, *Nor.* 62°11' N, 7°34' E **152**
Pyttis see Pyhtää, *Fin.* 60°29' N, 26°33' E **166**
Pyu, *Myanmar* 18°30' N, 96°25' E **202**

Q

Qaa, *Leb.* 34°22' N, 36°29' E **194**
Qaanaaq (Thule) 77°32' N, 69°13' W **106**
Qabanbay, *Kaz.* 45°49' N, 80°36' E **184**
Qabb Ilyās, *Leb.* 33°47' N, 35°49' E **194**
Qades, *Afghan.* 34°48' N, 63°26' E **186**
Qāḑub, *Yemen* 12°37' N, 53°50' E **182**
Qā'emshahr, *Iran* 36°30' N, 52°55' E **186**
Qā'en, *Iran* 33°44' N, 59°14' E **180**
Qagan Nur, *China* 43°18' N, 112°57' E **198**
Qagan Nur, lake, *China* 43°18' N, 114°17' E **198**
Qagcaka, *China* 32°33' N, 81°52' E **188**
Qahar Youyi Houqi, *China* 41°28' N, 113°11' E **198**
Qahar Youyi Zhongqi, *China* 41°15' N, 112°36' E **198**
Qaharir, oil field, *Oman* 17°55' N, 55°30' E **182**
Qaidam Pendi, *China* 37°41' N, 91°15' E **188**
Qaidam, river, *China* 36°29' N, 97°23' E **188**
Qairouan, *Tun.* 35°40' N, 10°5' E **156**
Qaiyara, oil field, *Iraq* 35°43' N, 43°6' E **180**
Qal 'at al Ḩasā, ruin(s), *Jordan* 30°49' N, 35°53' E **194**
Qala 'en Nahl, *Sudan* 13°36' N, 34°55' E **182**
Qalaa Kebira, *Tun.* 35°53' N, 10°31' E **156**
Qalansīyah, *Yemen* 12°38' N, 53°26' E **182**
Qalat, *Afghan.* 32°8' N, 66°58' E **186**
Qal'at al Azlam, ruin(s), *Saudi Arabia* 27°3' N, 35°55' E **180**
Qal'at al Maḑiq, *Syr.* 35°25' N, 36°22' E **194**
Qal'at Bīshah, *Saudi Arabia* 19°59' N, 42°37' E **182**
Qal'at Şahyūn, ruin(s), *Syr.* 35°34' N, 36°0' E **194**
Qal'at Şālī', ruin(s), *Syr.* 35°33' N, 35°59' E **156**
Qal'eh-ye Bar Panj, *Afghan.* 37°32' N, 71°27' E **184**
Qal'eh-ye Now, *Afghan.* 34°57' N, 63°11' E **186**
Qal'eh-ye Saber, *Afghan.* 34°3' N, 69°4' E **186**
Qal'eh-ye Sarkari, *Afghan.* 35°51' N, 67°16' E **186**
Qalhāt, *Oman* 22°40' N, 59°20' E **182**
Qallabat, *Sudan* 12°56' N, 36°6' E **182**
Qalqaman, *Kaz.* 51°57' N, 76°4' E **184**
Qalqīlyah, *West Bank, Israel* 32°11' N, 34°58' E **194**
Qaltat Bū as Su'ūd, spring, *Lib.* 27°39' N, 18°13' E **216**
Qalzhat, *Kaz.* 43°32' N, 80°35' E **184**
Qamar, Ghubbat al 15°45' N, 52°17' E **182**
Qamashi, *Uzb.* 38°49' N, 66°27' E **197**
Qamata, *S. Af.* 32°0' S, 27°26' E **227**
Qamdo, *China* 31°10' N, 97°6' E **188**
Qamīnis, *Lib.* 31°39' N, 20°1' E **216**
Qamystybas, *Kaz.* 46°13' N, 61°58' E **184**
Qanā, *Saudi Arabia* 27°44' N, 41°30' E **180**
Qanawāt, *Syr.* 32°45' N, 36°36' E **194**
Qandala, *Somalia* 11°23' N, 49°50' E **216**
Qanshenggel, *Kaz.* 44°18' N, 75°30' E **184**
Qapqal, *China* 43°49' N, 81°18' E **184**
Qapshaghay, *Kaz.* 43°54' N, 77°6' E **184**
Qaqortoq (Julianehåb) 60°47' N, 46°7' W **106**
Qāra, *Egypt* 29°38' N, 26°32' E **180**
Qarabey, *Kaz.* 48°46' N, 53°2' E **158**
Qarabulaq, *Kaz.* 44°53' N, 78°28' E **184**
Qarabulaq, *Kaz.* 42°32' N, 69°49' E **197**
Qarabutaq, *Kaz.* 49°57' N, 60°7' E **158**
Qaraghandy, *Kaz.* 49°49' N, 73°9' E **184**
Qaraghandy, adm. division, *Kaz.* 48°3' N, 68°19' E **184**
Qaraghayly, *Kaz.* 49°20' N, 75°43' E **184**
Qārah, *Syr.* 34°9' N, 36°44' E **194**
Qarah Bagh, *Afghan.* 33°9' N, 68°10' E **186**
Qaraoba, *Kaz.* 47°0' N, 56°14' E **158**
Qaraqalpakstan, *Uzb.* 44°49' N, 56°10' E **158**
Qarasū, *Kaz.* 52°39' N, 65°30' E **184**
Qaratal, river, *Kaz.* 45°59' N, 77°1' E **184**
Qarataū, *Kaz.* 43°5' N, 70°28' E **184**
Qarataū Zhotasy, *Kaz.* 42°32' N, 70°38' E **197**
Qaratöbe, *Kaz.* 49°43' N, 53°26' E **158**
Qaratoghay, *Kaz.* 48°24' N, 84°29' E **184**
Qaraton, *Kaz.* 46°20' N, 53°35' E **158**
Qaraūt, *Kaz.* 48°56' N, 79°15' E **184**
Qarazhal, *Kaz.* 48°1' N, 70°49' E **184**
Qarazhar, *Kaz.* 47°45' N, 56°8' E **158**
Qardho, *Somalia* 9°30' N, 49°7' E **216**
Qareh, river, *Iran* 38°31' N, 47°57' E **195**
Qarghaly, *Kaz.* 50°18' N, 57°17' E **158**
Qarn Alam, oil field, *Oman* 20°59' N, 57°3' E **182**
Qarokŭl, lake, *Taj.* 39°5' N, 73°10' E **197**
Qarqan, river, *China* 38°25' N, 86°14' E **188**
Qarqan, river, *China* 38°31' N, 85°47' E **190**
Qarqaraly, *Kaz.* 49°29' N, 75°23' E **184**
Qarsaqbay, *Kaz.* 47°47' N, 66°37' E **184**
Qarshi, *Uzb.* 38°51' N, 65°48' E **197**
Qarţabā, *Leb.* 34°5' N, 35°51' E **194**
Qaryah al 'Ulyā, *Saudi Arabia* 27°32' N, 47°40' E **196**
Qaryat abu Nujaym, *Lib.* 30°34' N, 15°21' E **216**
Qaryat al Qaddā'īyah, *Lib.* 31°21' N, 15°13' E **216**
Qaryat az Zuwaytīnah, *Lib.* 30°56' N, 20°8' E **216**
Qaryat Shumaykh, *Lib.* 31°21' N, 13°57' E **216**
Qarynzharyq, desert, *Kaz.* 42°45' N, 53°31' E **180**
Qasigiannguit (Christianshåb) 68°47' N, 51°7' W **106**
Qāsim, *Syr.* 32°59' N, 36°3' E **194**
Qaskeleng, *Kaz.* 43°12' N, 76°39' E **184**
Qaşr al Azraq, ruin(s), *Jordan* 31°51' N, 36°46' E **194**
Qaşr al Ḩallābāt, ruin(s), *Jordan* 32°3' N, 36°19' E **194**
Qaşr al Ḩammām, ruin(s), *Jordan* 31°31' N, 36°8' E **194**
Qaşr al Kharānah, ruin(s), *Jordan* 31°43' N, 36°26' E **194**
Qaşr al Mushayyish, ruin(s), *Jordan* 30°54' N, 36°5' E **194**
Qaşr 'Amrah, ruin(s), *Jordan* 31°47' N, 36°32' E **194**
Qaşr ash Shaqqah, ruin(s), *Lib.* 30°48' N, 24°52' E **180**
Qaşr aţ Ţūbah, ruin(s), *Jordan* 31°18' N, 36°31' E **194**
Qaşr Bū Hādī, ruin(s), *Lib.* 31°3' N, 16°20' E **216**
Qaşr Burqu', ruin(s), *Jordan* 32°34' N, 37°48' E **180**
Qaşr Farâfra, *Egypt* 27°2' N, 27°58' E **180**
Qaşr Ḩamām, *Saudi Arabia* 20°47' N, 45°51' E **182**
Qaşr Ibrîm, ruin(s), *Egypt* 22°30' N, 31°51' E **182**
Qaşr-e Qand, *Iran* 26°11' N, 60°50' E **182**
Qaşr-e Shīrīn, *Iran* 34°31' N, 45°34' E **180**
Qasserine (Kasserine), *Tun.* 35°9' N, 8°51' E **156**
Qatar 25°0' N, 51°0' E **196**
Qattara Depression see Qaţţâra, Munkhafad el, *Egypt* 29°32' N, 26°42' E **180**
Qaţţâra, Munkhafad el (Qattara Depression), *Egypt* 29°32' N, 26°42' E **180**
Qaţţâra, spring, *Egypt* 30°10' N, 27°9' E **180**
Qax, *Azerb.* 41°25' N, 46°55' E **195**
Qaynar, *Kaz.* 49°16' N, 77°29' E **184**
Qazakh, *Azerb.* 41°5' N, 45°21' E **195**
Qazaly, *Kaz.* 45°49' N, 62°7' E **184**
Qazaq Shyghanaghy 42°42' N, 51°45' E **158**
Qazbegi, *Ga.* 42°38' N, 44°40' E **195**
Qazimämmäd, *Azerb.* 40°2' N, 48°54' E **195**
Qazvīn, *Iran* 36°18' N, 49°59' E **195**
Qazyqurt, *Kaz.* 41°48' N, 69°27' E **197**
Qeissan, *Sudan* 10°47' N, 34°48' E **224**
Qelibia, *Tun.* 36°51' N, 11°5' E **156**
Qemult'a, *Asia* 42°26' N, 43°47' E **158**
Qena, *Egypt* 26°12' N, 32°40' E **180**
Qeqertarsuaq (Disko), island, *Den.* 69°31' N, 62°11' W **106**
Qeqertarsuaq (Godhavn), *Den.* 69°15' N, 53°30' W **106**
Qeqertarsuatsiaat (Fiskenæsset), *Den.* 63°6' N, 50°43' W **106**
Qeren Naftali, peak, *Israel* 33°3' N, 35°30' E **194**
Qerqenah Islands, *Tun.* 35°1' N, 11°13' E **214**
Qertassi see Qirzâs, ruin(s), *Egypt* 23°39' N, 32°43' E **182**
Qeshm, *Iran* 26°55' N, 56°12' E **196**
Qeshm, island, *Iran* 26°36' N, 56°3' E **180**
Qeys, island, *Iran* 26°22' N, 53°46' E **180**
Qeysar, *Afghan.* 35°42' N, 64°14' E **186**
Qezel Owzan, river, *Iran* 37°3' N, 48°34' E **195**
Qian Gorlos, *China* 45°3' N, 124°48' E **198**
Qian'an, *China* 44°58' N, 124°4' E **198**
Qianxi, *China* 27°3' N, 106°2' E **198**
Qianxian, *China* 34°31' N, 108°15' E **198**
Qianyang, *China* 34°38' N, 107°6' E **198**
Qiaowan, *China* 40°35' N, 96°43' E **188**
Qibā', *Saudi Arabia* 27°22' N, 44°23' E **180**
Qidaogou, *China* 41°32' N, 126°21' E **200**
Qidong, *China* 31°48' N, 121°38' E **198**
Qidong, *China* 26°44' N, 112°8' E **198**
Qiemo, *China* 38°12' N, 85°18' E **190**
Qijiang, *China* 28°58' N, 106°38' E **198**
Qikiqtarjuaq (Broughton Island), *Can.* 67°30' N, 63°52' W **73**
Qila Ladgasht, *Pak.* 27°49' N, 63°0' E **182**
Qila Safed, *Pak.* 28°58' N, 61°35' E **182**
Qilian Shan, *China* 39°14' N, 96°43' E **188**
Qimen, *China* 29°51' N, 117°40' E **198**
Qimusseriarsuaq 75°28' N, 66°10' W **106**
Qin'an, *China* 34°51' N, 105°40' E **198**
Qing, river, *China* 30°28' N, 110°40' E **198**
Qing'an, *China* 46°53' N, 127°30' E **198**
Qingchengzi, *China* 40°43' N, 123°37' E **200**
Qingdao, *China* 36°5' N, 120°24' E **198**
Qinggang, *China* 46°40' N, 126°7' E **198**
Qinghai, adm. division, *China* 35°28' N, 92°33' E **188**
Qinghai Hu, lake, *China* 36°45' N, 99°5' E **190**
Qinghe, *China* 42°32' N, 124°9' E **200**
Qingjian, *China* 37°8' N, 110°11' E **198**
Qingjiang, *China* 28°1' N, 115°30' E **198**
Qingshuihe, *China* 33°42' N, 97°4' E **188**
Qingshuihe, *China* 39°54' N, 111°40' E **198**
Qingtian, *China* 28°10' N, 120°17' E **198**
Qingtongxia, *China* 38°4' N, 106°3' E **198**
Qingxu, *China* 37°36' N, 112°19' E **198**
Qingyang, *China* 36°2' N, 107°54' E **198**
Qingyuan, *China* 42°6' N, 124°52' E **200**
Qingyuan, *China* 23°40' N, 113°2' E **198**
Qinhuangdao, *China* 39°56' N, 119°36' E **198**
Qinxian, *China* 36°45' N, 112°42' E **198**
Qinzhou, *China* 21°56' N, 108°34' E **198**
Qionghai, *China* 19°14' N, 110°31' E **198**
Qiqihar, *China* 47°21' N, 123°59' E **198**
Qira, *China* 37°2' N, 80°54' E **184**
Qir'awn, Bu'ayrat al, lake, *Leb.* 33°34' N, 35°35' E **194**
Qirzâs (Qertassi), ruin(s), *Egypt* 23°39' N, 32°43' E **182**
Qiryat Arba', *West Bank, Israel* 31°32' N, 35°7' E **194**
Qiryat Ata, *Israel* 32°47' N, 35°6' E **194**
Qiryat Gat, *Israel* 31°36' N, 34°46' E **194**
Qiryat Mal'akhi, *Israel* 31°43' N, 34°43' E **194**
Qiryat Motzkin, *Israel* 32°49' N, 35°3' E **194**
Qiryat Shemona, *Israel* 33°12' N, 35°34' E **194**
Qishn, *Yemen* 15°26' N, 51°39' E **182**
Qitaihe, *China* 45°49' N, 130°52' E **238**
Qixia, *China* 37°16' N, 120°47' E **198**
Qīyaly, *Kaz.* 54°11' N, 69°37' E **184**
Qiyang, *China* 26°38' N, 111°48' E **198**
Qızılağac Körfäzi 39°6' N, 48°36' E **195**
Qizilcha, *Uzb.* 40°42' N, 66°11' E **197**
Qizilqum, *Uzb.* 41°58' N, 64°9' E **197**
Qiziltepa, *Uzb.* 40°1' N, 64°50' E **197**
Qobda, *Kaz.* 50°8' N, 55°37' E **158**
Qoghaly, *Kaz.* 44°25' N, 78°37' E **184**
Qoghir see K2, peak, *Pak.* 35°51' N, 76°25' E **186**
Qom (Qum), *Iran* 34°39' N, 50°50' E **180**
Qom, river, *Iran* 34°17' N, 50°22' E **180**
Qomolangma see Everest, Mount, peak, *China-Nepal* 28°0' N, 86°53' E **197**
Qonaqkänd, *Azerb.* 41°3' N, 48°36' E **195**
Qonggyai, *China* 29°5' N, 91°37' E **197**
Qongyrat, *Kaz.* 46°59' N, 74°57' E **184**
Qoornoq 64°33' N, 51°9' W **106**
Qoow, *Somalia* 11°11' N, 48°57' E **216**
Qo'qon, *Uzb.* 40°31' N, 70°55' E **197**
Qorakŭl, *Uzb.* 39°30' N, 63°51' E **197**
Qorday, *Kaz.* 43°17' N, 74°54' E **184**
Qorghalzhyn, *Kaz.* 50°36' N, 69°50' E **184**
Qorovulbozor, *Uzb.* 39°31' N, 64°51' E **197**
Qorsaq, *Kaz.* 47°0' N, 53°18' E **158**
Qorveh, *Iran* 35°11' N, 47°44' E **180**
Qoryaale, *Somalia* 7°28' N, 49°11' E **218**
Qo'shrabot, *Uzb.* 40°15' N, 66°39' E **197**
Qosköl, *Kaz.* 49°36' N, 67°3' E **184**
Qosshaghyl, *Kaz.* 46°54' N, 53°54' E **158**
Qostanay, *Kaz.* 53°13' N, 63°35' E **184**
Qostanay, adm. division, *Kaz.* 52°2' N, 60°25' E **154**
Qotanqaraghay, *Kaz.* 49°10' N, 85°36' E **184**
Qoton, *Somalia* 9°30' N, 50°27' E **216**
Qoţūr, *Iran* 38°27' N, 44°23' E **195**
Qoubaiyat, *Leb.* 34°34' N, 36°17' E **194**
Qsar Ghilan, *Tun.* 33°3' N, 9°35' E **216**
Qsour Essaf, *Tun.* 35°26' N, 10°58' E **156**
Qu' Appelle Valley Dam, *Can.* 50°47' N, 106°26' W **90**
Quail Mountains, *Calif., U.S.* 35°39' N, 117°1' W **101**
Quakenbrück, *Ger.* 52°40' N, 7°58' E **163**
Qualicum Beach, *Can.* 49°20' N, 124°26' W **100**
Quan Hoa, *Vietnam* 20°25' N, 105°7' E **202**
Quanah, *Tex., U.S.* 34°16' N, 99°45' W **92**
Quang Ngai, *Vietnam* 15°7' N, 108°47' E **202**
Quang Tri, *Vietnam* 16°44' N, 107°12' E **202**
Quannan, *China* 24°41' N, 114°28' E **198**
Quantz Lake, *Can.* 51°7' N, 85°56' W **110**
Quanzhou, *China* 25°59' N, 111°4' E **198**
Quanzhou, *China* 24°58' N, 118°36' E **198**
Qu'Appelle, *Can.* 50°32' N, 103°54' W **90**
Qu'Appelle, river, *Can.* 50°40' N, 103°48' W **108**
Quaraí, *Braz.* 30°25' S, 56°24' W **139**
Quaraí, river, *South America* 30°8' S, 57°11' W **139**
Quaritoufoulout, spring, *Mali* 16°14' N, 3°17' E **222**
Quartz Hill, *Calif., U.S.* 34°39' N, 118°14' W **101**
Quartzite Mountain, peak, *Nev., U.S.* 37°29' N, 116°25' W **92**
Quartzsite, *Ariz., U.S.* 33°39' N, 114°15' W **101**
Quatsino, *Can.* 50°32' N, 127°38' W **90**
Quba, *Azerb.* 41°20' N, 48°32' E **195**
Qūchān, *Iran* 37°4' N, 58°29' E **180**
Que Son, *Vietnam* 15°40' N, 108°13' E **202**
Québec, *Can.* 46°47' N, 71°22' W **94**
Quebec, adm. division, *Can.* 53°50' N, 76°4' W **106**
Quebracho, *Uru.* 31°57' S, 57°52' W **139**
Quebracho Coto, *Arg.* 26°20' S, 64°28' W **132**
Quedal, Cabo, *Chile* 41°11' S, 75°34' W **134**
Queen Bess, Mount, peak, *Can.* 51°15' N, 124°39' W **90**
Queen Charlotte Islands, *Hecate Strait* 53°6' N, 132°30' W **98**
Queen Charlotte Sound 51°46' N, 130°1' W **108**
Queen City, *Tex., U.S.* 33°8' N, 94°10' W **103**
Queen Elizabeth Islands, *Northwest Passage* 76°21' N, 116°41' W **106**
Queen Elizabeth National Park, *Uganda* 0°25' N, 30°10' E **224**
Queen Elizabeth Shelf, *Arctic Ocean* 80°30' N, 100°0' W **255**
Queen Mary Coast, *Antarctica* 69°42' S, 97°55' E **248**
Queen Maud Gulf 67°52' N, 102°7' W **106**
Queen Maud Land, region, *Antarctica* 76°48' S, 8°55' E **248**
Queen Maud Mountains, *Antarctica* 86°1' S, 141°33' W **248**
Queen Victoria's Profile, site, *Hawai'i, U.S.* 21°55' N, 159°27' W **99**
Queens Channel 75°46' N, 100°43' W **106**
Queens Sound 51°48' N, 128°37' W **108**
Queensbury, *U.K.* 53°46' N, 1°52' W **162**
Queensland, adm. division, *Austral.* 23°32' S, 140°33' E **231**
Queenstown, *Austral.* 42°3' S, 145°33' E **231**
Queenstown, *N.Z.* 45°1' S, 168°39' E **240**
Queenstown, *S. Af.* 31°54' S, 26°45' E **207**
Queenstown, *S. Af.* 31°53' S, 26°51' E **227**
Queets, *Wash., U.S.* 47°31' N, 124°20' W **100**
Queets, river, *Wash., U.S.* 47°28' N, 124°16' W **100**
Queimadas, *Braz.* 11°2' S, 39°38' W **132**
Quela, *Angola* 9°17' S, 17°4' E **218**
Quelimane, *Mozambique* 17°55' S, 36°52' E **224**
Quellón, *Chile* 43°6' S, 73°39' W **134**
Quelo, *Angola* 6°28' S, 12°48' E **218**
Quemado, *N. Mex., U.S.* 34°19' N, 108°29' W **92**
Quemado, *Tex., U.S.* 28°56' N, 100°37' W **92**
Quemado de Güines, *Cuba* 22°47' N, 80°15' W **116**
Quembo, river, *Angola* 13°59' S, 19°30' E **220**
Quemoy see Kinmen, island, *Taiwan, China* 24°23' N, 118°32' E **198**
Quemú Quemú, *Arg.* 36°4' S, 63°33' W **139**
Quentin, *Miss., U.S.* 31°29' N, 90°45' W **103**
Quequén, *Arg.* 38°31' S, 58°43' W **139**
Quequeña, *Peru* 16°36' S, 71°26' W **137**
Querco, *Peru* 13°53' S, 74°52' W **137**
Quercy, *Fr.* 44°40' N, 1°10' E **165**
Querétaro, *Mex.* 20°34' N, 100°27' W **114**
Querétaro, adm. division, *Mex.* 20°44' N, 100°33' W **114**
Quesada, *Sp.* 37°51' N, 3°5' W **164**
Queshan, *China* 32°46' N, 114°2' E **198**
Quesnel, *Can.* 52°59' N, 122°31' W **106**
Quesnel Lake, lake, *Can.* 52°41' N, 121°20' W **108**
Quetico Lake, lake, *Can.* 48°32' N, 92°24' W **94**
Quetta, *Pak.* 30°13' N, 67°5' E **182**
Quetzaltenango, *Guatemala* 14°50' N, 91°31' W **115**
Queulat National Park, *Chile* 44°30' S, 72°44' W **122**
Queule, *Chile* 39°18' S, 73°12' W **134**
Quevedo, *Ecua.* 1°8' S, 79°37' W **130**
Quevedo, Península de, *Mex.* 23°56' N, 108°18' W **112**
Quévillon, Lac, lake, *Can.* 49°2' N, 77°31' W **94**
Quezon, *Philippines* 9°15' N, 118°2' E **203**
Quezon City, *Philippines* 14°43' N, 121°1' E **203**
Qufār, *Saudi Arabia* 27°24' N, 41°40' E **180**
Qufu, *China* 35°34' N, 116°54' E **198**
Qui Nhon, *Vietnam* 13°47' N, 109°12' E **202**
Quibala, *Angola* 10°45' S, 14°58' E **220**
Quibaxe, *Angola* 8°30' S, 14°36' E **220**
Quibdó, *Col.* 5°40' N, 76°38' W **136**
Quibell, *Can.* 49°57' N, 93°26' W **90**
Quiberon, Presqu'île de, *Fr.* 47°32' N, 3°9' W **150**
Quicabo, *Angola* 8°20' S, 13°47' E **220**
Quick, *Can.* 54°35' N, 126°58' W **108**
Quigley, *Can.* 56°5' N, 110°55' W **108**
Quiĩama National Park, *Angola* 9°57' S, 13°20' E **206**
Quiindy, *Parag.* 26°0' S, 57°14' W **139**
Quilá, *Mex.* 24°23' N, 107°13' W **112**
Quilán, Isla, island, *Chile* 43°34' S, 74°35' W **134**
Quilcene, *Wash., U.S.* 47°48' N, 122°53' W **100**
Quilengues, *Angola* 14°6' S, 14°3' E **220**
Quill Lake, *Can.* 52°4' N, 104°16' W **108**
Quillabamba, *Peru* 12°50' S, 72°43' W **137**
Quillacollo, *Bol.* 17°29' S, 66°13' W **137**
Quillagua, *Chile* 21°40' S, 69°33' W **137**
Quillaicillo, *Chile* 31°24' S, 71°37' W **134**
Quillan, *Fr.* 42°52' N, 2°9' E **164**
Quilpie, *Austral.* 26°37' S, 144°15' E **231**
Quilpué, *Chile* 33°3' S, 71°26' W **134**
Quimbele, *Angola* 6°32' S, 16°10' E **218**
Quime, *Bol.* 17°5' S, 67°18' W **137**
Quimilí, *Arg.* 27°38' S, 62°25' W **139**
Quimistán, *Hond.* 15°22' N, 88°22' W **116**
Quinault, *Wash., U.S.* 47°26' N, 123°51' W **100**
Quinault, river, *Wash., U.S.* 47°22' N, 124°9' W **100**
Quince Mil, *Peru* 13°15' S, 70°44' W **137**
Quincy, *Fla., U.S.* 30°34' N, 84°35' W **96**
Quincy, *Mass., U.S.* 42°14' N, 71°1' W **104**
Quincy, *Mich., U.S.* 41°56' N, 84°54' W **102**
Quincy, *Mo., U.S.* 39°55' N, 91°25' W **94**
Quincy, *Oreg., U.S.* 46°7' N, 123°10' W **100**
Quines, *Arg.* 32°15' S, 65°48' W **134**
Quinga, *Mozambique* 15°49' S, 40°11' E **224**
Quinhagak, *Alas., U.S.* 59°41' N, 161°45' W **106**
Quinigua, Serranía, peak, *Venez.* 4°19' N, 65°41' W **136**
Quintana Roo, adm. division, *Mex.* 19°18' N, 88°58' W **115**
Quintanar de la Orden, *Sp.* 39°35' N, 3°2' W **164**
Quinter, *Kans., U.S.* 39°3' N, 100°14' W **90**
Quintette Mountain, peak, *Can.* 54°51' N, 120°59' W **108**
Quintin, *Fr.* 48°24' N, 2°55' W **150**
Quinto, *Sp.* 41°24' N, 0°31' E **164**
Quinzau, *Angola* 6°50' S, 12°43' E **218**
Quionga, *Mozambique* 10°37' S, 40°33' E **224**
Quiquibey, river, *Bol.* 14°48' S, 67°39' W **137**
Quiriguá, ruin(s), *Guatemala* 15°15' N, 89°10' W **115**
Quirima, *Angola* 10°49' S, 18°4' E **220**
Quirinópolis, *Braz.* 18°35' S, 50°32' W **138**
Quirke Lake, *Can.* 46°27' N, 83°4' W **94**
Quiroga, *Arg.* 35°18' S, 61°27' W **139**
Quiroga, Punta, *Arg.* 42°23' S, 66°1' W **134**
Quirusillas, *Bol.* 18°23' S, 63°57' W **137**
Quisiro, *Venez.* 10°56' N, 71°18' W **136**
Quissanga, *Mozambique* 12°24' S, 40°30' E **224**
Quissico, *Mozambique* 24°40' S, 34°43' E **227**
Quitapa, *Angola* 10°23' S, 18°11' E **220**
Quitaque, *Tex., U.S.* 34°21' N, 101°4' W **92**
Quiterajo, *Mozambique* 11°45' S, 40°27' E **224**
Quitilipi, *Arg.* 26°53' S, 60°13' W **139**
Quitman, *Ga., U.S.* 30°46' N, 83°34' W **96**
Quitman, *La., U.S.* 32°20' N, 92°44' W **103**
Quitman, *Miss., U.S.* 32°2' N, 88°43' W **103**
Quitman, *Tex., U.S.* 32°47' N, 95°27' W **103**
Quito, *Ecua.* 0°17' N, 78°49' W **130**
Quitor, *Chile* 22°50' S, 68°14' W **137**
Quitovac, *Mex.* 31°30' N, 112°45' W **92**
Quixadá, *Braz.* 4°56' S, 39°4' W **132**
Quixaxe, *Mozambique* 15°16' S, 40°9' E **224**
Qujiang, *China* 24°38' N, 113°34' E **198**
Qulan (Lŭgovoy), *Kaz.* 42°54' N, 72°44' E **184**
Qulandy, *Kaz.* 46°6' N, 59°28' E **184**
Qulbān Layyah, spring, *Iraq* 29°47' N, 46°1' E **196**
Qullissat, *Den.* 70°3' N, 53°2' W **106**
Qulsary, *Kaz.* 46°58' N, 54°1' E **158**
Qum see Qom, *Iran* 34°39' N, 50°50' E **180**
Qumarlêb, *China* 34°27' N, 95°24' E **188**
Qumsay, *Kaz.* 49°27' N, 58°25' E **158**
Qunayyah, *Syr.* 34°30' N, 37°1' E **194**
Quneitra see Al Qunayţirah, *Syr.* 33°7' N, 35°49' E **194**
Qŭnghirot, *Uzb.* 43°1' N, 58°50' E **180**
Qu'nyido, *China* 31°18' N, 97°58' E **188**
Quogue, *N.Y., U.S.* 40°49' N, 72°36' W **104**
Quoin Point, *S. Af.* 35°3' S, 19°34' E **227**
Quorn, *Can.* 49°25' N, 90°54' W **94**
Qurayyāt, *Oman* 23°16' N, 58°54' E **182**
Qŭrghonteppa, *Taj.* 37°49' N, 68°48' E **197**
Quryq, *Kaz.* 43°11' N, 51°41' E **158**
Qûş, *Egypt* 25°54' N, 32°44' E **182**
Qusar, *Azerb.* 41°24' N, 48°27' E **195**
Quşeir, *Egypt* 26°8' N, 34°13' E **180**
Qusmuryn, *Kaz.* 52°27' N, 64°37' E **184**
Qusum, *China* 29°5' N, 92°12' E **197**
Quthing, *Lesotho* 30°25' S, 27°41' E **227**
Quttinirpaaq National Park, *Can.* 81°58' N, 73°8' W **72**
Quwo, *China* 35°40' N, 111°27' E **198**
Quxian, *China* 30°51' N, 106°52' E **198**
Qüxü, *China* 29°21' N, 90°39' E **197**
Quy Chau, *Vietnam* 19°32' N, 105°7' E **202**
Quzhou, *China* 36°49' N, 114°53' E **198**
Quzhou, *China* 28°56' N, 118°49' E **198**
Qvareli, *Ga.* 41°57' N, 45°48' E **195**
Qyyq, *Kaz.* 43°46' N, 70°57' E **184**
Qyzan, *Kaz.* 44°56' N, 52°45' E **158**
Qyzylkayyn, *Kaz.* 45°47' N, 80°14' E **184**
Qyzylorda, *Kaz.* 44°49' N, 65°34' E **184**
Qyzylorda, adm. division, *Kaz.* 42°40' N, 66°6' E **197**
Qyzylorda, adm. division, *Kaz.* 44°54' N, 61°41' E **184**
Qyzylqaq Köli, lake, *Kaz.* 53°27' N, 73°13' E **184**
Qyzylzhar, *Kaz.* 48°17' N, 69°38' E **184**

R

Raab, river, *Aust.* 47°2' N, 15°40' E **168**
Raahe (Brahestad), *Fin.* 64°41' N, 24°27' E **152**
Raanujärvi, *Fin.* 66°39' N, 24°41' E **152**
Raate, *Fin.* 64°47' N, 29°43' E **152**
Rab, *Croatia* 44°46' N, 14°45' E **156**
Raba, *Indonesia* 8°31' S, 118°52' E **192**
Rába, river, *Hung.* 47°26' N, 17°10' E **168**
Rábahídvég, *Hung.* 47°4' N, 16°45' E **168**
Rabai, *Kenya* 3°54' S, 39°35' E **224**
Rabak, *Sudan* 13°6' N, 32°46' E **182**
Rabast, Cap de, *Can.* 49°59' N, 64°15' W **111**
Rabastens, *Fr.* 43°48' N, 1°42' E **150**
Rabastens, *Fr.* 43°23' N, 0°8' E **164**
Rabat, *Mor.* 33°53' N, 7°7' W **214**
Rabaul, *P.N.G.* 4°15' S, 152°8' E **238**
Rabbit Ears Pass, *Colo., U.S.* 40°22' N, 106°38' W **90**
Rabbit Lake, *Can.* 53°8' N, 107°46' W **108**
Rabbit, river, *Can.* 59°25' N, 127°17' W **108**
Rabga Pass, *China* 27°51' N, 87°33' E **197**
Rābigh, *Saudi Arabia* 22°48' N, 39°0' E **182**
Rabrovo, *Serb.* 44°33' N, 21°32' E **168**
Rabyānah, spring, *Lib.* 24°16' N, 21°57' E **216**
Răcăşdia, *Rom.* 44°59' N, 21°37' E **168**
Racconigi, *It.* 44°45' N, 7°41' E **167**
Raccoon Point, *La., U.S.* 28°58' N, 91°7' W **103**
Race, Cape, *Can.* 46°41' N, 53°15' W **111**
Race Point, *Mass., U.S.* 42°3' N, 70°21' W **104**
Race Point, *N.Y., U.S.* 41°11' N, 72°2' W **104**
Race, The 41°11' N, 72°9' W **104**
Raceland, *La., U.S.* 29°42' N, 90°37' W **103**
Rach Gia, *Vietnam* 10°1' N, 105°5' E **202**
Raciąż, *Pol.* 52°46' N, 20°5' E **152**
Racine, *Wis., U.S.* 42°42' N, 87°48' W **102**
Racing, river, *Can.* 58°36' N, 125°4' W **108**
Raco, *Mich., U.S.* 46°22' N, 84°44' W **94**
Raczki, *Pol.* 53°58' N, 22°46' E **166**
Radan, *Serb.* 43°1' N, 21°22' E **168**
Radashkovichy, *Belarus* 54°9' N, 27°14' E **166**
Rădăuţi, *Rom.* 47°50' N, 25°55' E **152**
Radcliff, *Ky., U.S.* 37°50' N, 85°57' W **96**
Radebeul, *Ger.* 51°6' N, 13°37' E **152**
Radford, *Va., U.S.* 37°6' N, 80°35' W **96**
Radhanpur, *India* 23°49' N, 71°38' E **186**
Radio Beacon, site, *Can.* 43°55' N, 60°7' W **111**
Radishchevo, *Russ.* 52°49' N, 47°52' E **154**
Radisson, *Can.* 52°28' N, 107°23' W **108**
Radisson, *Can.* 53°44' N, 77°40' W **106**
Raditsa Krylovka, *Russ.* 53°17' N, 34°23' E **154**
Radlinski, Mount, peak, *Antarctica* 82°22' S, 102°9' W **248**
Radna, *Rom.* 46°6' N, 21°42' E **168**
Radojevo, *Serb.* 45°44' N, 20°47' E **168**
Radolfzell, *Ger.* 47°44' N, 8°57' E **150**
Radom, *Pol.* 51°23' N, 21°9' E **152**
Radom, *Sudan* 9°49' N, 24°50' E **224**
Radom National Park, *Sudan* 9°1' N, 23°41' E **224**
Radomiru, *Rom.* 44°8' N, 24°10' E **156**
Radomsko, *Pol.* 51°4' N, 19°27' E **152**
Radomyshl', *Ukr.* 50°29' N, 29°19' E **158**
Radovići, *Mont.* 42°23' N, 18°40' E **168**
Radoviš, *Maced.* 41°38' N, 22°27' E **168**
Radstock, *U.K.* 51°17' N, 2°27' W **162**
Raduzhnyy, *Russ.* 62°0' N, 77°39' E **169**
Radviliškis, *Lith.* 55°47' N, 23°30' E **166**
Radville, *Can.* 49°26' N, 104°19' W **90**
Raḑwá, Jabal, peak, *Saudi Arabia* 24°32' N, 38°11' E **182**
Radway, *Can.* 54°3' N, 112°57' W **108**
Radziwiłłówka, *Pol.* 52°22' N, 23°1' E **152**
Rae Bareli, *India* 26°13' N, 81°14' E **197**
Rae Isthmus, *Can.* 66°53' N, 91°0' W **106**
Rae, Mount, peak, *Can.* 50°36' N, 115°4' W **90**
Rae, river, *Can.* 68°7' N, 118°55' W **98**
Rae-Edzo, *Can.* 62°42' N, 116°26' W **106**
Raesfeld, *Ger.* 51°46' N, 6°51' E **167**
Raetihi, *N.Z.* 39°27' S, 175°15' E **240**

Rāf, Jabal, peak, *Saudi Arabia* 29°12' N, 39°47' E **180**
Rafaela, *Arg.* 31°14' S, 61°27' W **139**
Rafa', *Gaza Strip, Israel* 31°16' N, 34°15' E **194**
Rafaï, *Cen. Af. Rep.* 4°58' N, 23°58' E **224**
Rafalivka, *Ukr.* 51°18' N, 25°55' E **152**
Rafḥā', *Saudi Arabia* 29°41' N, 43°31' E **180**
Rafsanjān, *Iran* 30°22' N, 56°5' E **196**
Raft River Mountains, *Utah, U.S.* 41°48' N, 113°46' W **90**
Rafter, *Can.* 55°38' N, 101°11' W **108**
Rafz, *Switz.* 47°36' N, 8°32' E **150**
Raga, *Sudan* 8°25' N, 25°39' E **224**
Raga, river, *Sudan* 8°11' N, 25°30' E **224**
Ragachow, *Belarus* 53°5' N, 30°9' E **154**
Ragag, *Sudan* 10°56' N, 24°45' E **224**
Ragauka, *Latv.* 56°41' N, 27°24' E **166**
Ragay Gulf 13°35' N, 122°30' E **203**
Ragged, Mount, peak, *Austral.* 33°29' S, 123°13' E **230**
Raglan, *N.Z.* 37°51' S, 174°54' E **240**
Ragley, *La., U.S.* 30°29' N, 93°15' W **103**
Raguba, oil field, *Lib.* 29°1' N, 18°57' E **216**
Ragunda, *Nor.* 63°3' N, 16°23' E **154**
Ragusa, *It.* 36°54' N, 14°42' E **216**
Ragusa see Dubrovnik, *Croatia* 42°38' N, 18°5' E **156**
Rahad el Berdi, *Sudan* 11°16' N, 23°52' E **224**
Raheita, *Eritrea* 12°43' N, 43°5' E **218**
Rahib, Jebel, peak, *Sudan* 17°41' N, 27°5' E **226**
Rahimyar Khan, *Pak.* 28°24' N, 70°18' E **186**
Rahotu, *N.Z.* 39°20' S, 173°49' E **240**
Rahuri, *India* 19°25' N, 74°38' E **188**
Raíces, *Arg.* 31°53' S, 59°14' W **139**
Raichur, *India* 16°12' N, 77°20' E **188**
Raiganj, *India* 25°35' N, 88°6' E **197**
Raigarh, *India* 21°54' N, 83°22' E **197**
Rakiura National Park, *N.Z.* 47°25' S, 168°23' E **240**
Railroad Flat, *Calif., U.S.* 38°20' N, 120°32' W **100**
Railroad Pass, *Nev., U.S.* 39°22' N, 117°25' W **90**
Rainbach, *Aust.* 48°33' N, 14°28' E **156**
Rainbow, *Calif., U.S.* 33°24' N, 117°10' W **101**
Rainbow Falls, site, *Hawai'i, U.S.* 19°42' N, 155°10' W **99**
Rainbow Lake, *Can.* 58°28' N, 119°29' W **108**
Rainbow Springs, site, *Fla., U.S.* 29°6' N, 82°27' W **105**
Rainer, *Minn., U.S.* 48°35' N, 93°21' W **94**
Rainier, *Oreg., U.S.* 46°4' N, 122°57' W **100**
Rainier, Mount, peak, *Wash., U.S.* 46°49' N, 121°49' W **100**
Rainy Lake, *Can.* 48°41' N, 94°17' W **80**
Rainy River, *Can.* 48°44' N, 94°34' W **90**
Rainy, river, *Can.* 48°31' N, 94°41' W **82**
Raippaluoto see Replot, *Fin.* 63°13' N, 21°24' E **152**
Raipur, *India* 21°15' N, 81°38' E **197**
Rairakhol, *India* 21°4' N, 84°20' E **188**
Ra'īs, *Saudi Arabia* 23°33' N, 38°37' E **182**
Raisduoddarhaldde, peak, *Nor.* 69°19' N, 21°11' E **152**
Raisin, *Calif., U.S.* 36°36' N, 119°55' W **101**
Raisinghnagar, *India* 29°31' N, 73°27' E **186**
Raisio, *Fin.* 60°28' N, 22°10' E **166**
Raj Samund, *India* 25°1' N, 73°51' E **186**
Raja, *Est.* 58°46' N, 26°53' E **166**
Raja, Ujung, *Indonesia* 3°30' N, 96°14' E **196**
Rajada, *Braz.* 8°46' S, 40°50' W **132**
Rajahmundry, *India* 17°0' N, 81°48' E **190**
Rajamäki, *Fin.* 60°30' N, 24°44' E **166**
Rajapalaiyam, *India* 9°27' N, 77°33' E **188**
Rajampet, *India* 14°11' N, 79°8' E **188**
Rajanpur, *Pak.* 29°8' N, 70°21' E **186**
Rajasthan, adm. division, *India* 26°20' N, 70°59' E **186**
Rajasthan Canal, *India* 28°0' N, 72°30' E **186**
Rajbari, *Bangladesh* 23°40' N, 89°36' E **197**
Rajgarh, *India* 28°38' N, 75°24' E **197**
Rajin (Raseon), *N. Korea* 42°15' N, 130°19' E **200**
Rajka, *Hung.* 47°59' N, 17°12' E **168**
Rajkot, *India* 22°17' N, 70°46' E **186**
Rajshahi, *Bangladesh* 24°21' N, 88°33' E **197**
Raka, river, *China* 29°23' N, 85°57' E **197**
Rakai, *Uganda* 0°43' N, 31°22' E **224**
Rakaia, *N.Z.* 43°46' S, 172°0' E **240**
Rakamaz, *Hung.* 48°6' N, 21°27' E **152**
Rakaposhi, peak, *Pak.* 36°7' N, 74°22' E **186**
Rakaw, *Belarus* 53°58' N, 27°2' E **166**
Rakhshan, river, *Pak.* 26°58' N, 63°58' E **186**
Rakhyūt, *Oman* 16°41' N, 53°18' E **182**
Rakisvaara, peak, *Nor.* 68°13' N, 20°6' E **152**
Rakke, *Est.* 58°58' N, 26°13' E **166**
Rakops, *Botswana* 21°3' S, 24°24' E **227**
Rakovitsa, *Bulg.* 43°46' N, 22°27' E **168**
Rakovo, *Bulg.* 42°5' N, 22°43' E **168**
Rakow, *Ger.* 54°2' N, 13°2' E **152**
Rakula, *Russ.* 63°42' N, 41°36' E **154**
Rakulka, *Russ.* 61°50' N, 45°19' E **154**
Rakvere, *Est.* 59°20' N, 26°19' E **166**
Raleigh, *Miss., U.S.* 32°1' N, 89°31' W **103**
Raleigh, *N.C., U.S.* 35°45' N, 78°43' W **96**
Ralik Chain, islands, *North Pacific Ocean* 7°28' N, 166°35' E **238**
Ralja, *Serb.* 44°33' N, 20°32' E **168**
Ralls, *Tex., U.S.* 33°39' N, 101°23' W **92**
Ralston, *Can.* 50°15' N, 111°12' W **90**
Rām Allāh, *West Bank, Israel* 31°53' N, 35°11' E **194**
Rama, *Israel* 32°56' N, 35°22' E **194**
Rama, *Nicar.* 12°10' N, 84°10' W **115**
Ramādī Barrage, dam, *Iraq* 33°39' N, 42°10' E **180**
Ramage Point 73°23' S, 115°8' W **248**
Ramah, *Colo., U.S.* 39°6' N, 104°11' W **92**
Ramah, *N. Mex., U.S.* 35°7' N, 108°29' W **92**
Ramales de la Victoria, *Sp.* 43°14' N, 3°30' W **164**
Ramalho, Serra do, *Braz.* 14°0' S, 44°39' W **132**
Ramallo, *Arg.* 33°31' S, 60°1' W **139**
Raman, *Thai.* 6°24' N, 101°22' E **196**
Raman, oil field, *Turk.* 37°45' N, 41°29' E **195**
Ramanava, *Belarus* 53°56' N, 24°37' E **166**
Ramanuj Ganj, *India* 23°46' N, 83°39' E **197**
Ramat Magshimim, *Israel* 32°51' N, 35°49' E **194**
Ramatlabama, *Botswana* 25°38' S, 25°31' E **227**
Rambau, Lac, lake, *Can.* 53°39' N, 70°45' W **111**
Rambouillet, *Fr.* 48°38' N, 1°49' E **163**
Rambutyo, island, *P.N.G.* 2°44' S, 147°51' E **192**
Ramea, *Can.* 47°31' N, 57°24' W **111**
Ramerupt, *Fr.* 48°30' N, 4°17' E **163**
Rameshki, *Russ.* 57°18' N, 36°1' E **154**
Ramgarh, *India* 23°35' N, 85°32' E **197**
Ramgarh, *India* 27°22' N, 70°29' E **186**
Ramírez, Isla, island, *Chile* 51°49' S, 76°41' W **134**
Rāmis, river, *Eth.* 8°27' N, 41°27' E **224**
Ramla, *Israel* 31°55' N, 34°52' E **194**
Ramlu, peak, *Eritrea* 13°22' N, 41°38' E **182**
Ramnagar, *India* 25°14' N, 83°3' E **197**
Ramnagar, *India* 29°24' N, 79°6' E **197**
Ramnäs, *Nor.* 59°46' N, 16°10' E **152**
Râmnicu Vâlcea, *Rom.* 45°7' N, 24°21' E **156**
Ramon', *Russ.* 51°52' N, 39°13' E **158**
Ramon, Har, peak, *Israel* 30°29' N, 34°36' E **194**
Ramón Santamarina, *Arg.* 38°28' S, 59°21' W **139**
Ramón Trigo, *Uru.* 32°21' S, 54°39' W **139**
Ramona, *Calif., U.S.* 33°2' N, 116°53' W **101**
Ramonal, *Mex.* 18°25' N, 88°34' W **115**
Ramore, *Can.* 48°26' N, 80°20' W **94**
Ramos, *Mex.* 22°48' N, 101°56' W **114**
Ramos Arizpe, *Mex.* 25°32' N, 100°57' W **114**
Ramos, oil field, *Arg.* 22°41' S, 64°15' W **137**
Ramos, river, *Mex.* 25°13' N, 105°19' W **114**
Ramotswa, *Botswana* 24°52' S, 25°47' E **227**
Rampart, *Alas., U.S.* 65°19' N, 150°13' W **98**
Ramparts, river, *Can.* 66°25' N, 130°46' W **98**
Rampur, *India* 28°46' N, 79°3' E **197**
Rampur Hat, *India* 24°9' N, 87°48' E **197**
Ramsay, *Mich., U.S.* 46°28' N, 90°1' W **94**
Ramsele, *Nor.* 63°31' N, 16°29' E **152**
Ramsey, *Ill., U.S.* 39°8' N, 89°6' W **102**
Ramsey, *N.J., U.S.* 41°3' N, 74°9' W **104**
Ramsey Lake, *Can.* 47°9' N, 82°46' W **110**
Ramsgate, *U.K.* 51°20' N, 1°24' E **163**
Ramsjö, *Nor.* 62°11' N, 15°38' E **152**
Ramu, *Kenya* 3°50' N, 41°13' E **224**
Ramu, river, *P.N.G.* 5°7' S, 144°53' E **192**
Ramvik, *Nor.* 62°48' N, 17°49' E **152**
Rana, Cerro, peak, *Col.* 3°34' N, 68°9' W **136**
Ranaghat, *India* 23°7' N, 88°35' E **197**
Ranai, *Indonesia* 3°59' N, 108°23' E **196**
Ranau, *Malaysia* 5°57' N, 116°41' E **203**
Rancagua, *Chile* 34°11' S, 70°50' W **134**
Rance, *Belg.* 50°7' N, 4°17' E **163**
Rancharia, *Braz.* 22°14' S, 50°56' W **138**
Rancheria, river, *Can.* 60°0' N, 130°57' W **108**
Ranchester, *Wyo., U.S.* 44°54' N, 107°10' W **90**
Ranchi, *India* 23°22' N, 85°19' E **197**
Ranchita, *Calif., U.S.* 33°13' N, 116°33' W **101**
Rancho California, *Calif., U.S.* 33°30' N, 117°11' W **101**
Rancho Cordova, *Calif., U.S.* 38°35' N, 121°19' W **92**
Rancho de Caça dos Tapiúnas, *Braz.* 10°50' S, 56°2' W **130**
Rancho Mirage, *Calif., U.S.* 33°43' N, 116°26' W **101**
Rancho Santa Fe, *Calif., U.S.* 33°1' N, 117°13' W **101**
Ranchos de Taos, *N. Mex., U.S.* 36°20' N, 105°37' W **92**
Randa, *Nig.* 9°7' N, 8°27' E **222**
Randers, *Den.* 56°27' N, 10°0' E **152**
Randers Fjord 56°32' N, 9°59' E **152**
Randijaur, lake, *Nor.* 66°41' N, 18°35' E **152**
Randle, *Wash., U.S.* 46°31' N, 121°59' W **100**
Randolph, *Me., U.S.* 44°14' N, 69°46' W **104**
Randolph, *Nebr., U.S.* 42°21' N, 97°21' W **90**
Randolph, *N.H., U.S.* 44°22' N, 71°17' W **104**
Randolph, *Utah, U.S.* 41°40' N, 111°11' W **90**
Randolph, *Vt., U.S.* 43°55' N, 72°41' W **104**
Randolph, *Wis., U.S.* 43°32' N, 89°0' W **102**
Randolph Air Force Base, *Tex., U.S.* 29°28' N, 98°21' W **92**
Randolph Center, *Vt., U.S.* 43°56' N, 72°37' W **104**
Random Lake, *Wis., U.S.* 43°32' N, 87°58' W **102**
Randsburg, *Calif., U.S.* 35°21' N, 117°41' W **101**
Rånеå, *Nor.* 65°51' N, 22°16' E **152**
Ranérou, *Senegal* 15°19' N, 14°0' W **222**
Ranfurly, *N.Z.* 45°8' S, 170°6' E **240**
Rangae, *Thai.* 6°19' N, 101°45' E **196**
Rangamati, *Bangladesh* 22°37' N, 92°7' E **188**
Rangeley, *Me., U.S.* 44°57' N, 70°40' W **94**
Rangely, *Colo., U.S.* 40°4' N, 108°48' W **90**
Ranger, *Tex., U.S.* 32°27' N, 98°41' W **92**
Rangiora, *N.Z.* 43°20' S, 172°34' E **240**
Rangkŭl, *Taj.* 38°27' N, 74°25' E **184**
Rangoon see Yangon, *Myanmar* 16°45' N, 96°0' E **202**
Rangpur, *Bangladesh* 25°41' N, 89°12' E **197**
Rangsang, island, *Indonesia* 1°1' N, 103°5' E **196**
Raniganj, *India* 23°37' N, 87°7' E **197**
Ranikhet, *India* 29°40' N, 79°25' E **197**
Rāniyah, *Iraq* 36°15' N, 44°52' E **195**
Rankin, *Tex., U.S.* 31°12' N, 101°57' W **92**
Rankin Inlet, *Can.* 62°50' N, 92°9' W **106**
Rankūs, *Syr.* 33°45' N, 36°22' E **194**
Rann of Kutch 23°59' N, 69°56' E **186**
Rano, *Nig.* 11°32' N, 8°34' E **222**
Ranohira, *Madagascar* 22°36' S, 45°22' E **220**
Ranomafana, *Madagascar* 24°33' S, 46°59' E **220**
Ranomafana, *Madagascar* 21°13' S, 47°23' E **220**
Ranomena, *Madagascar* 23°24' S, 47°16' E **220**
Ranong, *Thai.* 9°54' N, 98°38' E **192**
Ranongga (Ganongga), island, *Solomon Islands* 8°5' S, 156°30' E **242**
Ranot, *Thai.* 7°48' N, 100°20' E **196**
Ransiki, *Indonesia* 1°27' S, 134°2' E **192**
Ransom, *Ill., U.S.* 41°9' N, 88°39' W **102**
Rantasalmi, *Fin.* 62°2' N, 28°15' E **166**
Rantau, oil field, *Indonesia* 4°23' N, 98°7' E **196**
Rantauprapat, *Indonesia* 2°6' N, 99°50' E **196**
Rantoul, *Ill., U.S.* 40°18' N, 88°9' W **102**
Rantsila, *Fin.* 64°30' N, 25°37' E **152**
Ranua, *Fin.* 65°53' N, 26°30' E **152**
Rao, *Senegal* 15°56' N, 16°26' W **222**
Raoui, Erg er, *Alg.* 30°3' N, 3°41' W **214**
Rapahoe, *N.Z.* 42°23' S, 171°17' E **240**
Raper, Cabo 46°54' S, 77°3' W **134**
Raper, Cape, *Can.* 69°39' N, 67°9' W **106**
Rapid City, *Can.* 50°9' N, 100°3' W **90**
Rapid City, *S. Dak., U.S.* 44°3' N, 103°15' W **90**
Rapid River, *Mich., U.S.* 45°55' N, 86°59' W **94**
Rapid, river, *Minn., U.S.* 48°16' N, 95°2' W **90**
Räpina, *Est.* 58°6' N, 27°27' E **166**
Rapla, *Est.* 59°0' N, 24°47' E **166**
Rappahannock, river, *Va., U.S.* 38°36' N, 77°58' W **80**
Rápulo, river, *Bol.* 14°24' S, 66°30' W **137**
Raqiq, ruin(s), *Israel* 31°16' N, 34°39' E **194**
Rara National Park, *Nepal* 29°29' N, 81°58' E **197**
Rarotonga, island, *N.Z.* 21°14' S, 159°47' W **241**
Ra's Abū Madd, *Saudi Arabia* 24°44' N, 37°10' E **182**
Ra's Abū Qumayyiş, *Saudi Arabia* 24°33' N, 51°30' E **196**
Ra's al Arḍ, *Kuwait* 29°19' N, 48°8' E **196**
Ra's al 'Ayn, *Syr.* 36°49' N, 40°7' E **195**
Ra's al Basīt 35°52' N, 35°13' E **156**
Ra's al Bayyāḑah, *Leb.* 33°9' N, 35°0' E **194**
Ra's al Ḩadd, *Oman* 22°33' N, 59°46' E **182**
Ra's al Hilāl, *Lib.* 33°2' N, 22°7' E **216**
Ra's al Kalb, *Yemen* 13°55' N, 48°41' E **182**
Ra's al Khaymah, *U.A.E.* 25°45' N, 55°57' E **196**
Ra's al Madrakah, *Oman* 18°59' N, 56°39' E **182**
Ra's al Mil', *Lib.* 32°1' N, 24°56' E **180**
Ra's al Mish'āb, *Saudi Arabia* 28°9' N, 48°36' E **196**
Ra's al Qulay'ah, *Kuwait* 28°53' N, 48°17' E **196**
Ra's al Unūf, *Lib.* 30°31' N, 18°31' E **216**
Ra's 'Āmir, *Lib.* 33°2' N, 20°43' E **216**
Ra's an Naqb, *Jordan* 29°57' N, 35°32' E **180**
Ra's as Sa'diyāt, *Leb.* 33°41' N, 35°14' E **194**
Ra's ash Shaqq, *Leb.* 34°19' N, 35°34' E **194**
Ra's ash Sharbatāt, *Oman* 17°42' N, 56°21' E **182**
Ra's aţ Ţarfā, *Saudi Arabia* 16°55' N, 41°35' E **182**
Ra's at Tīn, *Lib.* 32°41' N, 23°5' E **180**
Ra's az Zawr, *Saudi Arabia* 27°28' N, 49°0' E **196**
Rastu Ba'labakk, *Leb.* 34°15' N, 36°24' E **194**
Ra's Ḑarbat 'Alī, *Oman* 16°42' N, 52°15' E **182**
Râs el 'Ish, *Egypt* 31°8' N, 32°17' E **194**
Ras el Ma, *Alg.* 36°7' N, 5°31' E **150**
Râs el Mâ, *Alg.* 34°29' N, 0°48' E **214**
Râs el Mâ, *Mali* 16°36' N, 4°38' W **222**
Ra's Fartak, *Yemen* 15°38' N, 51°28' E **182**
Râs Ghârib, *Egypt* 28°21' N, 33°0' E **180**
Râs Ghârib, oil field, *Egypt* 27°56' N, 32°47' E **143**
Ra's Ḩāţibah, *Saudi Arabia* 21°55' N, 38°6' E **182**
Ra's Ibn Hānī', *Syr.* 35°35' N, 35°44' E **194**
Ra's Jibsh, *Oman* 21°28' N, 58°38' E **182**
Ra's Mirbāţ, *Oman* 16°48' N, 54°46' E **182**
Ras Muhammad National Park, *Egypt* 27°44' N, 33°47' E **182**
Ra's Musandam, *Oman* 26°18' N, 56°29' E **196**
Ra's Shamrah, site, *Mediterranean Sea* 35°35' N, 35°41' E **156**
Ra's Shamrah (Ugarit), site, *Syr.* 35°33' N, 35°44' E **194**
Ra's Sharwayn, *Yemen* 15°11' N, 51°29' E **182**
Ra's Shū'ab, *Yemen* 12°24' N, 52°34' E **182**
Ra's Tannūrah, *Saudi Arabia* 26°39' N, 50°7' E **196**
Rasa, Punta, *Arg.* 40°51' S, 62°17' W **134**
Raseiniai, *Lith.* 55°22' N, 23°5' E **166**
Raseon see Rajin, *N. Korea* 42°15' N, 130°19' E **200**
Rashaant, *Mongolia* 45°21' N, 106°14' E **198**
Rashad, *Sudan* 11°51' N, 31°4' E **216**
Rāshayyā, *Leb.* 33°29' N, 35°50' E **194**
Rashi, oil field, *Iraq* 30°9' N, 47°1' E **196**
Rashîd (Rosetta), *Egypt* 31°23' N, 30°21' E **180**
Rasht, *Iran* 37°15' N, 49°32' E **195**
Raška, *Serb.* 43°17' N, 20°36' E **168**
Raška, river, *Serb.* 43°7' N, 20°35' E **168**
Rasony, *Belarus* 55°53' N, 28°50' E **166**
Rasovo, *Bulg.* 43°42' N, 23°14' E **168**
Rășpopeni, *Mold.* 47°45' N, 28°37' E **156**
Rasskazovo, *Russ.* 52°37' N, 41°49' E **158**
Rastatt, *Ger.* 48°50' N, 8°10' E **150**
Rastede, *Ger.* 53°14' N, 8°11' E **163**
Rastigaissa, peak, *Nor.* 69°58' N, 26°5' E **152**
Rastu, *Rom.* 43°53' N, 23°17' E **168**
Rasua Garhi, *Nepal* 28°18' N, 85°24' E **197**
Rat, island, *Alas., U.S.* 51°33' N, 177°41' E **160**
Rat Islands, *Bering Sea* 51°41' N, 174°8' E **160**
Rat Lake, lake, *Can.* 56°23' N, 99°38' W **108**
Rat Rapids, *Can.* 51°10' N, 90°13' W **110**
Rat, river, *Can.* 56°8' N, 99°19' W **108**
Rat, river, *Wis., U.S.* 45°33' N, 88°38' W **94**
Rata, *N.Z.* 40°0' S, 175°30' E **240**
Rataje, *Serb.* 43°28' N, 21°7' E **168**
Ratak Chain, islands, *North Pacific Ocean* 9°43' N, 169°11' E **238**
Ratamka, *Belarus* 53°54' N, 27°21' E **166**
Ratangarh, *India* 28°3' N, 74°38' E **186**
Ratanpur, *India* 22°18' N, 82°10' E **197**
Ratcliff, *Tex., U.S.* 31°22' N, 95°8' W **103**
Rath, *India* 25°35' N, 79°34' E **197**
Rätikon, *Switz.* 46°55' N, 9°41' E **167**
Ratina, *Serb.* 43°42' N, 20°44' E **168**
Ratlam, *India* 23°18' N, 75°1' E **188**
Ratnagiri, *India* 17°0' N, 73°19' E **188**
Ratne, *Ukr.* 51°38' N, 24°32' E **152**
Raton, *N. Mex., U.S.* 36°53' N, 104°27' W **92**
Raton Pass, *N. Mex., U.S.* 36°58' N, 104°29' W **92**
Ratta, *Russ.* 63°34' N, 83°50' E **169**
Rattlesnake Hills, *Wash., U.S.* 46°30' N, 120°25' W **90**
Rattlesnake Hills, *Wyo., U.S.* 42°50' N, 107°40' W **90**
Rättvik, *Nor.* 60°52' N, 15°6' E **152**
Ratz, Mount, peak, *Can.* 57°23' N, 132°27' W **108**
Raub, *Malaysia* 3°47' N, 101°50' E **196**
Rauch, *Arg.* 36°47' S, 59°8' W **139**
Raudal Yupurari (Devils Cataract), fall(s), *Col.* 0°58' N, 71°28' W **136**
Raudhatain, oil field, *Kuwait* 29°51' N, 47°39' E **196**
Rauer Islands, *Indian Ocean* 68°54' S, 74°26' E **248**
Raufarhöfn, *Ice.* 66°28' N, 16°5' W **143**
Raul Soares, *Braz.* 20°7' S, 42°29' W **138**
Rauma, *Fin.* 61°7' N, 21°29' E **166**
Rauna, *Latv.* 57°19' N, 25°37' E **166**
Raupunga, *N.Z.* 39°3' S, 177°8' E **240**
Raurkela, *India* 22°14' N, 84°57' E **197**
Rautas, *Nor.* 67°59' N, 19°53' E **152**
Rautavaara, *Fin.* 63°28' N, 28°15' E **152**
Rautio, *Fin.* 64°4' N, 24°10' E **154**
Rautjärvi, *Fin.* 61°16' N, 29°7' E **166**
Ravānsar, *Iran* 34°43' N, 46°41' E **180**
Rāvar, *Iran* 31°12' N, 56°55' E **180**
Ravelo, *Bol.* 18°51' S, 65°36' W **137**
Ravena, *N.Y., U.S.* 42°28' N, 73°50' W **104**
Ravenglass, *U.K.* 54°21' N, 3°24' W **162**
Ravenna, *It.* 44°24' N, 12°11' E **167**
Ravenna, *Ky., U.S.* 37°40' N, 83°57' W **94**
Ravenna, *Nebr., U.S.* 41°1' N, 98°55' W **90**
Ravenna, *Ohio, U.S.* 41°8' N, 81°14' W **102**
Ravensthorpe, *Austral.* 33°35' S, 120°1' E **231**
Ravenswood, *W. Va., U.S.* 38°56' N, 81°46' W **94**
Ravi, river, *Pak.* 30°34' N, 71°52' E **186**
Ravn, Kap 68°9' N, 28°16' W **246**
Ravna Banja, *Serb.* 42°45' N, 21°40' E **168**
Ravne, *Slov.* 46°31' N, 14°57' E **156**
Ravno, *Bosn. and Herzg.* 43°50' N, 17°22' E **168**
Rawa Aopa Watumohai National Park, *Indonesia* 4°22' S, 121°38' E **238**
Rāwah, *Iraq* 34°30' N, 41°55' E **180**
Rawalpindi, *Pak.* 33°31' N, 73°4' E **186**
Rawandoz, *Iraq* 36°39' N, 44°31' E **195**
Rawene, *N.Z.* 35°26' S, 173°30' E **240**
Raw'ah, *Saudi Arabia* 19°28' N, 41°44' E **182**
Rawhide Lake, *Can.* 46°36' N, 83°11' W **94**
Rawi, Ko, island, *Thai.* 6°36' N, 98°58' E **196**
Rawicz, *Pol.* 51°36' N, 16°52' E **152**
Rawley Point, *Wis., U.S.* 44°7' N, 87°30' W **102**
Rawlinna, *Austral.* 31°0' S, 125°19' E **231**
Rawlins, *Wyo., U.S.* 41°48' N, 107°14' W **90**
Rawlinson Range, *Austral.* 25°29' S, 127°57' E **230**
Rawson, *Arg.* 43°16' S, 65°7' W **134**
Rawtenstall, *U.K.* 53°42' N, 2°17' W **162**
Raxaul, *India* 26°58' N, 84°48' E **197**
Ray, *N. Dak., U.S.* 48°19' N, 103°11' W **90**
Ray, Cape, *Can.* 47°39' N, 59°56' W **111**
Raya, peak, *Indonesia* 0°40' N, 112°25' E **192**
Rayachoti, *India* 14°2' N, 78°46' E **188**
Rayagada, *India* 19°10' N, 83°24' E **188**
Rayakoski, *Russ.* 68°56' N, 28°44' E **152**
Raychikhinsk, *Russ.* 49°52' N, 129°24' E **190**
Rayevskiy, *Russ.* 54°4' N, 54°54' E **154**
Raymond, *Calif., U.S.* 37°13' N, 119°56' W **100**
Raymond, *Can.* 49°27' N, 112°40' W **90**
Raymond, *N.H., U.S.* 43°2' N, 71°12' W **104**
Raymond, *Wash., U.S.* 46°41' N, 123°44' W **100**
Raymondville, *Tex., U.S.* 26°28' N, 97°47' W **114**
Raymore, *Can.* 51°24' N, 104°31' W **90**
Rayna, *India* 23°2' N, 87°52' E **197**
Rayne, *La., U.S.* 30°13' N, 92°17' W **103**
Rayner Peak, *Antarctica* 67°30' S, 55°30' E **248**
Raynham Center, *Mass., U.S.* 41°55' N, 71°4' W **104**
Rayón, *Mex.* 29°42' N, 110°34' W **92**
Rayón, *Mex.* 21°49' N, 99°39' W **114**
Rayón National Park, *Mex.* 19°58' N, 100°9' W **112**
Rayong, *Thai.* 12°41' N, 101°18' E **202**
Rayside-Balfour, *Can.* 46°35' N, 81°11' W **94**
Rayville, *La., U.S.* 32°27' N, 91°46' W **103**
Raz, Pointe du, *Fr.* 47°46' N, 4°59' W **150**
Razan, *Iran* 35°24' N, 49°2' E **180**
Ražana, *Serb.* 44°5' N, 19°54' E **168**
Ražanj, *Serb.* 43°40' N, 21°32' E **168**
Razbojna, *Serb.* 43°19' N, 21°10' E **168**
Razgrad, *Bulg.* 43°33' N, 26°31' E **156**
Razgrad, adm. division, *Bulg.* 43°33' N, 26°7' E **156**
Razhanka, *Belarus* 53°31' N, 24°46' E **158**
Razzaza Lake, *Iraq* 32°54' N, 42°53' E **180**
Re, Cu Lao, island, *Vietnam* 15°15' N, 109°10' E **202**
Readfield, *Me., U.S.* 44°23' N, 69°59' W **104**
Reading, *Mich., U.S.* 41°49' N, 84°46' W **102**
Reading, *Ohio, U.S.* 39°13' N, 84°27' W **102**
Reading, *U.K.* 51°27' N, 0°57' E **162**
Readsboro, *Vt., U.S.* 42°46' N, 72°58' W **104**
Real, Cordillera, *Bol.* 17°2' S, 67°51' W **132**
Real del Castillo, *Mex.* 31°55' N, 116°20' W **92**
Realicó, *Arg.* 35°2' S, 64°14' W **134**
Ream, *Cambodia* 10°30' N, 103°39' E **202**
Rhbków, *Pol.* 51°52' N, 21°33' E **152**
Rebojo, Cachoeira do, fall(s), *Braz.* 9°44' S, 59°8' W **130**
Reboly, *Russ.* 63°49' N, 30°47' E **152**
Rebouças, *Braz.* 25°37' S, 50°42' W **138**
Rebun Tō, island, *Japan* 45°31' N, 139°42' E **190**
Recalada, Isla, island, *Chile* 53°26' S, 76°1' W **134**
Recalde, *Arg.* 36°41' S, 61°9' W **139**
Recaș, *Rom.* 45°48' N, 21°30' E **168**
Recherche, Archipelago of the, islands, *Great Australian Bight* 34°52' S, 120°32' E **230**
Rechytsa, *Belarus* 52°19' N, 30°26' E **154**
Recife, *Braz.* 8°4' S, 34°57' W **132**
Recife, Cape, *S. Af.* 34°19' S, 25°42' E **227**
Recklinghausen, *Ger.* 51°36' N, 7°12' E **167**
Recoaro Terme, *It.* 45°43' N, 11°13' E **167**
Reconquista, *Arg.* 29°10' S, 59°39' W **139**
Recreo, *Arg.* 29°17' S, 65°6' W **134**
Recsk, *Hung.* 47°55' N, 20°7' E **168**
Red Bay, *Ala., U.S.* 34°26' N, 88°8' W **96**
Red Bay, *Can.* 51°44' N, 56°26' W **111**
Red Bluff, *Calif., U.S.* 40°11' N, 122°16' W **106**
Red Cedar Lake, lake, *Can.* 46°38' N, 80°30' W **94**
Red Cinder, peak, *Calif., U.S.* 40°29' N, 121°20' W **90**
Red Cliff, *Wis., U.S.* 46°51' N, 90°49' W **94**
Red Cloud, *Nebr., U.S.* 40°4' N, 98°33' W **90**
Red Deer, *Can.* 52°13' N, 113°48' W **108**
Red Deer Lake, lake, *Can.* 52°56' N, 101°58' W **108**
Red Deer Point, *Can.* 52°4' N, 99°51' W **108**
Red Deer, river, *Can.* 51°41' N, 115°26' W **108**
Red Devil, *Alas., U.S.* 61°48' N, 157°13' W **73**
Red Hill see Pu'u 'Ula'ula, peak, *Hawai'i, U.S.* 20°42' N, 156°18' W **99**
Red Hill, site, *Va., U.S.* 37°0' N, 78°58' W **96**
Red Hills, *Kans., U.S.* 37°28' N, 99°23' W **90**
Red Hook, *N.Y., U.S.* 41°59' N, 73°53' W **104**
Red Indian Lake, *Can.* 48°41' N, 57°34' W **111**
Red Lake, *Can.* 51°0' N, 93°50' W **90**
Red Lake, *Can.* 50°55' N, 95°1' W **90**
Red Lake, *Minn., U.S.* 47°50' N, 95°1' W **90**
Red Lake Falls, *Minn., U.S.* 47°50' N, 96°18' W **90**
Red Lake Road, *Can.* 49°57' N, 93°23' W **90**
Red Lick, *Miss., U.S.* 31°46' N, 90°58' W **103**
Red Mountain, *Calif., U.S.* 35°21' N, 117°38' W **101**
Red Mountain, peak, *Calif., U.S.* 41°30' N, 124°0' W **90**
Red Mountain, peak, *Mont., U.S.* 47°4' N, 112°49' W **90**
Red Oak, *Iowa, U.S.* 40°59' N, 95°12' W **94**
Red Pass, *Can.* 52°57' N, 119°3' W **108**
Red, river, *Can.* 59°17' N, 128°11' W **108**
Red, river, *Can.* 49°16' N, 97°12' W **90**
Red, river, *La., U.S.* 31°11' N, 92°26' W **103**
Red, river, *Okla., U.S.* 33°56' N, 97°49' W **80**
Red, river, *Tenn., U.S.* 36°26' N, 87°15' W **96**
Red Rock, *Can.* 48°56' N, 88°16' W **94**
Red Sea 18°15' N, 39°26' E **182**
Red Sea, adm. division, *Sudan* 19°37' N, 35°5' E **182**
Red Sucker Lake, *Can.* 54°8' N, 93°38' W **108**
Red Wing, *Minn., U.S.* 44°32' N, 92°32' W **94**
Redang, island, *Malaysia* 5°44' N, 103°4' E **196**
Redcar, *U.K.* 54°36' N, 1°5' W **162**
Redcliff, *Can.* 50°4' N, 110°46' W **90**
Redcliff, *Zimb.* 19°3' S, 29°47' E **224**
Redcliffe, Mount, peak, *Austral.* 28°27' S, 121°20' E **230**
Reddell, *La., U.S.* 30°39' N, 92°26' W **103**
Reddick, *Fla., U.S.* 29°22' N, 82°12' W **105**
Redding, *Calif., U.S.* 40°35' N, 122°24' W **90**
Redding, *Conn., U.S.* 41°18' N, 73°23' W **104**
Redditch, *U.K.* 52°18' N, 1°57' W **162**
Redeyef, *Tun.* 34°21' N, 8°7' E **214**
Redfield, *S. Dak., U.S.* 44°51' N, 98°33' W **90**
Redgranite, *Wis., U.S.* 44°1' N, 89°6' W **102**
Rédics, *Hung.* 46°36' N, 16°29' E **168**
Redig, *S. Dak., U.S.* 45°15' N, 103°33' W **90**
Redkey, *Ind., U.S.* 40°20' N, 85°9' W **102**
Redknife, river, *Can.* 60°49' N, 119°41' W **108**
Redlands, *Calif., U.S.* 34°3' N, 117°13' W **101**
Redmon, *Ill., U.S.* 39°38' N, 87°52' W **102**
Redmond, *Oreg., U.S.* 44°16' N, 121°9' W **238**
Redmond, *Wash., U.S.* 47°39' N, 122°7' W **100**
Redon, *Fr.* 47°39' N, 2°7' W **150**
Redonda Islands, *Strait of Georgia* 50°12' N, 124°55' W **100**
Redonda, Punta, *Arg.* 41°8' S, 62°40' W **134**
Redondeados, *Mex.* 25°51' N, 106°48' W **114**
Redondo, *Port.* 38°38' N, 7°34' W **150**
Redondo Beach, *Calif., U.S.* 33°50' N, 118°24' W **101**
Redondo, Pico, peak, *Braz.* 2°29' N, 63°33' W **130**
Redoubt Volcano, peak, *Alas., U.S.* 60°28' N, 152°55' W **98**
Redvers, *Can.* 49°34' N, 101°43' W **90**
Redwater, *Can.* 53°57' N, 113°7' W **108**
Redwater, *Tex., U.S.* 33°21' N, 94°16' W **103**
Redwood, *Miss., U.S.* 32°29' N, 90°48' W **103**
Redwood City, *Calif., U.S.* 37°29' N, 122°15' W **100**
Redwood Empire, region, *Calif., U.S.* 39°43' N, 123°40' W **92**
Redwood National Park, *Calif., U.S.* 41°20' N, 126°3' W **92**
Reed City, *Mich., U.S.* 43°52' N, 85°31' W **102**
Reeder, *N. Dak., U.S.* 46°6' N, 102°57' W **90**
Reedley, *Calif., U.S.* 36°35' N, 119°28' W **100**
Reedsburg, *Wis., U.S.* 43°32' N, 90°1' W **102**
Reedsport, *Oreg., U.S.* 43°41' N, 124°6' W **90**
Reedsville, *Wis., U.S.* 44°9' N, 87°58' W **102**
Reefton, *N.Z.* 42°7' S, 171°52' E **240**
Rees, *Ger.* 51°45' N, 6°24' E **167**
Reese, *Mich., U.S.* 43°26' N, 83°42' W **102**
Reeth, *U.K.* 54°23' N, 1°57' W **162**
Reeves, *La., U.S.* 30°30' N, 93°4' W **103**
Refahiye, *Turk.* 39°53' N, 38°47' E **180**
Reform, *Ala., U.S.* 33°21' N, 88°1' W **103**
Refuge Cove, *Can.* 50°7' N, 124°50' W **100**
Refugio, *Tex., U.S.* 28°18' N, 97°17' W **96**
Regbat, region, *Alg.* 26°23' N, 6°14' W **214**
Regência, *Braz.* 19°40' S, 39°54' W **138**
Regência, Pontal de, *Braz.* 20°0' S, 39°48' W **138**
Regeneração, *Braz.* 6°16' S, 42°43' W **132**
Regensburg, *Ger.* 49°0' N, 12°6' E **152**
Reggane, *Alg.* 26°42' N, 0°8' E **214**
Reggio di Calabria, *It.* 38°13' N, 15°40' E **143**
Regina, *Can.* 50°26' N, 104°46' W **90**
Régina, *South America* 4°21' N, 52°11' W **130**
Registro, *Braz.* 24°30' S, 47°48' W **138**
Registro do Araguaia, *Braz.* 15°45' S, 51°47' W **138**
Regocijo, *Mex.* 23°39' N, 105°9' W **114**
Regozero, *Russ.* 65°30' N, 31°17' E **152**
Rehoboth, *Namibia* 23°18' S, 17°3' E **227**
Reḥovot, *Israel* 31°53' N, 34°48' E **194**
Reïbell see Ksar Chellala, *Alg.* 35°12' N, 2°19' E **150**
Reidsville, *Ga., U.S.* 32°4' N, 82°7' W **96**
Reidsville, *N.C., U.S.* 36°21' N, 79°41' W **94**
Reigate, *U.K.* 51°14' N, 0°13' E **162**
Reims, *Fr.* 49°15' N, 4°2' E **163**
Reina Adelaida, Archipiélago, islands, *Chile* 52°7' S, 78°46' W **134**
Reina, Jardines de la, islands, *Caribbean Sea* 20°13' N, 79°3' W **115**
Reinbolt Hills, *Antarctica* 71°11' S, 72°8' E **248**

Reindeer Lake, Can. 57°3′ N, 111°32′ W 72
Reine, Nor. 67°55′ N, 13°4′ E 152
Reinga, Cape, N.Z. 34°27′ S, 172°19′ E 240
Reinhardswald, Ger. 51°28′ N, 9°23′ E 167
Reinosa, Sp. 43°0′ N, 4°9′ W 150
Reira, spring, Sudan 15°19′ N, 34°38′ E 182
Reisjärvi, Fin. 63°36′ N, 24°52′ E 154
Reitz, S. Af. 27°50′ S, 28°24′ E 227
Rejaf, Sudan 4°43′ N, 31°33′ E 224
Rekavice, Bosn. and Herzg. 44°40′ N, 17°7′ E 168
Reken, Ger. 51°50′ N, 7°3′ E 167
Rekinniki, Russ. 60°45′ N, 163°30′ E 160
Rekovac, Serb. 43°51′ N, 21°6′ E 168
Rėkyva, lake, Lith. 55°51′ N, 23°5′ E 166
Reliance, Can. 62°44′ N, 109°4′ W 106
Reliance, Wyo., U.S. 41°40′ N, 109°11′ W 90
Relizane, Alg. 35°44′ N, 0°33′ E 150
Remada, Tun. 32°21′ N, 10°24′ E 216
Remagen, Ger. 50°34′ N, 7°13′ E 167
Remansão, Braz. 4°28′ S, 49°35′ W 130
Remanso, Braz. 9°34′ S, 42°8′ W 132
Remarkables, The, peak, N.Z. 45°6′ S, 168°45′ E 240
Remate de Males, Braz. 4°25′ S, 70°13′ W 130
Remecó, Arg. 37°39′ S, 63°37′ W 139
Remer, Minn., U.S. 47°2′ N, 93°56′ W 90
Remeshk, Iran 26°48′ N, 58°51′ E 196
Remich, Lux. 49°33′ N, 6°21′ E 163
Remington, Ind., U.S. 40°45′ N, 87°10′ W 102
Rémire, South America 4°54′ N, 52°17′ W 130
Remmel Mountain, peak, Wash., U.S. 48°54′ N, 120°17′ W 90
Remontnoye, Russ. 46°30′ N, 43°34′ E 158
Remscheid, Ger. 51°10′ N, 7°11′ E 167
Remus, Mich., U.S. 43°36′ N, 85°9′ W 102
Rena, Nor. 61°8′ N, 11°19′ E 152
Renascença, Braz. 3°51′ S, 66°30′ W 130
Renaud Island, Antarctica 65°34′ S, 68°9′ W 134
Renca, Arg. 32°47′ S, 65°19′ W 134
Rencēni, Latv. 57°43′ N, 25°23′ E 166
Renda, Latv. 57°3′ N, 22°15′ E 166
Rendakoma, Eth. 14°25′ N, 40°2′ E 182
Rendova, island, Solomon Islands 8°35′ S, 157°15′ E 242
Renfrew, Can. 45°28′ N, 76°43′ W 94
Rengat, Indonesia 0°23′ N, 102°30′ E 196
Renholmen, Nor. 65°0′ N, 21°20′ E 152
Renhuai, China 27°46′ N, 106°24′ E 198
Reni, India 28°40′ N, 75°4′ E 186
Renison, Can. 50°58′ N, 81°9′ W 110
Renk, Sudan 11°44′ N, 32°48′ E 182
Renko, Fin. 60°53′ N, 24°16′ E 166
Rennell, island, Solomon Islands 11°41′ S, 160°19′ E 242
Rennell Sound 53°18′ N, 132°59′ W 108
Rennerod, Ger. 50°36′ N, 8°3′ E 167
Rennes, Fr. 48°6′ N, 1°42′ W 150
Reno, Nev., U.S. 39°32′ N, 119°50′ W 90
Reno, river, It. 44°34′ N, 11°58′ E 167
Rensselaer, Ind., U.S. 40°56′ N, 87°10′ W 102
Rensselaer, N.Y., U.S. 42°37′ N, 73°45′ W 104
Rentería, Sp. 43°17′ N, 1°54′ W 164
Renton, Wash., U.S. 47°28′ N, 122°14′ W 100
Renville, Minn., U.S. 44°46′ N, 95°13′ W 90
Reo, Indonesia 8°26′ S, 120°26′ E 192
Répcelak, Hung. 47°25′ N, 17°1′ E 168
Repino, Russ. 60°10′ N, 29°52′ E 166
Replot (Raippaluoto), Fin. 63°13′ N, 21°24′ E 152
Repossaari, Fin. 61°36′ N, 21°25′ E 166
Repparfjord, Nor. 70°26′ N, 24°19′ E 152
Republic, Mich., U.S. 46°24′ N, 87°58′ W 94
Republic, Ohio, U.S. 41°6′ N, 83°1′ W 102
Republican, river, Nebr., U.S. 40°17′ N, 100°48′ W 80
Repulse Bay, Can. 66°39′ N, 86°29′ W 73
Requa, Calif., U.S. 41°32′ N, 124°4′ W 90
Requena, Peru 5°5′ S, 73°50′ W 130
Requena, Sp. 39°30′ N, 1°7′ W 164
Requeña, Venez. 7°58′ N, 65°33′ W 136
Reşadiye, Turk. 40°23′ N, 37°19′ E 156
Resavica, Serb. 44°1′ N, 21°34′ E 168
Rescue, Punta, Chile 46°16′ S, 76°41′ W 134
Resende, Braz. 22°29′ S, 44°22′ W 138
Reserva, Braz. 24°41′ S, 50°55′ W 138
Reserve, N. Mex., U.S. 33°41′ N, 108°46′ W 92
Reshadat, oil field, Persian Gulf 25°57′ N, 52°43′ E 196
Reshety, Russ. 57°8′ N, 28°27′ E 166
Resia, It. 46°49′ N, 10°32′ E 167
Resistencia, Arg. 27°27′ S, 59°2′ W 139
Reşiţa, Rom. 45°18′ N, 21°53′ E 168
Resolute, Can. 74°39′ N, 94°58′ W 73
Resolution Island, Can. 61°20′ N, 64°59′ W 106
Restigouche, Can. 48°1′ N, 66°43′ W 94
Reston, Can. 49°32′ N, 101°7′ W 90
Restrepo, Col. 4°14′ N, 73°34′ W 136
Reszel, Pol. 54°2′ N, 21°8′ E 166
Retalhuleu, Guatemala 14°32′ N, 91°40′ W 115
Retezat, Munţii, Rom. 45°19′ N, 22°47′ E 168
Rethel, Fr. 49°30′ N, 4°21′ E 163
Rethondes, Fr. 49°24′ N, 2°56′ E 163
Reti, Pak. 28°4′ N, 69°49′ E 186
Retno, Russ. 57°59′ N, 30°12′ E 166
Rétság, Hung. 47°54′ N, 19°9′ E 168
Return Point, Antarctica 60°50′ S, 47°56′ W 134
Réunion, island, Fr. 21°9′ S, 55°35′ E 254
Reus, Sp. 41°8′ N, 1°6′ E 164
Reva, S. Dak., U.S. 45°32′ N, 103°6′ W 90
Reval see Tallinn, Est. 59°23′ N, 24°37′ E 166
Revda, Russ. 67°58′ N, 34°30′ E 152
Revda, Russ. 56°47′ N, 59°56′ E 154
Reveille Peak, Nev., U.S. 37°50′ N, 116°13′ W 90
Revelle Inlet 68°43′ S, 66°23′ W 248
Revelstoke, Can. 51°0′ N, 118°12′ W 90
Révfülöp, Hung. 46°50′ N, 17°38′ E 168
Revigny, Fr. 48°50′ N, 4°59′ E 163
Revillagigedo, Islas, islands, North Pacific Ocean 18°28′ N, 113°41′ W 112
Revin, Fr. 49°55′ N, 4°38′ E 163
Revivim, Israel 31°1′ N, 34°43′ E 194
Rewa, India 24°31′ N, 81°19′ E 197
Rex, Mount, peak, Antarctica 74°52′ S, 76°39′ W 248
Rexburg, Idaho, U.S. 43°49′ N, 111°48′ W 90
Rexford, Mont., U.S. 48°52′ N, 115°10′ W 90
Rexton, Mich., U.S. 46°9′ N, 85°15′ W 110
Rey, Iran 35°34′ N, 51°30′ E 180
Rey Bouba, Cameroon 8°38′ N, 14°12′ E 218
Rey, Isla del, island, Pan. 8°7′ N, 79°3′ W 115
Rey, river, Cameroon 8°10′ N, 14°26′ E 218
Reyes, Bol. 14°22′ S, 67°25′ W 137
Reyes, Point 38°2′ N, 123°22′ W 90
Reyes, Punta, Col. 2°40′ N, 78°24′ W 136
Reykjanes Ridge, North Atlantic Ocean 59°58′ N, 29°41′ W 253
Reykjavík, Ice. 64°4′ N, 22°23′ W 246
Reynoldsburg, Ohio, U.S. 39°56′ N, 82°49′ W 102
Rēzekne, Latv. 56°29′ N, 27°19′ E 166
Rezh, Russ. 57°23′ N, 61°22′ E 154
Rezh, river, Russ. 57°26′ N, 60°57′ E 154
Rezovo, Bulg. 41°59′ N, 28°1′ E 156
Rgotina, Serb. 44°0′ N, 22°16′ E 168
Rhaetian Alps, Switz. 46°22′ N, 9°21′ E 167
Rhafsaï, Mor. 34°39′ N, 4°55′ W 214
Rhame, N. Dak., U.S. 46°13′ N, 103°40′ W 90
Rhamnus, ruin(s), Gr. 38°12′ N, 23°56′ E 156
Rhayader, U.K. 52°17′ N, 3°31′ W 162
Rheda-Wiedenbrück, Ger. 51°51′ N, 8°17′ E 167
Rhede, Ger. 51°50′ N, 6°42′ E 167
Rheden, Neth. 52°0′ N, 6°3′ E 167
Rhein, river, Ger. 51°47′ N, 6°15′ E 167
Rheinbach, Ger. 50°37′ N, 6°57′ E 167
Rheinbrohl, Ger. 50°29′ N, 7°21′ E 167
Rheine, Ger. 52°16′ N, 7°26′ E 163
Rheinland-Palatinate, adm. division, Ger. 49°50′ N, 6°34′ E 150
Rhemilès, spring, Alg. 28°28′ N, 4°22′ W 214
Rhens, Ger. 50°16′ N, 7°37′ E 167
Rheydt, Ger. 51°9′ N, 6°26′ E 167
Rhinebeck, N.Y., U.S. 41°55′ N, 73°55′ W 104
Rhinelander, Wis., U.S. 45°38′ N, 89°23′ W 94
Rhineland-Palatinate, adm. division, Ger. 50°15′ N, 6°36′ E 167
Rhino Camp, Uganda 2°58′ N, 31°23′ E 224
Rhinocolura see El 'Arîsh, Egypt 31°6′ N, 33°46′ E 194
Rhiou, river, Alg. 35°59′ N, 0°58′ E 150
Rhir, Cap, Mor. 30°41′ N, 10°44′ W 214
Rho, It. 45°32′ N, 9°1′ E 167
Rhode Island, adm. division, R.I., U.S. 41°45′ N, 71°46′ W 104
Rhode Island Sound 41°14′ N, 71°13′ W 104
Rhodes Peak, Idaho, U.S. 46°38′ N, 114°53′ W 90
Rhodes see Ródos, Gr. 36°25′ N, 28°13′ E 156
Rhodes see Ródos, adm. division, Gr. 35°58′ N, 27°21′ E 156
Rhodes see Ródos, island, Gr. 35°44′ N, 27°53′ E 156
Rhodope Mountains, Bulg. 41°50′ N, 23°44′ E 156
Rhön, Ger. 50°36′ N, 9°54′ E 167
Rhône, river, Europe 46°10′ N, 7°16′ E 165
Rhône-Alpes, adm. division, Fr. 45°24′ N, 5°32′ E 156
Rhône-Alpes, adm. division, Fr. 45°41′ N, 4°23′ E 150
Rhourd el Baguel, oil field, Alg. 31°25′ N, 6°40′ E 214
Rhyl, U.K. 53°18′ N, 3°29′ W 162
Riachão, Braz. 7°22′ S, 46°41′ W 130
Riacho de Santana, Braz. 13°37′ S, 42°59′ W 138
Riachos, Isla de los, island, Arg. 40°12′ S, 62°5′ W 134
Rialma, Braz. 15°21′ S, 49°34′ W 138
Rialto, Calif., U.S. 34°6′ N, 117°23′ W 101
Rianápolis, Braz. 15°31′ S, 49°28′ W 138
Riangnom, Sudan 9°53′ N, 30°1′ E 224
Riaño, Sp. 42°57′ N, 5°2′ W 150
Riasi, India 33°4′ N, 74°51′ E 186
Riau, Kepulauan, islands, South China Sea 0°25′ N, 103°59′ E 196
Riaza, Sp. 41°16′ N, 3°29′ W 164
Rib Lake, Wis., U.S. 45°19′ N, 90°13′ W 94
Rib Mountain, peak, Wis., U.S. 44°54′ N, 89°47′ W 94
Riba de Saelices, Sp. 40°54′ N, 2°18′ W 164
Ribadavia, Sp. 42°16′ N, 8°11′ W 150
Ribadeo, Sp. 43°31′ N, 7°4′ W 150
Riba-roja d'Ebre, Sp. 41°13′ N, 0°28′ E 164
Ribarska Banja, Serb. 43°25′ N, 21°32′ E 168
Ribas do Rio Pardo, Braz. 20°27′ S, 53°49′ W 132
Ribáuè, Mozambique 14°57′ S, 38°21′ E 220
Ribe, Den. 55°19′ N, 8°45′ E 150
Ribécourt-Dreslincourt, Fr. 49°30′ N, 2°55′ E 163
Ribeira, Braz. 24°41′ S, 49°0′ W 138
Ribeira do Pombal, Braz. 10°49′ S, 38°34′ W 132
Ribeira, river, Braz. 24°43′ S, 48°18′ W 138
Ribeirão, Braz. 8°30′ S, 35°20′ W 132
Ribeirão do Salto, Braz. 15°48′ S, 40°17′ W 138
Ribeirão Preto, Braz. 21°11′ S, 47°50′ W 138
Ribemont, Fr. 49°47′ N, 3°27′ E 163
Riberalta, Bol. 11°2′ S, 66°7′ W 137
Ribes de Freser, Sp. 42°18′ N, 2°9′ E 164
Riblah, Syr. 34°27′ N, 36°33′ E 194
Rîbniţa, Mold. 47°44′ N, 29°0′ E 156
Ricardo Flores MagŽon, Mex. 29°56′ N, 106°58′ W 92
Ricaurte, Col. 1°10′ S, 70°14′ W 136
Riccione, It. 43°58′ N, 12°38′ E 167
Rice Lake, Wis., U.S. 45°30′ N, 91°45′ W 94
Rice Mountain, peak, N.H., U.S. 44°50′ N, 71°20′ W 94
Rice Valley, Calif., U.S. 34°1′ N, 114°52′ W 101
Rich, Mor. 32°20′ N, 4°31′ W 214
Rich Creek, Va., U.S. 37°22′ N, 80°50′ W 96
Rich Hill, Mo., U.S. 38°4′ N, 94°22′ W 94
Richan, Can. 49°59′ N, 92°49′ W 94
Richard Collinson Inlet 72°42′ N, 114°48′ W 106
Richard Toll, Senegal 16°28′ N, 15°44′ W 222
Richards Island, Can. 69°12′ N, 136°58′ W 98
Richardson Lake, Can. 58°18′ N, 111°58′ W 108
Richardson Mountains, Can. 68°35′ N, 136°39′ W 98
Richardson, river, Can. 58°6′ N, 111°0′ W 108
Richardton, N. Dak., U.S. 46°52′ N, 102°20′ W 90
Riche, Pointe, Can. 50°43′ N, 58°9′ W 111
Richey, Mont., U.S. 47°37′ N, 105°6′ W 90
Richfield, Utah, U.S. 38°46′ N, 112°5′ W 92
Richford, Vt., U.S. 44°59′ N, 72°41′ W 94
Richgrove, Calif., U.S. 35°48′ N, 119°7′ W 101
Richibucto, Can. 46°40′ N, 64°53′ W 111
Richland, Wash., U.S. 46°21′ N, 119°20′ W 246
Richland Center, Wis., U.S. 43°19′ N, 90°23′ W 94
Richland Springs, Tex., U.S. 31°15′ N, 98°57′ W 92
Richlands, Va., U.S. 37°5′ N, 81°49′ W 94
Richmond, Austral. 33°37′ S, 150°48′ E 231
Richmond, Calif., U.S. 37°56′ N, 122°21′ W 100
Richmond, Can. 45°39′ N, 72°8′ W 111
Richmond, Can. 49°9′ N, 123°10′ W 100
Richmond, Ill., U.S. 42°28′ N, 88°18′ W 102
Richmond, Ind., U.S. 39°48′ N, 84°52′ W 102
Richmond, Ky., U.S. 37°43′ N, 84°18′ W 96
Richmond, Me., U.S. 44°5′ N, 69°49′ W 104
Richmond, Mass., U.S. 42°21′ N, 73°23′ W 104
Richmond, Mo., U.S. 39°16′ N, 93°58′ W 94
Richmond, Mo., U.S. 42°28′ N, 88°18′ W 94
Richmond, N.H., U.S. 42°44′ N, 72°17′ W 104
Richmond, S. Af. 29°54′ S, 30°15′ E 227
Richmond, S. Af. 31°26′ S, 23°56′ E 227
Richmond, U.K. 54°24′ N, 1°45′ W 162
Richmond, Vt., U.S. 44°24′ N, 73°0′ W 104
Richmond, Va., U.S. 37°30′ N, 77°33′ W 96
Richmond Dale, Ohio, U.S. 39°12′ N, 82°49′ W 102
Richmond Hill, Can. 43°53′ N, 79°26′ W 94
Richtersveld National Park, S. Af. 28°14′ S, 16°16′ E 227
Richton, Miss., U.S. 31°20′ N, 88°56′ W 103
Richwood, Ohio, U.S. 40°25′ N, 83°17′ W 102
Ricla, Sp. 41°30′ N, 1°25′ W 164
Rico, Colo., U.S. 37°41′ N, 108°2′ W 92
Ridā', Yemen 14°26′ N, 44°49′ E 182
Ridanna, It. 46°54′ N, 11°17′ E 167
Riddell Nunataks, Antarctica 70°25′ S, 56°25′ E 248
Ridder, Kaz. 50°16′ N, 83°30′ E 190
Ridder (Leninogorsk), Kaz. 50°21′ N, 83°32′ E 184
Riddle, Idaho, U.S. 42°12′ N, 116°7′ W 90
Riderwood, Ala., U.S. 32°8′ N, 88°20′ W 103
Ridge Farm, Ill., U.S. 39°53′ N, 87°39′ W 102
Ridge, river, Can. 50°24′ N, 83°51′ W 110
Ridgecrest, Calif., U.S. 35°37′ N, 117°41′ W 101
Ridgefield, Conn., U.S. 41°17′ N, 73°30′ W 104
Ridgefield, Wash., U.S. 45°48′ N, 122°44′ W 100
Ridgeland, Miss., U.S. 32°24′ N, 90°9′ W 103
Ridgetown, Can. 42°25′ N, 81°53′ W 102
Ridgeville, Ind., U.S. 40°16′ N, 85°2′ W 102
Ridgewood, N.J., U.S. 40°58′ N, 74°8′ W 104
Riding Mountain National Park, Can. 50°49′ N, 101°3′ W 108
Riding Rocks, islands, North Atlantic Ocean 24°56′ N, 79°6′ W 116
Riedlingen, Ger. 48°9′ N, 9°29′ E 156
Rieneck, Ger. 50°5′ N, 9°39′ E 167
Ries, region, Ger. 48°44′ N, 10°30′ E 152
Riesco, Isla, island, Chile 52°41′ S, 71°24′ W 134
Rietavas, Lith. 55°44′ N, 21°56′ E 166
Rietberg, Ger. 51°47′ N, 8°25′ E 167
Rietfontein, Namibia 26°46′ S, 19°59′ E 227
Rievaulx, U.K. 54°15′ N, 1°7′ W 162
Riffe Lake, Wash., U.S. 46°28′ N, 122°21′ W 100
Rifle, Colo., U.S. 39°31′ N, 107°47′ W 90
Rig Rig, Chad 14°16′ N, 14°21′ E 216
Rīga, Latv. 56°55′ N, 24°1′ E 166
Riga, Gulf of 57°41′ N, 23°20′ E 166
Rīgān, Iran 28°38′ N, 59°3′ E 196
Riggins, Idaho, U.S. 45°24′ N, 116°19′ W 90
Rigolet, Can. 54°11′ N, 58°24′ W 111
Riguldi, Est. 59°6′ N, 23°31′ E 166
Rihand Dam, India 23°55′ N, 82°11′ E 197
Riihimäki, Fin. 60°44′ N, 24°44′ E 166
Riipi, Fin. 67°19′ N, 26°3′ E 152
Riiser-Larsen, Mount, peak, Antarctica 66°44′ S, 50°12′ E 248
Riisipere, Est. 59°6′ N, 24°17′ E 166
Riistavesi, Fin. 62°53′ N, 28°6′ E 154
Riíto, Mex. 32°5′ N, 114°55′ W 92
Rijau, Nig. 11°4′ N, 5°14′ E 222
Rijeća, Bosn. and Herzg. 44°1′ N, 18°40′ E 168
Rijeka (Fiume), Croatia 45°20′ N, 14°26′ E 156
Rijssen, Neth. 52°18′ N, 6°30′ E 163
Rila, Bulg. 41°59′ N, 23°11′ E 168
Rila, Bulg. 42°7′ N, 23°8′ E 168
Rila National Park, Bulg. 41°47′ N, 22°39′ E 180
Riley, Kans., U.S. 39°16′ N, 96°50′ W 90
Rilly, Fr. 49°9′ N, 4°2′ E 163
Rimā', Jabal ar, peak, Jordan 32°18′ N, 36°51′ E 194
Rimbey, Can. 52°37′ N, 114°14′ W 108
Rimbo, Sw. 59°44′ N, 18°21′ E 166
Rimini, It. 44°2′ N, 12°33′ E 167
Rîmnicu Sărat, Rom. 45°23′ N, 27°3′ E 156
Rimouski, Can. 48°26′ N, 68°31′ W 94
Rimpar, Ger. 49°51′ N, 9°57′ E 167
Rimrock, Wash., U.S. 46°39′ N, 121°8′ W 100
Rinbung, China 29°15′ N, 89°57′ E 197
Rinca, island, Indonesia 9°14′ S, 119°36′ E 192
Rincão, Braz. 21°33′ S, 48°5′ W 138
Rînceni, Rom. 46°23′ N, 28°7′ E 158
Rincon, Ga., U.S. 32°17′ N, 81°14′ W 96
Rincon, N. Mex., U.S. 32°40′ N, 107°5′ W 92
Rincón, Cerro, peak, Arg. 24°6′ S, 67°30′ W 132
Rincon de Guayabitos, Mex. 21°0′ N, 105°20′ W 114
Rincón de Romos, Mex. 22°13′ N, 102°19′ W 114
Rincón de Soto, Sp. 42°13′ N, 1°51′ W 164
Rincón del Atuel, Arg. 34°44′ S, 68°23′ W 134
Rincón del Bonete, Uru. 32°54′ S, 56°26′ W 139
Rincón del Bonete, Lago, lake, Uru. 32°30′ S, 56°26′ W 139
Rincón Hondo, Venez. 7°24′ N, 69°6′ W 136
Rincona, Sp. 37°11′ N, 4°28′ W 164
Rinconada, Arg. 22°27′ S, 66°13′ W 137
Rindge, N.H., U.S. 42°44′ N, 72°1′ W 104
Ringgold, La., U.S. 32°18′ N, 93°17′ W 103
Ringim, Nig. 12°9′ N, 9°9′ E 222
Ringkøbing, Den. 56°5′ N, 8°13′ E 150
Ringwood, U.K. 50°51′ N, 1°47′ W 162
Rini, spring, Mauritania 16°57′ N, 6°58′ W 222
Rinns Point 55°29′ N, 6°45′ W 150
Rio, Fla., U.S. 27°13′ N, 80°15′ W 105
Rio Abiseo National Park, Peru 8°0′ S, 77°34′ W 122
Rio Azul, Braz. 25°45′ S, 50°48′ W 138
Rio Branco, Braz. 9°58′ S, 67°49′ W 137
Rio Branco, Uru. 32°34′ S, 53°23′ W 139
Rio Branco do Sul, Braz. 25°10′ S, 49°21′ W 138
Rio Bravo, Mex. 26°0′ N, 98°8′ W 114
Rio Bravo del Norte see Rio Grande, river, North America 28°13′ N, 99°43′ W 80
Rio Brilhante, Braz. 21°50′ S, 54°32′ W 132
Rio Bueno, Chile 40°20′ S, 72°59′ W 134
Rio Caribe, Venez. 10°40′ N, 63°7′ W 116
Rio Chico, Venez. 10°21′ N, 65°59′ W 136
Rio Claro, Braz. 22°26′ S, 47°35′ W 138
Rio Colorado, Arg. 39°1′ S, 64°5′ W 139
Rio Corrientes, Ecua. 2°22′ S, 76°23′ W 136
Rio Cuarto, Arg. 33°10′ S, 64°21′ W 134
Rio das Mortes see Manso, river, Braz. 15°20′ S, 53°1′ W 138
Rio de Contas, Braz. 13°34′ S, 41°51′ W 138
Rio de Janeiro, Braz. 22°53′ S, 43°15′ W 138
Rio de Janeiro, adm. division, Braz. 22°4′ S, 42°44′ W 138
Rio de Jesús, Pan. 7°59′ N, 81°10′ W 115
Rio do Prado, Braz. 16°37′ S, 40°34′ W 138
Rio do Sul, Braz. 27°17′ S, 49°39′ W 138
Rio Gallegos, Arg. 51°37′ S, 69°17′ W 134
Rio Grande, Arg. 53°50′ S, 67°48′ W 123
Rio Grande, Bol. 20°52′ S, 67°16′ W 137
Rio Grande, Braz. 32°1′ S, 52°11′ W 139
Rio Grande, Mex. 23°47′ N, 103°2′ W 114
Rio Grande City, Tex., U.S. 26°24′ N, 98°49′ W 114
Rio Grande de Matagalpa, river, Nicar. 13°21′ N, 84°20′ W 115
Rio Grande do Norte, adm. division, Braz. 5°27′ S, 37°44′ W 132
Rio Grande do Sul, adm. division, Braz. 28°37′ S, 53°52′ W 138
Rio Grande (Rio Bravo del Norte), river, North America 28°13′ N, 99°43′ W 80
Rio Grande Rise, South Atlantic Ocean 31°19′ S, 35°27′ W 253
Rio Grande Wild and Scenic River, Tex., U.S. 29°51′ N, 102°10′ W 96
Rio Muerto, Arg. 26°19′ S, 61°40′ W 139
Rio Mulatos, Bol. 19°42′ S, 66°48′ W 137
Rio Muni, region, Equatorial Guinea 1°40′ N, 9°49′ E 218
Rio Negro, Braz. 26°4′ S, 49°45′ W 138
Rio Pardo, Braz. 29°59′ S, 52°22′ W 139
Rio Pardo de Minas, Braz. 15°39′ S, 42°35′ W 138
Rio Pico, Arg. 44°12′ S, 71°24′ W 134
Rio Pilcomayo National Park, Arg. 25°17′ S, 58°18′ W 122
Rio Pomba, Braz. 21°17′ S, 43°11′ W 138
Rio Sucio, Col. 5°25′ N, 75°42′ W 136
Rio Tercero, Arg. 32°13′ S, 64°8′ W 134
Rio Tigre, Ecua. 2°7′ S, 76°4′ W 136
Rio Tinto, Braz. 6°48′ S, 35°5′ W 132
Rio Tuba, Philippines 8°33′ N, 117°26′ E 203
Rio Verde, Braz. 17°50′ S, 50°57′ W 138
Rio Verde, Chile 52°34′ S, 71°28′ W 134
Rio Verde, Mex. 21°53′ N, 100°0′ W 114
Rio Verde de Mato Grosso, Braz. 18°57′ S, 54°53′ W 132
Rio Vista, Calif., U.S. 38°9′ N, 121°43′ W 100
Riobamba, Ecua. 1°47′ S, 78°47′ W 130
Riogordo, Sp. 36°54′ N, 4°18′ W 164
Riohacha, Col. 11°29′ N, 72°55′ W 136
Riom, Fr. 45°54′ N, 3°6′ E 150
Riomaggiore, It. 44°5′ N, 9°45′ E 167
Rion-des-Landes, Fr. 43°56′ N, 0°57′ E 150
Rionegro, Col. 6°10′ N, 75°21′ W 136
Rioni, river, Ga. 42°29′ N, 43°10′ E 195
Riosucio, Col. 7°29′ N, 77°9′ W 136
Riou Lake, lake, Can. 59°2′ N, 106°56′ W 108
Riozinho, Braz. 9°32′ S, 66°51′ W 137
Riozinho, river, Braz. 3°7′ S, 67°7′ W 136
Riozinho, river, Braz. 8°22′ S, 52°3′ W 130
Ripanj, Serb. 44°38′ N, 20°30′ E 168
Riparius, N.Y., U.S. 43°39′ N, 73°55′ W 104
Ripley, Calif., U.S. 33°31′ N, 114°40′ W 101
Ripley, Can. 44°3′ N, 81°34′ W 102
Ripley, Miss., U.S. 34°42′ N, 88°58′ W 96
Ripley, Ohio, U.S. 38°43′ N, 83°49′ W 102
Ripley, U.K. 53°3′ N, 1°25′ W 162
Ripoll, Sp. 42°12′ N, 1°11′ E 164
Ripon, Calif., U.S. 37°44′ N, 121°8′ W 100
Ripon, U.K. 54°8′ N, 1°32′ W 162
Ripon, Wis., U.S. 43°50′ N, 88°50′ W 102
Ripple Mountain, peak, Can. 49°0′ N, 117°10′ W 90
Risaralda, adm. division, South America 5°9′ N, 76°8′ W 136
Risbäck, Nor. 64°41′ N, 15°31′ E 154
Rīshahr, Iran 28°50′ N, 50°55′ E 196
Rishikesh, India 30°8′ N, 78°18′ E 197
Rishiri Tō, island, Japan 44°52′ N, 140°18′ E 190
Rishon Leẕiyyon, Israel 31°57′ N, 34°47′ E 194
Rising Star, Tex., U.S. 32°5′ N, 98°59′ W 92
Rising Sun, Ind., U.S. 38°56′ N, 84°52′ W 102
Rissani, Mor. 31°18′ N, 4°15′ W 214
Risti, Est. 58°59′ N, 24°3′ E 166
Ristiina, Fin. 61°29′ N, 27°14′ E 166
Ristna, Est. 58°53′ N, 21°42′ E 166
Risum-Lindholm, Ger. 54°46′ N, 8°52′ E 150
Ritscher Upland, Antarctica 74°5′ S, 11°15′ W 248
Ritter, Mount, peak, Calif., U.S. 37°41′ N, 119°15′ W 100
Rittman, Ohio, U.S. 40°57′ N, 81°47′ W 102
Ritva, Fin. 65°29′ N, 26°32′ E 152
Ritzville, Wash., U.S. 47°6′ N, 118°24′ W 90
Riva del Garda, It. 45°53′ N, 10°50′ E 167
Rivadavia, Arg. 35°28′ S, 62°58′ W 139
Rivadavia, Arg. 33°12′ S, 68°29′ W 134
Rivarolo Canavese, It. 45°19′ N, 7°43′ E 167
Rivas, Nicar. 11°26′ N, 85°51′ W 115
River Cess, Liberia 5°26′ N, 9°35′ W 222
River Jordan, Can. 48°25′ N, 124°2′ W 100
River Nile, adm. division, Sudan 18°30′ N, 32°31′ E 182
Rivera, Arg. 37°12′ S, 63°13′ W 139
Rivera, Uru. 30°53′ S, 55°35′ W 139
Riverbank, Calif., U.S. 37°43′ N, 120°58′ W 100
Riverdale, Calif., U.S. 36°25′ N, 119°53′ W 100
Riverdale, N. Dak., U.S. 47°28′ N, 101°23′ W 90
Riverhead, N.Y., U.S. 40°55′ N, 72°39′ W 104
Riverhurst, Can. 50°54′ N, 106°53′ W 90
Riverina, region, Austral. 33°35′ S, 146°11′ E 230
Rivero, Isla, island, Chile 45°34′ S, 75°39′ W 134
Rivers, Can. 50°2′ N, 100°15′ W 90
Riversdale, N.Z. 45°56′ S, 168°45′ E 240
Riversdale, S. Af. 34°5′ S, 21°14′ E 220
Riverside, Calif., U.S. 33°59′ N, 117°24′ W 101
Riverside, Tex., U.S. 30°50′ N, 95°24′ W 103
Riverside, Wash., U.S. 48°29′ N, 119°32′ W 90
Riverton, Can. 50°58′ N, 97°1′ W 90
Riverton, Conn., U.S. 41°57′ N, 73°1′ W 104
Riverton, Ill., U.S. 39°50′ N, 89°32′ W 102
Riverton, Wyo., U.S. 43°1′ N, 108°23′ W 90
Riverview, Can. 46°2′ N, 64°49′ W 111
Rivesaltes, Fr. 42°45′ N, 2°51′ E 164
Riviera, Ariz., U.S. 35°5′ N, 114°37′ W 101
Riviera Beach, Fla., U.S. 26°46′ N, 80°5′ W 105
Riviera, region, Mediterranean Sea 43°21′ N, 6°39′ E 165
Rivière au Serpent, river, Can. 50°29′ N, 71°42′ W 110
Rivière aux Rats, river, Can. 49°9′ N, 72°14′ W 94
Rivière-de-la-Chaloupe, site, Gulf of St. Lawrence 49°8′ N, 62°35′ W 111
Rivière-du-Loup, Can. 47°48′ N, 69°34′ W 94
Rivne, Ukr. 50°37′ N, 26°13′ E 152
Rivoli, It. 45°3′ N, 7°30′ E 167
Riwaka, N.Z. 41°6′ S, 172°59′ E 240
Riwoqê, China 31°8′ N, 96°33′ E 188
Riyadh see Ar Riyāḑ, Saudi Arabia 24°35′ N, 46°35′ E 186
Rīyāq, Leb. 33°51′ N, 36°0′ E 194
Rize, Turk. 41°2′ N, 40°29′ E 195
Rizhao, China 35°26′ N, 119°27′ E 198
Rizokarpaso (Dipkarpaz), Cyprus 35°36′ N, 34°22′ E 194
Rizzuto, Capo, It. 38°48′ N, 17°8′ E 156
Rkiz, Lac, lake, Mauritania 16°55′ N, 15°26′ W 222
Roa, Sp. 41°41′ N, 3°57′ W 164
Roachdale, Ind., U.S. 39°50′ N, 86°48′ W 102
Road Town, Tortola 18°27′ N, 64°38′ W 116
Roan, Nor. 64°10′ N, 10°14′ E 152
Roan Cliffs, Colo., U.S. 39°38′ N, 108°13′ W 90
Roan Cliffs, Utah, U.S. 39°29′ N, 110°17′ W 90
Roan Plateau, Colo., U.S. 39°44′ N, 108°50′ W 90
Roann, Ind., U.S. 40°54′ N, 85°54′ W 102
Roanne, Fr. 46°1′ N, 4°3′ E 150
Roanoke, Ind., U.S. 40°57′ N, 85°23′ W 102
Roanoke, La., U.S. 30°13′ N, 92°46′ W 103
Roanoke Island, N.C., U.S. 35°46′ N, 75°34′ W 80
Roatán, Isla de, island, Hond. 16°13′ N, 86°24′ W 115
Robaa Ouled Yahia, Tun. 36°5′ N, 9°34′ E 156
Robāt-e Khān, Iran 33°21′ N, 56°4′ E 180
Robāţ-e Tork, Iran 33°45′ N, 50°51′ E 180
Robbins Island, Austral. 41°2′ S, 142°8′ E 230
Robe, Mount, peak, Austral. 31°41′ S, 141°7′ E 230
Robeline, La., U.S. 31°40′ N, 93°19′ W 103
Robert, Cap, Can. 49°29′ N, 62°18′ W 111
Robert, Cape, Antarctica 66°26′ S, 137°47′ E 248
Robert Lee, Tex., U.S. 31°53′ N, 100°28′ W 92
Roberts, Arg. 35°8′ S, 61°59′ W 139
Roberts, Idaho, U.S. 43°43′ N, 112°7′ W 90
Roberts, Ill., U.S. 40°37′ N, 88°11′ W 102
Roberts Butte, peak, Antarctica 72°35′ S, 160°47′ E 248
Roberts Creek Mountain, peak, Nev., U.S. 39°51′ N, 116°23′ W 90
Roberts Knoll, peak, Antarctica 71°27′ S, 3°40′ W 248
Roberts Mountain, peak, Wyo., U.S. 42°54′ N, 109°22′ W 90
Roberts, Point, Wash., U.S. 48°53′ N, 122°45′ W 80
Robertsdale, Ala., U.S. 30°32′ N, 87°42′ W 103
Robertsganj, India 24°40′ N, 83°2′ E 197
Robertson, S. Af. 33°48′ S, 19°53′ E 227
Robertson Island, Antarctica 65°11′ S, 59°19′ W 134
Robertsport, Liberia 6°40′ N, 11°22′ W 222
Roberval, Can. 48°28′ N, 72°15′ W 82
Robin Hood's Bay, U.K. 54°26′ N, 0°33′ E 162
Robinson, Ill., U.S. 39°0′ N, 87°44′ W 102
Robinson Range, Austral. 26°23′ S, 118°37′ E 230
Robinsons, Me., U.S. 46°28′ N, 67°50′ W 111
Roblin, Can. 51°14′ N, 101°22′ W 90
Roboré, Bol. 18°25′ S, 59°43′ W 132
Robsart, Can. 49°23′ N, 109°17′ W 90
Robson, Can. 49°20′ N, 117°41′ W 90
Robson, Mount, peak, Can. 53°5′ N, 119°16′ W 108
Roby, Tex., U.S. 32°44′ N, 100°23′ W 92
Roca Partida, Isla, island, Isla Roca Partida 19°1′ N, 112°48′ W 112
Roca Partida, Punta, Mex. 18°43′ N, 95°14′ W 114
Rocamadour, Fr. 44°46′ N, 1°38′ E 214
Rocas, Atol das, island, Atol das Rocas 4°5′ S, 33°47′ W 132
Rocchetta Ligure, It. 44°42′ N, 9°3′ E 167

Rocha, Uru. 34°30′ S, 54°20′ W 139
Rochdale, Mass., U.S. 42°11′ N, 71°55′ W 104
Rochdale, U.K. 53°37′ N, 2°9′ W 162
Rochefort, Belg. 50°9′ N, 5°13′ E 167
Rochegda, Russ. 62°42′ N, 43°27′ E 154
Rochelle, Ga., U.S. 31°56′ N, 83°28′ W 96
Rochelle, Ill., U.S. 41°55′ N, 89°5′ W 102
Rocher, Lac, lake, Can. 50°28′ N, 77°0′ W 110
Roches, Lac des, lake, Can. 51°30′ N, 120°54′ W 90
Rochester, Can. 54°22′ N, 113°26′ W 108
Rochester, Ill., U.S. 39°44′ N, 89°32′ W 102
Rochester, Ind., U.S. 41°3′ N, 86°13′ W 102
Rochester, Minn., U.S. 44°1′ N, 92°30′ W 94
Rochester, N.H., U.S. 43°18′ N, 70°59′ W 104
Rochester, N.Y., U.S. 43°9′ N, 77°37′ W 110
Rochester, Pa., U.S. 40°41′ N, 80°17′ W 94
Rochester, U.K. 51°22′ N, 0°28′ E 162
Rochester, Vt., U.S. 43°52′ N, 72°49′ W 104
Rochester, Wash., U.S. 46°48′ N, 123°5′ W 100
Rock Falls, Ill., U.S. 41°45′ N, 89°42′ W 102
Rock Hill, S.C., U.S. 34°55′ N, 81°2′ W 96
Rock Island, Mo., U.S. 41°29′ N, 90°34′ W 110
Rock Lake, N. Dak., U.S. 48°45′ N, 99°15′ W 90
Rock Rapids, Iowa, U.S. 43°24′ N, 96°11′ W 90
Rock River, Wyo., U.S. 41°44′ N, 105°58′ W 90
Rock, river, Can. 60°24′ N, 127°14′ W 108
Rock, river, Wis., U.S. 42°48′ N, 89°12′ W 102
Rock Sound, Bahamas 24°55′ N, 76°10′ W 96
Rock Springs, Mont., U.S. 46°47′ N, 106°16′ W 90
Rock Springs, Wyo., U.S. 41°38′ N, 109°14′ W 106
Rockall, island, U.K. 57°36′ N, 13°41′ W 253
Rockdale, Ill., U.S. 41°29′ N, 88°7′ W 102
Rockefeller Plateau, Antarctica 79°52′ S, 104°57′ W 248
Rockenhausen, Ger. 49°37′ N, 7°48′ E 163
Rockford, Ill., U.S. 42°16′ N, 89°4′ W 102
Rockford, Mich., U.S. 43°7′ N, 85°33′ W 102
Rockford, Ohio, U.S. 40°40′ N, 84°39′ W 102
Rockglen, Can. 49°10′ N, 105°58′ W 90
Rockingham, Austral. 32°19′ S, 115°45′ E 231
Rockingham, N.C., U.S. 34°55′ N, 79°48′ W 96
Rockingham, Vt., U.S. 43°11′ N, 72°30′ W 104
Rockland, Can. 45°32′ N, 75°18′ W 94
Rockland, Idaho, U.S. 42°35′ N, 112°52′ W 90
Rockland, Mass., U.S. 42°7′ N, 70°55′ W 104
Rockledge, Fla., U.S. 28°19′ N, 80°44′ W 105
Rockport, Calif., U.S. 39°44′ N, 123°50′ W 90
Rockport, Ind., U.S. 37°52′ N, 87°4′ W 94
Rockport, Me., U.S. 44°11′ N, 69°5′ W 94
Rockport, Tex., U.S. 28°0′ N, 97°4′ W 96
Rockport, Wash., U.S. 48°29′ N, 121°36′ W 100
Rocksprings, Tex., U.S. 30°0′ N, 100°13′ W 92
Rockton, Ill., U.S. 42°27′ N, 89°5′ W 102
Rockville, Ind., U.S. 39°45′ N, 87°14′ W 102
Rockville, N.Z. 40°46′ S, 172°39′ E 240
Rockwell City, Iowa, U.S. 42°23′ N, 94°38′ W 94
Rockwood, Tenn., U.S. 35°52′ N, 84°41′ W 96
Rocky Ford, Colo., U.S. 38°3′ N, 103°44′ W 90
Rocky Hill, Conn., U.S. 41°39′ N, 72°39′ W 104
Rocky Lane, Can. 58°29′ N, 116°23′ W 108
Rocky Mount, N.C., U.S. 35°55′ N, 77°48′ W 96
Rocky Mountain House, Can. 52°21′ N, 114°53′ W 108
Rocky Mountain National Park, Colo., U.S. 40°33′ N, 105°37′ W 80
Rocky Mountain, peak, Mont., U.S. 47°46′ N, 112°52′ W 90
Rocky Mountains, Mont., U.S. 45°5′ N, 114°26′ W 72
Rocky Point, Calif., U.S. 41°9′ N, 124°26′ W 90
Rocky Point, Namibia 19°6′ S, 12°1′ E 220
Rocky Point, N.Y., U.S. 40°56′ N, 72°56′ W 104
Roda de Isabena, Sp. 42°16′ N, 0°31′ E 164
Rødby, Den. 54°42′ N, 11°23′ E 152
Roddickton, Can. 50°51′ N, 56°7′ W 111
Rodel 57°44′ N, 6°58′ W 150
Rodeo, Arg. 30°13′ S, 69°7′ W 134
Rodeo, Mex. 25°8′ N, 104°35′ W 114
Rodeo, N. Mex., U.S. 31°50′ N, 109°1′ W 92
Rodessa, La., U.S. 32°57′ N, 94°1′ W 103
Rodez, Fr. 44°21′ N, 2°35′ E 150
Rodi Garganico, It. 41°55′ N, 15°54′ E 156
Rodino, Russ. 52°28′ N, 80°18′ E 184
Rodnei, Munții, Rom. 47°28′ N, 24°19′ E 156
Rodney, Can. 42°33′ N, 81°41′ W 102
Rodniki, Kaz. 49°9′ N, 58°22′ E 158
Rodniki, Russ. 57°5′ N, 41°39′ E 154
Rodnîkovka, Kaz. 50°39′ N, 57°8′ E 158
Rodonit, Kepi i, Alban. 41°27′ N, 19°15′ E 168
Ródos, Gr. 36°20′ N, 28°10′ E 180
Ródos (Rhodes), Gr. 36°25′ N, 28°13′ E 156
Ródos (Rhodes), adm. division, Gr. 35°58′ N, 27°21′ E 156
Ródos (Rhodes), island, Gr. 35°44′ N, 27°53′ E 156
Rødøy, Nor. 66°39′ N, 13°3′ E 152
Rodrigues, Braz. 6°34′ S, 73°12′ W 130
Rodrigues, island, Mauritius 19°45′ S, 63°25′ E 254
Rodrigues Ridge, Indian Ocean 19°45′ S, 62°11′ E 254
Roebourne, Austral. 20°46′ S, 117°6′ E 231
Roebuck Bay 18°13′ S, 120°59′ E 230
Roes Welcome Sound 64°30′ N, 89°28′ W 106
Roeselare, Belg. 50°56′ N, 3°7′ E 163
Roetgen, Ger. 50°38′ N, 6°11′ E 167
Rogagua, Lago, lake, Bol. 13°40′ S, 67°19′ W 137
Rogaguado, Bol. 13°46′ S, 64°44′ W 137
Rogaguado, Laguna, lake, Bol. 12°56′ S, 65°54′ W 137
Rogaguado, Laguna, lake, Bol. 12°56′ S, 66°43′ W 130
Roganville, Tex., U.S. 30°47′ N, 93°55′ W 103
Rogatica, Bosn. and Herzg. 43°48′ N, 19°0′ E 168
Rogers, Ark., U.S. 36°18′ N, 94°7′ W 96
Rogers, Conn., U.S. 41°50′ N, 71°55′ W 104
Rogers, Tex., U.S. 30°54′ N, 97°13′ W 96
Rogers City, Mich., U.S. 45°25′ N, 83°50′ W 94
Rogers, Mount, peak, Va., U.S. 36°38′ N, 81°38′ W 96
Rogerson, Idaho, U.S. 42°13′ N, 114°36′ W 90
Rogersville, Tenn., U.S. 36°23′ N, 83°1′ W 94
Rognan, Nor. 67°5′ N, 15°19′ E 152
Rogun, Taj. 38°46′ N, 69°51′ E 197
Roha, India 18°25′ N, 73°8′ E 188
Rohault, Lac, lake, Can. 49°22′ N, 74°51′ W 94
Rohia, Tun. 35°39′ N, 9°3′ E 156
Röhlingen, Ger. 48°56′ N, 10°11′ E 152
Rohnerville, Calif., U.S. 40°34′ N, 124°9′ W 92
Rohri, Pak. 27°38′ N, 68°59′ E 186
Rohtak, India 28°54′ N, 76°34′ E 188
Rohtasgarh, India 24°36′ N, 83°56′ E 197
Roi Et, Thai. 16°3′ N, 103°41′ E 202
Roja, Latv. 57°30′ N, 22°46′ E 166
Roja, Punta, Sp. 38°26′ N, 1°36′ E 150
Rojas, Arg. 34°14′ S, 60°41′ W 139
Rojo, Cabo 17°49′ N, 67°45′ W 116
Rojo, Cabo, Mex. 21°36′ N, 97°23′ W 114
Rokan, river, Indonesia 0°57′ N, 100°36′ E 196
Rokeby National Park, Austral. 14°1′ S, 142°34′ E 238
Rokel, river, Sierra Leone 8°54′ N, 11°46′ W 222
Rokhmoyva, Gora, peak, Russ. 66°51′ N, 29°2′ E 152
Rokiškis, Lith. 55°57′ N, 25°34′ E 166
Rokytne, Ukr. 51°16′ N, 27°11′ E 152
Rola Co, lake, China 35°17′ N, 87°51′ E 188
Rolde, Neth. 52°59′ N, 6°37′ E 163
Rolette, N. Dak., U.S. 48°38′ N, 99°52′ W 90
Roll, Ariz., U.S. 32°44′ N, 113°59′ W 101
Rolla, Can. 55°53′ N, 120°10′ W 108
Rolla, Mo., U.S. 37°56′ N, 91°46′ W 96
Rolla, N. Dak., U.S. 48°50′ N, 99°38′ W 90
Rolle, Switz. 46°29′ N, 6°21′ E 167
Rolleston, N.Z. 43°35′ S, 172°21′ E 240
Rolling Fork, Miss., U.S. 32°53′ N, 90°53′ W 103
Rollins, Mont., U.S. 47°53′ N, 114°12′ W 90
Rom, Sudan 10°46′ N, 32°30′ E 182
Roma, Austral. 26°34′ S, 148°47′ E 231
Roma (Rome), It. 41°52′ N, 12°21′ E 156
Romain, Cape, S.C., U.S. 32°54′ N, 79°32′ W 96
Romakloster, Sw. 57°28′ N, 18°28′ E 166
Roma-Los Saenz, Tex., U.S. 26°26′ N, 98°59′ W 96
Roman, Rom. 46°56′ N, 26°56′ E 156
Romanche Fracture Zone, North Atlantic Ocean 0°8′ N, 16°37′ W 253
Romang, Arg. 29°29′ S, 59°50′ W 139
Români, Egypt 31°0′ N, 32°38′ E 194
Romania 45°55′ N, 24°6′ E 156
Romanija, peak, Bosn. and Herzg. 43°51′ N, 18°37′ E 168
Roman-Kosh, peak, Ukr. 44°37′ N, 34°8′ E 156
Romano, Cape, Fla., U.S. 25°54′ N, 82°1′ W 105
Romano, Cayo, island, Cuba 22°0′ N, 77°36′ W 116
Romanovce, Maced. 42°4′ N, 21°40′ E 168
Romanovka, Russ. 53°14′ N, 112°47′ E 238
Romanovka, Russ. 51°43′ N, 42°44′ E 158
Romans, Fr. 45°3′ N, 5°3′ E 150
Romanzof, Cape, Alas., U.S. 61°29′ N, 168°48′ W 98
Romblon, Philippines 12°35′ N, 122°17′ E 203
Rome, Ga., U.S. 34°15′ N, 85°10′ W 96
Rome, N.Y., U.S. 43°13′ N, 75°28′ W 94
Rome City, Ind., U.S. 41°29′ N, 85°23′ W 102
Rome see Roma, It. 41°52′ N, 12°21′ E 156
Romeo, Mich., U.S. 42°47′ N, 83°1′ W 102
Romford, U.K. 51°34′ N, 0°10′ E 162
Romilly, Fr. 48°31′ N, 3°44′ E 163
Romiton, Uzb. 39°56′ N, 64°22′ E 197
Rommani, Mor. 33°33′ N, 6°42′ W 143
Romnaes, Mount, peak, Antarctica 71°30′ S, 23°33′ E 248
Romney Marsh, U.K. 50°59′ N, 0°45′ E 162
Romny, Ukr. 50°45′ N, 33°28′ E 158
Romodanovo, Russ. 54°25′ N, 45°22′ E 154
Romont, Switz. 46°42′ N, 6°54′ E 167
Romsdal, Nor. 62°26′ N, 7°43′ E 152
Romsey, U.K. 50°59′ N, 1°30′ W 162
Røn, Nor. 61°3′ N, 9°3′ E 152
Ron, Mui, Vietnam 17°57′ N, 106°33′ E 198
Ronald, Wash., U.S. 47°13′ N, 121°2′ W 100
Ronan, Mont., U.S. 47°30′ N, 114°7′ W 90
Roncade, It. 45°37′ N, 12°21′ E 167
Roncador, Serra do, Braz. 11°42′ S, 52°48′ W 130
Ronceverte, W. Va., U.S. 37°45′ N, 80°28′ W 94
Ronchamp, Fr. 47°42′ N, 6°37′ E 150
Ronda, Sp. 36°44′ N, 5°9′ W 150
Rondane, peak, Nor. 61°54′ N, 9°43′ E 152
Rønde, Den. 56°18′ N, 10°28′ E 150
Rondón, Col. 6°15′ N, 71°7′ W 136
Rondônia, adm. division, Braz. 10°29′ S, 65°14′ W 137
Rondonópolis, Braz. 16°29′ S, 54°37′ W 132
Rong, Koh, island, Cambodia 10°41′ N, 102°33′ E 202
Rong Kwang, Thai. 18°22′ N, 100°19′ E 202
Rong'an, China 25°16′ N, 109°18′ E 198
Rongcheng (Yatou), China 37°10′ N, 122°26′ E 198
Rongjiang, China 25°56′ N, 108°27′ E 198
Rongshui, China 25°4′ N, 109°12′ E 198
Rõngu, Est. 58°7′ N, 26°13′ E 166
Rongxian, China 22°50′ N, 110°33′ E 198
Ronkonkoma, N.Y., U.S. 40°49′ N, 73°9′ W 104
Ronne Ice Shelf, Antarctica 77°54′ S, 68°27′ W 248
Rönnskär, Nor. 64°39′ N, 21°15′ E 152
Ronse, Belg. 50°44′ N, 3°35′ E 163
Ronuro, river, Braz. 13°7′ S, 54°31′ W 130
Roodhouse, Mo., U.S. 39°28′ N, 90°22′ W 94
Roof Butte, peak, Ariz., U.S. 36°26′ N, 109°9′ W 92
Roosendaal, Neth. 51°32′ N, 4°28′ E 167
Roosevelt, Utah, U.S. 40°17′ N, 110°0′ W 92
Roosevelt Island, Antarctica 78°13′ S, 162°49′ W 248
Roosevelt, Mount, peak, Can. 58°24′ N, 125°29′ W 108
Rooslepa, Est. 59°11′ N, 23°29′ E 166
Root, river, Can. 62°50′ N, 124°50′ W 98
Root, river, Minn., U.S. 43°32′ N, 92°10′ W 80
Ropaži, Latv. 56°56′ N, 24°40′ E 166
Ropcha, Russ. 63°2′ N, 52°29′ E 154
Roper, river, Austral. 15°13′ S, 134°30′ E 230
Ropi, Fin. 68°36′ N, 21°46′ E 152
Ropotovo, Maced. 41°28′ N, 21°22′ E 168
Roquefort, Fr. 44°1′ N, 0°19′ E 150
Roquetes, Sp. 40°49′ N, 0°29′ E 164
Roraima, adm. division, Braz. 2°16′ N, 63°20′ W 130
Roraima, Mount, peak, Venez. 5°12′ N, 60°51′ W 130
Rorketon, Can. 51°23′ N, 99°35′ W 90
Rørstad, Nor. 67°34′ N, 15°13′ E 152
Rosa, Zambia 9°40′ S, 31°21′ E 224
Rosa, Monte, peak, Switz. 45°56′ N, 7°49′ E 165
Rosa, Punta, Mex. 26°31′ N, 110°22′ W 112
Rosales, Arg. 34°10′ S, 63°10′ W 139
Rosales, Mex. 28°9′ N, 105°33′ W 92
Rosalia, Wash., U.S. 47°13′ N, 117°22′ W 90
Rosamond, Calif., U.S. 34°51′ N, 118°11′ W 101
Rosamorada, Mex. 22°7′ N, 105°12′ W 114
Rosario, Arg. 32°56′ S, 60°41′ W 139
Rosário, Braz. 2°57′ S, 44°16′ W 132
Rosario, Mex. 23°0′ N, 105°54′ W 114
Rosario, Parag. 24°26′ S, 57°7′ W 132
Rosario, Uru. 34°19′ S, 57°19′ W 139
Rosario, Venez. 10°18′ N, 72°24′ W 136
Rosario, Bahía del 29°53′ N, 116°22′ W 92
Rosario, Cayo del, island, Cuba 21°10′ N, 82°0′ W 116
Rosario de Lerma, Arg. 24°58′ S, 65°36′ W 134
Rosario del Tala, Arg. 32°18′ S, 59°6′ W 139
Rosário do Sul, Braz. 30°16′ S, 54°58′ W 139
Rosário d'Oeste, Braz. 14°51′ S, 56°26′ W 132
Rosarito, Mex. 26°29′ N, 111°40′ W 112
Rosas, Col. 2°13′ N, 76°45′ W 136
Roscoe, Tex., U.S. 32°26′ N, 100°34′ W 92
Roscoff, Fr. 48°43′ N, 4°0′ W 150
Roscommon, Ire. 53°38′ N, 8°12′ W 150
Roscommon, Mich., U.S. 44°29′ N, 84°36′ W 94
Rose Blanche, Can. 47°36′ N, 58°41′ W 111
Rose Harbour, Can. 52°6′ N, 131°5′ W 108
Rose Lake, Can. 54°24′ N, 126°4′ W 108
Rose Point, Can. 54°8′ N, 131°39′ W 108
Rose Prairie, Can. 56°29′ N, 120°50′ W 108
Rose Valley, Can. 52°16′ N, 103°48′ W 108
Roseau, Dominica 15°16′ N, 61°31′ W 116
Roseau, Minn., U.S. 48°49′ N, 95°49′ W 90
Roseau, river, North America 48°57′ N, 96°21′ W 94
Rosebud, Mont., U.S. 46°15′ N, 106°27′ W 90
Rosebud Mountains, Mont., U.S. 45°21′ N, 107°15′ W 90
Rosebud Peak, Nev., U.S. 40°48′ N, 118°45′ W 90
Roseburg, Oreg., U.S. 43°12′ N, 123°20′ W 82
Rosebush, Mich., U.S. 43°42′ N, 84°46′ W 102
Rosedale, Ind., U.S. 39°37′ N, 87°17′ W 102
Rosée, Belg. 50°13′ N, 4°40′ E 167
Roseires Dam, Sudan 11°39′ N, 34°2′ E 182
Roseland, La., U.S. 30°45′ N, 90°31′ W 103
Roselawn, Ind., U.S. 41°8′ N, 87°19′ W 102
Roselend, Lac de, lake, Fr. 45°40′ N, 6°28′ E 165
Rosenberg, Tex., U.S. 29°32′ N, 95°49′ W 96
Rosendal, Nor. 59°59′ N, 5°59′ E 152
Rosendale, N.Y., U.S. 41°50′ N, 74°7′ W 104
Rosepine, La., U.S. 30°54′ N, 93°18′ W 103
Roseto degli Abruzzi, It. 42°39′ N, 14°0′ E 156
Rosetown, Can. 51°33′ N, 108°0′ W 90
Rosetta see Rashîd, Egypt 31°23′ N, 30°21′ E 180
Roseville, Calif., U.S. 38°44′ N, 121°19′ W 90
Roseville, Mich., U.S. 42°29′ N, 82°57′ W 94
Roseville, Ohio, U.S. 39°48′ N, 82°5′ W 102
Rosharon, Tex., U.S. 29°20′ N, 95°27′ W 103
Roshchino, Russ. 60°14′ N, 29°36′ E 166
Rosholt, S. Dak., U.S. 45°51′ N, 96°45′ W 90
Roshtkala, Taj. 37°13′ N, 71°48′ E 186
Rosignol, Guyana 6°9′ N, 57°35′ W 130
Roşiori de Vede, Rom. 44°6′ N, 24°56′ E 143
Roskilde, Den. 55°37′ N, 12°4′ E 152
Roslavl', Russ. 53°54′ N, 32°55′ E 154
Roslyn, Wash., U.S. 47°12′ N, 121°0′ W 90
Rösrath, Ger. 50°53′ N, 7°10′ E 163
Ross, N.Z. 42°55′ S, 170°49′ E 240
Ross Bethio, Senegal 16°17′ N, 16°11′ W 214
Ross Dam, Wash., U.S. 48°50′ N, 121°5′ W 82
Ross Ice Shelf, Antarctica 81°35′ S, 166°21′ W 248
Ross Island, island, Antarctica 77°2′ S, 171°48′ E 248
Ross Lake National Recreation Area, Wash., U.S. 48°43′ N, 121°28′ W 100
Ross, Mount, peak, N.Z. 41°29′ S, 175°17′ E 240
Ross on Wye, U.K. 51°55′ N, 2°35′ W 162
Ross River, Can. 61°56′ N, 132°32′ W 98
Ross, river, Can. 62°6′ N, 131°21′ W 98
Ross Sea 74°54′ S, 179°17′ E 248
Rossburn, Can. 50°40′ N, 100°49′ W 90
Rosscarbery, Ire. 51°35′ N, 9°2′ W 150
Rossel Island, island, P.N.G. 11°15′ S, 154°4′ E 192
Rosses, The, Ire. 54°46′ N, 8°16′ W 150
Rossignol, Lac, lake, Can. 52°41′ N, 74°1′ W 111
Rossini Point 73°0′ S, 74°12′ W 248
Rossland, Can. 49°3′ N, 117°50′ W 82
Rosso, Mauritania 16°34′ N, 15°52′ W 222
Rosso, Capo, Fr. 42°9′ N, 7°58′ E 156
Rossosh', Russ. 50°13′ N, 39°32′ E 158
Rossville, Ill., U.S. 40°22′ N, 87°39′ W 102
Rossville, Ind., U.S. 40°24′ N, 86°36′ W 102
Røst Bank, Norwegian Sea 67°47′ N, 12°7′ E 255
Rosthern, Can. 52°39′ N, 106°20′ W 108
Rostock, Ger. 54°5′ N, 12°7′ E 152
Rostov, Russ. 57°12′ N, 39°19′ E 154
Rostov, adm. division, Russ. 47°19′ N, 38°14′ E 156
Rostov na Donu, Russ. 47°13′ N, 39°42′ E 156
Rostuša, Maced. 41°36′ N, 20°35′ E 168
Røsvassbukt, Nor. 65°52′ N, 14°4′ E 152
Roswell, N. Mex., U.S. 33°23′ N, 104°32′ W 92
Rota, Sp. 36°37′ N, 6°22′ W 164
Rotan, Tex., U.S. 32°50′ N, 100°29′ W 92
Rotenburg, Ger. 51°0′ N, 9°43′ E 167
Rothaargebirge, Ger. 51°4′ N, 8°8′ E 167
Rothera, U.K., station, Antarctica 67°32′ S, 68°18′ W 248
Rotherham, N.Z. 42°44′ S, 172°56′ E 240
Rotherham, U.K. 53°26′ N, 1°22′ W 162
Rothschild Island, Antarctica 69°22′ S, 77°37′ W 248
Roti, island, Indonesia 11°14′ S, 122°38′ E 192
Rotondo, Monte, peak, Fr. 42°12′ N, 8°59′ E 156
Rotorua, N.Z. 38°9′ S, 176°13′ E 240
Rotterdam, Neth. 51°54′ N, 4°29′ E 167
Rotterdam, N.Y., U.S. 42°48′ N, 74°0′ W 104
Rottneros, Nor. 59°49′ N, 13°5′ E 152
Rottnest Island, Austral. 32°39′ S, 114°32′ E 230
Rottumeroog, island, Neth. 53°29′ N, 6°32′ E 163
Rottumerplaat, island, Neth. 53°31′ N, 5°57′ E 163
Roubaix, Fr. 50°41′ N, 3°10′ E 163
Rouen, Fr. 49°26′ N, 1°6′ E 163
Rõuge, Est. 57°44′ N, 26°53′ E 166
Rouge, Pointe 49°20′ N, 68°5′ W 94
Rouina, Alg. 36°14′ N, 1°48′ E 150
Roumila, Alg. 37°2′ N, 6°20′ E 150
Round Mount, peak, Austral. 30°22′ S, 152°2′ E 230
Round Pond, Me., U.S. 43°57′ N, 69°28′ W 94
Round Rock, Tex., U.S. 30°29′ N, 97°41′ W 92
Roundstone, Ire. 53°23′ N, 9°57′ W 150
Roundup, Mont., U.S. 46°25′ N, 108°33′ W 90
Roura, South America 4°46′ N, 52°20′ W 130
Rous, Península, Chile 55°23′ S, 71°22′ W 134
Rouses Point, N.Y., U.S. 44°58′ N, 73°24′ W 94
Rouseville, Pa., U.S. 41°27′ N, 79°42′ W 110
Roussillon, region, Fr. 42°51′ N, 2°39′ E 165
Rouxville, S. Af. 30°25′ S, 26°50′ E 227
Rouyn-Noranda, Can. 48°14′ N, 79°2′ W 110
Rovaniemi, Fin. 66°26′ N, 25°38′ E 160
Rovde, Nor. 62°9′ N, 5°44′ E 152
Rovdino, Russ. 61°41′ N, 42°35′ E 154
Roven'ki, Russ. 49°58′ N, 38°54′ E 158
Rover, Mount, peak, Can. 66°38′ N, 141°0′ W 98
Rovereto, It. 45°53′ N, 11°3′ E 167
Roversi, Arg. 27°35′ S, 61°58′ W 139
Rovieng, Cambodia 13°21′ N, 105°5′ E 202
Rovigo, It. 45°4′ N, 11°47′ E 167
Rovinj, Croatia 45°5′ N, 13°38′ E 167
Rovišće, Croatia 45°56′ N, 16°43′ E 168
Rovkuly, Russ. 64°2′ N, 30°47′ E 152
Rovnoye, Russ. 50°43′ N, 46°5′ E 158
Rovuma, river, Africa 11°46′ S, 37°36′ E 224
Rowan Lake, Can. 49°15′ N, 94°4′ W 94
Rowd-e Lurah, river, Afghan. 31°31′ N, 66°49′ E 186
Rowletts, Ky., U.S. 37°13′ N, 85°54′ W 96
Rowley, Mass., U.S. 42°42′ N, 70°53′ W 104
Rowley Island, Can. 68°35′ N, 80°9′ W 106
Roxa, island, Guinea-Bissau 11°9′ N, 15°37′ W 222
Roxas, Philippines 10°18′ N, 119°16′ E 203
Roxas, Philippines 17°5′ N, 121°36′ E 203
Roxas, Philippines 11°33′ N, 122°43′ E 203
Roxas, Philippines 12°36′ N, 121°30′ E 203
Roxburgh, N.Z. 45°33′ S, 169°17′ E 240
Roxbury, Vt., U.S. 44°5′ N, 72°44′ W 104
Roxen, lake, Nor. 58°26′ N, 15°14′ E 152
Roxo, Cap, Senegal 12°26′ N, 17°12′ W 222
Roy, Mont., U.S. 47°18′ N, 108°58′ W 90
Roy, N. Mex., U.S. 35°56′ N, 104°13′ W 92
Roy, Utah, U.S. 41°9′ N, 112°1′ W 92
Royal Center, Ind., U.S. 40°51′ N, 86°30′ W 102
Royal Chitwan National Park, Nepal 27°14′ N, 83°51′ E 197
Royal Gorge, site, Colo., U.S. 38°27′ N, 105°26′ W 90
Royal Manas National Park, Bhutan 26°37′ N, 91°8′ E 197
Royal Natal National Park, S. Af. 28°52′ S, 28°0′ E 227
Royale, Isle, island, Mich., U.S. 47°37′ N, 89°34′ W 80
Royalton, Vt., U.S. 43°49′ N, 72°34′ W 104
Royalty, Tex., U.S. 31°21′ N, 102°52′ W 92
Royan, Fr. 45°39′ N, 1°3′ W 150
Roye, Fr. 49°41′ N, 2°48′ E 163
Røyrvik, Nor. 64°53′ N, 13°31′ E 152
Royston, Can. 49°38′ N, 124°57′ W 100
Royston, U.K. 52°2′ N, 1°59′ W 162
Rožaje, Mont. 42°50′ N, 20°9′ E 168
Rožanj, peak, Serb. 44°17′ N, 19°24′ E 168
Rožanstvo, Serb. 43°43′ N, 19°50′ E 168
Rozdil'na, Ukr. 46°53′ N, 30°3′ E 156
Rozewie, Przylądek, Pol. 54°51′ N, 17°52′ E 152
Rozhdestvenskoye, Russ. 58°7′ N, 45°38′ E 154
Rozhyshche, Ukr. 50°54′ N, 25°15′ E 152
Rozivka, Ukr. 47°21′ N, 37°3′ E 156
Rožňava, Slovakia 48°39′ N, 20°32′ E 152
Roznov, Rom. 46°51′ N, 26°29′ E 158
Rozoy, Fr. 49°42′ N, 4°7′ E 163
Roztocze, Pol. 50°37′ N, 22°29′ E 152
Rrëshen, Alban. 41°47′ N, 19°54′ E 168
Rtanj, mountains, Serb. 43°50′ N, 21°42′ E 168
Rtishchevo, Russ. 52°15′ N, 43°48′ E 158
Ruabon, U.K. 52°59′ N, 3°2′ W 162
Ruacaná Falls, Angola 17°54′ S, 12°59′ E 220
Ruaha, Tanzania 7°23′ S, 36°34′ E 224
Ruaha National Park, Tanzania 7°47′ S, 34°17′ E 224
Ruakituri, N.Z. 38°45′ S, 177°24′ E 240
Ruapehu, Mount, peak, N.Z. 39°20′ S, 175°28′ E 240
Ruatahuna, N.Z. 38°38′ S, 176°58′ E 240
Ruatoria, N.Z. 37°55′ S, 178°19′ E 240
Ruawai, N.Z. 36°9′ S, 174°2′ E 240
Rubafu, Tanzania 1°5′ S, 31°51′ E 224
Rubel', Belarus 51°57′ N, 27°5′ E 152
Rubene, Latv. 57°27′ N, 25°13′ E 166
Rubeži, Mont. 42°46′ N, 19°1′ E 168
Rubi, river, Dem. Rep. of the Congo 2°33′ N, 25°16′ E 224
Rubiataba, Braz. 15°11′ S, 49°51′ W 138
Rubielos de Mora, Sp. 40°10′ N, 0°40′ E 164
Rubim, Braz. 16°23′ S, 40°33′ W 138
Rubin, Mount, peak, Antarctica 73°31′ S, 64°58′ E 248
Rubio, Venez. 7°41′ N, 72°23′ W 136
Rubio, peak, Sp. 41°25′ N, 3°51′ W 164
Rubondo Island National Park, Tanzania 2°31′ S, 32°6′ E 224
Rubtsovsk, Russ. 51°31′ N, 81°11′ E 184
Ruby, Alas., U.S. 64°33′ N, 155°34′ W 98
Ruby Beach, site, Wash., U.S. 47°42′ N, 124°27′ W 100
Ruby Dome, peak, Nev., U.S. 40°36′ N, 115°33′ W 90
Ruby Mountains, Nev., U.S. 40°30′ N, 115°37′ W 90
Ruby Range, Mont., U.S. 44°58′ N, 112°50′ W 90
Rucava, Latv. 56°9′ N, 21°8′ E 166
Ruch'i, Russ. 66°2′ N, 41°6′ E 154
Ruch'i Karel'skiye, Russ. 66°59′ N, 32°10′ E 152
Ruda, Pol. 53°35′ N, 22°30′ E 152
Rudall River National Park, Austral. 22°34′ S, 122°13′ E 238
Rudan, Iran 27°26′ N, 57°18′ E 196
Rudauli, India 26°44′ N, 81°45′ E 188
Rudawka, Pol. 53°51′ N, 23°29′ E 166
Rudbar, Afghan. 30°6′ N, 62°37′ E 186
Rūdbār, Iran 36°50′ N, 49°21′ E 195
Rudinice, Mont. 43°4′ N, 18°50′ E 168
Rūdiškės, Lith. 54°30′ N, 24°48′ E 166
Rudky, Ukr. 49°38′ N, 23°28′ E 152
Rudne, Ukr. 49°50′ N, 23°51′ E 152
Rudnica, Serb. 43°13′ N, 20°43′ E 168
Rūdnîchnyy, Kaz. 44°39′ N, 78°55′ E 184
Rudnichnyy, Russ. 59°39′ N, 52°32′ E 154
Rudnichnyy, Russ. 59°40′ N, 60°17′ E 154
Rudnik, Serb. 44°3′ N, 20°26′ E 168
Rudnik, peak, Serb. 44°8′ N, 20°28′ E 168
Rudno, Russ. 58°57′ N, 28°15′ E 166
Rudnya, Russ. 54°57′ N, 31°11′ E 154
Rūdnyy, Kaz. 52°58′ N, 63°5′ E 184
Rudo, Bosn. and Herzg. 43°37′ N, 19°22′ E 168
Rudolf, Lake see Turkana, Lake, Kenya 2°32′ N, 34°10′ E 206
Rudolph, Ostrov, island, Russ. 81°54′ N, 59°19′ E 160
Rudong, China 32°18′ N, 121°11′ E 198
Rudyard, Mich., U.S. 46°13′ N, 84°36′ W 94
Rudzyensk, Belarus 53°35′ N, 27°53′ E 152
Rue, Fr. 50°15′ N, 1°39′ E 163
Rufa'a, Sudan 14°44′ N, 33°23′ E 182
Rufiji, river, Tanzania 8°14′ S, 37°49′ E 224
Rufino, Arg. 34°16′ S, 62°41′ W 139
Rufisque, Senegal 14°45′ N, 16°56′ W 214
Rufunsa, Zambia 15°4′ S, 29°36′ E 224
Rugāji, Latv. 57°0′ N, 27°4′ E 166
Rugby, N. Dak., U.S. 48°20′ N, 100°0′ W 90
Rugby, U.K. 52°22′ N, 1°16′ W 162
Rugei, oil field, Kuwait 29°10′ N, 46°47′ E 196
Rugeley, U.K. 52°45′ N, 1°57′ W 162
Rugozero, Russ. 64°5′ N, 32°42′ E 152
Ruhengeri, Rwanda 1°32′ S, 29°36′ E 224
Ruhla, Ger. 50°53′ N, 10°21′ E 167
Ruhnu Saar, island, Est. 57°41′ N, 23°5′ E 166
Ruhr, region, Ger. 51°38′ N, 7°7′ E 167
Ruhr, river, Ger. 51°21′ N, 8°10′ E 167
Ruhuhu, river, Tanzania 10°16′ S, 34°54′ E 224
Ruhuna National Park, Sri Lanka 6°21′ N, 81°4′ E 172
Rui Barbosa, Braz. 12°18′ S, 40°27′ W 132
Rui'an, China 27°45′ N, 120°39′ E 198
Ruidosa, Tex., U.S. 29°58′ N, 104°41′ W 92
Ruidoso, N. Mex., U.S. 33°19′ N, 105°41′ W 92
Ruidoso Downs, N. Mex., U.S. 33°19′ N, 105°35′ W 92
Ruijin, China 25°50′ N, 116°0′ E 198
Ruinas de Numancia, ruin(s), Sp. 41°48′ N, 2°30′ W 164
Ruinen, Neth. 52°45′ N, 6°21′ E 163
Ruiru, Kenya 1°9′ S, 36°56′ E 224
Ruivo, Pico, peak, Port. 32°38′ N, 17°4′ W 214
Ruíz, Mex. 21°57′ N, 105°8′ W 114
Ruj, peak, Bulg. 42°50′ N, 22°32′ E 168
Rujen, peak, Maced. 42°8′ N, 22°28′ E 168
Rūjiena, Latv. 57°54′ N, 25°18′ E 166
Ruker, Mount, peak, Antarctica 73°47′ S, 63°43′ E 248
Ruki, river, Dem. Rep. of the Congo 2°0′ N, 18°32′ E 218
Rukungiri, Uganda 0°51′ S, 29°55′ E 224
Rukwa, adm. division, Tanzania 6°54′ S, 30°38′ E 224
Rukwa, Lake, Tanzania 8°0′ S, 32°25′ E 224
Rule, Tex., U.S. 33°10′ N, 99°54′ W 92
Rum Cay, island, Bahamas 23°32′ N, 74°47′ W 116
Rum, river, Minn., U.S. 45°43′ N, 93°41′ W 94
Ruma, Serb. 45°0′ N, 19°49′ E 168
Rumā', Saudi Arabia 25°34′ N, 47°11′ E 196
Rumaila, oil field, Iraq 30°15′ N, 47°23′ E 196
Rumaylah, 'Urūqar, Saudi Arabia 23°47′ N, 47°58′ E 196
Rumaysh, Leb. 33°4′ N, 35°21′ E 194
Rumbek, Sudan 6°47′ N, 29°38′ E 224
Rumford, Me., U.S. 44°32′ N, 70°33′ W 104
Rumia, Pol. 54°34′ N, 18°24′ E 152
Rumija, peak, Mont. 42°5′ N, 19°9′ E 168
Rumilly, Fr. 45°51′ N, 5°56′ E 150
Rumney, N.H., U.S. 43°48′ N, 71°50′ W 104
Rumo, Fin. 63°49′ N, 28°31′ E 152
Rumonge, Burundi 3°59′ S, 29°24′ E 218
Rumphi, Malawi 11°1′ S, 33°49′ E 224
Rumput, peak, Indonesia 1°44′ N, 109°35′ E 196
Rumuruti, Kenya 0°15′ N, 36°32′ E 224
Runan, China 33°0′ N, 114°19′ E 198
Runaway, Cape, N.Z. 37°32′ S, 177°29′ E 240
Runcorn, U.K. 53°19′ N, 2°44′ W 162
Runde, river, Zimb. 21°15′ S, 31°22′ E 227
Rundeng, Indonesia 2°41′ N, 97°48′ E 196
Rundēni, Latv. 56°15′ N, 27°50′ E 166
Rundu, Namibia 17°54′ S, 19°44′ E 220
Rundvik, Nor. 63°30′ N, 19°24′ E 152
Runere, Tanzania 3°7′ S, 33°15′ E 224
Runge, Tex., U.S. 28°52′ N, 97°43′ W 92
Rungu, Dem. Rep. of the Congo 3°12′ N, 27°54′ E 224
Rungwa, Tanzania 6°58′ S, 33°32′ E 224

S

SAN-SAR

Sangaréd, Guinea 11°3′ N, 13°46′ W 222
Sangay National Park, Ecua. 1°58′ S, 78°42′ W 122
Sangay, peak, Ecua. 2°5′ S, 78°29′ W 136
Sangayan, Isla de, island, Peru 14°5′ S, 77°5′ W 130
Sangbé, Cameroon 6°1′ N, 12°28′ E 218
Sangbu, S. Korea 35°33′ N, 128°17′ E 200
Sang-e Masheh, Afghan. 33°16′ N, 67°7′ E 186
Sanger, Calif., U.S. 36°42′ N, 119°34′ W 100
Sanger, Tex., U.S. 33°21′ N, 97°9′ W 92
Sanggan, river, China 39°44′ N, 113°30′ E 198
Sanggou Wan 37°0′ N, 122°2′ E 198
Sanghar, Pak. 26°3′ N, 68°58′ E 186
Sangihe, Kepulauan, islands, Molucca Sea 2°38′ N, 125°59′ E 192
Sangiyn Dalay, Mongolia 46°0′ N, 104°58′ E 198
Sangju, S. Korea 36°23′ N, 128°11′ E 200
Sangkhla, Thai. 15°7′ N, 98°32′ E 202
Sangkulirang, Indonesia 0°56′ N, 117°52′ E 192
Sangla, Pak. 31°45′ N, 73°21′ E 186
Sangni, N. Korea 40°58′ N, 128°7′ E 200
Sangre de Cristo Mountains, N. Mex., U.S. 35°28′ N, 105°41′ W 112
Sangri, China 29°20′ N, 92°10′ E 197
Sangt'ong, N. Korea 40°5′ N, 127°20′ E 200
Sangue, river, Braz. 11°2′ S, 58°36′ W 130
Sanguinaires, Îles, islands, Mediterranean Sea 41°50′ N, 7°26′ E 156
Sangvor, Taj. 38°41′ N, 71°21′ E 197
Sangwŏn, N. Korea 38°50′ N, 126°6′ E 200
Sangzhi, China 29°24′ N, 110°10′ E 198
Sanhecun, China 42°30′ N, 129°42′ E 200
Sanibel Island, Fla., U.S. 26°20′ N, 82°10′ W 105
Sanikiluaq, Can. 56°20′ N, 79°9′ W 73
Saniquellie, Liberia 7°16′ N, 8°41′ W 222
Sanislău, Rom. 47°39′ N, 22°21′ E 168
Sāniyat ad Daffah, spring, Lib. 30°5′ N, 24°13′ E 180
Sanje, Uganda 0°50′ N, 31°29′ E 224
Sanjeong, S. Korea 34°21′ N, 126°33′ E 200
Sanjiang, China 25°52′ N, 109°39′ E 198
Sanjō, Japan 37°38′ N, 138°58′ E 201
Sankaty Head, Mass., U.S. 41°16′ N, 69°58′ W 104
Sankeyushu, China 41°44′ N, 125°21′ E 200
Sankt Augustin, Ger. 50°45′ N, 7°10′ E 167
Sankt Goar, Ger. 50°8′ N, 7°41′ E 167
Sankt Ingbert, Ger. 49°16′ N, 7°6′ E 163
Sankt Michael, Aust. 47°7′ N, 16°15′ E 168
Sankt Moritz, Switz. 46°30′ N, 9°49′ E 167
Sankt Pölten, Aust. 48°11′ N, 15°38′ E 143
Sankt Pölten, Aust. 48°12′ N, 15°37′ E 152
Sankt Ruprecht, Aust. 47°10′ N, 15°40′ E 168
Sankt Wendel, Ger. 49°27′ N, 7°10′ E 163
Sankt-Maurice, Switz. 46°13′ N, 7°1′ E 167
Sankt-Peterburg, adm. division, Russ. 59°55′ N, 30°15′ E 166
Sankt-Peterburg (Saint Petersburg, Leningrad), Russ. 59°55′ N, 30°17′ E 166
Sankuru, river, Dem. Rep. of the Congo 4°3′ S, 21°26′ E 218
Sankuru, river, Dem. Rep. of the Congo 5°56′ S, 23°37′ E 224
Şanlıurfa (Edessa), Turk. 37°6′ N, 38°45′ E 180
Sanlúcar de Barrameda, Sp. 36°46′ N, 6°22′ W 164
Sanmenxia, China 34°45′ N, 111°12′ E 198
Sanming, China 26°9′ N, 117°34′ E 198
Sannazzaro, It. 45°6′ N, 8°54′ E 167
Sannikova, Proliv 74°30′ N, 145°34′ E 246
Sano, Japan 36°18′ N, 139°36′ E 201
Sanquianga National Park, Col. 2°25′ N, 78°40′ W 122
Sans Sault Rapids, fall(s), Can. 65°13′ N, 128°46′ W 98
Sansanding, Mali 13°45′ N, 6°1′ W 222
Sansane, Niger 13°50′ N, 1°37′ E 222
Sansha, China 26°58′ N, 120°12′ E 198
Sanshui, China 23°10′ N, 112°55′ E 198
Sansui, China 27°1′ N, 108°40′ E 198
Sant' Antioco, island, It. 38°27′ N, 7°30′ E 214
Sant Antoni de Portmany, Sp. 38°58′ N, 1°17′ E 150
Sant Celoni, Sp. 41°41′ N, 2°29′ E 164
Sant Feliu de Guíxols, Sp. 41°46′ N, 3°1′ E 164
Sant Francesc de Formentera, Sp. 38°41′ N, 1°25′ E 150
Sant Jaume d'Enveja, Sp. 40°41′ N, 0°43′ E 164
Sant Joan d'Alacant, Sp. 38°23′ N, 0°26′ E 164
Sant Josep, Sp. 38°55′ N, 1°17′ E 150
Sant Llorenç de Morunys, Sp. 42°8′ N, 1°34′ E 164
Sant Quirze de Besora, Sp. 42°6′ N, 2°13′ E 164
Santa, Peru 9°2′ S, 78°38′ W 130
Santa Amelia, Guatemala 16°14′ N, 90°3′ W 115
Santa Ana, Bol. 15°32′ S, 67°30′ W 137
Santa Ana, Calif., U.S. 33°45′ N, 117°53′ W 101
Santa Ana, El Salv. 13°59′ N, 89°33′ W 115
Santa Ana, Mex. 30°32′ N, 111°6′ W 92
Santa Ana, Philippines 18°29′ N, 122°9′ E 203
Santa Ana, island, Solomon Islands 10°50′ S, 162°30′ E 242
Santa Ana Mountains, Calif., U.S. 33°40′ N, 117°36′ W 101
Santa Ana, river, Venez. 9°32′ N, 72°47′ W 116
Santa Barbara, Calif., U.S. 34°25′ N, 119°44′ W 100
Santa Bárbara, Mex. 26°47′ N, 105°50′ W 112
Santa Bárbara, Peru 12°53′ S, 75°2′ W 130
Santa Bárbara, Sp. 40°42′ N, 0°30′ E 164
Santa Bárbara, Venez. 3°54′ N, 67°5′ W 136
Santa Bárbara, Venez. 7°47′ N, 71°12′ W 136
Santa Barbara Channel 34°13′ N, 120°27′ W 100
Santa Barbara, island, Calif., U.S. 33°29′ N, 119°23′ W 101
Santa Bárbara, peak, Sp. 37°22′ N, 2°53′ W 164
Santa Catalina, Arg. 21°57′ S, 66°4′ W 137
Santa Catalina, Pan. 8°46′ N, 81°19′ W 115
Santa Catalina, Isla, island, Mex. 25°30′ N, 110°46′ W 112
Santa Catalina, island, Calif., U.S. 33°25′ N, 118°23′ W 101
Santa Catalina, island, Solomon Islands 10°53′ S, 162°30′ E 242
Santa Catarina, Mex. 25°39′ N, 100°29′ W 114
Santa Catarina, adm. division, Braz. 26°54′ S, 53°39′ W 139
Santa Catarina, Ilha de, island, Braz. 27°57′ S, 48°22′ W 132
Santa Clara, Calif., U.S. 37°21′ N, 121°57′ W 100
Santa Clara, Col. 2°45′ S, 69°43′ W 136
Santa Clara, Cuba 22°26′ N, 79°57′ W 116
Santa Clara, Mex. 24°27′ N, 103°22′ W 114
Santa Clara, Mex. 29°16′ N, 107°2′ W 92
Santa Clara, Uru. 32°55′ S, 54°58′ W 139
Santa Clara, Utah, U.S. 37°8′ N, 113°39′ W 101
Santa Clarita, Calif., U.S. 34°25′ N, 118°34′ W 101
Santa Claus Mountain, peak, Can. 54°11′ N, 61°31′ W 111
Santa Clotilde, Peru 2°32′ S, 73°41′ W 136
Santa Cruz, Angola 6°59′ S, 16°17′ E 218
Santa Cruz, Bol. 17°48′ S, 63°13′ W 137
Santa Cruz, Braz. 6°1′ S, 72°25′ W 130
Santa Cruz, Calif., U.S. 36°58′ N, 122°3′ W 100
Santa Cruz, Mex. 31°12′ N, 110°38′ W 92
Santa Cruz, Philippines 17°5′ N, 120°27′ E 203
Santa Cruz, Philippines 13°6′ N, 120°45′ E 203
Santa Cruz, Philippines 14°16′ N, 121°24′ E 203
Santa Cruz, Philippines 15°47′ N, 119°55′ E 203
Santa Cruz, Venez. 8°2′ N, 64°26′ W 130
Santa Cruz, adm. division, Arg. 48°26′ S, 71°7′ W 134
Santa Cruz, adm. division, Bol. 17°36′ S, 64°15′ W 137
Santa Cruz Cabrália, Braz. 16°18′ S, 39°3′ W 132
Santa Cruz Channel 33°57′ N, 120°5′ W 101
Santa Cruz de la Zarza, Sp. 39°59′ N, 3°13′ W 164
Santa Cruz de Moya, Sp. 39°57′ N, 1°17′ W 164
Santa Cruz de Mudela, Sp. 38°39′ N, 3°28′ W 164
Santa Cruz del Norte, Cuba 23°8′ N, 81°55′ W 112
Santa Cruz del Sur, Cuba 20°43′ N, 77°59′ W 116
Santa Cruz do Arai, Braz. 0°36′ N, 49°12′ W 130
Santa Cruz do Rio Pardo, Braz. 22°53′ S, 49°39′ W 138
Santa Cruz do Sul, Braz. 29°42′ S, 52°23′ W 139
Santa Cruz, Isla, island, Ecua. 0°40′ N, 90°9′ W 130
Santa Cruz, island, Calif., U.S. 34°4′ N, 119°42′ W 100
Santa Cruz Islands, Coral Sea 11°42′ S, 166°19′ E 238
Santa Cruz Mountains, Calif., U.S. 37°16′ N, 122°4′ W 100
Santa Elena, Arg. 30°56′ S, 59°46′ W 139
Santa Elena, Ecua. 2°18′ S, 80°48′ W 130
Santa Elena, Mex. 27°57′ N, 104°0′ W 92
Santa Elena, Venez. 4°36′ N, 61°7′ W 130
Santa Elena, Cabo, C.R. 10°50′ N, 87°0′ W 115
Santa Eulalia, Sp. 40°33′ N, 1°19′ W 164
Santa Eulalia del Río, Sp. 38°58′ N, 1°32′ E 150
Santa Fe, Arg. 31°37′ S, 60°42′ W 139
Santa Fe, N. Mex., U.S. 35°40′ N, 106°2′ W 92
Santa Fe, Philippines 12°10′ N, 121°59′ E 203
Santa Fé, Sp. 37°11′ N, 3°43′ W 164
Santa Fe, adm. division, Arg. 30°54′ S, 61°46′ W 139
Santa Filomena, Braz. 9°7′ S, 45°54′ W 130
Santa Helena, Braz. 24°56′ S, 54°26′ W 132
Santa Helena, Braz. 5°13′ S, 56°20′ W 130
Santa Helena de Goiás, Braz. 17°49′ S, 50°33′ W 138
Santa Inês, Braz. 3°43′ S, 45°26′ W 130
Santa Inês, Braz. 13°22′ S, 39°49′ W 138
Santa Inés, Isla, island, Chile 53°50′ S, 75°22′ W 134
Santa Inés, peak, Sp. 38°31′ N, 5°40′ W 164
Santa Isabel, Arg. 36°15′ S, 66°54′ W 134
Santa Isabel, Arg. 33°53′ S, 61°40′ W 139
Santa Isabel, Venez. 1°20′ N, 65°49′ W 136
Santa Isabel do Morro, Braz. 11°32′ S, 50°43′ W 130
Santa Isabel, Ilha Grande de, island, Braz. 3°25′ S, 42°32′ W 132
Santa Isabel, island, Solomon Islands 8°5′ S, 159°10′ E 242
Santa Juana, Venez. 7°0′ N, 67°33′ W 136
Santa Júlia, Braz. 7°48′ S, 58°14′ W 130
Santa Julia, Col. 1°34′ S, 72°18′ W 136
Santa Juliana, Braz. 19°19′ S, 47°32′ W 138
Santa Kurutze Kanpezu, Sp. 42°39′ N, 2°21′ W 164
Santa Lucía, Arg. 28°59′ S, 59°8′ W 139
Santa Lucía, Nicar. 12°30′ N, 85°41′ W 115
Santa Lucía, Uru. 34°28′ S, 56°22′ W 139
Santa Lucia Range, Calif., U.S. 35°58′ N, 121°22′ W 100
Santa Magdalena, Arg. 34°32′ S, 63°54′ W 139
Santa Margarita, Calif., U.S. 35°23′ N, 120°38′ W 100
Santa Margarita, Isla, island, Mex. 24°9′ N, 112°57′ W 112
Santa María, Arg. 26°43′ S, 66°2′ W 132
Santa Maria, Braz. 1°45′ S, 58°36′ W 130
Santa Maria, Braz. 2°57′ S, 60°25′ W 130
Santa Maria, Braz. 29°44′ S, 53°48′ W 139
Santa Maria, Calif., U.S. 34°57′ N, 120°27′ W 100
Santa María, Peru 1°25′ S, 74°38′ W 136
Santa Maria, Switz. 46°35′ N, 10°24′ E 167
Santa Maria, Zambia 11°9′ S, 29°58′ E 224
Santa María, Bahía 24°57′ N, 109°16′ W 80
Santa María, Cabo, Uru. 34°59′ S, 54°11′ W 139
Santa Maria, Cape, Bahamas 23°44′ N, 75°18′ W 80
Santa María, Cayo, island, Cuba 22°42′ N, 78°57′ W 116
Santa Maria da Vitória, Braz. 13°23′ S, 44°14′ W 138
Santa María de Huerta, Sp. 41°15′ N, 2°11′ W 164
Santa María de Ipire, Venez. 8°48′ N, 65°20′ W 136
Santa María de los Ángeles, Mex. 22°10′ N, 103°12′ W 114
Santa María de Nanay, Peru 3°54′ S, 73°45′ W 130
Santa María de Otáez, Mex. 24°40′ N, 106°0′ W 114
Santa María del Oro, Mex. 25°55′ N, 105°19′ W 114
Santa María del Oro, Mex. 21°20′ N, 104°36′ W 114
Santa María del Río, Mex. 21°47′ N, 100°44′ W 114
Santa Maria do Suaçuí, Braz. 18°12′ S, 42°26′ W 138
Santa María, Isla, island, Chile 37°8′ S, 75°29′ W 134
Santa María, Isla, island, Ecua. 1°54′ S, 90°21′ W 130
Santa María, river, Mex. 21°47′ N, 100°34′ W 114
Santa Marta, Col. 11°11′ N, 74°14′ W 136
Santa Marta, Sp. 38°36′ N, 6°38′ W 164
Santa Marta Grande, Cabo de, Braz. 28°34′ S, 48°43′ W 134
Santa Monica Mountains, Calif., U.S. 34°8′ N, 118°55′ W 101
Santa Olalla del Cala, Sp. 37°54′ N, 6°15′ W 164
Santa Pola, Sp. 38°11′ N, 0°34′ E 164
Santa Rita, Col. 4°54′ N, 68°22′ W 136
Santa Rita, Venez. 8°6′ N, 66°17′ W 136
Santa Rita, Venez. 10°33′ N, 71°32′ W 116
Santa Rita do Araguaia, Braz. 17°22′ S, 53°14′ W 138
Santa Rita do Weil, Braz. 3°31′ S, 69°20′ W 136
Santa Rita Park, Calif., U.S. 37°2′ N, 120°36′ W 100
Santa, river, Peru 8°55′ S, 78°46′ W 130
Santa Rosa, Arg. 28°3′ S, 67°37′ W 132
Santa Rosa, Arg. 36°37′ S, 64°18′ W 139
Santa Rosa, Arg. 40°0′ S, 66°33′ W 134
Santa Rosa, Arg. 32°21′ S, 65°9′ W 134
Santa Rosa, Ariz., U.S. 32°19′ N, 112°2′ W 92
Santa Rosa, Bol. 14°13′ S, 66°54′ W 137
Santa Rosa, Bol. 11°41′ S, 65°14′ W 137
Santa Rosa, Bol. 10°38′ S, 67°24′ W 137
Santa Rosa, Braz. 15°6′ S, 47°15′ W 138
Santa Rosa, Braz. 27°53′ S, 54°31′ W 139
Santa Rosa, Calif., U.S. 38°26′ N, 122°42′ W 90
Santa Rosa, N. Mex., U.S. 34°55′ N, 104°41′ W 92
Santa Rosa, Peru 14°39′ S, 70°46′ W 137
Santa Rosa, Peru 3°48′ S, 76°26′ W 136
Santa Rosa, Peru 3°1′ S, 73°13′ W 136
Santa Rosa, Venez. 8°30′ N, 69°43′ W 136
Santa Rosa de Amanadona, Venez. 1°25′ N, 66°53′ W 136
Santa Rosa de Cop'an, Hond. 14°46′ N, 88°46′ W 115
Santa Rosa de Rio Primero, Arg. 31°9′ S, 63°22′ W 139
Santa Rosa do Purus, Peru 9°28′ S, 70°33′ W 137
Santa Rosa, island, Calif., U.S. 34°3′ N, 120°7′ W 100
Santa Rosa Mountains, Calif., U.S. 33°29′ N, 116°25′ W 101
Santa Rosa National Park, North Pacific Ocean 10°46′ N, 85°46′ W 115
Santa Rosa Peak, Nev., U.S. 41°33′ N, 117°46′ W 90
Santa Rosa Range, Nev., U.S. 41°50′ N, 117°39′ W 90
Santa Rosalía, Mex. 27°20′ N, 112°17′ W 82
Santa Rosalía, Venez. 7°25′ N, 65°42′ W 136
Santa Rosalita, Mex. 28°40′ N, 114°19′ W 92
Santa Sylvina, Arg. 27°47′ S, 61°8′ W 139
Santa Teresa, Arg. 33°27′ S, 60°46′ W 139
Santa Teresa, Braz. 13°42′ S, 49°3′ W 138
Santa Teresa, Mex. 25°18′ N, 97°52′ W 114
Santa Teresa, river, Braz. 13°39′ S, 49°1′ W 138
Santa Terezinha, Braz. 10°28′ S, 50°35′ W 130
Santa Victoria, Arg. 22°16′ S, 62°45′ W 132
Santa Victoria, Arg. 22°16′ S, 64°59′ W 137
Santa Vitória do Palmar, Braz. 33°31′ S, 53°20′ W 139
Santa Ynez, Calif., U.S. 34°37′ N, 120°6′ W 100
Santa Ynez Mountains, Calif., U.S. 34°32′ N, 120°28′ W 100
Santai, China 31°2′ N, 105°0′ E 198
Santalpur, India 23°47′ N, 71°12′ E 186
Santana, Braz. 12°59′ S, 44°5′ W 138
Santana do Araguaia, Braz. 8°52′ S, 49°45′ W 130
Santana do Livramento, Braz. 30°53′ S, 55°29′ W 139
Santana, river, Braz. 10°0′ S, 51°14′ W 130
Santander, Col. 2°58′ N, 76°30′ W 136
Santander, Sp. 43°23′ N, 3°59′ W 214
Santander, Sp. 43°27′ N, 3°49′ W 164
Santander, adm. division, Col. 6°30′ N, 74°20′ W 136
Santander Jiménez, Mex. 24°11′ N, 98°30′ W 114
Sant'Angelo Lodigiano, It. 45°13′ N, 9°24′ E 167
Santanilla, Islas, islands, Caribbean Sea 17°40′ N, 84°22′ W 115
Santanyí, Sp. 39°20′ N, 3°7′ E 150
Santarcangelo di Romagna, It. 44°3′ N, 12°26′ E 167
Santarém, Braz. 2°29′ S, 54°48′ W 130
Santarém, Port. 39°13′ N, 8°42′ W 150
Santarém, adm. division, Port. 39°17′ N, 8°59′ W 150
Santaren Channel 23°42′ N, 79°35′ W 96
Santee, Calif., U.S. 32°50′ N, 116°59′ W 101
Santee Point 33°1′ N, 79°15′ W 96
Santee, river, S.C., U.S. 33°36′ N, 80°10′ W 80
Santena, It. 44°57′ N, 7°46′ E 167
Santhià, It. 45°22′ N, 8°10′ E 167
Santiago, Bol. 18°26′ S, 59°34′ W 132
Santiago, Braz. 29°12′ S, 54°50′ W 139
Santiago, Chile 33°30′ S, 70°56′ W 134
Santiago, Mex. 25°24′ N, 100°7′ W 114
Santiago, Cerro, peak, Pan. 8°32′ N, 81°48′ W 115
Santiago de Compostela, Sp. 42°51′ N, 8°34′ W 150
Santiago de Cuba, Cuba 20°1′ N, 75°50′ W 115
Santiago de Cuba, adm. division, Cuba 20°11′ N, 76°25′ W 115
Santiago de la Peña, Mex. 20°53′ N, 97°24′ W 114
Santiago del Estero, Arg. 27°48′ S, 64°19′ W 132
Santiago del Estero, adm. division, Arg. 28°2′ S, 63°30′ W 139
Santiago, Isla, island, Ecua. 0°21′ N, 90°34′ W 130
Santiago Mountains, Tex., U.S. 29°59′ N, 103°28′ W 92
Santiago Papasquiaro, Mex. 25°1′ N, 105°28′ W 114
Santiago, Region Metropolitana de, adm. division, Chile 33°45′ S, 72°16′ W 134
Santiago, Serranía de, Bol. 17°57′ S, 60°30′ W 132
Santiago Tuxtla, Mex. 18°27′ N, 95°19′ W 114
Santiaguillo, Laguna de, lake, Mex. 24°56′ N, 105°40′ W 81
Santiam Pass, Oreg., U.S. 44°24′ N, 121°52′ W 90
Santillana, Sp. 43°23′ N, 4°6′ W 164
Santo Amaro, Braz. 12°31′ S, 38°44′ W 132
Santo Anastácio, Braz. 21°58′ S, 51°42′ W 138
Santo André, Braz. 23°39′ S, 46°32′ W 138
Santo Ângelo, Braz. 28°22′ S, 54°18′ W 139
Santo Antônio, Braz. 2°0′ N, 68°29′ W 136
Santo Antônio do Içá, Braz. 3°5′ S, 67°58′ W 136
Santo Corazón, Bol. 18°0′ S, 58°49′ W 132
Santo Domingo, Dom. Rep. 18°26′ N, 70°3′ W 116
Santo Domingo, Mex. 23°18′ N, 101°44′ W 114
Santo Domingo de Acobamba, Peru 11°49′ S, 74°45′ W 137
Santo Domingo de los Colorados, Ecua. 0°16′ N, 79°13′ W 130
Santo Domingo Pueblo, N. Mex., U.S. 35°30′ N, 106°22′ W 92
Santo Hipólito, Braz. 18°17′ S, 44°16′ W 138
Santo Stefano, It. 44°32′ N, 9°26′ E 167
Santo Tomás, Mex. 31°32′ N, 116°25′ W 92
Santo Tomás, Peru 14°30′ S, 72°5′ W 137
Santo Tomás, Punta, Mex. 31°16′ N, 117°0′ W 92
Santo Tomé, Arg. 31°41′ S, 60°46′ W 139
Santo Tomé, Arg. 28°33′ S, 56°4′ W 139
Santok, Pol. 52°45′ N, 15°25′ E 152
Santong, river, China 42°4′ N, 125°59′ E 200
Santopitar, peak, Sp. 36°47′ N, 4°20′ W 164
Santos, Braz. 23°56′ S, 46°21′ W 138
Santos Dumont, Braz. 21°28′ S, 43°32′ W 138
Santos Dumont, Braz. 6°28′ S, 68°16′ W 130
Santos Plateau, South Atlantic Ocean 26°36′ S, 43°17′ W 253
Santos, Sierra de los, Sp. 37°57′ N, 5°14′ W 164
Santovenia de Pisuerga, Sp. 41°40′ N, 4°42′ W 150
Santuario del Moncayo, peak, Sp. 41°46′ N, 1°54′ W 164
Santurtzi, Sp. 43°18′ N, 3°2′ W 164
Sanya, China 18°13′ N, 109°30′ E 198
Sanyō-Onoda, Japan 33°58′ N, 131°11′ E 200
Sanyuan, China 34°38′ N, 108°56′ E 198
Sanza Pombo, Angola 7°21′ S, 15°59′ E 218
São Benedito, river, Braz. 9°16′ S, 57°29′ W 132
São Bento, Braz. 2°43′ S, 44°47′ W 132
São Borja, Braz. 28°41′ S, 56°3′ W 139
São Carlos, Braz. 22°2′ S, 47°55′ W 138
São Cristóvão, Braz. 11°2′ S, 37°11′ W 132
São Domingos, Braz. 19°14′ S, 40°38′ W 138
São Domingos, Braz. 13°24′ S, 46°23′ W 138
São Domingos, Guinea-Bissau 12°23′ N, 16°9′ W 222
São Fé de Minas, Braz. 16°42′ S, 45°25′ W 138
São Félix do Xingu, Braz. 6°39′ S, 52°0′ W 130
São Fidélis, Braz. 21°41′ S, 41°47′ W 138
São Francisco, Braz. 15°58′ S, 44°54′ W 138
São Francisco de Sales, Braz. 19°53′ S, 49°47′ W 138
São Francisco do Sul, Braz. 26°16′ S, 48°34′ W 138
São Francisco, Ilha de, island, Braz. 26°22′ S, 48°27′ W 132
São Francisco, river, Braz. 14°13′ S, 43°40′ W 138
São Gabriel, Braz. 30°22′ S, 54°20′ W 139
São Gabriel da Cachoeira, Braz. 0°8′ N, 67°5′ W 136
São Gabriel de Goiás, Braz. 15°13′ S, 47°34′ W 138
São Geraldo do Araguaia, Braz. 6°21′ S, 48°35′ W 130
São Gonçalo do Abaete, Braz. 18°21′ S, 45°52′ W 138
Sao Hill, Tanzania 8°23′ S, 35°13′ E 224
São João, Guinea-Bissau 11°36′ N, 15°26′ W 222
São João da Aliança, Braz. 14°44′ S, 47°31′ W 138
São João da Barra, Braz. 21°41′ S, 41°3′ W 138
São João da Boa Vista, Braz. 21°58′ S, 46°48′ W 138
São João da Ponte, Braz. 15°58′ S, 44°0′ W 138
São João de Cortes, Braz. 2°11′ S, 44°30′ W 132
São João del Rei, Braz. 21°9′ S, 44°16′ W 138
São João do Araguaia, Braz. 5°26′ S, 48°46′ W 130
São João do Paraíso, Braz. 15°21′ S, 42°6′ W 138
São João do Piauí, Braz. 8°22′ S, 42°14′ W 132
São João, Serra de, Braz. 8°22′ S, 62°44′ W 130
São Joaquim, Braz. 28°20′ S, 49°57′ W 138
São Joaquim, Braz. 2°119′ S, 67°19′ W 136
São Joaquim da Barra, Braz. 20°37′ S, 47°53′ W 138
São Joaquim National Park, Braz. 28°18′ S, 49°50′ W 138
São José, Braz. 9°40′ S, 67°10′ W 137
São José, Braz. 27°37′ S, 48°38′ W 138
São José de Anauá, Braz. 1°2′ N, 61°27′ W 130
São José do Norte, Braz. 32°2′ S, 52°3′ W 139
São José do Rio Pardo, Braz. 21°37′ S, 46°56′ W 138
São José do Rio Preto, Braz. 20°49′ S, 49°22′ W 138
São José dos Campos, Braz. 23°12′ S, 45°51′ W 138
São José dos Pinhais, Braz. 25°32′ S, 49°11′ W 138
São Leopoldo, Braz. 29°45′ S, 51°12′ W 139
São Lourenço, Braz. 22°8′ S, 45°4′ W 138
São Lourenço do Sul, Braz. 31°20′ S, 51°58′ W 139
São Luís, Braz. 2°33′ S, 44°15′ W 130
São Luís de Montes Belos, Braz. 16°33′ S, 50°21′ W 138
São Luís do Tocantins, Braz. 14°19′ S, 48°0′ W 138
São Luís Gonzaga, Braz. 28°27′ S, 54°59′ W 139
São Luís, Ilha de, island, Braz. 2°45′ S, 44°0′ W 132
São Manuel see Teles Pires, river, Braz. 9°30′ S, 55°14′ W 122
São Marcelino, Braz. 0°53′ N, 67°15′ W 136
São Marcos, river, Braz. 18°1′ S, 47°33′ W 138
São Mateus, Braz. 18°45′ S, 39°53′ W 138
São Mateus do Sul, Braz. 25°52′ S, 50°25′ W 138
São Miguel do Araguaia, Braz. 13°22′ S, 50°16′ W 138
São Miguel, river, Braz. 12°27′ S, 63°14′ W 132
São Paulo, Braz. 23°33′ S, 46°36′ W 138
São Paulo, adm. division, Braz. 21°42′ S, 49°43′ W 138
São Paulo de Olivença, Braz. 3°31′ S, 68°49′ W 136
São Pedro, Braz. 0°19′ N, 66°50′ W 136
São Pedro, Braz. 22°34′ S, 47°56′ W 138
São Pedro, Braz. 3°6′ S, 68°54′ W 136
São Raimundo do Araguaia, Braz. 5°40′ S, 48°14′ W 130
São Raimundo Nonato, Braz. 9°2′ S, 42°43′ W 132
São Romão, Braz. 5°51′ S, 67°48′ W 130
São Romão, Braz. 16°22′ S, 45°8′ W 138
São Roque do Paraguaçu, Braz. 12°54′ S, 38°54′ W 132
São Salvador, Braz. 7°28′ S, 73°13′ W 130
São Sebastião, Braz. 23°48′ S, 45°27′ W 138
São Sebastião do Paraíso, Braz. 20°55′ S, 46°59′ W 138
São Sebastião dos Poções, Braz. 14°34′ S, 44°24′ W 138
São Sebastião, Ilha de, island, Braz. 24°18′ S, 45°10′ W 132
São Sebastião, Ponta, Mozambique 22°35′ S, 35°29′ E 220
Sao Tome and Principe 1°0′ N, 7°0′ E 214
São Tomé, island, Sao Tome and Principe 0°12′ N, 6°39′ E 214
São Tomé, river, Braz. 8°29′ S, 57°57′ W 130
São Tomé & Principe 0°10′ N, 6°32′ E 218
São Vicente, Braz. 10°38′ S, 69°28′ W 137
São Vicente, Braz. 24°0′ S, 46°27′ W 138
São Vicente, Cabo de, Port. 36°57′ N, 11°3′ W 214
São Vicente do Sul, Braz. 29°42′ S, 54°43′ W 139
Saona, Isla, island, Dom. Rep. 17°48′ N, 68°52′ W 116
Saône, river, Fr. 45°58′ N, 4°39′ E 165
Saône, river, Fr. 47°32′ N, 5°41′ E 165
Saonek, Indonesia 0°23′ N, 130°43′ E 192
Saoner, India 21°22′ N, 78°54′ E 188
Saous, spring, Mali 17°45′ N, 5°296′ W 222
Sap, Tonle, lake, Cambodia 13°6′ N, 103°45′ E 202
Sapahaqui, Bol. 17°0′ S, 67°55′ W 137
Sapanca, Turk. 40°41′ N, 30°16′ E 156
Sapateiro, Lago, lake, Braz. 2°18′ S, 67°8′ W 136
Sapele, Nig. 5°59′ N, 5°41′ E 222
Şaphane Dağı, peak, Turk. 39°2′ N, 29°13′ E 156
Sapo, Serranía del, Pan. 7°38′ N, 78°2′ W 136
Sappada, It. 46°34′ N, 12°41′ E 167
Sapphire Mountains, Mont., U.S. 46°4′ N, 113°55′ W 90
Sappho, Wash., U.S. 48°3′ N, 124°18′ W 100
Sapporo, Japan 43°14′ N, 141°18′ E 190
Sapri, It. 40°5′ N, 15°37′ E 156
Sapt Kosi, river, India 26°10′ N, 86°44′ E 197
Sapulpa, Okla., U.S. 35°58′ N, 96°6′ W 96
Saqqez, Iran 36°17′ N, 46°14′ E 195
Šar Planina, Maced. 41°54′ N, 20°43′ E 168
Sara, Burkina Faso 11°44′ N, 3°50′ W 222
Sarāb, Iran 37°58′ N, 47°32′ E 195
Saraburi, Thai. 14°33′ N, 100°57′ E 202
Saraféré, Mali 15°48′ N, 3°42′ W 222
Sarahs, Turkm. 36°31′ N, 61°13′ E 180
Sarai, Russ. 53°41′ N, 40°58′ E 154
Sarajevo, Bosn. and Herzg. 43°51′ N, 18°22′ E 168
Sarakhs, Iran 36°33′ N, 61°4′ E 180
Saraktash, Russ. 51°46′ N, 56°16′ E 158
Sarala, Côte d'Ivoire 8°34′ N, 4°40′ W 222
Saraland, Ala., U.S. 30°48′ N, 88°4′ W 103
Saralzhyn, Kaz. 49°11′ N, 48°54′ E 158
Sarana, Russ. 56°29′ N, 57°46′ E 154
Saranac, Mich., U.S. 42°54′ N, 85°13′ W 102
Saranac Lake, N.Y., U.S. 44°19′ N, 74°9′ W 104
Saranda, Tanzania 5°41′ S, 34°56′ E 224
Sarandi, Braz. 27°58′ S, 52°56′ W 139
Sarandí del Yí, Uru. 33°19′ S, 55°39′ W 139
Sarandí Grande, Uru. 33°45′ S, 56°21′ W 139
Sarangani Bay 5°52′ N, 125°4′ E 203
Sarangani Islands, islands, Philippine Sea 4°20′ N, 123°17′ E 192
Saranpaul', Russ. 64°15′ N, 60°53′ E 169
Saransk, Russ. 54°9′ N, 45°7′ E 154
Sarapul, Russ. 56°28′ N, 53°47′ E 154
Sarasota, Fla., U.S. 27°21′ N, 82°31′ W 105
Saratoga, Tex., U.S. 30°17′ N, 94°32′ W 103
Saratoga, Wyo., U.S. 41°27′ N, 106°48′ W 90
Saratoga National Historical Park, N.Y., U.S. 42°58′ N, 73°42′ W 104
Saratoga Springs, N.Y., U.S. 43°4′ N, 73°48′ W 104
Saratoga Table, Antarctica 84°9′ S, 45°38′ W 248
Saratok, Malaysia 1°45′ N, 111°21′ E 192
Saratov, Russ. 51°29′ N, 45°56′ E 158
Saratov, adm. division, Russ. 52°44′ N, 47°53′ E 154
Saravan, Laos 15°43′ N, 106°22′ E 202

Selima Oasis, *Sudan* 21°22′ N, 29°21′ E **226**
Selinde, *Russ.* 57°16′ N, 132°39′ E **173**
Selinus, ruin(s), *It.* 37°34′ N, 12°43′ E **156**
Selitrennoye, *Russ.* 47°9′ N, 47°23′ E **158**
Seliyarovo, *Russ.* 61°17′ N, 70°16′ E **169**
Selizharovo, *Russ.* 56°50′ N, 33°38′ E **154**
Selje, *Nor.* 62°3′ N, 5°22′ E **152**
Selkirk, *Can.* 50°8′ N, 96°54′ W **90**
Selkirk Mountains, *Can.* 51°22′ N, 117°56′ W **108**
Selles, *Fr.* 47°16′ N, 1°33′ E **150**
Sells, *Ariz., U.S.* 31°54′ N, 111°52′ W **92**
Sellye, *Hung.* 45°51′ N, 17°51′ E **168**
Selma, *Ala., U.S.* 32°24′ N, 87°1′ W **96**
Selma, *Calif., U.S.* 36°34′ N, 119°37′ W **100**
Selma, *N.C., U.S.* 35°32′ N, 78°18′ W **96**
Selmer, *Tenn., U.S.* 35°9′ N, 88°35′ W **96**
Selous Game Reserve, *Tanzania* 9°29′ S, 36°6′ E **224**
Selous, Mount, peak, *Can.* 62°56′ N, 132°38′ W **98**
Sel'tso, *Russ.* 63°19′ N, 41°23′ E **154**
Selty, *Russ.* 57°19′ N, 52°8′ E **169**
Seluan, island, *Indonesia* 4°1′ N, 107°25′ E **196**
Selva, *Arg.* 29°45′ S, 62°3′ W **139**
Selvagens, Ilhas (Salvage Islands), *North Atlantic Ocean* 30°18′ N, 16°15′ W **214**
Selwyn Mountains, *Can.* 62°26′ N, 129°39′ W **98**
Selwyn Range, *Austral.* 21°1′ S, 139°47′ E **230**
Selyatyn, *Ukr.* 47°51′ N, 25°11′ E **156**
Semarang, *Indonesia* 7°5′ S, 110°15′ E **192**
Sembé, *Congo* 1°38′ N, 14°37′ E **218**
Sembo, *Eth.* 7°32′ N, 36°37′ E **224**
Şemdinli, *Turk.* 37°18′ N, 44°31′ E **195**
Semenov, *Russ.* 56°45′ N, 44°35′ E **154**
Semepalatinsk see Semey, *Kaz.* 50°23′ N, 80°14′ E **184**
Semeru, peak, *Indonesia* 8°5′ S, 112°44′ E **192**
Semey (Semepalatinsk), *Kaz.* 50°23′ N, 80°14′ E **184**
Semichi Islands, islands, *Alas., U.S.* 52°28′ N, 175°7′ E **160**
Sémien, *Côte d'Ivoire* 7°33′ N, 7°9′ W **222**
Semiluki, *Russ.* 51°40′ N, 38°58′ E **158**
Seminary, *Miss., U.S.* 31°33′ N, 89°29′ W **103**
Seminole, *Okla., U.S.* 35°13′ N, 96°41′ W **96**
Seminole, *Tex., U.S.* 32°42′ N, 102°38′ W **92**
Sémit, spring, *Mali* 16°43′ N, 0°41′ E **222**
Semizovac, *Bosn. and Herzg.* 43°55′ N, 18°17′ E **168**
Semmé, *Senegal* 15°11′ N, 13°0′ W **222**
Semmens Lake, lake, *Can.* 54°57′ N, 94°50′ W **108**
Semmering, pass, *Aust.* 47°37′ N, 15°47′ E **168**
Semmes, *Ala., U.S.* 30°46′ N, 88°15′ W **103**
Semna West, ruin(s), *Sudan* 21°30′ N, 30°49′ E **182**
Semnān, *Iran* 35°36′ N, 53°26′ E **180**
Semzha, *Russ.* 66°9′ N, 44°11′ E **154**
Sen, river, *Cambodia* 13°50′ N, 104°36′ E **202**
Sena, *Bol.* 11°31′ S, 67°11′ W **137**
Sena, *Mozambique* 17°27′ S, 34°59′ E **224**
Sena, *Sp.* 41°42′ N, 3°177′ W **164**
Sena Madureira, *Braz.* 9°8′ S, 68°41′ W **137**
Senador José Porfírio, *Braz.* 2°39′ S, 51°56′ W **130**
Senaja, *Malaysia* 6°50′ N, 117°3′ E **203**
Senanga, *Zambia* 16°8′ S, 23°16′ E **220**
Senatobia, *Miss., U.S.* 34°37′ N, 89°58′ W **96**
Sendai, *Japan* 31°47′ N, 130°19′ E **201**
Sendai, *Japan* 38°16′ N, 140°53′ E **201**
Senden, *Ger.* 51°51′ N, 7°29′ E **167**
Sendenhorst, *Ger.* 51°50′ N, 7°49′ E **167**
Senec, *Slovakia* 48°13′ N, 17°24′ E **152**
Seneca, *Ill., U.S.* 41°19′ N, 88°38′ W **102**
Seneca, *Kans., U.S.* 39°48′ N, 96°4′ W **90**
Seneca, *Oreg., U.S.* 44°8′ N, 118°58′ W **90**
Seneca, *Pa., U.S.* 41°23′ N, 79°42′ W **110**
Seneca, *S.C., U.S.* 34°40′ N, 82°58′ W **96**
Seneca Rocks, site, *W. Va., U.S.* 38°48′ N, 79°31′ W **82**
Senecaville Lake, *Ohio, U.S.* 39°52′ N, 81°41′ W **102**
Senegal 15°10′ N, 15°27′ W **214**
Sénégal, river, *Africa* 16°36′ N, 15°57′ W **206**
Seneki, *Ga.* 42°16′ N, 42°4′ E **195**
Senetosa, Punta di, *Fr.* 41°29′ N, 7°54′ E **156**
Senftenberg, *Ger.* 51°31′ N, 13°59′ E **152**
Sengés, *Braz.* 24°7′ S, 49°29′ W **138**
Sengiley, *Russ.* 53°54′ N, 48°47′ E **154**
Senguerr, river, *Arg.* 45°3′ S, 71°6′ W **134**
Sengwa, river, *Zimb.* 18°24′ S, 28°11′ E **224**
Senhor do Bonfim, *Braz.* 10°27′ S, 40°11′ W **132**
Senigallia, *It.* 43°42′ N, 13°12′ E **167**
Senkobo, *Zambia* 17°38′ S, 25°54′ E **224**
Senlin Shan, peak, *China* 43°10′ N, 130°35′ E **200**
Senlis, *Fr.* 49°12′ N, 2°35′ E **163**
Senmonorom, *Cambodia* 12°37′ N, 107°14′ E **202**
Sennar, *Sudan* 13°31′ N, 33°34′ E **182**
Senneterre, *Can.* 48°24′ N, 77°16′ W **94**
Sénoudébou, *Senegal* 14°21′ N, 12°18′ W **222**
Senozero, *Russ.* 66°9′ N, 31°44′ E **154**
Sens, *Fr.* 48°11′ N, 3°17′ E **163**
Sensuntepeque, *El Salv.* 13°52′ N, 88°38′ W **116**
Senta, *Serb.* 45°55′ N, 20°4′ E **168**
Sentein, *Fr.* 42°52′ N, 0°55′ E **164**
Sentinel, *Okla., U.S.* 35°7′ N, 99°10′ W **96**
Sentinel Peak, *Can.* 54°53′ N, 122°4′ W **108**
Senyavin Islands, *North Pacific Ocean* 7°29′ N, 156°35′ E **238**
Seocheon, *S. Korea* 36°4′ N, 126°43′ E **200**
Seogwipo, *S. Korea* 33°18′ N, 126°35′ E **198**
Seokjeong, *S. Korea* 34°53′ N, 127°0′ E **200**
Seomjin, river, *S. Korea* 35°11′ N, 127°28′ E **200**
Seonbong, *N. Korea* 42°20′ N, 130°25′ E **200**
Seongnae, *S. Korea* 36°30′ N, 129°26′ E **200**
Seoni, *India* 22°5′ N, 79°33′ E **197**
Seoni Malwa, *India* 22°27′ N, 77°28′ E **197**
Seonsan, *S. Korea* 36°13′ N, 128°19′ E **200**
Seosan, *S. Korea* 36°45′ N, 126°26′ E **200**
Seoul, *S. Korea* 37°33′ N, 126°54′ E **200**
Sepahua, *Peru* 11°7′ S, 73°4′ W **137**
Separation Point, *Can.* 53°36′ N, 57°26′ W **111**
Sepatini, river, *Braz.* 8°4′ S, 66°6′ W **132**
Sept Îles, Les, islands, *English Channel* 48°57′ N, 3°38′ W **150**
Sept-Îles, *Can.* 50°11′ N, 66°22′ W **111**
Sepupa, *Botswana* 18°48′ S, 22°10′ E **220**
Sequim, *Wash., U.S.* 48°3′ N, 123°6′ W **100**
Serafimovich, *Russ.* 49°32′ N, 42°41′ E **158**
Seraing, *Belg.* 50°35′ N, 5°30′ E **167**
Seram, *India* 17°11′ N, 77°18′ E **188**
Serang, *Indonesia* 6°13′ S, 106°7′ E **192**
Serasan, island, *Indonesia* 2°24′ N, 108°36′ E **196**
Seraya, island, *Indonesia* 2°33′ N, 108°11′ E **196**
Sērba, *Eth.* 13°12′ N, 40°32′ E **182**
Serbia 43°45′ N, 20°29′ E **168**
Sercaia, *Rom.* 45°50′ N, 25°9′ E **158**
Serdeles see Al 'Uwaynāt, *Lib.* 25°47′ N, 10°33′ E **216**
Serdo, *Eth.* 11°54′ N, 41°19′ E **182**
Serdobol see Sortavala, *Russ.* 61°42′ N, 30°39′ E **166**
Serdobsk, *Russ.* 52°28′ N, 44°13′ E **158**
Serebryanka, *Russ.* 57°6′ N, 70°43′ E **169**
Serebryansk, *Kaz.* 49°42′ N, 83°21′ E **184**
Seredka, *Russ.* 58°8′ N, 28°10′ E **166**
Şereflikoçhisar, *Turk.* 38°54′ N, 33°32′ E **156**
Seregno, *It.* 45°38′ N, 9°12′ E **167**
Seremban, *Malaysia* 2°45′ N, 101°55′ E **196**
Serena, *Ill., U.S.* 41°28′ N, 88°44′ W **102**
Serengeti National Park, *Tanzania* 2°26′ S, 34°26′ E **224**
Serengeti Plain, *Tanzania* 1°51′ S, 35°12′ E **224**
Serenje, *Zambia* 13°16′ S, 30°14′ E **224**
Serere, *Uganda* 1°29′ N, 33°25′ E **224**
Séres, *Gr.* 41°5′ N, 23°31′ E **180**
Serg Ozero, lake, *Russ.* 66°45′ N, 36°13′ E **154**
Ser'ga, *Russ.* 57°47′ N, 57°1′ E **154**
Sergach, *Russ.* 55°31′ N, 45°33′ E **154**
Sergeant Robinson, Mount, peak, *Alas., U.S.* 61°33′ N, 148°2′ W **98**
Sergeevka, *Kaz.* 53°53′ N, 67°23′ E **184**
Sergeyevo, *Russ.* 57°17′ N, 86°6′ E **169**
Sergino, *Russ.* 62°37′ N, 65°34′ E **169**
Sergipe, adm. division, *Braz.* 9°54′ S, 37°48′ W **132**
Sergiyev Posad, *Russ.* 56°19′ N, 38°7′ E **154**
Seria, *Brunei* 4°35′ N, 114°25′ E **192**
Serian, *Malaysia* 1°3′ N, 110°33′ E **192**
Seribudolok, *Indonesia* 2°56′ N, 98°36′ E **196**
Sérifontaine, *Fr.* 49°21′ N, 1°46′ E **163**
Sérignan, *Fr.* 43°16′ N, 3°15′ E **164**
Serik, *Turk.* 36°54′ N, 31°5′ E **156**
Seringa, Serra da, *Braz.* 7°31′ S, 51°0′ W **130**
Seripe, *Ghana* 8°55′ N, 2°24′ W **222**
Serkovo, *Russ.* 66°35′ N, 88°25′ E **169**
Sermata, island, *Indonesia* 8°38′ S, 128°59′ E **192**
Sermyle, ruin(s), *Gr.* 40°13′ N, 23°27′ E **156**
Sernur, *Russ.* 56°57′ N, 49°12′ E **154**
Séro, *Mali* 14°49′ N, 11°4′ W **222**
Seroglazovka, *Russ.* 46°56′ N, 47°27′ E **158**
Serón, *Sp.* 37°19′ N, 2°31′ W **164**
Seronera, *Tanzania* 2°28′ S, 34°50′ E **224**
Serov, *Russ.* 59°38′ N, 60°37′ E **154**
Serowe, *Botswana* 22°23′ S, 26°42′ E **227**
Serpent's Mouth 9°50′ N, 62°13′ W **116**
Serpukhov, *Russ.* 54°54′ N, 37°22′ E **154**
Serra Bonita, *Braz.* 15°16′ S, 46°50′ W **138**
Serra da Bocaina National Park, *Braz.* 23°22′ S, 44°57′ W **122**
Serra da Canastra National Park, *Braz.* 20°24′ S, 46°53′ W **138**
Serra da Capivara National Park, *Braz.* 8°44′ S, 42°32′ W **122**
Serra das Araras, *Braz.* 15°34′ S, 45°24′ W **138**
Serra do Divisor National Park, *Braz.* 9°11′ S, 73°16′ W **137**
Serra do Espinhaço, *Braz.* 17°53′ S, 43°58′ W **138**
Serra do Navio, *Braz.* 0°57′ N, 52°5′ W **130**
Serra Dourada, *Braz.* 12°45′ S, 43°59′ W **138**
Serrado Roncador, *Braz.* 14°7′ S, 53°7′ W **138**
Serranía de la Macarena National Park, *Col.* 2°33′ N, 73°56′ W **136**
Serranía de La Neblina National Park, *Venez.* 1°4′ N, 66°23′ W **136**
Serrano, *Arg.* 34°29′ S, 63°33′ W **139**
Serre, river, *Fr.* 49°41′ N, 3°44′ E **163**
Serrezuela, *Arg.* 30°39′ S, 65°23′ W **134**
Serrinha, *Braz.* 11°40′ S, 39°3′ W **132**
Serro, *Braz.* 18°38′ S, 43°25′ W **138**
Sertã, *Port.* 39°47′ N, 8°7′ W **150**
Sertânia, *Braz.* 8°5′ S, 37°16′ W **132**
Sertanópolis, *Braz.* 23°5′ S, 51°6′ W **138**
Serti, *Nig.* 7°30′ N, 11°20′ E **222**
Serui, *Indonesia* 1°48′ S, 136°11′ E **192**
Serule, *Botswana* 21°58′ S, 27°13′ E **227**
Sêrxü, *China* 33°0′ N, 98°5′ E **188**
Seryesik-Atyraū Qumy, *Kaz.* 46°3′ N, 75°39′ E **184**
Sesa, *Dem. Rep. of the Congo* 7°2′ S, 26°7′ E **224**
Sese Islands, *Uganda* 0°34′ N, 32°5′ E **224**
Seseganaga Lake, *Can.* 49°54′ N, 91°13′ W **94**
Sesfontein, *Namibia* 19°10′ S, 13°36′ E **220**
Sesheke, *Zambia* 17°28′ S, 24°17′ E **224**
Seskar, Ostrov, island, *Russ.* 60°0′ N, 28°26′ E **166**
Seskarö, *Sw.* 65°43′ N, 23°43′ E **152**
Sessa, *Angola* 13°57′ S, 20°37′ E **220**
Séssao, spring, *Mali* 16°59′ N, 4°5′ E **222**
Sestino, *It.* 43°43′ N, 12°16′ E **167**
Sesto Calende, *It.* 45°44′ N, 8°37′ E **167**
Sesto Fiorentino, *It.* 43°50′ N, 11°12′ E **167**
Sesto San Giovanni, *It.* 45°32′ N, 9°14′ E **167**
Šeštokai, *Lith.* 54°21′ N, 23°26′ E **166**
Sestola, *It.* 44°13′ N, 10°45′ E **167**
Sestri Ponente, *It.* 44°25′ N, 8°52′ E **167**
Sestroretsk, *Russ.* 60°4′ N, 29°55′ E **166**
Šėta, *Lith.* 55°16′ N, 24°13′ E **166**
Sete, *Angola* 14°56′ S, 21°44′ E **220**
Sète, *Fr.* 43°24′ N, 3°40′ E **164**
Sete Lagoas, *Braz.* 19°27′ S, 44°16′ W **138**
Sete Quedas, Cachoeira das, fall(s), *Braz.* 9°42′ S, 56°32′ W **130**
Setenil, *Sp.* 36°51′ N, 5°11′ W **164**
Setesdal, region, *Nor.* 58°58′ N, 7°4′ E **152**
Sétif, *Alg.* 36°13′ N, 5°25′ E **150**
Setit, river, *Africa* 14°20′ N, 37°5′ E **182**
Seto, *Japan* 35°10′ N, 137°6′ E **201**
Setonaikai National Park, *Japan* 34°16′ N, 134°16′ E **201**
Settat, *Mor.* 33°2′ N, 7°38′ W **214**
Setté Cama, *Gabon* 2°32′ S, 9°46′ E **218**
Settle, *U.K.* 54°4′ N, 2°16′ W **162**
Setúbal, *Port.* 38°31′ N, 8°54′ W **150**
Setúbal, adm. division, *Port.* 38°28′ N, 8°42′ W **150**
Seul Choix Point, *Mich., U.S.* 45°39′ N, 86°8′ W **110**
Seul, Lac, lake, *Can.* 50°33′ N, 93°10′ W **80**
Seulimeum, *Indonesia* 5°21′ N, 95°33′ E **202**
Seumanyam, *Indonesia* 3°47′ N, 96°37′ E **196**
Sevan, *Arm.* 40°33′ N, 44°56′ E **195**
Sevan National Park, *Arm.* 40°21′ N, 45°12′ E **195**
Sevana Lich, lake, *Arm.* 40°14′ N, 45°15′ E **195**
Sevar, *Bulg.* 43°50′ N, 26°36′ E **156**
Sevaruyo, *Bol.* 19°26′ S, 66°53′ W **137**
Sevastopol', *Ukr.* 44°34′ N, 33°28′ E **156**
Seven Heads, *Ire.* 51°22′ N, 8°41′ W **150**
Seven Sisters Peaks, *Can.* 54°56′ N, 128°18′ W **108**
Seven Stones, islands, *Celtic Sea* 50°5′ N, 7°11′ W **150**
Seven Troughs Range, *Nev., U.S.* 40°36′ N, 118°57′ W **90**
Sevenoaks, *U.K.* 51°16′ N, 0°11′ E **162**
Severn y ye Uvaly, *Russ.* 59°38′ N, 46°36′ E **169**
Severnaya Dvina, river, *Russ.* 62°37′ N, 43°16′ E **154**
Severnaya Osetiya-Alaniya, adm. division, *Russ.* 42°59′ N, 43°49′ E **195**
Severnaya, river, *Russ.* 63°21′ N, 41°46′ E **154**
Severnaya, river, *Russ.* 63°21′ N, 40°44′ E **246**
Severnaya Zemlya (North Land), islands, *Russ.* 80°22′ N, 102°0′ E **160**
Severnoye, *Russ.* 56°21′ N, 78°15′ E **169**
Severnoye Ust'ye, *Russ.* 57°34′ N, 30°16′ E **166**
Severnyy, *Russ.* 67°39′ N, 64°18′ E **169**
Severnyy Kommunar, *Russ.* 58°21′ N, 54°4′ E **154**
Severnyy Mayak, *Russ.* 65°19′ N, 43°39′ E **154**
Severnyye Uvaly, *Russ.* 60°56′ N, 51°45′ E **154**
Severo Kuril'sk, *Russ.* 50°35′ N, 155°59′ E **160**
Severo Yeniseyskiy, *Russ.* 60°23′ N, 93°13′ E **169**
Severobaykal'sk, *Russ.* 55°39′ N, 109°7′ E **190**
Severodvinsk, *Russ.* 64°34′ N, 39°52′ E **154**
Severomuysk, *Russ.* 56°20′ N, 113°25′ E **190**
Severoural'sk, *Russ.* 60°10′ N, 59°55′ E **154**
Seversk, *Russ.* 56°39′ N, 84°51′ E **169**
Sevettijärvi, *Fin.* 69°32′ N, 28°35′ E **152**
Sevier Desert, *Utah, U.S.* 39°38′ N, 113°0′ W **90**
Sevier, river, *Utah, U.S.* 38°27′ N, 112°24′ W **80**
Sevilla, *Col.* 4°14′ N, 75°57′ W **136**
Sevilla, *Sp.* 37°22′ N, 5°58′ W **214**
Sevilla (Seville), *Sp.* 37°23′ N, 6°0′ W **164**
Seville, *Fla., U.S.* 29°18′ N, 81°29′ W **105**
Seville see Sevilla, *Sp.* 37°23′ N, 6°0′ W **164**
Sevnica, *Slov.* 46°0′ N, 15°18′ E **156**
Sevsk, *Russ.* 52°7′ N, 34°30′ E **158**
Seward, *Alas., U.S.* 60°2′ N, 149°33′ W **98**
Seward, *Nebr., U.S.* 40°53′ N, 97°6′ W **90**
Seward Peninsula, *Alas., U.S.* 67°2′ N, 167°43′ W **160**
Seward Peninsula, *Alas., U.S.* 65°17′ N, 165°10′ W **98**
Sexsmith, *Can.* 55°20′ N, 118°47′ W **108**
Sexton Mountain Pass, *Oreg., U.S.* 42°34′ N, 123°25′ W **90**
Seyakha, *Russ.* 70°8′ N, 72°28′ E **169**
Seychelles 8°7′ S, 51°26′ E **173**
Seydi, *Turkm.* 39°25′ N, 62°55′ E **184**
Seydişehir, *Turk.* 37°24′ N, 31°51′ E **156**
Seyitgazi, *Turk.* 39°27′ N, 30°41′ E **156**
Seym, river, *Russ.* 51°24′ N, 36°36′ E **158**
Seym, river, *Ukr.* 51°19′ N, 33°0′ E **158**
Seymchan, *Russ.* 62°55′ N, 152°12′ E **160**
Seymour, *Conn., U.S.* 41°23′ N, 73°5′ W **104**
Seymour, *Ind., U.S.* 38°57′ N, 85°54′ W **102**
Seymour, *Tex., U.S.* 33°34′ N, 99°16′ W **92**
Seymour, *Wis., U.S.* 44°30′ N, 88°20′ W **94**
Seymour Island, *Antarctica* 64°25′ S, 56°33′ W **134**
Seyne, *Fr.* 44°21′ N, 6°19′ E **167**
Sézanne, *Fr.* 48°43′ N, 3°44′ E **163**
Sfax, *Tun.* 34°48′ N, 10°46′ E **156**
Sferracavallo, Capo, *It.* 39°44′ N, 9°42′ E **156**
Sfîntu Gheorghe, *Rom.* 45°52′ N, 25°47′ E **156**
Sfizef, *Alg.* 35°13′ N, 0°15′ E **150**
Sha, river, *China* 26°5′ N, 117°4′ E **198**
Shaanxi, adm. division, *China* 37°13′ N, 107°48′ E **198**
Shaar Mt. National Park, *Kosovo* 42°7′ N, 20°48′ E **168**
Shabasha, *Sudan* 14°7′ N, 32°11′ E **226**
Shabla, *Bulg.* 43°33′ N, 28°32′ E **156**
Shabla, Nos, *Bulg.* 43°34′ N, 28°38′ E **156**
Shabogamo Lake, *Can.* 53°13′ N, 67°37′ W **111**
Shabunda, *Dem. Rep. of the Congo* 2°41′ S, 27°19′ E **224**
Shaburovo, *Russ.* 59°40′ N, 62°8′ E **154**
Shabwah, *Yemen* 15°21′ N, 47°5′ E **182**
Shache (Yarkant), *China* 38°27′ N, 77°17′ E **184**
Shackleton Base (historic), site, *Weddell Sea* 78°21′ S, 37°47′ W **248**
Shackleton Coast, *Antarctica* 82°30′ S, 179°30′ E **248**
Shadehill Reservoir, lake, *S. Dak., U.S.* 45°46′ N, 102°37′ W **90**
Shadrinsk, *Russ.* 56°5′ N, 63°40′ E **184**
Shaduzup, *Myanmar* 25°56′ N, 96°40′ E **188**
Shadyside, *Ohio, U.S.* 39°57′ N, 80°46′ W **94**
Sha'f, *Syr.* 32°36′ N, 36°50′ E **194**
Shafer Peak, *Antarctica* 73°56′ S, 163°9′ E **248**
Shafter, *Calif., U.S.* 35°30′ N, 119°18′ W **100**
Shaftesbury, *U.K.* 51°0′ N, 2°12′ W **162**
Shaftsbury, *Vt., U.S.* 43°0′ N, 73°12′ W **104**
Shag Rocks, islands, *Scotia Sea* 54°7′ S, 42°46′ W **134**
Shagamu, *Nig.* 7°0′ N, 3°37′ E **222**
Shaghan, *Kaz.* 50°34′ N, 79°13′ E **184**
Shah Bandar, *Pak.* 24°10′ N, 67°58′ E **186**
Shah Juy, *Afghan.* 32°31′ N, 67°28′ E **186**
Shah Malan, *Afghan.* 31°11′ N, 64°5′ E **186**
Shahabad, *India* 27°38′ N, 79°54′ E **197**
Shahabad, *India* 25°16′ N, 77°10′ E **197**
Shahbā' (Philippopolis), *Syr.* 32°51′ N, 36°37′ E **194**
Shahdadkot, *Pak.* 27°51′ N, 67°55′ E **186**
Shahdol, *India* 23°18′ N, 81°22′ E **197**
Shahgarh, *India* 27°6′ N, 69°58′ E **186**
Sha"āt (Cyrene), *Lib.* 32°50′ N, 21°50′ E **216**
Shahimardan, *Uzb.* 39°56′ N, 71°45′ E **197**
Shāhīn Dezh, *Iran* 36°46′ N, 46°35′ E **195**
Shahjahanpur, *India* 27°51′ N, 79°54′ E **197**
Shahpur, *Pak.* 28°42′ N, 68°22′ E **186**
Shahpura, *India* 23°11′ N, 80°43′ E **197**
Shahrak, *Afghan.* 34°11′ N, 64°24′ E **186**
Shahr-e Bābak, *Iran* 30°7′ N, 55°9′ E **196**
Shahr-e Kord, *Iran* 32°19′ N, 50°51′ E **180**
Shahr-e Monjan, *Afghan.* 36°2′ N, 70°58′ E **186**
Shahrezā, *Iran* 32°1′ N, 51°51′ E **180**
Shahrisabz, *Uzb.* 39°5′ N, 66°51′ E **197**
Shahriston, *Taj.* 39°46′ N, 68°52′ E **197**
Shahrtuz, *Taj.* 37°14′ N, 68°9′ E **186**
Shāhrūd, *Iran* 36°27′ N, 54°59′ E **180**
Shaim, *Russ.* 60°15′ N, 64°16′ E **169**
Shajapur, *India* 23°24′ N, 76°16′ E **197**
Shakawe, *Botswana* 18°25′ S, 21°48′ E **220**
Shaker Heights, *Ohio, U.S.* 41°26′ N, 81°34′ W **102**
Shakespeare Cliff, *U.K.* 51°6′ N, 1°21′ E **163**
Shakhbuz, *Asia* 39°24′ N, 45°34′ E **195**
Shakhtakhty, *Asia* 39°19′ N, 45°7′ E **195**
Shakhtīnsk, *Kaz.* 49°44′ N, 72°37′ E **184**
Shakhty, *Russ.* 47°40′ N, 40°9′ E **156**
Shakhun'ya, *Russ.* 57°39′ N, 46°41′ E **154**
Shaki, *Nig.* 8°40′ N, 3°23′ E **222**
Shâkir, Gezîrat, island, *Egypt* 27°25′ N, 32°57′ E **180**
Shalaamboot, *Somalia* 1°38′ N, 44°41′ E **218**
Shalakusha, *Russ.* 62°11′ N, 40°18′ E **154**
Shalë, *Alban.* 42°18′ N, 19°48′ E **168**
Shali, *Russ.* 43°6′ N, 45°52′ E **195**
Shaling, *China* 41°19′ N, 123°5′ E **200**
Shalkar Yega Kara, Ozero, lake, *Russ.* 50°39′ N, 59°7′ E **158**
Shallowater, *Tex., U.S.* 33°41′ N, 101°59′ W **92**
Shalqar, *Kaz.* 50°29′ N, 51°49′ E **158**
Shalqar, *Kaz.* 47°50′ N, 59°39′ E **158**
Shalqar Köli, lake, *Kaz.* 50°35′ N, 51°20′ E **158**
Shalqīya, *Kaz.* 47°15′ N, 70°38′ E **184**
Shal'skiy, *Russ.* 61°48′ N, 36°4′ E **154**
Shām, Jabal ash, peak, *Oman* 23°10′ N, 57°11′ E **182**
Shamattawa, *Can.* 55°59′ N, 91°53′ W **106**
Shambe, *Sudan* 7°5′ N, 30°43′ E **224**
Shamīl, *Iran* 27°28′ N, 56°53′ E **196**
Shamkhor, *Azerb.* 40°49′ N, 46°0′ E **195**
Shammar, Jabal, *Saudi Arabia* 27°8′ N, 40°8′ E **180**
Shamokin, *Pa., U.S.* 40°47′ N, 76°34′ W **94**
Shamrock, *Fla., U.S.* 29°38′ N, 83°11′ W **105**
Shamrock, *Tex., U.S.* 35°12′ N, 100°15′ W **92**
Shamva, *Zimb.* 17°21′ S, 31°34′ E **224**
Shanchengzhen, *China* 42°22′ N, 125°27′ E **200**
Shandon, *Calif., U.S.* 35°39′ N, 120°24′ W **100**
Shandong, adm. division, *China* 36°25′ N, 116°37′ E **198**
Shandur Pass, *Pak.* 36°3′ N, 72°31′ E **186**
Shangalowe, *Dem. Rep. of the Congo* 10°50′ S, 26°30′ E **224**
Shangaly, *Russ.* 61°8′ N, 43°18′ E **154**
Shangani, *Zimb.* 19°48′ S, 29°21′ E **224**
Shangcai, *China* 33°17′ N, 114°17′ E **198**
Shangcheng, *China* 31°48′ N, 115°23′ E **198**
Shangchuan Dao, island, *China* 21°31′ N, 112°51′ E **198**
Shangdu, *China* 41°35′ N, 113°33′ E **198**
Shanghai, *China* 31°15′ N, 121°27′ E **198**
Shanghang, *China* 24°58′ N, 116°21′ E **198**
Shanghekou, *China* 40°25′ N, 124°49′ E **200**
Shanglin, *China* 23°29′ N, 108°35′ E **198**
Shangnan, *China* 33°32′ N, 110°55′ E **198**
Shangombo, *Zambia* 16°20′ S, 22°7′ E **220**
Shangqiu, *China* 34°27′ N, 115°34′ E **198**
Shangrao, *China* 28°27′ N, 117°56′ E **198**
Shangri-La, *China* 27°52′ N, 99°40′ E **190**
Shangsi, *China* 22°12′ N, 107°57′ E **198**
Shangxian, *China* 33°55′ N, 109°56′ E **198**
Shangyi, *China* 41°5′ N, 113°58′ E **198**
Shangyou, *China* 25°50′ N, 114°30′ E **198**
Shangyou Shuiku, lake, *China* 40°24′ N, 79°49′ E **184**
Shangzhi, *China* 45°12′ N, 127°53′ E **198**
Shani, *Nig.* 10°12′ N, 12°5′ E **218**
Shanidar Cave, ruin(s), *Iraq* 36°48′ N, 44°8′ E **195**
Shaniko, *Oreg., U.S.* 44°59′ N, 120°46′ W **90**
Shannock, *R.I., U.S.* 41°26′ N, 71°39′ W **104**
Shannon, *Ill., U.S.* 42°8′ N, 89°44′ W **102**
Shannon, *Ire.* 52°52′ N, 8°49′ W **143**
Shannon, *Miss., U.S.* 34°6′ N, 88°43′ W **96**
Shannon, *N.Z.* 40°35′ S, 175°25′ E **240**
Shannon Airport, *Ire.* 52°40′ N, 9°8′ W **150**
Shannon, island, *Shannon* 75°18′ N, 17°23′ W **246**
Shannon, Lake, *Wash., U.S.* 48°35′ N, 121°58′ W **100**
Shantarskiye Ostrova, islands, *Russ.* 54°31′ N, 138°48′ E **160**
Shantou (Swatow), *China* 23°23′ N, 116°40′ E **198**
Shanwa, *Tanzania* 3°8′ S, 33°45′ E **224**
Shanxi, adm. division, *China* 38°43′ N, 111°16′ E **198**
Shanxian, *China* 34°49′ N, 116°5′ E **198**
Shanyang, *China* 33°33′ N, 109°54′ E **198**
Shanyin, *China* 39°29′ N, 112°51′ E **198**
Shanyincheng, *China* 39°24′ N, 112°56′ E **198**
Shaoguan, *China* 24°52′ N, 113°32′ E **198**
Shaowu, *China* 27°14′ N, 117°27′ E **198**
Shaoxing, *China* 29°59′ N, 120°34′ E **198**
Shaoyang, *China* 27°15′ N, 111°29′ E **198**
Shap, *U.K.* 54°32′ N, 2°41′ W **162**
Shapa, *China* 21°32′ N, 111°28′ E **198**
Shapleigh, *Me., U.S.* 43°33′ N, 70°52′ W **104**
Shaqlāwah, *Iraq* 36°24′ N, 44°16′ E **195**
Shaqqā, *Syr.* 32°53′ N, 36°41′ E **194**
Shaqrā', *Saudi Arabia* 25°12′ N, 45°18′ E **182**
Shaqrā', *Yemen* 13°24′ N, 45°41′ E **182**
Shar, *Kaz.* 49°37′ N, 81°1′ E **184**
Shār, Jabal, peak, *Saudi Arabia* 27°36′ N, 35°40′ E **180**
Shar Space Launch Center, spaceport, *India* 13°36′ N, 80°5′ E **188**
Sharafkhāneh, *Iran* 38°17′ N, 45°26′ E **195**
Sharbaqty, *Kaz.* 52°30′ N, 78°11′ E **184**
Sharbatāt, *Oman* 17°53′ N, 56°18′ E **182**
Shardara, *Kaz.* 41°16′ N, 67°54′ E **197**
Sharg'un, *Uzb.* 38°21′ N, 68°0′ E **197**
Sharhulsan, *Mongolia* 44°37′ N, 104°1′ E **198**
Sharjah, *U.A.E.* 25°21′ N, 55°24′ E **196**
Shark Bay 25°46′ S, 113°18′ E **230**
Sharkan, *Russ.* 57°15′ N, 53°54′ E **154**
Sharkowshchyna, *Belarus* 55°22′ N, 27°24′ E **166**
Sharlawuk, *Turkm.* 38°14′ N, 55°42′ E **180**
Sharlyk, *Russ.* 52°55′ N, 54°46′ E **154**
Sharon, *Conn., U.S.* 41°52′ N, 73°29′ W **104**
Sharon, *Mass., U.S.* 42°7′ N, 71°11′ W **104**
Sharon, *Pa., U.S.* 41°13′ N, 80°31′ W **94**
Sharon, *Vt., U.S.* 43°47′ N, 72°28′ W **104**
Sharon, *Wis., U.S.* 42°30′ N, 88°44′ W **102**
Sharon Springs, *Kans., U.S.* 38°53′ N, 101°46′ W **90**
Sharp Top, peak, *Oreg., U.S.* 42°50′ N, 120°34′ W **90**
Sharpe, Lake, *S. Dak., U.S.* 43°9′ N, 99°14′ W **80**
Sharuhen, ruin(s), *Israel* 31°15′ N, 34°26′ E **194**
Shar'ya, *Russ.* 58°20′ N, 45°34′ E **154**
Sharypovo, *Russ.* 55°34′ N, 89°15′ E **169**
Shasha, *Eth.* 6°28′ N, 35°55′ E **224**
Shashe, river, *Africa* 21°47′ S, 28°27′ E **227**
Shashemenē, *Eth.* 7°12′ N, 38°32′ E **224**
Shashi, *China* 30°22′ N, 112°18′ E **198**
Shass Mountain, peak, *Can.* 54°25′ N, 124°58′ W **108**
Shasta, Mount, peak, *Calif., U.S.* 41°24′ N, 122°18′ W **90**
Shatsk, *Belarus* 53°25′ N, 27°42′ E **152**
Shatsk, *Russ.* 54°0′ N, 41°39′ E **154**
Shats'k, *Ukr.* 51°27′ N, 23°54′ E **152**
Shatskiy Rise, *North Pacific Ocean* 34°16′ N, 160°36′ E **252**
Shattuck, *Okla., U.S.* 36°15′ N, 99°53′ W **92**
Shatura, *Russ.* 55°33′ N, 39°31′ E **154**
Shaumyani, *Ga.* 41°20′ N, 44°44′ E **195**
Shaunavon, *Can.* 49°37′ N, 108°26′ W **90**
Shaver Lake, *Calif., U.S.* 37°6′ N, 119°20′ W **100**
Shaverki, *Russ.* 63°14′ N, 31°27′ E **154**
Shavikde, peak, *Ga.* 42°14′ N, 45°35′ E **195**
Shaw, *Miss., U.S.* 33°35′ N, 90°47′ W **96**
Shaw Air Force Base, *S.C., U.S.* 33°57′ N, 80°33′ W **96**
Shaw Island, *Austral.* 20°22′ S, 149°7′ E **230**
Shawan, *China* 44°20′ N, 85°39′ E **184**
Shawano, *Wis., U.S.* 44°46′ N, 88°37′ W **94**
Shawinigan, *Can.* 46°33′ N, 72°46′ W **94**
Shawinigan-Sud, *Can.* 46°30′ N, 72°45′ W **94**
Shawnee, *Ohio, U.S.* 39°35′ N, 82°13′ W **102**
Shawnee, *Wyo., U.S.* 42°44′ N, 105°1′ W **90**
Shawnigan Lake, *Can.* 48°38′ N, 123°37′ W **100**
Shaxian, *China* 26°24′ N, 117°44′ E **198**
Shaxrixon, *Uzb.* 40°41′ N, 72°4′ E **197**
Shaybah, oil field, *Saudi Arabia* 22°23′ N, 53°55′ E **182**
Shaybārā, island, *Saudi Arabia* 25°25′ N, 36°3′ E **182**
Shâyib el Banât, Gebel, peak, *Egypt* 26°58′ N, 33°22′ E **180**
Shaykh, Jabal ash (Hermon, Mount), peak, *Leb.* 33°24′ N, 35°49′ E **194**
Shaykh Miskīn, *Syr.* 32°50′ N, 36°10′ E **194**
Shaykh 'Uthmān, *Yemen* 12°52′ N, 44°59′ E **182**
Shaymak, *Taj.* 37°29′ N, 74°51′ E **184**
Shayrāt, *Syr.* 34°29′ N, 36°57′ E **194**
Shaytanovka, *Russ.* 62°2′ N, 58°6′ E **154**
Shchekino, *Russ.* 53°59′ N, 37°33′ E **154**
Shchel'yabozh, *Russ.* 66°17′ N, 56°23′ E **154**
Shchel'yayur, *Russ.* 65°18′ N, 53°26′ E **154**
Shchigry, *Russ.* 51°49′ N, 36°57′ E **158**
Shchuch'ye, *Russ.* 67°6′ N, 68°36′ E **169**
Shchūīnsk, *Kaz.* 52°52′ N, 70°14′ E **184**
Shchurovo, *Russ.* 55°1′ N, 38°49′ E **154**
Shchurovychi, *Ukr.* 50°16′ N, 25°0′ E **152**
Shchyrets', *Ukr.* 49°38′ N, 23°50′ E **152**
Shchytkavichy, *Belarus* 53°13′ N, 27°58′ E **154**
Shebar, Kowtal-e, pass, *Afghan.* 34°57′ N, 68°9′ E **186**
Shebekino, *Russ.* 50°24′ N, 36°56′ E **158**
Shebele, river, *Eth.* 5°47′ N, 42°0′ E **207**
Sheberghan, *Afghan.* 36°40′ N, 65°46′ E **186**
Sheboya, *Peru* 9°59′ S, 74°8′ W **137**
Sheboygan, *Wis., U.S.* 43°45′ N, 87°44′ W **102**
Shediac, *Can.* 46°12′ N, 64°32′ W **111**
Shedin Peak, *Can.* 55°56′ N, 127°36′ W **108**
Shedok, *Russ.* 44°12′ N, 40°44′ E **158**
Sheenjek, river, *Alas., U.S.* 66°50′ N, 144°27′ W **98**
Sheep Hole Mountains, *Calif., U.S.* 34°21′ N, 115°45′ W **101**
Sheep Mountain, peak, *Colo., U.S.* 39°54′ N, 107°13′ W **90**
Sheep Mountain, peak, *Mont., U.S.* 45°4′ N, 110°46′ W **90**
Sheep Peak, *Nev., U.S.* 36°34′ N, 115°18′ W **101**
Sheep Range, *Nev., U.S.* 36°44′ N, 115°13′ W **101**
Sheepeater Mountain, peak, *Idaho, U.S.* 45°22′ N, 115°25′ W **90**
Sheep's Head, *Ire.* 51°22′ N, 10°11′ W **150**
Sheerness, *U.K.* 51°25′ N, 0°45′ E **162**
Sheet Harbour, *Can.* 44°56′ N, 62°32′ W **111**
Sheffield, *Ala., U.S.* 34°45′ N, 87°41′ W **96**
Sheffield, *Ill., U.S.* 41°21′ N, 89°44′ W **102**
Sheffield, *Mass., U.S.* 42°6′ N, 73°22′ W **104**

Southport, *N.Y., U.S.* 42°3' N, 76°50' W **94**
Southport, *N.C., U.S.* 33°55' N, 78°2' W **96**
Southport, *U.K.* 53°38' N, 3°1' W **162**
Southwell, *U.K.* 53°4' N, 0°58' E **162**
Southwest Indian Ridge, *Indian Ocean* 39°49' S, 48°6' E **254**
Southwest Pacific Basin, *South Pacific Ocean* 40°58' S, 149°1' W **252**
Southwest Point, *Bahamas* 25°45' N, 77°12' W **96**
Southwold, *U.K.* 52°19' N, 1°40' E **163**
Soutpansberg, peak, *S. Af.* 23°2' S, 29°20' E **227**
Souvannakhili, *Laos* 15°25' N, 105°48' E **202**
Soveja, *Rom.* 45°59' N, 26°39' E **158**
Sovetsk, *Russ.* 55°4' N, 21°52' E **166**
Sovetsk, *Russ.* 57°35' N, 49°3' E **154**
Sovetskaya Gavan', *Russ.* 48°54' N, 140°9' E **238**
Sovetskaya Rechka, *Russ.* 66°41' N, 83°37' E **169**
Sovetskiy, *Russ.* 60°30' N, 28°41' E **166**
Sovetskiy, *Russ.* 61°26' N, 63°15' E **169**
Sovetskoye, *Russ.* 47°16' N, 44°28' E **158**
So'x, *Uzb.* 40°0' N, 71°7' E **197**
Soy, *Belg.* 50°16' N, 5°30' E **167**
Soyala, *Russ.* 64°28' N, 43°21' E **154**
Soyana, river, *Russ.* 65°35' N, 42°11' E **154**
Soymigora, *Russ.* 63°9' N, 31°50' E **154**
Soyo, *Angola* 6°12' S, 12°20' E **218**
Soyopa, *Mex.* 28°45' N, 109°40' W **92**
Sozh, river, *Belarus* 52°3' N, 30°59' E **158**
Sozimskiy, *Russ.* 59°44' N, 52°17' E **154**
Sozopol (Apollonia), *Bulg.* 42°25' N, 27°42' E **156**
Spa, *Belg.* 50°30' N, 5°52' E **167**
Spa, *Pol.* 51°32' N, 20°8' E **152**
Spaatz Island, *Antarctica* 74°21' S, 75°18' W **248**
Spackenkill, *N.Y., U.S.* 41°38' N, 73°56' W **104**
Spain 40°34' N, 3°17' W **150**
Spalatum see Split, *Croatia* 43°30' N, 16°26' E **168**
Spalding, *Nebr., U.S.* 41°40' N, 98°22' W **90**
Spalding, *U.K.* 52°47' N, 0°9' E **162**
Spanish Fork, *Utah, U.S.* 40°5' N, 111°37' W **90**
Spanish Head 53°51' N, 5°7' W **150**
Spanish Peak, *Oreg., U.S.* 44°22' N, 119°51' W **90**
Spanish Peaks, *Colo., U.S.* 37°9' N, 104°56' W **92**
Spanish Town, *Jam.* 17°59' N, 76°59' W **115**
Spann, Mount, peak, *Antarctica* 82°4' S, 42°47' W **248**
Sparkman, *Ark., U.S.* 33°54' N, 92°51' W **96**
Sparks, *Ga., U.S.* 31°9' N, 83°26' W **96**
Sparks Lake, lake, *Can.* 61°11' N, 110°10' W **108**
Sparland, *Ill., U.S.* 41°0' N, 89°28' W **102**
Sparta, *Can.* 42°41' N, 81°5' W **102**
Sparta, *Ga., U.S.* 33°16' N, 82°58' W **96**
Sparta, *Mo., U.S.* 38°6' N, 89°42' W **94**
Sparta, *Tenn., U.S.* 35°55' N, 85°28' W **96**
Sparta, *Wis., U.S.* 43°57' N, 90°49' W **94**
Spartanburg, *S.C., U.S.* 34°57' N, 81°56' W **96**
Spartel, Cap, *Mor.* 35°50' N, 7°13' W **214**
Spartivento, Capo, *It.* 37°51' N, 16°6' E **156**
Spartivento, Capo, *It.* 38°47' N, 8°52' E **156**
Sparwood, *Can.* 49°44' N, 114°53' W **90**
Spas Demensk, *Russ.* 54°28' N, 34°3' E **154**
Spas Klepiki, *Russ.* 55°9' N, 40°11' E **154**
Spasporub, *Russ.* 60°39' N, 48°57' E **154**
Spassk, *Russ.* 52°47' N, 87°48' E **184**
Spassk Dal'niy, *Russ.* 44°38' N, 132°48' E **160**
Spatsizi, river, *Can.* 57°14' N, 128°35' W **108**
Spearfish, *S. Dak., U.S.* 44°28' N, 103°53' W **82**
Spearman, *Tex., U.S.* 36°10' N, 101°12' W **92**
Spearsville, *La., U.S.* 32°54' N, 92°36' W **103**
Specter Range, *Nev., U.S.* 36°41' N, 116°17' W **101**
Speedway, *Ind., U.S.* 39°47' N, 86°14' W **102**
Speedwell Island, *Speedwell Island* 52°55' S, 59°49' W **248**
Speicher, *Ger.* 49°56' N, 6°39' E **167**
Speightstown, *Barbados* 13°12' N, 59°37' W **116**
Spencer, *Idaho, U.S.* 44°20' N, 112°10' W **90**
Spencer, *Ind., U.S.* 39°17' N, 86°47' W **102**
Spencer, *Iowa, U.S.* 43°8' N, 95°9' W **90**
Spencer, *Nebr., U.S.* 42°51' N, 98°43' W **90**
Spencer, *W. Va., U.S.* 38°48' N, 81°23' W **94**
Spencer, Cape, *Austral.* 35°9' S, 136°35' E **231**
Spencer Gulf 34°27' S, 135°22' E **230**
Spencerville, *Ohio, U.S.* 40°41' N, 84°21' W **102**
Spences Bridge, *Can.* 50°24' N, 121°21' W **108**
Spennymoor, *U.K.* 54°42' N, 1°37' W **162**
Sperlonga, *It.* 41°16' N, 13°26' E **156**
Sperone, Capo, *It.* 38°54' N, 7°43' E **156**
Sperrin Mountains, *U.K.* 54°46' N, 7°48' W **150**
Spessart, *Ger.* 50°7' N, 9°7' E **167**
Spezand, *Pak.* 29°58' N, 66°59' E **186**
Spicer Islands, islands, *Can.* 67°44' N, 80°35' W **106**
Spickard, Mount, peak, *Wash., U.S.* 48°57' N, 121°17' W **100**
Spieden, Cape 66°10' S, 129°48' E **248**
Spiess Seamount, *South Atlantic Ocean* 55°29' S, 1°19' W **255**
Spiez, *Switz.* 46°41' N, 7°40' E **167**
Spike Mountain, peak, *Alas., U.S.* 67°26' N, 142°2' W **98**
Spilsby, *U.K.* 53°10' N, 0°535' E **162**
Spin Buldak, *Afghan.* 31°1' N, 66°27' E **186**
Spincourt, *Fr.* 49°19' N, 5°39' E **163**
Spind, *Nor.* 58°5' N, 6°54' E **150**
Špionica, *Bosn. and Herzg.* 44°45' N, 18°31' E **168**
Spirit Lake, *Iowa, U.S.* 43°24' N, 95°7' W **90**
Spirit Lake, *Wash., U.S.* 46°15' N, 122°19' W **100**
Spirit River, *Can.* 55°46' N, 118°50' W **108**
Spiritwood, *Can.* 53°21' N, 107°28' W **108**
Spiro, *Okla., U.S.* 35°12' N, 94°38' W **96**
Spirovo, *Russ.* 57°24' N, 35°0' E **154**
Spišská Nová Ves, *Slovakia* 48°56' N, 20°33' E **152**
Spitsbergen Fracture Zone, *Greenland Sea* 81°13' N, 3°8' W **255**
Spitsbergen, island, *Nor.* 77°10' N, 3°50' E **160**
Spittal, *Aust.* 46°48' N, 13°29' E **167**
Splendora, *Tex., U.S.* 30°12' N, 95°10' W **103**
Split, Cape, *Can.* 45°20' N, 64°27' W **111**
Split Lake, *Can.* 56°14' N, 96°11' W **108**
Split Peak, *Nev., U.S.* 41°48' N, 118°31' W **90**
Split (Spalatum), *Croatia* 43°30' N, 16°26' E **168**
Splügen, *Switz.* 46°33' N, 9°17' E **167**
Splügen Pass, *Switz.* 46°31' N, 9°19' E **167**
Spogi, *Latv.* 56°3' N, 26°43' E **166**
Spokane, *Wash., U.S.* 47°40' N, 117°27' W **90**
Spokane, Mount, peak, *Wash., U.S.* 47°53' N, 117°12' W **90**
Spokane, river, *Wash., U.S.* 47°57' N, 118°41' W **80**
Spooner, *Wis., U.S.* 45°49' N, 91°54' W **94**
Sporyy Navolok, Mys, *Russ.* 75°20' N, 44°26' E **172**
Spotted Range, *Nev., U.S.* 36°45' N, 115°53' W **101**
Sprague, *Can.* 49°1' N, 95°36' W **90**
Sprague, *Wash., U.S.* 47°16' N, 117°59' W **90**
Spranger, Mount, peak, *Can.* 52°53' N, 120°50' W **108**
Spratly Islands, *South China Sea* 11°51' N, 112°52' E **238**
Spray, *Oreg., U.S.* 44°49' N, 119°48' W **90**
Spremberg, *Ger.* 51°34' N, 14°21' E **152**
Spring, *Tex., U.S.* 30°3' N, 95°25' W **103**
Spring Butte, peak, *Oreg., U.S.* 43°30' N, 121°26' W **90**
Spring Glen, *Utah, U.S.* 39°39' N, 110°51' W **92**
Spring Green, *Wis., U.S.* 43°10' N, 90°4' W **102**
Spring Grove, *Minn., U.S.* 43°33' N, 91°39' W **94**
Spring Hill, *Fla., U.S.* 28°26' N, 82°36' W **105**
Spring Lake, *Mich., U.S.* 43°3' N, 86°10' W **94**
Spring Mountains, *Nev., U.S.* 36°22' N, 115°51' W **101**
Spring Point, *Can.* 59°24' N, 109°46' W **108**
Spring Valley, *N.Y., U.S.* 41°6' N, 74°3' W **104**
Springbok, *S. Af.* 29°41' S, 17°52' E **227**
Springdale, *Ark., U.S.* 36°10' N, 94°9' W **96**
Springdale, *Can.* 49°30' N, 56°6' W **111**
Springdale, *Ohio, U.S.* 39°16' N, 84°29' W **102**
Springer, *N. Mex., U.S.* 36°21' N, 104°36' W **92**
Springer Mountain, peak, *Ga., U.S.* 34°37' N, 84°17' W **96**
Springfield, *Colo., U.S.* 37°23' N, 102°37' W **92**
Springfield, *Fla., U.S.* 30°8' N, 85°36' W **96**
Springfield, *Idaho, U.S.* 43°5' N, 112°41' W **90**
Springfield, *Ill., U.S.* 39°47' N, 89°41' W **102**
Springfield, *La., U.S.* 30°24' N, 90°33' W **103**
Springfield, *Mass., U.S.* 42°6' N, 72°36' W **104**
Springfield, *Minn., U.S.* 44°13' N, 95°0' W **90**
Springfield, *Mo., U.S.* 37°12' N, 93°18' W **96**
Springfield, *N.Z.* 43°21' S, 171°55' E **240**
Springfield, *Ohio, U.S.* 39°54' N, 83°48' W **102**
Springfield, *Oreg., U.S.* 44°2' N, 123°1' W **90**
Springfield, *S. Dak., U.S.* 42°50' N, 97°55' W **90**
Springfield, *Tenn., U.S.* 36°30' N, 86°52' W **94**
Springfield, *Vt., U.S.* 43°17' N, 72°29' W **104**
Springfontein, *S. Af.* 30°16' S, 25°42' E **227**
Springhill, *Can.* 45°38' N, 64°5' W **111**
Springhill, *La., U.S.* 32°59' N, 93°28' W **103**
Springport, *Mich., U.S.* 42°22' N, 84°42' W **102**
Springvale, *Me., U.S.* 43°27' N, 70°49' W **104**
Springview, *Nebr., U.S.* 42°48' N, 99°46' W **90**
Springville, *Calif., U.S.* 36°8' N, 118°50' W **101**
Spruce Home, *Can.* 53°23' N, 105°46' W **108**
Spruce Knob, peak, *W. Va., U.S.* 38°41' N, 79°37' W **94**
Spruce Knob-Seneca Rocks National Recreation Area, *W. Va., U.S.* 38°49' N, 87°57' W **80**
Spruce Mountain, peak, *Nev., U.S.* 40°32' N, 114°54' W **90**
Spruce Pine, *N.C., U.S.* 35°55' N, 82°5' W **96**
Spry, *Pa., U.S.* 39°54' N, 76°41' W **94**
Spulico, Capo, *It.* 39°57' N, 16°40' E **156**
Spur, *Tex., U.S.* 33°27' N, 100°51' W **92**
Spurger, *Tex., U.S.* 30°40' N, 94°11' W **103**
Spurn Head, *U.K.* 53°30' N, 0°7' E **162**
Spuž, *Mont.* 42°31' N, 19°13' E **168**
Spuzzum, *Can.* 49°41' N, 121°26' W **100**
Squamish, *Can.* 49°42' N, 123°8' W **100**
Squamish, river, *Can.* 50°7' N, 123°20' W **100**
Square Islands, *Can.* 52°43' N, 55°51' W **111**
Squires, Mount, peak, *Austral.* 26°15' S, 127°12' E **230**
Squirrel, river, *Can.* 50°25' N, 84°20' W **110**
Srbac, *Bosn. and Herzg.* 45°5' N, 17°31' E **168**
Srbica see Skënderaj, *Kosovo* 42°44' N, 20°46' E **168**
Srbobran, *Serb.* 45°33' N, 19°47' E **168**
Sre Umbell, *Cambodia* 11°6' N, 103°45' E **202**
Srebrenica, *Bosn. and Herzg.* 44°6' N, 19°19' E **168**
Sredinnyy Khrebet, *Russ.* 57°35' N, 160°3' E **160**
Srednekolymsk, *Russ.* 67°27' N, 153°21' E **160**
Sredneye Bugayevo, *Russ.* 66°0' N, 52°28' E **154**
Srednyaya Olekma, *Russ.* 55°20' N, 120°33' E **190**
Sremska Mitrovica, *Serb.* 44°58' N, 19°37' E **168**
Sremska Rača, *Serb.* 44°54' N, 19°19' E **168**
Sremski Karlovci, *Serb.* 45°11' N, 19°55' E **168**
Sretensk, *Russ.* 52°17' N, 117°45' E **190**
Sri Jayewardenepura Kotte, *Sri Lanka* 6°54' N, 79°57' E **188**
Sri Kalahasti, *India* 13°46' N, 79°40' E **188**
Sri Lanka 7°26' N, 80°15' E **188**
Sri Madhopur, *India* 27°28' N, 75°37' E **197**
Srikakulam, *India* 18°17' N, 83°55' E **188**
Srinagar, *India* 34°7' N, 74°48' E **186**
Srivardhan, *India* 18°5' N, 73°0' E **188**
Srnetica, *Bosn. and Herzg.* 44°26' N, 16°35' E **168**
Srokowo, *Pol.* 54°11' N, 21°31' E **166**
Srpska Crnja, *Serb.* 45°43' N, 20°42' E **168**
Srpski Itebej, *Serb.* 45°34' N, 20°43' E **168**
Ssanggyo, *N. Korea* 37°46' N, 125°26' E **200**
Staaten River National Park, *Austral.* 16°39' S, 142°26' E **238**
Staberhuk, *Kattegat* 54°18' N, 10°48' E **152**
Stack, Ben, peak, *U.K.* 58°19' N, 5°5' W **150**
Stade, *Ger.* 53°36' N, 9°28' E **150**
Städjan, peak, *Nor.* 61°54' N, 12°44' E **152**
Stadskanaal, *Neth.* 52°59' N, 6°57' E **163**
Stadtallendorf, *Ger.* 50°49' N, 9°0' E **167**
Stadtkyll, *Ger.* 50°20' N, 6°32' E **167**
Stadtlohn, *Ger.* 51°59' N, 6°54' E **167**
Stafford, *Kans., U.S.* 37°56' N, 98°36' W **90**
Stafford, *U.K.* 52°47' N, 2°7' W **162**
Stafford Springs, *Conn., U.S.* 41°57' N, 72°19' W **104**
Staffordsville, *Ky., U.S.* 37°49' N, 82°51' W **94**
Stage Road Pass, *Oreg., U.S.* 42°43' N, 123°22' W **90**
Stagira, ruin(s), *Gr.* 40°31' N, 23°38' E **156**
Stagnone, Isole dello, islands, *Mediterranean Sea* 37°35' N, 11°52' E **156**
Staicele, *Latv.* 57°51' N, 24°44' E **166**
Staigue Fort, site, *Ire.* 51°47' N, 10°7' W **150**
Staines, *U.K.* 51°26' N, 0°31' E **162**
Staithes, *U.K.* 54°33' N, 0°48' E **162**
Stalać, *Serb.* 43°41' N, 21°25' E **168**
Staldzene, *Latv.* 57°25' N, 21°35' E **166**
Stalham, *U.K.* 52°46' N, 1°31' E **163**
Stalingrad see Volgograd, *Russ.* 48°46' N, 44°28' E **158**
Stallo, *Miss., U.S.* 32°53' N, 89°6' W **103**
Stallworthy, Cape, *Can.* 81°41' N, 95°15' W **246**
Stalowa Wola, *Pol.* 50°33' N, 22°2' E **152**
Stamford, *Conn., U.S.* 41°2' N, 73°33' W **104**
Stamford, *N.Y., U.S.* 42°24' N, 74°39' W **110**
Stamford, *Tex., U.S.* 32°55' N, 99°49' W **92**
Stamford, *U.K.* 52°39' N, 0°29' E **162**
Stamford Bridge, *U.K.* 53°59' N, 0°55' E **162**
Stamovo, *Bulg.* 42°26' N, 25°50' E **156**
Stampriet, *Namibia* 24°18' S, 18°23' E **227**
Stamps, *Ark., U.S.* 33°21' N, 93°31' W **103**
Stanberry, *Mo., U.S.* 40°12' N, 94°32' W **94**
Standerton, *S. Af.* 26°57' S, 29°13' E **227**
Standish, *Me., U.S.* 43°43' N, 70°33' W **104**
Standish, *Mich., U.S.* 43°58' N, 83°58' W **102**
Standish Ranges, *Austral.* 21°44' S, 138°59' E **230**
Stanfield, *Oreg., U.S.* 45°46' N, 119°14' W **90**
Stanford, *Ky., U.S.* 37°31' N, 84°40' W **94**
Stanford, *Mont., U.S.* 47°7' N, 110°14' W **90**
Stånga, *Sw.* 57°16' N, 18°27' E **166**
Stanger, *S. Af.* 29°21' S, 31°15' E **227**
Staniard Creek, *Bahamas* 24°50' N, 77°55' W **96**
Stanišić, *Serb.* 45°55' N, 19°9' E **168**
Staňkov, *Czech Rep.* 49°33' N, 13°4' E **152**
Stanley, *Can.* 46°16' N, 66°45' W **111**
Stanley, *Falk. Is., U.K.* 51°42' S, 57°52' W **134**
Stanley, *Idaho, U.S.* 44°12' N, 114°56' W **90**
Stanley, *N. Dak., U.S.* 48°17' N, 102°24' W **90**
Stanley, *Wis., U.S.* 44°57' N, 90°56' W **94**
Stanley Falls see Boyoma Falls, *Dem. Rep. of the Congo* 0°14' N, 25°9' E **224**
Stanley Mission, *Can.* 55°25' N, 104°30' W **108**
Stanley, Mount, peak, *Austral.* 22°50' S, 130°28' E **230**
Stanley, Mount, peak, *Austral.* 40°6' S, 143°46' E **230**
Stanley Peak, *Can.* 51°11' N, 116°6' W **90**
Stanleyville see Kisangani, *Dem. Rep. of the Congo* 0°33' N, 25°16' E **224**
Stanovoy Khrebet, *Russ.* 54°46' N, 122°14' E **190**
Stanton, *Mich., U.S.* 43°17' N, 85°5' W **102**
Stanton, *Tex., U.S.* 32°7' N, 101°47' W **92**
Stanwick, *U.K.* 52°20' N, 0°33' E **162**
Stanwood, *Wash., U.S.* 48°13' N, 122°23' W **100**
Staphorst, *Neth.* 52°39' N, 6°12' E **163**
Staples, *Minn., U.S.* 46°20' N, 94°48' W **90**
Stapleton, *Nebr., U.S.* 41°28' N, 100°31' W **90**
Star, *Miss., U.S.* 32°5' N, 90°2' W **103**
Star City, *Ark., U.S.* 33°56' N, 91°51' W **96**
Star City, *Ind., U.S.* 40°58' N, 86°34' W **102**
Star Peak, *Nev., U.S.* 40°31' N, 118°16' W **90**
Star Valley, *Wyo., U.S.* 42°38' N, 111°3' W **90**
Stara Moravica, *Serb.* 45°52' N, 19°28' E **168**
Stara Pazova, *Serb.* 44°58' N, 20°9' E **168**
Stara Ushytsya, *Ukr.* 48°34' N, 27°5' E **152**
Stara Vyzhivka, *Ukr.* 51°25' N, 24°25' E **152**
Stara Zagora, *Bulg.* 42°25' N, 25°36' E **156**
Stara Zagora, adm. division, *Bulg.* 42°39' N, 25°6' E **156**
Staraya, *Russ.* 70°56' N, 112°20' E **173**
Staraya Poltavka, *Russ.* 50°28' N, 46°26' E **158**
Staraya Russa, *Russ.* 57°56' N, 31°23' E **152**
Starbuck, *Wash., U.S.* 46°30' N, 118°8' W **90**
Stare Pole, *Pol.* 54°3' N, 19°11' E **166**
Stargard Szczeciński, *Pol.* 53°19' N, 15°1' E **152**
Stari Bar, *Mont.* 42°6' N, 19°8' E **168**
Stari Mikanovci, *Croatia* 45°15' N, 18°33' E **168**
Starigrad, *Croatia* 43°10' N, 16°35' E **168**
Staritsa, *Belarus* 53°14' N, 27°15' E **154**
Staritsa, *Russ.* 56°28' N, 34°56' E **154**
Starke, *Fla., U.S.* 29°56' N, 82°8' W **96**
Starks, *La., U.S.* 30°17' N, 93°40' W **103**
Starksboro, *Vt., U.S.* 44°13' N, 73°4' W **104**
Starkville, *Colo., U.S.* 37°7' N, 104°33' W **92**
Starkville, *Miss., U.S.* 33°26' N, 88°48' W **103**
Starobaltachevo, *Russ.* 56°1' N, 55°56' E **154**
Starobil's'k, *Ukr.* 49°18' N, 38°53' E **158**
Starobin, *Belarus* 52°42' N, 27°27' E **152**
Starodub, *Russ.* 52°31' N, 32°51' E **154**
Starokostyantyniv, *Ukr.* 49°44' N, 27°12' E **152**
Starominskaya, *Russ.* 46°32' N, 39°1' E **156**
Staropol'ye, *Russ.* 59°1' N, 28°34' E **166**
Starorybnoye, *Russ.* 72°48' N, 104°49' E **173**
Staroshcherbinovskaya, *Russ.* 46°37' N, 38°38' E **156**
Staroye Syalo, *Belarus* 55°17' N, 29°58' E **166**
Start Point, *English Channel* 50°2' N, 3°37' W **150**
Starvyy Karabutak, *Kaz.* 49°49' N, 59°54' E **158**
Staryy Biryuzyak, *Russ.* 44°45' N, 46°47' E **158**
Staryy Krym, *Ukr.* 45°1' N, 35°0' E **156**
Staryy Kryvyn, *Ukr.* 50°21' N, 26°42' E **152**
Staryy Nadym, *Russ.* 65°36' N, 72°50' E **169**
Staryy Oskol, *Russ.* 51°17' N, 37°45' E **158**
Staryy Sambir, *Ukr.* 49°23' N, 22°55' E **152**
Staszów, *Pol.* 50°33' N, 21°10' E **152**
State Line, *Miss., U.S.* 31°24' N, 88°28' W **103**
Staten Island, *N.Y., U.S.* 40°27' N, 74°6' W **104**
Staten Island see de los Estados, Isla, *Arg.* 55°28' S, 64°48' W **134**
Statesboro, *Ga., U.S.* 32°25' N, 81°47' W **112**
Station 10, *Sudan* 19°41' N, 33°8' E **182**
Station 5, *Sudan* 21°2' N, 32°19' E **182**
Station 6, *Sudan* 20°44' N, 32°30' E **182**
Staunton, *Ill., U.S.* 39°0' N, 89°47' W **102**
Staunton, *Va., U.S.* 38°8' N, 79°5' W **94**
Stavanger, *Nor.* 58°56' N, 5°43' E **152**
Stave Lake, *Can.* 49°18' N, 122°30' W **100**
Stavelot, *Belg.* 50°23' N, 5°56' E **167**
Stavely, *Can.* 50°10' N, 113°39' W **90**
Staveren, *Neth.* 52°53' N, 5°22' E **163**
Stavnoye, *Ukr.* 48°56' N, 22°42' E **156**
Stavropol', *Russ.* 45°3' N, 41°58' E **158**
Stavropol', adm. division, *Russ.* 45°26' N, 41°12' E **160**
Stawiski, *Pol.* 53°22' N, 22°8' E **154**
Stayner, *Can.* 44°24' N, 80°6' W **110**
Steamboat, *Can.* 58°40' N, 123°45' W **108**
Steamboat Mountain, peak, *Wyo., U.S.* 41°57' N, 109°2' W **90**
Stederdorf, *Ger.* 52°21' N, 10°13' E **150**
Steele, *N. Dak., U.S.* 46°50' N, 99°56' W **108**
Steele Island, island, *Antarctica* 71°8' S, 60°19' W **248**
Steelpoort, *S. Af.* 24°46' S, 30°11' E **227**
Steelton, *Pa., U.S.* 40°13' N, 76°51' W **94**
Steelville, *Mo., U.S.* 37°57' N, 91°21' W **96**
Steen River, *Can.* 59°39' N, 117°11' W **108**
Steen, river, *Can.* 59°17' N, 118°21' W **108**
Steens Mountain, *Oreg., U.S.* 43°21' N, 118°14' W **90**
Steensby Inlet 69°57' N, 81°26' W **106**
Steenstrup Gletscher, glacier 74°42' N, 64°7' W **106**
Steenwijk, *Neth.* 52°46' N, 6°6' E **163**
Steep Rock, *Can.* 51°26' N, 98°48' W **90**
Steep Rock Lake, *Can.* 48°49' N, 91°38' W **94**
Steers Head 81°45' S, 164°32' W **248**
Stefansson Island, island, *Can.* 73°43' N, 112°11' W **106**
Stege, *Den.* 54°59' N, 12°17' E **152**
Steger, *Ill., U.S.* 41°27' N, 87°38' W **102**
Steigen, *Nor.* 67°55' N, 14°58' E **152**
Steigerwald, *Ger.* 49°45' N, 10°17' E **167**
Stein Pass, *Ger.* 47°39' N, 12°45' E **152**
Stein, river, *Can.* 50°10' N, 122°21' W **90**
Steinau, *Ger.* 50°18' N, 9°27' E **167**
Steinbach, *Can.* 49°31' N, 96°42' W **90**
Steinfeld, *Ger.* 52°36' N, 8°13' E **163**
Steinfort, *Lux.* 49°39' N, 5°55' E **163**
Steinfurt, *Ger.* 52°8' N, 7°19' E **163**
Steinhatchee, *Fla., U.S.* 29°40' N, 83°24' W **105**
Steinhausen, *Namibia* 21°49' S, 18°15' E **227**
Steinkjer, *Nor.* 63°57' N, 11°44' E **160**
Steinkopf, *S. Af.* 29°15' S, 17°42' E **227**
Stellaland, region, *S. Af.* 27°19' S, 24°2' E **227**
Stelle, *Ger.* 53°22' N, 10°6' E **152**
Stellenbosch, *S. Af.* 33°55' S, 18°48' E **227**
Stelvio, Passo dello, *It.* 46°31' N, 10°26' E **167**
Stenay, *Fr.* 49°29' N, 5°11' E **163**
Stende, *Latv.* 57°8' N, 22°32' E **166**
Stenstorp, *Nor.* 58°15' N, 13°41' E **152**
Stenträsk, *Nor.* 66°19' N, 19°50' E **152**
Stepanakert (Xankändi), *Asia* 39°48' N, 46°43' E **195**
Step'anavan, *Arm.* 41°0' N, 44°21' E **195**
Stepanci, *Maced.* 41°29' N, 21°38' E **168**
Stephen, *Minn., U.S.* 48°26' N, 96°53' W **94**
Stephens, *Ark., U.S.* 33°23' N, 93°5' W **103**
Stephens Lake, lake, *Can.* 56°42' N, 94°17' W **108**
Stephens Passage 57°46' N, 134°48' W **108**
Stephens, Port 32°50' S, 150°48' E **230**
Stephenson, *Mich., U.S.* 45°24' N, 87°36' W **94**
Stephenson, Mount, peak, *Antarctica* 69°49' S, 70°21' W **248**
Stephenville, *Can.* 48°31' N, 58°39' W **106**
Stephenville, *Tex., U.S.* 32°13' N, 98°13' W **92**
Stepnogorsk, *Kaz.* 52°23' N, 71°54' E **184**
Stepnoye, *Russ.* 44°15' N, 44°32' E **158**
Stepnyak, *Kaz.* 52°49' N, 70°47' E **184**
Stepojevac, *Serb.* 44°30' N, 20°18' E **168**
Steptoe Butte, peak, *Wash., U.S.* 46°59' N, 117°24' W **900**
Stereá Eláda, adm. division, *Gr.* 38°54' N, 22°26' E **156**
Sterling, *Colo., U.S.* 40°37' N, 103°14' W **90**
Sterling, *Ill., U.S.* 41°47' N, 89°42' W **102**
Sterling, *Kans., U.S.* 38°12' N, 98°13' W **90**
Sterling, *Mich., U.S.* 44°1' N, 84°2' W **102**
Sterling, *Mo., U.S.* 41°47' N, 89°42' W **94**
Sterling, *N. Dak., U.S.* 46°48' N, 100°18' W **90**
Sterling City, *Tex., U.S.* 31°49' N, 101°0' W **92**
Sterlington, *La., U.S.* 32°40' N, 92°5' W **103**
Sterlitamak, *Russ.* 53°39' N, 55°53' E **154**
Stettler, *Can.* 52°19' N, 112°42' W **108**
Stevenage, *U.K.* 51°54' N, 0°13' E **162**
Stevens Point, *Wis., U.S.* 44°31' N, 89°35' W **94**
Stevenson, *Wash., U.S.* 45°41' N, 121°54' W **100**
Stevenson Lake, lake, *Can.* 53°54' N, 96°43' W **108**
Stevenson Mountain, peak, *Oreg., U.S.* 44°33' N, 120°32' W **90**
Stevensville, *Mich., U.S.* 42°0' N, 86°30' W **102**
Stewardson, *Ill., U.S.* 39°15' N, 88°39' W **102**
Stewart, *Can.* 55°56' N, 130°1' W **108**
Stewart, *Miss., U.S.* 33°25' N, 89°26' W **103**
Stewart, *Ohio, U.S.* 39°18' N, 81°54' W **102**
Stewart Crossing, *Can.* 63°27' N, 136°41' W **98**
Stewart, Isla, island, *Chile* 54°51' S, 72°56' W **134**
Stewart Islands, *South Pacific Ocean* 8°0' S, 163°3' E **238**
Stewart River, *Can.* 63°21' N, 139°26' W **98**
Steynsburg, *S. Af.* 31°18' S, 25°47' E **227**
Steyr, *Aust.* 48°2' N, 14°24' E **152**
Steytlerville, *S. Af.* 33°20' S, 24°18' E **227**
Stia, *It.* 43°48' N, 11°41' E **167**
Stickney, *S. Dak., U.S.* 43°34' N, 98°26' W **90**
Stiene, *Latv.* 57°23' N, 24°33' E **166**
Stiens, *Neth.* 53°15' N, 5°44' E **163**
Stigler, *Okla., U.S.* 35°13' N, 95°9' W **96**
Stih, Hora, peak, *Ukr.* 48°35' N, 23°12' E **152**
Stikine, river, *Can.* 57°15' N, 131°59' W **108**
Stikine, river, *Can.* 58°11' N, 130°31' W **98**
Stikine, river, *Can.* 58°0' N, 129°22' W **108**
Stillman Valley, *Ill., U.S.* 42°6' N, 89°11' W **102**
Stillwater, *Can.* 49°46' N, 124°17' W **100**
Stillwater, *Minn., U.S.* 45°2' N, 92°50' W **94**
Stillwater, *N.Y., U.S.* 42°56' N, 73°40' W **104**
Stillwater, *Okla., U.S.* 36°5' N, 97°2' W **92**
Stillwater Range, *Nev., U.S.* 39°59' N, 118°14' W **90**
Stilo, Punta, *It.* 38°27' N, 16°35' E **156**
Stilton, *U.K.* 52°29' N, 0°17' E **162**
Stilwell, *Okla., U.S.* 35°46' N, 94°38' W **96**
Stine Mountain, peak, *Mont., U.S.* 45°41' N, 113°11' W **90**
Stinear, Mount, peak, *Antarctica* 73°18' S, 66°2' E **248**
Stinkingwater Pass, *Oreg., U.S.* 43°42' N, 118°32' W **90**
Stinnett, *Tex., U.S.* 35°47' N, 101°27' W **92**
Stinson Lake, *N.H., U.S.* 43°51' N, 71°50' W **104**
Štip, *Maced.* 41°44' N, 22°11' E **168**
Stiring-Wendel, *Fr.* 49°12' N, 6°55' E **163**
Stirling Island, *Solomon Islands* 7°20' S, 155°30' E **242**
Stirling, Mount, peak, *Nev., U.S.* 36°26' N, 116°1' W **101**
Stobi, ruin(s), *Maced.* 41°31' N, 21°54' E **168**
Stock Route, *Austral.* 19°46' S, 126°40' E **231**
Stockbridge, *Mass., U.S.* 42°16' N, 73°20' W **104**
Stockbridge, *Mich., U.S.* 42°25' N, 84°11' W **102**
Stockbridge, *U.K.* 51°6' N, 1°29' W **162**
Stockbridge, *Vt., U.S.* 43°47' N, 72°46' W **104**
Stockdale, *Tex., U.S.* 29°13' N, 97°57' W **96**
Stockholm, *Sw.* 59°19' N, 17°55' E **166**
Stockport, *U.K.* 53°23' N, 2°10' W **162**
Stockton, *Ala., U.S.* 30°58' N, 87°51' W **103**
Stockton, *Calif., U.S.* 37°57' N, 121°17' W **100**
Stockton, *Ill., U.S.* 42°20' N, 90°1' W **102**
Stockton, *Kans., U.S.* 39°26' N, 99°17' W **90**
Stockton, *Mo., U.S.* 37°40' N, 93°48' W **94**
Stockton on Tees, *U.K.* 54°34' N, 1°20' W **162**
Stockwell, *Ind., U.S.* 40°16' N, 86°46' W **102**
Stoddard, *N.H., U.S.* 43°4' N, 72°8' W **104**
Stöde, *Nor.* 62°24' N, 16°33' E **152**
Stogovo, *Maced.* 41°28' N, 20°32' E **168**
Stoke, *N.Z.* 41°21' S, 173°14' E **240**
Stoke Ferry, *U.K.* 52°34' N, 0°31' E **162**
Stoke on Trent, *U.K.* 53°0' N, 2°11' W **162**
Stokes, Bahia 54°9' S, 73°50' W **134**
Stokes, Mount, peak, *N.Z.* 41°8' S, 174°2' E **240**
Stokesay, *U.K.* 52°25' N, 2°50' W **162**
Stoksund, *Nor.* 64°2' N, 10°4' E **152**
Stolac, *Bosn. and Herzg.* 43°3' N, 17°57' E **168**
Stolberg, *Ger.* 50°46' N, 6°12' E **167**
Stolbovo, *Russ.* 55°59' N, 30°1' E **166**
Stolbovoy, Ostrov, island, *Russ.* 73°52' N, 128°4' E **160**
Stolin, *Belarus* 51°53' N, 26°49' E **152**
Stöllet, *Nor.* 60°23' N, 13°16' E **152**
Stolnici, *Rom.* 44°35' N, 24°47' E **156**
Stone, *U.K.* 52°54' N, 2°8' W **162**
Stone Lake, lake, *Can.* 50°34' N, 87°51' W **110**
Stonehenge, site, *U.K.* 51°9' N, 1°51' W **162**
Stoner, *Can.* 53°38' N, 122°40' W **108**
Stonewall, *Can.* 50°7' N, 97°19' W **108**
Stonewall, *La., U.S.* 32°16' N, 93°50' W **103**
Stonewall, *Miss., U.S.* 32°7' N, 88°46' W **103**
Stonglandet, *Nor.* 69°5' N, 17°12' E **152**
Stonington, *Ill., U.S.* 39°37' N, 89°12' W **102**
Stony Brook, *N.Y., U.S.* 40°55' N, 73°9' W **104**
Stony Creek, *N.Y., U.S.* 43°25' N, 73°57' W **104**
Stony Lake, *Can.* 58°53' N, 99°17' W **108**
Stony Plain, *Can.* 53°31' N, 114°3' W **108**
Stony Point, *N.Y., U.S.* 43°39' N, 76°34' W **94**
Stony Point, *N.Y., U.S.* 41°13' N, 74°0' W **104**
Stony Rapids, *Can.* 59°10' N, 106°0' W **106**
Stony River, *Alas., U.S.* 61°48' N, 156°33' W **98**
Stooping, river, *Can.* 51°19' N, 82°32' W **110**
Støren, *Nor.* 63°0' N, 10°18' E **152**
Storfjord, *Nor.* 69°16' N, 19°59' E **152**
Storfjorden 77°20' N, 7°31' E **172**
Storkerson Bay 72°55' N, 128°56' W **106**
Storlien, *Nor.* 63°18' N, 12°7' E **152**
Storm Berg, peak, *S. Af.* 31°22' S, 26°27' E **227**
Storm King Mountain, peak, *Colo., U.S.* 37°55' N, 106°29' W **90**
Storm Lake, *Iowa, U.S.* 42°38' N, 95°13' W **90**
Storozhevsk, *Russ.* 61°56' N, 52°20' E **154**
Storr, The, peak 57°29' N, 6°18' W **150**
Storriten, peak, *Nor.* 68°6' N, 17°7' E **152**
Storrs, *Conn., U.S.* 41°48' N, 72°16' W **104**
Storsjö, *Nor.* 62°47' N, 13°2' E **152**
Storskavlen, peak, *Nor.* 60°44' N, 7°10' E **152**
Storuman, *Nor.* 65°5' N, 17°6' E **152**
Storvätteshågna, peak, *Nor.* 62°7' N, 12°21' E **152**
Storvik, *Nor.* 60°34' N, 16°28' E **152**
Story, *Wyo., U.S.* 44°34' N, 106°53' W **90**
Story City, *Iowa, U.S.* 42°11' N, 93°36' W **94**
Stoughton, *Can.* 49°40' N, 103°4' W **90**
Stoughton, *Wis., U.S.* 42°54' N, 89°12' W **102**
Stour, river, *U.K.* 51°58' N, 0°47' E **162**
Stourbridge, *U.K.* 52°27' N, 2°9' W **162**
Stourport on Severn, *U.K.* 52°20' N, 2°16' W **162**
Stovepipe Wells, *Calif., U.S.* 36°36' N, 117°10' W **101**
Stow, *Ohio, U.S.* 41°8' N, 81°26' W **94**
Stow on the Wold, *U.K.* 51°55' N, 1°44' W **162**
Stowbtsy, *Belarus* 53°29' N, 26°45' E **154**
Stowe, *Vt., U.S.* 44°27' N, 72°42' W **104**
Stowell, *Tex., U.S.* 29°46' N, 94°24' W **103**
Stowmarket, *U.K.* 52°11' N, 0°59' E **162**
Stoyaniv, *Ukr.* 50°22' N, 24°39' E **158**
Stradella, *It.* 45°4' N, 9°17' E **167**
Strait 69°45' N, 84°55' W **106**
Straldzha, *Bulg.* 42°36' N, 26°41' E **158**
Stralsund, *Ger.* 54°16' N, 13°4' E **160**
Strand, *S. Af.* 34°6' S, 18°51' E **227**
Strandebarm, *Nor.* 60°16' N, 5°59' E **152**
Strasbourg, *Can.* 51°3' N, 104°57' W **90**
Strasbourg, *Fr.* 48°34' N, 7°44' E **163**
Strasburg, *N. Dak., U.S.* 46°7' N, 100°11' W **90**
Strasburg, *Ohio, U.S.* 40°35' N, 81°32' W **102**
Strasburg, *Va., U.S.* 38°59' N, 78°22' W **94**
Strășeni, *Mold.* 47°7' N, 28°38' E **156**

Swainsboro, Ga., U.S. 32°35′ N, 82°21′ W 96
Swakopmund, Namibia 22°31′ S, 14°28′ E 207
Swale, river, U.K. 54°23′ N, 1°51′ W 162
Swampscott, Mass., U.S. 42°28′ N, 70°56′ W 104
Swan Hills, Can. 54°43′ N, 115°35′ W 108
Swan Lake, S. Dak., U.S. 45°14′ N, 100°18′ W 90
Swan Lake, lake, Can. 55°45′ N, 129°7′ W 108
Swan Range, Mont., U.S. 47°43′ N, 113°44′ W 90
Swan River, Can. 52°4′ N, 101°15′ W 108
Swan, river, Can. 52°16′ N, 102°16′ W 108
Swanquarter, N.C., U.S. 35°24′ N, 76°21′ W 96
Swansea (Abertawe), U.K. 51°37′ N, 3°57′ W 162
Swanton, Ohio, U.S. 41°35′ N, 83°53′ W 102
Swanzey, N.H., U.S. 42°51′ N, 72°18′ W 104
Swartmodder, S. Af. 28°5′ S, 20°34′ E 227
Swartruggens, S. Af. 25°41′ S, 26°41′ E 227
Swartz, La., U.S. 32°33′ N, 91°59′ W 103
Swarzȩdz, Pol. 52°24′ N, 17°4′ E 152
Swasey Peak, Utah, U.S. 39°22′ N, 113°23′ W 90
Swat, river, Pak. 34°46′ N, 72°20′ E 186
Swatow see Shantou, China 23°23′ N, 116°40′ E 198
Swaziland 26°31′ S, 31°28′ E 227
Sweden 63°13′ N, 16°14′ E 152
Swedru, Ghana 5°32′ N, 0°44′ E 222
Sweeney Mountains, Antarctica 74°37′ S, 74°59′ W 248
Sweet Home, Oreg., U.S. 44°22′ N, 122°44′ W 90
Sweetgrass, Mont., U.S. 48°58′ N, 111°59′ W 90
Sweetwater, Tenn., U.S. 35°35′ N, 84°28′ W 96
Sweetwater, Tex., U.S. 32°27′ N, 100°24′ W 96
Sweetwater Summit, pass, Nev., U.S. 38°30′ N, 119°14′ W 100
Świdwin, Pol. 53°45′ N, 15°47′ E 152
Świebodzin, Pol. 52°15′ N, 15°31′ E 152
Świȩtokrzyskie, Pol. 51°5′ N, 19°47′ E 152
Świȩtokrzyskie, adm. division, Pol. 50°51′ N, 19°47′ E 152
Swift Current, Can. 50°17′ N, 107°49′ W 90
Swift River, Can. 60°2′ N, 131°13′ W 108
Swift, river, Can. 59°57′ N, 131°54′ W 108
Swindon, U.K. 51°33′ N, 1°47′ W 162
Świnoujście, Pol. 53°54′ N, 14°14′ E 152
Switz City, Ind., U.S. 39°1′ N, 87°3′ W 102
Switzerland 46°48′ N, 7°57′ E 156
Syamzha, Russ. 60°3′ N, 41°9′ E 154
Syanno, Belarus 54°48′ N, 29°46′ E 166
Syas′, river, Russ. 59°47′ N, 32°43′ E 154
Syas′stroy, Russ. 60°7′ N, 32°41′ E 154
Syava, Russ. 58°0′ N, 46°21′ E 154
Sycamore, Ga., U.S. 31°39′ N, 83°38′ W 96
Sycamore, Ill., U.S. 41°59′ N, 88°41′ W 102
Sycamore, Ohio, U.S. 40°56′ N, 83°10′ W 102
Sycewice, Pol. 54°25′ N, 16°51′ E 152
Sychevka, Russ. 55°49′ N, 34°21′ E 154
Sydney, Austral. 33°56′ S, 150°50′ E 230
Sydney, Can. 46°8′ N, 60°11′ W 111
Sydney Lake, Can. 50°40′ N, 94°47′ W 90
Syelishcha, Belarus 53°0′ N, 27°23′ E 154
Syghyndy, Kaz. 43°45′ N, 51°4′ E 195
Syktyvkar, Russ. 61°44′ N, 50°56′ E 154
Sylacauga, Ala., U.S. 33°9′ N, 86°20′ W 112
Sylarna, peak, Nor. 62°59′ N, 12°5′ E 152
Sylhet, Bangladesh 24°53′ N, 91°53′ E 197
Sylte, Nor. 62°50′ N, 7°15′ E 152
Sylva, Russ. 58°1′ N, 56°46′ E 154
Sylvan Lake, Can. 52°18′ N, 114°7′ W 108
Sylvan Pass, Wyo., U.S. 44°27′ N, 110°8′ W 90
Sylvania, Ga., U.S. 32°43′ N, 81°39′ W 96
Sylvania, Ohio, U.S. 41°42′ N, 83°42′ W 102
Sylvester, Tex., U.S. 32°43′ N, 100°17′ W 92
Sylvester, Mount, peak, Can. 48°9′ N, 55°11′ W 111
Sylvia, Mount, peak, Can. 58°5′ N, 124°32′ W 108
Sym, Russ. 60°19′ N, 88°25′ E 169
Sym, river, Russ. 60°42′ N, 87°3′ E 169
Synel′nykove, Ukr. 48°18′ N, 35°32′ E 158
Syngyrli, Mys, Kaz. 41°54′ N, 51°54′ E 158
Synnfjell, peak, Nor. 61°3′ N, 9°40′ E 152
Synnot, Mount, peak, Austral. 16°43′ S, 125°3′ E 230
Synya, Russ. 65°23′ N, 58°1′ E 154
Syowa, Japan, station, Antarctica 69°0′ S, 39°36′ E 248
Syr Darya, river, Kaz. 44°30′ N, 65°40′ E 184
Syracuse, Ind., U.S. 41°25′ N, 85°45′ W 102
Syracuse, Kans., U.S. 37°59′ N, 101°45′ W 90
Syracuse, Nebr., U.S. 40°38′ N, 96°11′ W 90
Syracuse, N.Y., U.S. 43°3′ N, 76°10′ W 94
Syracuse see Siracusa, It. 37°3′ N, 15°17′ E 156
Syria 34°59′ N, 38°11′ E 180
Syrian Desert, Iraq 32°22′ N, 37°50′ E 180
Syrian Gates, pass, Turk. 36°28′ N, 36°12′ E 156
Sýrna, island, Gr. 36°13′ N, 26°43′ E 180
Sysert′, Russ. 56°30′ N, 60°50′ E 154
Sysmä, Fin. 61°29′ N, 25°38′ E 166
Sysola, river, Russ. 61°2′ N, 50°31′ E 154
Systyg Khem, Russ. 52°52′ N, 95°43′ E 190
Sytomino, Russ. 61°18′ N, 71°21′ E 169
Syumsi, Russ. 57°5′ N, 51°42′ E 154
Syuneysale, Russ. 66°54′ N, 71°23′ E 169
Syutkya, peak, Bulg. 41°52′ N, 23°56′ E 156
Syzran′, Russ. 53°11′ N, 48°33′ E 154
Szabadszállás, Hung. 46°51′ N, 19°13′ E 168
Szabolcs-Szatmár-Bereg, adm. division, Hung. 48°6′ N, 21°43′ E 156
Szamotuły, Pol. 52°36′ N, 16°34′ E 152
Szarvas, Hung. 46°52′ N, 20°33′ E 168
Szczebra, Pol. 53°55′ N, 22°57′ E 166
Szczecin, Pol. 53°25′ N, 14°33′ E 152
Szczecinek, Pol. 53°42′ N, 16°42′ E 152
Szczuczyn, Pol. 53°33′ N, 22°14′ E 152
Szeged, Hung. 46°15′ N, 20°8′ E 168
Szeghalom, Hung. 47°1′ N, 21°9′ E 168
Szegvár, Hung. 46°35′ N, 20°14′ E 168
Székesfehérvár, Hung. 47°11′ N, 18°25′ E 168
Szekszárd, Hung. 46°20′ N, 18°42′ E 168
Szentendre, Hung. 47°39′ N, 19°6′ E 168
Szentes, Hung. 46°39′ N, 20°16′ E 168
Szentgotthárd, Hung. 46°56′ N, 16°16′ E 168
Szentl orinc, Hung. 46°2′ N, 17°59′ E 168
Szepietowo, Pol. 52°51′ N, 22°31′ E 152
Szigetvár, Hung. 46°2′ N, 17°48′ E 168
Szikszó, Hung. 48°12′ N, 20°56′ E 152
Szob, Hung. 47°48′ N, 18°54′ E 168
Szolnok, Hung. 47°11′ N, 20°11′ E 168
Szombathely, Hung. 47°14′ N, 16°39′ E 168
Szőny, Hung. 47°44′ N, 18°10′ E 168
Szőreg, Hung. 46°12′ N, 20°12′ E 168
Sztum, Pol. 53°54′ N, 19°0′ E 166
Sztutowo, Pol. 54°19′ N, 19°9′ E 166
Szulok, Hung. 46°3′ N, 17°32′ E 168
Szypliszki, Pol. 54°14′ N, 23°5′ E 166

T

Ta La, Vietnam 11°26′ N, 107°26′ E 202
Taalintehdas see Dalsbruk, Fin. 60°1′ N, 22°31′ E 166
Taavetti, Fin. 60°54′ N, 27°31′ E 166
Tab, Hung. 46°43′ N, 18°1′ E 168
Tabacal, Arg. 23°14′ S, 64°16′ W 132
Ţābah, Saudi Arabia 27°3′ N, 42°11′ E 180
Tabalak, Niger 15°3′ N, 6°0′ E 222
Tabane Lake, lake, Can. 60°33′ N, 102°21′ W 108
Tabankort, spring, Mali 17°49′ N, 0°15′ E 222
Tabanovce, Maced. 42°11′ N, 21°42′ E 168
Ţabaqat Fa'l, Jordan 32°26′ N, 35°36′ E 194
Tabar Islands, islands, P.N.G. 2°35′ S, 152°4′ E 192
Ţabas, Iran 33°35′ N, 56°54′ E 180
Ţabas, Iran 32°49′ N, 60°13′ E 180
Tabasará, Serranía de, Pan. 8°29′ N, 81°39′ W 115
Tabasco, Mex. 21°51′ N, 102°55′ W 114
Tabasco, adm. division, Mex. 18°12′ N, 93°42′ W 115
Tabatinga, Serra da, Braz. 10°53′ S, 45°27′ W 130
Tabelbala, Alg. 29°25′ N, 3°15′ W 143
Tabelkoza, Alg. 29°46′ N, 0°44′ E 214
Tabelot, Niger 17°34′ N, 8°55′ E 222
Taber, Can. 49°46′ N, 112°8′ W 90
Tabernas, Sp. 37°2′ N, 2°24′ W 164
Tabili, Dem. Rep. of the Congo 0°6′ N, 27°59′ E 224
Tablas Strait 12°28′ N, 121°16′ E 203
Tablat, Alg. 36°24′ N, 3°19′ E 150
Table, Cap de la, Can. 49°21′ N, 61°51′ W 111
Table Head, Can. 51°59′ N, 55°45′ W 111
Table Hill, peak, Austral. 14°33′ S, 129°35′ E 230
Table Mountain, peak, Alas., U.S. 68°12′ N, 144°2′ W 98
Table Mountain, peak, S. Dak., U.S. 45°51′ N, 103°46′ W 90
Table Point, Can. 50°23′ N, 58°21′ W 111
Table Rock, Nebr., U.S. 40°9′ N, 96°5′ W 94
Taboose Pass, Calif., U.S. 36°59′ N, 118°26′ W 101
Tábor, Czech Rep. 49°25′ N, 14°38′ E 152
Tabor, Russ. 71°9′ N, 150°45′ E 160
Tabor City, N.C., U.S. 34°8′ N, 78°54′ W 96
Tabora, Tanzania 5°2′ S, 32°49′ E 224
Tabora, adm. division, Tanzania 5°32′ S, 31°41′ E 224
Tabory, Russ. 58°31′ N, 64°28′ E 154
Taboshar, Taj. 40°35′ N, 69°37′ E 197
Tabou, Côte d'Ivoire 4°33′ N, 7°22′ W 222
Tabrīz, Iran 38°4′ N, 46°16′ E 195
Tabūk, Saudi Arabia 28°23′ N, 36°34′ E 180
Tabuleiro, Braz. 5°7′ S, 58°28′ W 130
Tabusintac Bay 47°18′ N, 65°36′ W 111
Tabusintac, river, Can. 47°18′ N, 65°51′ W 94
Tabuyung, Indonesia 0°51′ N, 98°59′ E 196
Täby, Sw. 59°29′ N, 18°2′ E 166
Tacalé, Braz. 1°37′ N, 54°46′ W 130
Tacámbaro, Mex. 19°13′ N, 101°28′ W 114
Tacaná, Volcán, peak, Mex. 15°8′ N, 92°14′ W 115
Tacheng, China 46°41′ N, 83°5′ E 184
Tachichilte, Isla de, island, Mex. 24°40′ N, 109°13′ W 112
Tachikawa, Japan 35°41′ N, 139°25′ E 201
Táchira, adm. division, Venez. 7°32′ N, 72°29′ W 136
Tacloban, Philippines 11°13′ N, 125°0′ E 203
Tacna, Ariz., U.S. 32°41′ N, 113°58′ W 101
Tacna, Col. 2°25′ S, 70°38′ W 136
Tacna, Peru 18°2′ S, 70°14′ W 137
Tacna, adm. division, Peru 17°46′ S, 70°53′ W 137
Taco Pozo, Arg. 25°38′ S, 63°16′ W 132
Tacoma, Wash., U.S. 47°13′ N, 122°26′ W 100
Tacuarembó, Uru. 31°45′ S, 55°59′ W 139
Tacubaya, Mex. 25°38′ N, 103°2′ W 114
Tacupeto, Mex. 28°47′ N, 109°9′ W 92
Tadami, Japan 37°21′ N, 139°18′ E 201
Tadcaster, U.K. 53°53′ N, 1°15′ W 162
Tadebyayakha, Russ. 70°26′ N, 74°21′ E 169
Tadélaka, spring, Niger 15°29′ N, 7°57′ E 222
Tademaït, Plateau du, Alg. 28°24′ N, 1°10′ E 214
Tadjakant, Mauritania 18°36′ N, 14°34′ W 222
Tadjetaret, spring, Alg. 22°39′ N, 7°52′ E 214
Tadjmout, Alg. 25°32′ N, 3°42′ E 214
Tadjoura, Djibouti 11°43′ N, 42°54′ E 216
Tadmor, N.Z. 41°28′ S, 172°46′ E 240
Tadmur, Syr. 34°32′ N, 38°19′ E 180
Tadoba National Park, India 20°18′ N, 79°12′ E 188
Tadoule Lake, Can. 58°32′ N, 99°4′ W 108
Tadoussac, Can. 48°8′ N, 69°43′ W 94
Taean, S. Korea 36°44′ N, 126°18′ E 200
T'aech'ŏn, N. Korea 39°55′ N, 125°29′ E 200
Taedong, N. Korea 40°37′ N, 125°27′ E 200
Taedong, river, N. Korea 39°51′ N, 126°37′ E 200
Taegu see Daegu, S. Korea 35°51′ N, 128°37′ E 200
Taegwan, N. Korea 40°11′ N, 125°10′ E 200
Taehŭng, N. Korea 40°5′ N, 126°56′ E 200
Taejŏn see Daejeon, S. Korea 36°18′ N, 127°27′ E 200
Taenarum see Akrotírio Ténaro, Gr. 36°13′ N, 21°38′ E 156
Ta'erqi, China 48°1′ N, 121°5′ E 198
T'aet'an, N. Korea 38°2′ N, 125°18′ E 200
Tafalla, Sp. 42°31′ N, 1°41′ W 164
Tafara, Mali 15°38′ N, 11°22′ W 222
Tafarit, Cap, Mauritania 20°0′ N, 16°12′ W 222
Ţafas, Syr. 32°43′ N, 36°3′ E 194
Tafí Viejo, Arg. 26°46′ S, 65°16′ W 134
Tafiré, Côte d'Ivoire 9°4′ N, 5°10′ W 222
Tafraout, Mor. 29°43′ N, 8°59′ W 214
Taft, Calif., U.S. 35°8′ N, 119°29′ W 100
Taft, Tex., U.S. 27°57′ N, 97°23′ W 96
Taftān, Kūh-e, peak, Iran 28°37′ N, 61°7′ E 182
Tagama, region, Niger 15°46′ N, 7°16′ E 222
Taganrog, Russ. 47°14′ N, 38°51′ E 156
Taganrogskiy Zaliv 47°0′ N, 38°41′ E 158
Tagant, region, Mauritania 17°21′ N, 12°13′ W 222
Tagarma, China 38°1′ N, 75°5′ E 184
Tagawa, Japan 33°37′ N, 130°49′ E 201
Tagbilaran, Philippines 9°40′ N, 123°52′ E 203
Taggafadi, Niger 18°31′ N, 9°14′ E 222
Taggia, It. 43°51′ N, 7°50′ E 167
Taghit, Alg. 30°58′ N, 2 0′ W 214
Tagil, river, Russ. 58°14′ N, 61°20′ E 154
Tagish, Can. 60°20′ N, 134°22′ W 108
Taglio di Po, It. 45°0′ N, 12°10′ E 167
Tagnout Chagguéret, spring, Mali 21°15′ N, 0°48′ E 222
Tagounit, Mor. 29°57′ N, 5°39′ W 214
Tagtabazar, Turkm. 35°55′ N, 62°56′ E 186
Tagua, Bol. 19°54′ S, 67°44′ W 137
Taguedoufat, spring, Niger 16°8′ N, 8°24′ E 222
Tagula, island, P.N.G. 11°20′ S, 153°16′ E 192
Tagum, Philippines 7°30′ N, 125°47′ E 203
Tagus see Tajo, river, Sp. 39°56′ N, 6°57′ W 214
Tahaetkun Mountain, peak, Can. 50°15′ N, 119°49′ W 90
Tahakopa, N.Z. 46°31′ S, 169°22′ E 240
Tahala, Mor. 34°6′ N, 4°25′ W 214
Tahan, peak, Malaysia 4°37′ N, 102°8′ E 196
Tahat, Mount, peak, Alg. 23°15′ N, 5°23′ E 214
Ţāherī, Iran 27°43′ N, 52°22′ E 196
Tahiti, island, French Polynesia, Fr. 17°38′ S, 149°25′ W 241
Tahkoluoto, Fin. 61°37′ N, 21°25′ E 166
Tahkuna Nina, Est. 59°5′ N, 22°35′ E 166
Tahlequah, Okla., U.S. 35°53′ N, 94°59′ W 96
Tahltan, Can. 58°1′ N, 131°1′ W 108
Tahltan Lake, Can. 57°56′ N, 132°22′ W 108
Tahoe City, Calif., U.S. 39°10′ N, 120°10′ W 90
Tahoka, Tex., U.S. 33°8′ N, 101°49′ W 92
Taholah, Wash., U.S. 47°18′ N, 124°17′ W 100
Tahoua, Niger 14°54′ N, 5°17′ E 222
Tahquamenon, river, Mich., U.S. 46°27′ N, 86°7′ W 94
Tahsis, Can. 49°55′ N, 126°40′ W 90
Tahtalı Dağ, peak, Turk. 38°45′ N, 36°42′ E 156
Tahtalıdaği, peak, Turk. 36°30′ N, 30°22′ E 156
Tahuamanu, river, Bol. 11°13′ S, 68°47′ W 137
Tahuamanu, river, Peru 11°7′ S, 70°52′ W 137
Tahuna, Indonesia 3°41′ N, 125°26′ E 192
Taï, Côte d'Ivoire 5°49′ N, 7°28′ W 222
Tai Hu, lake, China 31°13′ N, 120°0′ E 198
Taï National Park, Côte d'Ivoire 5°49′ N, 7°11′ W 222
Tai'an, China 36°12′ N, 117°8′ E 198
Taibai, China 34°0′ N, 107°19′ E 198
Taibei see Taipei, Taiwan, China 24°58′ N, 121°21′ E 198
Taibilla, Sierra de, Sp. 37°57′ N, 2°28′ W 164
Taibus Qi, China 41°52′ N, 115°15′ E 198
T'aichung, Taiwan, China 24°7′ N, 120°41′ E 198
Taigbe, Sierra Leone 7°25′ N, 12°23′ W 222
Taígetos, Óros, Gr. 37°10′ N, 22°10′ E 156
Taigu, China 37°26′ N, 112°30′ E 198
Taihape, N.Z. 39°42′ S, 175°46′ E 240
Taihe, China 26°47′ N, 114°50′ E 198
Taihe, China 33°12′ N, 115°36′ E 198
Taihu, China 30°26′ N, 116°15′ E 198
Taikkyee, Myanmar 17°20′ N, 95°56′ E 202
Tailai, China 46°18′ N, 123°27′ E 198
Taim, Braz. 32°30′ S, 52°38′ W 139
Taimana, Mali 13°55′ N, 6°45′ W 222
Tain, Fr. 45°4′ N, 4°50′ E 150
Tainan, Taiwan, China 22°59′ N, 120°12′ E 198
Taining, China 26°56′ N, 117°7′ E 198
Taiobeiras, Braz. 15°49′ S, 42°15′ W 138
Taipale, Fin. 62°38′ N, 29°9′ E 152
Taipei (Taibei), Taiwan, China 24°58′ N, 121°21′ E 198
Taiping, Malaysia 4°51′ N, 100°44′ E 196
Taiping Ling, peak, China 47°35′ N, 120°26′ E 198
Taipingshao, China 40°53′ N, 125°12′ E 200
Taipudia, India 27°49′ N, 94°35′ E 188
Taira, Japan 37°2′ N, 140°52′ E 201
Tairua, N.Z. 37°0′ S, 175°50′ E 240
Taisha, Japan 35°22′ N, 132°41′ E 201
Taishan, China 22°16′ N, 112°43′ E 198
Taitao, Cabo, Chile 46°0′ S, 76°26′ W 134
Taitao, Peninsula de, South America 46°27′ S, 75°28′ W 134
Taitung, Taiwan, China 22°44′ N, 121°6′ E 198
Taivalkoski, Fin. 65°34′ N, 28°13′ E 152
Taivassalo, Fin. 60°33′ N, 21°36′ E 166
Taiwan, special sovereignty, China 23°41′ N, 120°53′ E 198
Taiwan, island, Taiwan, China 24°25′ N, 121°54′ E 198
Taiwan Strait 23°49′ N, 118°3′ E 198
Taiyara, Sudan 13°8′ N, 30°45′ E 226
Taiyuan, China 37°52′ N, 112°35′ E 198
Taiyuan Space Launch Center, spaceport, China 37°33′ N, 112°32′ E 198
Taizhou, China 32°30′ N, 119°55′ E 198
Ta'izz, Yemen 13°35′ N, 44°1′ E 182
Tajar'ī, Lib. 24°21′ N, 14°12′ E 216
Tajerouine, Tun. 35°53′ N, 8°33′ E 156
Tajikistan 38°32′ N, 69°13′ E 184
Tajima, Japan 37°11′ N, 139°46′ E 201
Tajimi, Japan 35°18′ N, 137°10′ E 201
Tajo, river, Sp. 40°5′ N, 3°6′ W 164
Tajo (Tagus), river, Sp. 39°56′ N, 6°57′ W 214
Tajrīsh, Iran 35°52′ N, 51°35′ E 180
Tajumulco, Volcán, peak, Guatemala 15°0′ N, 92°0′ W 115
Tak, Thai. 16°52′ N, 99°7′ E 202
Takāb, Iran 36°27′ N, 47°5′ E 195
Takaba, Kenya 3°20′ N, 40°10′ E 224
Takahashi, Japan 34°48′ N, 133°37′ E 201
Takahe, Mount, peak, Antarctica 76°12′ S, 111°45′ W 248
Takajō, Japan 31°47′ N, 131°7′ E 201
Takaka, N.Z. 40°54′ S, 172°50′ E 240
Takamatsu, Japan 34°20′ N, 134°2′ E 201
Takamori, Japan 32°48′ N, 131°7′ E 201
Takanabe, Japan 32°7′ N, 131°29′ E 201
Takaoka, Japan 36°44′ N, 137°1′ E 201
Takapau, N.Z. 40°4′ S, 176°22′ E 240
Takasaki, Japan 36°18′ N, 139°0′ E 201
Takatsu, Japan 34°40′ N, 131°48′ E 200
Takaungu, Kenya 3°43′ S, 39°51′ E 224
Tā-kaw, Myanmar 21°15′ N, 98°39′ E 202
Takayama, Japan 36°8′ N, 137°16′ E 201
Takefu, Japan 35°53′ N, 136°10′ E 201
Takengon, Indonesia 4°38′ N, 96°49′ E 196
Takeo, Cambodia 10°58′ N, 104°47′ E 202
Takeo, Japan 33°11′ N, 130°1′ E 201
Tākestān, Iran 36°6′ N, 49°39′ E 180
Taketa, Japan 32°57′ N, 131°24′ E 201
Takhiatosh, Uzb. 42°20′ N, 59°36′ E 180
Takhini, Can. 60°51′ N, 135°25′ W 108
Takhta, Russ. 45°51′ N, 41°58′ E 158
Takiéta, Niger 13°41′ N, 8°31′ E 222
Takijuq Lake, Can. 66°22′ N, 115°33′ W 106
Takipy, Can. 55°24′ N, 100°58′ W 108
Takla Lake, Can. 55°9′ N, 126°12′ W 108
Takla Landing, Can. 55°28′ N, 125°59′ W 108
Taklimakan Shamo, China 39°27′ N, 77°39′ E 184
Takotna, Alas., U.S. 62°59′ N, 156°4′ W 98
Taksa Bor, Russ. 67°4′ N, 34°40′ E 152
Taku, river, Can. 58°39′ N, 133°35′ W 108
Takua Pa, Thai. 8°53′ N, 98°20′ E 202
Takum, India 27°48′ N, 93°37′ E 188
Takum, Nig. 7°13′ N, 9°57′ E 222
Takwa, river, Can. 51°32′ N, 72°10′ W 110
Tal, Pak. 35°28′ N, 72°14′ E 186
Tala, Mex. 20°38′ N, 103°40′ W 114
Tala, Tun. 35°32′ N, 8°38′ E 156
Talachyn, Belarus 54°24′ N, 29°42′ E 166
Talaimannar, Sri Lanka 9°6′ N, 79°42′ E 188
Talak, region, Niger 18°15′ N, 4°51′ E 222
Talara, Peru 4°37′ S, 81°13′ W 123
Talas, Kyrg. 42°27′ N, 72°33′ E 197
Talas, river, Kyrg. 42°37′ N, 71°44′ E 197
Talâta, Egypt 30°35′ N, 32°20′ E 194
Talata Mafara, Nig. 12°33′ N, 6°2′ E 222
Talaud, Kepulauan, islands, Philippine Sea 4°1′ N, 127°6′ E 192
Talavera de la Reina, Sp. 39°57′ N, 4°51′ W 150
Talavera la Real, Sp. 38°52′ N, 6°48′ W 164
Talayón, peak, Sp. 37°32′ N, 1°34′ W 164
Talayuelas, Sp. 39°51′ N, 1°17′ W 164
Talbahat, India 25°2′ N, 78°27′ E 197
Talbert, Sillon de, English Channel 48°54′ N, 3°10′ W 150
Talbot, Cape, Austral. 13°51′ S, 123°45′ E 172
Talbot, Mount, peak, Austral. 26°10′ S, 126°25′ E 230
Talca, Chile 35°25′ S, 71°41′ W 134
Talcahuano, Chile 36°45′ S, 73°7′ W 134
Talco, Tex., U.S. 33°20′ N, 95°6′ W 103
Taldyq, Kaz. 49°18′ N, 59°52′ E 158
Taldyqorghan, Kaz. 44°59′ N, 78°22′ E 184
Taleex, Somalia 9°10′ N, 48°25′ E 216
Talgarth, U.K. 51°59′ N, 3°13′ W 162
Talguharai, Sudan 18°14′ N, 35°52′ E 182
Tali Post, Sudan 5°54′ N, 30°48′ E 224
Taliabu, island, Indonesia 2°22′ S, 124°26′ E 192
Talibong, Ko, island, Thai. 7°10′ N, 98°36′ E 196
Talitsa, Russ. 61°8′ N, 60°28′ E 154
Talitsa, Russ. 58°2′ N, 51°32′ E 154
Talitsa, Russ. 56°59′ N, 63°44′ E 154
Talkot, Nepal 29°33′ N, 81°18′ E 197
Tall Abū Ẓahir, Iraq 36°29′ N, 42°23′ E 195
Tall 'Afar, Iraq 36°22′ N, 42°19′ E 195
Tall as Sulţān, ruin(s), West Bank, Israel 31°52′ N, 35°24′ E 194
Tall Birāk, Syr. 36°39′ N, 41°6′ E 195
Tall Bīsah, Syr. 34°50′ N, 36°43′ E 194
Tall Ḩalaf, ruin(s), Syr. 36°46′ N, 40°1′ E 195
Tall Kalakh, Syr. 34°40′ N, 36°16′ E 194
Tall Kayf, Iraq 36°30′ N, 43°1′ E 195
Tall Kūjik, Syr. 36°48′ N, 42°1′ E 195
Tall Tamir, Syr. 36°38′ N, 40°25′ E 195
Tall Trees Grove, site, Calif., U.S. 41°12′ N, 124°4′ W 90
Tallahassee, Fla., U.S. 30°24′ N, 84°23′ W 96
Tallaringa Well, spring, Austral. 29°0′ S, 133°24′ E 230
Tallassee, Ala., U.S. 32°31′ N, 85°54′ W 96
Tällberg, Nor. 60°48′ N, 14°59′ E 152
Talley, U.K. 51°58′ N, 3°59′ W 162
Tallinn, Est. 59°23′ N, 24°47′ E 160
Tallinn (Reval), Est. 59°23′ N, 24°37′ E 166
Tallmadge, Ohio, U.S. 41°5′ N, 81°26′ W 102
Tallulah, La., U.S. 32°23′ N, 91°12′ W 103
Talmage, Calif., U.S. 39°8′ N, 123°10′ W 90
Talmine, Alg. 29°21′ N, 0°29′ E 214
Talnakh, Russ. 69°28′ N, 88°34′ E 169
Tal'ne, Ukr. 48°51′ N, 30°49′ E 158
Talo, peak, Eth. 10°38′ N, 37°55′ E 224
Talodi, Sudan 10°35′ N, 30°24′ E 224
Taloga, Okla., U.S. 36°1′ N, 98°58′ W 92
Talon, Russ. 59°47′ N, 148°39′ E 173
Taloqan, Afghan. 36°45′ N, 69°31′ E 186
Talorha, Mauritania 18°52′ N, 12°23′ W 222
Talos Dome, Antarctica 73°6′ S, 161°47′ E 248
Taloyoak, Can. 69°25′ N, 93°20′ W 106
Talpa de Allende, Mex. 20°26′ N, 104°50′ W 114
Talshand, Mongolia 45°20′ N, 97°55′ E 190
Talsi, Latv. 57°14′ N, 22°34′ E 166
Talsint, Mor. 32°34′ N, 3°27′ W 214
Taltal, Chile 25°25′ S, 70°30′ W 132
Taltson, river, Can. 60°34′ N, 111°59′ W 108
Talu, Indonesia 0°14′ N, 100°0′ E 196
Taluk, Indonesia 0°33′ S, 101°33′ E 196
Talvik, Nor. 70°2′ N, 22°54′ E 152
Talybont, U.K. 52°28′ N, 3°59′ W 162
Talyllyn, U.K. 52°38′ N, 3°53′ W 162
Tam Ky, Vietnam 15°34′ N, 108°29′ E 202
Tam Quan, Vietnam 14°34′ N, 109°1′ E 202
Tamada, spring, Alg. 21°37′ N, 3°10′ E 222
Tamala, Russ. 52°32′ N, 43°14′ E 158
Tamalameque, Col. 8°51′ N, 73°48′ W 136
Tamale, Ghana 9°24′ N, 0°52′ E 222
Tamale Port see Yapei, Ghana 9°10′ N, 1°11′ W 222
Taman′, Russ. 45°13′ N, 36°40′ E 156
Taman Negara National Park, Malaysia 4°30′ N, 102°51′ E 196
Tamana, Japan 32°55′ N, 130°33′ E 201
Tamanar, Mor. 30°59′ N, 9°41′ W 214
Tamánco, Peru 5°48′ S, 74°18′ W 130
Tamano, Japan 34°29′ N, 133°55′ E 201
Tamanrasset, Alg. 22°48′ N, 5°18′ E 207
Támara, Col. 5°47′ N, 72°10′ W 136
Tamarugal, Pampa del, Chile 20°34′ S, 69°24′ W 132
Tamashima, Japan 34°32′ N, 133°39′ E 201
Tamási, Hung. 46°38′ N, 18°16′ E 168
Tamaulipas, adm. division, Mex. 24°20′ N, 99°35′ W 114
Tamaulipas, Sierra de, Mex. 23°9′ N, 98°45′ W 112
Tamaya, river, Peru 8°59′ S, 74°11′ W 137
Tamayya, Africa 23°56′ N, 15°42′ W 214
Tamazula, Mex. 19°39′ N, 103°15′ W 114
Tamazula, Mex. 24°55′ N, 106°57′ W 114
Tamazulapan, Mex. 17°38′ N, 97°34′ W 114
Tamazunchale, Mex. 21°12′ N, 98°48′ W 114
Tambach, Kenya 0°35′ N, 35°33′ E 224
Tambacounda, Senegal 13°46′ N, 13°43′ W 222
Tambaga, Mali 13°0′ N, 9°53′ W 222
Tambaqui, Braz. 5°15′ S, 62°50′ W 130
Tambelan Besar, island, Indonesia 0°49′ N, 106°57′ E 196
Tambey, Russ. 71°30′ N, 71°56′ E 173
Tambo de Mora, Peru 13°32′ S, 76°12′ W 130
Tambo, river, Peru 10°48′ S, 73°53′ W 137
Tambo, river, Peru 17°4′ S, 71°21′ W 137
Tamboril, Braz. 4°50′ S, 40°22′ W 132
Tambov, Russ. 52°41′ N, 41°19′ E 154
Tambov, adm. division, Russ. 53°5′ N, 40°14′ E 154
Tambunan, Malaysia 5°41′ N, 116°20′ E 203
Tambura, Sudan 5°34′ N, 27°29′ E 218
Tamchaket, Mauritania 17°16′ N, 10°44′ W 222
Tamel Aike, Arg. 48°18′ S, 70°57′ W 134
Tamesí, river, Mex. 22°26′ N, 98°27′ W 114
Tamesna, region, Niger 18°45′ N, 4°10′ E 222
Tamgak, Adrar, peak, Niger 19°11′ N, 8°37′ E 222
Tamgrout, Mor. 30°19′ N, 5°45′ W 214
Tamgué, Guinea 12°18′ N, 12°21′ W 222
Tamiahua, Mex. 21°14′ N, 97°27′ W 114
Tamiahua, Laguna de 21°29′ N, 98°2′ W 114
Tamil Nadu, adm. division, India 9°23′ N, 77°23′ E 188
Tamīnah, Lib. 32°16′ N, 15°3′ E 216
Tamins, Switz. 46°50′ N, 9°23′ E 167
Tamitatoala (Batovi), river, Braz. 14°11′ S, 53°58′ W 132
Tamitsa, Russ. 64°10′ N, 38°5′ E 154
Tammerfors see Tampere, Fin. 61°29′ N, 23°43′ E 166
Tammisaari see Ekenäs, Fin. 59°58′ N, 23°26′ E 166
Tampa, Fla., U.S. 27°58′ N, 82°26′ W 105
Tampa Bay 27°37′ N, 83°17′ W 80
Tampere, Fin. 61°23′ N, 23°51′ E 160
Tampere (Tammerfors), Fin. 61°29′ N, 23°43′ E 166
Tampico, Ill., U.S. 41°37′ N, 89°48′ W 102
Tampico, Mex. 22°11′ N, 97°51′ W 112
Tampin, Malaysia 2°29′ N, 102°12′ E 196
Tamrida see Hadīboh, Yemen 12°37′ N, 53°49′ E 173
Tamsagbulag, Mongolia 47°13′ N, 117°15′ E 198
Tamsalu, Est. 59°7′ N, 26°5′ E 166
Tamshiyacu, Peru 4°1′ S, 73°6′ W 130
Tamu, Myanmar 24°10′ N, 94°19′ E 188
Tamuín, Mex. 21°59′ N, 98°46′ W 114
Tamuning, U.S. 13°28′ N, 144°46′ E 242
Tamur, river, Nepal 26°56′ N, 87°39′ E 197
Tamworth, N.H., U.S. 43°51′ N, 71°17′ W 104
Tamworth, U.K. 52°39′ N, 1°42′ W 162
Tan An, Vietnam 10°32′ N, 106°25′ E 202
Tan Quang, Vietnam 22°30′ N, 104°51′ E 202
Tana, Nor. 70°27′ N, 28°15′ E 152
Tana, Lake, Eth. 11°57′ N, 35°26′ E 206
Tana, river, Europe 68°26′ N, 25°33′ E 160
Tana, river, Kenya 1°27′ S, 40°7′ E 224
Tanabe, Japan 33°43′ N, 135°23′ E 201
Tanacross, Alas., U.S. 63°14′ N, 143°23′ W 98
Tanafjorden 70°37′ N, 25°20′ E 160
Tanaga, island, Alas., U.S. 51°25′ N, 178°58′ W 160
Tanagra, ruin(s), Gr. 38°19′ N, 23°26′ E 156
Tanagura, Japan 37°1′ N, 140°23′ E 201
Tanah Merah, Malaysia 5°48′ N, 102°7′ E 196
Tanahbala, island, Indonesia 0°38′ N, 97°40′ E 196
Tanahgrogot, Indonesia 1°56′ S, 116°11′ E 192
Tanahmasa, island, Indonesia 0°18′ N, 98°33′ E 196
Tanahmerah, Indonesia 3°44′ N, 117°33′ E 192
Tanahmerah, Indonesia 6°14′ S, 140°17′ E 192
Tanakpur, India 29°4′ N, 80°3′ E 197
Tanalyk, river, Russ. 52°38′ N, 58°2′ E 154
Tanama, river, Russ. 69°45′ N, 78°33′ E 169
Tanami Desert, Austral. 19°13′ S, 130°40′ E 230
Tanami, Mount, peak, Austral. 19°59′ S, 129°25′ E 230
Tanana, Alas., U.S. 65°3′ N, 152°16′ W 98
Tanana, river, Alas., U.S. 63°31′ N, 144°53′ W 98
Tancheng, China 34°36′ N, 118°23′ E 198

Tigre, river, *Peru* 3°28′ S, 74°47′ W **136**
Tigre, river, *Venez.* 8°56′ N, 63°10′ W **116**
Tigris (Dicle, Dijlah), river, *Iraq* 32°8′ N, 46°36′ E **180**
Tiguent, *Mauritania* 17°17′ N, 16°7′ W **222**
Tiguentourine, oil field, *Alg.* 27°44′ N, 9°4′ E **214**
Tiguidit, Falaise de, region, *Niger* 16°40′ N, 6°58′ E **222**
Tigyaing, *Myanmar* 23°45′ N, 96°3′ E **202**
Tīh, Gebel el, *Egypt* 29°35′ N, 33°0′ E **180**
Tihany, *Hung.* 46°54′ N, 17°53′ E **168**
Tihosuco, *Mex.* 20°12′ N, 88°26′ W **115**
Tihuatlán, *Mex.* 20°41′ N, 97°33′ W **114**
Tijamré, spring, *Mauritania* 20°18′ N, 11°16′ W **222**
Tijesno, *Croatia* 43°47′ N, 15°38′ E **156**
Tíjola, *Sp.* 37°19′ N, 2°26′ W **164**
Tijti, spring, *Mauritania* 17°52′ N, 7°15′ W **222**
Tijuana, *Mex.* 32°31′ N, 117°4′ W **101**
Tijucas, *Braz.* 27°16′ S, 48°39′ W **138**
Tijucas do Sul, *Braz.* 25°57′ S, 49°12′ W **138**
Tikal National Park, *Guatemala* 17°13′ N, 90°10′ W **115**
Tikamgarh, *India* 24°44′ N, 78°50′ E **197**
Tikanlik, *China* 40°40′ N, 87°40′ E **188**
Tikaré, *Burkina Faso* 13°16′ N, 1°44′ W **222**
Tikattane, *Mauritania* 19°2′ N, 16°15′ W **222**
Tikhmanga, *Russ.* 61°14′ N, 38°31′ E **154**
Tikhoretsk, *Russ.* 45°52′ N, 40°5′ E **158**
Tikhtozero, *Russ.* 65°33′ N, 30°31′ E **154**
Tikhvin, *Russ.* 59°38′ N, 33°32′ E **154**
Tikitiki, *N.Z.* 37°48′ S, 178°23′ E **240**
Tikkurila, *Fin.* 60°16′ N, 24°58′ E **166**
Tiko, *Cameroon* 4°5′ N, 9°21′ E **222**
Tikshozero, *Russ.* 64°6′ N, 31°47′ E **152**
Tikshozero, *Russ.* 66°0′ N, 32°23′ E **152**
Tiksi, *Russ.* 71°22′ N, 128°46′ E **160**
Tilaiya Dam, *India* 24°20′ N, 85°35′ E **197**
Tilamuta, *Indonesia* 0°34′ N, 122°17′ E **192**
Tilatou, *Alg.* 35°19′ N, 5°47′ E **150**
Tilburg, *Neth.* 51°33′ N, 5°4′ E **163**
Tilbury, *Can.* 42°15′ N, 82°27′ W **102**
Tilbury, *U.K.* 51°27′ N, 0°21′ E **162**
Til-Châtel, *Fr.* 47°30′ N, 5°9′ E **150**
Tilden, *Nebr., U.S.* 42°1′ N, 97°50′ W **90**
Tileagd, *Rom.* 47°3′ N, 22°14′ E **168**
Tilemsoun, *Mor.* 28°13′ N, 10°57′ W **214**
Tilichiki, *Russ.* 60°28′ N, 165°53′ E **160**
Tillabéri, *Niger* 14°12′ N, 1°26′ E **222**
Tillamook, *Oreg., U.S.* 45°27′ N, 123°51′ W **90**
Tillamook Head, *Oreg., U.S.* 45°56′ N, 124°9′ W **100**
Tillanchang Dwip, island, *India* 8°34′ N, 93°43′ E **188**
Tillia, *Niger* 15°53′ N, 4°35′ E **222**
Tilloo Cay, island, *Bahamas* 26°33′ N, 76°56′ W **116**
Tillson, *N.Y., U.S.* 41°49′ N, 74°5′ W **104**
Tillsonburg, *Can.* 42°51′ N, 80°43′ W **102**
Tílos, island, *Gr.* 36°24′ N, 27°25′ E **180**
Tilpa, *Austral.* 30°56′ S, 144°26′ E **231**
Tilrhemt, *Alg.* 33°11′ N, 3°21′ E **214**
Tiltagals, *Latv.* 56°33′ N, 26°39′ E **166**
Tilton, *Ill., U.S.* 40°5′ N, 87°40′ W **102**
Tilton, *N.H., U.S.* 43°26′ N, 71°36′ W **104**
Tilža, *Latv.* 56°53′ N, 27°21′ E **166**
Tim, *Russ.* 51°34′ N, 37°9′ E **158**
Ţima, *Egypt* 26°55′ N, 31°21′ E **180**
Timanskiy Kryazh, *Russ.* 65°21′ N, 50°38′ E **154**
Timaru, *N.Z.* 44°24′ S, 171°13′ E **240**
Timashevo, *Russ.* 53°22′ N, 51°5′ E **154**
Timashevsk, *Russ.* 45°40′ N, 38°58′ E **156**
Timbáki, *Gr.* 35°2′ N, 24°44′ E **180**
Timbalier Bay 29°8′ N, 90°33′ W **103**
Timbalier Island, *La., U.S.* 28°57′ N, 90°34′ W **103**
Timbedgha, *Mauritania* 16°16′ N, 8°12′ W **222**
Timber, *Oreg., U.S.* 45°42′ N, 123°19′ W **100**
Timber Bay, *Can.* 54°9′ N, 105°40′ W **108**
Timber Lake, *S. Dak., U.S.* 45°25′ N, 101°6′ W **90**
Timber Mountain, peak, *Calif., U.S.* 41°37′ N, 121°23′ W **90**
Timber Mountain, peak, *Nev., U.S.* 37°2′ N, 116°30′ W **101**
Timbío, *Col.* 2°17′ N, 76°43′ W **136**
Timbiquí, *Col.* 2°41′ N, 77°45′ W **136**
Timbo, *Guinea* 10°37′ N, 11°52′ W **222**
Timbo, *Liberia* 5°31′ N, 9°42′ W **222**
Timbuktu see Tombouctou, *Mali* 16°44′ N, 3°2′ W **222**
Timeïaouine, spring, *Alg.* 20°28′ N, 1°48′ E **222**
Timelloukine, spring, *Alg.* 29°15′ N, 8°55′ E **214**
Timerein, *Sudan* 16°58′ N, 36°29′ E **182**
Timétrine, region, *Mali* 19°15′ N, 1°20′ W **222**
Tímfi, Óros, peak, *Gr.* 39°58′ N, 20°43′ E **156**
Timgad, ruin(s), *Alg.* 35°25′ N, 6°21′ E **150**
Timia, *Niger* 18°3′ N, 8°39′ E **222**
Timiş, adm. division, *Rom.* 45°49′ N, 20°44′ E **156**
Timimoun, *Alg.* 29°6′ N, 0°13′ E **207**
Timiris, Cap (Mirik), *Mauritania* 19°28′ N, 16°53′ W **222**
Timiryazevskiy, *Russ.* 56°28′ N, 84°44′ E **169**
Timiskaming, Lake, *Can.* 47°15′ N, 80°13′ W **94**
Timişoara, *Rom.* 45°46′ N, 21°14′ E **168**
Timkapaul', *Russ.* 61°29′ N, 62°16′ E **169**
Timmiarmiut 62°33′ N, 42°19′ W **106**
Timmins, *Can.* 48°29′ N, 81°16′ W **82**
Timms Hill, peak, *Wis., U.S.* 45°25′ N, 90°16′ W **94**
Timon, *Braz.* 5°6′ S, 42°53′ W **132**
Timor, island, *Indonesia* 9°36′ S, 122°49′ E **192**
Timor Sea 11°14′ S, 126°40′ E **192**
Timor-Leste (East Timor) 9°0′ S, 125°0′ E **192**
Timote, *Arg.* 35°20′ S, 62°15′ W **139**
Timpanogos Cave National Monument, *Utah, U.S.* 40°25′ N, 111°46′ W **90**
Timpson, *Tex., U.S.* 31°53′ N, 94°23′ W **103**
Timrå, *Nor.* 62°28′ N, 17°17′ E **152**
Tin Féraré, spring, *Mali* 15°6′ N, 0°53′ E **222**
Tin Fouye, oil field, *Alg.* 28°31′ N, 7°20′ E **214**
Tin Mountain, peak, *Calif., U.S.* 36°52′ N, 117°33′ W **92**
Tīna, Khalīg el 31°3′ N, 32°35′ E **194**
Tina, Mont, peak, *Dem. Rep. of the Congo* 2°56′ N, 28°32′ E **224**
Tinaca Point, *Philippines* 5°25′ N, 125°1′ E **203**
Tinaco, *Venez.* 9°41′ N, 68°28′ W **136**
Ti-n-Assamert, spring, *Mali* 16°12′ N, 0°30′ E **222**
Ti-n-Brahim, spring, *Mauritania* 19°31′ N, 15°58′ W **222**
Tinca, *Rom.* 46°46′ N, 21°58′ E **168**
Tinde see Jomu, *Tanzania* 3°53′ S, 33°11′ E **224**
Ti-n-Deïla, spring, *Mauritania* 17°59′ N, 15°32′ W **222**
Tindel, spring, *Mauritania* 17°0′ N, 12°57′ W **222**
Tindouf, *Alg.* 27°43′ N, 8°9′ W **143**
Tiné, *Chad* 14°59′ N, 22°47′ E **216**
Ti-n-Essako, spring, *Mali* 18°25′ N, 2°29′ E **222**
Ti-n-Ethisane, spring, *Mali* 19°2′ N, 0°50′ E **222**
Tinfouchy, spring, *Alg.* 28°53′ N, 5°49′ W **214**
Tinfunque National Park, *Parag.* 24°3′ S, 60°28′ W **122**
Tinggi, island, *Malaysia* 2°21′ N, 103°58′ E **196**
Tingo María National Park, *Peru* 9°13′ S, 76°11′ W **130**
Tingréla, *Côte d'Ivoire* 10°30′ N, 6°25′ W **222**
Tingri (Xêgar), *China* 28°40′ N, 87°3′ E **197**
Tingsryd, *Nor.* 56°31′ N, 14°59′ E **152**
Tingstäde, *Sw.* 57°44′ N, 18°36′ E **166**
Tinkisso, river, *Guinea* 11°27′ N, 10°6′ W **222**
Tinn, *Nor.* 59°58′ N, 8°44′ E **152**
Tinniswood, Mount, peak, *Can.* 50°18′ N, 123°52′ W **100**
Tinogasta, *Arg.* 28°5′ S, 67°34′ W **132**
Tinombo, *Indonesia* 0°24′ N, 120°13′ E **192**
Ti-n-Orfane, *Mali* 16°30′ N, 2°15′ W **222**
Tiñoso, Cabo, *Sp.* 37°25′ N, 1°15′ W **164**
Ti-n-Rerhoh, spring, *Alg.* 20°45′ N, 4°1′ E **222**
Tinrhert, Hamada de, *Lib.* 28°3′ N, 6°55′ E **206**
Tinsley, *Miss., U.S.* 32°42′ N, 90°28′ W **103**
Tinsukia, *India* 27°29′ N, 95°22′ E **188**
Tintagel (King Arthur's Castle), site, *U.K.* 50°39′ N, 4°49′ W **150**
Tintane, spring, *Mauritania* 20°51′ N, 16°32′ W **222**
Ti-n-Taourdi, spring, *Alg.* 22°46′ N, 8°0′ E **214**
Tintina, *Arg.* 27°1′ S, 62°43′ W **139**
Tinto Hills, peak, *U.K.* 55°34′ N, 3°47′ W **150**
Ti-n-Toumma, region, *Niger* 16°27′ N, 12°0′ E **222**
Tinui, *N.Z.* 40°54′ S, 176°5′ E **240**
Ti-n-Zaouâtene (Fort Pierre Bordes), *Alg.* 19°58′ N, 2°57′ E **222**
Tioga, *La., U.S.* 31°22′ N, 92°26′ W **103**
Tioga, *N. Dak., U.S.* 48°23′ N, 102°57′ W **90**
Tioga Pass, *Calif., U.S.* 37°54′ N, 119°16′ W **100**
Tioman, peak, *Malaysia* 2°47′ N, 104°4′ E **196**
Tionaga, *Can.* 48°5′ N, 82°6′ W **94**
Tip Top Mountain, peak, *Can.* 48°16′ N, 86°4′ W **94**
Tipitapa, *Nicar.* 12°9′ N, 86°4′ W **115**
Tipp City, *Ohio, U.S.* 39°57′ N, 84°10′ W **102**
Tippecanoe, *Ind., U.S.* 41°11′ N, 86°7′ W **102**
Tipton, *Calif., U.S.* 36°3′ N, 119°20′ W **100**
Tipton, *Ind., U.S.* 40°17′ N, 86°2′ W **102**
Tipton, *Iowa, U.S.* 41°45′ N, 91°8′ W **110**
Tipton, *Mich., U.S.* 42°0′ N, 84°4′ W **102**
Tipton, *Okla., U.S.* 34°28′ N, 99°9′ W **92**
Tipton, Mount, peak, *Ariz., U.S.* 35°31′ N, 114°13′ W **101**
Tipuani, *Bol.* 15°35′ S, 68°0′ W **137**
Tiputini, river, *Ecua.* 1°6′ S, 77°6′ W **136**
Tiquicheo, *Mex.* 18°52′ N, 100°45′ W **114**
Tiquié, river, *Braz.* 0°7′ N, 69°41′ W **136**
Tir Pol, *Afghan.* 34°38′ N, 61°20′ E **180**
Tiracambu, Serra do, *Braz.* 3°36′ S, 46°54′ W **130**
Tīrān, island, *Egypt* 27°57′ N, 34°5′ E **180**
Tirana see Tiranë, *Alban.* 41°19′ N, 19°41′ E **156**
Tiranë (Tirana), *Alban.* 41°19′ N, 19°41′ E **156**
Tirano, *It.* 46°12′ N, 10°9′ E **167**
Tiraspol, *Mold.* 46°49′ N, 29°37′ E **156**
Tirat Karmel, *Israel* 32°45′ N, 34°58′ E **194**
Tire, *Turk.* 38°3′ N, 27°42′ E **156**
Tiream, *Rom.* 47°37′ N, 22°29′ E **168**
Tirebolu, *Turk.* 41°0′ N, 38°46′ E **195**
Tirest, spring, *Mali* 20°21′ N, 1°6′ E **222**
Tîrgovişte, *Rom.* 44°57′ N, 25°26′ E **156**
Tîrgu Jiu, *Rom.* 45°1′ N, 23°18′ E **168**
Tîrguşor, *Rom.* 44°28′ N, 28°24′ E **158**
Tirich Mir, peak, *Pak.* 36°16′ N, 71°46′ E **186**
Tiririne, spring, *Alg.* 23°34′ N, 8°31′ E **214**
Tirlyanskiy, *Russ.* 54°14′ N, 58°28′ E **154**
Tîrnova, *Mold.* 48°9′ N, 27°39′ E **152**
Tîrnova, *Rom.* 45°19′ N, 21°59′ E **168**
Tiroungoulou, *Cen. Af. Rep.* 9°34′ N, 22°8′ E **216**
Tirthahalli, *India* 13°42′ N, 75°14′ E **188**
Tiruchchirappalli, *India* 10°48′ N, 78°41′ E **188**
Tirunelveli, *India* 8°44′ N, 77°40′ E **188**
Tiruntán, *Peru* 7°56′ S, 74°56′ W **130**
Tiryns, ruin(s), *Gr.* 37°35′ N, 22°42′ E **156**
Tisaiyanvilai, *India* 8°20′ N, 77°49′ E **188**
Tisdale, *Can.* 52°50′ N, 104°4′ W **108**
Tishomingo, *Okla., U.S.* 34°13′ N, 96°40′ W **92**
Tiskilwa, *Ill., U.S.* 41°17′ N, 89°31′ W **102**
Tissamaharama, *Sri Lanka* 6°17′ N, 81°18′ E **188**
Tissemsilt, *Alg.* 35°36′ N, 1°49′ E **150**
Tissint, *Mor.* 29°53′ N, 7°20′ W **214**
Tista, river, *India* 25°59′ N, 89°9′ E **197**
Tisul', *Russ.* 55°43′ N, 88°25′ E **169**
Tisza, river, *Hung.* 46°31′ N, 20°4′ E **156**
Tiszacsege, *Hung.* 47°40′ N, 20°58′ E **168**
Tiszaföldvár, *Hung.* 46°59′ N, 20°15′ E **168**
Tiszafüred, *Hung.* 47°37′ N, 20°45′ E **168**
Tiszakürt, *Hung.* 46°53′ N, 20°8′ E **168**
Tiszanána, *Hung.* 47°32′ N, 20°32′ E **168**
Tiszaug, *Hung.* 46°50′ N, 20°2′ E **168**
Tiszaújváros, *Hung.* 47°53′ N, 21°2′ E **168**
Tit, *Alg.* 26°56′ N, 1°30′ E **214**
Titaf, *Alg.* 27°27′ N, 0°12′ E **214**
Titan Dome, *Antarctica* 88°11′ S, 165°43′ W **248**
Titel, *Serb.* 45°12′ N, 20°17′ E **168**
Titicaca, Lago, lake, *Peru* 15°34′ S, 70°43′ W **122**
Titu, *Rom.* 44°40′ N, 25°31′ E **158**
Titule, *Dem. Rep. of the Congo* 3°12′ N, 25°32′ E **224**
Titusville, *Fla., U.S.* 28°36′ N, 80°50′ W **105**
Titusville, *Pa., U.S.* 41°37′ N, 79°41′ W **94**
Tivaouane, *Senegal* 14°57′ N, 16°38′ W **222**
Tivat, *Mont.* 42°26′ N, 18°41′ E **168**
Tiverton, *U.K.* 50°54′ N, 3°28′ W **162**
Tivissa, *Sp.* 41°2′ N, 0°44′ E **164**
Tivoli, *N.Y., U.S.* 42°3′ N, 73°55′ W **104**
Tiwai Point, *N.Z.* 46°35′ S, 168°23′ E **240**
Tiwanacu, *Bol.* 16°38′ S, 68°43′ W **137**
Tixtla, *Mex.* 17°32′ N, 99°23′ W **114**
Tizayuca, *Mex.* 19°49′ N, 98°57′ W **114**
Tizi Ouzou, *Alg.* 36°42′ N, 4°3′ E **150**
Tizimín, *Mex.* 21°7′ N, 88°11′ W **116**
Tiznit, *Mor.* 29°42′ N, 9°45′ W **214**
Tjåmotis, *Nor.* 66°54′ N, 18°39′ E **152**
Tlacotalpan, *Mex.* 18°37′ N, 95°40′ W **114**
Tlahualilo de Zaragoza, *Mex.* 26°6′ N, 103°27′ W **114**
Tlajomulco, *Mex.* 20°27′ N, 103°28′ W **114**
Tlalnepantla, *Mex.* 19°31′ N, 99°11′ W **114**
Tlapa, *Mex.* 17°31′ N, 98°34′ W **114**
Tlapacoyan, *Mex.* 19°57′ N, 97°13′ W **114**
Tlaquepaque, *Mex.* 20°37′ N, 103°19′ W **112**
Tlaxcala, *Mex.* 19°15′ N, 98°19′ W **114**
Tlaxcala, adm. division, *Mex.* 19°30′ N, 98°38′ W **114**
Tlaxiaco, *Mex.* 17°15′ N, 97°42′ W **114**
Tlell, *Can.* 53°36′ N, 131°59′ W **108**
Tlemcen, *Alg.* 34°51′ N, 1°18′ W **214**
Tleta, *Alg.* 36°47′ N, 5°52′ E **150**
Tlīsan, spring, *Lib.* 28°27′ N, 17°28′ E **216**
Tlyarata, *Russ.* 42°3′ N, 46°22′ E **195**
Tmassah, *Lib.* 26°22′ N, 15°46′ E **216**
Tni Haïa, spring, *Alg.* 24°20′ N, 2°45′ W **214**
Toad River, *Can.* 58°50′ N, 125°15′ W **108**
Toadlena, *N. Mex., U.S.* 36°13′ N, 108°53′ W **92**
Toahayana, *Mex.* 26°8′ N, 107°42′ W **112**
Toamasina, *Madagascar* 18°8′ S, 49°22′ E **220**
Toana Range, *Nev., U.S.* 40°45′ N, 114°29′ W **90**
Toano, *It.* 44°22′ N, 10°33′ E **167**
Toast, *N.C., U.S.* 36°28′ N, 80°39′ W **96**
Toay, *Arg.* 36°41′ S, 64°23′ W **134**
Toba, *Japan* 34°27′ N, 136°51′ E **201**
Toba, Danau, lake, *Indonesia* 2°47′ N, 98°39′ E **196**
Toba Inlet 50°19′ N, 124°52′ W **90**
Toba, river, *Can.* 50°35′ N, 124°16′ W **108**
Tobacco Root Mountains, *Mont., U.S.* 45°25′ N, 112°19′ W **90**
Tobago, island, *Trinidad and Tobago* 11°13′ N, 60°39′ W **118**
Tobarra, *Sp.* 38°35′ N, 1°42′ W **164**
Tobelo, *Indonesia* 1°41′ N, 127°54′ E **192**
Tobermory 56°37′ N, 6°5′ W **150**
Tobermory, *Can.* 45°13′ N, 81°40′ W **94**
Tobin, Mount, peak, *Nev., U.S.* 40°22′ N, 117°37′ W **90**
Tobli, *Liberia* 6°16′ N, 8°33′ W **222**
Toboali, *Indonesia* 3°3′ S, 106°26′ E **192**
Tobol, river, *Russ.* 56°41′ N, 66°37′ E **169**
Tobol'sk, *Russ.* 58°14′ N, 68°22′ E **169**
Tobruk, *Lib.* 31°52′ N, 23°50′ E **207**
Tobruk see Ţubruq, *Lib.* 32°3′ N, 23°57′ E **216**
Tobseda, *Russ.* 68°31′ N, 52°47′ E **160**
Toby, Mount, peak, *Mass., U.S.* 42°28′ N, 72°34′ W **104**
Tobyl, *Kaz.* 52°41′ N, 62°39′ E **184**
Tobyl, river, *Kaz.* 53°48′ N, 63°50′ E **184**
Tobysh, river, *Russ.* 66°21′ N, 50°21′ E **154**
Tocantínia, *Braz.* 9°36′ S, 48°23′ W **130**
Tocantinópolis, *Braz.* 6°19′ S, 47°28′ W **130**
Tocantins, adm. division, *Braz.* 12°57′ S, 48°39′ W **138**
Tocantins, river, *Braz.* 5°23′ S, 56°13′ W **132**
Tocantins, river, *Braz.* 11°43′ S, 48°39′ W **130**
Toccoa, *Ga., U.S.* 34°33′ N, 83°20′ W **96**
Tochigi, adm. division, *Japan* 36°37′ N, 139°24′ E **201**
Tochio, *Japan* 37°28′ N, 138°59′ E **201**
Toco, *Chile* 22°5′ S, 69°41′ W **137**
Toconao, *Chile* 23°12′ S, 68°2′ W **132**
Tocopilla, *Chile* 22°8′ S, 70°13′ W **137**
Tocuyo de la Costa, *Venez.* 11°1′ N, 68°25′ W **136**
Tocuyo, river, *Venez.* 10°43′ N, 69°31′ W **136**
Todal, *Nor.* 62°48′ N, 8°44′ E **152**
Todd, *Alas., U.S.* 57°29′ N, 135°5′ W **108**
Todenyang, *Kenya* 4°27′ N, 35°53′ E **224**
Todireni, *Rom.* 47°36′ N, 27°5′ E **156**
Todmorden, *U.K.* 53°43′ N, 2°6′ W **162**
Todo Santos, *Peru* 1°16′ S, 73°47′ W **136**
Todorovo, *Bulg.* 43°43′ N, 26°55′ E **156**
Todos Santos, *Bol.* 16°49′ S, 65°10′ W **137**
Todos Santos, *Mex.* 23°26′ N, 110°13′ W **112**
Toe Head 57°49′ N, 7°32′ W **150**
Tofield, *Can.* 53°21′ N, 112°40′ W **108**
Tofino, *Can.* 49°6′ N, 125°52′ W **82**
Töfsingdalens National Park, *Nor.* 62°11′ N, 12°23′ E **152**
Tōgane, *Japan* 35°30′ N, 140°19′ E **201**
Togi, *Japan* 37°7′ N, 136°44′ E **201**
Togiak, *Alas., U.S.* 59°3′ N, 160°25′ W **106**
Togian, Kepulauan, islands, *Indonesia* 0°10′ N, 122°30′ E **192**
Togliatti see Tol'yatti, *Russ.* 53°30′ N, 49°34′ E **154**
Togni, *Sudan* 18°2′ N, 35°9′ E **182**
Tognuf, *Eritrea* 16°8′ N, 37°23′ E **182**
Togo, *Can.* 51°24′ N, 101°37′ W **90**
Togo 8°41′ N, 1°2′ E **214**
Togobala, *Guinea* 9°17′ N, 7°57′ W **222**
Togtoh, *China* 40°17′ N, 111°8′ E **198**
Togur, *Russ.* 58°21′ N, 82°43′ E **169**
Toguskеn, *Kaz.* 43°34′ N, 67°24′ E **184**
Togwotee Pass, *Wyo., U.S.* 43°44′ N, 110°3′ W **90**
Togyz, *Kaz.* 47°36′ N, 60°30′ E **184**
Tohatchi, *N. Mex., U.S.* 35°51′ N, 108°46′ W **92**
Tohma, river, *Turk.* 38°58′ N, 37°29′ E **156**
Tohogne, *Belg.* 50°22′ N, 5°29′ E **167**
Toholampi, *Fin.* 63°45′ N, 24°11′ E **152**
Töhöm, *Mongolia* 44°26′ N, 108°17′ E **198**
Toibalawe, *India* 10°35′ N, 92°39′ E **188**
Toijala, *Fin.* 61°9′ N, 23°52′ E **166**
Toinya, *Sudan* 6°16′ N, 29°42′ E **224**
Toiyabe Range, *Nev., U.S.* 39°23′ N, 117°19′ W **90**
Tok, river, *Russ.* 52°40′ N, 52°27′ E **154**
Tōkamachi, *Japan* 37°6′ N, 138°45′ E **201**
Tokar, *Sudan* 18°26′ N, 37°41′ E **182**
Tokara Rettō, islands, *East China Sea* 29°46′ N, 128°15′ E **190**
Tokat, *Turk.* 40°18′ N, 36°34′ E **156**
Tŏkch'ŏn, *N. Korea* 39°44′ N, 126°18′ E **200**
Tokeland, *Wash., U.S.* 46°41′ N, 123°59′ W **100**
Tokelau, islands, *N.Z.* 8°1′ S, 173°11′ W **238**
Tokewanna Peak, *Utah, U.S.* 40°47′ N, 110°42′ W **90**
Tokhtamysh, *Taj.* 37°49′ N, 74°40′ E **184**
Toki, *Japan* 35°21′ N, 137°13′ E **201**
Tokmak, *Ukr.* 47°12′ N, 35°45′ E **156**
Tokmok, *Kyrg.* 42°48′ N, 75°17′ E **184**
Toko, *N.Z.* 39°21′ S, 174°22′ E **240**
Tokomaru Bay, *N.Z.* 38°8′ S, 178°17′ E **240**
Tokoroa, *N.Z.* 38°15′ S, 175°52′ E **240**
Toksova, *Russ.* 60°9′ N, 30°31′ E **166**
Toksu see Xinhe, *China* 41°35′ N, 82°38′ E **184**
Toktogul Reservoir, lake, *Kyrg.* 41°50′ N, 72°37′ E **197**
Tokuno Shima, island, *Japan* 27°22′ N, 129°2′ E **190**
Tokushima, *Japan* 34°4′ N, 134°32′ E **201**
Tokushima, adm. division, *Japan* 33°53′ N, 133°42′ E **201**
Tokuyama, *Japan* 34°4′ N, 131°50′ E **200**
Tōkyō, *Japan* 35°39′ N, 139°40′ E **201**
Tōkyō, adm. division, *Japan* 35°38′ N, 139°16′ E **201**
Tolaga Bay, *N.Z.* 38°21′ S, 178°17′ E **240**
Tôlañaro, *Madagascar* 24°56′ S, 46°58′ E **207**
Tolbo, *Mongolia* 48°22′ N, 90°16′ E **184**
Tolchin, Mount, peak, *Antarctica* 85°6′ S, 67°14′ W **248**
Töle Bī, *Kaz.* 43°36′ N, 73°47′ E **184**
Toledo, *Braz.* 24°41′ S, 53°46′ W **132**
Toledo, *Braz.* 5°56′ S, 73°6′ W **130**
Toledo, *Ill., U.S.* 39°16′ N, 88°15′ W **102**
Toledo, *Iowa, U.S.* 41°59′ N, 92°35′ W **94**
Toledo, *Ohio, U.S.* 41°38′ N, 83°32′ W **102**
Toledo, *Sp.* 39°52′ N, 4°2′ W **164**
Toledo, *Wash., U.S.* 46°25′ N, 122°52′ W **100**
Toledo Bend Reservoir, lake, *La., U.S.* 31°49′ N, 93°56′ W **103**
Toledo, Montes de, *Sp.* 39°29′ N, 4°52′ W **164**
Tolentino, *It.* 43°12′ N, 13°16′ E **156**
Tolentino, *Mex.* 22°14′ N, 100°34′ W **114**
Tolhuaca National Park, *Chile* 38°8′ S, 71°55′ W **134**
Tol'yatti (Togliatti), *Russia* 53°30′ N, 49°34′ E **154**
Toli, *China* 45°47′ N, 83°40′ E **184**
Toliara, *Madagascar* 23°18′ S, 43°50′ E **207**
Tolima, adm. division, *Col.* 4°1′ N, 75°40′ W **136**
Tolitoli, *Indonesia* 1°5′ N, 120°45′ E **192**
Tol'ka, *Russ.* 63°57′ N, 82°2′ E **169**
Tolkaboua, *Burkina Faso* 10°11′ N, 2°59′ W **222**
Tolkmicko, *Pol.* 54°18′ N, 19°32′ E **166**
Tollhouse, *Calif., U.S.* 37°1′ N, 119°25′ W **100**
Tollimarjon, *Uzb.* 38°17′ N, 65°33′ E **197**
Tollya, Zaliv 76°15′ N, 98°2′ E **160**
Tolmachevo, *Russ.* 58°51′ N, 29°52′ E **166**
Tolmin, *Slov.* 46°11′ N, 13°44′ E **167**
Tolna, *Hung.* 46°25′ N, 18°46′ E **168**
Tolna, adm. division, *Hung.* 46°26′ N, 18°4′ E **156**
Tolo, Teluk 2°28′ S, 121°52′ E **192**
Tolono, *Ill., U.S.* 39°58′ N, 88°16′ W **102**
Tolosa, *Sp.* 43°8′ N, 2°3′ W **164**
Tolstoi, *Can.* 49°5′ N, 96°49′ W **90**
Toltén, *Chile* 39°12′ S, 73°13′ W **134**
Tolti, *Pak.* 35°2′ N, 76°6′ E **186**
Tolú, *Col.* 9°31′ N, 75°34′ W **136**
Toluca, *Ill., U.S.* 41°0′ N, 89°8′ W **102**
Toluca, *Mex.* 19°14′ N, 99°43′ W **114**
Toluca, *Mo., U.S.* 41°0′ N, 89°8′ W **94**
Tom Burke, *S. Af.* 23°5′ S, 27°59′ E **227**
Tom, Mount, peak, *Mass., U.S.* 42°14′ N, 72°41′ W **104**
Tom Price, *Austral.* 22°41′ S, 117°49′ E **238**
Tom', river, *Russ.* 55°15′ N, 85°0′ E **160**
Tom White, Mount, peak, *Alas., U.S.* 60°38′ N, 143°50′ W **98**
Tomah, *Wis., U.S.* 43°58′ N, 90°30′ W **94**
Tomahawk, *Wis., U.S.* 45°27′ N, 89°43′ W **94**
Tomales Point, *Calif., U.S.* 38°13′ N, 122°57′ W **90**
Tomar, *Braz.* 0°25′ N, 63°54′ W **130**
Tómaros, peak, *Gr.* 39°28′ N, 20°43′ E **156**
Tomás Barrón, *Bol.* 17°41′ S, 67°29′ W **137**
Tomás Gomensoro, *Uru.* 30°24′ S, 57°27′ W **139**
Tomaševo, *Mont.* 43°4′ N, 19°39′ E **168**
Tomashevka, *Belarus* 51°32′ N, 23°35′ E **152**
Tomatin, *U.K.* 57°20′ N, 4°0′ W **150**
Tomatlán, *Mex.* 19°56′ N, 105°17′ W **114**
Tomatlán, river, *Mex.* 19°46′ N, 105°21′ W **114**
Tombador, Serra do, *Braz.* 10°46′ S, 58°16′ W **130**
Tombe, *Sudan* 5°47′ N, 31°39′ E **224**
Tombigbee, river, *Ala., U.S.* 31°46′ N, 88°8′ W **103**
Tomboco, *Angola* 6°51′ S, 13°17′ E **218**
Tombos, *Braz.* 20°54′ S, 42°3′ W **138**
Tombouctou (Timbuktu), *Mali* 16°44′ N, 3°2′ W **222**
Tombstone, *Ariz., U.S.* 31°41′ N, 110°4′ W **112**
Tombstone Mountain, peak, *Can.* 64°19′ N, 138°47′ W **98**
Tombua, *Angola* 15°52′ S, 11°50′ E **220**
Tomdibuloq, *Uzb.* 41°45′ N, 64°39′ E **197**
Tomé, *Chile* 36°35′ S, 72°57′ W **134**
Tomelloso, *Sp.* 39°9′ N, 3°2′ W **164**
Tomini, Teluk 0°22′ N, 120°27′ E **192**
Tomislavgrad, *Bosn. and Herzg.* 43°40′ N, 17°12′ E **168**
Tommot, *Russ.* 58°59′ N, 126°27′ E **160**
Tomo, river, *Col.* 5°29′ N, 68°18′ W **136**
Tomorit, Maja e, peak, *Alban.* 40°41′ N, 20°4′ E **156**
Tompa, *Hung.* 46°11′ N, 19°32′ E **168**
Tompkinsville, *Ky., U.S.* 36°41′ N, 85°42′ W **96**
Tomsino, *Russ.* 56°26′ N, 28°32′ E **166**
Tomsk, *Russ.* 56°30′ N, 85°3′ E **169**
Tomsk, adm. division, *Russ.* 58°34′ N, 80°3′ E **169**
Tonalá, *Mex.* 16°4′ N, 93°46′ W **115**
Tonale, Passo del, *It.* 46°16′ N, 10°34′ E **167**
Tonami, *Japan* 36°37′ N, 136°56′ E **201**
Tonantins, *Braz.* 2°45′ S, 67°46′ W **136**
Tonantins, river, *Braz.* 2°26′ S, 68°35′ W **136**
Tonasket, *Wash., U.S.* 48°41′ N, 119°27′ W **90**
Tonbridge, *U.K.* 51°11′ N, 0°16′ E **162**
Tondi Kiwindi, *Niger* 14°40′ N, 1°51′ E **222**
Tondou, Massif du, *Cen. Af. Rep.* 7°50′ N, 23°43′ E **224**
Tonekābon, *Iran* 36°47′ N, 50°54′ E **180**
Toney Mountain, peak, *Antarctica* 75°44′ S, 115°16′ W **248**
Tonga 22°46′ S, 174°39′ W **238**
Tonga, *Sudan* 9°30′ N, 31°3′ E **224**
Tonga, islands, *South Pacific Ocean* 20°25′ S, 173°49′ W **238**
Tonga Trench, *South Pacific Ocean* 21°53′ S, 172°51′ W **252**
Tong'an, *China* 24°43′ N, 118°9′ E **198**
Tongatapu Group, islands, *Tonga* 22°46′ S, 174°39′ W **238**
Tongatapu, island, *Tonga* 21°11′ S, 175°11′ W **241**
Tongcheng, *China* 31°3′ N, 116°56′ E **198**
Tongchuan, *China* 35°7′ N, 109°9′ E **198**
Tongdao, *China* 26°9′ N, 109°45′ E **198**
Tongeren, *Belg.* 50°46′ N, 5°27′ E **167**
Tonghe, *China* 46°0′ N, 128°45′ E **198**
Tonghua, *China* 41°42′ N, 125°54′ E **200**
Tonghua (Kuaidamao), *China* 41°41′ N, 125°45′ E **200**
Tongjiang, *China* 31°59′ N, 107°14′ E **198**
Tongjosŏn-man 39°23′ N, 128°10′ E **200**
Tongliang, *China* 29°50′ N, 106°4′ E **198**
Tongliao, *China* 43°35′ N, 122°17′ E **198**
Tongling, *China* 30°53′ N, 117°48′ E **198**
Tonglu, *China* 29°47′ N, 119°37′ E **198**
Tongnae, *S. Korea* 35°11′ N, 129°6′ E **200**
Tongobory, *Madagascar* 23°28′ S, 44°18′ E **220**
Tongren, *China* 27°45′ N, 109°13′ E **198**
Tongshi, *China* 18°43′ N, 109°29′ E **198**
Tongtian, river, *China* 33°51′ N, 93°30′ E **190**
Tongue of the Ocean 23°55′ N, 77°32′ W **96**
Tongue, river, *Mont., U.S.* 45°47′ N, 106°6′ W **90**
Tongwei, *China* 35°14′ N, 105°12′ E **198**
Tongxian, *China* 39°52′ N, 116°38′ E **198**
Tongxin, *China* 37°1′ N, 105°53′ E **198**
Tongyeong, *S. Korea* 34°50′ N, 128°26′ E **200**
Tongyu, *China* 44°47′ N, 123°4′ E **198**
Tongyuanpu, *China* 40°47′ N, 123°57′ E **200**
Tongzi, *China* 28°8′ N, 106°48′ E **198**
Tonica, *Ill., U.S.* 41°12′ N, 89°4′ W **102**
Tonichi, *Mex.* 28°35′ N, 109°33′ W **92**
Tönisvorst, *Ger.* 51°18′ N, 6°30′ E **167**
Tonj, *Sudan* 7°16′ N, 28°45′ E **224**
Tonj see Ibba, river, *Sudan* 6°16′ N, 28°21′ E **224**
Tonk, *India* 26°9′ N, 75°48′ E **197**
Tonkawa, *Okla., U.S.* 36°39′ N, 97°18′ W **92**
Tonkin, Gulf of 19°38′ N, 107°25′ E **190**
Tonneins, *Fr.* 44°23′ N, 0°17′ E **150**
Tonopah, *Nev., U.S.* 38°4′ N, 117°15′ W **92**
Tonota, *Botswana* 21°30′ S, 27°26′ E **227**
Tønsberg, *Nor.* 59°16′ N, 10°26′ E **152**
Tonsina, *Alas., U.S.* 61°38′ N, 145°11′ W **98**
Tonto National Monument, *Ariz., U.S.* 33°37′ N, 111°10′ W **92**
Tonya, *Turk.* 40°52′ N, 39°15′ E **195**
Tooele, *Utah, U.S.* 40°32′ N, 112°14′ W **106**
Toora Khem, *Russ.* 52°29′ N, 96°34′ E **190**
Toore, *Somalia* 1°21′ N, 44°22′ E **218**
Tootsi, *Est.* 58°34′ N, 24°47′ E **166**
Topaz Mountain, peak, *Utah, U.S.* 39°41′ N, 113°11′ W **90**
Topeka, *Kans., U.S.* 38°59′ N, 95°48′ W **90**
Topia, *Mex.* 25°9′ N, 106°33′ W **114**
Topki, *Russ.* 55°15′ N, 85°43′ E **169**
Topley, *Can.* 54°31′ N, 126°20′ W **108**
Topley Landing, *Can.* 54°47′ N, 126°11′ W **108**
Topli Do, *Serb.* 43°20′ N, 22°40′ E **168**
Topocalma, Punta, *Chile* 34°15′ S, 73°58′ W **134**
Topock, *Ariz., U.S.* 34°42′ N, 114°28′ W **101**
Topolobampo, Bahía de 25°32′ N, 110°21′ W **80**
Topolovăţu Mare, *Rom.* 45°47′ N, 21°38′ E **168**
Toppenish, *Wash., U.S.* 46°22′ N, 120°20′ W **90**
Topsfield, *Mass., U.S.* 42°38′ N, 70°58′ W **104**
Topsham, *Me., U.S.* 43°55′ N, 69°58′ W **104**
Toquepala, *Peru* 17°18′ S, 70°35′ W **137**
Toquima Range, *Nev., U.S.* 39°28′ N, 116°59′ W **90**
Tor, *Eth.* 7°48′ N, 33°32′ E **224**
Tor Bay 45°10′ N, 61°39′ W **111**
Torà, *Sp.* 41°48′ N, 1°23′ E **164**
Toragay, oil field, *Azerb.* 40°9′ N, 49°21′ E **195**
Toranou, *Côte d'Ivoire* 8°48′ N, 7°47′ W **222**
Torata, *Peru* 17°7′ S, 70°51′ W **137**
Torbalı, *Turk.* 38°10′ N, 27°20′ E **156**
Torbat-e Ḩeydarīyeh, *Iran* 35°17′ N, 59°13′ E **180**
Torbat-e Jām, *Iran* 35°16′ N, 60°34′ E **180**
Torbay, *U.K.* 50°27′ N, 3°34′ W **150**
Torbert, Mount, peak, *Antarctica* 83°32′ S, 55°58′ W **248**
Torch, river, *Can.* 53°33′ N, 104°9′ W **108**
Torchiara, *It.* 40°19′ N, 15°2′ E **156**
Torda, *Serb.* 45°35′ N, 20°26′ E **168**
Tordesillos, *Sp.* 40°39′ N, 1°35′ W **164**
Töre, *Nor.* 65°54′ N, 22°39′ E **152**
Töreboda, *Nor.* 58°41′ N, 14°7′ E **152**
Torelló, *Sp.* 42°2′ N, 2°15′ E **164**
Torere, *N.Z.* 37°59′ S, 177°30′ E **240**
Torez, *Ukr.* 48°3′ N, 38°37′ E **158**
Torgau, *Ger.* 51°34′ N, 12°59′ E **152**
Torghay, *Kaz.* 49°46′ N, 63°35′ E **184**
Torghay, river, *Kaz.* 48°34′ N, 62°27′ E **184**
Torhout, *Belg.* 51°3′ N, 3°6′ E **163**
Torija, *Sp.* 40°44′ N, 3°2′ W **164**
Torino (Turin), *It.* 45°4′ N, 7°40′ E **167**
Torit, *Sudan* 4°24′ N, 32°33′ E **224**

V

Vevey, Switz. 46°28′ N, 6°50′ E 167
Vévi, Gr. 40°46′ N, 21°36′ E 156
Veynes, Fr. 44°32′ N, 5°48′ E 150
Vézelise, Fr. 48°29′ N, 6°4′ E 163
Vezhen, peak, Bulg. 42°44′ N, 24°20′ E 156
Vezirköprü, Turk. 41°8′ N, 35°27′ E 156
Viacha, Bol. 16°42′ S, 68°21′ W 137
Viadana, It. 44°55′ N, 10°32′ E 167
Viale, Arg. 31°52′ S, 60°2′ W 139
Viamonte, Arg. 33°46′ S, 63°4′ W 139
Viana, Braz. 3°14′ S, 45°4′ W 132
Viana do Castelo, Port. 41°41′ N, 8°50′ W 150
Viana Do Castelo, adm. division, Port. 41°59′ N, 8°49′ W 150
Vianden, Lux. 49°55′ N, 6°11′ E 167
Viangchan (Vientiane), Laos 17°56′ N, 102°32′ E 202
Viareggio, It. 43°52′ N, 10°15′ E 167
Viaur, river, Fr. 44°5′ N, 2°10′ E 165
Vibank, Can. 50°19′ N, 103°57′ W 108
Viborg, Den. 56°26′ N, 9°23′ E 150
Vic, Sp. 41°55′ N, 2°14′ E 164
Vicálvaro, Sp. 40°23′ N, 3°35′ W 164
Vicdessos, Fr. 42°46′ N, 1°28′ E 164
Vicente Guerrero, Mex. 30°45′ N, 115°59′ W 112
Vicente Guerrero, Mex. 23°44′ N, 103°59′ W 114
Vicente Guerrero, Presa, lake, Mex. 23°56′ N, 99°20′ W 114
Vicente Pérez Rosales National Park, Chile 41°13′ S, 72°34′ W 122
Vicenza, It. 45°33′ N, 11°33′ E 167
Vic-Fézensac, Fr. 43°45′ N, 0°17′ E 150
Vichada, adm. division, Col. 4°52′ N, 70°21′ W 136
Vichada, river, Col. 4°55′ N, 68°23′ W 136
Vichadero, Uru. 31°48′ S, 54°42′ W 139
Vichuga, Russ. 57°11′ N, 41°56′ E 154
Vichy, Fr. 46°5′ N, 3°7′ E 143
Vici, Okla., U.S. 36°8′ N, 99°18′ W 96
Vick, La., U.S. 31°13′ N, 92°6′ W 103
Vicksburg, Mich., U.S. 42°7′ N, 85°32′ W 102
Vicksburg, Miss., U.S. 32°18′ N, 90°53′ W 103
Vicksburg National Military Park, La., U.S. 32°20′ N, 90°56′ W 103
Viçosa, Braz. 20°45′ S, 42°53′ W 138
Vicovu de Sus, Rom. 47°55′ N, 25°40′ E 158
Victor, Idaho, U.S. 43°35′ N, 111°6′ W 90
Victor Harbor, Austral. 35°33′ S, 138°36′ E 231
Victor, Mount, peak, Antarctica 72°39′ S, 30°58′ E 248
Victor Rosales, Mex. 22°57′ N, 102°42′ W 114
Victoria, Arg. 32°36′ S, 60°10′ W 139
Victoria, Can. 48°24′ N, 123°23′ W 100
Victoria, Chile 38°14′ S, 72°20′ W 134
Victoria, Ill., U.S. 41°1′ N, 90°7′ W 102
Victoria, Philippines 15°34′ N, 120°40′ E 203
Victoria, Seychelles 4°53′ S, 54°51′ E 172
Victoria, Tex., U.S. 28°47′ N, 97°0′ W 96
Victoria, Va., U.S. 36°59′ N, 78°14′ W 96
Victoria, adm. division, Austral. 36°44′ S, 141°23′ E 231
Victoria Beach, Can. 50°40′ N, 96°33′ W 90
Victoria Falls, Zimb. 17°21′ S, 20°52′ E 207
Victoria Falls National Park, Zimb. 17°55′ S, 25°40′ E 225
Victoria, Grand lac, lake, Can. 47°33′ N, 78°19′ W 94
Victoria, Isla, island, Chile 45°18′ S, 73°44′ W 134
Victoria Island, Can. 70°18′ N, 121°1′ W 106
Victoria, Lake, Africa 1°23′ S, 30°40′ E 218
Victoria Land, region, Antarctica 74°59′ S, 162°2′ E 248
Victoria, Mount, peak, Myanmar 21°27′ N, 93°33′ E 190
Victoria, Mount, peak, P.N.G. 8°54′ S, 147°21′ E 192
Victoria Strait 68°57′ N, 101°27′ W 106
Victoria West, S. Af. 31°24′ S, 23°5′ E 227
Victoriaville, Can. 46°3′ N, 71°59′ W 94
Victorica, Arg. 36°14′ S, 65°25′ W 134
Victorino, Venez. 2°49′ N, 67°49′ W 136
Victorio Peak, Tex., U.S. 31°17′ N, 104°57′ W 92
Victorville, Calif., U.S. 34°32′ N, 117°19′ W 101
Victory Peak see Pobedy Peak, China 42°2′ N, 80°3′ E 184
Vidal, Calif., U.S. 34°7′ N, 114°31′ W 101
Vidal, Peru 2°38′ S, 73°29′ W 136
Vidal Gormaz, Isla, island, Chile 52°17′ S, 76°29′ W 134
Vidalia, Ga., U.S. 32°12′ N, 82°25′ W 96
Videira, Braz. 27°1′ S, 51°9′ W 139
Videla, Arg. 30°57′ S, 60°41′ W 139
Videle, Rom. 44°17′ N, 25°32′ E 158
Vidin, Bulg. 43°59′ N, 22°51′ E 168
Vidin, adm. division, Bulg. 43°42′ N, 22°24′ E 168
Vidisha (Bhilsa), India 23°32′ N, 77°51′ E 197
Viditsa, Russ. 61°10′ N, 32°28′ E 152
Vidor, Tex., U.S. 30°6′ N, 94°1′ W 103
Vidriži, Latv. 57°19′ N, 24°36′ E 166
Vidsel, Nor. 65°50′ N, 20°28′ E 152
Vidzibor, Belarus 51°58′ N, 26°47′ E 152
Vidzy, Belarus 55°24′ N, 26°37′ E 166
Vidz′yuyar, Russ. 60°52′ N, 50°19′ E 154
Vie, river, Fr. 46°36′ N, 1°55′ W 150
Viedma, Arg. 40°51′ S, 63°1′ W 134
Viedma, Lago, lake, Arg. 49°34′ S, 73°52′ W 134
Vieja, Sierra, Tex., U.S. 30°42′ N, 105°1′ W 92
Viejo, Cerro, peak, Mex. 30°16′ N, 112°23′ W 92
Viekšniai, Lith. 56°15′ N, 22°31′ E 166
Vielha, Sp. 42°41′ N, 0°47′ E 164
Vielsalm, Belg. 50°16′ N, 5°55′ E 167
Vienna, Ga., U.S. 32°5′ N, 83°48′ W 96
Vienna, Mo., U.S. 38°12′ N, 91°57′ W 94
Vienna, W. Va., U.S. 39°19′ N, 81°33′ W 102
Vienna see Wien, Aust. 48°10′ N, 16°14′ E 152
Vienne, Fr. 45°31′ N, 4°52′ E 150
Vientiane, Laos 17°53′ N, 101°53′ E 172
Vientiane see Viangchan, Laos 17°56′ N, 102°32′ E 202
Vieques, island, U.S. 18°8′ N, 65°26′ W 118
Viersen, Ger. 51°15′ N, 6°23′ E 167
Viesca, Mex. 25°21′ N, 102°48′ W 114
Vieste, It. 41°52′ N, 16°10′ E 156
Vieste, Latv. 56°20′ N, 25°34′ E 166
Vietnam 21°0′ N, 105°0′ E 202
Vieux-Fort, Can. 51°25′ N, 57°49′ W 111
Vievis, Lith. 54°45′ N, 24°48′ E 166
Vif, Fr. 45°2′ N, 5°39′ E 150
Vigan, Philippines 17°33′ N, 120°24′ E 203
Vigeois, Fr. 45°22′ N, 1°30′ E 150
Vigevano, It. 45°18′ N, 8°50′ E 167
Vigía, Cabo, Arg. 48°46′ S, 66°49′ W 134
Vigía Chico, Mex. 19°46′ N, 87°38′ W 116
Vignacourt, Fr. 50°0′ N, 2°11′ E 163
Vignal, Lac, lake, Can. 53°15′ N, 68°51′ W 111
Vignale, It. 45°0′ N, 8°24′ E 167
Vignemale, Pic de, peak, Fr. 42°46′ N, 0°11′ E 164
Vignola, It. 44°29′ N, 11°0′ E 167
Vigo, Sp. 42°13′ N, 8°45′ W 150
Vigone, It. 44°50′ N, 7°29′ E 167
Vihanti, Fin. 64°29′ N, 24°58′ E 152
Vihorlat, peak, Slovakia 48°53′ N, 22°0′ E 152
Viiala, Fin. 61°12′ N, 23°43′ E 166
Viiksimo, Fin. 64°13′ N, 30°26′ E 154
Viipuri see Vyborg, Russ. 60°41′ N, 28°45′ E 166
Viiri, Fin. 66°23′ N, 26°38′ E 152
Vijayadurg, India 16°31′ N, 73°19′ E 188
Vijayanagar, ruin(s), India 15°16′ N, 76°17′ E 188
Vijayawada, India 16°34′ N, 80°33′ E 190
Vik, Ice. 63°28′ N, 18°59′ W 143
Vika, Fin. 66°35′ N, 26°23′ E 152
Vikhren, peak, Bulg. 41°45′ N, 23°19′ E 156
Viking, Can. 53°5′ N, 111°48′ W 108
Vikna, islands, Norwegian Sea 64°56′ N, 9°48′ E 152
Vikulovo, Russ. 56°47′ N, 70°37′ E 169
Vila Bela da Santíssima Trindade, Braz. 15°1′ S, 59°57′ W 132
Vila Bittencourt, Braz. 1°21′ S, 69°23′ W 136
Vila Conceição, Braz. 0°8′ N, 63°55′ W 130
Vila Coutinho, Mozambique 14°34′ S, 34°18′ E 224
Vila da Maganja, Mozambique 17°19′ S, 37°31′ E 224
Vila de Moura, Port. 38°7′ N, 7°29′ W 214
Vila de Sagres, Port. 37°0′ N, 8°57′ W 150
Vila do Conde, Port. 41°20′ N, 8°45′ W 150
Vila Gamito, Mozambique 14°11′ S, 33°0′ E 224
Vila Gomes da Costa, Mozambique 24°19′ S, 33°39′ E 227
Vila Junqueiro, Mozambique 15°29′ S, 36°58′ E 224
Vila Luísa, Mozambique 25°42′ S, 32°40′ E 227
Vila Machado, Mozambique 19°20′ S, 34°13′ E 224
Vila Murtinho, Braz. 10°23′ S, 65°17′ W 137
Vila Nova de Foz Côa, Port. 41°4′ N, 7°10′ W 150
Vila Nova de Gaia, Port. 41°6′ N, 8°39′ W 150
Vila Paiva de Andrada, Mozambique 18°40′ S, 34°4′ E 224
Vila Real, Port. 41°17′ N, 7°46′ W 150
Vila Real, adm. division, Port. 41°23′ N, 7°55′ W 150
Vila Real de Santo António, Port. 37°12′ N, 7°36′ W 214
Vila Vasco da Gama, Mozambique 14°54′ S, 32°15′ E 224
Vila Velha, Braz. 3°15′ N, 51°15′ W 130
Vila Velha (Espírito Santo), Braz. 20°25′ S, 40°21′ W 138
Vilafranca del Penedès, Sp. 41°20′ N, 1°41′ E 164
Viljaka, Latv. 57°10′ N, 27°37′ E 166
Vilaller, Sp. 42°26′ N, 0°42′ E 164
Vilán, Cabo, Sp. 43°10′ N, 9°27′ W 150
Viļāni, Latv. 56°32′ N, 26°56′ E 166
Vilanova i la Geltrú, Sp. 41°12′ N, 1°43′ E 164
Vilar Formoso, Port. 40°36′ N, 6°52′ W 150
Vilcabamba, Cordillera, Peru 13°0′ S, 73°16′ W 130
Vilcabamba, ruin(s), Peru 13°7′ S, 73°25′ W 137
Vileyka, Belarus 54°30′ N, 26°54′ E 166
Vil′gort, Russ. 60°35′ N, 56°25′ E 154
Vil′gort, Russ. 61°37′ N, 50°49′ E 154
Vilhelmina, Nor. 64°37′ N, 16°38′ E 152
Vilhena, Braz. 12°42′ S, 60°9′ W 130
Viliya, Ukr. 50°11′ N, 26°17′ E 152
Viliya, river, Belarus 54°49′ N, 25°58′ E 166
Viljandi, Est. 58°20′ N, 25°33′ E 166
Vilkaviškis, Lith. 54°40′ N, 23°1′ E 166
Vil′kitskogo, Proliv 76°58′ N, 84°44′ E 172
Villa Abecia, Bol. 21°0′ S, 65°24′ W 137
Villa Ahumada, Mex. 30°36′ N, 106°32′ W 92
Villa Alberdi, Arg. 27°35′ S, 65°37′ W 134
Villa Ana, Arg. 28°28′ S, 59°37′ W 139
Villa Ángela, Arg. 27°34′ S, 60°43′ W 139
Villa Bella, Bol. 10°29′ S, 65°24′ W 137
Villa Bens see Tarfaya, Mor. 27°55′ N, 12°54′ W 214
Villa Berthet, Arg. 27°16′ S, 60°25′ W 139
Villa Cañás, Arg. 34°1′ S, 61°37′ W 139
Villa Clara, adm. division, Cuba 22°39′ N, 80°15′ W 116
Villa Clara, island, Cuba 23°7′ N, 80°39′ W 116
Villa Constitución, Arg. 33°16′ S, 60°19′ W 139
Villa Cuauhtémoc, Mex. 22°9′ N, 97°49′ W 114
Villa de Cos, Mex. 23°17′ N, 102°21′ W 114
Villa de Guadalupe, Mex. 23°20′ N, 100°46′ W 114
Villa de Hidalgo, Mex. 22°24′ N, 100°41′ W 114
Villa de María, Arg. 29°54′ S, 63°42′ W 139
Villa de San Antonio, Hond. 14°20′ N, 87°36′ W 115
Villa del Río, Sp. 37°59′ N, 4°19′ W 164
Villa del Rosario, Arg. 31°37′ S, 63°32′ W 139
Villa Dolores, Arg. 31°56′ S, 65°9′ W 134
Villa Elisa, Arg. 32°9′ S, 58°23′ W 139
Villa Escobedo, Mex. 27°1′ N, 105°47′ W 112
Villa Florida, Parag. 26°26′ S, 57°6′ W 139
Villa Grove, Ill., U.S. 39°52′ N, 88°11′ W 102
Villa Guerrero, Mex. 21°57′ N, 103°35′ W 114
Villa Guillermina, Arg. 28°13′ S, 59°29′ W 139
Villa Hayes, Parag. 25°5′ S, 57°33′ W 132
Villa Hernandarias, Arg. 31°15′ S, 59°58′ W 139
Villa Hidalgo, Mex. 26°14′ N, 104°54′ W 114
Villa Ingavi (Caiza), Bol. 21°47′ S, 63°33′ W 137
Villa Iris, Arg. 38°12′ S, 63°13′ W 139
Villa Jesús María, Mex. 28°11′ N, 114°3′ W 92
Villa Juan José Pérez, Bol. 15°16′ S, 69°4′ W 137
Villa Juárez, Mex. 22°18′ N, 100°16′ W 114
Villa Mainero, Mex. 24°33′ N, 99°38′ W 114
Villa María, Arg. 32°25′ S, 63°14′ W 139
Villa Martín, Bol. 20°47′ S, 67°41′ W 137
Villa Minetti, Arg. 28°37′ S, 61°39′ W 139
Villa Nueva, Arg. 32°29′ S, 63°15′ W 139
Villa Ocampo, Arg. 28°28′ S, 59°22′ W 139
Villa Ocampo, Mex. 26°26′ N, 105°30′ W 114
Villa O'Higgins, Chile 48°28′ S, 72°38′ W 134
Villa Ojo de Agua, Arg. 29°27′ S, 63°45′ W 139
Villa Oliva, Parag. 26°0′ S, 57°50′ W 139
Villa Opicina, It. 45°41′ N, 13°46′ E 156
Villa Orestes Pereyra, Mex. 26°28′ N, 105°40′ W 114
Villa Pesqueira, Mex. 29°6′ N, 109°57′ W 92
Villa Ramírez, Arg. 32°10′ S, 60°12′ W 139
Villa Regina, Arg. 39°7′ S, 67°7′ W 134
Villa San José, Arg. 32°12′ S, 58°12′ W 139
Villa Serrano, Bol. 19°5′ S, 64°25′ W 137
Villa Talavera, Bol. 19°48′ S, 65°23′ W 137
Villa Tunari, Bol. 17°0′ S, 65°28′ W 137
Villa Unión, Arg. 29°25′ S, 62°47′ W 139
Villa Unión, Arg. 29°18′ S, 68°12′ W 134
Villa Unión, Mex. 23°10′ N, 106°14′ W 114
Villa Unión, Mex. 23°58′ N, 104°3′ W 114
Villa Unión, Mex. 28°12′ N, 100°45′ W 92
Villa Vaca Guzmán, Bol. 19°57′ S, 63°48′ W 137
Villacañas, Sp. 39°37′ N, 3°20′ W 164
Villacarrillo, Sp. 38°6′ N, 3°5′ W 164
Villach, Aust. 46°36′ N, 13°50′ E 156
Villada, Sp. 42°14′ N, 4°58′ W 150
Villadossola, It. 46°3′ N, 8°14′ E 167
Villafeliche, Sp. 41°12′ N, 1°30′ W 164
Villafranca, Sp. 42°16′ N, 1°45′ W 164
Villafranca de los Barros, Sp. 38°34′ N, 6°20′ W 164
Villafranca del Cid, Sp. 40°25′ N, 0°17′ E 164
Villafranca di Verona, It. 45°21′ N, 10°51′ E 167
Villagrán, Mex. 24°28′ N, 99°30′ W 114
Villaguay, Arg. 31°51′ S, 59°1′ W 139
Villaharta, Sp. 38°7′ N, 4°55′ W 164
Villahermosa, Mex. 17°56′ N, 93°2′ W 115
Villahermosa, Sp. 38°45′ N, 2°52′ W 164
Villajoyosa (La Vila Joiosa), Sp. 38°29′ N, 0°14′ E 164
Villaldama, Mex. 26°29′ N, 100°27′ W 114
Villalonga, Arg. 39°54′ S, 62°36′ W 139
Villamartín, Sp. 36°52′ N, 5°39′ W 164
Villamontes, Bol. 21°15′ S, 63°33′ W 137
Villanueva, Mex. 22°21′ N, 102°54′ W 114
Villanueva, N. Mex., U.S. 35°16′ N, 105°22′ W 92
Villanueva de Castellón, Sp. 39°4′ N, 0°31′ E 164
Villanueva de la Concepción, Sp. 36°55′ N, 4°33′ W 164
Villanueva de la Jara, Sp. 39°26′ N, 1°58′ W 164
Villanueva de la Serena, Sp. 38°58′ N, 5°48′ W 164
Villanueva de los Infantes, Sp. 38°44′ N, 3°2′ W 164
Villanueva del Arzobispo, Sp. 38°10′ N, 3°0′ W 164
Villanueva del Duque, Sp. 38°23′ N, 5°1′ W 164
Villanueva del Río y Minas, Sp. 37°39′ N, 5°43′ W 164
Villány, Hung. 45°52′ N, 18°27′ E 168
Villapalacios, Sp. 38°34′ N, 2°38′ W 164
Villaputzu, It. 39°27′ N, 9°35′ E 156
Villaquejida, Sp. 42°8′ N, 5°36′ W 150
Villar del Rey, Sp. 39°8′ N, 6°51′ W 164
Villarcayo, Sp. 42°55′ N, 3°34′ W 164
Villarino, Punta, Arg. 41°0′ S, 64°58′ W 134
Villarrica, Parag. 25°45′ S, 56°27′ W 132
Villarrica National Park, Chile 39°24′ S, 72°10′ W 134
Villarrobledo, Sp. 39°15′ N, 2°37′ W 164
Villarroya de la Sierra, Sp. 41°28′ N, 1°48′ W 164
Villasayas, Sp. 41°20′ N, 2°37′ W 164
Villavicencio, Col. 4°8′ N, 73°40′ W 136
Villaviciosa de Córdoba, Sp. 38°4′ N, 5°1′ W 164
Villavieja, Col. 3°13′ N, 75°13′ W 136
Villazón, Bol. 22°7′ S, 65°39′ W 137
Villé, Fr. 48°19′ N, 7°17′ E 163
Ville Platte, La., U.S. 30°40′ N, 92°17′ W 103
Villebon, Lac, lake, Can. 47°54′ N, 77°50′ W 94
Villefranche, Fr. 45°59′ N, 4°43′ E 150
Villefranche, Fr. 47°17′ N, 1°46′ E 150
Villefranche-de-Lauragais, Fr. 43°23′ N, 1°43′ E 164
Villel, Sp. 40°13′ N, 1°13′ W 164
Villemaur, Fr. 48°15′ N, 3°45′ E 163
Villena, Sp. 38°37′ N, 0°53′ E 164
Villenauxe, Fr. 48°35′ N, 3°32′ E 163
Villeneuve-Saint-Georges, Fr. 48°43′ N, 2°26′ E 163
Villers-Bretonneux, Fr. 49°52′ N, 2°30′ E 163
Villerupt, Fr. 49°27′ N, 5°55′ E 163
Villiers, S. Af. 27°7′ S, 28°36′ E 227
Villisca, Iowa, U.S. 40°56′ N, 94°59′ W 94
Villupuram, India 11°56′ N, 79°30′ E 188
Vilna, Can. 54°6′ N, 111°56′ W 108
Vilnius, Lith. 54°38′ N, 25°12′ E 166
Vilppula, Fin. 62°1′ N, 24°25′ E 166
Vilsandi Saar, island, Est. 58°23′ N, 21°35′ E 166
Vilshofen, Ger. 48°37′ N, 13°11′ E 152
Vilusi, Mont. 42°42′ N, 18°35′ E 168
Vilvoorde, Belg. 50°55′ N, 4°26′ E 167
Vilyuy, river, Russ. 62°48′ N, 120°41′ E 172
Vilyuy, river, Russ. 64°45′ N, 108°36′ E 160
Vilyuy, river, Russ. 63°0′ N, 115°4′ E 160
Vilyuysk, Russ. 63°38′ N, 121°30′ E 160
Vilyuyskoye Plato, Russ. 66°22′ N, 99°40′ E 172
Vilyuyskoye Vodokhranilishche, lake, Russ. 63°5′ N, 101°50′ E 172
Vimioso, Port. 41°34′ N, 6°32′ W 150
Vimpeli, Fin. 63°9′ N, 23°46′ E 152
Vina, Calif., U.S. 39°56′ N, 122°4′ W 90
Vina, Serb. 43°37′ N, 22°8′ E 168
Vinalhaven, Me., U.S. 44°2′ N, 68°50′ W 94
Vinaròs, Sp. 40°27′ N, 0°27′ E 150
Vinça, Fr. 42°39′ N, 2°29′ E 164
Vincennes, Ind., U.S. 38°40′ N, 87°31′ W 102
Vincent Lake, lake, Can. 50°34′ N, 91°27′ W 110
Vinchina, Arg. 28°46′ S, 68°14′ W 134
Vindeln, Nor. 64°11′ N, 19°43′ E 152
Vindrey, Russ. 54°15′ N, 43°0′ E 154
Vinegar Hill, peak, Oreg., U.S. 44°41′ N, 118°39′ W 90
Vineta, Namibia 22°34′ S, 14°30′ E 220
Vineyard Sound 41°24′ N, 70°48′ W 104
Vinga, Rom. 46°1′ N, 21°12′ E 168
Vinh, Vietnam 18°42′ N, 105°38′ E 202
Vinh Chau, Vietnam 9°21′ N, 105°59′ E 202
Vinh Long, Vietnam 10°13′ N, 105°57′ E 202
Vinica, Maced. 41°53′ N, 22°30′ E 168
Vinita, Okla., U.S. 36°37′ N, 95°10′ W 96
Vinje, Nor. 59°38′ N, 7°51′ E 152
Vinjeøra, Nor. 63°12′ N, 8°58′ E 152
Vînju Mare, Rom. 44°25′ N, 22°53′ E 168
Vinkovci, Croatia 45°16′ N, 18°46′ E 168
Vinnytsya, Ukr. 49°12′ N, 28°37′ E 152
Vinson Massif, peak, Antarctica 78°33′ S, 86°54′ W 248
Vinton, Iowa, U.S. 42°9′ N, 92°2′ W 110
Vinton, La., U.S. 30°11′ N, 93°36′ W 103
Violet Grove, Can. 53°8′ N, 115°4′ W 108
Vipiteno, It. 46°54′ N, 11°25′ E 167
Vir, Taj. 37°42′ N, 72°11′ E 197
Virac, Philippines 13°33′ N, 124°13′ E 203
Virachei, Cambodia 14°0′ N, 106°46′ E 202
Virachey National Park, Cambodia 14°12′ N, 106°23′ E 202
Viramgam, India 23°5′ N, 72°3′ E 186
Virandozero, Russ. 64°1′ N, 36°7′ E 154
Viranşehir, Turk. 37°12′ N, 39°46′ E 195
Virbalis, Lith. 54°38′ N, 22°48′ E 166
Virden, Can. 49°51′ N, 100°57′ W 90
Virden, Ill., U.S. 39°29′ N, 89°46′ W 102
Virden, Mo., U.S. 39°29′ N, 89°46′ W 94
Vire, Fr. 48°50′ N, 0°54′ E 150
Vireši, Latv. 57°27′ N, 26°21′ E 166
Vîrfurile, Rom. 46°18′ N, 22°33′ E 168
Virgem da Lapa, Braz. 16°48′ S, 42°23′ W 138
Virgin Gorda, island, U.K. 18°28′ N, 64°26′ W 118
Virgin Islands, Caribbean Sea 18°4′ N, 64°50′ W 118
Virgin Islands, adm. division, U.S. 18°20′ N, 64°50′ W 118
Virgin Mountains, Nev., U.S. 36°39′ N, 114°12′ W 101
Virgin, river, Can. 57°0′ N, 108°9′ W 108
Virgin, river, Nev., U.S. 36°39′ N, 114°20′ W 101
Virginia, Minn., U.S. 47°31′ N, 92°35′ W 82
Virginia, S. Af. 28°11′ S, 26°51′ E 227
Virginia, adm. division, Va., U.S. 37°56′ N, 79°15′ W 94
Virginia Beach, Va., U.S. 36°50′ N, 76°0′ W 96
Virginia Falls, Can. 61°52′ N, 128°14′ W 98
Virgolândia, Braz. 18°29′ S, 42°18′ W 138
Virje, Croatia 46°3′ N, 16°58′ E 168
Virmutjoki, Fin. 61°20′ N, 28°44′ E 166
Virojoki, Fin. 60°34′ N, 27°40′ E 166
Virolahti, Fin. 60°30′ N, 27°40′ E 166
Virovitica, Croatia 45°49′ N, 17°24′ E 168
Virpazar, Mont. 42°15′ N, 19°5′ E 168
Virrat, Fin. 62°12′ N, 23°43′ E 154
Vîrşolţ, Rom. 47°12′ N, 22°55′ E 168
Virtaniemi, Russ. 68°53′ N, 28°27′ E 152
Virton, Belg. 49°34′ N, 5°32′ E 163
Virtsu, Est. 58°33′ N, 23°30′ E 166
Virú, Peru 8°28′ S, 78°46′ W 130
Viru Roela, Est. 59°9′ N, 26°35′ E 166
Viru-Jaagupi, Est. 59°14′ N, 26°27′ E 166
Virunga, Dem. Rep. of the Congo 1°1′ S, 29°0′ E 224
Virunga National Park, Dem. Rep. of the Congo 0°40′ N, 29°47′ E 224
Vis, Croatia 43°2′ N, 16°10′ E 168
Vis (Lissa), island, Croatia 42°57′ N, 16°5′ E 168
Visaginas, Lith. 55°34′ N, 26°23′ E 166
Visalia, Calif., U.S. 36°20′ N, 119°18′ W 100
Visayan Sea 11°27′ N, 123°36′ E 203
Visbek, Ger. 52°50′ N, 8°19′ E 163
Visby, Sw. 57°37′ N, 18°17′ E 166
Visconde do Rio Branco, Braz. 2°54′ S, 69°39′ W 136
Viscount Melville Sound 74°17′ N, 105°54′ W 255
Visé, Belg. 50°44′ N, 5°42′ E 167
Višegrad, Bosn. and Herzg. 43°47′ N, 19°18′ E 168
Visegrád, Hung. 47°46′ N, 18°59′ E 168
Viseu, Braz. 1°13′ S, 46°10′ W 130
Viseu, Port. 40°39′ N, 7°56′ W 150
Viseu, adm. division, Port. 40°41′ N, 8°16′ W 150
Vishakhapatnam, India 17°44′ N, 83°18′ E 188
Vishera, river, Russ. 61°4′ N, 58°44′ E 154
Višķi, Latv. 56°1′ N, 26°46′ E 166
Vislanda, Nor. 56°46′ N, 14°25′ E 152
Viso del Marqués, Sp. 38°30′ N, 3°34′ W 164
Viso, Monte, peak, It. 44°39′ N, 7°4′ E 165
Visoko, Bosn. and Herzg. 43°58′ N, 18°9′ E 168
Visp, Switz. 46°17′ N, 7°53′ E 167
Vista, Calif., U.S. 33°12′ N, 117°16′ W 101
Vista Alegre, Braz. 4°21′ S, 56°17′ W 130
Vista Alegre, Braz. 6°18′ S, 68°10′ W 130
Vista Alegre, Braz. 1°27′ N, 68°14′ W 136
Vista, Cerro, peak, N. Mex., U.S. 36°13′ N, 105°29′ W 92
Vital Lake, lake, Can. 61°31′ N, 108°33′ W 108
Vitån, river, Nor. 66°17′ N, 21°49′ E 152
Viterbo, It. 42°25′ N, 12°5′ E 214
Viti Levu, island, Fiji Islands 17°50′ S, 178°0′ E 242
Vitichi, Bol. 20°16′ S, 65°29′ W 137
Vitim, Russ. 59°27′ N, 112°22′ E 160
Vitim, river, Russ. 53°53′ N, 114°38′ E 190
Vitina, Bosn. and Herzg. 43°13′ N, 17°29′ E 168
Vitor, Chile 18°48′ S, 70°22′ W 137
Vitor, Peru 16°29′ S, 71°48′ W 137
Vitória, Braz. 20°17′ S, 40°18′ W 138
Vitória, Braz. 2°56′ S, 52°3′ W 130
Vitória da Conquista, Braz. 14°52′ S, 40°52′ W 138
Vitória Seamount, South Atlantic Ocean 20°20′ S, 37°0′ W 253
Vitoria-Gasteiz, Sp. 42°50′ N, 2°41′ W 164
Vitorog, peak, Bosn. and Herzg. 44°6′ N, 17°2′ E 168
Vitry-le-François, Fr. 48°43′ N, 4°35′ E 163
Vitsyebsk, Belarus 55°12′ N, 30°20′ E 152
Vittangi, Nor. 67°40′ N, 21°37′ E 152
Vittel, Fr. 48°12′ N, 5°58′ E 163
Vittoria, It. 36°57′ N, 14°31′ E 156
Vittorio Veneto, It. 45°58′ N, 12°16′ E 167
Vitvattnet, Nor. 66°3′ N, 23°9′ E 152
Vityaz Trench, South Pacific Ocean 11°20′ S, 174°17′ E 252
Viveiro, Sp. 43°36′ N, 7°38′ W 214
Viver, Sp. 39°55′ N, 0°36′ E 164
Vivi, Ozero, lake, Russ. 66°19′ N, 92°55′ E 169
Vivi, river, Russ. 65°5′ N, 96°4′ E 169
Vivian, La., U.S. 32°51′ N, 93°59′ W 103
Vivoratá, Arg. 37°41′ S, 57°42′ W 139
Vizcachas, Meseta de las, Arg. 50°35′ S, 73°58′ W 134
Vizcaino, Cape, Calif., U.S. 39°45′ N, 124°16′ W 90
Vizcaíno, Desierto de, Mex. 27°41′ N, 113°54′ W 112
Vizcaíno, Sierra, Mex. 27°31′ N, 114°24′ W 112
Vize, Turk. 41°34′ N, 27°45′ E 156
Vizhas, Russ. 66°38′ N, 45°50′ E 154
Vizhay, Russ. 61°14′ N, 60°13′ E 154
Vizhevo, Russ. 64°41′ N, 43°55′ E 154
Vizianagaram, India 18°5′ N, 83°24′ E 188
Vizinga, Russ. 61°6′ N, 50°6′ E 154
Vlădeasa, peak, Rom. 46°44′ N, 22°46′ E 168
Vladičin Han, Serb. 42°42′ N, 22°3′ E 168
Vladikavkaz, Russ. 43°0′ N, 44°44′ E 195
Vladimir, Russ. 56°9′ N, 40°19′ E 154
Vladimir, adm. division, Russ. 56°2′ N, 39°15′ E 154
Vladimirci, Serb. 44°35′ N, 19°46′ E 168
Vladimirovac, Serb. 45°1′ N, 20°52′ E 168
Vladimirovka, Russ. 60°48′ N, 30°28′ E 166
Vladimirskiy Tupik, Russ. 55°40′ N, 33°25′ E 154
Vladivostok, Russ. 43°8′ N, 131°54′ E 200
Vlasenica, Bosn. and Herzg. 44°11′ N, 18°55′ E 168
Vlašić, Bosn. and Herzg. 44°18′ N, 17°21′ E 168
Vlasinje, Bosn. and Herzg. 44°26′ N, 17°12′ E 168
Vlasotince, Serb. 42°57′ N, 22°7′ E 168
Vlčany, Slovakia 48°0′ N, 17°57′ E 168
Vlieland, island, Neth. 53°18′ N, 4°49′ E 163
Vlissingen (Flushing), Neth. 51°27′ N, 3°34′ E 163
Vltava, river, Czech Rep. 49°29′ N, 14°4′ E 152
Vobkent, Uzb. 40°1′ N, 64°33′ E 197
Voćin, Croatia 45°37′ N, 17°31′ E 168
Voden, Bulg. 42°4′ N, 26°54′ E 156
Vodil, Uzb. 40°9′ N, 71°44′ E 197
Vodl Ozero, lake, Russ. 62°16′ N, 36°18′ E 154
Vodnyy, Russ. 63°31′ N, 53°28′ E 154
Voerde, Ger. 51°36′ N, 6°40′ E 167
Vogan, Togo 6°21′ N, 1°30′ E 222
Vogelsberg, Ger. 50°40′ N, 8°44′ E 167
Voghera, It. 44°58′ N, 9°0′ E 167
Võhandu, river, Est. 57°46′ N, 27°7′ E 166
Vohipeno, Madagascar 22°21′ S, 47°53′ E 220
Võhma, Est. 58°36′ N, 25°32′ E 166
Võhma, Est. 58°31′ N, 22°20′ E 166
Vöhringen, Ger. 48°16′ N, 10°4′ E 152
Voi, Kenya 3°23′ S, 38°35′ E 224
Void-Vacon, Fr. 48°41′ N, 5°36′ E 163
Voikoski, Fin. 61°14′ N, 26°47′ E 166
Vóïo, Óros, peak, Gr. 40°16′ N, 20°59′ E 156
Voislova, Rom. 45°31′ N, 22°27′ E 168
Voiteg, Rom. 45°28′ N, 21°14′ E 156
Vojmån, Nor. 64°47′ N, 16°48′ E 152
Vojmsjön, lake, Nor. 64°51′ N, 16°2′ E 152
Vojvodina, region, Serb. 45°21′ N, 19°4′ E 168
Voknavolok, Russ. 64°56′ N, 30°33′ E 152
Voláda, Gr. 35°32′ N, 27°11′ E 156
Volán Domuyo, peak, Arg. 36°44′ S, 70°47′ W 122
Volborg, Mont., U.S. 45°49′ N, 105°40′ W 90
Volcán, Arg. 23°54′ S, 65°29′ W 132
Volcán Isluga National Park, Chile 19°20′ S, 69°19′ W 122
Volcán Masaya National Park, Nicar. 11°56′ N, 86°13′ W 115
Volcán Nevado de Colima National Park, Mex. 19°27′ N, 103°57′ W 72
Volcán Poás National Park, C.R. 10°11′ N, 84°19′ W 115
Volcano Islands (Kazan Rettō), islands, Philippine Sea 23°11′ N, 139°38′ E 190
Volcano Peak, Calif., U.S. 35°57′ N, 117°53′ W 101
Volchansk, Russ. 59°57′ N, 60°3′ E 154
Voldi, Est. 58°32′ N, 26°35′ E 166
Vol′dino, Russ. 62°15′ N, 54°8′ E 154
Volga, Russ. 57°57′ N, 38°22′ E 154
Volga, S. Dak., U.S. 44°17′ N, 96°57′ W 90
Volga, river, Russ. 55°48′ N, 44°12′ E 160
Volga-Don Canal, Russ. 48°33′ N, 43°47′ E 158
Volgodonsk, Russ. 47°30′ N, 42°2′ E 158
Volgograd, adm. division, Russ. 49°28′ N, 42°54′ E 158
Volgograd (Stalingrad), Russ. 48°46′ N, 44°28′ E 158
Volgogradskoye Vodokhranilishche, lake, Russ. 50°16′ N, 45°9′ E 158
Volgorechensk, Russ. 57°27′ N, 41°16′ E 154
Volimes, Gr. 37°52′ N, 20°39′ E 156
Volintiri, Mold. 46°26′ N, 29°35′ E 156
Volkach, Ger. 49°51′ N, 10°13′ E 167
Volkhov, Russ. 59°55′ N, 32°25′ E 154
Volkhov, river, Russ. 58°34′ N, 31°39′ E 154
Volksrust, S. Af. 27°22′ S, 29°50′ E 227
Vollenhove, Neth. 52°40′ N, 5°58′ E 163
Volma, Belarus 53°52′ N, 26°57′ E 166
Volnovakha, Ukr. 47°36′ N, 37°29′ E 156
Volochanka, Russ. 71°2′ N, 94°36′ E 160
Volochys′k, Ukr. 49°30′ N, 26°11′ E 152
Volodarsk, Russ. 56°13′ N, 43°11′ E 154

Volodskaya, Russ. 62°22′ N, 41°56′ E 154
Vologda, Russ. 59°10′ N, 39°48′ E 154
Vologda, adm. division, Russ. 59°52′ N, 39°27′ E 154
Voloki, Belarus 54°35′ N, 28°11′ E 166
Volokonovka, Russ. 50°29′ N, 37°51′ E 158
Volonga, Russ. 67°3′ N, 47°52′ E 169
Vólos, Gr. 39°24′ N, 22°55′ E 180
Voloshka, Russ. 61°19′ N, 40°2′ E 154
Voloshovo, Russ. 58°42′ N, 29°17′ E 166
Volosovo, Russ. 59°26′ N, 29°28′ E 166
Volovo, Russ. 53°32′ N, 38°0′ E 154
Voloyarvi, Russ. 60°17′ N, 30°46′ E 166
Vol'sk, Russ. 52°5′ N, 47°22′ E 158
Volta, Calif., U.S. 37°5′ N, 120°56′ W 100
Volta, Lake, Ghana 8°15′ N, 1°21′ W 214
Volta Redonda, Braz. 22°27′ S, 44°6′ W 138
Volterra, It. 43°24′ N, 10°50′ E 156
Volubilis, ruin(s), Mor. 34°6′ N, 5°46′ W 214
Voluntown, Conn., U.S. 41°34′ N, 71°52′ W 104
Volzhsk, Russ. 55°52′ N, 48°25′ E 154
Volzhskiy, Russ. 48°49′ N, 44°50′ E 184
Vonavona, island, Solomon Islands 8°17′ S, 157°0′ E 242
Vonda, Can. 52°19′ N, 106°5′ W 108
Vondrozo, Madagascar 22°49′ S, 47°19′ E 220
Võnnu, Est. 58°16′ N, 27°3′ E 166
Voo, Kenya 1°41′ S, 38°20′ E 224
Voranava, Belarus 54°8′ N, 25°18′ E 166
Vorder-rhein, river, Switz. 46°40′ N, 8°52′ E 167
Vordingborg, Den. 55°0′ N, 11°55′ E 152
Vóreio Egéo, adm. division, Gr. 38°45′ N, 26°0′ E 156
Vorga, Russ. 53°42′ N, 32°45′ E 154
Vóries Sporádes, islands, Aegean Sea 39°8′ N, 23°37′ E 180
Voring Plateau, Norwegian Sea 67°13′ N, 4°23′ E 255
Vorkuta, Russ. 67°25′ N, 64°4′ E 169
Vorlich, Ben, peak, U.K. 56°20′ N, 4°20′ W 150
Vormsi, island, Est. 59°3′ N, 23°1′ E 166
Vorogovo, Russ. 60°57′ N, 89°25′ E 169
Vorona, river, Russ. 52°8′ N, 42°26′ E 158
Voronech', Belarus 55°18′ N, 28°35′ E 166
Voronezh, Russ. 51°38′ N, 39°11′ E 158
Voronezh, adm. division, Russ. 50°50′ N, 38°58′ E 158
Voronezh, river, Russ. 52°21′ N, 39°31′ E 158
Vorontsovka, Russ. 59°37′ N, 60°12′ E 154
Vorontsovo, Russ. 57°18′ N, 28°42′ E 166
Vorontsovo, Russ. 71°40′ N, 83°35′ E 160
Voron'ye, Russ. 68°28′ N, 35°20′ E 152
Vorposten Peak, Antarctica 71°31′ S, 14°56′ E 248
Vorskla, river, Ukr. 49°36′ N, 34°40′ E 158
Vørterkaka Nunatak, peak, Antarctica 72°42′ S, 27°23′ E 248
Võrts Järv, lake, Est. 58°19′ N, 25°43′ E 166
Võru, Est. 57°49′ N, 27°0′ E 166
Vorukh, Taj. 39°50′ N, 70°34′ E 197
Vosburg, S. Af. 30°35′ S, 22°49′ E 227
Vose, Taj. 37°46′ N, 69°41′ E 197
Vosges, Fr. 48°57′ N, 6°56′ E 163
Voskresensk, Russ. 55°19′ N, 38°43′ E 154
Voskresenskoye, Russ. 56°48′ N, 45°28′ E 154
Voskresenskoye, Russ. 59°25′ N, 37°56′ E 154
Voskresenskoye, Russ. 53°8′ N, 56°4′ E 154
Voss, Nor. 60°37′ N, 6°22′ E 152
Vostochnaya Guba, Russ. 67°24′ N, 32°38′ E 152
Vostok, Russia, station, Antarctica 78°31′ S, 107°1′ E 248
Võsu, Est. 59°33′ N, 25°56′ E 166
Votaw, Tex., U.S. 30°24′ N, 94°41′ W 103
Votice, Czech Rep. 49°38′ N, 14°37′ E 152
Votkinsk, Russ. 57°0′ N, 53°55′ E 154
Votuporanga, Braz. 20°25′ S, 49°59′ W 138
Voulgára, peak, Gr. 39°5′ N, 21°50′ E 156
Voulx, Fr. 48°14′ N, 2°59′ E 163
Vounása, peak, Gr. 39°56′ N, 21°41′ E 156
Voúrnios, Óros, Gr. 40°3′ N, 21°16′ E 156
Vouziers, Fr. 49°23′ N, 4°43′ E 163
Vovchans'k, Ukr. 50°16′ N, 36°57′ E 158
Voves, Fr. 48°15′ N, 1°38′ E 163
Vovodo, river, Cen. Af. Rep. 5°59′ N, 24°33′ E 218
Vowchyn, Belarus 52°17′ N, 23°17′ E 152
Voyageurs National Park, Minn., U.S. 48°14′ N, 94°58′ W 94
Voynitsa, Russ. 65°9′ N, 30°18′ E 152
Voyvozh, Russ. 62°54′ N, 55°5′ E 154
Vozhayel', Russ. 62°50′ N, 51°22′ E 154
Vozhe, Ozero, lake, Russ. 60°35′ N, 38°36′ E 154
Vozhega, Russ. 60°27′ N, 40°10′ E 154
Vozhgora, Russ. 64°34′ N, 48°21′ E 154
Vozhma, Russ. 58°55′ N, 46°47′ E 154
Vozh'yel', Russ. 63°14′ N, 49°37′ E 154
Voznesens'k, Ukr. 47°36′ N, 31°21′ E 156
Voznesen'ye, Russ. 61°1′ N, 35°30′ E 154
Vozvyahenka, Kaz. 54°28′ N, 70°52′ E 184
Vrachíonas, peak, Gr. 37°49′ N, 20°39′ E 156
Vrancea, adm. division, Rom. 45°41′ N, 26°29′ E 156
Vrancei, Munţii, Rom. 45°49′ N, 25°55′ E 156
Vrang, Taj. 37°1′ N, 72°22′ E 186
Vrangelya, Ostrov (Wrangel Island), island, Russ. 71°29′ N, 175°23′ E 160
Vranica, peak, Bosn. and Herzg. 43°56′ N, 17°40′ E 168
Vranje, Serb. 42°33′ N, 21°54′ E 168
Vranjska Banja, Serb. 42°32′ N, 22°1′ E 168
Vratsa, Bulg. 43°12′ N, 23°33′ E 156
Vratsa, adm. division, Bulg. 43°18′ N, 23°27′ E 156
Vrbanja, Croatia 44°58′ N, 18°55′ E 168
Vrbas, Serb. 45°33′ N, 19°38′ E 168
Vrbnik, Croatia 44°0′ N, 16°9′ E 168
Vrbnik, Croatia 45°4′ N, 14°39′ E 156
Vrboska, Croatia 43°9′ N, 16°40′ E 156
Vrbovec, Croatia 45°53′ N, 16°25′ E 168
Vrčin, Serb. 44°40′ N, 20°33′ E 168
Vrdnik, Serb. 45°7′ N, 19°47′ E 168
Vrede, S. Af. 27°27′ S, 29°8′ E 227
Vreden, Ger. 52°2′ N, 6°49′ E 167
Vredenburg, S. Af. 32°55′ S, 17°58′ E 227
Vrginmost, Croatia 45°20′ N, 15°52′ E 168
Vrgorac, Croatia 43°11′ N, 17°22′ E 168
Vrlika, Croatia 43°55′ N, 16°24′ E 168
Vrnograč, Bosn. and Herzg. 45°9′ N, 15°57′ E 168
Vršac, Serb. 45°7′ N, 21°18′ E 168
Vrtoče, Bosn. and Herzg. 44°38′ N, 16°10′ E 168
Vryburg, S. Af. 26°59′ S, 24°42′ E 227
Vryheid, S. Af. 27°48′ S, 30°45′ E 227
Vsevolodo Blagodatskiy, Russ. 60°28′ N, 59°59′ E 154
Vsheli, Russ. 58°10′ N, 29°50′ E 166
Vu Liet, Vietnam 18°42′ N, 105°22′ E 202
Vučitrn see Vushtrria, Kos. 42°49′ N, 20°58′ E 168
Vučja Luka, Bosn. and Herzg. 43°55′ N, 18°31′ E 168
Vučje, Serb. 42°51′ N, 21°54′ E 168
Vught, Neth. 51°38′ N, 5°17′ E 167
Vuka, river, Croatia 45°27′ N, 18°32′ E 168
Vuktyl, Russ. 63°54′ N, 57°28′ E 154
Vulcan, Can. 50°24′ N, 113°16′ W 90
Vulcan, Rom. 45°22′ N, 23°18′ E 168
Vulci, ruin(s), It. 42°23′ N, 11°31′ E 156
Vung Tau, Vietnam 10°21′ N, 107°4′ E 202
Vuntut National Park, Can. 68°11′ N, 139°49′ W 98
Vuoggatjålme, Nor. 66°33′ N, 16°21′ E 152
Vuohijärvi, Fin. 61°4′ N, 26°47′ E 166
Vuohijärvi, lake, Fin. 61°7′ N, 26°20′ E 166
Vuokatti, Fin. 64°7′ N, 28°13′ E 152
Vuollerim, Nor. 66°25′ N, 20°36′ E 152
Vuonislahti, Fin. 63°8′ N, 29°59′ E 152
Vuotso, Fin. 68°5′ N, 27°6′ E 152
Vurnary, Russ. 55°28′ N, 47°1′ E 154
Vushtrria (Vučitrn), Kos. 42°49′ N, 20°58′ E 168
Vwawa, Tanzania 9°6′ S, 32°55′ E 224
Vyartsilya, Russ. 62°10′ N, 30°41′ E 152
Vyatka, river, Russ. 59°20′ N, 52°0′ E 154
Vyatskiye Polyany, Russ. 56°11′ N, 51°11′ E 154
Vyazemskiy, Russ. 47°31′ N, 134°46′ E 190
Vyaz'ma, Russ. 55°13′ N, 34°21′ E 154
Vyazniki, Russ. 56°14′ N, 42°9′ E 154
Vybor, Russ. 57°13′ N, 29°7′ E 166
Vyborg (Viipuri), Russ. 60°41′ N, 28°45′ E 166
Vyborovo, Russ. 58°19′ N, 29°0′ E 166
Vychegda, river, Russ. 61°31′ N, 48°11′ E 154
Vyderta, Ukr. 51°43′ N, 25°1′ E 152
Vyerkhnyadzvinsk, Belarus 55°46′ N, 27°56′ E 166
Vyetryna, Belarus 55°24′ N, 28°26′ E 166
Vyg Ozero, lake, Russ. 63°48′ N, 33°40′ E 152
Vyksa, Russ. 55°18′ N, 42°12′ E 154
Vylkove, Ukr. 45°26′ N, 29°35′ E 156
Vylok, Ukr. 48°6′ N, 22°50′ E 156
Vym', river, Russ. 62°41′ N, 50°53′ E 154
Vym', river, Russ. 63°22′ N, 51°36′ E 154
Vymsk, Russ. 60°24′ N, 48°19′ E 154
Vyritsa, Russ. 59°24′ N, 30°17′ E 166
Vyshhorod, Ukr. 50°32′ N, 30°35′ E 158
Vyshniy Volochek, Russ. 57°34′ N, 34°38′ E 154
Vysočina, adm. division, Czech Rep. 49°10′ N, 15°21′ E 152
Vysokaye, Belarus 52°21′ N, 23°20′ E 152
Vysokovsk, Russ. 56°17′ N, 36°31′ E 154
Vysotsk, Russ. 60°36′ N, 28°34′ E 166
Vysotskoye, Russ. 56°49′ N, 29°1′ E 166
Vytegra, Russ. 61°1′ N, 36°30′ E 154

W

"W" National Park, Benin 11°49′ N, 2°27′ E 222
Wa, Ghana 10°2′ N, 2°30′ W 222
Wa, Pol. 50°45′ N, 16°16′ E 152
Waajid, Somalia 3°47′ N, 43°16′ E 218
Waal, river, Neth. 51°54′ N, 5°35′ E 167
Waalwijk, Neth. 51°41′ N, 5°5′ E 167
Waas, Mount, peak, Utah, U.S. 38°31′ N, 109°19′ W 90
Wa'at, Sudan 8°8′ N, 32°7′ E 224
Wababimiga Lake, Can. 50°18′ N, 87°9′ W 94
Wabakimi Lake, Can. 50°34′ N, 90°20′ W 110
Wabana, Can. 47°38′ N, 52°56′ W 111
Wabasca, river, Can. 56°15′ N, 113°42′ W 108
Wabasca-Desmarais, Can. 55°59′ N, 113°52′ W 108
Wabash, Ind., U.S. 40°48′ N, 85°50′ W 102
Wabash, river, Ind., U.S. 40°48′ N, 85°14′ W 102
Wabasha, Minn., U.S. 44°21′ N, 92°3′ W 110
Wabassi, river, Can. 51°46′ N, 87°39′ W 110
Wabasso, Fla., U.S. 27°44′ N, 80°27′ W 105
Wabē Gestro, river, Eth. 5°53′ N, 41°38′ E 224
Wabē Shebelē, river, Eth. 7°25′ N, 39°36′ E 224
Wabern, Ger. 51°6′ N, 9°21′ E 167
Wabimeig Lake, Can. 51°26′ N, 86°15′ W 110
Waboose Dam, Can. 50°51′ N, 88°0′ W 110
Wabowden, Can. 54°54′ N, 98°38′ W 108
Wabuk Point, Can. 55°18′ N, 87°23′ W 106
W.A.C. Bennett Dam, Can. 55°51′ N, 123°2′ W 108
Waccasassa Bay 29°6′ N, 82°54′ W 105
Wächtersbach, Ger. 50°15′ N, 9°17′ E 167
Waco, Can. 51°26′ N, 65°36′ W 111
Waco, Tex., U.S. 31°31′ N, 97°8′ W 96
Waconichi, Lac, lake, Can. 50°5′ N, 74°39′ W 94
Wad Abu Nahl, Sudan 13°6′ N, 34°53′ E 182
Wad Banda, Sudan 13°4′ N, 27°56′ E 216
Wad el Haddad, Sudan 13°48′ N, 33°30′ E 182
Wad Hamid, Sudan 16°27′ N, 32°45′ E 182
Wad Medani, Sudan 14°23′ N, 33°29′ E 182
Wadamago, Somalia 8°52′ N, 46°15′ E 216
Wadayama, Japan 35°19′ N, 134°48′ E 201
Waddān, Lib. 29°10′ N, 16°6′ E 216
Waddenzee 53°5′ N, 4°54′ E 163
Waddington, N.Y., U.S. 44°51′ N, 75°13′ W 94
Waddington, Mount, peak, Can. 51°22′ N, 125°21′ W 90
Wadena, Can. 51°56′ N, 103°48′ W 90
Wadena, Minn., U.S. 46°25′ N, 95°9′ W 94
Wadersloh, Ger. 51°44′ N, 8°14′ E 167
Wādī al Masīlah, river, Yemen 16°12′ N, 49°33′ E 182
Wādī as Sīr, Jordan 31°56′ N, 35°48′ E 194
Wâdi Gimâl, Gezîrat, island, Egypt 24°30′ N, 33°51′ E 182
Wadi Halfa, Sudan 21°46′ N, 31°20′ E 182
Wādīas Sir ḩān, Saudi Arabia 31°38′ N, 37°3′ E 194
Wadsworth, Nev., U.S. 39°38′ N, 119°19′ W 90
Wadsworth, Ohio, U.S. 41°0′ N, 81°44′ W 102
Wadu, island, Maldives 5°44′ N, 72°17′ E 188
Waelder, Tex., U.S. 29°40′ N, 97°18′ W 96
Waesche, Mount, peak, Antarctica 77°3′ S, 126°15′ W 248
Wafangdian, China 39°39′ N, 121°59′ E 198
Wafania, Dem. Rep. of the Congo 1°23′ S, 20°19′ E 218
Wafra, oil field, Kuwait 28°34′ N, 47°52′ E 196
Wagenia Fisheries, site, Dem. Rep. of the Congo 0°25′ N, 25°17′ E 224
Wageningen, Neth. 51°58′ N, 5°39′ E 167
Wager Bay 65°25′ N, 90°48′ W 106
Wager, Isla, island, Chile 47°34′ S, 75°43′ W 134
Waglisla, Can. 52°10′ N, 128°10′ W 108
Wagner, S. Dak., U.S. 43°3′ N, 98°19′ W 90
Wagner Nunatak, peak, Antarctica 83°59′ S, 68°23′ W 248
Wagon Mound, N. Mex., U.S. 36°0′ N, 104°43′ W 92
Wagontire Mountain, peak, Oreg., U.S. 43°20′ N, 119°58′ W 90
Wah Wah Range, Utah, U.S. 38°29′ N, 113°52′ W 90
Waha, oil field, Lib. 28°2′ N, 19°46′ E 216
Waha'ula Heiau, site, Hawai'i, U.S. 19°19′ N, 155°5′ W 99
Wahoo, Nebr., U.S. 41°12′ N, 96°38′ W 90
Wahpeton, N. Dak., U.S. 46°15′ N, 96°38′ W 90
Wai, India 17°58′ N, 73°55′ E 188
Wai'ale'ale, peak, Hawai'i, U.S. 22°4′ N, 159°33′ W 99
Wāīas Sir'ān, Jordan 31°26′ N, 36°56′ E 194
Waiau, N.Z. 42°40′ S, 173°3′ E 240
Waiau, river, N.Z. 45°42′ S, 167°34′ E 240
Waigeo, island, Indonesia 7°416′ N, 130°3′ E 192
Waihi, N.Z. 37°23′ S, 175°50′ E 240
Waihola, N.Z. 46°3′ S, 170°7′ E 240
Waikabubak, Indonesia 9°39′ S, 119°20′ E 192
Waikanae, N.Z. 40°54′ S, 175°6′ E 240
Waikawa, N.Z. 46°38′ S, 169°6′ E 240
Waikiwi, N.Z. 46°24′ S, 168°20′ E 240
Waikouaiti, N.Z. 45°35′ S, 170°40′ E 240
Waimamaku, N.Z. 35°34′ S, 173°28′ E 240
Waimangaroa, N.Z. 41°45′ S, 171°45′ E 240
Waimarama, N.Z. 39°49′ S, 176°58′ E 240
Waimate, N.Z. 44°45′ S, 171°2′ E 240
Wainfleet All Saints, U.K. 53°7′ N, 0°14′ E 162
Waingapu, Indonesia 9°41′ S, 120°4′ E 192
Waini Point, Guyana 8°25′ N, 59°51′ W 116
Wainwright, Alas., U.S. 70°37′ N, 160°3′ W 246
Wainwright, Can. 52°50′ N, 110°51′ W 108
Waiohonu Petroglyphs, site, Hawai'i, U.S. 20°42′ N, 156°3′ W 99
Wai'oli Mission, site, Hawai'i, U.S. 22°11′ N, 159°33′ W 99
Waiotira, N.Z. 35°57′ S, 174°12′ E 240
Waiouru, N.Z. 39°30′ S, 175°40′ E 240
Waipahi, N.Z. 46°9′ S, 169°14′ E 240
Waipara, N.Z. 43°4′ S, 172°45′ E 240
Waipawa, N.Z. 39°58′ S, 176°35′ E 240
Waipu, N.Z. 36°0′ S, 174°26′ E 240
Waipukurau, N.Z. 40°1′ S, 176°35′ E 240
Wairau Valley, N.Z. 41°36′ S, 173°31′ E 240
Wairoa, N.Z. 39°4′ S, 177°23′ E 240
Waitahanui, N.Z. 38°48′ S, 176°5′ E 240
Waitakaruru, N.Z. 37°16′ S, 175°24′ E 240
Waitara, N.Z. 39°2′ S, 174°13′ E 240
Waitati, N.Z. 45°46′ S, 170°34′ E 240
Waite, Cape, Antarctica 72°42′ S, 103°44′ W 248
Waitemata, N.Z. 36°52′ S, 174°37′ E 240
Waitoa, N.Z. 37°36′ S, 175°39′ E 240
Waitomo Caves, site, N.Z. 38°18′ S, 175°2′ E 240
Waitotara, N.Z. 39°49′ S, 174°43′ E 240
Wajima, Japan 37°23′ N, 136°53′ E 201
Wajir, Kenya 1°42′ N, 40°2′ E 224
Waka, Dem. Rep. of the Congo 0°50′ N, 20°3′ E 218
Waka, Dem. Rep. of the Congo 0°58′ N, 20°13′ E 218
Waka, Eth. 7°5′ N, 37°18′ E 224
Wakami Lake, Can. 47°27′ N, 83°25′ W 94
Wakasa, Japan 35°18′ N, 134°22′ E 201
Wakasa Wan 35°32′ N, 135°31′ E 201
Wakaw, Can. 52°39′ N, 105°45′ W 108
Wakayama, Japan 34°12′ N, 135°10′ E 201
Wakayama, adm. division, Japan 34°13′ N, 135°16′ E 201
Wake Forest, N.C., U.S. 35°58′ N, 78°31′ W 96
Wake Island, U.S. 19°19′ N, 166°31′ E 252
Wakeeney, Kans., U.S. 39°0′ N, 99°54′ W 90
Wakefield, Kans., U.S. 39°11′ N, 97°2′ W 90
Wakefield, Mich., U.S. 46°28′ N, 89°57′ W 94
Wakefield, Nebr., U.S. 42°15′ N, 96°52′ W 94
Wakefield, R.I., U.S. 41°26′ N, 71°30′ W 104
Wakefield, U.K. 53°41′ N, 1°30′ W 162
Wakema, Myanmar 16°36′ N, 95°9′ E 202
Wakenaam Island, Guyana 6°59′ N, 58°35′ W 130
Wakkanai, Japan 45°18′ N, 141°48′ E 190
Wakkerstroom, S. Af. 27°20′ S, 30°7′ E 227
Wakuach, Lac, lake, Can. 55°34′ N, 69°29′ W 106
Wakulla Springs, site, Fla., U.S. 30°12′ N, 84°23′ W 96
Walachia, region, Rom. 44°28′ N, 22°46′ E 168
Walberswick, U.K. 52°18′ N, 1°39′ E 163
Walcott, Can. 54°30′ N, 126°54′ W 108
Walcott Inlet 16°45′ S, 123°56′ E 230
Waldbröl, Ger. 50°52′ N, 7°36′ E 167
Waldeck, Ger. 51°12′ N, 9°4′ E 167
Walden, Vt., U.S. 44°26′ N, 72°14′ W 104
Waldfischbach-Burgalben, Ger. 49°16′ N, 7°38′ E 163
Waldheim, Can. 52°37′ N, 106°39′ W 108
Waldo, Ark., U.S. 33°20′ N, 93°18′ W 103
Waldo, Fla., U.S. 29°47′ N, 82°11′ W 105
Waldport, Oreg., U.S. 44°23′ N, 124°3′ W 90
Waldron, Ark., U.S. 34°52′ N, 94°6′ W 96
Waldron, Ind., U.S. 39°27′ N, 85°40′ W 102
Waldron, Cape, Antarctica 66°15′ S, 119°43′ E 248
Wales, Alas., U.S. 65°31′ N, 168°7′ W 98
Wales, Mass., U.S. 42°3′ N, 72°11′ W 104
Wales, adm. division, U.K. 52°21′ N, 3°52′ W 162
Wales Island, island, Can. 67°38′ N, 89°20′ W 106
Walewale, Ghana 10°21′ N, 0°49′ E 222
Walgreen Coast, Antarctica 75°29′ S, 102°49′ W 248
Walhalla, Mich., U.S. 43°56′ N, 86°7′ W 102
Walhalla, N. Dak., U.S. 48°54′ N, 97°56′ W 90
Walhalla, S.C., U.S. 34°45′ N, 83°5′ W 96
Walikale, Dem. Rep. of the Congo 1°30′ S, 28°5′ E 224
Walker, La., U.S. 30°29′ N, 90°52′ W 103
Walker, Mich., U.S. 42°59′ N, 85°43′ W 102
Walker, Minn., U.S. 47°4′ N, 94°37′ W 90
Walker, Lac, lake, Can. 50°24′ N, 67°30′ W 111
Walker Lake, Nev., U.S. 38°38′ N, 119°38′ W 80
Walker Lake, lake, Can. 54°36′ N, 97°31′ W 108
Walker Pass, Calif., U.S. 35°39′ N, 118°3′ W 101
Walkerton, Can. 44°7′ N, 81°9′ W 102
Walkerton, Ind., U.S. 41°28′ N, 86°29′ W 102
Walkerville, Mich., U.S. 43°42′ N, 86°7′ W 102
Wall, S. Dak., U.S. 43°59′ N, 102°16′ W 90
Wall, Mount, peak, Austral. 22°50′ S, 116°37′ E 230
Walla Walla, Wash., U.S. 46°4′ N, 118°22′ W 106
Wallabi Group, islands, Indian Ocean 28°15′ S, 113°42′ E 230
Wallace, Idaho, U.S. 47°26′ N, 115°54′ W 82
Wallace, Nebr., U.S. 40°50′ N, 101°11′ W 90
Wallace, N.C., U.S. 34°44′ N, 78°0′ W 96
Wallace Mountain, peak, Can. 54°55′ N, 115°56′ W 108
Wallaceburg, Can. 42°34′ N, 82°22′ W 102
Wallaroo, Austral. 33°55′ S, 137°39′ E 231
Wallasey, U.K. 53°25′ N, 3°2′ W 162
Walldorf, Ger. 50°36′ N, 10°23′ E 167
Wallenhorst, Ger. 52°20′ N, 7°59′ E 163
Wallingford, Conn., U.S. 41°27′ N, 72°50′ W 104
Wallingford, Vt., U.S. 43°28′ N, 72°59′ W 104
Wallis, Îles, islands, South Pacific Ocean 14°55′ S, 177°49′ W 238
Wallops Island, Va., U.S. 37°25′ N, 75°20′ W 80
Wallowa Mountains, Oreg., U.S. 45°28′ N, 117°49′ W 90
Walmer, U.K. 51°12′ N, 1°23′ E 163
Walnum, Mount, peak, Antarctica 72°8′ S, 23°50′ E 248
Walnut, Ill., U.S. 41°33′ N, 89°36′ W 102
Walnut Cove, N.C., U.S. 36°18′ N, 80°10′ W 94
Walnut Grove, Calif., U.S. 38°13′ N, 121°32′ W 100
Walnut Grove, Miss., U.S. 32°34′ N, 89°28′ W 103
Walnut Ridge, Ark., U.S. 36°3′ N, 90°58′ W 96
Walong, India 28°10′ N, 97°0′ E 188
Walpi, Ariz., U.S. 35°49′ N, 110°24′ W 92
Walpole, Mass., U.S. 42°5′ N, 71°16′ W 104
Walpole, N.H., U.S. 43°4′ N, 72°26′ W 104
Walsall, U.K. 52°35′ N, 2°0′ W 162
Walsenburg, Colo., U.S. 37°37′ N, 104°48′ W 92
Walsh, Colo., U.S. 37°22′ N, 102°17′ W 92
Walsingham, U.K. 52°53′ N, 0°52′ E 163
Walt Disney World, Fla., U.S. 28°23′ N, 81°34′ W 105
Walterboro, S.C., U.S. 32°54′ N, 80°41′ W 96
Walters Shoal, Indian Ocean 33°25′ S, 43°32′ E 254
Waltham, Mass., U.S. 42°22′ N, 71°15′ W 104
Walton, Ind., U.S. 40°39′ N, 86°14′ W 102
Walton, Ky., U.S. 38°51′ N, 84°36′ W 102
Walton, N.Y., U.S. 42°10′ N, 75°9′ W 94
Walton on the Naze, U.K. 51°50′ N, 1°15′ E 163
Walvis Bay, Namibia 23°0′ S, 14°33′ E 207
Walvis Ridge, South Atlantic Ocean 26°7′ S, 5°31′ E 253
Walyahmoning Rock, peak, Austral. 30°41′ S, 118°32′ E 230
Wamac, Ill., U.S. 38°29′ N, 89°8′ W 102
Wamba, Dem. Rep. of the Congo 1°37′ S, 22°28′ E 218
Wamba, Dem. Rep. of the Congo 2°9′ N, 27°57′ E 218
Wamba, Nig. 8°55′ N, 8°35′ E 222
Wampú, river, Hond. 15°0′ N, 85°36′ W 115
Wampusirpi, Hond. 15°11′ N, 84°38′ W 115
Wamsutter, Wyo., U.S. 41°40′ N, 107°58′ W 90
Wana, Pak. 32°19′ N, 69°40′ E 188
Wan'an, China 26°28′ N, 114°46′ E 198
Wandel Sea 82°11′ N, 24°59′ W 246
Wandering River, Can. 55°9′ N, 112°27′ W 108
Wando, S. Korea 34°17′ N, 126°47′ E 200
Wanfried, Ger. 51°11′ N, 10°10′ E 167
Wang Kai, Sudan 9°3′ N, 29°29′ E 224
Wang, river, Thai. 17°37′ N, 99°18′ E 202
Wanganui, N.Z. 39°57′ S, 175°2′ E 240
Wangcang, China 32°17′ N, 106°21′ E 198
Wangda see Zogang, China 29°42′ N, 97°53′ E 188
Wangdiphodrang, Bhutan 27°30′ N, 89°54′ E 197
Wangdu, China 38°40′ N, 115°6′ E 198
Wangkui, China 46°50′ N, 126°30′ E 198
Wangmo, China 25°10′ N, 106°6′ E 198
Wangou, China 42°4′ N, 126°56′ E 200
Wangpan Yang 30°22′ N, 120°37′ E 198
Wanham, Can. 55°43′ N, 118°22′ W 108
Wani, India 20°2′ N, 78°57′ E 188
Wanie Rukula, Dem. Rep. of the Congo 0°12′ N, 25°35′ E 224
Wankaner, India 22°35′ N, 70°56′ E 186
Wanning, China 18°48′ N, 110°19′ E 198
Wanow, Afghan. 32°37′ N, 65°55′ E 186
Wantage, U.K. 51°35′ N, 1°26′ W 162
Wantagh, N.Y., U.S. 40°40′ N, 73°30′ W 104
Wanxian, China 30°47′ N, 108°17′ E 198
Wanyuan, China 32°5′ N, 108°7′ E 198
Wanzai, China 28°5′ N, 114°27′ E 198
Wapakoneta, Ohio, U.S. 40°33′ N, 84°11′ W 102
Wapata Lake, lake, Can. 58°46′ N, 106°16′ W 108
Wapawekka Lake, lake, Can. 54°49′ N, 105°23′ W 108
Wapella, Can. 50°17′ N, 102°0′ W 90
Wapello, Iowa, U.S. 41°10′ N, 91°12′ W 110
Wapesi, river, Can. 50°25′ N, 92°17′ W 110
Wapiti, river, Can. 54°43′ N, 119°50′ W 108
Wapou, Côte d'Ivoire 4°38′ N, 7°12′ W 222
Wappingers Falls, N.Y., U.S. 41°35′ N, 73°56′ W 104
Wapta Icefield, glacier, Can. 51°44′ N, 117°0′ W 108
Wapusk National Park, Can. 57°35′ N, 93°37′ W 108
War, W. Va., U.S. 37°18′ N, 81°42′ W 96
War Galoh, Somalia 6°15′ N, 47°36′ E 218
Warab, Sudan 8°2′ N, 28°35′ E 224
Warab, adm. division, Sudan 7°50′ N, 28°24′ E 224
Warangal, India 17°59′ N, 79°33′ E 188
Warburg, Ger. 51°29′ N, 9°8′ E 167
Ward, N.Z. 41°51′ S, 174°7′ E 240
Ward Cove, Alas., U.S. 55°26′ N, 131°46′ W 108
Ward Hill, peak 58°52′ N, 3°28′ W 150
Ward, Mount, peak, Antarctica 71°45′ S, 66°36′ W 248
Ward Mountain, peak, Nev., U.S. 39°5′ N, 115°0′ W 90
Warden, S. Af. 27°53′ S, 28°55′ E 227
Warden, Wash., U.S. 46°56′ N, 119°3′ W 90
Wardenburg, Ger. 53°4′ N, 8°12′ E 163
Wardha, India 20°43′ N, 78°36′ E 188
Ward's Stone, peak, U.K. 54°1′ N, 2°40′ W 162
Wardsboro, Vt., U.S. 43°2′ N, 72°48′ W 104
Ware, Can. 57°26′ N, 125°37′ W 108
Ware, Mass., U.S. 42°15′ N, 72°15′ W 104
Ware Shoals, S.C., U.S. 34°23′ N, 82°16′ W 96
Waregem, Belg. 50°53′ N, 3°26′ E 163
Wareham, Mass., U.S. 41°45′ N, 70°45′ W 104
Warehouse Point, Conn., U.S. 41°55′ N, 72°37′ W 104
Waremme, Belg. 50°41′ N, 5°14′ E 167
Waren, Indonesia 2°27′ S, 136°18′ E 192
Warendorf, Ger. 51°57′ N, 7°59′ E 167
Warffum, Neth. 53°23′ N, 6°34′ E 163
Warka, Pol. 51°47′ N, 21°11′ E 152
Warkworth, U.K. 55°20′ N, 1°37′ W 150
Warlubie, Pol. 53°35′ N, 18°37′ E 152
Warm Springs, Ga., U.S. 32°53′ N, 84°41′ W 96
Warman, Can. 52°17′ N, 106°34′ W 108
Warmbad, Namibia 28°28′ S, 18°45′ E 227
Warmbaths see Bela-Bela, S. Af. 24°55′ S, 28°16′ E 227
Warmeriville, Fr. 49°21′ N, 4°13′ E 163
Warmińsko-Mazurskie, adm. division, Pol. 53°57′ N, 19°25′ E 152
Warminster, U.K. 51°12′ N, 2°12′ W 162
Warner, Can. 49°16′ N, 112°12′ W 90
Warner, N.H., U.S. 43°16′ N, 71°49′ W 104
Warner, Mount, peak, Can. 51°4′ N, 123°17′ W 90
Warner Mountains, Calif., U.S. 41°1′ N, 120°16′ W 90
Warner Robins, Ga., U.S. 32°32′ N, 83°36′ W 112
Warner Valley, Oreg., U.S. 42°48′ N, 119°59′ W 90
Warnes, Arg. 34°54′ S, 60°30′ W 139
Warora, India 20°13′ N, 79°0′ E 188
Warralu, Sudan 8°10′ N, 27°17′ E 224
Warrego Range, Austral. 25°4′ S, 145°24′ E 230
Warren, Ark., U.S. 33°35′ N, 92°5′ W 96
Warren, Ill., U.S. 42°29′ N, 89°59′ W 102
Warren, Ind., U.S. 40°40′ N, 85°25′ W 102
Warren, Mich., U.S. 42°30′ N, 83°3′ W 102
Warren, Minn., U.S. 48°9′ N, 96°47′ W 90
Warren, Ohio, U.S. 41°13′ N, 80°48′ W 102
Warren, Oreg., U.S. 45°48′ N, 122°52′ W 100
Warren, Pa., U.S. 41°51′ N, 79°10′ W 94
Warren, R.I., U.S. 41°43′ N, 71°17′ W 104
Warren, Tex., U.S. 30°36′ N, 94°24′ W 103
Warren, Vt., U.S. 44°6′ N, 72°52′ W 104
Warren Landing, Can. 53°41′ N, 97°56′ W 108
Warren Peak, Calif., U.S. 41°21′ N, 120°19′ W 90
Warren Point, Can. 69°43′ N, 134°16′ W 98
Warrender, Cape, Can. 74°24′ N, 80°17′ W 106
Warrensburg, N.Y., U.S. 43°29′ N, 73°47′ W 104
Warrenton, Ga., U.S. 33°23′ N, 82°40′ W 96
Warrenton, Oreg., U.S. 46°9′ N, 123°55′ W 100
Warrenton, S. Af. 28°11′ S, 24°50′ E 227
Warri, Nig. 5°32′ N, 5°42′ E 222
Warrington, U.K. 53°23′ N, 2°36′ W 162
Warrnambool, Austral. 38°21′ S, 142°29′ E 231
Warroad, Minn., U.S. 48°53′ N, 95°22′ W 90
Warsaw, Ind., U.S. 41°13′ N, 85°51′ W 102
Warsaw, Ky., U.S. 38°45′ N, 84°54′ W 102
Warsaw, N.C., U.S. 34°59′ N, 78°6′ W 96
Warsaw, Ohio, U.S. 40°20′ N, 82°1′ W 102
Warsaw see Warszawa, Pol. 52°12′ N, 20°50′ E 152
Warshiikh, Somalia 2°15′ N, 45°53′ E 218
Warsop, U.K. 53°12′ N, 1°9′ W 162
Warstein, Ger. 51°26′ N, 8°20′ E 167
Warszawa (Warsaw), Pol. 52°12′ N, 20°50′ E 152
Warton, U.K. 53°44′ N, 2°54′ W 162
Warwick, Austral. 28°12′ S, 152°3′ E 231
Warwick, R.I., U.S. 41°41′ N, 71°23′ W 104
Warwick, U.K. 52°16′ N, 1°36′ W 162
Wasagu, Nig. 11°20′ N, 5°51′ E 222
Wasam, Pak. 36°32′ N, 72°53′ E 186
Wasatch Range, Utah, U.S. 39°56′ N, 111°51′ W 90
Wasco, Calif., U.S. 35°36′ N, 119°21′ W 100
Wasco, Oreg., U.S. 45°34′ N, 120°43′ W 90
Wase, Nig. 9°5′ N, 9°58′ E 222
Wase, river, Nig. 9°8′ N, 9°47′ E 222

Waseca, *Minn., U.S.* 44°3' N, 93°33' W **82**
Wash, The 52°55' N, 0°9' E **162**
Washakie Needles, peak, *Wyo., U.S.* 43°44' N, 109°17' W **90**
Washburn, *Ill., U.S.* 40°54' N, 89°18' W **102**
Washburn, *N. Dak., U.S.* 47°17' N, 101°4' W **108**
Washburn, Mount, peak, *Wyo., U.S.* 44°46' N, 110°31' W **90**
Washington, *D.C., U.S.* 38°52' N, 77°9' W **94**
Washington, *Ga., U.S.* 33°43' N, 82°45' W **96**
Washington, *Ill., U.S.* 40°41' N, 89°25' W **102**
Washington, *Ind., U.S.* 38°39' N, 87°10' W **102**
Washington, *Kans., U.S.* 39°48' N, 97°3' W **90**
Washington, *Ky., U.S.* 38°36' N, 83°49' W **102**
Washington, *Md., U.S.* 38°38' N, 77°41' W **72**
Washington, *Miss., U.S.* 31°34' N, 91°18' W **96**
Washington, *Mo., U.S.* 38°32' N, 91°0' W **94**
Washington, *N.H., U.S.* 43°10' N, 72°7' W **104**
Washington, *N.C., U.S.* 35°33' N, 77°4' W **96**
Washington, *Pa., U.S.* 40°8' N, 80°15' W **82**
Washington, *R.I., U.S.* 41°40' N, 71°35' W **104**
Washington, *Utah, U.S.* 37°7' N, 113°31' W **101**
Washington, *Wis., U.S.* 45°23' N, 86°55' W **94**
Washington, adm. division, *Wash., U.S.* 47°10' N, 122°22' W **90**
Washington, Cape, *Antarctica* 74°14' S, 172°22' E **248**
Washington Court House, *Ohio, U.S.* 39°32' N, 83°26' W **102**
Washington Depot, *Conn., U.S.* 41°38' N, 73°20' W **104**
Washington Land 80°27' N, 66°2' W **246**
Washington, Mount, peak, *N.H., U.S.* 44°15' N, 71°20' W **104**
Washington, Mount, peak, *Oreg., U.S.* 44°18' N, 121°56' W **90**
Washita, river, *Okla., U.S.* 35°38' N, 99°16' W **80**
Washita, river, *Tex., U.S.* 35°36' N, 100°25' W **96**
Washtucna, *Wash., U.S.* 46°44' N, 118°20' W **90**
Wasior, *Indonesia* 2°39' S, 134°28' E **192**
Wasipe, *Ghana* 8°33' N, 2°14' W **222**
Waskaganish, *Can.* 51°27' N, 78°42' W **82**
Waskaiowaka Lake, *Can.* 56°28' N, 97°29' W **108**
Waskesiu Lake, *Can.* 53°55' N, 106°2' W **108**
Waskom, *Tex., U.S.* 32°29' N, 94°5' W **103**
Wasselonne, *Fr.* 48°37' N, 7°26' E **163**
Wasserkuppe, peak, *Ger.* 50°29' N, 9°54' E **167**
Wassuk Range, *Nev., U.S.* 38°57' N, 118°59' W **90**
Wassy, *Fr.* 48°30' N, 4°56' E **163**
Waswanipi, Lac, lake, *Can.* 49°22' N, 77°51' W **80**
Waţā al Khān, *Syr.* 35°40' N, 36°3' E **194**
Watamu Marine National Park, *Kenya* 3°20' S, 39°58' E **224**
Watapi Lake, lake, *Can.* 55°18' N, 110°3' W **108**
Watari, *Japan* 38°2' N, 140°51' E **201**
Watch Hill, *R.I., U.S.* 41°18' N, 71°52' W **104**
Watchet, *U.K.* 51°10' N, 3°19' W **162**
Water Cays, islands, *North Atlantic Ocean* 23°36' N, 79°7' W **80**
Waterboro, *Me., U.S.* 43°32' N, 70°43' W **104**
Waterbury, *Conn., U.S.* 41°33' N, 73°3' W **104**
Waterbury, *Vt., U.S.* 44°19' N, 72°46' W **104**
Waterbury Center, *Vt., U.S.* 44°22' N, 72°44' W **104**
Waterbury Lake, lake, *Can.* 58°2' N, 105°7' W **108**
Wateree Lake, *S.C., U.S.* 34°20' N, 81°49' W **80**
Waterford, *Calif., U.S.* 37°38' N, 120°47' W **100**
Waterford, *Conn., U.S.* 41°20' N, 72°9' W **104**
Waterford, *Wis., U.S.* 42°46' N, 88°14' W **102**
Waterford (Port Láirge), *Ire.* 52°15' N, 7°8' W **150**
Waterfound, river, *Can.* 58°27' N, 104°45' W **108**
Waterloo, *Can.* 45°20' N, 72°33' W **94**
Waterloo, *Can.* 43°27' N, 80°32' W **94**
Waterloo, *Ind., U.S.* 41°25' N, 85°2' W **102**
Waterloo, *Iowa, U.S.* 42°28' N, 92°22' W **94**
Waterloo, *Mo., U.S.* 38°19' N, 90°9' W **94**
Waterloo, *Sierra Leone* 8°20' N, 13°4' W **222**
Waterloo, *Wis., U.S.* 43°10' N, 89°0' W **102**
Waterman, *Ill., U.S.* 41°45' N, 88°48' W **102**
Waterman, Isla, island, *Chile* 55°22' S, 71°46' W **134**
Waterproof, *La., U.S.* 31°47' N, 91°24' W **103**
Watersmeet, *Mich., U.S.* 46°16' N, 89°11' W **94**
Waterton Lakes National Park, *Can.* 49°4' N, 113°35' W **80**
Watertown, *Conn., U.S.* 41°36' N, 73°7' W **104**
Watertown, *N.Y., U.S.* 43°58' N, 75°55' W **94**
Watertown, *S. Dak., U.S.* 44°52' N, 97°7' W **90**
Watertown, *Wis., U.S.* 43°10' N, 88°43' W **102**
Waterval Boven, *S. Af.* 25°40' S, 30°17' E **227**
Waterville, *Kans., U.S.* 39°40' N, 96°45' W **90**
Waterville, *Me., U.S.* 44°32' N, 69°39' W **104**
Waterville, *Minn., U.S.* 44°11' N, 93°35' W **94**
Waterville, *Ohio, U.S.* 41°29' N, 83°44' W **102**
Waterville, *Wash., U.S.* 47°38' N, 120°5' W **90**
Waterville Valley, *N.H., U.S.* 43°57' N, 71°31' W **104**
Watervliet, *Mich., U.S.* 42°10' N, 86°15' W **102**
Watervliet, *N.Y., U.S.* 42°43' N, 73°44' W **104**
Watford, *Can.* 42°56' N, 81°52' W **102**
Watford, *U.K.* 51°39' N, 0°25' E **162**
Watford City, *N. Dak., U.S.* 47°47' N, 103°18' W **90**
Wathaman Lake, lake, *Can.* 56°56' N, 104°28' W **108**
Wathena, *Kans., U.S.* 39°44' N, 94°57' W **94**
Watino, *Can.* 55°41' N, 117°41' W **108**
Watling see San Salvador, island, *Bahamas* 23°41' N, 74°29' W **116**
Watonga, *Okla., U.S.* 35°49' N, 98°24' W **92**
Watrous, *Can.* 51°41' N, 105°29' W **90**
Watrous, *N. Mex., U.S.* 35°46' N, 104°59' W **92**
Watsa, *Dem. Rep. of the Congo* 2°59' N, 29°31' E **224**
Watseka, *Ill., U.S.* 40°45' N, 87°44' W **102**
Watsi Kengo, *Dem. Rep. of the Congo* 0°47' N, 20°31' E **218**
Watson, *Can.* 52°7' N, 104°32' W **108**
Watson Lake, *Can.* 60°6' N, 128°46' W **98**
Watsonville, *Calif., U.S.* 36°54' N, 121°46' W **100**
Watton, *U.K.* 52°33' N, 0°51' E **162**
Wattwil, *Switz.* 47°19' N, 9°5' E **156**
Wau, *P.N.G.* 7°22' S, 146°41' E **192**
Wau, *Sudan* 7°39' N, 27°58' E **224**
Wau, river, *Sudan* 6°8' N, 27°1' E **224**
Waubay, *S. Dak., U.S.* 45°18' N, 97°19' W **90**
Wauchula, *Fla., U.S.* 27°33' N, 81°49' W **105**
Waucoba Mountain, peak, *Calif., U.S.* 37°1' N, 118°3' W **101**
Waugh, *Can.* 49°37' N, 95°13' W **90**
Waukena, *Calif., U.S.* 36°8' N, 119°31' W **100**
Waukesha, *Wis., U.S.* 43°1' N, 88°14' W **102**
Waupaca, *Wis., U.S.* 44°20' N, 89°6' W **94**
Waupun, *Wis., U.S.* 43°37' N, 88°44' W **102**
Wauregan, *Conn., U.S.* 41°44' N, 71°55' W **104**
Waurika, *Okla., U.S.* 34°8' N, 97°59' W **96**
Wausa, *Nebr., U.S.* 42°29' N, 97°33' W **90**
Wausau, *Wis., U.S.* 44°56' N, 89°37' W **94**
Wauseon, *Ohio, U.S.* 41°32' N, 84°9' W **102**
Wautoma, *Wis., U.S.* 44°4' N, 89°18' W **102**
Wauwinet, *Mass., U.S.* 41°19' N, 70°0' W **104**
Waveland, *Miss., U.S.* 30°16' N, 89°23' W **103**
Waverley, *N.Z.* 39°47' S, 174°37' E **240**
Waverly, *Ill., U.S.* 39°34' N, 89°58' W **102**
Waverly, *Iowa, U.S.* 42°42' N, 92°29' W **94**
Waverly, *Nebr., U.S.* 40°54' N, 96°33' W **90**
Waverly, *N.Y., U.S.* 42°0' N, 76°33' W **110**
Waverly, *Ohio, U.S.* 39°6' N, 83°0' W **102**
Waverly, *Va., U.S.* 37°2' N, 77°6' W **96**
Wavre, *Belg.* 50°42' N, 4°36' E **167**
Wāw al Kabīr, *Lib.* 25°20' N, 16°43' E **216**
Wāw an Nāmūs, spring, *Lib.* 24°58' N, 17°46' E **216**
Wawa, *Can.* 47°59' N, 84°47' W **94**
Wawa, *Nig.* 9°54' N, 4°24' E **222**
Wawa, river, *Nicar.* 14°1' N, 84°24' W **115**
Wawagosic, river, *Can.* 50°6' N, 79°5' W **94**
Wawona, *Calif., U.S.* 37°32' N, 119°40' W **100**
Waxahachie, *Tex., U.S.* 32°23' N, 96°51' W **96**
Waxweiler, *Ger.* 50°5' N, 6°22' E **167**
Waxxari, *China* 38°46' N, 87°29' E **188**
Way Archipelago, islands, *Antarctica* 66°37' S, 147°19' E **248**
Way Kambas National Park, *Indonesia* 5°4' S, 105°20' E **172**
Wayagamac, Lac, lake, *Can.* 47°20' N, 73°14' W **94**
Waycross, *Ga., U.S.* 31°11' N, 82°23' W **112**
Wayland, *Mich., U.S.* 42°39' N, 85°39' W **102**
Wayne, *Can.* 51°24' N, 112°42' W **90**
Wayne, *Me., U.S.* 44°20' N, 70°4' W **104**
Wayne, *Nebr., U.S.* 42°12' N, 97°1' W **90**
Wayne, *Ohio, U.S.* 41°17' N, 83°29' W **102**
Waynesboro, *Ga., U.S.* 33°4' N, 82°2' W **96**
Waynesboro, *Miss., U.S.* 31°40' N, 88°38' W **103**
Waynesboro, *Tenn., U.S.* 35°19' N, 87°45' W **96**
Waynesboro, *Va., U.S.* 38°4' N, 78°54' W **94**
Waynoka, *Okla., U.S.* 36°34' N, 98°54' W **92**
Wayside, *Miss., U.S.* 33°14' N, 91°2' W **103**
Waza, *Cameroon* 11°24' N, 14°35' E **216**
Waza National Park, *Cameroon* 11°12' N, 14°21' E **206**
Wazay, *Afghan.* 33°18' N, 69°27' E **186**
Wāzin, *Lib.* 31°57' N, 10°42' E **214**
Wazirabad, *Pak.* 32°24' N, 74°8' E **186**
We, island, *Indonesia* 5°52' N, 95°22' E **196**
Weagamow Lake, *Can.* 52°59' N, 91°20' W **82**
Weald, The, region, *U.K.* 51°0' N, 0°17' E **162**
Weare, *N.H., U.S.* 43°5' N, 71°45' W **104**
Wearhead, *U.K.* 54°45' N, 2°14' W **162**
Weatherford, *Okla., U.S.* 35°30' N, 98°43' W **92**
Weatherford, *Tex., U.S.* 32°46' N, 97°48' W **112**
Weaver Lake, lake, *Can.* 52°42' N, 97°13' W **108**
Webb, *Can.* 50°10' N, 108°13' W **90**
Webb City, *Okla., U.S.* 36°47' N, 96°42' W **92**
Webbwood, *Can.* 46°16' N, 81°53' W **94**
Weber Inlet 72°27' S, 74°30' W **248**
Weber Ridge, peak, *Antarctica* 84°21' S, 65°15' W **248**
Webster, *Fla., U.S.* 28°36' N, 82°4' W **105**
Webster, *Mass., U.S.* 42°2' N, 71°53' W **104**
Webster, *N.H., U.S.* 43°19' N, 71°44' W **104**
Webster, *S. Dak., U.S.* 45°18' N, 97°32' W **90**
Webster City, *Iowa, U.S.* 42°26' N, 93°50' W **94**
Weda, *Indonesia* 0°22' N, 127°46' E **192**
Weddell Island, *Falk. Is., U.K.* 51°50' S, 64°6' W **134**
Weddell Plain, *South Atlantic Ocean* 62°46' S, 4°49' W **255**
Weddell Sea 65°39' S, 58°34' W **134**
Wedge Mountain, peak, *Can.* 50°7' N, 122°53' W **108**
Weed, *Calif., U.S.* 41°25' N, 122°24' W **92**
Weed Patch, *Calif., U.S.* 35°13' N, 118°56' W **101**
Weed Patch Hill, peak, *Ind., U.S.* 39°8' N, 86°16' W **102**
Weekapaug, *R.I., U.S.* 41°19' N, 71°46' W **104**
Weekes, *Can.* 52°33' N, 102°54' W **108**
Weeki Wachee, *Fla., U.S.* 28°31' N, 82°34' W **105**
Weeki Wachee Spring, site, *Fla., U.S.* 28°29' N, 82°37' W **105**
Weems, Mount, peak, *Antarctica* 77°25' S, 87°1' W **248**
Weende, *Ger.* 51°33' N, 9°56' E **167**
Weener, *Ger.* 53°10' N, 7°21' E **163**
Weert, *Neth.* 51°14' N, 5°41' E **167**
Weeze, *Ger.* 51°37' N, 6°12' E **167**
Wegīdī, *Eth.* 9°25' N, 38°23' E **224**
Wei, river, *China* 34°27' N, 109°55' E **198**
Weichang, *China* 41°54' N, 117°43' E **198**
Weiden, *Ger.* 49°40' N, 12°9' E **152**
Weidman, *Mich., U.S.* 43°40' N, 84°58' W **102**
Weifang, *China* 36°42' N, 119°5' E **198**
Weihai, *China* 37°29' N, 122°8' E **198**
Weilburg, *Ger.* 50°29' N, 8°15' E **167**
Weilmünster, *Ger.* 50°27' N, 8°22' E **167**
Weimar, *Tex., U.S.* 29°41' N, 96°47' W **96**
Weinan, *China* 34°30' N, 109°28' E **198**
Weipa, *Austral.* 12°41' S, 142°4' E **238**
Weir, *Miss., U.S.* 33°14' N, 89°17' W **103**
Weir, river, *Can.* 56°58' N, 93°45' W **108**
Weirsdale, *Fla., U.S.* 28°58' N, 81°55' W **105**
Weirton, *W. Va., U.S.* 40°23' N, 80°37' W **94**
Weiser, *Idaho, U.S.* 44°15' N, 116°59' W **90**
Weishan, *China* 34°47' N, 117°11' E **198**
Weisshorn, peak, *Switz.* 46°6' N, 7°39' E **165**
Weissmies, peak, *Switz.* 46°7' N, 8°0' E **167**
Weitra, *Aust.* 48°42' N, 14°54' E **156**
Weitzel Lake, lake, *Can.* 57°39' N, 107°11' W **108**
Weixin, *China* 27°49' N, 105°3' E **198**
Weiya, *China* 42°7' N, 94°41' E **190**
Weizhou Dao, island, *China* 20°44' N, 108°55' E **198**
Wekusko, *Can.* 54°30' N, 99°46' W **108**
Wekusko Lake, lake, *Can.* 54°39' N, 100°27' W **108**
Wel Jara, spring, *Kenya* 0°28' N, 40°53' E **224**
Welaka, *Fla., U.S.* 29°28' N, 81°40' W **105**
Welbeck Abbey, site, *U.K.* 53°16' N, 1°10' W **162**
Welch, *W. Va., U.S.* 37°26' N, 81°36' W **96**
Welcome Mount, peak, *Antarctica* 72°13' S, 160°40' E **248**
Weldiya, *Eth.* 11°48' N, 39°33' E **182**
Weldon, *Calif., U.S.* 35°39' N, 118°18' W **101**
Weldon, *Ill., U.S.* 40°6' N, 88°45' W **102**
Weldon, *N.C., U.S.* 36°24' N, 77°36' W **96**
Weldon, *Tex., U.S.* 31°0' N, 95°34' W **103**
Welel, Tulu, peak, *Eth.* 8°51' N, 34°44' E **224**
Welk'īt'ē, *Eth.* 8°15' N, 37°48' E **224**
Welkom, *S. Af.* 28°1' S, 26°41' E **227**
Welland, *Can.* 42°52' N, 79°22' W **82**
Wellesley, *Mass., U.S.* 42°17' N, 71°18' W **104**
Wellesley Islands, *Gulf of Carpentaria* 16°33' S, 137°4' E **230**
Wellfleet, *Mass., U.S.* 41°56' N, 70°3' W **104**
Wellingborough, *U.K.* 52°18' N, 0°42' E **162**
Wellington, *Colo., U.S.* 40°42' N, 105°1' W **90**
Wellington, *Ill., U.S.* 40°31' N, 87°41' W **102**
Wellington, *N.Z.* 41°18' S, 174°39' E **240**
Wellington, *Ohio, U.S.* 41°9' N, 82°13' W **102**
Wellington, *S. Af.* 33°38' S, 18°59' E **227**
Wellington, *Tex., U.S.* 34°50' N, 100°14' W **96**
Wellington, *U.K.* 50°58' N, 3°13' W **162**
Wellington Channel 74°55' N, 95°14' W **106**
Wellington, Isla, island, *Chile* 49°48' S, 74°23' W **134**
Wells, *Can.* 53°5' N, 121°36' W **108**
Wells, *Me., U.S.* 43°19' N, 70°35' W **104**
Wells, *Mich., U.S.* 45°46' N, 87°5' W **94**
Wells, *Nev., U.S.* 41°6' N, 114°58' W **90**
Wells, *Tex., U.S.* 31°28' N, 94°57' W **103**
Wells, *Vt., U.S.* 43°24' N, 73°13' W **104**
Wells next the Sea, *U.K.* 52°56' N, 0°51' E **162**
Wells River, *Vt., U.S.* 44°8' N, 72°4' W **104**
Wellsboro, *Pa., U.S.* 41°44' N, 77°19' W **82**
Wellsford, *N.Z.* 36°18' S, 174°31' E **240**
Wellston, *Mich., U.S.* 44°12' N, 85°57' W **102**
Wellston, *Ohio, U.S.* 39°6' N, 82°32' W **102**
Wellsville, *N.Y., U.S.* 42°7' N, 77°58' W **94**
Wellsville, *Ohio, U.S.* 40°35' N, 80°39' W **94**
Wellton, *Ariz., U.S.* 32°39' N, 114°10' W **101**
Welmel, river, *Eth.* 6°7' N, 40°6' E **224**
Wels, *Aust.* 48°9' N, 14°1' E **152**
Welsh, *La., U.S.* 30°13' N, 92°50' W **96**
Welshpool, *U.K.* 52°39' N, 3°9' W **162**
Welwel, *Eth.* 7°6' N, 45°23' E **218**
Welwyn Garden City, *U.K.* 51°49' N, 0°14' E **162**
Wem, *U.K.* 52°51' N, 2°43' W **162**
Wembley, *Can.* 55°10' N, 119°9' W **108**
Wenatchee, *Wash., U.S.* 47°24' N, 120°19' W **90**
Wenatchee Mountains, *Wash., U.S.* 47°34' N, 121°49' W **100**
Wenchang, *China* 19°36' N, 110°43' E **198**
Wencheng, *China* 27°45' N, 120°3' E **198**
Wenchi, *Ghana* 7°45' N, 2°8' W **222**
Wendelstein, peak, *Ger.* 47°40' N, 11°55' E **156**
Wenden, *Ariz., U.S.* 33°48' N, 113°33' W **101**
Wendeng, *China* 37°11' N, 122°6' E **198**
Wendo, *Eth.* 6°38' N, 38°21' E **224**
Wendover, *Utah, U.S.* 40°43' N, 114°1' W **82**
Wenduine, *Belg.* 51°16' N, 3°4' E **163**
Wenebegon Lake, *Can.* 47°21' N, 83°46' W **94**
Wengyuan, *China* 24°14' N, 114°6' E **198**
Wenling, *China* 28°19' N, 121°24' E **198**
Wenona, *Ill., U.S.* 41°3' N, 89°4' W **102**
Wenquan, *China* 33°4' N, 91°54' E **188**
Wenquan, *China* 44°50' N, 80°57' E **184**
Wenshan, *China* 23°25' N, 104°18' E **202**
Wensu, *China* 41°16' N, 80°15' E **184**
Wentworth, *N.H., U.S.* 43°51' N, 71°55' W **104**
Wentzel Lake, lake, *Can.* 59°0' N, 115°2' W **108**
Wentzel, river, *Can.* 58°53' N, 114°49' W **108**
Wenxian, *China* 32°56' N, 104°40' E **198**
Wenzhou, *China* 27°57' N, 120°44' E **198**
Weobley, *U.K.* 52°9' N, 2°54' W **162**
Wepener, *S. Af.* 29°45' S, 27°0' E **227**
Wepusko Bay 56°59' N, 102°57' W **108**
Werbkowice, *Pol.* 50°44' N, 23°46' E **152**
Werda, *Botswana* 25°17' S, 23°14' E **227**
Werdau, *Ger.* 50°44' N, 12°23' E **152**
Werder, *Eth.* 7°0' N, 45°17' E **218**
Werder, *Ger.* 52°22' N, 12°56' E **152**
Werdohl, *Ger.* 51°15' N, 7°45' E **167**
Were Īlu, *Eth.* 10°35' N, 39°31' E **224**
Werl, *Ger.* 51°33' N, 7°54' E **167**
Wermelskirchen, *Ger.* 51°8' N, 7°13' E **167**
Werne, *Ger.* 51°39' N, 7°37' E **167**
Werneck, *Ger.* 49°59' N, 10°5' E **167**
Werota, *Eth.* 11°45' N, 37°31' E **182**
Wertheim, *Ger.* 49°44' N, 9°30' E **167**
Wervik, *Belg.* 50°47' N, 3°1' E **163**
Wesel, *Ger.* 51°39' N, 6°36' E **167**
Wesergebirge, *Ger.* 52°6' N, 8°54' E **150**
Weskan, *Kans., U.S.* 38°51' N, 101°58' W **90**
Weslaco, *Tex., U.S.* 26°9' N, 98°1' W **96**
Wesleyville, *Pa., U.S.* 42°7' N, 80°2' W **110**
Wessel Islands, *Arafura Sea* 10°56' S, 135°48' E **192**
Wesseling, *Ger.* 50°48' N, 6°58' E **167**
Wessex, region, *U.K.* 51°28' N, 2°20' W **162**
Wessington, *S. Dak., U.S.* 44°26' N, 98°43' W **90**
Wessington Springs, *S. Dak., U.S.* 44°3' N, 98°34' W **90**
Wesson, *Ark., U.S.* 33°5' N, 92°47' W **103**
Wesson, *Miss., U.S.* 31°41' N, 90°25' W **103**
West, *Miss., U.S.* 33°10' N, 89°48' W **103**
West, *Tex., U.S.* 31°46' N, 97°5' W **92**
West Acton, *Mass., U.S.* 42°28' N, 71°29' W **104**
West Allis, *Wis., U.S.* 43°0' N, 88°2' W **102**
West Baldwin, *Me., U.S.* 43°49' N, 70°47' W **104**
West Bank, special sovereignty, *Israel* 31°22' N, 35°0' E **194**
West Bay 29°12' N, 95°8' W **103**
West Bay 28°59' N, 89°38' W **103**
West Bay, *Fla., U.S.* 30°17' N, 85°52' W **96**
West Bend, *Wis., U.S.* 43°24' N, 88°13' W **102**
West Bengal, adm. division, *India* 24°8' N, 87°45' E **197**
West Berlin, *Vt., U.S.* 44°11' N, 72°38' W **104**
West Beskids, *Pol.* 49°32' N, 18°33' E **152**
West Bethel, *Me., U.S.* 44°23' N, 70°52' W **104**
West Boylston, *Mass., U.S.* 42°21' N, 71°48' W **104**
West Braintree, *Vt., U.S.* 43°58' N, 72°46' W **104**
West Branch, *Iowa, U.S.* 41°40' N, 91°21' W **110**
West Branch, *Mich., U.S.* 44°17' N, 84°14' W **94**
West Bridgford, *U.K.* 52°55' N, 1°7' W **162**
West Bromwich, *U.K.* 52°30' N, 2°0' W **162**
West Burlington, *Iowa, U.S.* 40°49' N, 91°10' W **110**
West Butte, peak, *Mont., U.S.* 48°54' N, 111°38' W **90**
West Buxton, *Me., U.S.* 43°39' N, 70°36' W **104**
West Caicos, island, *West Caicos* 21°35' N, 72°57' W **116**
West Camp, *N.Y., U.S.* 42°6' N, 73°57' W **104**
West Campton, *N.H., U.S.* 43°50' N, 71°41' W **104**
West Caroline Basin, *North Pacific Ocean* 3°16' N, 136°56' E **254**
West Carrollton City, *Ohio, U.S.* 39°39' N, 84°15' W **102**
West Castleton, *Vt., U.S.* 43°39' N, 73°15' W **104**
West Chicago, *Ill., U.S.* 41°52' N, 88°12' W **102**
West Coal, river, *Can.* 61°12' N, 128°15' W **108**
West Cornwall, *Conn., U.S.* 41°52' N, 73°22' W **104**
West Danville, *Vt., U.S.* 44°24' N, 72°12' W **104**
West Des Moines, *Iowa, U.S.* 41°33' N, 93°44' W **94**
West Dummerston, *Vt., U.S.* 42°55' N, 72°38' W **104**
West Elk Peak, *Colo., U.S.* 38°42' N, 107°17' W **90**
West End, *Bahamas* 26°40' N, 78°57' W **105**
West End Point, *Bahamas* 26°41' N, 78°58' W **105**
West End Point, *Little Cayman* 19°42' N, 81°6' W **115**
West Falkland, island, *Falk. Is., U.K.* 51°34' S, 62°18' W **134**
West Fayu Atoll see Pigailoe 8°36' N, 146°3' E **192**
West Frankfort, *Mo., U.S.* 37°53' N, 88°55' W **96**
West Glacier, *Mont., U.S.* 48°27' N, 113°59' W **108**
West Gouldsboro, *Me., U.S.* 44°27' N, 68°6' W **111**
West Granville, *Mass., U.S.* 42°4' N, 72°57' W **104**
West Group, islands, *Great Australian Bight* 33°43' S, 120°1' E **230**
West Ham, *U.K.* 51°30' N, 1°59' E **162**
West Hartford, *Conn., U.S.* 41°45' N, 72°45' W **104**
West Haven, *Conn., U.S.* 41°16' N, 72°57' W **104**
West Hazleton, *Pa., U.S.* 40°57' N, 76°1' W **94**
West Helena, *Ark., U.S.* 34°32' N, 90°40' W **96**
West Hurley, *N.Y., U.S.* 41°59' N, 74°7' W **104**
West Ice Shelf, *Antarctica* 66°37' S, 86°47' E **248**
West Island, *Austral.* 15°45' S, 135°31' E **231**
West Jefferson, *Ohio, U.S.* 39°55' N, 83°16' W **102**
West Keal, *U.K.* 53°8' N, 0°2' E **162**
West Lafayette, *Ohio, U.S.* 40°16' N, 81°45' W **102**
West Liberty, *Ky., U.S.* 37°55' N, 83°16' W **94**
West Liberty, *Ohio, U.S.* 40°15' N, 83°46' W **102**
West Lorne, *Can.* 42°35' N, 81°36' W **102**
West Lunga National Park, *Zambia* 12°45' S, 24°52' E **224**
West Lunga National Park, *Zambia* 13°10' S, 24°22' E **206**
West Lunga, river, *Zambia* 12°14' S, 24°21' E **220**
West Mariana Basin, *Philippine Sea* 17°0' N, 138°57' E **254**
West Milton, *Ohio, U.S.* 39°56' N, 84°20' W **102**
West Monroe, *La., U.S.* 32°29' N, 92°9' W **103**
West Newfield, *Me., U.S.* 43°38' N, 70°56' W **104**
West Nicholson, *Zimb.* 21°2' S, 29°18' E **227**
West Ossipee, *N.H., U.S.* 43°49' N, 71°13' W **104**
West Palm Beach, *Fla., U.S.* 26°43' N, 80°5' W **105**
West Paris, *Me., U.S.* 44°19' N, 70°35' W **104**
West Park, *N.Y., U.S.* 41°47' N, 73°59' W **104**
West Pawlet, *Vt., U.S.* 43°21' N, 73°16' W **104**
West Peru, *Me., U.S.* 44°30' N, 70°29' W **104**
West Pittston, *Pa., U.S.* 41°19' N, 75°49' W **94**
West Plains, *Mo., U.S.* 36°43' N, 91°52' W **96**
West Point 43°55' N, 60°58' W **111**
West Point, *Calif., U.S.* 38°23' N, 120°33' W **100**
West Point, *Can.* 46°37' N, 64°23' W **111**
West Point, *Ky., U.S.* 37°59' N, 85°58' W **94**
West Point, *Me., U.S.* 43°45' N, 69°52' W **104**
West Point, *Miss., U.S.* 33°35' N, 88°39' W **96**
West Point, *N.Y., U.S.* 41°23' N, 73°59' W **104**
West Point, *Va., U.S.* 37°32' N, 76°48' W **94**
West Portsmouth, *Ohio, U.S.* 38°45' N, 83°2' W **102**
West Quoddy Head, *Me., U.S.* 44°44' N, 66°55' W **111**
West Rumney, *N.H., U.S.* 43°48' N, 71°53' W **104**
West Salem, *Ill., U.S.* 38°31' N, 88°1' W **102**
West Southport, *Me., U.S.* 43°49' N, 69°41' W **104**
West Spanish Peak, *Colo., U.S.* 37°19' N, 105°4' W **80**
West Tanfield, *U.K.* 54°12' N, 1°35' W **162**
West Tavaputs Plateau, *Utah, U.S.* 39°48' N, 110°44' W **90**
West Terre Haute, *Ind., U.S.* 39°27' N, 87°27' W **102**
West Terschelling, *Neth.* 53°21' N, 5°12' E **163**
West Thornton, *N.H., U.S.* 43°56' N, 71°42' W **104**
West Topsham, *Vt., U.S.* 44°6' N, 72°19' W **104**
West Townsend, *Mass., U.S.* 42°40' N, 71°45' W **104**
West Union, *Ill., U.S.* 39°12' N, 87°40' W **102**
West Union, *Iowa, U.S.* 42°57' N, 91°47' W **110**
West Virginia, adm. division, *W. Va., U.S.* 38°34' N, 81°18' W **94**
West Wareham, *Mass., U.S.* 41°47' N, 70°46' W **104**
West Webster, *N.Y., U.S.* 43°12' N, 77°30' W **94**
West Wendover, *Nev., U.S.* 40°43' N, 114°4' W **90**
West Woodstock, *Vt., U.S.* 43°36' N, 72°34' W **104**
West Yarmouth, *Mass., U.S.* 41°38' N, 70°15' W **104**
Westbrook, *Conn., U.S.* 41°16' N, 72°27' W **104**
Westbrook, *Me., U.S.* 43°40' N, 70°22' W **104**
Westbrook, *Tex., U.S.* 32°21' N, 101°1' W **92**
Westbury, *U.K.* 51°15' N, 2°11' W **162**
Westend, *Calif., U.S.* 35°41' N, 117°24' W **101**
Westerburg, *Ger.* 50°33' N, 7°58' E **167**
Westerlo, *N.Y., U.S.* 42°30' N, 74°4' W **104**
Westerly, *R.I., U.S.* 41°22' N, 71°50' W **104**
Western Australia, adm. division, *Austral.* 25°2' S, 118°22' E **231**
Western Bahr Al Ghazal, adm. division, *Sudan* 7°22' N, 25°15' E **224**
Western Cape, adm. division, *S. Af.* 33°0' S, 19°18' E **227**
Western Darfur, adm. division, *Sudan* 14°27' N, 23°55' E **226**
Western Desert, *Egypt* 29°2' N, 24°32' E **142**
Western Equatoria, adm. division, *Sudan* 5°29' N, 27°18' E **224**
Western Ghats, *India* 21°0' N, 73°17' E **186**
Western Head, *Can.* 49°34' N, 58°48' W **111**
Western Kordofan, adm. division, *Sudan* 10°39' N, 27°40' E **224**
Western Port, *Austral.* 38°38' S, 143°33' E **230**
Western Sahara, special sovereignty, *Mor.* 21°39' N, 13°57' W **222**
Western Thebes, ruin(s), *Egypt* 25°43' N, 32°25' E **182**
Westerschelde 51°21' N, 3°54' E **163**
Westerville, *Ohio, U.S.* 40°7' N, 82°55' W **102**
Westerwald, *Ger.* 50°33' N, 7°25' E **167**
Westfield, *N.Y., U.S.* 42°19' N, 79°35' W **110**
Westfield, *Tex., U.S.* 30°0' N, 95°25' W **103**
Westfield, *Wis., U.S.* 43°53' N, 89°30' W **102**
Westhampton Beach, *N.Y., U.S.* 40°48' N, 72°39' W **104**
Westhope, *N. Dak., U.S.* 48°53' N, 101°3' W **90**
Westlake, *La., U.S.* 30°13' N, 93°16' W **103**
Westland (Tai Poutini) National Park, *N.Z.* 43°26' S, 168°39' E **240**
Westley, *Calif., U.S.* 37°32' N, 121°13' W **100**
Westlock, *Can.* 54°9' N, 113°52' W **108**
Westminster, *Colo., U.S.* 39°50' N, 105°3' W **90**
Westminster, *Vt., U.S.* 43°3' N, 72°28' W **104**
Westmorland, *Calif., U.S.* 33°2' N, 115°38' W **101**
Weston, *Malaysia* 5°14' N, 115°36' E **203**
Weston, *Mo., U.S.* 39°24' N, 94°55' W **94**
Weston, *Oreg., U.S.* 45°47' N, 118°26' W **90**
Weston, *Vt., U.S.* 43°17' N, 72°48' W **104**
Weston, *W. Va., U.S.* 39°2' N, 80°28' W **94**
Weston-super-Mare, *U.K.* 51°19' N, 2°58' W **162**
Westonzoyland, *U.K.* 51°6' N, 2°56' W **162**
Westover, *W. Va., U.S.* 39°37' N, 79°59' W **94**
Westoverledingen, *Ger.* 53°9' N, 7°27' E **163**
Westpoint, *Ind., U.S.* 40°20' N, 87°3' W **102**
Westport, *Calif., U.S.* 39°38' N, 123°47' W **90**
Westport, *Conn., U.S.* 41°8' N, 73°22' W **104**
Westport, *Ind., U.S.* 39°10' N, 85°34' W **102**
Westport, *N.Y., U.S.* 44°10' N, 73°28' W **104**
Westport, *N.Z.* 41°47' S, 171°38' E **240**
Westport, *Wash., U.S.* 46°52' N, 124°7' W **100**
Westport Point, *Mass., U.S.* 41°31' N, 71°6' W **104**
Westray, *Can.* 53°35' N, 101°23' W **108**
Westree, *Can.* 47°25' N, 81°33' W **94**
Westville, *Ill., U.S.* 40°2' N, 87°38' W **102**
Westward Ho!, *U.K.* 51°2' N, 4°13' W **150**
Westwego, *La., U.S.* 29°54' N, 90°9' W **103**
Westwood, *Calif., U.S.* 40°18' N, 121°0' W **92**
Wesuwe, *Ger.* 52°45' N, 7°12' E **163**
Wetar, island, *Indonesia* 7°40' S, 126°18' E **192**
Wetaskiwin, *Can.* 52°57' N, 113°23' W **108**
Wete, *Tanzania* 5°1' S, 39°45' E **224**
Wetetnagami, Lac, lake, *Can.* 48°53' N, 76°59' W **94**
Wetherby, *U.K.* 53°56' N, 1°23' W **162**
Wethersfield, *Conn., U.S.* 41°42' N, 72°41' W **104**
Wetter, *Ger.* 50°53' N, 8°42' E **167**
Wetteren, *Belg.* 50°59' N, 3°53' E **163**
Wettringen, *Ger.* 52°12' N, 7°19' E **163**
Wetumka, *Okla., U.S.* 35°13' N, 96°14' W **96**
Wetzlar, *Ger.* 50°33' N, 8°29' E **167**
Wevertown, *N.Y., U.S.* 43°37' N, 73°58' W **104**
Wewak, *P.N.G.* 3°36' S, 143°37' E **238**
Wewoka, *Okla., U.S.* 35°7' N, 96°29' W **92**
Wexford, *Ire.* 52°20' N, 6°29' W **150**
Weybourne, *U.K.* 52°56' N, 1°8' E **162**
Weybridge, *Vt., U.S.* 44°3' N, 73°13' W **104**
Weyburn, *Can.* 49°39' N, 103°52' W **90**
Weymouth, *Mass., U.S.* 42°13' N, 70°57' W **104**
Weymouth Bay 12°36' S, 142°4' E **230**

Whakapara, *N.Z.* 35°33′ S, 174°16′ E 240
Whakapunake, peak, *N.Z.* 38°50′ S, 177°31′ E 240
Whakatane, *N.Z.* 37°59′ S, 177°0′ E 240
Whale Bay 56°34′ N, 135°35′ W 108
Whale Cay, island, *Bahamas* 25°27′ N, 78°38′ W 80
Whale Cove, *Can.* 62°28′ N, 92°59′ W 73
Whangara, *N.Z.* 38°33′ S, 178°12′ E 240
Whangarei, *N.Z.* 35°46′ S, 174°18′ E 240
Wharfe, river, *U.K.* 53°55′ N, 1°21′ W 162
Wharton, *Tex., U.S.* 29°18′ N, 96°6′ W 96
Wharton Basin, *Indian Ocean* 20°5′ S, 100°10′ E 254
Wharton, Mount, peak, *Antarctica* 81°1′ S, 158°48′ E 248
Wharton, Peninsula, *Chile* 49°34′ S, 76°33′ W 134
Whataroa, *N.Z.* 43°17′ S, 170°21′ E 240
Whatcom, Lake, *Wash., U.S.* 48°41′ N, 122°34′ W 100
Whatley, *Ala., U.S.* 31°38′ N, 87°42′ W 103
Whatshan Lake, lake, *Can.* 50°0′ N, 118°40′ W 90
Wheatland, *Ind., U.S.* 38°39′ N, 87°19′ W 102
Wheatland, *Wyo., U.S.* 42°3′ N, 104°58′ W 90
Wheatley, *Can.* 42°6′ N, 82°28′ W 102
Wheaton, *Ill., U.S.* 41°51′ N, 88°6′ W 102
Wheaton, *Minn., U.S.* 45°47′ N, 96°30′ W 90
Wheeler, *Kans., U.S.* 39°45′ N, 101°43′ W 90
Wheeler, *Oreg., U.S.* 45°40′ N, 123°53′ W 100
Wheeler, *Tex., U.S.* 35°26′ N, 100°17′ W 92
Wheeler Mountain, peak, *Nev., U.S.* 41°16′ N, 116°7′ W 90
Wheeler Peak, *Nev., U.S.* 38°58′ N, 114°23′ W 90
Wheeler Peak, *N. Mex., U.S.* 36°32′ N, 105°29′ W 92
Wheeling, *W. Va., U.S.* 40°3′ N, 80°43′ W 94
Wheelwright, *Arg.* 33°49′ S, 61°12′ W 139
Whinham, Mount, peak, *Austral.* 26°5′ S, 129°59′ E 230
Whipple, Mount, peak, *Can.* 56°36′ N, 131°44′ W 108
Whipple Observatory, site, *Ariz., U.S.* 31°41′ N, 110°57′ W 92
Whirlwind Lake, *Can.* 60°15′ N, 109°15′ W 108
Whiskey Jack Lake, *Can.* 58°24′ N, 102°28′ W 108
Whistler, *Can.* 50°7′ N, 122°59′ W 100
Whitby, *U.K.* 54°29′ N, 0°38′ E 162
Whitchurch, *U.K.* 52°58′ N, 2°41′ W 162
Whitchurch, *U.K.* 51°13′ N, 1°21′ W 162
White Bay 49°57′ N, 56°42′ W 111
White Butte, peak, *N. Dak., U.S.* 46°22′ N, 103°23′ W 90
White Cap Mountain, peak, *Me., U.S.* 45°32′ N, 69°20′ W 94
White Castle, *La., U.S.* 30°9′ N, 91°9′ W 103
White City, *Fla., U.S.* 27°23′ N, 80°20′ W 105
White Cloud, *Mich., U.S.* 43°33′ N, 85°47′ W 102
White Deer, *Tex., U.S.* 35°24′ N, 101°11′ W 92
White Hall, *Ark., U.S.* 34°16′ N, 92°5′ W 96
White Heath, *Ill., U.S.* 40°4′ N, 88°30′ W 102
White Hills, *Ariz., U.S.* 35°47′ N, 114°27′ W 101
White Horse Beach, *Mass., U.S.* 41°55′ N, 70°35′ W 104
White Horse Pass, *Nev., U.S.* 40°20′ N, 114°15′ W 90
White Island, *Antarctica* 78°9′ S, 175°55′ E 248
White Island, *Antarctica* 66°45′ S, 45°32′ E 248
White Island, island, *Can.* 66°2′ N, 88°7′ W 246
White Lake, *La., U.S.* 29°41′ N, 92°41′ W 103
White Mount Peak, *Calif., U.S.* 37°37′ N, 118°21′ W 92
White Mountain, *Alas., U.S.* 64°40′ N, 163°26′ W 98
White Mountains, *Calif., U.S.* 37°10′ N, 118°10′ W 80
White Mountains, *Calif., U.S.* 37°46′ N, 118°28′ W 90
White Mountains, *N.H., U.S.* 44°2′ N, 72°0′ W 104
White Mountains National Park, *Austral.* 20°38′ S, 144°43′ E 238
White Nile, adm. division, *Sudan* 13°33′ N, 31°53′ E 182
White Nile Dam, *Sudan* 14°56′ N, 31°53′ E 226
White Oak, *Tex., U.S.* 32°32′ N, 94°52′ W 103
White Otter Lake, lake, *Can.* 49°3′ N, 92°29′ W 94
White Pigeon, *Mich., U.S.* 41°47′ N, 85°38′ W 102
White Pine Peak, *Utah, U.S.* 38°50′ N, 112°18′ W 90
White Pine Range, *Nev., U.S.* 39°4′ N, 115°37′ W 90
White Plains, *N.Y., U.S.* 41°1′ N, 73°47′ W 104
White River, *Can.* 48°35′ N, 85°16′ W 94
White River, *S. Dak., U.S.* 43°34′ N, 100°45′ W 90
White, river, *Ark., U.S.* 36°2′ N, 92°6′ W 80
White, river, *Ark., U.S.* 34°42′ N, 91°43′ W 80
White, river, *Can.* 48°30′ N, 86°2′ W 94
White, river, *Can.* 63°13′ N, 140°3′ W 98
White, river, *Colo., U.S.* 40°8′ N, 108°49′ W 90
White, river, *Colo., U.S.* 39°50′ N, 108°56′ W 80
White River Junction, *Vt., U.S.* 43°38′ N, 72°20′ W 104
White, river, *Nebr., U.S.* 42°55′ N, 103°10′ W 90
White River Plateau, *Colo., U.S.* 39°50′ N, 107°54′ W 90
White, river, *S. Dak., U.S.* 43°41′ N, 102°24′ W 82
White, river, *S. Dak., U.S.* 43°34′ N, 99°56′ W 90
White, river, *Tex., U.S.* 34°5′ N, 101°57′ W 112
White, river, *Utah, U.S.* 39°50′ N, 109°27′ W 90
White Rock, *Can.* 49°2′ N, 122°48′ W 100
White Rock Peak, *Nev., U.S.* 38°14′ N, 114°11′ W 90
White Rock, peak, *Oreg., U.S.* 43°6′ N, 123°7′ W 90
White Salmon, *Wash., U.S.* 45°43′ N, 121°30′ W 100
White Sands National Monument, *N. Mex., U.S.* 32°54′ N, 106°5′ W 80
White Sea see Beloye More 63°17′ N, 35°24′ E 160
White Volta, river, *Ghana* 9°39′ N, 0°54′ E 222
Whitecap Mountain, peak, *Can.* 50°42′ N, 122°36′ W 90
Whiteclay Lake, lake, *Can.* 50°49′ N, 89°14′ W 110
Whitecourt, *Can.* 54°7′ N, 115°42′ W 108
Whiteface Mountain, peak, *N.Y., U.S.* 44°21′ N, 73°56′ W 104
Whiteface, river, *Minn., U.S.* 47°4′ N, 92°51′ W 94
Whitefield, *Me., U.S.* 44°9′ N, 69°39′ W 104
Whitefield, *N.H., U.S.* 44°22′ N, 71°37′ W 104
Whitefish, *Mont., U.S.* 48°23′ N, 114°21′ W 90
Whitefish Bay, *Wis., U.S.* 43°6′ N, 87°55′ W 102
Whitefish Lake, lake, *Can.* 48°12′ N, 90°30′ W 110
Whitefish Point, *Mich., U.S.* 46°35′ N, 84°56′ W 94
Whitefish Range, *Mont., U.S.* 48°59′ N, 114°56′ W 90
Whitefish, river, *Can.* 60°42′ N, 125°12′ W 108
Whitehall, *Mich., U.S.* 43°22′ N, 86°21′ W 102
Whitehall, *Mont., U.S.* 45°51′ N, 112°6′ W 90
Whitehall, *N.Y., U.S.* 43°32′ N, 73°26′ W 104
Whitehall, *Ohio, U.S.* 39°57′ N, 82°53′ W 102
Whitehall, *Wis., U.S.* 44°21′ N, 91°20′ W 94
Whitehaven, *U.K.* 54°33′ N, 3°35′ W 162
Whitehorse, *Can.* 60°43′ N, 135°20′ W 98
Whitehouse, *Tex., U.S.* 32°12′ N, 95°14′ W 103
Whitemouth, *Can.* 49°55′ N, 95°59′ W 90
Whitemud, river, *Can.* 56°32′ N, 118°28′ W 108
Whiten Head, *U.K.* 58°36′ N, 4°54′ W 150
Whiteriver, *Ariz., U.S.* 33°50′ N, 109°58′ W 92
Whitesand, river, *Can.* 59°50′ N, 115°54′ W 108
Whitesboro, *Tex., U.S.* 33°38′ N, 96°55′ W 92
Whitesburg, *Ky., U.S.* 37°7′ N, 82°49′ W 94
Whitetail, *Mont., U.S.* 48°52′ N, 105°12′ W 90
Whiteville, *N.C., U.S.* 34°19′ N, 78°43′ W 96
Whiteville, *Tenn., U.S.* 35°18′ N, 89°9′ W 96
Whitewater, *Mont., U.S.* 48°44′ N, 107°37′ W 90
Whitewater, *Wis., U.S.* 42°50′ N, 88°45′ W 102
Whitewater Bay 25°16′ N, 81°13′ W 105
Whitewater Lake, *Can.* 50°42′ N, 89°52′ W 110
Whitewood, *Can.* 50°19′ N, 102°17′ W 90
Whitianga, *N.Z.* 36°50′ S, 175°40′ E 240
Whiting, *Vt., U.S.* 43°51′ N, 73°13′ W 104
Whiting, river, *Can.* 58°2′ N, 133°46′ W 108
Whitingham, *Vt., U.S.* 42°47′ N, 72°54′ W 104
Whitley Gardens, *Calif., U.S.* 35°39′ N, 120°32′ W 101
Whitman, *Nebr., U.S.* 42°1′ N, 101°32′ W 90
Whitmire, *S.C., U.S.* 34°29′ N, 81°37′ W 96
Whitney, Lake, *Tex., U.S.* 31°56′ N, 98°22′ W 80
Whitney, Mount, peak, *Calif., U.S.* 36°34′ N, 118°20′ W 101
Whitstable, *U.K.* 51°21′ N, 1°2′ E 162
Whitsunday Island National Park, *Austral.* 20°21′ S, 148°39′ E 238
Whittemore, *Mich., U.S.* 44°13′ N, 83°48′ W 102
Whittier, *Alas., U.S.* 60°40′ N, 148°51′ W 98
Whittier, *Calif., U.S.* 33°58′ N, 118°3′ W 101
Whittle, Cap, *Can.* 50°6′ N, 60°13′ W 111
Whittlesey, *U.K.* 52°32′ N, 0°8′ E 162
Wholdaia Lake, *Can.* 60°42′ N, 105°15′ W 108
Whyalla, *Austral.* 33°0′ S, 137°33′ E 231
Wiarton, *Can.* 44°43′ N, 81°9′ W 94
Wibaux, *Mont., U.S.* 46°57′ N, 104°13′ W 90
Wichita, *Kans., U.S.* 37°39′ N, 97°20′ W 90
Wichita Falls, *Tex., U.S.* 33°52′ N, 98°30′ W 92
Wichita, river, *Tex., U.S.* 33°47′ N, 99°19′ W 80
Wick, *U.K.* 58°27′ N, 3°9′ W 143
Wickede, *Ger.* 51°30′ N, 7°52′ E 167
Wickenburg, *Ariz., U.S.* 33°58′ N, 112°47′ W 112
Wickford see North Kingstown, *R.I., U.S.* 41°34′ N, 71°28′ W 104
Wickliffe, *Ky., U.S.* 36°58′ N, 89°4′ W 96
Wickliffe, *Ohio, U.S.* 41°35′ N, 81°28′ W 102
Wicklow, *Ire.* 52°58′ N, 6°4′ W 150
Wicklow Mountains, *Ire.* 53°1′ N, 6°59′ W 150
Wickrath, *Ger.* 51°7′ N, 6°24′ E 167
Widerøe, Mount, peak, *Antarctica* 72°7′ S, 22°53′ E 248
Widnes, *U.K.* 53°21′ N, 2°44′ W 162
Wiehl, *Ger.* 50°56′ N, 7°32′ E 167
Wielbark, *Pol.* 53°23′ N, 20°55′ E 152
Wielkopolskie, adm. division, *Pol.* 52°11′ N, 15°54′ E 152
Wien (Vienna), *Aust.* 48°10′ N, 16°14′ E 152
Wiener Neustadt, *Aust.* 47°48′ N, 16°14′ E 168
Wierden, *Neth.* 52°21′ N, 6°35′ E 163
Wiergate, *Tex., U.S.* 30°59′ N, 93°43′ W 103
Wiesbaden, *Ger.* 50°4′ N, 8°13′ E 167
Wiesmoor, *Ger.* 53°24′ N, 7°44′ E 163
Wieżyca, peak, *Pol.* 54°13′ N, 18°2′ E 152
Wigan, *U.K.* 53°32′ N, 2°38′ W 162
Wiggins, *Miss., U.S.* 30°50′ N, 89°6′ W 103
Wignes Lake, *Can.* 60°11′ N, 106°37′ W 108
Wigton, *U.K.* 54°49′ N, 3°10′ W 162
Wikieup, *Ariz., U.S.* 34°43′ N, 113°37′ W 101
Wil, *Switz.* 47°27′ N, 9°2′ E 156
Wilberforce, Cape, *Austral.* 11°50′ S, 136°37′ E 192
Wilbur, *Wash., U.S.* 47°44′ N, 118°42′ W 90
Wilcox, *Can.* 50°5′ N, 104°45′ W 90
Wilczek, Zemlya, islands, *Russ.* 79°47′ N, 64°40′ E 160
Wild, Cape, *Antarctica* 67°58′ S, 152°38′ E 248
Wild Rice, river, *Minn., U.S.* 46°57′ N, 96°45′ W 94
Wild Rose, *Wis., U.S.* 44°10′ N, 89°16′ W 102
Wildcat Peak, *Nev., U.S.* 39°0′ N, 116°55′ W 90
Wilder, *Vt., U.S.* 43°40′ N, 72°19′ W 104
Wildflicken, *Ger.* 50°23′ N, 9°55′ E 167
Wildomar, *Calif., U.S.* 33°36′ N, 117°17′ W 101
Wildon, *Aust.* 46°52′ N, 15°28′ E 156
Wildrose, *N. Dak., U.S.* 48°37′ N, 103°12′ W 90
Wildspitze, peak, *Aust.* 46°53′ N, 10°48′ E 167
Wildwood, *Can.* 53°35′ N, 115°16′ W 108
Wildwood, *Fla., U.S.* 28°51′ N, 82°3′ W 105
Wildwood, *N.J., U.S.* 38°59′ N, 74°50′ W 94
Wiley, *Colo., U.S.* 38°9′ N, 102°43′ W 90
Wilhelm, Mount, peak, *P.N.G.* 5°48′ S, 144°54′ E 192
Wilhelmina Gebergte, *Suriname* 3°44′ N, 56°34′ W 130
Wilhelmshaven, *Ger.* 53°31′ N, 8°8′ E 163
Wilhelmstal, *Namibia* 21°53′ S, 16°31′ E 227
Wilkes, U.S., station, *Antarctica* 66°5′ S, 110°43′ E 248
Wilkesboro, *N.C., U.S.* 36°8′ N, 81°10′ W 96
Wilkesland, region, *Antarctica* 69°56′ S, 132°51′ E 248
Wilkie, *Can.* 52°25′ N, 108°43′ W 108
Wilkinson, *Miss., U.S.* 31°13′ N, 91°14′ W 103
Will, Mount, peak, *Can.* 57°31′ N, 128°55′ W 108
Willacoochee, *Ga., U.S.* 31°20′ N, 83°3′ W 96
Willapa, *Wash., U.S.* 46°40′ N, 123°40′ W 100
Willapa Bay 46°32′ N, 125°1′ W 80
Willapa Bay, *Wash., U.S.* 46°40′ N, 124°4′ W 100
Willapa Hills, *Wash., U.S.* 46°20′ N, 123°12′ W 100
Willard, *N. Mex., U.S.* 34°35′ N, 106°2′ W 92
Willard, *Ohio, U.S.* 41°2′ N, 82°44′ W 102
Willaumez Peninsula, *P.N.G.* 5°15′ S, 149°24′ E 192
Willcox, *Ariz., U.S.* 32°14′ N, 109°51′ W 112
Willebroek, *Belg.* 51°2′ N, 4°21′ E 163
Willemstad, *Neth. Antilles, Neth.* 51°41′ N, 4°25′ E 167
William Lake, lake, *Can.* 53°49′ N, 99°46′ W 108
William Point, *Can.* 58°55′ N, 109°47′ W 108
William, river, *Can.* 58°9′ N, 109°0′ W 108
Williams, *Ariz., U.S.* 35°13′ N, 112°11′ W 82
Williams, *Calif., U.S.* 39°9′ N, 122°10′ W 90
Williams, *Ind., U.S.* 38°48′ N, 86°39′ W 102
Williams, *Minn., U.S.* 48°44′ N, 94°58′ W 90
Williams Bay, *Wis., U.S.* 42°34′ N, 88°33′ W 102
Williams Island, *Bahamas* 24°33′ N, 78°35′ W 105
Williams Lake, *Can.* 51°46′ N, 91°23′ W 110
Williams Lake, *Can.* 52°6′ N, 122°5′ W 106
Williams, Point, *Antarctica* 67°54′ S, 68°26′ E 248
Williamsburg, *Ky., U.S.* 36°44′ N, 84°10′ W 96
Williamsburg, *Mass., U.S.* 42°23′ N, 72°43′ W 104
Williamsburg, *Ohio, U.S.* 39°3′ N, 84°4′ W 102
Williamsburg, *Va., U.S.* 37°16′ N, 76°43′ W 94
Williamsfield, *Ill., U.S.* 40°54′ N, 90°2′ W 102
Williamson, *W. Va., U.S.* 37°40′ N, 82°17′ W 96
Williamson, Mount, peak, *Calif., U.S.* 36°39′ N, 118°21′ W 101
Williamsport, *Ind., U.S.* 40°16′ N, 87°18′ W 102
Williamsport, *Ohio, U.S.* 39°34′ N, 83°7′ W 102
Williamsport, *Pa., U.S.* 41°14′ N, 77°1′ W 94
Williamstown, *Ky., U.S.* 38°37′ N, 84°34′ W 102
Williamstown, *Vt., U.S.* 44°7′ N, 72°33′ W 104
Williamstown, *W. Va., U.S.* 39°23′ N, 81°28′ W 102
Williamsville, *Ill., U.S.* 39°56′ N, 89°33′ W 102
Willich, *Ger.* 51°15′ N, 6°33′ E 167
Willimantic, *Conn., U.S.* 41°42′ N, 72°13′ W 104
Willingdon, Mount, peak, *Can.* 51°46′ N, 116°20′ W 90
Willis, *Tex., U.S.* 30°24′ N, 95°28′ W 103
Willis Islands, *Scotia Sea* 53°50′ S, 39°43′ W 134
Willis Islets, islands, *Coral Sea* 15°9′ S, 149°13′ E 230
Williston, *Fla., U.S.* 29°22′ N, 82°28′ W 105
Williston, *N. Dak., U.S.* 48°7′ N, 103°39′ W 90
Williston, *S. Af.* 31°19′ S, 20°53′ E 227
Williston Lake, *Can.* 55°59′ N, 124°26′ W 108
Willits, *Calif., U.S.* 39°24′ N, 123°22′ W 90
Willmar, *Minn., U.S.* 45°6′ N, 95°3′ W 90
Willoughby, *U.K.* 53°13′ N, 0°12′ E 162
Willow, *Alas., U.S.* 61°44′ N, 150°4′ W 98
Willow Bunch, *Can.* 49°22′ N, 105°38′ W 90
Willow City, *N. Dak., U.S.* 48°34′ N, 100°19′ W 94
Willow Hill, *Ill., U.S.* 38°58′ N, 88°1′ W 102
Willow Island, *Nebr., U.S.* 40°53′ N, 100°5′ W 90
Willow Reservoir, lake, *Wis., U.S.* 45°42′ N, 90°22′ W 94
Willow River, *Can.* 54°2′ N, 122°31′ W 108
Willow Springs, *Mo., U.S.* 36°58′ N, 91°59′ W 96
Willowick, *Ohio, U.S.* 41°37′ N, 81°28′ W 102
Willowmore, *S. Af.* 33°17′ S, 23°29′ E 227
Willows, *Calif., U.S.* 39°31′ N, 122°13′ W 92
Wills Point, *Tex., U.S.* 32°41′ N, 96°1′ W 96
Willsboro, *N.Y., U.S.* 44°21′ N, 73°25′ W 104
Wilmer, *Ala., U.S.* 30°49′ N, 88°21′ W 103
Wilmer, *Can.* 50°32′ N, 116°4′ W 108
Wilmette, *Ill., U.S.* 42°4′ N, 87°42′ W 102
Wilmington, *Del., U.S.* 39°43′ N, 75°33′ W 94
Wilmington, *Ill., U.S.* 41°18′ N, 88°8′ W 102
Wilmington, *N.Y., U.S.* 44°23′ N, 73°50′ W 104
Wilmington, *N.C., U.S.* 34°14′ N, 77°55′ W 73
Wilmington, *Ohio, U.S.* 39°26′ N, 83°49′ W 102
Wilmington, *Vt., U.S.* 42°51′ N, 72°52′ W 104
Wilmot, *Ark., U.S.* 33°2′ N, 91°35′ W 103
Wilmot, *S. Dak., U.S.* 45°23′ N, 96°53′ W 90
Wilmot Flat, *N.H., U.S.* 43°25′ N, 71°54′ W 104
Wilmslow, *U.K.* 53°19′ N, 2°14′ W 162
Wilpattu National Park, *Sri Lanka* 8°19′ N, 79°37′ E 172
Wilsall, *Mont., U.S.* 45°58′ N, 110°40′ W 90
Wilseyville, *Calif., U.S.* 38°22′ N, 120°32′ W 100
Wilson, *Ark., U.S.* 35°33′ N, 90°3′ W 96
Wilson, *Kans., U.S.* 38°48′ N, 98°29′ W 92
Wilson, *La., U.S.* 30°54′ N, 91°7′ W 103
Wilson, *N.C., U.S.* 35°42′ N, 77°56′ W 96
Wilson, *Okla., U.S.* 34°8′ N, 97°25′ W 92
Wilson, *Tex., U.S.* 33°18′ N, 101°44′ W 92
Wilson Creek, *Wash., U.S.* 47°25′ N, 119°8′ W 90
Wilson Creek Range, *Nev., U.S.* 38°23′ N, 114°38′ W 90
Wilson Inlet 35°22′ S, 116°46′ E 230
Wilson, Mount, peak, *Colo., U.S.* 37°49′ N, 108°4′ W 92
Wilson, Mount, peak, *Nev., U.S.* 38°13′ N, 114°28′ W 90
Wilson, Mount, peak, *Oreg., U.S.* 45°2′ N, 121°45′ W 90
Wilsonville, *Ill., U.S.* 39°3′ N, 89°51′ W 102
Wilton, *Conn., U.S.* 41°11′ N, 73°27′ W 104
Wilton, *N.H., U.S.* 42°50′ N, 71°45′ W 104
Wilton, *N. Dak., U.S.* 47°8′ N, 100°49′ W 90
Wilton, *U.K.* 51°5′ N, 1°53′ W 162
Wilton, river, *Austral.* 13°31′ S, 133°56′ E 231
Wiluna, *Austral.* 26°36′ S, 120°13′ E 231
Wimauma, *Fla., U.S.* 27°43′ N, 82°17′ W 105
Wimbledon, *U.K.* 51°25′ N, 0°13′ E 162
Wimereux, *Fr.* 50°46′ N, 1°37′ E 163
Winam 0°21′ N, 34°13′ E 224
Winamac, *Ind., U.S.* 41°2′ N, 86°37′ W 102
Winburg, *S. Af.* 28°33′ S, 26°58′ E 227
Wincanton, *U.K.* 51°3′ N, 2°25′ W 162
Winchelsea, *U.K.* 50°55′ N, 0°43′ E 162
Winchelsea Island, *Austral.* 13°36′ S, 136°22′ E 230
Winchendon, *Mass., U.S.* 42°40′ N, 72°4′ W 104
Winchester, *Calif., U.S.* 33°42′ N, 117°6′ W 101
Winchester, *Ind., U.S.* 40°10′ N, 84°59′ W 102
Winchester, *N.H., U.S.* 42°45′ N, 72°23′ W 104
Winchester, *Ohio, U.S.* 38°55′ N, 83°38′ W 102
Winchester, *U.K.* 51°3′ N, 1°19′ W 162
Winchester, *Va., U.S.* 39°10′ N, 78°10′ W 94
Winchester Bay 43°35′ N, 125°25′ W 80
Wind Cave National Park, *S. Dak., U.S.* 43°29′ N, 103°16′ W 80
Wind Point, *Wis., U.S.* 42°46′ N, 87°46′ W 102
Wind, river, *Can.* 65°23′ N, 135°18′ W 98
Wind River Peak, *Wyo., U.S.* 42°42′ N, 109°13′ W 90
Wind River Range, *Wyo., U.S.* 42°39′ N, 109°21′ W 90
Wind, river, *Wyo., U.S.* 43°22′ N, 109°9′ W 80
Windeck, *Ger.* 50°48′ N, 7°36′ E 167
Winder, *Ga., U.S.* 33°58′ N, 83°44′ W 96
Windermere, *U.K.* 54°22′ N, 2°54′ W 162
Windfall, *Can.* 54°9′ N, 116°18′ W 108
Windfall, *Ind., U.S.* 40°21′ N, 85°58′ W 102
Windham, *Conn., U.S.* 41°41′ N, 72°10′ W 104
Windhoek, *Namibia* 22°34′ S, 16°56′ E 227
Windigo, river, *Can.* 48°22′ N, 73°33′ W 94
Windmill Islands, *Indian Ocean* 66°40′ S, 114°44′ E 248
Windom, *Minn., U.S.* 43°51′ N, 95°7′ W 90
Windom Peak, *Colo., U.S.* 37°36′ N, 107°41′ W 92
Window Rock, *Ariz., U.S.* 35°41′ N, 109°3′ W 92
Winds, Bay of 66°11′ S, 99°28′ E 248
Windsor, *Can.* 45°34′ N, 72°1′ W 94
Windsor, *Can.* 42°18′ N, 83°1′ W 102
Windsor, *Can.* 44°59′ N, 64°8′ W 111
Windsor, *Colo., U.S.* 40°28′ N, 104°55′ W 90
Windsor, *Conn., U.S.* 41°50′ N, 72°39′ W 104
Windsor, *Ill., U.S.* 39°25′ N, 88°36′ W 102
Windsor, *Mo., U.S.* 38°31′ N, 93°31′ W 94
Windsor, *N.C., U.S.* 35°59′ N, 77°0′ W 96
Windsor, *U.K.* 51°28′ N, 0°37′ E 162
Windsor, *Vt., U.S.* 43°28′ N, 72°24′ W 104
Windsorton, *S. Af.* 28°21′ S, 24°39′ E 227
Windward Islands, *Caribbean Sea* 13°41′ N, 61°20′ W 116
Windy Lake, *Can.* 60°18′ N, 100°44′ W 108
Windy Peak, *Wash., U.S.* 48°54′ N, 120°3′ W 90
Windy Point, *Can.* 50°56′ N, 55°48′ W 111
Winefred Lake, *Can.* 55°25′ N, 111°16′ W 108
Winfall, *N.C., U.S.* 36°13′ N, 76°29′ W 96
Winfield, *Can.* 52°56′ N, 114°27′ W 108
Winfield, *Tex., U.S.* 33°9′ N, 95°7′ W 103
Wingham, *Can.* 43°53′ N, 81°19′ W 102
Winifred, *Mont., U.S.* 47°31′ N, 109°23′ W 90
Winifreda, *Arg.* 36°15′ S, 64°15′ W 139
Winisk Lake, *Can.* 52°49′ N, 88°29′ W 80
Winisk, river, *Can.* 54°27′ N, 86°26′ W 106
Wink, *Tex., U.S.* 31°43′ N, 103°9′ W 92
Winkleigh, *U.K.* 50°51′ N, 3°57′ W 162
Winkler, *Can.* 49°10′ N, 97°56′ W 94
Winlock, *Wash., U.S.* 46°28′ N, 122°56′ W 100
Winn, *Me., U.S.* 45°28′ N, 68°23′ W 94
Winneba, *Ghana* 5°22′ N, 0°40′ E 222
Winnebago, *Ill., U.S.* 42°15′ N, 89°15′ W 102
Winnebago, *Minn., U.S.* 43°45′ N, 94°10′ W 94
Winnebago, Lake, *Wis., U.S.* 43°50′ N, 88°27′ W 102
Winneconne, *Wis., U.S.* 44°6′ N, 88°45′ W 102
Winner, *S. Dak., U.S.* 43°21′ N, 99°52′ W 90
Winnetka, *Ill., U.S.* 42°6′ N, 87°44′ W 102
Winnfield, *La., U.S.* 31°54′ N, 92°39′ W 103
Winnibigoshish, Lake, *Minn., U.S.* 47°21′ N, 96°1′ W 80
Winnie, *Tex., U.S.* 29°48′ N, 94°23′ W 103
Winnipeg, *Can.* 49°53′ N, 97°19′ W 90
Winnipeg Beach, *Can.* 50°29′ N, 97°2′ W 90
Winnipeg, Lake, *Can.* 53°1′ N, 98°32′ W 80
Winnipegosis, *Can.* 51°39′ N, 99°57′ W 90
Winnipegosis, Lake, *Can.* 52°3′ N, 99°36′ W 80
Winnisquam, *N.H., U.S.* 43°30′ N, 71°32′ W 104
Winnsboro, *La., U.S.* 32°9′ N, 91°44′ W 103
Winnsboro, *S.C., U.S.* 34°21′ N, 81°5′ W 96
Winnsboro, *Tex., U.S.* 32°57′ N, 95°17′ W 103
Winokapau Lake, *Can.* 53°13′ N, 63°41′ W 111
Winona, *Kans., U.S.* 39°3′ N, 101°15′ W 90
Winona, *Minn., U.S.* 44°2′ N, 91°38′ W 94
Winona, *Miss., U.S.* 33°27′ N, 89°44′ W 103
Winona, *Tex., U.S.* 32°29′ N, 95°10′ W 103
Winona Lake, *Ind., U.S.* 41°12′ N, 85°49′ W 94
Winschoten, *Neth.* 53°8′ N, 7°1′ E 163
Winsen, *Ger.* 53°22′ N, 10°12′ E 150
Winsford, *U.K.* 53°11′ N, 2°32′ W 162
Winslow, *Ariz., U.S.* 35°1′ N, 110°41′ W 92
Winslow, *Me., U.S.* 44°32′ N, 69°38′ W 94
Winstead, *S. Af.* 28°51′ S, 22°8′ E 227
Winsted, *Conn., U.S.* 41°55′ N, 73°4′ W 104
Winter Harbour, *Can.* 50°30′ N, 128°4′ W 90
Winter Haven, *Fla., U.S.* 28°1′ N, 81°44′ W 105
Winter Park, *Fla., U.S.* 28°35′ N, 81°22′ W 105
Winterberg, *Ger.* 51°11′ N, 8°32′ E 167
Winterhaven, *Calif., U.S.* 32°44′ N, 114°40′ W 101
Wintering Lake, lake, *Can.* 49°23′ N, 87°51′ W 94
Winters, *Tex., U.S.* 31°56′ N, 99°58′ W 96
Winterswijk, *Neth.* 51°58′ N, 6°43′ E 167
Winterton on Sea, *U.K.* 52°43′ N, 1°41′ E 163
Winterville, *Miss., U.S.* 33°29′ N, 91°3′ W 103
Winthrop, *Mass., U.S.* 42°22′ N, 71°0′ W 104
Winthrop, *Minn., U.S.* 44°32′ N, 94°23′ W 90
Winthrop, *Wash., U.S.* 48°27′ N, 120°10′ W 108
Winthrop Harbor, *Ill., U.S.* 42°28′ N, 87°50′ W 102
Winton, *Austral.* 22°25′ S, 143°2′ E 238
Winton, *Calif., U.S.* 37°23′ N, 120°38′ W 100
Winton, *Minn., U.S.* 47°54′ N, 91°49′ W 94
Winton, *N.Z.* 46°9′ S, 168°18′ E 240
Wipperfürth, *Ger.* 51°7′ N, 7°23′ E 163
Wis, river, *Pol.* 53°7′ N, 18°11′ E 142
Wis, river, *Pol.* 50°1′ N, 20°37′ E 152
Wisbech, *U.K.* 52°39′ N, 0°9′ E 162
Wiscasset, *Me., U.S.* 44°0′ N, 69°41′ W 94
Wisconsin, adm. division, *Wis., U.S.* 44°20′ N, 91°11′ W 94
Wisconsin Dells, *Wis., U.S.* 43°37′ N, 89°46′ W 102
Wisconsin, Lake, *Wis., U.S.* 43°21′ N, 89°53′ W 102
Wisconsin Range, *Antarctica* 84°42′ S, 105°9′ W 248
Wisconsin Rapids, *Wis., U.S.* 44°23′ N, 89°50′ W 110
Wisconsin, river, *Wis., U.S.* 42°45′ N, 91°14′ W 80
Wise Bay 82°34′ S, 170°4′ E 248
Wiseman, *Alas., U.S.* 67°18′ N, 150°16′ W 98
Wishek, *N. Dak., U.S.* 46°14′ N, 99°35′ W 90
Wishram, *Wash., U.S.* 45°39′ N, 120°58′ W 100
Wisner, *La., U.S.* 31°58′ N, 91°39′ W 103
Wissen, *Ger.* 50°46′ N, 7°43′ E 167
Wistaria, *Can.* 53°51′ N, 126°18′ W 108
Witbank, *S. Af.* 25°53′ S, 29°11′ E 227
Witdraai, *S. Af.* 27°1′ S, 20°41′ E 227
Witham, *U.K.* 51°48′ N, 0°38′ E 162
Witherbee, *N.Y., U.S.* 44°5′ N, 73°33′ W 104
Withernsea, *U.K.* 53°43′ N, 3°179′ E 162
Witney, *U.K.* 51°47′ N, 1°29′ W 162
Witry-lès-Reims, *Fr.* 49°17′ N, 4°7′ E 163
Witt, *Ill., U.S.* 39°14′ N, 89°21′ W 102
Wittdün, *Ger.* 54°37′ N, 8°23′ E 150
Witten, *Ger.* 51°25′ N, 7°19′ E 167
Witten, *S. Dak., U.S.* 43°25′ N, 100°6′ W 90
Wittenberge, *Ger.* 53°3′ N, 11°43′ E 160
Wittlich, *Ger.* 49°59′ N, 6°54′ E 167
Wittmund, *Ger.* 53°34′ N, 7°47′ E 163
Wittow, *Ger.* 54°38′ N, 13°6′ E 152
Witu, *Kenya* 2°23′ S, 40°26′ E 224
Witu Islands, islands, *Bismarck Sea* 4°24′ S, 148°22′ E 192
Witvlei, *Namibia* 22°24′ S, 18°32′ E 227
Witzenhausen, *Ger.* 51°20′ N, 9°51′ E 167
Wivenhoe, *Can.* 56°11′ N, 95°11′ W 108
Wiwŏn, *N. Korea* 40°53′ N, 126°2′ E 200
Wiżajny, *Pol.* 54°21′ N, 22°52′ E 166
Włocławek, *Pol.* 52°38′ N, 19°4′ E 152
Włodawa, *Pol.* 51°32′ N, 23°31′ E 152
Woburn, *Mass., U.S.* 42°28′ N, 71°10′ W 104
Woc, *Pol.* 54°16′ N, 18°45′ E 166
Wofford Heights, *Calif., U.S.* 35°43′ N, 118°28′ W 101
Wokam, island, *Indonesia* 5°44′ S, 134°34′ E 192
Woking, *Can.* 55°34′ N, 118°47′ W 108
Woking, *U.K.* 51°18′ N, 0°35′ E 162
Wokingham, *U.K.* 51°22′ N, 0°52′ E 162
Wolcott, *Ind., U.S.* 40°45′ N, 87°3′ W 102
Wolds, The, *U.K.* 53°56′ N, 0°40′ E 162
Woleai Atoll, *F.M.S.* 7°26′ N, 141°37′ E 192
Wolf Creek, *Mont., U.S.* 46°58′ N, 112°3′ W 90
Wolf Creek Pass, *Colo., U.S.* 37°29′ N, 106°49′ W 90
Wolf Lake, *Can.* 60°38′ N, 132°17′ W 108
Wolf Lake, *Mich., U.S.* 43°14′ N, 86°7′ W 102
Wolf Mountains, *Mont., U.S.* 45°9′ N, 107°18′ W 90
Wolf, river, *Miss., U.S.* 30°33′ N, 89°23′ W 103
Wolf, river, *Wis., U.S.* 45°17′ N, 89°0′ W 94
Wolfau, *Aust.* 47°15′ N, 16°5′ E 168
Wolfeboro, *N.H., U.S.* 43°34′ N, 71°13′ W 104
Wolfeboro Falls, *N.H., U.S.* 43°35′ N, 71°13′ W 104
Wolfen, *Ger.* 51°40′ N, 12°16′ E 152
Wolfforth, *Tex., U.S.* 33°29′ N, 102°1′ W 92
Wolfhagen, *Ger.* 51°19′ N, 9°10′ E 167
Wolfsburg, *Ger.* 52°25′ N, 10°47′ E 152
Wolfstein, *Ger.* 49°34′ N, 7°36′ E 163
Wolin, *Pol.* 53°51′ N, 14°36′ E 152
Wollaston Forland 74°31′ N, 18°52′ W 246
Wollaston, Islas, islands, *Chile* 56°6′ S, 67°3′ W 134
Wollaston Lake, *Can.* 57°56′ N, 103°5′ W 73
Wollaston Peninsula, *Can.* 69°41′ N, 121°29′ W 106
Wollongong, *Austral.* 34°24′ S, 150°50′ E 231
Wöllstein, *Ger.* 49°48′ N, 7°57′ E 167
Wolmaransstad, *S. Af.* 27°13′ S, 25°58′ E 227
Wolseley, *Can.* 50°25′ N, 103°17′ W 90
Wolsingham, *U.K.* 54°44′ N, 1°54′ W 162
Wolsztyn, *Pol.* 52°7′ N, 16°7′ E 152
Wolvega, *Neth.* 52°52′ N, 6°0′ E 163
Wolverhampton, *U.K.* 52°35′ N, 2°9′ W 162
Wolverine, river, *Can.* 57°46′ N, 116°59′ W 108
Wolverton, *U.K.* 52°3′ N, 0°49′ E 162
Wondong, *S. Korea* 34°21′ N, 126°42′ E 200
Wonewoc, *Wis., U.S.* 43°38′ N, 90°12′ W 102
Wonga Wongué National Park, *Gabon* 0°29′ N, 9°13′ E 206
Wonju, *S. Korea* 37°19′ N, 127°57′ E 200
Wonotobo Vallen, fall(s), *Suriname* 4°22′ N, 58°6′ W 130
Wonowon, *Can.* 56°43′ N, 121°48′ W 108
Wŏnsan, *N. Korea* 39°8′ N, 127°24′ E 200
Wonyulgunna Hill, peak, *Austral.* 24°53′ S, 119°34′ E 230

Wood Buffalo National Park, *Can.* 59°16' N, 114°1' W **72**
Wood Lake, *Nebr., U.S.* 42°37' N, 100°15' W **90**
Wood Lake, lake, *Can.* 55°13' N, 103°45' W **108**
Wood, Mount, peak, *Mont., U.S.* 45°14' N, 109°53' W **90**
Wood River, *Nebr., U.S.* 40°48' N, 98°37' W **90**
Wood, river, *Can.* 49°22' N, 107°21' W **80**
Woodah, Isle, island, *Austral.* 13°20' S, 134°37' E **230**
Woodall Mountain, peak, *Miss., U.S.* 34°43' N, 88°18' W **96**
Woodbine, *Ky., U.S.* 36°53' N, 84°6' W **96**
Woodbridge, *Calif., U.S.* 38°8' N, 121°19' W **100**
Woodbridge, *U.K.* 52°5' N, 1°17' E **162**
Woodburn, *Ind., U.S.* 41°6' N, 84°51' W **102**
Woodburn, *Oreg., U.S.* 45°7' N, 122°51' W **90**
Woodbury, *Conn., U.S.* 41°32' N, 73°13' W **104**
Woodbury, *N.J., U.S.* 39°50' N, 75°11' W **94**
Woodcock, Mount, peak, *Austral.* 19°17' S, 133°51' E **230**
Woodhall Spa, *U.K.* 53°9' N, 0°13' E **162**
Woodlake, *Calif., U.S.* 36°25' N, 119°7' W **101**
Woodland, *Calif., U.S.* 38°40' N, 121°47' W **90**
Woodland, *Wash., U.S.* 45°53' N, 122°46' W **100**
Woodlark, island, *P.N.G.* 9°5' S, 153°2' E **192**
Woodmont, *Conn., U.S.* 41°13' N, 73°0' W **104**
Woodpecker, *Can.* 53°30' N, 122°39' W **108**
Woodridge, *Can.* 49°15' N, 96°9' W **90**
Woodroffe, Mount, peak, *Austral.* 26°23' S, 131°32' E **230**
Woodruff, *Utah, U.S.* 41°31' N, 111°10' W **90**
Woods, Lake of the, *Can.* 49°4' N, 96°1' W **106**
Woodsboro, *Tex., U.S.* 28°13' N, 97°19' W **96**
Woodsfield, *Ohio, U.S.* 39°44' N, 81°7' W **102**
Woodstock, *Can.* 43°7' N, 80°44' W **102**
Woodstock, *Can.* 46°9' N, 67°36' W **94**
Woodstock, *Ill., U.S.* 42°18' N, 88°26' W **102**
Woodstock, *N.Y., U.S.* 42°2' N, 74°8' W **104**
Woodstock, *U.K.* 51°50' N, 1°22' W **162**
Woodstock, *Vt., U.S.* 43°37' N, 72°31' W **104**
Woodsville, *N.H., U.S.* 44°8' N, 72°3' W **104**
Woodville, *Calif., U.S.* 36°5' N, 119°13' W **101**
Woodville, *Ga., U.S.* 33°39' N, 83°7' W **96**
Woodville, *Miss., U.S.* 31°4' N, 91°18' W **103**
Woodville, *Tex., U.S.* 30°45' N, 94°26' W **103**
Woodward, *Okla., U.S.* 36°24' N, 99°23' W **96**
Woodworth, *La., U.S.* 31°8' N, 92°31' W **103**
Woody, *Calif., U.S.* 35°42' N, 118°51' W **101**
Woody Point, *Can.* 49°30' N, 57°56' W **111**
Woollard, Mount, peak, *Antarctica* 80°27' S, 95°39' W **248**
Woollett, Lac, lake, *Can.* 51°22' N, 74°22' W **110**
Woolpit, *U.K.* 52°13' N, 0°53' E **162**
Woolwich, *Me., U.S.* 43°55' N, 69°49' W **104**
Woolwich, *U.K.* 51°29' N, 6°357' E **162**
Woomera, *Austral.* 31°13' S, 136°55' E **231**
Woonsocket, *S. Dak., U.S.* 44°2' N, 98°18' W **90**
Wooster, *Ohio, U.S.* 40°47' N, 81°56' W **102**
Woosung, *Ill., U.S.* 41°53' N, 89°33' W **102**
Worbis, *Ger.* 51°25' N, 10°21' E **167**
Worcester, *Mass., U.S.* 42°16' N, 71°48' W **104**
Worcester, *S. Af.* 33°38' S, 19°23' E **227**
Worcester, *U.K.* 52°11' N, 2°12' W **162**
Worden, *Mont., U.S.* 45°57' N, 108°10' W **90**
Wordie Nunatak, peak, *Antarctica* 66°19' S, 51°16' E **248**
Workington, *U.K.* 54°38' N, 3°33' W **162**
Worksop, *U.K.* 53°17' N, 1°8' W **162**
Worland, *Wyo., U.S.* 44°0' N, 107°56' W **90**
World's View Hill, site, *Zimb.* 20°31' S, 28°29' E **227**
World War II Valor in the Pacific National Monument, *Calif., U.S.* 41°53' N, 121°22' W **90**
World War II Valor in the Pacific National Monument, *Hawai'i, U.S.* 21°21' N, 157°57' W **99**
Wormeldange, *Lux.* 49°37' N, 6°24' E **163**
Woronoco, *Mass., U.S.* 42°9' N, 72°51' W **104**
Wörrstadt, *Ger.* 49°49' N, 8°6' E **167**
Worsley, *Can.* 56°33' N, 119°8' W **108**
Wörth, *Ger.* 49°47' N, 9°10' E **167**
Wortham, *Tex., U.S.* 31°45' N, 96°28' W **96**
Worthing, *U.K.* 50°49' N, 0°23' E **162**
Worthington, *Ind., U.S.* 39°6' N, 86°59' W **102**
Worthington, *Minn., U.S.* 43°35' N, 95°37' W **90**
Worthington, *Ohio, U.S.* 40°5' N, 83°0' W **102**
Worthington Peak, *Nev., U.S.* 37°54' N, 115°42' W **90**
Worthville, *Ky., U.S.* 38°36' N, 85°4' W **102**
Wosi, *Indonesia* 0°10' N, 127°46' E **192**
Woumbou, *Cameroon* 5°15' N, 14°14' E **218**
Wounta, Laguna de, lake, *Nicar.* 13°34' N, 84°18' W **115**
Wour, *Chad* 21°21' N, 15°57' E **216**
Wowoni, island, *Indonesia* 4°20' S, 123°14' E **192**
Woyla, river, *Indonesia* 4°21' N, 96°4' E **196**
Wragby, *U.K.* 53°16' N, 0°19' E **162**
Wrangel Island see Vrangelya, Ostrov, island, *Russ.* 71°29' N, 175°23' E **160**
Wrangel Plain, *Arctic Ocean* 81°41' N, 157°4' E **255**
Wrangell, *Alas., U.S.* 56°28' N, 132°25' W **108**
Wrangell Mountains, *Alas., U.S.* 61°51' N, 144°32' W **98**
Wrangell-Saint Elias National Park and Preserve, *Alas., U.S.* 62°15' N, 143°49' W **98**
Wray, *Colo., U.S.* 40°3' N, 102°14' W **90**
Wreck Point, *S. Af.* 29°7' S, 16°12' E **227**
Wrekin, The, peak, *U.K.* 52°39' N, 2°36' W **162**
Wren, *Ala., U.S.* 34°25' N, 87°17' W **96**
Wrens, *Ga., U.S.* 33°11' N, 82°24' W **96**
Wrexham, *U.K.* 53°2' N, 2°59' W **162**
Wright, *Philippines* 11°47' N, 125°1' E **203**
Wright, *Wyo., U.S.* 43°42' N, 105°32' W **90**
Wright Hill, peak, *Antarctica* 79°36' S, 159°27' E **248**
Wright, Mont, peak, *Can.* 52°43' N, 67°27' W **111**
Wright Patman Lake, *Ark., U.S.* 33°1' N, 94°59' W **80**
Wright-Patterson Air Force Base, *Ohio, U.S.* 39°48' N, 84°6' W **102**
Wrightsville Beach, *N.C., U.S.* 34°12' N, 77°49' W **96**
Wrightwood, *Calif., U.S.* 34°21' N, 117°39' W **101**
Wrigley, *Can.* 63°19' N, 123°21' W **98**
Wrigley Gulf 73°35' S, 126°58' W **248**
Wrington, *U.K.* 51°21' N, 2°46' W **162**
Wroc, *Pol.* 51°6' N, 17°0' E **152**
Wrong Lake, lake, *Can.* 52°34' N, 96°38' W **108**
Wronki, *Pol.* 52°42' N, 16°23' E **152**
Wroxeter, *Can.* 43°51' N, 81°11' W **102**
Wroxham, *U.K.* 52°43' N, 1°24' E **163**
Wroxton, *Can.* 51°12' N, 101°54' W **90**
Wroxton, *U.K.* 52°4' N, 1°25' W **162**
Wu, river, *China* 28°38' N, 108°25' E **198**
Wu, river, *China* 27°14' N, 108°4' E **190**
Wu'an, *China* 36°42' N, 114°13' E **198**
Wubu, *China* 37°27' N, 110°40' E **198**
Wuchang, *China* 44°55' N, 127°8' E **198**
Wuchuan, *China* 41°7' N, 111°33' E **198**
Wuchuan, *China* 28°26' N, 108°1' E **198**
Wuchuan, *China* 21°24' N, 110°47' E **198**
Wuda, *China* 39°33' N, 106°44' E **198**
Wudalianchi, *China* 48°38' N, 126°10' E **198**
Wudaogou, *China* 42°5' N, 125°51' E **200**
Wudaoliang, *China* 35°13' N, 93°2' E **188**
Wudi, *China* 37°45' N, 117°35' E **198**
Wudu, *China* 33°25' N, 104°54' E **198**
Wufeng, *China* 30°14' N, 110°40' E **198**
Wugang, *China* 26°44' N, 110°34' E **198**
Wugong, *China* 34°17' N, 108°11' E **198**
Wuhai, *China* 39°39' N, 106°50' E **198**
Wuhan, *China* 30°30' N, 114°21' E **198**
Wuhe, *China* 33°9' N, 117°55' E **198**
Wuhu, *China* 31°23' N, 118°26' E **198**
Wüjang, *China* 33°36' N, 79°54' E **188**
Wukari, *Nig.* 7°49' N, 9°48' E **222**
Wulff Land 81°57' N, 58°19' W **246**
Wuli, *China* 34°22' N, 92°45' E **188**
Wulian, *China* 35°44' N, 119°13' E **198**
Wulongbei, *China* 40°15' N, 124°15' E **200**
Wum, *Cameroon* 6°19' N, 10°3' E **222**
Wuming, *China* 23°8' N, 108°18' E **198**
Wun Shwai, *Sudan* 8°1' N, 29°24' E **224**
Wuning, *China* 29°18' N, 115°1' E **198**
Wünnenberg, *Ger.* 51°30' N, 8°43' E **167**
Wunstorf, *Ger.* 52°25' N, 9°26' E **152**
Wuping, *China* 25°4' N, 116°4' E **198**
Wuppertal, *Ger.* 51°16' N, 7°10' E **167**
Wuqi, *China* 36°57' N, 108°14' E **198**
Wuqia, *China* 39°45' N, 75°6' E **184**
Wuqing, *China* 39°25' N, 117°0' E **198**
Wurno, *Nig.* 13°14' N, 5°27' E **222**
Würselen, *Ger.* 50°49' N, 6°7' E **163**
Würzburg, *Ger.* 49°47' N, 9°56' E **167**
Wusa'a, *Sudan* 13°0' N, 32°31' E **182**
Wushan, *China* 31°6' N, 109°51' E **198**
Wushi (Uqturpan), *China* 41°9' N, 79°17' E **184**
Wutai, *China* 38°41' N, 113°11' E **198**
Wuvulu Island, *P.N.G.* 2°23' S, 142°45' E **192**
Wuwei, *China* 38°0' N, 102°55' E **190**
Wuwei, *China* 31°17' N, 117°47' E **198**
Wuxi, *China* 31°23' N, 109°36' E **198**
Wuxi, *China* 31°37' N, 120°18' E **198**
Wuxue, *China* 29°54' N, 115°33' E **198**
Wuyi Shan, *China* 26°4' N, 116°25' E **198**
Wuyiling, *China* 48°37' N, 129°21' E **198**
Wuyuan, *China* 41°4' N, 108°19' E **198**
Wuzhai, *China* 38°54' N, 111°49' E **198**
Wuzhong, *China* 38°1' N, 106°12' E **198**
Wuzhou, *China* 23°34' N, 111°21' E **198**
Wyandotte, *Mich., U.S.* 42°11' N, 83°11' W **102**
Wyanet, *Ill., U.S.* 41°22' N, 89°34' W **102**
Wye, river, *U.K.* 52°15' N, 3°30' W **162**
Wyemandoo, peak, *Austral.* 28°36' S, 118°19' E **230**
Wylatowo, *Pol.* 52°36' N, 17°55' E **152**
Wymondham, *U.K.* 52°34' N, 1°6' E **163**
Wymore, *Nebr., U.S.* 40°5' N, 96°40' W **90**
Wyndham, *Austral.* 15°29' S, 128°14' E **238**
Wyndmere, *N. Dak., U.S.* 46°15' N, 97°10' W **90**
Wynne, *Ark., U.S.* 35°12' N, 90°49' W **96**
Wynnewood, *Okla., U.S.* 34°37' N, 97°9' W **96**
Wynyard, *Can.* 51°45' N, 104°11' W **90**
Wyoming, *Can.* 42°56' N, 82°7' W **102**
Wyoming, *Ill., U.S.* 41°3' N, 89°47' W **102**
Wyoming, adm. division, *Wyo., U.S.* 42°49' N, 108°38' W **90**
Wyoming Peak, *Wyo., U.S.* 42°36' N, 110°43' W **90**
Wyoming Range, *Wyo., U.S.* 42°46' N, 110°47' W **90**
Wysox, *Pa., U.S.* 41°46' N, 76°25' W **110**
Wytheville, *Va., U.S.* 36°56' N, 81°6' W **96**
Wyville Thomson Ridge, *North Atlantic Ocean* 59°30' N, 10°10' W **253**
Wyvis, Ben, peak, *U.K.* 57°39' N, 4°41' W **150**

X

X, Rock, *Antarctica* 66°2' S, 138°54' E **248**
Xá Muteba, *Angola* 9°33' S, 17°49' E **218**
Xaafuun, *Somalia* 10°21' N, 51°18' E **216**
Xaafuun, Raas, *Somalia* 10°26' N, 51°28' E **216**
Xàbia see Jávea, *Sp.* 38°47' N, 0°9' E **164**
Xaçmaz, *Azerb.* 41°27' N, 48°49' E **195**
Xaignabouri, *Laos* 19°16' N, 101°43' E **202**
Xainza, *China* 30°57' N, 88°37' E **197**
Xaitongmoin, *China* 29°27' N, 88°9' E **188**
Xai-Xai, *Mozambique* 25°3' S, 33°39' E **227**
Xalapa, *Mex.* 19°28' N, 96°59' W **114**
Xalin, *Somalia* 9°5' N, 48°37' E **216**
Xam Nua, *Laos* 20°27' N, 104°0' E **202**
Xamure, *Somalia* 7°11' N, 48°56' E **218**
Xamure, spring, *Somalia* 7°12' N, 48°55' E **216**
Xangongo, *Angola* 16°45' S, 15°0' E **220**
Xankändi see Stepanakert, *Asia* 39°48' N, 46°43' E **195**
Xanten, *Ger.* 51°39' N, 6°27' E **167**
Xánthi, *Gr.* 41°8' N, 24°54' E **180**
Xanthus, ruin(s), *Turk.* 36°19' N, 29°12' E **156**
Xanxerê, *Braz.* 26°52' S, 52°25' W **138**
Xapecó, river, *Braz.* 26°39' S, 52°30' W **139**
Xapuri, *Braz.* 10°42' S, 68°32' W **137**
Xapuri, river, *Braz.* 10°43' S, 69°13' W **137**
Xar Moron, river, *China* 43°17' N, 119°27' E **198**
Xarardheere, *Somalia* 4°38' N, 47°53' E **218**
Xassengue, *Angola* 10°26' S, 18°33' E **220**
Xàtiva, *Sp.* 38°58' N, 0°31' E **164**
Xavantina, *Braz.* 21°15' S, 52°50' W **138**
Xayar, *China* 41°14' N, 82°51' E **184**
Xcalak National Park, *Mex.* 18°20' N, 88°6' W **72**
Xêgar see Tingri, *China* 28°40' N, 87°3' E **197**
Xèng, river, *Laos* 20°10' N, 102°44' E **202**
Xenia, *Ill., U.S.* 38°37' N, 88°38' W **102**
Xenia, *Ohio, U.S.* 39°41' N, 83°56' W **102**
Xépôn, *Laos* 16°41' N, 106°15' E **202**
Xeriuini, river, *Braz.* 0°50' N, 62°15' W **130**
Xhora, *S. Af.* 31°59' S, 28°39' E **227**
Xi Ujimqin Qi, *China* 44°36' N, 117°36' E **198**
Xiachuan Dao, island, *China* 21°17' N, 112°22' E **198**
Xiajiang, *China* 27°35' N, 115°3' E **198**
Xiamen (Amoy), *China* 24°25' N, 118°6' E **198**
Xi'an, *China* 34°17' N, 108°57' E **198**
Xianfeng, *China* 29°41' N, 109°8' E **198**
Xiang, river, *China* 26°33' N, 112°13' E **198**
Xiangfan, *China* 32°6' N, 112°2' E **198**
Xianggang see Hong Kong, island, *China* 21°55' N, 114°15' E **198**
Xianghuang Qi (Hobot Xar), *China* 42°11' N, 113°53' E **198**
Xiangkhoang, *Laos* 19°20' N, 103°23' E **202**
Xiangning, *China* 35°57' N, 110°48' E **198**
Xiangshan, *China* 29°26' N, 121°52' E **198**
Xiangtan, *China* 27°54' N, 112°51' E **198**
Xiangyin, *China* 28°42' N, 112°50' E **198**
Xianju, *China* 28°53' N, 120°43' E **198**
Xiantao, *China* 30°19' N, 113°26' E **198**
Xianyou, *China* 25°22' N, 118°42' E **198**
Xiaogan, *China* 30°55' N, 113°55' E **198**
Xiaojiang, *China* 27°33' N, 120°28' E **198**
Xiaoshan, *China* 30°8' N, 120°18' E **198**
Xiaoyi, *China* 37°7' N, 111°46' E **198**
Xiapu, *China* 26°53' N, 119°59' E **198**
Xichang, *China* 27°53' N, 102°16' E **190**
Xichang Space Launch Center, spaceport, *China* 28°13' N, 101°49' E **190**
Xichú, *Mex.* 21°23' N, 100°5' W **114**
Xichuan, *China* 33°10' N, 111°31' E **198**
Xicoténcatl, *Mex.* 22°58' N, 98°56' W **114**
Xicotepec de Juárez, *Mex.* 20°16' N, 97°57' W **114**
Xié, river, *Braz.* 1°12' N, 67°15' W **136**
Xiejia, *China* 42°23' N, 125°43' E **200**
Xifeng, *China* 42°45' N, 124°39' E **200**
Xifeng, *China* 35°47' N, 107°39' E **198**
Xigazê, *China* 29°13' N, 88°53' E **190**
Xihe, *China* 33°59' N, 105°16' E **198**
Xihu, *China* 40°33' N, 95°1' E **188**
Xiis, *Somalia* 10°47' N, 46°52' E **216**
Xiji, *China* 36°0' N, 105°43' E **198**
Xijir Ulan Hu, lake, *China* 35°9' N, 89°12' E **188**
Xiliao, river, *China* 43°45' N, 122°32' E **198**
Xilinhot, *China* 43°56' N, 116°8' E **198**
Xilitla, *Mex.* 21°23' N, 98°58' W **114**
Ximeng, *China* 22°43' N, 99°25' E **202**
Xin Barag Youqi, *China* 48°39' N, 116°47' E **198**
Xin Barag Zouqi, *China* 48°10' N, 118°13' E **198**
Xin Hot see Abag Qi, *China* 44°1' N, 114°56' E **198**
Xinavane, *Mozambique* 25°2' S, 32°47' E **227**
Xinbin, *China* 41°43' N, 125°4' E **200**
Xincai, *China* 32°46' N, 114°53' E **198**
Xincheng, *China* 38°32' N, 106°11' E **198**
Xinchengzi, *China* 42°4' N, 123°33' E **200**
Xinfeng, *China* 25°24' N, 114°54' E **198**
Xinfeng, *China* 24°1' N, 114°10' E **198**
Xing'an, *China* 25°33' N, 110°37' E **198**
Xingcheng, *China* 40°39' N, 120°46' E **198**
Xingdi, *China* 41°17' N, 87°58' E **188**
Xinge, *Angola* 9°47' S, 19°11' E **220**
Xinghe, *China* 40°51' N, 113°54' E **198**
Xinghua, *China* 32°56' N, 119°53' E **198**
Xingning, *China* 24°6' N, 115°43' E **198**
Xingshan, *China* 31°22' N, 110°44' E **198**
Xingtai, *China* 37°1' N, 114°31' E **198**
Xingu, river, *Braz.* 5°8' S, 54°18' W **122**
Xingxian, *China* 38°28' N, 111°3' E **198**
Xingyi, *China* 25°1' N, 105°8' E **190**
Xingzi, *China* 29°27' N, 115°59' E **198**
Xinhe, *China* 37°31' N, 115°13' E **198**
Xinhe (Toksu), *China* 41°35' N, 82°38' E **184**
Xinhuang, *China* 27°20' N, 109°17' E **198**
Xinhui, *China* 22°26' N, 113°1' E **198**
Xining, *China* 36°30' N, 101°51' E **190**
Xinji, *China* 37°56' N, 115°15' E **198**
Xinjiang, *China* 35°38' N, 111°12' E **198**
Xinjiang, adm. division, *China* 41°27' N, 81°29' E **184**
Xinmin, *China* 41°59' N, 122°49' E **200**
Xinning, *China* 26°28' N, 110°48' E **198**
Xinpu see Lianyungang, *China* 34°38' N, 119°14' E **198**
Xinshao, *China* 27°21' N, 111°28' E **198**
Xinwen, *China* 35°53' N, 117°43' E **198**
Xinxiang, *China* 35°12' N, 113°48' E **198**
Xinxing, *China* 22°43' N, 112°9' E **198**
Xinyang, *China* 32°9' N, 114°6' E **198**
Xinye, *China* 32°31' N, 112°26' E **198**
Xinyi, *China* 34°19' N, 118°20' E **198**
Xinyu, *China* 27°46' N, 114°52' E **198**
Xinyuan, *China* 43°25' N, 83°25' E **184**
Xinzhou, *China* 38°24' N, 112°45' E **198**
Xique Xique, *Braz.* 10°51' S, 42°43' W **132**
Xiruá, river, *Braz.* 7°19' S, 68°34' W **130**
Xishui, *China* 30°27' N, 115°13' E **198**
Xishui, *China* 28°20' N, 106°11' E **198**
Xiushan, *China* 28°25' N, 108°59' E **198**
Xiushui, *China* 29°4' N, 114°30' E **198**
Xiuyan, *China* 40°16' N, 123°15' E **200**
Xiuying, *China* 19°59' N, 110°12' E **198**
Xixia, *China* 33°21' N, 111°30' E **198**
Xixian, *China* 32°22' N, 114°41' E **198**
Xixiang, *China* 33°4' N, 107°44' E **198**
Xizang (Tibet), adm. division, *China* 29°28' N, 87°1' E **197**
Xizhong Dao, island, *China* 39°8' N, 121°11' E **198**
Xocavand see Martuni, *Azerb.* 39°48' N, 47°5' E **195**
Xochihuehuetlán, *Mex.* 17°54' N, 98°28' W **114**
Xorkol, *China* 38°52' N, 91°10' E **188**
Xpuhil, ruin(s), *Mex.* 18°31' N, 89°33' W **115**
Xu, river, *China* 28°10' N, 116°2' E **198**
Xuan Loc, *Vietnam* 10°56' N, 107°14' E **202**
Xuan'en, *China* 30°1' N, 109°28' E **198**
Xuanhan, *China* 31°21' N, 107°36' E **198**
Xuanhua, *China* 40°38' N, 115°5' E **198**
Xuanzhou, *China* 30°54' N, 118°46' E **198**
Xuchang, *China* 34°3' N, 113°49' E **198**
Xudat, *Azerb.* 41°37' N, 48°41' E **195**
Xuddur (Oddur), *Somalia* 4°6' N, 43°55' E **218**
Xudun, *Somalia* 9°3' N, 47°29' E **216**
Xugou, *China* 34°41' N, 119°23' E **198**
Xulun Hoh see Zhenglan Qi, *China* 42°13' N, 116°2' E **198**
Xümatang, *China* 33°52' N, 97°21' E **188**
Xunwu, *China* 24°52' N, 115°37' E **198**
Xunyang, *China* 32°53' N, 109°22' E **198**
Xunyi, *China* 35°10' N, 108°18' E **198**
Xupu, *China* 27°56' N, 110°35' E **198**
Xuwen, *China* 20°18' N, 110°9' E **198**
Xuyong, *China* 28°9' N, 105°28' E **198**
Xuzhou, *China* 34°16' N, 117°7' E **198**
Xylofagou, *Cyprus* 34°58' N, 33°50' E **194**

Y

Yaak, *Mont., U.S.* 48°49' N, 115°43' W **90**
Yaak, river, *Can.* 48°43' N, 116°2' W **90**
Ya'an, *China* 30°2' N, 103°1' E **190**
Yabassi, *Cameroon* 4°25' N, 9°58' E **222**
Yabēlo, *Eth.* 4°51' N, 38°8' E **224**
Yablunyts'kyy, Pereval, pass, *Ukr.* 48°17' N, 24°27' E **152**
Yabrīn, spring, *Saudi Arabia* 23°11' N, 48°57' E **182**
Yabrūd, *Syr.* 33°58' N, 36°38' E **194**
Yachi, river, *China* 26°59' N, 106°14' E **198**
Yacimiento Río Turbio, *Arg.* 51°35' S, 72°21' W **134**
Yaco, *Bol.* 17°13' S, 67°34' W **137**
Yaco, river, *Peru* 10°47' S, 70°49' W **137**
Yacolt, *Wash., U.S.* 45°51' N, 122°25' W **100**
Yacuma, river, *Bol.* 14°6' S, 66°36' W **137**
Yadgir, *India* 16°46' N, 77°8' E **188**
Yaenengu, *Dem. Rep. of the Congo* 2°27' N, 23°11' E **218**
Yag, river, *China* 34°0' N, 93°55' E **188**
Yağca, *Turk.* 37°1' N, 30°32' E **156**
Yagodnoye, *Russ.* 62°34' N, 149°33' E **160**
Yagoua, *Cameroon* 10°22' N, 15°14' E **216**
Yagradagzê Shan, peak, *China* 35°8' N, 95°34' E **188**
Yaguarón, river, *South America* 32°0' S, 54°1' W **139**
Yaguas, river, *Peru* 3°11' S, 71°2' W **136**
Yahia Lehouas, *Alg.* 35°36' N, 4°55' E **150**
Yahk, *Can.* 49°5' N, 116°7' W **90**
Yahualica, *Mex.* 21°9' N, 102°54' W **114**
Yahuma, *Dem. Rep. of the Congo* 1°5' N, 23°5' E **218**
Yahyalı, *Turk.* 38°5' N, 35°21' E **156**
Yainax Butte, peak, *Oreg., U.S.* 42°19' N, 121°20' W **90**
Yaita, *Japan* 36°47' N, 139°56' E **201**
Yaizu, *Japan* 34°51' N, 138°18' E **201**
Yakeshi, *China* 49°15' N, 120°43' E **198**
Yakima, *Wash., U.S.* 46°35' N, 120°30' W **90**
Yakkabog', *Uzb.* 39°1' N, 66°41' E **197**
Yakmach, *Pak.* 28°43' N, 63°48' E **182**
Yakoma, *Dem. Rep. of the Congo* 4°2' N, 22°21' E **218**
Yakossi, *Cen. Af. Rep.* 5°37' N, 23°22' E **218**
Yakotoko, *Cen. Af. Rep.* 5°20' N, 25°16' E **224**
Yaksha, *Russ.* 61°49' N, 56°50' E **154**
Yaku Shima, island, *Japan* 29°39' N, 130°35' E **190**
Yakusu, *Dem. Rep. of the Congo* 0°35' N, 25°1' E **224**
Yakutsk, *Russ.* 62°2' N, 129°36' E **160**
Yala, *Ghana* 10°7' N, 1°52' W **222**
Yala, *Sri Lanka* 6°22' N, 81°31' E **188**
Yala, *Thai.* 6°30' N, 101°16' E **196**
Yalagüina, *Nicar.* 13°28' N, 86°28' W **115**
Yale, *Can.* 49°34' N, 121°26' W **100**
Yale, *Mich., U.S.* 43°8' N, 82°47' W **102**
Yale, *Okla., U.S.* 36°5' N, 96°41' W **92**
Yale Dam, *Wash., U.S.* 45°59' N, 122°25' W **100**
Yali, *Dem. Rep. of the Congo* 1°59' N, 21°5' E **218**
Yaligimba, *Dem. Rep. of the Congo* 2°11' N, 22°54' E **218**
Yalinga, *Cen. Af. Rep.* 6°30' N, 23°19' E **218**
Yalkubul, Punta, *Mex.* 21°34' N, 89°27' W **116**
Yalova, *Turk.* 40°38' N, 29°15' E **156**
Yalta, *Ukr.* 44°30' N, 34°5' E **156**
Yalu, river, *Asia* 41°46' N, 128°2' E **200**
Yalutorovsk, *Russ.* 56°40' N, 66°11' E **169**
Yalvaç, *Turk.* 38°17' N, 31°9' E **156**
Yamada, *Japan* 33°33' N, 130°45' E **201**
Yamaga, *Japan* 33°0' N, 130°41' E **201**
Yamagata, *Japan* 38°15' N, 140°20' E **201**
Yamagata, adm. division, *Japan* 38°22' N, 139°45' E **201**
Yamaguchi, *Japan* 34°11' N, 131°29' E **200**
Yamaguchi, adm. division, *Japan* 34°6' N, 131°0' E **200**
Yamal, Poluostrov, *Russ.* 70°23' N, 70°9' E **169**
Yamal-Nenets, adm. division, *Russ.* 66°22' N, 74°2' E **160**
Yamanaka, *Japan* 36°14' N, 136°22' E **201**
Yamanashi, adm. division, *Japan* 35°30' N, 138°17' E **201**
Yamato Mountains, *Antarctica* 71°23' S, 36°56' E **248**
Yambio, *Sudan* 4°32' N, 28°24' E **224**
Yambol, *Bulg.* 42°29' N, 26°30' E **156**
Yambol, adm. division, *Bulg.* 42°12' N, 26°17' E **156**
Yamburg, *Russ.* 68°18' N, 77°12' E **169**
Yamdena, island, *Indonesia* 7°13' S, 131°2' E **192**
Yamethinn, *Myanmar* 20°26' N, 96°7' E **202**
Yamkino, *Russ.* 57°53' N, 29°17' E **166**
Yamm, *Russ.* 58°24' N, 28°4' E **166**
Yammaw, *Myanmar* 26°15' N, 97°42' E **188**
Yamoussoukro, *Côte d'Ivoire* 6°44' N, 5°24' W **222**
Yampa, river, *Colo., U.S.* 40°33' N, 108°7' W **92**
Yampil', *Ukr.* 48°14' N, 28°20' E **156**
Yampol', *Ukr.* 49°57' N, 26°16' E **152**
Yamsay Mountain, peak, *Oreg., U.S.* 42°55' N, 121°27' W **90**
Yamsk, *Russ.* 59°35' N, 153°56' E **160**
Yamuna, river, *India* 29°23' N, 77°4' E **190**
Yamzho Yumco, lake, *China* 28°59' N, 90°26' E **197**
Yana, *Sierra Leone* 9°43' N, 12°22' W **222**
Yana, river, *Russ.* 69°54' N, 135°39' E **160**
Yanachaga Chemillén National Park, *Peru* 10°31' S, 75°37' W **122**
Yanagawa, *Japan* 33°9' N, 130°24' E **201**
Yanai, *Japan* 33°58' N, 132°7' E **201**
Yanam, *India* 16°45' N, 82°5' E **190**
Yan'an, *China* 36°33' N, 109°28' E **198**
Yanaoca, *Peru* 14°15' S, 71°25' W **137**
Yanaul, *Russ.* 56°16' N, 55°4' E **154**
Yanbu'al Ba'r, *Saudi Arabia* 24°5' N, 38°4' E **182**
Yanchang, *China* 36°36' N, 110°3' E **198**
Yancheng, *China* 33°21' N, 120°6' E **198**
Yanchi, *China* 37°46' N, 107°20' E **198**
Yanchuan, *China* 36°50' N, 110°10' E **198**
Yandoon, *Myanmar* 17°3' N, 95°37' E **202**
Yanfolila, *Mali* 11°11' N, 8°10' W **222**
Yangambi, *Dem. Rep. of the Congo* 0°47' N, 24°25' E **224**
Yangarey, *Russ.* 68°43' N, 61°29' E **169**
Yangasso, *Mali* 13°4' N, 5°20' W **222**
Yangbajain, *China* 30°11' N, 90°29' E **197**
Yangchun, *China* 22°8' N, 111°47' E **198**
Yanggu, *S. Korea* 38°7' N, 127°59' E **200**
Yanghe, *China* 40°4' N, 123°25' E **200**
Yangi-Nishon, *Uzb.* 38°37' N, 65°40' E **197**
Yangiqishloq, *Uzb.* 40°25' N, 67°13' E **197**
Yangiyer, *Uzb.* 40°12' N, 68°51' E **197**
Yangiyūl, *Uzb.* 41°9' N, 69°4' E **197**
Yangjiang, *China* 21°50' N, 111°59' E **198**
Yangon (Rangoon), *Myanmar* 16°45' N, 96°0' E **202**
Yangory, *Russ.* 62°46' N, 37°48' E **154**
Yangou Gala, *Cen. Af. Rep.* 7°21' N, 20°11' E **218**
Yangquan, *China* 37°52' N, 113°36' E **198**
Yangsan, *S. Korea* 35°20' N, 129°3' E **200**
Yangshan, *China* 24°29' N, 112°39' E **198**
Yangshuo, *China* 24°45' N, 110°26' E **198**
Yangtze, lake, *China* 30°23' N, 106°28' E **172**
Yangtze, river, *China* 27°59' N, 104°57' E **172**
Yangtze see Jinsha, river, *China* 25°47' N, 103°15' E **190**
Yangtze, Source of the, *China* 33°16' N, 90°53' E **188**
Yangudi Rassa National Park, *Eth.* 10°46' N, 41°7' E **224**
Yangxian, *China* 33°13' N, 107°31' E **198**
Yangxin, *China* 29°51' N, 115°6' E **198**
Yangyang, *S. Korea* 38°5' N, 128°37' E **200**
Yangyuan, *China* 40°7' N, 114°8' E **198**
Yangzhou, *China* 32°25' N, 119°27' E **198**
Yangzishao, *China* 42°25' N, 126°7' E **200**
Yanhe, *China* 28°32' N, 108°25' E **198**
Yanis'yarvi, Ozero, lake, *Russ.* 61°52' N, 29°54' E **152**
Yanji, *China* 42°55' N, 129°27' E **200**
Yanji (Longjing), *China* 42°46' N, 129°24' E **200**
Yankari National Park, *Nig.* 9°47' N, 9°50' E **222**
Yankeetown, *Fla., U.S.* 29°2' N, 82°44' W **105**
Yankovichi, *Belarus* 55°47' N, 28°48' E **166**
Yankton, *S. Dak., U.S.* 42°51' N, 97°24' W **90**
Yanonge, *Dem. Rep. of the Congo* 0°33' N, 24°39' E **224**
Yanqi, *China* 42°8' N, 86°39' E **184**
Yanrakynnot, *Russ.* 64°59' N, 172°39' W **98**
Yanshan, *China* 38°4' N, 117°13' E **198**
Yanshan, *China* 23°32' N, 104°20' E **202**
Yanshan, *China* 28°16' N, 117°38' E **198**
Yanshou, *China* 45°30' N, 128°21' E **198**
Yanskiy, *Russ.* 68°22' N, 135°8' E **160**
Yantai, *China* 37°32' N, 121°21' E **198**
Yantarnyy, *Russ.* 54°51' N, 19°56' E **166**
Yao, *Japan* 34°38' N, 135°35' E **201**
Yaoundé, *Cameroon* 3°55' N, 11°24' E **222**
Yaoxian, *China* 34°59' N, 109°0' E **198**
Yap Islands, *Philippine Sea* 9°43' N, 136°10' E **192**
Yap Trench, *North Pacific Ocean* 7°20' N, 137°57' E **254**
Yapacana National Park, *Venez.* 3°44' N, 66°47' W **136**
Yapacani, river, *Bol.* 15°52' S, 64°33' W **137**
Yapei (Tamale Port), *Ghana* 9°10' N, 1°11' W **222**
Yapele, *Dem. Rep. of the Congo* 0°12' N, 24°25' E **224**
Yapen, island, *Indonesia* 1°32' S, 135°43' E **192**
Yapeyú, *Arg.* 29°26' S, 56°53' W **139**
Yaptiksale, *Russ.* 69°20' N, 72°36' E **169**
Yaqui, river, *Mex.* 28°10' N, 110°3' W **112**
Yaquina Head, *Oreg., U.S.* 44°39' N, 124°22' W **90**
Yar, *Russ.* 58°13' N, 52°9' E **154**
Yar Sale, *Russ.* 66°49' N, 70°48' E **169**

Zakamensk, Russ. 50°22′ N, 103°22′ E 190
Zákány, Hung. 46°16′ N, 16°57′ E 168
Zakataly, Azerb. 41°38′ N, 46°37′ E 195
Zakho, Iraq 37°8′ N, 42°34′ E 195
Zakhodnyaya Dzvina, river, Belarus 54°48′ N, 30°6′ E 154
Zakhrebetnoye, Russ. 68°57′ N, 36°27′ E 152
Zákinthos, Gr. 37°45′ N, 20°51′ E 216
Zákinthos, island, Gr. 37°48′ N, 19°27′ E 216
Zakīyah, Syr. 33°19′ N, 36°8′ E 194
Zakouma National Park, Chad 10°24′ N, 19°17′ E 218
Zakum, oil field, Persian Gulf 24°46′ N, 53°41′ E 196
Zakwaski Mountain, peak, Can. 50°8′ N, 121°24′ W 108
Zala, Angola 7°52′ S, 14°2′ E 218
Zala, adm. division, Hung. 46°49′ N, 16°29′ E 156
Zalaegerszeg, Hung. 46°49′ N, 16°51′ E 168
Zalalöv o, Hung. 46°50′ N, 16°36′ E 168
Zalamea la Real, Sp. 37°40′ N, 6°40′ W 164
Zalanga, Nig. 10°36′ N, 10°10′ E 222
Zalangoye, Congo 1°22′ N, 14°48′ E 218
Zalantun, China 48°2′ N, 122°47′ E 198
Zalau, Nig. 10°22′ N, 8°59′ E 222
Zalău, Rom. 47°10′ N, 23°4′ E 168
Žalec, Slov. 46°15′ N, 15°8′ E 156
Zalim, Saudi Arabia 22°41′ N, 42°11′ E 182
Zalingei, Sudan 12°52′ N, 23°29′ E 216
Zalishchyky, Ukr. 48°38′ N, 25°44′ E 152
Zaltan, oil field, Lib. 28°47′ N, 19°44′ E 216
Zalve, Latv. 56°19′ N, 25°14′ E 166
Zama, Miss., U.S. 32°56′ N, 89°22′ W 103
Zama Lake, Can. 58°46′ N, 119°27′ W 108
Zamarte, Pol. 53°35′ N, 17°29′ E 152
Žamberk, Czech Rep. 50°4′ N, 16°27′ E 152
Zambezi, Zambia 13°33′ S, 23°9′ E 220
Zambezi National Park, Zimb. 18°30′ S, 25°12′ E 224
Zambezi, river, Zambia 16°33′ S, 23°28′ E 220
Zambézia, adm. division, Mozambique 16°33′ S, 35°52′ E 224
Zambia 15°2′ S, 26°18′ E 220
Zamboanga, Philippines 6°58′ N, 122°3′ E 203
Zamboanguita, Philippines 9°9′ N, 123°11′ E 203
Zâmbuè, Mozambique 15°9′ S, 30°47′ E 224
Zamezhnaya, Russ. 65°0′ N, 51°50′ E 154
Zamoge, Eth. 12°56′ N, 37°19′ E 182
Zamora, Ecua. 4°2′ S, 79°0′ W 130
Zamora, Mex. 19°59′ N, 102°17′ W 114
Zamora, Sp. 41°30′ N, 5°46′ W 150
Zamość, Pol. 50°42′ N, 23°14′ E 152
Zamoššа, Belarus 55°30′ N, 27°3′ E 166
Zamostoch'ye, Belarus 53°51′ N, 28°26′ E 166
Zamsheva, Russ. 59°4′ N, 89°14′ E 169
Zamuro, Sierra del, Venez. 4°48′ N, 63°53′ W 130
Zam'yany, Russ. 46°46′ N, 47°35′ E 158
Zanda, China 31°29′ N, 79°47′ E 188
Zandvoort, Neth. 52°22′ N, 4°31′ E 163
Zanesville, Ohio, U.S. 39°56′ N, 82°1′ W 102
Zangeza Bay 57°56′ N, 102°46′ W 108
Zanjān, Iran 36°42′ N, 48°29′ E 195
Zanjón, river, Mex. 29°24′ N, 110°58′ W 80
Zantiguila, Mali 11°37′ N, 5°21′ W 222
Zanzibar, Tanzania 6°7′ S, 39°16′ E 224
Zanzibar Island, Tanzania 6°36′ S, 39°36′ E 224
Zaouatallaz, Alg. 24°53′ N, 8°24′ E 214
Zaouiet Azmour, Tun. 36°55′ N, 11°0′ E 156
Zaoyang, China 32°6′ N, 112°43′ E 198
Zaozhuang, China 34°54′ N, 117°33′ E 198
Zapadnaya Dvina, Russ. 56°15′ N, 32°4′ E 154
Zapadno Sibirskaya Ravnina 61°31′ N, 62°50′ E 154
Zapala, Arg. 38°54′ S, 70°2′ W 123
Zapata, Tex., U.S. 26°53′ N, 99°16′ W 96
Zapata, Peninsula de, Cuba 22°23′ N, 82°2′ W 116
Zapatoca, Col. 6°47′ N, 73°16′ W 136
Zapiga, Chile 19°38′ S, 70°4′ W 137
Zapiola Ridge, South Atlantic Ocean 45°8′ S, 42°14′ W 253
Zapolyarnyy, Russ. 69°25′ N, 30°49′ E 152
Zapol'ye, Russ. 58°38′ N, 29°11′ E 166
Zaporizhzhya, Ukr. 47°48′ N, 35°11′ E 156
Zaporozhskoye, Russ. 60°33′ N, 30°32′ E 166
Zapotiltic, Mex. 19°36′ N, 103°26′ W 114
Zapug, China 33°16′ N, 80°51′ E 188
Zar, spring, Mauritania 18°0′ N, 14°39′ W 222
Zara, Turk. 39°54′ N, 37°44′ E 156
Zara see Zadar, Croatia 44°6′ N, 15°14′ E 156
Zarafshon, Taj. 39°8′ N, 68°39′ E 197
Zarafshon, Uzb. 41°31′ N, 64°14′ E 197
Zarafshon Range, Taj. 39°13′ N, 66°58′ E 184
Zarafshon, river, Taj. 39°20′ N, 69°7′ E 197
Zaragoza, Col. 7°28′ N, 74°49′ W 136
Zaragoza, Mex. 31°36′ N, 106°23′ W 112
Zaragoza, Mex. 28°28′ N, 100°56′ W 92
Zaragoza, Mex. 23°57′ N, 99°46′ W 114
Zaragoza, Mex. 22°0′ N, 100°45′ W 114
Zaragoza, Sp. 41°34′ N, 1°0′ E 214
Zarand, Iran 30°46′ N, 56°38′ E 180
Zarand, Munții, Rom. 46°8′ N, 22°4′ E 168
Zaranou, Côte d'Ivoire 6°23′ N, 3°23′ W 222
Zarasai, Lith. 55°44′ N, 26°16′ E 166
Zárate, Arg. 34°6′ S, 59°1′ W 139
Zarautz, Sp. 43°15′ N, 2°12′ W 164
Zaraysk, Russ. 54°45′ N, 38°52′ E 154
Zaraza, Venez. 9°20′ N, 65°21′ W 136
Zarcilla de Ramos, Sp. 37°50′ N, 1°53′ W 164
Zard Kūh, peak, Iran 32°21′ N, 49°58′ E 180
Zarech'ye, Belarus 54°8′ N, 29°49′ E 166
Zarghun Shahr, Afghan. 32°49′ N, 68°26′ E 186
Zaria, Nig. 11°2′ N, 7°43′ E 222
Zarichne, Ukr. 51°48′ N, 26°7′ E 152
Zaris Berge, Namibia 24°22′ S, 16°10′ E 227
Zarit, spring, Mali 16°4′ N, 3°50′ E 222
Żarnów, Pol. 51°14′ N, 20°11′ E 152
Zarqan, Iran 29°46′ N, 52°47′ E 196
Zarrarah, oil field, U.A.E. 22°42′ N, 54°2′ E 182
Zarubikha, Russ. 69°18′ N, 34°14′ E 152
Zarubino, Russ. 42°38′ N, 131°4′ E 200
Zaruma, Ecua. 3°49′ S, 79°37′ W 130
Żary, Pol. 51°37′ N, 15°8′ E 152
Zarya, Poluostrov, Russ. 75°5′ N, 70°47′ E 172
Zarzaïtine, oil field, Alg. 28°5′ N, 9°40′ E 214
Zarzal, Col. 4°21′ N, 76°6′ W 136
Zarzis, Tun. 33°31′ N, 11°5′ E 214
Zashaghan, Kaz. 51°9′ N, 51°20′ E 158
Zasheyek, Russ. 66°15′ N, 31°4′ E 152
Zaskevichi, Belarus 54°23′ N, 26°35′ E 166
Zaslawye, Belarus 54°0′ N, 27°14′ E 166
Zaslonava, Belarus 54°51′ N, 28°59′ E 166
Zastron, S. Af. 30°18′ S, 27°4′ E 227
Zatish'ye, Russ. 66°10′ N, 158°50′ E 160
Zatobyl, Kaz. 53°11′ N, 63°42′ E 184
Zatoka, Ukr. 46°4′ N, 30°28′ E 156
Zaturtsi, Ukr. 50°45′ N, 24°50′ E 152
Zavala, Bosn. and Herzg. 42°49′ N, 17°58′ E 168
Zavalla, Tex., U.S. 31°9′ N, 94°26′ W 103
Zavetnoye, Russ. 47°3′ N, 43°49′ E 158
Zavidovići, Bosn. and Herzg. 44°27′ N, 18°7′ E 168
Zavlaka, Serb. 44°27′ N, 19°29′ E 168
Zavolzhsk, Russ. 57°32′ N, 42°9′ E 154
Zav'yalovo, Russ. 56°47′ N, 53°24′ E 154
Zāwiyat al Mukhaylá, Lib. 32°11′ N, 22°17′ E 216
Zāwiyat Masūs, Lib. 31°33′ N, 21°0′ E 216
Zāwyet Shammâs, Egypt 31°28′ N, 26°27′ E 180
Zayāki Jangal, Pak. 27°52′ N, 65°49′ E 182
Zaymah, Saudi Arabia 21°36′ N, 40°8′ E 182
Zaysan, Kaz. 47°27′ N, 84°52′ E 184
Zaysan Köli, lake, Kaz. 47°57′ N, 83°47′ E 184
Zayü, China 28°37′ N, 97°30′ E 188
Zboriv, Ukr. 49°40′ N, 25°7′ E 152
Ždala, Croatia 46°9′ N, 17°7′ E 168
Zdolbuniv, Ukr. 50°31′ N, 26°14′ E 152
Zdziechowice, Pol. 50°47′ N, 22°7′ E 152
Zéalé, Côte d'Ivoire 6°51′ N, 8°9′ W 222
Zebla, Jebel, peak, Tun. 36°48′ N, 9°11′ E 156
Zednes, peak, Mauritania 23°44′ N, 10°46′ W 214
Zeeland, Mich., U.S. 42°48′ N, 86°1′ W 102
Ze'elim, Israel 31°12′ N, 34°31′ E 194
Zeerust, S. Af. 25°34′ S, 26°3′ E 227
Zefat, Israel 32°58′ N, 35°29′ E 194
Zeidab, Sudan 17°25′ N, 33°54′ E 182
Zeil, Mount, peak, Austral. 23°27′ S, 132°11′ E 230
Zeist, Neth. 52°5′ N, 5°14′ E 163
Zeitûn, Egypt 29°9′ N, 25°47′ E 180
Zejmen, Alban. 41°42′ N, 19°41′ E 168
Zela see Zile, Turk. 40°19′ N, 35°53′ E 156
Zelenchukskaya, Russ. 43°51′ N, 41°27′ E 195
Zelenikovo, Maced. 41°53′ N, 21°34′ E 168
Zelenoborskiy, Russ. 66°48′ N, 32°19′ E 152
Zelenoe, Kaz. 48°2′ N, 51°34′ E 158
Zelenogorsk, Russ. 60°11′ N, 29°42′ E 166
Zelenogradsk, Russ. 54°56′ N, 20°27′ E 166
Zelenokumsk, Russ. 44°22′ N, 43°55′ E 158
Zelfana, Alg. 32°27′ N, 4°5′ E 214
Zelina, Croatia 45°58′ N, 16°15′ E 168
Željin, Serb. 43°29′ N, 20°39′ E 168
Zell, Ger. 49°48′ N, 9°51′ E 167
Zell, Ger. 50°1′ N, 7°10′ E 167
Zellingen, Ger. 49°53′ N, 9°49′ E 167
Zellwood, Fla., U.S. 28°43′ N, 81°37′ W 105
Zeltiņi, Latv. 57°20′ N, 26°45′ E 166
Zel'va, Belarus 53°8′ N, 24°48′ E 152
Želva, Lith. 55°13′ N, 25°5′ E 166
Zemaitija National Park, Lith. 55°58′ N, 21°54′ E 166
Zemē, Eth. 9°53′ N, 37°45′ E 224
Zemen, Bulg. 42°29′ N, 22°45′ E 168
Zemetchino, Russ. 53°27′ N, 42°34′ E 154
Zemio, Cen. Af. Rep. 5°4′ N, 25°6′ E 224
Zemlya Frantsa Iosifa, islands, Barents Sea 82°32′ N, 4°43′ E 173
Zemlya Frantsa Iosifa see Franz Josef Land, islands, Barents Sea 82°32′ N, 4°43′ E 172
Zemongo, Cen. Af. Rep. 7°4′ N, 24°54′ E 224
Zempoala (Cempoala), ruin(s), Mex. 19°23′ N, 96°28′ W 114
Zempoaltepec, Cerro, peak, Mex. 17°8′ N, 96°2′ W 114
Zemun, Serb. 44°49′ N, 20°25′ E 168
Zencirli, site, Turk. 37°6′ N, 36°36′ E 156
Zengfeng Shan, peak, China 42°22′ N, 128°42′ E 200
Zenica, Bosn. and Herzg. 44°12′ N, 17°52′ E 168
Zenith Plateau, Indian Ocean 22°32′ S, 104°34′ E 254
Zenobia Peak, Colo., U.S. 40°35′ N, 108°57′ W 90
Zenobia, ruin(s), Syr. 35°39′ N, 39°45′ E 180
Zentsūji, Japan 34°14′ N, 133°47′ E 201
Zenza do Itombe, Angola 9°17′ S, 14°14′ E 218
Zenzontepec, Mex. 16°32′ N, 97°31′ W 112
Zepa, Bosn. and Herzg. 43°56′ N, 19°8′ E 168
Žepče, Bosn. and Herzg. 44°26′ N, 18°2′ E 168
Zephyrhills, Fla., U.S. 28°13′ N, 82°11′ W 105
Zepu, China 38°12′ N, 77°18′ E 184
Żerczyce, Pol. 52°28′ N, 23°3′ E 152
Zerendi, Kaz. 52°53′ N, 69°9′ E 184
Zerf, Ger. 49°35′ N, 6°41′ E 163
Zerhamra, Alg. 29°57′ N, 2°29′ W 214
Zerind, Rom. 46°38′ N, 21°32′ E 168
Zermatt, Switz. 46°1′ N, 7°44′ E 167
Zernez, Switz. 46°42′ N, 10°5′ E 167
Zernograd, Russ. 46°50′ N, 40°18′ E 158
Zerqan, Alban. 41°30′ N, 20°21′ E 168
Zestap'oni, Ga. 42°3′ N, 43°2′ E 195
Zetel, Ger. 53°25′ N, 7°59′ E 163
Zevio, It. 45°21′ N, 11°7′ E 167
Zeya, Russ. 53°51′ N, 127°9′ E 190
Zeysk, Russ. 54°51′ N, 129°16′ E 173
Zgharta, Leb. 34°23′ N, 35°54′ E 156
Zgierz, Pol. 51°50′ N, 19°25′ E 152
Zhabinka, Belarus 52°12′ N, 24°0′ E 152
Zhabye, Ukr. 48°9′ N, 24°48′ E 152
Zhag'yab, China 30°37′ N, 97°35′ E 188
Zhalangash, Kaz. 43°2′ N, 78°38′ E 184
Zhalauly, Kaz. 48°1′ N, 61°12′ E 184
Zhaldama, Kaz. 50°26′ N, 65°39′ E 184
Zhalpaqtal, Kaz. 49°40′ N, 49°28′ E 158
Zhaltyr, Kaz. 51°38′ N, 69°51′ E 184
Zhambyl, Kaz. 47°9′ N, 71°8′ E 184
Zhambyl, adm. division, Kaz. 42°45′ N, 70°19′ E 197
Zhanadarīya, Kaz. 44°43′ N, 64°45′ E 184
Zhanang, China 29°16′ N, 91°18′ E 197
Zhanaqala, Kaz. 44°46′ N, 63°11′ E 184
Zhanbīke, Kaz. 47°2′ N, 55°7′ E 158
Zhanga Qazan, Kaz. 48°57′ N, 49°35′ E 158
Zhangaly, Kaz. 47°2′ N, 50°46′ E 158
Zhangaözen, Kaz. 43°20′ N, 52°46′ E 158
Zhangaqala, Kaz. 49°13′ N, 50°19′ E 158
Zhangaqīma, Kaz. 51°36′ N, 67°35′ E 184
Zhangbei, China 41°11′ N, 114°40′ E 198
Zhangjiakou, China 40°48′ N, 114°51′ E 198
Zhangping, China 25°18′ N, 117°24′ E 198
Zhangpu, China 24°4′ N, 117°36′ E 198
Zhangwu, China 42°24′ N, 122°34′ E 200
Zhangye, China 38°51′ N, 100°33′ E 190
Zhangzhou, China 24°29′ N, 117°36′ E 198
Zhangzi, China 36°6′ N, 112°51′ E 198
Zhanhua, China 37°44′ N, 118°10′ E 198
Zhänibek, Kaz. 49°24′ N, 46°50′ E 158
Zhanjiang, China 21°10′ N, 110°20′ E 198
Zhansügirov, Kaz. 45°21′ N, 79°28′ E 184
Zhäntöbe, Kaz. 44°43′ N, 68°50′ E 184
Zhanyi, China 25°41′ N, 103°44′ E 190
Zhao'an, China 23°42′ N, 117°9′ E 198
Zhaodong, China 46°3′ N, 125°57′ E 198
Zhaosu, China 43°7′ N, 81°1′ E 184
Zhaotong, China 27°19′ N, 103°38′ E 190
Zhaoyuan, China 45°29′ N, 125°6′ E 198
Zhaozhou, China 45°41′ N, 125°17′ E 198
Zhapo, China 21°35′ N, 111°52′ E 198
Zhaqsy, Kaz. 51°55′ N, 67°20′ E 184
Zharbulaq, Kaz. 46°4′ N, 82°4′ E 184
Zharkamys, Kaz. 47°56′ N, 56°21′ E 158
Zharkent, Kaz. 44°8′ N, 79°58′ E 184
Zharkovskiy, Russ. 55°52′ N, 32°20′ E 154
Zharma, Kaz. 48°47′ N, 80°51′ E 184
Zharman Köli, lake, Kaz. 51°32′ N, 63°36′ E 184
Zharmysh, Kaz. 44°8′ N, 52°24′ E 158
Zhashui, China 33°42′ N, 109°7′ E 198
Zhaslyk, Uzb. 43°53′ N, 57°41′ E 158
Zhaxi Co, lake, China 32°5′ N, 84°27′ E 188
Zhayylma, Kaz. 51°33′ N, 61°39′ E 184
Zhayyq, river, Kaz. 50°40′ N, 51°12′ E 158
Zhdanov, Azerb. 39°47′ N, 47°36′ E 195
Zhecheng, China 34°3′ N, 115°16′ E 198
Zhejiang, adm. division, China 28°7′ N, 120°50′ E 198
Zhelezīnka, Kaz. 53°38′ N, 75°13′ E 184
Zheleznodorozhnyy, Russ. 54°20′ N, 21°16′ E 166
Zheleznodorozhnyy, Russ. 62°33′ N, 50°59′ E 154
Zheleznogorsk, Russ. 52°17′ N, 35°20′ E 158
Zheleznovodsk, Russ. 44°10′ N, 43°3′ E 158
Zhem, river, Kaz. 47°13′ N, 55°32′ E 160
Zhemgang, Bhutan 27°7′ N, 90°45′ E 197
Zhen'an, China 33°25′ N, 109°7′ E 198
Zhenba, China 32°32′ N, 107°53′ E 198
Zhenfeng, China 25°21′ N, 105°42′ E 198
Zheng'an, China 28°35′ N, 107°22′ E 198
Zhenghe, China 27°23′ N, 118°51′ E 198
Zhenglan Qi (Xulun Hoh), China 42°13′ N, 116°2′ E 198
Zhengxiangbai Qi, China 42°15′ N, 115°3′ E 198
Zhengzhou (Chengchow), China 34°46′ N, 113°36′ E 198
Zhenjiang, China 32°10′ N, 119°25′ E 198
Zhenlai, China 45°48′ N, 123°11′ E 198
Zhenning, China 26°5′ N, 105°44′ E 198
Zhenping, China 31°58′ N, 109°30′ E 198
Zhenping, China 33°4′ N, 112°16′ E 198
Zhenyuan, China 23°50′ N, 100°50′ E 202
Zhenyuan, China 27°3′ N, 108°26′ E 198
Zhenyuan, China 35°43′ N, 107°13′ E 198
Zherdevka, Russ. 51°52′ N, 41°21′ E 158
Zherino, Belarus 54°50′ N, 29°24′ E 166
Zheshart, Russ. 62°4′ N, 49°36′ E 154
Zhetibay, Kaz. 43°33′ N, 52°4′ E 158
Zhetiger, Kaz. 43°40′ N, 77°6′ E 184
Zhetiqara, Kaz. 52°11′ N, 61°13′ E 158
Zhezdi, Kaz. 48°2′ N, 67°1′ E 184
Zhezkent, Kaz. 50°54′ N, 81°24′ E 184
Zhezqazghan, Kaz. 47°46′ N, 67°31′ E 190
Zhicheng, China 30°18′ N, 111°28′ E 198
Zhidan, China 36°49′ N, 108°45′ E 198
Zhidoi, China 33°54′ N, 95°38′ E 188
Zhigalovo, Russ. 54°44′ N, 104°58′ E 160
Zhigansk, Russ. 66°44′ N, 123°6′ E 160
Zhigulevsk, Russ. 53°26′ N, 49°37′ E 158
Zhijiang, China 27°28′ N, 109°42′ E 198
Zhilichi, Belarus 53°28′ N, 24°8′ E 152
Zhilikhovo, Belarus 52°55′ N, 27°3′ E 152
Zhilinda, Russ. 70°9′ N, 113°46′ E 160
Zhirnovsk, Russ. 50°58′ N, 44°47′ E 158
Zhitkovo, Russ. 60°41′ N, 29°19′ E 166
Zhizdra, Russ. 53°41′ N, 34°49′ E 154
Zhlobin, Belarus 52°52′ N, 30°6′ E 154
Zhmerynka, Ukr. 49°3′ N, 28°19′ E 152
Zhob, Pak. 31°20′ N, 69°30′ E 186
Zhob, river, Pak. 30°50′ N, 68°17′ E 186
Zhodzina, Belarus 54°7′ N, 28°20′ E 166
Zhokhova, island, Russ. 76°1′ N, 152°19′ E 255
Zholymbet, Kaz. 51°45′ N, 71°44′ E 184
Zhongba, China 29°41′ N, 84°13′ E 197
Zhongning, China 37°30′ N, 105°38′ E 198
Zhongshan, China 24°28′ N, 111°17′ E 198
Zhongshan, China, station, Antarctica 69°24′ S, 76°11′ E 248
Zhongwei, China 37°32′ N, 105°9′ E 198
Zhongxian, China 30°21′ N, 107°57′ E 198
Zhongxiang, China 31°8′ N, 112°34′ E 198
Zhosaly, Kaz. 45°29′ N, 64°5′ E 184
Zhoukou, China 33°34′ N, 114°43′ E 198
Zhoushan Dao, island, China 30°5′ N, 122°19′ E 198
Zhovten', Ukr. 49°1′ N, 24°46′ E 152
Zhovti Vody, Ukr. 48°23′ N, 33°29′ E 156
Zhovtneve, Ukr. 46°53′ N, 32°1′ E 156
Zhuanghe, China 39°42′ N, 122°57′ E 200
Zhuanglang, China 35°11′ N, 106°2′ E 198
Zhucheng, China 36°3′ N, 119°26′ E 198
Zhugqu, China 33°40′ N, 104°15′ E 198
Zhuji, China 29°44′ N, 120°10′ E 198
Zhukovka, Russ. 53°29′ N, 33°49′ E 154
Zhumysker, Kaz. 47°5′ N, 51°48′ E 158
Zhuolu, China 40°23′ N, 115°10′ E 198
Zhuozhou, China 39°29′ N, 115°57′ E 198
Zhuozi, China 40°55′ N, 112°36′ E 198
Zhuozi Shan, peak, China 39°39′ N, 106°54′ E 198
Zhur (Žur), Kosovo 42°10′ N, 20°36′ E 168
Zhuryn, Kaz. 49°18′ N, 57°33′ E 158
Zhushan, China 32°16′ N, 110°14′ E 198
Zhuxi, China 32°20′ N, 109°42′ E 198
Zhuzhou, China 27°50′ N, 113°12′ E 198
Zhympity, Kaz. 50°15′ N, 52°37′ E 158
Zhytomyr, Ukr. 50°15′ N, 28°40′ E 152
Zi, river, China 32°39′ N, 96°11′ E 188
Zi, river, China 28°25′ N, 111°8′ E 198
Zibak, Afghan. 36°32′ N, 71°25′ E 186
Zibo, China 36°49′ N, 118°6′ E 198
Zichang, China 37°7′ N, 109°39′ E 198
Zierikzee, Neth. 51°39′ N, 3°55′ E 163
Žiežmariai, Lith. 54°49′ N, 24°25′ E 166
Zigana Geçidi, pass, Turk. 40°37′ N, 39°21′ E 195
Zigey, Chad 14°43′ N, 15°46′ E 216
Zigong, China 29°25′ N, 104°50′ E 198
Zigui, China 31°2′ N, 110°40′ E 198
Ziguinchor, Senegal 12°31′ N, 16°13′ W 222
Zihuatanejo, Mex. 17°36′ N, 101°33′ W 114
Zikhron Ya'aqov, Israel 32°33′ N, 34°57′ E 194
Zilair, Russ. 52°12′ N, 57°21′ E 154
Zile (Zela), Turk. 40°19′ N, 35°53′ E 156
Žilina, Slovakia 49°13′ N, 18°45′ E 152
Žilinský, adm. division, Slovakia 49°13′ N, 18°45′ E 152
Zillah, Lib. 28°32′ N, 17°33′ E 216
Zillah, Wash., U.S. 46°23′ N, 120°17′ W 90
Zilupe, Latv. 56°22′ N, 28°6′ E 166
Zima, Russ. 53°59′ N, 101°50′ E 190
Zimapán, Mex. 20°42′ N, 99°23′ W 114
Zimatlán, Mex. 16°51′ N, 96°45′ W 112
Zimba, Zambia 17°19′ S, 26°9′ E 224
Zimbabwe 19°5′ S, 29°8′ E 220
Zimmi, Sierra Leone 7°16′ N, 11°18′ W 222
Zimnicea, Rom. 43°41′ N, 25°20′ E 180
Zimovniki, Russ. 47°5′ N, 42°21′ E 158
Zina, Cameroon 11°16′ N, 14°56′ E 216
Zinapécuaro, Mex. 19°51′ N, 100°49′ W 114
Zinave National Park, Mozambique 21°47′ S, 33°31′ E 227
Zinder, Niger 13°46′ N, 8°59′ E 222
Zinguinasso, Côte d'Ivoire 10°3′ N, 6°22′ W 222
Zinjibār, Yemen 13°7′ N, 45°19′ E 182
Zion, Ill., U.S. 42°27′ N, 87°49′ W 102
Zion National Park, Utah, U.S. 37°15′ N, 114°31′ W 80
Zionsville, Ind., U.S. 39°57′ N, 86°17′ W 102
Zipaquirá, Col. 5°2′ N, 74°0′ W 136
Zirc, Hung. 47°15′ N, 17°53′ E 168
Žirče, Serb. 43°1′ N, 20°22′ E 168
Zirkel, Mount, peak, Colo., U.S. 40°49′ N, 106°44′ W 90
Zirkūh, island, U.A.E. 24°45′ N, 52°44′ E 182
Zitácuaro, Mex. 19°24′ N, 100°23′ W 114
Zitlala, Mex. 17°40′ N, 99°11′ W 114
Zitong, China 31°41′ N, 105°8′ E 198
Zitundo, Mozambique 26°37′ S, 32°53′ E 227
Živinice, Bosn. and Herzg. 44°28′ N, 18°38′ E 168
Zixi, China 27°39′ N, 117°2′ E 198
Zixing, China 26°0′ N, 113°21′ E 198
Ziya, river, China 38°30′ N, 116°41′ E 198
Ziyang, China 30°8′ N, 104°35′ E 198
Ziyang, China 32°34′ N, 108°33′ E 198
Ziyuan, China 26°2′ N, 110°41′ E 198
Ziyun, China 25°43′ N, 106°6′ E 198
Zizhou, China 37°37′ N, 110°5′ E 198
Zlatar, Croatia 46°6′ N, 16°4′ E 168
Zlatna, Rom. 46°7′ N, 23°15′ E 168
Zlatoust, Russ. 55°12′ N, 59°40′ E 154
Zlín, Czech Rep. 49°12′ N, 17°41′ E 152
Zlínský, adm. division, Czech Rep. 49°19′ N, 17°33′ E 152
Zlot, Serb. 44°1′ N, 21°59′ E 168
Zmeinogorsk, Russ. 51°10′ N, 82°17′ E 184
Żmigród, Pol. 51°28′ N, 16°55′ E 152
Zmiyev, Ukr. 49°40′ N, 36°18′ E 158
Znamenka, Kaz. 50°2′ N, 79°31′ E 184
Znamensk, Russ. 54°35′ N, 21°12′ E 166
Znam'yanka, Ukr. 48°43′ N, 32°39′ E 158
Zobia, Dem. Rep. of the Congo 3°0′ N, 25°58′ E 224
Zóbuè, Mozambique 15°35′ S, 34°24′ E 224
Zocca, It. 44°21′ N, 10°59′ E 167
Zodoke, Liberia 4°44′ N, 8°8′ W 214
Zoetermeer, Neth. 52°4′ N, 4°30′ E 163
Zofar, Israel 30°28′ N, 35°9′ E 194
Zogang (Wangda), China 29°42′ N, 97°53′ E 188
Zohor, Slovakia 48°18′ N, 16°59′ E 152
Zolfo Springs, Fla., U.S. 27°30′ N, 81°47′ W 105
Zolochiv, Ukr. 50°19′ N, 35°58′ E 158
Zolochiv, Ukr. 49°48′ N, 24°54′ E 152
Zolotarevka, Russ. 53°3′ N, 45°19′ E 154
Zolotonosha, Ukr. 49°38′ N, 32°3′ E 158
Zomba, Malawi 15°22′ S, 35°20′ E 224
Zongga see Gyirong, China 28°59′ N, 85°16′ E 197
Zongo, Dem. Rep. of the Congo 4°16′ N, 18°36′ E 218
Zonguldak, Turk. 41°27′ N, 31°48′ E 156
Zonhoven, Belg. 50°59′ N, 5°22′ E 167
Zoo Baba, spring, Niger 18°12′ N, 13°3′ E 222
Zoquiapan y Anexas National Park, Mex. 19°14′ N, 99°2′ W 72
Zor Dağ, peak, Turk. 39°43′ N, 43°53′ E 195
Zorita, Sp. 39°17′ N, 5°42′ W 164
Zorritos, Peru 3°45′ S, 80°40′ W 130
Żory, Pol. 50°3′ N, 18°41′ E 152
Zorzor, Liberia 7°41′ N, 9°28′ W 222
Zouar, Chad 20°28′ N, 16°31′ E 216
Zoucheng, China 35°24′ N, 117°0′ E 198
Zoug, Africa 21°37′ N, 14°9′ W 222
Zouîrat, Mauritania 22°46′ N, 12°27′ W 214
Zoushi, China 29°4′ N, 111°35′ E 198
Zoutkamp, Neth. 53°20′ N, 6°18′ E 163
Zrenjanin (Petrovgrad), Serb. 45°23′ N, 20°22′ E 168
Zrin, Croatia 45°11′ N, 16°24′ E 168
Zsira, Hung. 47°27′ N, 16°41′ E 168
Zubia, Sp. 37°7′ N, 3°35′ W 164
Zubovo, Russ. 60°16′ N, 37°0′ E 154
Zubtsov, Russ. 56°11′ N, 34°39′ E 154
Zudañez, Bol. 19°2′ S, 64°48′ W 137
Zuénoula, Côte d'Ivoire 7°21′ N, 6°3′ W 222
Zuera, Sp. 41°52′ N, 0°48′ E 164
Zufre, Sp. 37°49′ N, 6°21′ W 164
Zugdidi, Ga. 42°30′ N, 41°52′ E 195
Zugspitze, peak, Aust. 47°23′ N, 10°54′ E 156
Zuidhorn, Neth. 53°14′ N, 6°24′ E 163
Zújar, Sp. 37°32′ N, 2°51′ W 164
Zula, Eritrea 15°12′ N, 39°39′ E 182
Zulia, adm. division, Venez. 9°34′ N, 73°2′ W 136
Zülpich, Ger. 50°41′ N, 6°38′ E 167
Zululand, region, S. Af. 27°12′ S, 31°44′ E 227
Zumaia, Sp. 43°17′ N, 2°15′ W 150
Žumberačka Gora, Slov. 45°39′ N, 14°43′ E 156
Zumbo, Mozambique 15°37′ S, 30°28′ E 224
Zumpango, Mex. 19°45′ N, 99°3′ W 114
Zunape, Col. 4°12′ N, 70°28′ W 136
Zungeru, Nig. 9°47′ N, 6°9′ E 222
Zunhua, China 40°14′ N, 117°56′ E 198
Zuni, N. Mex., U.S. 35°4′ N, 108°51′ W 92
Zunyi, China 27°40′ N, 106°53′ E 198
Zuo, river, China 22°21′ N, 107°31′ E 198
Zuoz, Switz. 46°36′ N, 9°56′ E 167
Županja, Croatia 45°4′ N, 18°41′ E 168
Zūq Mīkhā'īl, Leb. 33°58′ N, 35°36′ E 194
Žur see Zhur, Kosovo 42°10′ N, 20°36′ E 168
Zūrābād, Iran 38°47′ N, 44°32′ E 195
Żurawica, Pol. 49°48′ N, 22°47′ E 152
Zureiqa, Sudan 13°32′ N, 32°1′ E 226
Zurich, Can. 43°25′ N, 81°37′ W 102
Zürich, Switz. 47°22′ N, 8°31′ E 150
Zuru, Nig. 11°24′ N, 5°12′ E 222
Zutiua, river, Braz. 5°8′ S, 46°19′ W 130
Zuwārah, Lib. 32°57′ N, 12°2′ E 216
Zuyevka, Russ. 58°24′ N, 51°15′ E 154
Zvenyhorodka, Ukr. 49°5′ N, 31°6′ E 158
Zvishavane, Zimb. 20°20′ S, 30°2′ E 227
Zvolen, Slovakia 48°34′ N, 19°7′ E 156
Zvonce, Serb. 42°55′ N, 22°34′ E 168
Zvornik, Bosn. and Herzg. 44°24′ N, 19°5′ E 168
Zvoz see Podsosan'ye, Russ. 63°17′ N, 42°2′ E 154
Zwedru, Liberia 5°57′ N, 8°9′ W 222
Zweibrücken, Ger. 49°14′ N, 7°21′ E 163
Zwickau, Ger. 50°43′ N, 12°29′ E 152
Zwijndrecht, Neth. 51°48′ N, 4°39′ E 167
Zwinge, Ger. 51°32′ N, 10°22′ E 167
Zwoleń, Pol. 51°21′ N, 21°34′ E 152
Zwolle, La., U.S. 31°36′ N, 93°39′ W 103
Zwolle, Neth. 52°31′ N, 6°5′ E 163
Zyembin, Belarus 54°21′ N, 28°11′ E 166
Zygi, Cyprus 34°43′ N, 33°19′ E 194
Żyrardów, Pol. 52°2′ N, 20°24′ E 152
Zyrya, Azerb. 40°22′ N, 50°16′ E 195
Zyryanka, Russ. 65°51′ N, 150°31′ E 160
Zyryanovo, Russ. 63°39′ N, 87°27′ E 169
Zyryanovsk, Kaz. 49°45′ N, 84°18′ E 184

CONSULTANTS

PHYSICAL and POLITICAL MAPS and EDITORIAL CONTENT

United States Government

Central Intelligence Agency
Departments of economic development in each state
Library of Congress, Geography and Map Division
National Aeronautics and Space Administration (NASA)
    Earth Observatory System (EOS)
    Goddard Space Flight Center (GSFC)
    Marshall Space Flight Center (MSFC)
National Geospatial-Intelligence Agency (NGA)
    Hydrographic and Topographic Center
Naval Research Laboratory
U.S. Board on Geographic Names (BGN)
U.S. Department of Agriculture (USDA)
U.S. Department of Commerce
    Bureau of Census
    Bureau of Economic Affairs
    National Oceanic and Atmospheric Administration (NOAA)
        National Marine Fisheries Service (NMFS)
        National Environmental Satellite, Data, and Information Service
        (NESDIS)
            National Climatic Data Center (NCDC)
            National Geophysical Data Center (NGDC)
            National Ocean Service (NOS)
U.S. Department of Defense
    Air Force Space and Missile systems Center (SMC)
    Defense Meteorological Satellite Program (DMSP)
U.S. Department of Interior
    Bureau of Land Management (BLM)
    Geological Survey (USGS)
        National Biological Survey
        EROS Data Center
    National Park Service
    National Wetlands Research Center
    Office of Territories
U.S. Department of State
U.S. Naval Oceanographic Office
U.S. Navy/NOAA Joint Ice Center

Government of Canada

Department of Energy, Mines and Resource
Canadian Permanent Committee on Geographic Names
Government du Québec
    Commission de toponymie
Offices of provincial premiers and of commissioners of the territories
Statistics Canada

Other

Embassies and statistical agencies of foreign nations
International Astronomical Union
    Working Group for Planetary System Nomenclature
International Telecommunication Union (ITU)
Norwegian Polar Institute
Population Reference Bureau (PRB)
Scripps Institution of Oceanography
State Economic Agencies
United Nations (UN)
    Cartography Unit, Map Library, Department of Technical
        Cooperation, Documentation, Reference
        and Terminology Section
    Department of Economic and Social Affairs, Statistics Division
    Environmental Program (UNEP), World Conservation Monitoring
        Centre (WCMC), Protected Areas Program
    Food and Agriculture Organization (FAO)
    Global Resources Information Database (GRID)
    United Nations High Commission on Refugees (UNHCR)
University of Cambridge, Scott Polar Research Institute
Wildlife Conservation Society (WCS), Human Footprint Project
World Bank
    Map Library, Statistical Office
    World Development Indicators
World Health Organization (WHO)
World Resources Institute (WRI), Global Forest Watch
World Wildlife Fund (WWF)

WORLD THEMATIC MAPS and EDITORIAL CONTENT

OVERALL CONSULTANTS

HARM J. DE BLIJ, John A. Hannah Professor of Geography,
    Michigan State University
ROGER M. DOWNS, Pennsylvania State University

THEMATIC CONSULTANTS

World From Above
ROBERT STACEY, WorldSat International Inc.

Geospatial Concepts
STEVEN STEINBERG, Humboldt State University

Tectonics
SETH STEIN, Northwestern University

Geomorphology
STEPHEN CUNHA, Humboldt State University

Earth's Surface
PETER SLOSS, NOAA

JONATHAN T. OVERPECK, Department of Geosciences,
    The University of Arizona

JEREMY L. WEISS, Department of Geosciences, The University of Arizona

Climate and Weather
JOHN OLIVER, Indiana State University

Biosphere
GENE CARL FELDMAN, SeaWiFs, NASA/Goddard Space Flight Center

Water
AARON WOLF, Oregon State University

Land Cover
PAUL DAVIS, University of Maryland, Global Land Cover Facility

Biodiversity
JOHN KUPTER, University of South Carolina

Land Use
NAVIN RAMANKUTTY, University of Wisconsin, Madison

Human Population and Population Trends
CARL HAUB, Population Reference Bureau

Cultures
BERNARD COMRIE, Max Planck Institute for Revolutionary
Anthropology
DENNIS COSGROVE, University of California, Los Angeles

Health & Literacy
MICHAEL REICH, Harvard University

Economy
AMY GLASMEIER, Pennsylvania State University

Food
GIL LATZ, Portland State University

Trade & Globalization
AMY GLASMEIER, Pennsylvania State University

Transportation
JEAN-PAUL RODRIGUE, Hofstra University

Communication
GREG DOWNEY, University of Wisconsin, Madison

Energy
BARRY D. SOLOMON, Michigan Technological University

Defense & Conflict
ALEXANDER MURPHY, University of Oregon

Environment
TANIA DEL MAR LÓPEZ MARRERO, Pennsylvania State University

Protected Lands
PHILIP DEARDEN, University of Victoria
ERIC SANDERSON, Wildlife Conservation Society

Geographic Comparisons
DAVID DIVINS, NOAA/NGDC
ROBERT FISHER, Scripps Institute of Oceanography
CARL HAUB, Population Reference Bureau
MARTIN JAKOBSSON, University of New Hampshire
CHARLES O'REILLY, Canadian Hydrographic Service
RON SALVASON, Canadian Hydrographic Service
HANS WERNER SCHENKE, Alfred Wegener Institute
    for Polar and Marine Research

CREDITS and SOURCES

Abbreviations: Advanced Very High Resolution
Radiometer (AVHRR); Digital Elevation Model (DEM);
Moderate Resolution Imaging Spectroradiometer (MODIS);
Shuttle Radar Topography Mission (SRTM).

Cover
(Photo: Mt. Everest) Jim Surette; (Photo: Panda from Wolong Nature
Reserve, China) Daniel J. Cox, Natural Exposures; (Photo: Tree frog from
Gunung Palung National Park, Indonesia) Tim Laman; (Political Maps)
National Geographic Maps; (Ocean Circulation) Don Foley; (Lights at
Night Data) NOAA/NGDC; DMSP; (Human Footprint) Human
Footprint Project, ©WCS and Center for International Earth Science
Information Network (CIESIN), Columbia University; (Surface Elevation)
ETOPO2 data rendered by Peter W. Sloss, Ph.D., NOAA, NGDC.

Preface: (Map: World) MODIS, ETOPO-2, Lights at Night data;
NOAA/NGDC; DMSP.

CHAPTER OPENERS

The World, pages 18-19: (Map: World) Human Footprint Project
© Wildlife Conservation Society (WCS) and Center for International
Earth Science Information Network (CIESIN) 2006; Project leads:
Eric Sanderson, Kent Redford, WCS; Marc Levy, CIESIN; Funding:
Center for Environmental Research and Conservation (CERC) at Columbia
University, ESRI Conservation Program, Prospect Hill Foundation.

The Human Footprint Project illustrates the application of geographic information systems (GIS) as a way to combine diverse geographic data to reveal
new patterns on the land. The authors of the study from the Wildlife
Conservation Society and Columbia University combined nine global data
layers to create this "human footprint" map. The layers covered the following themes: human population density, human land use and infrastructure,
and human access. They concluded that 83% of the earth's land surface is
influenced directly by human beings, whether through human land uses,
human access from roads, railways, or major rivers, electrical infrastructure
(indicated by lights detected at night), or direct occupancy by human populations at densities above one person per square kilometer. The researchers
scored each of the variables on a one to ten scale, summed the numbers, and
mapped
the results. The lower the score, the lesser the degree of human influence.
Antarctica was not mapped in the original study, but human influence there
is known to be quite low, so it is shown in a uniform green color.

**Continental Images: North America, pages 70-71; South America,
pages 120-121; Europe, pages 140-141; Asia, pages 170-171; Africa,
pages 204-205; Australia & Oceania, pages 228-229; Polar Regions,
pages 244-245:** (All Imagery) Landsat, AVHRR, Lights at Night data
rendered by Robert Stacey, WorldSat International Inc.;
NOAA/NGDC; DMSP.

To "paint" the images of continents, polar regions, and oceans which open
the chapters, data from multiple passes of numerous satellites, Space Shuttle,
and sonar soundings—recorded at varying scales and levels of resolution—
were combined digitally to form mosaics. This level of detail, rendered cloud
free, captured nighttime lights of populated areas, flares from natural gas
burning above oil wells, and lights from fishing fleets. The images were further enhanced and blended to approximate true color. Shaded relief, as if the
sun were shining from the northwest, was added for realism, and elevation
was exaggerated twenty times to make variations in elevation easily visible.
The images were then reproduced as if viewed from space.

Oceans, pages 250-251: (All Globes) Gregory W. Shirah,
NASA/GSFC Scientific Visualization Studio; David W. Pierce,
Scripps Institution of Oceanography.

The speed and direction of ocean currents can be computed from small variations in the height of the sea surface just as the speed and direction of the
wind is computed from surface air pressure differences. Satellite-derived
images depict a ten-year average of the hills and valleys, or shape, of the
changing ocean surface. These undulations range over a few meters in
height, and flow occurs along the color contours. The vectors (white arrows)
show ocean velocity caused exclusively by the effect of wind on the top layer
of the ocean (called the Ekman Drift). Estimates of the Ekman Drift are
used by ocean researchers to determine the shape of the sea surface and as a
component of the overall surface current (which also includes thermal,
saline, tidal, and wave-driven components).

WORLD THEMATIC SECTION

World From Above, pages 14-15: (Aerial Photographs: Washington,
D.C.) National Capital Planning Commission and District of Columbia,
processed by Photo Science, Gaithersburg, Maryland; (Radar Imagery,
Rio de Janeiro) Radar data by Canadian Space Agency, processed by
Radarsat International; (Imagery: Rio de Janeiro) Landsat/Thermal, Near
Infrared, Visible data from Brazilian Ministry of Science and Technology's
National Institute for Space Research, processed by Stephen W. Stetson,
Systems for World Surveillance; (Globes) Nimbus satellite data processed
by Laboratory for Oceans and Ice, NASA/GSFC; (Map: North America)
Landsat, AVHRR, and Lights at Night data rendered by Robert Stacey,
WorldSat International Inc.; NOAA/NGDC; DMSP; (Imagery: Beaufort
Sea) Landsat, SPOT, and RADARSAT data processed by Canada Centre
for Remote Sensing; (Imagery: North Carolina Flooding in 1999)
RADARSAT ScanSAR data processed by Canada Centre for Remote
Sensing; (Imagery: Southern California Wildfire) Landsat-5 data courtesy
of USGS; (Imagery: Ancient Footpaths, Arenal, Costa Rica) NASA/MSFC.

Geospatial Concepts, pages 16-17: (Map series: California) © National
Geographic Society; (GIS Application: Urban Planning) Community
Cartography; (GIS Application Sample: TransCAD Transportation
Planning) Caliper Corporation; (GIS Application: Emergency
Management) CalMAST and the San Bernadino County Sheriff used
ESRI's ArcGIS technology to visualize a 3-D flyover of the Old and Grand
Prix Fire perimeters (data provided courtesy of CalMAST and USGS);
(GIS Application: Demographic/Census) Courtesy of CBS News and ESRI;
(GIS Application: Health) Copyright © 2001-2005 ESRI. All rights
reserved. Used by permission; (GIS Application: Conservation) National
Zoological Park, Smithsonian Institution.

Tectonics, pages 24-25: (Map series: Paleogeography) Christopher R.
Scotese, PALEOMAP project ; (Map: Earth Tectonics) Seth Stein,
Northwestern University; USGS Earthquake Hazard Program; Global
Volcanism Program, Smithsonian Institution; (Artwork: "Tectonic Block
Diagrams") Susan Sanford.

COLLEGE
ATLAS OF THE WORLD

SECOND EDITION

Published by THE NATIONAL GEOGRAPHIC SOCIETY

John M. Fahey, Jr.	*President and Chief Executive Officer*
Gilbert M. Grosvenor	*Chairman of the Board*
Tim T. Kelly	*President, Global Media Group*
John Q. Griffin	*Executive Vice President; President, Publishing*
Nina D. Hoffman	*Executive Vice President; President, Book Publishing Group*

Prepared by NATIONAL GEOGRAPHIC MAPS

Paul Levine	*Senior Vice President, Interactive Platforms*
Charles D. Regan, Jr.	*Vice President, General Manager, NG Maps*
Allen T. Carroll	*Chief Cartographer*
Kevin P. Allen	*Vice President, Mapping Services*

NATIONAL GEOGRAPHIC MAPS ATLAS STAFF

Juan José Valdés	*Project Manager, Director of Editorial and Research*
Richard W. Bullington	*Director of GIS*
Debbie J. Gibbons	*Director of Production*
James E. McClelland, Jr.	*Senior Production Cartographer*
Stephen P. Wells	*Map Production*
Maureen J. Flynn	*Map Editor*
Julie A. Ibinson	*Map Editor*
Evan Feeney, Alissa M. Ferry, Ewa K. Wieslaw	*Interns*

ADDITIONAL STAFF

Glenn C. Caillouet	*Map Production*
Nicholas P. Rosenbach	*Map Editor*
Mapping Specialists Limited	*Production*

MANUFACTURING and QUALITY MANAGEMENT

Christopher A. Liedel	*Chief Financial Officer*
Phillip L. Schlosser	*Vice President*
Chris Brown	*Technical Director*
Michael G. Lappin	*Printing and Quality Control*

Printed and bound by RR Donnelley & Sons Company
Willard, Ohio

Printed in the U.S.A.